AWE

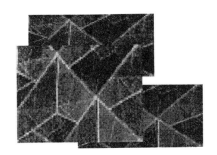

Proceedings

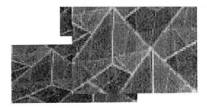

2002 IEEE International Conference on Data Mining

ICDM 2002

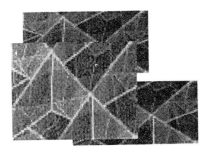

Proceedings

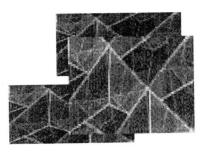

2002 IEEE International Conference on Data Mining

ICDM 2002

9-12 December 2002 • Maebashi City, Japan

Editors

Vipin Kumar, University of Minnesota, USA
Shusaku Tsumoto, Shimane Medical University, Japan
Ning Zhong, Maebashi Institute of Technology, Japan
Philip S. Yu, IBM T. J. Watson Research Center, USA
Xindong Wu, University of Vermont, USA

Sponsored by

IEEE Computer Society Technical Committee on
Pattern Analysis and Machine Intelligence (TCPAMI)
IEEE Computer Society Technical Committee on Computational Intelligence (TCCI)

IEEE

COMPUTER
SOCIETY
Los Alamitos, California

Washington • Brussels • Tokyo

IEEE Computer Society Order Number PR01754
ISBN 0-7695-1754-4
Library of Congress Number 2002109464

Additional copies may be ordered from:

IEEE Computer Society
Customer Service Center
10662 Los Vaqueros Circle
P.O. Box 3014
Los Alamitos, CA 90720-1314
Tel: + 1-714-821-8380
Fax: + 1-714-821-4641
E-mail: cs.books@computer.org

IEEE Service Center
445 Hoes Lane
P.O. Box 1331
Piscataway, NJ 08855-1331
Tel: + 1-732-981-0060
Fax: + 1-732-981-9667
http://shop.ieee.org/store/
customer-service@ieee.org

IEEE Computer Society
Asia/Pacific Office
Watanabe Bldg., 1-4-2
Minami-Aoyama
Minato-ku, Tokyo 107-0062
JAPAN
Tel: + 81-3-3408-3118
Fax: + 81-3-3408-3553
tokyo.ofc@computer.org

Editorial production by Stephanie Kawada
Cover art production by Joe Daigle/Studio Productions
Printed in the United States of America by The Printing House

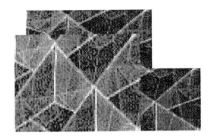
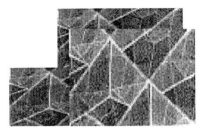

Proceedings

ICDM 2002

Table of Contents

Main-Track Regular Papers

Main-Track Short Papers

Industry-Track Papers

Welcome from the Conference Chairs and Program Chairs

Welcome to IEEE Data Mining 2002, the second IEEE International Conference on Data Mining (ICDM '02). On behalf of the ICDM '02 Conference Committee, we would like to thank you for coming to ICDM '02, and we hope you enjoy the technical and social programs of the conference as well as the local nature and culture of Maebashi City, Gumma Prefecture, Japan.

The second meeting of the IEEE ICDM conference series follows the success of ICDM '01 in San Jose, California, USA, in 2001. ICDM '02 brought together researchers and practitioners to share their original research and practical development experiences in Data Mining technology. The most important feature of this conference is that it emphasizes a multifaceted, holistic view of this emerging technology—from its computational foundations, in terms of models, methodologies, and tools for developing a variety of embodiments of data mining systems to its practical impact on tackling real-world problems in the industry and timely applications such as bioinformatics and Web intelligence.

Data mining is an emerging and interdisciplinary field. ICDM '02 covers broad and diverse topics related to the design, analysis, and implementation of data mining theory, systems, and applications. These include, but are not limited to, the following areas:

- Foundations and principles of data mining
- Data mining algorithms and methods in traditional areas (such as classification, clustering, probabilistic modeling, and association analysis), and in new areas
- Data and knowledge representation for data mining
- Modeling of structured, textual, temporal, spatial, multimedia, and Web data to support data mining
- Complexity, efficiency, and scalability issues in data mining
- Data preprocessing, data reduction, feature selection, and feature transformation
- Statistics and probability in large-scale data mining
- Soft computing (including neural networks, fuzzy logic, evolutionary computation, and rough sets) and uncertainty management for data mining
- Integration of data warehousing, OLAP, and data mining
- Man-machine interaction in data mining and visual data mining
- Artificial intelligence contributions to data mining
- High performance and distributed data mining
- Machine learning, pattern recognition, and automated scientific discovery
- Quality assessment and interestingness metrics of data mining results
- Process centric data mining and models of data mining process
- Security and social impact of data mining
- Emerging data mining applications, such as electronic commerce, bioinformatics, Web intelligence, and intelligent learning database systems

With the support of both world-renowned experts and new researchers from the international data mining community, the conference has received an overwhelming response compared with any other data mining-related conference this year, and achieved a truly international status. The conference received 347 submissions to the regular track and 22 submissions to the industry track from 36 different countries and regions. The distribution of these submitted papers is as follows: Australia (24), Austria (3), Belgium (3), Brazil (1), Canada (22), Catalonia (1), China (31), Czech Republic (1), Egypt (3), Finland (9), France (12), Germany (9), Greece (5), Hong Kong (17), India (2), Iran (1), Israel (2), Italy (6), Japan (22), Korea (5), Macao (1), Malaysia (3), Portugal (2), Romania (1), Russia (2), Singapore (6), Slovenia (2), Spain (7), Sweden (2), Switzerland (1), Taiwan (32), Thailand (2), UK (11),

USA (94), Venezuela (1), and Yugoslavia (1). In addition, we received 9 workshop proposals and 39 tutorial proposals this year.

Each of the 369 submissions went through the following rigorous reviewing process. First, each paper was reviewed by three Program Committee members. Second, any inconsistencies in these reviews were resolved through discussions among Program Committee members and were moderated by Vice Chairs over a period of two weeks. Thirdly, if some conflicts were still observed in the reviews, Vice Chairs or Program Chairs provided a fourth review. Approximately 20% of the 369 submissions were accepted as regular papers and an additional 12% were accepted as short papers.

Concerning the trends and characteristics of the paper submissions this year, we have discovered several changes, compared with ICDM '01. Thus, we have decided to compare these two meetings by using "data mining" methods, and will present a detailed analysis at the conference.

A successful conference requires enormous time commitment from a large number of volunteers. First, we would like to thank the Program Vice Chairs (Masaru Kitsurgawa, Bing Liu, Ken Satoh, Kyuseok Shim, Hannu Toivonen, and Geoff Webb), Industry Track Chairs (Koji Sasaki and Gregory Piatetsky-Shapiro), Workshop Chair Einoshin Suzuki, Tutorial Chair Takashi Washio, Panel Chair Katharina Morik, Publicity Chair Jiming Liu, Finance Chair Xindong Wu, Local Arrangements Chair Nobuo Otani, members of the Program Committee, and additional reviewers for the countless hours they devoted to various conference activities. The Steering Committee provided valuable feedback and discussions on many important aspects of the conference during the course of the year. We reserve special thanks for the fine overall advice and the specific help with the proceedings publication that Xindong Wu has provided.

We are honored to have Jaime Carbonell (Carnegie Mellon University), Satoru Miyano (University of Tokyo), Hiroshi Motoda (Osaka University), Stephen Muggleton (Imperial College, UK), Steve Smale (University of California at Berkeley), and Jeffrey D. Ullman (Stanford University) as invited speakers to present keynote talks that will cover different perspectives of data mining.

The conference Web support team at the Knowledge Information Systems Laboratory, Maebashi Institute of Technology did a terrific job of putting together and maintaining the home page for the conference as well as building a software package, namely, Cyberchair, that is an intelligent agent and interface among conference organizers, program committee members, authors, and conference attendees.

We are very grateful to the ICDM '02 cooperative sponsors: Maebashi Convention Bureau, Maebashi City Government, Gunma Prefecture Government, Maebashi Institute of Technology, AdIn Research, Inc., Japan, The Japan Research Institute, Limited, Support Center for Advanced Telecommunications Technology Research, US AFOSR/AOARD, AROFE, The SAS Institute, Japan, SPSS Japan Inc., KANKODO, Japan, System Alpha, Inc., Japan, GCC Inc., Japan, Yamato Inc., Japan, Daiei Dream Co., LTD, Japan, and Fressay, Japan, for their generous support. We also thank the Japanese Society for Artificial Intelligence (JSAI) for their cooperation and support of the conference.

Last but not the least, we would like to thank all authors of the submitted papers, and all conference attendees for their contribution and participation. Without them, we would not have this conference.

Ning Zhong and Philip S. Yu
ICDM '02 Conference Chairs

Vipin Kumar and Shusaku Tsumoto
ICDM '02 Program Chairs

Conference Organization

Honorary Chair
Setsuo Ohsuga, *Waseda University, Japan*

Conference Chairs
Ning Zhong, *Maebashi Institute of Technology, Japan*
Philip S. Yu, *IBM T. J. Watson Research Center, USA*

Program Committee Chairs
Vipin Kumar, *University of Minnesota, USA*
Shusaku Tsumoto, *Shimane Medical University, Japan*

Industry Track Chairs
Koji Sasaki, *AdIn Research, Inc., Japan*
Gregory Piatetsky-Shapiro, *KDnuggets, USA*

Workshops Chair
Einoshin Suzuki, *Yokohama National University, Japan*

Tutorials Chair
Takashi Washio, *Osaka University, Japan*

Panels Chair
Katharina Morik, *University of Dortmund, Germany*

Publicity Chair
Jiming Liu, *Hong Kong Baptist University, Hong Kong*

Finance Chair
Xindong Wu, *University of Vermont, USA*

Local Arrangements Chair
Nobuo Otani, *Maebashi Institute of Technology, Japan*

Steering Committee

Xindong Wu (Chair), *University of Vermont, USA*
Max Bramer, *University of Portsmouth, UK*
Nick Cercone, *University of Waterloo, Canada*
Ramamohanarao Kotagiri, *University of Melbourne, Australia*
Katharina Morik, *University of Dortmund, Germany*
Gregory Piatetsky-Shapiro, *KDnuggets, USA*
Benjamin W. Wah, *University of Illinois, Urbana-Champaign, USA*
Philip S. Yu, *IBM T.J. Watson Research Center, USA*
Ning Zhong, *Maebashi Institute of Technology, Japan*

Program Committee

Program Chairs
Vipin Kumar, *University of Minnesota, USA*
Shusaku Tsumoto, *Shimane Medical University, Japan*

Vice Chairs
Foundations
Ken Satoh, *National Institute for Informatics, Japan*
AI Issues
Hannu T. T. Toivonen, *University of Helsinki, Finland*
Database Issues
Kyuseok Shim, *Seoul National University, Korea*
Statistics/Probability and Soft-Computing
Geoff Webb, *Deakin University, Australia*
High-Performance and Distributed Data Mining
Masaru Kitsuregawa, *University of Tokyo, Japan*
Applications and Emerging Topics
Bing Liu, *University of Illinois at Chicago, USA*

Program Committee
Dimitris Achlioptas, *Microsoft Research, USA*
Chid Apte, *IBM T. J. Watson Research Center, USA*
Hiroki Arimura, *Kyushu University, Japan*
Serafim Batzoglou, *Stanford University, USA*
Roberto Bayardo, *IBM Almaden Research Center, USA*
Paul Bradley, *digiMine Inc., USA*
Juan Pedro Caraca-Valente, *University Politecnica De Madrid, Spain*
Nick Cercone, *University of Waterloo, Canada*
Philip Chan, *Florida Institute of Technology, USA*
Arbee L. P. Chen, *National Tsing Hua University, Taiwan*
Ming-Syan Chen, *National Taiwan University, Taiwan*
Alok Choudhary, *Northwestern University, USA*
Gautam Das, *Microsoft Research, USA*
Luc De Raedt, *Albert-Ludwigs-Universitat Freiburg, Germany*
Vasant Dhar, *New York University, USA*
Guozhu Dong, *Wright State University, USA*
Usama M. Fayyad, *digiMine Inc., USA*
Ada Fu, *Chinese University of Hong Kong, China*
Johannes Gehrke, *Cornell University, USA*
Joydeep Ghosh, *University of Texas, USA*
Ananth Grama, *Purdue University, USA*
Robert Grossman, *University of Illinois at Chicago, USA*
Yike Guo, *Imperial College, UK*
Petr Hajek, *Academy of Sciences of the Czech Republic, Czech Republic*
Howard J. Hamilton, *University of Regina, Canada*

Non-PC Reviewers

Adina Costea
Aleksandar Lazarevic
Alfredo Garro
Alin Dobra
Amit Mandvikar
Amit Shirsat
Andrew Foss
Anthony Rowe
Antonin Rozsypal
April Kontostathis
B. L. Narayan
Bianca Zadrozny
C. J. Liau
Carlo Mastroianni
Chien-Chung Cha
Christoph Helma
Clara Pizzuti
Cory Butz
Dan Oblinger
Ernestina Menasalvas
Eugene Davydov
Faisal Khan
Filippia Emmanouil
Giuseppe Amato
Giuseppe Manco
Huiyuan Shan
Huma Lodhi
Hung-Chen Chen
Hwanjo Yu
Iko Pramudiono
Ioannis Ioannidis
Irene Liu
Jan Ramon
Jean-Francois Boulicaut
Jeffrey Xu Yu
Jia Li
Jian Pei
Jian Tang
Jianghui Liu
Jianyong Wang

Jie Chi
JingTao Yao
Jirong Yang
Jiye Li
Katherine G. Herbert
Ke Wang
Ken Ding-Ying Chiu
Lars Holzman
Leon Galitsky
Liadan OCallaghan
Liqiang Geng
Luiza Antonie
Malu Castellanos
Manoranjan Dash
Martin Scholz
Masashi Toyoda
Matt Mahoney
Matthew Richardson
Mayank Bawa
Mehmet Koyuturk
Michael M. Yin
Michael Steinbach
Miho Ohsaki
Mike Brudno
Minos Garofalakis
Mirco Nanni
Mitchell Tsai
Mohamed Ali Jafri
Moustafa Ghanem
Murali Mani
Narasimha Deepak
Kolippakkam
Noriaki Izumi
Pabitra Mitra
Pang-Ning Tan
Paolo Palmerini
Patrick Wendel
Peter Au
Raffaele Perego
Ralf Klinkenberg

Raymond Wong
Relly Brandman
Ricardo Vilalta
Robert Chun
Ronnie Fanguy
Ryan G. Benton
Salvatore Orlando
Sam Sung
Samer Nassar
Sau Dan Lee
Sen Zhang
Shenzhi Li
Shichao Zhang
Soma Roy
Sreangsu Acharyya
Stefan Roeping
Suin Lee
Thomas Johnsten
Tianhao Wu
Timm Euler
Tong Zhang
Tony Abou-Assaleh
Vasa Curcin
Vlado Keselj
Wen Wen Hsieh
William Cheung
Xia Yi
Xiaohua Hu
Xiaoxin Yin
Xifeng Yan
Xin Wang
Yanqing Zhang
Yi-Hung Wu
Ying Xie
YingWei Wang
Yirong Yang
Yong Zhan
Yun Chi
Zhenmei Gu

Corporate Sponsors

Maebashi Convention Bureau

Maebashi City Government

Gunma Prefecture Government

Maebashi Institute of Technology

AdIn Research, Inc., Japan

The Japan Research Institute, Limited

Support Center for Advanced Telecommunications Technology Research

US AFOSR/AOARD, AROFE

The SAS Institute, Japan

SPSS Japan Inc.

KANKODO, Japan

System Alpha, Inc., Japan

GCC Inc., Japan

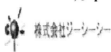

Yamato Inc., Japan

Daiei Dream Co., LTD, Japan

Fressay, Japan

ICDM '02 in cooperation with
JSAI

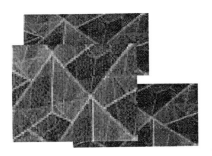
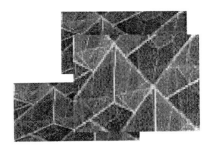

Main-Track Regular Papers

Empirical Comparison of Various Reinforcement Learning Strategies for Sequential Targeted Marketing

Naoki Abe, Edwin Pednault, Haixun Wang, Bianca Zadrozny,* Wei Fan, Chid Apte
Math. Sci. Dept. and Dist. Comp. Dept.
I.B.M. T. J. Watson Research Center
Yorktown Heights, NY 10598

Abstract

We empirically evaluate the performance of various reinforcement learning methods in applications to sequential targeted marketing. In particular, we propose and evaluate a progression of reinforcement learning methods, ranging from the "direct" or "batch" methods to "indirect" or "simulation based" methods, and those that we call "semi-direct" methods that fall between them. We conduct a number of controlled experiments to evaluate the performance of these competing methods. Our results indicate that while the indirect methods can perform better in a situation in which nearly perfect modeling is possible, under the more realistic situations in which the system's modeling parameters have restricted attention, the indirect methods' performance tend to degrade. We also show that semi-direct methods are effective in reducing the amount of computation necessary to attain a given level of performance, and often result in more profitable policies.

1. Introduction

Recently there has been a growing interest in the issues of cost-sensitive learning and decision making, in the data mining community. Various authors have noted the limitations of classic supervised-learning methods for use in cost sensitive decision making (e.g., [13, 4, 5, 17, 8]), and a number of cost sensitive learning methods have been developed [4, 17, 6] that out-perform classification based methods. The problem of optimizing a *sequence* of cost-sensitive decisions, however, has rarely been addressed.

In a companion paper [10], we proposed to apply the framework of reinforcement learning to address the issue of sequential cost-sensitive decision making. In the past, reinforcement learning has been applied mostly in domains in which satisfactory modeling of the environment is possible, which can then be used by a learning algorithm to experiment with and learn from. This type of methods, known as "indirect" or "simulation based" learning methods, would be difficult to apply in the domain of business intelligence, since customer behavior is too complex to allow reliable modeling. For this reason we proposed to apply so-called "direct" reinforcement learning methods, or those that do not estimate an environment model used for experimentation, but directly estimate the values of actions from given data. It was left for future research, however, to verify whether direct methods work better than indirect methods.

In the present paper, we examine this question by conducting a number of controlled experiments in the domain of targeted marketing. Targeted marketing is a proto-typical application area of cost-sensitive learning (e.g. [17]) and it is also *sequential* in nature, namely marketing decisions are made over time, and the interactions among them affect the overall, cumulative profits. Our experiments were conducted using a couple of different scenarios, each derived using the well-known donation data set from the KDD Cup 1998 competition, which contains direct-mail promotional history data. The results of our experiments show that, while indirect methods can work very well and in particular better than direct methods if the modeling of the simulation model is nearly perfect, in situations in which the modeling is less than perfect, the direct methods perform much better.

We also propose reinforcement learning methods that fall between the direct and indirect methods. Since they are essentially direct methods but mirror some aspects of the indirect methods by means of sampling and use of estimated rewards, we refer to them as "semi-direct" methods. Our experimental results show that semi-direct methods are effective in reducing the amount of computation necessary to attain a given level of performance, and often result in

---

* This author's present address: Dept. of Comp. Sci. and Eng. U.C.S.D., La Jolla, CA 92093. The work was performed while this author was visiting IBM T.J.Watson Research Center.

3

more profitable policies. The rest of the paper is organized as follows. In Section 2, we describe our proposed approach to sequential targeted marketing by reinforcement learning, including direct, semi-direct and indirect methods of reinforcement learning. In Section 3, we describe the various experiments we conducted to compare the performance of these competing approaches. In Section 4, we present the experimental results. We conclude with some discussion of future research directions in Section 5.

2. Reinforcement Learning Methods for Sequential Targeted Marketing

We adopt the popular Markov Decision Process (MDP) model in reinforcement learning. For an introduction to reinforcement learning see, for example, [12, 7]. For self-containment, we briefly explain MDP below, and then go on to describe various concrete methods we consider in this paper.

2.1. Markov Decision Processes

In a Marko Decision Process, the environment is assumed to be in one of a set of possible states, at any point in time. At each time clock (we assume a discrete time clock), the environment is in some state s, the learner takes one of several possible actions a, receives a finite reward (i.e., a profit or loss) r, and the environment makes a transition to another state s'. Here, the reward r and the transition state s' are both obtained with probability distributions that depend on the state s and action a.

Suppose that the environment starts in some initial state s_0 and the learner repeatedly takes actions indefinitely. This process results in a sequence of actions $\{a_t\}_{t=0}^{\infty}$, rewards $\{r_t\}_{t=0}^{\infty}$, and transition states $\{s_t\}_{t=1}^{\infty}$. The goal of the learner is to maximize the total rewards accrued over time, usually with future rewards discounted. That is, the goal is to maximize the cumulative reward R,

$$R = \sum_{t=0}^{\infty} \gamma^t r_t , \qquad (1)$$

where r_t is the reward obtained at the t-th time step and γ is some positive constant less than 1.

Generally speaking, a learner follows a certain policy to make decisions about its actions. This policy can be represented as a function π mapping states to actions such that $\pi(s)$ is the action the learner would take in state s. A theorem of Markov Decision Processes is that an optimum policy π^* exists that maximizes the cumulative reward given by Equation 1 for every initial state s_0.

In order to find an optimal policy π^*, a useful quantity to define is what is known as the *value function* Q^{π} of a policy. A value function maps a state s and an action a to the expected value of the cumulative reward that would be obtained if the environment started in state s, and the learner performed action a and then followed policy π forever after. $Q^{\pi}(s, a)$ is thus defined as

$$Q^{\pi}(s, a) = E_{\pi}\left[\sum_{t=0}^{\infty} \gamma^t r_t \;\middle|\; s_0 = s, a_0 = a\right] , \qquad (2)$$

where E_{π} denotes the expectation with respect to the policy π that is used to define the actions taken in all states except the initial state s_0.

A remarkable property of Markov Decision Processes is that the value function Q^* of an optimal policy π^* satisfies the following recurrence relation, known as the *Bellman optimality equation*:

$$\begin{aligned} Q^*(s, a) &= E_r\left[r \mid s, a\right] \\ &+ \gamma E_{s'}\left[\max_{a'} Q^*(s', a') \;\middle|\; s, a\right] , \end{aligned} \qquad (3)$$

where $E_r[r \mid s, a]$ is the expected immediate reward obtained by performing action a in state s, and $E_{s'}[\max_{a'} Q^*(s', a') \mid s, a]$ is the expected cumulative reward of performing the optimum action in the state s' that results when action a is performed in state s. The policy determined as follows is then optimal.

$$\pi^*(s) = \arg\max_a Q^*(s, a)$$

In learning situations, both the expected reward for each state-action pair as well as the state transition probabilities are unknown. The problem faced by a learner is to infer a (near) optimal policy over time through observation and experimentation. Several learning methods are known in the literature. A popular method known as *Q-learning*, due to Watkins [15], is based on the Bellman equation(Equation 3), and the process known as the *value iteration*. Q-learning estimates value functions in an on-line fashion when the sets of possible states and actions are both finite. The method starts with some initial estimates of the Q-values for each state and then updates them at each time step according to the following equation:

$$Q(s_t, a_t) \leftarrow Q(s_t, a_t) + \alpha(r_{t+1} + \gamma \max_{a'} Q(s_{t+1}, a') - Q(s_t, a_t)) . \qquad (4)$$

It is known that, with some technical conditions, the above procedure probabilistically converges to the optimal value function [16].

Another popular learning method, known as *sarsa* [11], is less aggressive than Q-learning. Like Q-learning, Sarsa-learning starts with some initial estimates for the Q-values that are then dynamically updated, but there is no maximization over possible actions in the transition state s_{t+1}.

$$Q(s_t, a_t) \leftarrow Q(s_t, a_t) + \alpha\left(r_{t+1} + \gamma Q(s_{t+1}, a_{t+1}) - Q(s_t, a_t)\right) . \qquad (5)$$

4

Instead, the current policy π is used without updating to determine both a_t and a_{t+1}.

2.2. Reinforcement Learning with Function Approximation

In the foregoing description, a simplifying assumption was made that is not satisfied in most practical applications. The assumption is that the problem space consists of a reasonably small number of atomic states and actions. In many practical applications, including targeted marketing, it is natural to treat the state space as a feature space, and the state space becomes prohibitively large to represent explicitly. For this reason, we employ reinforcement learning methods with *function approximation*, that is, we estimate and represent the value function as a function of state features and actions (e.g. [3, 14]). For this purpose, we employ the multivariate linear regression tree method implemented in the IBM ProbE data mining engine.[1]

2.3. Direct (Batch) Reinforcement Learning

Direct or batch reinforcement learning attempts to estimate the value function $Q(s, a)$ by reformulating value iteration as a supervised learning problem. In particular, on the first iteration, an estimate of the expected immediate reward function $R(s, a)$ is obtained by using supervised learning methods to predict the value of $R(s, a)$ based on the features that characterize the input state s and the input action a. On the second and subsequent iterations, the same supervised learning methods are used again to obtained successively improved predictions of $Q(s, a)$ by using a variant of sarsa-learning (Equation 5) to recalculate the target values that are used in the training data for each iteration.

Figure 1 presents a pseudo-code for a version of batch reinforcement learning based on sarsa-learning. Here the input training data D is assumed to consist of, or contain enough information to recover, *episode* data. An episode is a sequence of *events*, where each event consists of a state, an action, and a reward. An episode is a sequence of events in the order that they were observed. States $s_{i,j}$ are feature vectors that contain numeric and/or categorical data fields. Actions $a_{i,j}$ are assumed to be members of some prespecified finite set. Rewards $r_{i,j}$ are real-valued. The base learning module, Base, takes as input a set of event data and outputs a regression model Q_k that maps state-action pairs (s, a), to their estimated Q-values, $Q_k(s, a)$. In the experiments reported on in this paper, we set α_k to be α/k for some positive constant $\alpha < 1$.

---

1 This learning method produces decision trees with multivariate linear regression models at the leaves. For details, see, for example [9, 1].

Procedure Direct-RL(sarsa)
Premise:
  A base learning module, Base, for regression is given.
Input data: $D = \{e_i | i = 1, ..., N\}$ where
    $e_i = \{\langle s_{i,j}, a_{i,j}, r_{i,j} \rangle | j = 1, ..., l_i\}$
    (e_i is the i-th episode, and l_i is the length of e_i.)
  1. For all $e_i \in D$
     $D_{0,i} = \{\langle s_{i,j}, a_{i,j}, r_{i,j} \rangle | j = 1, ..., l_i\}$
  2. $D_0 = \bigcup_{i=1,...,N} D_{0,i}$
  3. $Q_0 = \text{Base}(D_0)$.
  4. For $k = 1$ to $final$
     4.1 For all $e_i \in D$
       4.1.1 For $j = 1$ to $l_i - 1$
         4.1.1.1 $v_{i,j}^{(k)} = Q_{k-1}(s_{i,j}, a_{i,j})$
                   $+\alpha_k(r_{i,j} + \gamma Q_{k-1}(s_{i,j+1}, a_{i,j+1})$
                   $-Q_{k-1}(s_{i,j}, a_{i,j}))$
         4.1.1.2 $D_{k,i} = \{\langle s_{i,j}, a_{i,j}, v_{i,j}^{(k)} \rangle | j = 1, ..., l_i - 1\}$
     4.2 $D_k = \bigcup_{i=1,...,N} D_{k,i}$
     4.3 $Q_k = \text{Base}(D_k)$
  5. Output the final model, Q_{final}.

Figure 1. Direct reinforcement learning (sarsa-learning)

2.4. Indirect Reinforcement Learning via Simulation

Indirect, or simulation-based methods of reinforcement learning first build a model of Markov Decision Process by estimating the transition probabilities and expected immediate rewards, and then learn from data generated using the model and a policy that is updated based on the current estimate of the value function. The crucial difference from the direct method is that by using an estimated optimal policy to generate training data in each stage of value iteration, it can learn from types of data that are not in the original data and are tailored to the optimal policy being learned. With function approximation, the transition probabilities and expected rewards are estimated as functions of the state vectors as well.

Figure 2 shows a pseudo code for a generic indirect method of reinforcement learning.

2.5. Semi-direct Reinforcement Learning

One feature of indirect methods that distinguish them significantly from direct methods is the way they use the estimated value function to change and guide the sampling or control policy. In direct reinforcement learning, training is done from data that have already been collected, presumably using some fixed policy. In a domain that involves a

Procedure Indirect-RL

Premise:

A base learning module, Base, for regression is given.
Probabilistic state transition function $\hat{T} : S \times A \to S$
as well as the expected reward function $\hat{R} : S \times A \to \mathcal{R}$
have been estimated using input data.
A set of initial states indexed by individuals,
$IS = \{s(i)|i = I\}$, is given.
Input data: $D = \{e_i|i = 1, ..., N\}$ where
  $e_i = \{\langle s_{i,j}, a_{i,j}, r_{i,j}\rangle|j = 1, ..., l_i\}$
  (e_i is the i-th episode, and l_i is the length of e_i.)
1. For all $e_i \in D$
   $D_{0,i} = \{\langle s_{i,j}, a_{i,j}, r_{i,j}\rangle|j = 1, ..., l_i\}$
2. $D_0 = \bigcup_{i=1,...,N} D_{0,i}$
3. $Q_0 = \text{Base}(D_0)$.
4. For $k = 1$ to $final$
   4.1 For all $i \in I$
      $e_{k,i} = Simulate(s(i), l, \hat{T}, \hat{R}, Q_{k-1})$
   4.2 For all $e_{k,i} = \{\langle s_{i,j}, a_{i,j}, r_{i,j}\rangle|j = 1, ..., l\}$
      4.2.1 For $j = 1$ to $l - 1$
         4.2.1.1 $v_{i,j}^{(k)} = Q_{k-1}(s_{i,j}, a_{i,j})$
            $+\alpha_k(r_{i,j} + \gamma Q_{k-1}(s_{i,j+1}, a_{i,j+1})$
            $-Q_{k-1}(s_{i,j}, a_{i,j}))$
      4.2.1.2 $D_{k,i} = \{\langle s_{i,j}, a_{i,j}, v_{i,j}^{(k)}\rangle|j = 1, ..., l-1\}$
   4.3 $D_k = \bigcup_{i=1,...,N} D_{k,i}$
   4.4 $Q_k = \text{Base}(D_k)$
5. Output the final model, Q_{final}.

Subprocedure Simulate

Input data:
  s: an initial state
  l: episode length
  $\hat{T}$: probabilistic state transition function
  $\hat{R}$: expected reward function
  $\hat{Q}$: estimated Q-value function
1. $s_1 = s$
2. For $j = 1$ to $l - 1$
   2.1 $a_j = \arg\max_a \hat{Q}(s_j, a)$
   2.2 $r_{j+1} = \hat{R}(s_j, a_j)$
   2.3 $s_{j+1} = \hat{T}(s_j, a_j)$
End For
3. Output $\langle\langle s_1, a_1, r_1\rangle, \langle s_2, a_2, r_2\rangle, ..., \langle s_l, a_l, r_l\rangle\rangle$

Figure 2. Indirect method of reinforcement learning.

huge amount of data, however, it is often practical to perform selective sampling to effectively change the sampling policy over the course of value iteration. For example, one method would be to select only those data that conform to the estimated policy from the previous iteration, thereby partially realizing the effect of employing an updated sampling policy as in indirect learning methods.

A second aspect in which indirect methods differ from direct methods is that, since they learn from data generated from an estimated model, learning tends to be stable. One way to mimic this aspect in a direct method is to use estimated immediate rewards in place of the actual observed rewards in the data, in the learning steps. (Equation 5 and 4.) In the present paper, we propose reinforcement learning methods having these two features, which we call "semi-direct" methods of reinforcement learning.

The semi-direct method we consider employs a version of sampling method we call *Q-sampling* in which only those states are selected, from within randomly sampled sub-episodes, that conform to the condition that the action taken in the next state is the best action with respect to the current estimate of the Q-value function. The value update is akin to Equation 5 used in sarsa-learning, but the effect of the learning that occurs corresponds to Equation 4 used in Q-learning because the sampling strategy ensures that $Q(s_{t+1}, a_{t+1}) = \max_a Q(s_{t+1}, a)$. Figures 3 shows a pseudo code for this method.

3. Empirical Evaluation

We conducted a number of controlled experiments to compare the performance of competing approaches of direct, semi-direct and indirect methods of reinforcement learning, in the domain of sequential targeted marketing. As we briefly mentioned in Introduction, our experiments were run with two different set-ups. In the first set-up, we assumed a nearly perfect modeling, in which the reinforcement learning methods have access to all features that characterize the nature of data. That is, the reinforcement learning methods make use of all the features in their learning process, and their performance is measured using a simulation model which is also built using the same set of features. In particular, the indirect learning method builds its model of MDP using the same feature set as the simulation model used for evaluation, and is likely to learn from training data that closely mirror the evaluation model. In the second setting, we assume imperfect modeling. That is, the learning methods have access to a restricted subset of the features. More precisely, we first build a simulation model of the MDP from the original batch data, using all of the features. We then *pretend* this model to be the real environment, and generate hypothetical training data via simulation using that model. The competing learning methods

6

Procedure Semidirect-RL

Premise:

A base learning module, Base, for regression is given. The expected immediate reward function, $\hat{R}$, has been estimated from data.

Input data: $D = \{e_i | i = 1, ..., N\}$ where

$e_i = \{\langle s_{i,j}, a_{i,j}, r_{i,j} \rangle | j = 1, ..., l_i\}$

(e_i is the i-th episode, and l_i is the length of e_i. A subepisode of e_i is any sub-sequence of e_i.)

1. For all e_i in a *randomly selected* subset R_0 of D
$D_{0,i} = \{\langle s_{i,j}, a_{i,j}, r_{i,j} \rangle | j = 1, ..., l_i\}$

2. $D_0 = \bigcup_{e_i \in R_0} D_{0,i}$

3. $Q_0 = \text{Base}(D_0)$.

4. For $k = 1$ to $final$

    4.1. For all e_i in a *randomly selected* set R_k of sub-episodes of length l from D

        4.1.1 $D_{k,i} = \emptyset$

        4.1.2 For $j = 1$ to $l - 1$

        If $Q_{k-1}(s_{i,j+1}, a_{i,j+1})) = \max_a Q_{k-1}(s_{i,j+1}, a)$ Then

        4.1.2.1 $v_{i,j}^{(k)} = Q_{k-1}(s_{i,j}, a_{i,j})$
$+\alpha_k(\hat{R}(s_{i,j}, a_{i,j}) + \gamma Q_{k-1}(s_{i,j+1}, a_{i,j+1})$
$-Q_{k-1}(s_{i,j}, a_{i,j}))$

        4.1.2.2 $D_{k,i} = D_{k,i} \cup \{\langle s_{i,j}, a_{i,j}, v_{i,j}^{(k)} \rangle\}$

    4.2 $D_k = \bigcup_{e_i \in R_k} D_{k,i}$

    4.3 $Q_k = \text{Base}(D_k)$

5. Output the final model, Q_{final}.

Figure 3. Semidirect reinforcement learning (Q-sampling)

then learn from this data set, using a restricted feature set. So in particular, the simulation model built by the indirect method is built with the restricted feature set, and thus is limited in its ability to mirror the real environment. The performance of the learning methods is then evaluated using a simulation model that was estimated using all of the feature set. Below we will give more details of these experimental set-ups.

3.1. Data Set

All of the training data we used were generated from the donation data set from KDD Cup 1998, which is available from the UCI KDD repository [2]. This data set concerns direct mail promotions for soliciting donations, and contains demographic data as well as promotion history of 22 campaigns, conducted monthly over an approximately two year period. The campaign information contained includes whether an individual was mailed or not, whether he or she responded or not and how much was donated. Additionally, if the individual was mailed, the date of the mailing

is available (month and year), and if the individual has responded, the date of the response is available. We used the training data portion of the original data set, which contains data for approximately 100 thousand selected individuals.[2] Out of the large number of demographic features contained in the data set, we selected only the age and income bracket. Based on the campaign information in the data, we generated a number of temporal features that are designed to capture the *state* of that individual at the time of each campaign. These include the frequency of gifts, recency of gift and promotion, number of recent promotions in the last 6 months, etc., and are summarized in Table 1.

Of particular interest are two types of features that we introduce specifically to capture the temporal aspects of the customer behavior. These are what we call "mailedbits" and "respondedbits" at the bottom of the list in the table. Both types of features are concerned with the retailer's actions and customer's behavior from a number of months ago. More precisely, mailedbit[n] takes on the value 1 just in case donation solicitation mail was mailed to that customer n months ago, and 0 otherwise. Similarly, respondedbit[n] assumes the value 1 if the customer responded n months ago, and 0 otherwise. Linear approximation of the expected cumulative profits as a function of the mailedbits essentially corresponds to the assertion that the expected profits made in any period has as its additive component responses to each of mailings in the past several months. A (possibly negatively weighted) linear combination of respondedbits would account for the so-called "saturation effects" due to a customer's limited capacity to respond or purchase in any given period of time.

It should be noted that many of these features are not explicitly present in the original data set, and need to be calculated from the data by traversing through the campaign history data. For example, the feature named *numprom* in the original KDD Cup data takes on a single value for each individual, and equals the total number of promotions mailed to that individual prior to the last campaign. In our case, *numprom* is computed for *each campaign* by traversing the campaign history data backwards from the last campaign, subtracting one every time a promotion was mailed in a campaign.[3]

3.2. The First Experiment Set-up

In the first set-up, episode data that were obtained from the original KDD cup data, having all of the features in

---

2   This is contained in "cup98lrn.zip" on the URL "http://kdd.ics.uci.edu/databases/kddcup98/kddcup98.html".

3   We note that we did not make use of the RFA codes included in the original data, which contain the so-called Recency/Frequency/Amount information for the individuals, since they did not contain enough information to recover their values for each campaign.

Features	Descriptions
age	individual's age
income	income bracket
ngiftall	number of gifts to date
numprom	number of promotions to date
frequency	ngiftall / numprom
recency	number of months since last gift
lastgift	amount in dollars of last gift
ramntall	total amount of gifts to date
nrecproms	num. of recent promotions (last 6 mo.)
nrecgifts	num. of recent gifts (last 6 mo.)
totrecamt	total amount of recent gifts (6 mo.)
recamtpergift	recent gift amount per gift (6 mo.)
recamtpergift	recent gift amount per prom (6 mo.)
promrecency	num. of months since last promotion
timelag	num. of mo's from first prom to gift
recencyratio	recency / timelag
promrecratio	promrecency / timelag
respondedbit[1]*	whether responded last month
respondedbit[2]*	whether responded 2 months ago
respondedbit[3]*	whether responded 3 months ago
mailedbit[1]*	whether promotion mailed last month
mailedbit[2]*	whether promotion mailed 2 mo's ago
mailedbit[3]*	whether promotion mailed 3 mo's ago
action	whether mailed in current promotion

Table 1. Features Used in Our Experiments

Table 1, were used by the various reinforcement learning methods. Therefore, the obtained models of the value function are all functions of these features. The performance of these methods was then evaluated via simulation using a model of MDP, also estimated essentially from the same data set, using the same set of features.

The MDP we constructed consists of two estimation models: one model $P(s, a)$ for the probability of response as a function of the state features and the action taken, and the other $A(s, a)$ for the expected amount of donation *given* that there is a response, as a function of the state features and the action. The $P(s, a)$ model was constructed using ProbE's naive-Bayes tree modeling capability, while $A(s, a)$ was constructed using linear-regressions tree modeling. Given these two models, it is easy to construct an MDP. The reward obtained is the amount of donation, as determined by $P(s, a)$ and $A(s, a)$, minus the mailing cost. The state transition function can be obtained by calculating the transition of each feature using the two models. Updates for other features can be computed similarly.

Given the above functional definition of an MDP, the evaluation by simulation was conducted as follows. Initially, we selected a subset (5,000) of the individuals, and set their initial states to be the states corresponding to their

states prior to a fixed campaign number (in experiments reported here, campaign number 1 was used). Starting with these initial states, we perform simulation using the MDP and the policy derived from the value function output by a reinforcement learning procedure. Utilizing the response probability model and the expected amount model, we compute the rewards and next states for all of them. We record the rewards thus obtained, and then go on to the next campaign. We repeat this procedure 20 times, simulating a sequence of 20 virtual campaigns.

3.3. The Second Experiment Set-up

In the second set-up, episode data obtained from the original KDD cup data, having all the features in Table 1, were used to obtain the same MDP that was used as an evaluation model in the first set-up. This model was then used to generate a set of episode data consisting of a restricted feature set, which we pretend to be a real world data set for this set-up. That is, this data set was used as input data set to various reinforcement learning methods, except those features with "*" in Table 1, the mailedbits and respondedbits, were masked out. Notice that the simulation model used internally by the indirect method only use this restricted feature set. The performance of the competing learning methods was then evaluated in the same way as in the first set-up, using the MDP built on the *entire* feature set. The intention behind this set-up is that detailed temporal features, such as mailedbits and respondebits, are pivotal in determining the actual customer behavior, but may be latent and not be available for use in analysis. The actual choice of these "latent" features are immaterial to the claims made in this paper - it is an example of what we consider to be a typical situation in the real world in which only a restricted subset of the features determining customer's behavior are visible and available for use in analysis and decision making.

4. Experimental Results

4.1. Direct v.s. Indirect Methods: First Set-up

We compared the performance of direct and indirect methods by the total (life time) profits obtained by the output policies, evaluated using the simulation model estimated from the same data. Figure 4 shows the total profits obtained by the direct (sarsa) and indirect methods, plotted as a function of the number of value iterations performed. The plots were obtained by averaging over 4 runs. Both the direct and indirect methods used as training data a subsample consisting of 10 thousand episodes, giving rise to 160 thousand event data. (The first 6 campaigns in each episode were discarded, due to lack of information regarding some of the temporal features.) The total profits are obtained us-

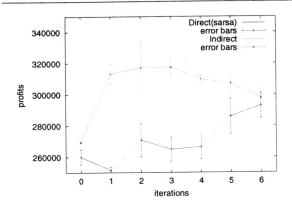

Figure 4. Total profits obtained by Direct and Indirect Methods in Experiment 1.

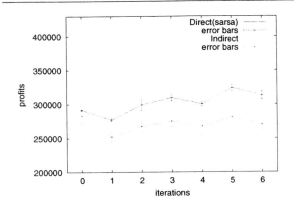

Figure 5. Total profits obtained by Direct and Indirect Methods in Experiment 2.

ing the simulation model as described in the previous section, and totaled over 20 campaigns. The error bars shown in the graph are the *standard errors* calculated from the total profits obtained in the four independent runs, namely

$$\sigma = \sqrt{\frac{\sum_{i=1}^{n}(P_i - \bar{P})^2/n - 1}{n}} \qquad (6)$$

where P_i is the total profit obtained in the i-th run, $\bar{P}$ is the average total profit, and n is the number of runs (4 in this case).

As one can see in Figure 4, in Experiment 1 in which the learning algorithms are given access to all features that characterize customer behavior, the indirect method performs better than the direct method. Recall that the above evaluation is conducted using a simulation model trained using the same features and is very closely mirrored by the internal simulation model used during learning of the indirect model, giving the indirect method an unfair advantage over the direct method. The direct method learned using only the original data set, which was generated presumably by a significantly different process in the real world.

4.2. Direct v.s. Indirect Methods: Second Set-up

We also compared the total (life time) profits obtained by the direct and indirect methods in the second set-up. The two methods were again run on training data consisting of 10 thousand episodes, or 160 thousand event data. The episode data were generated using a simulator, using a policy that was obtained by the Base method, one that tries to maximize the immediate rewards.

The results of these experiments are shown in Figure 5. These plots were obtained by averaging over 6 runs. As one can see in the graph, these results exhibit a rather striking contrast from the results in the first set-up. When learning is

performed with restricted attention, the performance of the indirect method degrades significantly. It seems to support the thesis that, in practical situations in which not all the relevant features are available for analysis, the direct methods are more likely to generate more reliable policies.

4.3. Effect of Semi-direct Methods

The performance of the semi-direct methods was compared against that of direct and semi-direct methods in the second set-up. The semi-direct method was run, performing sampling from a larger data set containing 50 thousand episodes, corresponding to 800 thousand event data, generated again using the same simulator. This is because the situation we suppose for the semi-direct methods is when we have abundance of training data, and not all of them can be used in each iteration of the value iteration in the interest of computational efficiency. It started with the same number (10 thousand) of episode data, corresponding to 160 thousand event data, sampled from this larger data in the initial iteration, and in the subsequent iterations selectively sampled event data from randomly selected sub-episodes containing 320 thousand events. We note that it used training data of comparable size to the direct and indirect methods in these subsequent iterations, by the nature of its selective sampling strategy.

Figure 6 shows the total profits obtained by two semi-direct methods, as well as by the direct (sarsa) and indirect methods (averaged over 6 runs). The results indicate that, while the profitability of the policies output by the semi-direct methods can become more unstable as the number of value iterations increases, well-performing policies can be obtained at earlier stages of value iteration. While CPU time used by the respective methods would be a more direct measure of computation time, it is also sensitive to the exact im-

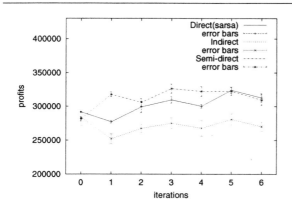

Figure 6. Total profits obtained by Direct, Indirect and Semi-direct Methods in Experiment 2.

plementation details, including the scalability properties of the base method. The data size is almost always a dominant factor in determining the computation time of the training process, and is a more robust measure. Since comparable data sizes were used by the respective methods, one can see that the semi-direct methods can be quite effective in reducing the computational requirement for obtaining policies of comparable profitability.

5. Conclusions

We proposed and evaluated a series of reinforcement learning methods for sequential targeted marketing. Our experimental results verify our initial premise that, in this application domain, direct methods of reinforcement learning are better suited than indirect methods. We also demonstrated that the "semi-direct" methods can be effective in reducing the computational burden. Our experiments were admittedly preliminary in nature. In the future, we plan to verify these claims in real world applications.

6. Acknowledgments

We thank Fateh Tipu for his help in carrying out our experiments.

References

[1] C. Apte, E. Bibelnieks, R. Natarajan, E. Pednault, F. Tipu, D. Campbell, and B. Nelson. Segmentation-based modeling for advanced targeted marketing. In *Proceedings of the Seventh ACM SIGKDD International Conference on Knowledge Discovery and Data Mining (SIGKDD)*, pages 408–413. ACM, 2001.

[2] S. D. Bay. UCI KDD archive. Department of Information and Computer Sciences, University of California, Irvine, 2000. http://kdd.ics.uci.edu/.

[3] D. P. Bertsekas and J. N. Tsitsiklis. *Neuro-Dynamic Programming*. Athena Scientific, 1996.

[4] P. Domingos. MetaCost: A general method for making classifiers cost sensitive. In *Proceedings of the Fifth International Conference on Knowledge Discovery and Data Mining*, pages 155–164. ACM Press, 1999.

[5] C. Elkan. The foundations of cost-sensitive learning. In *Proceedings of the Seventeenth International Joint Conference on Artificial Intelligence*, Aug. 2001.

[6] W. Fan, S. J. Stolfo, J. Zhang, and P. K. Chan. AdaCost: misclassification cost-sensitive boosting. In *Proc. 16th International Conf. on Machine Learning*, pages 97–105. Morgan Kaufmann, San Francisco, CA, 1999.

[7] L. P. Kaelbling, M. L. Littman, and A. W. Moore. Reinforcement learning: A survey. *Journal of Artificial Intelligence Research*, 4, 1996.

[8] D. D. Margineantu and T. G. Dietterich. Bootstrap methods for the cost-sensitive evaluation of classifiers. In *Proc. 17th International Conf. on Machine Learning*, pages 583–590. Morgan Kaufmann, San Francisco, CA, 2000.

[9] R. Natarajan and E. Pednault. Segmented regression estimators for massive data sets. In *Second SIAM International Conference on Data Mining*, Arlington, Virginia, 2002. to appear.

[10] E. Pednault, N. Abe, B. Zadrozny, H. Wang, W. Fan, and C. Apte. Sequential cost-sensitive decision making with reinforcement learning. In *Proceedings of the Eighth ACM SIGKDD International Conference on Knowledge Discovery and Data Mining*. ACM Press, 2002. To appear.

[11] G. A. Rummery and M. Niranjan. On-line q-learning using connectionist systems. Technical Report CUED/F-INFENG/TR 166, Cambridge University Engineering Department, 1994. Ph.D. thesis.

[12] R. S. Sutton and A. G. Barto. *Reinforcement Learning: An Introduction*. MIT Press, 1998.

[13] P. Turney. Cost-sensitive learning bibliography. Institute for Information Technology, National Research Council, Ottawa, Canada, 2000. http://extractor.iit.nrc.ca/bibliographies/cost-sensitive.html.

[14] X. Wang and T. Dietterich. Efficient value function approximation using regression trees. In *Proceedings of the IJCAI Workshop on Statistical Machine Learning for Large-Scale Optimization*, 1999.

[15] C. J. C. H. Watkins. *Learning from Delayed Rewards*. PhD thesis, Cambridge University, Cambridge, 1989.

[16] C. J. C. H. Watkins and P. Dayan. Q-learning. *Machine Learning*, 8:279–292, 1992.

[17] B. Zadrozny and C. Elkan. Learning and making decisions when costs and probabilities are both unknown. In *Proceedings of the Seventh International Conference on Knowledge Discovery and Data Mining*, 2001.

Investigative Profiling with Computer Forensic Log Data and Association Rules

Tamas Abraham and Olivier de Vel
Information Networks Division,
Defence Science and Technology Organisation,
PO Box 1500, Edinburgh SA 5111, Australia
{tamas.abraham,olivier.devel}@dsto.defence.gov.au

Abstract

Investigative profiling is an important activity in computer forensics that can narrow the search for one or more computer perpetrators. Data mining is a technique that has produced good results in providing insight into large volumes of data. This paper describes how the association rule data mining technique may be employed to generate profiles from log data and the methodology used for the interpretation of the resulting rule sets. The process relies on background knowledge in the form of concept hierarchies and beliefs, commonly available from, or attainable by, the computer forensic investigative team. Results obtained with the profiling system has identified irregularities in computer logs.

1 Introduction

Computer Forensics undertakes the *post-mortem*, or "after-the-event" analysis of computer crime. Of particular importance is the requirement to successfully narrow the potentially large search space often presented to investigators of such crimes. This usually involves some form(s) of guided processing of the data collected as evidence in order to produce a shortlist of suspicious activities. Investigators can subsequently use this shortlist to examine related evidence in more detail [6].

Investigative profiling is an important activity in computer forensics that can significantly narrow the search for the perpetrator and reason about the perpetrator's behaviour. This is analogous to criminal profiling which focuses on establishing personality characteristics of an offender in order to identify the type of person involved in the crime under investigation (e.g., arson). Profiling can also aid in identifying the type of activity the perpetrator is engaged in e.g., e-mail authorship analysis may identify the educational level or gender of the offender and may, consequently, be able to establish if an e-mail has been masqueraded [8].

Data Mining is employed to analyse large data sets, as might occur in a typical computer forensics investigation, in order to discover potentially useful, previously unknown regularities within data. In contrast to other, more conventional technologies, it has been able to produce good results on large data sets where both incompleteness and noise may be present, e.g., [9].

Data mining for the more specific purpose of constructing personal profiles has been used in the context of customer personalisation. Here, marketing content and services are tailored to an individual on the basis of knowledge about their preferences and behaviour. Applications include content-based and collaborative filtering-based recommendation systems, customer profiling [2, 1, 13], fraud detection [10], web browsing activities [7, 18, 23, 17]. Content-based recommendation systems model the link between data content and a person's preferences for that content whereas collaborative recommendation systems model the link between a person's preferences and other persons' preferences for the given data content [15, 19]. Customer profiling is growing in importance in e-commerce. Both factual and individual behavioural information are derived from the customer's e-transactional history. The personalisation of web browsing activities for the purpose of improving the user's access to the web has also attracted interest recently. Techniques for the modeling of the user's web access behaviour are varied including; the use of a page content interestingness metric (N-grams) for capturing a user's interests [7], web page navigation dependencies for page predictive pre-fetching [18], web page clustering for deriving aggregate user profiles [17], sequential web page patterns for discovering negatively-correlated components within a web site structure [23]. However, most web personalisation applications deal with aggregate or classes of user profiles rather than individual user profiles.

In this paper, we describe techniques to profile and analyse computer forensic data. We use a combination of existing techniques not yet employed in this application domain, modified where necessary to accommodate the particular environment. In Section 2, we introduce the elements

11

used in our approach to computer forensic profiling. Further details are given in Section 3 about data preparation and the need for guiding the investigative process. Section 4 describes the algorithms we use and how they have been adopted for our needs. Tests performed on actual computer log data are detailed in Section 5, followed by our conclusions in Section 6.

2 Background to Investigative Profiling

An offender profile consists of two components, namely the factual component and behavioural component. The factual profile (FP) consists of factual background knowledge about the offender such as their name, employee status, computer user name(s), relationships with other employees and organisations etc. The behavioural profile (BP) incorporates knowledge about an offender's crime scene-related behaviour. Behaviour profile knowledge is derived from a variety of sources namely, log file transactions, header and body of e-mails, telecommunications call-record data patterns and so on.

The behavioural profile, BP, can be modeled in different ways. For example, a BP can be represented as a union of sub-profile hierarchies (PH_j) such as, authorship profile, software application usage profile, log-in profile etc, or

$$BP \leftarrow \bigcup_j^M PH_j$$

A profile hierarchy is a knowledge representation scheme using a hierarchy of multi-slot frames, similar to a concept hierarchy (described in Section 3.1), that characterises a behavioural profile.

Alternatively, BP can also be modeled as a set of association rules:

$$BP \leftarrow \{R_i | i = 1, 2, \ldots N\}$$

Here, the rule attributes can be obtained from the raw data and/or selected from the profile hierarchy nodes. For example, the rule "If user X is a system administrator, then the application $Y = nmap$ (a stealth port scanner) executed" may be a valid rule in a system administrator profile (assuming that port scanning, as used in his/her current job context, is employed for system hardening), but probably not in a finance contractor profile.

In this paper we study user behavioural profiles derived from event data in log files. These profiles are conveniently represented by a set of implications or association rules $\{R_i | i = 1, 2, \ldots N\}$ of the form

$$R_i : antecedent \Rightarrow consequent$$

These rules provide an intuitive and declarative way to describe user behaviour [10]. For example, the rule

$R_0 :$ (**StaffType** $= admin$) $\wedge$ (**DayOfWeek** $= tuesday$) $\wedge$ (**Application** $= database$) $\Rightarrow$ (**Access** $= valid$)

states that "Administration staff that work on Tuesday have

a valid access to a database application". Note that an association rule indicates the presence of some correlation between the rule's antecedent and consequent, but does not necessarily imply any causality.

2.1 Profiling with Association Rules

Association rule generation has been one of the most successful techniques in data mining. It originated as a tool for discovering sets of items that occur together in supermarket basket data [4]. Since then, it has evolved to address a multitude of other types of problems, to a point where it can even be used for purposes such as multi-dimensional inter-transaction mining [16]. Supposing $\mathcal{I} = \{i_1, i_2, \ldots, i_m\}$ is a set of items occurring in a data set, an association rule can be expressed by the formula $A \Rightarrow B : (s, c)$, where $A, B \subseteq \mathcal{I}$ are groups of items of size k_A and k_B, respectively, where $k_A + k_B \leq m$ and $A \cap B = \emptyset$. We refer to the combined collection of items in A and B as an *itemset* of length $k = k_A + k_B$. The variables s and c express support and confidence percentages for the rule, where support s indicates how frequently the items in A and B occur together in the data, while confidence c is the conditional probability $P(B|A)$ where the probability $P(x)$ is estimated using the support percentage of the set x. For example, the rule $(bread \wedge butter) \rightarrow (milk) : (15\%, 70\%)$ produced from a supermarket transactional database states that customers that buy bread and butter together are also 70% likely to purchase milk, with 15% of the total number of records supporting this claim.

One of the potential uses for associations is the building of rule sets that describe behavioural data [2, 1, 3]. This may be data collected about people or the operation of some systems. Often in computer forensic investigations, this information could be found in log files on a computer system. The rule sets generated from this data can be considered to describe a profile contained within the data set. Profiles produced this way, however, are usually not complete. The support percentage parameter used in association mining introduces loss into the rule set. This is because only data that occurs frequently enough (that is, satisfies a pre-defined minimum support) is used in the rule generation process. In the forensic sense, however, this is not necessarily a disadvantage. Regularities that are not picked up in the profile due to not satisfying support may be looked at as non-habitual and can be investigated as contrary to regular behaviour, if necessary.

Another important aspect of forensic profiling is that a user profile is generated using available evidence and does not change once produced. Additional evidence may be added later, but this should be regarded as the incompleteness of initial evidence rather than the evolution of an existing profile. In this case, the profile should be re-generated.

Recognising temporal segments, or evolution *within* a profile, however, is quite important and analysis of such phenomena can be a major part of the profile evaluation process.

2.2 Deviation in Association Rule Profiles

One of the first steps in a computer forensic investigation is to look for unusual events. For example, if an attacker gains super-user privileges on a computer system, he may use them to perform actions not normally instigated by the real super-user(s). This would clearly be a deviation from the super-user profile as supported by data up to the time of intrusion. There are two ways this may be evidenced in the data and the profile generated on the full data set:

1. As data entries with not enough support to be represented as association rules: In order to find such entries, there must exist a mechanism for the investigator to query the data set for entries not fitting the profile.

2. As association rules making up part of the profile: It would hence be important to identify this section of the profile as being anomalous, or at least different from other parts of the profile. Assigning a temporal scope to rules making up the profile could help an investigator recognise that something potentially unusual may have occurred at a certain time in the life of the system being investigated.

There are, of course, caveats to the above. The attacker may have covered his/her tracks, for example, by removing entries from the log files. If he/she was thorough, he/she may have only removed entries corresponding to his/her own actions, or, alternatively, may have removed all records, or every record stored during the period of the criminal activity. In this case, the lack of evidence may warrant further investigation.

3 Building Profiles

The data obtained for computer forensic investigations are usually information stored on computers and networks. They range from system log files to databases, personal user files and other items that may be located on a computer. To build a profile for a particular user, many of these items may need to be examined both individually and as a collection of interrelated items with potential relationships existing between recorded activities. Profiling algorithms are therefore expected to be of varying complexity. A simple algorithm may produce rules based on the sporadic occurrences of data observed in a single file, another may be required to recognise temporal dependencies or causal relationships in user activity recorded across several files.

Since computer forensics undertakes the post-mortem analysis of computer crime, much of the analysis is done off-line. Therefore, emphasis is more often on effectiveness than efficiency in order to produce a smaller set of targeted conclusions, and reduce overall human investigation time. For example, it is preferable to achieve a low rate of false negatives at the expense of increased computational time and number of false positives.

Much of the information found on a computer is expected to be in a format not suited for immediate analysis. An investigator must facilitate this by providing details on the subsets of data intended for analysis, their format and conversion requirements, and available background knowledge. Some of this can be achieved through automated means. Filtering, the removal of unwanted information and the aggregation of separate data items are some of the more important activities during this stage of the analytical process.

3.1 Concept Hierarchies and Beliefs

Background knowledge in data mining is popularly expressed in the form of concept hierarchies and is often used in the rule generation process [21, 11]. The hierarchies convey a generalisation of concepts from node to root (which is usually the concept any) and can be represented as a set of parent-child relationships in a data file. An investigator may be prompted with a set of node level concepts found in the data and asked to abstract it to higher level ones according to his/her liking. This hierarchy, which is generally domain-dependent in forensics investigations, can then be used in the mining process to produce a profile that contains rules with elements at an arbitrary level of abstraction. There should be no requirement for a concept hierarchy to be complete for profiling to operate correctly. A set of hierarchy fragments is often more desirable as it helps to avoid over-generalisation by not including very high level concepts in the search process.

Concept hierarchies may be employed in two different ways during profile generation. In a *drill-down* approach, rules are initially generated for high concept levels. Interesting high-level rules can be further investigated by descending the concept hierarchies for some attributes. In a *drill-up* approach, a larger number of rules are produced with a potentially low support level requirement using the attribute values present in the data. By ascending concept hierarchies, higher level rules with increased support levels may be obtained.

Evolution within a profile is an important indicator of potentially irregular activities. A profiling algorithm is expected to be able to attach temporal tags to rules indicating intervals of validity if so required. Concept hierarchies, therefore, must accommodate such functionality. This hap-

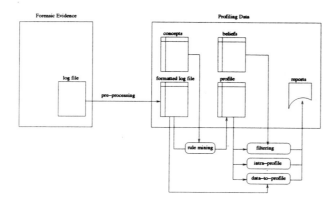

Figure 1. Data flow diagram of the profiling process.

pens at two levels – changes in the structure of concept hierarchy over time, and changes in the position of a leaf node value over time.

In addition to using hierarchical abstraction of attribute values, investigators may have pre-conceived beliefs about a case being investigated. A separate collection of rules can be used to describe a set of such beliefs. These can be used to focus the investigation by searching for specific regularities in profiles, or may also be used to reduce the profile by discarding rules that are defined as trivial [1]. Furthermore, the use of these rules may allow a post-processing algorithm to identify rules that contradict existing beliefs.

4   The Profiling Process

The data flow diagram in Figure 1 describes the data, rules and processes used for profiling purposes. It incorporates references to background knowledge such as concept hierarchies and beliefs, and the final conclusions resulting from the forensic analysis (detailed in Section 4.2).

4.1   Basic Profile Generation Algorithm

The association mining algorithm implemented for forensic analysis is designed to generate a profile using a single input file. Depending on the desired level of background knowledge to be employed, three approaches can be distinguished:

- Generating rules with no concept hierarchies and beliefs. This method is likely to produce a large set of rules that may require extensive user analysis [1].

- Generating rules with concept hierarchies but no beliefs. This solution allows for production of high-level rules and/or generalisation of lower level rules permitting both *drill-down* and *drill-up*.

- Generating rules with concept hierarchies and beliefs. This permits the same possibilities as above, as well as

filtering made possible by the availability of existing beliefs.

The usual steps of *data filtering*, *data conversion*, and, when background knowledge is used, the creation of *concept hierarchies* and *beliefs* precedes profiling.

The association mining algorithm M2IS-c (*Matrix to Itemsets using concepts*) we employ, shown in Algorithm 1, is a version of the classic *Apriori* association mining algorithm [5]. Note that the algorithm is not a new, improved implementation, and was mainly selected because it suits our analytical environment. Its novelty lies in the fact that it performs binary mining in memory in conjunction with concept hierarchy ascension. Details of this process are outlined below.

Let $\mathbb{A} = \{\mathbf{A}_1, \mathbf{A}_2, \ldots, \mathbf{A}_l\}$ be a set of l attributes. Each attribute $\mathbf{A}_i$, $i = 1, \ldots, l$, can take on a discrete set of mutually exclusive values. Let a record r be a conjunction of values taken from each available attribute. Let $\mathbb{R}$ be a collection of n records. In this finite collection, each attribute $\mathbf{A}_i$ may take on a finite number of discrete values. Let the number of these values be denoted by m_i for attribute $\mathbf{A}_i$. The total number of distinct attribute values that appear in $\mathbb{R}$ is then $\sum_{i=1}^{l} m_i$. Let $\mathbb{H} = \{H_1, H_2, \ldots, H_N\}$ be a set of domain-dependent *concept hierarchies* or *attribute taxonomies*. Each concept hierarchy H_j, $j \in \{1, 2, \ldots, N\}$ in the concept forest is formulated as a direct acyclic graph (DAG), with none, one or more hierarchies assigned to each attribute $\mathbf{A}_i$, $i = 1, \ldots, l$. Concept hierarchies are structurally similar to profile hierarchies discussed in Section 2. The main difference is that each pair of adjacent nodes in a DAG H_j represents an "*is-a*" or generalisation-specialisation relationship, rather than multi-slot frame profile content relationship. Examples of concept hierarchies are the IP (Internet Protocol) domain name hierarchy, the functional directory of an organisation, etc. Leaf nodes in concept hierarchies belonging to attribute $\mathbf{A}_i$ therefore generally (but not necessarily) represent values occurring in $\mathbb{R}$. Non-leaf-nodes in concept hierarchies represent higher level abstractions of leaf-nodes and can not be values that occur in the original data. Denote the collection of concept hierarchies with these leaf-nodes removed by $\hat{\mathbb{H}} = \{\hat{H}_1, \hat{H}_2, \ldots, \hat{H}_N\}$. Let $\hat{m}_i$ denote the number of non-leaf concept nodes defined in all hierarchies for attribute $\mathbf{A}_i$ in $\mathbb{H}$, or equivalently, the number of nodes in $\hat{\mathbb{H}}$. Let $m = \sum_{i=1}^{l} m_i + \hat{m}_i$ be the length of a binary vector $v = \{b_1, \ldots, b_m\}$ where bit $b_i \in \{0, 1\}$ uniquely corresponds to an attribute value or concept occurring in $\mathbb{R} \cup \hat{\mathbb{H}}$. Require that bits corresponding to values and concepts of a given attribute be consecutive, with concepts having higher indexes than attribute values. That is,

$$v = \{\underbrace{b_1, \ldots, b_{m_1}, b_{m_1+1}, \ldots, b_{m_1+\hat{m}_1}}_{\mathbf{A}_1}, \ldots, \underbrace{b_{m-m_l-\hat{m}_l+1}, \ldots, b_m}_{\mathbf{A}_l}\}$$

14

Let $M : r \to v$ be a mapping of an actual record r in $\mathbb{R}$ to a binary vector v such that each attribute value and its higher level concepts in corresponding hierarchies are represented by 1 in v with all other values set to 0. Let the function $attr(b_i)$ for bit $b_i \in v$ return the attribute $\mathbf{A}_j$, $j \in \{1, \ldots, l\}$, to which b_i was mapped to. According to the consecutiveness requirement above this means that if $attr(b_i) \neq attr(b_j)$ for some pair $(i, j) \in \{1, \ldots, m\}$, and $i < j$, then the indexes for all bit-pairs for the two attributes involved will exhibit the same *less than* relationship. This property is utilised in the algorithm below.

Algorithm 1: M2IS-c

Inputs: An $(n \times m)$ bit-matrix $\mathcal{M}$; an $(m \times m)$ concept relationship bit-matrix $\mathcal{C}$; $minsup \in [0,1]$
Outputs: A collection of itemsets $\mathcal{I}$ satisfying $minsup$, $\mathcal{I} = \bigcup_k I^k$

1. Initialise $k := 1$
2. For each column $i = 1, \ldots, m$ of $\mathcal{M}$,
   2.1. Initialise support $sup_i := \sum_{j=0}^{n} b_{ji}, b_{ij} \in \{0,1\}$
3. Add 1-itemsets I_1^i to $\mathcal{I}$ where $sup_i / n \geq minsup$
4. Increment k. Stop if $k > l$, otherwise for the current k:
   4.1. Initialise k-itemset count $count_k := 0$
   4.2. Generate potential k-itemset from existing $(k-1)$-itemsets by finding next pair $\{I_i^{k-1} = \{i_i^1, \ldots, i_i^{k-1}\}, I_j^{k-1} = \{i_j^1, \ldots, i_j^{k-1}\}\}$ so that $i_i^o = i_j^o, o = 1, \ldots, k-2, i_i^{k-1} < i_j^{k-1}$, and i_i^{k-1} is not in a concept relationship with i_j^{k-1}
   4.3. For potential itemset $I_{ij}^k = \{i_i^1, \ldots, i_i^{k-1}, i_j^{k-1}\}$ calculate support sup in $\mathcal{M}$ by counting the rows where all bits appearing in I_{ij}^k are set.
   4.4. If $sup/n \geq minsup$, add I_{ij}^k into $\mathcal{I}$ as a k-itemset and increment $count_k$
   4.5. Go to Step 4.1 until all potential k-itemsets are found.
5. Stop if $count_k = 0$, otherwise go to Step 4.

An extension to the *Apriori* algorithm in M2IS-c is the incorporation of concept hierarchy values into the mining process by including them in the binary mapping[1]. This is desirable in cases where individual values may not have enough support to be represented in a profile, but their higher level equivalents have. A consequence of this approach is the introduction of potential itemsets with both child and parent concepts present. Itemsets containing such pairs express trivial relationships and need to be pruned as they dilute the final rule set. The removal of itemsets containing child-parent pairs is an additional feature of the modified algorithm used in the profiling process. This ensures that the maximum length of any itemset produced is limited to the number of attributes l in the original data set. Child-parent relationships can be represented by a bit-matrix with ones indicating relationship and zeroes not[2]. As this lookup can be achieved in a single step, we refer the

---

[1] Note that the use of memory for storage of the main bit-matrix may be problematic for large data sets on non-specialised systems.

[2] A single matrix would suffice for this purpose. Individual matrices for each attribute could be preferable for memory efficiency as ones can only

reader to the original article for discussion of the complexity of the algorithm [5].

4.2 Profile Analysis Algorithms

The generation of profiles is only the first step in an investigation. Algorithms for analysing the profiles need to be provided and utilised either interactively or by automated means. Some of the functionality required can be described by the following list:

- *Filtering* profiles. This process allows investigators to reduce the profile set to concentrate on subsets that may be of higher interest. It can be guided by a previously defined set of beliefs about the expected behaviour of the profile. Rules complying with beliefs may automatically be dropped, while rules in contradiction with beliefs may be assigned higher priority in the investigative process.

- Contrasting raw *data to profiles*. This produces a list or summary of data entries that deviate from the profile. It is generated for data that did not have enough support to be part of the profile, but convey potentially unexpected information different from the profile.

- Generating *intra-profile* contrasts. This means finding rules in a profile that are in contradiction with other rules in the same profile. These rules may indicate a shift in behaviour, whose causes may need to be investigated. To measure difference between rules, a distance metric will be required.

We propose a simple profile analysis algorithm to measure the degree of anomalies in the profile elements.

4.3 A Metric for Profile Element Distance

One of the more interesting and complex issues in the analysis of a profile is the discovery of contradicting elements within the profile. These contradictions may be identified both at the itemset level and in the final ruleset. In this paper, we concentrate on contradictions in itemsets, using a Manhattan distance based metric that makes differences easy to detect. For example, some of the characteristics of a particular person may be repeated in several itemsets with only a single attribute value being different. This difference can be attributed to:

- *Repetition*. In this case, the attribute represents a value (for example, day of the week), that indicates that the same set of characteristics is valid for multiple occasions.

---

appear along the diagonal in $(m_i + \hat{m}_i) \times (m_i + \hat{m}_i)$ subsets for attributes $\mathbf{A}_i, i = 1, \ldots, l$.

- *Generalisation.* The attribute value has been replaced by the higher level concept that retains the same set of characteristics, but possibly with larger support.
- *Contradiction.* The attribute value is in contradiction with another, potentially pre-defined as a belief. For example, a user may be allocated a particular computer but the profile indicates the use of a different one.

The recognition of the occurrences of these differences may be automated. Some may be combined (repetition) or discarded as unimportant (generalisation or trivial beliefs). Others may require inspection by investigators to decide if they are worth following up. Algorithm 2 (*Itemset to itemset distance*) describes the calculation of a metric that indicates the closeness or similarity of two k-itemsets by comparing their elements. It employs the $attr()$ function defined prior to presenting Algorithm 1 and assumes that the itemsets to be compared are represented by bits from the bit-vector v format defined there. Because of the consecutiveness requirement, it follows that the bits at position o in a k-itemset be in three distinct relationships:

1. They may belong to different attributes $\mathbf{A}_i \neq \mathbf{A}_j$.
2. They may belong to the same attribute $\mathbf{A}_i$ and be the same attribute value or concept, or have a child-parent relationship.
3. They may belong to the same attribute $\mathbf{A}_i$ but be different values/concepts with no relationship.

Algorithm 2: IS2IS-dist

Inputs: K-itemsets $I_i = \{b_1^i, \ldots, b_k^i\}$ and $I_j = \{b_1^j, \ldots, b_k^j\}$; an $(m \times m)$ concept relationship bit-matrix $\mathcal{C}$; attribute function $attr(b)$

Outputs: Distance $d \in [0, \ldots, k+1]$
1. Initialise $d := 0$
2. For $o := 1$ to k
   2.1. If $attr(b_i^o) \neq attr(b_j^o)$, set $d := k+1$ and stop
   2.2. If $(b_i^o \neq b_j^o) \wedge (b_i^o$ not in child-parent relationship with $b_j^o)$, increment d

---

It can be seen that distance d of Algorithm 2 can be less than the length of the itemset k only if the same attribute value/concept is found duplicated (i.e. equals or is in a concept relationship with) at least once in the two itemsets being compared. It also follows that the total number of such duplicates found and d equals k, with $d = 0$ only if the respective elements of the two itemsets are the same or are in a concept relationship. Thus, the metric is a non-negative integer $d \in [0, \ldots, k+1]$, from which only values $0 < d < k$ are of interest.

A similar algorithm can be devised to calculate the distance between a k-itemset and a data record (IS2DAT-dist)[3]. This can be achieved by expanding the itemset to

---

[3]This algorithm is not presented due to its similarity to Algorithm 2.

User	Console	Origin	Weekday	Date	Time	Duration
samson	ftp	cpe-203-21-225-3	Mon	Apr 16	21:24 - 21:31	(00:07)
ftp	ftp	c81010.upc-c.che	Mon	Apr 16	20:58 - 20:59	(00:00)
everett	ttyp1	host-216-252-150	Mon	Apr 16	20:24 - 22:25	(02:01)
max	ftp	max2.cs.xyu.edu	Mon	Apr 16	15:59 - 16:00	(00:00)
evelyn	ttyp1	marlin.xyu.edu.a	Mon	Apr 16	15:07 - 15:12	(00:05)
joseph	ftp	188.191.47.170	Mon	Apr 16	14:23 - 14:23	(00:00)
joseph	ttyp1	188.191.47.170	Mon	Apr 16	13:05 - 14:45	(01:40)
pedro	ftp	188.191.47.157	Mon	Apr 16	12:49 - 13:05	(00:15)
pedro	ftp	188.191.47.157	Mon	Apr 16	12:15 - 12:38	(00:23)
robert	ttyp1	hamilton.cs.xyu.	Mon	Apr 16	11:03 - 11:03	(00:00)
pedro	ftp	188.191.47.157	Mon	Apr 16	10:58 - 11:09	(00:10)
robert	ttyp3	hamilton.cs.xyu.	Mon	Apr 16	10:45 - 10:58	(00:13)

Figure 2. Example time slice of past and current user login information as obtained by executing the UNIX last command.

hold *nil* values for attributes not originally in the itemset, then comparing this itemset with the data record the same way as comparing two l-itemsets. The difference between Algorithm 2 and this modified version is that d is not incremented for attributes where the itemset holds a *nil* value. This limits d to a maximum value of k.

5 Data, Experiments and Results

To evaluate the profiling methodology proposed in this paper, a number of experiments have been performed. Both Algorithms 1 and 2 have been implemented as well as IS2DAT-dist. As input, log files captured by executing the UNIX **last** command were used, which searches the *wtmp* system log file and lists past and current user login information for a computer. An example output from executing the **last** command is shown in Figure 2.

Note that the data used in our experiments are actual log data recorded by a UNIX-based computer set up as a server with remote login access. However, in order to preserve anonymity, the data attribute name instances have been modified. Furthermore, there was no implication of inappropriate behaviour in the data set.

Of several columns of information generated, six attributes were copied or composed into a table containing formatted input. Some filtering was performed at this stage to remove incomplete (current) and non-user (e.g. *shutdown*) logins. The table, using additional higher level concepts from attribute hierarchies, was then mined to produce a profile containing association rules. Intra-profile and data-to-profile contrasting was then performed.

The distance metric of IS2IS-dist and IS2DAT-dist was employed to produce reports for both contrasting methods.

5.1 Intra-Profile Experiments

Intra-profile contrasts were calculated only for itemsets of the same length. For example, in one test, from about 2000 original data records, approximately 2200 itemsets with more than 1 element were produced. Intra-profile contrasting produced roughly 43000 distances that were less than the lengths of the itemsets being compared. Although this is a far smaller number than what it potentially could have been, it is still more than what can be perused manually. To reduce this set further, additional strategies need to be devised. One option is to prioritise attributes. That is, if difference is measured only in a particular attribute that may not be carrying important information (such as day of the week), then pairs exhibiting distance only in such attributes may be dropped. Similarly, a strategy may be employed to drop contrasts that are too "high". That is, the distance metric for a particular itemset length may be regarded as high, even though it satisfies the initial constraint of being less than the length. This may, for example, render all distances produced for 2-itemsets unnecessary. Finally, focusing techniques may be provided to filter the distances for certain attributes or attribute values. One of the more interesting contrasts produced by IS2IS-dist during testing was the 1-distance pair

$$I_0 : (\textbf{User} = miami) \wedge (\textbf{Origin} = miami)$$
$$I_1 : (\textbf{User} = pedro) \wedge (\textbf{Origin} = adelaide)$$

which indicates that the same user has been logging in from two very different geographic locations. Further inspection of this contrast revealed that the user in question left his place of work in Adelaide for another in Miami while still regularly accessing his old Adelaide account.

5.2 Data-to-Profile Experiments

The filtering requirement to reduce the set of distances to manageable proportions becomes even more evident with data-to-profile contrasts. Without pre-processing, each itemset needs to be compared to every data record, potentially producing a much larger result set than for intra-profile contrasts. This is partly due to the fact that a number of records are not included in the profile due to unsatisfactory support. Each of these records could produce small distances to itemsets similar to it that made it into the profile. As in the case of intra-profile contrasts, measures can be taken to reduce the final result set. In addition to the strategies outlined in Section 5.1, duplicate records may be removed by post-processing the results. Also, data-to-profile distances may be zero, if a particular data record was one of those used to generate the itemset it is being compared to. These distances should also be pruned from the results.

Figure 3 shows some of the distances from a test calculated for a particular itemset of length 5 (top row). Non-zero distances up to a maximum value of 2 were allowed in order to list contrasts where difference is present in not too many attributes. Duplicates were removed and as mentioned, some attributes were sanitised to remove confidential information from the data. The itemset contains generalised concepts for both the *User* and *Origin* attributes, while *Duration* is represented by concepts categorising a

Dist	Duration	User	Console	Origin	Weekday
-	UpToHalfHour	lecturer	ftp	cs.xyu.edu.au	Mon
1	UpToHalfHour	clyde	ftp	188.191.47.160	Mon
2	FewMinutes	clyde	ftp	188.191.47.160	Mon
2	UpToHalfHour	ftp	ftp	lizard.cs.xyu.ed	Fri
2	FewMinutes	everett	ftp	host-216-252-150	Mon
2	UpToHalfHour	john	ftp	188.191.47.161	Thu
2	NoMinutes	joseph	ftp	188.191.47.170	Mon
1	NoMinutes	max	ftp	max2.cs.xyu.edu	Mon
1	UpToHalfHour	max	ftp	max2.cs.xyu.edu	Tue
1	UpToHalfHour	max	ftp	max2.cs.xyu.edu	Thu
1	UpToHalfHour	max	ftp	max2.cs.xyu.edu	Fri
2	FewMinutes	max	ftp	max2.cs.xyu.edu	Thu
2	FewMinutes	milo	ftp	bet.cs.xyu.edu.a	Fri
2	NoMinutes	milo	ftp	bet.cs.xyu.edu.a	Sun
2	UpToHalfHour	milo	ttyp1	bet.cs.xyu.edu.a	Fri
1	UpToHalfHour	pedro	ftp	188.191.47.157	Thu
1	UpToHalfHour	pedro	ftp	188.191.47.157	Fri
2	FewMinutes	pedro	ftp	188.191.47.157	Fri
2	NoMinutes	pedro	ftp	188.191.47.157	Thu
2	30-60Minutes	pedro	ftp	188.191.47.157	Wed
2	UpToHalfHour	pedro	ttyp1	cay.cs.xyu.edu.a	Wed
2	NoMinutes	pedro	ftp	188.191.47.157	Wed
2	NoMinutes	stuart	ftp	sloth.cs.xyu.edu	Tue
2	UpToHalfHour	stuart	ttyp2	1cust81.tnt2.tow	Mon
2	FewHours	stuart	ftp	1cust81.tnt2.tow	Mon
2	UpToHalfHour	vernon	ttyp2	barn.cs.xyu.edu.	Mon

Figure 3. Example data-to-profile distances from IS2DAT-dist for a sample profile element and a collection of data records, ordered by *User* for readability

potentially large number of discrete values. From the definition of the metric, values/concepts in the same hierarchy have a distance of zero, which explains the diversity of rows of (non-generalised) values in the data having similar distances. For readability, we give here some of the concept relationships from the otherwise rather large hierarchies that exist for *User* and *Origin*:

$$\{max, milo, pedro, stuart\} \subset lecturer,$$
$$\{*.cs.xyu.edu.au, 188.191.47.*\} \subset cs.xyu.edu.au \subset$$
$$xyu.edu.au \subset adelaide,$$
$$\{*.tnt2.tow.net.au, 198.twn0103.twn.net.au\} \subset$$
$$ISP.adelaide \subset adelaide.$$

Using this information, the first data row with $d = 1$ shows that user *clyde* is not a *lecturer*, whilst for *lecturers max* and *pedro*, who log onto university computers, we can observe that the same *wtmp* login information is valid for several weekdays other than Monday.

Figure 3, as is, contains superfluous information. Depending on the support used in mining the profile, some or most of the data records contribute to itemsets generated by the algorithm. Comparing a k-itemset to data that contributes to another k-itemset is a repetition of comparing an itemset with another. Crosschecking a data record against every other k-itemset prior to calculating a distance would, however, be even less cost-effective. Instead, a strategy of producing distances in a matrix form for k-itemsets, $k = 2, \ldots, l$, then discarding rows with at least one zero in it, would be a better solution. Alternatively, a separate algorithm may parse the data set to locate individual occurrences of records that do not contribute to any itemset of a given length, and then run the contrasting algorithm against this filtered data set only. This is indeed the requirement proposed in Section 4.2 for data-to-profile contrasting.

6 Conclusions and Future Directions

The initial implementation of the profiling analysis process described in this paper has resulted in promising results capable of identifying irregularities in computer logs that can serve as useful evidence in computer crime investigations. Profile analysis, however, forms only a part of the investigative process and relies heavily on expert knowledge. It is therefore best perceived as a component in a larger collection of tools designed to aid the forensic investigator.

The profiling tool presented in this paper presents further opportunities for enhancement. One such area is the handling of multiple log information in a single process. Multidimensional mining may offer a solution for this problem, with some interesting work already found in the literature [16, 20]. Alternatively, it may be possible to "flatten" several logs into a sequence of "events", for which more traditional sequential mining techniques can be applied. Further improvements may be achieved by replacing the mining algorithm used in profiling. One obvious candidate is the attribute-oriented induction technique [14]. This technique compacts a collection of records into a generalised relation, or a conjunction of generalised records where individual attribute values are replaced by higher level concepts by ascending concept hierarchies. One of the advantages of this technique is that the final rule set incorporates information about every record in the original data set. Further work is also to be carried out in the intelligent presentation of results, notably in the provision of appropriate visual interpretation of the profiles and its potential contrasts. Contrast measures currently used are itemset-specific. Deriving distance measures for rules, such as the value distance metric (VDM) [22] may yield better results in identifying discrepancies. Some of the better known data mining interestingness measures [12], or variations of, may also be adopted for this purpose.

References

[1] G. Adomavicius and A. Tuzhilin. Expert-driven validation of rule-based user models in personalization applications. *Data Mining and Knowledge Discovery*, 5(1/2):33–58, 2001.

[2] G. Adomavicius and A. Tuzhilin. Using data mining methods to build customer profiles. *Computer*, 34(2):74–82, 2001.

[3] C. Aggarwal, Z. Sun, and P. Yu. Online algorithms for finding profile association rules. In *Proceedings of the ACM International Conference on Information and Knowledge Management (CIKM-98)*, Bethesda, MD, USA, 1998.

[4] R. Agrawal, T. Imielinski, and A. Swami. Mining associations between sets of items in massive databases. In *Proceedings of the ACM SIGMOD Int. Conference on Management of Data*, Washington, DC, USA, May 1993.

[5] R. Agrawal, H. Mannila, R. Srikant, H. Toivonen, and A. Verkamo. *Advances in Knowledge Discovery and Data Mining*, chapter Fast discovery of association rules. AAAI Press, 1996.

[6] E. Casey. *Digital Evidence and Computer Crime*. Academic Press, 2000.

[7] P. K. Chan. A non-invasive learning approach to building web user profiles. In *Proceedings of the Workshop on Web Usage Analysis and User Profiling (WEBKDD'99)*, 1999.

[8] O. de Vel, A. Anderson, M. Corney, and G. Mohay. Mining e-mail content for author identification forensics. *SIGMOD Record*, 30(4), 2001.

[9] M. Ester, H.-P. Kriegel, J. Sander, and X. Xu. A density-based algorithm for discovering clusters in large spatial databases with noise. In *Proceedings of the Second Int. Conference on Knowledge Discovery and Data Mining*, 1996.

[10] T. Fawcett and F. Provost. Adaptive fraud detection. *Data Mining and Knowledge Discovery*, 1(3):291–316, 1997.

[11] J. Han and Y. Fu. Discovery of multiple-level association rules from large databases. In *Proceedings of 21st VLDB Conference*, September 1995.

[12] R. J. Hilderman and H. J. Hamilton. Knowledge discovery and interestingness measures: A survey. Technical Report CS-99-04, Dept of Computer Science, University of Regina, 1999.

[13] M. Hirsh, C. Basu, and B. Davidson. Learning to personalize. *Communications of the ACM*, 43(8):102–106, 2000.

[14] H. J, Y. Cai, and N. Cercone. Knowledge discovery in databases: an attribute-oriented approach. In *Proceedings of 18th Int. Conference on Very Large Databases*, 1992.

[15] J. Konstan, B. Miller, D. Maltz, J. Herlocker, L. Gordon, and J. Riedl. Grouplens: Applying collaborative filtering to usenet news. *Communications of the ACM*, 40(3):77–87, 1997.

[16] H. Lu, L. Feng, and J. Han. Beyond intra-transaction association analysis: mining multi-dimensional inter-transaction rules. *ACM Transactions on Information Systems*, 18(4):423–454, 2000.

[17] B. Mobasher, H. Dai, T. Luo, Y. Sun, and J. Wiltshire. Discovery of aggregate usage profiles for web personalization. In *Proceedings of the Workshop on Web Mining for E-Commerce (WEBKDD'00)*, August 2000.

[18] A. Nanopoulos, D. Katsaros, and Y. Manolopoulos. Effective prediction of web-user accesses: a data mining approach. In *Proceedings of the Workshop on Mining Logdata Accross All Customer Touchpoints (WEBKDD'01)*, 2001.

[19] S. Nesbitt and O. de Vel. A collaborative filtering agent system for dynamic virtual communities on the web. In *Proceedings of the Conference on Learning and Discovery (CONALD98)*, June 1998.

[20] T. Oates and P. R. Cohen. Searching for structure in multiple streams of data. In *Proceedings of the Thirteenth International Conference on Machine Learning*, 1996.

[21] R. Srikant and R. Agrawal. Mining generalized association rules. In *Proceedings of 21st VLDB Conference*, 1995.

[22] C. Stanfill and D. Waltz. Toward memory-based reasoning. *Communications of the ACM*, 29(12):1213–1228, 1986.

[23] P. N. Tan and V. Kumar. Mining indirect associations in web data. In *Proceedings of the Workshop on Mining Logdata Accross All Customer Touchpoints (WEBKDD'01)*, 2001.

Text Document Categorization by Term Association

Maria-Luiza Antonie
University of Alberta, Canada
luiza@cs.ualberta.ca

Osmar R. Zaïane
University of Alberta, Canada
zaiane@cs.ualberta.ca

Abstract

A good text classifier is a classifier that efficiently categorizes large sets of text documents in a reasonable time frame and with an acceptable accuracy, and that provides classification rules that are human readable for possible fine-tuning. If the training of the classifier is also quick, this could become in some application domains a good asset for the classifier. Many techniques and algorithms for automatic text categorization have been devised. According to published literature, some are more accurate than others, and some provide more interpretable classification models than others. However, none can combine all the beneficial properties enumerated above. In this paper, we present a novel approach for automatic text categorization that borrows from market basket analysis techniques using association rule mining in the data-mining field. We focus on two major problems: (1) finding the best term association rules in a textual database by generating and pruning; and (2) using the rules to build a text classifier. Our text categorization method proves to be efficient and effective, and experiments on well-known collections show that the classifier performs well. In addition, training as well as classification are both fast and the generated rules are human readable.

1 Introduction

Automatic text categorization has always been an important application and research topic since the inception of digital documents. Today, text categorization is a necessity due to the very large amount of text documents that we have to deal with daily. A text categorization system can be used in indexing documents to assist information retrieval tasks as well as in classifying e-mails, memos or web pages in a yahoo-like manner. Needless to say, automatic text categorization is essential.

The text classification task can be defined as assigning category labels to new documents based on the knowledge gained in a classification system at the training stage. In the training phase we are given a set of documents with class labels attached, and a classification system is built using a learning method. Classification is an important task in both data mining and machine learning communities, however, most of the learning approaches in text categorization are coming from machine learning research.

Recent studies in the data mining community proposed new methods for classification employing association rule mining [12, 13]. These associative classifiers have proven to be powerful and achieve high accuracy. However, they were only implemented and tested on small numerical datasets from the UCI archives [19].

In this work we present a new classification method for text that takes advantage of association rule mining in the learning phase and makes the following contributions: First, *a new technique for text categorization that makes no assumption of term independence is proposed. This method proves to perform as well as other methods in the literature.* Second, *it is fast during both training and categorization phases.* Third, *the classifier that is built using our approach can be read, understood and modified by humans.* Experiments show that the effectiveness of the classifier can be improved by manually fine tuning the classification rules generated during the training phase. The resulting classifier is able to perform both single-class classification, by which each document is assigned a unique class label, and multiple-class classification, by which a document could be classified in many classes simultaneously. Our experiments are performed on text databases, however, this doesn't limit the use of our classifier to text documents. It can be applied in addition to images or any other database that can be modelled as a transactional database [2].

The remainder of the paper is organized as follows: Section 2 gives an overview of related work in automatic text categorization and in association rule mining. In Section 3 we introduce our new text categorization approach. Experimental results are described in Section 4 along with the performance of our system compared to known systems. We summarize our research and discuss some future work directions in Section 5.

19

2 Related work

Many text classifiers have been proposed in the literature using machine learning techniques, probabilistic models, etc. They often differ in the approach adopted: decision trees, naïve-Bayes, rule induction, neural networks, nearest neighbors, and lately, support vector machines. Although many approaches have been proposed, automated text categorization is still a major area of research primarily because the effectiveness of current automated text classifiers is not faultless and still needs improvement.

A classifier is built by applying a learning method to a training set of objects. This model is further used to predict the labels to new incoming objects. With all the effort in this domain there is still place for improvement and a great deal of attention is paid to developing highly accurate classifiers.

The use of association rule mining for building classification models is very new. Recent studies have proposed the use of association rules in building effective classifiers for numerical data. These classification systems discover the strongest association rules in the database and use them to build a categorizer.

In the following subsections a more detailed overview of the related work is presented from both domains that merge in our research: text categorization and association rule mining.

2.1 Text categorization

The automatic text classification problem can be defined as building a classification model to assign one or more predefined classes to new documents. Text categorization research has a long history, starting in the early 1960s. Nowadays, with all the textual information on the Web or in companies' intranets, text categorization has revived and there is more demand for effective and efficient classification models.

Most of the research in text categorization comes from the machine learning and information retrieval communities. Rocchio's algorithm [8] is the classical method in information retrieval, being used in routing and filtering documents. Researchers tackled the text categorization problem in many ways. Classifiers based on probabilistic models have been proposed starting with the first presented in literature by Maron in 1961 and continuing with naïve-Bayes [10] that proved to perform well. ID3 and C4.5 are well-known packages whose cores are making use of decision trees to build automatic classifiers [5, 6, 9]. K-nearest neighbor (k-NN) is another technique used in text categorization [20]. Another method to construct a text categorization system is by an inductive rule learning method. This type of classifiers is represented by a set of rules in disjunctive normal form that best cover the training set [14, 11, 3].

As reported in [18] the use of bigrams improved text categorization accuracy as opposed to unigrams use. In addition, in the last decade neural networks and support vector machines (SVM) were used in text categorization and they proved to be powerful tools [16, 21, 9].

2.2 Association Rule Mining

2.2.1 Association Rules Generation

Association rule mining is a data mining task that discovers relationships among items in a transactional database. Association rules have been extensively studied in the literature. The efficient discovery of such rules has been a major focus in the data mining research community. From the original *apriori* algorithm [1] there has been a remarkable number of variants and improvements culminated by the publication the FP-Tree growth algorithm [7]. However, most popular algorithms designed for the discovery of all types of association rules, are apriori-based.

Formally, association rules are defined as follows: Let $\mathcal{I} = \{i_1, i_2, ...i_m\}$ be a set of items. Let $\mathcal{D}$ be a set of transactions, where each transaction T is a set of items such that $T \subseteq \mathcal{I}$. Each transaction is associated with a unique identifier TID. A transaction T is said to contain X, a set of items in $\mathcal{I}$, if $X \subseteq T$. An *association rule* is an implication of the form "$X \Rightarrow Y$", where $X \subseteq \mathcal{I}, Y \subseteq \mathcal{I}$, and $X \cap Y = \emptyset$. The rule $X \Rightarrow Y$ has a *support s* in the transaction set $\mathcal{D}$ if $s\%$ of the transactions in $\mathcal{D}$ contain $X \cup Y$. In other words, the support of the rule is the probability that X and Y hold together among all the possible presented cases. It is said that the rule $X \Rightarrow Y$ holds in the transaction set $\mathcal{D}$ with *confidence c* if $c\%$ of transactions in $\mathcal{D}$ that contain X also contain Y. In other words, the confidence of the rule is the conditional probability that the consequent Y is true under the condition of the antecedent X. The problem of discovering all association rules from a set of transactions $\mathcal{D}$ consists of generating the rules that have a *support* and *confidence* greater than given thresholds. These rules are called *strong rules*.

The main idea behind apriori algorithm is to scan the transactional database searching for k-itemsets (k items belonging to the set of items I). As the name of the algorithm suggests, it uses prior knowledge for discovering frequent itemsets in the database. The algorithm employs an iterative search and uses k-itemsets discovered to find (k+1)-itemsets. The frequent itemsets are those that have the support higher than a minimum threshold.

2.2.2 Associative classifiers

Besides the classification methods described above, recently, and parallel to our work on associative text categorization, a new method that builds associative general clas-

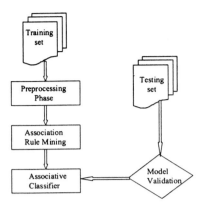

Figure 1. Construction phases for an association-rule-based text categorizer

sifiers has been proposed. In this case the learning method is represented by the association rule mining. The main idea behind this approach is to discover strong patterns that are associated with the class labels. The next step is to take advantage of these patterns such that a classifier is built and new objects are categorized in the proper classes.

Two such models were presented in the literature: CMAR [12] and CBA [13]. Although both of them proved to be effective and achieve high accuracy on relatively small UCI datasets [19], they have some limitations. Both models perform only single-class classification and were not implemented for text categorization. In many applications, however, and in text categorization in particular, multiple-class classification is required. In our paper we try to overcome this limitation and construct an associative classification model that allows single and multiple-class categorizations of text documents based on term co-frequency counts (i.e. a probabilistic technique that doesn't assume term independence).

3 Building an Associative Text Classifier

In this paper we present a method to build a categorization system that merges association rule mining task with the classification problem. This model is graphically presented in Figure 1.

Given a data collection, a number of steps are followed until the classification model is found. Data preprocessing represents the first step. At this stage cleaning techniques can be applied such as stopwords removal, stemming or term pruning according to the TF/IDF values (term frequency/inverse document frequency). The next step in building the associative classifier is the generation of association rules using an apriori-based algorithm. Once the entire set of rules has been generated an important step is

to apply some pruning techniques for reducing the set of association rules found in the text corpora. The last stage in this process is represented by the use of the association rules set in the prediction of classes for new documents. The first three steps belong to the training process while the last one represents the testing (or classification) phase. More details on the process are given in the subsections below. If a document D_i is assigned to a set of categories $C = \{c_1, c_2, ...c_m\}$ and after word pruning the set of terms $T = \{t_1, t_2, ...t_n\}$ is retained, the following transaction is used to model the document: $D_i : \{c_1, c_2, ...c_m, t_1, t_2, ...t_n\}$ and the association rules are discovered from such transactions representing all documents in the collection. The association rules are, however, constrained in that the antecedent has to be a conjunction of terms from T, while the consequent of the rule has to a member of C.

3.1 Data Collection Preprocessing

In our approach, we model text documents as transactions where items are words or phrases from the document as well as the categories to which the document belongs, as described above. A data cleaning phase is required to weed out those words that are of no interest in building the associative classifier. We consider stopwording and term pruning as well as the transformation of documents into transactions as a pre-processing phase. Stopword removal and term pruning is done according to the TF/IDF values and a given list of stopwords. We have opted to selectively turn on and off stopwording depending upon the data set to categorize. It is only after the terms are selected from the cleansed documents that the transactions are formed. The subsequent phase consists of discovering association rules from the set of cleansed transactions.

3.2 Association Rule Generation

In our algorithm, as we shall see in this section, we take advantage of the apriori algorithm to discover frequent term-sets in documents. Eventually, these frequent itemsets associated with text categories represent the discriminate features among the documents in the collection. The association rules discovered in this stage of the process are further processed to build the associative classifier.

Using the apriori algorithm on our transactions representing the documents would generate a very large number of association rules, most of them irrelevant for classification. We use an apriori-based algorithm that is guided by the constraints on the rules we want to discover. Since we are building a classifier, we are interested in rules that indicate a category label, rules with a consequent being a category label. In other words, given the document model described above, we are interested in rules of the form $T \Rightarrow c_i$ where $T \subseteq \mathcal{T}$ and $c_i \subseteq C$. To discover these interesting rules efficiently we push the rule shape constraint in the candidate generation phase of the apriori algorithm in order to retain only the suitable candidate itemsets. Moreover, at the phase for rule generation from all the frequent k-itemsets, we use the rule shape constraint again to prune those rules that are of no use in our classification.

There are two approaches that we have considered in building an associative text classifier. The first one ARC-AC (Association Rule-based Classifier with All Categories) [22] is to extract association rules from the entire training set following the constraints discussed above. As a result of discrepancies among the categories in a text collection of a real-world application, we discovered that it is difficult to handle some categories that have different characteristics (small categories, overlapping categories or some categories having documents that are more correlated than others). As a result we propose a second solution ARC-BC (Associative Rule-based Classifier By Category) that solves such problems. In this approach we consider each set of documents belonging to one category as a separate text collection to generate association rules from. If a document belongs to more than one category this document will be present in each set associated with the categories that the document falls into. The ARC-BC algorithm is described in more detail below.

Algorithm ARC-BC Find association rules on the training set of the text collection when the text corpora is divided in subsets by category

Input A set of documents (D) of the form D_i : $\{c_i, t_1, t_2, ...t_n\}$ where c_i is the category attached to the document and t_j are the selected terms for the document; A minimum support threshold; A minimum confidence threshold;

Output A set of association rules of the form $t_1 \wedge t_2 \wedge ... \wedge t_n \Rightarrow c_i$ where c_i is the category and t_j is a term;

Method:

(1) $C_1 \leftarrow \{$Candidate 1 term-sets and their $support\}$
(2) $F_1 \leftarrow \{Frequent$ 1 term-sets and their $support\}$
(3) for $(i \leftarrow 2; F_{i-1} \neq \emptyset; i \leftarrow i + 1)$ $do\{$
(4) $C_i \leftarrow (F_{i-1} \bowtie F_{i-1})$
(5) $C_i \leftarrow C_i - \{c \mid (i - 1)$ item-set of $c \notin F_{i-1}\}$
(6) $\mathcal{D}_i \leftarrow FilterTable(\mathcal{D}_{i-1}, F_{i-1})$
(7)   foreach document d in $\mathcal{D}_i$ do $\{$
(8)   foreach c in C_i do $\{$
(9) $c.support \leftarrow c.support + Count(c, d)$
(10) $\}$
(11) $\}$
(12) $F_i \leftarrow \{c \in C_i \mid c.support > \sigma\}$
(13) $\}$
(14) Sets $\leftarrow \bigcup_i \{c \in F_i \mid i > 1\}$
(15) R= $\emptyset$
(16) foreach itemset I in Sets do $\{$
(17) $R \leftarrow R + \{I \Rightarrow Cat\}$
(18) $\}$

In ARC-BC algorithm step (2) generates the frequent 1-itemset. In steps (3-13) all the k-frequent itemsets are generated and merged with the category in C_1. Steps (16-18) generate the association rules. The document space is reduced in each itereation by eliminating the transactions that do not contain any of the frequent itemsets. This step is done by $FilterTable(\mathcal{D}_{i-1}, F_{i-1})$ function.

Table 1 presents a set of rules that are discovered in the text collection. Such rules are composing the classifier. Although the rules are human readable and understandable if the amount of rules generated is too large it is time consuming to read the set of rules for further tuning of the system. This problem leads us to the next subsection where pruning methods are presented. Although the rules are similar to those produced using a rule-based induced system, the approach is different. In addition, the number of words belonging to the antecedent could be large (in our experiments up to 10 words), while in some studies with rule-based induced systems, the rules generated have only one or a pair of words as antecedent [3].

3.3 Pruning the Set of Association Rules

The number of rules that can be generated in the association rule mining phase could be very large. There are two issues that must be addressed in this case. One of them is that such a huge amount of rules could contain noisy information which would mislead the classification process. Another is that a huge set of rules would make the classification time longer. This could be an important problem in applications where fast responses are required.

The pruning methods that we study in this paper are the following: eliminate the specific rules and keep only those that are more general and with high confidence, and prune unnecessary rules by database coverage. Let us introduce the notions used in this subsection by the following definitions:

Definition 1 Being given two rules $T_1 \Rightarrow C$ and $T_2 \Rightarrow C$ we say that the first rule is more general if $T_1 \subseteq T_2$.

The first step of this process is to order the set of rules. This is done accordingly to the following ordering definition.

Definition 2 Being given two rules R_1 and R_2, R_1 is higher ranked than R_2 if:

(1) R_1 has higher confidence than R_2

(2) if the confidences are equal, supp(R_1) must exceed supp(R_2)

(3) both confidences and support are equal, but R_1 has less attributes in left hand side than R_2

With the set of association rules sorted, the goal is to select a subset that will build an efficient and effective classifier. In our approach we attempt to select a high quality subset of rules by selecting those rules that are general and

22

net ∧ profit ⇒ earn
agriculture ∧ department ∧ grain ⇒ corn
assistance ∧ bank ∧ england ∧ market ∧ money ⇒ interest
acute ∧ coronary ∧ function ∧ left ∧ ventricular ⇒ myocardial-infarction
ambulatory ∧ ischemia ∧ myocardial ⇒ coronary-disease
antiarrhythmic ∧ effects ⇒ arrhythmia

Table 1. Examples of association rules composing the classifier.

have high confidence. The most significant subset of rules is finally selected by applying the database coverage. The algorithm for building this set of rules is described below.

Algorithm Pruning the set of association rules

Input The set of association rules that were found in the association rule mining phase (S) and the training text collection (D)

Output A set of rules used in the classification process

Method:

(1)   sort the rules according to **Definition 1**
(2)   **foreach** rule in the set S
(3)   find all those rules that are more specific according to (**Definition 2**)
(4)   prune those that have lower confidence
(5)   a new set of rules S' is generated
(6)   **foreach** rule R in the set S'
(7)   go over D and find those transactions that are covered by the rule R
(8)   **if** R classifies correctly at least one transaction
(9)   select R
(10)   remove those cases that were covered by R

3.4 Prediction of Classes Associated with New Documents

The set of rules that were selected after the pruning phase represent the actual classifier. This categorizer will be used to predict to which classes new documents are attached. Given a new document, the classification process searches in this set of rules for finding those classes that are the closest to be attached with the document presented for categorization. This subsection discusses the approach for labelling new documents based on the set of association rules that forms the classifier.

A trivial solution would be to attach to the new document the class that has the most rules matching this new document or the class associated with the first rule that apply to the new object. However, in the text categorization domain, multi-class categorization is an important and challenging problem that needs to be solved. In our approach we give a solution to this problem by introducing the *dominance factor*. By employing this variable we allow our system to assign more than one category. The dominance factor δ is the proportion of rules of the most dominant category in the

applicable rules for a document to classify. Given a document to classify, the terms in the document would yield a list of applicable rules. If the applicable rules are grouped by category in their consequent part and the groups are ordered by the sum of rules' confidences, the ordered groups would indicate the most significant categories that should be attached to the document to be classified. We call this order category dominance, hence the dominance factor δ. The dominance factor allows us to select among the candidate categories only the most significant. When δ is set to a certain percentage a threshold is computed as the sum of rules' confidences for the most dominat category times the value of the *dominance factor*. Then, only those categories that exceed this threshold are selected. TakeKClasses(S,δ) function selects the most k significant classes in the classification algorithm.

The next algorithm describes the classification of a new document.

Algorithm Classification of a new object

Input A new object to be classified o; The associative classifier (ARC); The dominance factor δ; The confidence threshold τ;

Output Categories attached to the new object

Method:

(1) $S \leftarrow \emptyset$ /*set of rules that match o*/
(2)   **foreach** rule r in ARC (the sorted set of rules)
(3)   **if** ($r \subset o$) { count++ }
(4)   **if** (count == 1)
(5)   fr.conf $\leftarrow$ r.conf /*keep the first rule confidence*/
(6) $S \leftarrow S \cup r$
(7)   **else if** (r.conf $>$ fr.conf-τ)
(8) $S \leftarrow S \cup r$
(9)   **else** exit
(10) divide S in subsets by category: $S_1, S_2...S_n$
(11) **foreach** subset $S_1, S_2...S_n$
(12)   sum the confidences of rules and divide by the number of rules in S_k
(13) **if** it is single class classification
(14)   put the new document in the class that has the highest confidence sum
(15) **else** /*multi-class classification*/
(16)   TakeKClasses(S,δ)
(17)   assign these k classes to the new document

4 Experimental Results and Performance Study

4.1 Text Corpora

In order to be able to objectively evaluate our algorithm vis-a-vis other approaches, like other researchers in the field of automatic text categorization, we used the Reuters-21578 text collection [15] as benchmarks. This text database is described below. Text collections for experiments are usually split into two parts: one part for training or building the classifier and a second part for testing the effectiveness of the system.

There are many splits of the Reuters collection; we chose to use the *ModApte* version. This split leads to a corpus of 12,202 documents consisting of 9,603 training documents and 3,299 testing documents. There are 135 topics to which documents are assigned. However, only 93 of them have more than one document in the training set and 82 of the categories have less than 100 documents [22]. Obviously, the performances in the categories with just a few documents would be very low, especially for those that do not even have a document in the training set. Among the documents there are some that have no topic assigned to them. We chose to ignore such documents since no knowledge can be derived from them. Finally we decided to test our classifiers on the ten most populated categories with the largest number of documents assigned to them in the training set. Other researchers have used the same strategy [17], which constrained us to do the same for the sake of comparison. By retaining only the ten most populated categories we have 6488 training documents and 2545 testing documents. On these documents we performed stopword elimination but no stemming.

4.2 Experimental Results

On this data set we tested our classification system ARC-BC on a Pentium III 700MHz dual processor machine running Linux. Several measurements have been used in previous studies for evaluation. Some measures, as well as those used in our evaluation, can be defined in terms of precision and recall. The formulae for precision and recall are given below: $R = \frac{a}{a+c}$ and $P = \frac{a}{a+b}$. The terms used to express precision and recall are given in the contingency table Table 2.

For evaluating the effectiveness of our system, we used the breakeven points. The breakeven point is the point at which precision equals recall and it is obtained as reported in [4].

When dealing with multiple classes there are two possible ways of averaging these measures, namely, macro-average and micro-average. In the macro-averaging, one

Category *cat*		human assignments	
		Yes	No
classifier	Yes	a	b
assignments	No	c	d

Table 2. Contingency table for category *cat*

contingency table per class is used, the performance measures are computed on each of them and then averaged. In micro-averaging only one contingency table is used for all classes, an average of all the classes is computed for each cell and the performance measures are obtained therein. The macro-average weights equally all the classes, regardless of how many documents belong to it. The micro-average weights equally all the documents, thus favoring the performance on common classes.

In Table 3 we report the micro-averages for ARC-BC when both support and dominance factor were varied. The results are computed on the ten most populated categories in Reuters dataset. As described in Section 3.3 we applied some pruning techniques on the discovered association rule set. Table 3 reports micro-averages when the classifier is built by employing the pruning methods (i.e. no pruning at all (without pruning), removing specific rules (rm-s) and removing specific rules plus database coverage applied (rm-s + db-cov).

micro BEP	supp=10%			supp=15%			supp=20%		
	δ=50	δ=70	δ=90	δ=50	δ=70	δ=90	δ=50	δ=70	δ=90
without pruning	82.0	84.6	85.6	81.8	84.4	85.8	81.0	86.3	84.0
rm-s	65.5	72.9	76.3	68.2	75.0	78.8	68.2	76.1	79.7
rm-s + db-cov	71.0	79.0	82.3	71.4	79.6	73.1	70.1	70.4	84.1

Table 3. Precision/Recall-breakeven point micro-averages for ARC-BC

Table 4 (the results for the other classification systems are reported as given in [9]) shows a comparison between our ARC-BC classifier and other well-known methods. The measures used are precision/recall-breakeven point, micro-average and macro-average on ten most populated Reuters categories. Our system proves to perform well as compared to the other methods. It outperforms most of the conventional methods, but it does not perform better than SVM. In addition to these results, our system has two more features. First, it is very fast in both training and testing phases (see Table 6). The times reported are for all training and testing documents. Second, it produces readable and understandable rules that can be easily modified by humans (see Table 1). Table 5 reports the improvements in the response of the system when human tuning was applied. The support was set to 20% which made *corn* and *wheat* categories to perform very poor. By reading the rules we noticed that by adding 4 more rules for each of these categories the perfor-

BEP	ARC-BC with δ=50			Bayes	Rocchio	C4.5	k-NN	bigrams	SVM (poly)	SVM (rbf)
	10%	15%	20%							
acq	**90.9**	89.9	87.8	91.5	92.1	85.3	92.0	73.2	94.5	95.2
corn	69.6	**82.3**	70.9	47.3	62.2	87.7	77.9	60.1	85.4	85.2
crude	77.9	77.0	**80.7**	81.0	81.5	75.5	85.7	79.6	87.7	88.7
earn	**92.8**	89.2	86.6	95.9	96.1	96.1	97.3	83.7	98.3	98.4
grain	68.8	72.1	**73.1**	72.5	79.5	89.1	82.2	78.2	91.6	91.8
interest	70.5	70.1	**75.3**	58.0	72.5	49.1	74.0	69.6	70.0	75.4
money-fx	70.5	**72.4**	70.5	62.9	67.6	69.4	78.2	64.2	73.1	75.4
ship	**73.6**	73.2	63.0	78.7	83.1	80.9	79.2	69.2	85.1	86.6
trade	68.0	69.7	**69.8**	50.0	77.4	59.2	77.4	51.9	75.1	77.3
wheat	84.8	**86.5**	85.3	60.6	79.4	85.5	76.6	69.9	84.5	85.7
micro-avg	**82.1**	81.8	81.1	72.0	79.9	79.4	82.3	73.3	85.4	86.3
macro-avg	76.74	**78.24**	76.32	65.21	79.14	77.78	82.05	67.07	84.58	86.01

Table 4. Precision/Recall-breakeven point on ten most populated Reuters categories for ARC-BC and most known classifiers

ARC-BC supp=20% δ=90 rm-s+db-cov		
BEP	initial set of rules	manual tuned set of rules
acq	89.6	89.6
corn	2.0	63.6
crude	80.0	80.0
earn	92.7	92.7
grain	92.5	81.9
interest	57.7	57.7
money-fx	77.9	77.9
ship	61.3	61.3
trade	75.5	75.5
wheat	6.0	63.5
micro-avg	84.14	84.62
macro-avg	63.55	74.41

Table 5. Micro-average Precision/Recall-breakeven point for ten most populated Reuters categories - manual tuning of the classifier

support	training	testing
10%	18	3
15%	9	2
20%	8	2

Table 6. Training and testing time (in seconds) with respect to the support threshold for Reuters-21578 dataset

set.

The experimental results show that the association rule-based classifier performs well and its effectiveness is comparable to most well-known text classifiers. One major advantage of the association rule-based classifier is its relatively fast training time. Moreover, the rules generated are understandable and can easily be manually updated or adjusted if necessary. The maintenance of the classifier is straight forward. In the case of ARC-BC, when new documents are presented for retraining, only the concerned categories are adjusted and the rules could be incrementally updated.

The introduction of the dominance factor δ allowed multi-class categorization. However, other feature selection techniques, such as latent semantic analysis could improve the results by giving an insight on the discriminative feature among classes. We are working on reducing the number of features, thus better discrimination among classes is expected. Currently the discovered rules consider the presence of terms in documents to categorize. We are studying possibilities to take into account the absence of terms in the classification rules as well.

mances improved as presented in Table 5.

A comparison between the pruning methods is given in Table 7. By applying the pruning methods the accuracy of the classifier is not improved. However, the reduction in number of rules represents a step further in manually or automatically tuning of the system.

5 Conclusion and Future Work

This paper introduced a new technique for text categorization. It employs the use of association rules. Our study provides evidence that association rule mining can be used for the construction of fast and effective classifiers for automatic text categorization. We have presented an association rule-based algorithm for building the classifier: **ARC-BC** that considers categories one at a time. The algorithm assume a transaction-based model for the training document

BEP	ARC-BC with $\delta = 50$ and supp=15%		
	w/o pruning	rm-s	rm-s + db-cov
	3072 rules	383 rules	127 rules
acq	89.9	84.2	76.6
corn	82.3	62.7	2.8
crude	77.0	58.4	64.8
earn	89.2	85.6	78.0
grain	72.1	56.4	71.8
interest	70.1	60.8	63.6
money-fx	72.4	62.3	68.7
ship	73.2	67.6	59.0
trade	69.7	59.2	73.5
wheat	86.5	46.9	24.7
micro-avg	81.8	68.2	71.4
macro-avg	78.24	64.40	58.53

Table 7. Precision/Recall-breakeven point for ten most populated Reuters categories with different pruning methods

References

[1] R. Agrawal, T. Imielinski, and A. Swami. Mining association rules between sets of items in large databases. In *Proc. 1993 ACM-SIGMOD Int. Conf. Management of Data*, pages 207–216, Washington, D.C., May 1993.

[2] M.-L. Antonie, O. R. Zaïane, and A. Coman. Application of data mining techniques for medical image classification. In *Second International ACM SIGKDD Workshop on Multimedia Data Mining*, pages 94–101, San Francisco, USA, August 2001.

[3] C. Apte, F. Damerau, and S. Weiss. Automated learning of decision rules for text categorization. *ACM Transactions on Information Systems*, 12(3):233–251, 1994.

[4] R. Bekkerman, R. El-Yaniv, N. Tishby, and Y. Winter. On feature distributional clustering for text categorization. In *Proceedings of SIGIR-01, 24th ACM International Conference on Research and Development in Information Retrieval*, pages 146–153, New Orleans, US, 2001.

[5] W. Cohen and H. Hirsch. Joins that generalize: text classification using whirl. In *4th International Conference on Knowledge Discovery and Data Mining (SigKDD'98)*, pages 169–173, New York City,USA, 1998.

[6] W. Cohen and Y. Singer. Context-sensitive learning methods for text categorization. *ACM Transactions on Information Systems*, 17(2):141 –173, 1999.

[7] J. Han, J. Pei, and Y. Yin. Mining frequent patterns without candidate generation. In *ACM-SIGMOD*, Dallas, 2000.

[8] D. A. Hull. Improving text retrieval for the routing problem using latent semantic indexing. In *17th ACM International Conference on Research and Development in Information Retrieval (SIGIR-94)*, pages 282–289, 1994.

[9] T. Joachims. Text categorization with support vector machines: learning with many relevant features. In *10th European Conference on Machine Learning (ECML-98)*, pages 137–142, 1998.

[10] D. Lewis. Naïve (bayes) at forty: The independence assumption in information retrieval. In *10th European Conference on Machine Learning (ECML-98)*, pages 4–15, 1998.

[11] H. Li and K. Yamanishi. Text classification using esc-based stochastic decision lists. In *8th ACM International Conference on Information and Knowledge Management(CIKM-99)*, pages 122 –130, Kansas City,USA, 1999.

[12] W. Li, J. Han, and J. Pei. CMAR: Accurate and efficient classification based on multiple class-association rules. In *IEEE International Conference on Data Mining (ICDM'01)*, San Jose, California, Novermber 29-December 2 2001.

[13] B. Liu, W. Hsu, and Y. Ma. Integrating classification and association rule mining. In *ACM Int. Conf. on Knowledge Discovery and Data Mining (SIGKDD'98)*, pages 80–86, New York City, NY, August 1998.

[14] I. Moulinier and J.-G. Ganascia. Applying an existing machine learning algorithm to text categorization. In S.Wermter, E.Riloff, and G.Scheler, editors, *Connectionist statistical,and symbolic approaches to learning for natural language processing*. Springer Verlag, Heidelberg, Germany, 1996. Lecture Notes for Computer Science series, number 1040.

[15] The reuters-21578 text categorization test collection. http://www.research.att.com/~lewis/reuters21578.html.

[16] M. Ruiz and P. Srinivasan. Neural networks for text categorization. In *22nd ACM SIGIR International Conference on Information Retrieval*, pages 281–282, Berkeley, CA, USA, August 1999.

[17] F. Sebastiani. Machine learning in automated text categorization. Technical Report IEI-B4-31-1999, Consiglio Nazionale delle Ricerche, Pisa, Italy, 1999.

[18] C. M. Tan, Y. F. Wang, and C. D. Lee. The use of bigrams to enhance text categorization. *Journal of Information Processing and Management*, 2002. http://www.cs.ucsb.edu/ yfwang/papers/ig&m.pdf.

[19] University of california irvine knowledge discovery in databases archive. http://kdd.ics.uci.edu/.

[20] Y. Yang. An evaluation of statistical approaches to text categorization. Technical Report CMU-CS-97-127, Carnegie mellon University, April 1997.

[21] Y.Yang and X.Liu. A re-examination of text categorization methods. In *22nd ACM International Conference on Research and Development in Information Retrieval (SIGIR-99)*, pages 42–49, Berkeley,US, 1999.

[22] O. R. Zaïane and M.-L. Antonie. Classifying text documents by associating terms with text categories. In *Thirteenth Australasian Database Conference (ADC'02)*, pages 215–222, Melbourne, Australia, January 2002.

Online Algorithms for Mining Semi-structured Data Stream

Tatsuya Asai   Hiroki Arimura[†]   Kenji Abe   Shinji Kawasoe   Setsuo Arikawa

Department of Informatics, Kyushu University, Fukuoka 812–8581, JAPAN

{t-asai,arim,k-abe,s-kawa,arikawa}@i.kyushu-u.ac.jp

† PRESTO, JST, JAPAN

Abstract

In this paper, we study an online data mining problem from streams of semi-structured data such as XML data. Modeling semi-structured data and patterns as labeled ordered trees, we present an online algorithm StreamT that receives fragments of an unseen possibly infinite semi-structured data in the document order through a data stream, and can return the current set of frequent patterns immediately on request at any time. A crucial part of our algorithm is the incremental maintenance of the occurrences of possibly frequent patterns using a tree sweeping technique. We give modifications of the algorithm to other online mining model. We present theoretical and empirical analyses to evaluate the performance of the algorithm.

1. Introduction

Recently, a new class of data-intensive applications such as network monitoring, web site management, sensor networks, and e-commerce emerged with the rapid growth of network and web technologies. In these applications, the data are modeled not as static collections but as transient *data streams*, where the data source is an unbounded stream of individual data items, e.g., transaction records or web page visits, which may arrive continuously in rapid, time-varying way [18].

Particularly in data communication through internet, it is becoming popular to use *semi-structured data*-based communication technologies [2], e.g., SOAP [19], to send heterogeneous and ill-structured data through networks. Since traditional database technologies are not directly applicable to such data streams, it is important to study efficient information extraction methods for semi-structured data streams.

In this paper, we model such semi-structured data streams by sequences of *labeled ordered trees*, and study the frequent pattern discovery problem in online setting. We model a semi-structured data stream as an infinite sequence of the nodes generated by the depth-first scanning of a possibly infinite data tree. An online algorithm has to continuously work on the data stream, and has to quickly

answer queries on request based on the portion of the data received so far. This formulation captures typical situations for web applications reading a sequence of XML tags or SAX events element by element from a data stream. Since this is a finest-grained online model, the results of this paper can be easily generalized to coarser-grained models where, e.g., XML documents are processed page by page.

We present an online algorithm StreamT for discovering labeled ordered trees with frequency at least a given minimum threshold from an unbounded data stream. A difficulty lies in that we have to continuously work with unbounded data streams using only bounded resources. A key idea is a technique of sweeping a branch, called the *sweep branch*, over the whole virtual data tree to find all embeddings of candidate patterns intersecting it. Using this sweep branch as a synopsis data structure, we achieve incremental and continuous computation of all occurrences of patterns with bounded working space.

As another idea, we adopt a candidate management policy similar to Hidber [11] for online association mining to limit the number of candidate patterns as small as possible. We also use the enumeration technique for labeled ordered trees that we recently proposed in [4], a generalization of a technique by Bayardo [6]. Combining these ideas, our algorithm StreamT works efficiently in both time and space complexities in online manner. Furthermore, we extend our algorithm to the *forgetting model* of online data stream mining, where the effect of a past data item decays exponentially fast in its age. We also give theoretical analysis on the accuracy of the discovered patterns as well as an empirical analysis on the scalability of the algorithms.

The rest of this paper is organized as follows. In Section 2, we give basic definitions, and in Section 3, we present our online algorithm. In Section 4, we modify this algorithm in the forgetting model. In Section 5, we report experimental results, and in Section 6, we conclude. For proofs not found here, see [5].

1.1. Related Works

Emerging technologies of semi-structured data have attracted wide attention of networks, e-commerce, information retrieval and databases [2, 19]. In contrast, there have not been many studies on *semi-structured data mining* [1, 4, 7, 9, 13, 15, 16, 20, 22]. There are a body of researches on online data processing and mining [10, 14, 18]. Most related work is Hidber [11], who proposed a model of continuous pattern discovery from unbounded data stream, and presented adaptive online algorithm for mining association rules. Parthasarathy *et al.* [17] and Mannila *et al.* [14] studied mining of sequential patterns and episode patterns. Yamanishi *et al.* [21] presented an efficient online-outlier detection system *SmartSifter* with a forgetting mechanism.

Zaki [22] and Asai *et al.* [4] independently developed efficient pattern search techniques, called *rightmost expansion*, for semi-structured data, which is a generalization of the set-enumeration tree technique [6]. Although our algorithm partly uses this technique, its design principle is different from previous semi-structured data mining algorithms [4, 7, 9, 13, 15, 16, 20, 22]

2. Preliminaries

2.1. Model of Semi-Structured Data

Semi-structured data are heterogeneous collections of weakly structured data [2], which are typically encoded in a markup language such as XML [19]. We model semi-structured data and patterns [2] by labeled ordered trees. For the basic terminologies on trees, we refer to, e.g. [3].

Labeled Ordered Trees. We define labeled ordered trees according to [4, 12]. Let $\mathcal{L} = \{\ell, \ell_0, \ell_1, \ldots\}$ be a fixed alphabet of *labels*. Then, a *labeled ordered tree on $\mathcal{L}$ (tree, for short)* is a labeled, rooted, connected directed acyclic graph $T = (V, E, B, L, v_0)$ with the following properties [3]. Each node $v \in V$ of T is labeled by an element $L(v)$ of $\mathcal{L}$, and all node but the root v_0 have the unique parent by the child relation $E \subseteq V^2$. For each node v, its children are ordered from left to right by an indirect sibling relation $B \subseteq V^2$ [3]. Note that the term *ordered* means the order *not* on labels but on children.

The size of a tree T is the number of its nodes $|T| = |V|$. Throughout this paper, we assume that a tree of size k has the node set $V = \{1, \ldots, k\}$ and the nodes are ordered in the pre-order by the depth-first search order on T. We refer to the node i as the *i-th node* of T. This assumption is crucial in our discussion. By this assumption, the root and the rightmost leaf of T, denoted by $root(T)$ and $rml(T)$, are always 1 and k, respectively. For a tree T of size k, the *rightmost branch* of T, denoted by $RMB(T)$, is the path from the root 1 to the rightmost leaf k of T.

We denote by $\mathcal{T}$ the class of all labeled ordered trees on $\mathcal{L}$. We also refer to V, E, B and L as V_T, E_T, B_T and L_T, respectively, if it is clear from context.

Matching and Occurrences. Next, we define the notion of *matching* between two labeled ordered trees T and D. A *pattern tree T matches a data tree D* if T can be embedded in D with preserving the labels, the (direct) child relation, the (indirect) sibling relation by a non-collapsing mapping, that is, there exists some function $\varphi : V_T \to V_D$ that satisfies the following (i)–(iv) for any $v, v_1, v_2 \in V_T$:

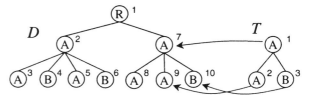

Figure 1. A data tree D and a pattern tree T on the set $\mathcal{L} = \{A, B\}$ of labels

(i) φ is one-to-one.

(ii) $L_T(v) = L_D(\varphi(v))$.

(iii) $(v_1, v_2) \in E_T$ iff $(\varphi(v_1), \varphi(v_2)) \in E_D$.

(iv) $(v_1, v_2) \in B_T$ iff $(\varphi(v_1), \varphi(v_2)) \in B_D$.

Then, we say that φ is a *matching function of T to D,* or *T occurs in D.* We assume the *empty tree* $\bot$ such that $|\bot| = 0$ and $\bot$ matches to any tree at any node. An *embedding* of T in D w.r.t. φ is the image $\varphi(T) \subseteq V_D$ of T into D, whose induced subgraph is isomorphic to T. We define the *root occurrence* and the *rightmost leaf occurrence* of T in D w.r.t. φ by the nodes $\varphi(1)$ and $\varphi(k)$ of D to which the root and the rightmost leaf of T map, respectively. If φ is not irrelevant then we simply omit φ.

For example, Fig. 1 shows examples of labeled ordered trees D and T on $\mathcal{L} = \{A, B\}$. We see that the pattern tree T matches the data tree D, where the matching is designated with a set of arrows from T to D. The root occurrences of T in D are 2 and 7, while the rightmost occurrences are 4, 6, and 10.

Semi-structured Data Streams. Let D be a labeled ordered tree, called a *data tree* with finite depth and possibly infinite width. Given a collection of trees as a data source, we always treat them as a single tree by combining trees with appending the imaginary common root. Recall that the nodes of D are numbered in the preorder traversal of D.

We introduce a convenient sequential representation of labeled ordered trees. The *depth* of node v of tree T is the number of edges on the path from the root to v. The *depth-label representation* of a node v of D is the pair $(d, \ell) \in \mathbf{N} \times \mathcal{L}$ of the depth d and the label ℓ of v. Then, a data tree D is encoded as the sequence $\pi = ((d_1, \ell_1), (d_2, \ell_2), \ldots)$ of depth-label pairs corresponding to the nodes on the preorder traversal of T. This depth-label representation π also linearly related to the *open-close parentheses* representation as in XML [19].

Conversely, we can uniquely decode a depth-label representation π into a labeled ordered tree as follows.

Definition 4 ([4, 22]) Let S be a tree of size $k \geq 1$. Then, a *rightmost expansion* of S is any tree T of size $k+1$ obtained from S by (i) attaching a new node w with a label in $\mathcal{L}$ as a child of a parent node p on the rightmost branch of S so that (ii) w is the rightmost sibling of p. Then, we say that T is a *successor* of S, or S is a *predecessor* of T. If the depth and the label of w is $d \in \mathbf{N}$ and $\ell \in \mathcal{L}$, resp., then T is called the (d, ℓ)-*expansion* of S. The $(0, \ell)$-expansion of $\perp$ is the single node tree with label ℓ.

Thus, the empty sequence ε transforms to the empty tree $\perp$, and if the sequence π transforms to a tree S, then the sequence $\pi \cdot (d, \ell)$ to the (d, ℓ)-expansion of S. The notion of depth-label representation is motivated by the tree expansion technique [4, 22], and plays an important role in the following discussion.

For example, in the previous example of Fig. 1, the data tree D transforms to the depth-label representation $\pi = (0, R), (1, A), (2, A), (2, B), (2, A), (2, B), (1, A), (2, A), (2, A), (2, B)$, and *vice versa*.

We model a semi-structured data stream as an infinite sequence of the nodes generated by the depth-first scanning of a possibly infinite data tree as follows. For a set A, we denote by A^∞ the sets of all infinite sequences on A. A *semi-structured data stream* for D is an infinite sequence $S = (\boldsymbol{v}_1, \boldsymbol{v}_2, \ldots, \boldsymbol{v}_i, \ldots) \in (\mathbf{N} \times \mathcal{L})^\infty$, where for every $i \geq 1$, the i-th element $\boldsymbol{v}_i = (d_i, \ell_i)$ is the depth-label representation of the i-th node $v_i = i$ of D. Then, $\boldsymbol{v}_i$ is called the i-th *node* of S and i is called the *time stamp*. The i-th *left-half tree*, denoted by D_i, is the labeled ordered tree that is the induced subgraph of D consisting of the first i nodes $(v_1, v_2, \ldots, v_i)$ of the traversal.

Online Data Mining Problems. Now, our online data mining problem is stated as follows. The definition of the frequency of a pattern T at time i will be specified later.

Definition 5 (Online Frequent Pattern Discovery from Semi-structured Data Streams) Let $0 \leq \sigma \leq 1$ be a non-negative number called the *minimum support*. In our online mining protocol, for stages $i = 1, 2, \ldots$, an *online mining algorithm* $\mathcal{A}$ iterates the following process: $\mathcal{A}$ receives the i-th node $\boldsymbol{v}_i$ from the stream S, updates its internal state based on the first i nodes $\boldsymbol{v}_1, \ldots, \boldsymbol{v}_i$ received so far, and then on request by a user $\mathcal{A}$ reports a set $\mathcal{F}_i$ of frequent patterns that appears in D_i with frequency no less than σ.

The goal of an online algorithm is to continuously work on unbounded stream for arbitrary long time with bounded resources, and to quickly answer user's queries at any time.

We define the models of the frequency of patterns as follows. Let $i \geq 1$ be any time. For every $1 \leq j \leq i$, we define the indicator function $hit_j^{(i)}(T) = 1$ if the pattern T has a root occurrence at the node v_j in D_i. Otherwise, we define $hit_j^{(i)}(T) = 0$. For a technical reason, we require not only $\varphi(1)$ but also the whole $\varphi(T)$ to be contained in D_i.

Definition 6 Let S be a given semi-structured data stream and $T \in \mathcal{T}$ be any pattern. Below, $count_i(T)$ and $freq_i(T)$ denote the *count* and the *frequency* of T at time i, resp.

- **Online Model (OL).** In this model motivated by Hidber [11], we count the number of distinct root occurrences of T in D_i. The *frequency* of T at time i is:

$$freq_i(T) = \tfrac{1}{i} count_i(T) = \tfrac{1}{i} \textstyle\sum_{j=1}^{i} hit_j^{(i)}(T)$$

- **Forgetting Model (FG).** In the forgetting model, e.g., [21], the contribution of the past event decays exponentially fast. For positive number $0 < \gamma < 1$ called a *forgetting factor*, the *frequency* of T is defined by:

$$freq_{\gamma,i}^{\text{fg}}(T) = \tfrac{1}{Z_i} \textstyle\sum_{j=1}^{i} \gamma^{i-j} hit_j^{(i)}(T). \quad (1)$$

Although we used a simplified normalization factor $Z_i = i$ instead of a more precise one $Z_i = \sum_{j=1}^{i} \gamma^{i-j}$, most of the discussion in the later sections also holds.

A difference of above models is the speed of decay. Since the effect of a past event decays exponentially faster in FG than in OL, the former is more trend conscious than the latter. We can deal with the *sliding window model* in this framework in a similar manner. For details, see [5].

3. Online Mining Algorithms

In this section, we present an online algorithm StreamT for solving the online frequent pattern discovery problem from semi-structured data stream.

3.1. Overview of the Algorithm

In Fig. 2, we show our algorithm StreamT in the online model. Let $S = (\boldsymbol{v}_1, \boldsymbol{v}_2, \ldots, \boldsymbol{v}_i, \ldots) \in (\mathbf{N} \times \mathcal{L})^\infty$ be a possibly infinite data stream for a data tree D. Through the stages $i = 1, 2, \ldots$, StreamT receives the i-th node $\boldsymbol{v}_i = (d_i, \ell_i)$ from S, updates a pool $\mathcal{C} \subseteq \mathcal{T}$ of candidate patterns and the internal state, and on request reports a set of frequent labeled ordered trees $\mathcal{F}_i \subseteq \mathcal{T}$ with frequency no less than a given threshold $0 \leq \sigma \leq 1$.

To continuously compute the set of frequent patterns on an unbounded stream, the algorithm uses a technique, similar to *plane sweeping* in computational geometry [8], to find all root occurrences of candidate patterns in D. A basic idea of our algorithm is explained as follows. To detect all embeddings of a set of patterns in D, we sweep a path from the root to the currently scanned node v_i, called the *sweep branch*, rightwards over the data tree D by increasing the stage $i = 1, 2, \ldots$. While we sweep the plane, we keep track of all embedding of patterns that intersect the current sweep branch.

Algorithm StreamT

Input: A set $\mathcal{L}$ of labels, a data stream $(\boldsymbol{v}_1, \boldsymbol{v}_2, \ldots, \boldsymbol{v}_i, \ldots)$ of a data tree D, and a frequency threshold $0 \leq \sigma \leq 1$.

Output: A sequence $(\mathcal{F}_1, \mathcal{F}_2, \ldots, \mathcal{F}_i, \ldots)$ of sets of frequent patterns, where $\mathcal{F}_i$ is the set of frequent patterns for every i.

Variables: The candidate pool $\mathcal{C} \subseteq \mathcal{T}$, and the bucket stack $B = (B[0], \ldots, B[Top])$.

Method:

1. $\mathcal{C}$:= the class of all single node patterns;
   $B := \emptyset$ and $Top = -1$; $i := 1$;

2. While there is the next node $\boldsymbol{v}_i = (d, \ell)$, do the followings:

   (a) Update the bucket stack $B[0] \cdots B[d-1]$:
   $$(B, EXP) := \mathsf{UpdateB}(B, \mathcal{C}, (d, \ell), i);$$

   (b) Update the candidate pool $\mathcal{C}$ and the bucket $B[d]$:
   $$(B, \mathcal{C}) := \mathsf{UpdateC}(EXP, B, \mathcal{C}, (d, \ell), i);$$

   (c) Output the set $\mathcal{F}_i = \{\, T \in \mathcal{C} \mid freq_i(T) \geq \sigma \,\}$ of frequent patterns; $i = i + 1$;

Figure 2. An online mining algorithm for semi-structured data stream

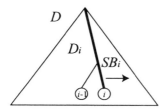

Figure 3. The i-th left-half tree D_i and i-th sweep branch SB_i for the data tree D

The algorithm incrementally maintains the following data structures during the computation.

- A set $\mathcal{C} \subseteq \mathcal{T}$ of patterns, called the *candidate pool*.

- A stack $B = (B[0], B[1], \ldots, B[Top])$ of buckets, called the *sweep branch stack* (*SB-stack*, for short).

For each candidate $T \in \mathcal{C}$, the following features are associated: A counter $count(T)$ of the root occurrences of T in D_i. A vector $Rto_T = (Rto_T[0], Rto_T[1], \ldots)$ of the latest root occurrences $Rto_T[d] = \rho$ of T with depth d.

3.2. Incremental Pattern Discovery Using Tree Sweeping

To keep track of all embeddings of candidate patterns, we do not need the whole information on them. Instead, we record the information on the intersections of these embedding and the current sweep branch at every stage.

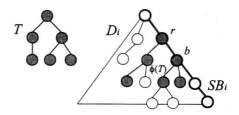

Figure 4. The root and the bottom occurrences r and b of pattern T on D_i w.r.t the sweep branch SB_i with matching ϕ.

Let $i \geq 1$ be any stage. In what follows, we denote by v_i, D_i and SB_i the present node, the left-half tree and the sweep branch at stage i. In other words, SB_i is the rightmost branch of D_i.

For pattern T, let $\varphi(T)$ be an embedding of T with some matching $\varphi : V_T \to V_D$ of T to D_i. Since an embedding of a tree is also an ordered tree in D_i, we can define the rightmost branch, denoted by $RMB(\varphi(T)) \subseteq V_D$, of $\varphi(T)$ in D_i. During the scan of D, the sweep branch $SB_i \subseteq V_D$ may have nonempty intersection $SB_i \cap RMB(\varphi(T))$ with $RMB(\varphi(T))$.

Lemma 1 *For any embedding $\varphi(T)$ of a pattern T and the sweep branch SB_i, the intersection $SB_i \cap RMB(\varphi(T))$ is a consecutive path in D.*

From the above lemma, we define the *root* and the *bottom occurrences* of T w.r.t. φ to be the highest and the lowest nodes in the intersection $SB_i \cap RMB(\varphi(T))$ (Fig. 4). We can easily see that if the intersection $SB_i \cap RMB(\varphi(T))$ is contained in SB_i then the corresponding bottom occurrence becomes the rightmost occurrence of T w.r.t. φ. The next lemma gives an incremental characterization of the rightmost occurrences, which enables us to detect all rightmost occurrences of candidate patterns by maintaining all bottom occurrences of their predecessors on the sweep branch using the SB-stack.

Lemma 2 *Let $T \in \mathcal{T}$ be any pattern of size $k > 1$. At every time $i \geq 1$, T has a rightmost occurrence at the current node v_i in D_i iff there exists some pattern S of size $(k-1)$ that has a bottom occurrence at the parent of v_i in D_i and such that T is the (d, ℓ)-expansion of S, where d is the depth of the rightmost leaf k of T from its root and $\ell = L(v_i)$ is the label of v_i. This is also true even if $k = 1$.*

To implement this idea, we use the sweep branch stack $B = (B[0], B[1], \ldots, B[Top])$ to record the intersections of embeddings of patterns with the current sweep branch SB_i. $Top \geq 0$ is the length of SB_i. Each bucket $B[b]$ ($0 \leq b \leq Top$) contains a set of triples of the form $\tau = (T, r, b)$ such that pattern T has the root and the bottom occurrences of the depths r and b, respectively, on SB_i. For each bucket $B[d]$, the time stamp $B[d].time \in \mathbf{N}$ of the last time is associated with the bucket.

For any stage $i \geq 1$, the SB-stack $B = (B[0], B[1], \ldots, B[Top])$ is said to be *up-to-date w.r.t.* the present sweep branch SB_i if Top is the length of SB_i, and for every $0 \leq b \leq Top$, the bucket $B[b]$ contains all triples $(T, r, b) \in \mathcal{T} \times \mathbf{N} \times \mathbf{N}$ for some $T \in \mathcal{C}$ and $r \in \mathbf{N}$ such that the pattern T appears in D_i and has the root and the bottom occurrences on SB_i of the depths r and b, respectively (Fig. 4). Then, we also say that each bucket $B[b]$ is up-to-date if no confusion arises. Note that the up-to-date stack is unique at time i. Now, we give a characterization of the contents of the current SB-stack B_i inductively.

Lemma 3 *Let $i \geq 1$ and $v_i = (d, \ell)$ be the current node of the data stream S for D. Let $B_k = (B_k[0], B_k[1], \ldots, B_k[Top_k])$ be the SB-stack at time $k \in \{i-1, i\}$. Suppose that both of the SB-stacks B_i and B_{i-1} are up-to-date. Then, the following 1 – 4 hold:*

1. For any $0 \leq b < d-1$, $\tau \in B_i[b]$ if and only if $\tau \in B_{i-1}[b]$.

2. For $b = d-1$, $\tau \in B_i[d-1]$ if and only if either (i) or (ii) below holds:

   (i) $\tau \in B_{i-1}[d-1]$.

   (ii) τ is represented as $\tau = (T, r, d-1)$ for some tuple $(T, r, b) \in B_{i-1}[d] \cup \cdots \cup B_{i-1}[Top_{i-1}]$ such that $r \leq d \leq b$.

3. $\tau \in B_i[d]$ if and only if $\tau = (T, r, b)$ and either (i) or (ii) below holds:

   (i) T is the single node tree with the label ℓ.

   (ii) T is the $(d-r, \ell)$-expansion of S for some triple $(S, r, d-1) \in B_i[d-1]$.

4. For any $b > d$, $B_i[b]$ is undefined.

Proof. Case 1, 2, 3(i) and 4 are obvious. For case 3(ii), suppose that E_T is an embedding of T in D and its right-branch embedding intersects SB_i with the bottom depth $b = d$. Then, T has the rightmost occurrence at the current node $v_i = i$. Let C_T is the tree obtained from E_T by removing v_i. Then, C_T is an embedding of the predecessor of T with the rightmost occurrence at the parent, say w, of $v_i = i$. Since the depth of the parent w is $d-1$, the corresponding triple $(S, r, d-1)$ for C_T belongs to $B_i[d-1]$ where T is the $(d-r, \ell)$-expansion of S. □

Fig. 5 illustrates how to update the sweep branch stack B_{i-1} based on Lemma 3. Suppose that we receive the i-th node (d, ℓ) from a data stream. Then, the triples in UN-CHANGE buckets, i.e., $B[0] \cup \cdots \cup B[d-1]$, stay unchanged. The buckets in $B[d] \cup \cdots \cup B[Top]$ are partitioned

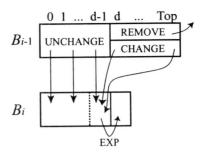

Figure 5. SB-stacks from time $i-1$ to i

Algorithm UpdateB$(B, \mathcal{C}, (d, \ell), i)$

Input: A bucket stack $B = (B[0], B[1], \ldots, B[Top])$, a candidate pool $\mathcal{C}$, a depth-label representation $v_i = (d, \ell) \in \mathbf{N} \times \mathcal{L}$ of the ith node of the data stream S, and the current time i;

Output: A set $EXP \subseteq \mathcal{T} \times \mathbf{N} \times \mathbf{N}$ of triples ;

Method:

1. If $d \leq Top$, then do the followings:
   - $BELOW := B[d] \cup \ldots \cup B[Top]$;
   - /* *Discard the triples below the branching point* */
     $REMOVE := \{ (T, r, b) \in BELOW \mid r \geq d \}$;
   - /* *Collect the triples across the branching point* */
     $CHANGE := \{ (T, r, b) \in BELOW \mid r \leq d-1 \}$;
   - /* *Change the bottom occurrences of the triples* */
     $B[d-1] := B[d-1] \cup \{ (T, r, d-1) \mid (T, r, b) \in CHANGE \}$;

2. $EXP := \{(T_\ell, d, d)\}$, where T_ℓ is the single node tree with the label ℓ;

3. For each $(S, r, d-1) \in B[d-1]$ do the followings:
   - T is the $(d-r, \ell)$-expansion of S;
   - $EXP := EXP \cup \{ (T, r, d) \}$;

4. Return (B, EXP);

Figure 6. Updating the SB-stack

---

into REMOVE and CHANGE. The triples in REMOVE buckets are discarded, and triples in CHANGE buckets move to the bucket $B[d-1]$. For all triples in $B[d-1]$, we apply the rightmost expansion and then insert obtained expansions into EXP.

In Fig. 6, we show the algorithm UpdateB for incrementally updating the SB-stack. At any stage $i \geq 1$, UpdateB updates the first $d-1$ buckets $B_i[0] \cdots B_i[d-1]$ of new one. The d-th bucket is not immediately updated, but the updated contents are separately returned as EXP for computing the bucket $B_i[d]$ in further processing. The following corollary is immediately from Lemma 3.

Corollary 4 *For every time invoked in the while loop in* StreamT *of Fig. 2 at time $i \geq 1$ with the current node $v_i = (d, l)$, the algorithm* UpdateB$(B, \mathcal{C}, (d, \ell), i)$ *returns* *the followings: (i) The sequence $B[0], \ldots, B[d-1]$ of buckets that are up-to-date at time i up to depth $d - 1$. (ii) The set EXP of all triples corresponding to the bottom occurrences on SB_i whose depth is d and predecessors belong to C.*

3.3. Duplicate Detection for the Root Occurrences

From the observations above, the algorithm UpdateB (Fig. 6) detects all rightmost leaf occurrences of the patterns whose predecessors belong to C at Step 2 and Step 3.

Then, the next step is to compute the corresponding root occurrences from these rightmost occurrences. Let $b \in V_D$ be a rightmost occurrence of pattern T whose triple (T, r, b) is detected at Step 2 or Step 3 of UpdateB. Recall that a list $Rto_T = (Rto_T[0], Rto_T[1], \ldots)$ is associated with each $T \in C$ and it is initially empty. Then, we can obtain the root occurrence corresponding to the triple by the following procedure FindRootOcc:

FindRootOcc$(B, (T, r, b))$
- Let $t := B[r].time$ and $\rho := v_t$;
- If $Rto_T[r] = \rho$ then return UNDEF;
- Otherwise, $Rto_T[r] := \rho$ and return ρ as the root occurrence of T; (Duplicate check)

Figure 7. Finding root occurrences

It is easy to observe that FindRootOcc correctly finds the root occurrence as follows. If the sweep branch SB_i intersects an embedding of T w.r.t. a matching φ then it also intersects the root occurrence of T w.r.t. φ, and thus the component r of (T, r, b) correctly gives the depth of a root occurrence, say, $w \in V_D$. By definition, $B[r].time$ stores the time stamp, say t, of the node on SB_i whose depth is r when it is first encountered. Thus, $v_t = w$ gives the root occurrence corresponding to the triple.

Furthermore for a fixed r, any node w' occupies the bucket $B[r]$ in a consecutive period during the scanning of S. Thus, it is sufficient to record the last root occurrence of depth r for each depth $r \geq 0$ in order to check the duplication of the occurrences. Hence, we see that FindRootOcc correctly detect the root occurrence of candidate patterns without duplicates.

3.4. Candidate Management

The algorithm StreamT stores candidate patterns in a candidate pool $C \subseteq T$. Fig. 8 shows an algorithm UpdateC for managing C by updating the frequency count of each patterns. A root occurrence has monotonicity that if pattern T is a rightmost most expansion of pattern S then the root count of S is greater than or equal to the root count of T. Based on this observation, the algorithm UpdateC uses a

---

Algorithm UpdateC$(EXP, B, C, (d, \ell), i)$

Input: A set EXP of triples, a bucket stack $B = (B[0], B[1], \ldots, B[Top])$, a candidate pool C, the i-th node $v_i = (d, \ell) \in \mathbf{N} \times \mathcal{L}$ of the data stream, and the time i;

Output: The updated pair (B, C);

Method:

1. /* Increment candidates */
   For each triple $(T, r, b) \in EXP$, do:
   If $\rho := $ FindRootOcc(B, (T, r, b)) is not UNDEF then
   – If $T \in C$ then $count(T) := count(T) + 1$;
   – If $T \notin C$ and the predecessor of T is frequent, then $count(T) := 1$ and $C := C \cup \{T\}$;

2. $B[d] := \emptyset$; $Top := d$; $B[d].time := i$;
   $freq(T) := count(T)/i$;

3. /* Delete candidates */
   For each pattern $T \in C$ and the predecessor of T is infrequent at time i and frequent at time $i - 1$,
   – $C = C \setminus \{T\}$;

4. /* Insert candidates in $B[d]$ */
   For each triple $(T, r, b) \in EXP$,
   – If $T \in C$ then $B[d] := B[d] \cup \{(T, r, b)\}$;

5. Return (B, C);

Figure 8. Updating the candidate pool

candidate management policy similar to Hidber [11], which is summarized as follows.

- **Initialize.** We insert all single node patterns into C. This is done at Step 1 of the algorithm StreamT

- **Increment.** We increment $count(T)$ for all pattern trees $T \in C$ that has the rightmost occurrence at the current node v_i, i.e., $count(T) = count(T) + 1$.

- **Insert.** We insert a pattern of size more than one if its unique predecessor S is already contained in C and becomes frequent, i.e., $freq(S) \geq \sigma$ based on the monotonicity of $freq(S)$ w.r.t. rightmost expansion. This is an on-demand version of the insertion policy of [11]. If some pattern becomes frequent then insert *all* of its successors to the candidate pool.

- **Delete.** We delete a pattern T from C when its unique predecessor P becomes infrequent, i.e., $freq(T) < \sigma$. To be consistent to the initialization and the insertion policy, we do not delete any single nodes. As suggested in [11], we postpone the deletion of the patterns from C until the algorithm requires additional space.

As summary, our algorithm StreamT tries to maintain the *negative border* [17], the set of all patterns that are infrequent but whose predecessors are frequent.

IncFreq(T, i)

- If $hit_i(T) = 1$ then $Fr(T) := \frac{lt(T)}{i-1}\gamma^{i-lt(T)} fr(T) + \frac{1}{i}hit_i(T)$ and $lt(T) := i$;
- If $T \notin \mathcal{C}$ then $ft(T) := i$;

GetFreq(T, i)

- If $hit_i(T) = 1$ then IncFreq(T, i) and return $Fr(T)$;
- Otherwise, return $\frac{lt(T)}{i-1}\gamma^{i-lt(T)} fr(T)$;

Figure 9. Updating and Computing the Frequency

3.5. Time Analysis

We give theoretical analysis of the update time of the algorithm **StreamT** at stage i. Let B_{i-1} be the previous SB-stack of top Top and $N_j = |B_{i-1}[j]|$ be the number of triples in the j-th bucket. If a node of depth d is received, then **UpdateB** updates the SB-stack in $O(\sum_{j=d-1}^{Top} N_j)$ time. Then, **UpdateC** updates pattern pool $\mathcal{C}$ in $O(kC+D)$ time, where k is the maximum pattern size, C is the number of candidates in $\mathcal{C}$ that occur at the current node v_i by the rightmost leaf occurrence, and D is the number of removed candidates in the stage.

4. Modification to the Forgetting Model

The algorithm **StreamT** in Fig. 2 is an online algorithm for the online frequent pattern discovery problem in the *online model* of Definition 6. Now we present modification of **StreamT** to the *forgetting model* also introduced in Definition 6.

Recall that in the forgetting model, the contribution of the past event decays exponentially fast. For a forgetting factor $0 < \gamma < 1$, the frequency of T at time i is given by Eq. 1 in Section 2. At first look, implementation of the forgetting model is as easy as the online model above because they only differ in the definition of the frequency. In the forgetting model, however, the frequency at time i depends on all of the weights γ^{i-j} of past events changing as $i \geq 1$ goes larger. Thus, it seems that an algorithm have to maintain all of these weights at every time. Fortunately, this is not true.

We abbreviate the frequency $freq_{\gamma,i}^{fg}(T)$ and the event $hit_j^{(i)}(T)$, respectively, to fr_i and hit_j. Below, we give an incremental method to compute the frequency. Let $lt(i) = \max\{ j \leq i \mid hit_j = 1 \}$ be the last time stamp at which T appeared. Then, we have the following lemma.

Lemma 5 *For every $T \in \mathcal{T}$ and every $i \geq 1$, we have the recurrence*

$$
\begin{aligned}
fr_0 &= 0, \\
fr_i &= \frac{lt(i)}{i-1}\gamma^{i-lt(i)} fr_{lt(i)} + \frac{1}{i}hit_i \quad (i > 0)
\end{aligned}
\tag{2}
$$

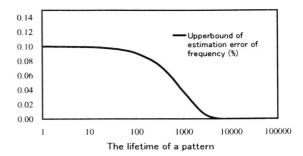

Figure 10. The upper bound of the frequency error against the life time with $\gamma = 0.999$

Proof. We first derive the recurrence for the consecutive steps. Then, derive the recurrence of the lemma by expanding fr_i using $lt(i)$. Since $hit_u = 0$ for any u with $lt(i) < u < i$, the claim immediately follows. $\square$

Now, we present a modified version of **StreamT** in the forgetting model. We modify the algorithms **StreamT** and **UpdateC** (Fig. 8) as follows. **StreamT** maintains the three parameters $fr(T), ft(T), lt(T)$, the frequency, the first and the last time stamps of the updates for T. **UpdateC** uses IncFreq to update these parameters whenever a root occurrence of pattern T is detected at Step 1, and **Stream** uses GetFreq to compute the frequency of T whenever it receives a request at Step 2(c). We can see IncFreq(T, i) and GetFreq(T, i) can be executed in constant time when invoked by these procedures.

Then, we will present an upper bound of the error to estimate the true frequency of a pattern in this model. The *life time* of a pattern T is the period $\Delta i = i - ft(T) \geq 0$. The following theorem says that the error becomes exponentially smaller in the forgetting model as the life time Δi of T goes longer.

Theorem 6 *Let $i \geq 1$, $0 < \gamma < 1$, and $\varepsilon = 1 - \gamma$. For any $T \in \mathcal{C}$ with the life time $\Delta i = i - ft(T)$ at time i, the following inequality holds:*

$$
GetFreq(T, i) \leq freq_{\gamma,i}^{fg}(T) \leq GetFreq(T, i) + \frac{1}{\varepsilon i}e^{-\varepsilon \Delta i}.
$$

Proof. By standard arguments using elementary calculus, Eqs. $1 - \gamma^x \leq 1$ and $(1 - \varepsilon)^x \leq e^{-\varepsilon x}$ $(x \geq 0)$. $\square$

In Fig. 10, we plot the upper bound of the frequency error given by Theorem 6 varying the life time from $\Delta i = 1$ to $\Delta i = 100,000$, where $\gamma = 0.999$ and $i = 1000,000$. A half-value period is about seven thousands for γ.

5. Experimental Results

In this section, we present preliminary experimental results on real-life datasets to evaluate the algorithm

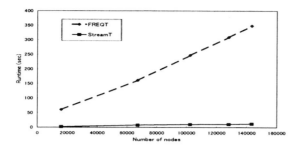

Figure 11. the online scale-up experiment

StreamT. We prepared a dataset *Citeseers* by collecting cgi-generated Web pages from an online bibliographic archive Citeseers [1]. This dataset consists of 189 HTML documents of 5.6MB and its data tree had 143,250 nodes. All experiments were performed on PC (PentiumIII 500MHz, 512MB RAM, Windows2000) and the algorithm was implemented in Java (SUN JDK1.3.1, JIT compiler).

We studied the scalability of StreamT. Fig. 11 shows the running times of the online version StreamT and the offline version FREQT [4] of frequent tree miners with the same frequency threshold $\sigma = 2(\%)$ on the data stream for the dataset *Citeseers* varying the data size from 16K(nodes) to 143K(nodes).

From this experiment, the proposed online algorithm StreamT seems to be much more efficient than the offline algorithm FREQT. However, this is possibly because our algorithm computes approximate answers due to candidate management policy in Sec. 3.4 due to [11] and two algorithms may generate different sets of patterns. Therefore, to compare the performance of those algorithms, we require further research.

6. Conclusion

In this paper, we studied an online data mining problem from unbounded semi-structured data stream. We presented efficient online algorithms that are continuously working on an unbounded stream of semi-structured data with bounded resources, and find a set of frequent ordered tree patterns from the stream on request at any time.

Our labeled ordered trees can be seen as a generalization of serial episodes of Mannila *et al.* [14], and of itemsets and sequential patterns with a pre-processing of data as used for encoding XML-attributes in [4]. Thus, it will be an interesting problem to study the relationship of our algorithms to other online algorithms for classes of patterns such as sequential patterns and episodes.

It is also a future problem to examine the online property of the proposed algorithms using long and trend-changing semi-structured data streams in the real world.

---

[1] http://citeseer.nj.nec.com/

Acknowledgments

Hiroki Arimura is grateful to Masaru Kitsuregawa for his direction of the author's interests to online data processing. The authors would like to thank Hiroshi Motoda, Takeshi Tokuyama, Akihiro Yamamoto, Yoshiharu Ishikawa, and Mohammed Zaki for fruitful discussions on web mining.

References

[1] K. Abe, S. Kawasoe, T. Asai, H. Arimura, and S. Arikawa. Optimized Substructure Discovery for Semi-structured Data, In *Proc. PKDD'02*, 1–14, LNAI 2431, Springer, 2002.

[2] S. Abiteboul, P. Buneman, D. Suciu, *Data on the Web*, Morgan Kaufmann, 2000.

[3] Aho, A. V., Hopcroft, J. E., Ullman, J. D., *Data Structures and Algorithms*, Addison-Wesley, 1983.

[4] T. Asai, K. Abe, S. Kawasoe, H. Arimura, H. Sakamoto, and S. Arikawa. Efficient Substructure Discovery from Large Semi-structured Data. In *Proc. the 2nd SIAM Int'l Conf. on Data Mining (SDM2002)*, 158–174, 2002.

[5] T. Asai, K. Abe, S. Kawasoe, H. Arimura, H. Sakamoto, and S. Arikawa. Online Algorithms for Mining Semi-structured Data Stream, *DOI Technical Report*, Dept. of Informatics, Kyushu Univ., DOI-TR 211, June 2002. ftp://ftp.i.kyushu-u.ac.jp/pub/tr/trcs211.ps.gz

[6] R. J. Bayardo Jr., Efficiently Mining Long Patterns from Databases, In *Proc. SIGMOD98*, 85–93, 1998.

[7] G. Cong, L. Yi, B. Liu, K. Wang, Discovering Frequent Substructures from Hierarchical Semi-structured Data, In *Proc. SDM2002*, 175–192, 2002.

[8] M. de Berg, M. van Kreveld, M. Overmars, O. Schwarzkopf, Computational Geometry, Algorithms and Applications, Springer, 2000.

[9] L. Dehaspe, H. Toivonen, R. D. King, Finding Frequent Substructures in Chemical Compounds, In *Proc. KDD-98*, 30–36, 1998.

[10] P. B. Gibbons and Y. Matias, Synopsis Data Structures for Massive Data Sets, In *External Memory Algorithms*, DIMACS Series in Discr. Math. and Theor. Compt. Sci., Vol. 50, AMS, 39–70, 2000.

[11] C. Hidber, Online Association Rule Mining, In *Proc. SIGMOD'99*, 145–156, 1999.

[12] P. Kilpelainen, H. Mannila, Ordered and Unordered Tree Inclusion, SIAM J. Comput, 24(2), 340–356, 1995.

[13] M. Kuramochi, G. Karypis, Frequent Subgraph Discovery, In *Proc. ICDM'01*, 313–320, 2001.

[14] H. Mannila, H. Toivonen, and A. I. Verkamo, Discovering Frequent Episode in Sequences, In *Proc. KDD-95*, 210–215, AAAI, 1995.

[15] T. Matsuda, T. Horiuchi, H. Motoda, T. Washio, K. Kumazawa, N. Arai, Graph-Based Induction for General Graph Structured Data, In *Proc. DS'99*, 340–342, 1999.

[16] T. Miyahara, Y. Suzuki, T. Shoudai, T. Uchida, K. Takahashi, H. Ueda, Discovery of Frequent Tag Tree Patterns in Semistructured Web Documents. In *Proc. PAKDD-2002*, 341–355, 2002.

[17] S. Parthasarathy, M. J. Zaki, M. Ogihara, S. Dwarkadas, Incremental and Interactive Sequence Mining, In *CIKM'99*, 251–258, 1999.

[18] R. Rastogi, Single-Path Algorithms for Querying and Mining Data Streams, In *Proc. SDM2002 Workshop HDM'02*, 43–48, 2002.

[19] W3C, Extensive Markup Language (XML) 1.0 (Second Edition), *W3C Recommendation*, 06 October 2000. http://www.w3.org/TR/REC-xml

[20] K. Wang, H. Liu, Discovering Structural Association of Semistructured Data, TKDE, 12(2), 353-371, 2000.

[21] K. Yamanishi, J. Takeuchi, A Unifying Framework for Detecting Outliers and Change Points from Non-Stationary Time Series Data, In *Proc. SIGKDD-2002*, ACM, 2002.

[22] M. J. Zaki. Efficiently mining frequent trees in a forest, In *Proc. SIGKDD-2002*, ACM, 2002.

A Lazy Approach to Pruning Classification Rules

Elena Baralis
Politecnico di Torino
Dipartimento di Automatica e Informatica
baralis@polito.it

Paolo Garza
Politecnico di Torino
Dipartimento di Automatica e Informatica
garza@polito.it

Abstract

Associative classification is a promising technique for the generation of highly precise classifiers. Previous works propose several clever techniques to prune the huge set of generated rules, with the twofold aim of selecting a small set of high quality rules, and reducing the chance of overfitting.

In this paper, we argue that pruning should be reduced to a minimum and that the availability of a large rule base may improve the precision of the classifier, without affecting its performance. In L^3 (Live and Let Live), a new algorithm for associative classification, a lazy pruning technique iteratively discards all rules that only yield wrong case classifications.

Classification is performed in two steps. Initially, rules which have already correctly classified at least one training case, sorted by confidence, are considered. If the case is still unclassified, the remaining rules (unused during the training phase) are considered, again sorted by confidence.

Extensive experiments on 26 databases from the UCI machine learning database repository show that L^3 improves the classification precision with respect to previous approaches.

1. Introduction

An important class of data mining problems is represented by association rule discovery [2]. Association rules describe the co-occurrence among data items in a large amount of collected data. Recently, association rules have been also considered a valuable tool for classification purposes.

Classification rule mining is the discovery of a small set of rules in the training database to form a model of the data, the classifier. The classifier is then used to classify appropriately new data for which the class label is unknown [9].

Association rules are usually extracted without previous definition of the set of labels that belong to the domain of the head of the rules, while for classification rules this domain corresponds to the set of class labels. Differently from decision trees, association rules consider the simultaneous correspondence of values of different attributes, hence allowing to achieve better accuracy in general, as shown by a number of experiments [3, 6, 7, 11].

Recent approaches to associative classification (e.g., CAEP [3], CMAR [6], CBA [7] and ADT [11]) extract a small set of high quality association rules, with specified thresholds for support and confidence. Since association mining may yield a huge number of classification rules, the rule base obtained by association mining is then pruned to reduce its size. Several different methods have been proposed for performing pruning, all achieving a good accuracy. However, we argue that most pruning techniques may go too far, by discarding also useful knowledge together with low quality rules. Hence, we propose a novel two steps classification technique, in which only a very reduced amount of pruning is performed, by eliminating only "harmful" rules, i.e., rules that only produce wrong classification results in the training data.

The contribution of this paper is as follows. First, we customized a good association rule extraction algorithm [6] to extract rules with variable support threshold, in order to generate a similar number of rules for all classes, including those that may have a small number of cases. Second, we designed a lazy pruning technique that only discards "harmful" rules from the rule base. Third, we developed a two steps classification approach, in which "first" class rules (i.e, rules used in the classification of training cases) are considered first, and second class rules (i.e., rules not used during the training phase) are used next for the same task of classification. Second class rules are considered only when a test case cannot be classified by means of first class rules.

In the following Section, we show by means of a motivating example how previous approaches fail the classification of a new test case because of excessive pruning. Section 2 discusses the problem of associative classification. In Section 3 we present the generation of the L^3 classifier by means of multiple support thresholds and lazy pruning.

35

Housing	Finance	Social	Health	Class
h:c	f:c	s:np	he:r	recommended
h:c	f:c	s:sp	he:r	recommended
h:lc	f:ic	s:np	he:nr	not recommended

Figure 1. Example training data set

Attribute	Domain	Attribute	Domain
Housing	convenient, less_conv	Social	nonprob, slightly_prob
Finance	convenient, inconvenient, less_conv	Health	not_rec, recommended

Figure 2. Domains of attributes

Section 4 describes how L^3 classifies test data by means of its two levels. Section 5 provides an extensive suite of experiments to validate the L^3 approach. Finally, in Section 6 we discuss the main differences between our approach and previous work on associative classification, and Section 7 draws conclusions.

1.1. Motivating Example

Current approaches to associative classification, albeit to a different extent, select association rules for the classifier by matching them with training set cases. Once one (e.g., CBA [7]) or more rules (e.g., CMAR [6]) cover a case, the case is discarded. Hence, all other rules that were covering (only) the same case will not be included in the classifier.

Consider the example training dataset in Fig. 1, which describes the characteristics of two classes of nurses: recommended and not recommended. Values of attributes have been abbreviated, for the sake of rule representation. The actual domains of attributes are given in Fig. 2.

Given this training data, the extraction of all rules, without using support and confidence constraints, yields 38 rules. In Fig. 3 are reported some of the extracted rules, sorted by descending confidence, descending support, and increasing length.

We now apply the pruning techniques proposed in previous approaches to derive the classifier rules. A first pruning technique, applied by most previous approaches (e.g., CMAR [6], CBA [7] and ADT [11]) uses general rules to prune more specific rules with lower confidence. The rules remaining after this pruning are 9.

CMAR next applies a pruning technique based on χ^2 coefficient. Let all rules be positively correlated and not pruned by this technique. Finally, the last pruning technique adopted by CBA and CMAR is the *database coverage* technique. In particular, CBA extracts the minimal number of

Rule	Conf	Supp
{f:c} → rec.	100.00%	66.67%
{h:c} → rec.	100.00%	66.67%
{he:r} → rec.,	100.00%	66.67%
{f:ic} → not rec.	100.00%	33.33%
{he:nr} → not rec.	100.00%	33.33%
{he:r,s:np} → rec.	100.00%	33.33%
{he:r,s:sp} → rec.	100.00%	33.33%
......	......	......
{s:np} → rec.	50.00%	33.33%

Figure 3. Some of the example generated rules

Rule	Conf	Supp
{f:c} → rec.	100.00%	66.67%
{f:ic} → not rec.	100.00%	33.33%

Figure 4. Example CBA classifier

rules necessary to cover each case in the training data. After this pruning, the rules in Fig. 4 compose the final CBA classifier.

Differently from CBA, CMAR selects at least δ rules before discarding any training case. This allows the generation of a "richer" classifier containing more rules, which will be able to cover a wider spectrum of test data. By using $\delta = 2$ (adequate for such a small training dataset), CMAR yields a classifier composed by the rules in Fig. 5.

Now consider the following new (test) tuple: (h:lc, f:lc, s:sp, he:r). Both CBA and CMAR classifiers are not able to classify this tuple because of an excessive pruning. Indeed, e.g., rule $\{he : r, s : sp\} \rightarrow rec.$ (and several others which would cover the case) has been discarded, although with high confidence (100%)[1].

Excessive pruning affects (albeit to a different extent) all previous proposals of associative classifiers. The database coverage technique used by CMAR is a first step towards a reduction of the negative effect of excessive pruning, but still useful knowledge is lost. We argue that rules may be useful to cover new cases even if they have not been used to cover training data and should not be discarded. However,

---

[1]Support is only 33.33%, low with respect to other rules, so a simple threshold on support may have discarded this rule as well.

Rule	Conf	Supp
{f:c} → rec.	100.00%	66.67%
{h:c} → rec.	100.00%	66.67%
{f:ic} → not rec.	100.00%	33.33%
{he:nr} → not rec.	100.00%	33.33%

Figure 5. Example CMAR classifier

since the quality of these rules has not been verified during the training phase (they have not been used), these rules should be treated differently from the high quality rules selected during the training phase. To this end, we propose a two steps classification process, in which the second step considers rules usually pruned by the other algorithms.

2. Problem Statement

The database is represented as a relation R, whose schema is given by k distinct attributes $A_1 \ldots A_k$ and a class attribute C. The attributes may have either a categorical or a continuous domain. For categorical attributes, all values in the domain are mapped to consecutive positive integers. In the case of continuous attributes, the value range is discretized into intervals, and the intervals are also mapped into consecutive positive integers.[2] In this way, all attributes are treated uniformly.

Each tuple in R can be described as a collection of pairs *(attribute, integer value)*, plus a class label (a value belonging to the domain of class attribute C). Each pair *(attribute, integer value)* will be called *item* in the reminder of the paper. A training case is a tuple in relation R, where the class label is known, while a test case is a tuple in R where the class label is unknown.

A classifier is a function from $A_1, \ldots, A_n$ to C, that allows the assignment of a class label to a test case. Given a collection of training cases, the classification task is the generation of a classifier able to predict the class label for test cases with high accuracy.

Association rules extraction is a recently proposed approach for the classification task. Association rules are rules in the form $X \rightarrow Y$. When using them for classification purposes, X is a set of items, while Y is a class label. A case d is said to match a collection of items X when $X \subseteq d$. The quality of an association rule is measured by two parameters, its support, given by the number of cases matching $X \cup Y$ over the number of cases in the database, and its confidence given by the the number of cases matching $X \cup Y$ over the number of cases matching X. Hence, the classification task can be reduced to the generation of the most appropriate set of association rules for the classifier. Our approach to such task is described in the next Section.

3. Mining classification rules

In our approach, abundance of classification rules is important, to allow a wider selection of rules when classification is performed. Hence, our aim is to extract a large number of rules, by setting rather low support and confidence

---

[2]The problem of discretization has been widely dealt with in the machine learning community (see, e.g., [4]) and will not be discussed further in this paper.

thresholds. Ideally, setting the support threshold close to zero could be considered, together with a limitation on the number of generated rules by screening rules on the confidence value. An attempt in this direction has been proposed in [10], where classification rules are extracted only with a confidence threshold, but it is unclear how well the approach scales on training cases characterized by a large number of items.

Currently, the most efficient approach to the extraction of classification rules is proposed in CMAR [6], which is based on the well-known FP-growth[5] algorithm. To perform classification rule extraction, we use a variation of the rule extraction part of the CMAR algorithm, with a variable support threshold, that allows us to treat uniformly classes characterized by an uneven number of training cases. In the remainder of this Section, we discuss the use of multiple support thresholds for rule extraction and the lazy pruning technique applied by L^3.

3.1. Multiple support thresholds

Most algorithms for the extraction of classification rules, set only one fixed threshold *minsup* for the minimum support value. As already stated in [8], this is not the best choice when the training cases are unevenly distributed among classes. In [8], the extraction algorithm uses a different support threshold for each class c_i given by $minsup_i = minsup * freq(c_i)$, where $freq(c_i)$ is the frequency of class c_i. However, the number of extracted association rules depends also significantly on the characteristics of the data distribution in class c_i. Hence, this definition of $minsup_i$ does not guarantee that a sufficient number of rules for classes having low frequency will be generated.

We use an iterative approach, in which the appropriate support threshold $minsup_i$ for each class is selected by analyzing the result of the previous extraction cycle. As an initial value for support, analogously to [8], we set $minsup_i^{(0)} = minsup * freq(c_i)$. After this first step, since the availability for all classes of some rules with high confidence is important, we check the following two conditions for each class c_i: (a) an excessively low number of high confidence rules has been extracted for class c_i with respect to the average number of rules (less than 15%), or (b) class c_i is characterized by a significantly smaller number of rules with respect to the average number of rules in classes (less than 20%). If any of the above conditions is true, $minsup_i$ is further lowered as $minsup_i^{(k)} = 0.9 * minsup_i^{(k-1)}$ where k is the iteration number. We have found after several experiments that the constant value 0.9 allowed us to gradually decrease the support threshold. Furthermore, only a few iterations were necessary before both above conditions became false. The effect of variable support thresholds is further discussed in Section 5.

3.2. Lazy Pruning

Although the number of association rules generated by rule extraction can be huge, we argue that most rules can provide useful knowledge for the classification of test cases. Hence, in L^3 *lazy* pruning is proposed, to limit the number of pruned rules to a minimum, as described below. This technique yields good precision results only if it is coupled with the novel classification technique described in Section 4, as shown by the experiments presented in Section 5.

Before performing lazy pruning, a global order is imposed on the rule base (similar to [6, 7]). Let r_1 and r_2 be two rules. Then r_1 precedes r_2, denoted as $r_1 > r_2$ if (1) $\text{conf}(r_1) > \text{conf}(r_2)$, or (2) $\text{conf}(r_1) = \text{conf}(r_2)$ and $\text{sup}(r_1) > \text{sup}(r_2)$, or (3) $\text{conf}(r_1) = \text{conf}(r_2)$ and $\text{sup}(r_1) = \text{sup}(r_2)$ and $\text{len}(r_1) > \text{len}(r_2)$, or (4) if $\text{conf}(r_1) = \text{conf}(r_2)$ and $\text{sup}(r_1) = \text{sup}(r_2)$ and $\text{len}(r_1) = \text{len}(r_2)$ and $\text{lex}(r_1) > \text{lex}(r_2)$, where $\text{len}(r)$ denotes the number of items in the body of r, and $\text{lex}(r)$ denotes the position of r in the lexicographic order on items.

The only significant difference with respect to previous work is that in point (3) we sort rules in decreasing length order, while previous approaches prefer short rules over long rules. The reason for this choice is to give a higher rank in the ordering to more specific rules (rules with a larger number of items in the body) over generic rules, which may lead to misclassification. Note that, since shorter rules are not pruned, they can be considered anyway, when specific rules are not applicable.

The idea behind lazy pruning is to discard from the classifier only the rules that do not correctly classify any training case, i.e., the rules that only negatively contribute to the classification of training cases. To this end, after rule sorting, we cover the training cases to detect "harmful" rules. Lines 1-24 of the pseudocode in Figure 6 show our approach. For each training case, we assign it to the first rule in the sort order that covers it (lines 2-17), and we check if the assigned class label was correct or wrong (lines 9-10). The case is then discarded (line 16).[3] After all cases have been considered, the pruning step discards rules that only classified training cases wrongly (lines 18-23). Training cases classified by discarded rules enter again the assignment loop (lines 1-24), and the cycle is repeated until no training case is covered by discarded rules.

After having discarded "harmful" rules, the remaining rules are divided in two groups (lines 25-30):

used rules which have already correctly classified at least one training case,

spare rules which have not been used during the training phase, but may become useful later.

---

[3]Note that the case is discarded also if it is not covered by any rule.

Procedure generateClassifier(*rules,data*)
1. while *data* not empty {
2.   for each *d* in *data* {
3.   covered=false;
4.   NR = number of *rules*;
5.   *r* = first rule of *rules*;
6.   while (covered==false) and (NR>0) {
7.   if *r* covers *d* {
8.   *r*.dataClassified = *r*.dataClassified ∪ *d*;
9.   if (*d*.class==*r*.class) *r*.right++;
10.   else *r*.wrong++;
11.   covered=true;
12.   }
13.   NR- -;
14.   *r*=next rule from *rules*;
15.   }
16.   delete *d* from *data*;
17. }
18. for each *r* in *rules* {
19.   if *r*.wrong>0 and *r*.right==0 {
20.   delete *r* from *rules*;
21.   *data = data* ∪ *r*.dataClassified;
22.   }
23. }
24. }
25. for each *r* in *rules* {
26.   if *r*.right>0
27.   *usedRules = usedRules* ∪ *r*;
28.   else
29.   *spareRules = spareRules* ∪ *r*;
30. }

Figure 6. L^3 classifier generation

Used rules are generated with a database coverage technique similar to other approaches [6, 7] and provide a high level model of each class. Spare rules, instead, allow us to increase the precision of the classifier by capturing "special" cases which are not covered by used rules (see Section 1.1). Both groups of rules are used to create the classifier. In particular, used rules are assigned to the first level of the classifier, while spare rules yield the second level. Rules in each level are ordered following the global order described above. Our pruning technique is very simple, compared with previous proposals (see, e.g., [6, 7, 11]), but it is very effective, as shown by the experiments in Section 5. It eliminates from the rule base only those rules which yield negative effects on the classification of training cases. As discussed in Section 5, we observe that such a simple pruning is not adequate if the classifier is to be generated only with used rules. Hence, more tolerance in pruning is effective only if coupled with more tolerance in the generation of the classifier.

38

We finally note that pruning of more specific classification rules as suggested in [6, 7], even with a lower confidence, is not performed. Indeed, if the iterative rule deletion loop eliminates a general rule, the specific rule may remain and if it does not generate erroneous classifications, be assigned to spare rules and become useful for test cases.

4. Classification

In this Section we describe the classification of test cases by means of the two levels L^3 classifier. When a test case is to be classified, rules of level I of the classifier are considered. If no rule in this level matches the test case, then rules in level II are considered. If again no rule matches the test case, the case is assigned to the default class.

Differently from previously proposed associative classifiers, L^3 usually contains a large number of rules. In particular, level I of the classifier, containing rules used in the training phase to cover some training case, is characterized by a small number of rules, analogously to previous approaches. As shown in Section 5, this level performs the "heavy duty" classification of most test cases and can provide a general model of each class. By contrast, level II of the classifier may contain a large number of rules which are seldom used. These rules allow the classification of some more cases, which cannot be covered by rules in the first level. Hence, the few used rules in the second level allow a significant increase in classification precision, as shown in Section 5.

Since level I usually contained about 10^2-10^3 rules, it can easily fit in main memory. Thus, the main classification task can be performed efficiently. Level II, in our experiments, included around 10^5 rules. Rules were organized in a compact list, sorted as described in Section 3.2. Hence, level II of L^3 could be loaded in main memory as well, as discussed in more detail in Section 5. Of course, if the number of rules in the second level further increases (e.g., because the support threshold is further lowered to capture more rules with high confidence), efficient access may become difficult. We are currently considering a more compact representation of rules, based on the relationship between a generic rule and its specializations.

We finally note that, similarly to [7, 11], we only consider the first rule matching the test case to classify it, but a further increase in precision may be obtained by performing classification with multiple rules, as described in [6]. Indeed, this technique is orthogonal to our approach and can be separately applied to each L^3 level.

5. Experimental Results

In this Section, we describe the experiments to measure accuracy, classification efficiency, and memory consumption for L^3. We have performed a large set of experiments using 26 data sets downloaded from UCI Machine Learning Repository [1]. We compared L^3 with the classification algorithms CBA [7], CMAR [6], and C4.5 [9]. The experiments show that L^3 outperforms all previous approaches, by achieving a larger average accuracy (+0.63% over the best previous, i.e., CMAR), and improving accuracy on 14 data sets over 26.

The confidence constraint has not been enforced, i.e., $minconf$=0. The value of the lowest $minsup_i$ (column 5), and the average value of $minsup_i$ (column 6) for each data set are shown in Table 1. We have adopted the same technique used by CBA to discretize continuous attributes. A 10 fold cross validation test has been used to compute the accuracy of the classifier. All the experiments have been performed on a 1000Mhz Pentium III PC with 1.5G main memory, running RedHat Linux 7.2.

Table 1 compares the accuracy of L^3 with the accuracy of C4.5, CBA and CMAR, obtained using standard values for all the parameters. In particular, the columns of Table 1 are: (1) name of data set, (2) number of attributes, (3) number of classes, (4) number of cases (records), (7) accuracy of C4.5, (8) accuracy of CBA, (9) accuracy of CMAR, and (10) accuracy of L^3.

L^3 has best average accuracy (+0.63% with respect to CMAR) and best accuracy on 14 of the 26 UCI data sets (over 50% of the data sets). The improvement in accuracy may be due to several factors: (a) the use of multiple support thresholds, (b) the lazy pruning technique, and (c) the use of rules included in the second level of the classifier.

It has not been necessary to adopt multiple support thresholds in most of the 14 cases in which L^3 achieves better accuracy than previous approaches. Hence, multiple support thresholds only have a limited effect on the average accuracy value.

To observe the effect of rules in level II of L^3, we compare the accuracy obtained by only using rules in level I of L^3 with the accuracy obtained by using both levels. The result of the experiment is reported in Table 1. The related columns of Table 1 are: (11) number of rules in the first level of L^3, (12) number of rules in the second level, (13) accuracy of L^3 using only rules in the first level, (14) difference between L^3 with both levels (column (10)) and L^3 with only first level (column (13)).

By considering only rules in the first level, L^3 achieves best accuracy on only 6 of the UCI data sets and an average accuracy somewhat lower than CBA and CMAR. In particular, the average accuracy is about 1% less in the worst case (i.e., with respect to CMAR [6]). Hence, the first level already captures most fundamental characteristics of each class, thus providing a model of reasonable quality. However, this experiment also shows the importance of rules stored in the second level. Indeed, lazy pruning

Name	a	c	r	Min	Av.	C4.5	CBA	CMAR	L^3	I level	II level	Only I level	Δacc
Anneal	38	6	898	1	1	94.8	**97.9**	97.3	96.10	73	128784	95.43	+0.67
Austral	14	2	690	1	1	84.7	84.9	86.1	**86.23**	142	46909	85.07	+1.16
Auto	25	7	205	0.48	0.9	**80.1**	78.3	78.1	77.56	30	233832	75.12	+2.44
Breast	10	2	699	1	1	95	96.3	**96.4**	95.99	66	22117	95.57	+0.42
Cleve	13	2	303	1	1	78.2	82.8	82.2	**85.15**	62	6937	84.49	+0.66
Crx	15	2	690	1	1	84.9	84.7	84.9	**85.80**	131	23587	85.36	+0.44
Diabetes	8	2	768	0.9	0.9	74.2	74.5	75.8	**78.39**	82	9765	78.39	0.00
German	20	2	1000	0.3	1.4	72.3	73.4	**74.9**	72.50	57	175308	70.20	+2.30
Glass	9	7	214	1	1	68.7	73.9	70.1	**77.57**	34	11027	66.82	+10.75
Heart	13	2	270	1	1	80.8	81.9	82.2	**82.96**	57	40012	82.59	+0.37
Hepatic	19	2	155	1	1	80.6	81.8	80.5	**86.45**	26	76648	86.45	0.00
Horse	22	2	368	1	1	82.6	82.1	82.6	**83.15**	110	125134	81.79	+1.36
Hypo	25	2	3163	1	1	**99.2**	98.9	98.4	95.23	6	393843	95.23	0.00
Iono	34	2	351	0.7	0.9	90	92.3	91.5	**92.88**	40	60405	91.45	+1.43
Iris	4	3	150	0.5	0.5	**95.3**	94.7	94	93.33	11	179	93.33	0.00
Labor	16	2	57	1	1	79.3	86.3	89.7	**92.98**	17	7950	87.72	+5.26
Led7	7	10	3200	0.8	0.8	**73.5**	71.9	72.5	72.00	100	5760	71.78	+0.22
Lymph	18	4	148	1	1	73.5	77.8	83.1	**84.46**	41	86876	80.41	+4.05
Pima	8	2	768	1	1	75.5	72.9	75.1	**77.99**	84	9758	77.99	0.00
Sick	29	2	2800	2	2	**98.5**	97	97.5	93.89	8	143444	93.86	+0.03
Sonar	60	2	208	2	2	70.2	77.5	79.4	**80.77**	52	135889	77.40	+3.37
Tic-tac	9	2	958	0.5	0.5	99.4	**99.6**	99.2	99.48	30	41793	99.48	0.00
Vehicle	18	4	846	0.8	1.3	**72.6**	68.7	68.8	68.56	104	67730	67.38	+1.18
Waveform	21	3	5000	0.7	0.8	78.1	80	**83.2**	82.52	354	41342	81.48	+1.04
Wine	13	3	178	1	1	92.7	95	95	**97.19**	11	40764	94.94	+2.25
Zoo	16	7	101	0.8	1.1	92.2	96.8	**97.1**	93.07	9	380912	89.11	+3.96
Average				0.94	1.04	83.34	84.69	85.22	**85.85**			84.18	+1.67

Table 1. Comparison of L^3 accuracy with respect to C4.5, CBA, CMAR

by itself (considering only level I rules) yields a "medium" quality classifier, while the joint effect with the presence of level II rules allows a significant gain in average accuracy (+1.67%). This result shows that the small number of rules used for covering training data (rules in level I), albeit very effective, is not sufficient. A significant improvement in accuracy is obtained by exploiting the knowledge contained in rules which have not been used for covering training cases (i.e., level II rules). We observe that, usually, the number of test cases correctly classified by the second level is rather small, but sufficient to obtain a better accuracy for L^3. For example, for data set *labor* level II correctly classifies just 3 more test cases, but since the data set is composed by 57 cases, this allows a +5.26% in accuracy. In the case of data set *glass* the improvement obtained by the second level is more evident. Indeed, 23 more cases are correctly classified over a total of 214 cases (+10.75% in accuracy).

To verify if lazy pruning affected classification accuracy, we also ran tests (not reported here) using two level classification without performing any pruning of rules. For these experiments, each training case is considered only once for matching (lines 2-17 in Fig. 6). Rules that matched at least one training case (disregarding correctness of the match) are assigned to the first level, while the second level contains all remaining rules. These tests resulted in lower average precision (-1.44%) with respect to the value reported for L^3 in Table 1, showing that also two level classification by itself is not an effective classification technique.

Since the number of rules in the two levels of L^3 is significantly different (see Table 1), we analyzed the performance of L^3 during the classification of test data. The results are reported in column (5) of Table 2, which shows the CPU time required by the classification of the whole data set as a test set using L^3. We have also make a test using only the first level, but we have not reported those times because they are very closed to the ones showed in Table 2. A larger time is necessary for the generation of the classifier with respect to previous approaches, owing to the lower (and variable) support threshold for association rule extraction. However, we observe that the generation of the classifier is a task that takes place very rarely, as opposed to the classification of new cases. Thus, a longer generation time may be acceptable, in order to increase significantly the precision of the classification step. Table 2 also shows the number of cases classified by rules of the first level (column (3) rightly classified + wrongly classified) and by rules of the second level + unclassified data (column (4)). The number of cases in each data set is reported in column (2). We observe that a vast majority of cases is classified by rules of the first level, while only a minimal number of accesses to the second level is required. Furthermore, rules of second level usually correctly classified each considered case. Only in very few cases rules of the second level are not able to classify a case, or wrongly classify it. Hence, although the number of rules in the second level can be quite large, accessing it is a rare event that does not significantly affect performance, while it significantly improves accuracy.

To obtain efficent classification, it is important that rules in both levels can be stored in memory. Hence, we analyzed main memory usage of L^3 for the storage of the rule base during the classification phase. Table 2 reports the results. The columns of table 2 are: (6) number of rules in the first level of L^3, (7) number of rules in the second level of L^3, (8) memory used to store the rules of the first level (in Kbyte), (9) memory used to store the rules of the second level (in Kbyte). As expected, the memory required for storing first level rules is negligible, while the second level rules need significantly more memory, especially for some data sets (up to 50Mbyte). Hence, on currently available machines (512Mbyte main memory is a standard today) we are able to store second level rules in main memory. The ability of storing second level rules is closely related to the value of the support threshold. Since we believe that second level rules have to be stored in main memory, we selected support threshold values that did not generate an excessive number of rules, such that main memory storage becomes impossible. For the presence of the second level L^3 required more memory of CBA and CMAR, and so L^3 memory performance is worse than the previous ones.

6. Previous Related Work

Associative classification has been first proposed in CBA [7]. CBA, based on the Apriori association rules mining algorithm [2], extracts a limited number of association rules (max 80000). A weakness of this approach is the reduced number of rules extracted by means of Apriori, because long and interesting rules are usually not generated, thus losing some relevant knowledge. Furthermore, as discussed in Section 1.1, after sorting on descending confidence, a pruning technique is applied, and only the minimal number of rules necessary to cover training data is used to create the classifier. A new version of the algorithm has been presented [8], in which the use of multiple supports is proposed to increase accuracy in presence of uneven class distributions, together with a combination of C4.5 and Naive-Bayes classifiers, to be used when CBA rules wrongly classify training cases. While using multiple support thresholds permits to overcome to some extent the limitations due to the use of the Apriori algorithm, it does not address the overpruning problem described in Section 1.1.

ADT [11] is a different classification algorithm based on association rules, combined with decision tree pruning techniques. All rules with a confidence greater or equal to a given threshold are extracted and more specific rules are pruned. A decision tree is created based on the remaining association rules, on which classical decision tree pruning techniques are applied. Analogously to other algorithms, the classifier is composed by a small number of rules and prone to the overpruning problem.

CMAR[6] is the latest classification algorithm based on association rules proposed in literature. CMAR proposes a suite of different pruning techniques: pruning of specialistic rules, use of the χ^2 coefficient, and database coverage. As already noted, the database coverage technique is more tolerant than the coverage technique adopted by CBA, and allows more (but not all) rules to cover the same training case. Again, useful rules may be pruned, thus yielding the same overpruning problem. A further technique applied in CMAR to increase average accuracy is the classification of test cases by means of more than one rule. This technique is independent of the adopted pruning techniques, and is likely to be profitable in our setting as well. Hence, we are considering it as a further improvement of our classifier.

7. Conclusions

In this paper we have described L^3, a novel approach to classification by means of association rules. While previous approaches suggested various techniques to generate a classifier containing a very limited number of rules, we believe that it is important to exploit all the knowledge that can be extracted from the training cases. Hence, we propose a lazy pruning technique, which only discards "harmful" rules, coupled with a two levels classification approach, in which rules normally discarded in previous approaches are included in the second level of the classifier and used only when first level rules are not able to classify a test case.

We observe that, even in presence of a large number of rules into the second level of L^3 classifier, the interpretability of techniques based on classification rules is not lost. Indeed, used rules (rules in the first level of the classifier) capture recurring properties of the data, thus providing a high level model of each class, composed of just a few rules.

Furthermore, we note that overfitting is avoided by the second level of the classifier. Indeed, as shown in Section 5,

Name	#cases	#level I	#level II	Time(s)	Rules I	Rules II	Mem. I(K)	Mem. II(K)
Anneal	898	857+29	11+1	0.935	73	128784	100	696
Austral	690	587+95	8	0.616	142	46909	100	6908
Auto	205	154+33	17+1	0.250	30	233832	96	13360
Breast	699	668+29	2	0.660	66	22117	96	7680
Cleve	303	256+44	3	0.286	62	6937	96	492
Crx	690	589+91	10	0.656	131	23587	104	43680
Diabetes	768	602+166	0	0.695	82	9765	96	716
German	1000	702+263	35	0.949	57	175308	116	40436
Glass	214	143+48	23	0.192	34	11027	92	704
Heart	270	223+43	4	0.270	57	40012	100	2964
Hepatic	155	134+21	0	0.147	26	76648	92	4184
Horse	368	301+62	5	0.345	110	125134	96	8420
Hypo	3163	3012+151	0	3.132	6	393843	96	45964
Iono	351	321+22	8	0.343	40	60405	92	4612
Iris	150	140+10	0	0.125	11	179	100	16
Labor	57	50+2	5	0.055	17	7950	92	552
Led7	3200	2297+896	7	2.918	100	5760	100	896
Lymph	148	119+11	18	0.175	41	86876	92	6528
Pima	768	599+169	0	0.735	84	9758	104	704
Sick	2800	2628+171	1	2.601	8	143444	92	47576
Sonar	208	161+39	8	0.207	52	135889	100	9612
Tic-tac	958	953+5	0	0.871	30	41793	92	3716
Vehicle	846	570+266	10	0.858	104	67730	104	14040
Waveform	5000	4074+838	88	4.834	354	41342	152	27212
Wine	178	169+3	6	0.162	11	40764	92	3120
Zoo	101	90+0	4+7	0.093	9	380912	100	27008

Table 2. Classification time and memory usage of L^3

this level forces a priority ordering among rules that avoids considering a "medium" quality rule belonging to the second level, when a better rule is available for classification in the first level. Hence, considering second level rules can never cause a reduction in precision, since cases classified by these rules would be otherwise unclassified (or assigned to the default class).

The lazy pruning approach allowed us to significantly increase average classification precision over previous approaches. In particular, the experiments show that the presence of the second level provides a major enhancement in the classification quality, without reducing the efficiency of the classification activity.

References

[1] http://www1.ics.uci.edu/ mlearn/MLRepository.html, UCI Machine Learning Repository, University of California, Irvine.

[2] R. Agrawal and R. Srikant. Fast algorithm for mining association rules. In VLDB'94, Santiago, Chile, Sept. 1994.

[3] G. Dong, X. Zhang, L. Wong, and J. Li. CAEP: Classification by aggregating emerging patterns. In International Conference on Discovery Science, Tokyo, Japan, Dec. 1999.

[4] U. Fayyad and K. Irani. Multi-interval discretization of continuos-valued attributes for classification learning. In IJ-CAI'93, 1993.

[5] J. Han, J. Pei, and Y. Yin. Mining frequent patterns without candidate generation. In SIGMOD'00, Dallas, TX, May 2000.

[6] W. Li, J. Han, and J. Pei. CMAR: Accurate and efficient classification based on multiple class-association rules. In ICDM'01, San Jose, CA, November 2001.

[7] B. Liu, W. Hsu, and Y. Ma. Integrating classification and association rule mining. In KDD'98, New York, NY, August 1998.

[8] B. Liu, Y. Ma, and K. Wong. Improving an association rule based classifier. In PKDD'00, Lyon, France, Sept. 2000.

[9] J. Quinlan. C4.5: program for classification learning. Morgan Kaufmann, 1992.

[10] K. Wang, Y. He, D. W. Cheung, and F. Y. L. Chin. Mining confident rules without support requirement. In CIKM'01, Atlanta, GA, November 2001.

[11] K. Wang, S. Zhou, and Y. He. Growing decision trees on support-less association rules. In KDD'00, Boston, MA, August 2000.

High Performance Data Mining Using the Nearest Neighbor Join

Christian Böhm
University for Health Informatics and Technology
Christian.Boehm@umit.at

Florian Krebs
University of Munich
krebs@dbs.informatik.uni-muenchen.de

Abstract

The similarity join has become an important database primitive to support similarity search and data mining. A similarity join combines two sets of complex objects such that the result contains all pairs of similar objects. Well-known are two types of the similarity join, the distance range join where the user defines a distance threshold for the join, and the closest point query or k-distance join which retrieves the k most similar pairs. In this paper, we investigate an important, third similarity join operation called k-nearest neighbor join which combines each point of one point set with its k nearest neighbors in the other set. It has been shown that many standard algorithms of Knowledge Discovery in Databases (KDD) such as k-means and k-medoid clustering, nearest neighbor classification, data cleansing, postprocessing of sampling-based data mining etc. can be implemented on top of the k-nn join operation to achieve performance improvements without affecting the quality of the result of these algorithms. We propose a new algorithm to compute the k-nearest neighbor join using the multipage index (MuX), a specialized index structure for the similarity join. To reduce both CPU and I/O cost, we develop optimal loading and processing strategies.

1. Introduction

KDD algorithms in multidimensional databases are often based on similarity queries which are performed for a high number of objects. Recently, it has been recognized that many algorithms of similarity search [2] and data mining [3] can be based on top of a single join query instead of many similarity queries. Thus, a high number of single similarity queries is replaced by a single run of a *similarity join*. The most well-known form of the similarity join is the distance range join $R \bowtie_\varepsilon S$ which is defined for two finite sets of vectors, $R = \{r_1,...,r_n\}$ and $S = \{s_1,...,s_m\}$, as the set of all pairs from $R \times S$ having a distance of no more than ε:

$$R \bowtie_\varepsilon S := \{(r_i,s_j) \in R \times S \mid \|p_i - q_j\| \le \varepsilon\}$$

E.g. in [3], it has been shown that density based clustering algorithms such as DBSCAN [25] or the hierarchical cluster analysis method OPTICS [1] can be accelerated by high factors of typically one or two orders of magnitude by the range distance join. Due to its importance, a large number of algorithms to compute the range distance join of two sets have been proposed, e.g. [27, 19, 5]

Another important similarity join operation which has been recently proposed is the incremental distance join [16]. This join operation orders the pairs from $R \times S$ by increasing distance and returns them to the user either on a give-me-more basis, or based on a user specified cardinality of k best pairs (which corresponds to a k-closest pair operation in computational geometry, cf. [23]). This operation can be successfully applied to implement data analysis tasks such as noise-robust catalogue matching and noise-robust duplicate detection [11].

In this paper, we investigate a third kind of similarity join, the k-nearest neighbor similarity join, short k-nn join. This operation is motivated by the observation that many data analysis and data mining algorithms is based on k-nearest neighbor queries which are issued separately for a large set of *query points* $R = \{r_1,...,r_n\}$ against another large set of *data points* $S = \{s_1,...,s_m\}$. In contrast to the incremental distance join and the k-distance join which choose the best pairs from the complete pool of pairs $R \times S$, the k-nn join combines each of the points of R with its k nearest neighbors in S. The differences between the three kinds of similarity join operations are depicted in figure 1.

Applications of the k-nn join include but are not limited to the following list: k-nearest neighbor classification, k-means and k-medoid clustering, sample assessment and sample postprocessing, missing value imputation, k-distance diagrams, etc. In [8] we have shown that k-means clustering, nearest neighbor classification, and various other algorithms can be transformed such that they operate exclusively on top of the k-nearest neighbor join. This transformation typically leads to performance gains up to a factor of 8.5.

Our list of applications covers all stages of the KDD process. In the preprocessing step, data cleansing algorithms are typically based on k-nearest neighbor queries for each of the points with NULL values against the set of complete vectors. The missing values can be computed e.g. as the weighted means of the values of the k nearest neighbors. A k-distance diagram can be used to determine suitable parameters for data mining. Additionally, in the core step, i.e. data mining, many algorithms such as clustering and classification are based on k-nn queries. As such algorithms are often time consuming and have at least a linear, often $n \log n$ or even quadratic complexity they typically run on a sample set rather than the complete data set. The k-nn-queries are used to assess the quality of the sample set (preprocessing). After the run of the data mining algorithm, it is necessary to relate the result to the complete set of database points [10]. The typical method for doing that is again a k-nn-query for each of the database points with respect to the set of classified sample points. In all these algorithms, it is possible to replace a large number of k-nn queries which are originally issued separately, by a single run of a k-nn join. Therefore, the k-nn join gives powerful support for all stages of the KDD process.

The remainder of the paper is organized as follows: In section 2, we give a classification of the well-known similarity join operations and review the related work. In section 3, we define the new operation, the k-nearest neighbor join. In section 4, we develop an algorithm for the k-nn join which applies matching loading and processing strategies on top of the multipage index [7], an index structure which is particularly suited for high-dimensional similarity joins, in order to reduce both CPU and I/O cost and efficiently compute the k-nn join. The experimental evaluation of our approach is presented in section 5 and section 6 concludes the paper.

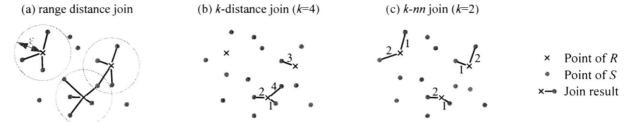

(a) range distance join   (b) *k*-distance join (*k*=4)   (c) *k-nn* join (*k*=2)

×	Point of *R*
•	Point of *S*
×—•	Join result

Figure 1. Difference between similarity join operations

2. Related work

In the relational data model a join means to combine the tuples of two relations *R* and *S* into pairs if a *join predicate* is fulfilled. In multidimensional databases, *R* and *S* contain points (feature vectors) rather than ordinary tuples. In a *similarity join*, the join predicate is similarity, e.g. the Euclidean distance between two feature vectors.

2.1 Distance range based similarity join

The most prominent and most evaluated similarity join operation is the distance range join. Therefore, the notions *similarity join* and *distance range join* are often used interchangeably. Unless otherwise specified, when speaking of *the similarity join*, often the distance range join is meant by default. For clarity in this paper, we will not follow this convention and always use the more specific notions. As depicted in figure 1a, the distance range join $R \bowtie_\epsilon S$ of two multidimensional or metric sets *R* and *S* is the set of pairs where the distance of the objects does not exceed the given parameter ϵ:

Definition 1 Distance Range Join (ϵ-Join)
The distance range join $R \bowtie_\epsilon S$ of two finite multidimensional or metric sets *R* and *S* is the set

$$R \bowtie_\epsilon S := \{(r_i, s_j) \in R \times S : \|r_i - s_j\| \le \epsilon\}$$

The distance range join can also be expressed in a SQL like fashion:

SELECT * FROM *R, S* **WHERE** $\|R.\text{obj} - S.\text{obj}\| \le \epsilon$

In both cases, $\|\cdot\|$ denotes the distance metric which is assigned to the multimedia objects. For multidimensional vector spaces, $\|\cdot\|$ usually corresponds to the Euclidean distance. The distance range join can be applied in density based clustering algorithms which often define the local data density as the number of objects in the ϵ-neighborhood of some data object. This essentially corresponds to a self-join using the distance range paradigm.

Like for plain range queries in multimedia databases, a general problem of distance range joins from the users' point of view is that it is difficult to control the result cardinality of this operation. If ϵ is chosen too small, no pairs are reported in the result set (or in case of a self join: each point is only combined with itself). In contrast, if ϵ is chosen too large, each point of *R* is combined with every point in *S* which leads to a quadratic result size and thus to a time complexity of any join algorithm which is at least quadratic; more exactly $o(|R| \cdot |S|)$. The range of possible ϵ-values where the result set is non-trivial and the result set size is sensible is often quite narrow, which is a consequence of the curse of dimensionality. Provided that the parameter ϵ is chosen in a suitable range and also adapted with an increasing number of objects such that the result set size remains approximately constant, the typical complexity of advanced join algorithms is better than quadratic.

Most related work on join processing using multidimensional index structures is based on the *spatial join*. We adapt the relevant algorithms to allow distance based predicates for multidimensional point databases instead of the intersection of polygons. The most common technique is the *R-tree Spatial Join (RSJ)* [9] which processes R-tree like index structures built on both relations *R* and *S*. RSJ is based on the lower bounding property which means that the distance between two points is never smaller than the distance (the so-called mindist, cf. figure 2) between the regions of the two pages in which the points are stored. The RSJ algorithm traverses the indexes of *R* and *S* synchronously. When a pair of directory pages (P_R, P_S) is under consideration, the algorithm forms all pairs of the child pages of P_R and P_S having distances of at most ϵ. For these pairs of child pages, the algorithm is called recursively, i.e. the corresponding indexes are traversed in a depth-first order. Various optimizations of RSJ have been proposed such as the *BFRJ-algorithm* [14] which traverses the indexes according to a breadth-first strategy.

Recently, index based similarity join methods have been analyzed from a theoretical point of view. [7] proposes a cost model based on the concept of the Minkowski sum [4] which can be used for optimizations such as page size optimization. The analysis reveals a serious optimization conflict between CPU and I/O time. While the CPU requires fine-grained partitioning with page capacities of only a few points per page, large block sizes of up to 1 MB are necessary for efficient I/O operations. Optimizing for CPU deteriorates the I/O performance and vice versa. The consequence is that an index architecture is necessary which allows a separate optimization of CPU and I/O operations. Therefore, the authors propose the *Multipage Index (MuX)*, a complex index structure with large pages (optimized for I/O) which accommodate a secondary search structure (optimized for maximum CPU efficiency). It is shown that the resulting index yields an I/O performance which is similar to the I/O optimized R-tree similarity join and a CPU performance which is close to the CPU optimized R-tree similarity join.

If no multidimensional index is available, it is possible to construct the index on the fly before starting the join algorithm. Several techniques for bulk-loading multidimensional index structures

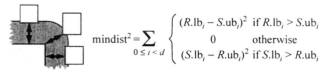

$$\text{mindist}^2 = \sum_{0 \le i < d} \begin{cases} (R.\text{lb}_i - S.\text{ub}_i)^2 & \text{if } R.\text{lb}_i > S.\text{ub}_i \\ 0 & \text{otherwise} \\ (S.\text{lb}_i - R.\text{ub}_i)^2 & \text{if } S.\text{lb}_i > R.\text{ub}_i \end{cases}$$

Figure 2. mindist for the similarity join on R-trees

have been proposed [17, 12]. The *seeded tree method* [20] joins two point sets provided that only one is supported by an R-tree. The partitioning of this R-tree is used for a fast construction of the second index on the fly. The *spatial hash-join* [21, 22] decomposes the set R into a number of partitions which is determined according to given system parameters.

A join algorithm particularly suited for similarity self joins is the ε-*kdB-tree* [27]. The basic idea is to partition the data set perpendicularly to one selected dimension into stripes of width ε to restrict the join to pairs of subsequent stripes. To speed up the CPU operations, for each stripe a main memory data structure, the ε-kdB-tree is constructed which also partitions the data set according to the other dimensions until a defined node capacity is reached. For each dimension, the data set is partitioned at most once into stripes of width ε. Finally, a tree matching algorithm is applied which is restricted to neighboring stripes. Koudas and Sevcik have proposed the *Size Separation Spatial Join* [18] and the *Multidimensional Spatial Join* [19] which make use of space filling curves to order the points in a multidimensional space. An approach which explicitly deals with massive data sets and thereby avoids the scalability problems of existing similarity join techniques is the *Epsilon Grid Order (EGO)* [5]. It is based on a particular sort order of the data points which is obtained by laying an equi-distant grid with cell length ε over the data space and then compares the grid cells lexicographically.

2.2 Closest pair queries

It is possible to overcome the problems of controlling the selectivity by replacing the range query based join predicate using conditions which specify the selectivity. In contrast to range queries which retrieve potentially the whole database, the selectivity of a (k-) closest pair query is (up to tie situations) clearly defined. This operation retrieves the k pairs of $R \times S$ having minimum distance. (cf. figure 1b) Closest pair queries do not only play an important role in the database research but have also a long history in computational geometry [23]. In the database context, the operation has been introduced by Hjaltason and Samet [16] using the term (k-) *distance join*. The (k-)closest pair query can be formally defined as follows:

Definition 2 (k-) Closest Pair Query $R \underset{k\text{-CP}}{\bowtie} S$

$R \underset{k\text{-CP}}{\bowtie} S$ is the smallest subset of $R \times S$ that contains at least k pairs of points and for which the following condition holds:

$$\forall\, (r,s) \in R \underset{k\text{-CP}}{\bowtie} S,\ \forall\, (r',s') \in R \times S \setminus R \underset{k\text{-CP}}{\bowtie} S:\ \|r-s\| < \|r'-s'\| \quad (1)$$

This definition directly corresponds to the definition of (k-) nearest neighbor queries, where the single data object o is replaced by the pair (r,s). Here, tie situations are broken by enlargement of the result set. It is also possible to change definition 2 such that the tie is broken non-deterministically by a random selection. [16] defines the closest pair query (non-deterministically) by the following SQL statement:

    SELECT * FROM R, S
    ORDER BY $\|R.\text{obj} - S.\text{obj}\|$
    STOP AFTER k

We give two more remarks regarding self joins. Obviously, the closest pairs of the selfjoin $R \underset{k\text{-CP}}{\bowtie} R$ are the n pairs (r_i, r_i) which have trivially the distance 0 (for any distance metric), where $n = |R|$ is the cardinality of R. Usually, these trivial pairs are not needed, and, therefore, they should be avoided in the **WHERE** clause. Like the

distance range selfjoin, the closest pair selfjoin is symmetric (unless nondeterminism applies). Applications of closest pair queries (particularly self joins) include similarity queries like

- find all stock quota in a database that are similar to each other
- find music scores which are similar to each other
- noise-robust duplicate elimination in multimedia applications
- match two collections of arbitrary multimedia objects

Hjaltason and Samet [16] also define the distance semijoin which performs a GROUP BY operation on the result of the distance join. All join operations, k-distance join, incremental distance join and the distance semijoin are evaluated using a pqueue data structure where node-pairs are ordered by increasing distance.

The most interesting challenge in algorithms for the distance join is the strategy to access pages and to form page pairs. Analogously to the various strategies for single nearest neighbor queries such as [24] and [15], Corral et al. propose 5 different strategies including recursive algorithms and an algorithm based on a pqueue [13]. Shin et al. [26] proposed a plane sweep algorithm for the node expansion for the above mentioned pqueue algorithm [16, 13]. In the same paper [26], Shim et al. also propose the *adaptive multi-stage algorithm* which employs aggressive pruning and compensation methods based on statistical estimates of the expected distance values.

3. The *k*-nn-join

The range distance join has the disadvantage of a result set cardinality which is difficult to control. This problem has been overcome by the closest pair query where the result set size (up to the rare tie effects) is given by the query parameter k. However, there are only few applications which require the consideration of the k best pairs of two sets. Much more prevalent are applications such as classification or clustering where each point of one set must be combined with its k closest partners in the other set, which is exactly the operation that corresponds to our new k-nearest neighbor similarity join (cf. figure 1c). Formally, we define the k-nn join as follows:

Definition 3 k-nn Join $R \underset{k\text{-nn}}{\bowtie} S$

$R \underset{k\text{-nn}}{\bowtie} S$ is the smallest subset of $R \times S$ that contains for each point of R at least k points of S and for which the following condition holds:

$$\forall\, (r,s) \in R \underset{k\text{-nn}}{\bowtie} S,\ \forall\, (r,s') \in R \times S \setminus R \underset{k\text{-nn}}{\bowtie} S:\ \|r-s\| < \|r'-s'\| \quad (2)$$

In contrast to the closest pair query, here it is guaranteed that each point of R appears in the result set exactly k times. Points of S may appear once, more than once (if a point is among the k-nearest neighbors of several points in R) or not at all (if a point does not belong to the k-nearest neighbors of any point in R). Our k-nn join can be expressed in an extended SQL notation:

    SELECT * FROM R,
    (**SELECT * FROM** S
        ORDER BY $\|R.\text{obj} - S.\text{obj}\|$
        STOP AFTER k)

The closest pair query applies the principle of the nearest neighbor search (finding k best *things*) on the basis of the pairs. Conceptually, first all pairs are formed, and then, the best k are selected. In contrast, the k-nn join applies this principle on a basis "per point of the first set". For each of the points of R, the k best join partners are searched. This is an essential difference of concepts.

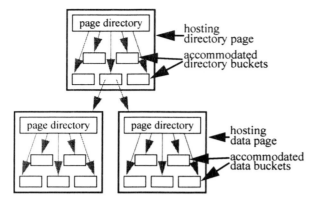

Figure 3. Index architecture of the multipage index

Again, tie situations can be broken deterministically by enlarging the result set as in this definition or by random selection. For the selfjoin, we have again the situation that each point is combined with itself which can be avoided using the WHERE clause. Unlike the ε-join and the k-closest pair query, the k-nn selfjoin is not symmetric as the nearest neighbor relation is not symmetric. Equivalently, the join $R \underset{k\text{-}nn}{\bowtie} S$ which retrieves the k nearest neighbors for each point of R is essentially different from $S \underset{k\text{-}nn}{\bowtie} R$ which retrieves the nearest neighbors of each S-point. This is symbolized in our symbolic notation which uses an *asymmetric* symbol for the k-nn join in contrast to the other similarity join operations.

4. Fast index scans for the k-nn join

In this section we develop an algorithm for the k-nn join which applies suitable loading and processing strategies on top of a multidimensional index structure, the multipage index [7], to efficiently compute the k-nn join. In [7] we have shown for the distance range join that it is necessary to optimize index parameters such as the page capacity separately for CPU and I/O performance. We have proposed a new index architecture (Multipage Index, MuX) depicted in figure 3 which allows such a separate optimization. The index consists of large pages which are optimized for I/O efficiency. These pages accommodate a secondary R-tree like main memory search structure with a page directory (storing pairs of MBR and a corresponding pointer) and data buckets which are containers for the actual data points. The capacity of the accommodated buckets is much smaller than the capacity of the hosting page. It is optimized for CPU performance. We have shown that the distance range join on the Multipage Index has an I/O performance similar to an R-tree which is purely I/O optimized and has a CPU performance like an R-tree which is purely CPU optimized. Although this issue is up to future work, we assume that also the k-nn join clearly benefits from the separate optimization (because optimization trade-offs are very similar).

In the following description, we assume for simplicity that the hosting pages of our Multipage Index only consist of one directory level and one data level. If there are more directory levels, these levels are processed in a breadth first approach according to some simple strategy, because most cost arise in the data level. Therefore, our strategies focus on the last level.

4.1 The fast index scan

In our previous work [6] we have already investigated fast index scans, however not in the context of a join operation but in the context of single similarity queries (range queries and nearest neighbor queries) which are evaluated on top of an R-tree like index structure, our IQ tree. The idea is to chain I/O operations for subsequent pages on disk. This is relatively simple for range queries: If the index is traversed breadth-first, then the complete set of required pages at the next level is exactly known in advance. Therefore, pages which have adjacent positions on disk can be immediately grouped together into a single I/O request (cf. figure 4, left side). But also pages which are not direct neighbors but only close together can be read without disk head movement. So the only task is to sort the page requests by (ascending) disk addresses before actually performing them. For nearest neighbor queries the trade-off is more complex: These are usually evaluated by the HS-algorithm [15] which has been proven to be optimal, w.r.t. the *number* of accessed pages. Although the algorithm loses its optimality by I/O chaining of page requests, it pays off to chain pages together which have a low probability of being pruned before their actual request is due. We have proposed a stochastical model to estimate the probability of a page to be required for a given nearest neighbor query. Based on this model we can estimate the cost for various chained and unchained I/O requests and thus optimize the I/O operations (cf. figure 4, right side).

Take a closer look at the trade-off which is exploited in our optimization: If we apply no I/O chaining or too careful chaining, then the *number* of processed pages is optimal or close to optimal but due to heavy disk head movements these accesses are very expensive. If considerable parts of the data set are needed to answer the query, the index can be outperformed by the sequential scan. In contrast, if too many pages are chained together, many pages are processed unnecessarily before the nearest neighbor is found. If only a few pages are needed to answer a query, I/O chaining should be carefully applied, and the index should be traversed in the classical way of the HS algorithm. Our probability estimation grasps this rule of thumb with many gradations between the two extremes.

4.2 Optimization goals of the nearest neighbor join

Shortly speaking, the trade-off of the nearest neighbor search is between (1) getting the nearest neighbor *early* and (2) limiting the cost for the single I/O operations. In this section, we will describe a similar trade-off in the k-nearest neighbor join. One important goal of the algorithm is to get a good approximation of the nearest neighbor (i.e. a point which is not necessarily *the* nearest neighbor

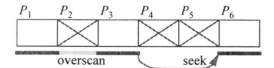

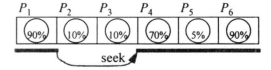

Figure 4. The fast index scan for single range queries (l.) and for single nearest neighbor queries (r.)

but a point which is not much worse than the nearest neighbor) for each of these active queries as early as possible. With a good conservative approximation of the *nearest neighbor distance*, we can even abstain from our probability model of the previous paragraph and handle nearest neighbor queries furtheron like range queries. Only few pages are processed too much.

In contrast to single similarity queries, the seek cost do not play an important role in our join algorithm because our special index structure, MuX, is optimized for disk I/O. Our second aspect, however, is the CPU performance which is negligible for single similarity queries but not for join queries. From the CPU point of view, it is not a good strategy to load a page and immediately process it (i.e. join it with all pages which are already in main memory, which is usually done for join queries with a range query predicate). Instead, the page should be paired only with those pages for which one of the following conditions holds:

- It is probable that this pair leads to a considerable reduction of some nearest neighbor distance
- It is improbable that the corresponding mate page will receive any improvements of its nearest neighbor distance in future

While the first condition seems to be obvious, the second condition is also important because it ensures that unavoidable workloads are done before other workloads which are avoidable. The cache is primarily loaded with those pages of which it is most unclear whether or not they will be needed in future.

4.3   Basic algorithm

For the k-nn join $R \bowtie_{k\text{-}nn} S$, we denote the data set R for each point of which the nearest neighbors are searched as the outer point set. Consequently, S is the inner point set. As in [7] we process the hosting pages of R and S in two nested loops (obviously, this is not a *nested loop join*). Each hosting page of the outer set R is accessed exactly once. The principle of the nearest neighbor join is illustrated in figure 5. A hosting page PR_1 of the outer set with 4 accommodated buckets is depicted in the middle. For each point stored in this page, a data structure for the k nearest neighbors is allocated. Candidate points are maintained in these data structures until they are either discarded and replaced by new (better) candidate points or until they are *confirmed* to be the actual nearest neighbors of the corresponding point. When a candidate is *confirmed*, it is guaranteed that the database cannot contain any closer points, and the pair can be written to the output. The distance of the last (i.e. k-th or worst) candidate point of each R-point is the pruning distance: Points, accommodated buckets and hosting pages beyond that pruning distance need not to be considered. The pruning distance of a *bucket* is the *maximum* pruning distance of all points stored in this bucket, i.e. all S-buckets which have a distance from a given R-bucket that exceeds the pruning distance of the R-bucket, can be safely neglected as join-partners of that R-bucket. Similarly, the pruning distance of a *page* is the maximum pruning distance of all accommodated buckets.

In contrast to conventional join methods we reserve only one cache page for the outer set R which is read exactly once. The remaining cache pages are used for the inner set S. For other join predicates (e.g. relational predicates or a distance range predicate), a strategy which caches more pages of the outer set is beneficial for I/O processing (the inner set is scanned fewer times) while the CPU performance is not affected by the caching strategy. For the k-nn join predicate, the cache strategy affects both I/O *and* CPU performance. It is important that for each considered point of R good can-

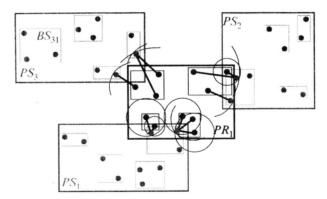

Figure 5. *k-nn* join on the multipage index (here *k*=1)

didates (i.e. near neighbors, not necessarily the nearest neighbors) are found as early as possible. This is more likely when reserving more cache for the inner set S. The basic algorithm for the k-nn join is given below.

```
1   foreach PR of R do
2       cand : PQUEUE [|PR|, k] of point := {⊥,⊥,...,⊥} ;
3       foreach PS of S do PS.done := false ;
4       while ∃ i such that cand [i] is not confirmed do
5           while ∃ empty cache frame ∧
6                 ∃ PS with (¬PS.done ∧ ¬ IsPruned(PS)) do
7               apply loading strategy if more than 1 PS exist
8               load PS to cache ;
9               PS.done := true ;
10          apply processing strategy to select a bucket pair ;
11          process bucket pair ;
```

A short explanation: (1) Iterates over all hosting pages PR of the outer point set R which are accessed in an arbitrary order. For each point in PR, an array for the k nearest neighbors (and the corresponding candidates) is allocated and initialized with empty pointers in line (2). In this array, the algorithm stores candidates which may be replaced by other candidates until the candidates are *confirmed*. A candidate is confirmed if no unprocessed hosting page or accommodated bucket exists which is closer to the corresponding R-point than the candidate. Consequently, the loop (4) iterates until all candidates are confirmed. In lines 5-9, empty cache pages are filled with hosting pages from S whenever this is possible. This happens at the beginning of processing and whenever pages are discarded because they are either processed or pruned for all R-points. The decision which hosting page to load next is implemented in the so-called loading strategy which is described in section 4.4. Note that the actual page access can also be done asynchronously in a multithreaded environment. After that, we have the accommodated buckets of one hosting R-page and of several hosting S-pages in the main memory. In lines 10-11, one pair of such buckets is chosen and processed. For choosing, our algorithm applies a so-called *processing strategy* which is described in section 4.5. During processing, the algorithm tests whether points of the current S-bucket are closer to any point of the current R-bucket than the corresponding candidates are. If so, the candidate array is updated (not depicted in our algorithm) and the pruning distances are also changed. Therefore, the current R-bucket can safely prune some of the S-buckets that formerly were considered join partners.

4.4 Loading strategy

In conventional similarity search where the nearest neighbor is searched only for one query point, it can be proven that the optimal strategy is to access the pages in the order of increasing distance from the query point [4]. For our *k-nn join*, we are simultaneously processing nearest neighbor queries for all points stored in a hosting page. To exclude as many hosting pages and accommodated buckets of S from being join partners of one of these simultaneous queries, it is necessary to decrease all pruning distances as early as possible. The problem we are addressing now is, what page should be accessed next in lines 5-9 to achieve this goal.

Obviously, if we consider the complete set of points in the current hosting page PR to assess the quality of an unloaded hosting page PS, the effort for the optimization of the loading strategy would be too high. Therefore, we do not use the complete set of points but rather the accommodated buckets: the pruning distances of the accommodated buckets have to decrease as fast as possible.

In order for a page PS to be good, this page must have the power of *considerably improving* the pruning distance of at least one of the buckets BR of the current page PR. Basically there can be two obstacles that can prevent a pair of such a page PS and a bucket BR from having a high improvement power: (1) the distance (mindist) between this page-bucket pair is large, and (2) the bucket BR has *already* a small pruning distance. Condition (1) corresponds to the well-known strategy of accessing pages in the order of increasing distance to the query point. Condition (2), however, intends to avoid that the same bucket BR is repeatedly processed before another bucket BR' has reached a reasonable pruning distance (having such buckets BR' in the system causes much avoidable effort).

Therefore, the *quality* $Q(PS)$ of a hosting page PS of the inner set S is not only measured in terms of the distance to the current buckets but the distances are also related to the current pruning distance of the buckets:

$$Q(PS) = \max_{BR \in PR} \left\{ \frac{prunedist(BR)}{mindist(PS, BR)} \right\} \quad (3)$$

Our *loading strategy* applied in line (7) is to access the hosting pages PS in the order of decreasing quality $Q(PS)$, i.e. we always access the unprocessed page with the highest quality.

4.5 Processing strategy

The processing strategy is applied in line (10). It addresses the question in what order the accommodated buckets of R and S that have been loaded into the cache should be processed (joined by an in-memory join algorithm). The typical situation found at line (10) is that we have the accommodated buckets of *one* hosting page of R and the accommodated buckets of *several* hosting pages of S in the cache. Our algorithm has to select a pair of such buckets (BR,BS) which has a high quality, i.e. a high potential of improving the pruning distance of BR. Similarly to the quality $Q(PS)$ of a page developed in section 4.4, the quality $Q(BR,BS)$ of a bucket pair rewards a small distance and punishes a small pruning distance:

$$Q(BR,BS) = \frac{prunedist(BR)}{mindist(BS, BR)} \quad (4)$$

We process the bucket pairs in the order of decreasing quality. Note that we do not have to redetermine the quality of every bucket pair each time our algorithm runs into line (10) which would be prohibitively costly. To avoid this problem, we organize our current buck-

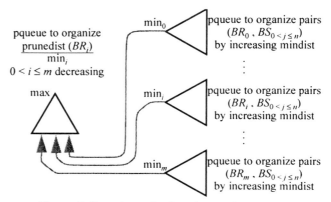

Figure 6. Structure of a fractionated pqueue

et pairs in a tailor-made data structure, a fractionated pqueue (half sorted tree). By *fractionated* we mean a pqueue of pqueues, as depicted in figure 6. Note that this tailor-cut structure allows efficiently (1) to determine the pair with maximum quality, (2) to insert a new pair, and in particular (3) to update the prunedist of BR_i which affects the quality of a large number of pairs.

Processing bucket pairs with a high quality is highly important at an early stage of processing until all R-buckets have a sufficient pruning distance. Later, the improvement power of the pairs does not differ very much and a new aspect comes into operation: The pairs should be processed such that one of the hosting S pages in the cache can be replaced as soon as possible by a new page. Therefore, our processing strategy switches into a new mode if the last c (given parameter) processing steps did not lead to a considerable improvement of any pruning distance. The new mode is to select one hosting S-page PS in the cache and to process all pairs where one of the buckets BS accommodated by PS appears. We select that hosting page PS with the fewest active pairs (i.e. the hosting page that causes least effort).

5. Experimental evaluation

We implemented the k-nearest neighbor join algorithm, as described in the previous section, based on the original source code of the Multipage Index Join [7] and performed an experimental evaluation using artificial and real data sets of varying size and di-

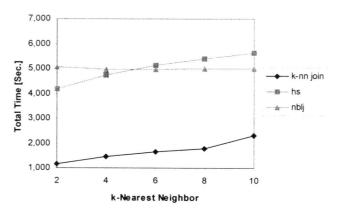

Figure 7. Varying k for 8-dimensional uniform data

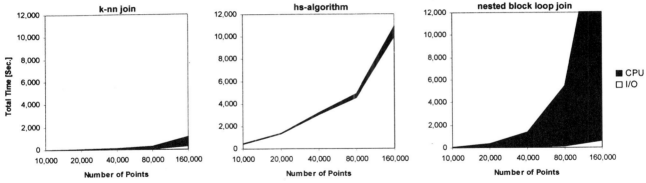

Figure 8. Total time, CPU-time and I/O-time for hs, *k-nn* join and nblj for varying size of the database

mension. We compared the performance of our technique with the nested block loop join (which basically is a sequential scan optimized for the *k*-nn case) and the *k*-nn algorithm by Hjaltason and Samet [15] as a conventional, non-join technique.

All our experiments were carried out under Windows NT4.0 SP6 on Fujitsu-Siemens Celsius 400 machines equipped with a Pentium III 700 MHz processor and at least 128 MB main memory. The installed disk device was a Seagate ST310212A with a sustained transfer rate of about 9 MB/s and an average read access time of 8.9 ms with an average latency time of 5.6 ms.

We used synthetic as well as real data. The synthetic data sets consisted of 4, 6 and 8 dimensions and contained from 10,000 to 160,000 uniformly distributed points in the unit hypercube. Our real-world data sets are a CAD database with 16-dimensional feature vectors extracted from CAD parts and a 9-dimensional set of weather data. We allowed about 20% of the database size as cache resp. buffer for either technique and included the index creation time for our *k*-nn join and the hs-algorithm, while the nested block loop join (nblj) does not need any pre-constructed index.

The Euclidean distance was used to determine the k-nearest neighbor distance. In order to show the effects of varying the neighboring parameter k we include figure 7 with varying k (from 4-nn to 10-nn) while all other charts show results for the case of the 4-nearest neighbors. In figure 7 we can see, that except for the nested block loop join all techniques perform better for a smaller number of nearest neighbors and the hs-algorithm starts to perform worse than the nblj if more than 4 nearest neighbors are requested. This is a well known fact for high dimensional data as the pruning power of the directory pages deteriorates quickly with increasing dimension and parameter k. This is also true, but far less dramatic for the *k*-nn join because of the use of much smaller buckets which still perserve pruning power for higher dimensions and parameters k. The size of the database used for these experiments was 80,000 points.

The three charts in figure 8 show the results (from left to right) for the hs-algorithm, our *k*-nn join and the nblj for the 8-dimensional uniform data set for varying size of the database. The total elapsed time consists of the CPU-time and the I/O-time. We can observe that the hs-algorithm (despite using large block sizes for optimization) is clearly I/O bound while the nested block loop join is clearly CPU bound. Our *k*-nn join has a somewhat higher CPU cost than the hs-algorithm, but significantly less than the nblj while it produces almost as little I/O as nblj and as a result clearly outperforms both, the hs-algorithm and the nblj.

This balance between CPU and I/O cost follows the idea of MuX to optimize CPU and I/O cost independently. For our artificial data the speed-up factor of the *k*-nn join over the hs-algorithm is 37.5 for the small point set (10,000 points) and 9.8 for the large point set (160,000 points), while compared to the nblj the speed-up factor increases from 7.1 to 19.4. We can also see, that the simple, but optimized nested block loop join outperforms the hs-algorithm for smaller database sizes because of its high I/O cost.

One interesting effect is, that our MUX-algorithm for *k*-nn joins is able to prune more and more bucket pairs with increasing size of

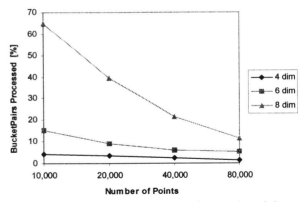

Figure 9. Pruning of bucket pairs for the *k-nn* join

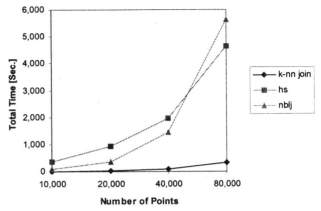

Figure 10. Results for 9-dimensional weather data

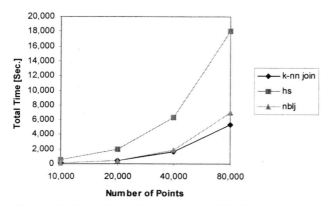

Figure 11. Results for 16-dimensional CAD data

the database i.e. the percentage of bucket pairs that can be excluded during processing increases with increasing database size. We can see this effect in figure 9. Obviously, the k-nn join scales much better with increasing size of the database than the other two techniques.

Figure 10 shows the results for the 9-dimensional weather data. The maximum speed-up of the k-nn join compared to the hs-algorithm is 28 and the maximum speed-up compared to the nested block loop join is 17. For small database sizes, the nested block loop join outperforms the hs-algorithm which might be due to the cache/buffer and I/O configuration used. Again, as with the artificial data, the k-nn join clearly outperforms the other techniques and scales well with the size of the database.

Figure 11 shows the results for the 16-dimensional CAD data. Even for this high dimension of the data space and the poor clustering property of the CAD data set, the k-nn join still reaches a speed-up factor of 1.3 for the 80,000 point set (with increasing tendency for growing database sizes) compared to the nested block loop join (which basically is a sequential scan optimized for the k-nn case). The speed-up factor of the k-nn join over the hs-algorithm is greater than 3.

6. Conclusions

In this paper, we have proposed an algorithm to efficiently compute the k-nearest neighbor join, a new kind of similarity join. In contrast to other types of similarity joins such as the distance range join, the k-distance join (k-closest pair query) and the incremental distance join, our new k-nn join combines each point of a point set R with its k nearest neighbors in another point set S. We have seen that the k-nn join can be a powerful database primitive which allows the efficient implementation of numerous methods of knowledge discovery and data mining such as classification, clustering, data cleansing, and postprocessing. Our algorithm for the efficient computation of the k-nn join uses the Multipage Index (MuX), a specialized index structure for similarity join processing and applies matching loading and processing strategies in order to reduce both CPU and I/O cost. Our experimental evaluation proves high performance gains compared to conventional methods.

References

[1] Ankerst M., Breunig M. M., Kriegel H.-P., Sander J.: *OPTICS: Ordering Points To Identify the Clustering Structure*, ACM SIGMOD Int. Conf. on Management of Data, 1999.
[2] Agrawal R., Lin K., Sawhney H., Shim K.: *Fast Similarity Search in the Presence of Noise, Scaling, and Translation in Time-Series Databases*, Int. Conf on Very Large Data Bases (VLDB), 1995.
[3] Böhm C., Braunmüller B., Breunig M. M., Kriegel H.-P.: *Fast Clustering Based on High-Dimensional Similarity Joins*, Int. Conf. on Information Knowledge Management (CIKM), 2000.
[4] Berchtold S., Böhm C., Keim D., Kriegel H.-P.: *A Cost Model For Nearest Neighbor Search in High-Dimensional Data Space*, ACM Symposium on Principles of Database Systems (PODS), 1997.
[5] Böhm C., Braunmüller B., Krebs F., Kriegel H.-P.: *Epsilon Grid Order: An Algorithm for the Similarity Join on Massive High-Dimensional Data*, ACM SIGMOD Int. Conf. on Management of Data, 2001.
[6] Berchtold S., Böhm C., Jagadish H. V., Kriegel H.-P., Sander J.: *Independent Quantization: An Index Compression Technique for High Dimensional Data Spaces*, IEEE Int. Conf. on Data Engineering (ICDE), 2000.
[7] Böhm C., Kriegel H.-P.: *A Cost Model and Index Architecture for the Similarity Join*, IEEE Int. Conf on Data Engineering (ICDE), 2001.
[8] Böhm C., Krebs F.: *The k-Nearest Neighbor Join: Turbo Charging the KDD Process*, submitted.
[9] Brinkhoff T., Kriegel H.-P., Seeger B.: *Efficient Processing of Spatial Joins Using R-trees*, ACM SIGMOD Int. Conf. Management of Data, 1993.
[10] Breunig M. M., Kriegel H.-P., Kröger P., Sander J.: *Data Bubbles: Quality Preserving Performance Boosting for Hierarchical Clustering*, ACM SIGMOD Int. Conf. on Management of Data, 2001.
[11] Böhm C.: *The Similarity Join: A Powerful Database Primitive for High Performance Data Mining*, tutorial, IEEE Int. Conf. on Data Engineering (ICDE), 2001.
[12] van den Bercken J., Seeger B., Widmayer P.: *A General Approach to Bulk Loading Multidimensional Index Structures*, Int. Conf. on Very Large Databases, 1997.
[13] Corral A., Manolopoulos Y., Theodoridis Y., Vassilakopoulos M.: *Closest Pair Queries in Spatial Databases*, ACM SIGMOD Int. Conf. on Management of Data, 2000.
[14] Huang Y.-W., Jing N., Rundensteiner E. A.: *Spatial Joins Using R-trees: Breadth-First Traversal with Global Optimizations*, Int. Conf. on Very Large Databases (VLDB), 1997.
[15] Hjaltason G. R., Samet H.: *Ranking in Spatial Databases*, Int. Symp. on Large Spatial Databases (SSD), 1995.
[16] Hjaltason G. R., Samet H.: *Incremental Distance Join Algorithms for Spatial Databases*, SIGMOD Int. Conf. on Management of Data, 1998.
[17] Kamel I., Faloutsos C.: *Hilbert R-tree: An Improved R-tree using Fractals*. Int. Conf. on Very Large Databases, 1994.
[18] Koudas N., Sevcik K.: *Size Separation Spatial Join*, ACM SIGMOD Int. Conf. on Management of Data, 1997.
[19] Koudas N., Sevcik K.: *High Dimensional Similarity Joins: Algorithms and Performance Evaluation*, IEEE Int. Conf. on Data Engineering (ICDE), Best Paper Award, 1998.
[20] Lo M.-L., Ravishankar C. V.: *Spatial Joins Using Seeded Trees*, ACM SIGMOD Int. Conf., 1994.
[21] Lo M.-L., Ravishankar C. V.: *Spatial Hash Joins*, ACM SIGMOD Int. Conf. on Management of Data, 1996.
[22] Patel J.M., DeWitt D.J., *Partition Based Spatial-Merge Join*, ACM SIGMOD Int. Conf., 1996.
[23] Preparata F. P., Shamos M. I.: *Computational Geometry*, Springer 1985.
[24] Roussopoulos N., Kelley S., Vincent F.: *Nearest Neighbor Queries*, ACM SIGMOD Int. Conf., 1995.
[25] Sander J., Ester M., Kriegel H.-P., Xu X.: *Density-Based Clustering in Spatial Databases: The Algorithm GDBSCAN and its Applications*, Data Mining and Knowledge Discovery, Kluwer Academic Publishers, Vol. 2, No. 2, 1998.
[26] Shin H., Moon B., Lee S.: *Adaptive Multi-Stage Distance Join Processing*, ACM SIGMOD Int. Conf., 2000.
[27] Shim K., Srikant R., Agrawal R.: *High-Dimensional Similarity Joins*, IEEE Int. Conf. on Data Engineering, 1997.

Mining Molecular Fragments:
Finding Relevant Substructures of Molecules

Christian Borgelt
School of Computer Science
University of Magdeburg, Universitätsplatz 2
D-39106 Magdeburg, Germany
e-mail: borgelt@iws.cs.uni-magdeburg.de

Michael R. Berthold
Data Analysis Research Lab
Tripos, Inc., 601 Gateway Blvd, Suite 720
South San Francisco, CA 94080, USA
e-mail: berthold@tripos.com

Abstract

We present an algorithm to find fragments in a set of molecules that help to discriminate between different classes of, for instance, activity in a drug discovery context. Instead of carrying out a brute-force search, our method generates fragments by embedding them in all appropriate molecules in parallel and prunes the search tree based on a local order of the atoms and bonds, which results in substantially faster search by eliminating the need for frequent, computationally expensive reembeddings and by suppressing redundant search. We prove the usefulness of our algorithm by demonstrating the discovery of activity-related groups of chemical compounds in the well-known National Cancer Institute's HIV-screening dataset.

1. Introduction

Many data mining tasks in bioinformatics consist in analyzing large collections of molecules with the goal to find some regularity among molecules of a specific class. Possible applications are manifold. One example is drug discovery, where the biologist wants to find new drug candidates based on experimental evidence of activity against a certain disease gathered by screening hundreds of thousands of molecules. A second, more recent emphasis comes from chemical synthesis success prediction, where the goal is to find molecular features that inhibit the desired reaction.

Current approaches to find regularities among molecules are often based on so-called descriptors, which usually consist of thousands of binary features, representing (sometimes in a hashed manner) certain substructures of interests, such as aromatic rings or some other predefined small group of atoms [4]. Other descriptors model pairwise atom distances or 3D molecule arrangements. Prediction algorithms then simply use a distance function on these descriptors to define similarity between molecules. More sophisticated algorithms attempt to find boolean combinations of some of these features that are related to different classes [10]. Approaches that try to regard molecules as graphs and de-

rive similarity measures based on transformations of these graphs were also proposed [9]. However, such notions of similarity, based on a particular descriptor with a corresponding metric, only model limited aspects of molecular similarity well. Therefore attempts to directly extract relevant substructures from a collection of molecules are of persistent interest.

Recently an approach was presented that finds linear fragments [7], i.e. chains of atoms, using an algorithm similar to the well-known Apriori association rule mining method [1]. However, the restriction to linear fragments is limiting in many real-world applications, since substructures of interest often contain rings or branching points. Nevertheless, the idea to use an association rule mining algorithm by regarding the molecules as a set of nodes (instead of the usual bit sets) has sparked considerable interest. A more recent approach [5] finds arbitrary connected substructures by deriving canonical labels for each graph. The search is again based on the Apriori algorithm and hence still relies on frequent reembeddings of fragments in order to determine valid intermediate candidates throughout the search.

In this paper we present an algorithm that also finds arbitrary connected substructures but avoids frequent reembeddings by using a different search strategy. The algorithm maintains parallel embeddings of a fragment into all molecules throughout the growth process and exploits a local order of the atoms and bonds of a fragment to prune the search tree, which results in faster search and allows for a restricted depth first search algorithm, similar to the Eclat association rule mining algorithm [12].

We first present the main algorithm, followed by a discussion of results obtained on the HIV-screening dataset from the National Cancer Institute [11] and conclude with a brief discussion of possible extensions of our method.

2. The Induction Algorithm

In this section we describe our algorithm by developing it from algorithms for the well-known task of association rule induction. We start by reviewing the search schemes for fre-

51

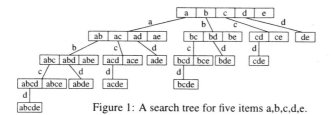

Figure 1: A search tree for five items a,b,c,d,e.

quent itemsets in Section 2.1 and then transfer their ideas to the more complicated case of finding molecular substructures in Section 2.2. In Section 2.3 we describe how our algorithm prunes the search tree based on a local order of the atoms and bonds of a fragment. In section 2.4 we discuss a simple example and in Section 2.5 we study why it is impossible to avoid *all* redundant search. Finally, in Sections 2.6 and 2.7, we describe how to embed core structures to start the search from and how to find contrast structures that distinguish between groups of molecules.

2.1. Association Rules and Frequent Itemsets

The induction of association rules is a powerful method for *market basket analysis*, which aims at finding regularities in the shopping behavior of customers of supermarkets, mailorder companies, on-line shops and the like. With it one tries to find sets of products that are frequently bought together, so that from the presence of certain products in a shopping cart one can infer (with a high probability) that certain other products are present. The main difference to our task of finding frequent substructures of molecules is that in market basket analysis we have only simple *sets of items* to deal with, while in molecular substructure analysis we have to take the chemical connectivity, i.e. the bonds connecting individual atoms, into account as well.

The best-known association rule algorithms are *Apriori* [1] and *Eclat* [12]. Both work in two steps: First the *frequent itemsets* (often misleadingly called *large itemsets*) are determined. These are sets of items that have at least a given minimum support, i.e., occur in at least a given percentage of all transactions. In the second step association rules are generated from these frequent itemsets. Here we focus on the first step, because we are not concerned with generating rules. However, research in association rule induction usually does the same, because finding the frequent itemsets accounts for the greater part of the processing time.

In order to find frequent itemsets, one has to count the transactions different itemsets are contained in. This task consists in traversing a tree like the one shown in Figure 1 and determining the values of the counters in its nodes. Each box represents a counter. The edge labels on a path from the root to a node indicate the common part of the itemsets for which there are counters in that node. The tree is unbalanced, because we are dealing with sets, not sequences: *abc*, for instance, is the same as *bca* and thus

only one of these counters is needed. Mathematically, the search tree is a substructure of the subset lattice, having exactly one path to any itemset. In addition, both Apriori and Eclat exploit the simple observation that no superset of an infrequent itemset can be frequent. This observation can be used to further prune the tree, because all counters for itemsets having an infrequent subset can be discarded.

The main differences between Apriori and Eclat are how they traverse this tree and how they determine the counter values. Apriori does a breadth first search and determines the support of an itemset by explicit subset tests on the transactions. An efficient implementation can use a data structure like the tree shown in Figure 1 to store the counters [2, 3]. However, the need to build a data structure like this can also be a severe disadvantage, as it can consume a lot of memory. Furthermore, the subset tests can be costly.

On the other hand, Eclat does a depth first search and determines the support of an itemset by intersecting the transaction lists for two subsets, the union of which is the itemset. The advantage is that not all counters have to be kept in memory, especially if one allows for some unnecessary tests, which could be avoided only by checking *all* subsets. A disadvantage is that several transaction lists have to be kept in memory at the same time—lists that can be very long, especially for small itemsets. More sophisticated approaches try to combine the advantages, using Apriori for the first levels of the tree (usually only 2 or 3) and Eclat as soon as the transaction lists are short enough [12, 6].

2.2. Frequent Substructures of Molecules

In order to capture the bond structure of molecules, we model them as attributed graphs, in which each vertex represents an atom and each edge a bond between atoms. Each vertex carries attributes that indicate the atom type (i.e., the chemical element), a possible charge, and whether it is part of an aromatic ring. Each edge carries an attribute that indicates the bond type (single, double, triple, or aromatic).

Our goal is to find substructures that have a certain minimum support in a given set of molecules, i.e., are part of at least a certain percentage of the molecules. However, in order to restrict the search space, we consider only *connected substructures*, i.e., graphs having only one connected component. For most applications, this restriction is harmless, because connected substructures are most often exactly what is desired. We do *not* constrain the connectivity of the graph in any other way: The graphs may be chains or trees or may contain an arbitrary number of cycles. With this we go beyond [7], who considered only *linear substructures*, i.e., simple chains of atoms without branches. Such simple chains are rarely sufficient in real-world applications.

Most naturally, the search is carried out by traversing a tree of fragments of molecules, similar to the tree of itemsets shown in figure 1. The root of the tree is the core structure to start from, which for now we assume to be a single atom (more complex cores are discussed below). Going down one level in the search tree means to extend a substructure by a bond (and maybe an atom, if the bond does not close a ring), just like going down in the tree shown in Figure 1 means adding an item to an itemset. That is, with a single atom at the root of the tree, the root level contains the substructures with no bonds, the second level those with one bond, the third level those with two bonds and so on.

As indicated above, there are basically two ways in which the search tree can be traversed: We can use either a breadth first search and explicit subset tests (Apriori) or a depth first search and intersections of transaction lists (Eclat). For our task the Eclat approach is clearly preferable, because the disadvantages of the Apriori approach become considerably more severe: Even subset tests can be costly, but substructure tests, which consist mathematically in checking whether a given attributed graph is a subgraph of another attributed graph, are extremely costly. Furthermore, the number of small substructures (1 to 4 atoms) can be enormous, so that even storing only the topmost levels of the tree can require a prohibitively large amount of memory.

Of course, the Eclat approach also suffers, because the transaction lists are now lists of embeddings of a substructure into the given molecules. Since there can be several embeddings of the same substructure into one molecule, these lists tend to get longer. This drawback can make it necessary to start from a reasonably sized core structure (see below).

To be more specific, our algorithm searches as follows: The given core structure is embedded into all molecules, resulting in a list of embeddings. Each embedding consists of references into a molecule that point out the atoms and bonds that form the substructure. Remember that a list of embeddings may contain several embeddings for the same molecule if the molecule contains the substructure in more than one place or if the substructure is symmetric.

In a second step each embedding is extended in every possible way. This is done by adding all bonds in the corresponding molecule that start from an atom already in the embedding (to ensure connectedness and, of course, to reduce the number of bonds that have to be considered). This may or may not involve adding the atom the bond leads to, because this atom may or may not be part of the embedding already. More technically, by following the references of an embedding the atoms and bonds of the corresponding molecule are marked and only unmarked bonds emanating from marked atoms are considered as possible extensions.

The resulting extended embeddings are then sorted into equivalence classes, each of which represents a new substructure. This sorting is very simple, because only the added bond and maybe the added atom have to be compared. In our implementation we use a hash table and an array of lists of embeddings to sort the extensions. The hash table associates an embedding with an array index, using a hash code that is computed from the type of the bond that was added in the preceding step, the position (in the substructure) of the atom it starts from, and the position and

the type of the atom it leads to. After all extended embeddings have been processed, each array element contains the list of embeddings of a new substructure. Each of these new substructures corresponds to a child node in the search tree, each of which is then processed in turn by searching recursively on the list of embeddings corresponding to it.

2.3. Search Tree Pruning

Of course, subtrees of the search tree can be pruned if they refer to substructures not having enough support, i.e., if too few molecules are referred to in the associated list of embeddings. We call this *support based pruning*. We may also prune the search tree if a user-defined threshold for the number of atoms in a fragment has been reached. We call this *size based pruning*. However, when we reviewed the search for frequent itemsets, we also considered a third type of pruning, which we refer to as *structural pruning*. It is responsible for the unbalancedness of the search tree shown in Figure 1: As pointed out above, we do not need a counter for bca, because it is the same itemset as abc. Structural pruning ensures that every itemset is considered in one branch only, even though adding items in different orders can yield the same itemset. In the following we consider how such structural pruning can be done in the search for frequent substructures of molecules, because, obviously, adding bonds in different orders can result in the same substructure.

In order to find a structural pruning scheme, let us analyze the structural pruning of the itemset tree in more detail. Figure 1 shows the basic idea very clearly. The items are ordered, which is indicated by the symbols a, b, etc. This order is, of course, arbitrary. But once it is fixed, the itemsets processed in a node can be constructed as follows: Extend the set of items used as edge labels on the path to the node with an item following the last edge label. Consider, for example, the second node on the third level (count from top to bottom and from left to right): The path to this node has labels a and c. Therefore the set $\{a, c\}$ has to be extended by items following c, i.e. by d and e. Consequently there are counters for the sets $\{a, c. d\}$ and $\{a, c, e\}$ in this node. The same holds for any other node. Obviously, this scheme fixes an order in which items can be added and thus each itemset can be reached only in one possible way.

We organize the nodes of the search tree for molecular substructures in a very similar way. The main difference is that we cannot define a *global* order of the atoms of the molecules, which would correspond directly to the order of the items. Rather, we number the atoms *in a substructure* and record how a substructure was constructed in order to constrain its extensions. The number we assign to an atom reflects the step in which it was added. That is, the core atom is numbered 0, the atom added with the first bond is numbered 1 and so on. Note that this number does not tell anything about the type of the atom, as two completely different atoms may receive the same number, simply because they were added in the same step.

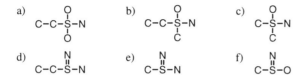

Figure 2: A set of six example molecules.

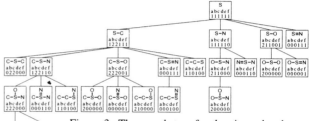

Figure 3: The search tree for the six molecule example. The tables below the fragments indicate the numbers of embeddings per molecule.

Whenever an embedding is extended, we record in the resulting extension the number of the atom from which the added bond started. When the extended embedding is to be extended itself, we consider only bonds that start from atoms having numbers no less than this recorded number. That is, only the atom extended in the preceding step and atoms added later than this atom can be the starting point of a new bond. This rule is directly analogous to the rule that only items following the item added last may be added to an itemset. With this simple scheme we immediately avoid that two bonds, call them A and B, which start from different atoms, are added in the order A, B in one branch of the search tree and in the order B, A in another. Since either the atom A starts from or the atom B starts from must have a smaller number, one of the orders is ruled out.

However, two or more bonds can start from the same atom. Therefore we also have to define an order on bonds, so that we do not add two different bonds A and B that start from the same atom in the order A, B in one branch of the search tree and in the order B, A in another. This order on bonds is, of course, arbitrary. In our implementation, single bonds precede aromatic bonds, which precede double bonds, which precede triple bonds. Finally, within extensions by bonds of the same type starting from the same atom, the order is determined by (1) whether the atom the bond leads to is already in the substructure or not and (2) the type of this atom. To take care of the bond type etc., we record in each embedding which bond was added last.

The above rules provide us with a structural pruning scheme, but unfortunately this scheme is not perfect and making it perfect would be very expensive computationally. The problem is that we do not have any precedence rule for two bonds of the same type starting from an atom with the same number and leading to atoms of the same type, and that it is not possible to give any precedence rule for this case that is based exclusively on locally available information. We consider the problems that result from this imperfection and our solution below, but think it advisable to precede this consideration by an illustrative example of the search process as we defined it up to now.

2.4. An Illustrative Example

As an illustration we consider how our algorithm finds the frequent substructures of the six example molecules shown in Figure 2[1], starting from a sulfur atom. We use a minimum support of 50%, i.e., a substructure must occur in at least three of the six molecules to qualify as frequent.

First the sulfur atom is embedded into the six molecules. This results in six embeddings, one for each molecule, which form the root of the search tree (see Figure 3; the table in the root node records that there is one embedding for each molecule). Then the embeddings are extended in all possible ways, which leads to the four different substructures shown on the second level (i.e., S–C, S–N, S–O, S=N). These substructures are ordered, from left to right, as they are considered by our algorithm, i.e., extensions by single bonds precede extensions by double bonds, and within extensions by bonds of the same type the element type of the atom a bond leads to determines the order. Note that there are two embeddings of S–C into both the molecules b and c and two embeddings of S–O into the molecule a.

In the third step the extensions of the substructure S–C are constructed. This leads to the first five substructures on the third level (i.e., C–S–C, C–S–N, C–S–O, C–S=N and C–C–S). Again the order of these substructures, from left to right, reflects the order in which they are considered. Since we search depth first, the next substructure to be extended is C–S–C.[2] However, this substructure does not have enough support and therefore the subtree is pruned.

The substructure C–S–N is considered next etc. However, we confine ourselves to pointing out situations in which specific aspects of our method become obvious. Effects of the structural pruning can be seen, for instance, at the fragment C–S–N, which does not have a child in which a second carbon atom is attached to the sulfur atom. The reason is that the extension by the bond to the nitrogen atom rules out all single bonds leading to atoms of a type preceding nitrogen (like carbon). Similarly, C–S=N does not have children with another atom attached to the sulfur atom by a single bond, not even an oxygen atom, which follows nitrogen in the periodic table of elements. The reason is that

---

[1] Please note that these structures were made up to demonstrate certain aspects of the search scheme. None of them has any real meaning.

[2] It may seem strange that there are two embeddings of this substructure into both the molecules b and c. The reason for this is explained below.

1) $\overset{\overset{O}{|}}{C-S-N}$
3 (50%)

2) C–C–S–N
3 (50%)

3) C–S–N
5 (83%)

4) C–S–O
4 (67%)

5) C–S=N
3 (50%)

6) C–S
6 (100%)

Figure 4: The six frequent substructures that are found in the example in the order in which they are generated.

a double bond succeeds a single bond and thus the extension by the double bond to the nitrogen atom rules out all single bonds emanating from the sulfur atom. Finally, the structure C–C–S has no children at all, even though it has enough support. The reason is that in this substructure a bond was added to the carbon atom adjacent to the sulfur atom. This carbon atom is numbered 1 and thus no bonds can be added to the sulfur atom, which has number 0. Only the carbon atoms can be starting points of a new bond, but there are no such bonds in the molecules a, b, and d.

During the recursive search all frequent substructures encountered are recorded. The resulting set of six frequent substructures, together with their absolute and relative support is shown in Figure 4. Note that C–C–S is not reported, because it has the same support as its superstructure C–C–S–N. Likewise, O–S–N, S=N, and S are not reported. This example makes it clear that our algorithm can find arbitrary substructures, even though it does not show how cyclic structures are treated. Unfortunately, search trees for cyclic structures are too big to be depicted here.

2.5. Incomplete Structural Pruning

We indicated above that our structural pruning is not perfect. In order to understand the problems that can arise, consider two molecules A and B with the common substructure N–C–S–C–O. We try to find this substructure starting from the sulfur atom. Since the two bonds emanating from the sulfur atom are equivalent, we have no precedence rule and thus the order in which they are added to an embedding depends on the order in which they occur in the corresponding molecule. Suppose that in molecule A the bond going to the left precedes the bond going to the right, while in molecule B it is the other way round. As a consequence, in embeddings into molecule A the left carbon atom will precede the right one, while in embeddings into molecule B it will be the other way round. Now consider the substructure C–S–C and its extensions. In molecule A the carbon numbered 1 (the left one) will be extended by adding the nitrogen atom and thus the oxygen atom can be added in the next step (to the carbon on the right, which is numbered 2), resulting in the full substructure. However, in molecule B the nitrogen atom has to be added by extending the carbon atom numbered 2 (again the left one; in embeddings into molecule B the right carbon is numbered 1). Hence it is not

possible to add the oxygen atom in the next step, because this would mean adding a bond starting at an atom with a lower number than the atom extended in the preceding step. Therefore the common substructure is not found. This example also shows that it does not help to look "one step ahead" to the next atom, because there could be arbitrarily long equivalent chains, which differ only at the ends.

If, however, we accept to reach identical substructures in different branches of the search tree in cases like this, we can correct the imperfection of our structural pruning. Whenever we have extended an embedding by following a bond, we allow adding an equivalent bond in the next step, regardless of whether it precedes or succeeds, in the corresponding molecule, the bond added in the preceding step. This relaxation explains why there are two embeddings of the substructure C–S–C into both the molecules b and c of our example. In one embedding the left carbon atom is numbered 1 and the one at the bottom is numbered 2, while in the other it is the other way round (cf. Figure 2).

Note that considering the same substructure several times cannot lead to wrong results, only to multiple reporting of the same substructure. Multiple reporting, however, can be suppressed by maintaining a list of frequent substructures and suppressing new ones that are identical to already known ones. It is more important that the missing rule for equivalent bonds can lead to considerable redundant search in certain structures, especially molecules containing one or more aromatic rings. We are currently trying to tackle this problem by collapsing rings into special vertices.

However, it should be noted that even if we could amend the weakness of our structural pruning, we would still be unable to guarantee that each substructure is considered in only one branch. If, for instance, some substructure X can be embedded twice into some molecules and if there are frequent substructures that contain both embeddings (and thus X twice), then these substructures can be grown from either embedding. If the connection between the two embeddings of X is not symmetric, the same substructure is reached in two different branches of the search tree in this case. Obviously, there is no simple way to avoid such situations.

2.6. Embedding a Core Structure

Up to now we assumed that we start the search from a single atom. This usually works fairly well as long as this atom is rare in the molecules to work on. For example, sulfur or phosphorus are often good starting points in biochemical applications, while starting with carbon is a bad idea: Every organic molecule contains several carbon atoms, often twenty or more, and thus we end up with an already very high number of embeddings of the initial atom. As a consequence, the algorithm is likely to run out of memory before reaching substructures of reasonable size.

However, if we cannot start from a rare element, it is sometimes possible to specify a core—for instance, an aromatic ring with one or two side chains—from which the search can be started. Provided the core structure is specific enough, there are only few, at best only one embedding per molecule, so that the list of embeddings is short.

While it is trivial to embed a single atom into a molecule, embedding a core structure can be much more difficult. In our implementation we rely on the following simple observation: Embedding a core structure is the same as finding a common substructure of the molecule and the core that is as big as the core itself. This leads to the idea to grow a substructure into both the core and the molecule until it completely covers the core. That is, we do a substructure search for the core and the molecule starting from an arbitrary atom of the core and requiring a support of 100% (i.e., both the core and the molecule must contain the substructure). In addition, we can restrict the search to one embedding of a substructure into the core at all times, since we know that it must be completely covered in the end. (For the molecule, however, we must consider all possible embeddings.)

Note that the same mechanism of growing a substructure into two molecules can also be used for substructure tests as they are needed to suppress multiple reporting of the same fragment (see above) as well as reporting redundant fragments (fragments that are substructures of some other fragment and have the same support as this fragment).

2.7. Finding Contrast Structures

Our approach to find frequent substructures can easily be extended to find *contrast structures*, that is, substructures that are frequent in a predefined subset of the molecules and infrequent in the complement of this subset. Finding contrast structures requires two parameters: a minimum support for the focus subset and a maximum support for the complement. The search is carried out in exactly the same way as described above. The only difference is that two support numbers are determined: one for the focus subset and one for the complement. Only the support in the focus subset is used to prune the search tree. The support in the complement determines whether a frequent substructure is recorded or not, thus filtering out those substructures that do not satisfy the requirements for a contrast structure.

3. Experimental Results

We applied the presented approach to a number of confidential data sets with substantial success. In order to be able to report results in more detail, we used a well-known, publicly available dataset from the National Cancer Institute, the DTP AIDS Antiviral Screen dataset. This screen utilized a soluble formazan assay to measure protection of human CEM cells from HIV-1 infection. Full details were published in [11]. Compounds able to provide at least 50% protection to the CEM cells were retested. Compounds that provided at least 50% protection on retest were listed as moderately active (**CM**). Compounds that reproducibly

Atom		CA	CM and CI
C	Carbon	325 (100.0%)	36828 (99.95%)
O	Oxygen	311 (95.7%)	33029 (89.64%)
N	Nitrogen	276 (84.9%)	29234 (79.34%)
S	Sulfur	143 (44.0%)	10926 (29.65%)
...	...		
Se	Selenium	6 (1.9%)	132 (0.36%)

Table 1: Some single-atom fragments occurring in molecules of the HIV database, together with their occurrence frequencies.

provided 100% protection were listed as confirmed active (**CA**). Compounds not meeting these criteria were listed as confirmed inactive (**CI**). Available online [8] are screening results and chemical structural data on compounds that are not covered by a confidentiality agreement. Available are 41,316 compounds of which we used 37,171. Out of these, a total of 325 belongs to class **CA**, 877 are of class **CM** and the remaining 35,969 are of class **CI**.

NCI lists 75 known active compounds, which are grouped into seven classes: (1) Azido Pyrimidines, (2) Natural Products or Antibiotics, (3) Benzodiazepines, Thiazolobenzimidazoles and related Compounds, (4) Pyrimidine Nucleosides, (5) Dyes and Polyanions, (6) Heavy Metal Compounds, and (7) Purine Nucleosides.

As described above, our molecular fragment mining algorithm requires a seed fragment, which may be empty. For the HIV dataset an empty core results in numerous embeddings of trivial fragments, such as single carbon atoms or small combinations of carbon atoms only. However, fragments of interest contain at least one non-carbon atom, which enabled us to seed the algorithm using the remaining atoms. The list of atoms can be obtained through various methods. We simply started from an empty core, restricted the fragment size to one atom, and ran our molecular fragment miner. Parts of the resulting list of atoms together with their occurrence frequencies are listed in Table 1.

Obviously, due to space constraints, we cannot report in detail about seeding the algorithm with each of these atoms. In the following we therefore concentrate on a few experiments to demonstrate how the proposed method picks out relevant fragments in some of these groups.

3.1. Nitrogen based Fragments

First we focus on compounds containing a nitrogen atom. We used a minimum support of 15.0% for compounds of class **CA** and a maximum support of 0.1% for the complement[3] (classes **CM** and **CI**). 171 fragments were generated

---

[3]Thresholds were selected "top-down", i.e., starting with large settings (that quickly resulted in no reported fragments) the thresholds were subsequentially lowered until a small number of fragments was reported.

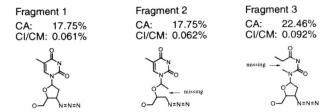

Fragment 1
CA: 17.75%
CI/CM: 0.061%

Fragment 2
CA: 17.75%
CI/CM: 0.062%

Fragment 3
CA: 22.46%
CI/CM: 0.092%

Figure 5: The three largest fragments containing a nitrogen atom.

#254064   #602670

Figure 6: One particular compound (#254064) along with a representative of the normal structure (#602670).

within approximately 20 minutes.[4] The three largest fragments found are shown in Figure 5.

Note how the first two fragments have essentially the same coverage. The only difference is one additional compound of class **CI** that contains fragment 2. In this compound the three nitrogen atoms are connected to the 4-carbon-oxygen ring through an intermediate carbon. This results in a fragment where the carbon connected to the three nitrogen atoms is part of a ring in all cases but one, which prevents the search algorithm from closing the ring. The ring was closed in the first fragment, however, resulting in one less inactive compound being covered. Figure 6 shows this specific compound along with another compound of class **CA** that exhibits the more typical structure.

The third fragments coverage is substantially different, even though its structure is almost identical. The only difference is the double bond between two carbons that closes the second ring in the first fragment, which is missing in Fragment 3. However, some active compounds have a single bond instead of a double bond between these carbons and hence not closing this ring results in a slightly smaller fragment with a much higher coverage. This fragment successfully picks out compounds of class Azido Pyrimidines, a well-known inhibitor of HIV-1. Below we will discuss how "softening" the matching criteria allows us to tolerate such small differences between otherwise identical fragments, which makes this approach also more useful for chemists, who tend to regard such structures as similar.

3.2. Sulfur based Fragments

Next we seeded the algorithm with a sulfur atom. We chose the thresholds support=10% and complement=0.5%, which

---

[4]We used a Java implementation of our algorithm on a 1Ghz Xeon Dual-Processor machine with 1GB of main memory using jre1.3.1.

Fragment 1: CA: 11.9%
                  CI/CM: 0.3%

Fragment 2: CA: 11.9%
                  CI/CM: 0.4%

Figure 7: The two largest fragments with a sulfur atom. These fragments are common to 11 of the 13 Dyes and Polyanions.

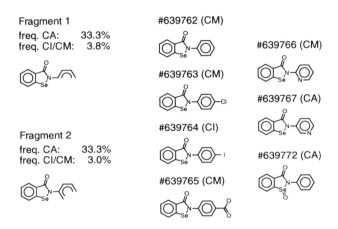

Fragment 1
freq. CA: 33.3%
freq. CI/CM: 3.8%

Fragment 2
freq. CA: 33.3%
freq. CI/CM: 3.0%

#639762 (CM)
#639763 (CM)
#639764 (CI)
#639765 (CM)
#639766 (CM)
#639767 (CA)
#639772 (CA)

Figure 8: Fragments (left) and corresponding compounds (right) containing a Selenium atom. The two compounds of class **CA** are members of the group of Heavy Metal Compounds.

generated a list of 122 fragments in under one minute. The first two (which also happen to be the largest ones with 18 atoms and 19 bonds, resp.) are shown in Figure 7.

Note how these two fragments differ only in the location of the SO_3 group. Both fragments exhibit a lift of well above 25 and pick out 11 of the 13 molecules listed as Dyes and Polyanions. We miss only two of the remaining Dyes and Polyanions (#9617 and #65849), which contain uncommon structures for this family of compounds.

3.3. Selenium based Fragments

An interesting effect of the current method to find fragments can be seen when seeding the algorithm with a Selenium atom (**Se**). Figure 8 (left) shows the two fragments that are found for a minimum support of 30% and a maximum complement support of 5%.

Clearly the first fragment is sufficient to pick out all 7 compounds from the database (shown on the right of Figure 8). However, the second fragment covers one compound less (#639766) and tries to complete the aromatic ring in both directions in parallel. This results in a conflict with the nitrogen atom in compound #639766 and a fragment which is neither a subset of the other fragment nor has exactly the same coverage. For our algorithm these two fragments are therefore unique and are not pruned.

single bond ≠ aromatic bond   single bond = aromatic bond

Figure 9: Two fragments extracted from a set of steroids. On the left, single and aromatic bonds were treated as different bond types, on the right, they were treated as the same bond type.

3.4. Treatment of Aromatic Bonds

An important aspect of molecular fragment mining is the treatment of aromatic rings. Since aromaticity is not clearly defined and can be modeled differently (i.e. explicit aromatic bonds vs. alternating single and double bonds) it is desirable to be able to take it into account throughout the mining process itself. We achieve this by modeling aromatic bonds as either single or double bonds with a flag that indicates aromaticity. This allows us to choose to ignore this flag during mining and hence to find fragments that contain either aromatic or single resp. double bonds. The following example illustrates why this is desirable.

Using a small set of steroid compounds we derived fragments that occur in all of them (support=100%) using the standard algorithm. Figure 9 (left) shows the corresponding fragment. Note how only two rings with an incomplete third ring are discovered of the four ring structure that is typical for steroids. However, if we model aromatic bonds as single+flag and allow the algorithm to ignore this flag, the resulting fragment contains all four rings (see Figure 9 (right)). For some steroids this fourth ring consists of single bonds, while others have an aromatic ring at this position. However, most chemists still regard this as the same 4-ring structure. Such selective "tolerance" against some mismatches can therefore make the presented algorithm more useful for real applications.

4. Conclusions

We presented an algorithm to find relevant molecular fragments in large chemical structure databases. The algorithm allows us to focus on fragments that help to discriminate between different classes of molecules. The underlying search method, which is based on a depth first search with structural pruning, makes it possible to find such fragments efficiently, without the need for frequent reembeddings of fragment candidates, which is a known problem of previously reported approaches. We have shown how the proposed method finds relevant fragments using data from a well-known HIV-screening compound database. The extracted fragments successfully model several of the activity classes known for this dataset.

Future work will focus on making the presented approach more meaningful for the underlying application. In partic-

ular, finding fragments that match exactly is not of prime interest to chemists. As demonstrate above, some types of ring structures are considered functionally equivalent, which should be taken into account by the search algorithm as well. We are currently exploring ways to include such "fuzziness" into the underlying search algorithm directly.

References

[1] R. Agrawal, T. Imielienski, and A. Swami. Mining Association Rules between Sets of Items in Large Databases. *Proc. Conf. on Management of Data*, 207–216. ACM Press, New York, NY, USA 1993

[2] C. Borgelt. Apriori — Finding Association Rules with the Apriori Algorithm (free computer software under the GLPL). http://fuzzy.cs.uni-magdeburg.de/~borgelt/apriori/

[3] C. Borgelt and R. Kruse. Induction of Association Rules: Apriori Implementation. *Proc. 14th Conf. on Computational Statistics (COMPSTAT)*. Berlin, Germany 2002

[4] R.D. Clark. Relative and Absolute Diversity Analysis of Combinatorial Libraries. *Combinatorial Library Design and Evaluation*, 337–362. Dekker, New York, NY, USA 2001

[5] M. Desphande, M. Kuramochi, and G. Karypis. Automated Approaches for Classifying Structures. *Proc. Workshop on Data Mining in Bioinformatics, BioKDD*, 11-18, 2002

[6] J. Hipp, A. Myka, R. Wirth, and U. Güntzer. A New Algorithm for Faster Mining of Generalized Association Rules. *Proc. 2nd Europ. Symp. on Principles of Data Mining and Knowledge Discovery (PKDD'98, Nantes, France)*, 74–82. LNAI 1510, Springer, Heidelberg, Germany 1998

[7] S. Kramer, L. de Raedt, and C. Helma. Molecular Feature Mining in HIV Data. *Proc. 7th Int. Conf. on Knowledge Discovery and Data Mining (KDD-2001, San Francisco, CA)*, 136–143. ACM Press, New York, NY, USA 2001

[8] http://dtp.nci.nih.gov/docs/aids/aids_data.html

[9] J. W. Raymond, E. J. Gardiner, and P. Willett. Heuristics for Similarity Searching of Chemical Graphs using a Maximum Common Edge Subgraph Algorithm. *Journal of Chemical Information and Computer Sciences*, 42(2):305–316. American Chemical Society, Columbus, OH, USA 2002

[10] W. J. Streich and R. Franke. Topological Pharmacophores, New Methods and Their Application to a Set of Antimalarials, Part 1: The Methods LOGANA and LOCON. *Quant. Struct.-Act. Relat.*, 4:13–18. J. Wiley & Sons, Chichester, United Kingdom 1985

[11] O. Weislow, R. Kiser, D. Fine, J. Bader, R. Shoemaker, and M. Boyd. New Soluble Formazan Assay for HIV-1 Cytopathic Effects: Application to High Flux Screening of Synthetic and Natural Products for AIDS Antiviral Activity. *Journal of the National Cancer Institute*, 81:577–586. Oxford University Press, Oxford, United Kingdom 1989

[12] M. Zaki, S. Parthasarathy, M. Ogihara, and W. Li. New Algorithms for Fast Discovery of Association Rules. *Proc. 3rd Int. Conf. on Knowledge Discovery and Data Mining (KDD'97)*, 283–296. AAAI Press, Menlo Park, CA, USA 1997

Mining General Temporal Association Rules for Items with Different Exhibition Periods

Cheng-Yue Chang, Ming-Syan Chen and Chang-Hung Lee
Department of Electrical Engineering
National Taiwan University
Taipei, Taiwan, ROC
Email: {cychang, chlee}@arbor.ee.ntu.edu.tw; mschen@cc.ee.ntu.edu.tw

Abstract

In this paper, we explore a new model of mining general temporal association rules from large databases where the exhibition periods of the items are allowed to be different from one to another. Note that in this new model, the downward closure property which all prior Apriori-based algorithms relied upon to attain good efficiency is no longer valid. As a result, how to efficiently generate candidate itemsets form large databases has become the major challenge. To address this issue, we develop an efficient algorithm, referred to as algorithm SPF (standing for Segmented Progressive Filter) in this paper. The basic idea behind SPF is to first segment the database into sub-databases in such a way that items in each sub-database will have either the common starting time or the common ending time. Then, for each sub-database, SPF progressively filters candidate 2-itemsets with cumulative filtering thresholds either forward or backward in time. This feature allows SPF of adopting the scan reduction technique by generating all candidate k-itemsets (k > 2) from candidate 2-itemsets directly. The experimental results show that algorithm SPF significantly outperforms other schemes which are extended from prior methods in terms of the execution time and scalability.

1. Introduction

In recent years, a significant amount of research effort has been elaborated upon deriving data mining techniques to discover useful but unknown knowledge from large databases. The knowledge discovered includes those on association rules, classification rules, sequential patterns, path traversal patterns, user moving patterns, and etc. Among others, mining of association rules is a well addressed important problem, i.e., "Given a database of sales transactions, one would like to discover the important associations among items such that the presence of some items in a transaction will imply the presence of other items in the same transaction."

The problem of mining association rules was first explored by [2]. Following this pioneering work, several fast algorithms based on the level-wise Apriori framework [3, 15] and partitioning [12] are proposed to remedy the performance bottleneck of Apriori. In addition, several novel mining techniques, including TreeProjection [1] and FP-growth algorithms [10], also receive a significant amount of research attention. On the other hand, many variants of mining association rules are studied to explore more mining capabilities, such as incremental updating [5, 11], mining of generalized and multi-level rules [8, 16], mining of quantitative rules [17], mining of multi-dimensional rules [14], constraint-based rule mining [9] and mining with multiple minimum supports [13, 18], mining associations among correlated or infrequent items [7], and temporal association rule discovery [4, 6].

While these are important results toward enabling the integration of association mining and fast searching algorithms, their mining methods, however, cannot be effectively applied to the transaction database where the exhibition periods of the items are different from one to another. As a matter of fact, it is a common phenomenon that the items in a real transaction database have different exhibition periods. The problem can be best understood by the following example.

Example 1.1: Consider the transaction database $\mathcal{D}$ as shown in Figure 1. A set of time series database indicates the transaction records from January 2002 to April 2002. The exhibition period of each item is given in the right of Figure 1. Assume that the minimum support and the minimum confidence required are $min\_supp = 30\%$ and $min\_conf = 75\%$, respectively. By conventional mining algorithms, with respect to the same support counting

		Date	TID	Itemset
$\mathcal{D}$	P1	Jan-02	T01	A C F
			T02	A D F
			T03	C F
			T04	A D
	P2	Feb-02	T05	BCD F
			T06	C
			T07	BCD
			T08	AB
	P3	Mar-02	T09	C EF
			T10	AB F
			T11	EF
			T12	B
	P4	Apr-02	T13	A E
			T14	B E
			T15	AB
			T16	AB

(Transaction Database)

Item	start	end
A	Jan-02	Apr-02
B	Feb-02	Apr-02
C	Jan-02	Mar-02
D	Jan-02	Feb-02
E	Mar-02	Apr-02
F	Jan-02	Mar-02

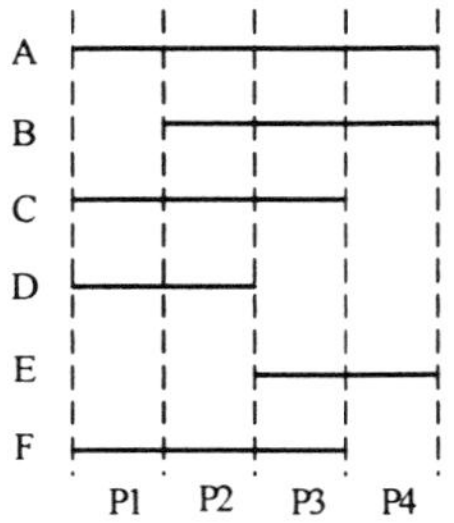

Figure 1. An illustrative database where the items have individual exhibition periods.

basis $|\mathcal{D}|$, only the itemsets $\{A\}$, $\{B\}$, $\{C\}$ and $\{F\}$ will be termed as frequent itemsets. Thus, no rule will be discovered in this case. However, as will be shown later in Example 1.2, some rules do exist in the illustrative database when the individual exhibition periods of items are taken into consideration.

From Example 1.1, we can observe that the problem of conventional mining algorithms lies in their absence of equitable support counting basis for each itemset. It is noted that the itemsets with longer exhibition periods (e.g., A, B, C and F) are more likely to be frequent than those with shorter exhibition periods (e.g., D and E). As a result, the association rules we usually discover will be those composed of long-term items (e.g., milk and bread are frequently purchased together, which is, however, of less interest to us). In contrast, some short-term itemsets, such as those composed of seasonal food or clothes, which may be really "frequent" and interesting in their exhibition periods are less likely to be identified as frequent ones if a conventional mining process is employed. To address this issue, we explore in this paper a new model of mining general temporal association rules where the items are allowed to have different exhibition periods, and the determination of their supports is made in accordance with their exhibition periods. Explicitly, we introduce the notion of *maximal common exhibition period* (abbreviated as *MCP)* and define the *relative support* to provide an equitable support counting basis for each itemset. The *MCP* of the itemset X, denoted by $[p, q]$, is defined as the period between the *latest-exhibition-start time* p and the *earliest-exhibition-end time* q of all items belonging to X. For example, for the itemset BC in Figure 1, its *MCP* is $[2, 3]$ since the *latest-exhibition-start time* of the items B and C is 2 and the *earliest-exhibition-end time* of the items B and C is 3. The relative support of the itemset X is given by $supp(X^{p,q}) = \frac{|\{T \in \mathcal{D}^{p,q} | X \subseteq T\}|}{|\mathcal{D}^{p,q}|}$ where $\mathcal{D}^{p,q}$ indicates the partial database bounded by $[p, q]$, and $|\{T \in \mathcal{D}^{p,q} | X \subseteq T\}|$ indicates the number of transactions that contain X in $\mathcal{D}^{p,q}$. The general temporal association rule $(X \Longrightarrow Y)^{p,q}$ is termed to be frequent within its *MCP* $[p, q]$ if and only if its relative support is not smaller than the minimum support required (i.e., $supp((X \cup Y)^{p,q}) \geq min_supp$), and its confidence is not smaller than the minimum confidence needed (i.e., $conf((X \Longrightarrow Y)^{p,q}) = \frac{supp((X \cup Y)^{p,q})}{supp(X^{p,q})} \geq min_conf$).

Example 1.2: Based on the definitions above, the frequent general temporal association rules in Example 1.1 can be identified as follows:

(1) $(A \Longrightarrow B)^{2,4}$ with $supp(AB^{2,4}) = \frac{4}{12} > 30\%$ and $conf((A \Longrightarrow B)^{2,4}) = \frac{supp(AB^{2,4})}{supp(A^{2,4})} = \frac{4}{5} > 75\%$;

(2) $(D \Longrightarrow B)^{2,2}$ with $supp(BD^{2,2}) = \frac{2}{4} > 30\%$ and $conf((D \Longrightarrow B)^{2,2}) = \frac{supp(BD^{2,2})}{supp(D^{2,2})} = \frac{2}{2} > 75\%$;

(3) $(E \Longrightarrow F)^{3,3}$ with $supp(EF^{3,3}) = \frac{2}{4} > 30\%$ and $conf((E \Longrightarrow F)^{3,3}) = \frac{supp(EF^{3,3})}{supp(E^{3,3})} = \frac{2}{2} > 75\%$;

(4) $(D \Longrightarrow BC)^{2,2}$ with $supp(BCD^{2,2}) = \frac{2}{4} > 30\%$ and $conf((D \Longrightarrow BC)^{2,2}) = \frac{supp(BCD^{2,2})}{supp(D^{2,2})} = \frac{2}{2} > 75\%$.

It is important to note that in this new model, the downward closure property which all prior Apriori-based algorithms relied upon to attain good efficiency is no longer valid. Recall that the downward closure property guarantees that all sub-itemsets of a frequent itemset are frequent. Based on this property, all prior Apriori-based algorithms are allowed to limit their attention to those candidates whose sub-itemsets are frequent and to prune the searching space effectively. However, once this property is not valid anymore, the searching space will explode and become difficult to tackle.

Example 1.3: From the illustrative database in Example 1.1, we can find that although the itemset BCD is frequent in its maximal common exhibition period, the itemsets BC, BD and CD are not all frequent in their corresponding maximal common exhibition periods. Explicitly, the itemset BC is infrequent in its maximal common exhibition period $[2, 3]$ since its relative support is only 25% (< 30%). Similarly, the itemset CD is infrequent in its maximal common exhibition period $[1, 2]$. Hence, to determine if an itemset is frequent, without the downward closure property, we are not allowed anymore to limit our attention to those whose subitemsets are frequent.

To address this issue, we develop an efficient algorithm, referred to as algorithm SPF (standing for *Segmented Progressive Filter)* in this paper. In essence, algorithm SPF consists of two major procedures, i.e., *Segmentation* (abbreviated as *ProcSG*) and *Progressively Filtering* (abbreviated as *ProcPF*). The basic idea behind SPF is to first divide the database into partitions according to the time granularity imposed. Then, in light of the exhibition period of each item, SPF employs *ProcSG* to segment the database into sub-databases in such a way that items in each sub-database will have *either* the common starting time *or* the common ending time. Note that such a segmentation will allow us of counting the itemsets in each sub-database either forward or backward (in time) efficiently. Then, for each sub-database, SPF utilizes *ProcPF* to progressively filter candidate 2-itemsets with cumulative filtering thresholds from one partition to another. Since infrequent 2-itemsets are hence filtered out in the early processed partitions, the resulting candidate 2-itemsets will be very close to the frequent 2-itemsets. This feature allows us of adopting the scan reduction technique by generating all candidate k-itemsets ($k > 2$) from candidate 2-itemsets directly [15]. The experimental results show that algorithm SPF significantly outperforms other schemes which are extended from prior methods in terms of the execution time and scalability. The advantage of SPF becomes even more prominent as the size of the database increases.

The rest of this paper is organized as follows. Section 2 describes the problem of mining general temporal association rules. The proposed algorithm SPF is presented in Section 3. The performance of algorithm SPF is empirically evaluated in Section 4. We conclude this paper with Section 5.

2. Problem Description

As described in Section 1, the items in a transaction database may have different exhibition periods. Without loss of generality, it is assumed that a certain time granularity, e.g., *week, month, quarter* or *year*, is imposed by the application database. Let n be the number of partitions divided by the time granularity imposed. In the model considered, $db^{p,q}$ ($1 \leq p \leq q \leq n$) denotes the portion of the transaction database formed by a continuous region from the partition P_p to the partition P_q, and $X^{p,q}$ denotes the *temporal itemset* whose items are commonly exhibited from the partition P_p to the partition P_q.

As such, we can define the maximal temporal itemset $X^{p,q}$ and the corresponding temporal sub-itemsets as follows.

Definition 1: *The temporal itemset $X^{p,q}$ is called a maximal temporal itemset (TI) if P_p is the latest starting partition and P_q is the earliest ending partition of all items belonging to X. $[p,q]$ is referred to as the maximal common exhibition period (MCP) of the itemset X, denoted by $MCP(X)$.*

Definition 2: *The temporal itemset $Y^{p,q}$ is called a tempo-*

ral sub-itemset (SI) of the maximal temporal itemset $X^{p,q}$ if $Y \subset X$.

Based on Definition 1, the temporal itemset $BCD^{2,2}$ in Figure 1 is deemed a maximal temporal itemset since the latest starting partition and the earliest ending partition of the items B, C and D are both P_2. In addition, the temporal itemsets $BC^{2,2}$, $BD^{2,2}$ and $CD^{2,2}$ are the corresponding temporal sub-itemsets of $BCD^{2,2}$ according to Definition 2. Note that $BD^{2,2}$ is also a maximal temporal itemset itself, but $BC^{2,2}$ is not since the earliest ending partition of the items B and C is P_3 rather than P_2.

In the conventional problem of mining association rules, the support of the itemset X is determined by $supp(X) = \frac{|\{T \in db^{1,n}|X \subseteq T\}|}{|db^{1,n}|}$, which is referred to as the *absolute* support in this paper. However, as explained in Section 1, we shall provide an equitable support counting basis for each temporal itemset. To this end, we define the relative support for a temporal itemset below.

Definition 3: *The relative support of the temporal itemset $X^{p,q}$ is defined as*

$$supp(X^{p,q}) = \frac{|\{T \in db^{p,q}|X \subseteq T\}|}{|db^{p,q}|}$$

which is the fraction of the transactions supporting the itemset X in $db^{p,q}$.

With the equitable support counting basis defined in Definition 3, we can then determine whether a maximal temporal itemset is frequent by the following definition.

Definition 4: *The maximal temporal itemset $X^{MCP(X)}$ is termed to be frequent iff $supp(X^{MCP(X)}) \geq min\_supp$ where min_supp is the minimum support required.*

Property 1: *All temporal sub-itemsets of a frequent maximal temporal itemset are frequent.*

As will be explained later, Property 1 is very important for us to determine the confidence of a general temporal association rule defined below.

Definition 5: *The rule $(Y \implies Z)^{MCP(X)}$ derived from the maximal temporal itemset $X^{MCP(X)}$ is called a general temporal association rule if $Y \subset X$ and $Z = X - Y$.*

Definition 6: *The confidence of the general temporal association rule $(Y \implies Z)^{MCP(Y \cup Z)}$ is defined as*

$$conf((Y \implies Z)^{MCP(Y \cup Z)}) = \frac{supp((Y \bigcup Z)^{MCP(Y \cup Z)})}{supp(Y^{MCP(Y \cup Z)})}.$$

Note that the calculation of the confidence of a general temporal association rule not only depends on the relative support of the corresponding maximal temporal itemset but also relys on the relative supports of the corresponding temporal sub-itemsets. Property 1 ensures that the relative supports of the corresponding temporal sub-itemsets can be obtained without extra database scans since all temporal sub-itemsets of the frequent maximal temporal itemset are also frequent.

Finally, given a pair of min_conf and min_supp required, we can define the frequent general temporal association rule below.

Definition 7: *The general temporal association rule* $(Y \implies Z)^{MCP(Y \cup Z)}$ *is termed to be frequent iff* $supp((Y \cup Z)^{MCP(Y \cup Z)}) \geq min\_supp$ *and* $conf((Y \implies Z)^{MCP(Y \cup Z)}) \geq min\_conf$.

With these definitions, the problem of mining general temporal association rules is to discover all frequent general temporal association rules from the large database. Similarly, the problem of mining general temporal association can be decomposed into two steps: (1) Generate all frequent maximal temporal itemsets (TIs) and the corresponding temporal sub-itemsets (SIs) with their relative supports; (2) Derive all frequent general temporal association rules that satisfy min_conf from these frequent TIs.

Note that once the frequent TIs and SIs with their supports are obtained, deriving the frequent general temporal association rules is straightforward. Therefore, in the rest of this paper we concentrate our discussion on the algorithms for mining frequent TIs and SIs.

3. Mining General Temporal Association Rules

We present the proposed algorithm, SPF, for mining general temporal association rules in this section. A detailed description of algorithm SPF is given in Section 3.1. In Section 3.2, we use an example to illustrate the operations of SPF.

3.1. Algorithm SPF

The major challenge of mining general temporal association rules is that the exhibition periods of the items in the transaction database are allowed to be different from one to another. In such a circumstance, it is very difficult to efficiently generate candidate itemsets since the downward closure property is no longer valid as explained in Section 1. To address this problem, a novel algorithm, SPF, is proposed in this section to discover general temporal association rules efficiently.

In essence, algorithm SPF consists of two major procedures, i.e., *Segmentation* (abbreviated as *ProcSG*) and *Progressively Filtering* (abbreviated as *ProcPF*). The basic idea behind SPF is to first divide the database into partitions according to the time granularity imposed. Then, in light of the exhibition period of each item, SPF employs *ProcSG* to segment the database into sub-databases in such a way that items in each sub-database will have *either* the common starting time *or* the common ending time. For each sub-database, SPF utilizes *ProcPF* to progressively filter candidate 2-itemsets with cumulative filtering thresholds from

one partition to another. After all sub-databases are processed, SPF unions all candidate 2-itemsets generated in each sub-database. As pointed out earlier, since infrequent 2-itemsets will be filtered out in the early processed partitions, the resulting candidate 2-itemsets will be very close to the frequent 2-itemsets. This feature allows us of adopting the scan reduction technique by generating all candidate k-itemsets ($k > 2$) from candidate 2-itemsets directly. After all candidate itemsets are generated, they are transformed to TIs, and the corresponding SIs are generated based on these TIs. Finally, the frequent TIs and SIs with their supports can be obtained by scanning the whole database once.

3.1.1. Description of *ProcSG* for *Segmentation*

The motivation of *ProcSG* is to first reduce the problem of mining general temporal association rules to the one in which the exhibition periods of the items are only allowed to be *either* different in the starting time *or* different in the ending time. After such a reduction, we are able to employ *ProcPF*, in each sub-database, to progressively filter candidate 2-itemsets either forward or backward (in time) efficiently. However, as mentioned above, the advantageous feature of *ProcPF* is that it can progressively filter out infrequent 2-itemset in the early processed partitions. Thus, the more segments the whole database is divided into, the less significant the filtering effect will be. In view of this, *ProcSG* is devised to segment the whole database into the minimal number of sub-databases as required for items in each sub-database to have either the common starting partition or the common ending partition.

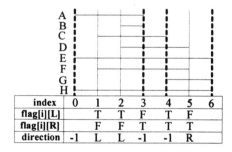

Figure 2. An example illustrating the execution of *ProcSG*.

Figure 2 illustrates the execution of *ProcSG*. Operations in lines 1-3 initialize the parameters used in the procedure. The **for** loop in lines 4-8, for each item, sets the left flag of the starting partition and the right flag of the ending partition to be *true*. The resulting values in *flag* array are shown in the bottom of Figure 2. With these flags, the **for** loop in lines 9-31 scans the partitions from the first to the last. Once the value of $direction$ is reversed, one segmentation has to be made, and the value of $direction$ is reset. From the example in Figure 2, the value of $direction$ is reversed twice, meaning that two times of segmentation are needed. Consequently, the original database $db^{1,6}$ is divided into $db^{1,3}$, $db^{4,4}$ and $db^{5,6}$.

Procedure ProcSG(n)

1. $SM = \emptyset;\ direction = -1;\ head = 1;$
2.   **for** $(index = 0$ **to** $n)$
3. $flag[i][L] = false;\ flag[i][R] = false;$
4.   **for** (each item $i \in \mathcal{I}$) {
5. $(p, q) = MCP(i);$
6. $flag[p - 1][L] = true;$
7. $flag[q][R] = true;$
8.   }
9.   **for** $(i = 1$ **to** $n - 1)$ {
10.   **if** $(direction == -1)$ {
11.   **if** $(flag[i][L] == true$ **and** $flag[i][R] == true)$ {
12. $SM = SM \cup \{(head, index, direction)\};$
13. $head = index + 1;$
14.   } **elseif** $(flag[i][L] == true$ **and** $flag[i][R] == false)$
15. $direction = L;$
16.   **elseif** $(flag[i][L] == false$ **and** $flag[i][R] == true)$
17. $direction = R;$
18.   } **elseif** $(direction == L)$ {
19.   **if** $(flag[index][R] == true)$ {
20. $SM = SM \cup \{(head, index, direction)\};$
21. $head = index + 1;$
22. $direction = -1;$
23.   }
24.   } **elseif** $(direction == R)$ {
25.   **if** $(flag[i][L] == true)$ {
26. $SM = SM \cup \{(head, index, direction)\};$
27. $head = index + 1;$
28. $direction = -1;$
29.   }
30.   }
31.   }
32. $SM = SM \cup \{(head, n, direction)\};$
33.   **return** $SM;$

3.1.2. Description of *ProcPF* for *Progressively Filtering*

After the entire database is segmented by *ProcSG*, *ProcPF* is designed to progressively filter candidates 2-itemsets from one partition to another in each sub-database. Specifically, *ProcPF* generates all 2-itemsets and counts their occurrences in the first partition. For those 2-itemsets whose numbers of occurrences are not smaller than the filtering threshold (i.e., $min\_supp * |P_1|$), they are viewed as candidate 2-itemsets and will be brought to the next partition for further processing. Then, *ProcPF* will generate new

2-itemsets in the second partition and count their occurrences as well. However, for those candidate 2-itemsets brought from the previous partition, their numbers of occurrences will be cumulated from the previous partition to the current one. Note that the filtering threshold (i.e., $min\_supp * (|P_1| + |P_2|)$) for them will also be cumulated. Similarly, those 2-itemsets whose numbers of occurrences are not smaller than their corresponding filtering thresholds will be brought to the next partition for further processing until there is no partition to be processed any more.

Let PS denote the cumulative set of candidate 2-itemsets. It is noted that PS is composed of the following two types of candidate 2-itemsets: (1) the candidate 2-itemsets that were carried over from the previous partition and remain as candidate 2-itemsets after the current partition is included into consideration; and (2) the candidate itemsets that were not in the cumulative candidate set in the previous partition but are newly selected after taking the current partition into account. Since a significant number of 2-itemsets will be filtered out in the early partitions, the resulting PS will be very close to the set of frequent 2-itemsets after processing all partitions. Taking advantage of this feature, we can employ the scan reduction technique to generate all candidate k-itemsets where $k > 2$ from (k-1)-itemsets at the same time [15].

The procedure to progressively filter out infrequent 2-itemsets is shown in *ProcPF*. *ProcPF* takes three arguments p, q and $direction$ as the inputs, where p and q are the starting and ending partitions to be processed ($p \leq q$), and $direction$ indicates the scanning direction, i.e., either forward (i.e., from p to q) or backward (i.e., from q to p) in time. If the items in the sub-database have the same ending partition, the direction is forward. Otherwise, the direction is backward. As shown in *ProcPF*, operations in lines 1-5 initially set PS to be an empty set and determine the scanning sequence. The **for** loop, in lines 6-17, finds out all 2-itemsets with their numbers of occurrences in each partition, and employs the corresponding filtering threshold (i.e., $min\_supp * \sum_{m=X.start,h} |P^m|$) to filter out infrequent ones. After processing all partitions, the cumulative set of candidate 2-itemsets, PS, is returned in line 18.

Procedure ProcPF($p, q, direction$)

1. $PS = \emptyset;$
2.   **if** $(direction == left)$
3. $head = p;\ tail = q;$
4.   **else**
5. $head = q;\ tail = p;$
6.   **for** $(h = head$ **to** $tail)$
7.   **for** (each 2-itemset X_2 in P_h)
8.   **if** $(X_2 \notin PS)$ {
9. $X_2.count = N_{P_h}(X_2);$
10. $X_2.start = h;$
11.   **if** $(X_2.count \geq min\_supp * |P_h|)$

12. $PS = PS \cup X_2$;

13.   } else {

14. $X_2.count = X_2.count + N_{P_h}(X_2)$;

15. $\mathbf{if}\,(X_2.count < \lceil min\_supp * \sum_{m=X_2.start,h} |P_m| \rceil)$

16. $PS = PS - X_2$;

17.   }

18. **return** PS;

Finally, algorithm SPF is completed by the integration of *ProcSG* and *ProcPF*. At first, algorithm SPF segments the database into sub-databases by *ProcSG*. Then, for each sub-database, algorithm SPF employs *ProcPF* to progressively filter out candidate 2-itemsets. Using the scan reduction technique [15], SPF generates all candidate k-itemsets from (k-1)-itemsets. Thereafter, the candidate k-itemsets are transformed to TIs, and the corresponding SIs are generated. Finally, the database is scanned once to determine all frequent TIs and SIs.

3.2. An Illustrative Example of Algorithm SPF

The operation of algorithm SPF can be best understood by an illustrative example as shown in Figure 1. Suppose that the minimum support and confidence required are 30% and 75%, respectively, i.e., $min\_supp = 30\%$ and $min\_conf = 75\%$. As explained in Section 3.1, SPF first segments the database into several sub-databases by *ProcSG*. In our example, the transaction database, $db^{1,4}$, is segmented into two sub-databases, $db^{1,2}$ and $db^{3,4}$ as shown in Figure 3. The scanning direction of $db^{1,2}$ is from the left to the right whereas the scanning direction of $db^{3,4}$ is from the right to the left.

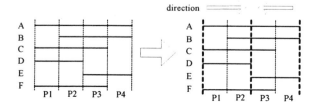

Figure 3. Segmenting the illustrative database.

After the database is segmented into sub-databases where the items in each sub-database have either the same starting or ending partition., algorithm SPF employs *ProcPF* to progressively filter the candidate 2-itemsets in each of these two sub-databases. The execution of *ProcPF* in sub-database $db^{1,2}$ is shown in the upper-left part of Figure 4. Five 2-itemsets are first considered in the partition P_1, and their numbers of occurrences and the partition in which they are first considered (i.e., P_1) are also

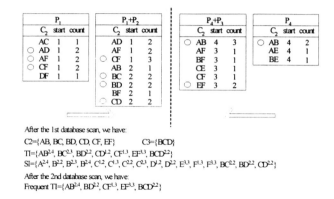

After the 1st database scan, we have:
C2={AB, BC, BD, CD, CF, EF}   C3={BCD}
TI={AB²⁴, BC²³, BD²², CD¹², CF¹³, EF³³, BCD²²}
SI={A²⁴, B²², B²³, B²⁴, C¹², C¹³, C²², C²³, D¹², D²², E³³, F¹³, F³³, BC²², BD²², CD²²}
After the 2nd database scan, we have:
Frequent TI={AB²⁴, BD²², CF¹³, EF³³, BCD²²}

Figure 4. Progressively Filtering candidate 2-itemsets in each sub-database.

recorded. The corresponding filtering threshold for each of them is equal to $2 = \lceil 4 * 0.3 \rceil$ since there are four transactions in P_1. As a result, only the 2-itemsets AD, AF and CF are viewed as the candidate 2-itemsets and brought to the next partition for further processing. In the partition P_2, the 2-itemsets AC, BC, BD, BF and CD are newly generated, and their numbers of occurrences and the partition in which they are first considered (i.e., P_2) are also recorded. Since AD, AF and CF are brought from the previous partition, their numbers of occurrences are cumulated. So are the corresponding filtering thresholds for them (i.e., $3 = \lceil 0.3 * (4 + 4) \rceil$). Thus, only the 2-itemsets CF, BC, BD and CD are viewed as candidate 2-itemsets after processing P_2. The execution of *ProcPF* in the sub-database $db^{3,4}$ works similarly and is shown in the upper-right part of Figure 4. Note that the scanning direction in the sub-database $db^{3,4}$ is from the right to the left, i.e., from P_4 to P_3. After scanning the sub-databases $db^{1,2}$ and $db^{3,4}$, the resulting candidate set C_2 becomes $\{AB, BC, BD, CD, CF, EF\}$. Using the scan reduction technique, we generate all candidate k-itemsets from candidate (k-1)-itemsets where $k > 2$. In our case, only one candidate 3-itemset BCD is generated. Then, these candidates are transformed to the TIs (i.e., $\{AB^{2,4}, BC^{2,3}, BD^{2,3}, CD^{1,2}, CF^{1,3}, EF^{3,3}, BCD^{2,2}\}$), and the corresponding SIs (i.e., $\{A^{2,4}, B^{2,2}, B^{2,3}, B^{2,4}, C^{1,2}, C^{1,3}, C^{2,2}, C^{2,3}, D^{1,2}, D^{2,2}, E^{3,3}, F^{1,3}, F^{3,3}, BC^{2,2}, BD^{2,2}, CD^{2,2}\}$) are generated as shown in the bottom of Figure 4. By scanning the entire database again, we can have the relative supports of all temporal itemsets in $TI \cup SI$ and then determine the frequent TIs. From the frequent TIs determined (i.e., $\{AB^{2,4}, BD^{2,2}, CF^{1,3}, EF^{3,3}, BCD^{2,2}\}$), we can thus derive all frequent general temporal association rules as shown in Example 1.2.

4. Performance Analysis

To assess the performance of algorithm SPF, we compare algorithm SPF with $Apriori^{IP}$, which is extended from algorithm Apriori to deal with the problem of mining general temporal association rules. $Apriori^{IP}$ first transforms each item to the temporal 1-itemsets with all possible exhibition periods. Then, based on the anti-monotone Apriori-like heuristic, it generates candidate temporal k-itemsets from frequent temporal (k-1)-itemsets until no candidate temporal itemset can be generated any more. The simulation program is coded in C++. The experiments are run on a computer with Pentium III CPU and 512MB RAM. As will be shown later, algorithm SPF outperforms $Apriori^{IP}$ in terms of execution time and scalability. We describe the method used to generate synthetic databases in Section 4.1. The execution time of algorithm SPF and $Apriori^{IP}$ is compared in Section 4.2. Results of scaleup experiments are presented in Section 4.3.

4.1. Generation of Synthetic Workload

The method used in this paper to generate synthetic databases is similar to the one used in [3, 15] with some modifications. In order to mimic various exhibition periods of the items in a realistic database, the modifications are made as follows. Initially, we still employ the method used in [3, 15] to generate a synthetic database. Then, we equally divide the synthetic database into P partitions to simulate the phenomenon of the time granularity required. In addition, to model the exhibition periods of the items in a realistic database, we randomly select a starting partition s in the range $[1, P]$ and the ending partition e in range $[s, P]$ for each item in the synthetic database. Finally, we scan the database once to remove the items in the transactions which are not within their exhibition periods. For example, the item A would be removed from the transaction ABC in partition 1 if the exhibition period of the item A were $[2, 4]$.

Based on such a modified method, we generate several different synthetic databases to evaluate the performance of algorithm SPF. Each of the generated database consists of $|D|$ transactions with average size of $|T|$ items. The number of different items in each database is N. The average size of the potential frequent itemsets is set to $|I|$, and the number of the potential frequent itemsets is set to $|L|$. The mean correlation level between the potential frequent itemsets is set to 0.25 in our experiments. In addition, for the simplicity of presentation, we use the notation $Tx - Iy - Dz(Nm - Ln - Po)$ to represent a database in which $|T| = x$, $|I| = y$, $D = z$ (K), $N = m$ (K), $|L| = n$ and $|P| = o$ in the following subsections.

4.2. Execution Time

In the first experiment, we investigate the execution time of algorithm SPF and $Apriori^{IP}$ by varying minimum supports. The experimental results on various synthetic databases are shown in Figure 5. As shown in Figure 5, algorithm SPF consistently outperforms $Apriori^{IP}$ in terms of the execution time. Specifically, the execution time of algorithm SPF is in orders of magnitude smaller than that of $Apriori^{IP}$. The margin even grows as the minimum support decreases.

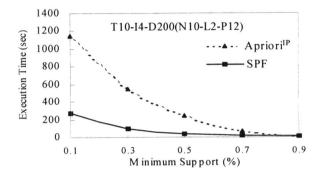

Figure 5. The execution time under various minimum supports.

The advantage of SPF over $Apriori^{IP}$ can be explained below. First, the number of candidates generated by $Apriori^{IP}$ increases exponentially as the number of items or the number of partitions increases. In contrast, the number of candidates generated by algorithm SPF is in proportion to the number of items or the number of partitions in the synthetic database. Second, $Apriori^{IP}$ needs to scan the database multiple times to determines frequent k-itemsets. However, by the technique of scan reduction, algorithm SPF only needs to scan the database twice. These two factors will be further explored in the second experiment in Section 4.3.

4.3. Scaleup Experiments

In the fourth experiment, we investigate the scalability of algorithm SPF by varying the number of transactions in the synthetic database ($|D|$). Three different minimum supports are considered in this experiment set, i.e., 0.2%, 0.4%, 0.8% respectively. The experimental result is shown in Figure 6. Note that the execution time under various numbers of transactions are normalized with respect to the time for $T10 - I4 - D100$. As shown in Figure 6, the execution time of algorithm SPF increases linearly while the number

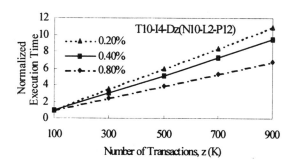

Figure 6. Normalized execution time under various numbers of transactions

of transactions in the synthetic database increases. It shows that algorithm SPF is of good scalability.

5. Conclusion

In this paper, we explored a new model of mining general temporal association rules, i.e., $(X \Rightarrow Y)^{MCP(X \cup Y)}$, from large databases where the exhibition periods of the items are allowed to be different from one to another. We developed an efficient algorithm, referred to as algorithm SPF in this paper to discover general temporal association rules effectively. The experimental results showed that algorithm SPF significantly outperforms other schemes which are extended from prior methods in terms of the execution time and scalability. With the capability of mining general temporal association rules for items with different exhibition periods, algorithm SPF outperforms prior methods in its generality and superiority.

Acknowledgment

The authors are supported in part by the National Science Council, Project No. NSC 91-2213-E-002-034 and NSC 91-2213-E-002-045, Taiwan, Republic of China.

References

[1] R. Agarwal, C. Aggarwal, and V. Prasad. A Tree Projection Algorithm for Generation of Frequent Itemsets. *Jornal of Parallel and Distributed Computing (Special Issue on High Performance Data Mining)*, 2000.

[2] R. Agrawal, T. Imielinski, and A. Swami. Mining Association Rules between Sets of Items in Large Databases. *Proc. of ACM SIGMOD*, pages 207–216, May 1993.

[3] R. Agrawal and R. Srikant. Fast Algorithms for Mining Association Rules in Large Databases. *Proc. of the 20th International Conference on Very Large Data Bases*, pages 478–499, September 1994.

[4] J. Ale and G. Rossi. An Approach to Discovering Temporal Association Rules. *ACM Symposium on Applied Computing*, 2000.

[5] A. M. Ayad, N. M. El-Makky, and Y. Taha. Incremental Mining of Constrained Association Rules. *Proc. of the First SIAM Conference on Data Mining*, 2001.

[6] X. Chen and I. Petr. Discovering Temporal Association Rules: Algorithms, Language and System. *Proc. of 2000 Int. Conf. on Data Engineering*, 2000.

[7] E. C. et.al. Finding Interesting Associations without Support Pruning. *IEEE Transactions on Knowledge and Data Engineering*, pages 64–78, January/February 2001.

[8] J. Han and Y. Fu. Discovery of Multiple-Level Association Rules from Large Databases. *Proc. of the 21th International Conference on Very Large Data Bases*, pages 420–431, September 1995.

[9] J. Han, L. V. S. Lakshmanan, and R. T. Ng. Constraint-Based, Multidimensional Data Mining. *COMPUTER (special issues on Data Mining)*, pages 46–50, 1999.

[10] J. Han, J. Pei, and Y. Yin. Mining Frequent Patterns without Candidate Generation. *Proc. of 2000 ACM-SIGMOD Int. Conf. on Management of Data*, pages 486–493, May 2000.

[11] C.-H. Lee, C.-R. Lin, and M.-S. Chen. Sliding-Window Filtering: An Efficient Algorithm for Incremental Mining. *Proc. of the Tenth ACM International Conference on Information and Knowledge Management*, November, 2001.

[12] J.-L. Lin and M. Dunham. Mining Association Rules: Anti-Skew Algorithms. *Proc. of 1998 Int'l Conf. on Data Engineering*, pages 486–493, 1998.

[13] B. Liu, W. Hsu, and Y. Ma. Mining Association Rules with Multiple Minimum Supports. *Proc. of 1999 Int. Conf. on Knowledge Discovery and Data Mining*, August 1999.

[14] R. Ng and J. Han. Efficient and Effective Clustering Methods for Spatial Data Mining. *Proc. of the 18th International Conference on Very Large Data Bases*, pages 144–155, September 1994.

[15] J.-S. Park, M.-S. Chen, and P. S. Yu. Using a Hash-Based Method with Transaction Trimming for Mining Association Rules. *IEEE Transactions on Knowledge and Data Engineering*, 9(5):813–825, October 1997.

[16] R. Srikant and R. Agrawal. Mining Generalized Association Rules. *Proc. of the 21th International Conference on Very Large Data Bases*, pages 407–419, September 1995.

[17] R. Srikant and R. Agrawal. Mining quantitative association rules in large relational tables. *Proc. of 1996 ACM-SIGMOD Conf. on Management of Data*, 1996.

[18] K. Wang, Y. He, and J. Han. Mining Frequent Itemsets Using Support Constraints. *Proc. of 2000 Int. Conf. on Very Large Data Bases*, September 2000.

Learning with Progressive Transductive Support Vector Machine

Yisong Chen, Guoping Wang, Shihai Dong
HCI & Multimedia Laboratory of Peking University, Beijing, 100871, P.R.China
Email:cys@graphics.pku.edu.cn

Abstract

Support Vector Machine (SVM) is a new learning method developed in recent years based on the foundations of statistical learning theory. By taking a transductive approach instead of an inductive one in support vector classifiers, the test set can be used as an additional source of information about margins. Intuitively, we would expect transductive learning to yield improvements when the training sets are small or when there is a significant deviation between the training and working set subsamples of the total population. In this paper, a progressive transductive support vector machine is addressed to extend Joachims' Transductive SVM to handle different class distributions. It solves the problem of having to estimate the ratio of positive/negative examples from the working set. The experimental results show that the algorithm is very promising.

Keywords: Statistical learning, Pattern recognition, Support vector machine, Transductive inference.

1. Introduction

The foundations of Support Vector Machines (SVM) have been developed by V. Vapnik [1] and are gaining popularity due to many attractive features and promising empirical performance [2][3]. Support vector machines perform structural risk minimization (SRM), which has been shown to be superior to traditional empirical risk minimization (ERM). SVMs were developed to solve the classification problem, but recently they have been extended to the domain of function regression and density estimation problems.

By explicitly including the working set data in problem formulation, a better generalization can be expected on some problems with insufficient labeled points [4][5]. Transductive support vector machine is a well-known algorithm that realizes transductive learning in the field of support vector classification [6].

In this paper, a progressive transductive support vector machine (PTSVM) model is designed to implement effective transductive inference in support vector learning. In the PTSVM learning algorithm, the unlabeled working set data are labeled and modified iteratively with the rule of pairwise labeling and dynamical adjusting, until a final solution is progressively reached. The idea of progressive labeling makes PTSVM achieve better generalization performance than the original TSVM approach.

The remainder of the paper is organized as follows. Section 2 offers a brief introduction to the theory of support vector classification. Section 3 addresses the concept and importance of transductive inference, together with the review of a well-known transductive support vector machine provided by T. Joachims. In Section 4, a progressive transductive support vector machine is detailed out, which can effectively overcome the shortcoming of TSVM. Section 5 analyzes the performance of PTSVM with the experimental results in detail, and indicates some further possible improvement. Section 6 summarizes and concludes the paper.

2. Support vector machine for classification

Consider the problem of separating the set of training set vectors belonging to two separate classes in some feature space. Given one set of training example vectors,

$$(x_1, y_1),...,(x_l, y_l), x_i \in R^n, y_i \in \{-1,+1\} \quad (1)$$

where the vectors x_i can be constructed by extracting some features from the target samples or by mapping the original vectors to their associated kernel space. We try to separate the vectors with a hyperplane

$$(w \cdot x) + b = 0 \quad (2)$$

so that

$$y_i[(w \cdot x_i) + b] \geq 1, (i = 1,2,...,l) \quad (3)$$

The hyperplane with the largest margin is known as the optimal separating hyperplane. It separates all vectors without error and the distance between the closest vectors to the hyperplane is maximal. The distance is given by

$$\min_{\{x_i|y_i=1\}} \frac{w \cdot x_i + b}{|w|} - \max_{\{x_i|y_i=-1\}} \frac{w \cdot x_i + b}{|w|} = \frac{2}{|w|} \quad (4)$$

Hence the hyperplane that separates the data optimally is the one that minimizes

$$\Phi(w) = \frac{1}{2}\|w\|^2 \quad (5)$$

subject to the constraints of (3).

To solve above problem, introduce lagrange multipliers $\alpha_i, i = 1,2,...,l$, and define

$$w(\alpha) = \sum_{i=1}^{l} \alpha_i y_i x_i \qquad (6)$$

With Wolfe theory the problem can be transformed to its dual problem.

$$MaxW(\alpha) = \sum_i \alpha_i - \frac{1}{2} w(\alpha) \cdot w(\alpha),$$
$$s.t.\ \alpha_i \geq 0, \sum_i a_i y_i = 0 \qquad (7)$$

With the optimal separating hyperplane $(w_0 \cdot x) + b_0 = 0$ found, the decision function can be written as

$$f(x) = w_0 \cdot x + b_0 \qquad (8)$$

Then the test data can be labeled with

$$label(x) = \mathrm{sgn}(f(x)) = \mathrm{sgn}(w_0 \cdot x + b_0) \qquad (9)$$

Training vectors that satisfy $y_i[(w_0 \cdot x_i) + b_0] = 1$ are termed support vectors, which are always corresponding to nonzero α_i s. The region between the hyperplanes through the support vectors on each side is called the margin band.

In the case of linearly non-separable training data, by introducing slack variables ξ_i, the primal problem can be rewritten as

$$Min(\frac{1}{2} \|w\|^2 + C \sum_i \xi_i),$$
$$s.t.\ y_i(w \cdot x_i + b) \geq 1 - \xi_i, \xi_i \geq 0 \qquad (10)$$

Similarly, we can get the corresponding dual problem

$$MaxW(\alpha) = \sum_i \alpha_i - \frac{1}{2} w(\alpha) \cdot w(\alpha),$$
$$s.t.\ 0 \leq \alpha_i \leq C, \sum_i a_i y_i = 0 \qquad (11)$$

All the training vectors corresponding to nonzero α_i s are called support vectors.

Problems described as in equation (7) and (11) are typical quadratic optimization questions. Recent advances in optimization methods have made support vector learning in large-scale training data possible [7][8][9].

3. Transductive support vector machine

3.1 Transductive inference for pattern recognition

The concept of transductive inference in pattern recognition comes mainly from the following two facts.

Firstly, in many learning applications, obtaining classification labels is expensive, while large quantities of unlabeled examples are readily available. Because the quantity of the labeled examples is relatively small, they cannot describe the global data distribution well. This possibly leads to a classifier with poor generalization performance. Considering the fact that unlabeled examples are significantly easier to obtain than labeled ones, we would like our learning algorithm to take as much advantages of unlabeled examples as possible [10].

Secondly, in many situations, we do not care about the general decision function. Our goal is to classify a given set of examples with as few errors as possible. In such cases, inductive learning is unnecessary. If we incorporate part or all of the particular examples of interest in the designing and training processes of the classifier, it is quite possible that not only the test data can be classified with enough accuracy, but also the generalization performance can be dramatically improved [11].

Transductive learning often uses a small number of labeled examples and a large number of unlabeled examples. A large number of unlabeled examples often provide enough information about the joint probability distribution of the whole sample space. This remedies the disadvantage of the small number of the labeled examples. Transductive inference has been researched and applied in many fields of pattern recognition [12][13].

3.2 Transductive support vector machine

Currently, the most important work of transductive inference in the field of support vector learning is T. Joachims's Transductive Support Vector Machine(TSVM), which will be briefly discussed in the remainder of this section. Detailed descriptions can be found in [6].

Given a set of independent, identically distributed labeled examples

$$(x_1, y_1), ..., (x_n, y_n), x_i \in R^m, y_i \in \{-1, +1\} \qquad (12)$$

and another set of unlabeled examples from the same distribution,

$$x_1^*, x_2^*, x_3^*, ..., x_k^* \qquad (13)$$

in a general linearly non-separable data case, the learning process of transductive SVM can be formulated as the following optimization problem.

$$Over\ (y_1^*, ..., y_k^*, w, b, \xi_1, ..., \xi_n, \xi_1^*, ..., \xi_k^*)$$
$$Minimize\ \frac{1}{2} \|w\|^2 + C \sum_{i=1}^{n} \xi_i + C^* \sum_{j=1}^{k} \xi_j^*$$
$$subject\ to : \forall_{i=1}^n : y_i[w \cdot x_i + b] \geq 1 - \xi_i \qquad (14)$$
$$\forall_{j=1}^k : y_j^*[w \cdot x_j^* + b] \geq 1 - \xi_j^*$$
$$\forall_{i=1}^n : \xi_i \geq 0$$
$$\forall_{j=1}^k : \xi_j^* \geq 0$$

where C and C^* are user-specified parameters. C^* is called the "effect factor" of the unlabeled examples and $C^* \xi_i^*$ is called the "effect term" of the i-th unlabeled example in the objective function of (14).

Above formulation is similar to the earlier one presented by K. Bennett *et al.* in their semi-supervised support vector machine (S3VM) method [10]. The main contribution of TSVM lies in that it supplies an optimization algorithm that effectively handles large-scale datasets.

Training the TSVM amounts to solving process of above optimization problem. TSVM training algorithm can be roughly outlined as the following steps:

Step 1, Specify the parameter C and C^*, execute an initial learning with inductive learning using all labeled examples, and produce an initial classifier. Assign a number N as the estimated number of the positive-labeled examples in the unlabeled examples.

Step 2, Compute the decision function values of all the unlabeled examples with the initial classifier. Label N examples with the largest decision function values as positive, and the others as negative. Set a temporary effect factor C^*_{tmp}.

Step 3, Retrain the support vector machine over all the examples. For the newly yielded classifier, switch labels of one pair of different-labeled unlabeled examples using a certain rule to make the value of the objective function in (14) decrease as much as possible. This step is repeated until no pair of examples satisfying the switching condition is found.

Step 4, Increase the value of C^*_{tmp} slightly and return to step 3. When $C^*_{tmp} \geq C^*$, the algorithm is finished and the result is output.

The label switching operation in Step 3 guarantees that the objective function will decrease after switching. The successive increase of the temporary effect factor in Step 4 tries to pursue a reasonable error control by adding the effect of the unlabeled examples on the objective function little by little. The algorithm can finish after finite iterations because C^* is a finite number.

4. Progressive Transductive Support Vector Learning

TSVM can achieve better performance than inductive learning because it successfully takes into account the distribution information implicitly embodied in the large quantity of the unlabeled examples. However, TSVM algorithm has one drawback. The parameter N has to be specified at the beginning of the learning. Nonetheless, in general cases it is often difficult to estimate the value of N

correctly. In TSVM, the fraction of the positive examples in the labeled ones is used to estimate N. This method may lead to a fairly large estimating error, especially when the number of the labeled examples is small. When the estimated N has a big deviation from the actual number of the positive examples, the performance of the learner may decrease significantly.

A simple example may help to understand the above statements. When the positive examples and the negative examples in the labeled data are approximately equal. TSVM will presume that there are about half positive examples in the unlabeled data, and set the value of N according to this assumption. However, it often occurs that the actual distribution of the positive and negative examples in the unlabeled data is completely unbalanced. It may happen that there are much more examples in one class than the other. Although this imbalance is embodied in the large quantity of the unlabeled examples, it is unknown to the learner. TSVM may estimate N incorrectly and yield a classifier that cannot describe the actual distribution of the data. This drawback limits the usage and the extension of TSVM in practice.

A new transductive learning method is proposed in this section to solve the above problem. In this scheme, the number of the positive unlabeled examples is not specified a priori, and the unlabeled examples will not be labeled altogether at the same time. Instead, all the unlabeled examples are labeled gradually in the process of the learning and an approximate solution to equation (14) is progressively reached. We call this algorithm Progressive Transductive Support Vector Machine (PTSVM).

The basic idea of PTSVM is as follows. At the beginning of the algorithm, no estimation about the number of the positive unlabeled examples is made. In each iteration, one or two unlabeled examples that can be labeled with the strongest confidence are chosen and labeled. Roughly speaking, the newly labeled examples will affect the learning process of the next iteration, and cause a small shift of the separating hyperplane. This shifting of the separating hyperplane may indicate that some earlier labeling is not proper. When this happens, all improper labeling are canceled and the corresponding examples are restored as unlabeled. If this progressive labeling and dynamical adjusting is carefully arranged, we expect that the separating hyperplane will approach the final optimal one little by little in the training process, and the final classifier will describe the data distribution better than TSVM.

In this algorithm, every labeling should be as accurate as possible to guarantee the correct progress of the later process, i.e. we hope that the early labeled examples will have enough ability to move the current separating hyperplane in the correct orientation. For this reason, we stop using the method of successively increasing the effect factor of the unlabeled examples, but instead give C^* a moderate value in the beginning of the learning. A moderate effect factor means a greater influence ability of the later learning process. At the same time it keeps the risk of misclassification under certain control.

A simple and natural scheme of progressive labeling is as follows. In every iteration of the learning, do inductive learning with all current labeled examples and figure out a separating hyperplane, compute the decision function values of all unlabeled examples, and label the one in the margin band having the maximal absolute decision function value with the sign of its decision function. i.e. choose the example of the unlabeled examples with the index i that satisfies

$$i = \arg\max_{j:|f(x_j^*)|<1} \left| f(x_j^*) \right| \qquad (15)$$

and label the corresponding example with

$$Label(x_i^*) = \text{sgn}(w \cdot x_i^* + b) \qquad (16)$$

This method has a potential drawback. In some data distributions, after the first unlabeled example is labeled, the new separating hyperplane is likely to move towards the other side of the newly labeled example because of its influence. This may cause the result that the next labeled example has the same label as the previous one. This phenomenon may accumulate and the separating plane keeps moving in the same direction, which probably results in some unlabeled examples being misclassified by the final classifier.

To overcome this shortcoming, a new labeling method is used in PTSVM. For each iteration, one positive example and one negative example are labeled simultaneously according to equation (17) and (18).

$$i_1 = \arg\max_{j:0<|f(x_j^*)|<1} \left| f(x_j^*) \right| \qquad (17)$$

$$i_2 = \arg\max_{j:-1<|f(x_j^*)|<0} \left| f(x_j^*) \right| \qquad (18)$$

If no unlabeled example satisfying (17) or (18) exists in the current iteration, the corresponding labeling is not done. The process continues until all the unlabeled examples are outside the margin band of the separating hyperplane after several iterations. At this point, the algorithm labels all remaining unlabeled examples with the current separating hyperplane, and the learning finishes. This scheme not only effectively avoids the disadvantage mentioned above, but also speeds up the convergence of the algorithm.

The goal of pairwise labeling is to do a reasonable guess based on the current learning result. The method stems from the intuition that unlabeled points with larger absolute decision function values are more possible to be labeled correctly. This idea is a little like the idea of the query learning with large margin classifiers [14]. Both algorithms involve progressively selecting the most informative data during the solution process. However, it is worth noting that in the query-learning algorithm, to achieve a more informative query, the strategy is to select the point nearest to the separating hyperplane. This is just opposite to the strategy in PTSVM, where the margin point farthest to the hyperplane is selected.

In the progress of pairwise labeling, it is possible to find out that some labeling done earlier are not consistent with the classification result of the current classifier. This phenomenon denotes a possible mislabeling in the earlier learning period. In such a case, the inconsistent examples are reset as unlabeled and the training goes on. We expect that these examples may be labeled in some future iteration with more confidence. We call this method dynamical adjusting. Dynamical adjusting makes PTSVM easier to recover from some early classification errors.

Now we can write the major steps of PTSVM as follows.

Step 1, Specify the parameter C and C^*. Execute an initial learning with inductive learning using all labeled examples and generate an initial classifier.

Step 2, Compute the decision function values of all unlabeled examples. Label one positive example and one negative example using pairwise labeling.

Step 3, Retrain the support vector machine over all labeled examples. Compute the decision function values of all unlabeled examples. Cancel all inconsistent labeling by dynamical adjusting.

Step 4, Add one or two new labels through pairwise labeling, and return to step 3. If no unlabeled example remains in the margin band, label all remaining unlabeled examples with current separating hyperplane, then output the result and finish the training.

The rules of pairwise labeling and dynamical adjusting are very important in PTSVM and deserve more explanations.

To show the rationality of pairwise labeling, note that although there are many possible methods to label the unlabeled examples in the margin band, pairwise labeling seems to be the most reasonable scheme to label one new positive example and one new negative example. This can be illustrated with Figure 1. The figure shows that, labeling the two "x" examples will lead to a wider resulted margin band than labeling the two "*" examples.

To show the rationality of dynamical adjusting, note that every unlabeled example should have been set a label that is consistent with its corresponding decision function value under the final solution. Otherwise, switching the label of the inconsistent example will surely lead to a smaller objective function, which contradicts the assumption that the objective function has been minimized. This strongly implies that it is reasonable to cancel inconsistent labeling during the training process.

An inconsistency denotes that the earlier labeling is not appropriate and may need modification. Nonetheless, it is not necessarily true that the labeling is surely wrong. It only indicates that current knowledge of the learner is not sufficient to give the example a convincing labeling then, and more information is needed. For this reason, in PTSVM, the label of the example is not modified immediately. Instead, the earlier labeling is canceled and delayed. A more confident decision may come by in the future, after more information about the distribution of the data is accumulated.

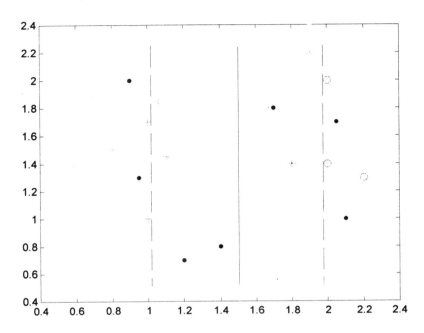

Figure 1. Illustration of pairwise labeling
"+"s are positive labeled points, "o"s are negative labeled points, others are all unlabeled points

5 Experimental results

We implement PTSVM based on T. Joachims's SVMLight, which is a popular shareware [8]. Two different data sets are tested and the results are given in section 5.1 and section 5.2 respectively.

5.1 Tutorial data set

The first test data set, Tutorial, is a simple linearly separable two-dimensional point set. The goal of designing this data set is to address the virtue of PTSVM more intuitively. There are altogether 6 labeled examples and 20 unlabeled examples in the original training data, as shown in Figure 2. The three "+" points in the figure are positive and the three "o" points are negative. All other points are unlabeled examples. In Figure 2 we can see that the training set can be easily separated into two different classes in the 2-d space. One feature of the Tutorial Training data is that the unlabeled examples are much more than the labeled examples and can describe the global data distribution much better. So, the Tutorial data set is good for testing of transductive inference.

In Figure 2 the actual positive examples are much more than the negative ones in the training set. So the ratio estimation method in TSVM will lead to a big estimating error, and can hardly achieve a satisfactory learning result. Therefore TSVM is not appropriate for the learning of this mixed training set. In contrast, estimation of the number of the positive points in the unlabeled examples is not necessary in PTSVM, so better learning process and test result are expected.

In our experiment, 100 examples are tested, with a similar distribution as the training set. The training and testing results are offered in table 1.

Table 1. Results comparison on the Tutorial dataset

	Training time	Training errors	Testset Size	Test errors	Test accuracy
TSVM	0.67	4	100	15	85%
PTSVM	0.17	0	100	0	100%

Table 1 shows that the test accuracy of PTSVM is much higher than TSVM. The reason is that PTSVM makes use of the information about the data distribution implicitly carried in the unlabeled examples more reasonably. We will offer a more rigorous analysis below.

There are 3 positive labeled examples and 3 negative labeled examples in the training set. Since the number of the labeled examples is small, it is not a good indication of the global data distribution. TSVM assumes that 10 of the 20 unlabeled examples should be positive. This is a high deviation because the actual number of positives is 14. TSVM tries to label 10 unlabeled examples as positive and adjust the separating hyperplane under this wrong assumption. It is not surprising that this will lead to the result that some unlabeled examples labeled as negative by the learning algorithm are actually positive. As shown in table 1, four unlabeled training examples are ultimately misclassified in training. Because of these erroneously labeled examples, the final separating hyperplane is also not satisfactory. This is the reason of the low testing accuracy of TSVM.

PTSVM uses a different training method. The number of the examples to be positive-labeled is not fixed, but changed dynamically in the process of training. Obviously, this method can adapt to more general data distribution and thus yield better generalization performance. A trace into learning of PTSVM discovers that every pairwise labeling makes the separating hyperplane shift in the right direction. This shifting may correct some misclassification in the earlier learning period. For instance, notice the lowest unlabeled example in Figure 2 with the coordinate about (1.6, 0.5). An inductive learning will misclassify this point as negative and the error persists in TSVM.

Nevertheless, in PTSVM the shifting of the separating hyperplane caused by pairwise labeling will eventually label this example correctly. This process intuitively presents the virtue of PTSVM.

Figure 2 also illustrates the training results of TSVM and PTSVM on the Tutorial data set. The solid line is the final hyperplane found by PTSVM and the dashed line is the final hyperplane found by TSVM. As shown in the figure, the wrong estimation for the value of N leads to the bad performance of TSVM. This problem is successfully avoided in PTSVM.

We can also find out that the training time of PTSVM is much shorter than TSVM. This is mainly due to the fact that TSVM need to successively increase the value of C^{*}_{tmp} and the calculation has to be done for every C^{*}_{tmp} value. In PTSVM, the calculation is only done for one fixed C^{*}. It is worth noting that this acceleration is not always true. Acceleration only occurs in cases where the scale of the training set is comparatively small.

The above experiment shows that for the case of linearly separable dataset in a low dimensional space, PTSVM can be very efficient. One would ask what happens if the training and testing data come from a high dimensional space, or are more sparsely distributed? Although it is not easy to imagine these cases intuitively, we do expect that the superiority will still take effect in such cases. We try to confirm this statement with the second experiment.

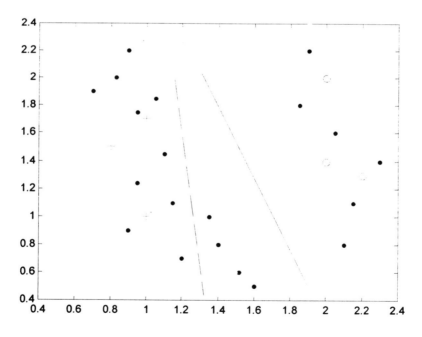

Figure 2. Training data and results of the Tutorial dataset

5.2 Reuters dataset

In the second experiment, we utilize the well-known Reuters-21578 dataset, which is collected from Reuters newswire in 1987. Documents are represented using feature vectors with each feature corresponding to a word stem. The task is to learn which Reuters articles are about "corporate acquisitions".

Three kernel functions are tested in the experiments, namely, linear kernel, polynomial kernel and Gaussian radial basis function kernel. All three kernels yield comparable results. The following results are generated by the use of linear kernel function. The values of C and C^* are set heuristically. Our test founds that 1.0 is a good empirical value for C. C^*_{tmp} in TSVM increases progressively from 0.00001. C^* in PTSVM takes a moderate value 0.5, which can control the influence of the effect terms of (14) fairly well, as mentioned earlier.

All following experiments use a common labeled example set in the training set, i.e. 5 positive examples and 5 negative examples artificially classified a priori. The unlabeled examples are selected with different numbers and different positive-negative ratios to test the performance of the algorithm in various data distributions. We reasonably assume that the more unlabeled examples in the training set, the better they can reflect the actual distribution of the whole data set. A common test set composed of 300 positive examples and 300 negative examples is used in all the test jobs.

Results of 8 different experiments are given in Table 2. The first training set contains no unlabeled examples. That is, for this training set, both TSVM and PTSVM perform conventional inductive learning, so the learning process and the result are exactly the same. The other 7 training sets contain unlabeled examples of different numbers and positive-negative ratios.

Table 2 shows that both TSVM and PTSVM result in better performance compared to the original inductive learning. This is because unlabeled examples provide useful information in transductive learning. The more unlabeled examples used in the training, the better the classifier yielded by the learning.

When comparing TSVM and PTSVM on the same training set, we can see that when the actual number of positive and negative examples is approximately equal, TSVM may give a better test result than PTSVM because positive estimation is done correctly. However, in more general cases, where there is a big difference between the number of positive and negative examples, PTSVM outperforms TSVM because its ability to dynamically adjust the positive fraction in the unlabeled examples to simulate the actual distribution better. Except for the cases where the number of positive and negative examples is approximately equal in the training set, training results of PTSVM are always better approximations to the actual situation.

Finally, we briefly compare the computational cost of TSVM with that of PTSVM. As mentioned earlier in Section 5.1, when the number of the unlabeled examples is small, PTSVM has faster execution speed. When the number of the unlabeled examples becomes larger, frequent operations of pairwise labeling and dynamical adjusting make the complexity of PTSVM grow quickly and exceed TSVM. This is one disadvantage of PTSVM that may be improved by using some faster learning algorithms, such as the incremental and decremental learning methods [15].

Table 2. Results comparison of TSVM and PTSVM on the Reuters dataset

Unlabeled examples	Train algorithm	Training time (s)	SV nums	Test errors	Precision (POS)	Recall (POS)	Test accuracy
Pos=0	TSVM	0.01	10	165	64.64%	99.33%	72.50%
Neg=0	PTSVM	0.01	10	165	64.64%	99.33%	72.50%
Pos=10	TSVM	0.77	30	125	71.19%	98.00%	79.17%
Neg=10	PTSVM	0.30	30	91	77.43%	98.33%	84.83%
Pos=20	TSVM	0.82	39	91	90.98%	77.33%	84.83%
Neg=10	PTSVM	0.35	39	79	89.35%	83.00%	86.83%
Pos=100	TSVM	5.17	181	43	89.78%	96.67%	92.83%
Neg=100	PTSVM	3.62	184	46	87.57%	98.67%	92.33%
Pos=50	TSVM	4.19	146	109	73.46%	99.67%	81.83%
Neg=100	PTSVM	2.40	140	93	76.61%	99.33%	84.50%
Pos=1000	TSVM	58.87	768	54	97.67%	84.00%	91.00%
Neg=500	PTSVM	167.60	805	41	97.44%	88.67%	93.17%
Pos=500	TSVM	110.72	697	87	77.66%	99.67%	85.50%
Neg=1000	PTSVM	175.48	770	80	80.22%	97.33%	86.67%
Pos=1000	TSVM	69.96	826	19	95.47%	98.33%	96.83%
Neg=1000	PTSVM	303.05	894	36	90.74%	98.00%	94.00%

5.3 Further discussions

A comparative study of the two experiments discussed in section 5.1 and 5.2 reveals the following observation. Although in more general cases PTSVM outperforms TSVM on the Reuters dataset, the superiority is not as notable as it is on the Tutorial dataset. This can be explained using the different characteristics of the two datasets. Note that the dimension of the vector space is 2 for the Tutorial dataset, but nearly 10000 for the Reuters dataset. The situation of a high dimensional space is much more complex, and we are far less familiar with the data distribution feature of the Reuters dataset than its lower dimensional counterpart. Firstly, the examples in the Reuters dataset may not be linearly separable. Secondly, the examples in the Reuters dataset may not have as compact a distribution as the Tutorial dataset. With such a disadvantageous distribution, the training algorithm of PTSVM may yield some labeling errors and these errors may affect the subsequent training and reduce the performance. Although dynamical adjusting offers some sort of error recovery function, its capacity is limited and not able to handle large-scale errors. The authors believe that the improper data distribution is the major reason for performance decrease, i.e. PTSVM is more suitable to linearly separable datasets or datasets with compact distribution characteristics.

One possible improvement is to properly use the effect factor increasing method of TSVM in PTSVM. For example, use a small effect factor to control the influence of the examples with uncertain labeling to the later training process, thus depressing the accumulation and propagation of errors. However, a small effect factor conflicts with the idea of progressive labeling to some degree. This contradiction should be carefully treated and some tradeoff may be necessary.

Another attractive approach comes from the use of kernel functions. Notice that a linearly inseparable data set may be mapped to a kernel space with some kernel function and become linearly separable. This means that a proper kernel function can improve the distribution of the original data set. So for some data set with bad or even unknown distribution, we can proceed by finding such a kernel function. Then the transductive inference is done in the kernel space, where the distribution situation is improved.

6. Conclusion

A progressive transductive support vector machine (PTSVM) is presented in this paper as a new attempt in the field of support vector machine and transductive inference. PTSVM can automatically adapt to different data distributions and realize a transductive learning of support vectors in a more general sense.

Still many open questions are left regarding SVM and transductive inference. How well does the algorithm presented here approximate the global optimal solution? How is a proper transductive inference algorithm for dataset with different features chosen? How can PTSVM be improved with different approaches to work with different data distribution? All these questions are very interesting and each deserves further effort.

References

[1] V. Vapnik, The Nature of Statistical Learning Theory. Springer-Verlag, New York, 1995

[2] M.O. Stitson, J. Weston, A. Gammerman, V. Vovk, and V. Vapnik, Theory of Support Vector Machines. Technical Report CSD-TR-96-17, Computational Intelligence Group, Royal Holloway, University of London, 1996.

[3] C. Cortes, V. Vapnik, Support Vector Networks. Machine Learning, 1995, 20:273-297.

[4] V. Vapnik, Statistical learning theory, Wiley, 1998.

[5] A. Gammerman, V. Vapnik, and V. Vowk, Learning by transduction, in Conference On Uncertainty in Artificial Intelligence, 1998, pp. 148-156.

[6] T. Joachims, Transductive Inference for Text Classification using Support Vector Machines. International Conference on Machine Learning (ICML), 1999, pp. 200-209.

[7] E. Osuna, R. Freund, and G. Girosi, An Improved Training Algorithm for Support Vector Machines. Proc. of IEEE NNSP'97, Amelia Island, FL, 24-26 Sep., 1997, pp. 276-285.

[8] T. Joachims, 11 in: Making large-Scale SVM Learning Practical. Advances in Kernel Methods - Support Vector Learning, B. Schölkopf and C. Burges and A. Smola (ed.), MIT Press, 1999.

[9] J. Platt, Sequential minimal optimization: A fast algorithm for training support vector machines. Technical Report MSR-TR-98-14, Microsoft Research, 1998.

[10] K. Bennet, A. Demiriz, Semi-Supervised Support Vector Machines Advances in Neural Information Processing Systems, 12, M. S. Kearns, S. A. Solla, D. A. Cohn, editors, MIT Press, Cambridge, MA, 1998, pp 368-374.

[11] K. Branson, A Naive Bayes Classifier Using Transductive Inference for Text Classification, 2001, http://www-cse.ucsd.edu/users/elkan/254/reports.html.

[12] A. Blum, T. Mitchell, Combining labeled and unlabeled data with co-training, In Annual Conference on Computational Learning Theory(COLT-98), 1998, pp. 92-100.

[13] K. Nigam, A. McCallum, and T. Mitchell, Learning to classify text from labeled and unlabeled documents, in Proceedings of AAAI-1998, pp. 792-799.

[14] C. Campbell, N. Cristianini, and A. Smola, Query Learning with Large Margin Classifiers.. Proceedings of the 17th International Conference on Machine Learing, (ICML2000, Stanford, CA, 2000), Morgan Kaufmann, pp. 111-118.

[15] G. Cauwenberghs, T. Poggio, Incremental and decremental support vector machine learning, in Adv. Neural Information Processing Systems (NIPS*2000), Cambridge MA: MIT Press, vol. 13, 2001, pp. 409-415.

Towards Automatic Generation of Query Taxonomy: A Hierarchical Query Clustering Approach

Shui-Lung Chuang
Institute of Information Science
Academia Sinica
Taipei 115, Taiwan
slchuang@iis.sinica.edu.tw

Lee-Feng Chien
Institute of Information Science
Academia Sinica
Taipei 115, Taiwan
lfchien@iis.sinica.edu.tw

Abstract

Previous works on automatic query clustering most generate a flat, un-nested partition of query terms. In this work, we are pursuing to organize query terms into a hierarchical structure and construct a query taxonomy in an automatic way. The proposed approach is designed based on a hierarchical agglomerative clustering algorithm to hierarchically group similar queries and generate the cluster hierarchies by a novel cluster partition technique. The search processes of real-world search engines are combined to obtain highly ranked Web documents as the feature source for each query term. Preliminary experiments show that the proposed approach is effective to obtain thesaurus information for query terms, and is also feasible to construct a query taxonomy which provides a basis for in-depth analysis of users' search interests and domain-specific vocabulary on a larger scale.

1. Introduction

As Web searching has grown, research interests on mining search engine logs to discover users' search patterns and information requests have increased. Query clustering is a research task aiming to group similar user queries together. This task is important to discover the common interests among the users and to exploit the experience of previous users for the others [10]. Knowledge obtained with query clustering can be used in the development of thesauri and recommending systems [9]. The discovered clusters of queries can assist users in reformulating refined queries, discovering users' FAQs for question answering systems [10], and performing more effective query expansion and term suggestion routines in search engines [1].

Previous works on automatic query clustering most organize query terms into flat clusters. In this work, we are pursuing to organize users' query terms into a hierarchical

structure and construct a query taxonomy in an automatic way. The query taxonomy is defined as the classification tree constituted by the concept hierarchies of users' requests and categorized query terms that are automatically generated. As the example illustrated in Figure 1, a query taxonomy is a classification tree in which similar user queries (as leaf nodes) are grouped to form basic query clusters (as interior nodes), and similar query clusters form super clusters recursively to characterize the associations between composed clusters. Each of the query clusters can represent a certain concept of users' information requests.

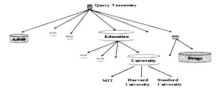

Figure 1. An example query taxonomy.

With the query taxonomy, deeper analysis of domain-specific terminology and further discovery of term relationships can then be performed under the corresponding subject domain of each cluster. Manually collecting and organizing such term vocabularies is cost-ineffective and inapplicable especially for organizing Web queries. For the above purpose, this paper presents a hierarchical query clustering approach. The proposed approach is extended from Hierarchical Agglomerative Clustering algorithm (HAC) to cluster similar queries and to generate appropriate cluster hierarchies. Since a query term is short in length and simple in structure, there is a lack of information to judge the query term's corresponding subject domains. The proposed approach combines with the search processes of real-world search engines to obtain the highly ranked Web documents from which the features for each query term are extracted. With the huge amount of Web pages indexed by the search

75

engines, most of the users' query terms can retrieve relevant documents and create feature sets, and therefore be clustered properly. A hierarchical cluster partitioning technique based on a heuristic quality measure of any particular partition is further applied on the binary-tree hierarchy produced by the HAC algorithm to generate a natural and comprehensive multi-way-tree hierarchy. The preliminary experiments and observations also show the promising results.

In the rest of this paper, we first review some related work and introduce the proposed approach. Then the conducted experiments and their results are presented. Finally, we discuss some applications and conclude our results.

2. Related Work

Some researches on clustering indexed terms are in certain degree related to our research, such as the works on latent semantics, SVD, term relationship analysis, etc [3, 6]. Most of them dealt with the automatic clustering of controlled indexed terms into clusters and used them to assist information retrieval systems in the query expansion process to improve the precision and recall ratios. Query clustering and the construction of concept hierarchies for users' queries were not the main subjects of these investigations.

The characteristics of short Web query and noisy search results have led researchers to investigate the query clustering problem. Beeferman and Berger [1] proposed a query clustering method based on "click-through data," which is a collection of user transactions with queries and their corresponding clicked URLs, to discover correlations between queries and the clicked pages. Query terms with more common clicked URLs were taken as similar and being grouped. Without merely using the clicked URLs, Wen et. al. [10] developed a similar method to combine the indexed terms from the clicked pages to estimate the similarity between queries and achieved better performance. However, the number of distinct URLs is often huge in a Web search service. This might cause many similar queries not to be grouped together due to a lack of common clicked URLs. With fewer clicked URLs as the feature sets, it is more difficult to find similar terms for those new query terms or queries with lower usages. To allow most of users' queries with appropriate features to characterize intended search interests, the proposed approach exploits the highly ranked documents retrieved by a query term as the data source and designs an effective algorithm for query clustering.

3. Overview of the Proposed Approach

Hierarchical query clustering is loosely defined as a problem of automatically grouping similar query terms into disjoint clusters and organizing them into a hierarchical

structure with the association strengths between clusters. The diagram depicted in Figure 2 shows the overall concept of the proposed approach, which is mainly composed of three computational processes: relevant document retrieval, feature extraction, and query clustering. The relevant document retrieval process is to retrieve the most relevant document sets for candidate query terms by combining with the search processes of real-world search engines. The retrieved document set is then passed to the feature extraction process to extract the features for each candidate query term. The query clustering process is to cluster similar queries and generate appropriate cluster hierarchies. It consists of two cascaded processing steps: generation of a binary-tree hierarchy and hierarchical cluster partitioning. The former step is to construct an initial binary-tree hierarchy by HAC algorithm to organize query clusters for the input query terms, and the latter step is to partition the hierarchy into a more natural multi-way tree according to the quality of each sub-hierarchy. In the following paragraphs, we will describe the details of these computational processes.

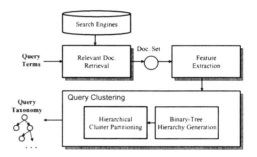

Figure 2. An abstract diagram showing the concept of the proposed approach.

4. Data Set

To instantiate the research, a three-month query term log collected in 1998 from Dreamer search engine[1] in Taiwan is used as the basis for our analysis. This data set contains 228,566 distinct query terms with total frequency 2,184,256. The most-frequent 18,017 queries have been manually categorized into a two-level hierarchy, consisting of fourteen major categories together with one hundred subcategories, by five Library & Information Science students together with a professional reference librarian for three months. This most-frequent query set, which only represented 8% of the distinct queries, totally formed 81% of the

---

[1]http://www.dreamer.com.tw/

search requests in the test log and has been used on analysis of search behavior and several research studies [9].

4.1. Collecting Retrieval Documents

As we mentioned previously, a query term is short in length and simple in structure. In order to judge the relevance of query terms, we take the highly-ranked documents retrieved from on-line search engines by the query terms as their feature source. To collect the contents each query term can retrieve, we adopt Google Chinese[2] as the back-end engine. Each query term is submitted to Google, and then up to 100 search result entries are collected. The title and description of each entry are extracted as the representation of the corresponding document. In the final result, only 107 queries among 18,017 total queries have no retrieved documents. By combining the search processes of real-world search engines, our query clustering hypothesis can be intuitively stated as: That two queries are clustered together is due to that they can retrieve similar contents.

4.2. Feature Set

It is a crucial step to determine a set of feature terms for characterizing the feature space of users' queries. The feature term set should be both as broad in coverage and as modest in size as possible. Query terms from search engine logs or the document terms extracted from the retrieved Web documents are two alternatives that can be taken as feature terms.

Since many queries may be related to ephemeral interests, such as a new movie or some recent events, the feature terms are pursuing to be sustainable. Another two-week query term log collected in 1999 from GAIS search engine[3] is used to filter out those ephemeral queries. Only 9,751 queries among our 18,017 queries still appear in the new query log. It is also found that query terms affected by time are mostly proper nouns. On the other hand, terms not affected by time, except for some proper nouns like the names of famous websites and people, are mostly subject terms like "movie," "baseball," or "flight ticket." These terms are considered to be core terms because they are long-lasting, modest in size, and rich in content. From our observations, core terms are more comprehensive in meaning and are often used by Web users to express popular search interests. Using them as features is believed to be more effective.

In order to reveal the effects of different feature sets, we prepare four kinds of features: (1) the 9,751 core terms (coreterm); (2) 10,000 most-frequent query terms in our data set (freqterm); (3) randomly-selected 10,000 terms

[2]http://www.google.com/
[3]http://www.gais.cs.ccu.edu.tw

from the 18,017 queries (randterm); (4) the Chinese character bi-, tri-grams and English words extracted from the retrieved documents (2,3-gram). The comparison will be made in a later section.

5. The Query Clustering Algorithm

Clustering can be loosely defined as the process of organizing objects into groups whose members are closely associated in some way. The problem has been studied extensively in the literature, and there exist many different clustering algorithms. They are mainly in two major styles: partitioning and hierarchical clustering. K-means and hierarchical agglomerative clustering (HAC) are representatives of these two styles [4].

According to the literature, the HAC approach is more common and well-performed on the problems dealing with text-represented data such as clustering documents or Web search results [11, 12]. Hence we adopt HAC as the basic mechanism to our on-hand clustering problem. Perhaps one of the most important criteria to choose a clustering algorithm is the nature of the data and the anticipated clusters. Except common and extensive adoption of the algorithm, there are other considerations that lead us to this decision, and they will be briefly mentioned furthermost in the next subsection.

5.1. HAC Algorithm

An HAC algorithm operates on a set of objects with a matrix of inter-object distances and builds a binary-tree hierarchy where each node is a cluster and the clusters corresponding to the node's immediate children form a complete partition of that cluster [8]. First, the objects are placed into a list of singleton clusters $C_1, C_2, \ldots, C_n$. Then the closest pair of clusters $\{C_i, C_j\}$ from the list is chosen to merge. Finally, C_i and C_j are removed from the list and replaced with a new cluster $\{C_i \cup C_j\}$ (here we treat clusters as sets). This process is repeated until there is only one cluster remaining.

Inter-object distance
For the clustering approach, we have to measure the distances between instances to be grouped. We adopt the vector-space model as our data representation. As stated previously, each candidate query term is converted to a bag of feature terms via the content retrieved from on-line search engines by the query term. Let T be the feature term vocabulary, i.e., the set of all distinct terms in the whole data collection, and t_j be the j-th term in T. With simple processing, the i-th query term can be represented as a term vector v_i in a $|T|$-dimensional space. Let V be the set of all distinct query term vectors $v_1, v_2, \ldots, v_n$ and $v_{i,j}$ be the

weight t_j in v_i. The term weights in this work are determined according to the conventional *tf-idf* term weighting scheme,in which each term weight $v_{i,j}$ is defined as:

$$v_{i,j} = \left(0.5 + 0.5 \frac{tf_{i,j}}{\max_{t_k \in T} tf_{i,k}} \right) \log \frac{n}{n_j}$$

where $tf_{i,j}$, the term frequency, is the number of occurrences of term t_j in the v_i's corresponding feature term bag, n is the total number of query terms, and n_j is the number of query terms which contain t_j in their corresponding bags of feature terms. The similarity between a pair of query terms is computed as the cosine of the angle between the corresponding vector ($cos\theta$), i.e.,

$$sim(v_a, v_b) = \frac{\sum_{t_j \in T} v_{a,j} v_{b,j}}{\sqrt{\sum_{t_j \in T} v_{a,j}^2} \sqrt{\sum_{t_j \in T} v_{b,j}^2}}.$$

In this study, the distance between a pair of candidate query terms is defined as one minus the cosine measure:

$$dist(v_a, v_b) = 1 - sim(v_a, v_b).$$

Inter-cluster distance
The core of an HAC algorithm is to choose a specific distance function for clusters. Table 1 lists three most well-known inter-cluster distance functions.

Table 1. Three well-known cluster distance functions.

Method	Distance function
Single-linkage (SL)	$\min\limits_{v_a \in C_i, v_b \in C_j} dist(v_a, v_b)$
Average-linkage (AL)	$\frac{1}{|C_i||C_j|} \sum\limits_{v_a \in C_i} \sum\limits_{v_b \in C_j} dist(v_a, v_b)$
Complete-linkage (CL)	$\max\limits_{v_a \in C_i, v_b \in C_j} dist(v_a, v_b)$

Intuitively speaking, the single-linkage method defines the distance between two clusters as the smallest distance between two objects in both clusters, and the complete-linkage uses the largest distance instead. Usually, the clusters produced by the single-linkage method are isolated but not cohesive, and there may be some undesirably "elongated" clusters. On the other extreme, the complete-linkage method produces cohesive clusters that may not be isolated at all. The average-linkage method represents a compromise between the two extremes.

To choose a feasible distance measure for our term-clustering problem, a major consideration is the heterogeneous and diverse nature of Web contents. Many traditional information retrieval problems such as text categorization

meet big challenges when dealing with Web contents by directly applying their traditional well-performed methods. This is because Web in particular encourages diverse authorship, navigational and citation links, and short, fragmented documents with objects in various media types. All of these make the content data in Web noisy. In our approach, we extract the features from the snippets returned from search engines, whose quality may be worse and less trustful. Besides, term-vector-based data representation makes our clustering problem naturally a data-sparseness problem with high dimensional feature space. Some noisy features may make the distance measure not so reliable. So the method with nature to produce cohesive clusters is preferred, and the complete- and average-linkage methods are preferred mainly based on this consideration. The comparison of these methods will be made in a later section.

Before we move ahead, let's define some notations and formalization of the HAC algorithm for further illustration. In the HAC clustering process, at each iteration step, two clusters are merged as a new one, and the whole process halts when there exists only one un-merged cluster, i.e., the root node in the binary-tree hierarchy. Let $v_1, v_2, \ldots, v_n$ be the initial input object vectors, and $C_1, C_2, \ldots, C_n$ be the corresponding singleton clusters. Also let C_{n+i} be the new cluster created at the i-th step. The output binary-tree cluster hierarchy of the HAC algorithm can be undoubtedly and unambiguously expressed as a list $C_1, C_2, \ldots, C_n, C_{n+1}, \ldots, C_{2n-1}$ with two functions $left(C_{n+i})$ and $right(C_{n+i})$, $1 \le i < n$, indicating the left and right child of internal cluster node C_{n+i}, respectively. Figure 3 shows this detailed algorithmic procedure.

HAC$(v_1, v_2, \ldots, v_n)$
$v_i, 1 \le i \le n$: the vectors of the objects
1: **for all** $v_i, 1 \le i \le n$ **do**
2:    $C_i \leftarrow \{v_i\}$
3:    $f(i) \leftarrow true$ \{f: whether a cluster can be merged\}
4: calculate the pairwise cluster distance matrix
5: **for all** $1 \le i < n$ **do**
6:    choose the closest pair $\{C_a, C_b\}$ with $f(a) \wedge f(b) \equiv true$
7:    $C_{n+i} \leftarrow C_a \cup C_b$, $left(C_{n+i}) \leftarrow C_a$, $right(C_{n+i}) \leftarrow C_b$
8:    $f(n+i) \leftarrow true$, $f(a) \leftarrow false$, $f(b) \leftarrow false$
9:    update the distance matrix with new cluster C_{n+i}
10: return $C_1, C_2, \ldots, C_{2n-1}$ together with functions $left$ and $right$

Figure 3. The hierarchical agglomerative clustering procedure.

5.2. Hierarchical Cluster Partitioning

The HAC algorithm produces a binary-tree hierarchy of clusters. However, we are more interested in an approach to producing a natural and comprehensive hierarchical organization such as Yahoo!, in which there are 13-15 major categories and each sub-category also contains an appropriate number of sub-categories. This multi-way-tree representation, instead of the binary-tree one, is believed to be more natural, easier, and more suitable for human to browse, interpret, and do some deeper analysis.

To generate a multi-way-tree hierarchy from a binary-tree one, a top-down approach is to decompose the hierarchy into several major sub-hierarchies first, and then, recursively apply the same procedure to each sub-hierarchy. To create a particular major sub-hierarchy partition from the binary-tree hierarchy, our approach is to determine a suitable level to cut the hierarchy at it. Before we describe our cutting criterion, let's illustrate some notations and the formalization of the problem. The problem of cutting at a suitable level can be taken as to determine which pair of adjacent clusters $\{C_{n+i-1}, C_{n+i}\}$, $1 \leq i < n$, in the binary-tree hierarchy $C_1, C_2, \ldots, C_n, C_{n+1}, \ldots, C_{2n-1}$ to put the partition point in between. Let the cut level l between $\{C_{n+i-1}, C_{n+i}\}$, $1 \leq i < n$, be indexed as number $n - i$, e.g., $\{C_{2n-2}, C_{2n-1}\}$ means cut level $l = 1$, and so on (referred to Figure 4). To simplify the further illustration, we also let $clusters(l)$ be the clusters produced at cut level l, which is the set of remaining unmerged clusters after $n - l - 1$ iterations of the HAC procedure, and $CH(C_i)$ be the cluster hierarchy rooted at node C_i, i.e., $CH(C_i) = C_1^i, C_2^i, \ldots, C_{n_i}^i, C_{n_i+1}^i, \ldots, C_{2n_i-1}^i$ where C_1^i, $\ldots, C_{n_i}^i$ are the leaf, singleton clusters, $C_{n_i+1}^i, \ldots, C_{2n_i-1}^i$ are the internal, merged clusters, and $C_{2n_i-1}^i = C_i$,. For example, in Figure 4, $clusters(2)$ is $\{C_5, C_6, C_7\}$, and $CH(C_8)$ is $\{C_3, C_4, C_5, C_6, C_8\}$. Note that all the above information could be obiter collected while the HAC clustering process is proceeding, so they are available without too much extra computational efforts.

The idea of our approach to this cluster partitioning problem is to find a proper cut level whose corresponding unmerged clusters are most qualified. Let $QC(C)$ be a function to measure the quality of a set of clusters C. Then, to determine a proper partition level is transfered to the problem of finding a cut level l with the best quality measure of clusters at that cut level, i.e., with the maximum value of $QC(clusters(l))$. This problem can be easily determined if the QC function is defined, and next, we will describe our

definition of QC.

The generally accepted requirement of "natural" clusters is that they must be cohesive and isolated from the other clusters [8]. Our criterion to determine the proper cut level given a binary-tree cluster hierarchy is to heuristically realize this intuition. Our definition of $QC(C)$ is a product of three components: (a) $F(C)$: A function to measure the cohesion of the clusters; (b) $S(C)$: A function to measure the isolation of the clusters; And (c) $M(C)$: A function to measure whether the number of clusters are proper, i.e., the number of clusters should be neither too few nor too many. Thus the formula of $QC(C)$ is defined as

$$QC(C) = F(C)S(C)M(C).$$

Next, we will give the definition to each component.

Given a cluster C_i with n_i objects, we define the cohesion measure of the cluster as the average similarity measure of all its object pairs. For a singleton cluster, we define its cohesion measure as one because a singleton cluster is undoubtedly most cohesive. The overall cohesion measure of a set of clusters is defined as the weighted average cohesion measure and its formal definition is given by

$$F(C) = \frac{1}{n} \sum_{C_i \in C} n_i f(C_i)$$

$$f(C_i) = \begin{cases} \frac{2}{n_i(n_i-1)} \sum_{\substack{v_a, v_b \in C_i \\ v_a \neq v_b}} sim(v_a, v_b), & \text{if } n_i > 1; \\ 1 & \text{otherwise.} \end{cases}$$

where n_i is the number of objects contained in C_i and n is the total number of objects in cluster set C.

Given two clusters C_i and C_j, we define the isolation measure between them as the smallest distance between two objects in both clusters. Notice that this definition is equivalent to their single-linkage distance measure, and its formula is shown in Table 1. Let it be notated as $mindist(C_i, C_j)$. The overall isolation measure of a cluster set $C = \{C_1, C_2, \ldots, C_k\}$ is defined as the average of this distance measure of all cluster pairs in C:

$$S(C) = \frac{2}{k(k-1)} \sum_{1 \leq i < k} \sum_{i < j \leq k} mindist(C_i, C_j)$$

Usually, a partition with neither too few nor too many clusters are preferred. Given n objects, there are at least one cluster and at most n clusters . In a hierarchical partitioning approach, we expect that the number of top-level clusters should be small, but a proper number is really hard to anticipate automatically because we have no idea of how many meaningful groups exist among the objects. Here, we take the square root of n as the expected cluster number. And then, an ellipse function is used to measure the degree

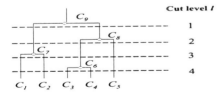

Figure 4. An illustrative example for cluster partitioning.

of preference on the number of the given clusters. Its definition is given as follows:

$$M(C) = \sqrt{1 - \frac{(|C| - en)^2}{n^2}}$$

where n is the total number of objects contained in C and en is set as $\sqrt{n}$.

Now, all three components of our QC measure are defined. To choose a suitable cut level, we just need to compute QC value for each cut level and then select the one with maximum QC value. Figure 5 shows the detailed algorithmic procedure of the whole hierarchical clustering process, which first constructs a binary-tree cluster hierarchy of given objects and then, recursively applies the partitioning procedure to determine most appropriate cut level on each sub-hierarchy. To avoid performing the partitioning procedure on the cluster with too few objects, a constant ϵ is provided to restrict the size of a cluster to be further processed.

HierarchicalClustering$(v_1, v_2, \ldots, v_n)$
$v_i, 1 \leq i \leq n$: the vectors of the objects
  1: $C_1, C_2, \ldots, C_{2n-1} \leftarrow$ **HAC**$(v_1, v_2, \ldots, v_n)$
  2: return **HierarchicalPartitioning**$(C_1, C_2, \ldots, C_{2n-1})$
HierarchicalPartitioning$(C_1, C_2, \ldots, C_n, C_{n+1}, \ldots, C_{2n-1})$
$C_i, 1 \leq i \leq 2n-1$: the binary-tree hierarchy
  1: **if** $n < \epsilon$ **then**
  2:    return $C_1, C_2, \ldots, C_n$
  3: $maxqc \leftarrow 0, bestcut \leftarrow 0$
  4: **for all** cut level $l, 1 \leq l < n$ **do**
  5:    $qc \leftarrow QC(clusters(l))$
  6:    **if** $maxqc < qc$ **then**
  7:      $maxqc \leftarrow qc, bestcut \leftarrow l$
  8: **for all** $C_i \in clusters(bestcut)$ **do**
  9:    $children(C_i) \leftarrow$ **HierarchicalPartitioning**$(CH(C_i))$
10: return $clusters(bestcut)$

Figure 5. Hierarchical clustering algorithm.

In the literature, several criteria to determine the number of clusters for HAC algorithms have been suggested [7], but they are typically based on predetermined constants, e.g., the number of final clusters or a threshold for distance measure. Relying on predefined constants is practically harmful in applying the clustering algorithm because these criteria are very sensitive to the data set on-hand and hard to be properly determined. Our approach is automatic to determine the proper level to cut only based on the data set itself.

5.3. Cluster Naming

It is not easy to determine an appropriate name for a cluster. There are different alternative methods. In our current stage, we take the most high-frequency co-occurred feature terms from the composed query terms to name the cluster.

6. Experiment

To assess the performance of the proposed approach, two categories of experiments have been conducted. The first one was performed to test the accuracy of query clustering compared with human analysis under various feature sets and distance measure strategies, and the second one is to examine the quality of the hierarchical structure generation.

Two test query term sets are prepared from our data set: (1) the most-frequent 1,000 query terms (HF) and (2) randomly selected 1,000 query terms from the most-frequent 10,000 queries (RD). Notice that all 18,017 query terms in our data set (ref. Section 4) have been manually categorized into a two-level subject hierarchy, and this class information will be treated as the external information for us to evaluate the clustering results.

With the available external class information, we adopt F-measure [5] as the evaluation metric for the generated clusters. The F-measure of cluster j with respect to class i is defined as:

$$F_{i,j} = \frac{2R_{i,j}P_{i,j}}{R_{i,j} + P_{i,j}}$$

where $R_{i,j}$ and $P_{i,j}$ are recall and precision and been defined as $n_{i,j}/n_i$ and $n_{i,j}/n_j$, respectively, in which $n_{i,j}$ is the number of members of class i in cluster j, n_j is the number of members in cluster j, and n_i is the number of members of class i. For an entire hierarchical clustering, the F-measure of any class is the maximum value it attains at any node in the tree, and an overall F-measure is computed by taking the weighted average of all values for the F-measure as given by the following:

$$F = \sum_i \frac{n_i}{n} \max\{F_{i,j}\}$$

where the maximum is taken over all clusters at all levels, n is the total number of query terms, and n_i is the number of query terms in class i.

Table 2 shows the experimental results on the two test query sets by variant feature term sets and variant distance measure strategies. This category of experiments was performed by fixing the final cluster number to 100, and the performance measures were achieved based on the human-assigned 100 second-level category information. Besides, in order to reveal the effects of variant size of feature set, we ran another experiment on HF test set with complete-linkage method and different core term sets: top 100, 500, 1,000, 3,000, 5,000, and 9,751 core terms in accordance with the term frequency.

From the experimental results, we found that the average- and complete-linkage methods perform much better than the single-linkage one under the F-measure metric, and the average-linkage method is even slightly better. Also using core terms as features is stabler in the two

Table 2. The experimental results.

(A) With variant feature sets and distance measures.

HF	randterm	freqterm	coreterm	2,3-gram
SL	.1277	.1181	.1221	.1421
AL	.5217	.4955	.4921	.4977
CL	.4757	.4882	.4794	.4390

RD	randterm	freqterm	coreterm	2,3-gram
SL	.1092	.1049	.1200	.1295
AL	.4370	.3795	.4394	.3732
CL	.4097	.2288	.4043	.3747

(B) With variant size of core-term feature set.

HF	100	500	1,000	3,000	5,000	9,751
CL	.3443	.4547	.4562	.4634	.4851	.4767

Cluster 44 (Airlines class, Precision: 1, Recall: 1)	Cluster 28 (Security software class, Precision: 0.78, Recall: 0.55)	Cluster 38 (Job class, Precision: 0.8, Recall: 0.75)
Eva (Airline name) tp	病毒 (Virus) cd	履歷表 (Resume) lj
長榮航空 (Airline) tp	norton cd	自傳 (Bio) lj
長榮 (EVA) tp	掃毒 (Virus Scanning) cd	就業 (Employment) lj
機票 (Flight Ticket) tp	病毒碼 (Virus Code) cd	徵才 (Job Opportunities) lj
遠東航空 (FAT Airline) tp	防毒軟體 (Anti -virus SW) cd	千里馬 (Taiwan Job Online) lj
復興航空 (Formosa Airline) tp	防毒 (Anti -virus) cd	工作 (Job) lj
華航 (China Airline ab) tp	電腦病毒 (Computer Virus) cd	找工作 (Job Finding) lj
中華航空 (China Airline) tp	趨勢科技 (Trends, Inc.) cg	人力 (Human Resource) lj
飛機 (Airplane) tp	pc-cillin cd	104 (HR site) lj
航空公司 (Airway Co) tp	cih cd	104 人力銀行 (HR site) lj
航空 (Airway) tp	sscan cd	人力銀行 (HR site) lj
	桃絲 cd	人力資源 (HR) lj
	駭客 (Hacker) ck	job lj
	駭客帝國 (The Matrix) en	求職 (Job Hunting) lj
		求才 (Head Hunting) lj
		青輔會 (National Youth Commission) pl
		勞委會 (Bureau of Labor) pl
		職訓局 (Vocational Training Department) pl

Major category	/	Sub-category	:	ID
Computer&Network	/	Security Software	:	cd
	/	Software Company	:	cg
	/	Hacker/Crack	:	ck
Entertainment	/	Movie	:	en
Life Information	/	Job	:	lj
Politics	/	Local Government	:	pl
Travel	/	Airlines	:	tp

Figure 6. Several example clusters of query terms.

test sets, which confirms our consideration on feature selection stated in Section 4.2. To provide the readers a more comprehensive and clearer clustering result, Figure 6 lists three selected query clusters generated in the experiment. The headlines of the columns are the cluster IDs which are attached with the corresponding manually-assigned class names, achieved precision and recall rates respectively. The second lines of the columns are clustered query terms. The class ID assigned by humans is attached after each query term, and English translations are provided for the Chinese queries. The meanings of the class IDs could refer to the bottom part of the figure, in which it lists some of manual classes with their names of major classes, sub-classes, and symbols, respectively. It would be easy to see that the terms grouped in the same clusters are most highly relevant. Although some of the terms whose corresponding classes are not matched with the generated classes, e.g., "Trend, Inc." in Cluster 28 and "Vocational Training Department" in Cluster 38, their classes "Software Company" and "Local Government" are related to the automatically-assigned classes "Security Software" and "Job" respectively, and might not be considered as incorrect clustering.

On the other hand, the second category of experiments was performed to test the quality of the hierarchical structure generation. Table 3 shows some statistics on the hierarchies generated from the two test sets based on core-term feature set and average-linkage distance measure. The depth of the hierarchy and the number of clusters at each level seem appropriate. Notice that the F-measure values are better than the ones in the previous experiments. The achieved high F-measures reveal that hierarchically grouping the query terms seem more suitable to capture hidden associations among the query terms than the flat approach. Although it's hard to have a quantitative approach to measure the goodness of the generated hierarchy structure, we believe this multi-way-tree representation is more natural

and easier for human to browse and interpret than a deep binary-tree hierarchy.

7. Discussions and Applications

Query clustering serves as a first step toward the construction of thesaurus for Web search. For those query terms grouped in the same clusters, we found they contain many abbreviations, synonyms, related terms, and even translations that are hard to be manually organized. In fact, the proposed approach is very effective and can compete with conventional document-based methods to obtain thesaurus information for query terms. Conventional approaches rely on extracting co-occurring terms from documents and suffer from term segmentation difficulty. However, more accurate analysis on the relationships between the clustered terms need to be further discovered.

Table 3. Results of hierarchical structure generation.

	HF	RD
Hierarchy depth	6	5
# 1st-level clusters	34	35
# 2nd-level clusters	164	132
# 3rd-level clusters	206	216
# 4th-level clusters	79	93
# 5th-level clusters	25	40
# 6th-level clusters	14	
F-measure	.6048	.5532

One of the reasons that increases the robustness of the proposed approach is the representative of the selected feature sets and the co-occurring feature terms extracted from the highly ranked documents. It is worthy to note that the F-measure value can achieve 0.3443 by only using the top 100 core terms as the feature set. This reveals that these most-frequent core terms might represent some major search interests and are effective features in determining the query terms into certain clusters. In fact, a small set of core terms, e.g., 500, is useful to obtain an acceptable performance. This size is relatively much smaller than the total number of query terms.

However, there exist weaknesses in our initial study. In fact, some other factors may affect the accuracy of query clustering and need to be further studied, such as the relevance and the numbers of the retrieved documents, and the sufficiency of the surrogates of these documents as described in the previous paragraphs etc. Another challenge is the ambiguous nature of terms. Query terms are usually very short. This means that some terms might have multiple information requests. The proposed query clustering approach only groups such ambiguous query terms into one appropriate cluster. Clustering ambiguous query terms into multiple clusters is still unexplored. There are other challenges regarding the class size of query terms. With the automatic approach, we found both too large classes and too small classes are difficult to be successfully grouped. A larger class is easier to be clustered into separate clusters, such as adult classes. A small class is easier to be merged with other larger classes, such as academic-related classes. These classes will decrease the obtained F-measure value compared with the manual classes.

By the proposed query clustering approach for real-world query terms, there are some applications that can benefit from. Our work provides a good startup for constructing Web thesauri. With such thesaurus information, several applications, such as term suggestion for interactive Web search, can be applied in the search process. On the other hand, our approach is very helpful to know more about the information needs of Web users. With our approach to subject clustering of query terms, it's straightforward to construct an automatic system for Web search engines or digital library systems to monitor the changes of users' search requests, such as the distributions of users' search subject categories, and up-to-date frequencies of query terms in each class. The proposed approach has been successful applied to some of the above applications [2].

8. Concluding Remarks

In this work, we have proposed a hierarchical query clustering approach to organizing users' query terms into a hierarchical structure and construct a query taxonomy in an automatic way. To assess the performance of the proposed approach, two categories of experiments have been conducted. The first one was performed to test the accuracy of the query clustering compared with human analysis, and the second one is to test the quality of the hierarchical structure generation. The obtained experimental results have shown the possibility of the automatic approach to grouping similar query terms and generate concept hierarchies of users' search interests. The approach was also proven useful in various Web information retrieval applications.

References

[1] D. Beeferman and A. Berger. Agglomerative clustering of a search engine query log. In *Proceedings of the Sixth ACM SIGKDD International Conference on Knowledge Discovery and Data Mining*, pages 407–416, New York, NY, 2000. ACM Press.

[2] S.-L. Chuang and L.-F. Chien. Enriching web taxonomies through subject categorization of query terms from search engine logs. To appear in *Decision Support Systems, Special Issue on Web Retrieval and Mining*, 2002.

[3] S. Deerwester, S. T. Dumais, G. W. Furnas, T. K. Landauer, and R. A. Harshman. Indexing by latent semantic analysis. *Journal of American Society for Information Science*, 41(6):391–407, 1990.

[4] R. C. Dubes and A. K. Jain. *Algorithms for Clustering Data*. Prentice-Hall, Englewood Cliffs, NJ,, 1988.

[5] B. Larsen and C. Aone. Fast and effective text mining using linear-time document clustering. In *Proceeding of KDD-99*, San Diego, California, 1999.

[6] R. Mandata, T. Tokunaga, and H. Tanaka. Combining multiple evidence from different types of thesaurus for query expansion. In *Proceeding of the 22nd ACM International Conference on Research and Development in Information Retrieval*, pages 191–197, New York, NY, 1999. ACM Press.

[7] G. W. Milligan and M. C. Cooper. An examination of procedures for detecting the number of clusters in a data set. *Psychometrika*, 50:159–179, 1985.

[8] B. Mirkin. *Mathematical Classification and Clustering*. Kluwer, 1996.

[9] H.-T. Pu, S.-L. Chuang, and C. Yang. Subject categorization of query terms for exploring web users' search interests. *Journal of the American Society for Information Science and Technology*, 53(8):617–630, June 1 2002.

[10] J.-R. Wen, J.-Y. Nie, and H.-J. Zhang. Clustering user queries of a search engine. In *Proceedings of the 10th International World Wide Web Conference*, pages 162–168, 2001.

[11] P. Willet. Recent trends in hierarchical document clustering: a critical review. *Information Processing and Management*, 24:577–597, 1988.

[12] O. Zamir, O. Etzioni, O. Madani, and R. M. Karp. Fast and intuitive clustering of web documents. In *Proceedings of the Third International Conference on Knowledge Discovery and Data Mining*, pages 287–290, 1997.

Evolutionary Time Series Segmentation for Stock Data Mining

Fu-lai Chung[1], Tak-chung Fu, Robert Luk and Vincent Ng
Department of Computing
Hong Kong Polytechnic University
Hunghom, Kowloon, Hong Kong.
{cskchung, cstcfu, csrluk, cstyng}@comp.polyu.edu.hk

Abstract

Stock data in the form of multiple time series are difficult to process, analyze and mine. However, when they can be transformed into meaningful symbols like technical patterns, it becomes an easier task. Most recent work on time series queries only concentrates on how to identify a given pattern from a time series. Researchers do not consider the problem of identifying a suitable set of time points for segmenting the time series in accordance with a given set of pattern templates (e.g., a set of technical patterns for stock analysis). On the other hand, using fixed length segmentation is a primitive approach to this problem; hence, a dynamic approach (with high controllability) is preferred so that the time series can be segmented flexibly and effectively according to the needs of the users and the applications. In view of the facts that such a segmentation problem is an optimization problem and evolutionary computation is an appropriate tool to solve it, we propose an evolutionary time series segmentation algorithm. This approach allows a sizeable set of stock patterns to be generated for mining or query. In addition, defining the similarity between time series (or time series segments) is of fundamental importance in fitness computation. By identifying the perceptually important points directly from the time domain, time series segments and templates of different lengths can be compared and intuitive pattern matching can be carried out in an effective and efficient manner. Encouraging experimental results are reported from tests that segment the time series of selected Hong Kong stocks.

1. Introduction

Recently, the increasing use of temporal data has initiated various research and development efforts in the field of data mining. Time series are an important class of temporal data objects and they can be easily obtained from financial and scientific applications. They are, in fact, major sources of temporal databases and, undoubtedly, discovering useful time series patterns is of fundamental importance. Unlike transactional databases with discrete items, time series data are characterized by their numerical and continuous nature. It is suggested in [1] to divide the sequences into meaningful subsequences and represent them using real-valued functions. Furthermore, there is a need to discretize a continuous time series into meaningful labels/symbols [2,3]. We express this process as "numeric-to-symbolic" (N/S) conversion, and consider it to be one of the most fundamental components in time series data mining systems.

In [2], a simple N/S conversion method is proposed. A fixed length window is used to segment a time series into subsequences, based upon those a time series is represented by the primitive shape patterns that are formed. This discretization process mainly depends on the choice of the window width, w. However, using fixed length segmentation is a primitive approach to solving the problem. There are at least two identified disadvantages. First, with fixed length subsequences, only patterns with such a length will be considered in the mining process. However, meaningful patterns typically appear with different lengths throughout a time series. Second, as a result of the even segmentation of a time series, meaningful patterns may be missed if they are split across time points. Thus, a dynamic approach is preferred to identify the time points in a more flexible way [4] (i.e., using different window widths), but this is certainly not a trivial segmentation problem.

In [5, 6], it is suggested to identify the time points at which behavior changes occur in a time series. In the statistics literature, this is called the change-point detection problem. The standard solution involves fixing the number of change-points beforehand, identifying their positions, and then determining functions for curve fitting the intervals between successive change-points. In [7], an iterative algorithm is proposed that fits a model to a time segment and then uses a likelihood criterion to determine if the segment should be partitioned further. In [8], it is suggested to discover the underlying switching process in a time series, which entails identifying the number of sub-processes and the dynamics of each sub-process. The nonlinear gated experts concept from statistical physics was proposed to perform the segmentation. In [9,10], dynamic programming is proposed to determine the total number of

* *Acknowledgement: This work was supported by the RGC CERG grant under project PolyU 5065/98E*
[1] *Corresponding author*

intervals within the data, the location of these intervals and the order of the model within each segment. In [11], the segmentation problem is considered with a new tool for exploratory data analysis and data mining, called the scale-sensitive gated experts (SSGE), which can partition a complex nonlinear regression surface into a set of simpler surfaces (which are called features).

The segmentation problem has also been considered from the perspective of finding cyclic periodicity for all of the segments. In [12,13], the data cube and Apriori data mining techniques were used for mining segment-wise periodicity using a fixed length period. An off-line technique for the competitive identification of piecewise stationary time series is described in [14]. In addition to performing piecewise segmentation and identification, the proposed technique maps similar segments of a time series as neighbors on a neighborhood map.

As we can see, much of the recent data mining research on this problem, or similar ones, can be characterized procedurally in the following general manner [15]: (i) find an approximation and robust representation for a time series, for example, Fourier coefficients, piecewise linear models, etc.; (ii) define a flexible matching function that can handle various pattern deformations (scaling, transformations, etc.); and (iii) provide an efficient scalable algorithm, using the adopted representation and matching function, for massive time-series data sets. Although these approaches can generally identify the given pattern from a time series, they do not consider the problem of identifying a suitable set of time points in a time series when a set of pattern templates are given; for example, the technical patterns (e.g., head-and-shoulder, double top, etc.) for stock analysis. Further, in order to form a versatile mining space, a variety of patterns (e.g., in different resolutions) have to be identified. The aforementioned segmentation task can be considered as an optimization problem where evolutionary computation can contribute. In this paper, an evolutionary time series segmentation algorithm for stock data mining is proposed. With respect to the target application, for fitness evaluation we have adopted the perceptually important point (PIP) based subsequence-matching scheme [16]. In addition, parameters are introduced to control the identification of subsequence patterns with different characteristics (i.e., in different temporal scales). The paper is organized into six sections. In next section, the PIP based pattern-matching scheme for fitness evaluation is described. The proposed segmentation algorithm is introduced in Section 3. The simulation results are reported in Section 4 and the final section provides the conclusions of the paper.

2. A Flexible Pattern Matching Scheme for Fitness Evaluation

To facilitate evolutionary time series segmentation, defining a distance measure or the similarity between time series (or time series segments) is of fundamental importance for fitness evaluation. In [16], we proposed a flexible time series pattern-matching scheme that was based on the fact that interesting and frequently appearing patterns are typically characterized by a few critical points. For example, the head-and-shoulder pattern consists of a head point, two shoulder points and a pair of neck points. These points are perceptually important in the human visual identification process; therefore, they should similarly be taken into account in the pattern matching process. The proposed scheme follows this idea by locating those perceptually important points in a data sequence, P, in accordance with a query sequence, Q. The location process works as follows.

2.1 Identification of Perceptually Important Points

With sequences P and Q being normalized to a unit square (for shifting and uniform amplitude scaling invariant), the perceptually important points (PIPs) are located in order according to the pseudo-code described in Fig. 1. Currently, the first two PIPs that are found will be the first and last points of P. The next PIP that is found will be the point in P with maximum distance to the first two PIPs. The fourth PIP that is found will then be the point in P with maximum distance to its two adjacent PIPs, either in-between the first and second PIPs or in-between the second and the last PIPs. The process of locating the PIPs continues until the number is equal to the length of the query sequence, Q. To determine the maximum distance to the two adjacent PIPs, we calculate the vertical distance between a test point p_3 and a line connecting the two adjacent PIPs (see Fig. 2), that is,

$$VD(p_3, p_c) = |y_c - y_3| = \left| \left(y_1 + (y_2 - y_1) \cdot \frac{x_c - x_1}{x_2 - x_1} \right) - y_3 \right| \quad (1)$$

where $x_c = x_3$. Such a function is intended to capture the fluctuation in the sequence, and those highly fluctuating points are considered as PIPs.

```
Function PIPlocate (P,Q)
    Input: sequence p[1..m], length of Q[1..n]
    Output: pattern sp[1..n]
Begin
    Set sp[1]=p[1], sp[n]=p[m]
    Repeat until sp[1..n] all filled {
        Select point p[j] with maximum distance to
        the adjacent points in sp
        Add p[j] To sp }
    Return sp
End
```

Figure 1. Pseudo code of the PIP identification process

To demonstrate the identification process, the 'head-and-shoulder' pattern is used. Fig. 3 shows the result when the number of data points in the input sequence, P, and the query sequence, Q, is 29 and 7, respectively (i.e., $m = 29$ and $n = 7$).

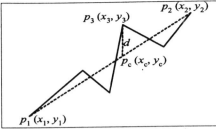

Figure 2. Vertical distance metric

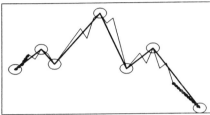

Figure 3. Identification of 7 PIPs (head-and-shoulder pattern)

2.2 Distance Measure

After identifying the PIPs in the data sequence, the amplitude distance (AD) between P and Q can be computed using direct point-to-point comparison, that is,

$$AD(SP,Q) = \sqrt{\frac{1}{n}\sum_{k=1}^{n}(sp_k - q_k)^2} \tag{2}$$

for all query patterns, Q, in the predefined set. Here, SP and (sp_k) denote the PIPs found in P. However, the measure in Eqn. (2) has not yet taken the horizontal scale (time dimension) into consideration. So, it is preferable to consider the horizontal distortion of the pattern against the pattern templates. The temporal distance (TD) between P and Q is defined as follows:

$$TD(SP,Q) = \sqrt{\frac{1}{n-1}\sum_{k=2}^{n}(sp_k{}^t - q_k{}^t)^2} \tag{3}$$

where $sp_k{}^t$ and $q_k{}^t$ denote the time coordinate of the sequence points sp_k and q_k, respectively. To take into consideration both horizontal and vertical distortion in our fitness evaluation, the distance measure (DM) (or similarity) could be modified as follows:

$$DM(SP,Q) = w_1 \times AD(SP,Q) + (1-w_1) \times TD(SP,Q) \tag{4}$$

where w_1 denotes the weighting for the amplitude distance and the temporal distance, and this can be specified by the users.

3. Evolutionary Time Series Segmentation

Obviously, static N/S conversion is only a basic conversion approach. A dynamic approach can be derived if the time points can be identified in an irregular way. This is an optimization problem where evolutionary computation [17,18] can contribute. In this section, we propose an evolutionary time series segmentation algorithm for stock price data. A set of pattern templates $\{Q\}$, particularly the technical patterns, is assumed to have been given for fitness

evaluation purposes. The evolutionary segmentation process can be described as follows.

3.1 Chromosome Representation

Unlike the traditional genetic algorithms (GAs) that adopt binary bit strings to encode a chromosome, a more direct representation is used in our approach. The time points identified in each individual will form the genes themselves, for example, $P_a = \{4, 9, 14, 16, 19\}$ represents a time series being cut at time points 4, 9, 14, 16, and 19. In other words, the first segment lasts from data point 1 to data point 4, the second segment starts at data point 5 and ends at data point 9, and so on. Note here that the variable length of individuals (chromosomes) can be represented.

3.2 Algorithmic Framework

Initially, a set of user-defined parameters has to be set as follows:

PopSize: size of the population.
MaxGen: maximum number of generations.
MinFitness: minimum fitness value.
dlen: desired segment length.

The evolutionary segmentation process is executed according to the pseudo-code given in Fig. 4. The fittest individual, $P_{fittest}$, with minimum fitness value[2] in the last generation will be the final segmentation result.

```
Initialization of population P(1)
For t = 1 to MaxGen
    Evaluate the fitness of each individual Pi    in P(t) with
    the given set of pattern   templates Q
    If min(fitness(Pi)) < MinFitness then Stop
    Else
       Apply the following steps to produce   the next
       generation P(t+1):
         - Selection
         - Genetic Operations (Crossover & Mutation)
    End If
End For
```

Figure 4. Overall evolutionary segmentation process

3.3 Initialization of the Population

The first step of the evolutionary segmentation process is to initialize a set of time points (the genes) for the chromosomes in the first generation. Here, we have adopted a user-oriented approach—users specify the desired segment length *dlen* during the evolutionary process. It is a reasonable assumption that users can specify whether they want to investigate a long-term or a short-term period/pattern. Moreover, it is only an approximate parameter for the initialization process. With this parameter, the approximate number of time points (ds) for a chromosome is given by

$$ds = L / dlen \tag{5}$$

where L is the length of the whole time series. The initial population, $P(1)$, can be generated as described in the pseudo-code of Fig. 5. Using such a scheme, the initial time

---

[2] *In this paper, fitter individuals are having lower fitness values.*

points will be distributed quite evenly within the chromosome.

```
For Each individual P_i in P(1) (where i = 1 to PopSize)
   Evenly distribute the set of time points  (D_1^i, ..., D_{n_i}^i)
   where n_i=ds
   For Each D_j^i in P_i (where j = 1 to n_i)
      Randomly Move it between D_{j-1}^i and D_{j+1}^i
   End For
   The time series s is segmented as
   s = [s(1)...s(D_1^i), s(D_1^i +1)...s(D_2^i), ..., s(D_{n_i}^i +1)...s(L)]
End For
```

Figure 5. Initialization process of population *P(1)*

3.4 Selection

Selection in GAs is aimed at giving a higher probability for reproduction to fitter individuals in a population so that their favorable characteristic can be inherited by even fitter offspring. This is where the principle of "survival of the fittest" applies. Here, we keep the best parent (based on the fitness value) from the current population, $P(t)$, as one of the candidates in the next generation. For the other candidates, the roulette selection scheme [18] is applied. The idea is to give good candidates a higher chance of passing their genes to the following generation. The individuals selected, based on a selection probability P_{sel}, will then go through the genetic operations of crossover and mutation.

3.5 Genetic Operation: Crossover

The essence of any crossover operator is to exchange the components of two parents to form new offspring, which is based on a crossover rate R_c (it is recommended that $R_c = 0.6$, or higher). Single-point crossover is realized by cutting the chromosomes at a randomly chosen position and then swapping the segments between the two parents. We formulate the single-point crossover as:.

Crossover Procedure
1. Choose two individuals P_a and P_b from the pool of selected parents.
2. Randomly pick a crossover-point (*CutPt*).
3. Select those time points $(D_1^a, ..., D_x^a)$ from P_a, where $x \leq CutPt$, as the new genes.
4. Select those time points $(D_y^b, ..., D_{n_b}^b)$ from P_b, where $CutPt < y$, as the new genes.
5. Combine the two sets of new genes to form an offspring, i.e., a new individual $P_{new} = (D_1^a, ..., D_x^a, D_y^b, ..., D_{n_b}^b)$

Figure 6. Crossover operation in evolutionary segmentation process

For example, if we have two individual P_a and P_b:

$P_a = \{4, 6, 9, 14, 16, 20\}$
$P_b = \{2, 7, 12, 16, 19\}$

and (the crossover-point) *CutPt = 10*. The new individual (offspring) will then be either

$P_{new} = \{4, 6, 9\} \cup \{12, 16, 19\} = \{4, 6, 9, 12, 16, 19\}$

or

$P_{new} = \{2, 7\} \cup \{14, 16, 20\} = \{2, 7, 14, 16, 20\}$

Such a crossover operation can be easily generalized to k-point crossover by cutting the chromosomes at k randomly chosen positions and swapping the corresponding segments between the two parents.

3.6 Genetic Operation: Mutation

Mutation in GAs is generally regarded as a background operation. Its main function is to introduce new genetic material and maintain a certain level of diversity in a population since crossover does not introduce any new genetic material. In our approach, the remaining candidates of the next generation are formed by selecting a candidate from the current generation based on the value of P_{sel}. Then, mutation is carried out on the selected individual according to the algorithm described in Fig. 7.

Mutation Procedure
1. Set the user-defined parameters
   R_a: probability of adding a time point during mutation (probability of dropping a time point = $1 - R_a$)
2. Choose an individual P_i from the pool of selected parents based on P_{sel}.
3. Add or drop a time point in P_i. The probability of adding a time point is R_a; otherwise a time point is dropped.

Figure 7. Mutation operation in evolutionary segmentation process

3.7 Fitness Evaluation

With a set of pattern templates $\{Q\}$, the proposed PIP-based similarity measure (from Section 2) can be adopted to evaluate the fitness of each subsequence segmented by the identified time points. Thus, the fitness of the individuals in a population can be computed as:

```
For Each individual P_i in P
   For Each segment P_{i,j} in P_i
      fitness(P_{i,j}) = min_{∀Q} {DM(P_{i,j}, Q)}      ; see Eqn.(4)
   End For

   fitness(P_i) = (1/(n_i+1)) Σ_{j=1}^{n_i+1} fitness(P_{i,j})

End For
```

Figure 8. Fitness evaluation in evolutionary segmentation process

3.8 Weighting Different Pattern Templates

With the distance measure defined in Eqn.(4), we found that the pattern templates having more data points around the middle amplitude level, i.e., 0.5 in the unit square, were favored in the fitness evaluation. It is because the expected error of those data points, arising from Eqn.(2), is smaller. The expected error of data point q_k can be calculated by:

$$E_{Err}(q_k) = \Pr(sp_k > q_k) \times E_{Err}(q_k \mid sp_k > q_k) + \Pr(sp_k < q_k) \times E_{Err}(q_k \mid sp_k < q_k) \quad (6)$$

where $\Pr(sp_k > q_k)$ denotes the probability of $sp_k > q_k$ and $E_{Err}(q_k \mid sp_k > q_k)$ is the expected error of data point q_k

given $sp_k > q_k$. If we assume that sp_k is evenly distributed in the unit range, $E_{Err}(q_k | sp_k > q_k)$ will be equal to $0.5 \times (1 - q_k)$ while $E_{Err}(q_k | sp_k < q_k)$ will be equal to $0.5 \times q_k$. By estimating the expected error of each data point in a pattern template Q, the expected error for such pattern template can be computed by:

$$E_{Err}(Q) = \frac{1}{n} \sum_{i=1}^{n} E_{Err}(q_k) \qquad (7)$$

To take the expected errors of different pattern templates into considerations, we introduce a template weighting term and formulate it as:

$$TW(Q) = 1 + \left(1 - \frac{E_{Err}(Q) - \min_{\forall Q}\{E_{Err}(Q)\}}{\max_{\forall Q}\{E_{Err}(Q)\} - \min_{\forall Q}\{E_{Err}(Q)\}} \right) \qquad (8)$$

with values in the range of 1 to 2. Thus, the distance measure in Eqn.(4) is redefined as:

$$DM(SP,Q) = w_1 \times AD(SP,Q) \times TW(Q) + \qquad (9)$$
$$(1 - w_1) \times TD(SP,Q).$$

to make it unbiased to different pattern templates.

3.9 Segmentation with Temporal Control

As mentioned in Section 3.3, users may prefer to investigate a specific resolution for patterns in a time series (i.e., long-term or short-term). For stock data mining, creating a huge pattern space with a wide variety of patterns (e.g., the co-existence of long-term and short-term patterns) is very important. Thus, we propose the introduction of controllability in temporal domains of our evolutionary segmentation scheme. By setting different parameters, users can have more control over the desired time series segmentation results.

In the temporal domain, the length of the segments (and also the number of time points) is uncontrollable once we start the evolutionary (iterative) process of the proposed segmentation scheme. Therefore, we prefer a mechanism that can control the length of the segments towards the length specified by the users during the evolutionary process. To achieve this goal, a temporal control penalty function is proposed and defined as follows:

$$TC(SP) = 1 - \exp^{-(d_l / \theta_l)^2} \qquad (10)$$

where $d_l = slen - dlen$, that is, the difference between segment length (slen) and the desired segment length (dlen) specified by the users. The parameter θ_1 is used to control the sharpness of the function, hence the strength of the temporal control. It is defined as follows:

$$\theta_1 = dlen / dlc \qquad (11)$$

where dlc is the desired length control parameter. Larger dlc values will lead to smaller θ_1 values and this will strengthen the temporal control (i.e., a segment length closer to the desired length is greatly preferred).

For example, if the desired segment length dlen is 180 (e.g., 180 trading days) and dlc is set to 2, then $\theta_1 = 90$, and the temporal control penalty function will look like Fig. 9a.

However, if dlc is set to 6 ($\theta_1 = 30$), the temporal control is strengthened (see Fig. 9b) by adding a greater penalty to the fitness evaluations for patterns with a length different to the desired one.

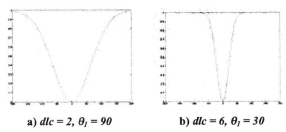

| a) $dlc = 2$, $\theta_l = 90$ | b) $dlc = 6$, $\theta_l = 30$ |

Figure 9. Temporal control penalty function (dlen = 180)

4. Simulation Results

In this section, we report the performance of the proposed evolutionary time series segmentation algorithm. Two sets of experiments were conducted. The first set was used to demonstrate the segmentation effects using time series generated artificially with 500 data points, whereas the second set was designed to validate the affects of the temporal control during the segmentation process. In the second experiment, the time series data used was taken from the daily closing price of the Hong Kong Hang Seng Index from March 1989 to March 1999 (i.e., 2532 data points). In addition, several closing price time series from stocks of different sectors of the Hong Kong stock market were tested. Due to the paper length limit, only two are selected to report here and furthermore the parameter analysis of the proposed algorithm is omitted. Twenty-two technical patterns were used as the pattern templates, i.e., the cardinality of {Q} is 22. Fig. 10 shows half of them and the other half are simply their inverted patterns. The length of the pattern templates is 9 (i.e., 9 points). All parameters are set to the default values shown in Table 1 if they are not specified.

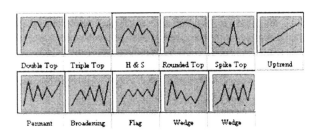

Figure 10. Typical technical patterns

Table 1. Parameter value adopted

Parameter		Value
PopSize	Size of population	50
MaxGen	Maximum number of generation	500
MinFitness	Minimum fitness value	0.0
R_c	Crossover rate	0.4
R_a	Probability of adding a time point during mutation	0.5

4.1 Segmentation of Artificial Time Series

In this experiment, the performance of segmenting artificial time series is demonstrated. Fig.11(a) and 12(a) show the two artificial time series (consisting of 500 data points) generated by random combination of resized technical pattern templates. Fig. 11(b) and 12(b) are the segmentation results using the proposed algorithm. We can see that most of the patterns, especially those reversal patterns, can be identified even in different resolutions (see the spike top and reversed spike top in Fig.11(b)). Note here that consecutive up-trend or downtrend patterns are quite common and they can be combined to form larger patterns. Fig.11(c) and Fig.12(c) are the segmentation results of the artificial time series with noise added. Although the results are not as good as that of the clean series, most of involved technical patterns can still identified.

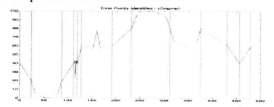

(a) Original artificial time series formed by cascading different technical patterns of different resolutions

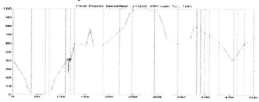

(b) Segmentation result by the proposed algorithm

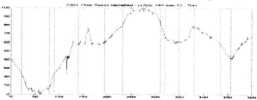

(c) Segmentation result of the noisy time series

Figure 11. Segmentation results of an artificial time series

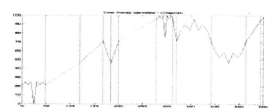

(a) Original artificial time series formed by cascading different technical patterns of different resolutions

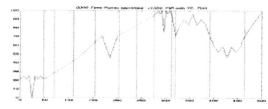

(b) Segmentation result by the proposed algorithm

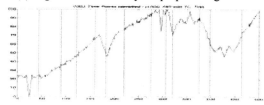

(c) Segmentation result of the noisy time series

Figure 12. Segmentation results of another artificial time series

4.2 Analysis of the Temporal Control

With the desired segment length *dlen* = *180*, Fig.13 shows the standard deviation of the segment length when using different desired length control, *dlc*, values. As expected, the standard deviation will become small when *dlc* is large, (i.e., a sharp temporal control penalty function is used). Fig.14 shows that the number of time points obtained is relatively insensitive to different values of *dlc*. If *dlc* increases, the number of time points tends to become the number that can segment the time series evenly (in this case, 2532 data points are divided by the desired segment length 180, i.e., 14 time points). From the segmentation results shown in Fig.15, increasing *dlc* will lead to a segment length that is much closer to the *dlen* specified by the users. When *dlc* is increased beyond 0.2, the time points are close to being evenly distributed across the time series, as shown in Fig.15(c).

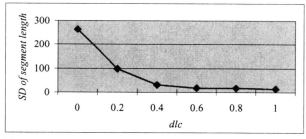

Figure 13. Std. Dev. of segment length for different *dlc* values

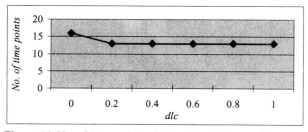

Figure 14. No. of time points obtained for different *dlc* values

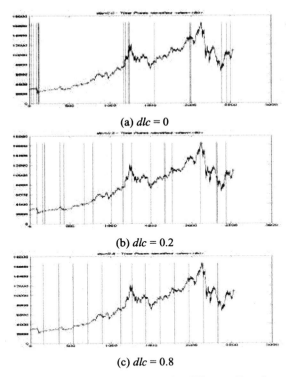

(a) $dlc = 0$

(b) $dlc = 0.2$

(c) $dlc = 0.8$

Figure 15. Segmentation results for different *dlc* values

By fixing $dlc = 0.2$ and setting $dlen = 90$ and 180, the average segment lengths are 73 and 134, respectively. Fig.16 shows their corresponding segmentation results.

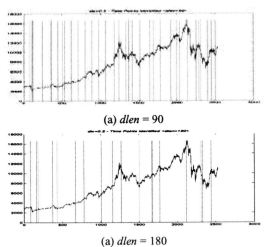

(a) $dlen = 90$

(a) $dlen = 180$

Figure 16. Segmentation results of the Hong Kong Hang Seng Index time series for different *dlen*

4.2 Examples of Other Stocks

In this section, we report the investigation of two more closing price time series from the property and public affairs sectors of the Hong Kong stock market. The same 22 technical patterns (Fig.10) are used as the pattern templates $\{Q\}$. All parameters are set to the default values shown in

Table I if they are not specified. From the estimation in the experiments, *dlc* is set to 0.3. By setting different *dlen* values (i.e., 90 and 180), different segmentation results with different considerations are shown in Figs.17 and 18. With larger *dlen*, long-term stock price movement is considered because larger segments are produced with a smaller number of time points (Fig.17(b) and 18(b)). We observe that most segments found when examining long-term patterns are related to the overall up or down trend in that period, whereas other technical patterns are found during short-term investigations. Moreover, the time points identified using different *dlen* are independent (comparing Fig.17(a) with Fig.17(b) and Fig.18(a) with Fig.18(b)). The time points are identified for the best matching of the segments with pattern templates.

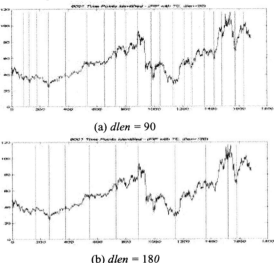

(a) $dlen = 90$

(b) $dlen = 180$

Figure 17. Segmentation results of a property stock time series for different *dlen*

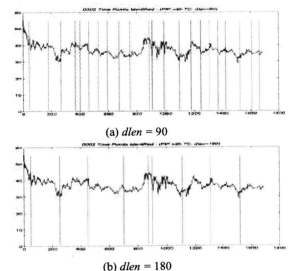

(a) $dlen = 90$

(b) $dlen = 180$

Figure 18. Segmentation results of a public affairs stock series for different *dlen*

5. Conclusions

In this paper, we proposed an evolutionary segmentation algorithm for dividing a given time series into subsequence for further manipulation. Encouraging results were reported. Although this paper has focused on stock time series, the proposed algorithm can also be applied to other domains with a given set of pattern templates. In addition, a flexible time series pattern matching method based on perceptually important points is introduced for fitness evaluations. This method follows the time domain approach to carry out the matching process and it is intuitive to ordinary data analysts. One may find it particularly attractive in applications like stock data analysis. The new method is efficient and yet effective for fitness evaluation in the evolutionary segmentation algorithm. Moreover, parameters are introduced to control the temporal scale of the final segments obtained. This will help to create an informative pattern space for subsequent mining activities.

References

[1]   H. Shatkay and S. B. Zdonik, "Approximate queries and representations for large data sequences," *Proc. Int. Conf. on Data Engineering (ICDE'96)*, 1996.

[2]   G. Das, K.I. Lin and H. Mannila, "Rule discovery from time series," *Proc. ACM SIGKDD Int. Conf. on Knowledge Discovery and Data Mining (KDD'98)*, pp.16-22, 1998.

[3]   O .Y. Kai, W. Jia, P. Zhou and X. Meng, "A new approach to transforming time series into symbolic sequences," *Proc. First Joint BMES/EMBS Conference*, October 1999.

[4]   T.C. Fu, F.L. Chung, V. Ng and R. Luk, "Evolutionary Segmentation of Financial Time Series into Subsequences," *Proc. Congress on Evolutionary Computation (CEC'2001)*, Seoul, Korea, pp.426-430, 2001.

[5]   J.J. Oliver, R.A. Baxter and C.S. Wallace, "Minimum message length segmentation," *Proc. Pacific-Asia Conference on Knowledge Discovery and Data Mining (PAKDD'98)*, pp.222-233, 1998.

[6]   J.J. Oliver and C.S. Forbes, "Bayesian approaches to segmenting a simple time series," *Technical Reports 97/336, Department of Computer Science*, Monash University, Melbourne, Australia, pp.1-20, 1997.

[7]   V. Guralnik and J. Srivastava, "Event detection from time series data," *Proc. 5th ACM SIGKDD International Conference on Knowledge Discovery and Data mining (KDD'99)*, pp.33-42, 1999.

[8]   A.N. Srivastava and A. Weigend, "Improving time series segmentation with gated experts through annealing," *Technical Reports CU-CS-795-95, Department of Computer Science and Institute of Cognitive Science*, University of Colorado, USA, 1996.

[9]   G.F. Bryant, S.R. Duncan, "A solution to the segmentation problem based on dynamic programming," *Proc. 3rd IEEE Conference on Control Applications*, Vol.2, pp.1391-1396, 1994.

[10] Duncan, S.R.; Bryant, G.F., "A new algorithm for segmenting data from time series," *Proc. of the 35th IEEE Conference on Decision and Control*, Vol.3, p.p.3123-3128, 1996.

[11] A.N. Srivastava, R. Su and A.S. Weigend, "Data mining for features using scale-sensitive gated experts," *IEEE Trans. on Pattern Analysis and Machine Intelligence*, vol.21, no.12, pp.1268 –1279, Dec. 1999.

[12] J. Han, W. Gong and Y. Tin, "Mining segment-wise periodic patterns in time-related databases," *Proc. Int. Conf. on Knowledge Discovery and Data Mining (KDD'98)*, New York City, NY, pp.214-218, 1998.

[13] J. Han, G. Dong and Y. Yin, "Efficient mining of partial periodic patterns in time series database," *Proc. 15th Int. Conf. on Data Engineering*, pp.106-115, 1999.

[14] C.L. Fancoua, J.C. Principe, "A neighborhood map of competing one step predictors for piecewise segmentation and identification of time series," *Proc. IEEE Int. Conf. on Neural Networks*, Vol.4, pp.1906-1911, 1996.

[15] X. Ge and P. Smyth, "Deformable Markov model templates for time-series pattern matching," *Proc. ACM SIGKDD Int. Conf. on Knowledge Discovery and Data Mining (KDD'2000)*, pp.81-90, 2000.

[16] F.L. Chung, T.C. Fu, R. Luk and V. Ng, "Flexible time series pattern matching based on perceptually important points," *accepted by Workshop on Learning from Temporal and Spatial Data in International Joint Conference on Artificial Intelligence (IJCAI'01)*, Seattle, Washington, 4-10 August, 2001.

[17] T. Back and H.P. Schwefel, "Evolutionary computation: An overview," *Proc. IEEE Int. Conf. on Evolutionary Computation*, pp.20-29, 1996.

[18] T. Back, U. Hammel and H.P. Schwefel, "Evolutionary computation: Comments on the history and current state," *IEEE Trans. on Evolutionary Computation*, vol.11, pp.3-17, April 1997.

Using functional PCA for cardiac motion exploration

Denis Clot
Université Claude Bernard Lyon 1
LASS UMR CNRS 5823
Bât. 101, 43 Bd du 11 novembre 1918, Villeurbanne 69622, France
clot@univ-lyon1.fr

Abstract

Principal component analysis (PCA) [14, 6] is a main tool in multivariate data analysis. Its paradigms are also used in the Karhunen-Loeve decomposition [5], a standard tool in image processing. Extensions of PCA to the framework of functional data have been proposed. The analysis provided by the functional PCA seems to be a powerful tool to find principal sources of variability in curves or images, but it fails in providing us with easy interpretations in the case of multifunctional data. Guide lines aiming at spot information from the outputs of PCA applied to functionals with values in space of continuous functions upon a bounded domain are proposed. An application to cardiac motion analysis illustrates the complexity of the multifunctional framework and the results provided by functional PCA.

1. Introduction

With [7] in 1973, it has been proven that PCA could be applied to random variables with values in Hilbert spaces, but one had to wait a long time before observing some applications of PCA to variables such as continuous functions upon a bounded time interval or more general curves. Even if PCA seems to be a powerful method to investigate major source of variability in functional data, it fails in providing us with easy interpretations, at least in the case of multi-functional data. The strategies to handle results of PCA should be adapted to this "new" framework. We believe that the number of graphics as well as their contents deserve particular attention. On the one hand, usual results become too numerous (e.g. graphics) and lose their synthetic nature so that the analyst can not infer global and structural information about the variables and their relations. On the other hand, results should be expressed in an adequat maneer, since data are much richer and more complex: correlations, directions of variation or oppositions

are now properties to be studied upon a continuous domain. Difficulties of interpreting the results may be charged to these facts : one can observe that PCA involving functional data appears mainly within mono-functional or at most bi-functional frameworks, where functionals have their values in simple spaces such as $\mathcal{C}(T)$ (T denotes a bounded real interval and $\mathcal{C}(T)$ the set of continuous functions upon T).

After a reminder of the concepts of principal component analysis applied to real random variables, we expose how this method has been extended to functional data. We then propose a methodology that aims at spot important information from the calculations of the PCA when the set of functionals have values in $\mathcal{C}(T)$. The illustrations given along rely on meteorological data. An application to cardiac motion analysis reveals the wide scope of the functional PCA as well as the complexity of its outputs and highlights the benefits of our approach.

2. Linear PCA

There are several manners to motivate a PCA. We introduce this method by the research of the subspace which gives us the "best insight" of the information carried by some data, in order to catch easily structures and patterns present in the data. Indeed, we are looking to express this information in a graphical way.

2.1. Problem of linear PCA

Given p quantitative measured variables, let us consider each individual as a point of $\mathbb{R}^p$ whose coordinates are given by the values of the p variables. This space can be regarded as an euclidian space with the inner product

$$\langle x, y \rangle = x'My$$

where M is a symmetric positive definite matrix and x' is the transpose of x. Let us denote by

- $X^1, \ldots, X^p$ the p variables which are random vectors of $\mathbb{R}^n$, $x_1, \cdots, x_n$ the n points of $\mathbb{R}^p$ representing the individuals and $X = (X^1, \ldots, X^p) = (x_i^j)$ the $n \times p$ matrix of data

- w_i the weight associated with the ith individual, satisfying $w_i \geq 0$ and $\sum_i w_i = 1$, $W = (w_i)$ the diagonal matrix whose i^{th} diagonal element is w_i.

We are looking for a subspace H of dimension $d << p$ such that the quantity $\sum_i w_i \|\widehat{x_i^H}\|^2$ is maximum (where $\widehat{x_i^H}$ denotes the orthogonal projection of x_i on H). From a physical point of view, the problem is to find the projection of the population that maximizes its inertia.

This problem reduces to finding the orthonormal vectors that constitute the basis of H, whereas its origin is known to be the point $g = \sum_i w_i x_i$. Considering, without loss of generality, that $g = 0$, so that x_{ij} is the value of variable X^j measured about its mean $\overline{X^j}$, we simplify our problem by working with centered variables.

In practical situations, we often work with the data of a sampled population, so one might wonder how these results are linked with these corresponding to the whole population. According to [1], results obtained from a sample converge to "real" results under certain assumptions we will not care about here.

2.2. Solution of linear PCA

For a given d, it is well known that a basis of H is given by the d first eigenvectors $e_1, \ldots, e_d$ corresponding to the d largest eigenvalues of $VM = X'WXM$, where V is the variance-covariance matrix. The initial problem

$$\max_{\substack{e_1, \ldots, e_d \\ \langle e_k, e_l \rangle = \delta_{kl}}} \sum_i w_i \|\widehat{x_i^H}\|^2 \qquad (1)$$

can be rewritten

$$\max_{\substack{e_1, \ldots, e_d \\ \langle e_k, e_l \rangle = \delta_{kl}}} \sum_j e_j' MVM e_j \qquad (2)$$

where $e_1, \ldots, e_d$ form an orthonormal basis for H. An axis following the direction of an eigenvector is called a principal axis. Moreover, the eigenvalue λ_j is the part of inertia associated with the subspace spanned by e_j (i.e. $\frac{\lambda_j}{\sum_{k=1}^p \lambda_k}$ gives its proportion).

Hence the optimisation part of the analysis is solved. Choosing a suitable d is often a part of the problem of PCA. Many criterions exist to select d [14, 6], as many as one can feel interest for a part of inertia. This point is put aside.

Before going into the details of interpretation that constitute the main part of the art of PCA, we point out another side of the result of the optimisation part of the problem: the first eigenvector can be interpreted as the vector of coefficients of XMe_1, the linear combination of the

initial variables with the highest variance under the constraint $\|e_1\| = 1$, the second eigenvector as the vector of coefficients of XMe_2, the linear combination of the initial variables with the highest variance under the constraints $\|e_2\| = 1$ and $\mathrm{cov}(XMe_1, XMe_2) = 0$, etc. These linear combinations are the so-called principal components.

2.3. Interpreting the outputs of linear PCA

Interpretations of PCA results are mainly based on two types of graphics and on additional indicators. The first type of graphics is the projection of individuals on subspace spanned by the couples of principal axes. The second type is the projection of variables on two dimensional subspace of the vector space spanned by the principal components found. Those graphics are meant to bring to the fore some visual information about correlations between variables and their intensities and directions. These informations are helpful to interpret principal components.

Let us consider for example the following couple of graphics :

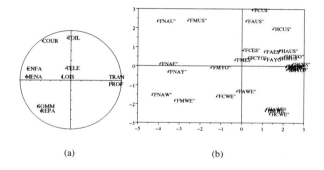

(a)   (b)

Figure 1. Projections of normalized variables onto the correlation circle associated with the two major principal components and projections of individuals given by the first two principal components

Fig. 1(a) shows us that the major source of variability in the data is strongly linked with four variables (whose labels are: MENA, ENFA, TRAN and PROF) while some other variables seem to be uncorrelated to them (e.g. TOIL). We also observe opposite directions of variation within the four variables.

Fig. 1(b) is used to complete interpretation that can be proposed about the principal components. It sometimes provides us with a more obvious interpretation of a latent structure. It can also be used to incorporate more information coming from qualitative variables for example.

Additional indicators provide more accurate information about quality of projections, importance of individuals, but also about individual contributions to inertia for the whole bunch of variables or for a single principal component. They are sometimes necessary when the distribution of the weights is so heterogeneous that interpretation can hardly be infered from graphics of projections of individual. The reader can refer to [15] and [6] for further reading.

3. Functional PCA

3.1. Functional data

It is usual to handle a set of variables measured on the individuals of a population. Each individual is associated with a finite vector of various elements. In the functional context, variables are replaced by functionals: thus scalar values of individual vectors are replaced by functions. These functions are generaly continuous upon a bounded time interval, but they can depend on more than one variable and assumptions about their smoothness are contextual [13, 12]. As shown by our application to cardiac motion exploration, functional data embrace more general objects than multivariate time series which are a particular case.

There are two problems that are often encountered with functional data. The first one is to rebuilt the whole data from discrete data since the process of measuring a time function can hardly ever be continuous. The functions are never known exactly and particular care is required in formulating hypothesis about their properties in order to put to good use their discretization. These assumptions also guide the choice for a technic such as interpolation or roughness penalty smoothing, that is often the first step of the analysis. The second problem is data alignment. It appears when the analysis is based on pointwise comparison of curves. In the case of time dependant function, if the landmarks on the curves are not synchronic, one has to transform curves with time transformation to align all the curves on those particular points to recover the time process. Typically, this problem is encountered for the estimation of mean curves [11].

3.2. The problem of functional PCA

Let us see now how the PCA concepts are used for functional data according to [13].

As in the multivariate case, we consider p variables measured on a population, but here, these variables are functional. For convenience, we will assume that our functional values are real continuous functions upon a bounded interval of time T and elements of $L_2(T)$, the set of square integrable functions over T. So the individuals can be identified to points of $L_2^p(T) \cap \mathcal{C}^p(T)$, where $L_2^p(T) \cap \mathcal{C}^p(T)$

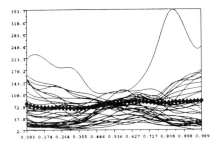

Figure 2. Data and their pointwise mean ♦

stands for $\underbrace{(L_2(T) \times \cdots \times L_2(T))}_{p \text{ times}} \cap \underbrace{(\mathcal{C}(T) \times \cdots \times \mathcal{C}(T))}_{p \text{ times}}$.
This space supplies structures, inner product and distance (defined using those of the p spaces $L_2(T)$), that are essential to express the classical PCA problem. Let us denote by

- $F^1, \ldots F^p$ the p functionals, $f_i = \left(f_i^1 f_i^2 \cdots f_i^p \right)$ the ith individual and $F = (F^1, \ldots, F^p) = (f_i^j)$ the $n \times p$ matrix of data

- w_i the weight associated with the ith individual, satisfying $w_i \geq 0$ and $\sum_i w_i = 1$ and $W = (w_i)$ the diagonal matrix whose i^{th} diagonal element is w_i.

As before, f_i^j is the value for F^j about its mean $\overline{F^j}$ corresponding to the ith individual.

A quick way to describe how PCA is extended is to say that the discrete index j used in the multivariate case is substituted by the continuous index t of the time. Assuming that we are working with no more that one functional (see 3.3 for the general case), the formulation of the problem becomes :

$$\max_{\substack{u_1,\ldots,u_d \in L_2(T) \cap \mathcal{C}(T) \\ \langle u_l, u_k \rangle_{L_2(T)} = \delta_{lk}}} \sum_i w_i \|\widehat{f_i^H}\|_{L_2(T)}^2 \qquad (3)$$

where H is the subspace spanned by $u_1, \ldots, u_d$.

For $d = 1$, u_1 is corresponding to the element of $L_2(T) \cap \mathcal{C}(T)$ whose shape shows the most important mode of variation around the mean $\overline{F^1}$ in the population. For $d = 2$, u_1 and u_2 are the two most important modes of variation in the curves f_i^1, and they are orthonormal in the sense of $L_2(T)$ inner product.

The following example should give the reader an insight of the analysis in the univariate case : the set of curves to analyse is shown on Fig. 2. Most of the individual curves can be well approached by the sum of the mean and a well chosen linear combination of u_1 and u_2. PCA reveals that the two major modes of variation around the mean , u_1 and u_2, enable an approximation that restores 95% of the information brought by the set of curves (87% by the first mode and 8% by the second). The shape of u_1 is shown on figure 3. According to this decomposition of the variation, approx-

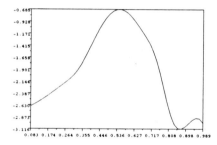

Figure 3. First mode of variation

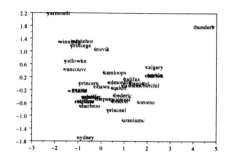

Figure 4. Projections of the individuals given by the two first principal components

imations of individual curves can be visualized as points of the subspace spanned by the couple $(u1, u2)$ (see Fig. 4).

This shortened example provides a rough overview of what univariate functional PCA resembles: multivariate PCA with the difference that interpretations of the modes of variation include dynamic aspects (developed below). But how does this apply to the analysis of several functionals? One could think of using PCA upon the separate functionals, since functional PCA provides smart decomposition for a functional. This would lead to several independant sets of results which would not tell anything about common features, independance or structural links of the functionals. PCA applied to several functionals helps in analysing co-variations as PCA does in the multivariate context.

A rigorous description of the PCA relies on more specifications about function spaces and other concepts we are using. The reader can refer to [10] for a detailed statement.

Before switching to the interpretation of the results, we should notice an important point for the effectiveness of functional PCA. As for the multivariate case, analysis are often driven by sampled data. Results drawn from sampled data are linked to results of the whole population in a good manner according to [4]. So working with sampled data may lead to satisfactory results under certain conditions.

3.3. Pointing out spots of valuable information

We shall now focus on the multivariate (we should rather say multifunctional) case, since it is where functional PCA fails in providing us with easy interpretations. Let us consider $p > 2$ functionals with values in $\mathcal{C}(T) \cap L_2(T)$. Illustrations coming along are derived from an analysis of meteorological data. These data involve four functionals: two of them were retrieved from the link `ftp://ego.psych.mcgill.ca` in the folder `/pub/ramsay/FDAfuns/`. The first one, denoted $F1$, gives monthly measures of the temperature in 35 weather stations. $F2$ gives the corresponding precipitations. $F3$

and $F4$ were build for illustrative purpose: $F3 = 50(1 - \cos(\frac{2\pi t}{12})) - 4F1 + 3F2$ and $F4 = \sin(F1F2)$. The measure of each F^i on some individuals of a population brings us to work within the usual setting of the PCA. Each individual is represented by an element of $\mathcal{C}^p(T) \cap L_2^p(T)$, which forms a separable Hilbert space with the inner product defined by

$$\langle x, y \rangle = \sum_{1..p} \int_T x_j(t) y_j(t) dt = \sum_{1..p} \langle x_j, y_j \rangle_{L_2(T)} \quad (4)$$

The decomposition, limited to the d first terms, provides the following approximation for the data :

$$\begin{pmatrix} f_1^1 \cdots f_1^p \\ \vdots \\ f_n^1 \cdots f_n^p \end{pmatrix} \approx \sum_{k=1..d} \begin{pmatrix} \sum_{j=1}^p \left\langle f_1^j, u_k^j \right\rangle_{L_2(T)} \\ \vdots \\ \sum_{j=1}^p \left\langle f_n^j, u_k^j \right\rangle_{L_2(T)} \end{pmatrix} \begin{pmatrix} u_k^1 \\ \vdots \\ u_k^p \end{pmatrix}'$$

$$(5)$$

where the kth term can be rewritten

$$\begin{pmatrix} \langle f_1, u_k \rangle_{L_2^p(T)} \\ \vdots \\ \langle f_n, u_k \rangle_{L_2^p(T)} \end{pmatrix} u_k \quad (6)$$

Abiding by old habits, one should firstly examine the eigenvalues to observe how inertia is restored by each principal axis, bearing in mind the initial inertia (Fig.5(a) shows eigenvalues accrued taken in decreasing order). Ordinary criterions should help to guess how developed should the approximation (5) be. But whereas PCA upon real random variables would straightly focus on several graphics of projection, here analysis shall be pursued with a scrutiny of the structure of eigenvector-space. [13] suggests to have a look at the shapes of the coordinates, but also to plot those curves around the means of the functionals. Indeed, the way a phenomenon is perceived may implicitly take into account the mean. But for some p greater than say 4, the systematic examination of those graphics may only confuse the analyst, since there may be an awful lot of these graphics ($2 \times p \times d$ to be precise). Before investigating them, we should learn how to pick the right ones. For example, quality of the approximation may be considered relatively to each functional by assessing the inertia of the approximation of F^j stemming from u_k: Fig. 5(b) shows the part of inertia restored by the ith coordinate of u_1 for F_i. All but the fourth coordinate seem to deserve attention.

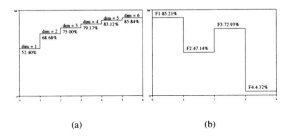

(a)   (b)

Figure 5. Cumulative parts of inertia and inertia for each functional

Supposing that some of the F^j are of similar nature and that the corresponding coordinates for some eigenvector are also close, one can imagine that the information brought by these coordinates is highly redundant! Grouping functionals relatively to some mode of variation should help the analyst to reduce the dimensionality intrinsic to the coordinates. Using the coordinates of the eigenvector as inputs for a univariate functional PCA seems advisable since it provides us an idea of how many groups are to be formed (the number of PC of this last PCA) but also the modes of variation those groups represent (the eigenvectors).

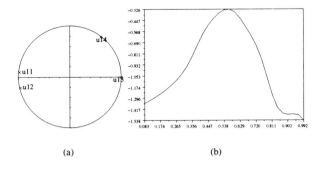

(a)   (b)

Figure 6. Projections of normalized u_1^j and first mode of variation

Applied to the coordinates of u_1, PCA reveals that they can be expressed simply with their mean and a single mode of variation: Fig. 6(a) synthetise the fact that the u_1^j are well represented by two modes of deviation from their mean. Each point represents the projection of a $\|.\|_{L^2}$-normalized coordinate; the closer a point is from the unit circle, the better the quality of this projection is. Since information related to $F4$ is of minor interest and only $F4$ gives a reason to consider the second mode of variation, we can consider that only the first mode of variation (see Fig.6(b)) is worth being considered. The approximations of the u_1^j look quite good (Figs 7(a)&7(b)). We will see below how these informations help in interpreting the first principal axis.

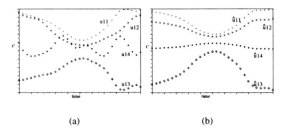

(a)   (b)

Figure 7. Original coordinates and their approximations

Another interesting ability for the analyst whould be to discriminate between the coordinates in order to discard from analyse directions that weakly contribute to the inertia restored by the corresponding axis. The expression of the inertia restored by the eigenvector u_k can be written

$$\sum_i w_i \left(\langle f_i^1, u_k^1 \rangle + \cdots + \langle f_i^p, u_k^p \rangle \right)^2 \qquad (7)$$

whose terms can be regrouped as follows:

$$\sum_l \left(\sum_i w_i \langle f_i^l, u_k^l \rangle^2 \right) + \sum_{l<j} \left(2 \times \sum_i w_i \langle f_i^l, u_k^l \rangle \langle f_i^j, u_k^j \rangle \right) \qquad (8)$$

A rapid step towards the analysis of these quantities is to take a glance at the following $p \times p$-matrix, giving the percentages of the inertia of u_k associated to them:

$$\frac{100}{\lambda_k} \times \begin{pmatrix} \sum_i w_i \langle f_i^1, u_k^1 \rangle^2 & \cdots & 2\sum_i w_i \langle f_i^1, u_k^1 \rangle \langle f_i^p, u_k^p \rangle \\ 0 & \ddots & \vdots \\ \vdots & & \cdot 2\sum_i w_i \langle f_i^{p-1}, u_k^{p-1} \rangle \langle f_i^p, u_k^p \rangle \\ 0 & 0 & \sum_i w_i \langle f_i^p, u_k^p \rangle^2 \end{pmatrix} \qquad (9)$$

Coordinates with preponderant or worthwhile contribution to quantity (8) should show up in matrix (9) with high-valued diagonal term and attract attention for correlation analysis on corresponding coefficients. The corresponding matrix (10) for u_1 shows that the terms linked to u_1^4 represent 4.32% of the inertia of the first principal axis. As felt earlier, one shall not pay much attention to u_1^4.

$$\begin{pmatrix} 16.91 & 15.73 & 30.03 & 1.77 \\ 0 & 9.20 & 9.63 & 0.79 \\ 0 & 0 & 14.19 & 1.59 \\ 0 & 0 & 0 & 0.17 \end{pmatrix} \quad (10)$$

Let us now focus on the interpretation that can be proposed for the first principal axis in our example. As shown by some stations well represented by this axis (see Fig. 8), stations with a high value upon the first principal axis will be dryer, colder and more sunny than the mean out of summer. These departures from their respective mean will all have dynamics stemming from the shape of the first mode of variation revealed by the PCA of the u_1^j (fig.6(b)). We observe that Rainfall and Temperatures are strongly positively correlated upon the year whereas u_{13} appears opposed to them.

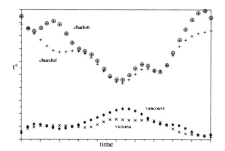

Figure 8. Temperature in well chosen stations

4. Application to cardiac motion analysis

4.1. Introduction

Cardiology is an active area of medical research. Tagged magnetic resonance imaging (MRI) allows 2D or 3D acquisitions upon a short interval of time of the heart motion from which various parameters can be extracted [9]. Among these parameters, those linked with the cardiac dynamic are of particular interest for the detection and the treatment of the pathologies of the heart. As tagged MRI becomes a popular technic, tools enabling the analysis of its outputs becomes a priority. Some analysis of certain parameters have already been undertaken [2, 8] , with some limitations : the parameters were considered in turn, only at few locations of the heart and at precise physiological instants. [3] proposes an approach for systematic and exhaustive analysis

of spatio-temporal deformation parameters (STDP) of the myocardium of the left ventricule during the systolic phase. Although time is treated as a continuous parameter and each region of the left ventricule is considered, information is infered without considering the set of tags as a spatial continuum. Our contribution is to show that functional PCA brings some information while spatio-temporal parameters are taken as continuous parameters. Thus, the analysis is shifted to a more global level : the level of the heart.

4.2. Applying functional PCA to the STDPs of the heart

The data analysed here are 28 STDPs extracted from 3D acquisitions of the left ventricule upon a short interval of time containing one systolic phase. Thus, for each individual, 28 parameters are known for a finite number of instants at each point of a given 3D-mesh of the left ventricule, as well as the motion of each point of the mesh. It is important to understand that a point of the mesh correspond to an anatomical location which plays the role of a landmark that is followed upon the time. We assume for simplicity that the measures during the tagged MRI and the process of extraction of the various parameters from MRI data leads to common features : the dimensions of the mesh defining the heart wall are identical, and the measure instants, identical in number, respectively correspond to the same physiological times for each individual. Another important hypothesis is that the tags correspond to the same anatomical locations accros the individuals : this is a necessary condition for the definition of a domain of integration common to all individuals.

Let us denote Ω a subset of $\mathbb{R}^3$ representing a model for the material configuration of the left ventricule of the heart (Fig. 9) and T the interval of physiological time. Given an

Figure 9. The material configuration Ω

anatomical landmark represented by $X \in \Omega$, its position at the time t for the ith individual is given by

$$x_i(X, t) = \begin{pmatrix} \alpha_i(X, t) \\ \beta_i(X, t) \\ \gamma_i(X, t) \end{pmatrix} \quad (11)$$

where α_i, β_i and γ_i are the coordinates in the chosen referential.

Differentiability and square integrability upon $\Omega \times T$ are natural features of the functions x_i. It is also true for the functions f_i^j which are realisations of the F^j since each F^j is a PSTD. Therefore individuals can be considered as points of $L_2^{28}(\Omega \times T) \cap C^{28}(\Omega \times T)$.

We define the inertia of the ith individual with

$$\sum_{j=1..28} \int_T \int_{\Omega_t} f_{ij}^2 (x_i, t)\, dx_i dt \qquad (12)$$

where $\Omega_t = x_i(\Omega, t)$. Eq. 12 can be rewriten, using the substitution formula

$$\sum_{j=1..28} \int_T \int_{\Omega} f_{ij}^2 (x_i(X, t), t) \left| \det J_{x_i(.,t)}(X) \right| dX dt \quad (13)$$

where $J_{x_i(.,t)}$ is the jacobian matrix of the function $x_i(.,t) : \mathbb{R}^3 \to \mathbb{R}^3$. From this definition of inertia we derive the following inner product for the individuals i and i'

$$\langle f_i, f_{i'} \rangle = \sum_{j=1}^{28} \int_T \int_{\Omega} f_{ij} (x_i(X, t), t)\, f_{i'j}(x_{i'}(X, t), t) \times$$
$$\left| \det J_{x_i(.,t)}(X) \det J_{x_{i'}(.,t)}(X) \right| dX dt \quad (14)$$

With this inner product, $L_2^{28}(\Omega \times T) \cap C^{28}(\Omega \times T)$ is a separable Hilbert space. Thus, functional PCA applies to our framework.

4.3. Insight of the results

$\Omega \times T$ is a subset of a $4D$ (or $3D + T$) space (Fig. 10). Visualizing the elements of $L_2(\Omega \times T) \cap C(\Omega \times T)$ may lead to unusual representation but remains possible. The

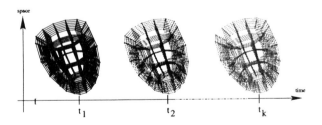

Figure 10. Representation of the domain $\Omega \times T$

proposed representation here relies on the use of color and transparency over our material configuration Ω within an animated graphic (Fig. 11). More accurately, it consists of the animation of the colors upon Ω, where transparency allows an insight through the whole ventricule. Given f,

an element of $L_2(\Omega \times T) \cap C(\Omega \times T)$, its value at a fixed location of the domain is represented by a point at the same spacio-temporal location with a color defined as follows :

- The value 0 corresponds to white

- Let us denote M the maximum value of $abs(f)$ over $\Omega \times T$. If $M \neq 0$, then a positive (resp. negative) value of f will be subsituted by a mixed color of white and red (resp. blue). The closer to M (resp. $-M$) the value is, the more red (resp. blue) the point will be.

Of course, this substitution involves a loss of precision, since values are replaced by colors, but it allows an overview of what happens over the ventricule during the systolic phase in a way that is easily understandable.

Figure 11. Extracts of the representation of element of $L_2(\Omega \times T) \cap C(\Omega \times T)$

4.4. Mining functional PCA results

The visualization of elements of $L_2(\Omega \times T) \cap C(\Omega \times T)$ such as the pointwise means of the functionals or the coordinates of eigenvectors is complex. To consider 28 functions at a glance and to infer something about their covariation is here impossible. This comes from the complexity of the studied objects and expecting graphics that would drastically simplify these objects is something of an illusion.

Applying the guide lines proposed in 3.3 helps in focusing the concentration of the analyst : Fig. 12 shows what functionals are well approximated by the first eigenvector and the evaluation of the matrix 9 is useful to differentiate among these the ones which also have a strong covariation with the others functional from those which weakly covariate with some others.

Thus, for a given eigenvalue, it is possible to discard some functionals before analysing the structure of the associated eigenvector. Applying functional PCA to the coordinates of a given eigenvector also prevents from dissipating attention. It provides the dimensionality of the modes of variations present in the coordinates as well as the groups of coordinates that should be considered as close from each other.

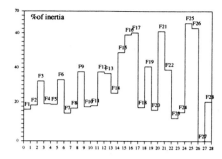

Figure 12. Inertia restored by u_1 for each F^j

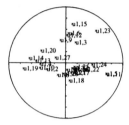

Figure 13. Projections of the coordinates

5. Concluding remarks

What makes the application of PCA to functional data so different is the care to take about each principal axis i.e each eigenvector and specially about its coordinates. Each coordinate is a complex object on its own. Its shape and its contribution to variability should be finely analysed twice: separately and together with the other coordinates. Outcomes from the processes proposed should help to:

- discard worthless part of information,

- outline important coordinates (relatively to their contribution to inertia)

- shrink results about eigenvector-space structure

- make easier the interpretation of principal axes

Our proposals for mining the raw outputs of the functional PCA have been illustrated within the original framework of the cardic motion analysis, where the considered functionals F^i have their values in $L_2(\Omega \times T) \cap \mathcal{C}(\Omega \times T)$, with $\Omega \subset \mathbb{R}^3$. These guide lines have revealed themselves as an efficient way to face the complexity of the objects under study. An application to the detection of abnormal motion of the heart is under progress.

Functional PCA is like a second wind in the area of data analysis. New perspectives for data mining systems seem to appear whereas the growth of the complexity of the studied objects widens the scope of the possible analysis.

References

[1] T. Anderson. Asymptotic theory for principal component analysis. *Ann. Math. Statis*, pages 122–148, 1963.

[2] N. Clark, N. Reichek, P. Bergey, H. E.A., B. D., P. L., and A. L. Circumferential myocardial shortening in the normal human left ventricle. assesment by magnetic resonance imaging using spatial modulation of magnetisation. *Circulation*, pages 67–74, 1991.

[3] P. Clarysse, M. Han, P. Croisille, and I. Magnin. Esploratory analysis of the spatio-temporal deformation of the myocardium during systole from tagged mri. *IEEE Transactions on biomedical engineering*, To appear.

[4] J. DAUXOIS, A. POUSSE, and Y. Romain. Asymptotic theory for the principal component analysis of a vector random function : some applications to statistical inference. *Journal of multivariate analysis*, pages 136–154, 1982.

[5] A. Jain. *Fundamentals of digital image processing*. Prentice-Hall International Editions, 1989.

[6] I. Jolliffe. *Principal componant analysis*. Springer, 1986.

[7] J. Kleffe. Principal components of random variables with values in a separable hilbert space. *Mathematische operationsforchung und statistik*, pages 391–406, 1973.

[8] J. Marcus, M. Götte, A. Van Rossum, J. Kuijer, R. Heethaar, L. Axel, and C. Visser. Myocardial function in infarcted and remote regions early after infarction in man : assesment by magnetic resonance tagging and strain analysis. *Magn. Res. Med.*, pages 803–810, 1997.

[9] J. Montagnat. *Modèles déformables pour la ségmentation et la modélisation d'images médicales 3D et 4D*. PhD thesis, INRIA and Université de Nice Sophia-Antipolis, 1999.

[10] F. Ocana, A. Aguilera, and M. Valderrama. Functional principal components analysis by choice of norm. *Journal of multivariate analysis*, pages 262–276, 1999.

[11] J. Ramsay, R. Bock, and T. Gasser. Comparison of height acceleration curves in the fels, zurich, and berkeley growth data. *Annals of Human Biology*, pages 413–426, 1995.

[12] J. Ramsay and C. Dalzel. Some tools for functionnal data analysis (with discussion). *Journal of the Royal Statistical Society*, pages 539–572, 1991.

[13] J. Ramsay and B. Silverman. *Functional Data Analysis*. Springer Series in Statistics, 1997.

[14] G. Saporta. *Probabilités, analyse des données et statistique*. EditionsTechnip, 1990.

[15] M. Volle. *Analyse des données*. Economica, 1991.

Unsupervised Segmentation of Categorical Time Series into Episodes

Paul Cohen, Brent Heeringa
Department of Computer Science
University of Massachusetts, Amherst
Amherst, MA 01003
{cohen, heeringa}@cs.umass.edu

Niall Adams
Department of Mathematics
Imperial College
London, UK
n.adams@ic.ac.uk

Abstract

This paper describes an unsupervised algorithm for segmenting categorical time series into episodes. The VOTING-EXPERTS algorithm first collects statistics about the frequency and boundary entropy of ngrams, then passes a window over the series and has two "expert methods" decide where in the window boundaries should be drawn. The algorithm successfully segments text into words in four languages. The algorithm also segments time series of robot sensor data into subsequences that represent episodes in the life of the robot. We claim that VOTING-EXPERTS finds meaningful episodes in categorical time series because it exploits two statistical characteristics of meaningful episodes.

1 Introduction

Though we live in a continuous world, we have the impression that experience comprises episodes: writing a paragraph, having lunch, going for a walk, and so on. Episodes have hierarchical structure; for instance, writing a paragraph involves thinking of what to say, saying it, editing it; and these are themselves episodes. Do these examples of episodes have anything in common? Is there a domain-independent, formal notion of episode sufficient, say, for an agent to segment continuous experience into meaningful units?

One can distinguish three ways to identify episode boundaries: First, they may be *marked*, as spaces mark word boundaries and promoters mark coding regions in DNA. Second, episodes may be *recognized*. For instance, we recognize nine words in the sequence "itwasabright-colddayinapriland". Third we might *infer* episode boundaries given the statistical structure of a series. For example, "juxbtbcsjhiudpmeebzjobqsjmboe" is formally (statistically) identical with "itwasabrightcolddayinapriland" — one is obtained from the other by replacing each letter with

the adjacent one in the alphabet — however, the latter is easily segmented by recognition whereas the former requires inference.

This paper proposes two statistical characteristics of episode boundaries and reports experiments with an unsupervised algorithm called VOTING-EXPERTS based on these characteristics. We offer the conjecture that these characteristics are domain-independent and illustrate the point by segmenting text in four languages.

2 The Episode Boundary Problem

Suppose we remove all the spaces and punctuation from a text, can an algorithm figure out where the word boundaries should go? Here is the result of running VOTING-EXPERTS on the first 500 characters of George Orwell's *1984*. The ⋆ symbols are induced boundaries:

Itwas ⋆ a ⋆ bright ⋆ cold ⋆ day ⋆ in ⋆ April ⋆ andthe ⋆ clock-
swere ⋆ st ⋆ ri ⋆ king ⋆ thi ⋆ rteen ⋆ Winston ⋆ Smith ⋆ his
⋆ chin ⋆ nuzzl ⋆ edinto ⋆ his ⋆ brea ⋆ st ⋆ in ⋆ aneffort ⋆ to
⋆ escape ⋆ the ⋆ vilewind ⋆ slipped ⋆ quickly ⋆ through ⋆ the
⋆ glass ⋆ door ⋆ sof ⋆ Victory ⋆ Mansions ⋆ though ⋆ not ⋆
quickly ⋆ en ⋆ ought ⋆ oprevent ⋆ aswirl ⋆ ofgrit ⋆ tydust ⋆
from ⋆ ent ⋆ er ⋆ inga ⋆ long ⋆ with ⋆ himThe ⋆ hall ⋆ ways
⋆ meltof ⋆ boiled ⋆ cabbage ⋆ and ⋆ old ⋆ ragmatsA ⋆ tone ⋆
endof ⋆ it ⋆ acoloured ⋆ poster ⋆ too ⋆ large ⋆ for ⋆ indoor ⋆
dis ⋆ play ⋆ hadbeen ⋆ tack ⋆ ed ⋆ tothe ⋆ wall ⋆ It ⋆ depicted
⋆ simplya ⋆ n ⋆ enormous ⋆ face ⋆ more ⋆ than ⋆ ametre ⋆
widethe ⋆ faceof ⋆ aman ⋆ of ⋆ about ⋆ fortyfive ⋆ witha ⋆
heavy ⋆ black ⋆ moustache ⋆ and ⋆ rugged ⋆ ly ⋆ handsome ⋆
featur

The segmentation is imperfect: Words are run together (*Itwas, aneffort*) and broken apart (*st ⋆ ri ⋆ king*). Occasionally, words are split between segments (*to in en ⋆ ought ⋆ oprevent*). Still, the segmentation is surprisingly good when one considers that it is based on nothing more than statistical features of subsequences of letters — not words, as no word boundaries are available — in Orwell's text.

How can an algorithm identify subsequences that are *meaningful* in a domain lacking any knowledge about the domain; and particularly, lacking positive and negative training instances of meaningful subsequences? VOTING-EXPERTS must somehow detect *domain-independent* indicators of the boundaries of meaningful subsequences. In fact, this is a good description of what it does. It implements a weak theory of domain-independent features of meaningful units. The first of these features is that entropy remains low inside meaningful units and increases at their boundaries; the second is that high-frequency subsequences are more apt to be meaningful than low-frequency ones.

3   Characteristics of Episodes

The features of episodes that we have implemented in the VOTING-EXPERTS algorithm are called *boundary entropy* and *frequency*:

Boundary entropy. Every unique subsequence is characterized by the distribution of subsequences that follow it; for example, the subsequence "en" in this sentence repeats seven times and is followed by tokens c (4 times), t, s and ", a distribution of symbols with an entropy value (1.66, as it happens). In general, every subsequence S has a boundary entropy, which is the entropy of the distribution of subsequences of length m that follow it. If S is an episode, then the boundary entropies of subsequences of S will have an interesting profile: They will start relatively high, then sometimes drop, then peak at the last element of S. The reasons for this are first, that the predictability of elements within an episode increases as the episode extends over time; and second, the elements that immediately follow an episode are relatively uncertain. Said differently, within episodes, we know roughly what will happen, but at episode boundaries we become uncertain.

Frequency. Episodes, recall, are meaningful sequences. They are patterns in a domain that we call out as special, important, valuable, worth committing to memory, worth naming, etc. One reason to consider a pattern meaningful is that one can use it for something, like prediction. (Predictiveness is another characteristic of episodes nicely summarized by entropy.) Rare patterns are less useful than common ones simply because they arise infrequently, so all human and animal learning places a premium on frequency. In general, episodes are common patterns, but not all common patterns are episodes.

4   Related work

Many methods have been developed for segmenting time series. Of these, many deal with continuous time series (e.g., [11]) and are not directly applicable to the problem we consider here. Some methods for categorical series are based on compression (e.g., [10]), but compression alone

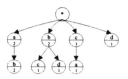

Figure 1. A trie having depth 3.

finds common, not necessarily meaningful, subsequences. Some methods are trained to find instances of patterns or templates (e.g., [9, 5]) or use a supervised form of compression (e.g., [12]), but we wanted an unsupervised method. There is some work on segmentation in the natural language and information retrieval literature, for instance, techniques for segmenting Chinese, which has no word boundaries in its orthography, but again, these methods are often supervised. The method in [14] is similar to ours, though it requires supervised training on very large corpora. Parsing based on mutual information used in [8] is similar to our notion of boundary entropy. [6] and [7] use boundary entropy (but not frequency information) to find separators, but we're interested in categorical data where explicit boundary demarcations are removed. [2] provides a developmentally plausible unsupervised algorithm for word segmentation, but the procedure assumes known utterance boundaries. [1] give an unsupervised segmentation procedure for Japanese, however it too supposes known sequence boundaries. With minor alterations, their segmentation technique is applicable to our domain, but we found that VOTING-EXPERTS consistently outperforms it. We know of no related research on characteristics of meaningful episodes, that is, statistical markers of boundaries of meaning-carrying subsequences.

5   The Voting Experts Algorithm

VOTING-EXPERTS includes experts that attend to boundary entropy and frequency and is easily extensible to include experts that attend to other characteristics of episodes. The algorithm simply moves a window across a time series and asks for each location in the window whether to "cut" the series at that location. Each expert casts a single vote. Each location takes n steps to traverse a window of size n, and is seen by the experts in n different contexts, and may accrue up to n votes from each expert. Given the results of voting, we cut the series at locations with high vote counts. Here are the steps of the algorithm:
Build an ngram trie of depth $n + 1$. Nodes at level $i + 1$ of the trie represent ngrams of length i. The children of a node are the extensions of the ngram represented by the node. For example, $a\ b\ c\ a\ b\ d$ produces the depth 3 trie in Figure 1
Every ngram of length 2 or less in the sequence $a\ b\ c\ a\ b$

d is represented by a node in this tree. The numbers in the lower half of the nodes represent the frequencies of the subsequences. For example, the subsequence ab occurs twice, and every occurrence of a is followed by b.

For the first 10,000 characters in Orwell's text, an ngram trie of depth 8 includes 33774 nodes, of which 9109 are leaf nodes. That is, there are over nine thousand unique subsequences of length 7 in this sample of text, although the average frequency of these subsequences is 1.1—most occur exactly once. The average frequencies of subsequences of length 1 to 7 are 384.4, 23.1, 3.9, 1.8, 1.3, 1.2, and 1.1.

Calculate boundary entropy. The boundary entropy of an ngram is the entropy of the distribution of tokens that can extend the ngram. The entropy of a discrete random variable X is

$$H(X) = - \sum_{x \in X} p(x) \log p(x)$$

Boundary entropy is easily calculated from the trie. For example, the node a in the tree above has entropy equal to zero because it has only one child, ab, whereas the entropy of node b is 1.0 because it has two equiprobable children, bc and bd. Clearly, only the first n levels of the ngram tree of depth $n + 1$ can have node entropy scores.

Standardize frequencies and boundary entropies. In most domains, there is a systematic relationship between the length and frequency of patterns; in general, short patterns are more common than long ones (e.g., on average, for subsets of 10,000 characters from Orwell's text, 64 of the 100 most frequent patterns are of length 2; 23 are of length 3, and so on). Our algorithm will compare the frequencies and boundary entropies of ngrams of different lengths, but in all cases we will be comparing how *unusual* these frequencies and entropies are, relative to other ngrams of the same length. To illustrate, consider the words "a" and "an." In the first 10000 characters of Orwell's text, "a" occurs 743 times, "an" 124 times, but "a" occurs only a little more frequently than other one-letter ngrams, whereas "an" occurs much more often than other two-letter ngrams. In this sense, "a" is ordinary, "an" is unusual. Although "a" is much more common than "an" it is much less unusual relative to other ngrams of the same length. To capture this notion, we standardize the frequencies and boundary entropies of the ngrams. To standardize a value in a sample, subtract the sample mean from the value and divide by the sample standard deviation. This has the effect of expressing the value as the number of standard deviations it is away from the sample mean. Standardized, the frequency of "a" is 1.1, whereas the frequency of "an" is 20.4. In other words, the frequency of "an" is 20.4 standard deviations above the mean frequency for sequences of the same length. We standardize boundary entropies in the same way, and for the same reason.

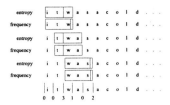

Figure 2. Sample execution of VOTING-EXPERTS.

Score potential segment boundaries. In a sequence of length k there are $k - 1$ places to draw boundaries between segments, and, thus, there are 2^{k-1} ways to divide the sequence into segments. Our algorithm is greedy in the sense that it considers just $k - 1$, not 2^{k-1}, ways to divide the sequence. It considers each possible boundary in order, starting at the beginning of the sequence. The algorithm passes a window of length n over the sequence, halting at each possible boundary. All of the locations within the window are considered, and each garners zero or one vote from each expert. Because we have two experts, for boundary entropy and frequency respectively, each location may accrue a maximum of $2n$ votes. This is illustrated in Figure 2. A window of length 3 is passed along the sequence itwasacold. Initially, the window covers itw. The entropy and frequency experts each decide where they could best insert a boundary within the window (more on this, below). The entropy expert favors the boundary between t and w, while the frequency expert favors the boundary between w and whatever comes next. Then the window moves one location to the right and the process repeats. This time, both experts decide to place the boundary between t and w. The window moves again and both experts decide to place the boundary after s, the last token in the window. Note that each potential boundary location (e.g., between t and w) is seen n times for a window of size n, but it is considered in a slightly different context each time the window moves. The first time the experts consider the boundary between w and a, they are looking at the window itw, and the last time, they are looking at was. In this way, each boundary gets up to $2n$ votes, or $n = 3$ votes from each of two experts. The wa boundary gets one vote, the tw boundary, three votes, and the sa boundary, two votes.

The experts use slightly different methods to evaluate boundaries and assign votes. Consider the window itw from the viewpoint of the boundary entropy expert. Each location in the window bounds an ngram to the left of the location; the ngrams are i, it, and itw, respectively. Each ngram has a standardized boundary entropy. The boundary entropy expert votes for the location that produces the ngram with the highest standardized boundary entropy. As it happens, for the ngram tree produced from Orwell's text, the standardized boundary entropies for i, it, and itw are 0.2, 1.39 and 0.02, so the boundary entropy expert opts to put a boundary after the ngram it.

The frequency expert places a boundary so as to maximize the sum of the standardized frequencies of the ngrams to the left and right of the boundary. Consider the window itw again. If the boundary is placed after i, then (for Orwell's text) the standardized frequencies of i and tw sum to 1.73; if the boundary is placed after it, then the standardized frequencies of it and w sum to 2.9; finally, if it is placed after itw, the algorithm has only the standardized frequency of itw to work with; it is 4.0. Thus, the frequency expert opts to put a boundary after itw.

Segment the sequence. Each potential boundary in a sequence accrues votes, as described above, and now we must evaluate the boundaries in terms of the votes and decide where to segment the sequence. Our method is a familiar "zero crossing" rule: If a potential boundary has a locally maximum number of votes, split the sequence at that boundary. In the example above, this rule causes the sequence itwasacold to be split after it and was. We confess to one embellishment on the rule: The number of votes for a boundary must exceed an absolute threshold, as well as be a local maximum. We found that the algorithm splits too often without this qualification.

Let us review the design of the experts and the segmentation rule, to see how they test the characteristics of episodes described earlier. The boundary entropy expert assigns votes to locations where the boundary entropy peaks locally, implementing the idea that entropy increases at episode boundaries. The frequency expert tries to find a "maximum likelihood tiling" of the sequence, a placement of boundaries that makes the ngrams to the left and right of the boundary as likely as possible. When both experts vote for a boundary, and especially when they vote repeatedly for the same boundary, it is likely to get a locally-maximum number of votes, and the algorithm is apt to split the sequence at that location.

6 Evaluation

In these experiments, induced boundaries stand in six relationships to episodes.

1. The boundaries coincide with the start and end of the episode;

2. The episode falls entirely within the boundaries and begins or ends at one boundary.

3. The episode falls entirely within the boundaries but neither the start nor the end of the episode correspond to a boundary.

4. One or more boundaries splits an episode, but the start and end of the episode coincide with boundaries.

5. Like case 4, in that boundaries split an episode, but only one end of the episode coincides with a boundary.

6. The episode is split by one or more boundaries and neither end of the episode coincides with a boundary.

These relationships are illustrated graphically in Figure 3, following the convention that horizontal lines denote actual episodes, and vertical lines denote induced boundaries. The cases can be divided into three groups. In cases 1 and 4, boundaries correspond to both ends of the episode; in cases 2 and 5, they correspond to one end of the episode; and in cases 3 and 6, they correspond to neither end. We call these cases *exact*, *dangling*, and *lost* to evoke the idea of episodes located exactly, dangling from a single boundary, or lost in the region between boundaries.

We use both hit and false-positive rates to measure the accuracy of our episode finding algorithms. To better explain the trade-off between hits and false-positives we employ the F-measure [13]. This standard comparison metric finds the harmonic mean between precision and recall and is defined as

$$\text{F-measure} = \frac{2 \times \text{Precision} \times \text{Recall}}{\text{Precision} + \text{Recall}}$$

where Recall is the hit-rate and Precision is the ratio of correct hits to proposed hits. Note that the difference in proposed and correct hits yields the number of false positives. Higher F-measures often indicate better overall performance.

For control purposes we compare VOTING-EXPERTS with two control conditions. The first generates a random, sorted sequence of boundaries that is equal in size to the actual number of episodes. We call this procedure RANDOM-SAMPLE. The second control condition induces a boundary at every location. We call this procedure ALL-LOCATIONS.

In many of the experiments, we compare the results of VOTING-EXPERTS with another unsupervised algorithm, SEQUITUR, which also finds structure in categorical time series. SEQUITUR is a compression-based algorithm that builds a context-free grammar from a string of discrete tokens [10]. It has successfully identified structure in both

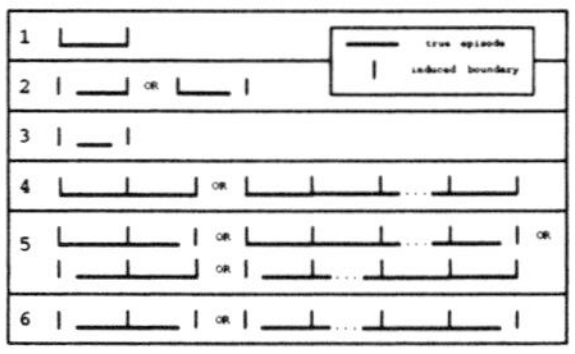

Figure 3. A graphical depiction of the relationships between boundaries and episodes.

102

text and music. This structure is denoted by the rules of the induced grammar. Expanding the rules reveals boundary information. In our experiments, expanding only the rule associated with the start symbol – what we refer to as level 1 expansion – most often gives the highest F-measure.

6.1 Word Boundaries

We removed spaces and punctuation from texts in four languages and accessed how well VOTING-EXPERTS could induce word boundaries. We take word boundaries as our gold standard for meaning-carrying units in text because they provide, in most cases, the most unambiguous and un-contentious denotation of episodes. Clearly word prefixes and suffixes might also carrying meaning, but most humans would likely segment a discrete stream of text into words.

6.1.1 English

We ran VOTING-EXPERTS, SEQUITUR, and both control conditions on the first 50,000 characters of Orwell's *1984*. The detailed results are given in Table 1. VOTING-EXPERTS performs best when the window length is 7 and the threshold 4. The algorithm induced 12153 boundaries, for a mean episode length of 4.11. The mean word length of the text is 4.49. The algorithm induces boundaries at 80% of the true word boundaries (the hit rate) missing 20% of the word boundaries. 27% of the induced boundaries did not correspond to word boundaries (the false positive rate). Exact cases, described above, constitute 62.6% of all cases; that is, 62.6% of the words were bounded at both ends by induced boundaries. Dangling and lost cases constitute 33.9% and 3.3% of all cases, respectively. Said differently, only 3.3% of all words in the text got lost between episode boundaries. These tend to be short words, in fact, 59% of the lost words have length 3 or shorter and 85% have length 5 or shorter. In contrast, all 89% of the words for which the algorithm found exact boundaries have length 3 or longer.

SEQUITUR performs best when expanding only to the level 1 boundaries. That is, it achieves its highest F-measure by not further expanding any non-terminals off the sentential rule. Expanding to further levels leads to a substantial increase in the false positive rate and hence an overall decrease in F-measure. For example, when expanding to level 5, SEQUITUR identified 78% of the word boundaries correctly, 20% dangling and only 2% missed. This happens because it is inducing more boundaries. In fact, at level 5, the false-positive rate of 68% is near the 78% maximum false positive rate achieved by ALL-LOCATIONS. The same behavior occurs to a smaller extent in VOTING-EXPERTS when the splitting threshold is decreased. For example, with a window length of 4 and a threshold of 2, VOTING-EXPERTS finds 74% of the word boundaries exactly but the

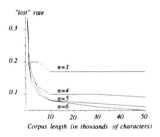

Figure 4. The proportion of "lost" words as a function of corpus length.

F-measure decreases because of a corresponding increase in the false-positive rate. In general, SEQUITUR finds likely patterns, but these patterns did not always correspond to word boundaries.

It is easy to ensure that all word boundaries are found, and no word is lost: use ALL-LOCATIONS to induce a boundary between each letter. However, this strategy induces a mean episode length of 1.0, much shorter than the mean word length. The false-positive count equals the total number of non-boundaries in the text and the false-positive rate converges to the ratio of non-boundaries to total locations (.78). In contrast, VOTING-EXPERTS finds roughly the same number of episodes as there are words in the text and loses very few words between boundaries. This success is evident in the high F-measure (.76) achieved by VOTING-EXPERTS. Not surprisingly, RANDOM-SAMPLE performed poorest on the text.

The appropriate control conditions for this experiment were run and yielded the expected results: VOTING-EXPERTS performs marginally less well when it is required to segment text it has not seen. For example, if the first 10,000 characters of Orwell's text are used to build the ngram tree, and then the algorithm is required to segment the next 10,000 characters, there is a very slight decrement in performance. The algorithm performs very poorly given texts of random words, that is, subsequences of random letters. The effects of the corpus size and the window length are shown in Figure 4. The proportion of "lost" words (cases 3 and 6, above) is plotted on the vertical axis, and the corpus length is plotted on the horizontal axis. Each curve in the graph corresponds to a window length, k. The proportion of lost words becomes roughly constant for corpora of length 10,000 and higher.

Said differently, corpora of this length seem to be required for the algorithm to estimate boundary entropies and frequencies accurately. As to window length, recall that a window of length n means each potential boundary is considered n times by each expert, in n different contexts. Clearly, it helps to increase the window size, but the benefit

Algorithm	F-measure	Hit Rate	F.P. Rate	Exact %	Dangling %	Lost %
VOTING-EXPERTS	.76	.80	.27	.63	.34	.03
SEQUITUR	.58	.58	.43	.30	.56	.14
ALL-LOCATIONS	.36	1.0	.78	1.0	0.0	0.0
RANDOM-SAMPLE	.21	.22	.79	.05	.34	.61

Table 1. Results of running four different algorithms on George Orwell's *1984*.

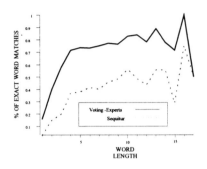

Figure 5. A comparison of exact match-rate on a per-word basis between SEQUITUR and VOTING-EXPERTS.

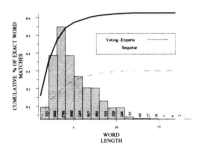

Figure 6. A comparison of cumulative exact match-rate over word length for SEQUITUR and VOTING-EXPERTS. The background histogram depicts the distribution of word lengths in the Orwell corpus.

diminishes.

Further evidence of VOTING-EXPERTS ability to find meaningful word boundaries is given in Figures 5 and 6. In Figure 5 we graph the percentage of exact word matches as a function of word length. For example, SEQUITUR exactly matches 30% of words having length 15 while VOTING-EXPERTS matches 70%. The curves converge at word length 17 because only two words in our corpus have length 17 and both algorithms find only one of them. The curves roughly mimic each other except in the word length interval from 2 to 4. In this period, VOTING-EXPERTS accelerates over SEQUITUR because it finds disproportionately more exact matches than SEQUITUR. This phenomenon is even easier to see in Figure 6. Here cumulative percentage of exact word matches is plotted as a function of word lengths and the distribution of word lengths is given behind the curves. The slope of VOTING-EXPERTS is steeper than SEQUITUR in the interval from 2 to 4 revealing the success it has on the most frequent word lengths. Furthermore, words with length 2, 3, and 4 comprise over 57% of the Orwell corpus, so at places where accuracy is perhaps most important, VOTING-EXPERTS performs well.

6.1.2 Chinese, German and Roma-ji

As a test of the generality of VOTING-EXPERTS, we ran it on corpora of Roma-ji, Chinese and German texts. Roma-ji

is a transliteration of Japanese into roman characters. The Roma-ji corpus was a set of Anime lyrics comprising 19163 characters. The Chinese text comes from Guo Jim's Mandarin Chinese PH corpus. The PH corpus is taken from stories in newspaper texts and is encoded in in the standard GB-scheme. Franz Kafka's *The Castle* in the original German comprised the final text. For comparison purposes we selected the first 19163 characters of Kafka's text and the same number of characters from *1984* and the PH corpus. As always, we stripped away spaces and punctuation, and the algorithm induced word boundaries. The window length was 6. The results are given in Table 2.

Clearly the algorithm is not biased to do well on English. In particular, it performs very well on Kafka's text, losing only 4% of the words and identifying 61% exactly. The algorithm performs less well with the Roma-ji text; it identifies fewer boundaries accurately (i.e., places 34% of its boundaries within words) and identifies fewer words exactly. VOTING-EXPERTS performed worst on Chinese corpus. Only 42% of the boundaries were identified although the false positive rate is an extremely low 7%. The explanation for these results has to do with the lengths of words in the corpora. We know that the algorithm loses disproportionately many short words. Words of length 2 make

VOTING-EXPERTS	F-measure	Hit Rate	F.P. Rate	Exact %	Dangling %	Lost %
German	.75	.79	.31	.61	.25	.04
English	.71	.76	.33	.58	.38	.04
Roma-ji	.65	.64	.34	.37	.53	.10
Chinese	.57	.42	.07	.13	.57	.30

Table 2. Results of running VOTING-EXPERTS **on Franz Kafka's** *The Castle*, **Orwell's** *1984*, **a subset of the Chinese PH corpus of newspaper stories, and a set of Roma-ji Anime lyrics.**

up 39% of the Chinese corpus, 32% of the Roma-ji corpus, 17% of the Orwell corpus, and 10% of the Kafka corpus, so it is not surprising that the algorithm performs worst on the Chinese corpus and best on the Kafka corpus.

If we incorporate the knowledge that Chinese words are rather short in length by decreasing the splitting threshold, we can increase the F-measure of VOTING-EXPERTS to 77% on the PH corpus. In general, knowledge of the mean episode length can help improve the boundary detection of VOTING-EXPERTS. Like [1], pretraining on a small amount of segmented text may be sufficient to find suitable window and threshold values.

6.2 Robot Episodes

We ran VOTING-EXPERTS and SEQUITUR on a multivariate timeseries of robot controller data comprising 17788 time steps and 65 unique states. Each state was mapped to a unique identifier, and these tokens were given to the algorithm as input. The timeseries data was collected with a Pioneer 2 mobile robot, equipped with sonar and a Sony pan-tilt-zoom camera. The robot, under control of a hybrid subsumption architecture, wandered around a room-size playpen for 30 minutes looking for interesting objects. Upon finding an object, the robot orbited it for a few minutes. The multivariate timeseries consisted of eight binary variables representing different controllers in our agent architecture. Each variable is 1 when its corresponding controller is active and 0 when its inactive, so potentially, we have $2^8 = 256$ different states, but as mentioned earlier, only 65 manifested during the experiment.

- MOVE-FORWARD
- TURN
- COLLISION-AVOIDANCE
- VIEW-INTERESTING-OBJECT
- RELOCATE-INTERSTING-OBJECT
- SEEK-INTERESTING-OBJECT
- CENTER-CHASIS-ON-OBJECT
- CENTER-CAMERA-ON-OBJECT

This timeseries can be broken up into five different observable robot behaviors. Each behavior represents a quali-

tatively different episode in the timeseries. We denote these episodes as

- FLEEING
- WANDERING
- AVOIDING
- ORBITING-OBJECT
- APPROACHING-OBJECT

Table 3 summarizes the results of running VOTING-EXPERTS and SEQUITUR on the robot controller data. The definition of hit-rate and false-positive rate is slightly different here. Because the controller data can be noisy at the episode boundaries, we allow *hits* a window of length 1 in either temporal direction. For example, if we induce a boundary at location 10, but the actual boundary is at location 9, we still count it as a hit. We also enforce a rule that actual boundaries can only count once toward induced boundaries. For example, if we induce a boundary at 8 and count it as a hit toward the actual boundary 9, the induced boundary at 10 can no longer count toward 9.

The mean episode length in the robot controller data is 7.13. This length is somewhat smaller than expected because the robot often gets caught up in the corners of its playpen for periods of time and performs a series of wandering, avoiding, and fleeing behaviors to escape. The total number of true episodes was 2491. VOTING-EXPERTS induced 3038 episodes with a hit rate of 66% and a false-positive rate of 46% for a combined F-measure of 59%. Like on Orwell, VOTING-EXPERTS consistently outperforms SEQUITUR on the F-measure. SEQUITUR does best when expanding to the level 1 boundaries. The transition from level 1 to level 2 produces a sharp increase in the false-positive rate with a corresponding increase in hit rate, however the F-measure decreases slightly. At level 5, SEQUITUR loses only 8% of the episodes but its false-positive rate is 78%, which is near the maximum possible rate of 86%.

7 Conclusion

For an agent to generalize its experiences, it must divide them into meaningful units. The VOTING-EXPERTS

Robot Data	F-measure	Hit Rate	F.P. Rate	Exact %	Dangling Rate	Lost Rate
SEQUITUR						
Level 1	.55	.57	.47	.17	.37	.46
Level 2	.51	.77	.62	.34	.37	.29
Level 3	.32	.88	.71	.48	.33	.19
Level 4	.38	.94	.76	.56	.32	.12
Level 5	.36	.97	.78	.63	.29	.08
VOTING-EXPERTS						
Depth 7, Threshold 4	.59	.66	.46	.20	.39	.41
Depth 9, Threshold 6	.59	.60	.41	.18	.38	.44
Depth 5, Threshold 2	.56	.80	.56	.27	.42	.31

Table 3. Results of running SEQUITUR **and** VOTING-EXPERTS **on 30 minutes of robot controller data.**

algorithm uses statistical properties of categorical time series to segment them into episodes without supervision or prior training. Although the algorithm does not use explicit knowledge of words or robot behaviors, it detects episodes in these domains. The algorithm successfully segments texts into words in four languages. With less success, VOTING-EXPERTS segments robot controller data into activities. In the future we will examine how other, domain-independent experts can help improve performance. Additionally we are interested in unifying the frequency and boundary entropy experts to more accurately capture the balance of strengths and weaknesses of each method. On a related note, we could employ supervised learning techniques to learn a weigh parameter for the experts, however we favor the unification approach because it removes a parameter from the algorithm and keeps the method completely unsupervised, The idea that meaningful subsequences differ from meaningless ones in some formal characteristics—that syntactic criteria might help us identify semantic units—has practical as well as philosophical implications.

Acknowledgments

We are grateful to Ms. Sara Nishi for collecting the corpus of Anime lyrics. This research is supported by DARPA under contract numbers DARPA/USASMDCDASG60-99-C-0074 and DARPA/AFRLF30602-01-2-0580. The U.S. Government is authorized to reproduce and distribute reprints for governmental purposes notwithstanding any copyright notation hereon. The views and conclusions contained herein are those of the authors and should not be interpreted as necessarily representing the official policies or endorsements either expressed or implied, of DARPA or the U.S. Government.

References

[1] R. K. Ando and L. Lee. Mostly-unsupervised statistical segmentation of japanese: Application to kanji. In *Proceedings of North American Association for Computational Linguistics (NAACL)*, pages 241–248, 2000.

[2] M. R. Brent. An efficient, probabilistically sound algorithm for segmentation and word discovery. *Machine Learning*, 45(1–3):71–105, 1999.

[3] P. Cohen and N. Adams. An algorithm for segmenting categorical time series into meaningful episodes. In *Proceedings of Fourth Symposium on Intelligent Data Analysis*, pages 198–207. Springer, 2001.

[4] P. R. Cohen, B. Heeringa, and N. Adams. An unsupervised algorithm for segmenting categorical time series into episodes. In *Working Notes of the 2002 ESF Exploratory Workshop on Pattern Detection and Discovery in Data Mining (to appear)*, 2002.

[5] M. N. Garofalakis, R. Rastogi, and K. Shim. SPIRIT: Sequential pattern mining with regular expression constraints. In *The VLDB Journal*, pages 223–234, 1999.

[6] J. L. Hutchens and M. D. Alder. Finding structure via compression. In D. M. W. Powers, editor, *Proceedings of the Joint Conference on New Methods in Language Processing and Computational Natural Language Learning: NeMLaP3/CoNLL98*, pages 79–82. Association for Computational Linguistics, Somerset, New Jersey, 1998.

[7] A. Kempe. Experiments in unsupervised entropy?based corpus segmentation. In *Proc. Workshop on Computational Natural Language Learning (CoNLL)*, pages 7–13, Bergen, Norway, June 1999. SIGNLL/ACL.

[8] D. Magerman and M. Marcus. Parsing a natural language using mutual information statistics. In *Proceedings, Eighth National Conference on Artificial Intelligence (AAAI 90)*, pages 984–989, 1990.

[9] H. Mannila, H. Toivonen, and A. I. Verkamo. Discovery of frequent episodes in event sequences. *Data Mining and Knowledge Discovery*, 1(3):259–289, 1997.

[10] C. G. Nevill-Manning and I. H. Witten. Identifying hierarchical structure in sequences: A linear-time algorithm. *Journal of Artificial Intelligence Research*, 7(1):67–82, 1997.

[11] J. T. Oates. *Grounding Knowledge in Sensors: Unsupervised Learning for Language and Planning*. PhD thesis, Department of Computer Science, University of Massachusetts, 2001.

[12] W. J. Teahan, Y. Wen, R. J. McNab, and I. H. Witten. A compression-based algorithm for chinese word segmentation. *Computational Linguistics*, 26(3):375–393, 2000.

[13] C. J. Van Rijsbergen. *Information Retrieval, 2nd edition*. Dept. of Computer Science, University of Glasgow, 1979.

[14] G. M. Weiss and H. Hirsh. Learning to predict rare events in event sequences. In *Knowledge Discovery and Data Mining*, pages 359–363, 1998.

Speed-up Iterative Frequent Itemset Mining with Constraint Changes

Gao Cong   Bing Liu
School of Computing, National University of Singapore, Singapore 117543
E-mail: {conggao, liub}@comp.nus.edu.sg

Abstract

Mining of frequent itemsets is a fundamental data mining task. Past research has proposed many efficient algorithms for the purpose. Recent work also highlighted the importance of using constraints to focus the mining process to mine only those relevant itemsets. In practice, data mining is often an interactive and iterative process. The user typically changes constraints and runs the mining algorithm many times before satisfied with the final results. This interactive process is very time consuming. Existing mining algorithms are unable to take advantage of this iterative process to use previous mining results to speed up the current mining process. This results in enormous waste in time and in computation. In this paper, we propose an efficient technique to utilize previous mining results to improve the efficiency of current mining when constraints are changed. We first introduce the concept of tree boundary to summarize the useful information available from previous mining. We then show that the tree boundary provides an effective and efficient framework for the new mining. The proposed technique has been implemented in the contexts of two existing frequent itemset mining algorithms, FP-tree and Tree Projection. Experiment results on both synthetic and real-life datasets show that the proposed approach achieves dramatic saving in computation.

1. Introduction

Frequent itemset mining plays an essential role in mining association rules [3], correlations, sequential patterns, maximal patterns [4], etc. Although many efficient algorithms [3, 16, 1, 9] have been developed, mining of frequent itemsets remains to be a time consuming process [10], especially when the data size is large. To make the matter worse, in most practical applications, the user often needs to run the mining algorithm many times before satisfied with the final results. In each process, the user typically changes some parameters or constraints.

Considering a mining task with only the *minimum support* constraint (also called the *frequency* constraint), the user may initially set the minimum support to 5% and run a mining algorithm. After inspecting the returned

results, s/he finds that 5% is too high. S/he then decides to reduce the minimum support to 3% and runs the algorithm again. Usually, this process is repeated many times before s/he is satisfied with the final mining results.

This interactive and iterative mining process is very time consuming. Mining the dataset from scratch in each iteration is clearly inefficient because a large portion of the computation from previous mining is repeated in the new mining process. This results in enormous waste in computation and time. So far, limited work has been done to address this problem, and to the best of our knowledge there is still no effective and efficient solution.

In recent years, many constraints (apart from the traditional support and confidence constraints) are introduced into frequent itemset mining in order to find only those relevant itemsets [13, 10, 12]. On one hand, these additional constraints give the user more freedom to express his/her preferences. On the other hand, however, it often prolongs the mining process because the user may want to see the results of various combinations of constraint changes by running the mining algorithm more times. This makes mining using previous results for efficiency even more important.

Constraint changes can mean *tightening constraints* and *relaxing constraints*. Let us use an example to start the discussion.

Example: Consider that one sets the constraint that the average price of the items in an itemset is less than $100 in the old mining process (for a market basket problem). After inspecting the mining results, one finds that the results are not satisfactory. There are possible two reasons: (1) $100 is too low (many useful itemsets may not be discovered), and (2) $100 is too high (too many itemsets are generated). One may wish to change the average price to $150 or to $80 for the new mining. The question is "can we make use of the results from the old mining to speed up the new mining?"

It is straightforward to answer part of the question, i.e., when constraints are *tightened* (the solution space is reduced), e.g., when the average price of frequent itemsets is decreased. To obtain the new set of frequent itemsets under the new constraints, we can simply check the frequent itemsets from the old mining to filter out those itemsets that do not satisfy the new constraints. This filtering process is sufficient because the set of new frequent itemsets is only a subset of the old set.

When constraints are *relaxed* (the solution space is

0-7695-1754-4/02 $17.00 © 2002 IEEE   107

expanded), the problem becomes non-trivial as re-running the mining algorithm is needed to find those additional frequent itemsets. For instance, in the above example, when the average price of frequent itemsets is increased, more itemsets may be generated. The problem becomes even more complicated when multiple constraints are changed at the same time. The objective of this work is to study how to make use of the previous mining results to speed up re-mining when constraints are changed.

In this paper, we propose a novel technique to solve this problem. Using the relaxation of frequency constraint (the decrease of *minimum support*) as an example, we first propose the concept of *tree boundary* to summarize and to reorganize the previous mining results. We then show that the additional frequent itemsets can be generated in the new mining process by extending only the itemsets on the *tree boundary* without re-generating the frequent itemsets produced in the previous mining (note that our tree boundary based technique is quite different from the incremental mining approaches based on negative border). The proposed technique has been implemented in the contexts of two frequent itemset mining algorithms, FP-tree [9] and Tree Projection [1]. This results in two augmented itemset mining algorithms RM-FP (re-mining using FP-tree) and RM-TP (re-mining using Tree Projection). Extensive experiments on both synthetic data and real-life data show that RM-FP and RM-TP dramatically outperform FP-tree and Tree Projection algorithm respectively. Finally, we also address how the proposed technique can be applied to handle the changes of other types of constraints given in previous studies [13, 10, 12].

2. Related work

Frequent itemset mining has been studied extensively in the past e.g. in [3, 16, 1, 9, 15, 4, 5]. Most current algorithms are variations of the Apriori algorithm [3]. They use support-based generate-and-test approach to find all the frequent itemsets. Recently, some tree-based algorithms were also proposed, e.g., the FP-tree algorithm [9], which is based on the frequent pattern tree, and Tree Projection algorithm [1], which is based on the lexicographic tree. Both algorithms do not strictly follow the Apriori-like candidate generate-and-test approach and were shown to be more efficient than the Apriori algorithm [3].

Since [13] first introduced item constraints to produce only those useful itemsets, many other types of constraints have been integrated into itemset mining algorithms [10, 12]. Although many efficient algorithms for mining frequent itemsets with constraints exist, user interaction is at the minimum level. To remedy this situation, [10] proposes to establish breakpoints in the mining process to accept user feedback to guide the mining. Furthermore, online association rule mining also allows the user to increase minimum support during the mining process [2]. However, [2] does not allow decreasing of minimum support. Similarly, the support threshold used in [11] for incremental and interactive sequence pattern mining can also be increased but not decreased.

The closely related work to ours is the incremental mining, where the concept of *negative border* (proposed in [16]) is utilized to update the mining results when additional data becomes available [14, 15, 8, 11]. A negative border consists of all the itemsets that are candidates of the Apriori algorithm that do not have sufficient support. Although the methods in [14, 15, 8] only need one scan of the updated dataset, they could not avoid the disadvantage of negative border, i.e., maintaining a negative border is very memory consuming and is not well adapted for very large databases [11].

The approach in [14, 15, 8] seemingly can be adapted for handling constraint relaxation. [15] actually mentions the possibility but no detailed algorithm is proposed. However, one significant shortcoming of the approach is that generating candidates under new constraints using the negative border under old constraints usually result in over-generation of a huge number of useless candidates. This makes the approach in [14, 15, 8] impractical for our constraint relaxation problem for large datasets, especially when the minimum support is low. For example, if 10^5 frequent itemsets are obtained given minimum support of 1% and 50 1-itemsets become frequent after minimum support is reduced to 0.9%, the number of candidate itemsets generated using the above approach is $(2^{50}-1)*10^5$ $\approx 10^{20}$ even if we do not consider the expansions of 10^5 frequent itemsets themselves. This is clearly impractical.

FUP in [6] is another incremental mining method that follows the Apriori framework. FUP is not for mining with constraint changes. If it is applied to our task, it basically re-runs the Apriori algorithm without re-counting the supports of those itemsets generated previously (they still need to be re-generated). The computation saving is thus very limited, if any, because of some overheads (see [7] for more details).

3. Problem statement

Let I be the set of all items, and Γ be a transaction database. Each transaction in Γ consists of a subset of items in I. Let S $(\subseteq I)$ be an itemset. The **support** of S (denoted by *Support(S)*) is defined as in [3]. Given a *minimum support MinSup*, an itemset S is **frequent** in Γ if *Support(S)* $\geq$ *MinSup*. With a transaction set Γ and a *MinSup*, the problem of **frequent itemset mining** is to find the complete set of frequent itemsets in Γ.

Constraints can be imposed on both itemset S itself and its attributes (e.g., *price*, *type*, etc) in frequent itemset mining. There are many types of constraints that can be imposed on frequent itemset mining. Four categories of constraints: *anti-monotone, monotone, succinct,* and *convertible* constraints have been effectively integrated into some mining algorithms [10, 12].

***Iterative mining of frequent itemsets with constraint changes*:** Given a transaction database Γ, the whole process of *iterative (and interactive) mining of frequent itemsets with constraint changes* is captured with the following iterative steps:

(1) specify the initial set of constraints *SC*.

(2) run the mining algorithm

(3) check the returned results to determine whether they are satisfactory. If so, the mining process ends. Otherwise, the user changes one or more constraints in *SC* (including deletion and addition of constraints), and the process then goes to (2).

(1) and (3) will not be discussed further in the paper as it is the user's responsibility to devise and to change constraints. Our objective is to design a framework for the mining algorithm in (2) so that it is able to leverage on the mining results from the previous mining iteration to improve the efficiency of the current mining, and consequently speed up the whole data mining process.

***Constraint changes*:** Change of a constraint includes two cases:

(1) Tighten the constraint: The solution space is reduced. For example, when the *minimum support* is increased.

(2) Relax the constraint: The solution space is expanded. For example, the *minimum support* is decreased.

Constraint changes mean changes to one or several constraints in a set of pre-defined constraints. The changes cover deletion or addition of constraints. Adding a new constraint corresponds to tightening the constraint, while deleting an existing constraint corresponds to relaxing the constraint.

As discussed earlier, if a constraint C is tightened to C', the set of itemsets that satisfy the new constraint C' is only a subset of the itemsets that satisfy the old constraint C. Thus, the set of itemsets that satisfy C' can be obtained by filtering the set of itemsets that satisfy C. The challenge comes when a constraint C is relaxed to C'. The set of itemsets that satisfy the old constraint C is only a subset of the itemsets that satisfy the new constraint C'. The problem is how to efficiently discover the set of itemsets F_n that satisfy the new constraint C' but not the old constraint C. The rest of the paper focuses on this problem. We also study how to utilize the previous mining results to efficiently discover the set of itemsets when multiple constraints are changed at the same time.

4. The proposed technique

We use the minimum support constraint as an example to present the proposed technique for finding the set of itemsets F_n that satisfy the new but not the old *minimum support* when the *minimum support* is reduced (relaxed) from one mining process to the next. The relaxation problems of the other constraints can be solved within the proposed framework (to be discussed in Section 7), although the technical details may vary.

Let $MinSup_{old}$ be the minimum support used in the previous (or old) mining, and $MinSup_{new}$ be the relaxed (or new) minimum support. This section first introduces the useful information that can be obtained from the previous mining process using a *tree-based* itemset mining framework. The reason that we use a tree-based framework will become clear later. We then describe a method to represent the old information for the purpose of mining under $MinSup_{new}$. Next, we present a naïve approach and the proposed technique for discovering the set of itemsets F_n that are frequent under $MinSup_{new}$ but not $MinSup_{old}$.

4.1. Useful information from previous mining

After running a mining algorithm using $MinSup_{old}$, we find the set of frequent itemsets. One byproduct of the process is the set of itemsets that are checked against $MinSup_{old}$ (supports are counted) but are not frequent. Let L_f be the set of frequent itemsets under $MinSup_{old}$, and L_{if} be the set of itemsets that are counted, but found infrequent (the byproduct). Although all frequent itemset mining algorithms generate the same set L_f, the set of infrequent itemsets L_{if} checked in the process varies according to algorithms.

Algorithms, such as those in [4, 1, 9], do not strictly follow the candidate generation of Apriori-like algorithms [3, 16, 10]. Instead, they are based on some kinds of tree. We classify these algorithms as tree-based algorithms. Tree-based algorithms will count the support of an itemset $S = \{i_1, i_2, ..., i_k\}$ if two proper subsets of S, namely $S_1 = \{i_1, ..., i_{k-2}, i_{k-1}\}$ and $S_2 = \{i_1, ..., i_{k-2}, i_k\}$, are frequent.

We use tree-based mining algorithms as the underlying mining framework of our proposed technique because tree-based mining algorithms give us sufficient information, while Apriori-like algorithms do not (see the end of the Section). [1,9] also show that tree-based algorithms are actually more efficient in many cases.

As in [1], we use a lexicographic tree to represent the set of frequent itemsets L_f. Given the set of items I, it is assumed that a lexicographic order R exists among the items in I. The order R is important for efficiency and for the organization of mining results. We use the notation $i \leq_L j$ to denote that item i occurs lexicographically earlier than j.

Definition 4.1 (Lexicographic Tree) A node in a lexicographic tree corresponds to a frequent itemset. The root of the tree corresponds to the *null* itemset.

We extend Definition 4.1 to also represent those itemsets in L_{if} with a lexicographic tree. An example lexicographic tree is shown in Figure 1. Those nodes enclosed in circles are frequent itemsets under $MinSup_{new}$

but not $MinSup_{old}$, which are in F_n. Those nodes enclosed by dotted squares are the itemsets in L_{if} that are not frequent under either $MinSup_{old}$ or $MinSup_{new}$. The other nodes are itemsets that are frequent under both $MinSup_{old}$ and $MinSup_{new}$. Let P and Q be two itemsets and Q be the parent of P.

Definition 4.2 (Tree Extensions) A frequent 1-extension of an itemset such that the last item is the contributor to the extension is called a *tree extension*. The list of *tree extensions* of a node P is denoted by $E(P)$.

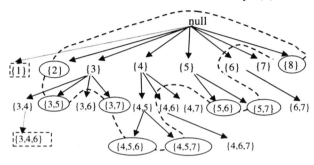

Figure 1. A lexicographic tree

In Figure 1, under $MinSup_{old}$, the list of tree extensions of node 3 $E(3) = <4, 6>$.

Definition 4.3 (Candidate Extensions) The list of candidate extensions of a node P is defined to be those items in $E(Q)$ that occur lexicographically after the node P. We denote the list by $C(P)$. Note that $E(P)$ is a subset of $C(P)$.

Items in $C(P)$ are possible frequent extensions of P. Under $MinSup_{old}$, the tree extensions of *null* node $E(null) = <3, 4, 5, 6, 7>$ (note that 2 is not frequent under $MinSup_{old}$), and the candidate extensions of node 3 $C(3) = <4, 5, 6, 7>$.

4.2. Extensions of lexicographic tree

This subsection extends the lexicographic tree with some new conceptions, which will be used in our proposed technique.

Definition 4.4 (Infrequent Borders) If a 1-extension i of itemset P is not frequent, i is called an *infrequent border*. The list of *infrequent borders* of a node P is denoted by $IB(P)$. We have the relationship: $IB(P) = C(P) - E(P)$.

In Figure 1, under $MinSup_{old}$, the infrequent borders of node 3 $IB(3) = <5, 7>$.

Definition 4.5 (New Tree Extensions) If itemset $P \cup \{i\}$, $i \in IB(P)$, becomes frequent after $MinSup$ is reduced from $MinSup_{old}$ to $MinSup_{new}$, i is called a new tree extension of node P w.r.t. $MinSup_{new}$. The list of new tree extensions of node P w.r.t. $MinSup_{new}$ is denoted by $NTE(P)$.

In Figure 1, the list of new tree extensions of node 3 w.r.t. $MinSup_{new}$ $NTE(3) = <5, 7>$.

For any frequent itemset P (can be *null*) under $MinSup_{old}$, its *tree extensions* $E(P)$ and *infrequent borders* $IB(P)$ are stored for mining under $MinSup_{new}$. Its *new tree extensions* $NTE(P)$ w.r.t. $MinSup_{new}$ can be obtained by checking the list of infrequent borders of P, $IB(P)$. Under $MinSup_{old}$, the set of *tree extensions* of all frequent tree nodes makes up L_f, and the set of *infrequent borders* of all frequent nodes in the tree makes up L_{if}.

4.3. A naïve approach

With the two sets L_f and L_{if} from the mining under $MinSup_{old}$, we first look at a naïve approach to making use of previous mining results for the new mining. We then present the proposed approach based on *tree boundary*.

The naïve approach checks all itemsets in L_f and L_{if} one by one to find the change of their candidate extensions under $MinSup_{new}$, and to extend them to obtain the complete set F_n (in which itemsets are frequent under $MinSup_{new}$ but not $MinSup_{old}$). Figure 2(a) shows the children itemsets of *null* node and the children itemsets of itemset $\{3\}$ in the naïve approach. To make the figure manageable, we assume that itemset $\{3, 8\}$ is frequent under $MinSup_{new}$ but $\{4, 8\}$, $\{5, 8\}$, $\{6, 8\}$, and $\{7, 8\}$ are not. Candidate extensions of each node are shown under the node in Figure 2(a). The only saving in the new mining is that we can utilize the count information saved previously for those itemsets in L_f and L_{if}.

However, this saving in computation is very limited in a tree-based algorithm. Thus, the computation is basically the same as re-mining from scratch. In tree-based algorithms, the main computation comes from the generation of projected transactions for each node. Project transactions for an itemset S are the set of transactions containing S. Tree-based algorithms use this sub-transaction set for counting support and for all subsequent itemset (containing S) generations. This naïve approach still requires the same computation to generate the projected transactions as running a tree-based algorithm from scratch. For instance in Figure 2(a), we still need to create projected transactions for $\{3\}$ to count the support for itemset $\{3, 8\}$ although the supports of its other children itemsets $\{3, 4\}$, $\{3, 5\}$, $\{3, 6\}$ and $\{3, 7\}$ are known previously (the projected transactions for $\{3\}$ are also used to generate the projected transactions for children itemsets of $\{3\}$). Similar computation is required for creating projected transactions for $\{2\}$, $\{3\}$, $\{4\}$, $\{5\}$, $\{6\}$ and $\{7\}$.

Another shortcoming of the naive approach is that it cannot avoid re-generating itemsets in L_f because they need to be extended in the new mining. For example, in Figure 2(a), itemsets $\{3\}$, $\{4\}$, $\{5\}$, $\{6\}$ and $\{7\}$ still need to be generated to check whether item 8 is in their tree extensions although their supports are already counted in previous mining.

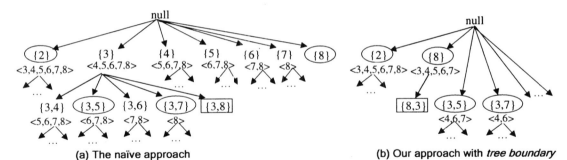

(a) The naïve approach   (b) Our approach with *tree boundary*

Figure 2. Part of mining results under $MinSup_{new}$

Based on the above discussion, we see that saving by the naïve approach is limited. It is thus not efficient.

4.4. The proposed approach

Definition 4.6 (Tree Boundary) A tree boundary *w.r.t.* $MinSup_{new}$ is defined to be the set of itemsets $TB = \{tb \mid tb \in L_{if}, Support(tb) \geq MinSup_{new}\}$, where L_{if} is the set of counted but infrequent itemsets under $MinSup_{old}$, and $Support(tb)$ is the *support* of itemset tb.

For example, the itemsets on the dotted line shown in Figure 1 make up the *tree boundary w.r.t. $MinSup_{new}$*. Itemsets $\{1\}$ and $\{3, 4, 6\}$ are not in TB although they are in L_{if} because they are not frequent under $MinSup_{new}$.

Our proposed approach discovers the complete set of F_n by extending only the itemsets on the *tree boundary*. The basic idea is to eliminate the effect of $MinSup$ decrease on itemsets in L_f, i.e., no itemset will be extended if it has been extended in previous mining. This is achieved by changing the order of *tree extensions* of every node (including the *null* node) in L_f (under $MinSup_{old}$).

Let S_p be *null* node or any itemset in L_f. Tree extensions of S_p under $MinSup_{new}$, denoted by $E_{new}(S_p)$, contains two parts:

- tree extensions of S_p under $MinSup_{old}$, $E_{old}(S_p)$, e.g., $E_{old}(3) = <4, 6>$, and
- new tree extensions of S_p (w.r.t. $MinSup_{new}$), $NTE(S_p)$, e.g., $NTE(3) = <5, 7>$.

We change the item order of $E_{new}(S_p)$ as follows: move items from the new tree extensions, $NTE(S_p)$, to the front of the (old) tree extensions of S_p under $MinSup_{old}$, $E_{old}(S_p)$. For example, in Figure 1, we change the tree extensions of *null* under $MinSup_{new}$ from $<2, 3, 4, 5, 6, 7, 8>$ to $<2, 8, 3, 4, 5, 6, 7>$.

With the new ordering, for a child itemset of S_p such that $S_c = S_p \cup \{i\}$, where $i \in E_{old}(S_p)$ ($S_c \in L_f$), the *candidate extensions* of S_c are the same under $MinSup_{old}$ and $MinSup_{new}$. For a child itemset of S_p such that $S_n = S_p \cup \{i\}$, where $i \in NTE(S_p)$, the *candidate extensions* of S_n consists of :

(1) those items j such that $i \leq_L j$, where $j \in NTE(S_p)$,

and (2) those items j, $j \in E_{old}(S_p)$.

Due to the re-ordering, candidate extensions of the itemsets in L_f are not affected. For instance, after we change the tree extensions of *null* node under $MinSup_{new}$ into $<2, 8, 3, 4, 5, 6, 7>$, the tree extensions of itemsets $\{3\}$, $\{4\}$, $\{5\}$, $\{6\}$ and $\{7\}$ under $MinSup_{new}$ are the same with those under $MinSup_{old}$. The tree extensions of itemset $\{8\}$ become $<3, 4, 5, 6, 7>$ from $\emptyset$ under $MinSup_{old}$. We compute the projected transactions for itemset $\{8\}$ to decide whether items 3, 4, 5, 6, and 7 are tree extensions of $\{8\}$. There is no need to compute projected transactions for $\{3\}$, $\{4\}$, $\{5\}$, $\{6\}$ and $\{7\}$ (they were computed in previous mining).

Another example is given in Figure 2(b), which shows the corresponding part of Figure 2(a) in our approach. After we change the order of tree extensions of *null* node, there is no need to extend itemsets $\{3\}$, $\{4\}$, $\{5\}$, $\{6\}$ and $\{7\}$ with 8. We change tree extensions of itemset $\{3\}$ from $<4, 5, 6, 7>$ to $<5, 7, 4, 6>$. The candidate extensions of node $\{3, 5\}$ are $<4, 6, 7>$. The candidate extensions of node $\{3, 7\}$ are $<4, 6>$. As a result, we only need to compute projected transactions for itemsets $\{3, 5\}$ and $\{3, 7\}$ (which are not computed in previous mining) while the naïve approach needs to compute projected transactions for itemsets $\{3, 4\}$, $\{3, 5\}$, $\{3, 6\}$ and $\{3, 7\}$.

Notice that those itemsets on the *tree boundary* whose candidate extensions are empty can be removed from the *tree boundary*, e.g., itemsets $\{4, 5, 7\}$ and $\{5, 7\}$ in Figure 1.

Let us summarize the advantages of our *tree boundary* based extension with ordering change.

1) Our approach is able to avoid the computation of counting the supports of itemsets in L_f and L_{if}. We do not re-generate the itemsets in L_f to extend them in the new mining process.

2) Our approach is able to avoid the generation of projected transactions that were done in previous mining while the naïve approach is unable to.

The ordering change is the key of our technique. It also brings some additional benefits when integrating tree-based algorithms with *tree boundary*. Refer to [7].

Now, let us prove the correctness and completeness of *tree boundary* approach.

111

Property 4.1 Given *tree boundary TB* w.r.t. $MinSup_{new}$, extending the itemsets in *TB* is able to generate the complete set of itemsets F_n (frequent under $MinSup_{new}$ but not $MinSup_{old}$).

Interested readers can refer to [7] for proof.

Remark: In Apriori-like algorithms, previous mining results under $MinSup_{old}$ do not provide sufficient information to build the *tree boundary* for re-mining under $MinSup_{new}$. Moreover, even if we could build a *tree boundary*, Apriori-like algorithms could not be easily modified to extend itemsets on *tree boundary* to discover F_n.

Interested readers can refer to [7] for proof.

5. Tree boundary based re-mining

We realized the proposed technique using the FP-tree frequent itemset mining and the Tree Projection algorithms. The algorithm using FP-tree is called Re-Mining using FP-tree (in short RM-FP), and the algorithm using Tree Projection is called RM-TP (Re-Mining using Tree Projection). Interested readers can refer to [7] for the algorithms RM-FP and RM-TP.

6. Experimental evaluation

This section presents performance comparison of FP-tree algorithm with RM-FP on both synthetic and real-life data sets. The comparison of Tree Projection algorithm with RM-TP achieves similar results, and is given in [7]. All experiments are performed on a 750-Mhz Pentium PC with 512 MB main memory, running on Microsoft Windows 2000. All the programs are written in Microsoft Visual C++ 6.0.

The synthetic datasets were generated using the procedure described in [3]. We report experiments results on two synthetic datasets: One is T25.I20.D200k [9] with 1K items, which is denoted as D1. In D1, the average transaction size and the average maximal potentially frequent itemset size are 25 and 20 respectively. The number of transactions is 200k. The other dataset is T20.I6.D100k [3] also with 1K items, denoted as D2.

We also tested our approaches on two real-life datasets obtained from the UC-Irvine Machine Learning Database Repository(http://www.ics.uci.edu/~mlearn/MLRepository.html). One is the *Connect*-4 dataset the other is the *Mushroom* dataset.

Figures 3 and 5 show the comparisons of RM-FP with FP-tree algorithm on datasets D1 and *Connect*-4. In the curves for RM-FP, the CPU time for each point (except the first point) is obtained by running RM-FP (with the value of that point as $MinSup_{new}$) based on the previous mining results under $MinSup_{old}$ just before that point. For example in Figure 3, the CPU time of RM-FP at $MinSup_{new}$ = 1.75% is based on the old mining results with $MinSup_{old}$ = 2%, and the CPU time for RM-FP at $MinSup_{new}$ = 1.5% is

based on the old mining results with $MinSup_{old}$ = 1.75%, and so on. Note that when $MinSup_{new}$ of RM-FP is the same as $MinSup_{old}$ of the previous mining, e.g., at $MinSup$ = 2% in Figure 3, the extra running time of RM-FP against FP-tree shows the overhead of RM-FP to output itemsets in L_{if}. The time is very small as shown in Figures 3-9. The results on D2 and *Mushroom* are not shown due to space limitations. Actually, readers can see them based on Figures 7 and 9.

From Figures 3 and 5, we observe that RM-FP is able to save more than 40% running time of FP-tree in each iteration. The saving is very significant in practice. In fact, RM-FP can achieve even better results if the decrease of $MinSup$ is smaller in each iteration as shown in Figure 4. In Figure 4, the $MinSup$ is reduced by 10% each time (the decrease is smaller than that in Figures 3 and 5). At each point, again RM-FP is run based on the mining results of the previous point except for 2%. In each iteration, we can save more than 70% of the running time.

More performance curves on datasets D1, D2, *Mushroom* and *Connect*-4 are given in Figure 6, 7, 8 and 9 respectively. In Figure 6, RM-FP was run based on the initial mining results of the FP-tree algorithm with $MinSup_{old}$ = 2%, 1.5% and 0.75%. In each case, a few decreased $MinSup_{new}$ values are used. In Figure 7, RM-FP was run based on the mining results of $MinSup_{old}$ = 2%, 1% and 0.5%. In Figure 8, RM-FP was run based on the mining results of $MinSup_{old}$ = 60%, 50%, and 45% (we use very high minimum support because the dataset is very dense). In Figure 9, RM-FP was run based on the mining results at $MinSup_{old}$ = 2%, 1%, and 0.5%. In each of these figures, we show results with different $MinSup_{new}$ values.

All the experiments show that RM-FP consistently outperforms the FP-tree algorithm even when $MinSup$ drops to a very low level from a very high level. Using the same initial (old) mining results, we observe that the lower the $MinSup_{new}$ is in the new mining, the smaller is the percentage of saving in computation. This is clear because the number of frequent itemsets at $MinSup_{new}$ is much larger than the number of itemsets in L_f from old mining. For example, for D2, the discovered frequent itemsets at 2% is 381 while the number at 0.15% is 558,834. However, in practice, the user typically will not reduce the $MinSup$ so drastically from one mining process to the next. For example, in most cases, it is quite unlikely that the user uses $MinSup_{old}$ = 2% first, and then changes it to $MinSup_{new}$ = 0.15% suddenly for the next mining. Instead, the decrease each time is usually small as in the cases of Figures 3, 4, and 5.

Note that in Figure 9, RM-FP based on 1% support takes more time than RM-FP based on 2% support at $MinSup_{new}$ = 0.75%. This is because the time used to check previous mining results offsets part of the benefit from utilizing previous mining results when the previous mining results are very large.

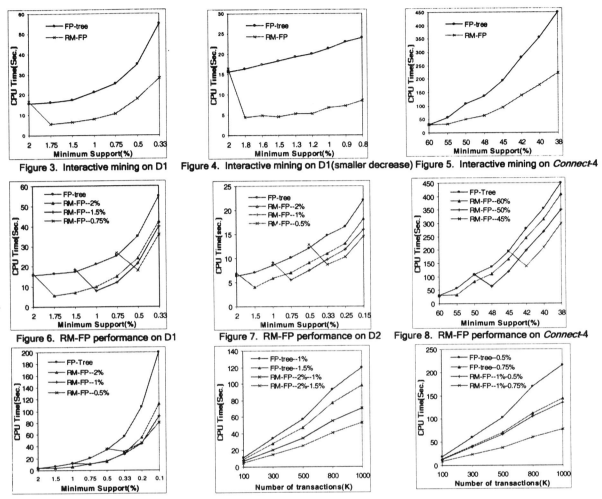

Figure 3. Interactive mining on D1   Figure 4. Interactive mining on D1(smaller decrease) Figure 5. Interactive mining on *Connect-4*

Figure 6. RM-FP performance on D1   Figure 7. RM-FP performance on D2   Figure 8. RM-FP performance on *Connect-4*

Figure 9. RM-FP performance on *Mushroom*   Figure 10. Scalability with the number of transactions

The scalability experiments are conducted by increasing the number of transactions on dataset D1. As shown in Figure 10, both FP-tree and RM-FP have linear scalability with the number of transactions, but RM-FP is more scalable.

7. Application to other constraints

This section shows that the proposed approach is also applicable to discovering the set F_n when any other single or multiple constraints are changed. The detailed techniques for handing changes of these constraints differ. We only present methods for dealing with the change of individual constraints and multiple constraints intuitively. Interested readers may refer to our technical report [7] for additional details and examples.

7.1. Dealing with Individual Constraint Changes

We discuss the methods for discovering the set F_n when a single constraint is changed.

Method 1: Filtering previous mining results

The set F_n can be obtained by filtering previous results in the following two cases: (1) tightening of a constraint of any kind; (2) relaxation of a convertible monotone or monotone constraint.

Method 2: Tree boundary based re-mining

This method as discussed in Section 4 applies to the relaxation of a convertible anti-monotone or anti-monotone constraint although it is a bit different when applying to anti-monotone constraint relaxation due to the special property of convertible constraints [7].

Method 3: Simpler tree boundary based re-mining

Tree boundary in this method is easier to devise than

that for Method 2 and usually contains only 1-itemsets. It applies to the relaxation of a succinct and anti-monotone constraint, or a succinct and monotone constraint. When one of such constraints is relaxed, it can be dealt with as follows: Let $E(null)$ be the list of frequent items that satisfy the old constraint. By checking the old mining results, we first find the list of frequent items $NTE(null)$ that satisfy the new constraint but not the old constraint. Itemsets made of individual items in $NTE(null)$ make up the *tree boundary*.

Constraint 1	Constraint 2	Tighten 1&2	Relax 1 tighten 2	Tighten 1 relax 2	Relax 1&2
Succinct & Anti-mono.	Succ. & Anti.	M1	M1&M3	M1&M3	M3
	Succ. & Mono.	M1	M1&adapted M3	M1&M3	adapted M3
	Anti.	M1	M1&M3	M1&M2	M2&M3
	Mono.	M1	M1&M3	M1	M1&M3
	Convert. Anti.	M1	depends	M1&M2	depends
	Convert. Mono.	M1	depends	M1	depends
Succ.&Mono.	Succ. & Mono.	M1	M1&M3	M1&M3	M3
	Anti.	M1	M1&M3	M1&M2	M2&M3
	Mono.	M1	M1&M3	M1	M1&M3
	Convert. Anti.	–\M1	–\M1&M3	–\M1&M2	–\M2&M3
	Convert. Mono.	–\M1	–\M1&M3	–\M1	–\M1&M3
Anti-mono.	Anti.	M1	M1&M2	M1&M2	adapted M2
	Mono.	M1	M1&M2	M1	M1&M2
	Convert. Anti.	M1	violates	M1&M2	violates
	Convert. Mono.	M1	violates	M1	violates
Monotone	Mono.	M1	M1	M1	M1
	Convert. Anti.	M1	M1	M1&M2	M1&M2
	Convert. Mono.	M1	M1	M1	M1
Convertible Anti-mono.	Convert. Anti.	–\M1	–\M1&M2	–\M1&M2	–\M2
	Convert. Mono.	–\M1	–\M1&M2	–\M1	–\M1&M2
Convert. Mono.	Convert. Mono.	–\M1	–\M1	–\M1	–\M1

Table 1. Handling the change of two combined constraints

7.2. Dealing with multiple constraint changes

Although users usually change one constraint at a time to see the effect of the change, it is also possible that multiple constraints are changed at the same time. Table 1 shows the methods for discovering F_n when two constraints are changed at the same time. Most of the combined cases can be handled by combining the approaches to handling the change of individual constraints. For example, tightening a succinct & anti-monotone constraint and relaxing a succinct & monotone constraint requires Method 1 (handling the tightening) and 3 (handling the relaxation). Interested readers can refer to [7] for the meanings of those exceptional cases including "Adapted", "Violates", "Depends" and "–".

Finally, when more than two constraints are changed at the same time, they can be handled by combining the methods for their respective changes in consideration of the exceptional cases in table 1.

8. Conclusions

Practical data mining is often a highly interactive and iterative process. Users change constraints and run the mining algorithm many times before satisfied with the final results. Current mining algorithms are unable to take advantage of the previous mining results to speed up the new mining process. Motivated by this problem and using the minimum support constraint as an example, this paper first proposed the concept of *tree boundary* to summarize and reorganize the previous mining results. It then presents an effective and efficient framework for re-mining under the reduced minimum support. Experiment results demonstrate that the proposed technique is highly effective. Finally, we also show that when any other individual constraint is changed or multiple constraints are changed at the same time, the new set of frequent itemsets can also be mined efficiently using the proposed technique.

References

[1] R. Agarwal, C. Aggarwal, and V. Prasad. A Tree Projection algorithm for generation of frequent itemsets. In J. Parallel and Distributed Computing, 2000.

[2] C. Aggarwal and P. Yu. Online generation of association rules. In Proc. of 14th ICDE, 1998.

[3] R. Agrawal and R. Srikant. Fast algorithm for mining association rules. In Proc. of the 20th VLDB, 1994.

[4] R. J. Bayardo. Efficiently mining long patterns from database. In Proc. of the SIGMOD, 1998.

[5] A. Bykowski, C. Rigotti. A condensed representation to find frequent patterns. In Proc. of PODS, 2001.

[6] D. W. Cheung, J. Han, V. Ng, and C.Y. Wong. Maintenance of discovered association rules in large databases: An incremental updating technique. In Proc. of ICDE, 1996

[7] G. Cong, B. Liu, Interactive mining of frequent itemsets with constraint changes. Technical report, National Univ. of Singapore, 2002.

[8] R. Feldman, Y. Aumann, A. Amir, and H. Manila. Efficient algorithm for discovering frequent sets in incremental databases. In 2nd SIGMOD workshop DMKD, 1997.

[9] J. Han, J. Pei, and Y.Yin. Mining Frequent Patterns without Candidate Generation. In SIGMOD, 2000.

[10] R. Ng, L.V.S. Lakshmanan, J.Han, and A.Pang. Exploratory mining and pruning optimizations of constrained association rules. In Proc. of SIGMOD, 1998.

[11] S. Parthasarathy, M. J. Zaki, M. Ogihara, and S. Dwarkadas. Incremental and interactive sequence mining. In Proc. of the 8th CIKM, Kansas City, MO, USA, November 1999.

[12] J. Pei, J. Han, and L.V.S.Lakshmanan. Mining frequent itemsets with convertible constraints. In Proc. ICDE, 2001.

[13] R. Srikant, Q, Vu, and R. Agrawal. Mining association rules with item constraints. In Proc. of KDD, CA, 1997.

[14] S. Thomas, S. Chakravarthy. Incremental mining of constrained associations. In HiPC2000.

[15] S. Thomas, S. Bodagala, K. Alsabti, and S. Ranka. An efficient algorithm for the incremental updation of association rules in large databases. In Proc. KDD, 1997.

[16] H. Toivonen. Sampling large databases for association rules. In Proc. of the 22th VLDB, 1996.

Feature Selection for Clustering – A Filter Solution

Manoranjan Dash   Kiseok Choi   Peter Scheuermann
Dept of Elect & Comp Eng
Northwestern University
Evanston, IL 60208
{manoranj,kchoi,peters}@ece.northwestern.edu

Huan Liu
Dept of Comp Sci & Eng
Arizona State University
Tempe, AZ 85287
hliu@asu.edu

Abstract

Processing applications with a large number of dimensions has been a challenge to the KDD community. Feature selection, an effective dimensionality reduction technique, is an essential pre-processing method to remove noisy features. In the literature there are only a few methods proposed for feature selection for clustering. And, almost all of those methods are 'wrapper' techniques that require a clustering algorithm to evaluate the candidate feature subsets. The wrapper approach is largely unsuitable in real-world applications due to its heavy reliance on clustering algorithms that require parameters such as number of clusters, and due to lack of suitable clustering criteria to evaluate clustering in different subspaces. In this paper we propose a 'filter' method that is independent of any clustering algorithm. The proposed method is based on the observation that data with clusters has very different point-to-point distance histogram than that of data without clusters. Using this we propose an entropy measure that is low if data has distinct clusters and high otherwise. The entropy measure is suitable for selecting the most important subset of features because it is invariant with number of dimensions, and is affected only by the quality of clustering. Extensive performance evaluation over synthetic, benchmark, and real datasets shows its effectiveness.

1 Introduction

Many real-world applications deal with high dimensional data. Feature selection that chooses the important original features is an effective dimensionality reduction technique. An important feature for a learning task can be defined as one whose removal degrades the learning accuracy. By removing the unimportant features, data sizes reduce, while learning accuracy and comprehensibility improve. Learning can be supervised or unsupervised. In supervised learning a class label is specified for each instance while unsupervised learning uses no class label. The literature for feature selection for classification, which is a supervised learning task, is very vast (see a review in [7]). On the other hand, there are only a few, mostly recent, feature selection methods for clustering, which is a unsupervised task. Arguably, the reason behind this gap in research is due to the fact that it is easier to select features for classification than for clustering.

Feature selection for clustering is the task of selecting important features for the underlying clusters. Among the methods proposed [8, 9, 11, 17, 20] most of them are 'wrapper' methods for feature selection. A wrapper method for feature selection evaluates the candidate feature subsets by the learning algorithm itself which uses the selected features later for efficient learning. The term wrapper was extensively used in [15] for feature selection for classification. In clustering, a wrapper method evaluates the candidate feature subsets by a clustering algorithm. For example in [8, 17] the K-means clustering algorithm is used for evaluation, while in [11] EM – Expectation Maximization – is used for evaluation. Although wrapper methods for classification have several disadvantages such as lack of robustness across different learning algorithms, they are still preferable in applications where accuracy is an important criterion. But, unlike classification which has a very quantifiable way of evaluating accuracy, there is no generally acceptable criterion to estimate the accuracy of clustering (see [14] for a partial list of clustering criteria). To make matters worse, feature selection for clustering requires that the evaluation functions be able to distinguish among clustering in different subspaces. The above limitations make wrapper methods for clustering disadvantageous.

In this paper we propose and evaluate a 'filter' method for feature selection. A filter method, by definition, is independent of clustering algorithms, and thus completely avoids the issue about lack of unanimity in the choice of clustering criterion. The proposed method is based on the observation that data with clusters has very different point-to-point distance histogram than data without clusters. Using this observation we propose an entropy measure that is low if data has distinct clusters and high otherwise. The entropy measure is suitable for selecting the most important subset of features because it is invariant with number of dimensions, and is affected only by the quality of clustering. Experiments over real, benchmark, and synthetic datasets show the effectiveness of the proposed method.

2 Properties of Feature Selection

Let us assume that our dataset consists of N data points or instances each with M dimensions or features. We shall denote X_i as the ith data point, X_{i_k} as the kth feature value of the ith point, and F_k as the kth feature for $i = 1...N$ and $k = 1...M$. Also $D_{i1,i2}$ denotes the distance between points X_{i1} and X_{i2}, and χ_j denotes the jth cluster for $j = 1...c$ where c is the number of clusters. Below we discuss two important properties of unsupervised data that affect feature selection.

Importance of Features over Clustering Typically, while gathering information for a particular application, one tends to gather as much information as possible without considering the significance of each feature over the underlying clusters. It is an essential data mining pre-processing task to remove unwanted features before performing other KDD tasks such as clustering.

In Figure 1(a,b,c) we show an example using synthetic data in (3,2,1)-dimensional spaces respectively. There are a total of 75 points in three dimensions; there are three clusters in the $F1$-$F2$ dimensions with each cluster having 25 points. Values in $F1$ and $F2$ features follow Gaussian distribution within each of the three clusters while values in feature $F3$, that does not define any cluster, follow a uniform distribution. When we take all three features the clusters are unnecessarily complex (see Figure 1(a)), whereas no clusters can be found when we visualize using only one feature, say $F1$ (Figure 1(c)). Figure 1(b) with $F1$-$F2$ features shows three well-formed clusters. Selecting features $F1$ and $F2$ reduces the dimensionality of the data while forming well separated clusters. This is basically the goal of this paper, i.e., to select the important original features for clustering thus reducing the data size (and the computation time) and at the same time improving the knowledge discovery performance and comprehensibility.

In a single dimensional dataset clusters can be formed if the single feature takes values in separate ranges. In a multi-dimensional dataset, however, clusters can be formed from combination of feature values although the single features by themselves alone may not define clusters. Below we have noted down two distinct scenarios.

Scenario 1 *A single feature defines clusters independently.*

Consider Figure 1(e) where feature $F2$ is uniformly distributed while $F1$ takes values in two separate ranges. It can be clearly seen that $F1$ is more important for defining the two clusters than $F2$.

Scenario 2 *Individual features do not define clusters but correlated features do.* Consider Figure 1(f) where features $F1$ and $F2$ are uniformly distributed. Note that $F1$ and $F2$ alone cannot define the clusters, but by their correlation they define two distinct clusters.

Any feature selection algorithm for clustering must take into account these two scenarios while selecting features.

Distance Histogram In Figure 2 we show the histogram of point-to-point distances for two datasets: one with clusters and the other without clusters. The histogram has b (=100) buckets. Distance are normalized in the interval [0...1] and the bucket# is determined by multiplying the normalized value by b in order to select a bucket. A counter is maintained for each bucket by incrementing it each time a distance belongs to the particular bucket. In the histogram plots, each plotted point corresponds to a single bucket. X value of the plotted point is the bucket number and Y value is the frequency or the counter value of bucket X.

An important distinction between the two histograms is that histogram for data without clusters has a predictable shape similar to a bell shape (see Figure 2(b)). But the histogram for data with clusters has a very different distribution (see Figure 2(a) where the dataset has 20 clusters in 2-D). The early buckets (or distances) are mostly intra-cluster while the latter ones are mostly inter-cluster. *Typically, if the dataset consists of some clusters then, the majority of the intra-cluster distances will be smaller than the majority of the inter-cluster distances.* This observation is true for a wide range of data types. When clusters are very distinct intra-cluster and inter-cluster distances are quite distinguishable. In this paper we propose a method that, without doing clustering, can distinguish between data with clusters and data without clusters. In the next section we introduce such a method which is then applied in Section 4 to select a subset of important features.

3 Distance-based Entropy Measure and Its Efficient Calculation

As stated, we want to develop a method that can distinguish between data with clusters and data without clusters. Entropy theory says that entropy of a system measures the disorder in the system. Mathematically:

$$E = -\sum_{X_i} p(X_{i_1}, ..., X_{i_M}) \log p(X_{i_1}, ..., X_{i_M}) +$$

$$-\sum_{X_i} (1 - p(X_{i_1}, ..., X_{i_M})) \log(1 - p(X_{i_1}, ..., X_{i_M}))$$

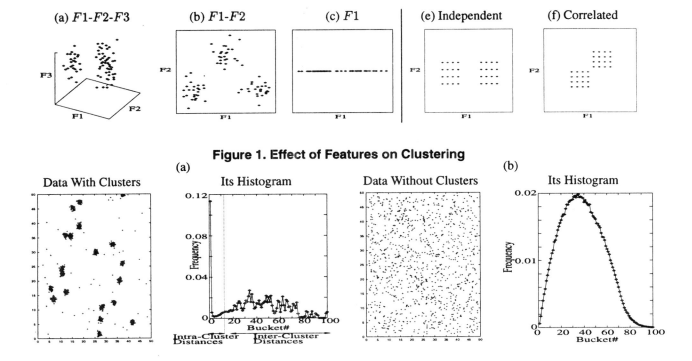

(a) F1-F2-F3 (b) F1-F2 (c) F1 (e) Independent (f) Correlated

Figure 1. Effect of Features on Clustering

(a) Data With Clusters Its Histogram (b) Data Without Clusters Its Histogram

Figure 2. Distance histograms of data *with* and *without* clusters

where $p(X_{i_1}, ..., X_{i_M})$ is the probability or density at the point $(X_{i_1}, ..., X_{i_M})$. The second term in the expression inside summation is used to make the expression symmetric. If the probability of each point is equal we are most uncertain about the outcome, and entropy is the maximum. This will happen when the data points are uniformly distributed in the feature space. On the other hand, when the data has well-formed clusters the uncertainty is low and so also the entropy. So, the entropy can be used to distinguish between data with clusters and data without clusters.

But as we do not know the probability of points, we propose the following proxy method to estimate the entropy. *The **goal** of this method is to assign low entropy to intra- and inter-cluster distances, and to assign a higher entropy to noisy distances.* A straight-forward method is obtained by substituting probability with distance:

$$E = -\sum_{X_i}\sum_{X_j} [D_{ij} \log D_{ij} + (1 - D_{ij}) \log(1 - D_{ij})] \quad (1)$$

where D_{ij} is the normalized distance [1] in the range [0.0 − 1.0] between instances X_i and X_j. E is normalized to the range [0.0 − 1.0]. Entropy is 0.0 for the minimum (0.0) or the maximum (1.0) distance and it is 1.0 for the mean distance (0.5). A plot showing entropy-distance relationship looks similar to the dotted curve of Figure 3(a). Although,

[1] We use Euclidean measure although other distances such as Manhattan can be used.

to some extent, it works well in distinguishing data with clusters from data without clusters, considering its stated goal it suffers from the following two drawbacks. (a) The mean distance of 0.5, the meeting point (μ) of the two sides (i.e., left and right) of the plot, can be an inter-cluster distance, but still it is assigned the highest entropy. (b) Entropy increases rapidly for very small distances thus assigning very different entropy values for intra-cluster distances. In summary, this measure does not fulfill its stated goal of assigning small entropy for both intra- and inter-cluster distances. The second drawback can be easily overcome by incorporating a coefficient (β) in the equation and by using an exponential function in place of logarithmic function. Regarding the first drawback, we can set the meeting point (μ) so as to separate the intra-cluster and inter-cluster distances more accurately. Considering all these we propose the following method:

$$\mathbf{E} = \sum_{X_i}\sum_{X_j} E_{ij} \quad (2)$$

$$E_{ij} = \begin{cases} \frac{exp(\beta * D_{ij}) - exp(0)}{exp(\beta * \mu) - exp(0)} & : \quad 0 \le D_{ij} \le \mu \\ \frac{exp(\beta * (1.0 - D_{ij})) - exp(0)}{exp(\beta * (1.0 - \mu)) - exp(0)} & : \quad \mu \le D_{ij} \le 1.0 \end{cases} \quad (3)$$

where E_{ij} is normalized to the range [0.0 − 1.0].

Setting β and μ Figure 3(a) shows that increasing the β value will decrease the entropy. An effective β is a pos-

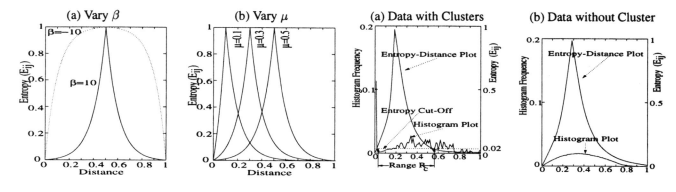

Figure 3. Relationship between entropy and distance with varying β and μ values

Figure 4. Illustrating the effectiveness of the proposed method

itive value (> 0) because a -ve β will lead to the second drawback. A very large +ve β will fail to distinguish between intra- and inter-cluster distances. A very small +ve β will not assign sufficiently small entropy to intra- and inter-cluster distances. Among different +ve β's that we experimented, it works well when it is set to a value around 10 (as shown in the Figure 3(a) bold curve).

Varying μ has the effect of shifting the meeting point of the two sides of the entropy – distance plot (see Figure 3(b)). The value of μ affects the total entropy. According to the histogram plots of Figure 2, it is easy to see that if the μ is set properly then we can distinguish between data with and data without clusters. The method we propose here is based on the observation that it is easy and more accurate to estimate the range of intra-cluster than inter-cluster distances. This is due to the fact that intra-cluster distances typically occupy the lowest portion of the complete range of distances. Below we describe an easy and robust estimation of μ using the intra-cluster distance range (R_I).

1. Starting with the first bin of the histogram, reject all bins of frequencies less than a very low frequency Q_{Min} until a bin with higher frequency occurs.

2. Starting from the bin with frequency more than Q_{Min} find the bin (B_I) with highest frequency in range R_I.

3. Calculate the μ value by setting other unknowns in the Equation 3 for the range $0 \leq D_{ij} \leq \mu$ as follows: set E to a small value E_T, set β, and set distance D_{ij} corresponding to the bin B_I.

Step 1 This step is useful when dimensionality (M) is very large. As shown in [4], for data with large M, if the points are uniformly distributed then all distances approach the maximum distance, i.e., the histogram plot will be effectively shifted towards the right forcing the frequencies of the

lower bins to be very small. So, to make a more effective estimation of μ we reject these initial bins with frequency less than a very small frequency Q_{Min}. In the experiments we set Q_{Min} to 0.5% of the total frequency 1.

Step 2 We tested for various R_Is. It is found that the results remain insensitive if it is set to the initial 5% to 30% of the over-all distance range. The reason is if the data has clusters then the intra-cluster distances are very small and the maximum intra-cluster frequency will typically occur for a very small distance.

Step 3 E_T is set to 2% of the maximum entropy 1, i.e. 0.02. Setting of β is discussed earlier in this section.

We explain the above procedure pictorially in Figure 4. Datasets with and without cluster are taken from Figure 2. Figure 4(a) superimposes the entropy-distance relationship plot over histogram plot for the data with clusters (do not be distracted by the entropy cut-off line and label "Range R_c" in the figure whose significances are explained in the next sub-section). For super-imposition, the bucket numbers of the histogram plot are converted to a range [0.0 – 1.0]. The step 1 is not required for this low-dimensional data. The step 2 yields bin B_I as 1 corresponding to the maximum frequency in the range R_I. Finally step 3 calculates μ as 0.185. Using this information the total entropy (E) for the data with clusters is calculated to be 93433.9. Similarly Figure 2(b) shows the estimation of μ for data without clusters. Using this information E is calculated to be 174723.0 which is much larger than 93433.9. A notable difference between the two figures is: in case of data with clusters entropy is low for many bins (or distances) having considerably high frequency counts (signifying intra- and inter-cluster distances), but for data without clusters entropy is large for most of the bins with considerably high frequency counts. *The proposed method is able to exploit the shape of the histogram plots to assign a low entropy for data with clusters and a high entropy otherwise.*

A Fast Method Number of distance calculations required to calculate the entropy for a subset of features is $O(\frac{N^2-N}{2})$ where N is the number of points and computation required to calculate the distance between a pair of points is taken as unit. Obviously quadratic run times are impractical for large datasets.

A much faster method to calculate entropy is described here. The basic idea is as follows. Until now, in this and the previous sections, a major concern was how to assign low entropy to intra-cluster and inter-cluster distances. In other words, *this approach tries to minimize the entropy for data with clusters.* So, typically a large portion of distances have very low entropy whose total make a less than significant contribution to the over-all entropy. By considering only those distances having entropy higher than a threshold entropy E_{thres} we are able to find a range of distance R_C with higher entropy than E_{thres}, that spreads equally on both sides of the meeting point μ. Entropy for any distance outside this range can be set to a very low constant value C_E less than or equal to E_{thres}. Figure 4(a) illustrates the above observation. A range of distance R_C is shown having entropy above a minimum threshold E_{thres} which is set to 2% of the maximum entropy 1. Note that only 62% of the distances fall in the range R_C, i.e., approximately 38% entropy calculations can be avoided. The total entropy is little affected if, for distances outside R_C, we replace all entropy calculations by a constant entropy (C_E) value less than or equal to E_{thres}.

To exploit this observation, we propose an algorithm based on grid-blocks where data space is partitioned into equal size grid-blocks by dividing each dimension using axis-parallel partitions.
1. For data size that can fit into the main memory we read the data into main memory and separate them into grid-blocks. For large data residing in disk we create an index such that data can be read by grid-blocks.
2. For each pair of blocks, minimum distance is calculated and stored either in memory or disk depending on its size.
3. For each point whose entropy (or distance) is being calculated, its block is determined. For each of the remaining blocks, minimum distance from this block is obtained. If this distance falls in the range R_C then entropy between the candidate point and all points in the block are calculated in the usual way. Otherwise, for all points in the block entropy is pre-assigned to C_E.
For very high-dimensional data where most grid-blocks will be sparse or empty, we consider only those blocks that have considerable number of data points. This way the number of grid-blocks will not grow in an exponential manner which has been a curse for high-dimensional partitioning. For uniformly distributed data, most grid blocks may be sparse. We decide to go for grid block computation if total number of sparse blocks contain less than a threshold number of

points, otherwise a full computation is done.

For very large datasets where even the above fast method is prohibitive, we use sampling. Sampling works well because the entropy measure, to work well, requires the underlying cluster structure to be retained, which a sample is particularly good at.

4 Feature Selection Algorithm

In the previous section we discussed how to distinguish between data with and data without clusters by using an entropy measure. In this section we propose a feature selection algorithm based on this measure. Feature selection process has two main steps: search or generation and evaluation of subsets of features. The entropy measure can be directly used as an evaluation technique to compare subsets of features. This is possible because it is independent of the cardinality of the subsets and comparison is made on how well the subspaces define clusters. So, irrespective of the cardinalities of subsets, low entropy is output for subset defining well-formed clusters while high entropy is output otherwise. Regarding the other important step of feature selection, namely search method, efficiency is measured by *optimality*. In the present context, optimality is defined as that subset for which the entropy is minimum. In the literature, particularly for classification, many search techniques are proposed. See [7] for a list of these techniques. Prominent among these methods are exhaustive, heuristic, random, or some hybrid of these techniques. Exhaustive methods guarantee optimality but are impractical due to their exponential complexity in number of features M, i.e., $O(2^M)$. Random methods that generate subsets randomly are anytime algorithm in that they can return the best subset at any point of time, and moreover they asymptotically approach the optimal subset. A variation of pure random methods is probabilistic method where the probability of generating a subset varies by some rules. Examples of such rules are genetic algorithm and simulated annealing. Commonly used heuristic methods for feature selection are forward or backward selection or some combination of both. A forward selection method first finds the best feature among all features, and then using the already selected features finds the next best feature, and so on. The subset that outputs the least entropy is output as the best subset. Backward selection algorithm is the opposite of the forward selection algorithm. There are many other search techniques that can be applied to feature selection. As our goal in this paper is to propose an evaluation method that can correctly compare data with and data without clusters, we do not go into the details about these search methods. In the experiments we use a forward selection algorithm (ForwardSelect) and compare its output with the exhaustive method. A forward selection algorithm has two loops: the outer loop iterates M – total number of

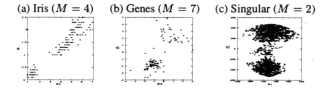

(a) Iris ($M = 4$) (b) Genes ($M = 7$) (c) Singular ($M = 2$)

Figure 5. Subspace showing clusters

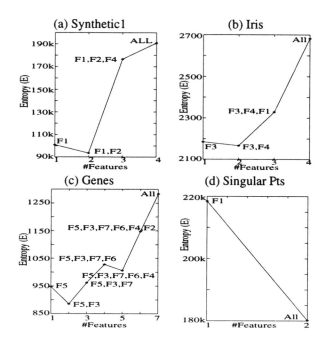

Figure 6. Results of ForwardSelect

features – times, and selects the overall best subset of features while the inner loop selects the best feature for each iteration of the outer loop.

5 Experimental Evaluation

Evaluation of a unsupervised learning task such as clustering is arguably more difficult than a supervised task such as classification for the simple reason that in clustering there is no commonly accepted evaluation approach unlike classification where accuracy of the classifier is a commonly accepted evaluation measure. Feature selection for clustering has the additional disadvantage that the clusters depend on the dimensionality of the selected features and that any given feature subset may have its own clusters, which may well be incompatible with those formed based on different feature subsets. Considering these aspects, the best way of evaluating a feature selection method for clustering is to check the correctness of the selected features, i.e., how well the selected features match with the actual important features. According to this evaluation criterion, we first evaluate the proposed method over synthetic datasets for which we know the important features. Next we evaluate over benchmark and real datasets for which important features are known or can be found out by visualization. We run forward selection method and validate its result by running exhaustive search method to check if ForwardSelect selected the optimal subset that has the overall minimum entropy. If not stated otherwise, the results of the forward selection matches that of exhaustive method, i.e., the forward selection method outputs the optimal subset. Next, we compare a wrapper method with the proposed filter method. In all experiments we follow the guidelines of Section 3 on how to set the two parameters β and μ.

5.1 Synthetic Datasets

Synthetic datasets are generated by using a simple data generation algorithm which can be run from the web-site http://i2s.kisti.re.kr/c̄hoi/choi/proj/gen-data.html. Clusters can be defined by two distributions: Gaussian and Uniform. If k features define a Gaussian cluster, then each feature will have a mean and a standard deviation randomly chosen

from a given range. Similarly, for a uniformly distributed cluster, the lower and the higher ranges are randomly chosen from the range. A noisy point will have all of its features uniformly distributed. The above information is kept in a configuration file that also contains information about the number of clusters, the number of points per each cluster, and the number of noisy points.

An Example The first synthetic dataset (Synthetic1) has 4 features and 1050 points in 20 clusters with 5% noise. Features {F1,F2} define the clusters while {F3,F4} are noise. This is taken from Figure 2(a) after adding {F3,F4}. Figure 6(a) shows that {F1,F2} has the minimum entropy. When we re-checked using exhaustive search, the entropy is also minimum for {F1,F2}.

Other Datasets Other datasets with varying number of features and clusters are generated similarly. Experiments are conducted for $M = 4, 10, 20,$ and 100 features in 2, 5, 10, 20 and 50 clusters. First half of the features i.e. {F1,...,F$_{\frac{M}{2}}$} are important whereas the last half, i.e. {F$_{\frac{M}{2}+1}$,...,F$_M$}, are noisy features. For example, for data with 4 features, {F1,F2} is the best subset. Each data has 5-10% noisy points. Out of these 20 (4 × 5) datasets, except for 10 features – 10 clusters, 10 features – 50 clusters, and 20 features – 20 clusters datasets, the results are correct for the remaining 17 datasets, i.e. subset {F1,...,F$_{\frac{M}{2}}$} has the lowest entropy. The results for these three datasets are almost correct as well as the selected features are all important and it missed out only one important feature.

5.2 Benchmark and Real Datasets

Iris dataset, popularly used for testing clustering and classification algorithms, is taken from UCI ML repository [5]. It contains 3 classes of 50 instances each, where each class refers to a type of Iris plant. One class is linearly separable from the other two; the latter are not linearly separable from each other (see Figure 5(a)). Out of the four it is known that F3 (petal length) and F4 (petal width) features are more important for the underlying clusters because of their very high correlation with the three classes. Before performing experiments we removed the class labels. In Figure 6(b) we plot the entropy values for the subsets of features selected by ForwardSelect. For the subset consisting of the two most important features ({F3,F4}) the entropy is minimum and is correctly selected by the algorithm.

Genes dataset is taken from the recently publicized clustering software CLUTO available from the web site http://www-users.cs.umn.edu/karypis/cluto/. In this, there is a dataset called Genes2 which has 99 yeast genes (or data points) described using 7 profiles (or features). When ForwardSelect is run over this data, it shows the minimum entropy for subset {F3,F5} (see Figure 6(c)). When we checked the data, as shown in Figure 5(b), it showed two clusters in this two-dimensional subspace. Exhaustive search also returned this subset as the best. With the help of domain experts, we are in the process of finding the significance of these clusters in this subspace. *This experiment shows that the proposed method can be used to uncover clusters from datasets with previously unknown clusters hidden in subspaces of features.*

Singular Points of Parallel Manipulator We obtained data of an experiment conducted in a robotics laboratory to test the singularity points of a parallel manipulator. A parallel manipulator is a closed-loop mechanism in which a moving platform is connected to the base by at least two serial kinematics chains (legs). Singularity is a point inside the workspace where the manipulator moves in a random direction even if all joints are locked. In order to avoid it one approach is to cluster them and find paths in the empty space among the clusters. The data, shown in Figure 5(c), is a good example of *scenario 2* (Section 2) where clusters are defined by the correlation of features and not by individual features. The result shows that the entropy for the subset consisting of both features is smaller than the entropy for any other subset (see Figure 6(d)).

5.3 Comparison with Wrapper Method

We compared the results with a wrapper method described in [11]. Data points are first clustered using a partitional clustering algorithm EM – Expectation Maximization – and then evaluated by using an invariant criterion *trace*.

The $trace(S_w^{-1}S_b)$ is the chosen criterion because it is invariant under any non-singular linear transformation [10]. S_w ($\sum_{j=1}^{c} \sum_{X_i \in \chi_j} (X_i - m_j)(X_i - m_j)^t$) is the within-cluster scatter matrix and S_b ($\sum_{j=1}^{c} (m_j - m)(m_j - m)^t$) is the between cluster scatter matrix where χ_j is the jth cluster, m is the total mean vector of the data and m_j is the mean vector for j^{th} cluster, $(X_i - m_j)^t$ is the matrix transpose of the column vector $(X_i - m_j)$, and *trace* of a matrix is the sum of its diagonal elements. The larger the $trace(S_w^{-1}S_b)$, the larger the normalized distance between clusters which results in better cluster discrimination. In order to test whether the wrapper method is able to select features correctly, we evaluate subsets exhaustively.

For all datasets we set the number of clusters correctly to run EM. Results show that (1) for the example dataset with clusters, (shown in Figure 2), the maximum trace occurs for the subset {F1} while the trace for the important subset {F1,F2} is much lower than that for {F1}, (2) for the Iris dataset the maximum trace occurs for the subset {F2,F3,F4} which is higher than the actual important subset {F3,F4}, (3) for the Genes dataset the maximum trace occurs for the subset {F1,F2} (visualization shows no clusters in this subspace) which is much higher than the trace for the important subset {F3,F5}, and (4) for the singular points the maximum trace occurs for the subset {F2} although the clusters are most distinct in {F1,F2}.

Sensitivity of Parameters Among the parameters of the proposed algorithm, μ affects the outcome more directly than β. Setting of μ depends on finding the maximum intra-cluster frequency which in turn depends on the setting of the higher range of intra-cluster distances. In the experiments we set it to the smallest 10% of the total range of distances. For all experiments we varied it from 5% to 30% and still the results are same as 10%. But note that by varying the number of clusters even very slightly for wrapper methods, the results change drastically. We can explain the robustness of the proposed method as follows. If a subspace contains some clusters then, typically, majority of the intra-cluster distances will be smaller than majority of the inter-cluster distances. So setting any value less than 30% is robust enough because the maximum frequency found are the same most of the time.

6   Related Work and Conclusion

Earliest methods for reducing dimensionality for unsupervised learning are feature extraction methods such as Principal Components Analysis, Karhunen-Loeve transformation, or Singular Value Decomposition [10, 13]. These methods do not reduce the number of the original features, instead they create extracted features or principal components from the original ones. In the last several years a number of methods for feature selection for clustering are proposed most of which are 'wrapper' in approach. In clustering, a wrapper method uses a clustering algorithm to evaluate the candidate feature subsets. Wrapper methods can be categorized based on whether they select features for the whole data (*global type*) or just for a fraction of the data in a cluster (*local type*). The global type assumes a subset of features to be more important than others for the whole data while the local type assumes each cluster to have a subset of important features. Examples of global methods are [8, 9, 11, 17, 20, 21] and the proposed method in this paper. The method described in [17] uses K-means for evaluation of subsets of features. In [11] EM (Expectation–Maximization) and trace measure are used for evaluation. The authors also propose visual aids for the user to decide the optimal number of features. In [9, 19] features are ranked and selected for categorical data. Forward and backward search techniques are used to generate candidate subsets. To evaluate each candidate subset, these methods measure the category utility of the clusters by applying COBWEB [12]. [2] In [21] authors proposed an objective function for choosing the feature subset and finding the optimal number of clusters for a document clustering problem using a Bayesian statistical estimation framework.

Examples of local wrapper methods are [1, 2, 6]. Projected clustering (ProClus [1]) finds subsets of features defining (or important for) each cluster. ProClus first finds clusters using K-medoid [16] considering all features and then finds the most important features for each cluster using Manhattan distance. The algorithm called CLIQUE in [2] divides each dimension into a user given divisions. It starts with finding dense regions (or clusters) in 1-dimensional data and works upward to find j-dimensional dense regions using candidate generation algorithm Apriori [3].

In this paper we proposed a filter method to evaluate feature subsets and choose the best subset for clustering by considering their effect on the underlying clusters. Earlier methods proposed for clustering were mostly wrapper methods which require some clustering algorithm and some invariant clustering criterion to evaluate feature subsets. A main drawback of this approach is the lack of unanimous agreement in evaluating the clusters. Furthermore, running a clustering algorithm is very sensitive on some parameters such as the number of clusters or some equivalent of it. For real-world data this information is usually hard to obtain, making it unusable in most cases. But in contrast the proposed method largely depends on a parameter (range of intra-cluster distance) which is easier to set because the proposed method is quite insensitive to it. We performed experiments over benchmark, synthetic and real datasets and results show that the proposed method correctly finds the most important subsets. Comparison with a wrapper method showed the superior evaluation accuracy of the pro-

posed method. Without performing clustering, the proposed method can discover clusters in subspaces even if no *a priori* information about such clusters is available. This is evident in the experimental study of the Genes dataset.

References

[1] C. C. Aggarwal, C. Procopiuc, J. L. Wolf, P. S. Yu, and J. S. Park. Fast algorithms for projected clustering. In *Proc. of ACM SIGMOD*, 1999.

[2] R. Agrawal, J. Gehrke, D. Gunopulos, and P. Raghavan. Automatic subspace clustering of high dimensional data for data mining applications. In *Proc. of ACM SIGMOD*, 1998.

[3] R. Agrawal and R. Srikant. Fast algorithm for mining association rules. In *Proc. of VLDB*, 1994.

[4] K. Beyer, J. Goldstein, R. Ramakrishnan, and U. Shaft. When is "nearest neighbor" meaningful? In *Proc. of ICDT*, 1999.

[5] C. Blake and C. Merz. UCI ML repository. http://www.ics.uci.edu/~mlearn/MLRepository.html, 1998.

[6] C. Cheng, A. W. Fu, and Y. Zhang. Entropy-based subspace clustering for mining numerical data. In *Proc. of KDD*,1999.

[7] M. Dash and H. Liu. Feature selection for classification. *Intl J. of Intelligent Data Analysis*, 1(3), 1997.

[8] M. Dash and H. Liu. Feature selection for clustering. In *Proc. of PAKDD*, 2000.

[9] M. Devaney and A. Ram. Efficient feature selection in conceptual clustering. In *Proc. of ICML*, 1997.

[10] R. O. Duda and P. E. Hart. *Pattern Classification and Scene Analysis*. John Wiley & Sons, 1973.

[11] J. G. Dy and C. E. Brodley. Visualization and interactive feature selection for unsupervised data. In *Proc. of ACM SIGKDD*, 2000.

[12] D. H. Fisher. Knowledge acquisition via incremental conceptual clustering. *Machine Learning*, 2:139–172, 1987.

[13] K. Fukunaga. *Introduction to Statistical Pattern Recognition*. Academic Press, 1990.

[14] A. K. Jain and R. C. Dubes. *Algorithm for Clustering Data*. Prentice-Hall Advanced Reference Series, 1988.

[15] G. H. John. *Enhancements to the data mining process*. PhD thesis, Dept of Comp Sci, Stanford Univ, 1997.

[16] L. Kaufman and P. Rousseuw. *Finding Groups in Data - An Introduction to Cluster Analysis*. Wiley Series in Probability and Mathematical Statistics, 1990.

[17] Y. S. Kim, W. N. Street, and F. Menczer. Feature selection in unsupervised learning via evolutionary search. In *Proc. of ACM SIGKDD*, 2000.

[18] R. Motwani and P. Raghavan, editors. *Randomized Algorithms*. Cambridge University Press, 1995.

[19] L. Talavera. Feature selection as a preprocessing step for hierarchical clustering. In *Proc. of ICML*, 1999.

[20] L. Talavera. Feature selection and incremental learning of probabilistic concept hierarchies. In *Proc. of ICML*, 2000.

[21] S. Vaithyanathan and B. Dom. Model selection in unsupervised learning with applications to document clustering. In *Proc. of ICML*, 1999.

---

[2] COBWEB is a hierarchical clustering algorithm for categorical data.

A Theory of Inductive Query Answering

Luc DE RAEDT[†]   Manfred JAEGER[†,‡,*]   Sau Dan LEE[†]   Heikki MANNILA[‡]

[†]Inst. für Informatik
University of Freiburg
Georges Koehler Allee 79
D-79110 Freiburg, Germany
deraedt@informatik.uni-freiburg.de
danlee@informatik.uni-freiburg.de

[‡] Helsinki Institute of
Information Technology
PO Box 26
FIN-00014 Univ. of Helsinki
Finland
mannila@cs.helsinki.fi

[*] MPI Informatik
Stuhlsatzenhausweg 85
D-66123 Saarbrücken
Germany
jaeger@mpi-sb.mpg.de

Abstract

We introduce the boolean inductive query evaluation problem, which is concerned with answering inductive queries that are arbitrary boolean expressions over monotonic and anti-monotonic predicates. Secondly, we develop a decomposition theory for inductive query evaluation in which a boolean query Q is reformulated into k sub-queries $Q_i = Q_A \wedge Q_M$ that are the conjunction of a monotonic and an anti-monotonic predicate. The solution to each subquery can be represented using a version space. We investigate how the number of version spaces k needed to answer the query can be minimized. Thirdly, for the pattern domain of strings, we show how the version spaces can be represented using a novel data structure, called the version space tree, and can be computed using a variant of the famous Apriori algorithm. Finally, we present some experiments that validate the approach.

1. Introduction

Many data mining problems address the problem of finding a set of patterns that satisfy a constraint. Formally, this can be described as the task of finding the set of patterns $Th(Q, \mathcal{D}, \mathcal{L}) = \{\varphi \in \mathcal{L} \mid Q(\varphi, \mathcal{D})$, i.e. those patterns φ satisfying query Q on database $\mathcal{D}\}$. Here $\mathcal{L}$ is the language in which the patterns or rules are described and Q is a predicate or constraint that determines whether a pattern φ is a solution to the data mining task or not [15]. This framework allows us to view the predicate or the constraint Q as an *inductive query* to an *inductive database system*. It is then the task of the inductive database management system to efficiently generate the answers to the query. This view of data mining as a declarative querying process is also appealing

as the basis for a theory of data mining. Such a theory would be analogous to traditional database theory in the sense that one could study properties of different pattern languages $\mathcal{L}$, different types of queries (and query languages), as well as different types of databases. Such a theory could also serve as a sound basis for developing algorithms that solve inductive queries.

It is precisely such a theory that we introduce in this paper. More specifically, we study inductive queries that are boolean expressions over monotonic and anti-monotonic predicates. An example query could ask for molecular fragments that have frequency at least 30 per cent in the active molecules or frequency at most 5 per cent in the inactive ones [14]. To the best of our knowledge this type of boolean inductive query is the most general type of inductive query that has been considered so far in the data mining literature. Indeed, most contemporary approaches to constraint based data mining use either single constraints (such as minimum frequency), e.g. [2], a conjunction of monotonic constraints, e.g. [17, 10], or a conjunction of monotonic and anti-monotonic constraints, e.g. [4, 14]. However, [6] has studied a specific type of boolean constraints in the context of association rules and item sets. It should also be noted that even these simpler types of queries have proven to be useful across several applications, which in turn explains the popularity of constraint based mining in the literature.

Our theory of boolean inductive queries is first of all concerned with characterizing the solution space $Th(Q, \mathcal{D}, \mathcal{L})$ using notions of convex sets (or version spaces [13, 12, 16]) and border representations [15]. This type of representations have a long history in the fields of machine learning [13, 12, 16] and data mining [15, 3]. These data mining and machine learning viewpoints on border sets have recently been unified by [4, 14], who introduced the level-wise version space algorithm that computes the S and G set w.r.t. a conjunction of monotonic and anti-monotonic constraints.

In the present paper, we build on these results to develop a decomposition approach to solving arbitrary boolean queries over monotonic and anti-monotonic predicates. More specifically, we investigate how to decompose arbitrary queries Q into a set of sub-queries Q_k such that $Th(Q, \mathcal{D}, \mathcal{L}) = \bigcup_i Th(Q_i, \mathcal{D}, \mathcal{L})$, k is minimal, and each $Th(Q_i, \mathcal{D}, \mathcal{L})$ can be represented using a single version space. This results in an operational and effective decomposition procedure for solving queries. Indeed, the overall query Q is first reformulated into the sub-queries Q_i, which can then be solved by existing algorithms such as the levelwise version space algorithm of [4].

Our theory is then instantiated to answer boolean queries about string patterns. String patterns are widely applicable in the many string databases that exist today, e.g. in DNA or in proteins. Furthermore, the present work is to a large extent motivated by the earlier MolFea system [14, 4], in which conjunctive queries (over anti-monotonic and monotonic constraints) for molecular features were solved using a version space approach. MolFea features are essentially strings that represent sequences of atoms and bonds. For string patterns, we introduce a novel data structure, i.e. version space trees, for compactly representing version spaces of strings. Version space trees combine ideas of version spaces with those of suffix trees. They have various desirable properties. Most notably, they can be computed using a variant of traditional level wise algorithms for tries, recognizing whether a string belongs to the version space is linear in the size of the string, and the size of the version space tree is at most quadratic in the size of the elements in the S set of the version space.

This paper is organized as follows. In Section 2, we define the inductive query evaluation problem and illustrate it on the pattern domains of strings and item-sets; in Section 3, we introduce a decomposition approach to reformulate the original query in simpler sub-queries; in Section 4, we introduce version space trees that compactly represent the solutions to a sub-query in the pattern domain of strings; in Section 5, we report on some experiments in this domain, and, finally, in Section 6, we conclude.

2 Boolean Inductive Queries

A pattern language $\mathcal{L}$ is a formal language for specifying patterns. Each pattern $\phi \in \mathcal{L}$ matches (or covers) a set of examples ϕ_e, which is a subset of the universe $\mathcal{U}$ of possible examples. In general, pattern languages will not allow to represent all subsets $\mathcal{P}(\mathcal{U})$ of the universe[1].

Example 2.1 *Let $\mathcal{I} = \{i_1, \dots, i_n\}$ be a finite set of possible items, and $\mathcal{U_I} = 2^{\mathcal{I}}$ be the universe of item sets*

---

[1]The terminology used here is similar to that in concept-learning, where $\mathcal{U}$ would be the space of examples, $\mathcal{P}(\mathcal{U})$ the set of possible concepts, and $\mathcal{L}$ the set of concept-descriptions.

over $\mathcal{I}$. The traditional pattern language for this domain is $\mathcal{L_I} = \mathcal{U_I}$. A pattern $\phi \in \mathcal{L_I}$ covers the set $\phi_e := \{\psi \subseteq \mathcal{I} \mid \phi \subseteq \psi\}$. An alternative, less expressive, pattern language is the language $\mathcal{L}_{\mathcal{I},k} \subseteq \mathcal{L_I}$ of item sets of size at most k.

Example 2.2 *Let Σ be a finite alphabet and $\mathcal{U}_\Sigma = \Sigma^*$ the universe of all strings over Σ. We will denote the empty string with ϵ. The traditional pattern language in this domain is $\mathcal{L}_\Sigma = \mathcal{U}_\Sigma$. A pattern $\phi \in \mathcal{L}_\Sigma$ covers the set $\phi_e = \{\psi \in \Sigma^* \mid \phi \sqsubseteq \psi\}$, where $\phi \sqsubseteq \psi$ denotes that ϕ is a substring of ψ. An alternative, more expressive, language is the language of all regular expressions over Σ.*

One pattern ϕ is *more general* than a pattern ψ, written $\phi \succeq \psi$, if and only if $\phi_e \supseteq \psi_e$.

A pattern *predicate* defines a primitive property of a pattern, usually relative to some data set D (a set of examples), and sometimes other parameters. For any given pattern, it evaluates to either *true* or *false*.

We now introduce a number of pattern predicates that will be used for illustrative purposes throughout this paper. Most of these predicates are inspired by MolFea [14]. Our first pattern predicates are very general in that they can be used for arbitrary pattern languages:

- min_freq(p,n,D) evaluates to true iff p is a pattern that occurs in database D with frequency at least $n \in \mathbb{N}$. The frequency $f(\phi, D)$ of a pattern ϕ in a database D is the (absolute) number of data items in D covered by ϕ. Analogously, the predicate max_freq(p, n, D) is defined.

- ismoregeneral(p,ψ) is a predicate that evaluates to true iff pattern p is more general than pattern ψ. Dual to the ismoregeneral predicate one defines the ismorespecific predicate.

The following predicate is an example predicate tailored towards the specific domain of string-patterns over $\mathcal{L}_\Sigma$.

- length_atmost(p,n) evaluates to true for $p \in \mathcal{L}_\Sigma$ iff p has length at most n. Analogously the length_atleast(p,n) predicate is defined.

In all the preceding examples the pattern predicates have the form pred($p,params$) or pred($p,D,params$), where *params* is a tuple of parameter values, D is a data set and p is a pattern variable.

We also speak a bit loosely of pred alone as a pattern predicate, and mean by that the collection of all pattern predicates obtained for different parameter values *params*.

We say that m is a *monotonic* predicate, if for all possible parameter values *params* and all data sets D:

$$\forall \phi, \psi \in \mathcal{L} \text{ such that } \phi \succeq \psi :$$
$$\mathsf{m}(\psi, D, params) \rightarrow \mathsf{m}(\phi, D, params)$$

The class of *anti-monotonic* predicates is defined dually. Thus, min_freq, ismoregeneral, and length_atmost are monotonic, their duals are anti-monotonic.

A pattern predicate pred(p,D,*params*) that can be applied to the patterns from a language $\mathcal{L}$ defines relative to D the *solution set* $Th(\text{pred}(p, D, params), \mathcal{L}) = \{\phi \in \mathcal{L} \mid \text{pred}(\phi, D, params) = true\}$. Furthermore, for monotonic predicates m these sets will be monotone, i.e. for all $\phi \succeq \psi \in \mathcal{L} : \psi \in Th(\text{m}, \mathcal{L}) \to \phi \in Th(\text{m}, \mathcal{L})$.

Example 2.3 *Consider the string data set* $D = \{abc, abd, cd, d, cd\}$. *Here we have pattern frequencies* $f(abc, D) = 1$, $f(cd, D) = 2$, $f(c, D) = 3$, $f(abcd, D) = 0$. *And trivially,* $f(\epsilon, D) = |D| = 5$. *Thus, the following predicates evaluate to true:* min_freq(c; 2; D), min_freq(cd; 2; D), max_freq(abc; 2; D), max_freq(cd; 2; D).

The pattern predicate m $:=$ min_freq($p, 2, D$) *defines* $Th(\text{m}, \mathcal{L}_\Sigma) = \{\epsilon, a, b, c, d, ab, cd\}$, *and the pattern predicate* a $:=$ max_freq($p, 2, D$) *defines the infinite set* $Th(\text{a}, \mathcal{L}_\Sigma) = \mathcal{L}_\Sigma \setminus \{\epsilon, c, d\}$.

The definition of $Th(\text{pred}(\text{p}, D, params), \mathcal{L})$ is extended in the natural way to a definition of the solution set $Th(Q, \mathcal{L})$ for boolean combinations Q of pattern predicates over a unique pattern variable: $Th(\neg Q, \mathcal{L}) := \mathcal{L} \setminus Th(Q, \mathcal{L})$, $Th(Q_1 \vee Q_2, \mathcal{L}) := Th(Q_1, \mathcal{L}) \cup Th(Q_2, \mathcal{L})$. The predicates that appear in Q may reference one or more data sets $D_1, \ldots, D_n$. To emphasize the different data sets that the solution set of a query depends on, we also write $Th(Q, D_1, \ldots, D_n, \mathcal{L})$ or $Th(Q, \mathcal{D}, \mathcal{L})$ for $Th(Q, \mathcal{L})$.

We are interested in computing solution sets $Th(Q, \mathcal{D}, \mathcal{L})$ for boolean queries Q that are constructed from monotonic and anti-monotonic pattern predicates. As anti-monotonic predicates are negations of monotonic predicates, we can, in fact, restrict our attention to monotonic predicates. We can thus formally define the *boolean inductive query evaluation problem* addressed in this paper.

Given

- a language $\mathcal{L}$ of patterns,

- a set of monotonic predicates
  $\mathcal{M} = \{\text{m}_1(p, D_1, params_1), ..., \text{m}_n(p, D_n, params_n)\}$,

- a query Q that is a boolean expression over the predicates in $\mathcal{M}$ (and over a single pattern variable),

Find the set of patterns $Th(Q, D_1, \ldots, D_n, \mathcal{L})$, i.e. the solution set of the query Q in the language $\mathcal{L}$ with respect to the data sets $D_1, \ldots, D_n$.

3 A decomposition approach

The query evaluation problem for a query Q will be solved by decomposing Q into k sub-queries Q_i such that Q is equivalent to $Q_1 \vee \ldots \vee Q_k$, and then computing $Th(Q, \mathcal{D}, \mathcal{L})$ as $\cup_i Th(Q_i, \mathcal{D}, \mathcal{L})$. Furthermore, each of the sub-queries Q_i will be such that $Th(Q_i, \mathcal{D}, \mathcal{L})$ is a version space (also called a convex space), and therefore can be efficiently computed for a wide class of pattern languages $\mathcal{L}$, and queries Q_i.

Definition 3.1 *Let* $\mathcal{L}$ *be a pattern language, and* $I \subseteq \mathcal{L}$. *I has dimension 1, if* $\forall \phi, \phi', \psi \in \mathcal{L} : \phi \preceq \psi \preceq \phi'$ *and* $\phi, \phi' \in I \implies \psi \in I$. *$I$ has dimension k if it is the union of k subsets of dimension 1, but not the union of $k - 1$ subsets of dimension 1.*

A query Q has dimension k (with respect to the pattern language $\mathcal{L}$) if k is the maximal dimension of any solution set $Th(Q, \mathcal{D}, \mathcal{L})$ of Q (where the maximum is taken w.r.t. all possible data sets $\mathcal{D}$ and w.r.t. the fixed language $\mathcal{L}$).

If Q has dimension 1 w.r.t. $\mathcal{L}$, then $Th(Q, \mathcal{D}, \mathcal{L})$ is a version space [16] or a convex space [13]. Version spaces are particularly useful when they can be represented by boundary sets, i.e. by the sets $G(Q, \mathcal{D}, \mathcal{L})$ of their maximally general elements, and $S(Q, \mathcal{D}, \mathcal{L})$ of their minimally general elements. For the theoretical framework of the present section we need not assume boundary representability for convex sets. However, concrete instantiations of the general method we here develop, like the one described in sections 4 and 5, usually will assume pattern languages in which convexity implies boundary representability.

Example 3.2 *Reconsider the string domain. Let*

$$Q_1 = \text{ismoregeneral}(p, abcde) \wedge \text{length\_atleast}(p, 3)$$
$$Q_2 = \text{ismorespecific}(p, ab) \wedge \text{ismorespecific}(p, uw)$$
$$\wedge (\text{length\_atleast}(p, 6) \vee \text{min\_freq}(p, 3, D))$$

The query Q_1 does not reference any dataset, and $Th(Q_1, \mathcal{L}_\Sigma) = \{abcde, abcd, bcde, abc, bcd, cde\}$. This set of solutions is completely characterized by $S(Q_1, \mathcal{L}_\Sigma) = \{abcde\}$ and $G(Q_1, \mathcal{L}_\Sigma) = \{abc, bcd, cde\}$. $Th(Q_2, D, \mathcal{L}_\Sigma)$ cannot in general be represented using a single version space. However, as our general method will show, the dimension of $Th(Q_2, D, \mathcal{L}_\Sigma)$ is at most two, so that it can be represented as the union of two version spaces.

With the following definition and lemma we provide an alternative characterization of dimension k sets.

Lemma 3.3 *Let* $I \subseteq \mathcal{L}$. *Call a chain* $\phi_1 \preceq \phi_2 \preceq \ldots \preceq \phi_{2k-1} \subseteq \mathcal{L}$ *an* alternating chain (of length k) for I *if* $\phi_i \in I$ *for all odd i, and* $\phi_i \notin I$ *for all even i. Then the dimension of I is equal to the maximal k for which there exists in $\mathcal{L}$ an alternating chain of length k for I.*

Example 3.4 *Consider the following queries:*
$Q_3 = ismoregeneral(p, abc) \land ismorespecific(p, a)$,
$Q_4 = ismoregeneral(p, c)$, *and* $Q_5 = Q_3 \lor Q_4$.
Then c, bc, abc *is an alternating chain of length 2 for*
$Th(Q_5, \mathcal{L}_\Sigma)$.

Given Q and $\mathcal{L}$ we are now interested in computing the dimension k of Q, and transforming Q into a disjunction $\lor_{h=1}^k Q_i$, such that each $Th(Q_i, \mathcal{D}, \mathcal{L})$ is a version space. The approach we take is to first evaluate Q in a reduced pattern language $\mathcal{L}^{adm}_{\mathcal{M}(Q)}$, so that the desired partition $\lor Q_i$ can be derived from the structure of $Th(Q, \mathcal{L}^{adm}_{\mathcal{M}(Q)})$. The solution set $Th(Q, \mathcal{L}^{adm}_{\mathcal{M}(Q)})$ does not depend on the datasets $\mathcal{D}$ that Q references, and the complexity of its computation only depends on the size of Q, but not on the size of any datasets.

Definition 3.5 *For a query Q, let $\mathcal{M}(Q) = \{m_1, \ldots, m_n\}$ be the set of monotonic predicates contained in Q (where predicates that only differ with respect to parameter values also are considered distinct). Define $\mathcal{L}_{\mathcal{M}(Q)} := 2^{\mathcal{M}(Q)}$. A subset $\phi \subseteq \mathcal{M}(Q)$ is called* admissible *if there exists data sets $\mathcal{D}$ such that $Th(\land_{m_i \in \phi} m_i \land_{m_j \notin \phi} \neg m_j, \mathcal{D}, \mathcal{L})$ is not empty. Let $\mathcal{L}^{adm}_{\mathcal{M}(Q)} = \{\phi \in \mathcal{L}_{\mathcal{M}(Q)} \mid \phi$ admissible$\}$.*

For the predicates m_i we define $Th(m_i, \mathcal{L}_{\mathcal{M}(Q)})$, respectively $Th(m_i, \mathcal{L}^{adm}_{\mathcal{M}(Q)})$, as the set of (admissible) ϕ that contain m_i. By the general definition this also determines $Th(Q, \mathcal{L}_{\mathcal{M}(Q)})$ and $Th(Q, \mathcal{L}^{adm}_{\mathcal{M}(Q)})$.

Example 3.6 *Using only monotonic predicates, the query Q_2 from example 3.2 can be rewritten as $\neg m_1 \land \neg m_2 \land (\neg m_3 \lor m_4)$, with*

$$m_1 = not\text{-}ismorespecific(p, ab)$$
$$m_2 = not\text{-}ismorespecific(p, uw)$$
$$m_3 = not\text{-}length\_atleast(p, 6)$$
$$m_4 = min\_freq(p, 3, D)$$

(where e.g. not-ismorespecific is the (monotonic) complement of the anti-monotonic predicate ismorespecific; note that this is distinct from ismoregeneral).

Here every $\phi \subseteq \{m_1, \ldots, m_4\}$ is admissible (a witness for the admissibility of $\{m_3, m_4\}$, for instance, is a dataset D in which the string abuw appears at least three times, i.e. abuw $\in Th(\neg m_1 \land \neg m_2 \land m_3 \land m_4, D, \mathcal{L}_\Sigma)$).

Figure 1 (a) shows $\mathcal{L}_{\mathcal{M}(Q_2)} = \mathcal{L}^{adm}_{\mathcal{M}(Q_2)}$, where e.g. pattern $\{m_3, m_4\}$ is just represented by its "index string" 34.

Now consider a variant Q_6 of Q_2 obtained by replacing m_3 with $m_3' := not\text{-}length\_atleast(p, 4)$. Here not every $\phi \subseteq \{m_1, m_2, m_3', m_4\}$ is admissible: as ismorespecific$(p, ab) \land$ ismorespecific(p, uw) implies lengthatleast$(p, 4)$, we have that neither $\{m_3'\}$ nor $\{m_3', m_4\}$ are admissible. These are the only two inadmissible subsets of $\mathcal{M}(Q)$, so that $\mathcal{L}^{adm}_{\mathcal{M}(Q_6)}$ here is as in figure 1 (b).

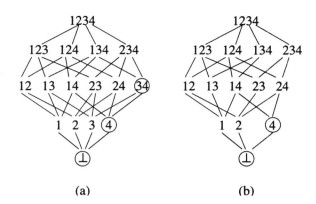

Figure 1. Pattern languages $\mathcal{L}^{adm}_{\mathcal{M}(Q)}$

Assuming that we can decide admissibility of subsets of $\mathcal{M}(Q)$ (for the types of pattern languages and predicates we have considered so far admissibility can always be decided), we can construct $\mathcal{L}^{adm}_{\mathcal{M}(Q)}$ and compute $Th(Q, \mathcal{L}^{adm}_{\mathcal{M}(Q)})$. These solution sets are indicated for the queries Q_2 and Q_6 in their respective languages $\mathcal{L}^{adm}_{\mathcal{M}(Q)}$ by circles in figure 1. One sees that $Th(Q_2, \mathcal{L}^{adm}_{\mathcal{M}(Q_2)})$ has dimension 2, and $Th(Q_6, \mathcal{L}^{adm}_{\mathcal{M}(Q_6)})$ has dimension 1. This gives an upper bound for the dimensions of the solutions to the query:

Theorem 3.7 *The dimension of $Th(Q, \mathcal{L}^{adm}_{\mathcal{M}(Q)})$ is an upper bound for the dimension of $Th(Q, \mathcal{D}, \mathcal{L})$ for all datasets $\mathcal{D}$.*

The dimension of $Th(Q, \mathcal{L}_{\mathcal{M}(Q)})$ is greater or equal the dimension of $Th(Q, \mathcal{L}^{adm}_{\mathcal{M}(Q)})$, and therefore also can serve as an upper bound for the dimension of $Th(Q, \mathcal{D}, \mathcal{L})$. In general, this will be a coarser bound: for Q_6, for instance, we obtain for $Th(Q, \mathcal{L}_{\mathcal{M}(Q_6)})$ the same structure as shown for Q_2 in figure 1 (a), and therefore only the bound 2.

When $Th(Q, \mathcal{L}^{adm}_{\mathcal{M}(Q)})$ is of dimension k, we can define each of its convex components I_h as a solution to a query Q_h in the predicates m_i: if $\phi_1, \ldots, \phi_l$ are the maximal and $\psi_1, \ldots, \psi_m$ the minimal elements of I_h, then $I_h = Th(Q_h, \mathcal{L}^{adm}_{\mathcal{M}(Q)})$ for

$$Q_h := (\lor_{i=1}^l \land_{m_j \notin \phi_i} \neg m_j) \land (\lor_{i=1}^m \land_{m_j \in \psi_i} m_j) \quad (1)$$

Theorem 3.8 *$Th(Q_h, \mathcal{D}, \mathcal{L})$ is convex for all datasets $\mathcal{D}$, and $Th(Q, \mathcal{D}, \mathcal{L}) = Th(\lor_{h=1}^k Q_h, \mathcal{D}, \mathcal{L}) = \cup_{h=1}^k Th(Q_h, \mathcal{D}, \mathcal{L})$.*

Example 3.9 *Continuing from example 3.6, we can partition $Th(Q_2, \mathcal{L}^{adm}_{\mathcal{M}(Q_2)})$ into two convex components $I_1 = \{\{m_4\}, \{m_3, m_4\}\}$ and $I_2 = \{\bot\}$. We thus obtain the de-*

composition of the query Q_2 into the two subqueries

$$Q_{2_1} = \text{ismorespecific}(p, ab) \wedge \text{ismorespecific}(p, uw)$$
$$\wedge \text{min\_freq}(p, 3, D)$$
$$Q_{2_2} = \text{ismorespecific}(p, ab) \wedge \text{ismorespecific}(p, uw)$$
$$\wedge \text{length\_atleast}(p, 6) \wedge \neg \text{min\_freq}(p, 3, D)$$

For Q_6 we have that $\text{Th}(Q_6, \mathcal{L}^{\text{adm}}_{\mathcal{M}(Q_6)})$ consists of one version space $\{\bot, \{m_4\}\}$, so that Q_6 is equivalent to the query

$$Q_{6_1} = \text{ismorespecific}(p, ab) \wedge \text{ismorespecific}(p, uw)$$
$$\wedge \text{length\_atleast}(p, 4)$$

The sub-queries (1) to which the original query Q is reduced not only are known to have convex solution sets $Th(Q_h, \mathcal{D}, \mathcal{L})$, they also are of a special syntactic form $Q_h = Q_{h,M} \wedge Q_{h,A}$, where $Q_{h,M}$ defines a monotone set $Th(Q_{h,M}, \mathcal{D}, \mathcal{L})$, and $Q_{h,A}$ defines an anti-monotone set $Th(Q_{h,A}, \mathcal{D}, \mathcal{L})$. This factorization of Q_h facilitates the computation of the border sets $G(Q_h, \mathcal{D}, \mathcal{L})$ and $S(Q_h, \mathcal{D}, \mathcal{L})$, for which the level wise version space algorithm [4, 14] can be used. In the following section we will present an algorithm that for queries in the string domain uses the syntactic form of the Q_h for efficiently computing and representing the solution sets $Th(Q_h, \mathcal{D}, \mathcal{L})$ with *version space trees*.

4. Version space trees

In this section, we introduce a novel data structure, called the version space tree, that can be used to elegantly represent and index a version space of strings, e.g. the $Th(Q_h, \mathcal{D}, \mathcal{L}_\Sigma)$ introduced in the previous section. Furthermore, we present effective algorithms that compute version space trees containing all strings that satisfy the conjunction of a monotonic and an anti-monotonic predicate (as in the queries Q_h).

4.1. The data structure

A *trie* is a tree where each edge is labelled with a symbol from the alphabet Σ. Moreover, the labels on every edge emerging from a node must be unique. Each node n in a trie thus uniquely represents the string $s(n)$ containing the characters on the path from the root r to the node n. The root node itself represents the empty string ϵ.

A *suffix trie* is a trie with the following properties:

- For each node n and for each suffix t of $s(n)$, there is also a node n' in the trie representing t, i.e. $t = s(n')$.

- Each node n has a *suffix link* $suffix(n) = n'$, where $s(n')$ represents the suffix obtained from $s(n)$ by dropping the first symbol. The root node represents ϵ, which has no suffixes. We define $suffix(root) = \bot$, where $\bot$ is a unique entity.

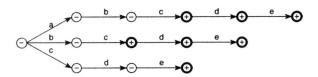

Figure 2. An example version space tree

Suffix tries have been well studied in the literature [18, 19]. However, we make some important deviations from the main stream approach:

- instead of building a suffix trie on all the suffixes of a *single* string, we are indexing all the suffixes of a *set of strings*; thus multiple strings are stored in the trie.

- we use *fully labelled* tries, in which each node is labelled with either "$\oplus$" or "$\ominus$"; the $\oplus$ label to indicate nodes that are interesting to us (say: belong to the version space) and $\ominus$ for those that are not.

- because we need to store labels and counts for all substrings represented in the trie, we do not coalesce chains of nodes with only one out-going edge into a single edge label.

Note that a fully labelled trie may contain nodes for which its label as well as those of its descendants are all $\ominus$. Thus the node as well as the subtrie below it are uninteresting. Therefore, in practice we will often use a *pruned labelled trie*. This is a fully labelled trie with the additional property that all leaf nodes have the sign $\oplus$. Both trees have the same semantics and each fully labelled tree has a unique equivalent pruned tree. Furthermore, as most of our results are valid for both types of trees, we will often employ the term "labelled trie".

Now *a version space tree V* is a labelled trie that represents a version space of strings over $\mathcal{L}_\Sigma$. More formally, let V be a set of strings of dimension 1. Then the corresponding (pruned) version space trie T is such that $V = \{v \mid n \text{ is a node in } T \text{ with label } \oplus \text{ and } s(n) = v\}$. Figure 2 illustrates the (pruned) version space tree representing $Th(Q_7, \mathcal{D}, \mathcal{L}_\Sigma)$, where $Q_7 = \text{is\_more\_general}(t, abcde) \wedge (\text{is\_more\_specific}(t, bc) \vee \text{is\_more\_specific}(t, cde))$.

A version space tree VST representing version space V has the following properties:

1. All leaf nodes are labelled $\oplus$.

2. Along every path from root to a leaf there is at most one sign change (from $\ominus$ to $\oplus$); cf. Lemma 3.3.

3. If $S = \min V$ then VST will 1) have a leaf corresponding to each $s \in S$ and 2) have a node corresponding to each suffix s' of each $s \in S$ for which $s' \in V$.

127

4. Therefore, the number of nodes in the version space tree VST is at most $\Sigma_{i \in S}|s_i|^2$, where $|s|$ denotes the length of the string. However, the size of a VST is usually much smaller.

5. Testing whether a string s belongs to the version space represented by a version space VST is linear in $|s|$, as the VST can be interpreted as a deterministic automaton on input s.

6. Property 3 can be used as the basis for an algorithm for constructing a version space tree based on S and G.

7. For a given version space tree, one can easily and efficiently construct the S and G-sets. Indeed, the S-set will contain all leafs l of the version space tree to whom no suffix pointer points; and the G-set will contain all nodes g with label $\oplus$ whose parent node has label $\ominus$ and for which the node $suffix(g)$ either does not exist or also has the label $\ominus$.

As one can see, there is a close correspondence between version spaces of strings and version space trees. We will now show that there is also a close correspondence between version space trees and algorithms such as Apriori [2].

4.2. The algorithms

In this section, we sketch the VST algorithm to build a version space tree that satisfies the conjunction $Q_A \wedge Q_M$ of an anti-monotonic predicate Q_A and a monotonic one Q_M. This form of query corresponds to the one of the queries Q_h that would be generated by our decomposition (over anti-monotonic and monotonic constraints) approach. Algorithm VST is a level-wise algorithm based on the well-known Apriori [2] algorithm. The algorithm assumes 1) that the version space tree to be computed is finite and 2) that the alphabet Σ is given. It consists of two phases:

DESCEND: top-down growing of the version space tree using the monotonic predicate Q_M.

ASCEND: bottom-up marking of the version space tree using the anti-monotonic predicate Q_A.

Both phases are designed to minimize the number of database scans[2]. As such, they both exhibit the cyclic pattern: candidate generation, candidate testing (database scan) and pruning. The cycle terminates when no more new candidates patterns are generated.

Since only the monotonic pattern predicate is handled in the descend phase, we can reuse the idea of Apriori. The algorithm searches the strings satisfying Q_M in a top-down,

breadth-first manner. At each depth level k, the descend algorithm first expands the $\oplus$ nodes found in the previous iteration (L_{k-1}). The nodes resulting from the expansion constitute the set C_k. These candidate nodes are then tested against the predicate Q_M. The testing involves one database scan for the whole iteration. The candidate patterns in C_k that satisfy the constraints are put into L_k. Those that do not are pruned away from the tree. This process is repeated in a level wise fashion until C_k becomes empty. All generated nodes are labelled with $\oplus$ and the necessary suffix links are set up during this phase.

Note that the sets C_k and L_k are the same as the candidate sets and "large" sets in the Apriori algorithm. Moreover, the generation of C_k from L_{k-1} also mimics the Apriori-join operation in the Apriori algorithm.[3] The descend algorithm makes use of the suffix like and parent-child relationship of a suffix trie to perform the join efficiently. More specifically, the candidate child nodes of a node n in L_{k-1} (as well as the edges) correspond to the children of the node $suffix(n)$. So, the major difference between DESCEND and Apriori is that the former also organizes the discovered strings into a suffix trie, facilitating the join operation and the second phase of the VST algorithm.

The second phase is implemented with algorithm AS-CEND. This phase handles the anti-monotonic constraint Q_A. Here we assume that we have the set F_0 of leaf nodes in the tree T generated during the descend phase. While DESCEND works top-down, ASCEND starts from the leaves and works upwards. It first checks the leaf nodes against the predicate Q_A. The labels of all the nodes n that do not satisfy Q_A, are changed into $\ominus$. In addition, all their ancestors are also labelled as $\ominus$. This is sound due to the anti-monotonicity. So, we can propagate these $\ominus$ marks upwards until we have marked the root with $\ominus$. Actually, we can stop as soon as we reach an ancestor already marked with $\ominus$, as another such leaf node n' may share some ancestors with n. So, all the ancestors from that point upwards have already been marked with $\ominus$. Secondly, for those nodes p in F_0 that satisfy Q_A, the label remains unchanged (i.e. $\oplus$). Furthermore, we will enter their parent into the set F_1 (and remove possible duplicates). F_1 contains the nodes to be considered at the next iteration. This process is then repeated until F_k becomes empty.

So, after these two phases, namely DESCEND and then ASCEND, both the monotonic and the anti-monotonic constraints are handled. With a simple tree traversal, we can prune away those subtrees that contain only $\ominus$ labels. The

---

[2]As in Apriori, one only needs to scan the data sets at most once for each level of the tree.

[3]There are some differences here since we are dealing with strings instead of sets. E.g., while Apriori-join generates item set {a, b, c} from {a, b} and {a, c}, the descend algorithm generates abc from ab and bc, because these are the *only* immediately shorter *substrings* of abc. At the same time, it is not hard to imagine a variant of the version space tree algorithm for use with item sets. Indeed, the kind of trie searched is quite similar to some of the data structures used by e.g. [3, 11].

result is a tree that is a pruned suffix trie representing the version space of strings that satisfy the query $Q_A \wedge Q_M$.

Theorem 4.1 *The VST algorithm performs at most $2m$ database scans, where m is length of the longest strings satisfying the monotonic query Q_M.*

5. Experiments

We have implemented the VST algorithm and performed experiments on datasets of command histories collected from 168 Unix users over a period of time [7]. The users are divided into four groups: computer scientists, experienced programmers, novice programmers and non-programmers. The corresponding data sets are denoted "sci", "exp", "nov" and "non", respectively. When each user accesses the Unix system, he first logs in, then types in a sequence of commands, and finally logs out. Each command is recorded as a symbol in the database. The sequence of commands from log in to log out constitutes a login session, and is mapped to a string in our experiment. Each user contributes to many login sessions in the database. Table 1 gives some statistics on the data.

In the first set of experiments we determined solutions of queries min_freq(p, n, D) for the four different datasets and for thresholds n that were selected so as to produce solution sets of around 300 frequent string patterns. Table 1 summarizes the datasets, the queries, and their solutions. Timings (wall-clock time on a Pentium III 600 Mhz) are reported as well.

Whereas the first set of experiments only used the min_freq predicate, the second set of experiments involves the computation of two version space trees T_1 and T_2 corresponding to the queries Q_8 and Q_9:

$$Q_8 : \text{min\_freq}(p, non, 24) \wedge \text{max\_freq}(p, sci, 60)$$

$$Q_9 : \text{min\_freq}(p, nov, 80) \wedge \text{max\_freq}(p, exp, 36)$$

Q_8 and Q_9 are conjunctions of an anti-monotonic predicate and a monotonic one, thus their solution space is a version space. Furthermore, they are the sub-queries that are generated for the query $Q_{10} = Q_8 \vee Q_9$ using the decomposition approach outlined in Section 3.

The results of the second experiment are shown in Table 2. Each row shows the time the algorithm spent on building that tree. The columns of the table show the number of nodes and total length of strings represented by those nodes. Each of the five sub-column in each case shows the number for a subset of the nodes in the final trie. The column "all" shows the figure for all trie nodes. The columns "⊕" and "⊖" show the figure aggregated over nodes with the respective labels only. The columns "S" and "G" show the figures for the maximally specific strings and the minimally specific strings, respectively. For what concerns the

query Q_{10}, there are in total 401 strings in its answer set, and together they have length 1953.

Our experimental results confirm our claim that the sets S and G constitute a compact representation of the set of all patterns satisfying the given constraints Q_M and Q_A. From Table 2, it can be seen that the total length of strings for S and G together is always smaller than that for all interesting patterns (i.e. ⊕). In the case of T_2, the space saving is significant. Moreover, algorithm VST is also very efficient in terms of time and space. This shows that using suffix tries in the mining of string patterns is a promising approach.

The longest pattern found (represented by the deepest node in either T_1 or T_2 having a ⊕ label) was "pix umacs pix umacs pix umacs pix umacs pix umacs pix umacs pix umacs pix umacs pix umacs pix", which has a length of 19.

6. Conclusions

We have described an approach to the general pattern discovery problem in data mining. The method is based on the decomposition of the answer set to a collection of components defined by monotonic and anti-monotonic predicates. Each of the components is a convex set or version space, the borders of which can be computed using the level wise version space algorithm or - for the pattern domain of strings - using the VST algorithm, which employs a novel data structure called the version space tree. Experiments have been presented that validate the approach.

The results we have presented in this paper are by no means complete, a lot of open problems and questions remain. First, it seems possible to adapt the version space trees and algorithm for use in other domains (such as itemsets). However, at present it is unclear how to do this for some more expressive domains such as Datalog queries or even the string domain where one is using a coverage relation based on subsequence matching rather than substring matching. Secondly, for the string domain, it is possible to further optimize these algorithms for specific predicates (e.g. involving frequency counting on a database of strings). Thirdly, we are at present also studying set operations on version space trees. Such operations would allow us to perform some of the logical operations directly on solution spaces. Fourthly, the framework seems also useful in the context of optimizing a sequence of inductive queries. Here, it would be interesting to see how the results to previous (sub) queries could be reused for more efficiently answering the next question.

Although there are many remaining questions, the authors hope that the introduced framework provides a sound theoretical framework for studying these open questions as well as for developing practical inductive database systems based on the idea of inductive querying.

Table 1. Summary statistics of the data

Data set (D)	number of users	number of sequences	minimum frequency (n)	frequent strings found	execution time (seconds)	memory used (bytes)
nov	55	5164	24	294	3.24	56994
exp	36	3859	80	292	2.88	88706
non	25	1906	80	293	0.72	59754
sci	52	7751	48	295	4.89	94290

Table 2. Results on finding the union of two version spaces

Suffix Trie	Time (sec)	number of nodes					total length of strings				
		$\oplus$	$\ominus$	all	S	G	$\oplus$	$\ominus$	all	S	G
T_1	2.55	166	40	206	104	68	472	75	547	305	147
T_2	5.51	237	18	255	85	15	1489	23	1512	416	24

Acknowledgements

This work was partly supported by the European IST FET project cInQ.

References

[1] R. Agrawal and R. Srikant. Fast algorithms for mining association rules. In *Proc. VLDB*, 1994.

[2] R. Agrawal, T. Imielinski, A. Swami. Mining association rules between sets of items in large databases. In *Proc. SIGMOD*, pp. 207-216, 1993.

[3] R. Bayardo. Efficiently mining long patterns from databases. In *Proc. SIGMOD*, 1998.

[4] L. De Raedt, S. Kramer. The level wise version space algorithm and its application to molecular fragment finding. In *Proc. IJCAI*, 2001.

[5] L. De Raedt. Query evaluation and optimisation in inductive databases using version spaces. In *Proc. EDBT Workshop on DTDM*, 2002.

[6] B. Goethals, J. Van den Bussche. On supporting interactive association rule mining. In *Proc. DAWAK*, LNCS Vol. 1874, Springer Verlag, 2000.

[7] S. Greenberg. Using unix: Collected traces of 168 users. Research Report 88/333/45, Department of Computer Science, University of Calgary, Canada, 1988.

[8] D. Gunopulos, H. Mannila, S. Saluja. Discovering All Most Specific Sentences by Randomized Algorithms. In *Proc. ICDT*, LNCS Vol. 1186, Springer Verlag, 1997.

[9] J. Han, Y. Fu, K. Koperski, W. Wang, and O. Zaiane. DMQL: A Data Mining Query Language for Relational Databases.In *Proc. SIGMOD'96 Workshop on Research Issues on Data Mining and Knowledge Discovery*, Montreal, Canada, June 1996.

[10] J. Han, L. V. S. Lakshmanan, and R. T. Ng. Constraint-Based, Multidimensional Data Mining, *Computer*, Vol. 32(8), pp. 46-50, 1999.

[11] J. Han, J. Pei, and Y. Yin. Mining frequent patterns without candidate generation. In *Proc. SIGMOD*, 2000.

[12] H. Hirsh. Generalizing Version Spaces. *Machine Learning*, Vol. 17(1): 5-46 (1994).

[13] H. Hirsh. Theoretical underpinnings of versionspaes. In *Proc. IJCAI*, 1991.

[14] S. Kramer, L. De Raedt, C. Helma. Molecular Feature Mining in HIV Data. In *Proc. SIGKDD*, 2001.

[15] H. Mannila and H. Toivonen. Levelwise search and borders of theories in knowledge discovery, *Data Mining and Knowledge Discovery*, Vol. 1, 1997.

[16] T. Mitchell. Generalization as Search, *Artificial Intelligence*, Vol. 18 (2), pp. 203-226, 1980.

[17] R. T. Ng, L. V.S. Lakshmanan, J. Han, and A. Pang. Exploratory mining and pruning optimizations of constrained associations rules. In *Proc. SIGMOD*, 1998.

[18] E. Ukkonen. On-line construction of suffix trees. *Algorithmica*, 14(3):249–260, 1995.

[19] P. Weiner. Linear pattern matching algorithm. In *Proc. 14th IEEE Symposium on Switching and Automata Theory*, pages 1–11, 1973.

Iterative Clustering of High Dimensional Text Data Augmented by Local Search

Inderjit S. Dhillon* and Yuqiang Guan*
Department of Computer Sciences
University of Texas
Austin, TX 78712-1188, USA
inderjit, yguan@cs.utexas.edu

J. Kogan
Department of Mathematics and Statistics
University of Maryland Baltimore County
Baltimore, MD 21228, USA
kogan@math.umbc.edu

Abstract

The k-means algorithm with cosine similarity, also known as the spherical k-means algorithm, is a popular method for clustering document collections. However, spherical k-means can often yield qualitatively poor results, especially when cluster sizes are small, say 25-30 documents per cluster, where it tends to get stuck at a local maximum far away from the optimal solution. In this paper, we present a local search procedure, which we call "first-variation" that refines a given clustering by incrementally moving data points between clusters, thus achieving a higher objective function value. An enhancement of first variation allows a chain of such moves in a Kernighan-Lin fashion and leads to a better local maximum. Combining the enhanced first-variation with spherical k-means yields a powerful "ping-pong" strategy that often qualitatively improves k-means clustering and is computationally efficient. We present several experimental results to highlight the improvement achieved by our proposed algorithm in clustering high-dimensional and sparse text data.

1. Introduction

Clustering or grouping document collections into conceptually meaningful clusters is a well-studied problem. A starting point for applying clustering algorithms to unstructured document collections is to create a *vector space model*, alternatively known as a *bag-of-words model* [16]. The basic idea is (a) to extract unique content-bearing words from the set of documents treating these words as *features* and (b) to then represent each document as a vector of certain weighted word frequencies in this feature space. Typically, a large number of words exist in even a moderately sized set of documents where a few thousand words or more are common; hence the document vectors are very high-dimensional. In addition, a single document typically contains only a small fraction of the total number of words in the entire collection; hence, the document vectors are generally very sparse, i.e., contain a lot of zero entries.

The k-means algorithm is a popular method for clustering a set of data vectors [5]. The classical version of k-means uses squared Euclidean distance, however this distance measure is often inappropriate for its application to document clustering [18]. An effective measure of similarity between documents, and one that is often used in information retrieval, is cosine similarity, which uses the cosine of the angle between document vectors [16]. The k-means algorithm can be adapted to use the cosine similarity metric to yield the *spherical k-means* algorithm, so named because the algorithm operates on vectors that lie on the unit sphere [4]. Since it uses cosine similarity, spherical k-means exploits the sparsity of document vectors and is highly efficient [3].

The spherical k-means algorithm, similar to the Euclidean algorithm, is a hill-climbing procedure and is prone to getting stuck at a local optimum (finding the global optimum is NP-complete). For large document clusters, it has been found to yield good results in practice, i.e., the local optimum found yields good conceptual clusters [4, 18, 3]. However, as we show in Section 3, spherical k-means often produces poor results on small and moderately sized clusters where it tends to get stuck in a qualitatively inferior local optimum.

In this paper, we present an algorithm that uses local search to refine the clusters produced by spherical k-means. Our refinement algorithm alternates between two phases: (a) first-variation and (b) spherical k-means itself. A first-variation step moves a single document from one cluster to another, thereby increasing the objective function value. A sequence of first-variation moves allows an escape from a local maximum, so that fresh iterations of spherical k-means can be applied to further increase the objective function value. This ping-pong strategy yields a powerful refinement algorithm which often qualitatively improves k-means clustering and is computationally efficient. Note that our refinement algorithm *always* improves upon the input clustering in terms of the objective function value.

Many variants of k-means, such as "batch" and "incre-

---
*This research was supported by NSF Grant No. ACI-0093404.

mental" versions have been proposed in the literature, see Section 6 for a discussion. The main contribution of this paper is our use of local search for document clustering. Our strategy leads to a "ping-pong" algorithm which alternates between "batch" k-means and first-variation iterations, thereby harnessing the power of both in terms of improved quality of results and computational speed.

We now give an outline of the paper. In Section 2, we present the spherical k-means algorithm while Section 3 presents scenarios in which this algorithm performs poorly. In Section 4, we introduce the first-variation method and present our proposed refinement algorithm. Experimental results in Section 5 show that our algorithm yields qualitatively better results giving higher objective function values. In Section 6 we discuss related work and finally, in Section 7 we present our conclusions and future work.

2. Spherical k-means algorithm

We start with some necessary notation. Let d be the number of documents, w be the number of words and let $\mathbf{X} = \{\mathbf{x}_1, \mathbf{x}_2, \dots, \mathbf{x}_d\}$ denote the set of non-negative document vectors, where each $\mathbf{x}_i \in R^w$ and $\|\mathbf{x}_i\|(\equiv \|\mathbf{x}_i\|_2) = 1$, i.e., each $\mathbf{x}_i$ lies on the unit sphere. A clustering of the document collection is its partitioning into disjoint subsets $\pi_1, \pi_2, \dots, \pi_k$, i.e., $\bigcup_{j=1}^{k} \pi_j = \mathbf{X}$ and $\pi_j \cap \pi_l = \phi, j \neq l$. For a cluster π we denote the sum $\sum_{\mathbf{x} \in \pi} \mathbf{x}$ by $\mathbf{s}(\pi)$. The concept vector of the cluster π is defined by

$$\mathbf{c}(\pi) = \frac{\mathbf{s}(\pi)}{\|\mathbf{s}(\pi)\|},$$

i.e., the concept vector of the cluster is its normalized expectation. We define the "quality" or "coherence" of a non-empty cluster π as

$$q(\pi) = \sum_{\mathbf{x} \in \pi} \mathbf{x}^T \mathbf{c}(\pi) = \|\mathbf{s}(\pi)\|. \tag{1}$$

We set $q(\phi) = 0$ for convenience. Finally, for a partition $\{\pi_j\}_{j=1}^{k}$ we define the objective function to be the sum of the qualities of the k clusters:

$$\mathcal{Q}\left(\{\pi_j\}_{j=1}^{k}\right) = \sum_{j=1}^{k} q(\pi_j) = \sum_{j=1}^{k} \sum_{\mathbf{x} \in \pi_j} \mathbf{x}^T \mathbf{c}_j,$$

where we have written $\mathbf{c}_j$ for $\mathbf{c}(\pi_j)$. The goal is to find a clustering that maximizes the value of the above objective function. In what follows we present the spherical k-means algorithm which is an iterative process that generates a sequence of partitions $\{\pi_l^{(t)}\}_{l=1}^{k}$, $t = 0, 1, \dots$, such that

$$\mathcal{Q}\left(\{\pi_j^{(t+1)}\}_{j=1}^{k}\right) \geq \mathcal{Q}\left(\{\pi_j^{(t)}\}_{j=1}^{k}\right). \tag{2}$$

To emphasize the relationship between successive partitions we shall denote the "next" partition generated by k-means,

$\{\pi_j^{(t+1)}\}_{j=1}^{k}$, by $\texttt{nextKM}\left(\{\pi_l^{(t)}\}_{l=1}^{k}\right)$. With the above notation, we now present the spherical k-means algorithm. Given a user supplied tolerance $\texttt{tol} > 0$ do the following:

1. Start with a partitioning $\{\pi_l^{(0)}\}_{l=1}^{k}$ and the concept vectors $\mathbf{c}_1^{(0)}, \mathbf{c}_2^{(0)}, \dots, \mathbf{c}_k^{(0)}$ associated with the partitioning. Set the index of iteration $t = 0$.

2. For each document vector $\mathbf{x} \in \mathbf{X}$ find the concept vector $\mathbf{c}_{l^*(\mathbf{x})}$ closest in cosine similarity to $\mathbf{x}$ (unless stated otherwise we break ties arbitrarily), i.e.,

$$l^*(\mathbf{x}) = \arg\max_j \mathbf{x}^T \mathbf{c}_j^{(t)}.$$

Next, compute the new partitioning $\{\pi_l^{(t+1)}\}_{l=1}^{k} = \texttt{nextKM}\left(\{\pi_l^{(t)}\}_{l=1}^{k(t)}\right)$ induced by the old concept vectors $\{\mathbf{c}_l^{(t)}\}_{l=1}^{k}$:

$$\pi_l^{(t+1)} = \{\mathbf{x} \in \mathbf{X} : l^*(\mathbf{x}) = l\}, \ 1 \leq l \leq k. \tag{3}$$

3. Compute the new concept vectors corresponding to the partitioning computed in (3):

$$\mathbf{c}_l^{(t+1)} = \frac{\mathbf{s}(\pi_l^{(t+1)})}{\|\mathbf{s}(\pi_l^{(t+1)})\|}.$$

4. If $\mathcal{Q}\left(\texttt{nextKM}\left(\{\pi_l^{(t)}\}_{l=1}^{k(t)}\right)\right) - \mathcal{Q}\left(\{\pi_l^{(t)}\}_{l=1}^{k}\right)$ is greater than $\texttt{tol}$, increment t by 1 and go to step 2 above. Otherwise, stop.

As noted in (2), it can be shown that the above algorithm is a gradient-ascent scheme, i.e., the objective function value increases from one iteration to the next. For details, including a proof, see [4]. However, like any gradient-ascent scheme, the spherical k-means algorithm is prone to local maxima.

3 Inadequacy of k-means

We now present some scenarios in which spherical k-means can get stuck in a qualitatively poor local maximum.

Example 3.1 *Consider the three unit vectors in* $\mathbf{R}^2$:

$$\mathbf{x}_1 = (1,0)^T, \ \mathbf{x}_2 = (\cos\theta, \sin\theta)^T, \ \mathbf{x}_3 = (0,1)^T.$$

Let the initial partition be $\pi_1^{(0)} = \{\mathbf{x}_1, \mathbf{x}_2\}$, $\pi_2^{(0)} = \{\mathbf{x}_3\}$. *The value of the objective function for this partition is* $\mathcal{Q}_0 = 2\cos(\theta/2) + 1$. *When* $0 \leq \theta \leq \pi/3$ *the concept vector* $\mathbf{c}_1 = \cos(\theta/2)$ *of the cluster* $\pi_1^{(0)}$ *is closest in cosine similarity to vectors* $\mathbf{x}_1$ *and* $\mathbf{x}_2$. *Hence, an application of spherical k-means does not change the partition(see figure below).*

The partition $\pi_1^{(1)} = \{\mathbf{x}_1\}$, $\pi_2^{(1)} = \{\mathbf{x}_2, \mathbf{x}_3\}$, has the objective function value $\mathcal{Q}_1 = 2\cos(\pi/4 - \theta/2) + 1$. If $\theta = \pi/3$, then $\mathcal{Q}_0 = 2\cos(\pi/6) + 1 < 2\cos(\pi/12) + 1 = \mathcal{Q}_1$, and so the optimal partition is missed by k-means.

In Section 4, we show that a "first variation" iteration corrects the above problem and generates the optimal partition $\pi_1^{(1)} = \{\mathbf{x}_1\}$, $\pi_2^{(1)} = \{\mathbf{x}_2, \mathbf{x}_3\}$ starting from $\pi_1^{(0)}$ and $\pi_2^{(0)}$.

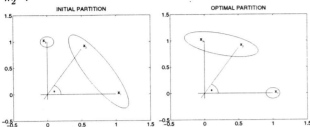

Example 3.2 *Consider the set of vectors arranged as columns of the $(k^2 + k) \times k$ matrix:*

$$\mathbf{X} = [\mathbf{x}_1, \mathbf{x}_2, \ldots, \mathbf{x}_{k^2}] = \begin{bmatrix} \mathbf{K}_1 & \mathbf{K}_2 & \ldots & \mathbf{K}_k \\ \mathbf{I} & 0 & \ldots & 0 \\ 0 & \mathbf{I} & \ldots & 0 \\ \ldots & \ldots & \ldots & \ldots \\ 0 & \ldots & \ldots & \mathbf{I} \end{bmatrix},$$

where $\mathbf{I}$ is the $k \times k$ identity matrix and $\mathbf{K}_l$ is the $k \times k$ matrix with entries $\frac{1}{k}$ in the lth row and 0's elsewhere. Note that all vectors $\mathbf{x}_i \in R^{k^2+k}$ have the same norm, $\|\mathbf{x}_i\| = \sqrt{1 + 1/k^2}$, and they form k natural clusters with $\mathbf{x}_{ik+j}$ being placed in cluster $i + 1$.

The intra-cluster and inter-cluster dot products are respectively given by

1. $\mathbf{x}_i^T \mathbf{x}_j = \frac{1}{k^2}$, where $(l-1)k < i < j \leq lk$ and $l = 1, \ldots, k$,

2. $\mathbf{x}_i^T \mathbf{x}_j = 0$, otherwise.

As mentioned above, the best clustering would have $\mathbf{x}_1, \ldots, \mathbf{x}_k$ in the first cluster, $\mathbf{x}_{k+1}, \ldots, \mathbf{x}_{2k}$ in the second cluster, and so on. For this optimal clustering, the cosine of any $\mathbf{x}_i$ with its own concept vector is $\frac{1 + \frac{1}{k}}{\sqrt{1 + \frac{1}{k^2}}\sqrt{k+1}} = \sqrt{\frac{k+1}{k^2+1}}$, and 0 with any other concept vector.

But suppose we initialize the k clusters as follows: cluster 1 consists of $\mathbf{x}_1, \mathbf{x}_{k+1}, \ldots, \mathbf{x}_{k^2-k+1}$, cluster 2 consists of $\mathbf{x}_2, \mathbf{x}_{k+2}, \ldots, \mathbf{x}_{k^2-k+2}$, and generally cluster l consists of $\mathbf{x}_l, \mathbf{x}_{k+l}, \ldots, \mathbf{x}_{k^2-k+l}$, for $1 \leq l \leq k$. Then it can be seen that spherical k-means does not change this initial clustering at all. This is because the cosine of $\mathbf{x}_i$ with its own concept vector is $\frac{1 + \frac{1}{k^2}}{\sqrt{1 + \frac{1}{k^2}}\sqrt{k + \frac{1}{k}}} = \frac{1}{\sqrt{k}}$, and $\frac{1}{k^2\sqrt{1 + \frac{1}{k^2}}\sqrt{k + \frac{1}{k}}} = \frac{1}{\sqrt{k^2+1}\sqrt{k}}$ with any other concept vector. The situation is similar with most other starting partitions. In a set of experiments for $k = 5$, we observed that all 100 runs of spherical k-means with random initializations stopped without a change in the initial clustering.

Example 3.3 *The above behavior is often seen in real-life applications. As a concrete example, we took a collection of 30 documents consisting of 10 documents each from the three distinct classes MEDLINE, CISI and CRAN (see Section 5 for more details). These 30 documents contain a total of 1073 words (after removing stop words). Due to this high-dimensionality, the cosine similarities between the 30 document vectors are quite low. The average cosine similarity between all documents is 0.025; however the average cosine between documents in the same class is 0.294 while the average inter-class cosine is 0.0068. Thus there is a clear separation between intra-class cosines and inter-class cosines and so it seems that a good clustering algorithm should be easily able to recover the original class structure.*

However, when we run spherical k-means on this data set, there is hardly any movement of document vectors between clusters irrespective of the starting partition — indeed we observed that 96% of 1000 different starting partitions resulted in no movement at all, i.e., k-means returned a final partition that was identical to the initial partition. This behavior is unusual; in contrast, for large data sets the first few iterations of spherical k-means typically lead to a lot of movement of data points between clusters [4, 3]. However, a closer look reveals the reasons for this failure. Consider a document vector $\mathbf{x}$, and consider an initial cluster π_i such that $\mathbf{x} \notin \pi_i$. Due to the small number of data points and the small average cosine similarity between documents, $\mathbf{x}^T \mathbf{c}_i$ turns out to be quite small in magnitude for an arbitrary initial partitioning. However, it is instructive to take a closer look at $\mathbf{x}$ and its own cluster. If $\mathbf{x} \in \pi_l$, the cosine similarity $\mathbf{x}^T \mathbf{c}_l$ may be broken down into two parts:

$$\mathbf{x}^T \mathbf{c}_l = \frac{1}{\|\mathbf{s}(\pi_l)\|} + \sum_{y \in \pi_l - \{\mathbf{x}\}} \frac{\mathbf{x}^T \mathbf{y}}{\|\mathbf{s}(\pi_l)\|}$$

where the first term has 1 in the numerator since $\mathbf{x}^T \mathbf{x} = 1$ (due to the contribution of $\mathbf{x}$ in $\mathbf{c}_l$). For data sets that are high-dimensional and contain a small number of points, this first term itself is typically much larger in magnitude than $\mathbf{x}^T \mathbf{c}_i$, $\mathbf{x} \notin \pi_i$. As a result, a spherical k-means iteration retains each document vector in its original cluster. Thus, in this case we start with an arbitrarily poor clustering and the k-means algorithm returns this poor clustering as the final output. We now see how to overcome this difficulty.

4 Refinement Algorithm

This section describes algorithms to "fix" the above problems.

4.1 First Variation

Definition 4.1 *A first variation of a partition $\{\pi_l\}_{l=1}^k$ is a partition $\{\pi_l'\}_{l=1}^k$ obtained by removing a single vector $\mathbf{x}$ from a cluster π_i of $\{\pi_l\}_{l=1}^k$ and assigning this vector to an existing cluster π_j of $\{\pi_l\}_{l=1}^k$.*

We denote the set of all first variation partitions of $\{\pi_l\}_{l=1}^k$ by $\mathcal{FV}\left(\{\pi_l\}_{l=1}^k\right)$. Among all the elements of this set, we seek to select the "steepest ascent" partition. The formal definition of this partition is given next.

Definition 4.2 *The partition* $\texttt{nextFV}\left(\{\pi_l\}_{l=1}^k\right)$ *is a first variation of* $\{\pi_l\}_{l=1}^k$ *so that for each first variation* $\{\pi_l'\}_{l=1}^k$,

$$\mathcal{Q}\left(\texttt{nextFV}\left(\{\pi_l\}_{l=1}^k\right)\right) \geq \mathcal{Q}\left(\{\pi_l'\}_{l=1}^k\right).$$

The proposed first variation algorithm generates a sequence of partitions $\{\pi_l^{(t)}\}_{l=1}^k, t \geq 0$, so that

$$\{\pi_l^{(t+1)}\}_{l=1}^k = \texttt{nextFV}\left(\{\pi_l^{(t)}\}_{l=1}^k\right), \quad t = 0, 1, \ldots.$$

We now pause briefly to illustrate differences between first variation iterations and the spherical k-means iterations. To simplify the presentation we consider a two cluster partition $\{\mathbf{Z}, \mathbf{Y}\}$ where $\mathbf{Z} = \{\mathbf{z}_1, \ldots, \mathbf{z}_n\}$, and $\mathbf{Y} = \{\mathbf{y}_1, \ldots, \mathbf{y}_m\}$. Our goal is to examine whether a single vector, say $\mathbf{z}_n$, should be removed from $\mathbf{Z}$, and assigned to $\mathbf{Y}$. We denote the potential new clusters by $\mathbf{Z}^-$ and $\mathbf{Y}^+$, i.e., $\mathbf{Z}^- = \{\mathbf{z}_1, \ldots, \mathbf{z}_{n-1}\}$ and $\mathbf{Y}^+ = \{\mathbf{y}_1, \ldots, \mathbf{y}_m, \mathbf{z}_n\}$. Note that spherical k-means examines the quantity

$$\Delta_{kmeans} = \mathbf{z}_n^T\left[\mathbf{c}(\mathbf{Y}) - \mathbf{c}(\mathbf{Z})\right]. \tag{4}$$

If $\Delta_{kmeans} > 0$, then the spherical k-means algorithm moves $\mathbf{z}_n$ from $\mathbf{Z}$ to $\mathbf{Y}$. Otherwise $\mathbf{z}_n$ remains in $\mathbf{Z}$.

Unlike k-means, first variation computes

$$\Delta = \left[q\left(\mathbf{Z}^-\right) - q(\mathbf{Z})\right] + \left[q\left(\mathbf{Y}^+\right) - q(\mathbf{Y})\right],$$

where the quality q is as in (1). A straightforward computation shows that

$$\Delta = \left[\sum_{i=1}^{n-1}\mathbf{z}_i^T\mathbf{c}(\mathbf{Z}^-) - \sum_{i=1}^{n-1}\mathbf{z}_i^T\mathbf{c}(\mathbf{Z}) - \mathbf{z}_n^T\mathbf{c}(\mathbf{Z})\right] +$$
$$\left[\sum_{i=1}^{m}\mathbf{y}_i^T\mathbf{c}(\mathbf{Y}^+) + \mathbf{z}_n^T\mathbf{c}(\mathbf{Y}^+) - \sum_{i=1}^{m}\mathbf{y}_i^T\mathbf{c}(\mathbf{Y})\right]$$
$$= \sum_{i=1}^{m}\mathbf{y}_i^T\left[\mathbf{c}(\mathbf{Y}^+) - \mathbf{c}(\mathbf{Y})\right] + \mathbf{z}_n^T\left[\mathbf{c}(\mathbf{Y}^+) - \mathbf{c}(\mathbf{Y})\right] +$$
$$\sum_{i=1}^{n-1}\mathbf{z}_i^T\left[\mathbf{c}(\mathbf{Z}^-) - \mathbf{c}(\mathbf{Z})\right] + \Delta_{kmeans}, \tag{5}$$

where Δ_{kmeans} is defined in (4). By the Cauchy-Schwarz inequality, we have

$$\sum_{i=1}^{n-1}\mathbf{z}_i^T\mathbf{c}(\mathbf{Z}^-) \geq \sum_{i=1}^{n-1}\mathbf{z}_i^T\mathbf{c}(\mathbf{Z}), \quad \text{and so}$$
$$\sum_{i=1}^{n-1}\mathbf{z}_i^T\left[\mathbf{c}(\mathbf{Z}^-) - \mathbf{c}(\mathbf{Z})\right] \geq 0.$$

For the same reason,

$$\sum_{i=1}^{m}\mathbf{y}_i^T\left[\mathbf{c}(\mathbf{Y}^+) - \mathbf{c}(\mathbf{Y})\right] + \mathbf{z}_n^T\left[\mathbf{c}(\mathbf{Y}^+) - \mathbf{c}(\mathbf{Y})\right] \geq 0.$$

These two inequalities along with (5) imply that:

$$\Delta \geq \Delta_{kmeans}.$$

The last inequality shows that even when $\Delta_{kmeans} \leq 0$ and cluster affiliation of $\mathbf{z}_n$ is not changed by spherical k-means, the quantity Δ may still be positive. Thus, while $\mathcal{Q}\left(\{\mathbf{Z}^-, \mathbf{Y}^+\}\right) > \mathcal{Q}\left(\{\mathbf{Z}, \mathbf{Y}\}\right)$, the partition $\{\mathbf{Z}^-, \mathbf{Y}^+\}$ will be missed by spherical k-means (see Example 3.1). We now turn to the magnitude of $\Delta - \Delta_{kmeans}$. From (5),

$$0 \leq \Delta - \Delta_{kmeans} = \mathbf{s}(\mathbf{Z}^-)^T\left[\mathbf{c}(\mathbf{Z}^-) - \mathbf{c}(\mathbf{Z})\right] + \mathbf{s}(\mathbf{Y}^+)^T\left[\mathbf{c}(\mathbf{Y}^+) - \mathbf{c}(\mathbf{Y})\right].\tag{6}$$

Since the vectors $\mathbf{s}(\mathbf{Z}^-)$ and $\mathbf{c}(\mathbf{Z}^-)$ are proportional, a large value of $\mathbf{c}(\mathbf{Z}^-) - \mathbf{c}(\mathbf{Z})$ results in a large dot product $\mathbf{s}(\mathbf{Z}^-)^T\left[\mathbf{c}(\mathbf{Z}^-) - \mathbf{c}(\mathbf{Z})\right]$. A similar argument holds for the second term on the right hand side of (6). Hence we can expect a "substantial" difference between Δ and Δ_{kmeans} when removing a vector from cluster $\mathbf{Z}$ and assigning it to cluster $\mathbf{Y}$ "significantly" changes locations of the corresponding concept vectors. This phenomenon is unlikely to happen when clusters are large. However, first variation iterations become effective in the case of small clusters (clusters of size 100 or less in our experience). The "spherical first variation" algorithm is formally presented below. Given a user supplied tolerance $\texttt{tol} > 0$ do the following:

1. Start with a partitioning $\{\pi_l^{(0)}\}_{l=1}^k$. Set the index of iteration $t = 0$.

2. Generate $\{\pi_l^{(t+1)}\}_{i=1}^k = \texttt{nextFV}(\{\pi_l^{(t)}\}_{l=1}^k)$.

3. If $\mathcal{Q}\left(\texttt{nextFV}\left(\{\pi_l^{(t)}\}_{l=1}^k\right)\right) - \mathcal{Q}\left(\{\pi_l^{(t)}\}_{l=1}^k\right)$ is greater than $\texttt{tol}$, increment t by 1, and go to step 2. Otherwise, stop.

It is easy to see that a single "spherical first variation" iteration applied to the initial partition of Example 3.1 generates the "optimal partition".

We now address the time and memory complexity of first variation iterations. The computational bottleneck is in computing $q(\pi_i^{(t)} - \{\mathbf{x}\}) - q(\pi_i^{(t)})$ and $q(\pi_j^{(t)} \cup \{\mathbf{x}\}) - q(\pi_j^{(t)})$ for all the document vectors $\mathbf{x} \in \mathbf{X}$. Note that

$$q\left(\pi_i^{(t)} - \{\mathbf{x}\}\right) - q\left(\pi_i^{(t)}\right) =$$
$$\left(\|\mathbf{s}(\pi_i^{(t)})\|^2 - 2\|\mathbf{s}(\pi_i^{(t)})\|\mathbf{x}^T\mathbf{c}(\pi_i^{(t)}) + 1\right)^{1/2} - \|\mathbf{s}(\pi_i^{(t)})\|\tag{7}$$

and

$$q\left(\pi_j^{(t)} \cup \{\mathbf{x}\}\right) - q\left(\pi_j^{(t)}\right) =$$

$$\left(\|\mathbf{s}(\pi_j^{(t)})\|^2 + 2\|\mathbf{s}(\pi_j^{(t)})\|\mathbf{x}^T\mathbf{c}(\pi_j^{(t)}) + 1\right)^{1/2} - \|\mathbf{s}(\pi_j^{(t)})\| \quad (8)$$

We remark that computation of the quantities $\|\mathbf{s}(\pi_l^{(t)})\|$, and $\mathbf{x}^T\mathbf{c}(\pi_l^{(t)})$, $\mathbf{x} \in \mathbf{X}$, $l = 1, \ldots, k$ are needed for iterations of the spherical k-means algorithm as well. When these quantities are available, a first variation iteration can be completed in $O(d + k)$ amortized time, where d is the number of document vectors.

4.2 Kernighan-Lin Chains

A first variation iteration moves a single vector that maximally increases the objective function value. One way to enhance first variation is by expanding the local search to seek a chain of moves instead of just one move. Note that the first few moves in this chain might lead to a temporary decrease in objective function value, but overall we seek the chain that leads to a maximal increase. We implement this idea by following the well known Kernighan-Lin heuristic for graph partitioning [10].

The search for the optimal chain proceeds as follows. We generate a first variation move, record the improvement in objective function value, and then "mark" the moved vector so that it is not moved again in this chain. We repeat this step, say, f times where f is a user defined parameter. Finally, we search for that prefix of moves that leads to the greatest increase in objective function value. This idea is formally described below (the notation $\texttt{nextFV}\left(\{\pi_l\}_{l=1}^k, \mathbf{U}\right)$ restricts the search for the vector to be moved to the set of unmarked vectors $\mathbf{U}$).

Given a user supplied tolerance $\texttt{tol} > 0$ and a number f, do the following:

1. Start with a partitioning $\{\pi_l^{(0)}\}_{l=1}^k$. Set the index of iteration $t = 0$.
2. Set $j = 0, \mathbf{U} = \mathbf{X}$ and do the following f times:
   (a) Set $\{\pi_l^{(t+j+1)}\}_{l=1}^k = \texttt{nextFV}\left(\{\pi_l^{(t+j)}\}_{l=1}^k, \mathbf{U}\right)$. Mark the vector moved and delete it from $\mathbf{U}$.
   (b) Record $\quad \mathcal{Q}\left(\texttt{nextFV}\left(\{\pi_l^{(t+j)}\}_{l=1}^k, \mathbf{U}\right)\right) - \mathcal{Q}\left(\{\pi_l^{(t+j)}\}_{l=1}^k\right)$ in $\texttt{ObjChange[j]}$. Increment j by 1.
3. Set $\texttt{MaxChange} = \max_i \sum_{j=0}^i \texttt{ObjChange[j]}$ and $\texttt{MaxI} = \arg\max_i \sum_{j=0}^i \texttt{ObjChange[j]}$, $i = 0, 1, \ldots, f - 1$.
4. If $\texttt{MaxChange} \geq \texttt{tol}$, increment t by $\texttt{MaxI+1}$, and go to step 2. Otherwise, output the partition $\{\pi_l^{(t)}\}_{l=1}^k$ and $\texttt{MaxI}$, and then stop.

Given an initial partitioning $\{\pi_l\}_{l=1}^k$, $\texttt{tol}$ and f, this KL-chain first variation algorithm outputs the partition $\texttt{nextKLFV}\left(\{\pi_l\}_{l=1}^k\right)$.

4.3 The Refinement Algorithm

The advantage of "spherical first variation" is that it computes an exact change in the value of the objective function; however these iterations lead to small increases in the objective function value. On the other hand, k-means iterations typically lead to larger increases. To achieve best results we combine these iterations. Our "ping-pong" refinement algorithm is a two step procedure — the first step runs spherical k-means; if the first step fails the second step runs the Kernighan-Lin heuristic outlined in the previous section. The proposed refinement algorithm is as follows. Given a user supplied tolerance $\texttt{tol} > 0$ do the following:

1. Start with a partitioning $\{\pi_l^{(0)}\}_{l=1}^k$. Set the index of iteration $t = 0$.
2. Generate the partition $\texttt{nextKM}\left(\{\pi_l^{(t)}\}_{l=1}^k\right)$. If $\mathcal{Q}\left(\texttt{nextKM}\left(\{\pi_l^{(t)}\}_{l=1}^k\right)\right) - \mathcal{Q}\left(\{\pi_l^{(t)}\}_{l=1}^k\right)$ is greater than $\texttt{tol}$, set $\{\pi_l^{(t+1)}\}_{l=1}^k = \texttt{nextKM}\left(\{\pi_l^{(t)}\}_{l=1}^k\right)$, increment t by 1 and repeat step 2.
3. Generate the partition $\texttt{nextKLFV}\left(\{\pi_l^{(t)}\}_{l=1}^k\right)$. If $\mathcal{Q}\left(\texttt{nextKLFV}\left(\{\pi_l^{(t)}\}_{l=1}^k\right)\right) - \mathcal{Q}\left(\{\pi_j^{(t)}\}_{j=1}^k\right)$ is greater than $\texttt{tol}$, increment t by $\texttt{MaxI+1}$, set $\{\pi_l^{(t)}\}_{l=1}^k = \texttt{nextKLFV}\left(\{\pi_l^{(t)}\}_{l=1}^k\right)$, and go to step 2. Otherwise, stop.

We emphasize that most of the computations associated with step 3 above have already been performed in step 2, see (7) and (8). Hence the computational overhead of running a first variation iteration just after an iteration of spherical k-means is small. Note also that the above algorithm can do no worse than spherical k-means. Indeed, as we show below, in many cases the quality of clusters produced is much superior.

5 Experimental Results

In this section, we present experimental results which demonstrate that our proposed algorithm often qualitatively improves k-means clustering results. In all our experiments with spherical k-means, we tried several initialization schemes varying from random initial partitions to choosing the initial centroids as data vectors that are "maximally" far apart from each other [2].

For our first experiment we created the data set described in Example 3.2 setting $k = 5$. We observed that all 100 runs of spherical k-means with different initializations stopped without changing the initial partition. However, on applying our refinement algorithm to this initial partitioning and

Table 1. Confusion matrices for Example 3.2 ($k = 5$).

π_1	2	0	0	0	1	π_1	5	0	0	0	0
π_2	0	2	2	0	1	π_2	0	5	0	0	0
π_3	0	0	1	0	0	π_3	0	0	5	0	0
π_4	0	1	1	4	1	π_4	0	0	0	5	0
π_5	3	2	1	1	2	π_5	0	0	0	0	5

Obj. fun. value for spherical
k-means partition:**10.8193**

Obj. fun. value for final
partition:**12.0096**

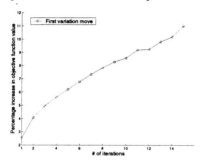

Figure 1. Increase in objective function value for Example 3.2 ($k = 5$, $f = 1$).

setting $f = 1$, i.e. only one first variation move is allowed in the KL chain, we were able to recover the optimal clustering in *all* 100 cases. For a particular run, Table 1 shows the confusion matrices for the initial and final partitions. Note that entry(i, j) in a confusion matrix gives the number of vectors in cluster i that belong to the true class j; thus, a diagonal confusion matrix is desirable. Figure 1 shows the percentage increase in objective function value as our algorithm progresses.

For experiments with real-life text data, we used the MEDLINE, CISI, and CRANFIELD collections (available from ftp://ftp.cs.cornell.edu/pub/smart). MEDLINE consists of 1033 abstracts from medical journals, CISI consists of 1460 abstracts from information retrieval papers, while CRANFIELD consists of 1400 abstracts from aerodynamical systems papers.

For our experiments we created three data sets of 30, 150, and 300 documents respectively (see Example 3.3). Each data set was created by an equal sampling of the three collections. After removing stopwords, the document vectors obtained are very high-dimensional and sparse. The dimensions for the 30, 150 and 300 document data sets are 1073, 3658 and 5577 respectively. In all runs the spherical k-means algorithm *did not change the initial partition*. We then applied our refinement algorithm to generate the final partitions (using $f = 1$). These results are summarized in Tables 2, 3 and 4 by the resulting confusion matrices. In addition, Figures 2, 3 and 4 plot the percentage increase in

Table 2. Confusion matrices for 30 documents with 1073 words.

π_1	5	1	2	π_1	9	1	0
π_2	2	7	1	π_2	0	9	0
π_3	3	2	7	π_3	1	0	10

Obj. fun. value for spherical
k-means partition:**11.0422**

Obj. fun. value for final
partition:**11.9669**

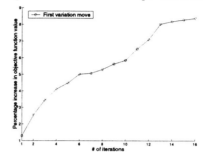

Figure 2. Increase in objective function value for 30 documents ($k = 3$, $f = 1$).

objective function values.

All the final partitions generated have almost diagonal confusion matrices and about $8\% - 25\%$ higher objective function values, which shows that our ping-pong strategy qualitatively improves spherical k-means clustering. The confusion matrices in Table 2 and 3 are almost optimal, while the final partition generated in Table 4 is qualitatively better than the spherical k-means result, but is not optimal. As testified by Figures 2, 3 and 4, the significant fraction of the clustering work is done by first variation iterations.

To improve the final partitioning of the 300 documents and show how KL-chain moves lead to a better local optimum, we applied our refinement algorithm with KL-chains to the partitioning of the 300 documents in Table 4 by setting $f = 30$. Figure 5 shows that during the first 18 moves there is a steady decrease in the objective function value. But from moves 22 to 30 the objective function value increases and becomes greater than the starting value. If we set $f < 22$, then the refinement algorithm will quit without changing the input partition. Figure 5 shows that the first KL-chain of 30 moves triggers a fresh spherical k-means iteration, which substantially increases the objective function value. In the second KL-chain, the maximum increase occurs at the 10th first variation and all the subsequent moves decrease the objective function value. The resulting confusion matrix shown in Table 5 is almost diagonal.

The following experiment shows that our algorithm is more beneficial as the number of clusters k increases. For this experiment we used a much larger collection — the 20-newsgroup data set consists of approximately 20,000 newsgroup postings collected from 20 different usenet news-

Table 3. Confusion matrices for 150 documents with 3652 words.

π_1	25	10	17
π_2	5	18	10
π_3	20	22	23

π_1	49	0	0
π_2	1	49	0
π_3	0	1	50

Obj. fun. value for spherical k-means partition:**28.1934**

Obj. fun. value for final partition:**35.0355**

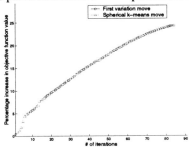

Figure 3. Increase in objective function value for 150 documents ($k = 3$, $f = 1$).

Table 4. Confusion matrices for 300 documents with 5577 words.

π_1	31	28	49
π_2	26	36	34
π_3	43	36	17

π_1	99	0	0
π_2	1	100	19
π_3	0	0	81

Obj. fun. value for spherical k-means partition:**52.7753**

Obj. fun. value for final partition:**58.7598**

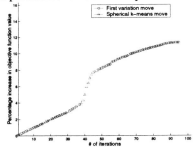

Figure 4. Increase in objective function value for 300 documents ($k = 3$, $f = 1$).

Table 5. Confusion matrices for the 300 documents. using KL-chains with $f = 30$. The objective function values for the *final* partition 59.5886.

π_1	99	0	0
π_2	1	100	19
π_3	0	0	81

π_1	99	0	0
π_2	1	100	0
π_3	0	0	100

Obj. fun. value for *initial* partition:**58.7598**

Obj. fun. value for *final* partition:**59.5886**

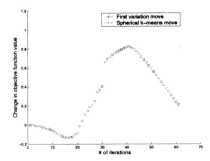

Figure 5. KL-chain moves and change in objective function value for 300 documents ($k = 3$, $f = 30$).

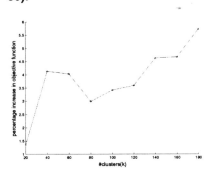

Figure 6. The percentage increase in objective function value of our refinement algorithm over spherical k-means on the 20-newsgroup data set ($f = 20$).

groups [12]. Some of the newsgroups are closely related to each other (e.g., comp.graphics, comp.os.ms-windows.misc and comp.windows.x), while others are unrelated (e.g., alt.atheism, rec.sport.baseball and sci.space). The headers for each of the messages were removed so that they do not bias clustering results, and 1169 duplicate messages were also taken out of the collection. After removing common stopwords and words that occur in less than 2 documents, the documents are represented by 59534-dimensional vectors, which are more than 99.87% sparse.

Figure 6 shows the percentage increase in objective function due to the refinement algorithm over spherical k-means as k increases. The main trend is that as k increases, i.e., when the average cluster size becomes smaller our refinement algorithm leads to greater improvement.

6 Related Work

The k-means algorithm has been well-studied and is one of the most widely used clustering methods [5]. Some of the important early work is due to Forgy[6] and MacQueen[13]. In the vector quantization literature, k-means clustering is also referred to as the Lloyd-Max algorithm[7]; see [8] for a comprehensive history of quantization and its relations to statistical clustering. Many variants of k-means exist; the version we presented in Section 2 is generally attributed to Forgy (see [6, 13]) and is similar to the one given in [5, 10.4.3]; we call this "batch" k-means since the centroids are updated after a batch of points has been reassigned. Another version, which we call "incremental" k-means, randomly selects a single vector $\mathbf{x}$ whose re-assignment from a cluster π_i to a cluster π_j leads to a better objective function value (see [5, 10.8] where this incremental algorithm is referred to as "Basic Iterative Minimum-Squared-Error Clustering"). Incremental k-means is similar to our first-variation iterations. The ISODATA algorithm introduces an additional step in each k-means iteration, in which the number of clusters is adjusted[1].

However, as we have found, neither the batch nor the incremental version is satisfactory for our purposes. As shown in Section 3, batch k-means can give poor results in high-dimensional settings. On the other hand, the incremental version can be computationally expensive. Our main contribution in the paper is the "ping-pong" strategy which exploits the strong points of both batch and incremental k-means.

Other clustering algorithms use "medoids" instead of centroids for clustering, for example, the PAM clustering algorithm swaps a single medoid with a non-selected object as long as the swap results in an improvement of the quality of the clustering (see [9, 14]).

7 Conclusions and Future Research

In this paper, we have presented a refinement algorithm that uses local search after completion of spherical k-means iterations. The resulting improvements in the quality of clustering can be substantial, especially when the data is highly dimensional and sparse and when clusters contain a small number of data vectors. Note that while many implementations of k-means can return empty clusters, our refinement strategy guarantees that all k clusters will be non-empty.

Future enhancement of our algorithm will allow variable number of clusters at each iteration [11]. To accomplish this we plan to modify the objective function as follows:

$$Q_\omega \left(k, \{\pi_j\}_{j=1}^k \right) = \sum_{j=1}^k \left[\sum_{\mathbf{x} \in \pi_j} \mathbf{x}^T \mathbf{c}_j \right] + f(k)\omega$$

where ω is a scalar parameter and $f(k)$ is an increasing function of k. When $\omega = 0$ the trivial partition maximizes the objective function. A negative ω imposes a penalty on the number of clusters, and prevents the trivial partition from becoming the optimal one.

We plan to push this idea further. Instead of keeping ω constant, we plan to select ω at each iteration. The selection will be based on the current partition, and the parameter ω will then become a feedback, and the iterative process can considered to be a discrete control system (see e.g. [17]).

We also plan to explore the use of MDL and MML principles to decide on the "right" number of clusters [15].

References

[1] G. Ball and D. Hall. ISODATA: a novel method of data analysis and pattern classification. Technical report, Stanford Research Institute, Menlo Park, CA, 1965.

[2] P. Bradley, U. Fayyad, and C. Reina. Scaling clustering algorithms to large databases. In *Proceedings of Fourth International Conference on Knowledge Discovery and Data Mining.* AAAI Press, 1998.

[3] I. S. Dhillon, J. Fan, and Y. Guan. Efficient clustering of very large document collections. In R. Grossman, C. Kamath, P. Kegelmeyer, V. Kumar, and R. Namburu, editors, *Data Mining for Scientific and Engineering Applications*, pages 357–381. Kluwer Academic Publishers, 2001.

[4] I. S. Dhillon and D. S. Modha. Concept decompositions for large sparse text data using clustering. *Machine Learning*, 42(1):143–175, January 2001.

[5] R. O. Duda, P. E. Hart, and D. G. Stork. *Pattern Classification.* John Wiley & Sons, 2nd edition, 2000.

[6] E. Forgy. Cluster analysis of multivariate data: Efficiency vs. interpretability of classifications. *Biometrics*, 21(3):768, 1965.

[7] A. Gersho and R. M. Gray. *Vector quantization and signal compression.* Kluwer Academic Publishers, 1992.

[8] R. M. Gray and D. L. Neuhoff. Quantization. *IEEE Trans. Inform. Theory*, 44(6):1–63, 1998.

[9] L. Kaufman and P. Rousseeuw. *Finding Groups in Data.* Wiley, New York, 1990.

[10] B. Kernighan and S. Lin. An efficient heuristic procedure for partitioning graphs. *The Bell System Technical Journal*, 49(2):291–307, 1970.

[11] J. Kogan. Means clustering for text data. In M.W.Berry, editor, *Workshop on Text Mining at the 1st SIAM International Conference on Data Mining*, pages 47–54, 2001.

[12] K. Lang. News Weeder: Learning to filter netnews. In *Proc. 12th Int'l Conf. Machine Learning*, San Francisco, 1995.

[13] J. MacQueen. Some methods for classification and analysis of multivariate observations. In *Proceedings of the Fifth Berkeley Symposium on Math., Stat. and Prob.*, pages 281–296, 1967.

[14] R. Ng and J. Han. Efficient and effective clustering methods for spatial data mining. In *Proc. of the 20th Int'l Conf. on Very Large Data Bases (VLDB)*, pages 144–155, Santiago, Chile, 1994.

[15] J. Rissanen. *Stochastic Complexity in Statistical Inquiry.* Series in Computer Science -Vol. 15. World Scientific, Singapore, 1989.

[16] G. Salton and M. J. McGill. *Introduction to Modern Retrieval.* McGraw-Hill Book Company, 1983.

[17] E. D. Sontag. *Mathematical Control Theory: Deterministic Finite Dimensional Systems.* Springer, New York, second edition, 1998.

[18] A. Strehl, J. Ghosh, and R. Mooney. Impact of similarity measures on web-page clustering. In *AAAI 2000 Workshop on AI for Web Search*, pages 58–64, July 2000.

Cluster merging and splitting in hierarchical clustering algorithms

Chris Ding and Xiaofeng He

NERSC Division, Lawrence Berkeley National Laboratory
University of California, Berkeley, CA 94720. {chqding,xhe}@lbl.gov

Abstract

Hierarchical clustering constructs a hierarchy of clusters by either repeatedly merging two smaller clusters into a larger one or splitting a larger cluster into smaller ones. The crucial step is how to best select the next cluster(s) to split or merge. Here we provide a comprehensive analysis of selection methods and propose several new methods. We perform extensive clustering experiments to test 8 selection methods, and find that the average similarity is the best method in divisive clustering and the MinMax linkage is the best in agglomerative clustering. Cluster balance is a key factor to achieve good performance. We also introduce the concept of objective function saturation and clustering target distance to effectively assess the quality of clustering.

1 Introduction

Hierarchical clustering methods are among the first methods developed and analyzed for clustering problems[5]. There are two main approaches. (i) The agglomerative approach, which builds a larger cluster by merging two smaller clusters in a bottom-up fashion. The clusters so constructed form a binary tree; individual objects are the leaf nodes and the root node is the cluster that have all data objects. (ii) The divisive approach, which splits a cluster into two smaller ones in a top-down fashion. All clusters so constructed also form a binary tree.

The hierarchical cluster structure provides a comprehensive description of the data, which is quite useful for a number of applications. Given a dataset, however, the hierarchical cluster structure is not unique. It depends crucially on the criterion of choosing the clusters to merge or split. This is the main subject of this paper.

Besides hierarchical methods, there are many other clustering methods[5, 4]. A popular method is the K-means method, which is essentially a function minimization, where the objective function is the squared error. In most applications, one initializes K mean-vectors and directly optimize the objective function to obtain the optimal clusters. One can also follow a hierarchical divisive approach, and split a current cluster into two using the K-means method [7]. The gaussian mixture model using EM algorithm directly improves over the K-means

method by using a probabilistic model of cluster membership of each object.

Both K-means method and Gaussian mixtures utilize directly the coordinates (attributes or variables) of the data points. From a general data clustering perspective, given all distances between data points, the cluster structure of the dataset is uniquely determined. Using the concept of *similarity*, we can equivalently say that given all pairwise similarities, the clustering is uniquely decided.

Recently, a MinMaxCut algorithm[3] is developed using similarity concepts. It is based on a min-max clustering principle: data should be grouped into clusters such that similarity between different clusters is minimized while the similarities within each clusters are maximized individually. MinMaxCut is extensively analyzed and experimented on two-cluster problems in [3], and is shown to be more effective than other current competitive methods such as the normalized cut [8] and PDDP [1]. Here we analyze the MinMaxCut on multi-cluster problems using hierarchical approaches.

2 Clustering objective functions

In this paper, we emphasize the view that clustering is an objective function optimization problem. This is a consistent and useful viewpoint. For example, we believe that after hierarchical clustering, one round of refinement of the leaf clusters based on an objective function will improve the clustering. The results of all 40 clustering experiments support this view.

2.1 K-means

The popular K-means algorithm is an error minimization algorithm where the objective function is the sum of error squared, sometimes called distorsion,

$$J_{\mathrm{Kmeans}}(K) = \sum_{k=1}^{K} \sum_{i \in C_k} (\mathbf{x}_i - \mathbf{c}_k)^2$$

where $\mathbf{c}_k = \sum_{i \in C_k} \mathbf{x}_i / n_k$ is the centroid of cluster C_k and $n_k = |C_k|$. When objects within each cluster are distributed according to a spherical Gaussian, with the same covariance for all clusters, J_{Kmeans} is a good measure.

2.2 Gaussian mixture model using EM

Both the K-means and MinMaxCut algorithms produce *hard* clustering, i.e., each data object belongs to exactly one cluster. For real life data, many points are situated near the boundaries between different clusters; it would be more natural to assign them fractionally to different clusters. A popular probabilistic model to allow this partial cluster membership is the Gaussian mixtures,

$$p(\mathbf{x}_i; K) = \pi_1 g_1(\mathbf{x}_i) + \cdots + \pi_K g_K(\mathbf{x}_i) \qquad (1)$$

where each component $g_k(\mathbf{x})$ is a Gaussian distribution, and π_k are prior distributions, satisfying $\sum_k \pi_k = 1$. The model parameters and cluster membership are determined by maximize the log-likelihood

$$\ell(K) = \sum_i \log(p(\mathbf{x}_i; K))$$

An efficient algorithm to achieve this is the Expectation-Maximization (EM) algorithm [2].

2.3 MinMax Cut

We briefly describe the MinMaxCut algorithm. Given n data objects and the pairwise similarity matrix $W = (w_{ij})$ where w_{ij} is the similarity between i, j, we wish to partition the data into two clusters C_1, C_2 using the min-max clustering principle. The similarity between C_1, C_2 is defined to be $s(C_1, C_2) \equiv \sum_{i \in C_1} \sum_{j \in C_2} w_{ij}$, which is also called the *overlap* between C_1, C_2. The similarity within a cluster C_1 is the sum of pairwise similarities within C_1: $s(C_1, C_1)$. We call $s(C_1, C_1)$ self-similarity of cluster C_1. The clustering principle requires minimizing $s(C_1, C_2)$ while maximizing $s(C_1, C_1)$ and $s(C_2, C_2)$ simultaneously. These requirements lead to the minimization of the MinMaxCut objective function,

$$J_{\mathrm{MMC}} = \frac{s(C_1, C_2)}{s(C_1, C_1)} + \frac{s(C_1, C_2)}{s(C_2, C_2)}. \qquad (2)$$

Finding a partition to minimize J_{MMC} is NP-hard. However, an order $O(n^2)$ method exists that computes a globally near-optimal solution. A clustering is represented by an indicator vector $\mathbf{q}$, where $q(i) = a$ if $i \in C_1$; $-b$ if $i \in C_2$, and a, b are constants. One can show

$$\min_{\mathbf{q}} J_{\mathrm{MMC}}(C_1, C_2) \Rightarrow \min_{\mathbf{q}} \frac{\mathbf{q}^T (D - W) \mathbf{q}}{\mathbf{q}^T D \mathbf{q}}, \qquad (3)$$

subject to $\mathbf{q}^T W \mathbf{e} = \mathbf{q}^T D \mathbf{e} = 0$, where $D = \mathrm{diag}(d_i)$ is a diagonal matrix and $d_i = \sum_j w_{ij}$, and $\mathbf{e} = (1, \cdots, 1)^T$. We relax $q(i)$ from discrete indicators $\{a, -b\}$ to continuous values in $(-1, 1)$. The solution of $\mathbf{q}$ for minimizing

the Rayleigh quotient of Eq.(3) is given by $(D - W)\mathbf{q} = \lambda D \mathbf{q}$. Since $\mathbf{q}_1 = \mathbf{e}^T$ is the eigenvector corresponding to the lowest eigenvalue, the second lowest eigenvector $\mathbf{q}_2$ is the desired solution (details and references are given in [3]). For $K \geq 3$, we define $J_{\mathrm{MMC}}(C_1, \cdots, C_K) \equiv J_{\mathrm{MMC}}(K)$,

$$J_{\mathrm{MMC}}(K) = \sum_{p,q} J_{\mathrm{MMC}}(C_p, C_q) = \sum_k \frac{s(C_k, \bar{C}_k)}{s(C_k, C_k)} \qquad (4)$$

where $\bar{C}_k = \sum_{p \neq k} C_p$ is the complement of C_k. In this paper, we use hierarchical approach to optimize this K-way clustering objective function.

3 Cluster merging and splitting

In hierarchical clustering, clusters are either merged into larger clusters or split to smaller clusters. It is instructive to see how clustering objective functions change with respect to the change of K, the number of clusters. Here we point out a fundamental difference between the graph-based MinMaxCut and the Euclidean distance based the K-means and Gaussian mixture.

Given the dataset and similarity measure (Euclidean distance in K-means and similarity graph weight in MinMaxCut), the global optimal value of the objective function is a function of K. An important property of these clustering objective functions is the monotonicity. We can prove that as K increases $K = 2, 3, \cdots$, the MinMaxCut objective increases monotonically, while the K-means objective decreases monotonically.

Theorem 1. Given the dataset and the similarity metric, as K increases, (i) the optimal value of the K-means objective function decreases monotonically:

$$J_{\mathrm{Kmeans}}^{\mathrm{opt}}(K) > J_{\mathrm{Kmeans}}^{\mathrm{opt}}(K + 1)$$

(ii) the maximun log-likelihood of the Gaussian mixture increases monotonically:

$$\ell^{\mathrm{opt}}(K) < \ell^{\mathrm{opt}}(K + 1)$$

(iii) the optimal value of the MinMax Cut objective function increases monotonically:

$$J_{\mathrm{MMC}}^{\mathrm{opt}}(K) < J_{\mathrm{MMC}}^{\mathrm{opt}}(K + 1)$$

Proof. It is sometimes assumed that (i) is obvious, based on the arguments that for $K + 1$ clusters, there are more parameters (than K cluster case) in the function optimization. This argument is incorrect, since it can be equally appled to (iii) and obtain wrong conclusion. We prove it for $K = 2$ by considering the 2-cluster problem. Assume we have found the optimal clustering for $K = 2$ and denote the clusters as A, B, with

$$J_{\mathrm{Kmeans}}^{\mathrm{opt}}(A, B) = \sum_{i \in A} (\mathbf{x}_i - \mathbf{c}_A)^2 + \sum_{i \in B} (\mathbf{x}_i - \mathbf{c}_B)^2.$$

Now we fix A and split B into B_1, B_2 in an optimal way using K-means:

$$J_{\text{Kmeans}}^{\text{B-split}}(A, B_1, B_2) = \sum_{i \in A} (\mathbf{x}_i - \mathbf{c}_A)^2$$

$$+ \sum_{i \in B_1} (\mathbf{x}_i - \mathbf{c}_{B_1})^2 + \sum_{i \in B_2} (\mathbf{x}_i - \mathbf{c}_{B_2})^2.$$

It is easy to show that

$$\sum_{i \in B_1} (\mathbf{x}_i - \mathbf{c}_B)^2 \geq \sum_{i \in B_1} (\mathbf{x}_i - \mathbf{c}_{B_1})^2$$

$$\sum_{i \in B_2} (\mathbf{x}_i - \mathbf{c}_B)^2 \geq \sum_{i \in B_2} (\mathbf{x}_i - \mathbf{c}_{B_2})^2;$$

This is because for any $\mathbf{c}$, the quadratic function $f(\mathbf{c}) = \sum_{i \in B_1} (\mathbf{x}_i - \mathbf{c})^2$ achieves its minimum at $\mathbf{c} = \mathbf{c}_{B_1} = \sum_{i \in B_1} \mathbf{x}_i / n_{B_1}$, n_{B_1} is the size of B_1. Similar results hold for B_2. Note that the equality sign can not hold simultaneously for B_1, B_2. Therefore, we have

$$J_{\text{Kmeans}}^{\text{B-split}}(A, B_1, B_2) < J_{\text{Kmeans}}^{\text{opt}}(A, B) \qquad (5)$$

Now the true global minimum $J_{\text{Kmeans}}^{\text{opt}}(K = 3)$ must be lower than or equal to the particular instance of A, B_1, B_2. Thus we have

$$J_{\text{Kmeans}}^{\text{opt}}(K = 3) \leq J_{\text{Kmeans}}^{\text{B-split}}(A, B_1, B_2) < J_{\text{Kmeans}}^{\text{opt}}(K = 2)$$

This proves (i) for $K = 2$. For $K = 3$, we fix A, B and split C; the proof goes through similarly. By induction, this holds for arbitrary K.

We can follow the same steps to prove (ii); details are omitted here.

To prove (iii), we assume A, B_1, B_2 are the optimal clusters for $K = 3$ for a given dataset. Now we merge B_1, B_2, and show that

$$J_{\text{MMC}}^{\text{B-merge}}(A, B) < J_{\text{MMC}}^{\text{opt}}(A, B_1, B_2). \qquad (6)$$

This is because

$$J_{\text{MMC}}^{\text{opt}}(A, B_1, B_2) - J_{\text{MMC}}^{\text{B-merge}}(A, B) = -\frac{s(A, B)}{s(B, B)}$$

$$+ \frac{s(B_1, A) + s(B_1, B_2)}{s(B_1, B_1)} + \frac{s(B_2, A) + s(B_2, B_1)}{s(B_2, B_2)}$$

$$= \left[\frac{s(B_1, A)}{s(B_1, B_1)} - \frac{s(B_1, A)}{s(B, B)} \right] + \left[\frac{s(B_2, A)}{s(B_1, B_1)} - \frac{s(B_2, A)}{s(B, B)} \right]$$

$$+ \left[\frac{s(B_2, B_1)}{s(B_1, B_1)} + \frac{s(B_2, B_1)}{s(B_2, B_2)} \right] \qquad (7)$$

Since $s(B_1, B_1) < s(B, B)$ and $s(B_2, B_2) < s(B, B)$, every term is positive; thus we have Eq.(6). Now the

true global minimum for $K = 2$ must be lower than or equal to the particular instance of A, B. Thus we have

$$J_{\text{MMC}}^{\text{opt}}(K = 2) \leq J_{\text{MMC}}^{\text{B-merge}}(A, B) < J_{\text{MMC}}^{\text{opt}}(K = 3)$$

This proves (iii) for $K = 2$, which can be generalized to any K. $\qquad \square$

We note that (i) and (ii) in Theorem 1 are previously known, although we are not aware of a concrete proof. However, they are generally considered true based on the arguments of number of parameters involved. We make two contributions in Theorem 1: (1) prove the monotonicity of MinMaxCut; (2) the proof of (1) shows that the general arguments based on the number of parameters are incorrect, and we provide a concrete proof of (i) and (ii).

Theorem 1 shows the fundamental difference between graph-based MinMaxCut objective function and the K-means and Gaussian mixture. If we use the optimal value of the objective function to judge what is the optimal K, then K-means and Gaussian mixture favor large number of clusters while MinMaxCut favors small number of clusters. The monotonic increase or decrease indicate that one cannot determine optimal K from objective function alone. This is a well-known fact in data mining and Theorem 1 is a concise proof in support of this fact.

Another consequence of Theorem 1 is that in the top-down hierarchical divisive clustering, as clusters are split into more clusters, the K-means objective will steadily decrease while the MinMaxCut objective will steadily increase.

4   Objective function saturation

If a dataset has K reasonably distinguishable clusters, these natural clusters could have many different shapes and sizes. But in many datasets, clusters overlap substantially and natural clusters cannot be defined clearly. Therefore, in general, a single (even the "best" if exists) objective function J can not effectively model the vast different types of datasets. For many datasets, as J is optimized, the accuracy (quality) of clustering is usually improved. But this works only up to a point. Beyond that, further optimization of the objective will not improve the quality of clustering because the objective function does not necessarily model the data in fine details. We here formalize this characteristics of clustering objective function as the *saturation* of objective function.

Definition. For a given measure η of quality of clustering (i.g, accuracy), the saturation objective, J_{sat}, is defined to be the value when J is further optimized beyond J_{sat}, η is no longer improved. We say η reaches its saturation value η_{sat}.

Saturation accuracy is a useful concept and also a useful measure. Given a dataset with known class labels, there is a unique saturation accuracy for a clustering method. Saturation accuracy gives a good sense on how well the clustering algorithm will do on the given dataset.

In general we have to use the clustering method to do extensive clustering experiments to compute saturation accuracy. Here we propose an effective method to compute an upper bound on saturation accuracy for a clustering method. The method is the following. (a) Initialize with the perfect clusters constructed from the known class labels. At this stage, the accuracy is 100%. (b) Run the refinement algorithm on this clustering until convergence. (c) Compute accuracy and other measures. These values are the upper bounds on saturation values.

5 Hierarchical divisive clustering

Divisive clustering starts from the top, treating the whole dataset as a cluster. It repeatedly partitions a current cluster (a leaf node in a binary tree) until the number of clusters reaches a predefined value K, or some other stopping criteria are met. The most important issue here is how to select the next candidate cluster to split. After discussing the size-priority selection, we introduce 4 new selection methods.

5.1 Size-priority cluster split

A common approach is to select the cluster with largest size to split [5]. This approach gives priority to produce size-balanced clusters. This can be written as choose p according to $p = \arg \min_k (1/n_k)$. This is a reasonable approach. However, natural clusters are not restricted to the situation where each cluster has the same size. Thus this approach is not necessarily the optimal approach.

5.2 Average similarity

Here we propose a new cluster choice. The idea is from the min-max clustering principle. The self-similarity of cluster C_k is $s(C_k, C_k) \equiv s_{kk}$, which is to be maximized during clustering. Define *average* self-similarity for each cluster, computed as $\bar{s}_{kk} = s_{kk}/n_k^2$. A cluster C_k with large $\bar{s}_{kk}$ implies that cluster members are more homogeneous; if we define similarity as the inverse of distance, $w_{ij} = 1/d_{ij}$, we may say that cluster members are more close to each other in Euclidean space, i.e., C_k is compact or tight. A cluster with small $\bar{s}_{kk}$ is less homogeneous or loose. A goal of min-max clustering principle is to produce clusters as compact and balanced as possible. Therefore, our priority in splitting clusters is to increase average similarity for all clusters. Our criterion is to choose the loosest (smallest average similarity) cluster p to split, $p = \arg \min_k (s_{kk}/n_k^2)$. Our experiments (§7) show that this choice works well when natural clusters have either similar or different sizes.

5.3 Cluster cohesion

For a cluster with a given average similarity, there could be many different shapes. An elongated cluster (or a cluster consisting of two well-separated subclusters) could have the same average similarity as a highly spherical cluster. We introduce a new quantity to measure the difficulty for breaking the cluster into two:
Definition. Cluster cohesion is the smallest value of the MinMaxCut objective function when the cluster is split into two sub-clusters.
A quantity similar to the idea of cluster cohesion is implicitly used in [6].

A cluster k with small cohesion h_k implies it can be meaningfully split into two. Therefore a cohesion-based criterion is to choose the cluster p with the smallest cohesion among the current leaf clusters: $p = \arg \min_k h_k$.

The arguments above also suggest the combination of cohesion with average similarity could be a good cluster selection criterion. In this similarity-cohesion criterion, we select the cluster p according to

$$p = arg \min_k \left(s_{kk}/n_k^2 \right)^\gamma h_k^{(1-\gamma)}. \tag{8}$$

by setting $\gamma = 1/2$. Note that setting $\gamma = 1$, we get similarity criterion; setting $\gamma = 0$, we get cohesion criterion.

5.4 Temporary objective

All above cluster choices are based on cluster characteristics and do not involve the clustering objective Eq.(4). Since the goal of clustering is to optimize the objective function, we can choose the cluster C_k such that the split of C_k leads to the smallest increase in the overall objective temporarily. This step-wise greedy approach is similar to the cohesion criterion, since the cohesion, the last term in Eq.(7), is the dominant contribution to the increase in J_{MMC}.

5.5 Stopping criteria

There are two stopping criterion for terminating the divisive procedure. (i) Terminate when the number of leaf nodes reaches the pre-defined K. (ii) Terminate when J_{MMC} computed based on current clusters on leaf nodes goes above a threshold value J_{stop}. Theorem 1 indicates that as the divisive process continues and the number of leaf clusters increase, J_{MMC} increases. Since J_{MMC} measures the overlop between different clusters (properly weighted against self-similarities), a large J_{MMC} (above J_{stop}) indicates that the current cluster is already highly homogeneous and it is better not to cut it further.

In applications where we do not know the correct K, we prefer to use (ii) as stopping criterion. In this paper, K is already known for the datasets, thus we use (i).

5.6 Refinement

In standard hierarchical clustering, clusters are taken as they are in the clustering tree. However, one can improve the clusters by refining them according to a proper clustering objective function. In this paper, we use MinMaxCut to split clusters, and thus we optimize the multi-K MinMaxCut objective function on the clusters produced by the divisive process.

Cluster refinement based on MinMax objective for $K = 2$ is discussed in [3]. Here we extend to $K > 2$. We use a greedy procedure. For each data point $\mathbf{x}_i$, we move it from its current cluster C_k to the new cluster C_p that gives the smallest objective function value. Note that often $p = k$, i.e., $\mathbf{x}_i$ should stay with C_k. Only those points near the boundaries are likely to be moved to other clusters.

6 Clustering quality measures

The results for clustering are specified by the $m \times n$ confusion matrix, $Z = (z_{pq})$, where z_{pq} is the number of data points in the discovered cluster C_q (column q) which are in fact belongs to the true cluster R_p (row p). Therefore, $n_k = \sum_{p=1}^{m} z_{pk}$ (sum of column k) is the size of discovered cluster C_k, while $m_k = \sum_{q=1}^{n} z_{kq}$ (sum of row k) is the size of true cluster R_k. Note that $\sum_{k=1}^{m} m_k = \sum_{k=1}^{n} n_k = N$, total number of data points.

The standard accuracy for k-th cluster is $q_k = z_{kk}/m_k$ (when $n = m$), the fraction of C_k that truly belongs to R_k. Since each true cluster contribute m_k to the total N data points, i.e, their contribution has a weight m_k/N, the usual global accuracy is the weighted sum of $Q = \sum_k (m_k/N) q_k = \sum_k z_{kk}/N$.

Accuracy measures only use the diagonal elements in Z. To account for the off-diagonal entries in Z, the mutual information (quotient) is often used,

$$I(Z) = \frac{1}{H(R)} \sum_{pq} \frac{z_{pq}}{N} \log(\frac{z_{pq}N}{m_p n_q}) = 1 - \frac{H(R|C)}{H(R)}, \quad (9)$$

where $H(R)$ is the entropy over the row distribution $(m_1, \cdots, m_K)$, and $H(R|C) = \sum_k (n_k/N)H(R|C_k)$, where $H(R|C_k)$ is the conditional entropy for column C_k. Note that we include $H(R)$ in the denominator, such that (i) for perfect clustering, $I(Z) = 1$; (ii) for random clustering, $I(Z) = 0$. Since $H(R)$ is fixed for a given dataset, $H(R|C)$ is sometimes used instead[10]. I is also useful when $n \neq m$.

Here we argue that there are certain desirable characteristics of clustering (and classification) that are not captured by mutual information. We further propose a new metric, *target distance*, which correctly captures these desirable features and is also more sensitive than accuracy. The first cluster feature is illustrated by two clustering results represented by contingency tables Z_A

and Z_B,

$$Z_A = \begin{bmatrix} 20 & 20 \\ 20 & 20 \end{bmatrix}, \ Z_B = \begin{bmatrix} 39 & 1 \\ 39 & 1 \end{bmatrix}.$$

They both have same mutual information $I = 0$ and the same accuracy $Q = 50\%$. However, we believe that the results of Z_A is better, because the two clusters obtained are more balanced; the two clusters obtained in Z_B are highly unbalanced (one has 78 points and the other has 2 points). The desired (target) contingency table for perfect clustering is $T = \begin{bmatrix} 40 & \cdot \\ \cdot & 40 \end{bmatrix}$. We thus define the *target distance* as

$$d(Z) = ||Z - T||_F/||T||_F = (\Sigma_{ij}(z_{ij} - t_{ij})^2/\Sigma_{ij}t_{ij}^2)^{1/2},$$

where the Frobenius norm of T is $||T||_F^2 = \sum_{ij} t_{ij}^2$. One can show that (i) $d = 0$ for perfect clustering; (ii) $0 \le d \le 2$. For the contingency tables Z_A, Z_B, $d(Z_A) = 0.707$ is lower than $d(Z_B) = 0.975$, indicating Z_A is better. Clearly, $d(Z)$ captures the desired feature of balanced clustering. Also note that both $d(Z_A)$ and $d(Z_B)$ are far above 0, indicating poor clustering.

The second clustering feature is illustrated in the clustering of contingency tables Z_A and Z_B,

$$Z_A = \begin{bmatrix} 10 & 1 & 1 & 1 \\ \cdot & 10 & 1 & 1 \\ \cdot & \cdot & 10 & 1 \\ \cdot & \cdot & \cdot & 10 \end{bmatrix}, Z_B = \begin{bmatrix} 10 & \cdot & \cdot & 3 \\ \cdot & 10 & 2 & \cdot \\ \cdot & \cdot & 10 & 1 \\ \cdot & \cdot & \cdot & 10 \end{bmatrix}.$$

The accuracy are 0.93% for both. Mutual information $I(Z_A) = 0.678$ and $I(Z_B) = 0.748$, indicating Z_B is better. However, we believe Z_A is better because there are 6 small errors in Z_A (six 1's), whereas there are 3 larger errors in Z_B (3, 2 and 1). In other words, we prefer *many but small* random errors, instead of *fewer but large* errors. The target distance, $d(Z_A) = 0.194, d(Z_B) = 0.229$ correctly asserts that Z_A is better.

The fundamental reason is due to squares of off-diagonal entries in Z: a larger error get squared ($3^2 = 9$) is much larger than the sum of small errors squared ($1^2 + 1^2 + 1^2 = 3$). Thus target distance captures the desired clustering feature. However, mutual information (entropy) gives opposite results: given two distributions $p_A = \{4, 0, 0, 0, 4\}$ and $p_B = \{4, 1, 1, 1, 1\}$ (the corresponding columns in two different contingency tables for clustering same data). $H(p_A|C) = \log(2)$ whereas $H(p_B|C) = 2\log(2)$. Since $H(R)$ is same (see Eq.9), the mutual information criteria favor the clustering p_A with one large error, instead of the clustering p_B with 4 small errors.

7 Clustering Internet newsgroups

We apply the MinMaxCut with the divisive clustering algorithm to document clustering. We perform experiments on Internet newsgroup articles in 20 newsgroups.

Dataset	MB		MU	
method	t-dist	acc(%)	t-dist	acc(%)
Saturation	0.111(26)	92.5(2.0)	0.117(26)	91.7(1.6)
Size-P I	0.259(75)	82.8(3.4)	0.371(191)	77.1(10.8)
Size-P F	0.121(25)	91.8(1.7)	0.309(194)	81.7(9.9)
cohesion I	0.594(200)	66.1(10.6)	0.374(214)	75.6(13.8)
cohesion F	0.531(233)	73.0(10.8)	0.355(227)	78.8(13.2)
Tmp-obj I	0.300(167)	80.3(9.0)	0.481(28)	70.9(2.2)
Tmp-obj F	0.218(238)	87.0(11.6)	0.454(23)	75.0(1.3)
avg-sim I	0.246(47)	83.5(2.0)	0.168(29)	88.4(1.8)
avg-sim F	0.124(21)	91.7(1.1)	0.114(22)	91.7(1.3)
sim-coh I	0.246(47)	83.5(2.0)	0.168(29)	88.4(1.8)
sim-coh F	0.120(17)	91.8(1.2)	0.122(17)	91.0(1.0)

Table 1: Clustering results of the divisive MinMaxCut for the datasets MB and MU. Errors are in parenthesis.

Dataset	LB		LU	
method	t-dist	acc(%)	t-dist	acc(%)
Saturation	0.249(26)	81.4(2.1)	0.292(72)	79.0(4.4)
Size-P I	0.509(54)	67.2(2.9)	0.536(113)	62.9(6.7)
Size-P F	0.429(109)	71.8(4.8)	0.465(47)	68.4(1.9)
Cohesion I	0.891(140)	46.3(11.6)	0.722(209)	50.9(14.7)
Cohesion F	0.822(37)	49.6(5.3)	0.622(206)	58.1(13.8)
Tmp-obj I	0.652(54)	56.9(4.9)	0.597(96)	60.1(4.2)
Tmp-obj F	0.651(48)	58.7(5.6)	0.466(35)	68.8(2.8)
avg-sim I	0.469(27)	69.3(2.3)	0.345(47)	74.8(4.6)
avg-sim F	0.395(71)	72.4(4.1)	0.344(32)	74.1(2.5)
sim-coh I	0.601(134)	63.5(5.4)	0.428(38)	71.0(2.3)
sim-coh F	0.502(181)	67.1(8.0)	0.354(32)	72.6(2.3)

Table 2: Clustering results of divisive MinMaxCut for the datasets LB and LU.

We focus on two sets of 5-cluster cases. The choice of $K = 5$ is to have enough levels in the cluster tree; we avoid $K = 4, 8$ where the clustering results are less sensitive to cluster selection. The first dataset includes

```
NG2:   comp.graphics
NG9:   rec.motorcycles
NG10:  rec.sport.baseball
NG15:  sci.space
NG18:  talk.politics.mideast
```

In this dataset, cluster overlap at medium level. The second dataset includes

```
NG2:   comp.graphics
NG3:   comp.os.ms-windows
NG8:   rec.autos
NG13:  sci.electronics
NG18:  talk.politics.mideast
```

Here the overlaps among different clusters are large.

The newsgroup dataset is from www.cs.cmu.edu/afs /cs/project/theo-11/www/naive-bayes.html. Word - document matrix is first constructed. 2000 words are selected according to the mutual information between words and documents. Standard `tf.idf` term weighting is used. Cosine similarities between all pair of document are calculated and stored in W. We perform the clustering as explained above.

From each set of newsgroups, we construct two datasets of different sizes: (A) randomly select 100 articles from each newsgroup. (B) randomly select 200, 140, 120, 100, 60 from the 5 newsgroups, respectively. Dataset (A) has clusters of equal sizes, which is presumably easier to cluster. Dataset (B) has clusters of significantly varying sizes, which is presumably difficult to cluster. Therefore, we have 4 newsgroup - cluster size combination categories

LB: large overlapping clusters of balanced sizes
LU: large overlapping clusters of unbalanced sizes
MB: medium overlapping clusters of balanced sizes
MU: medium overlapping clusters of unbalanced sizes

For each category, 5 different random datasets are generated and the divisive MinMaxCut clustering algorithm using the 4 cluster selection methods is applied to each of them. The final results are the average of these 5 random datasets in each categories. The results of clustering on the four datasets are listed in Tables 1,2. Two quality measures are computed: the target distance (t-dist) and accuracy (acc). The upper bounds of saturation values are computed as described in §4. Clustering results for each cluster selection method, size-priority (Size-P), average similarity (avg-sim), cohesion and similarity-cohesion (sim-coh) (see Eq.8) and temporary objective (tmp-obj) are given in 2 rows: "I" (initial) are the results immediately after divisive cluster; "F" (final) are the results after two rounds of greedy refinements.

A number of observations can be made from these extensive clustering experiments. (1) The best results are obtained by average similarity cluster selection. This is consistent for all 4 datasets. (2) The similarity-cohesion cluster selection gives very good results, statistically no different from average similarity selection method. (3) Cluster cohesion alone as the selection method gives consistently poorest results. The temporary objective choice performs slightly better than cohesion criterion, but still substantially below avg-sim and sim-coh choices. These results are somehow unexpected. We checked the details of several divisive processes. The temporary objective and cohesion often lead to unbalanced clusters because of the greedy nature and unboundedness of these choices[1]. (4) Size-priority selection method gives good results for datasets with balanced sizes, but not as

---

[1]A current cluster C_k is usually split into balanced clusters C_{k1}, C_{k2} by the MinMaxCut [3]. However, C_{k1} and C_{k2} may be quite smaller than other current clusters, because no mechanism exists in the divisive process to enforce cluster balances. After several divisive steps, they could become substantially out of balance. In contrast, avg-similarity and size-priority choices prevent large unbalance to occur.

good results for datasets with unbalanced cluster sizes. These are as expected.

(5) The refinement based on MinMaxCut objective improves the accuracy about 9%, and improve the target distances about 50% for dataset MB for avg-sim and sim-coh selection methods. For other datasets, the improvements are less profound, but can be clearly recognized for all cluster selection methods on all datasets. This indicates the importance of refinements in hierarchical clustering. (6) In all datasets and all methods, target distances are more sensitive than accuracies in showing the improvements due to refinements. This fact, together with the discussions in §6, that indicates target distance is a good metric for assessing the quality of clustering. (7) Both accuracies and target distances of the final clustering with avg-sim and sim-coh choices are very close to the saturation values, indicating the obtained clusters are as good as the MinMax cut objective function could provide.

Dataset MB has been studied in [9] using K-means methods. The standard K-means method achievers an accuracy of 66%, while two improved K-means methods achieve 76-80% accuracy. In comparison, the divisive MinMaxCut achieves 92% accuracy (Table 1).

8 Agglomerative clustering

In hierarchical agglomerative clustering, clusters are built from bottom up. During each recursive procedure, we merge two *current* clusters C_p and C_q that has the largest pairwise linkage between C_p and C_q:

$$\max_{\langle pq \rangle} \ell(C_p, C_q)$$

among all pairs of clusters. The key here is the choice of pairs, based on the *linkage* function. Using similarity measure $W = (w_{ij})$, we can translate standard linkage functions[5] using *distance* into those using *similarity*: (i) the single linkage, defined as the closest distance (largest similarity) among points in C_p, C_q,

$$\ell_{\text{single}}(C_p, C_q) = \max_{i \in C_p \, j \in C_q} w_{ij}.$$

(ii) the complete linkage, defined as the fartherest distance (smallest similarity) among points in C_p, C_q,

$$\ell_{\text{complete}}(C_p, C_q) = \min_{i \in C_p \, j \in C_q} w_{ij}$$

(iii) the average linkage, defined as the average of all distances (similarities) among points in C_p, C_q,

$$\ell_{\text{average}}(C_p, C_q) = \frac{s(C_p, C_q)}{|C_p||C_q|}.$$

(iv) the MinMax linkage, proposed and analyzed in [3], is defined as

$$\ell_{\text{MinMax}}(C_p, C_q) = \frac{s(C_p, C_q)}{s(C_p, C_p) s(C_q, C_q)}.$$

It is motivated by min-max principle : given the same overlap $s(C_p, C_q)$, we want to merge the pair of clusters that has small self-similarities (or loose clusters); in this way, clusters with larger similarities are retained and the final clusters have larger self-similarities.

At start, each data object is a cluster. The similarity or linkage between objects $\mathbf{x}_i, \mathbf{x}_j$ is w_{ij}. As cluster gets merged, we need a linkage between a single object and a cluster of several objects. All 4 linkages above have unique extension to this point-cluster linkage. For cluster with one point $\mathbf{x}_i$, $s(\mathbf{x}_i, \mathbf{x}_i) \equiv 1$, and $s(\mathbf{x}_i, C_k) \equiv \sum_{j \in C_k} w_{ij}$.

In our experiments, we stop the agglomerative process when the current number of cluster reaches K, the known number of clusters in the dataset. In applications when K is unknown, one may set a threshold J_{stop}. As the number of current clusters is reduced during the cluster merging process, J_{MMC} gradually decreases(Theorem 1). The process is terminated when J_{MMC} reaches J_{stop}.

Agglomerative clustering is uniquely determined for a given linkage, independent of any objective function. But, as in divisive clustering, we can refine the clusters according to MinMaxCut objective once the agglomerative process terminates. This improves the clustering results in all 4 linkages in all experiments we performed.

We perform agglomerative clustering using all 4 linkages on the datasets MB and LB in §7. The same 5 random samples for each datasets are used for clustering. The agglomerative process is terminated when the number of total current clusters reaches 5. The clustering results of this initial clustering and those after two rounds of greedy refinements are shown in Table 3.

Several observations from Table 3 are obtained. (1) Complete linkage performs worst consistently. and average linkage performs slightly better. (2) The Min-Max linkage leads to the best initial and final clustering in all experiments. (3) Based on target distance, single linkage out-performs complete linkage and average linkage, but substantially less well compared to Min-Max linkage. After examining several cases, we believe

Dataset	MB		LB	
method	t-dist	acc(%)	t-dist	acc(%)
Single I	0.791(73)	35.4(3.7)	0.763(70)	33.6(5.8)
Single F	0.283(113)	80.0(7.9)	0.485(69)	69.5(6.1)
Complet I	1.248(03)	20.6(0.3)	1.034(04)	32.4(0.2)
Complet F	0.952(202)	40.2(16.0)	0.809(140)	46.7(9.8)
Average I	1.145(175)	28.2(14.7)	0.877(161)	45.8(13.5)
Average F	1.086(197)	31.9(16.4)	0.733(178)	53.2(14.4)
MinMax I	0.315(72)	77.0(4.6)	0.490(72)	67.7(3.3)
MinMax F	0.124(32)	91.6(1.9)	0.453(54)	74.5(2.9)

Table 3: Clustering results of agglomarative MinMax-Cut with 4 different linkage functions.

the reason for these points. are due to cluster balance. For complete linkage and average linkage, large clusters tend to merge to form even larger clusters, while smaller clusters tend to be left alone. This snow-ball effect leads to high unbalanced clusters as observed in experiments. Single linkage can sometime link small clusters to larger ones; MinMax linkage weighs inversely with self-similarities; thus small clusters can produce large linkage, which cause them to merge with other clusters and lead to balanced clusters. Producing balanced clusters was one motivation for MinMaxCut algorithm[3].

(4) Comparing results in Table 3 with those in Tables 1 and 2, the agglomerative clustering appears to be substantially less effective than divisive clustering. Even in the best cases, the initial clustering obtained in agglomerative clustering is substantially poorer than the initial clustering obtained in divisive clustering.

Observation (4) is somehow unexpected. One would think that since in agglomerative clustering, each data point is individually compared to all existing clusters and is assigned to the best cluster, the final clustering should be better than those from divisive clustering, where no individual points are carefully considered. Observation (4) suggests that the collective optimizations (overlap vs self-similarities of clusters, etc) in divisive clustering is more important than the optimizations of individual points in a greedy fashion.

We also note that agglomerative clustering is much slower to run; its complexity is $O(n^3 \log(n))$, in contrast to $O(n^2)$ for divisive clustering. All these suggest that agglomerative clustering is not as competitive as the divisive clustering method.

9   Summary and discussions

In this paper, we provide a comprehensive analysis and experiments on divisive and agglomerative clustering. We use *similarities* instead of the traditional *distances*. We study the effects of merging and splitting clusters on clustering objective functions of MinMaxCut, K-means and gaussian mixture. The monotonicity property provides a general guidance about the changes of objective functions during divisive or agglomerative process, which is useful for stopping criteria.

For divisive clustering, we introduce 4 new cluster selection criteria, the average similarity, the cluster cohesion avg-cohesion, and temporary objective. Extensive experiments on internet newsgroups show that average similarity and similarity-cohesion selection perform well. For agglomerative clustering, we introduce the MinMax linkage and compared with single-linkage, complete linkage and average linkage. The MinMax linkage for merging clusters is found to be most effective. We found that maintaining cluster balance during divisive or agglomerative process is a key factor for good performance.

Besides algorithmic studies, we introduce two use-ful new concepts, the objective function saturation and cluster target distance. These concepts provide concrete and more effective means to assess the quality of clustering provided.

Although the cluster choices are specified in *similarity*, they can be converted to *distances*. For example, the average similarity in §5.2 is converted into

$$p = \arg\max_k \sum_{i,j \in C_k} \frac{(\mathbf{x}_i - \mathbf{x}_j)^2}{n_k^2} = \arg\max_k \sum_{i \in C_k} \frac{(\mathbf{x}_i - \mathbf{c}_k)^2}{n_k}$$

and the MinMax linkage of §8 is converted into two

$$\ell_{\mathrm{MinMax}}(C_p, C_q) = \frac{d_{pq}}{d_{pp}^{1/2} d_{qq}^{1/2}}, \quad d_{pq} = \sum_{i \in C_p} \sum_{j \in C_q} \frac{(\mathbf{x}_i - \mathbf{x}_j)^2}{n_p n_q}.$$

Acknowledgments. This work is supported by U.S. Department of Energy, Office of Science (MICS Office and LDRD) under contract DE-AC03-76SF00098.

References

[1] D. Boley. Principal direction divisive partitioning. *Data mining and knowledge discovery*, 2:325–344, 1998.

[2] A.P. Dempster, N.M. Laird, and D.B. Rubin. Maximum-likelihood from incomplete data via em algorithm. *J. Royal Stat. Soc. B.*, pages 1–38, 1977.

[3] C. Ding, X. He, H. Zha, M. Gu, and H. Simon. A min-max cut algorithm for graph partitioning and data clustering. *Proc. IEEE Int'l Conf. Data Mining*, pages 107–114, 2001.

[4] J. Han and M. Kamber. *Data Mining: Concepts and Techniques*. Morgan Kaufmann, 2000.

[5] A.K. Jain and R.C. Dubes. *Algorithms for clustering data*. Prentice Hall, 1988.

[6] G. Karypis, E.-H. Han, and V. Kumar. Chameleon: Hierarchical clustering using dynamic modeling. *IEEE Computer*, 32:68–75, 1999.

[7] S.M. Savaresi and D. Boley. On the performance of bisecting K-means and PDDP. *Proc. SIAM Data Mining Conf*, 2001.

[8] J. Shi and J. Malik. Normalized cuts and image segmentation. *IEEE. Trans. on Pattern Analysis and Machine Intelligence*, 22:888–905, 2000.

[9] H. Zha, C. Ding, M. Gu, X. He, and H.D. Simon. Spectral relaxation for k-means clustering. *Proc. Neural Info. Processing Systems (NIPS 2001)*, Dec. 2001.

[10] Y. Zhao and G. Karypis. Criterion functions for document clustering: Experiments and analysis. *Univ Minnesota, CS, Tech Report*, 2001.

Adaptive dimension reduction for clustering high dimensional data

Chris Ding[a], Xiaofeng He[a], Hongyuan Zha[b] and Horst D. Simon[a]

[a] NERSC Division, Lawrence Berkeley National Laboratory
University of California, Berkeley, CA 94720
[b] Department of Computer Science and Engineering
Pennsylvania State University, University Park, PA 16802
{chqding,xhe,hdsimon}@lbl.gov, zha@cse.psu.edu

Abstract

It is well-known that for high dimensional data clustering, standard algorithms such as EM and the K-means are often trapped in local minimum. Many initialization methods were proposed to tackle this problem , but with only limited success. In this paper we propose a new approach to resolve this problem by repeated dimension reductions such that K-means or EM are performed only in very low dimensions. Cluster membership is utilized as a bridge between the reduced dimensional subspace and the original space, providing flexibility and ease of implementation. Clustering analysis performed on highly overlapped Gaussians, DNA gene expression profiles and internet newsgroups demonstrate the effectiveness of the proposed algorithm.

1 Introduction

In many application areas, such as information retrieval, image processing, computational biology and global climate research, analysis of high dimensional datasets is frequently encountered. For example, in text processing, typical dimension of a word vector is of the size of the vocabulary of a document collection and tens of thousands of words/phrases are used routinely; in molecular biology, human gene expression profile analysis typically involves thousands of genes; and in image processing, a typical 2-dim image has $128^2 = 16,384$ pixels or dimensions.

Developing effective clustering methods to handle high dimensional dataset is a challenging problem. Popular clustering methods such as the K-means and EM methods suffer from the well-known local minima problem: as iterations proceed, they are often trapped in the local minima in the configuration space, due to the greedy nature of these algorithms. In high dimensional space, the equi-potential (cost function) surface is very rugged. The iterations almost always get trapped somewhere close to the initial starting configuration. In other words, it is difficult to sample through a large configuration (parameter) space. The conventional approach is to do a large number of runs with random initial starts and pick up the best one as the result [24, 26]. Besides random starts, there are a number of initialization methods, most of which concentrate on how to intelligently choose the starting configurations (the K centers) in order to be as close to the global minima as possible [5, 25, 22, 17]. However, these approaches are limited by the inherent difficulty of finding global minima in high dimensional space in the first place. Monte Carlo methods are also used [28].

In this paper, we propose a new approach to solve this problem. Our approach utilizes the idea of dimension reduction. Dimension reduction is often used in clustering, classification, and many other machine learning and data mining applications. It usually retains the most important dimensions (attributes), removes the noisy dimensions (irrelevant attributes) and reduces computational cost.

In most applications, dimension reduction is carried out as a *preprocessing* step. The selection of the dimensions using principal component analysis (PCA) [20, 14] through singular value decomposition (SVD) [15] is a popular approach for numerical attributes. In information retrieval, latent semantic indexing uses SVD to project textual documents represented as document vectors [7]; SVD is shown to be the optimal solution for a probablistic model for document/word occurrence [12]. Random projections to subspaces have also been used [13, 6].

In all those applications, however, once the dimensions are selected, they stay fixed during the entire clustering process. The dimension reduction process is decoupled from the clustering process. If the data distribution is far from Gaussian, for example, the dimensions selected using PCA may deviate substantially from the optimal.

Here (i) we approach dimension reduction as a *dynamic* process that should be adaptively adjusted and integrated with the clustering process; (ii) we make effective use of cluster membership as the bridge connecting the clusters defined in the reduced dimensional space (subspace) and those defined in the full dimensional space; (iii) using this connection, clusters are discovered in the low dimensional subspace to avoid the curse of dimensionality [27] and are adaptively re-adjusted in the full dimension space for global optimality. This process is repeated until convergence.

In this paper we focus on the K-means and EM algorithms using the mixture model of spherical Gaussian components. Using marginal distributions, the gaussian mixtures retain identical model parameters in reduced low-dimensional subspace as in the original high dimensional space, providing a theoretical justification for dimension reduction. The objective function for the K-means has the same property.

K-centroid classification on text are studied via dimension reduction in [18], where K centroids are used to define the subspace projection. Dimension reduction in text processing has been extensively studied [4, 12, 9, 21]. All of above studies use dimension reduction as preprocessing; while in our approach, dimension reduction is performed adaptively.

In this paper, we consider projection methods in which the new projected dimensions are linear combination of old dimensions. Optimal selection of a subset of existing dimensions (attributes) is a substantially different approach. Selection of a subset of attributes in the context of clustering are studied in [2, 1]. In the context of classification, subset selection has been extensively studied [19].

2 Effective Dimension for Clustering

Our approach is to perform clustering in low dimensional subspaces. EM, in essence, is fitting a density functional form and is sensitive to local density variations. In the much reduced-dimension subspaces, we have a much smoother density [27], therefore reducing the chances of being trapped in the local minima.

We may interpret the low dimensional subspace as containing the relevant attributes (linear combinations

of coordinates). What is the dimensionality r of the reduced-dimension subspace for clustering? We argue that $r \leq K - 1$ based on linear discriminant analysis: Given two gaussian distributions with means μ_1, μ_2, and pooled covariance matrix Σ in d-dim space, a point x is classified to belong to class 1 or 2 depending upon

$$x^T \Sigma^{-1}(\mu_1 - \mu_2) \geq \text{threshold}$$

For spherical Gaussian, $\Sigma = \sigma^2 I$ (I is the identity matrix), thus the $d - 1$ subspace perpendicular to the direction $\mu_1 - \mu_2$ does not enter the consideration. The effective dimension for 2 clusters is 1. For $K > 2$, we may consider all pairs of two-class classifications, and the dimensions perpendicular to all $\mu_i - \mu_j$ directions ($i \neq j$) are irrelevant. Thus the effective clustering dimensions for the K spherical gaussians are spanned by the K centers $\mu_1, \cdots, \mu_K$, for which $r = K - 1$. We call the relevant dimensions passing through all K centers the r-dim subspace. This conclusion is essentially a geometric point of view. If Euclidean distances are the main factors in clustering, the dimensions perpendicular to the relevant subspace are clearly irrelevant.

The effective dimensionality of the relevant subspace could be less than $K - 1$. This happens when the K cluster centers lie in a subspace with dimension $r < K - 1$. For example, there could be 5 clusters with all their centroids lie on a 2-dim plane. In summary, the effective dimension for clustering is $r \leq K - 1$.

3 EM in relevant subspace

Our algorithm can be easily and naturally incorporated into Expectation-Maximization (EM) algorithm [8, 23] applied to spherical Gaussian mixtures. The idea is that the irrelevant dimensions can be integrated out, and the resulting marginal distribution follows the same Gaussian mixture functional form. Then we can freely move between the reduced-dimension subspace and the original space. In this approach, cluster membership information (posterior probabilities of the indicator variables) plays a critical role. Knowing them in the reduced-dimension subspace we can directly infer the centers in the original space. We assume the following mixture model

$$p(\mathbf{x}) = \pi_1 g_1^d(\mathbf{x} - \mu_1) + \cdots + \pi_K g_K^d(\mathbf{x} - \mu_K) \quad (1)$$

where each component is a spherical Gaussian distribution,

$$g_k^d(\mathbf{x}) = \frac{1}{(\sqrt{2\pi}\sigma_k)^d} \exp(-\frac{\|\mathbf{x} - \mu_k\|^2}{2\sigma_k^2})$$

and $\mathbf{x}, \mu_k$ are vectors in d-dim space. We denote it as $N^{(d)}(\mu_k, \sigma_k)$. Note that the spherical gaussian function has two invariant properties that will be important later on: (i) they are invariant under any orthogonal coordinate rotation operation $R : \mathbf{x} \to R\mathbf{x}$:

$$g_k^d(R\mathbf{x}|R\theta) = g_k^d(\mathbf{x}|\theta)$$

where R is a $d \times d$ orthonormal matrix and $\theta = \{\mu_1, \cdots, \mu_\kappa, \sigma_1, \cdots, \sigma_\kappa\}$ are the model parameters. (ii) they are invariant under coordinate translation (shift) operation $L : \mathbf{x} \to \mathbf{x} + \ell$: we have

$$g_k^d(L\mathbf{x}|L\theta) = g_k^d(\mathbf{x}|\theta)$$

Given the gaussian mixture model, dimension reduction can be properly studied in a probabilistic framework using marginal distributions. For this reason, we need to split the space into an r-dim space which contains all the relevant dimensions (attributes), and an s-dim space ($s = d - r$) which contains all the irrelevant dimensions (noises). We split the coordinates into $\mathbf{y} = R^T \mathbf{x} = (R_r, R_s)^T \mathbf{x}$, or more explicitly,

$$\begin{pmatrix} \mathbf{y}^\| \\ \mathbf{y}^\perp \end{pmatrix} = \begin{pmatrix} R_r^T \mathbf{x} \\ R_s^T \mathbf{x} \end{pmatrix}, \quad \begin{pmatrix} \nu^\| \\ \nu^\perp \end{pmatrix} = \begin{pmatrix} R_r^T \mu \\ R_s^T \mu \end{pmatrix} \quad (2)$$

where $\mathbf{y}^\|, \nu^\|$ are in r-dim relevant space, and $\mathbf{y}^\perp, \nu^\perp$ are in s-dim subspace of noise, orthogonal to the r-dim relevant space. R is the coordinate rotation, such as the coordinate transformation used in PCA, to clearly separate those relevant and noisy dimensions.

The marginal distribution is defined as

$$p(\mathbf{y}^\|) \equiv \int p(\mathbf{x}) J d\mathbf{y}^\perp = \int p(\mathbf{y}^\|, \mathbf{y}^\perp) J d\mathbf{y}^\perp.$$

where $J = \det(\partial \mathbf{x}/\partial \mathbf{y}) = \det(R)$ is the Jacobian related to coordinate transformation. For orthonormal rotations such as U and V in PCA, $R^T R = R^T R = I_k$ and $\det(R) = 1$. Splitting coordinates, we have

$$\begin{aligned} \|\mathbf{x} - \mu\|_d^2 &= \left\| \begin{bmatrix} R_r^T(\mathbf{x} - \mu) \\ R_s^T(\mathbf{x} - \mu) \end{bmatrix} \right\|_d^2 \\ &= \|\mathbf{y}^\| - \nu^\|\|_r^2 + \|\mathbf{y}^\perp - \nu^\perp\|_s^2 \quad (3) \end{aligned}$$

Thus we have $g_k^d(\mathbf{x} - \mu) = g_k^r(\mathbf{y}^\| - \nu_k^\|) \cdot g_k^s(\mathbf{y}^\perp - \nu_k^\perp)$. The marginal distribution of $g_k^d(\mathbf{x})$ becomes

$$\int g_k^d(\mathbf{x} - \mu) d\mathbf{y}^\perp = g_k^r(\mathbf{y}^\| - \nu^\|), \quad (4)$$

which is exactly the standard spherical Gaussian in the r-dim subspace. For this reason, we simply use $\mathbf{y}$ for

$\mathbf{y}^\|$ and ν for $\nu^\|$ in the r-dim subspace. Therefore we conclude that

Theorem 1. In EM clustering using spherical Gaussian mixture models in d-dimensions, after integrating out irrelevant dimensions, the marginal probability becomes

$$p(\mathbf{y}) = \pi_1 g_1^r(\mathbf{y} - \nu_1) + \cdots + \pi_\kappa g_\kappa^r(\mathbf{y} - \nu_\kappa), \quad (5)$$

exactly the same type of Gaussian distribution as in r-dim space. All relevant attributes for clustering are retained in the r-dim subspace.

4 Adaptive Dimension Reduction for EM

For real-world clustering problems where clusters are not well-separated, the r-dim subspace initially obtained using PCA does not necessarily coincide with the subspace spanned by the K cluster centers. Therefore, the centers, and cluster memberships, in the usual dimension reduction clustering are not necessarily the correct (or accurate) results. One can correct this by adaptively modifying the r-dim subspace using the most current clustering results, and do another round of clustering in the modified subspace. One can repeat this process several times to improved the results.

Given a point or a cluster centroid in the r-dim subspace, mapping back to the original d-dim space is not *unique*. In fact, there are infinite number of points in the d-dim space, all of which project into one point in the r-dim subspace (all points on a vertical line project into a single point in x-y plane). However, the centers (or centroids in the K-means) obtained in clustering in the r-dim subspace can be *uniquely* traced back to the original d-dim space by using the cluster membership of each data point. This observation is the basis of our ADR-EM clustering.

The cluster membership information is contained in the posterior probability h_i^k,

$$h_i^k = \Pr(c_i = k|y_i, \theta)$$

the probability of point i belongs to cluster c_k given current model (parameters) and the evidence (value of y_i). EM algorithm is the following: (i) initialize model parameters $\{\pi_k, \nu_k, \sigma_k\}$; (ii) compute $\{h_i^k\}$, $h_i^k = \pi_k g_k^r(y)/\sum_k \pi_k g_k^r(y)$; (iii) update: (1) compute the number of points belonging to cluster c_k: $n_k = \sum_i h_i^k$; (2) update priors: $\pi_k = n_k/N$; (3) update centers: $\nu_k = \sum_i h_i^k y_i/n_k$; (4) update covariances: $\sigma_k = \sum_i h_i^k \|y_i - \mu_k\|^2/rn_k$. Steps (ii) and (iii) are repeated until convergence. Once EM converges, the final cluster information is contained in $\{h_i^k\}$. Using this information, the centers in the original d-dim space can be computed as

$$\mu_k = \sum_i h_i^k x_i / n_k.$$

Once the locations of the K cluster centers in the original d-dim space are known, expressed as the $d \times K$ matrix

$$C_K = (\mu_1, \mu_2, \cdots, \mu_K), \tag{6}$$

and we can easily find the new $r = K - 1$ dimensional subspace spanned by these K centers. The new subspace is defined by a set of $K - 1$ orthonormal vectors $U_r = (u_1, u_2, \cdots, u_r)$. Note that this orthonormal basis is not unique: any rotation of it is an equally good basis. Here we present two methods to compute the basis. Both have the same $O(r^2 \cdot N)$ computational complexity where N is the number of data vectors in the dataset.

4.1 SVD Basis

We compute the singular value decomposition (SVD) [15] of C as: $C = \sum_\ell \mathbf{u}_\ell \lambda_\ell \mathbf{v}_\ell^T$. Since the data is centered, $\sum_k \pi_k \mu_k = \sum_i \mathbf{x}_i / n = 0$, $\{\mu_1 \cdots \mu_K\}$ are linearly dependent. Therefore C has rank $r = K - 1$. The $d \times r$ matrix $U_r = (u_1, u_2, \cdots, u_r)$ is the orthogonal basis of the new subspace. The SVD basis has a useful property that it automatically orders the dimensions according to their importance. For example, the last dimension u_r is not as important as the first sub-dimension u_1, as in principal component analysis.

Now we project the original data into the new subspace using $y_i = U_r^T x_i$ and do another round of EM clustering, with the starting cluster centers from the projections $\nu_i = U_r^T \mu_i$ and information on priors $\{\pi_k\}$.

4.2 QR basis

Another way to build the orthogonal basis is to use QR or Gram-Schmidt on the K centroids [18]. Without loss of generality, we let μ_K be the one with the smallest magnitude, and form a $d \times (K - 1)$ matrix

$$C_{K-1} = (\mu_1 - \mu_K, \mu_2 - \mu_K, \cdots, \mu_{K-1} - \mu_K). \tag{7}$$

Note that vectors in C_r are not necessarily orthogonal to each other. We use the Gram-Schmidt procedure, or equivalently, the QR factorization in linear algebra,

$$C_{k-1} = Q \begin{bmatrix} P \\ 0 \end{bmatrix} = [Q_r, Q^\perp] \begin{bmatrix} P \\ 0 \end{bmatrix} = Q_r P,$$

where the $d \times r$ matrix $Q_r = (\mathbf{q}_1, \cdots, \mathbf{q}_r)$ is the orthonormal basis for the subspace. P is an $r \times r$ upper triangle matrix, containing the projections of components in the C_r basis. This QR basis has the property that $\mathbf{q}_k$ will be close to the μ_k centers if they are reasonably orthogonal to each other.

Now we use Q_r to project the original data into the new subspace by $y_i = Q_r^T x_i$, etc. Note that by construction, no centers can coincide with each other in either SVD or QR basis.

4.3 The complete ADR-EM algorithm

The complete Adaptive Dimension Reduction Expectation Maximization (ADR-EM) algorithm is described as follows.

1. Preprocessing data to fit better the spherical Gaussian model. Center the data such that $\sum_i \mathbf{x}_i = 0$. Rescale the data such that the variance in every dimension is 1. Choose appropriate K as input parameter. Choose dimensionality r for the reduced dimension subspace. In general, we recommend $r = K - 1$. But $r = K$ or $r < K - 1$ are also appropriate.

2. Do the first dimension reduction using PCA or any other methods, including random starts.

3. Run EM in the r-dim subspace to obtain clusters. Use cluster membership to construct cluster centroids in the original space. Check convergence. If yes, go to step 5.

4. Compute the new r-dim subspace spanned by the K centroids using either SVD or QR basis. Project data into this new subspace. Go to step 3.

5. Output results and converting posterior probabilities to discrete indicators. The relevant attributes (coordinates) are also identified.

If accurate results are necessary, one may run one final round of EM in the original data space starting with existing parameters (see section 7).

A key feature of ADR is that no matter how the data are projected and transformed (shifted, rotated, etc) in subspaces, once the cluster memberships in the subspace are computed, we can always use them to construct clusters in the original space, no need for book-keeping of the details of data transformations and/or reductions. One can easily design hybrid schemes of different data projections and use the obtained cluster membership as the bridge between them to form an integrated clustering method.

4.4 Relevant dimensions

In general, $r = K - 1$ is the optimal choice. However, $r = K$ is also a good choice in many cases: (i) when using QR basis, the QR can be applied to C_K (cf. Eq.6) instead of C_{K-1} (cf. Eq.7) and obtain K basis vectors; (ii) in either SVD basis or QR basis, we can add one or even more additional basis vectors which are orthogonal to existing basis. These additional basis vectors can be either chosen for a particular emphasis or chosen randomly. Randomly choosing additional basis vector could help to search for broader configuration space, making sure we are not stuck in a local minimum.

Sometimes we can also choose $r < K - 1$. Although K centers define a $(K - 1)$-dim subspace, they can sometimes locate on or near an r-dim subspace where $r < K - 1$. For example, 4 points in a 3-dim space could lie on a 2-dim plane or even on a 1-dim line. In these cases, C is rank deficient, i.e., the rank of C will be less than $K - 1$ and the singular values in SVD basis will drop to near zero; we should choose the appropriate $r < K - 1$.

Even if C is not rank deficient, we may still set r to be less than $K - 1$ for computational efficiency and effectiveness. This is especially important if we are dealing with a large and complex dataset and somehow we believe there should be, for example, $K = 10$ clusters. Due to the curse of dimensionality, 9-dim space may still be too high, so we may set $r = 3$ and find 10 clusters in 3-dim space where EM or K-means are typically more effective. Also in 3-dim space, computation is more efficient (than in 9-dim) and the results can be inspected using 3-dim graphics or other visualization tools. In this case, after the best 10 clusters are discovered using $r = 3$, we may further refine the results by setting $r = 9$ and re-run the algorithm, using cluster membership as the bridge.

In all the test examples below, we have tested this $r < K - 1$ (over-reduced) method and the results are generally the same as the $r = K - 1$ method. However, we do notice the slower convergence of the EM method.

5 Adaptive Dimension Reduction for K-means

The ADR method can also be applied to the K-means clustering as well. Given a set of data vectors $X = [x_1, \ldots, x_n]$, the K-means for K clusters seeks to find a set of centers $C_\mu = [\mu_1, \ldots, \mu_K]$ so as to minimize

$$J_d(X, C_\mu) = \sum_{k=1}^{K} \sum_{i \in c_k} \|x_i - \mu_k\|_d^2. \qquad (8)$$

Each cluster c_i is represented by a center μ_i and consists of the data vectors that are closest to it in Euclidean distance, and the center of a cluster is the centroid of its data vectors. The K-means clustering can be viewed as a special case of EM with three simplifications (i) $\sigma_1 = \cdots = \sigma_K = \sigma$; (ii) $\pi_1 = \cdots = \pi_K$; (iii) with $\sigma \to 0$ so that $h_i^k = 1$ or 0.

As before, the key is to find the relevant r-dim reduced space, specified by the projection matrix R_r. We have the following.

Theorem 2. Suppose we somehow know the correct r-dim relevant subspace defined by R_r. Let $Y = R_r^T X = R_r^T(x_1, \ldots, x_n)$ and $C_\nu = [\nu_1, \ldots, \nu_K]$ be K centroids in r-dim subspace. Solve the K-means problem in r-dim subspace,

$$\min_{C_\nu} J_r(Y, C_\nu).$$

Use the cluster membership $H = (h_i^k)$ obtained to reconstruct the K centers $C_\mu^* = [\mu_1^*, \ldots, \mu_K^*]$ in the full dimensional space. Then C_μ^* are the exact optimal solution to the the full-dimension K-means problem.

Proof. Assume the centroid matrix C_μ^* are the minimum for K cluster K-means in (8). Construct projection matrix R_r that spans the subspace for C_μ^*. Use Gram-Schmit procedure to construct R_s such that $R = [R_r, R_s]$ is orthonormal matrix. Since R_r spans the subspace for C_μ^*, $R_s^T \mu_k^* = 0$. Using this fact and Eq.(2), we have

$$\|x_i - \mu_k^*\|_d^2 = \|y_i - \nu_k^*\|_r^2 + \|R_s^T x_i\|_s^2$$

This indicates that among all K centers, if c_k^* is closest to x_i in the d-sim space, then $R_r^T c_k^*$ is closest to $R_r^T x_i$ in the r-dim space, independent of R_s. We can write $J_d(X, C) = J_r(Y, C_\nu) + \text{const}$. $\qquad \square$

If we know the final solution C_μ^*, we can easily construct R_r. For any $r \times r$ orthonormal matrix S, $R_r S$ still spans the correct subspace. In practice we do not know C_μ^* until after the problem is solved. By Theorem 2, we only need to find the relevant subspace. Because of the large flexibility in defining R_r, finding the relevant subspace is much easier than finding C_μ^* directly. This is the usefulness of Theorem 2. Our adaptive dimension reduction K-means is based on the theorem. The complete ADR-Kmeans algorithm is identical to ADR-EM algorithm in §4.3.

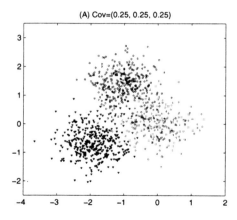

(A) Cov=(0.25, 0.25, 0.25)

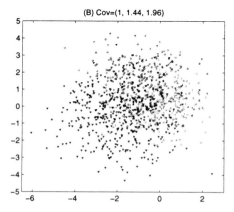

(B) Cov=(1, 1.44, 1.96)

Figure 1: Three Gaussian clusters in 4-dim space. (A) covariances (0.25, 0.25, 0.25). (B) covariances (1, 1.44, 1.96). Data points are shown in the first 2 PCA components. From (A) to (B), variance increases $(1/0.5)^2$ for the 1st cluster (red squares), $(1.2/0.5)^2$ for the 2nd cluster (blue circles), and $(1.4/0.5)^2$ for the 3rd cluster (black triangles).

6   Applications

6.1   Highly overlapping Gaussian mixtures

The first example is a 1000-point synthetic dataset of 3 gaussians in 4-dim with centers $(\mathbf{c}_1, \mathbf{c}_2, \mathbf{c}_3)$, listed below

$$(\mathbf{c}_1, \mathbf{c}_2, \mathbf{c}_3) = \begin{bmatrix} 0 & 0 & 1 \\ 0 & 1 & 1 \\ 0 & 1 & -1 \\ 0 & 1 & 1 \end{bmatrix}, \qquad (9)$$

covariances $(\sigma_1^2, \sigma_2^2, \sigma_3^2) = (1, 1.44, 1.96)$, and prior distributions $(\pi_1, \pi_2, \pi_3) = (0.25, 0.35, 0.4)$. The 3 gaussians are highly overlapped (see Fig.1) The results of

ADR-EM are shown below,

$$(\mathbf{c}_1^*, \mathbf{c}_2^*, \mathbf{c}_3^*) = \begin{bmatrix} 0.03 & 0.06 & 1.04 \\ 0.23 & 1.18 & 0.99 \\ -0.03 & 1.02 & -1.32 \\ 0.12 & 1.16 & 1.00 \end{bmatrix}$$

quite close to the correct results. Repeated runs show that the method is quite robust. If we run EM directly in 4-dim space, the EM will have difficulty finding the correct clusters. Results change for each different run. After 10 runs, the best results are shown below

$$(\mathbf{c}_1^*, \mathbf{c}_2^*, \mathbf{c}_3^*) = \begin{bmatrix} 0.38 & 0.12 & 1.44 \\ 0.20 & 0.97 & 1.76 \\ -0.69 & 0.72 & -1.96 \\ 0.30 & 0.91 & 1.38 \end{bmatrix}$$

Dimension reduction is essential in this highly-overlapped situation.

6.2   DNA Microarray gene expression profiling

This example is from molecular biology. High density DNA microarray technology can simultaneously monitor the expression level of thousands of genes which determines different pathological states of the same tissue drawn from different patients [16, 3]. Here we study gene expression profiles of non-Hodgkin lymphoma cancer data from [3]. Among the 96 samples of 9 phenotypes (classes), we pick the 4 largest classes with a total of 76 samples(see Fig.2): (1) 46 samples of diffuse large B-cell lymphoma ($\circ$), (2) 10 samples of Activated Blood cell B-cell ($\triangledown$), (3) 9 samples of chronic lymphocytic leukemia ($\triangle$), (4) 11 samples of follicular lymphoma ($+$).

Each sample contains expression levels of 4026 genes (variables). The question we ask: could we discover these phenotypes from data directly, without human expertise?

We use t-test statistic criteria to select top 100 genes. The clustering problem is focused on the 76 samples in 100-dim space with K=4. This is still a high dimensional problem. We use ADM-EM algorithm on this dataset, setting r=3. The clustering result is shown in the following contingency table

$$T = \begin{bmatrix} 39 & 3 & 4 & \cdot \\ \cdot & 10 & \cdot & \cdot \\ \cdot & \cdot & 9 & \cdot \\ \cdot & \cdot & \cdot & 11 \end{bmatrix}$$

where $T = (t_{ij})$, t_{ij} is the number of data points which are observed to be in cluster i, but was computed via the clustering method to belong to cluster j. The accuracy is 69/76=0.91% (accuracy is defined as $\sum_k t_{kk}/N$ [11]). If we perform the clustering directly in the 100-dim space, the runs are often trapped in local minimum. The usefulness of PCA on gene expression analysis were noted in [10].

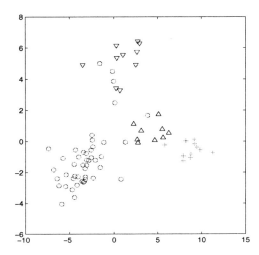

Figure 2: Gene expression profiles for lymphoma cancer dataset. Shown are the data in the first 2 PCA components.

6.3 Internet newsgroups clustering

We use the Internet newsgroups dataset [1] to illustrate the process of adaptive dimension reduction. We use five news groups NG2/NG9/NG10/NG15/NG18 with 50 news articles from each group (see [29] for details). NG2: `comp.graphics`; NG9: `rec.motorcycles`; NG10: `rec.sport.baseball`; NG15: `sci.space`; NG18: `talk.politics.mideast`.

Words with document frequency less than 3 are removed, and a total of 2731 distinct words are retained. Each document is represented by a vector in this d=2731 dimensional space. We set $r = 5$ (relevant dimension is a 5-dim subspace). We start with a *random* initial 5-dim subspace. In Table 1, we list the accuracy and J at the end of each adaptive iteration. Repeated adaptive dimension reduction gradually converges to the correct subspace. As a comparison, we run K-means algorithm in the original d=2731 space with the same initial clusters and obtain accuracy 50.40% and J=227.83. This indicates the effectiveness of our adaptive method.

[1] The newsgroups dataset together with the bow toolkit for processing it can be downloaded from http://www.cs.cmu.edu /afs/cs/project/theo-11/www/naive-bayes.html.

iteration	accuracy	min(J)
1	25.60	235.58
2	34.40	233.11
3	44.80	231.01
4	52.80	229.68
5	60.40	228.19
6	63.60	227.47
7	66.00	227.06
8	67.20	226.86

Table 1: Clustering results of ADM-Kmeans algorithm.

7 Discussions

We introduced a new method for clustering high dimensional data using adaptive dimension reductions. The key to the effectiveness of this method lies in (Theorems 1 and 2) that working in the subspace containing true cluster centers is sufficient to find the cluster centers. The subspace containing cluster centers is of dimension K, far smaller than the original dimension in many applications. Adaptive dimension reduction is an effective way to converge to this subspace. Note that finding the subspace is much easier than finding cluster centers directly, due to the flexibility in defining subspace.

Although we concentrate on EM and K-means algorithm here, the adaptive dimension reduction approach could be extended to other clustering methods. Using cluster membership as the bridge to connect subspaces of different dimensions makes these extensions easy to implement. For example, one may construct a number of subspaces based on different feature selection methods and apply different clustering methods on these subset of features and move or combine them to satisfy some optimal conditions.

Another interesting subtle point is that although the functional form in d-dim space [cf. Eq.(1)] is very much the same as that in r-dim subspace [cf. Eq.(5)], the final parameters are *not* the same: the priors π_k differ in the two spaces in the case of highly overlapped clusters with different covariances. The reason is that the probability can not be separated into a product of P(relevant coordinates)*P(irrelevant coordinates): $p(\mathbf{x}) = p(\mathbf{y}, \mathbf{y}^\perp) \neq p(\mathbf{y}) \cdot p(\mathbf{y}^\perp)$, even if each mixture component is separable. Therefore, the standard practice of reporting the results directly obtained in the reduced-dimension subspace is not accurate enough. For this reason, we suggest the EM in the d-dim space be run once using those parameters obtained in the r-dim subspace to get more accurate final parameters.

Acknowledgments. This work is supported by U.S. Department of Energy (Office of Science, Office of Advanced Scientific Research, MICS Division, and Office of Laboratory Policy and Infrastructure) under contract DE-AC03-76SF00098.

References

[1] C.C. Aggarwal, C. Procopiuc, J.L. Wolf, P.S. Yu, and J.S. Park. Fast algorithms for projected clustering. pages 61–72, 1999.

[2] R. Agrawal, J. Gehrke, D. Gunopulos, and P. Raghavan. Automatic subspace clustering of high dimensional data for data mining applications. pages 94–105, 1998.

[3] A.A. Alizadeh, M.B. Eisen, et al. Distinct types of diffuse large B-cell lymphoma identified by gene expression profiling. *Nature*, 403:503–511, 2000.

[4] M.W. Berry, S.T. Dumais, and Gavin W. O'Brien. Using linear algebra for intelligent information retrieval. *SIAM Review*, 37:573–595, 1995.

[5] P. Bradley and U. Fayyad. Refining initial points for k-means clustering. In *Proc. 15th International Conf. on Machine Learning*, 1998.

[6] S. Dasgupta. Experiments with random projection. In *Proc. 16th Conf. Uncertainty in Artificial Intelligence (UAI 2000)*, 2000.

[7] S. Deerwester, S.T. Dumais, T.K. Landauer, G.W. Furnas, and R.A. Harshman. Indexing by latent semantic analysis. *J. Amer. Soc. Info. Sci*, 41:391–407, 1990.

[8] A.P. Dempster, N.M. Laird, and D.B. Rubin. Maximum-likelihood from incomplete data via em algorithm. *J. Royal Stat. Soc. B.*, pages 1–38, 1977.

[9] I. Dhillon and D. Modha. Concept decomposition for large sparse text data using clustering. *Machine Learning*, 42:143–175, 2001.

[10] C. Ding. Analysis of gene expression profiles: class discovery and leaf ordering. In *Proc. 6th Int'l Conf. Research in Comp. Mol. Bio.(RECOMB 2002)*, pages 127–136, April 2002.

[11] C. Ding and I. Dubchak. Multi-class protein fold recognition using support vector machines and neural networks. *Bioinformatics*, 17:349–358, 2001.

[12] C.H.Q. Ding. A similarity-based probability model for latent semantic indexing. *Proc. 22nd ACM SIGIR Conference*, pages 59–65, Aug. 1999.

[13] P. Drineas, A. Frieze, R. Kannan, S. Vempala, and V. Vinay. Clustering in large graphs and matrices. In *Proc. 19th ACM-SIAM Symposium on Discrete Algorithms*, 1999.

[14] R. O. Duda, P. E. Hart, and D. G. Stork. *Pattern Classification, 2nd ed.* Wiley, 2000.

[15] G. Golub and C. Van Loan. *Matrix Computations, 3rd edition.* Johns Hopkins, Baltimore, 1996.

[16] T.R. Golub, D.K. Slonim, P. Tamayo, et al. Molecular classification of cancer: class discovery and class prediction by gene expression monitoring. *Science*, 286:531–537, 1999.

[17] J. Grim, J Novovicova, P. Pudil, P. Somol, and F. Ferri. Initialization normal mixtures of densities. *Proc. Int'l Conf. Pattern Recognition (ICPR 1998)*, Dec. 1998.

[18] M. Jeon, H. Park, and J.B. Rosen. Dimension reduction based on centroids and least squares for efficient processing of text data. *Proc. SIAM Conf. on Data Mining*, 2001.

[19] G.H. John, R. Kohavi, and K. Pfleger. Irrelevant features and the subset selection problem. In *Int'l Conf. Machine Learning*, pages 121–129, 1994.

[20] I.T. Jolliffe. *Principal Component Analysis.* Springer Verlag, 1986.

[21] G. Karypis and E.-H. Han. Concept indexing: A fast dimensionality reduction algorithm with applications to document retrieval and categorization. *Proc. 9th Int'l Conf. Information and Knowledge Management (CIKM 2000)*, 2000.

[22] R. Kothari and D. Pitts. On finding the number of clusters. *Pattern Recognition Letters*, 50:405–416, 1999.

[23] G. McLachlan and T. Krishnan. *The EM Algorithm and Extensions.* John Wiley, 1997.

[24] M. Meila and D. Heckerman. An experimental comparison of several clustering and initialization methods. *Proc. 14th Conf. Uncertainty in Artificial Intelligence (UAI 98)*, pages 386–395, 1998.

[25] A.W. Moore. Very fast em-based mixture model clustering using multiresolution kd-trees. *Proc. Neural Info. Processing Systems (NIPS 1998)*, Dec. 1998.

[26] J. Pena, J. Lozano, and P. Larranaga. An empirical comparison of four initialization methods for the k-means algorithm. *Pattern Recognition Letters*, 50:1027–1040, 1999.

[27] D. W. Scott. *Multivariate Density Estimation: Theory, Practice, and Visualization.* John Wiley, 1992.

[28] C.K.I. Williams. A MCMC approach to hierarchical mixture modeling. *Proc. Neural Info. Processing Systems (NIPS 2000)*, Dec. 2000.

[29] H. Zha, C. Ding, M. Gu, X. He, and H.D. Simon. Spectral relaxation for k-means clustering. *Proc. Neural Info. Processing Systems (NIPS 2001)*, Dec. 2001.

Modal–style operators in qualitative data analysis *

Ivo Düntsch[†]

Department of Computer Science

Brock University

St. Catherines, Ontario, Canada, L2S 3A1

duentsch@cosc.brocku.ca

Günther Gediga[‡]

Institut für Evaluation und Marktanalysen

Brinkstr. 19

49143 Jeggen, Germany

gediga@eval-institut.de

Abstract

We explore the usage of the modal possibility operator (and its dual necessity operator) in qualitative data analysis, and show that it – quite literally – complements the derivation operator of formal concept analysis; we also propose a new generalization of the rough set approximation operators. As an example for the applicability of the concepts we investigate the Morse data set which has been frequently studied in multidimensional scaling procedures.

1 Introduction

A frequently used operationalisation of data is an

$$Object \mapsto Attribute$$

relationship. Such operationalisation comes in various flavours: Examples include deterministic information systems a la Pawlak [16], the many–valued tables of Lipski [11] and Orłowska & Pawlak [15], in which each object is assigned a set of attribute values, the property systems of Vakarelov [21], or the relational attribute systems of Düntsch et al. [5] which incorporate semantical constraints. In its most general form, each object of the universe of discourse is related to one or more attribute values. Mathematically, one considers structures $\langle U, V, R \rangle$, where U and V are sets, and $R \subseteq U \times V$ is a binary relation between elements of U and elements of V. Based on the existential and universal quantifiers, one can define mappings $2^U \to 2^V$ in a natural way, namely,

$$\langle R \rangle(X) = \{y \in V : (\exists x \in X) xRy\} = \bigcup_{x \in X} R(x),$$

$$[[R]](X) = \{y \in V : (\forall x \in X) xRy\} = \bigcap_{x \in X} R(x),$$

where $R(x) = \{y \in V : xRy\}$. In a general mathematical setting, the mapping $[[R]]$ has been called a *polarity* [1]; it is also the *derivation operator* of formal concept analysis (FCA) [22]. While $[[R]]$ has received some prominence via FCA, the operator $\langle R \rangle$ seems to have been largely neglected in the study of object–attribute relations. Interestingly, it is the reverse in logical systems, where $\langle R \rangle$ became the widely studied possibility operator of modal logics associated with Kripke frames $\langle U, R \rangle$, the roots of which go back to the seminal paper by Jónsson & Tarski [10]. The operator $[[R]]$ was introduced to modal logics by Humberstone [9] and Gargov et al. [6], who called it a "sufficiency operator". Their aim was to be able to express "negative" properties of relations such as irreflexivity, which could not be expressed by the common modal operators "possibility" and its dual, "necessity". Apart from the sufficiency operator in FCA, modal–style operators have been used in data analysis in connection with rough set approximation [13, 17], where R is an equivalence relation on U; here, $\langle R \rangle$ can be interpreted as an upper approximation, and its dual as a lower approximation, based on the knowledge of the world given by the classification induced by R. There is a rich literature on binary relations among objects, induced by information systems, and we invite the reader to consult [14] for many examples and details.

Our aim in this note is to explore the possibilities of the $\langle R \rangle$ operator and its dual necessity operator $[R]$ in relational attribute systems, and we shall show that it (quite literally) complements the derivation operator of FCA. Along the way, we will propose a new generalization for the rough set approximation operators. The paper closes with an application of the concepts to the Morse data set [18].

*Co-operation for this paper was supported by EU COST Action 274 "Theory and Applications of Relational Structures as Knowledge Instruments" (TARSKI); http://www.tarski.org/

[†]The ordering of authors is alphabetical and equal authorship is implied.

2 Definitions and notation

Throughout this paper, U and V are nonempty sets, and $R \subseteq U \times V$. For unexplained notation and concepts in lattices and order theory we refer the reader to [4].

A *closure operator* on U is a mapping $\mathrm{cl} : 2^U \to 2^U$ such that for all $X, Y \subseteq U$,

$X \subseteq Y \subseteq U \Rightarrow \mathrm{cl}(X) \subseteq \mathrm{cl}(Y)$,   i.e. cl is monotone,

$X \subseteq \mathrm{cl}(X)$,   i.e. cl is expanding,

$\mathrm{cl}(X) = \mathrm{cl}(\mathrm{cl}(X))$ i.e. cl is idempotent.

Dually, an *interior operator* is a mapping $\mathrm{int} : 2^U \to 2^U$ such that for all $X, Y \subseteq U$,

$X \subseteq Y \subseteq U \Rightarrow \mathrm{int}(X) \subseteq \mathrm{int}(Y)$,   i.e. int is monotone,

$\mathrm{int}(X) \subseteq X$,   i.e. int is contracting,

$\mathrm{int}(X) = \mathrm{int}(\mathrm{int}(X))$,   i.e. int is idempotent.

If L is a lattice and $M \subseteq L$, then M is called *join–dense* (*meet–dense*), if every $x \in L$ is a join (meet) of elements of M.

For each $x \in U$ we let

$$R(x) = \{y \in V : xRy\}$$

be the *R-range of x*, and

$$\mathrm{dom}\, R = \{x \in U : xRy \text{ for some } y \in V\}$$

is the *domain of R*. Furthermore,

$$R^{\smile} = \{\langle y, x \rangle \subseteq V \times U : xRy\}$$

is the *converse of R*. If $f : 2^U \to 2^V$, then the *dual of f* is the mapping $f^{\partial} : 2^U \to 2^V$ defined by

$$f^{\partial}(X) = V \setminus f(U \setminus X).$$

The operators $2^U \to 2^V$ which we want to consider are the following:

$\langle R \rangle(X) = \{y \in V : X \cap R^{\smile}(y) \neq \emptyset\}$,   (possibility)

$[R](X) = \{y \in V : R^{\smile}(y) \subseteq X\}$,   (necessity)

$[[R]](X) = \{y \in V : X \subseteq R^{\smile}(y)\}$,   (sufficiency)

$\langle\langle R \rangle\rangle(X) = \{y \in V : (-R)^{\smile}(y) \cap (U \setminus X) \neq \emptyset\}$,

     (dual suff.)

Here, $(-R) = \{\langle x, y \rangle \in U \times V : \langle x, y \rangle \notin R\}$ is the complement of the relation R in $U \times V$. It is well known that these mappings have the following structural properties: Let $\mathfrak{X} \subseteq 2^U, x \in U$; then

$$\langle R \rangle(\{x\}) = R(x) = [[R]](\{x\}),$$
$$[R](U \setminus \{x\}) = V \setminus R(x) = \langle\langle R \rangle\rangle(U \setminus \{x\}),$$
$$\langle R \rangle \left(\bigcup_{X \in \mathfrak{X}} X \right) = \bigcup_{X \in \mathfrak{X}} \langle R \rangle(X),$$
$$[R] \left(\bigcap_{X \in \mathfrak{X}} X \right) = \bigcap_{X \in \mathfrak{X}} [R](X),$$
$$[[R]] \left(\bigcup_{X \in \mathfrak{X}} X \right) = \bigcap_{X \in \mathfrak{X}} [[R]](X),$$
$$\langle\langle R \rangle\rangle \left(\bigcap_{X \in \mathfrak{X}} X \right) = \bigcup_{X \in \mathfrak{X}} \langle\langle R \rangle\rangle(X).$$

Hence, the mappings $\langle R \rangle$ and $[[R]]$ are determined by their action on the singleton sets, and $[R]$ as well as $\langle\langle R \rangle\rangle$ are determined by their action on the complements of singletons.

As an example, suppose that U is a set of students, V is a set of problems, and aRb is interpreted as "Student a solves problem b" [7]. If $X \subseteq U$ is a set of students, then for a problem b we have

$b \in \langle R \rangle(X) \iff$ Some student in X solves b,

$b \in [R](X) \iff$ Each student who solves b is in X,

$b \in [[R]](X) \iff b$ is solved by each student in X,

$b \in \langle\langle R \rangle\rangle(X) \iff$ Not all students in $U \setminus X$ solve b.

If we think of qRs as "s is a property which q has", then, for each $Y \subseteq V$, the set $[R^{\smile}](Y)$ collects those objects all of whose properties are in Y, and $[[R^{\smile}]](Y)$ is the set of objects which possess all properties of Y (and possibly more).

It is not hard to see (and well known) that $\langle R \rangle$ and $[R]$, as well as $[[R]]$ and $\langle\langle R \rangle\rangle$ are dual to each other. Furthermore,

(1) $[[R]](X) = [(-R)](U \setminus X), \quad \langle\langle R \rangle\rangle(X) = \langle(-R)\rangle(U \setminus X).$

We see from (1) that each of the four operators, along with the complements on U and $U \times V$ and the converses, defines all others. It may be argued that, in principle, everything is already said, when we consider, for example, the sufficiency operator $[[R]]$. As far as the formal Mathematics and the computational aspects go, this may be true; however, the semantic interpretations of the various operators differ widely, and it is useful to start with the other operators if the situation so requires. Indeed, considering complementation on the relational level adds another level to the underlying logic; in order to avoid this, the sufficiency operator was introduced on the language level.

3 Modal operators in data analysis

In the realm of data analysis the sufficiency operator has received the widest attention of all four modal–style operators via the context of formal concept analysis [22]. There, a *context* is a triple $\langle U, V, R \rangle$, where U, V are sets, and $R \subseteq U \times V$. If $X \subseteq U$, $Y \subseteq V$, the set $[[R]](X)$ is called *intent of X* and $[[R^{\smile}]](Y)$ is called the *extent of Y*. Here, we think of Y as a set of properties, and X as the set of objects (of our set U of discourse) which possess these properties. A *concept* is defined as a pair $\langle X, Y \rangle \in 2^U \times 2^V$ such that $[[R]](X) = Y$ and $[[R^{\smile}]](Y) = X$. The main theorem of FCA is the following:

Proposition 1. *[22] Let $M = \langle U, V, R \rangle$ be a context, and set*

$$C_M = \{\langle X, Y \rangle \in 2^U \times 2^V : [[R]](X) = Y, [[R^{\smile}]](Y) = X\}.$$

Then, C_M can be made into a complete lattice by setting

$$\sum_{i \in I} \langle X_i, Y_i \rangle = \langle [[R^{\smile}]][[R]](\bigcup_{i \in I} X_i), \bigcap_{I \in I} Y_i \rangle,$$

$$\prod_{i \in I} \langle X_i, Y_i \rangle = \langle \bigcap_{i \in I} X_i, [[R]][[R^{\smile}]](\bigcup_{i \in I} Y_i) \rangle.$$

Conversely, a complete lattice L is isomorphic to some C_M, if and only if there are mappings $\gamma : U \to L$, $\mu : V \to L$ such that

$$\{\gamma(x) : x \in U\} \text{ is join–dense in } L,$$
$$\{\mu(y) : y \in V\} \text{ is meet–dense in } L,$$
$$xRy \iff \gamma(x) \leq \mu(y) \text{ for all } x \in U, y \in V.$$

C_M is called the *concept lattice of M*.

Concept lattices have proved to be quite useful in qualitative data analysis, but they are not a panacea, as the following example shows [7]: Let U be a set of problems, V be a set of skills, and $R \subseteq U \times V$ such that qRs is interpreted as

Skill s is necessary to solve q, and

the skill set $R(q)$ is minimally sufficient to solve q.

Suppose that $X \subseteq U$ is the set of all problems which some student t has solved in a test. If one assumes that X is a true representation of the student's state of knowledge, then

1. For each $q \in X$, the student has all the skills to solve q (no lucky guesses). By our operationalization, these are given by $R(q)$; thus, the student possesses all skills in $\bigcup_{q \in X} R(q) = \langle R \rangle(X)$. This is a somewhat conservative interpretation, since the student may possess other skills that are necessary, but not sufficient, to solve an additional problem not in X.

2. The student actually has solved all problems which can be solved with the skills in $\langle R \rangle(X)$ (no careless errors). Thus, for each $q \in U$, $R(q) \subseteq \langle R \rangle(X)$ implies $q \in X$; in other words, $[R^{\smile}]\langle R \rangle(X) \subseteq X$.

We shall see in Lemma 2 that $[R^{\smile}]\langle R \rangle(X)$ is actually a closure operator; thus, we have $[R^{\smile}]\langle R \rangle(X) = X$ in this case, and the true knowledge states are the closed sets with respect to this operator. More generally, we can regard $[R^{\smile}]\langle R \rangle(X)$ as an upper bound of the collection of problems which t is capable of solving. Similarly, if qRs is interpreted as

It is possible to solve problem q with skill s,

then $\langle R^{\smile} \rangle[R](X)$ is a lower bound of the collection of problems which t is capable of solving.

The usefulness of $[[R^{\smile}]]$ or $[[R]]$ is somewhat limited in this context, since $[[R]](X)$ will be small or empty, in case the student has managed to solve problems which test different skills.

These considerations lead to the following: If $X \subseteq U$ and $Y \subseteq V$ we call $\langle R \rangle(X)$ the *span of X*, and $[R^{\smile}](Y)$ the *content of Y*. The span of X is the set of all properties which are related to some element of X, and the content of Y is the set of those objects which can be completely described by the properties in Y. These operators have the following properties:

Lemma 2. *1. $[R^{\smile}]\langle R \rangle$ is a closure operator on 2^U.*

2. $\langle R \rangle[R^{\smile}]$ is an interior operator on 2^V.

3. $x \in [R^{\smile}]\langle R \rangle(\emptyset) \iff x \notin \text{dom} R$.

Proof. 1. Using (1) and the fact that $\langle S \rangle$ and $[S]$ as well as $[[S]]$ and $\langle\langle S \rangle\rangle$ are dual to each other, we obtain

$$[R^{\smile}]\langle R \rangle(X) = [[(-R)^{\smile}]](V \setminus \langle R \rangle(X))$$
$$= [[(-R)^{\smile}]]([R](V \setminus X)) = [[(-R)^{\smile}]][[-R]](X).$$

It is well known that $[[S^{\smile}]][[S]]$ is a closure operator for any $S \subseteq U \times V$ [22], and thus, so is $[R^{\smile}]\langle R \rangle$.

2. follows from the fact that $\langle R \rangle[R^{\smile}]$ is the dual of $[R]\langle R^{\smile} \rangle$.

3. $x \in [R^{\smile}]\langle R \rangle(\emptyset) \iff R(x) \subseteq \langle R \rangle(\emptyset) \iff R(x) \subseteq \emptyset \iff x \notin \text{dom} R$. $\square$

We call $[R^{\smile}]\langle R \rangle(X)$ the *upper bound of X* and $\langle R^{\smile} \rangle[R](X)$ the *lower bound of X*, both with respect to R.

In related development, Wong et al. [23] define an interval structure as a pair $\langle f, g \rangle$ of mappings between two Boolean algebras which have approximately the properties of the pair of operators $\langle [R], \langle R \rangle \rangle$.

If $U = V$ and R is a transitive relation on U, then $[R^\lnot]\langle R\rangle = \langle R\rangle$ and $\langle R\rangle[R^\lnot] = [R^\lnot]$; therefore, $[R^\lnot]\langle R\rangle$ coincides with the upper approximation operator and $\langle R\rangle[R^\lnot]$ with the lower approximation operator of rough set theory.

For reflexive relations, Słowiński & Vanderpooten [20] propose $\langle R\rangle$ as an upper approximation operator. This definition has the drawback that, unless R is also transitive, $\langle R\rangle$ is not idempotent, so that we may have the situation that $\langle R\rangle(X) \subsetneq \langle R\rangle\langle R\rangle(X)$. On the contrary, $[R^\lnot]\langle R\rangle$ is a closure operator regardless of the properties of R.

Let us denote the set of all pairs $\langle X, Y\rangle$ with $X = [R^\lnot](Y)$, $Y = \langle R\rangle(X)$ by SC_M. We now have a fundamental theorem for SC_M, analogous to Proposition 1:

Proposition 3. *SC_M becomes a complete lattice by setting*

$$(2) \qquad \sum_{i \in I}\langle X_i, Y_i\rangle = \langle [R^\lnot]\langle R\rangle(\bigcup_{i \in I} X_i), \bigcup_{i \in I} Y_i\rangle,$$

$$(3) \qquad \prod_{i \in I}\langle X_i, Y_i\rangle = \langle \bigcap_{i \in I} X_i, \langle R\rangle[R^\lnot](\bigcap_{i \in I} Y_i)\rangle$$

Conversely, a complete lattice L is isomorphic to some SC_M if and only if there are mappings $\gamma: U \to L$, $\mu: V \to L$ such that

$$\{\gamma(x) : x \in U\} \cup \{0\} \text{ is join–dense in } L,$$
$$\{\mu(y) : y \in V\} \cup \{1\} \text{ is meet–dense in } L,$$
$$xRy \Longleftrightarrow \gamma(x) \not\leq \mu(y) \text{ for all } x \in U, y \in V.$$

Proof. This can be inferred from Proposition 1 and the fact that $[R^\lnot]\langle R\rangle(X) = [[(-R)^\lnot]][[-R]](X)$. □

The result shows that $SC_{\langle U,V,R\rangle}$ is isomorphic to the concept lattice $C_{\langle U,V,-R\rangle}$. The internal structure, as well as the semantic interpretation of the two lattices are, however, different. Unlike the extent–intent operators of FCA, our construction is asymmetric, since we use one operator into one direction, and its dual in the opposite direction. Furthermore, for $\langle X_0, Y_0\rangle$, $\langle X_1, Y_1\rangle \in SC_M$, we have

$$\langle X_0, Y_0\rangle \leq \langle X_1, Y_1\rangle \Longleftrightarrow X_0 \subseteq X_1 \Longleftrightarrow Y_0 \subseteq Y_1,$$

so that $\leq$ is isotone in both components.

4 The Morse data

In this Section we will give an example how the modal-style operators can be applied to relations of similarity. For related work in a similar context we invite the reader to consult [2]. The data under investigation, a flagship of multidimensional scaling, were originally collected by Rothkopf [18] in the following context:

"The S[ubject]s of this experiment were exposed to pairs of aural Morse signals sent at a high tone speed. The signals of each pair were separated by a short temporal interval. The S[ubject]s were asked to indicate whether they thought the signals were the same (or different) by making the appropriate remark on an IBM True–False Answer sheet. Each S[ubject] was asked to respond in this fashion to 351 different pairs of Morse signals."

The data is given as a matrix, with rows and columns labeled by the alphanumeric characters[1]. An entry s in cell $\langle p, q\rangle$ means that $s\%$ of subjects regarded the code for p and q as the same signal. In the sequel, we will refer to p as the *first stimulus* or as being *in the first position*, and to q as the *second stimulus*, or as being *in the second position*. We use upper case letters for first stimuli and lower case letters for second stimuli; the numeric characters are prefixed by a $*$, if they occur as second stimuli. We emphasize that these are only notational conveniences, so that e.g. a and A or 1 and $*1$ correspond to the same code sequence. The matrix diagonal corresponds to pairs which are truly the same, the off-diagonal entries correspond to pairs which are truly different. It should be noted that the matrix is not symmetric, and that the entries in the diagonal are always less than 100. Thus, we have an example of a non-reflexive asymmetric relation which expresses some form of similarity.

Shepard [19] describes the data using the dimensions

1. Length of the signal,
2. Distribution of dots and dashes in the signal, going from only dots to only dashes.

The distances between the points in a plane spanned by these dimensions reflect (partially) the ordinal relation among the given proximities.

For various "cut points " s we consider the relation

$$R_s = \{\langle p, q\rangle : \text{At least } s\% \text{ of the subjects responded "same",}$$
$$\text{when } \langle p, q\rangle \text{ was presented}\}.$$

Observe that $R_s \subseteq R_t$ in case $t \leq s$.

As the length of the signal is one of the dimension identified in [19] (and also in [3]), we are interested in the behavior of the modal–style operators on the sets

$$X_n = \{p : \text{The length of the Morse code for first stimulus } p \text{ is } n\},$$
$$Y_n = \{q : \text{The length of the Morse code for second stimulus } q \text{ is } n\},$$

which are given in Table 1.

---

[1]The data are available from http://www.eval-institut.de/data/ morsedat.html

Table 1. Distinguished sets

Stimulus (first position)	Stimulus (second position)
$X_1 = \{E, T\}$	$Y_1 = \{e, t\}$
$X_2 = \{A, I, M, N\}$	$Y_2 = \{a, i, m, n\}$
$X_3 = \{D, G, K, O, R, S, U, W\}$	$Y_3 = \{d, g, k, o, r, s, u, w\}$
$X_4 = \{B, C, F, H, J, L, P, Q, V, X, Y, Z\}$	$Y_4 = \{b, c, f, h, j, l, p, q, v, x, y, z\}$
$X_5 = \{0, 1, 2, 3, 4, 5, 6, 7, 8, 9\}$	$Y_5 = \{*0, *1, *2, *3, *4, *5, *6, *7, *8, *9\}$

Disregarding for the moment the cut off parameter, the equality interpretation of the operators is as follows: If we start with the first stimuli, in particular the sets X_n, then

$q \in \langle R \rangle (X_n) \iff q$ was gauged to be the same as some first stimulus of length n.

$q \in [R](X_n) \iff q$ was gauged to be the same only as first stimuli of length n.

$q \in [[R]](X_n) \iff q$ was gauged to be the same to all first stimuli of length n, and possibly others.

If we start with a set Y of stimuli at the second position, we replace R by $R\check{}$, which means that "first" is replace by "second" in the definition of the sets. Putting these together, we obtain

$p \in [R\check{}]\langle R \rangle (X_n) \iff$ Every signal, which cannot be distinguished from p cannot be distinguished from some stimulus of length n.

$p \in \langle R\check{} \rangle [R](X_n) \iff$ Some signals, which cannot be distinguished from p were gauged to be the same only to stimuli of length n.

$p \in [[R\check{}]][[R]](X_n) \iff$ Whenever q cannot be distinguished from all stimuli of length n, then q cannot be distinguished from p.

If we consider cut off points s and t, we interpret, for example, for a first stimulus p,

$p \in [R_s\check{}]\langle R_t \rangle (X_n) \iff$ Every second stimulus which could not be distinguished from p by at least $s\%$ of all subjects could not be distinguished from some first stimulus of length n by at least $t\%$ of all subjects.

$p \in \langle R_s\check{} \rangle [R_t](X_n) \iff$ There is a second stimulus q such that at least $s\%$ of subjects gauged q to be the same as p, and at least $t\%$ of subjects gauged q to be the same only as stimuli of length n.

A first impression of the difficulties encountered by the subjects when discriminating the first and second stimuli is offered by the binary relations R_{50} and $R_{50}\check{}$, which are generated, when the probability cut point $p = 0.5$ is used. Table 2 presents the results of the operators applied to the sets X_n of first and Y_n of second stimuli. One can see that applying the sufficiency operators is not suitable for this situation, since the results are too coarse (see the last column of Table 2). The combination of content and span operators seem to be more promising in either direction.

Each signal can be interpreted in two ways – as confusing the first stimulus with the second one and vice versa–, and we can apply the operators starting with either case.

Stimuli of length 1 or 2 are easily distinguished from those of different length. Starting with second stimuli of length 3, we see that none of d, k, s, u is contained in the lower bound $\langle R \rangle [R\check{}](Y_3)$. When we consider these signals as first stimuli, then this is not the case, since $\langle R\check{} \rangle [R](X_3) = X_3$. This result is hard to present in geometrical terms, as the scaling proposed by Shepard [19] uses a non-metric MDS approach.

Signals of length 4 and 5 are harder to distinguish. We observe that the signals H and h of length 4, and 6, $*6$, 7, $*7$ of length 5 cause considerable confusion. This cannot be determined from the geometrical MDS representation. Indeed, the first stimulus H seems to have the largest distance of any element of set X_4 to the set X_5, and thus, according to the model, not much confusion should arise.

Another interesting stimulus seems to be the Morse code

$\cdots\underline{}$ of character V, because this code of length 4 is confused with stimuli of length 3 and 5. Therefore, V should be presented in a "bridging position" in a geometrical presentation.

Variation of the cut point offers further insights. In Tab. 3 we present the set differences of lower and upper bound of the signal sets for $s = 80, 70, 60, 40$. The first entry in a cell $\langle Z, s \rangle$ is the set of elements which are in the set Z, but not in the lower bound, and the second entry is the set of those elements which are not in Z, but belong to the upper bound of Z. Inspecting the result in Tab. 3, we observe that the signals 6 and $*6$ seem to be very hard to distinguish

Table 2. Modal-style operators applied to Morse data (Cut point p=0.5)

X_n	$[R^\neg]\langle R\rangle$	$\langle R^\neg\rangle[R]$	$[[R^\neg]][[R]]$
E T	e t E T	e t E T	t E T
A I M N	a i m n A I M N	a i m n A I M N	∅ 1
D G K O R S U W	b d g h k l o p r s u v w x D G K O R S U V W	d g o r s u w D G K O R S U W	∅ 1
B C F H J L P Q V X Y Z	b c f h j k l p q v x y z *1 *2 *5 *6 *7 *8 B C F H J L P Q V X Y Z **67**	c f j q y C F J P Q X Y Z	∅ 1
1 2 3 4 5 6 7 8 9 0	b h v x z *1 *2 *3 *4 *5 *6 *7 *8 *9 *0 **B H V** 1 2 3 4 5 6 7 8 9 0	*3 *4 *9 *0 1 2 3 4 5 8 9 0	∅ 1
Y_n	$[R]\langle R^\neg\rangle$	$\langle R\rangle[R^\neg]$	$[[R]][[R^\neg]]$
e t	E T e t	E T e t	E e t
a i m n	A I M N a i m n	A I M N a i m n	∅ 1
d g k o r s u w	D G K O R S U W X d g k o r s u w	O R W g o r w	∅ 1
b c f h j l p q v x y z	B C D F G H J K L P Q S U V X Y Z 4 5 6 7 8 b c **d** f h j k l p q s **u** v x y z *4 *5 *6 *7	C F L P V Y b c f j l p q v x y z	∅ 1
*1 *2 *3 **4 **5 **6 **7 *8 *9 *0	B H J Q X Z 1 2 3 4 5 6 7 8 9 0 *1 *2 *3 *4 *5 *6 *7 *8 *9 *0	1 2 3 9 0 *1 *2 *3 *8 *9 *0	∅ 1

Bold letter in "codes": Letter does not appear in the lower bound.
Bold letter in "$[R^\neg]\langle R\rangle$", resp. "$[R]\langle R^\neg\rangle$": Letter is added in the upper bound.
The first line in a second column cell is the result when applying the inner operator to the original set, the second line is the result when applying the outer operator to the first line.

Table 3. Difference of lower and upper bound given varied cut points in Morse Data

Codes	Cut = 0.8	Cut = 0.7	Cut = 0.6	Cut = 0.5	Cut = 0.4
ET	0,0	0,0	0,0	0,0	0,0
et	0,0	0,0	0,0	0,0	0,0
AIMN	0,0	0,0	0,0	0,0	0,0
aimn	0,0	0,0	0,0	0,0	0,0
DGKORSUW	0,0	0,0	0,0	−,V	K,−
dgkorsuw	0,0	0,0	{d,k},0	{d,k,s,u},0	{d,k,s,u},0
BCFHJLPQVXYZ	0,0	0,{5,6}	{B,H},{1,2,6}	{B,H,L,V},{6,7}	{B,F,H,L,V},{K,2,3,4,5,6,7}
bcfhjlpqvxyz	0,{*6}	{b,h},{*6}	{h},{d,k,*4,*5}	{h},{d,k,s,u,*4,*5,*6,*7}	{b,f,h,j,l,q,v,x,z},{d,k,s,u,*4,*5}
1234567890	0,0	{5,6},0	{1,2,6},{H}	{6,7},{B,H,V}	{2,3,4,5,6,7},{B,H,V}
*1*2*3*4*5*6*7*8*9*0	{*6},0	{*6},{b,h}	{*4,*5},{h}	{*4,*5,*6,*7},0	{*4,*5},{f,j,q}

from the signals of length 4, – an effect which is worse for *6. Furthermore, 5 and *5 frequently appear in one of the differences.

Summarising, we recognize the troublesome first stimuli 5,6,7 of length 5, B,H,V of length 4 and their second position counterparts, and, in addition, the second stimuli {d,k,s,u}.

With respect to the second dimension of the MDS model, namely, the distribution of dots and dashes, we see that, except for k, the problematic signals contain more short than long impulses. A geometric representation has to present the data in a "long–short" dimension, but – since the result pattern is asymmetric – the representation cannot deal with the data in an adequate manner. It was shown in [12] that in fact an asymmetric "drift" from short to long can be

extracted, when MDS is applied to "residual proximities"; these can be computed by the difference of the original data and the estimated symmetric proximity matrix, which is the base of the classical MDS approach.[2]

Therefore, our operator–based qualitative analysis supports the findings of the MDS model, and offers some additional explanations. These are, in short,

- The signal length is the first determining factor for the discrimination of the stimuli, because:
  - Signals of length 1 or 2 are easy to discriminate from other stimuli.

---

[2]It is interesting to note that the first MDS approach [19] was published in 1963, and the "asymmetric extensions" by Möbus [12] appeared 16 years later.

– Signals of length 3 are easy to discriminate from other stimuli, if they are located at the first position.

– Signals of length 3 in the second position overlap with signals of length 4. Signals of length 4 overlap mainly with signals of length 5.

- The character of the impulses is of less effect because a signal must contain mainly short Morse impulses, and should contain at least 4 (first stimuli) or 3 (second stimuli) Morse impulses to be hard to discriminate.

- Asymmetric features of the data are reflected by the construction. There is no need for an extra analysis of method–dependent "residual matrices".

5 Discussion

The presented modal operator approach offers a complementary view of data with respect to derivation operator of formal concept analysis. In principle, the proposed operators can be derived from concept analysis by applying the intent–extent operators to $-R$, and building complements of the resulting concept sets. This is nice, because the computation of convolutions of possibility and necessity operators can be performed by programs for concept analysis, and using the de Morgan rules. Of course, this does not mean that the proposed analysis based on possibility and necessity operators is the same as applying concept analysis, because

- Both proposed operators act asymmetrically, while intent and extent of FCA are symmetric.

- The combination of $\langle R \rangle$ and $[R]$ can be interpreted as a generalization of rough sets approximations, which are based on equivalence relations.

Comparing the proposed theory with MDS, we observe that it offers comparable results, and that these results are presented in a direct manner: There is no need for a 2-dimensional representation (which is not even adequate for Morse data as Shepard [19] remarks), and the risk of so called *divergence artifacts* [8] is reduced. It should be noted, however, that the proposed theory offers a literally "rough approximation" to the data: Once a cut point p is chosen, all differences below this cut point are neglected: It has to be assumed that these differences are not relevant for further interpretation. This is different to the MDS approach; there, the rank order of the proximities is used, which contains more information than taking a simple cut.

Although the proposed theory is nice, handy and applicable from scratch, there is an observation which opens a box of further questions: Unlike for equivalence relations, the $\subseteq$ ordering on relations is not reflected by the new definition of lower and upper bounds, i.e. $R \subseteq S$ does not necessarily imply $[R^\smile]\langle R \rangle(X) \subseteq [S^\smile]\langle S \rangle(X)$. The question arises, which kind of compatibility assumptions must hold in order for the structural properties of the relations to generate comparable properties in the results of the operators.

References

[1] Birkhoff, G. (1948). Lattice Theory, vol. 25 of *Am. Math. Soc. Colloquium Publications*. Providence: AMS, 2nd Edn.

[2] Bisdorff, R. & Roubens, M. (2002). Clustering with null kernels for a valued similarity relation: Application to the Morse data. Presented at the l'Aquila workshop of COST Action 274.

[3] Buja, A. & Swayne, D. F. (2001). Visualization methodology for multidimensional scaling. Preprint.

[4] Davey, B. A. & Priestley, H. A. (1990). Introduction to Lattices and Order. Cambridge University Press.

[5] Düntsch, I., Gediga, G. & Orłowska, E. (2001). Relational attribute systems. *International Journal of Human Computer Studies*, **55**, 293–309.

[6] Gargov, G., Passy, S. & Tinchev, T. (1987). Modal environment for Boolean speculations. In D. Skordev (Ed.), *Mathematical Logic and Applications*, 253–263, New York. Plenum Press.

[7] Gediga, G. & Düntsch, I. (2002). Skill set analysis in knowledge structures. *British Journal of. Mathematical and Statistical Psychology*. To appear.

[8] Gigerenzer, G. (1981). Messung und Modellbildung in der Psychologie. Basel: Birkhäuser.

[9] Humberstone, I. L. (1983). Inaccessible worlds. *Notre Dame Journal of Formal Logic*, **24**, 346–352.

[10] Jónsson, B. & Tarski, A. (1951). Boolean algebras with operators I. *American Journal of Mathematics*, **73**, 891–939.

[11] Lipski, W. (1976). Informational systems with incomplete information. In S. Michaelson & R. Milner (Eds.), *Third International Colloquium on Automata, Languages and Programming*, 120–130, University of Edinburgh. Edinburgh University Press.

[12] Möbus, C. (1979). Zur Analyse nichtsymmetrischer Ähnlichkeitsurteile: Ein dimensionales Driftmodell, eine Vergleichshypothese, Tversky's Kontrastmodell und seine Fokushypothese. *Archiv für Psychologie*, **131**, 105–136.

[13] Orłowska, E. (1988). Logical aspects of learning concepts. *Journal of Approximate Reasoning*, **2**, 349–364.

[14] Orłowska, E. (Ed.) (1998). Incomplete Information – Rough Set Analysis. Heidelberg: Physica – Verlag.

[15] Orłowska, E. & Pawlak, Z. (1984). Representation of nondeterministic information. *Theoretical Computer Science*, **29**, 27–39.

[16] Pawlak, Z. (1973). Mathematical foundations of information retrieval. ICS Research Report 101, Polish Academy of Sciences.

[17] Pawlak, Z. (1982). Rough sets. *Internat. J. Comput. Inform. Sci.*, **11**, 341–356.

[18] Rothkopf, E. Z. (1957). A measure of stimulus similarity and errors in some paired-associate learning tasks. *Journal of Experimental Psychology*, **53**, 94–101.

[19] Shepard, R. N. (1963). Analysis of proximities as a technique for the study of information processing in man. *Human Factors*, **5**, 33–48.

[20] Słowiński, R. & Vanderpooten, D. (2000). A generalized definition of rough approximations based on similarity. *IEEE Transactions on Knowledge and Data Engineering*, **12**, 331–336.

[21] Vakarelov, D. (1998). Information systems, similarity relations and modal logics. In [14], 492–550.

[22] Wille, R. (1982). Restructuring lattice theory: An approach based on hierarchies of concepts. In I. Rival (Ed.), *Ordered sets*, vol. 83 of *NATO Advanced Studies Institute*, 445–470. Dordrecht: Reidel.

[23] Wong, S., Wang, L. & Yao, Y. (1995). On modeling uncertainty with interval structures. *Computational Intelligence*, **11**, 406–426.

Progressive Modeling

Wei Fan[1]   Haixun Wang[1]   Philip S. Yu[1]   Shaw-hwa Lo[2]   Salvatore Stolfo[3]

[1]IBM T.J.Watson Research
Hawthorne, NY 10532
{weifan,haixun,psyu}@us.ibm.com

[2]Dept. of Statistics, Columbia Univ.
New York, NY 10027
slo@stats.columbia.edu

[3]Dept. of Computer Science, Columbia Univ.
New York, NY 10027
sal@cs.columbia.edu

Abstract

Presently, inductive learning is still performed in a frustrating batch process. The user has little interaction with the system and no control over the final accuracy and training time. If the accuracy of the produced model is too low, all the computing resources are misspent. In this paper, we propose a progressive modeling framework. In progressive modeling, the learning algorithm estimates online both the accuracy of the final model and remaining training time. If the estimated accuracy is far below expectation, the user can terminate training prior to completion without wasting further resources. If the user chooses to complete the learning process, progressive modeling will compute a model with expected accuracy in expected time. We describe one implementation of progressive modeling using ensemble of classifiers.

Keywords: estimation

1 Introduction

Classification is one of the most popular and widely used data mining methods to extract useful information from databases. ISO/IEC is proposing an international standard to be finalized in August 2002 to include four data mining types into database systems; these include association rules, clustering, regression, and classification. Presently, classification is performed in a "capricious" batch mode even for many well-known commercial data mining software. An inductive learner is applied to the data; before the model is completely computed and tested, the accuracy of the final model is not known. Yet, for many inductive learning algorithms, the actual training time is not known prior to learning either. It depends on not only the size of the data and the number of features, but also the combination of feature values that utimately determines the complexity of the model. During this possibly long waiting period, the only interaction between the user and program is to make sure that the program is still running and observe some status reports. If the final accuracy is too low after some long training time,

Figure 1. An interactive scenario where both accuracy and remaining training time are estimated

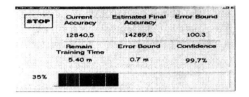

all the computing resources become futile. The users either have to repeat the same process using other parameters of the same algorithm, choose a different feature subset, select a completely new algorithm or give up. There are many learners to choose from, a lot of parameters to select for each learner, countless ways to construct features, and exponential ways for feature selection. The unpredictable accuracy, long and hard-to-predict training time, and endless ways to run an experiment make data mining frustrating even for experts.

1.1 Example of Progressive Modeling

In this paper, we propose a "progressive modeling" concept to address the problems of batch mode learning. We illustrate the basic ideas through a cost-sensitive example even though the concept is applicable to both cost-sensitive and traditional accuracy-based problems.

We use a charity donation dataset (KDDCup 1998) that chooses a subset of population to send campaign letters. The cost of a campaign letter is $0.68. It is only beneficial to send a letter if the solicited person will donate at least $0.68. As soon as learning starts, the framework begins to compute intermediate models, and report current accuracy as well as estimated final accuracy on a hold-out validation set and estimated remaining training time. For cost-sensitive problem, accuracy is measured in benefits such as dollar amounts. We use the term accuracy to mean traditional accuracy and benefits interchangeably where the meaning is clear from the context. Figure 1 shows a snap shot of the new learning process. It displays that the accuracy on the hold out validation set (total donated charity minus the cost of mailing to both donors and non-donors) for the algorithm using the current intermediate model is $12840.5. The accuracy of the complete model on the hold-out validation set when learning completes is *estimated* to be $14289.5±100.3 with at least 99.7% confidence. The additional training time to generate the complete model is *estimated* to be 5.40±0.70 minutes with at least 99.7% confidence. This information continuously refreshes whenever a new intermediate model is produced, until the user explicitly terminates the learning or the complete model is generated.

The user may stop the learning process mainly due to the following reasons - i) intermediate model has enough accuracy, ii) its accuracy is not significantly different from that of the complete model, iii) the estimated accuracy of the complete model is too low, or iv) the training time is unexpectedly long. For the example shown in Figure 1, we would continue, since it is worthwhile to spend 6 more minutes to receive at least $1400 more donation with at least 99.7% confidence. In this example, we illustrated progressive modeling applied to *cost-sensitive* learning. For *cost-insensitive* learning, the algorithm reports traditional accuracy in place of dollar amounts.

Progressive modeling is significantly more useful than a batch mode learning process, especially for very large dataset. The user can easily experiment with different algorithms, parameters, and feature selections without waiting for a long time for a failure result.

2 Our Approach

We propose an implementation of progressive modeling based on ensembles of classifiers that can be applied to several inductive learning algorithms. The basic idea is to generate a small number of base classifiers to estimate the performance of the entire ensemble when all base classifiers are produced.

2.1 Main Algorithm

Assume that a training set S is partitioned into K disjoint subsets S_j with equal size. When the distribution of the dataset is uniform, each subset can be taken sequentially. Otherwise, we can either completely "shuffle" the dataset or use random sampling without replacement to draw S_j. A base level model C_j is trained from S_j. Given an example x from a validation set S_v (it can be a different dataset or the training set), C_j outputs probabilities for all possible class labels that x may be an instance of, i.e., $p_j(\ell_i|x)$ for class label ℓ_i. Details on how to calculate $p_j(\ell_i|x)$ can be found in [5]. In addition, we have a benefit matrix $b[\ell_i, \ell_j]$

that records the benefit received by predicting an example of class ℓ_i to be an instance of class ℓ_j. For cost-insensitive (or accuracy-based) problems, $\forall i, b[\ell_i, \ell_i] = 1$ and $\forall i \neq j, b[\ell_i, \ell_j] = 0$. Since traditional accuracy-based decision making is a special case of cost-sensitive problem, we only discuss the algorithm in the context of cost-sensitive decision making. Using benefit matrix $b[\ldots]$, each model C_j will generate an expected benefit or risk $e_j(\ell_i|x)$ for every possible class ℓ_i.

Expected Benefit: $$e_j(\ell_i|x) = \sum_{\ell_{i'}} b[\ell_{i'}, \ell_i] \cdot p_j(\ell_{i'}|x) \tag{1}$$

Assume that we have trained $k \leq K$ models $\{C_1, \ldots, C_k\}$. Combining individual expected benefits, we have

Average Expected Benefit: $$E_k(\ell_i|x) = \frac{\sum_j e_j(\ell_i|x)}{k} \tag{2}$$

We then use optimal decision policy to choose the class label with the maximal expected benefit

Optimal Decision: $$L_k(x) = \operatorname{argmax}_{\ell_i} E_k(\ell_i|x) \tag{3}$$

Assuming that $\ell(x)$ is the true label of x, the accuracy of the ensemble with k classifiers is

$$A_k = \sum_{x \in S_v} b[\ell(x), L_k(x)] \tag{4}$$

For accuracy-based problems, A_k is usually normalized into percentage using the size of the validation set $|S_v|$. For cost-sensitive problems, it is customary to use some units to measure benefits such as dollar amounts. Besides accuracy, we also have the total time to train C_1 to C_k.

$$T_k = \text{the total time to train}\{C_1, \ldots, C_k\} \tag{5}$$

Next, based on the performance of $k \leq K$ base classifiers, we use statistical techniques to estimate both the accuracy and training time of the ensemble with K models.

We first summarize some notations. A_K, T_K and M_K are the true values to estimate. Respectively, they are the accuracy of the complete ensemble, the training time of the complete ensemble, and the remaining training time after k classifiers. Their estimates are denoted in lower case, i.e., a_K, t_K and m_K. An estimate is a range with a mean and standard deviation. The mean of a symbol is represented by a bar ($\bar{\ }$) and the standard deviation is represented by a sigma (σ). Additionally, σ_d is standard error or the standard deviation of a sample mean.

2.2 Estimating Accuracy

The accuracy estimate is based on the probability that ℓ_i is the predicted label by the ensemble of K classifiers for example x.

$$P\{L_K(x) = \ell_i\} \text{ the probability that}$$
$$\ell_i \text{ is the prediction by the ensemble of size } K \quad (6)$$

Since each class label ℓ_i has a probability to be the predicted class, and predicting an instance of class $\ell(x)$ as ℓ_i receives a benefit $b[\ell(x), \ell_i]$, the expected accuracy received for x by predicting with K base models is

$$\bar{\alpha}(x) = \sum_{\ell_i} b[\ell(x), \ell_i] \cdot P\{L_K(x) = \ell_i\} \quad (7)$$

with standard deviation of $\sigma(\alpha(x))$. To calculate the expected accuracy on the validation set S_v, we sum up the expected accuracy on each example x

$$\bar{a}_K = \sum_{x \in S_v} \bar{\alpha}(x) \quad (8)$$

Since each example is independent, according to multinomial form of central limit theorem (CLT), the total benefit of the complete model with K models is a normal distribution with mean value of Eq[8] and standard deviation of

$$\sigma(a_K) = \sqrt{\sum_{x \in S_v} \sigma(\alpha(x))^2} \quad (9)$$

Using confidence intervals, the accuracy of the complete ensemble A_K falls within the following range:

$$\text{With confidence } p, A_K \in \bar{a}_K \pm \mathbf{t} \cdot \sigma(a_K) \quad (10)$$

When $\mathbf{t} = 3$, the confidence p is approximately 99.7%.

Next we discuss how to derive $P\{L_K(x) = \ell_i\}$. If $E_K(\ell_i|x)$ are known, there is only one label, $L_K(x)$ whose $P\{L_K(x) = \ell_i\}$ will be 1, and all other labels will have probability equal to 0. However, $E_K(\ell_i|x)$ are not known, we can only use its estimate $E_k(\ell_i|x)$ measured from k classifiers to derive $P\{L_K(x) = \ell_i\}$. From random sampling theory [2], $E_k(\ell_i|x)$ is an unbiased estimate of $E_K(\ell_i|x)$ with standard error of

$$\sigma_d(E_k(\ell_i|x)) = \frac{\sigma(E_k(\ell_i|x))}{\sqrt{k}} \cdot \sqrt{1-f} \text{ where } f = \frac{k}{K} \quad (11)$$

According to central limit thereon, the true value $E_K(\ell_i|x)$ falls within a normal distribution with mean value of $\mu = E_k(\ell_i|x)$ and standard deviation of $\sigma = \sigma_d(E_k(\ell_i|x))$. If $E_k(\ell_i|x)$ is high, it is more likely for $E_K(\ell_i|x)$ to be high, and consequently, for $P\{L_k(x) = \ell_i\}$ to be high. For the time being, we ignore correlation among different class labels, and compute naive probability $P'\{L_K(x) = \ell_i\}$. Assuming that r_t is an approximate of $\max_{\ell_i}\left(E_K(\ell_i|x)\right)$, the

area in the range of $[r_t, +\infty)$ is the probability $P'\{L_K(x) = \ell_i\}$.

$$P'\{L_K(x) = \ell_i\} = \int_{r_t}^{+\infty} \frac{1}{\sqrt{2\pi}\sigma} \exp\left[-\frac{1}{2}\left(\frac{z-\mu}{\sigma}\right)^2\right] dz \quad (12)$$

where $\sigma = \sigma_d(E_k(\ell_i|x))$ and $\mu = E_k(\ell_i|x)$. When $k \le 30$, to compensate the error in standard error estimation, we use *Student-t* distribution with $df = k$. We use the average of the two largest $E_k(\ell_i|x)$'s to approximate $\max_{\ell_i}\left(E_K(\ell_i|x)\right)$. The reason not to use the maximum itself is that if the associated label is not the predicted label of the complete model, the probability estimate for the true predicted label may be too low.

On the other hand, $P\{L_k(x) = \ell_i)$ is inversely related to the probabilities for other class labels to be the predicted label. When it is more likely for other class labels to be the predicted label, it will be less likely for ℓ_i to be the predicted label. A common method to take correlation into account is to use normalization,

$$P\{L_K(x) = \ell_i\} = \frac{P'\{L_K(x) = \ell_i\}}{\sum_j P'\{L_K(x) = \ell_j\}} \quad (13)$$

Thus, we have derived $P\{L_K(x) = \ell_i\}$ in order to estimate the accuracy in Eq[7].

Estimating Training Time Assuming that the training time for the sampled k models are τ_1 to τ_k. Their mean and standard deviation are $\bar{\tau}$ and $\sigma(\tau)$. Then the total training time of K classifiers is estimated as

With confidence p, $T_K \in \bar{t}_K \pm \mathbf{t} \cdot \sigma(t_K)$, where

$$\bar{t}_K = K \cdot \bar{\tau} \text{ and } \sigma(t_K) = \frac{\mathbf{t} \cdot K \cdot \sigma(\tau)}{\sqrt{k}} \cdot \sqrt{1-f} \quad (14)$$

To find out remaining training time M_K, we simply deduct $k \cdot \bar{\tau}$ from Eq[14].

With confidence p, $M_K \in \bar{m}_K \pm \mathbf{t} \cdot \sigma(m_K)$, where
$$\bar{m}_K = \bar{t}_K - k \cdot \bar{\tau} \text{ and } \sigma(m_K) = \sigma(t_K) \quad (15)$$

2.3 Progressive Modeling

We request the first random sample from the database and train the first model. Then it requests the second random sample and train the second model. From this point on, the user will be updated with estimated accuracy, remaining training time and confidence levels. We have the accuracy of the current model (A_k), and the estimated accuracy of the complete model (a_K) as well as estimated remaining training time (m_K). From these statistics, the user decides to continue or terminate. The user normally terminates learning if one of the following *Stopping Criteria* are met:

```
Data      : benefit matrix b[ℓ_i, ℓ_j], training set S, vali-
            dation set S_v and K
Result    : k ≤ K classifiers
begin
    partition S into K disjoint subsets of equal size
    {S_1, ..., S_K};
    train C_1 from S_1, and τ_1 is the training time;
    k ← 2;
    while k ≤ K do
        train C_k from S_k and τ_k is the training time;
        for x ∈ S_v do
            calculate P{L_K = ℓ_i} (Eq[13]);
            calculate ᾱ(x) and its standard deviation
            σ(α(x)) (Eq[7]);
        end
        estimate accuracy a_K (Eq[8] and Eq[9]) and
        remaining training time m_K (Eq[15]);
        if a_K and m_K satisfy stopping criteria then
            return C_1, ..., C_k;
        end
        k ← k + 1;
    end
    return C_1, ..., C_k;
end
```

Algorithm 1: Progressive Modeling Based on Averaging Ensemble

- The accuracy of the current model is sufficiently high. Assume that θ_A is the target accuracy.

- The accuracy of the current model is sufficiently close to that of the complete model. There won't be significant improvement by training the model to the end. Formally, $\mathbf{t} \cdot \sigma(a_K) \leq \epsilon$.

- The estimated accuracy of the final model is too low to be useful. Formally, if $(\bar{a}_K + \mathbf{t} \cdot \sigma(a_K)) \ll \theta_A$, stop the learning process.

- The estimated training time is too long, the user decides to abort. Formally, assume that θ_T is the target training time, if $(\bar{m}_K - \mathbf{t} \cdot \sigma(m_K)) \gg \theta_T$, cancel the learning.

As a summary of all the important steps of progressive modeling, the complete algorithm is outlined in Algorithm 1.

2.4 Efficiency

Computing K base models sequentially has complexity of $K \cdot O(f(\frac{N}{K}))$. Both the average and standard deviation can be incrementally updated linearly in the number of examples.

3 Experiment

There are two main issues - the accuracy of the ensemble and the precision of estimation. The accuracy and training time of a single model computed from the entire dataset is regarded as the baseline. To study the precision of the estimation methods, we compare the upper and lower error bounds of an estimated value to its true value. We have carefully selected three datasets. They are from real world applications and significant in size. We use each dataset both as a traditional problem that maximizes traditional accuracy as well as a cost-sensitive problem that maximizes total benefits. As a cost-sensitive problem, the selected datasets differ in the way how the benefit matrices are obtained.

3.1 Datasets

The first one is the donation dataset that first appeared in KDDCUP'98 competition. Suppose that the cost of requesting a charitable donation from an individual x is \$0.68, and the best estimate of the amount that x will donate is $Y(x)$. Its benefit matrix is:

	predict *donate*	predict ¬*donate*
actual *donate*	Y(x) - \$.0.68	0
actual ¬*donate*	-\$0.68	0

As a cost-sensitive problem, the total benefit is the total amount of received charity minus the cost of mailing. The data has already been divided into a training set and a test set. The training set consists of 95412 records for which it is known whether or not the person made a donation and how much the donation was. The test set contains 96367 records for which similar donation information was not published until after the KDD'98 competition. We used the standard training/test set splits to compare with previous results. The feature subsets were based on the KDD'98 winning submission. To estimate the donation amount, we employed the multiple linear regression method. As suggested in [10], to avoid over estimation, we only used those contributions between \$0 and \$50.

The second data set is a credit card fraud detection problem. Assuming that there is an overhead \$90 to dispute and investigate a fraud and $y(x)$ is the transaction amount, the following is the benefit matrix:

	predict *fraud*	predict ¬*fraud*
actual *fraud*	y(x) - \$90	0
actual ¬*fraud*	-\$90	0

As a cost-sensitive problem, the total benefit is the sum of recovered frauds minus investigation costs. The dataset was sampled from a one year period and contains a total of 5M transaction records. The features record the time of the transaction, merchant type, merchant location, and past payment and transaction history summary. We use data of the last month as test data (40038 examples) and data of previous months as training data (406009 examples). Details about this dataset can be found in [9].

The third dataset is the adult dataset from UCI repository. It is a widely used dataset to compare different algorithms on traditional accuracy. For cost-sensitive studies, we artificially associate a benefit of $2 to class label **F** and a benefit of $1 to class label **N**, as summarized below:

	predict **F**	predict **N**
actual **F**	$2	0
actual **N**	0	$1

We use the natural split of training and test sets, so the results can be easily duplicated. The training set contains 32561 entries and the test set contains 16281 records.

3.2 Experimental Setup

We have selected three learning algorithms, decision tree learner C4.5, rule builder RIPPER, and naive Bayes learner. We have chosen a wide range of partitions, $K \in \{8, 16, 32, 64, 128, 256\}$. The accuracy and estimated accuracy is the test dataset.

3.3 Accuracy

Since we study the capability of the new framework for both traditional accuracy-based problems as well as cost-sensitive problems, each dataset is treated both as a traditional and cost-sensitive problem. The baseline traditional accuracy and total benefits of the batch mode single model are shown in the two columns under accuracy for traditional accuracy-based problem and benefits for cost-sensitive problem respectively in Table 1. These results are the baseline that the multiple model should achieve.[1]

For the multiple model, we first discuss the results when the complete multiple model is fully constructed, then present the results of partial multiple model. Each result is the average of different multiple models with K ranging from 2 to 256. In Table 2, the results are shown in two columns under accuracy and benefit. As we compare the respective results in Tables 1 and 2, the multiple model consistently and significantly beat the accuracy of the single model for all three datasets using all three different inductive learners. The most significant increase in both accuracy and total benefits is for the credit card dataset. The total benefits have been increased by approximately $7,000 \sim $10,000; the accuracy has been increased by approximately 1% $\sim$ 3%. For the KDDCUP'98 donation dataset, the total benefit has been increased by $1400 for C4.5 and $250 for NB.

---

[1] Please note that we experimented with different parameters for RIPPER on the donation dataset. However, the most specific rule produced by RIPPER contains only one rule that covers 6 donors and one default rule that always predict ¬donate. This succinct rule will not find any donor and will not receive any donations. However, RIPPER performs reasonably well for the credit card and adult datasets.

C4.5

	Accuracy Based accuracy	Cost-sensitive benefit
Donation	94.94%	$13292.7
Credit Card	87.77%	$733980
Adult	84.38%	$16443

RIPPER

	Accuracy Based accuracy	Cost-sensitive benefit
Donation	94.94%	$0
Credit Card	90.14%	$712541
Adult	84.84%	$19725

NB

	Accuracy Based accuracy	Cost-sensitive benefit
Donation	94.94%	$13928
Credit Card	85.46%	$704285
Adult	82.86%	$16269

Table 1. Baseline accuracy and total benefits

We next study the trends of accuracy when the number of partitions K increases. In Figure 2, we plot the accuracy and total benefits for the credit card datasets, and the total benefits for the donation dataset with increasing number of partitions K. C4.5 was the base learner for this study. As we can see clearly that for the credit card dataset, the multiple model consistently and significantly improve both the accuracy and total benefits over the single model by at least 1% in accuracy and $40000 in total benefits for all choices of K. For the donation dataset, the multiple model boosts the total benefits by at least $1400. Nonetheless, when K increases, both the accuracy and total tendency show a slow decreasing trend. It would be expected that when K is extremely large, the results will eventually fall below the baseline.

3.4 Accuracy Estimation

The current and estimated final accuracy are continuously updated and reported to the user. The user can terminate the learning based on these statistics. As a summary, these include the accuracy of the current model A_k, the true accuracy of the complete model A_K and the estimate of the true accuracy $\bar{a}_K$ with $\sigma(a_K)$. If the true value falls within the error range of the estimate with high confidence and the error range is small, the estimate is good. Formally, with confidence p, $A_K \in \bar{a}_K \pm \mathbf{t} \cdot \sigma(a_K)$. Quantitatively, we say an estimate is good if the error bound $(t \cdot \sigma)$ is within 5% of the mean and the confidence is at least 99%. We chose $k = 20\% \cdot K$. In Table 3, we show the average of estimated accuracy of multiple models with different number of partitions $K = \{8, \ldots, 256\}$. The true value A_K all fall within

Figure 2. Plots of accuracy and total benefits for credit card datasets, and plot of total benefits for donation dataset with respect to K

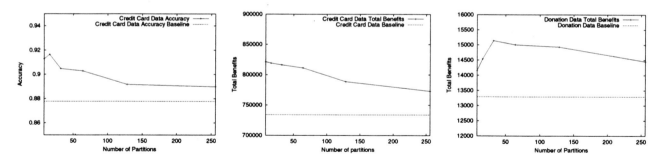

C4.5

	Accuracy Based	Cost-sensitive
	accuracy	benefit
Donation	94.94± 0%	$14702.9± 458
Credit Card	90.37±0.5%	$804964± 32250
Adult	85.6±0.6%	$16435±150

RIPPER

	Accuracy Based	Cost-sensitive
	accuracy	benefit
Donation	94.94±0%	$0±0
Credit Card	91.46±0.6%	$815612±34730
Adult	86.1±0.4%	$19875±390

NB

	Accuracy Based	Cost-sensitive
	accuracy	benefit
Donation	94.94±0%	$14282±530
Credit Card	88.64±0.3%	$798943± 23557
Adult	84.94±0.3%	$16169± 60

Table 2. Average accuracy and total benefits by complete multiple model with different number of partitions.

C4.5

	Accuracy Based		Cost-sensitive	
	True Val	Estimate	True Val	Estimate
Donation	94.94%	94.94%±0%	$14702.9	$14913±612
Credit Card	90.37%	90.08%±1.5%	$804964	$799876±3212
Adult	85.6%	85.3%±1.4%	$16435	$16255±142

RIPPER

	Accuracy Based		Cost-sensitive	
	True Val	Estimate	True Val	Estimate
Donation	94.94%	94.94%±0%	$0	$0±0
Credit Card	91.46%	91.24%±0.9%	$815612	$820012±3742
Adult	86.1%	85.9%±1.3%	$19875	$19668±258

NB

	Accuracy Based		Cost-sensitive	
	True Val	Estimate	True Val	Estimate
Donation	94.94%	94.94%±0%	$14282	$14382±120
Credit Card	88.64%	89.01%±1.2%	$798943	$797749±4523
Adult	84.94%	85.3%±1.5%	$16169	$16234±134

Table 3. True accuracy and estimated accuracy.

the error range.

To see how quickly the error range converges with increasing sample size, we draw the entire process to sample up to $K = 256$ for all three datasets as shown in Figure 3. There are four curves in each plot. The one on the very top and the one on the very bottom are the upper and lower error bounds. The current benefits and estimated total benefits are within the higher and lower error bounds. Current benefits and estimated total benefits are very close especially when k becomes big. As shown clearly in all three plots, the error bound decreases exponentially. When k exceeds 50 (approximately 20% of 256), the error range is already within 5% of the total benefits of the complete model. If we are satisfied with the accuracy of the current model, we can dis-

continue the learning process and return the current model. For the three datasets under study and different number of partitions K, when $k > 30\% \cdot K$, the current model is usually within 5% error range of total benefits by the complete model. For traditional accuracy, the current model is usually within 1% error bound of the accuracy by the complete model (detailed results not shown).

Next, we discuss an experiment under extreme situations. When K becomes too big, each dataset becomes trivial and will not be able to produce an effective model. If the esti-

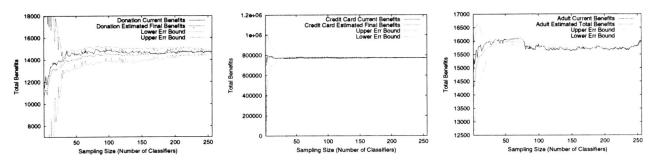

Figure 3. Current benefits and estimated final benefits when sampling size k increases up to $K = 256$ for all three datasets. The error range is $3 \cdot \sigma(a_K)$ for 99.7% confidence.

mation methods can effectively detect the inaccuracy of the complete model, the user can choose a smaller K. We partitioned all three dataset into $K = 1024$ partitions. For the adult dataset, each partition contains only 32 examples but there are 15 attributes. The estimation results are shown in Figure 4. The first observation is that the total benefits for donation and adult are much lower than the baseline. This is obviously due to the trivial size of each data partition. The total benefits for the credit card dataset is $750,000, which is still higher than the baseline of $733980. The second observation is that after the sampling size k exceeds around as small as 25 (out of $K = 1024$ or 0.5%), the error bound becomes small enough, implying that the total benefits by the complete model is very unlikely (99.7% confidence) to increase. At this point, the user should cancel the learning for both donation and adult datasets. The reason for the "bumps" in the adult dataset plot is that each dataset is too small and most decision trees will always predict **N** most of the time. At the beginning of the sampling, there is no variations or all the trees make the same predictions; when more trees are introduced, it starts to have some diversities. However, the absolute value of the bumps are less than $50 as compared to $12435.

3.5 Training Efficiency

We recorded both the training time of the batch mode single model plus the time to classify the test data, and the training time of the multiple model with $k = 30\% \cdot K$ classifiers plus the time to classify the test data k times. We then computed ratio of the recorded time of the single and multiple models, called serial improvement. It is the number of times that training the multiple model is faster than training the single model. In Figure 5, we plot the serial improvement for all three datasets using C4.5 as the base learner. When $K = 256$, using the multiple model not only provide higher accuracy, but the training time is also 80 times faster for credit card, 25 times faster for both adult and donation.

4 Related Work

Online aggregation has been well studied in database community. It estimates the result of an aggregate query such as avg(AGE) during query processing. One of the most noteworthy work is due to [7], which provides an interactive and accurate method to estimate the result of aggregation. One of the earliest work to use data reduction techniques to scale up inductive learning is due to Chan [1], in which he builds a tree of classifiers. In BOAT [6], Gehrke et al build multiple bootstrapped trees in memory to examine the splitting conditions of a coarse tree. There has been several advances in cost-sensitive learning [3]. Meta-Cost [4] takes advantage of purposeful mis-labels to maximize total benefits. In [8], Provost and Fawcett study the problem on how to make optimal decision when cost is not known precisely.

5 Conclusion

In this paper, we have demonstrated the need for a progressive and interactive approach of inductive learning where the users can have full control of the learning process. An important feature is the ability to estimate the accuracy of complete model and remaining training time. We have implemented a progressive modeling framework based on averaging ensembles and statistical techniques. One important result of this paper is the derivation of error bounds used in performance estimation. We empirically evaluated our approaches using several inductive learning algorithms. First, we find that the accuracy and training time by the progressive modeling framework maintain or greatly improve over batch mode learning. Second the precision of estimation is high. The error bound is within 5% of the true value when the model is approximately $25\% \sim 30\%$ complete. Based on our studies, we conclude that progressive modeling based on ensemble of classifiers provide an effective

Figure 4. Current benefits and estimated final estimates when sampling size k **increases up to** $K = 1024$ **for all three datasets. To enlarge the plots when** k **is small, we only plot up to** $k = 50$. **The error range is** $3 \cdot \sigma(a_K)$ **for 99.7% confidence.**

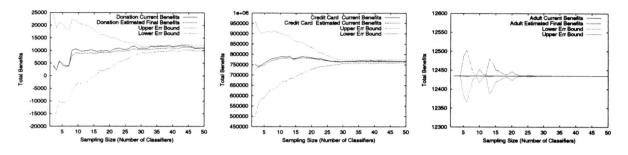

Figure 5. Serial improvement for all three datasets when early stopping is used

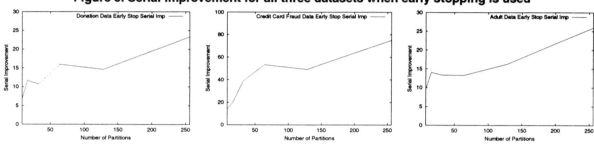

solution to the frustrating process of batch mode learning.

References

[1] P. Chan. *An Extensible Meta-learning Approach for Scalable and Accurate Inductive Learning*. PhD thesis, Columbia University, Oct 1996.

[2] W. G. Cochran. *Sampling Techniques*. John Wiley and Sons, 1977.

[3] T. Dietterich, D. Margineatu, F. Provost, and P. Turney, editors. *Cost-Sensitive Learning Workshop (ICML-00)*, 2000.

[4] P. Domingos. MetaCost: a general method for making classifiers cost-sensitive. In *Proceedings of Fifth International Conference on Knowledge Discovery and Data Mining (KDD-99)*, San Diego, California, 1999.

[5] W. Fan, H. Wang, P. S. Yu, and S. Stolfo. A framework for scalable cost-sensitive learning based on combining probabilities and benefits. In *Second SIAM International Conference on Data Mining (SDM2002)*, April 2002.

[6] J. Gehrke, V. Ganti, R. Ramakrishnan, and W.-Y. Loh. BOAT-optimistic decision tree construction. In *Proceedings of ACM SIGMOD International Conference on Management of Data (SIGMOD 1999)*, 1999.

[7] J. M. Hellerstein, P. J. Haas, and H. J. Wang. Online aggregation. In *Proceedings of ACM SIGMOD International Conference on Management of Data (SIGMOD'97)*, 1997.

[8] F. Provost and T. Fawcett. Robust classification for imprecise environments. *Machine Learning*, 42:203–231, 2000.

[9] S. Stolfo, W. Fan, W. Lee, A. Prodromidis, and P. Chan. Credit card fraud detection using meta-learning: Issues and initial results. In *AAAI-97 Workshop on Fraud Detection and Risk Management*, 1997.

[10] B. Zadrozny and C. Elkan. Obtaining calibrated probability estimates from decision trees and naive bayesian classifiers. In *Proceedings of Eighteenth International Conference on Machine Learning (ICML'2001)*, 2001.

Unsupervised Clustering of Symbol Strings and Context Recognition

John A. Flanagan, Jani Mäntyjarvi and Johan Himberg
Nokia Research Center, PO BOX 407,
FIN-00045 NOKIA GROUP, Finland
{Adrian.Flanagan, Jani.Mantyjarvi, Johan Himberg} @nokia.com

Abstract

The representation of information based on symbol strings has been applied to the recognition of context. A framework for approaching the context recognition problem has been described and interpreted in terms of symbol string recognition. The Symbol String Clustering Map (SCM) is introduced as an efficient algorithm for the unsupervised clustering and recognition of symbol string data. The SCM can be implemented in an on line manner using a computationally simple similarity measure based on a weighted average. It is shown how measured sensor data can be processed by the SCM algorithm to learn, represent and distinguish different user contexts without any user input.

1 Introduction

Context awareness is an emerging application area with the aim of easing man-machine interaction. For example in the case of a mobile device the man-machine interaction can be tedious given the physical size limitations both in the keyboard and screen. If the mobile terminal is aware of or recognizes the user's current context then it could react in some appropriate manner to suit the user without the need of user interaction. The user's context is inferred by the device based on information coming from various different sources. Thus the first step in context recognition is the sensing of the user's physical environment using various sensing systems. The second step is the exploitation of context information sources located in the interactive environment, and the acquisition of terminal specific knowledge from applications and operating networks. The ultimate stage comprises a fusion of these information sources and the extraction of the useful information needed to determine the user's context. As such the implementation of context aware computing requires sophisticated computing methods that can process information from a large and diverse number of sources. In the case of a mobile device

a further challenge is that these methods must be efficient in terms of memory and computational power. The efficient determination, combination and extraction of relevant information from time varying information sources is therefore a must in the area of context awareness.

Various research efforts investigating the development of various context recognition and extraction systems have been carried out. These efforts include context recognition experiments with Hidden Markov Models (HMMs) to determine the occurrence of audio-visual contextual events [4], [3], and a combination of the Self-Organizing Map (SOM) with Markov Chains has been used in [13], [16]. In another approach the information from multiple sensors can be processed to generate multidimensional context feature vectors, from which relevant context information can be extracted and compressed by using statistical methods [10]. For extracting high level descriptions of contexts, clustering and time series segmentation can be utilized [9], [14]. Applying known data mining methods in mobile environment has been shown to have potential [9] and not just for context awareness [11].

In this work context recognition is carried out using clustering. Clustering is a very well known approach to the pattern recognition problem and a vast literature exists describing the theory and applications of clustering [5]. However the clustering used here is quite different from other clustering algorithms in that classical clustering is generally applied to multivariate data, that is the data is generally taken from R^n, an n-dimensional real, vector space. Here it is shown how clustering can be applied to symbol strings where the symbol string represents context. Classical approaches to clustering symbol strings however the computational effort can be quite large. Projected clustering has been shown to reduce the computational effort required in this case [1]. Here instead of adapting the data to fit to the classical clustering paradigm, the classical clustering paradigm is adapted to the nature of the data. This approach has been taken in [2] where symbol strings have been modelled as finite state Markov models and clustered using a generative model and the Expectation Maximization

(EM) algorithm. This approach works quite well when the order of the symbols in the symbol string is important, however the Markov model does not apply when the order of the symbols in the symbol string is not important. A much simpler approach is to use a clustering algorithm. Using this type of algorithm means that some form of similarity measure between symbol strings is required and this in itself is difficult. One of the main problems in clustering is the determination of the number, if any, of natural clusters in the data. This is a problem for any type of data, symbol string or multivariate. An unsupervised algorithm for determining the number of natural clusters in a data set has been shown in [8] based on the Self-Organizing Map (SOM) [12]. In this work an algorithm, referred to as the Symbol String Clustering Map (SCM), is introduced and used to recognize different levels of context based on an unsupervised clustering of a symbol string representation of context. Unsupervised in this sense means that no user interaction is required to determine the number of clusters and neither is the number of clusters an explicit parameter of the clustering. The SCM is a learning algorithm comprising a simple similarity measure based on averages and simple update rules for sets of coefficients. It should be noted that in some respects the structure of the SCM is similar to the SOM, however the SCM is very different in its aim which is clustering of the data and not the self-organization that happens in the SOM.

To understand the context recognition problem based on clustering of symbol strings it is first necessary to discuss our definition of context. This discussion is in section 2. In section 3 this conceptual description of context is translated into a symbolic representation of context and how it can be recognized based on the clustering of symbol strings. Section 4 explains the algorithm for clustering symbol strings. In section 5 an implementation of the framework to context recognition is described with a concrete example. Section 6 concludes and summarizes the work.

2 Understanding Context

Intuitively context can be defined as any information that describes the relevant elements of a given situation [6]. This information can be derived from many different sources and in different ways. Consider first the case where there are several independent sensors. At any time instant, combining the information from the different sensors can define a context. This is the problem of fusion of multiple information sources. These sources of information could be for example audio, time, or accelerometer sensor signals. At the given time instant using these information sources it would be possible to say for example that the user's context is walking in the evening in a busy street. However this represents one level of the user's context. Maybe the user is speaking on the phone with a friend. Thus the user's context

is defined as walking in the evening in a busy street speaking on the phone with a friend. By combining different sources of context information a better, and truer, description of the user's context is obtained. Generalizing this example we say that higher level context can be obtained from the simultaneous fusion of context information from lower level context sources. Note in the example that the lower level sources of context information, "walking in the evening in a busy street" and "talking on the phone with a friend" are in turn generated from lower level sources of information, the sensors and the phone. In fact sensor information and other general sources of external information, for this discussion, can be considered simply as sources of lower level context information. This interpretation of context is therefore consistent from the lowest to the highest level of context. This approach thus provides a definition of context in terms of lower level context, where the lowest level of context information is derived from external sources of information. Time t generates another aspect of context, in other words context is dynamic, it changes with time. This change over time leads to another mechanism for generating higher level context.

Consider a single source of context, its output at any time t is referred to here as the context state. Now fuse the different states of context over time. In keeping with the example of the user walking in the street, assume that previously the users context was identified as "at work". Combining the two contexts, "at work", "walking in the evening in a busy street", the user's context could be considered as going home from work. Generalizing this idea, each context state in the sequence represents a lower context level and a fusion of a sequence of lower context states generates a higher context level. Thus from a single source of context information it is possible to generate higher levels of context over time.

It now becomes clear that the recognition of context consists of generating higher level context from lower level context. The lower level context states have been "recognized", their combination constitutes a new context. Thus in general an algorithm that can recognize context is a transformation from a collection of low level context states to a higher level context state. As discussed earlier, the lower level states are either taken at the same time instant from several different context sources or are time consecutive states from the same source.

3 Symbolic Representation of Context

The definition of context at the beginning of section 2 is an intuitive definition and gives no indication as to how context could be processed. The simplest most general form is to represent a context state by a symbol. For example let $S_j^i(t)$ represent the context state, at level i, of context source *j* at time *t*.

Now consider the problem of context recognition, using the framework described in the previous section, based on the context derived from the fusion of n sources of context. It is assumed that the state of each of the n sources have been assigned a symbolic representation, and therefore, they have been "recognized". As discussed in section 2 the recognition and fusion of the context sources to generate a single context state are the same operation. Hence the context generated and represented by the fusion of the n context states $S_j^i(t), j = 1, \ldots, n$ is denoted by $S_k^{i+1}(t)$, a context state from source k at context level $i + 1$, and is given simply by,

$$S_k^{i+1}(t) = (S_1^i(t), S_2^i(t), \ldots, S_n^i(t)). \quad (1)$$

Now the context state $S_k^{i+1}(t)$ has been recognized and assigned with a symbolic representation. In a similar manner the recognition and segmentation problem for a time sequence of context states generated from the same source can be described using this symbolic representation. The sequence of context states from source j at context level i is given by,

$$(S_j^i(t_1), S_j^i(t_2), S_j^i(t_3), \ldots) \quad (2)$$

where $t_1 < t_2 < t_3 < \ldots$. Once again the recognition of the context is similar to the previous case except this time the higher level context is given by, $(l, m > 0)$

$$S_k^{i+1}(t_{l+m}) = (S_j^i(t_l), S_j^i(t_{l+1}), \ldots, S_j^i(t_{l+m})) \quad (3)$$

While the recognition and generation of higher level context are the same in both cases in this last case before the recognition can take place the limits $l, l + m$ must be determined. Another very important distinction between the two cases must be made. In equation (1) it is likely that the ordering of the symbols is not important. However in the second case given by equation (3) it is very likely that the ordering of the symbols is highly important in determining the context.

Given a set of n sources of context information that produce the context states as in equation (1) at time t, then recognizing the context could be simply a lookup table where the resulting context state $S_k^{i+1}(t)$ is listed as the resulting context. However the mobile terminal is personal to the user, and the user's context is defined by the user. This implies that any sort of lookup table would be personalized to the user. Secondly in any real world situation there will always be noise. This implies that there will not be a unique one to one relationship between a set of symbols and their higher level context representation. Well known methods for clustering data cannot be applied in an efficient, on-line manner to the clustering of symbolic data as described here. In the next section a method for clustering noisy symbol strings is described.

4 Unsupervised Clustering of Symbol Strings

A complete description of the SCM algorithm has been given in [7] and now the algorithm is described briefly. The SCM is based on a lattice structure, generally 2 dimensional with a total of $M \times M$ lattice points. Associated with each node k of the lattice is a symbol string $\mathbf{S}_k$, from now on referred to as the "node string" and associated with the node string is a weight vector $\mathbf{X}_k$ where,

$$\mathbf{S}_k(t) = (s_1(t), \ldots, s_{n(k,t)}(t)) \quad (4)$$

$$\mathbf{X}_k(t) = (x_1(t), \ldots, x_{n(k,t)}(t)), \ x_j(t) \in [0, 1] \quad (5)$$

where $n(k, t)$ is the number of symbols in the node string $\mathbf{S}_k(t)$ and is the same as the number of weights in the weight vector $\mathbf{X}_k(t)$. Note that $x_j(t)$ of $\mathbf{X}_k(t)$ is directly associated with the symbol $s_j(t)$ of $\mathbf{S}_k(t)$ and the ordering of the symbols in $\mathbf{S}_k$ is not important. Initially the weight vectors $\mathbf{X}_k$ and node strings $\mathbf{S}_k$ are set to random values with $x_j(0) \in [0, 1], \forall k, j$. At time step t there is an input symbol string

$$\hat{\mathbf{S}}(t) = (\hat{s}_1(t), \hat{s}_1(t), \ldots, \hat{s}_{\hat{n}(t)}(t)). \quad (6)$$

For this given input the similarity between $\hat{\mathbf{S}}(t)$ and each of the nodes k, is calculated and given by an activation function $\mathcal{A}_k(t)$. The activation $\mathcal{A}_k(t)$ is defined as $\mathcal{A}_k(t) =$,

$$\sum_{j=1}^{n(k,t)} \frac{\delta_{k,j}(t) * x_j(t) * (1.0 - \alpha(t)x_j(t))}{n(k,t)} * \sum_{j=1}^{\hat{n}(t)} \frac{\delta_{k,j}(t)}{\hat{n}(t)} \quad (7)$$

and for $s_j(t) \in \mathbf{S}_k(t)$, the $\delta_{k,j}(t)$ function is defined as,

$$\delta_{k,j}(t) = \begin{cases} 1 & \text{if } s_j(t) \in \hat{\mathbf{S}}(t) \\ 0 & \text{if } s_j(t) \notin \hat{\mathbf{S}}(t) \end{cases} \quad (8)$$

The activation function for each node is therefore a weighted average of the weights of the node, where the weights are either 1 if the associated symbol of the node is in the input string and 0 if the associated symbol of the node is not in the input string. The weights are further weighted by the term $(1.0 - \alpha(t)x_j(t))$ which goes to 1.0 as the function $\alpha(t) \to 0$ as $t \to \infty$. It was found necessary to include this term to generate a good clustering. This weighted average of the node weights is then multiplied by a second term, given by the ratio of the number of matched symbols between the node and the input and the total number of symbols in the input string. The winner node $v(t)$ at time t is chosen as the one with maximum activation, hence

$$v(t) = \underset{1 \leq k \leq M \times M}{\arg \max} \mathcal{A}_k(t) \quad (9)$$

This represents the first step of the clustering algorithm, deciding on the winner node that best represents the input.

173

The second stage is the updating of the nodes. For each node $k = 1, 2, \ldots, M \times M$ the following is the update rule for the node string $\mathbf{S}_k(t)$ and the node weight vector $\mathbf{X}_k(t)$,

1. if $s_j(t) \in \hat{\mathbf{S}}(t)$,

$$x_j(t) = x_j(t) + \alpha(t) \, h_m(v(t), k) \left(1.0 - x_j(t)\right) \tag{10}$$

2. if $s_j(t) \notin \hat{\mathbf{S}}(t)$,

$$x_j(t) = x_j(t)\left(1.0 - \alpha(t) \, |h_m(v(t), k)|\right) \tag{11}$$

3. if $\hat{s}_j(t) \notin \mathbf{S}_k(t)$ and $h_m(v(t), k) > 0$,

$$n(t) = n(t) + 1 \tag{12}$$
$$s_{n(t)}(t) = \hat{s}_j(t) \tag{13}$$
$$x_{n(t)}(t) = \alpha(t) \, h_m(v(t), k) \tag{14}$$

4. if $x_j(t) < \beta(t)$ then remove $s_j(t)$ from $\mathbf{S}_k(t)$ and $x_j(t)$ from $\mathbf{X}_i(t)$ and

$$n(t) = n(t) - 1 \tag{15}$$

These steps are repeated for each symbol in the input string and each symbol and weight coefficient of the node and then $\mathbf{S}_k(t+1) = \mathbf{S}_k(t)$, $\mathbf{X}_k(t+1) = \mathbf{X}_k(t)$, and $n(t+1) = n(t)$. In these rules, $\alpha(t) \in [0, 1]$ is a gain function that decreases towards 0, $h_m(v(t), k)$ is a Mexican hat as a function of the lattice distance d_L between the winner $v(t)$ and the node k being updated.

What rule 1 does is increase the weight component $x_j(t)$ towards 1 if the symbol $s_j(t)$ is present in the input $\hat{\mathbf{S}}(t)$ and the value of the Mexican hat function is positive. Otherwise if the Mexican hat is negative the $x_j(t)$ is driven towards 0. The first part corresponds to a reinforcement learning while the second is an inhibition. In rule 2, if the symbol $s_j(t)$ is not present in the input $\hat{\mathbf{S}}(t)$ then the weight $x_j(t)$ is driven towards 0 irrespective of whether the Mexican hat function is positive or negative. This can be considered a form of unlearning. In rule 3, if there is an element $\hat{s}_j(t)$ of the input that is not in $\mathbf{S}_k(t)$ then it is added into $\mathbf{S}_k(t)$ and given an initial weight value proportional to $\alpha(t)$ and $h_m(v(t), k)$. If $h_m(v(t), k) \leq 0$ then the symbol is not added. Finally rule 4, decides whether a symbol should remain part of the symbol string, where $\beta(t) \in [0, 1]$. It can be shown that even if the update rule tends to increase and decrease the weight values towards, 1 and 0 respectively, in general it does tend to increase the activation function for the winner node and its neighbors. The same process is repeated over for each input pattern.

Intuitively what the algorithm does is determine patterns of frequently occurring symbols in the input. The weights of the weight vector associated with a node string indicate the level of probability of the symbol occurring in the symbol string. The cutoff function $\beta(t)$ increases in time, for example from $0.1 \rightarrow 0.3$ and removes less frequently occurring symbols from the node string. In this sense the node strings represent average values of the input strings. This means the most frequently occurring symbols strings occur at the cluster centers of the input. It has been found that the algorithm can cluster data with very high levels of noise.

5 Context Recognition : An Example

In this section an experiment is described showing how the symbolic representation of context can be used with a symbol string clustering algorithm for recognizing and generating higher level context in a practical situation. The available data was derived from sensors. The first level of context came from sensors in a mobile terminal, the second level of context was generated by a fusion of the sensor data. By fusing these second level contexts over time a third level of context was generated. The second level of context corresponds to a user activity at a particular time, for example, walking outside, the third level corresponded to a scenario where the user walked from the office, outside, came back inside etc.

5.1 Experimental Setup

A small mobile device was equipped with a set of sensors described in Table 1. A user then went through one of the 5 scenarios described in Table 2. When the terminal was not on the table it was hanging in front, from the user's neck. The sensor signals were logged by using a laptop carried by the user. As the sensor signals arrived they were processed to generate context atoms [15]. A total of 10 context atom classes were used in the experiment and are listed in Table 1 along with the sensor signal from which the context atom is derived. Each context atom class has several different associated context atoms [14], for example, device orientation has 6 possible context atoms corresponding to each orientation. Similarly "type of light" can have two possible context atoms, one for natural light and the other for artificial light. Each context atom is assigned a symbol, in this case an integer value, also shown in Table 1. The symbols in "not assigned" were used when it was not possible to determine the context atom for the context class with confidence. During the experiment, and once every second, a 10 dimensional vector of context atoms was produced, with only one context atom taken from each context atom class. A symbol string with 10 symbols was produced every second for example, $(4, 9, 12, 14, 18, 23, 25, 29, 33, 37)$ could be interpreted as the mobile terminal with antenna up, unstable, not in hand in artificial light at 50 Hz etc.

Table 1. Taxonomy of the context atoms and their symbolic representation as integer values 1 – 40. ND represents not defined and means that the context atom could not be readily classified. DD=display down, DU=display up, AD=antenna down, AU=antenna up, SR=sideways right, SL=sideways left.

Context Atom Class	Sensor	Context Atom
1. Orientation	Accelerometer	(1=DD), (2=DU), (3=AD), (4=AU), (5=SR), (6=SL), (7=ND)
2. Stability	Accelerometer	(8=Stable), (9=Unstable), (10=ND)
3. In Hand	Touch	(11=In Hand), (12=Not In Hand), (13=ND)
4. Light Freq.	Ambient light	(14=50Hz), (15=60Hz), (16=ND)
5. Illumination level	Ambient light	(17=Bright), (18=Normal), (19=Dim), (20=Dark), (21=ND)
6. Type of Light	Ambient light	(22=Natural), (23=Artificial)
7. Temperature level	Temperature	(24=Hot), (25=Warm), (26=Cool), (27=Cold), (28=ND)
8. Humidity level	Humidity	(29=Humid), (30=Normal), (31=Dry), (32=ND)
9. Loudness level	Microphone	(33=Silent), (34=Modest), (35=Loud), (36=ND)
10. Activity level	Accelerometer	(37=Walking), (38=Walking Fast), (39=Running), (40=ND)

Each scenario was repeated about 25 times for two test persons. The data consist of a total of 241 repetitions of the scenarios 1-5. Each test lasted about 3–4 minutes depending on the testee and on the environment. In total there were approximately 50000 symbol string vectors.

5.2 Context Recognition

The context atoms represent the first level of context, the second level of context is generated by combining the context atoms into the 10 dimensional symbol string described in the previous section, and then recognizing each 10 dimensional symbol string as a particular context. During the repetitions of the scenarios shown in Table 2 the user spends more time on some activities than others, for example a lot of time is for walking, but little time for when the terminal is in hand. In order to obtain a more uniformly distributed probability for each user activity for the learning process, the segmentation algorithm of [9] was used to automatically segment each repetition of each scenario into 14 segments. The segmentation algorithm detects changes in the context atom classes and inserts a segment when there is a significant change in one or several values of the context atom classes. This change indicates a different user context. One sample symbol string from each segment was randomly chosen as a representative of the segment. With a total of 241 repetitions of the 5 scenarios, and 14 segments for each scenario, a total of 3374 = 241 × 14 symbol strings were used in the off line training of the SCM algo-

Table 2. A brief description of the sequence of actions carried out during each of the 5 scenarios.

	Activities		Location
Scenario 1 44 recordings	device on table	inside	office room
	device in hand	inside	office room
	walking	inside	corridor
	walking	inside	down the stairs, lobby
	walking	outside	street
	walking	inside	lobby
	walking	inside	up the stairs, corridor
	device in hand	inside	office room
	device on table	inside	office room
Scenario 2 48 recordings	device on table	inside	office room
	device in hand	inside	office room
	walking	inside	corridor, down stairs
	halt	inside	mail lockers
	walking	outside	backyard
	halt	inside	mail lockers
	walking	inside	up the stairs, corridor
	device in hand	inside	office room
	device on table	inside	office room
Scenario 3 49 recordings	device on table	inside	office room
	device in hand	inside	office room
	walking	inside	corridor
	halt	inside	lift upstairs
	walking	inside	corridor
	halt	outside	balcony
	walking	inside	corridor
	halt	inside	lift downstairs
	walking	inside	corridor
	device in hand	inside	office room
	device on table	inside	office room
Scenario 4 50 recordings	device on table	inside	office room
	device in hand	inside	office room
	walking	inside	corridor
	sitting+talking	inside	meeting room
	walking+talking	inside	corridor
	sitting+talking	inside	coffee room
	walking	inside	corridor
	device in hand	inside	office room
	device on table	inside	office room
Scenario 5 50 recordings	device on table	inside	office room
	device in hand	inside	office room
	walking	inside	corridor
	halt	inside	lift upstairs
	walking	inside	corridor
	halt	inside	lift downstairs
	walking	inside	corridor
	device in hand	inside	office room
	device on table	inside	office room

rithm. The training was carried out by randomly selecting one of the 3374 symbol strings as input to the SCM. The resulting SCM after 10000 iterations is shown in figure 1(a), (b). Figure 1(a) shows the symbol string associated with each node of the SCM lattice and figure 1(b) shows the associated weight vectors. There are 5 clearly distinguishable clusters separated by nodes with null symbol strings and weight vectors. Each cluster can be seen from Table 1 to correspond to a different user context. It is possible to manually label the nodes as belonging to different clusters, however figure 1(c) shows the cluster labels generated automatically for each node using a learning algorithm described in [7] the relevant cluster labels being $199, 19, 281, 49, 379$.

For example the cluster with $[4, 9, 12, 16, 17, 22, 25, 29, 33, 38]$, indicates the user's action, such that the antenna is up (4) and not in hand (12) and unstable (9). Hence the user is most likely moving with the terminal hanging in front. Furthermore the light is natural and bright (16, 17, 22) and it is warm and humid with a low sound level (25, 29, 33) and finally the user is walking fast (38). Obviously this cluster corresponds to a context where the user is walking outside. However included in the same cluster is node strings containing 37, 40 indicating that the cluster corresponds to any form of walking slow or fast. All other clusters have similar and most importantly, different, interpretations.

Now consider generating a second set of symbol strings which describe each repetition of each scenario. At each time instant the symbol string generated from the context atoms is clustered and the user's context at that time instant is denoted by the cluster number to which the symbol string was clustered. This results in a second set of symbol strings for each repetition of the scenarios, for example, $199, 199, 19, 19, 281, 19, 281, \ldots$ The symbol strings were reduced so that adjacent repeating symbols were only listed once, for example the previous symbol string was reduced to, $199, 19, 281, 19, 281, \ldots$. An important difference between this symbol string and that of strings used in the first clustering is that the order of the symbols in this sequence are important and contain information. The SCM algorithm as described here and the similarity measure does not apply to this type of symbol string, but only to the case when the ordering of the symbol strings is not important. At this point a Markov model approach could be used to model and classify the evolution of the time series of symbols generated by the first clustering. However a hash coding of the symbol sequence is used to convert the sequence of symbols from one where the ordering of the symbols is important into a sequence where the ordering of the symbols is not important while still maintaining the information of the ordering in the original sequence. The transformation is quite simple and in a simple form is applied as follows. Assuming the symbols are integers then the triplet $s(t-2), s(t-1), s(t)$

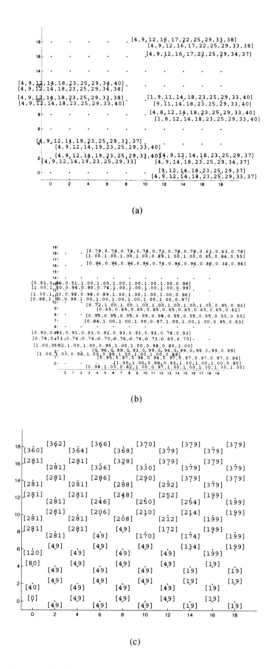

Figure 1. (a) symbols strings for every second node of the SCM lattice. (b) the corresponding coefficients for each symbol of the symbol strings. (c) cluster labels for each node. Every second node string, weight vector and cluster label is plotted for ease of illustration.

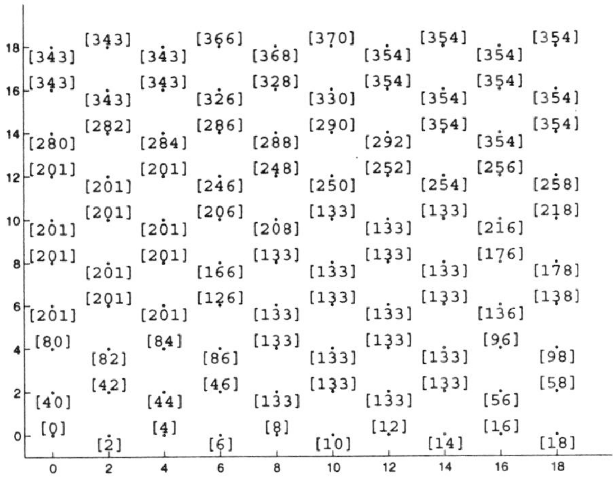

```
18  [343]   [343]   [366]   [368]   [370]   [354]   [354]   [354]
16  [343]   [343]   [326]   [328]   [330]   [354]   [354]   [354]
14  [280]   [282]   [284]   [286]   [288]   [290]   [292]   [354]   [354]
12  [201]   [201]   [201]   [246]   [248]   [250]   [252]   [254]   [256]   [258]
10  [201]   [201]   [201]   [206]   [208]   [133]   [133]   [133]   [216]   [218]
 8  [201]   [201]   [201]   [166]   [133]   [133]   [133]   [133]   [176]   [178]
 6  [201]   [201]   [201]   [126]   [133]   [133]   [133]   [133]   [136]   [138]
 4  [80]    [82]    [84]    [86]    [133]   [133]   [133]   [133]   [96]    [98]
 2  [40]    [42]    [44]    [46]    [133]   [133]   [133]   [133]   [56]    [58]
 0  [0]     [2]     [4]     [6]     [8]     [10]    [12]    [14]    [16]    [18]
     0       2       4       6       8       10      12      14      16      18
```

Figure 2. The cluster labels assigned to each node of the SCM for the clustering of the different scenarios.

is coded into a single symbol,

$$\bar{s}(t) = s(t-2) * N^2 + s(t-1) * N + s(t) \quad (16)$$

where N is the total number of symbols in the alphabet. This coding is carried out for every symbol $s(t)$ in the sequence resulting in a second symbol string in which the ordering of the symbols can be considered not important. This assumption is exactly the same as that used in Markov chains where it is assumed the value of the current state is dependent only on the previous state. Note that for every triplet there is a unique coded representation. In this case there were 5 clusters in the first clustering, hence the alphabet size $N = 5$. This second set of coded symbol strings was then used to train a second SCM and consisted of 241 coded symbol strings generated from each repetition of a scenario. As a result a total of 4 clusters were found and automatically labelled by the clustering algorithm as shown in figure 2 with the relevant clusters being 133, 354, 343, 201.

The length of the cluster centers generated by the SCM are quite long and not reproduced here. However using the clustering algorithm, each of the symbol strings associated with each of the repetitions were classed to a particular cluster. Table 3 shows the results. The results suggest that scenarios, 1, 2 are quite similar with little similarity between scenarios 1, 2, scenario 3, scenario 4, and scenario 5. From the description of the scenarios in Table 2 it is clear that scenarios 1, 2, 3 all have in common that the user goes outside for some time, while in scenarios 4, 5 at no time does the user goes outside. Scenarios 1, 2 are actually quite similar and different from scenario 3 in that in scenarios 1, 2 the user walks outside, whereas in scenario 3 the user is

Table 3. The number of the repetitions of each of the scenarios assigned to each cluster in the second clustering stage

Cluster	Scen. 1	Scen. 2	Scen. 3	Scen. 4	Scen. 5
133	43	47	4	0	0
354	1	1	45	0	0
343	0	0	0	43	4
201	0	0	0	7	46

moving about on a small balcony. From scenarios 4, 5 it is seen from Table 2 that in scenario 4 there is talking while in scenario 5 there is none. There is some classification of scenarios 4, 5 to the others main cluster however this could be due to the fact that the sound context atoms, define the loudness of sound and cannot identify speech, hence the value of loudness is relative and even when there is speech it may be recorded as low level sound. Furthermore the speech was conversational and hence did not create a continuous sound wave.

This second clustering shows a higher level of context than the first clustering. It has been possible to cluster different repetitions of the scenarios, using symbol strings generated from the first clustering and define which scenario the repetition was for. It seems that the level of information from the context atoms and the differences between the scenarios is not big enough to completely separate the different scenarios, but the principle of generating higher level context and recognizing context has been demonstrated using a real data set and unsupervised clustering of symbol strings.

The complete process for the context recognition is shown in figure 3. In summary data from a set of sensors was processed to generate context atoms subdivided into 10 different context atom classes. Each context atom was represented by a symbol. At every one second interval the context atom classes where sampled to find their current state. The result was a symbol string of 10 symbols. These first symbol strings where automatically clustered and labelled. Clustering any of the symbol strings results in a label which is a symbolic representation of the current context of the user, and hence one level of context higher than that described by any one of the context atoms. At each time interval, for all repetitions of all scenarios, these first symbol strings are clustered and automatically labelled with a symbol (i.e. the number of the cluster) to produce a sequence of symbols for each repetition. Automatically clustering and labelling these symbol strings allows for each repetition to be clustered, thus generating a higher level of the user's context than that represented by the symbol strings generated from the context atoms.

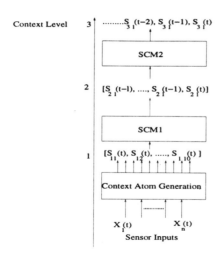

Context Level

3 ·········$S_{3_1}(t-2), S_{3_1}(t-1), S_{3_1}(t)$

SCM2

2 $[S_{2_1}(t-1), ..., S_{2_1}(t-1), S_{2_1}(t)]$

SCM1

1 $[S_{1_1}(t), S_{1_2}(t), ..., S_{1_{10}}(t)]$

Context Atom Generation

$X_1(t)$ ·········· $X_n(t)$

Sensor Inputs

Figure 3. Various stages of the context recognition method based on the SCM

6 Conclusion

The problem of context recognition has been shown to provide an ideal application for the use of data mining algorithms. By using a symbolic representation of context and combining and generating context based on symbol strings, context recognition becomes a problem of pattern recognition in symbol strings. The approach taken here is to use a clustering algorithm to extract the patterns. The SCM, an efficient algorithm for the unsupervised clustering and cluster labelling of symbol string data, has been introduced and applied to this clustering of symbol string data. The algorithm is memory efficient as it is on-line and does not require the storage of input data. It is also computationally efficient as a very simple similarity measure based on a weighted average of coefficients is used to compare symbol strings. It has been shown how data from very different sensors can be fused together using a symbol string representation. This representation is then recognized using clustering. A first clustering of the context atom symbol strings generates a time sequence of symbols. This time series constitutes another symbol string. For different time series of symbols representing different scenarios a second SCM can be used for clustering and the resulting clusters distinguishes between different scenarios.

Acknowledgements

The authors would like to thank Urpo Tuomela, Petri Kangas and Heikki Mannila for their contribution and support in this work.

References

[1] C. C. Aggarwal, J. L. Wolf, P. S. Yu, C. Procopiuc, and J. S. Park. Fast algorithms for projected clustering. In *Proceedings of the 1999 ACM SIGMOD international conference on Management of data*, pages 61–72. ACM Press, 1999.

[2] I. V. Cadez, S. Gaffney, and P. Smyth. A general probabilistic framework for clustering individuals and objects. In *Proceedings of the sixth ACM SIGKDD international conference on Knowledge discovery and data mining*, pages 140–149. ACM Press, 2000.

[3] B. Clarkson, K. Mase, and A. Pentland. Recognizing User Context via Wearable Sensors. In *Digest of Papers, The fourth International Symposium on Wearable Computers*, pages 69–76, 2000.

[4] B. Clarkson and A. Pentland. Extracting Context from Environmental Audio. In *Proceedings on 2nd International Symposium on Wearable Computers*, 1998.

[5] P. S. D. Hand, H. Mannila. *Principles of Data Mining*. MIT Press, Cambridge, Massachusetts, London, England, 2001.

[6] A. Dey. Understanding and Using Context. *Personal and Ubiquitous Computing*, 5, 2001.

[7] J. A. Flanagan. The symbol string clustering map : A method for clustering and segmenting sequences of symbols. To be Submitted, 2002.

[8] J. A. Flanagan. Unsupervised clustering of a data set based on the self-organizing map. Submitted to Neural Computation, 2002.

[9] J. Himberg, K. Korpiaho, H. Mannila, J. Tikanmäki, and H. Toivonen. Time Series Segmentation for Context Recognition in Mobile Devices. In *Proc. of the 1st IEEE Conference on Data Mining (ICDM2001)*, pages 203–210, 2001.

[10] J. Himberg, J. Mäntyjärvi, and P. Korpipää. Using PCA and ICA for Exploratory, Data Analysis in Situation Awareness. In *Proc. of IEEE Conference on Multisensor Fusion and Integration for Intelligent Systems (MFI2001)*, pages 127–131, 2001.

[11] H. Kargupta, B. Park, S. Pittie, L. Liu, D. Kushraj, and K. Sarkar. MobiMine: Monitoring the Stock Market from a PDA. *ACM SIGKDD Explorations*, 3(2):37–46, 2002.

[12] T. Kohonen. *Self-Organizing Maps*. Springer, Berlin, Heidelberg, 2001. (Third Extended Edition).

[13] K. V. Laerhoven and O. Cakmakci. What Shall We Teach Our Pants? In *Digest of Papers of the Fourth International Symposium on Wearable Computers*, pages 77–83. IEEE, 2000.

[14] J. Mäntyjärvi, J. Himberg, P. Korpipää, and H. Mannila. Extracting the Context of a Mobile Device User. In *Proc. of 8th IFAC/IFIP/IFORS/IEA Symposium on Analysis, Design, and Evaluation of Human-Machine System*, 2001.

[15] V.-M. Mäntylä, J. Mäntyjärvi, T. Seppänen, and E. Tuulari. Hand Gesture Recognition of a Mobile Device User. In *Proceedings of the IEEE International Conference on Multimedia and Expo*, volume 1, pages 281–284, 2000.

[16] A. Schmidt, K. Aidoo, A. Takaluoma, U. Tuomela, K. V. Laerhoven, and W. V. de Velde. Advanced Interaction in Context. In *Hand Held and Ubiquitous Computing*, number 1707 in Lecture Notes in Computer Science, pages 89–101. Springer-Verlag, 1999.

A Parameterless Method for Efficiently Discovering Clusters of Arbitrary Shape in Large Datasets

Andrew Foss
University of Alberta, Canada
afoss@cs.ualberta.ca

Osmar R. Zaïane
University of Alberta, Canada
zaiane@cs.ualberta.ca

Abstract

Clustering is the problem of grouping data based on similarity and consists of maximizing the intra-group similarity while minimizing the inter-group similarity. The problem of clustering data sets is also known as unsupervised classification, since no class labels are given. However, all existing clustering algorithms require some parameters to steer the clustering process, such as the famous k for the number of expected clusters, which constitutes a supervision of a sort. We present in this paper a new, efficient, fast and scalable clustering algorithm that clusters over a range of resolutions and finds a potential optimum clustering without requiring any parameter input. Our experiments show that our algorithm outperforms most existing clustering algorithms in quality and speed for large data sets.

1. Introduction

There exist a multitude of algorithms for clustering data. Basically, they each try to concentrate on some important issues in clustering, such as high dimensionality problems, efficiency, scalability with data size, sensitivity to noise in data, identification of clusters with various cluster shapes, etc. However, none has managed to take all these factors into account at once. The major drawbacks of existing clustering algorithms include the splitting of large genuine clusters, which is the case for partitional approaches such as k-means [6]; failure to handle convex and elongated shapes of clusters as is the case with most hierarchical approaches such as CURE [11] and ROCK [4]; and the sensitivity to noise in the data such as in CHAMELEON's case [7] or DBSCAN [2], a density-based clustering algorithm.

The greatest difficulty in the field of data clustering is the need for input parameters. Many algorithms, especially the hierarchical methods [5, 11], require the initial choice of the number of clusters to find. Even where this is not required or the algorithm can stop automatically before that number is reached, other parameters greatly influence the output.

One can argue that for some applications parameters are a means to incorporate domain knowledge into the clustering process and thus are beneficial in some circumstances. This is particularly true when the number of clusters to be discovered is predetermined and fixed by the application. However, in many applications the optimal values of these parameters are very difficult to determine. Often a long and tedious trial-and-error process is used to tune these parameters. However, when the number of dimensions is larger than three, this becomes extremely difficult or unpractical, and an automated process is desirable. On the other hand, domain knowledge could be expressed in the definition of similarity functions used to measure how similar or dissimilar data points are in order to group them in clusters.

In this paper, we present a novel clustering algorithm called *TURN** which does not require the input of any parameter and still efficiently discovers clusters of complex shapes in very large data sets. We report the efficiency and demonstrate the effectiveness of *TURN** on large and complex data sets containing points in 2D space borrowed from [7, 13] for comparison reasons.

Section 2 gives an overview of existing, well-known clustering algorithms and Section 3 describes our clustering algorithm *TURN**. Section 4 presents some experimental results for *TURN** and six established clustering algorithms. Finally, Section 5 concludes and discusses future work.

2. Related Work

There are mainly four groups of clustering methods: partitioning methods, hierarchical methods, density-based methods and grid-based methods. We give a brief introduction to these existing methods in this section.

Supposing there are n objects in the original data set, partitioning methods break the original data set into k partitions. The basic idea of partitioning is very intuitive, and the process of partitioning is typically to achieve certain optimal criterion iteratively.

The most classical and popular partitioning methods are k-means and k-medoid, where each cluster is represented by the gravity centre of the cluster in k-means method or by one of the "central" objects of the cluster in k-medoid method.

All the partitioning methods have a similar clustering quality and the major difficulties with these methods include: (1) The number k of clusters to be found needs to be known prior to clustering requiring at least some domain knowledge which is often not available; (2) it is difficult to identify clusters with large variations in sizes (large genuine clusters tend to be split); (3) the method is only suitable for concave clusters.

A hierarchical clustering algorithm produces a dendrogram representing the nested grouping relationship among objects. In the past few years, many new hierarchical algorithms have been published. The major difference between all these hierarchical algorithms is the measure of similarity between each pair of clusters and the underlying modelling of the clusters. Because these algorithms are typically computationally expensive, many proceed by sampling the data and clustering only a representative sample of the data points, which puts the effectiveness of the clustering at the mercy of the goodness of the sampling method.

Instead of using a single point to represent a cluster as in centroid/medoid based methods, CURE [11] uses a constant number of representative points to represent a cluster. These are selected so that they are well scattered and then "shrunk" towards the centroid of the cluster according to a shrinking factor α. Cluster similarity is measured by the similarity of the closest pair of the cluster's representative points The problem with CURE is its global similarity measure which makes it ineffective with complex data distributions and it can cause false outliers (See Figure 4).

The same authors developed ROCK [4]. ROCK operates on a derived similarity graph and is thus suiteable for both numerical and categorical data. ROCK measures the similarity between pairs of clusters by the normalized number of total links between them. This is given as a fixed global parameter (θ). However, ROCK is extremely sensitive to θ, which reflects a fixed modeling of clusters. ROCK's clustering result is not good for complex clusters with various data densities, and the algorithm is sensitive to noise.

A recent state-of-art clustering method is CHAMELEON [7] which considers both relative connection and relative closeness. The algorithm operates on a derived similarity graph allowing the clustering of numerical as well as categorical data like ROCK. Phase one of the algorithm uses a graph partitioning method to pre-cluster objects into a set of small clusters. The second phase merges these small clusters based on their similarity measure. CHAMELEON has been found to be very effective in clustering convex shapes. However, the algorithm cannot handle outliers and needs parameter setting in order to work effectively.

Density-based methods identify clusters through the data point density and can usually discover clusters with arbitrary shapes without a pre-set number of clusters. DBSCAN is a typical density-based method which connects regions with sufficiently high density into clusters. Each cluster is a maximum set of density-connected points. Points are connected when they are density-reachable from one neighbourhood to the other. A neighbourhood is a circle of a radius (ϵ) and reachability is defined based on a minimum number of points ($MinPts$) contained in a radius ϵ. DBSCAN, however, is very sensitive to the selection of ϵ and $MinPts$ and it cannot identify clusters with different densities. The problem of discovering clusters with different densities and clusters within clusters was alleviated in OPTICS [9] by the same authors. However, the parameter $MinPts$ still needs to be defined.

Grid-based methods first discretize the clustering space into a finite number of cells, and perform clustering on the gridded cells. The main advantage of grid-based methods is that the processing speed only depends on the resolution of griding and not on the size of the data set. The grid-based methods are more suitable for high density data sets with huge number of data objects in limited space.

Representative grid-based algorithms include CLIQUE [1] and, recently, WaveCluster [12] which applies a noise filter and wavelet transformation. Grid-based quantization of the data space speeds up the processing, but due to the rectangular structure, the algorithm represents a much coarser approach to levels of resolution than that adopted by our algorithm *TURN** presented herein, or DBSCAN, and is much more likely to lead to the misclassification of data points. The algorithm requires this quantization so one does not have the option of classifying the data at full resolution. WaveCluster offers multiresolution by skipping "rows" of the quantized data (i.e. down sampling), a much cruder approach than that used by the other algorithms that use all the data and simply expand the nearest neighbour definition or equivalent of each point. WaveCluster's main benefits are speed and scalability since the data is read in and quantized and then subsequent processing is on a much smaller effective data size.

While WaveCluster claims to be parameter free, our research showed that its clustering results are quite sensitive to the settings that have to be made. In fact [12] points out that knowing the number of clusters to be found is very helpful for choosing the parameters for WaveCluster.

2.1. Unsupervised Method: TURN

Previously, we have devised a non-parametric approach to categorical data clustering in a non-Euclidean space called TURN that we used for clustering web access transactions [3]. Here we present a non-parametric approach suited to spatial data as well as higher dimensional spaces. TURN operates on a derived similarity graph allowing any similarity function to be plugged in. The basic idea of TURN is to identify natural boundaries between clusters instead of spotting clusters themselves. This amounts to searching for the minima in the distribution of points, which represent turning points. TURN proceeds by iteratively selecting a non assigned object p and computing the similarity between p and all non-assigned objects. After sorting the similarities and differencing them 3 times, the algorithm looks for a change of sign (i.e. turning point) in the differenced number series. All objects that appear before the turning point are assigned to the same cluster as p and their direct neighbours are also pulled in. The process repeats until all objects are assigned [3]. TURN has been tested on categorical data only and experimentally it outperformed ROCK in clustering web usage data.

3. TURN* Algorithm

In this section we introduce our new clustering algorithm *TURN**, a non-parametric clustering approach that efficiently discovers clusters of arbitrary shapes.

*TURN** consists of an overall algorithm and two component algorithms, one, an efficient resolution dependent clustering algorithm TURN-RES which returns both a clustering result and certain global statistics (cluster features) from that result and two, TurnCut, an automatic method for finding the important or "optimum" resolutions from a set of resolution results from TURN-RES. To date, clustering algorithms have returned clustering results for a given set of parameters, as TURN-RES does, and some have presented graphs or dendograms of cluster features from which the user may be able to adjust or select the parameters to optimize the clustering. *TURN** takes clustering into new territory by automating this process removing the need for input parameters. Clustering Validation is a field where attempts have been made to find rules for quantifying the quality of a clustering result. Though developed independently, Turn-Cut could be seen as an advance in this field which has been integrated into the clustering process.

3.1. TURN-RES: Clustering at one resolution

This is a fast, efficient, scaleable clustering algorithm for a single resolution. While little discussed, except in papers such as [12], resolution is a key concept in clustering. When a radius is defined, as in DBSCAN, or some related parameter, a particular view is being set that has an equivalence to viewing a density plot with a microscope or telescope at a certain magnification. The night sky is one example; as the magnification level is adjusted, one will identify different groupings or clusters. The CHAMELEON data set (Figure

1) is another example. It looks like there are nine clusters but given a magnifying glass, the large clusters will be seen to have their own sub-clusters.

TURN-RES is resolution or scale dependent because of its definition of "close" neighbours. Two points are considered "close" only if they are separated by a distance $d \leq 1.0$, at a given resolution, along all dimensional axes. For example, points x_0 (1, 1) and x_1 (3, 3) are not neighbours unless the scale is reduced (e.g. $\div$ 2 giving x_0 (.5, .5) and x_1 (1.5, 1.5)). We compute a density value t_P for each point P based on its distance to its nearest neighbours, irrespective of their closeness, which, in our approach, is a maximum of 2 per dimension, one on each side. t_P allows us to determine how closely packed the points are locally and a threshold ϕ is set as a cut-off to differentiate between points that are to be treated as internal or external to a cluster. Points that fall on the edge of a cluster will not be marked as internal but they get included because close neighbours to internal points are pulled into the cluster. ϕ is not a function of the data set but rather of the method employed and a single value sufficed for all data sets tested so this is not a user input parameter.

As noise typically can create small clusters, we defined small clusters as noise or outliers. Small is defined as $\min(100, N/100)$ where N is the number of data points. TURN-RES collects certain global statistics or cluster features, being k, the number of clusters, n, the number of points assigned to clusters (not considering outliers), t, total density and t_m, mean density ($t \div n$). Our interest is to characterize the resolution level in such a way that levels of particular interest can be determined automatically. t is the sum over n of t_P that is defined for point P as:

$$t_P = 1 \div \sum_{i=1}^{2} \sqrt{(d_{L_i}^2 + d_{R_i}^2)} \qquad (1)$$

Note: d_L and d_R are the distances to the 'left' and 'right' side neighbours along a dimensional axis i.

Once the data points have been characterized as internal or external, they are simply agglutinated into clusters. An unclassified internal point is selected, a new cluster number is assigned to it and all of its "close" neighbours are similarly classified. For each of those that are also internal, the process is repeated. Not incorporating "close" neighbours of external points stops clusters growing across 'noise' bridges.

To quickly determine the nearest neighbour ids of each point a single sort is performed on each dimension. Building the clusters requires one further sort by id. Each sort is followed by a single scan giving a computational complexity of $O(N \log(N))$.

TURN-RES Algorithm

Input: 2D data points and resolution level r

Output: Clustered data points

1. For each data point P, scale coordinates of P to resolution r and find the two nearest neighbours on each dimensional axis, and the distance d of each from P; if $d \leq 1.0$ assign the point as a "close" neighbour;

2. compute the density t_P; set P as internal if $t_P > \phi$ (ϕ is fixed and not an input parameter)

3. For each non assigned internal data point P do

    (a) add P to new cluster C;

    (b) add all "close" neighbours of P to C;

    (c) for all m added points that are internal add all their "close" neighbours to C and repeat until $m = 0$;

TURN* Algorithm

Input: 2D data points

Output: "Best" clustering of data points

1. start at resolution r=1:1. Seek S_∞ by increasing/decreasing the resolution by step $p_{2.5}$ (multiplying or dividing by $2.5, 5.0, ...$) and clustering at each resolution until all points are labelled as outliers;

2. scan from S_∞ towards S_1 ($k = 1$) by repeating.

    (a) decrease the resolution r by step $p_{0.5}$;

    (b) cluster at r with TURN-RES;

    (c) store clustering result and statistics t, t_m, k, and n for r;

    (d) stop if $k = 1$ else call TurnCut to determine if r is an "optimum" clustering result and stop on success.

3.2. TurnCut

TurnCut uses the core of the TURN algorithm described in Section 2.1, from our previous work in [3], detecting a change in the third differential of a series to identify important areas in a cluster feature across resolution series built by repeated calls to TURN-RES by the *TURN** algorithm. Single and double differencing are routinely used in time series analysis ([10]) to render a series stationary. Differencing amounts to a highpass filter which we have employed, differencing thrice (double differencing the change values of the series), as we found it to be most effective way to reveal meaningful change in the underlying trend.

Though developed independently of work on Clustering Validation, TurnCut automates other authors' concept of finding the "knee" in the cluster feature graph [8]. It picks out the first (and subsequent) "abrupt" change in the overall trend of the curve - acceleration or reversal of the

rate of change of the clustering feature studied. If the data points being clustered are homogenously distributed, no "turn" will be found. If clusters exist, TurnCut will pick out the point where stabilization occurs in the clustering process, which will often coincide with a level that an observer would identify as a clustering result (almost by definition - we would never pick out a level that did not appear to represent a certain plateau). In general there can be several of these and the algorithm can find them all even though in this paper the algorithm given for *TURN** stops at the first found. In effect, TurnCut is detecting plateaus in the entropy curve.

Other authors only analyzed a feature versus cluster number (k) graph [8]. We evaluated k and found better results with mean density and often further improvements with total density (as defined above) across resolutions. In most algorithms data can only be collected for a particular value of k. In *TURN** we can study as fine a resolution step size as we choose, several steps often yielding the same value of k. Our result makes sense because each statistic has more information than the previous - k is a fairly coarse statistic compared with those we defined that change with every point added to the clustering result.

3.3. TURN*: Finding the best clustering

The algorithm proceeds by detecting clusters across a range of different resolutions stopping (or at least flagging) what is considered as the "optimal" clustering using Turn-Cut. A resolution is simply a scale by which all data point values are multiplied (see TURN-RES above).

Naturally, TURN-RES will return a clustering result only within a certain range of resolutions. On one end of the range every data point will be classified as noise/outlier. Moving in the direction of increasing k, the first resolution level at which this occurs we call S_∞. Moving in the other direction a point is reached where all points are included in a single cluster (S_1). First, the algorithm seeks S_∞ starting by clustering with TURN-RES at resolution 1:1 and then stepping out at a large geometric increment ($p_{2.5} = \times 2.5$ where the scale $> 1:1$; $\div 2.5$ where the scale $< 1:1$) clustering until S_∞ is found. Then the step size is reduced ($\times.5, \div.5$) and a scan over $S_\infty \rightarrow S_1$ is performed. Geometric steps sizes are used as: a) this ensures quickly finding S_∞ and traversing the range to S_1, and b) optical magnification steps are always given in geometric values.

At each step, TURN-RES is called and the clustering result and global features/statistics are stored and TurnCut is called to assess if an "optimum" clustering has been achieved. If so, either *TURN** stops as we did in this research or it can be allowed to continue, collecting information for all the key resolutions flagged by TurnCut.

No sampling takes place, however the scalability of

TURN* is evidenced by the performance on small and large data sets (Table 2). The space complexity is straightforward. For each object, a simple data structure is needed to store coordinates in the $D = 2$ dimensional space, the nearest neighbours on each dimensional axis, and some specific data such as cluster label, type of point etc. Thus, the memory space needed is $O(DN)$.

3.4. Parameter Free?

The parameters involved in the component algorithms are 1) ϕ, that defines if a point is to be treated as internal, 2) the resolution level given to TURN-RES, 3) the definition of a "small" cluster, and 4) the step size(s) used between resolutions at which TURN-RES is run.

Our implementation is parameter free in so far as 1) ϕ is part of the concept of closeness for a resolution level and thus should not need to be varied as proved to be the case; 2) *TURN** feeds TURN-RES a series of resolutions starting from the extreme case (S_∞) where all points are identified as outliers so the user is never asked to enter a resolution; 3) we found that only very small data sets would need this modifying and *TURN** is not intended for such sets; 4) the step size starts large until S_∞ is found and is then reduced. In choosing the step size there is a trade-off between fineness and speed. We found the step size we chose to be robust across varied data set types but if the differentiation between cluster densities in the data was small, a key resolution could be missed. However, to be secure against this the algorithm could be extended as follows: Once TurnCut flags a resolution of interest the range across the previous step can be scanned by further reducing the step size giving finer resolving power. It is most unlikely that any user input would be needed in this case and the speed of the algorithm makes this additional processing reasonable.

While there will never be a perfect parameter free solution, our implementation proved robust across a wide range of different data set types with differing cluster densities, closeness of clusters, arbitrary shaped clusters and noise levels including many examples of noise "bridges".

4. Experimental Results

In this section, we present experimental results to evaluate *TURN** and compare the performance of our algorithm with other well-known clustering algorithms: k-Means, DBSCAN, CURE, ROCK, CHAMELEON and WaveCluster. The implementation of DBSCAN was obtained from the authors of the algorithm (University of Munich, Germany), while the implementation of ROCK and CURE was obtained from the authors of CHAMELEON (University of Minnesota, USA) written for the evaluation of their own algorithm [7]. However, as they could not provide

the CHAMELEON code for legal reasons, this was implemented locally. We believe that our implementation and optimization of CHAMELEON is similar to the one published by the authors in [7] since we get the same performance on the same data sets as that presented in [7]. WaveCluster [13] was also implemented locally for the same reasons with equal success.

We tested *TURN** on data sets provided by the developers of CHAMELEON [7] and WaveCluster [13]. Due to CHAMELEON's computational intensity, their files are rather small: 8K to 10K. The main benefit claimed in the WaveCluster paper is its effectiveness on large data sets and their data is 100K+ points. We chose these data sets because they are publicly available and they have been used to evaluate other algorithms. Moreover, these data sets are 2-dimensional making it easier to visualize and provide comparisons. We have experimented with various data sets with sizes varying from 8k to more than 575K data points and our algorithm performed well in all cases.

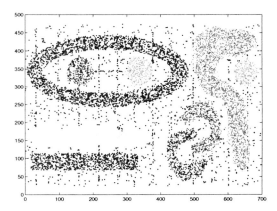

Figure 1. *TURN**'s clustering result on t7.10k.dat before cleaning

On a 10K data set (t7.10k) Figure 1, TURN-RES computed a single resolution in 0.26 seconds and the total process of *TURN** to find the optimum resolution took 3.90 seconds. A single run of CHAMELEON took 28 minutes with the parameter $MinSize$ set to 4%. $MinSize$ is the size of the graph partition in the first phase of the algorithm. Selecting a different value would slow down CHAMELEON or degrade the results. The process of finding the correct parameters to give a good clustering result took several hours. DBSCAN is nearly as fast as *TURN** for a single resolution/parameter setting but also required many runs to find the optimal input variables as it is very sensitive to its parameters. We effectively spent hours tuning the parameters and found out that the best values for the t7.10k.dat dataset were $MinSize = 4$ and $\epsilon = 5.9$. This would have been impossible with a higher dimensionality

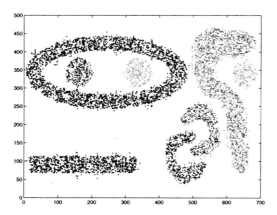

Figure 2. *TURN**'s **cleaned clustering result on t7.10k.dat after removal of points identified as noise**

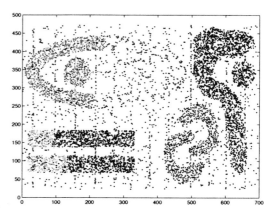

Figure 4. CURE's clustering result on t7.10k.dat with $k = 9$, $\alpha = 0.3$, **and number_of_representative_points** $= 10$

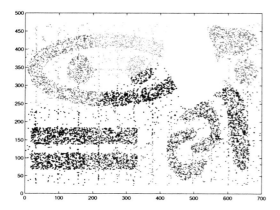

Figure 3. K-means's clustering result on t7.10k.dat with $k = 9$

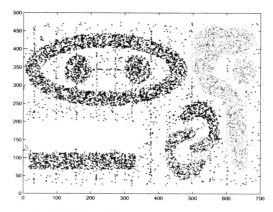

Figure 5. ROCK's clustering result on t7.10k.dat with $\theta = 0.975$ **and** $k = 1000$

data space since validation is difficult if not impossible.

For the data sets chosen, *TURN** took typically 10-20 resolution tests, performed automatically, to find an "optimum" resolution. In our research, *TURN** found the resolution that a human observer would tend to choose in 80% of cases, and in the other cases, it stopped one or two resolutions away on what was identifiably a meaningful clustering result. It can also be allowed to run on, collecting data at each "turn" or key resolution level building the equivalent of a dendogram that reveals the clustering structure at different densities.

As can be seen from Figures 3, 5 and 4, k-means, ROCK and CURE perform relatively poorly on these difficult data sets due to the complex shape of the clusters and the large amount of noise. DBSCAN, CHAMELEON and *TURN** work well. WaveCluster, after much tweaking of its settings, came close to finding the visually obvious clusters.

DBSCAN proved very sensitive to the parameter settings. CHAMELEON requires the setting of the number of clusters to be sought, which is generally not known. It also fails to separate out noise. Combined with its high complexity , this makes it a weak contender.

TURN* provides fast, efficient, scaleable clustering and identifies outliers allowing for the optional removal of noise as has been done in the *TURN** output presented in Figure 2. This would be useful in many applications such as OCR preprocessing, image enhancement, etc. It can stop at or flag interesting levels of granularity identified by the behaviour of global clustering features as discussed.

Here we show our experimental results of each algorithm on the DS4 data set from the CHAMELEON paper [7], also known as t7.10k. This data set was chosen because it has several features which challenge a clustering algorithm. It has nine clusters of different shapes, sizes and orientations,

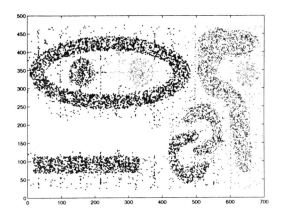

Figure 6. CHAMELEON's clustering result on t7.10k.dat with $nb\_clossest\_neighbor$ = 10, **MinSize** = 2.5% **and** $k = 9$

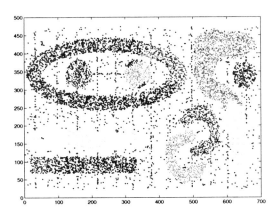

Figure 7. DBSCAN's clustering result on t7.10k.dat with $\epsilon = 5.5$ **and MinPts** = 4

and the density within and between the clusters varies. In addition, there are clusters within clusters, non-spherical shapes and a large amount of random noise which could create artificial "bridges" between the clusters. In all the clustering result figures, black points indicate data points identified by the algorithm as noise.

4.1. Clustering Effectiveness Comparison

Clustering results of *TURN** are shown in Figure 1. *TURN** correctly identified the nine principal clusters as shown in Figure 2 This cluster result shows that *TURN** can effectively identify all the 9 clusters and filter out noise. This result was found by *TURN**'s automatic resolution scan process and did not require any parameter tuning.

K-mean's result is shown in Figure 3. From here we see that k-means tends to find spherical clusters. It is obvious

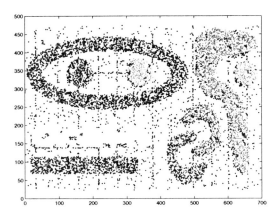

Figure 8. WaveCluster's clustering result on t7.10k.dat with $resolution = 5$ **and** $\tau = 1.5$

that it is not well suited to find arbitrary shaped clusters. Our experiments showed that CURE has similar problems to k-means: it tends to find spherical clusters (Figure 4). ROCK is designed for clustering categorical data but can, in theory, handle numerical data like the $t7.10k.dat$ data set. Its result for clustering this spatial data set is, however, not good. After adjusting the parameters for a long time, the best clustering result found is presented in Figure 5. For this result, we set the number of clusters to be 1000, and among the resulting 1000 clusters, we got five large clusters. The remaining 995 can be considered as noise and they all group around the upper crescent in Figure 5.

Algorithm	Clustering time (secs)	Complexity	Memory Usage
K_means	8.44	$O(N)$	5.5MB
CURE	155.59	$\geq O(N^2)$	4.6MB
ROCK	526.19	$> O(N^2)$	1.145GB
CHAMELEON	1667.86	$> O(NlogN)$	8.6MB
DBSCAN	10.53	$O(NlogN)$	1.4MB
WaveCluster	0.82	$O(N)$	0.8MB
TURN-RES	0.26	$O(NlogN)$	1.4MB
*TURN**	3.90	$O(NlogN)$	1.4MB

Table 1. Clustering Speed and Memory Size Results upon a 10K data set

CHAMELEON's result is shown in Figure 6, which is very close to the result in the CHAMELEON paper. Compared with *TURN**'s result, we see that CHAMELEON includes all the noise points in the neighbouring clusters. In addition, we needed to set several parameters for CHAMELEON to obtain this quality of clustering.

DBSCAN could give a good result if the adequate parameters are known. We found that the only problem of

Data Set Size	Clustering time (seconds)
10,000	0.26
100,000	3.70
228,828	8.29
275,429	9.15
574,499	22.18

Table 2. Average clustering speed of TURN-RES on one resolution across dataset sizes

DBSCAN is that it is indeed very sensitive to the two parameters ϵ and $MinPts$. Figure 7 shows the results of DBSCAN with ϵ set at 5.5 and $MinPts$ at 4. At $\epsilon = 5.9$ the result is similar to $TURN*$'s but any small change in ϵ or $MinPts$ causes splitting or merging of clusters. WaveCluster's best result on t7.10k.dat was with the signal threshold on the transformed frequency domain $\tau = 1.5$ and $resolution = 5$ (Figure 8). Two clusters are joined due to the strength of the bridge in the averaged signal output. Adjusting τ (for example) resolves this problem but breaks other genuine clusters.

$TURN*$ was applied on both the CHAMELEON data sets [7] and the large data sets available from the WaveCluster authors (100K - 575K points) [13], and the test results are shown in Table 2 showing that the algorithm scales nearly linearly with the data set size.

5. Conclusion

The efficiency and effectiveness of clustering algorithms keeps improving. Our research confirms the weakness in the older methods and the relative benefits of the more recent algorithms. While OPTICS [9], WaveCluster [12], and other algorithms provide information at different resolution levels through dendograms or related graphs, it is left to the user to find what resolution to choose. Also, all the algorithms have certain choices - parameters - to set requiring at least some domain knowledge which is often not available to the user. Note that while our approach is non-pararametric and fully unsupervised, the user can still opt for a given resolution if desired.

In this paper, we have proposed a new clustering method called $TURN*$ that can build clustering information for a data set across resolutions including the equivalent of the dendograms built by other algorithms. The TURN algorithm allows us to automatically identify and, if desired, stop on the important resolution level(s) for clustering. An extension, Fuzzy TURN, not discussed here due to limits of space, permits flattening of the dendogram to identify clusters containing areas of differing densities. Together, we have a complete clustering solution which can operate unsupervised. It is fast, scales well with increasing data size, discovers clusters of arbitrary shape and is free of input parameters. It is well suited to a parallel implementation making it even faster with a near linear speedup. Our solution can also scale to higher dimensions, as will be reported elsewhere, but here we emphasise the utility in the area of two-dimensional spatial clustering. For the sake of argument and visual validation, we have used, as did other authors of clustering algorithms, two-dimensional datasets to illustrate effectiveness.

References

[1] R. Agrawal, J. Gehrke, D. Gunopulos, and P. Raghavan. Automatic subspace clustering of high dimensional data for data mining applications. In *Proc. 1998 ACM-SIGMOD Int. Conf. Management of Data (SIGMOD'98)*, pages 94–105, 1998.

[2] M. Ester, H.-P. Kriegel, J. Sander, and X. Xu. A density-based algorithm for discovering clusters in large spatial databases with noise. In *Proc. 1996 Int. Conf. Knowledge Discovery and Data Mining (KDD'96)*, pages 226–231, 1996.

[3] A. Foss, W. Wang, and O. R. Zaïane. A non-parametric approach to web log analysis. In *Web Mining Workshop in conjunction with the SIAM International Conference on Data Mining*, pages 41–50, Chicago, IL, USA, April 2001.

[4] S. Guha, R. Rastogi, and K. Shim. ROCK: a robust clustering algorithm for categorical attributes. In *15th Int'l Conf. on Data Eng.*, 1999.

[5] J. Han and M. Kamber. *Data Mining, Concepts and Techniques*. Morgan Kaufmann, 2001.

[6] A. Jain and R. Dubes. *Algorithms for Clustering Data*. Prentice Hall, 1988.

[7] G. Karypis, E.-H. Han, and V. Kumar. CHAMELEON: A hierarchical clustering algorithm using dynamic modeling. *IEEE Computer*, 32(8):68–75, August 1999.

[8] M. V. M. Halkidi, Y. Batistakis. On clustering validation techniques. *Journal of Intelligent Information Systems*, 17(2-3):107–145, December 2001.

[9] M.Ankerst, M.Breunig, H.-P. Kriegel, and J.Sander. OPTICS: Ordering points to identify the clustering structure. In *Proc. 1999 ACM-SIGMOD Conf. on Management of Data (SIGMOD'99)*, pages 49–60, 1999.

[10] T. Masters. *Neural, Novel & Hybrid Algorithms for Time Series Prediction*. John Wiley and Sons, 1995.

[11] K. S. S. Guha, R. Rastogi. CURE: An efficient clustering algorithm for large databases. In *SIGMOD'98*, Seattle, Washington, 1998.

[12] G. Sheikholeslami, S. Chatterjee, and A. Zhang. Wavecluster: a multi-resolution clustering approach for very large spatial databases. In *24th VLDB Conference*, New York, USA, 1998.

[13] G. Sheikholeslami, S. Chatterjee, and A. Zhang. A wavelet-based clustering approach for spatial data in very large databases. *The International Journal on Very Large Databases*, 8(4):289–304, February 2000.

Discriminative Category Matching: Efficient Text Classification for Huge Document Collections

Gabriel Pui Cheong Fung
Dept. of Sys. Eng. & Eng. Management
The Chinese University of Hong Kong
Hong Kong, China
pcfung@se.cuhk.edu.hk

Jeffrey Xu Yu
Dept. of Sys. Eng. & Eng. Management
The Chinese University of Hong Kong
Hong Kong, China
yu@se.cuhk.edu.hk

Hongjun Lu
Dept. of Computer Science
The Hong Kong Uni. of Science & Technology
Hong Kong, China
luhj@cs.ust.hk

Abstract

With the rapid growth of textual information available on the Internet, having a good model for classifying and managing documents automatically is undoubtly important. When more documents are archived, new terms, new concepts and concept-drift will frequently appear. Without a doubt, updating the classification model frequently rather than using the old model for a very long period is absolutely essential. Here, the challenges are: a) obtain a high accuracy classification model; b) consume low computational time for both model training and operation; and c) occupy low storage space. However, none of the existing classification approaches could achieve all of these requirements. In this paper, we propose a novel text classification approach, called Discriminative Category Matching, which could achieve all of the stated characteristics. Extensive experiments using two benchmarks and a large real-life collection are conducted. The encouraging results indicated that our approach is hignhly feasible.

1 Introduction

With the tremendous growth in the volume of information represented in textual format on the Internet, such as news articles, government reports, company announcements, product promotions, etc., new terms and new concepts are more likely to appear than ever. Concept of a collection may easily drift from one aspect to another also. Boardly speaking, the general requirements for a model to classify a huge document collection under the assumption of possible concept drift are as follows:

§1. High classification accuracy.

§2. Low computational cost and storage requirements for: a) constructing the initial model; b) updating the model after the model is built; and c) operation.

§3. No parameter tuning and highly adaptable in any domains.

While the existing approaches have shown their effectiveness in text classification [9, 10, 14, 21, 22, 23], none of them are able to achieve all of the stated requirements. In particular, §1 is, somehow, conflict with §2, while §3 is difficult to achieve.

For the existing techniques, SVM is properly the best in term of accuracy. However, its training cost is quadratic with the number of training instances [14]. In term of computational cost, Naive Bayes should be the best. However, its accuracy is not high [23]. Besides, most of the approaches require performance tuning, such as feature selection, threshold decision, parameter setting, etc [7, 15, 22, 23], which leads to the difficulty for handling a huge document collection with frequently model updating.

In this paper, we propose a novel text classification approach, called Discriminative Category Matching (DCM), which could satisfy all of the stated requirements by using a new weighting scheme. Here, we argue that none of the existing weighting schemes are suitable for text classification. In fact, all of them are designed for information retrieval but not for classification. Their motivation is: features which

187

appear frequently in many documents will have limited discrimination power, and therefore have to be de-emphasized [4, 17]. However, this is not the case for text classification. In addition, most of them have the difficulty in updating the feature domain once the model is built [4, 8].

Our new weighting scheme aims at discriminating a category from others by assigning the features with higher weights if they appear in fewer categories. Extensive experiments are conducted using two benchmarks (*Reuters-21578* and *TREC9-MeSH*) and a very large collection of articles (namely, *Reuters News Collection*). Our experimental results show that DCM achieves high accuracy and low computational cost and storage requirement, which make it feasible for online classification.

The rest of the paper is organized as follows. Section 2 discusses the related work. Section 3 describes DCM in details. Evaluations and experimental results are reported in Section 4. Finally, a summary and conclusion is given in Section 5.

2 Related Work

In this section, we briefly discuss the merits and limitations of two popular approaches: Naive Bayes (NB) and Support Vector Machines (SVM).

2.1 Naive Bayes

NB is a probabilistic-base algorithm in which its basic idea is to compute the posterior probability of the incoming document given a particular category [11, 12]. Mathematically, it is calculated by the Bayes rule:

$$P(d_i|c_j) = \frac{P(c_j) \cdot P(d_i|c_j)}{P(d_i)} \quad (1)$$

where d_i is the incoming document and c_j is the category j. $P(c_j)$ is computed by the maximum likelihood estimator and $P(d_i|c_j)$ is computed under the word independent assumption.

There are two versions of NB: Multivariate Bernoulli and Multinomial Mixture. The former one only takes the term occurrence into account, while the later one further takes the term frequency into consideration. In general, Multinomial Mixture model performs better [13, 23]. An efficient implementation of NB is the Rainbow package by McCallum.[1]

The merit of NB lies on its robustness and consumes little computational resources. Its major criticism is the word independence assumption. Several research tries to address this problem by generating some association-like

[1] http://www.cs.cmu.edu/ mccallum/bow

Symbol	Meaning
d	A document
k	Category k
f_i	Feature i
$f_{i,x}$	Feature i in x, where $x \in [d, k]$
l_d	Length of document d (i.e. the total number of features)
N_k	Total number of documents in category k
N	Total number of categories in the collection
$nf_{i,d}$	Number of time feature f_i appear in document d
$df_{i,k}$	Number of documents contain feature f_i in category k
$\beta_{i,k}$	The risk estimator of feature f_i in category k
C_i	The set of categories contain feature f_i
$w_{i,d}$	The weight of feature f_i in document d
$W_{i,k}$	The weight of feature f_i in category k

Table 1. Symbols and their meanings

rules [3, 14, 15]. Although an improvement on classification accuracy is obtained, the computational cost is far more expensive then before.

2.2 Support Vector Machines

SVM is developed based on statistical learning theory for solving two-class pattern recognition problem [18]. Conceptually, it tries to generate a decision hyperplane that maximizes the margin between the positive and the negative examples in a training set. Mathematically, it requires minimizing the following quadratic programming [1]:

$$W(\alpha) = \frac{1}{2} \sum_{i,j} \alpha_i Q_{ij} \alpha_i - \sum_i \alpha_i + b \sum_i y_i \alpha_i \quad (2)$$

where Q_{ij} is the symmetric positive definite kernel matrix, b is the Lagrange multiplier and y_i equals 1 for positive training example and 0 otherwise.

The algorithm used for solving linearly separable case can be extended to solve linearly non-separable case by either introducing some soft margin hyperplans or mapping the original vectors to a higher dimensional space. Some efficient implementation of it include SVM^{light} by Joachims[2] and Sequential Minimal Optimization by Platt[3] [16].

Recent research shows that SVM achieves very high accuracy for text classification [9]. The major draw back of it is the very expensive training cost which is quadratic to the number of training instances. This leads to the problem for very large-scale learning or updating.

3 Discriminative Category Matching (DCM)

In this section, we introduce our novel text classification approach, the Discriminative Category Matching (DCM). Table 1 shows a list of symbols and their corresponding

[2] SVM^{light} is available at: http://svmlight.joachims.org/
[3] SMO is available at: http://research.microsoft.com/ jplatt/smo.html

meanings that will be used in the following discussions. Like existing works, we use a vector space model to represent a document and a category:

$$d = \langle f_{1,d} : w_{1,d}, f_{2,d} : w_{2,d}, \ldots, f_{n,d} : w_{n,d} \rangle \quad (3)$$
$$k = \langle f_{1,k} : W_{1,k}, f_{2,k} : W_{2,k}, \ldots, f_{m,k} : W_{m,k} \rangle (4)$$

Classification is achieved by finding the maximum similarity between d and k among all of the categories. The similarity is measured by the Jaccard coefficient:

$$S(d,k) = \frac{\sum_{i \in d}(w_{i,d} \cdot W_{i,k})}{\sum_{i \in d} w_{i,d}^2 + \sum_{i \in d} W_{i,k}^2 - \sum_{i \in d}(w_{i,d} \cdot W_{i,k})} \quad (5)$$

Jaccard coefficient expresses the degree of overlapping between the document and the category as the proportion of overlapping from the whole. It provides both intuitive and practical fitness to our model – matching a document with a category. Other measurements, such as cosine coefficient, may not be suitable as they will take the size of document and category into account.

Note that, in Equation (5), not all of the features in both the document and the category are compared. Only the features appearing in the document will be considered. In the following subsections, we present all other components in Equation (5) in details.

3.1 Weighting a Feature within a Document

The weight for the relative importance of f_i in d is:

$$w_{i,d} = \frac{\log_2(nf_{i,d} + 1)}{\log_2(l_d + 1)} \quad (6)$$

Here, the feature is assigned a higher weight if it appears frequently within a document. As pointed out in [2], a feature appearing n times cannot imply that it is n times more important. Thus, a logarithmic relationship rather than a linear relationship is taken. This actually follows the results in other studies [2, 4, 17], especially the one from Harman [5].

3.2 Weighting a Feature within a Category

The weight of f_i in k is:

$$W_{i,k} = AI_{i,k} \cdot \left(\frac{WC_{i,k}^2 \cdot CC_i^2}{\sqrt{WC_{i,k}^2 + CC_i^2}} \cdot \sqrt{2} \right) \quad (7)$$

Here, $\sqrt{2}$ is used for normalization such that $0 \leq W_{i,k} \leq 1$. The main components are: 1) the relative importance of $f_{i,k}$ ($WC_{i,k}$); 2) the relative importance of f_i among all categories (CC_i); and 3) the average importance of $f_{i,k}$ ($AI_{i,k}$). These components are further computed as follows:

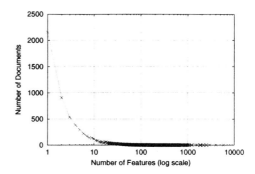

Figure 1. The distribution of $d_{i,k}$. Here k is the category *EARN* in *Reuters-21578*

$$WC_{i,k} = \frac{\log_2(df_{i,k} + 1)}{\log_2(N_k + 1)} \quad (8)$$

$$CC_i = \log \frac{N \cdot \max_{k \in C_i}\{WC_{i,k}\}}{\sum_{k=1}^{N} WC_{i,k}} \cdot \frac{1}{\log N} \quad (9)$$

$$AI_{i,k} = \left(\frac{\sum_{d \in k} w_{i,d}}{df_{i,k}} \right)^{\beta_{i,k}} \quad (10)$$

$$\beta_{i,k} = 2 - WC_{i,k} \quad (11)$$

The motivations of these equations are explained below. In order to demonstrate the effectiveness of DCM, the benchmark *Reuters-21578* is used for illustration and explanation. Extensive experiments have also been conducted, and are presented in Section 4.

3.2.1 The Relative Importance of a Feature in a Category ($WC_{i,k}$)

Documents belonging to the same category should inherit some common themes in nature, otherwise they would have no reasons to be grouped together. In other words, features that appear frequently within a category should be critical in term of classification. As a result, Equation (8) is formulated.

In Equation (8), both numerator and denominator are logarithmic. This is based on our observation that the frequency of a feature appearing over many documents is rare. Figure 1 illustrates this using the category *EARN* in *Reuters-21578*. In Figure 1, the probability of a feature that appears in many documents is very low. Similar finding is also reported in [6]. Figure 2 shows $d_{i,k}$ versus $WC_{i,k}$, where a linear shape is obtained. It shows that the number of features which appears in many documents and their corresponding importance form a logarithmic relationship.

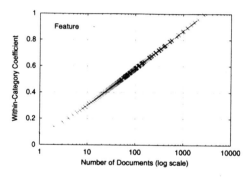

Figure 2. The relationship between $d_{i,k}$ and $WC_{i,k}$. Here k is the category *EARN* in *Reuters-21578*

Feature: *BARREL*			Feature: *REGULATION*		
Category	Occ.	Doc.	Category	Occ.	Doc.
ACQ	5	1595	ACQ	12	1595
CPU	1	54	CPI	1	54
CRUDE	140	253	CRUDE	1	253
EARN	7	2840	EARN	3	2840
FUEL	4	4	GAS	1	10
GAS	2	10	GOLD	1	70
GNP	2	59	GRAIN	3	41
HEAT	2	6	INTEREST	2	191
NAT-GAS	2	24	MONEY-FX	6	222
RETAIL	1	19	SUGAR	4	97
WPI	1	14	TRADE	7	251

Table 2. The distribution of two features, BARREL and REGULATION, in *Reuters-21578*.

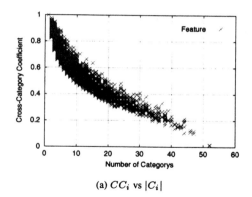

(a) CC_i vs $|C_i|$

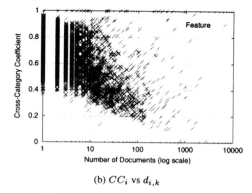

(b) CC_i vs $d_{i,k}$

Figure 3. The properties of CC_i

3.2.2 The Relative Importance of a Feature Across Categories (CC_i)

$WC_{i,k}$ above is designed to capture the information within category, but it cannot gain any global information about the feature distribution in the whole collection. However, having a global view across categories is very important. For instance, given two features, f_i and f_j, where f_i appears in more than half of the categories and f_j appears only in a few categories. Obviously, f_j provides far more precious information for text classification than f_i, because f_j has much higher discriminative power.

To be more specific, consider the feature REUTERS which appears over 5930 out of 6560 documents in 53 categories. Obviously, it does not have any value for classification. In other words, a feature is more valuable if its occurrence is skewed.

However, in computing the importance of a feature across categories, we argue that it is not realistic to weight the importance it by simply counting the number of categories that the feature appeared as suggested in [20]. As an example, the distribution of two features, BARREL and

REGULATION, is shown in Table 2. Both of them appeared in 11 categories. If we weight their importance by simply counting the number of categories they appeared, then both of them will be assigned to the same weight.

However, note that the occurrence of BARREL is skewed in the category *CRUDE*, whereas REGULATION is more or less evenly distributed. In other words, BARREL has a much higher discriminative power than REGULATION. Thus, BARREL should receive much higher weight. Unfortunately, there are no reported studies on how to weight the discriminative power of a feature for classification purposes. In this paper, we first propose a formula which weights features based on their discriminative power.

In Equation (9), the summation is used for gathering the total importance of a feature across all categories, while the maximum is used for averaging the summation value. If a feature is regarded as important in many categories, then this feature is obviously not important for classification. In other words, the higher the value of the numerator, the smaller the discriminative power is. The term, $1/\log(N)$, is used for normalization such that $0 \leq CC_i \leq 1$.

Figure 3 (a) shows the relationship between CC_i and $|C_i|$ and Figure 3 (b) shows the relationship between CC_i

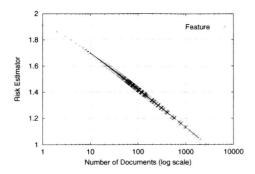

Figure 4. Risk estimator (β) versus document frequency ($d_{i,k}$)

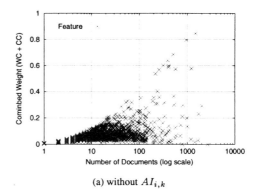

(a) without $AI_{i,k}$

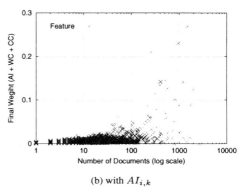

(b) with $AI_{i,k}$

Figure 5. The Effectiveness of $AI_{i,k}$

	with $AI_{i,k}$	without $AI_{i,k}$
Standard Dev.	0.008199	0.041573

Table 3. The standard deviation of $W_{i,k}$ with and without $AI_{i,k}$.

and $d_{i,k}$. The category *EARN* is used for illustration.

Figure 3 (a) shows a number of important properties of CC_i. First, CC_i tends to decrease while $d_{i,k}$ increases, as expected from Equation (9). Second, $CC_i \neq CC_j$ even if $|C_i| = |C_j|$. It is because the two features, f_i and f_j, appearing in the same number of categories do not necessarily have the same discriminative power. For references, CC_{BARREL} and $CC_{REGULATION}$ are 0.61 and 0.29, respectively.

Finally, although CC_i is computed by $WC_{i,k}$, which, in turn, depends on $d_{i,k}$, CC_i is in fact independent on $d_{i,k}$. No trends could be seen in Figure 3 (b). It is very important because if CC_i depends on $d_{i,k}$, the system may bias for those large size categories.

3.2.3 The Average Importance of a Feature in a Category ($AI_{i,k}$)

$WC_{i,k}$ and CC_i above are computed at the category level. However, the importance of a feature within an individual document has not yet been addressed. Thus, average-importance of a feature, is introduced. In Equation (10), the term within the bracket is to average the weights of f_i among all documents in k. The risk estimator, β, is used to determine the suitability of this average. The motivation of this estimator is based on the observation that: if there are more documents containing f_i, then this averaged value can be a better estimator for its true importance.

For instance, given two features: f_i and f_j, f_i appears in most documents but f_j appears in only a few documents. It is more confident to declare that the average for f_i is more likely to reflect the true status of it than that of f_j. Thus, the higher the β is, the higher the risk will be, and fewer documents will contain the corresponding feature.

Figure 4 shows the β values versus the number of documents containing f_i, which is decreasing linearly. If we remove β from the equation, a deteriorate result will be obtained. More details are given in Section 4.

Figure 5 shows the effectiveness of $AI_{i,k}$. The overall shape of both figures is very similar, but the points (features) in Figure 5 (b) are much denser. This is very important as the standard deviation of the weights among different features will be lowered. In other words, $AI_{i,k}$ can reduce the discrepancy among weights. This can increase the recall and precision of the model. Table 3 shows the effectiveness, with and without using of $AI_{i,k}$.

4 Experimental Studies

All of the experiments are conducted on a Sun Blade-1000 workstation with 512MB physical memory and a 750MHz Ultra-SPARC-III CPU running Solaris 2.8. All features are stemmed and converted to lower case, in which punctuation marks are removed, numbers and web page addresses are ignored.

Dataset	Training	Testing	Cat.	Features
Reuters-21578	6,560	2,568	52	13,270
TREC9-MeSH	5,182	26,327	154	25,245
Reuters News Collection	133,380	33,345	38	206,897

Table 4. A summary of the corpora used.

We compare DCM with NB and SVM. The standard measurement of recall and precision [2] are used. In order to have a harmonic average of them, F_1-measure is taken [21]:

$$F_1 = \frac{2 \times precision \times recall}{precision + recall} \quad (12)$$

We restrict the evaluation to single category classification: assigning a document to only one category. The full advantage of DCM is that it can continuous to learn whenever there is any new document arrives. We implement two versions of DCMs. The first version, denoted DCM, does not update once it is built. The second version, denoted DCM+, continues to learn whenever a new document is classified.

4.1 Datasets

The corpora used for evaluations are: *Reuters-21578*[4], *TREC9-MeSH*[5] and *Reuters News Collection*. They are summarized in Table 4 and their details are as follows:

- *Reuters-21578*: We take the ModApte-split and select documents that are assigned to one category such that each category has at least one document for training and one document for testing. Note that this collection is highly skewed: the largest category contains 2,840 training documents, while the smallest category contains only 1. About 85% of the categories contain less than 100 documents.
- *TREC9-MeSH*: It is a selected subset of *MeSH* categories in *Ohsumed233445*. The selection criteria are: 1) at least four relevant documents in the 1987 training data set; and 2) at least one relevant document in each year of the testing set. We further select documents that are assigned to one disease category.
- *Reuters News Collection*: It is a set of news articles that we have archived from Reuters directly from October 2000 to March 2002. Our task is to assign the news articles to one of the 38 Morgan Stanley Capital International (MSCI) category. Note that Reuters has already classified the articles to the correct categories. The news articles are ordered by broadcasting time. The first 80% is used for training while the remaining 20% is used for testing.

---

[4]http://kdd.ics.uci.edu
[5]http://trec.nist.gov

Method	M-Precision	M-Recall	M-F_1	m-F_1
NB	0.603	0.565	0.544	0.863
SVM	0.791	0.681	0.712	0.914
DCM	0.775	0.750	0.720	0.910
DCM+	**0.837**	**0.762**	**0.749**	**0.933**

Table 5. A summary of the evaluation results for *Reuters-21578*.

Method	M-Precision	M-Recall	M-F_1	m-F_1
NB	0.492	0.374	0.386	0.577
SVM	**0.662**	0.495	0.525	**0.692**
DCM	0.579	0.579	0.529	0.598
DCM+	0.595	**0.592**	**0.542**	0.600

Table 6. A summary of the evaluation results for *TREC9-MeSH*.

4.2 Evaluation using benchmarks

Table 5 and Table 6 summarized the accuracy for *Reuters-21578* and *TREC9-MeSH*, respectively. Four standard measurements are: macro-precision (M-Precision), macro-recall (M-Recall), macro-F_1 and micro-F_1 [21].

As shown in the tables, SVM outperforms NB significantly in both benchmarks. This replicates previous findings [9, 14, 23]. Comparing with SVM, DCM outperforms it in *Reuters-21578*. For *TREC9-MeSH*, DCM performs better at macro level, whereas SVM is better at micro level. This can be explained by the performance consistence of DCM over all categories with different sizes, as macro-measure looks at the global picture of the performance of all categories, while micro-measure favors the performance on large sized categories. However, a direct comparison between them is inappropriate as they focus on different aspects. Since neither SVM nor DCM dominate in both measures, we cannot conclude which approach is better in *TREC9-MeSH*. It all depends on which measurement one may concern with.

4.3 Scalability

In order to evaluate the scalability, CPU time in both training and operation phrase are measured by scaling up the *Reuters-21578* corpus with a factor of 10. Figure 6 shows the model training and testing CPU time (second).

In Figure 6 (a), the training time of SVM increases significantly with the number of training examples. This definitely leads to the problem of model updating for huge document collections. For NB, its advantages are the very low training and operational costs. However, the accuracy of it is the worst among all classifiers. For DCM, although its

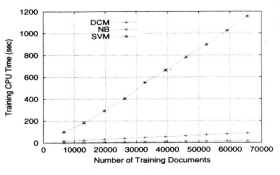

(a) Training Time

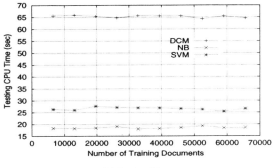

(b) Testing Time

Figure 6. The training and testing CPU time.

operational cost is highest, it still performs well.

4.4 Evaluation using real-life large collection

The scalability study in Section 4.3 shows the effectiveness and efficiency of DCM using *Reuters-21578*. However, as listed in Table 4, this dataset is rather small in size. The number of features are only 13,270. We further conducted another experiment using our *Reuters News Collection* which contains over 206,897 features. The numbers of training and testing documents are 133,380 and 33,345, respectively. Table 7 shows a summary of the classification accuracy.

NB does not perform well, as both F_1 values are less than 0.5. Among all, SVM performs the best in term of M-Precision and micro-F_1 measure, whereas DCM+ performs the best in term of M-Recall and macro-F_1 measure. In fact, in all of the corpora used, DCM always performs excellent with macro-measure. This gives a suggestion that those small-size categories may be more beneficial using DCM.

Method	M-Precision	M-Recall	M-F_1	m-F_1
NB	0.617	0.329	0.336	0.465
SVM	**0.758**	0.667	0.667	**0.779**
DCM	0.677	0.589	0.603	0.706
DCM+	0.721	**0.678**	**0.687**	0.730

Table 7. A summary of the evaluation results for *Reuters News Collection*.

Exp. No.	use $WC_{i,k}$	use CC_i	use $AI_{i,k}$
1	√	√	×
2	√	×	√
3	×	√	√
4	√	×	×
5	×	√	×
6	×	×	√
7	√	√	+
8	√	√	√

Table 8. $W_{i,k}$ Analysis.

4.5 The Combined Effectiveness of the Three Components Used in $W_{i,k}$

In this section, we examine the importance of each of the components, $WC_{i,k}$, CC_i and $AI_{i,k}$, in Equation (5). Eight experiments are conducted using *Reuters-21578* shown in Table 8. Here, a tick denotes that the corresponding component is included, whereas a cross denotes for ignorance. Experiment 7 is set up such that the three components are included but the risk estimator, β, is ignored. Experiment 8 uses all of the coefficients including the risk estimator.

The results of these experiments are shown in Table 9. Obviously, none of the settings can outperform Experiment 8 – using all of the components. Experiment 4 and 5 use either $WC_{i,k}$ or CC_i, and obtain extremely poor results. However, the accuracy of using both $WC_{i,k}$ and CC_i (Experiment 1) improves dramatically. For Experiment 7, ignoring the the risk estimator obtains inferior result, which explains the importance of it.

5 Conclusion

In this paper, we proposed a novel text classification approach, called discriminative category matching (DCM). DCM does not need to generate any sophisticated models but only requires simple statistical data. Furthermore, DCM can be updated immediately whenever a new document arrives.

For the computational time, DCM depends on the number of categories and the number of features in the collection. Online classification is highly feasible as the respond time is very short. For the data storage, DCM does not need

Method	M-Precision	M-Recall	M-F_1	m-F_1
1	0.797	0.589	0.650	0.892
2	0.772	0.589	0.637	0.903
3	0.808	0.657	0.709	0.911
4	0.213	0.183	0.158	0.136
5	0.143	0.068	0.075	0.142
6	0.736	0.548	0.603	0.898
7	0.626	0.390	0.452	0.820
8	**0.837**	**0.762**	**0.749**	**0.933**

Table 9. A comparison of using different combination of the coefficients.

to store the whole documents and only requires simple statistical data.

Two main advantages of DCM are: 1) it can train the model very efficiently regardless the size of the collection; and 2) it is able to deal with concept-drift by updating the newly received features with higher weights. Further investigations on these areas will be done.

In fact, most text classification approaches focus on the model generation and performance tuning. None of them try to discover the feature distribution within a collection. The detailed analysis on the characteristics of features presented here will certainly provide valuable guildlines for developing weighting schemes in text classification applications.

Acknowledgments

The work described in this paper was partially supported by grants from the Research Grants Council of the Hong Kong Special Administrative Region, China (CUHK4229/01E, DAG01/02.EG14).

References

[1] G. Cauwenberghs and T. Poggio. Incremental and decremental support vector machine learning. In *Proceedings of Advances in Neural Information Processing Systems*, pages 409–105, 2000.

[2] W. B. Frakes and R. Baeza-Yates. *Information Retrieval: Data Structures and Algorithms*. Prentice Hall PTR, 1992.

[3] N. Friedman, D. Giger, and M. Goldszmidt. Bayesian network classifiers. *Machine Learning*, 29(203):131–163, 1997.

[4] W. R. Greiff. A theory of term weighting based on exploratory data analysis. In *Proceedings of SIGIR-98 21th ACM International Conference on Research and Development in Information Retrieval*, pages 11–19, 1998.

[5] D. Harman. An experimental study of factors important in document ranking. In *Proceedings of SIGIR-86 9th International Conference on Research and Development in Information Retrieval*, pages 186–193, 1986.

[6] J. D. Holt and S. M. Chung. Efficient mining of association rules in text databases. In *Proceedings of 8th International Conference on Information and Knowledge Management*, pages 234–242, 1999.

[7] D. J. Ittner, D. D. Lewis, and D. D. Ahn. Text categorization of low quality images. In *Symposium on Document Analysis and Information Retrieval*, pages 301–315, 1995.

[8] T. Joachims. Text categorization with support vector machines: Learning with many relevant features. Technical Report LS-8-23, University of Dortmund, 1997.

[9] T. Joachims. Text categorization with support vector machines: Learning with many relevant features. In *Proceedings of 13th European Conference on Machine Learning*, pages 137–142, 1998.

[10] W. Lam and C. Y. Ho. Using a generalized instance set for automatic text categorization. In *Proceedings of SIGIR-98 21th ACM International Conference on Research and Development in Information Retrieval*, pages 81–89, 1998.

[11] D. D. Lewis. An evaluation of phrasal and clustered representations on a text categorization task. In *Proceedings of SIGIR-92 15th ACM International Conference on Research and Development in Information Retrieval*, pages 37–50, 1992.

[12] D. D. Lewis. Naive (bayes) at forty: The independence assumption in information retrieval. In *Proceedings of 13th European Conference on Machine Learning*, pages 4–15, 1998.

[13] A. McCallum and K. Nigam. A comparison of event models for naive bayes text classification. In *AAAI 1998 Workshop on Learning for Text Categorization*, 1998.

[14] D. Meretakis, D. Fragoudis, H. Lu, and S. Likothanassis. Scalable association-based text classification. In *Proceedings of 10th International Conference on Information and Knowledge Management*, pages 5–11, 2001.

[15] D. Meretakis, H. Lu, and B. Wuthrich. A study on the performance of large bayes classifier. In *Proceedings of 15th European Conference on Machine Learning*, pages 271–279, 2000.

[16] J. Platt. Sequential minimal optimization: A fast algorithm for training support vector machines. Technical Report MST-TR-98-14, Microsoft Research, 1998.

[17] G. Salton and C. Buckley. Term-weighting approaches in automatic text retrieval. *Information Processing and Management*, 24(5):513–523, 1988.

[18] V. Vapnik. *The Nature of Statistical Learning Theory*. Springer, 1995.

[19] I. H. Witten and E. Frank. *Data Mining: Practical Machine Learning Tools and Techniques with Java Implementations*. Morgan Kaufmann Publishers, 2000.

[20] K. Yamamoto, S. Masuyama, and S. Naito. Automatic text classification method with simple class-weighting approach. In *Natural Language Processing Pacific Rim Symposium*, 1995.

[21] Y. Yang. An evaluation of statistical approaches to text categorization. *Information Retrieval*, 1-2(1):69–90, 1999.

[22] Y. Yang. A study on thresholding strategies for text categorization. In *Proceedings of SIGIR-01 24th ACM International Conference on Research and Development in Information Retrieval*, pages 137–145, 2001.

[23] Y. Yang and X. Liu. A re-examination of text categorization methods. In *Proceedings of SIGIR-99 22th ACM International Conference on Research and Development in Information Retrieval*, pages 42–49, 1999.

Using Text Mining to Infer Semantic Attributes for Retail Data Mining

Rayid Ghani and Andrew E. Fano
Accenture Technology Labs,
161 N Clark St, Chicago, IL 60601
Rayid.Ghani, Andrew.E.Fano@accenture.com

Abstract

Current Data Mining techniques usually do not have a mechanism to automatically infer semantic features inherent in the data being "mined". The semantics are either injected in the initial stages (by feature construction) or by interpreting the results produced by the algorithms. Both of these techniques have proved effective but require a lot of human effort. In many domains, semantic information is implicitly available and can be extracted automatically to improve data mining systems. In this paper, we present a case study of a system that is trained to extract semantic features for apparel products and populate a knowledge base with these products and features. We show that semantic features of these items can be successfully extracted by applying text learning techniques to the descriptions obtained from websites of retailers. We also describe several applications of such a knowledge base of product semantics that we have built including recommender systems and competitive intelligence tools and provide evidence that our approach can successfully build a knowledge base with accurate facts which can then be used to create profiles of individual customers, groups of customers, or entire retail stores.

1 Introduction

Current Data Mining techniques usually do not automatically take into account the semantic features inherent in the data being "mined". In most data mining applications, a large amount of transactional data is analyzed without a systematic method for "understanding" the items in the transactions or what they say about the customers who purchased those items. The majority of algorithms used to analyze transaction records from retail stores treat the items in a market basket as objects and represent them as categorical values with no associated semantics. For example, in an apparel retail store transaction, a basket may contain a shirt, a tie and a jacket. When data mining algorithms such as association rules, decision trees, neural networks etc. are applied to this basket, they completely ignore what these items "mean" and the semantics associated with them. Instead, these items could just be replaced by distinct symbols, such as A, B and C or with apple, orange and banana for that matter, and the algorithms would produce the same results. The semantics of particular domains are injected into the data mining process in one of the following two stages: In the initial stage where the features to be used are constructed e.g. for decision trees or neural networks, feature engineering becomes an essential process that uses the domain knowledge of experts and provides it to the algorithm . The second instance where semantics are utilized is in interpreting the results. Once association rules or decision trees are generated and A and B are found to be correlated, the semantics are then used by humans to interpret them. Both of these methods of injecting semantics have been proved to be effective but at the same time are very costly and require a lot of human effort.

In many domains, semantic information is implicitly available and can be automatically extracted. In this paper, we describe a system that extracts semantic features for apparel products and populates a knowledge base with these products and features. We use apparel products and show that semantic features of these items can be successfully extracted by applying text learning techniques to the product names and descriptions obtained from websites of retailers. We also describe several applications of such a knowledge base of product semantics including recommender systems and competitive intelligence and provide evidence that our approach can successfully build a knowledge base with accurate facts which can then be used to create profiles of individual customers, groups of customers, or entire retail stores.

The work presented in this paper was motivated by discussions with CRM experts and retailers who currently analyze large amounts of transactional data but are unable to systematically understand the semantics of an item. For example, a clothing retailer would know that a particular customer bought a shirt and would also know the SKU, date, time, price, size, and color of a particular shirt that was purchased. While there is some value to this data, there is a lot of information not being captured that would facilitate understanding the tastes of the customer and enable a variety of applications. For example, is the shirt flashy or conservative? How trendy is it ? Is it casual or formal? These "softer" attributes that characterize products and the people who buy them tend not to be available for analysis in a systematic way.

In this paper, we describe our work on a system capable of inferring these kinds of attributes to enhance product databases. The system learns these attributes by applying text learning techniques to the product descriptions found on retailer web sites. This knowledge can be used to create profiles of individuals that can be used for recommendation systems that improve on traditional collaborative filtering approaches and can also be used to profile a retailer's positioning of their overall product assortment, how it changes over time, and how it compares to their competitors. Although the work described here is limited to the apparel domain and a particular set of features, we believe that this approach is relevant to a wider class of data mining problems and that extracting semantic clues and using them in data mining systems can add a potentially valuable dimension which existing data mining algorithms are not explicitly designed to handle.

2 Related Work

There has been some work in using textual sources to create knowledge bases consisting of objects and features associated with these objects. Craven et al.[3], as part of the WebKB group at Carnegie Mellon University built a system for crawling the Web (specifically, websites of CS departments in universities) and extract names of entities (students, faculty, courses, research projects, departments) and relations (course X is taught by faculty Y, faculty X is the advisor of student Y, etc.) by exploiting the content of the documents, as well as the link structure of the web. This system was used to populate a knowledge base in an effort to organize the Web into a more structured data source but the constructed knowledge base was not used to make any inferences. Recently, Ghani et al. [6] extended the WebKB framework by creating a knowledge base consisting of companies and associated features such as address, phone numbers, employee names, competitor names etc. extracted from semi-structured and free-text sources on the Web. They applied association rules, decision trees, relational learning algorithms to this knowledge base to infer facts about companies. Nahm & Mooney [11] also report some experiments with a hybrid system of rule-based and instance-based learning methods to discover soft-matching rules from textual databases automatically constructed via information extraction.

3 Overview of our approach

At a high level, our system deals with text associated with products to infer a predefined set of semantic features for each product. These features can generally be extracted from any information related to the product but in this paper, we only use the descriptions associated with each item. The features extracted are then used to populate a knowledge base, which we call the product semantics knowledge base. The process is described below.

1. Collect information about products

2. Define the set of features to be extracted

3. Label the data with values of the features

4. Train a classifier/extractor to use the labeled training data to now extract features from unseen data

5. Extract Semantic Features from new products by using the trained classifier/extractor

6. Populate a knowledge base with the products and corresponding features

4 Data Collection

We constructed a web crawler to visit web sites of several large apparel retail stores and extract names, urls, descriptions, prices and categories of all products available. This was done very cheaply by exploiting regularities in the html structure of the websites and manually writing wrappers[1]. We realize that this restricts the collection of data from websites where we can construct wrappers and although automatically extracting names and descriptions of products from arbitrary websites would be an interesting application area for information extraction or segmentation algorithms[14], we decided to take the manual approach. The extracted items and features were placed in a database and a random subset was chosen to be labeled.

5 Defining the set of features to extract

After discussions with domain experts, we defined a set of features that would be useful to extract for each product. We believe that the choice of features should be made with particular applications in mind and that extensive domain knowledge should be used. We currently infer values for 8 kinds of attributes for each item but are in the process of identifying more features that are potentially interesting. The features we use are Age Group, Functionality,

---

[1]In our case, the wrappers were simple regular expressions that took the html content of web pages into account and extracted specific pieces of information

196

Price point, Formality, Degree of Conservativeness, Degree of Sportiness, Degree of Trendiness, and Degree of Brand Appeal. More details including the possible values for each feature are given in Table 1.

The last four features (conservative, sportiness, trendiness, and brand appeal) have five possible values 1 to 5 where 1 corresponds to low and 5 is the highest (e.g. for trendiness, 1 would be not trendy at all and 5 would be extremely trendy).

6 Labeling Training Data

The data (product name, descriptions, categories, price) collected by crawling websites of apparel retailers was placed into a database and a small subset (600 products) was given to a group of fashion-aware people to label with respect to each of the features described in the previous section. They were presented with the description of the predefined set of features and the possible values that each feature could take (listed in Table 1).

7 Verifying Training Data

Since the data was divided into disjoint subsets and each subset was labeled by a different person, we wanted to make sure that the labeling done by each expert was consistent with the other experts and there were no glaring errors. One way to do that would be to now swap the subsets for each person and ask the other labelers to repeat the process on the other set. Obviously, this can get very expensive and we wanted to find a cheaper way to get a general idea of the consistency of the labeling process. For this purpose, we decided to generate association rules on the labeled data. We pooled all the data together and generated association rules between features of items using the apriori algorithm[1]. The particular implementation that we used was [2]. By treating each product as a transaction (basket) and the features as items in the basket, this scenario becomes analogous to the traditional market-basket analysis. For example, a product with some unique ID, say Polo V-Neck Shirt, which was labeled as Age Group: Teens, Functionality: Loungewear, Pricepoint: Average, Formality: Informal, Conservative: 3, Sportiness: 4, Trendiness:4, Brand Appeal: 4 becomes a basket with each feature value as an item. By using Apriori algorithm, we can derive a set of rules which relate multiple features over all products that were labeled. We ran apriori with both single and two-feature antecedents and consequents. Table 2 shows some sample rules that were generated.

By analyzing the association rules, we found a few inconsistencies in the labeling process where the labelers misunderstood the features. As we can see from Table 2, the

Table 2. Sample Association Rules

Rule	Support	Confidence
Informal <- Sportswear	24.5%	93.6%
Informal <- Loungewear	16.1%	82.3%
Informal <- Juniors	12.1%	89.4%
PricePoint=Ave <- BrandAppeal=2	8.8%	79.0%
BrandAppeal=5 <- Trendy=5	16.3%	91.2%
Sportswear <- Sporty=4	9.0%	85.7%
AgeGroup=Mature <- Trendy=1	9.4%	78.8%

association rules match our general intuition e.g. Apparel items labeled as informal were also labeled as sportswear and loungewear. Items with average prices did not have high brand appeal - this was probably because items with high brand appeal are usually more expensive. An interesting rule that was discovered was that items that were labeled as belonging to Mature Age group were also labeled as being not trendy at all.

Using association rules over the entire labeled data proved to be very useful in verifying the consistency of the labeling process done by several different labelers and we believe would be a useful tool for data verification in general where the labeling is performed by multiple people.

8 Training from the Labeled Data

We treat the learning problem as a traditional text classification problem and create one text classifier for each "semantic feature". For example, in the case of the Age Group feature, we classify the product into one of five classes (Juniors, Teens, GenX, Mature, All Ages). The initial algorithm used to perform this classification was Naive Bayes and a description is given below.

8.1 Naive Bayes

Naive Bayes is a simple but effective text classification algorithm[10, 9]. Naive Bayes defines an underlying generative model where, first a class is selected according to class prior probabilities. Then, the generator creates each word in a document by drawing from a multinomial distribution over words specific to the class. Thus, this model assumes each word in a document is generated independently of the others given the class. Naive Bayes forms maximum a posteriori estimates for the class-conditional probabilities for each word in the vocabulary V from labeled training data D. This is done by counting the frequency that word w_t occurs in all word occurrences for documents d_i in class c_j, supplemented with Laplace smoothing to avoid probabilities of zero:

Table 1. Details of features extracted from each product description

Feature Name	Possible Values	Description
Age Group	Juniors, Teens, GenX, Mature, All Ages	For what ages is this item most appropriate?
Functionality	Loungewear, Sportswear, Eveningwear, Business Casual, Business Formal	How will the item be used?
Pricepoint	Discount, Average, Luxury	Compared to other items of this kind is this item cheap or expensive?
Formality	Informal , Somewhat Formal, Very Formal	How formal is this item?
Conservative	1(gray suits) to 5 (Loud, flashy clothes)	Does this suggest the person is conservative or flashy?
Sportiness	1 to 5	
Trendiness	1 (Timeless Classic) to 5 (Current favorite)	Is this item popular now but likely to go out of style? or is it more timeless?
Brand Appeal	1(Brand makes the product unappealing) to 5 (high brand appeal)	Is the brand known and makes it appealing?

$$\Pr(w_t|c_j) = \frac{1 + \sum_{i=1}^{|\mathcal{D}|} N(w_t, d_i) \Pr(c_j|d_i)}{|V| + \sum_{s=1}^{|V|} \sum_{i=1}^{|\mathcal{D}|} N(w_s, d_i) \Pr(c_j|d_i)},$$

(1)

where $N(w_t, d_i)$ is the count of the number of times word w_t occurs in document d_i, and where $\Pr(c_j|d_i) \in \{0, 1\}$ as given by the class label.

At classification time we use these estimated parameters by applying Bayes' rule to calculate the probability of each class.

$$\begin{aligned} \Pr(c_j|d_i) &\propto \Pr(c_j) \Pr(d_i|c_j) \\ &= \Pr(c_j) \prod_{k=1}^{|d_i|} \Pr(w_{d_{i,k}}|c_j). \end{aligned}$$

(2)

8.2 Incorporating Unlabeled Data using EM

In our initial data collection phase, we collected names and descriptions of thousands of women's apparel items from websites. Since the labeling process was expensive, we only labeled about 600 of those, leaving the rest as unlabeled. Recently, there has been much recent interest in supervised learning algorithms that combine information from labeled and unlabeled data. Such approaches include using Expectation-Maximization to estimate maximum a posteriori parameters of a generative model [12], using a generative model built from unlabeled data to perform discriminative classification [7], and using transductive inference for support vector machines to optimize performance on a

specific test set [8]. These results have shown that using unlabeled data can significantly decrease classification error, especially when labeled training data are sparse.

For the case of textual data in general, and product descriptions in particular, obtaining the data is very cheap. A simple crawler can be build and large amounts of unlabeled data can be collected for very little cost. Since we had a large number of product descriptions that were collected but unlabeled, we decided to use the Expectation-Maximization algorithm to combine labeled and unlabeled data for our task.

8.2.1 Expectation-Maximization

If we extend the supervised learning setting to include unlabeled data, the naive Bayes equations presented above are no longer adequate to find maximum a posteriori parameter estimates. The Expectation-Maximization (EM) technique can be used to find locally maximum parameter estimates.

EM is an iterative statistical technique for maximum likelihood estimation in problems with incomplete data [4]. Given a model of data generation, and data with some missing values, EM will locally maximize the likelihood of the parameters and give estimates for the missing values. The naive Bayes generative model allows for the application of EM for parameter estimation. In our scenario, the class labels of the unlabeled data are treated as the missing values.

EM is an iterative two-step process. Initial parameter estimates are set using standard naive Bayes from just the labeled documents. Then we iterate the E- and M-steps. The E-step calculates probabilistically-weighted class labels, $\Pr(c_j|d_i)$, for every unlabeled document using Equation 2. The M-step estimates new classifier parameters using all the documents, by Equation 1, where $\Pr(c_j|d_i)$ is now continuous, as given by the E-step. We iterate the E- and M-steps until the classifier converges.

9 Experimental Results

In order to evaluate the effectiveness of the algorithms described above for building an accurate knowledge base, we calculated classification accuracies using the labeled product descriptions and 5 fold cross-validation. The evaluation was performed for each attribute and the table below reports the accuracies. The first row in the table (baseline) gives the accuracies if the most frequent attribute value was predicted as the correct class. The experiments with Expectation-Maximization were run with the same amount of labeled data as Naive Bayes but with an additional 3500 unlabeled product descriptions.

Looking at Table 3, we can see that Naive Bayes outperforms our baseline for all the attributes. Using unlabeled data and combining it from the initially labeled product descriptions with EM helps improve the accuracy even further. To get a qualitative and intuitive feel for the performance of these algorithms and for the effectiveness of our approach, Table 4 gives a list of words which had high weights for some of the features that we used the naive bayes classifier to extract. There words were selected by scoring all the words according to their log-odds-ratio scores and picking the top 10 words. Looking at the words gives us a qualitative and intuitive idea of what type of words are indicative of each attribute and verifies our initial hypothesis that the marketing language associated with product does correspond to these softer attributes that we are trying to infer.

9.1 Results on a new test set

The results reported earlier in Table 3 are extremely encouraging but are indicative of the performance of the algorithms on a test set that follows a similar distribution as the training set. Since we first extracted and labeled product descriptions from a retail website and then used subsets of that data for training and testing (using 5 fold cross-validation), the results may not hold for test data that is drawn from a different distribution or a different retailer.

The results we report in Table 5 are obtained by training the algorithm on the same labeled data set as before but testing it on a small (125 items) new labeled data set collected from a variety of retailers. As we can observe, the results are consistently better than baseline and in some cases, even better than in Table 3. This results enables us to hypothesize that our system can be applied to a wide variety of data and can adapt to different distributions of test sets using the unlabeled data.

10 Applications

The knowledge base (KB) constructed by labeling unseen products has several applications. In this section, we describe some concrete applications that we have developed. The KB can be used to create profiles of individuals that can be used for recommender systems that improve on traditional collaborative filtering approaches and can also be used to profile a retailer's positioning of their overall product assortment, how it changes over time, and how it compares to their competitors.

10.1 Recommender systems

Being able to analyze the text associated with products and map it to the set of predefined semantic features in real-time gives us the ability to create instant profiles of customers shopping in an online store. As the shopper browses products in a store, the system running in the background can extract the name and description of the items and using the trained classifiers, can infer semantic features of that product. This process can be used create instant profiles based on viewed items without knowing the identity of the shopper or the need to retrieve previous transaction data. This can be used to suggest subsequent products to new and infrequent customers for whom past transactional data may not be available. Of course, if historical data is available, our system can use that to build a better profile and recommend potentially more targeted products. We believe that this ability to engage and target new customers tackles one of the challenges currently faced by commercial recommender systems [13] and can help retain new customers.

We have built a prototype of a recommender system for women's apparel items by using our knowledge base of product semantics. More details about the recommender system can be found in [5].The knowledge base is populated with thousands of items and their associated semantic attributes inferred by the learning algorithm described in earlier sections. Our system monitors the browsing behavior of user browsing a retailer's website and in real-time, extracts names and descriptions of products that they browse. The description text is then passed through our learned models and the semantic attributes of the products are inferred. For each product browsed, our system calculates $P(A_{i,j}|Product)\forall i, j$, where $A_{i,j}$ is the jth value of the ith attribute. The attributes are the semantic features described in Table 1 and the possible values for each attribute are also listed in the table. The user profile is constructed by combining these probabilities for each product browsed: User Profile =

$$\Pr(U_{i,j}|PastNItems) = \frac{1}{N}\sum_{k=1}^{N}\Pr(A_{i,j}|Item_k) \quad (3)$$

Table 3. Classification accuracies for each attribute using 5 fold cross-validation. Naive Bayes uses only labeled data and EM uses both labeled and unlabeled data.

Algorithm	AgeGroup	Functionality	Formality	Conservative	Sportiness	Trendiness	BrandAppeal
Baseline	29%	24%	68%	39%	49%	29%	36%
Naive Bayes	66%	57%	76%	80%	70%	69%	82%
EM	78%	70%	82%	84%	78%	80%	91%

Table 4. For each class, the table shows the ten words that are most highly weighted by one of our learned models. The weights shown represent the weighted log-odds ratio of the words given the class.

Brand Appeal=5(high)	Conservative=5(high)	Conservative=1(low)	Formality=Informal	Somewhat Formal
lauren	lauren	rose	jean	jacket
ralph	ralph	special	tommy	fully
dkny	breasted	leopard	jeans	button
kenneth	seasonless	chemise	denim	skirt
cole	trouser	straps	sweater	lines
imported	jones	flirty	pocket	york
	sport	spray	neck	seam
	classic	silk	tee	crepe
	blazer	platform	hilfiger	leather

agegroup=juniors	Functionality=Loungewear	Functionality=Partywear	Sportiness=5(high)	Trendiness=1(low)
jrs	chemise	rock	sneaker	lauren
dkny	silk	dress	camp	seasonless
jeans	kimono	sateen	base	breasted
tee	calvin	length:	rubber	trouser
collegiate	klein	skirt	sole	pocket
logo	august	shirtdress	white	carefree
tommy	lounge	open	miraclesuit	ralph
polo	hilfiger	platform	athletic	blazer
short	robe	plaid	nylon	button
sneaker	gown	flower	mesh	

Table 5. Classification accuracies when trained on the same labeled data as before but tested on a new set of test data that is collected from a new set of retailers

Algorithm	AgeGroup	Functionality	Formality	Conservative	Sportiness	Trendiness	BrandAppeal
Naive Bayes	83%	45%	61%	70%	81%	80%	87%

The user profile is stored in terms of probabilities for each attribute value which allows us flexibility to include mixture models in future work in addition to being more robust to changes over time.

As the user browses products, the system compares the evolving profile against the products in the knowledge base, which has products classified into the same taxonomy of semantic features, and recommends the closest matching ones. Currently, we give equal weight to all products browsed when constructing the profile. In future work, we plan to experiment with different weighting schemes such as weighting recent items more than older ones.

There are two prevalent approaches to building recommender systems : Collaborative Filtering and Content-based. Collaborative Filtering systems work by collecting user feedback in the form of ratings for items in a given domain and exploit similarities and differences among profiles of several users to recommend an item. It recommends other items bought by people who also bought the current item of interest and completely ignores "what" the current item of interest was. Collaborative Filtering approaches suffer from two main problems: the "sparsity" problem that most customers do not browse or buy most products in a store and the "New Item" problem that a new product cannot be recommended to any customer until it has been browsed by a large enough number of customers. On the other hand, content-based methods provide recommendations by comparing representations of content contained in an item to representations of content that interests the user. A main criticism of content-based recommendation systems is that the recommendations provided are not very diverse. Since the system is powered solely by the user's preferences and the descriptions of the items browsed, it tends to recommend items "too" similar to the previous items of interest.

This type of recommender system improves on collaborative filtering as it would work for new products which users haven't browsed yet and can also present the user with explanations as to why they were recommended certain products (in terms of the semantic attributes). We believe that our system also performs better than standard content-based systems. Although content-based systems also use the words in the descriptions of the items, they traditionally use those words to learn one scoring function. For example, a classical content-based recommendation engine takes the text from the descriptions of all the items that user has browsed or bought and learns a model (usually a binary target function: "recommend" or "not recommend"). In contrast, our system changes the feature space from words (thousands of features) to the eight semantic attributes. This still enables us to recommend a wide variety of products unlike most content-based systems. Another potential advantage of our system is its ability to suggests products across categories (i.e. apparel styles may be predictive of furniture,

for example) which content-based systems are not able to do.

Since our goal was not to build the best recommendation system but rather to demonstrate the potential of a knowledge base of product semantics, we did not explore many approaches to building a user's profile. In future work, we plan to tackle the cases where a user's profile consists of a number of separate profiles. For example, if a user is looking for something for herself and also for her son, our system should be able to recognize that the items that the user is buying or browsing are inherently different. This could be done through mixture models where we construct a profile using a mixture of different profiles. Another potential solution is to monitor the users profile as they browse more and more products. Since each product can be though of as a point in an n-dimensional Euclidean space (where n is the number of features, in our case, 8), we can calculate the distance of a new product from the current profile of the user. If a new product is "very" different from the current profile of the user (using thresholds based on cross-validation), it can be placed in a separate profile or treated as an outlier. We also plan to conduct user studies to validate the effectiveness of such a recommendation system based on these intermediate-level semantic features.

10.2 Store Profiling

Product recommendations are just one application that we have built so far. We also have a prototype that profiles retailers to build competitive intelligence applications. For example, by closely tracking the product offerings we can notice changes in the positioning of a retailer. We can track changes in the industry as a whole or specific competitors and compare it to the performance of retailers. By profiling their aggregate offerings, our system can enable retailers to notice changes in the positioning of product lines by competitor retailers and manufacturers. This ability to profile retailers enables strategic applications such as competitive comparisons, monitoring brand positioning, tracking trends over time, etc.

11 Conclusions and Future Work

We described our work on a system capable of inferring semantic attributes of products enabling us to enhance product databases for retailers. The system learns these attributes by applying supervised and semi-supervised learning techniques to the product descriptions found on retailer web sites. One of the main assumptions we make is the descriptions associated with the products accurately convey the semantic attributes. We believe that this assumption is justified because in most cases these descriptions are written by marketers to position the product in the consumer's mind in a manner that implicitly suggests these softer attributes. The system can be bootstrapped from a small number of labeled training examples utilizes the large number of cheaply obtainable unlabeled examples (product descriptions) available from retail websites.

In the prototype we have built at Accenture Technology Labs, we currently have several applications for this type of a knowledge base. We use it to create profiles of individuals that can be used for recommendation systems that improve on traditional collaborative filtering approaches. The ability to infer the semantics of products can also be used to profile a retailer's positioning of their overall product assortment, how it changes over time, and how it compares to their competitors. Although the work described here is limited to the apparel domain and a particular set of features, we believe that this approach is relevant to a wider class of data mining problems. We believe that by going beyond the immediately available data, such as the fact that a customer is looking at or bought a product, and paying attention to what these products mean, we can increase the effectiveness of data mining applications.

References

[1] R. Agrawal, H. Mannila, R. Srikant, H. Toivonen, and A. I. Verkamo. Fast discovery of association rules. In U. Fayyad, G. Piatetsky-Shapiro, P. Smyth, and R. Uthurusamy, editors, *Advances in Knowledge Discovery and Data Mining, AAAI Press/The MIT Press*, pages 307–328, 1996.

[2] C. Borgelt. apriori. `http://fuzzy.cs.Uni-Magdeburg.de/~borgelt/`.

[3] M. Craven, D. DiPasquo, D. Freitag, A. McCallum, T. Mitchell, K. Nigam, and S. Slattery. Learning to construct knowledge bases from the world wide web. *Artificial Intelligence*, 118(1-2):69–114, 2000.

[4] A. P. Dempster, N. M. Laird, and D. B. Rubin. Maximum likelihood from incomplete data via the EM algorithm. *Journal of the Royal Statistical Society, Series B*, 39(1):1–38, 1977.

[5] R. Ghani and A. E. Fano. Building recommender systems using a knowledge base of product semantics. In *Proceedings of the Workshop on Recommendation and Personalization in ECommerce at the 2nd International Conference on Adaptive Hypermedia and Adaptive Web based Systems*, 2002.

[6] R. Ghani, R. Jones, D. Mladenic, K. Nigam, and S. Slattery. Data mining on symbolic knowledge extracted from the web. In *Workshop on Text Mining at the Sixth ACM SIGKDD International Conference on Knowledge Discovery and Data Mining*, 2000.

[7] T. Jaakkola and D. Haussler. Exploiting generative models in discriminative classifiers. In *Advances in NIPS 11*, 1999.

[8] T. Joachims. Transductive inference for text classification using support vector machines. In *Machine Learning: Proceedings of the Sixteenth International Conference*, 1999.

[9] D. D. Lewis. Naive (Bayes) at forty: The independence assumption in information retrieval. In *Machine Learning: ECML-98, Tenth European Conference on Machine Learning*, pages 4–15, 1998.

[10] A. McCallum and K. Nigam. A comparison of event models for naive Bayes text classification. In *Learning for Text Categorization: Papers from the AAAI Workshop*, pages 41–48, 1998. Tech. rep. WS-98-05, AAAI Press.

[11] U. Y. Nahm and R. J. Mooney. Text mining with information extraction. In *AAAI 2002 Spring Symposium on Mining Answers from Texts and Knowledge Bases*, 2002.

[12] K. Nigam, A. McCallum, S. Thrun, and T. Mitchell. Text classification from labeled and unlabeled documents using EM. *Machine Learning*, 39(2/3):103–134, 2000.

[13] J. Schafer, J. Konstan, and J. Riedl. Electronic commerce recommender applications. *Journal of Data Mining and Knowledge Discovery*, 5:115–152, 2000.

[14] K. Seymore, A. McCallum, and R. Rosenfeld. Learning hidden Markov model structure for information extraction. In *Machine Learning for Information Extraction: Papers from the AAAI Workshop*, 1999. Tech. rep. WS-99-11, AAAI Press.

Phrase-based Document Similarity Based on an Index Graph Model

Khaled M. Hammouda   Mohamed S. Kamel

Department of Systems Design Engineering
University of Waterloo
Waterloo, Ontario, Canada N2L 3G1
E-mail: {hammouda,mkamel}@pami.uwaterloo.ca

Abstract

Document clustering techniques mostly rely on single term analysis of the document data set, such as the Vector Space Model. To better capture the structure of documents, the underlying data model should be able to represent the phrases in the document as well as single terms. We present a novel data model, the Document Index Graph, which indexes web documents based on phrases, rather than single terms only. The semi-structured web documents help in identifying potential phrases that when matched with other documents indicate strong similarity between the documents. The Document Index Graph captures this information, and finding significant matching phrases between documents becomes easy and efficient with such model. The similarity between documents is based on both single term weights and matching phrases weights. The combined similarities are used with standard document clustering techniques to test their effect on the clustering quality. Experimental results show that our phrase-based similarity, combined with single-term similarity measures, enhances web document clustering quality significantly.

1. Introduction

In an effort to keep up with the tremendous growth of the World Wide Web, many research projects target the organization of such information in a way that will make it easier for the end users to find the information they want efficiently and accurately. Information on the web is present in the form of text documents (formatted in HTML), and that is the reason many web document processing systems are rooted in text data mining techniques.

Text data mining shares many concepts with traditional data mining methods. Data mining includes many techniques that can unveil inherent structure in the underlying data. One of these techniques is clustering. Applied to text data, clustering methods try to identify inherent groupings of the text documents so that a set of clusters are produced in which clusters exhibit high intra-cluster similarity and low inter-cluster similarity [2]. Generally speaking, text document clustering methods attempt to segregate the documents into groups where each group represents some topic that is different than those topics represented by the other groups [3]. By applying text mining in the web domain, the process becomes what is known as *web mining*. There are three types of web mining in general, according to Kosala *et al* [9]: (1) web structure mining; (2) web usage mining; and (3) web content mining. We are mainly interested in the last type, web content mining.

Any clustering technique relies on four concepts: (1) a data representation model, (2) a similarity measure, (3) a cluster model, and (4) a clustering algorithm that builds the clusters using the data model and the similarity measure. Most of the document clustering methods that are in use today are based on the Vector Space Model [1, 14, 13], which is a very widely used data model for text classification and clustering. The Vector Space Model represents documents as a feature vector of the terms (words) that appear in all the document set. Each feature vector contains term-weights (usually term-frequencies) of the terms appearing in that document. Similarity between documents is measured using one of several similarity measures that are based on such a feature vector. Examples include the *cosine* measure and the *Jaccard* measure. Clustering methods based on this model make use of single-term analysis only, they do not make use of any word proximity or phrase-based analysis[1]. The motivation behind the work in this paper is that we believe that document clustering should be based not only on single word analysis, but on phrases as well.

The work that has been reported in literature about using phrases in document clustering is limited. Most efforts have been targeted toward single-word analysis. The methods used for text clustering includes decision trees [11], statistical analysis [4], neural nets [5], inductive logic program-

---

[1] Throughout this paper the term "phrase" means a sequence of words, and not the grammatical structure of a sentence.

ming [8], and rule-based systems [15] among others. These methods are at the cross roads of more than one research area, such as database (DB), information retrieval (IR), and artificial intelligence (AI) including machine learning (ML) and Natural Language Processing (NLP).

The most relevant work to what is presented here is that of Oren Zamir *et al* [19, 20]. They proposed a phrase-based document clustering approach based on Suffix Tree Clustering (STC). The method basically involves the use of a "trie" (a compact tree) structure to represent shared suffixes between documents. Based on these shared suffixes they identify base clusters of documents, which are then combined into final clusters based on a connected-component graph algorithm. They claim to achieve $n \log(n)$ performance and produce high quality clusters. The results they showed were encouraging, but the suffix tree model could be argued to have a high number of redundancies in terms of the suffixes stored in the tree.

In this paper we propose a novel document representation model, the Document Index Graph (DIG) that captures the structure of sentences in the document set, rather than single words only. The DIG model is based on graph theory and utilizes graph properties to match any-length phrase from a document to any number of previously seen documents in a time nearly proportional to the number of words of the new document. This means that when a new document is introduced to the system, we can detect any-length phrase match from this document to all the previously seen documents in the data set by just scanning the new document and extracting the matching phrases from the document index graph.

The above model is used to measure the similarity between the documents using a new similarity measure that makes use of phrase-based matching. This similarity measure over-performs similarity measures that are based on single-word models only. The similarity calculation between documents is based on a combination of single-term similarity and phrase-based similarity. Similarity based on matching phrases between documents is proved to have a more significant effect on the clustering quality due to its insensitivity to noisy terms that could lead to incorrect similarity measure. Phrases are less sensitive to noise when it comes to calculating document similarity; this is due to the fact that it is less likely to find matching phrases in non-related documents (see section 4.1).

The clusters produced using this similarity combination were of higher quality than those produced using single-term similarity only. We relied on two clustering quality measures, the F-measure, and the Entropy of the clusters. Both of these quality measures were improved when phrase-similarity was introduced to the different clustering algorithms.

The rest of this paper is organized as follows. Section 2 discusses the important features of the semi-structured web documents. Section 3 introduces the Document Index Graph model. Section 4 presents the phrase-based similarity measure. Section 5 presents our experimental results. Finally we conclude and discuss future work in the last section.

2. Web document structure analysis

Web documents are known to be semi-structured. Since the HTML language is meant for specifying the layout of the document, it is used to present the document to the user in a friendly manner, rather than specify the structure of the data in the document, hence they are semi-structured. However, it is still possible to identify key parts of the document based on this structure. The idea is that some parts of the document are more informative than other parts, thus having different levels of significance based on where they appear in the document and the tags that surround them. It is less informing to treat the title of the document, for example, and the text body equally.

The proposed system analyzes the HTML document and restructures the document according into a predetermined structure that assigns different levels of significance to different document parts. The result is a well structured XML document that corresponds to the original HTML document, but with the significance levels assigned to the different parts of the original document.

Currently we assign one of three levels of significance to the different parts; HIGH, MEDIUM, and LOW. Examples of HIGH significance parts are the title, meta keywords, meta description, and section headings. Example of MEDIUM significance parts are text that appear in bold, italics, colored, hyper-linked text, image alternate text, and table captions. LOW significance parts are usually comprised of the document body text that was not assigned any of the other levels.

This structuring scheme is exploited in measuring the similarity between two documents (see section 4 for details). For example, if we have a phrase match of HIGH significance in both documents, the similarity is rewarded more than if the match was for LOW significance phrases. This is justified by arguing that a phrase match in titles, for example, is much more informative than a phrase match in body text.

A sentence boundary detector algorithm was developed to locate sentence boundaries in the documents. The algorithm is based on a finite state machine lexical analyzer with heuristic rules for finding the boundaries. Finally, a document cleaning step is performed to remove stop-words that have no significance, and to stem the words using the popular Porter Stemmer algorithm [12].

3. Document index graph

The vector space model does not represent any relation between the words, so sentences are broken down into their individual components without any representation of the sentence structure. On the other hand, the proposed Document Index Graph (DIG for short) indexes the documents while maintaining the sentence structure in the original documents. This allows us to make use of more informative phrase matching rather than individual words matching. Moreover, the DIG also captures the different levels of significance of the original sentences, thus allowing us to make use of sentence significance as well.

3.1. DIG structure

The DIG is a directed graph (digraph) $G = (V, E)$

where V: is a set of *nodes* $\{v_1, v_2, \ldots, v_n\}$, where each node v represents a unique word in the entire document set; and

E: is a set of *edges* $\{e_1, e_2, \ldots, e_m\}$, such that each edge e is an ordered pair of nodes (v_i, v_j). Edge (v_i, v_j) is from v_i to v_j, and v_j is adjacent to v_i. There will be an edge from v_i to v_j if, and only if, the word v_j appears successive to the word v_i in any document.

The above definition of the graph suggests that the number of nodes in the graph is the number of unique words in the document set; *i.e.* the vocabulary of the document set, since each node represents a single word in the whole document set.

Nodes in the graph carry information about the documents they appeared in, along with the sentence path information. Sentence structure is maintained by recording the edge along which each sentence continues. This essentially creates an inverted list of the documents, but with sentence information recorded in the inverted list.

Assume a sentence of m words appearing in one document consists of the following word sequence: $\{v_1, v_2, \ldots, v_m\}$. The sentence is represented in the graph by a path from v_1 to v_m, such that $(v_1, v_2)(v_2, v_3), \ldots, (v_{m-1}, v_m)$ are edges in the graph. Path information is stored in the vertices along the path to uniquely identify each sentence. Sentences that share sub-phrases will have shared parts of their paths in the graph that correspond to the shared sub-phrase.

The structure maintained in each node is a table of documents. Each document entry in the document table records the term frequency of the word in that document. Since words can appear in different parts of a document with different level of significance, the recorded term frequency is

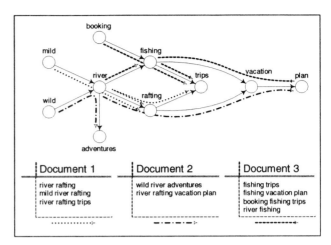

Figure 1. Example of the Document Index Graph

actually broken into those levels of significance, with a frequency count per level per document entry. This structure helps in achieving a more accurate similarity measure based on level of significance later on.

Since the graph is directed, each node maintains a list of an outgoing edges per document entry. This list of edges tells us which sentence continues along which edge. The task of creating a sentence path in the graph is thus reduced to recording the necessary information in this edge table to reflect the structure of the sentences.

To better illustrate the graph structure, Figure 1 presents a simple example graph that represents three documents. Each document contains a number of sentences with some overlap between the documents. As seen from the graph, an edge is created between two nodes only if the words represented by the two nodes appear successive in any document. Thus, sentences map into paths in the graph. Dotted lines represent sentences from document 1, dash-dotted lines represent sentences from document 2, and dashed lines represent sentences from document 3. If a phrase appears more than once in a document, the frequency of the individual words making up the phrase is increased, and the sentence information in the nodes reflects the multiple occurrence of such phrase. As mentioned earlier, matching phrases between documents becomes a task of finding shared paths in the graph between different documents.

The example presented here is a simple one. Real web documents will contain hundreds or thousands of words. With a very large document set, the graph could become more complex in terms of memory usage. Typically, the number of graph nodes will be exactly the same as the number of unique words in the data set. The number of edges is

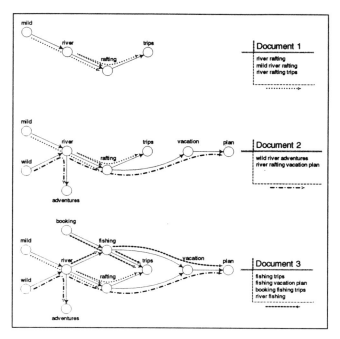

Figure 2. Incremental construction of the Document Index Graph

Algorithm 1 Document Index Graph construction and phrase matching

1: $D \leftarrow$ New Document
2: **for** each sentence s in D **do**
3:     $w_1 \leftarrow$ first word in s
4:     **if** w_1 is not in G **then**
5:         Add w_1 to G
6:     **end if**
7:     $L \leftarrow$ Empty List $\{L$ is a list of matching phrases$\}$
8:     **for** each word $w_i \in \{w_2, w_3, \ldots, w_k\}$ in s **do**
9:         **if** (w_{i-1}, w_i) is an edge in G **then**
10:             Extend phrase matches in L for sentences that continue along (w_{i-1}, w_i)
11:             Add new phrase matches to L
12:         **else**
13:             Add edge(w_{i-1}, w_i) to G
14:             Update sentence path in nodes w_{i-1} and w_i
15:         **end if**
16:     **end for**
17: **end for**
18: Output matching phrases in L

about 4 to 6 times the number of nodes (that is the average degree of a node).

3.2. Constructing the graph

The DIG is built incrementally by processing one document at a time. When a new document is introduced, it is scanned in sequential fashion, and the graph is updated with the new sentence information as necessary. New words are added to the graph as necessary and connected with other nodes to reflect the sentence structure. The graph building process becomes less memory demanding when no new words are introduced by a new document (or very few new words are introduced). At this point the graph becomes more stable, and the only operation needed is to update the sentence structure in the graph to accommodate for the new sentences introduced. It is very critical to note that introducing a new document will only require the inspection (or addition) of those words that appear in that document, and not every node in the graph. This is where the efficiency of the model comes from.

Along with indexing the sentence structure, the level of significance of each sentence is also recorded in the graph. This allows us to recall such information when we match sentences from other documents.

Continuing from the example introduced earlier, the process of constructing the graph that represents the three documents is illustrated in Figure 3.1. The emphasis here is on the incremental construction process, where new nodes are added and new edges are created incrementally upon introducing a new document.

Unlike traditional phrase matching techniques that are usually used in information retrieval literature, the DIG provides complete information about full phrase matching between *every* pair of documents. While traditional phrase matching methods are aimed at searching and retrieval of documents that have matching phrases to a specific query, the DIG is aimed at providing information about the degree of overlap between every pair of documents. This information will help in determining the degree of similarity between documents as will be explained in section 4.

3.3. Detecting matching phrases

Upon introducing a new document, finding matching phrases from previously seen documents becomes an easy task using the DIG. Algorithm 1 describes the process of both incremental graph building and phrase matching.

The procedure starts with a new document to process (line 1). We expect the new document to have well defined sentence boundaries; each sentence is processed individually. This is important because we do not want to match a phrase that spans two sentences (which could break the local context we are looking for.) It is also important to know the original sentence length so that it will be used in the similarity calculation (section 4). For each sentence (for loop at line 2) we process the words in the sentence sequentially, adding new words as new nodes to the graph, and constructing a path in the graph (by adding new edges if necessary) to represent the sentence we are processing. At the beginning of each sentence we locate the first word of the sentence in the graph by consulting a hash table. If the word is in the graph, we continue from that node, otherwise we add it to the graph and link it to other nodes as necessary.

Matching the phrases from previous documents is done by keeping a list L that holds an entry for every previous document that shares a phrase with the current document D. As we continue along the sentence path, we update L by adding new matching phrases and their respective document identifiers, and extending phrase matches from the previous iteration (lines 10 and 11). If there are no matching phrases at some point, we just update the respective nodes of the graph to reflect the new sentence path (lines 13 and 14). After the whole document is processed L will contain all the matching phrases between the current document and any previous document that shared at least one phrase with the new document. Finally we output L as the list of documents with matching phrases and all the necessary information about the matching phrases.

The above algorithm is capable of matching *any-length* phrase between a new document D and all previously seen documents in roughly $O(m)$ time, where m is the number of words in document D. Some could argue that the step at line 10 in the algorithm, where we extend the matching phrases as we continue along an existing path, is not actually a constant time step, because when the graph starts building up, the number of matching phrases becomes larger, and consequently when moving along an existing path we have to match more phrases. However, it turns out that the size of the list of matching phrases becomes roughly constant even with very large document sets, due to the fact that a certain phrase will be shared by only a small set of documents; which on average tends to be a constant number.

4. A phrase-based similarity measure

As mentioned earlier, phrases convey local context information, which is essential in determining an accurate similarity between documents. Towards this end we devised a similarity measure based on matching phrases rather than individual terms. This measure exploits the information extracted from the previous phrase matching algorithm to better judge the similarity between the documents. This is related to the work of Isaacs *et al* [6] who used a pair-wise probabilistic document similarity measure based on Information Theory. Although they showed it could improve on traditional similarity measures, but it is still fundamentally based on the vector space model representation.

The phrase similarity between two documents is calculated based on the list of matching phrases between the two

documents. This similarity measure is a function of four factors:

- The number of matching phrases P,

- The lengthes of the matching phrases ($l_i : i = 1, 2, \ldots, P$),

- The frequencies of the matching phrases in both documents (f_{i1} and $f_{i2} : i = 1, 2, \ldots, P$), and

- The levels of significance (*weight*) of the matching phrases in both document (w_{i1} and $w_{i2} : i = 1, 2, \ldots, P$).

Frequency of phrases is an important factor in the similarity measure. The more frequent the phrase appears in both documents, the more similar they tend to be. Similarly, the level of significance of the matching phrase in both documents should be taken into consideration.

The phrase similarity between two documents, $\mathbf{d_1}$ and $\mathbf{d_2}$, is calculated using the following empirical equation:

$$\text{sim}_p(\mathbf{d_1}, \mathbf{d_2}) = \frac{\sqrt{\sum_{i=1}^{P}[g(l_i) \cdot (f_{i1}w_{i1} + f_{i2}w_{i2})]^2}}{\sum_j |s_{j1}| \cdot w_{j1} + \sum_k |s_{k2}| \cdot w_{k2}} \quad (1)$$

where $g(l_i)$ is a function that scores the matching phrase length, giving higher score as the matching phrase length approaches the length of the original sentence; $|s_{j1}|$ and $|s_{k2}|$ are the original sentence lengths from document $\mathbf{d_1}$ and $\mathbf{d_2}$, respectively. The equation rewards longer phrase matches with higher level of significance, and with higher frequency in both documents. The function $g(l_i)$ in the implemented system was used as: $g(l_i) = (|ms_i|/|s_i|)^\gamma$, where $|ms_i|$ is the matching phrase length, and γ is a sentence fragmentation factor with values greater than or equal to 1. If γ is 1, two halves of a sentence could be matched independently and would be treated as a whole sentence match. However, by increasing γ we can avoid this situation, and score whole sentence matches higher than fractions of sentences. A value of 1.2 for γ was found to produce best results.

The normalization by the length of the two documents in equation (1) is necessary to be able to compare the similarities from other documents.

4.1. Combining single-term and phrase similarities

If the similarity between documents is based solely on matching phrases, and not single-terms at the same time, related documents could be judged as non-similar if they do not share enough phrases (a typical case that could happen in many situations.) Shared phrases provide important local context matching, but sometimes similarity based on phrases only is not sufficient. To alleviate this problem, and to produce high quality clusters, we combined single-term similarity measure with our phrase-based similarity measure. We used the *cosine correlation* similarity measure [14], with TF-IDF (Term Frequency–Inverse Document Frequency) term weights, as the single-term similarity measure. The cosine measure was chosen due to its wide use in the document clustering literature, and since it is described as being able to capture human categorization behavior well [17]. The TF-IDF weighting is also a widely used term weighting scheme [18].

Recall that the cosine measure calculates the cosine of the angle between the two document vectors. Accordingly our term-based similarity measure (sim_t) is given as:

$$\text{sim}_t(\mathbf{d_1}, \mathbf{d_2}) = \cos(\mathbf{d_1}, \mathbf{d_2}) = \frac{\mathbf{d_1} \cdot \mathbf{d_2}}{\|\mathbf{d_1}\| \|\mathbf{d_2}\|} \quad (2)$$

where the vectors $\mathbf{d_1}$ and $\mathbf{d_2}$ are represented as term weights calculated using TF-IDF weighting scheme.

The combination of the term-based and the phrase-based similarity measures is a weighted average of the two quantities from equations (1) and (2), and is given by equation (3).

$$\text{sim}(\mathbf{d_1}, \mathbf{d_2}) = \alpha \cdot \text{sim}_p(\mathbf{d_1}, \mathbf{d_2}) + (1 - \alpha) \cdot \text{sim}_t(\mathbf{d_1}, \mathbf{d_2}) \quad (3)$$

where α is a value in the interval $[0, 1]$ which determines the weight of the phrase similarity measure, or, as we call it, the *Similarity Blend Factor*.

5. Experimental results

In order to test the effectiveness of phrase matching in determining an accurate measure of similarity between documents, we conducted a set of experiments using our proposed data model and similarity measure.

Our experimental setup consisted of 314 web documents collected from University of Waterloo various web sites, such as the Graduate Studies Office, Information Systems and Technology, Health Services, Career Services, Co-operative Education, and other Canadian web sites. The documents were classified according to their content into 10 different categories. In order to allow for independent testing and the reproduction of the results presented here, we decided to make the data available to others. The document collection can be downloaded at: http://pami.uwaterloo.ca/~hammouda/webdata/.

The similarities calculated by our algorithm were used to construct a similarity matrix between the documents. We elected to use three standard document clustering techniques for testing the effect of phrase similarity on clustering [7]: (1) Hierarchical Agglomerative Clustering (HAC), (2) Single Pass Clustering, and (3) k-Nearest Neighbor

Clustering (k-NN)[2]. For each of the algorithms, we constructed the similarity matrix and let the algorithm cluster the documents based on the presented similarity matrix.

In order to evaluate the quality of the clustering, we adopted two quality measures widely used in the text mining literature for the purpose of document clustering [16]. The first is the **F-measure**, which combines the *Precision* and *Recall* ideas from the Information Retrieval literature. The precision and recall of a cluster j with respect to a class i are defined as:

$$P = \text{Precision}(i, j) = \frac{N_{ij}}{N_i} \quad (4a)$$

$$R = \text{Recall}(i, j) = \frac{N_{ij}}{N_j} \quad (4b)$$

where N_{ij}: is the number of members of class i in cluster j,
N_j: is the number of members of cluster j, and
N_i: is the number of members of class i.

The F-measure of class i is $F(i) = 2PR/(P + R)$. With respect to class i we consider the cluster with the highest F-measure to be the cluster j that maps to class i, and that F-measure becomes the score for class i. The overall F-measure for the clustering result C is the weighted average of the F-measure for each class i:

$$F_C = \frac{\sum_i (|i| \times F(i))}{\sum_i |i|} \quad (5)$$

where $|i|$ is the number of objects in class i. The higher the overall F-measure, the better the clustering, due to the higher accuracy of the clusters mapping to the original classes.

The second measure is the **Entropy**, which provides a measure of "goodness" for un-nested clusters or for the clusters at one level of a hierarchical clustering. Entropy tells us how homogeneous a cluster is. The higher the homogeneity of a cluster, the lower the entropy is, and vice versa. The entropy of a cluster containing only one object (perfect homogeneity) is zero.

For every cluster j in the clustering result C we compute p_{ij}, the probability that a member of cluster j belongs to class i. The entropy of each cluster j is calculated using the standard formula $E_j = -\sum_i p_{ij} \log(p_{ij})$, where the sum is taken over all classes. The total entropy for a set of clusters is calculated as the sum of entropies for each cluster weighted by the size of each cluster:

$$E_C = \sum_{j=1}^{m} \left(\frac{N_j}{N} \times E_j \right) \quad (6)$$

where N_j is the size of cluster j, and N is the total number of data objects.

---

[2]Although k-NN is mostly known to be used for classification, it has also been used for clustering (example could be found in [10]).

208

Table 1. Phrase-based clustering improvement

	Single-Term Similarity		Combined Similarity		Improvement
	F-measure	Entropy	F-measure	Entropy	
HAC [a]	0.709	0.351	0.904	0.103	+19.5%F, -24.8%E
Single Pass [b]	0.427	0.613	0.817	0.151	+39.0%F, -46.2%E
k-NN[c]	0.228	0.173	0.834	0.082	+60.6%F, -9.1%E

[a]Complete Linkage was used as the cluster distance measure for the HAC method since it tends to produce tight clusters with small diameter.

[b]A document-to-cluster similarity threshold of 0.25 was used.

[c]A k of 5 and a cluster similarity threshold of 0.25 were used.

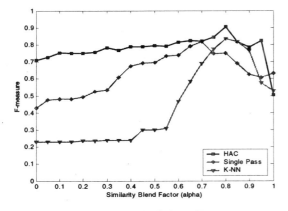

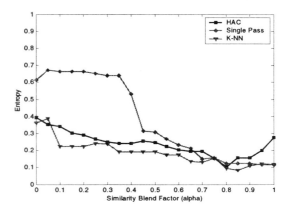

(a) Effect of phrase similarity on F-measure

(b) Effect of phrase similarity on Entropy

Figure 3. Effect of phrase similarity on clustering quality

Basically we would like to maximize the F-measure, and minimize the Entropy of clusters to achieve high quality clustering.

The results listed in Table 1 show the improvement on the clustering quality using a combined similarity measure. The improvements shown were achieved at a similarity blend factor between 70% and 80% (phrase similarity weight—see section 4.1 for details on combining phrase-based similarity and single-term similarity.) The parameters chosen for the different algorithms were the ones that produced best results. The percentage of improvement ranges from 19.5% to 60.6% increase in the F-measure quality, and 9.1% to 46.2% drop in Entropy (lower is better for Entropy). It is obvious that the phrase based similarity plays an important role in accurately judging the relation between documents. It is known that Single Pass clustering is very sensitive to noise; that is why it has the worst performance. However, when the phrase similarity was introduced, the quality of clusters produced was pushed close to that produced by HAC and k-NN.

In order to better understand the effect of the phrase similarity on the clustering quality, we generated a clustering quality profile against the similarity blend factor.

Figure 3(a) illustrates the effect of introducing the phrase similarity on the F-measure of the resulting clusters. It is obvious that the phrase similarity enhances the F-measure of the clustering until a certain point (around a weight of 80%) and then its effect starts bringing down the quality. As we mentioned in section 4.1 that phrases alone cannot capture all the similarity information between documents, the single-term similarity is still required, but to a smaller degree. The same can be seen from the Entropy profile in Figure 3(b), where Entropy is minimized at around 80% contribution of phrase similarity against 20% for the single-term similarity.

6. Conclusion and future research

We presented a system composed of three components in an attempt to improve the document clustering problem in the web domain. By exploiting the semi-structure inherent in web documents we can achieve better clustering results. We presented a web document analysis component that is capable of identifying the structure in web documents, and building structured documents out of it.

The second component, and perhaps the most important one that has most of the impact on performance, is the new document model introduced in this paper, the Document Index Graph. This model is based on indexing web documents using phrases and their levels of significance. Such a model enables us to perform phrase matching and similarity calculation between documents in a very robust and accurate way. The quality of clustering achieved using this model significantly surpasses the traditional vector space model based approaches.

The third component is the phrase-based similarity measure. By carefully examining the factors affecting the degree of overlap between documents, we devised a phrase-based similarity measure that is capable of accurate calculation of pair-wise document similarity.

The merits of such a design is that each component could be utilized independent of the other. But we have confidence that the combination of these components leads to better results, as justified by the results presented in this paper. By adopting different standard clustering techniques to test against our model, we are very confident that this model is well justified, and not biased.

There are a number of future research directions to extend and improve this work. One direction that this work might continue on is to improve on the accuracy of similarity calculation between documents by employing different similarity calculation strategies.

Although the work presented here is aimed at web document clustering, it could be easily adapted to any document type as well. However, it will not benefit from the semi-structure found in web documents. Our intention is to investigate the usage of such model on standard corpora and see its effect on clustering compared to traditional methods.

An important part of the clustering process is the clustering algorithm itself. One important benefit of the presented model is that we can use it with any clustering algorithm that can make use of the accurate pair-wise document similarity. We are currently working on an incremental clustering algorithm based on maintaining high cluster coherency, which looks promising and suitable for online clustering.

References

[1] K. Aas and L. Eikvil. Text categorisation: A survey. Technical Report 941, Norwegian Computing Center, June 1999.

[2] K. Cios, W. Pedrycs, and R. Swiniarski. *Data Mining Methods for Knowledge Discovery*. Kluwer Academic Publishers, Boston, 1998.

[3] W. B. Frakes and R. Baeza-Yates. *Information Retrieval: Data Structures and Algorithms*. Prentice Hall, Englewood Cliffs, N.J., 1992.

[4] T. Hofmann. The cluster-abstraction model: Unsupervised learning of topic hierarchies from text data. In *Proceedings*

of the *16th International Joint Conference on Artificial Intelligence IJCAI-99*, pages 682–687, 1999 .

[5] T. Honkela, S. Kaski, K. Lagus, and T. Kohonen. WEBSOM—self-organizing maps of document collections. In *Proceedings of WSOM'97, Workshop on Self-Organizing Maps*, pages 310–315, Espoo, Finland, June 1997.

[6] J. D. Isaacs and J. A. Aslam. Investigating measures for pairwise document similarity. Technical Report PCS-TR99-357, Dartmouth College, Computer Science, Hanover, NH, June 1999.

[7] A. K. Jain and R. C. Dubes. *Algorithms for Clustering Data*. Prentice Hall, Englewood Cliffs, N.J., 1988.

[8] M. Junker, M. Sintek, and M. Rinck. Learning for text categorization and information extraction with ILP. In J. Cussens, editor, *Proceedings of the 1st Workshop on Learning Language in Logic*, pages 84–93, Bled, Slovenia, 1999.

[9] R. Kosala and H. Blockeel. Web mining research: a survey. *ACM SIGKDD Explorations Newsletter*, 2(1):1–15, 2000.

[10] S. Y. Lu and K. S. Fu. A sentence-to-sentence clustering procedure for pattern analysis. *IEEE Transactions on Systems, Man, and Cybernetics*, 8:381–389, 1978.

[11] U. Y. Nahm and R. J. Mooney. A mutually beneficial integration of data mining and information extraction. In *17th National Conference on Artificial Intelligence (AAAI-00)*, pages 627–632, 2000.

[12] M. F. Porter. An algorithm for suffix stripping. *Program*, 14(3):130–137, July 1980.

[13] G. Salton and M. J. McGill. *Introduction to Modern Information Retrieval*. McGraw-Hill computer science series. McGraw-Hill, New York, 1983.

[14] G. Salton, A. Wong, and C. Yang. A vector space model for automatic indexing. *Communications of the ACM*, 18(11):613–620, November 1975.

[15] S. Soderland. Learning information extraction rules for semi-structured and free text. *Machine Learning*, 34(1-3):233–272, 1999.

[16] M. Steinbach, G. Karypis, and V. Kumar. A comparison of document clustering techniques. *KDD-2000 Workshop on TextMining*, August 2000.

[17] A. Strehl, J. Ghosh, and R. Mooney. Impact of similarity measures on web-page clustering. In *Proceedings of the 17th National Conference on Artificial Intelligence: Workshop of Artificial Intelligence for Web Search (AAAI 2000)*, pages 58–64, Austin, TX, July 2000. AAAI.

[18] Y. Yang and J. P. Pedersen. A comparative study on feature selection in text categorization. In *Proceedings of the 14th International Conference on Machine Learning (ICML'97)*, pages 412–420, Nashville, TN, 1997.

[19] O. Zamir, O. Etzioni, O. Madanim, and R. M. Karp. Fast and intuitive clustering of web documents. In *Proceedings of the 3rd International Conference on Knowledge Discovery and Data Mining*, pages 287–290, Newport Beach, CA, August 1997. AAAI.

[20] O. Zamir and O. Etzioni. Web document clustering: A feasibility demonstration. In *Proceedings of the 21st Annual International ACM SIGIR Conference*, pages 46–54, Melbourne, Australia, 1998.

Mining Top-K Frequent Closed Patterns without Minimum Support·

Jiawei Han   Jianyong Wang   Ying Lu   Petre Tzvetkov

University of Illinois at Urbana-Champaign, Illinois, U.S.A.

{hanj, wangj, yinglu, tzvetkov}@cs.uiuc.edu

ABSTRACT

In this paper, we propose a new mining task: mining top-k frequent closed patterns of length no less than min_ℓ, where k is the desired number of frequent closed patterns to be mined, and min_ℓ is the minimal length of each pattern. An efficient algorithm, called TFP, is developed for mining such patterns *without* minimum support. Two methods, *closed_node_count* and *descendant_sum* are proposed to effectively raise support threshold and prune FP-tree both *during* and *after* the construction of FP-tree. During the mining process, a novel *top-down and bottom-up combined* FP-tree mining strategy is developed to speed-up support-raising and closed frequent pattern discovering. In addition, a fast hash-based closed pattern verification scheme has been employed to check efficiently if a potential closed pattern is really closed.

Our performance study shows that in most cases, TFP outperforms CLOSET and CHARM, two efficient frequent closed pattern mining algorithms, even when both are running with the best tuned *min_support*. Furthermore, the method can be extended to generate association rules and to incorporate user-specified constraints. Thus we conclude that for frequent pattern mining, mining top-k frequent closed patterns without *min_support* is more preferable than the traditional *min_support*-based mining.

1. INTRODUCTION

As one of several essential data mining tasks, mining frequent patterns has been studied extensively in literature. From the implementation methodology point of view, recently developed frequent pattern mining algorithms can be categorized into three classes: (1) Apriori-based, horizontal formatting method, with Apriori [1] as its representative, (2) Apriori-based, vertical formatting method, such as CHARM [8], and (3) projection-based pattern growth method, which may explore some compressed data structure such as FP-tree, as in FP-growth [3].

The common *framework* is to use a *min_support* threshold to ensure the generation of the correct and complete set of frequent patterns, based on the popular Apriori property [1]: *every subpattern of a frequent pattern must be frequent* (also called the *downward closure property*). Unfortunately, this framework, though simple, leads to the following two problems that may hinder its popular use.

First, Setting *min_support* is quite subtle: *a too small*

threshold may lead to the generation of thousands of patterns, whereas a too big one may often generate no answers. Our own experience at mining shopping transaction databases tells us this is by no means an easy task.

Second, frequent pattern mining often leads to the generation of a large number of patterns (and an even larger number of mined rules). And mining a long pattern may unavoidably generate an exponential number of subpatterns due to the downward closure property of the mining process.

The second problem has been noted and examined by researchers recently, proposing to mine (frequent) closed patterns [5, 7, 8] instead. Since a closed pattern is the pattern that covers all of its subpatterns with the same support, one just need to mine the set of closed patterns (often much smaller than the whole set of frequent patterns), without losing information. Therefore, mining closed patterns should be the default task for mining frequent patterns.

The above observations indicate that it is often preferable to change the task of *mining frequent patterns* to mining top-k frequent closed patterns of minimum length min_ℓ, where k is a user-desired number of frequent closed patterns to be mined (which is easy to specify or set default), *top-k* refers to the k most frequent closed patterns, and min_ℓ, the minimal length of closed patterns, is another parameter easy to set. Notice that without min_ℓ, the patterns found will be of length one (or their corresponding closed superpatterns) since a pattern can never occur more frequently than its corresponding shorter ones (i.e., subpatterns) in any database.

In this paper, we study the problem of mining top-k frequent closed patterns of minimal length min_ℓ efficiently without *min_support*, i.e., starting with *min_support = 0*. Our study is focused on the FP-tree-based algorithm. An efficient algorithm, called TFP, is developed by taking advantage of a few interesting properties of top-k frequent closed patterns with minimum length min_ℓ, including (1) any transactions shorter than min_ℓ will not be included in the pattern mining, (2) *min_support* can be raised dynamically in the FP-tree construction, which will help pruning the tree before mining, and (3) the most promising tree branches can be mined first to raise *min_support* further, and the raised *min_support* is then used to effectively prune the remaining branches.

Performance study shows that TFP has surprisingly high performance. In most cases, it is better than two efficient frequent closed pattern mining algorithms, CLOSET and CHARM, with the best tuned *min_support*.

Moreover, association rules can be extracted by minor extension of the method, and constraints can also be incorpo-

* The work was supported in part by U.S. National Science Foundation, University of Illinois, and Microsoft Research.

rated into top-k closed pattern mining.

Therefore, we conclude that mining top-k frequent closed patterns without minimum support is more preferable (from both usability and efficiency points of view) than traditional $min\_support$-based mining.

The remaining of the paper is organized as follows. In Section 2, the basic concept of top-k closed pattern mining is introduced, and the problem is analyzed with the related properties identified. Section 3 presents the algorithm for mining top-k closed patterns. A performance study of the algorithm is reported in Section 4. Extensions of the method are discussed in Section 5, and we conclude our study in Section 6.

2. PROBLEM DEFINITION

In this section, we first introduce the basic concepts of top-k closed patterns, then analyze the problems and present an interesting method for mining top-k closed patterns.

Let $I = \{i_1, i_2, \ldots, i_n\}$ be a set of **items**. An **itemset** X is a non-empty subset of I. The **length of itemset** X is the number of items contained in X, and X is called an l-**itemset** if its length is l. A tuple $\langle tid, X \rangle$ is called a **transaction** where tid is a transaction identifier and X is an itemset. A **transaction database** TDB is a set of transactions. An itemset X is **contained** in transaction $\langle tid, Y \rangle$ if $X \subseteq Y$. Given a transaction database TDB, the **support** of an itemset X, denoted as $sup(X)$, is the number of transactions in TDB which contain X.

DEFINITION 1. (**top-k closed itemset**) *An itemset X is a **closed itemset** if there exists no itemset X' such that (1)$X \subset X'$, and (2) $\forall$ transaction T, $X \in T \rightarrow X' \in T$. A closed itemset X is a **top-k closed itemset** of minimal length min_ℓ if there exist[1] no more than $(k-1)$ closed itemsets of length at least min_ℓ whose support is higher than that of X.* ∎

Our task is to mine top-k closed itemsets of minimal length min_ℓ efficiently in a large transaction database.

EXAMPLE 1 (**A transaction dataset example**). *Let Table 1 be our transaction database TDB. Suppose our task is to find top-4 frequent closed patterns with $min\_\ell = 4$.* ∎

TID	Items	Ordered Items
T100	i, c, d, e, g, h	d, c, e, h, i, g
T200	m, a, p, c, e, d	d, c, e, a, p, m
T300	a, i, b, d, e, g	d, e, a, b, i, g
T400	b, a, d, h, c, n	d, c, a, h, b, n
T500	a, e, c	c, e, a
T600	n, a, c, d, e	d, c, e, a, n
T700	p, a, b, c, d, e, h	d, c, e, a, h, b, p

Table 1: A transaction database TDB.

Our first question is "*which mining methodology should be chosen from among the three choices:* Apriori, CHARM, *and*

---

[1]Since there could be more than one itemset having the same support in a transaction database, to ensure the set mined is independent of the ordering of the items and transactions, our method will mine every closed itemset whose support is no less than the k-th frequent closed itemset.

FP-growth*?*" Without min_support threshold, one can still use Apriori to mine all the l-itemsets level-by-level for l from 1 to min_ℓ. However, since one cannot use the downward closure property to prune *infrequent* l-itemsets for generation of $(l+1)$-itemset candidates, Apriori has to join all the length l itemsets to generate length $l+1$ candidates for all l from 1 to $min\_\ell - 1$. This is inefficient. CHARM loses its pruning power as well since it has to generate transaction id_list for every item, and find their intersected transaction id_list for every pair of such items since there is no itemset that can be pruned. Will the fate be the same for FP-growth? Since FP-growth uses a compressed data structure FP-tree to register TDB, all the possible itemsets of a transaction and their corresponding length information are preserved in the corresponding branch of the FP-tree. Moreover, FP-tree preserves the support information of the itemsets as well. Thus it is possible to utilize such information to speed up mining. Of the three possible methods, we will examine FP-growth in detail.

The question then becomes, "*how can we extend FP-growth for efficient top-k frequent closed pattern mining?*" We have the following ideas: (1) 0-$min\_support$ forces us to construct the "full FP-tree", however, with top-k in mind, one can capture sufficient higher support closed nodes in tree construction and dynamically raise $min\_support$ to prune the tree; and (2) in FP-tree mining, one can first mine the most promising subtrees so that high support patterns can be derived earlier, which can be used to prune low-support subtrees. In the following section, we will develop the method step-by-step.

3. MINING TOP-K FREQUENT CLOSED PATTERNS: METHOD DEVELOPMENT

In this section, we perform step-by-step analysis to develop an efficient method for mining top-k frequent closed patterns.

3.1 Short transactions and l-counts

Before studying FP-tree construction, we notice,

REMARK 3.1 (**Short transactions**). *If a transaction T contains less than min_ℓ distinct items, none of the items in T can contribute to a pattern of minimum length min_ℓ.*

For the discussions below, we will consider only the transactions that satisfy the minimum length requirement.

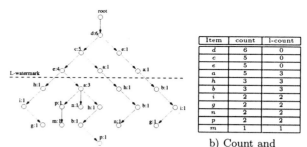

Item	count	l-count
d	6	0
c	5	0
e	5	0
a	5	3
h	3	3
b	3	3
i	2	2
g	2	2
n	2	2
p	2	2
m	1	1

a) The FP-tree constructed from TDB. b) Count and l-count of items.

Figure 1: FP-tree and its header table.

Let the occurrence frequency of each item be stored as *count* in the *(global) header table*. Here we introduce in the header table another counter, l(ow)-count, which records the total occurrences of an item at the level no higher than min_ℓ in the FP-tree, as shown in Figure 1 b).

REMARK 3.2 (*l*-**count**). *If the l-count of an item t is lower than min_support, t cannot be used to generate frequent itemset of length no less than min_ℓ.*

Rationale. *Based on the rules for generation of frequent itemset in FP-tree [3], only a node residing at the level min_ℓ or lower (i.e., deeper in the tree) may generate a prefix path no shorter than min_ℓ. Based on Remark 3.1, short prefix paths will not contribute to the generation of itemset with length greater or equal to min_ℓ. Thus only the nodes with l-count no lower than min_support may generate frequent itemset of length no less than min_ℓ.* ∎

People may wonder that our assumption is to start with $min\_support = 0$, how could we still use the notion of $min\_support$? Notice that if we can find a good number (i.e., no less than k) of closed nodes with nontrivial support during the FP-tree construction or before tree mining, the $min\_support$ can be raised, which can be used to prune other items with low support.

3.2 Raising $min\_support$ **for pruning** FP-tree

Since our goal is to mine top-k frequent closed nodes, in order to raise $min\_support$ effectively, one must ensure that the nodes taken into count are closed.

LEMMA 3.1 (**Closed node**). *At any time during the construction of an FP-tree, a node n_t is a closed node (representing a closed itemset) if it falls into one of the following three cases: (1) n_t has more than one child and n_t carries more count than the sum of its children, (2) n_t carries more count than its child, and (3) n_t is a leaf node.*

Rationale. *This can be easily derived from the definition of closed itemset and the rules for construction of FP-tree [3]. As shown in Figure 2 a), a node ($n_t : t$) denotes an itemset $n_1, \ldots, n_t$ with support t. Any later transaction (or prefix-path) that contains exactly the same set of items will be represented by the same node in the tree with increased support. If n_t has more than one child and n_t carries more count than the sum of its children, then n_t cannot carry the same support as any of its children, and thus n_t must be a closed node. The same reason holds if n_t carries more count than its child. If n_t is a leaf node, the future insertion of branches will make the node either remain as a leaf node or carry more count than its children, thus n_t must be a closed node as well.* ∎

To raise $min\_support$ dynamically during the FP-tree construction, a simple data structure, called $closed\_node\_count$ array, can be used to register the current count of each closed l-node with support node#, as illustrated in the left. The array is constructed as follows. Initially, all the count of each node# is initialized to 0 (or only the non-zero l-node is registered, depending on the implementation). Each closed l-node with support m in the FP-tree has one count in the *count* slot of node# m. During the construction of an FP-tree, suppose inserting one transaction into a branch makes the support of a closed l-node P increases from m to

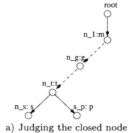

l-node#	count
95	1
⋮	⋮
5	9
4	7
3	17
2	32
1	86

a) Judging the closed node b) Count of closed l-nodes with support node#.

Figure 2: Closed node and closed node count array.

$m + 1$. Then the *count* corresponding to the node# $m + 1$ in the array is increased by one whereas that corresponding to the node# m is decreased by one.

Based on how the $closed\_node\_count$ array is constructed, one can easily derive the following lemma.

LEMMA 3.2 (**Raise** $min\_support$ **using** $closed\_node$). *At any time during the construction of an FP-tree, the minimum support for mining top-k closed itemsets will be at least equal to the node# if the sum of the closed_node_count array from the top to node# is no less than k.* ∎

Besides using the $closed\_node\_count$ array to raise minimum support, there is another method to raise $min\_support$ with FP-tree, called anchor-node descendant-sum, or simply descendant-sum, as described below. An anchor-node is a node at level $min\_\ell - 1$ of an FP-tree. It is called an *anchor-node* since it serves as an anchor to the (descendant) nodes at level min_ℓ and below. The method is described in the following example.

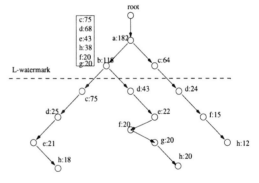

Figure 3: Calculate $descendant\_sum$ **for an anchor node of an** FP-tree.

EXAMPLE 2. *As shown in Figure 3, node b is an anchor node since it resides at level $min\_\ell - 1 = 2$. At this node, we collect the sum of the counts for each distinct itemset of b's descendants. For example, since b has two descendant d-nodes, $(d : 25)$ and $(d : 43)$, b's descendant_sum for d is $(d : 68)$ (which means that the support of itemset abd contributed from b's descendants is 68). From the FP-tree presented in Figure 3, it is easy to figure out that b's descendant_sum should be $\{(c : 75), (d : 68), (e : 43), (h : 38), (f : 20), (g : 20)\}$. Such summary information may raise min_support* *effectively. For example, min_support for top-3 closed nodes should be at least 43 based on b's descendant_sum.* ∎

LEMMA 3.3 (descendant_sum). *Each distinct count in descendant_sum of an anchor node represents the minimum count of one distinct closed pattern that can be generated by the FP-tree.*

Rationale. *Let the path from the root of the FP-tree to an anchor node b be β. Let a descendant of b be d and its count be count_d. Then based on the method for FP-tree construction, there must exist an itemset β · d whose count is count_d. If β · d is a closed node, then it is the unique closed node in the FP-tree with count count_d; otherwise, there must exist a closed pattern which is its super-pattern with support count_d. Since another node in b's descendant_sum with the same support count_d may share such a closed node with β · d, and also another branch may contribute additional count to such a closed node, thus only a distinct count in descendant_sum of b may represent the minimum count of a distinct closed pattern generated by the FP-tree.* ∎

We have the following observations regarding the two support raising methods. First, the *closed_node_count* method is cheap (only one array) and is easy to implement, and it can be performed at any time during the tree insertion process. Second, comparing with *closed_node_count*, *descendant_sum* is more effective at raising *min_support*, but is more costly since there could be many $(min\_\ell - 1)$ level nodes in an FP-tree, and each such node will need a *descendant_sum* structure. Moreover, before fully scanning the database, one does not know which node may eventually have a very high count. Thus it is tricky to select the appropriate anchor nodes for support raising: too many anchor nodes may waste storage space, whereas too few nodes may not be able to register enough count information to raise *min_support* effectively. Computing *descendant_sum* structure for low count nodes could be a waste since it usually derives small *descendant_sum* and may not raise *min_support* effectively.

Based on the above analysis, our implementation explores both techniques but at different times: During the FP-tree construction, it keeps an *closed_node_count* array which raises *min_support*, dynamically prunes some infrequent nodes, and reduces the size of the FP-tree to be constructed. After scanning the database (i.e., the FP-tree is constructed), we traverse the subtree of the level $(min\_\ell - 1)$ node with the highest support to calculate *descendant_sum*. This will effectively raise *min_support*. If the so-raised *min_support* is still less than the highest support of the remaining level $(min\_\ell - 1)$ nodes, the remaining node with the highest support will be traversed, and this process continues. Based on our experiments, only a small number of nodes need to be so traversed (if k for top-k is less than 1000) in most cases.

3.3 Efficient mining of FP-tree for top-k patterns

The raise of *min_support* prunes the FP-tree and speeds up the mining. However, the overall critical performance gain comes from efficient FP-tree mining.

We have the following observations.

REMARK 3.3 (Item skipping). *If the count of an item in the global header table is less than min_support, then it is infrequent and its nodes should be removed from the FP-tree.*

Moreover, if the l-count of an item in the global header table is less than min_support, the item should not be used to generate any conditional FP-tree. ∎

The TFP-mining with FP-tree is similar to FP-growth. However, there are a few subtle points.

1. "Top-down" ordering of the items in the global header table for the generation of conditional FP-trees.

The first subtlety is in what order the conditional FP-trees should be generated for top-k mining. Notice since FP-growth in [3] is to find the complete set of frequent patterns, its mining may start from any item in the header table. For top-k mining, our goal is to *find only the patterns with high support and raise the min_support as fast as possible to avoid unnecessary work*. Thus mining should start from the item that has the first non-zero l-count (which usually carries the highest l-count) in the header table, and walk down the header table entries to mine subsequent items (i.e., in the sorted_item_list order). This ordering is based on that items with higher l-count usually produce patterns with higher support. With this ordering, *min_support* can be raised faster and the top-k patterns can be discovered earlier. In addition, an item with l-count less than *min_support* do not have to generate conditional FP-tree for further mining (as stated in Remark 3.2). Thus, the faster the *min_support* can be raised, the more and earlier pruning can be done.

2. "Bottom-up" ordering of the items in a local header table for mining conditional FP-trees.

The second subtlety is how to mine conditional FP-trees. We have shown that the generation of conditional FP-trees should follow the order of the sorted_item_list, which can be viewed as top-down walking through the header table. However, it is often more beneficial to mine a conditional pattern tree in the "bottom-up" manner in the sense that we first mine the items that are located at the low end of a tree branch since it tends to produce the longest patterns first then followed by shorter ones. It is more efficient to first generate long closed patterns since the patterns containing only the subset items can be absorbed by them easily.

3. Efficient searching and maintaining of closed patterns using a pattern-tree structure.

The third subtle point is how to efficiently maintain the set of current frequent closed patterns and check whether a new pattern is a closed one.

During the mining process, a pattern-tree is used to keep the set of current frequent closed patterns. The structure of pattern-tree is similar to that of FP-tree. Recall that the items in a branch of the FP-tree are ordered in the support-decreasing order. This ordering is crucial for closed pattern verification (to be discussed below), thus we retain this item ordering in the patterns mined. The major difference between FP-tree and pattern-tree is that the former stores transactions in compressed form, whereas the latter stores potential closed frequent patterns.

The bottom-up mining of the conditional FP-trees generates patterns in such an order: for patterns that share prefixes, longer patterns are generated first. In addition, there is a total ordering over the patterns generated. This leads to our **closed frequent pattern verification scheme**, presented as follows.

Let $(i_1, \ldots, i_l, \ldots, i_j, \ldots, i_n)$ be the *sorted_item_list*, where i_l is the first non-zero l-count item, and i_j be the item whose conditional FP-tree is currently being mined. Then the set of already mined closed patterns, S, can be split into two subsets: (1) S_{old}, obtained by mining the conditional trees corresponding to items from i_l to i_{j-1} (i.e., none of the itemsets contains item i_j), and (2) S_{i_j}, obtained so far by mining i_j's conditional tree (i.e., every itemset contains item i_j). Upon finding a new pattern p during the mining of i_j's conditional tree, we need to perform new pattern checking (checking against S_{i_j}) and old pattern checking (checking against S_{old}).

The new pattern checking is performed as follows. Since the mining of the conditional tree is in a bottom-up manner, just like CLOSET, we need to check whether (1) p is a subpattern of another pattern p_{i_j} in S_{i_j}, and (2) $supp(p) \equiv supp(p_{i_j})$. If the answer is no, i.e., p passes new pattern checking, p becomes a new closed pattern with respect to S. Note that because patterns in S_{old} do not contain item i_j, there is no need to check if p is a subpattern of the patterns in S_{old}.

The old pattern checking is performed as follows. Since the global FP-tree is mined in a top-down manner, pattern p may be a super-pattern of another pattern, p_{old}, in S_{old} with $supp(p) \equiv supp(p_{old})$. In this case, p_{old} cannot be a closed pattern since it is absorbed by p. Therefore, if p has passed both new and old pattern checking, it can be used to raise the support threshold. Otherwise, if p passes only the new pattern checking, then it is inserted into the pattern-tree, but it cannot be used to raise the support threshold.

The correctness of the above checking is shown in the following lemmas.

LEMMA 3.4 (**New pattern checking**). *If a pattern p cannot pass the new pattern checking, there must exist a pattern, p_{i_j}, in S_{i_j}, which must also contain item i_j with $supp(p_{i_j}) \equiv supp(p)$.*

Rationale. *This can be obtained directly from the new pattern checking method.* ∎

Let $prefix(p)$ be the prefix pattern of a pattern p (i.e., obtained by removing the last item i_j from p).

LEMMA 3.5 (**Old pattern checking**). *For old pattern checking, we only need to check if there exists a pattern $prefix(p)$ in S_{old} with $supp(prefix(p)) \equiv supp(p)$.*

Rationale. *Since a pattern in S_{old} does not contain item i_j, it cannot become a super-pattern of p. Thus we only need to check if it is a subpattern of p. In fact we only need to check if there is a pattern $prefix(p)$ in S_{old} with the same support as p. We can prove this by contradiction. Let us assume there is another subpattern of $prefix(p)$ that can be absorbed by p. If this is the case, according to our mining order, we know this subpattern must have been absorbed by $prefix(p)$ either via new pattern checking or old pattern checking.* ∎

LEMMA 3.6 (**Support raise**). *If a newly mined pattern p can pass both new pattern checking and old pattern checking, then it is safe to use p to raise min_support.*

Rationale. *From Lemma 3.5, there will be two possibilities for p. First, it is a real closed pattern, i.e., it will not be absorbed by any patterns later. Second, it will be absorbed by a later found pattern, and this pattern can only absorb pattern p. In this case, we will not use the later found pattern to raise support because it has already been used to raise*

support when we found pattern p (or p's precedents). Thus it is safe to use p to raise min_support. ∎

To accelerate both new and old pattern checking, we introduce a two-level index header table into the pattern-tree structure. Notice that if a pattern can absorb (or be absorbed by) another pattern, the two patterns must have same support. Thus, our first index is based on the support of a pattern. In addition, for new pattern checking, we only need to check if pattern p can be absorbed by another pattern that also contains i_j; and for old pattern checking, we need to check if p can absorb $prefix(p)$ that ends with the second-last item of p. To speed up the checking, our second level indexing uses the last *item_ID* in a closed pattern as the index key. At each pattern-tree node, we also record the length of the pattern, in order to judge if the corresponding pattern needs to be checked.

The two-level index header table and the checking process are shown in the following example.

EXAMPLE 3 (**Closed pattern verification**). *Figure 4 shows a two-level indexing structure for verification of closed patterns. Based on the lemmas, we only need to index into*

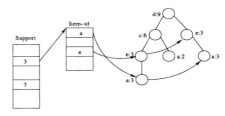

Figure 4: Two-level indexing for verification of closed patterns.

the first structure based on the itemset support, and based on its matching of the last two items in the index structure to find whether the corresponding closed node is in the tree. ∎

3.4 Algorithm

Now we summarize the entire mining process and present the mining algorithm.

ALGORITHM 1. *Mining top-k frequent closed itemsets with minimal length min_ℓ in a large transaction database.*

Input: *(1) A transaction database DB, (2) an integer k, i.e., the k most frequent closed itemsets to be mined, and (3) min_ℓ, the minimal length of the frequent closed itemsets.*

Output. *The set of frequent closed itemsets which satisfy the requirement.*

Method.

1. *Initially, min_support = 0;*

2. *Scan DB once[2], Collect the occurrence frequency (count)*

---

[2] This scan can be replaced by a sampling process, which reduces one database scan but increases the chance that items may not be ordered very well due to biased sampling, which may hurt performance later. Thus such scan reduction may or may not improve the performance depending on the data characteristics and the ordering of transactions.

of every item in transactions and sort them in frequency descending order, which forms sorted_item_list *and the header of* FP-tree.

3. *Scan DB again, construct* FP-tree, *update the l-count in the header of the* FP-tree, *use closed node count array to raise min_support, and use this support to prune the tree. After scanning DB, traverse* FP-tree *with descendant_sum check, which raises min_support further, and the raised min_support is used to prune the tree.*

4. *Tree mining is performed by traversing down the header table, starting with the item with the first non-zero l-count and generate the conditional* FP-tree *for each item, as along as its l-count is no less than the current min_support. Each conditional* FP-tree *is mined in "bottom-up" (i.e., long to short) manner. Each mined closed pattern is inserted into a pattern-tree.*

5. *Output patterns from pattern-tree in the order of their support. Stop when it outputs k patterns.*

∎

4. EXPERIMENTAL EVALUATION

In this section, we report our performance study of TFP over a variety of datasets.

In particular, we compare the efficiency of TFP with CHARM and CLOSET, two well known algorithms for mining frequent closed itemsets. To give the best possible credit to CHARM and CLOSET, our comparison is always based on assigning the best tuned *min_support* (which is difficult to obtain in practice) to the two algorithms so that they can generate the same top-k closed patterns for a user-specified k value (under a condition of *min_ℓ*). These optimal *min_support* are obtained by running TFP once under each experimental condition. This means that even if TFP has only comparable performance with those algorithms, it will still be far more useful than the latter due to its usability and the difficulty to speculate *min_support* without mining. In addition, we also study the scalability of TFP.

The experiments show that (1) the running time of TFP is shorter than CLOSET and CHARM in most cases when *min_ℓ* is long, and is comparable in other cases; and 2) TFP has nearly linear scalability.

4.1 Datasets

Both real and synthetic datasets are used in experiments, and they can be grouped into the following two categories.

1. Dense datasets that contain many long frequent closed patterns: 1) *pumsb* census data, which consists of 49,044 transactions, each with an average length of 74 items; 2) *connect-4* game state information data, which consists of 67,557 transactions, each with an average length of 43 items, and 3) *mushroom* characteristic data, which consists of 8,124 transactions, having an average length of 23 items. All these datasets are obtained from the UC-Irvine Machine Learning Database Repository.

2. Sparse datasets: 1) *gazalle* click stream data, which consists of 59,601 transactions with an average length of 2.5 items, and contains many short (length below 10) and

some very long closed patterns, (obtained from BlueMartini Software Inc.), and 2) *T10I4D100K* synthetic data from the IBM dataset generator, which consists of 100,000 transactions with an average length of 10· items, and with many closed frequent patterns having average length of 4.

4.2 Performance Results

All experiments were performed on a 1.7GHz Pentium-4 PC with 512MB of memory, running Windows 2000. The CHARM code was provided to us by its author. The CLOSET is an improved version that uses the same index-based closed node verification scheme as in TFP.

We compared the performance of TFP with CHARM and CLOSET on the 5 datasets by varying *min_ℓ* and K. In most cases K is selected to be either 100 or 500 which covers the range of typical K values. We also evaluated the scalability of TFP with respect to the size of database.

Dense Datasets: For the dense datasets with many long closed patterns, TFP performs consistently better than CHARM and CLOSET for longer *min_ℓ*.

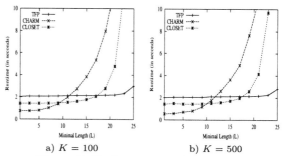

a) $K = 100$ b) $K = 500$

Figure 5: Performance on Connect-4 (I)

Figure 5 shows the running time of the three algorithms on the connect-4 dataset for K fixed at 100 and 500 respectively and *min_ℓ* ranging from 0 to 25. We observe that, TFP's running time for K at 100 and 500 remains stable over the range of *min_ℓ*. When *min_ℓ* reaches 11 or 12, TFP starts to outperform CHARM and the same for CLOSET when *min_ℓ* reaches 17 or 18. The reason is that for long patterns, the *min_support* is quite low. In this case, CHARM has to retain many short frequent patterns before forming the required longer patterns, and the FP-tree of CLOSET would also contain a large number of items that takes up much mining time. On the other hand, TFP is able to use the *min_ℓ* length restriction to cut many short frequent patterns early, thus reduce the total running time.

Figure 6 shows the running time of the three algorithms on the connect-4 dataset with *min_ℓ* set to 10 and 20 respectively and K ranging from 100 to 2000. For the connect-4 dataset, the average length of the frequent closed patterns is above 10, thus *min_ℓ* at 10 is considered to be a very low length restriction for this dataset. From a) we can see that even for very low length restriction such as 10, TFP's performance is comparable to that of CLOSET and CHARM when it runs without giving support threshold. For *min_ℓ* equal to 20, the running time for TFP is almost constant over the full range, and on average 5 times faster than CHARM and 2 to 3 times faster than CLOSET. We also noticed that, even for very low *min_ℓ* as K increases, the performance gap between TFP, CLOSET, and CHARM gets smaller.

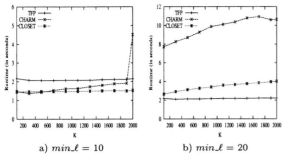

a) $min\_\ell = 10$ b) $min\_\ell = 20$

Figure 6: Performance on Connect-4 (II)

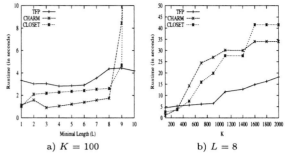

a) $K = 100$ b) $L = 8$

Figure 8: Performance on T10I4D100K

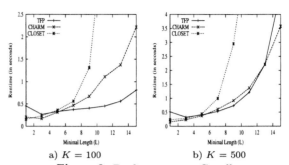

a) $K = 100$ b) $K = 500$

Figure 9: Performance on Gazelle

Figure 7 shows the running time of the three algorithms on the mushroom and pumsb datasets with K set to 500 and min_ℓ ranges from 0 to 25. For the mushroom dataset, when min_ℓ is less than 6 all three algorithms have similar low running time. TFP keeps its low running time for the whole range of min_ℓ and starts to outperform CHARM when min_ℓ is as low as 6 and starts to outperform CLOSET when min_ℓ is equal to 8. Pumsb has very similar results as connect-4 and mushroom datasets.

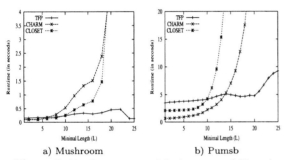

a) Mushroom   b) Pumsb

Figure 7: Performance on Mushroom and Pumsb

Sparse Dataset: Experiments show that TFP can efficiently mine sparse datasets without $min\_support$. It has comparable performance with CHARM and CLOSET for low min_ℓ, and outperforms both on higher min_ℓ.

Figure 8a) shows the running times of TFP, CHARM, and CLOSET on T10I4D100K with K fixed at 100 and min_ℓ ranges from 1 to 10. Again, it demonstrates TFP's strength in dealing with long min_ℓ. At $min\_\ell = 8$, the performance of CHARM and CLOSET starts deteriorating, while TFP retains its good performance. Figure 8b) shows the performance on the same dataset but with min_ℓ fixed at 8 and varying K from 200 to 2000. The curves show that when K is above 400, the running times of CHARM and CLOSET are around 3 times slower than TFP.

The experiments on the gazelle dataset are shown in Figure 9. For smaller K, TFP outperforms both CHARM and CLOSET for min_ℓ greater than or equal to 5. For $K = 500$, TFP continues to outperform CLOSET for min_ℓ greater than or equal to 5, and has similar performance as CHARM.

From this performance study, we conclude that TFP has good overall performance for both dense and sparse datasets. Its running time is nearly constant over a wide range of K and min_ℓ values for dense data. Unlike CHARM and CLOSETwhose performance deteriorates as min_ℓ increases,

TFP's running time stays low. The reason is inherent from the mining strategy of TFP, CHARM, and CLOSET. In most time, the support for long patterns is lower than that of short patterns. Thus even with the optimal support given, both CLOSET and CHARM are unable to prune short frequent patterns early, thus causing much time spent on mining useless patterns. On the other hand, TFP is able to use the min_ℓ length restriction to cut many short frequent patterns early, thus improves its running time instantly. In addition, TFP does not include any nodes that reside above min_ℓ level to participate in the mining process. As min_ℓ increases, more nodes reside above the min_ℓ level of the tree means that less conditional FP-trees need to be built, thus keeps the running time low.

Besides the good performance over long min_ℓ values, the performance of TFP over short min_ℓ values (even when $min\_\ell = 1$, i.e., no length constraint) is still comparable to that of CLOSET and CHARM. In such cases, the running times between the three do not differ much, and both CLOSET and CHARM were run with the optimal support threshold while TFP was not given any support threshold.

Scalability Test: Our performance tests showed that the running time of TFP increases linearly with increased dataset size.

5. DISCUSSION

In this section, we discuss the related work, how to generate association rules from the mined top-k frequent patterns, and how to push constraints into the mining process.

5.1 Related work

Recent studies have shown that closed patterns are more desirable [5] and efficient methods for mining closed patterns, such as CLOSET [7] and CHARM [8], have been developed. However, these methods all require a user-specified support threshold. Our algorithm does not need the user to provide any minimum support and in most cases runs faster than two efficient algorithms, CHARM and CLOSET, which in turn outperform Apriori substantially [7, 8].

Fu, et al. [2] studied mining N most interesting itemsets for every length l, which is different from our work in several aspects: (1) they mine all the patterns instead of only the closed ones ; (2) they do not have minimum length constraints—since it mines patterns at all the lengths, some heuristics developed here cannot be applied; and (3) their philosophy and methodology of FP-tree modification are also different from ours. To the best of our knowledge, this is the first study on mining top-k frequent closed patterns with length constraint, therefore, we only compare our method with the two best known and well-performed closed pattern mining algorithms.

5.2 Generation of association rules

Although top-k frequent itemsets could be all that a user wants in some mining tasks, in some other cases, s/he wants to mine strong association rules from the mined top-k frequent itemsets. We examine how to do this efficiently.

Items in the short transactions, though not contributing to the support of a top-k itemset of length no less than min_ℓ, may contribute to the support of the items in it. Thus they need to be included in the computation which has minimal influence on the performance. To derive correct confidence, we have the following observations: (1) The support of every 1-itemset is derived at the start of mining. (2) The set of top-k closed itemsets may contain the items forming subset/superset relationships, and the rules involving such itemsets can be automatically derived. (3) For rules in other forms, one needs to use the derived top-k itemsets as probes and the known $min\_support$ as threshold, and perform probe constrained mining to find the support only related to those itemsets. (4) As an alternative to the above, one can set $min\_\ell = 2$, which will derive the patterns readily for all the combinations of association rules.

5.3 Pushing constraints into TFP mining

Constraint-based mining [4, 6] is essential to top-k mining since users may always want to put constraints on the data and rules to be mined. We examine how different kinds of constraints can be pushed into the top-k frequent closed pattern mining.

First, succinct and anti-monotone constraints can be pushed deep into the TFP-mining process. he succint constraints should be pushed deep to select only those itemsets before mining starts and the anti-monotonic constraint should be pushed into the iterative TFP-mining process in a similar way as FP-growth.

Second, for monotone constraints, the rule will also be similar to that in traditional frequent pattern mining, i.e, if an itemset mined so far (e.g., $abcd$) satisfies a constraint "$sum \geq 100$", adding more items (such as e) still satisfies it and thus the constraints checking can be avoided in further expansion.

Third, for convertible constraints, one can arrange items in an appropriate order so that the constraint can be transformed into an anti-monotone one and the anti-monotone constraint pushing can be applied.

Interested readers can easily prove such properties for top-k frequent closed pattern mining.

6. CONCLUSIONS

We have studied a practically interesting problem, mining top-k frequent closed patterns of length no less than min_ℓ, and proposed an efficient algorithm, TFP, with several optimizations: (1) using $closed\_node\_count$ and $descendant\_sum$ to raise $min\_support$ before tree mining, (2) exploring the top-down and bottom-up combined FP-tree mining to first mine the most promising parts of the tree in order to raise $min\_support$ and prune the unpromising tree branches, and (3) using a special indexing structure and a novel closed pattern verification scheme to perform efficient closed pattern verification. Our experiments and performance study show that TFP has high performance. In most cases, it outperforms two efficient frequent closed pattern mining algorithms, CLOSET and CHARM, even when they are running with the best tuned $min\_support$. Furthermore, the method can be extended to generate association rules and to incorporate user-specified constraints.

Based on this study, we conclude that mining top-k frequent closed patterns without $min\_support$ should be more preferable than the traditional $min\_support$-based mining for frequent pattern mining. More detailed study along this direction is needed, including further improvement of the performance and flexibility at mining top-k frequent closed patterns, as well as mining top-k frequent closed sequential patterns or structured patterns.

Acknowledgements. We are grateful to Dr. Mohammed Zaki for providing the code and data conversion package of CHARM and promptly answering many questions .

7. REFERENCES

[1] R. Agrawal and R. Srikant. Fast algorithms for mining association rules. VLDB'94.

[2] A. W.-C. Fu, R. W.-W. Kwong, and J. Tang. Mining n-most interesting itemsets. ISMIS'00.

[3] J. Han, J. Pei, and Y. Yin. Mining frequent patterns without candidate generation. SIGMOD'00.

[4] R. Ng, L. V. S. Lakshmanan, J. Han, and A. Pang. Exploratory mining and pruning optimizations of constrained associations rules. SIGMOD'98.

[5] N. Pasquier, Y. Bastide, R. Taouil, and L. Lakhal. Discovering frequent closed itemsets for association rules. ICDT'99.

[6] J. Pei, J. Han, and L. V. S. Lakshmanan. Mining frequent itemsets with convertible constraints. ICDE'01.

[7] J. Pei, J. Han, and R. Mao. CLOSET: An efficient algorithm for mining frequent closed itemsets. DMKD'00.

[8] M. J. Zaki and C. J. Hsiao. CHARM: An efficient algorithm for closed itemset mining. SDM'02.

Mining Similar Temporal Patterns in Long Time-Series Data and Its Application to Medicine

Shoji Hirano and Shusaku Tsumoto
Department of Medical Informatics, Shimane Medical University, School of Medicine
89-1 Enya-cho, Izumo, Shimane 693-8501, Japan
hirano@ieee.org, tsumoto@computer.org

Abstract

Data mining in time-series medical databases has been receiving considerable attention since it provides a way of revealing useful information hidden in the database; for example relationships between temporal course of examination results and onset time of diseases. This paper presents a new method for finding similar patterns in temporal sequences. The method is a hybridization of phase-constraint multiscale matching and rough clustering. Multiscale matching enables us cross-scale comparison of the sequences, namely, it enable us to compare temporal patterns by partially changing observation scales. Rough clustering enable us to construct interpretable clusters of the sequences even if their similarities are given as relative similarities. We combine these methods and cluster the sequences according to multiscale similarity of patterns. Experimental results on the chronic hepatitis dataset showed that clusters demonstrating interesting temporal patterns were successfully discovered.

1 Introduction

Recent advances in medical devices and networking technology enable us to automatically collect huge amount of temporal data on medical laboratory tests, for example blood tests and urinalysis. Analysis of such temporal databases has attracted much interests because it might reveal underlying relationships between temporal patterns of examination results and onset time of diseases. However, despite of its importance, large-scale analysis of time-series medical databases has rarely been performed. This is primarily due to the following problems: (1) in order to capture all of the events that have different durations, sequence should be compared in multiple observation scales. (2) such comparison scheme imposes similarity of sequences to be relative, in which triangular inequality may not hold; this property limits selection of clustering methods.

This research aims at establishing a new scheme of time-series data analysis that overcomes the above problems and enables us to discover interesting knowledge from time-series medical databases, for example common patterns appeared before/after applying some drags or treatments. It also aims at implementing the concept of active user reaction [1] on medical data analysis, in which the feedback from users will be further used to determine strategies for the subsequent phases of data analysis and data collection.

In this paper, we propose a new methodology of data analysis that is a hybridization of multiscale matching [2] and rough clustering [3]. Multiscale matching is a method that compares similarity of sequences by partly changing observation scales and thus has an ability to capture both long- and short-term events. Since matching is performed on the basis of similarity of segments, which are subsequences between adjacent inflection points, it can be used to represent common increase/decrease patterns of the measurements. It also has a very important advantage that the connectivity of subsequences is preserved in the resultant sequence because it checks hierarchy of inflection points. While, rough clustering is a clustering method that groups up sequences based on their indiscernibility, which is defined in the context of rough set theory [4]. It does not use any distance-related features, therefore, is able to produce interpretable clusters even when similarity of sequences is defined as relative ones. In our method, multiscale matching is used to calculate similarity of the sequences, and rough clustering is used to cluster the sequences according to the derived similarity. The common patterns in the clustered sequences are then visualized using the result of multiscale matching to support visual inspection of the results by experts.

The remaining part of this paper is organized as follows. In Section 2 we summarize the problems in time-series data mining and introduce some related work. In Section 3 we describe the procedure of our method including explanation of multiscale structure matching and rough sets-based clustering. Then in Section 4 we show some experimental results on the chronic hepatitis dataset and finally conclude the technical results.

2 Problems and Related Works

2.1 Problems

1. Selection of appropriate observation scales

   Usually, a long time-series sequence contains some events that have different durations. Let us consider the case of chronic virus hepatitis as example. The hepatitis C virus chronically inflames the liver from several years to more than 20 years. Therefore, to evaluate progress of the disease, the change should be observed in long-term observation scales. On the other hand, the antiviral treatment with interferon is usually applied to the patient during 6 month. Therefore, the change induced by the treatment should be observed in short-term scales. In order to capture both long-term and short-term events, observation scales should be changed partly in the sequence.

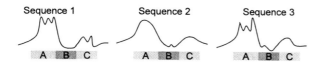

Figure 1. Example sequences.

Figure 1 shows an example of this case. Sequences 1, 2 and 3 are different but they have similar global patterns of increase(A) - decrease(B) - increase(C) when observed in long-term scales. Sequences 1 and 3 have further similar subpatterns in part A. Therefore, when comparing sequences 1 and 3, observation scales at part A should be changed to be shorter than those in sequences 1 and 2 or 2 and 3.

2. Selection of the appropriate clustering method

   Appropriate observation scales are different for each pair of sequences. This means that similarity of the sequences should be treated as relative similarity, in which triangular inequality is not guaranteed to hold among any three pairs of the sequences. In this case, applicable clustering methods are limited because clusters should be generated without using geometric measures such as centroids.

2.2 Related Work

A widely used approach in time-series data mining is to cluster sequences based on the similarity of their primary coefficients. Agrawal et al. [5] utilize discrete Fourier transformation (DFT) coefficients to evaluate similarity of sequences. Chan et al. [6] obtain the similarity based on the frequency components derived by the discrete wavelet transformation (DWT). Korn et al. [7] use singular value decomposition (SVD) to reduce complexity of sequences and compare the sequences according to the similarity of their eigenwaves. Another approach includes comparison of sequences based on the similarity of forms of partial segments. Morinaka et al. [8] propose the L-index, which performs piecewise comparison of linearly approximated subsequences. Keogh et al. [9] propose a method called piecewise aggregate approximation (PAA), which performs fast comparison of subsequences by approximating each subsequence with simple box waves having constant length.

These methods can compare the sequences in various scales of view by choosing proper set of frequency components, or by simply changing size of the window that is used to translate a sequence into a set of simple waves or symbols. However, they are not designed to perform cross-scale comparison. In cross-scale comparison, connectivity of subsequences should be preserved across all levels of discrete scales. Such connectivity is not guaranteed in the existing methods because they do not trace hierarchical structure of partial segments. Therefore, subsequences obtained on the different scales can not be directly merged into the resultant sequences. In other words, one can not capture similarity of sequences by partially changing scales of observation.

On the other hand, clustering has a rich history and a lot of methods have been proposed. They include, for example, k-means [10], fuzzy c-means [11], EM algorithm [12], CLIQUE [13], CURE [14] and BIRCH [15]. However, the similarity provided by multiscale matching is relative and not guaranteed to satisfy triangular inequality. Therefore, the methods based on the center, gravity or other types of topographic measures can not be applied to this task. Although classical agglomerative hierarchical clustering [16] can treat such relative similarity, in some case it has a problem that the clustering result depends on the order of handling objects.

3 Methods

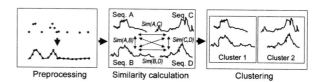

Figure 2. Overview of the method.

Figure 2 shows an overview of the proposed method.

First, we apply pre-processing to all the input sequences and obtain the interpolated sequences resampled at a regular interval. This procedure rearranges all data on the same time-scale and is required to compare long- and short-term difference using their length of trajectory. Simple linear interpolation of the nearest neighbors is used to fill in a missing value. Next, we apply multiscale structure matching to all possible combinations of two sequences and obtain their similarity as a matching score. We here restricted combinations of pairs so that they have the same attributes such as GPT-GPT, because our interest is not on the cross-attributes relationships. After obtaining similarity of the sequences, we cluster the sequences by using rough-set based clustering. Consequently, the similar sequences are clustered into the same clusters and their features are visualized.

3.1 Phase-constraint Multiscale Structure Matching

Multiscale structure matching, proposed by Mokhtarian [17], is a method to describe and compare objects in various scales of view. Its matching criterion is similarity between partial contours. It seeks the best pair of partial contours throughout all scales, not only in the same scale. This enables matching of object not only from local similarity but also from global similarity. The method required much computation time because it should continuously change the scale, however, Ueda et al. [2] solved this problem by introducing a segment-based matching method which enabled the use of discrete scales. We use Ueda's method to perform matching of time sequences between patients. We associate a convex/concave structure in the time-sequence as a convex/concave structure of partial contour. Such a structure can be generated by increase/decrease of examination values. Then we can compare the sequences from different terms of observation.

Now let $x(t)$ denote a time sequence where t denotes time of examination. The sequence at scale σ, $X(t, \sigma)$, can be represented as a convolution of $x(t)$ and a Gauss function with scale factor σ, $g(t, \sigma)$, as follows:

$$
\begin{aligned}
X(t, \sigma) &= x(t) \otimes g(t, \sigma) \\
&= \int_{-\infty}^{+\infty} x(u) \frac{1}{\sigma \sqrt{2\pi}} e^{-(t-u)^2/2\sigma^2} du.
\end{aligned}
$$

Figure 3 shows an example of sequences in various scales. From Figure 3 and the function above, it is obvious that the sequence will be smoothed at higher scale and the number of inflection points is also reduced at higher scale. Curvature of the sequence can be calculated as

$$
K(t, \sigma) = \frac{X''}{(1 + X'^2)^{3/2}},
$$

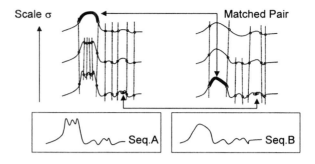

Figure 3. Multiscale matching.

where X' and X'' denotes the first- and second-order derivative of $X(t, \sigma)$, respectively. The m-th derivative of $X(t, \sigma)$, $X^{(m)}(t, \sigma)$, is derived as a convolution of $x(t)$ and the m-th order derivative of $g(t, \sigma)$, $g^{(m)}(t, \sigma)$, as

$$
X^{(m)}(t, \sigma) = \frac{\partial^m X(t, \sigma)}{\partial t^m} = x(t) \otimes g^{(m)}(t, \sigma).
$$

The next step is to find inflection points according to change of the sign of the curvature and to construct segments. A segment is a partial contour whose ends correspond to the adjacent inflection points. Let $\mathbf{A}^{(k)}$ be a set of N segments that represents the sequence at scale $\sigma^{(k)}$ as

$$
\mathbf{A}^{(k)} = \left\{ a_i^{(k)} \mid i = 1, 2, \cdots, N^{(k)} \right\}.
$$

Then, for a given pair of sequences $\mathbf{A}$ and $\mathbf{B}$, difference between segments $a_i^{(k)}$ and $b_i^{(h)}$, $d(a_i^{(k)}, b_j^{(h)})$ is defined as follows:

$$
d(a_i^{(k)}, b_j^{(h)}) = \frac{\mid \theta_{a_i}^{(k)} - \theta_{b_j}^{(h)} \mid}{\theta_{a_i}^{(k)} + \theta_{b_j}^{(h)}} \left| \frac{l_{a_i}^{(k)}}{L_A^{(k)}} - \frac{l_{b_j}^{(h)}}{L_B^{(h)}} \right|,
$$

where $\theta_{a_i}^{(k)}$ and $\theta_{b_j}^{(h)}$ denote rotation angles of tangent vectors along the contours, $l_{a_i}^{(k)}$ and $l_{b_j}^{(h)}$ denote length of the contours, $L_A^{(k)}$ and $L_B^{(h)}$ denote total segment length of the sequences A and B at scales $\sigma^{(k)}$ and $\sigma^{(h)}$. According to the above definition, large differences can be assigned when difference of rotation angle or relative length is large. Continuous $2n-1$ segments can be integrated into one segment at higher scale. Difference between the replaced segments and another segment can be defined analogously, with additive replacement cost that suppresses excessive replacement.

The above similarity measure can absorb shift of time and difference of sampling duration. However, we should suppress excessive back-shift of sequences in order to correctly distinguish the early-phase events from late-phase events. Therefore, we extend the definition of similarity as follows.

$$d(a_i^{(k)}, b_j^{(h)}) =$$

$$\frac{1}{3} \left(\left| \frac{d_{a_i}^{(k)}}{D_A^{(k)}} - \frac{d_{b_j}^{(h)}}{D_B^{(h)}} \right| + \frac{|\theta_{a_i}^{(k)} - \theta_{b_j}^{(h)}|}{\theta_{a_i}^{(k)} + \theta_{b_j}^{(h)}} + \left| \frac{l_{a_i}^{(k)}}{L_A^{(k)}} - \frac{l_{b_j}^{(h)}}{L_B^{(h)}} \right| \right)$$

where $d_{a_i}^{(k)}$ and $d_{b_j}^{(h)}$ denote dates from first examinations, $D_A^{(k)}$ and $D_B^{(h)}$ denote durations of examinations. By this extension, we simultaneously evaluate the following three similarities: (1)dates of events (2) velocity of increase/decrease (3) duration of each event.

The remaining procedure of multiscale structure matching is to find the best set of segment pairs that minimizes the total difference. Figure 3 illustrates the process. For example, five contiguous segments at the lowest scale of Sequence A are integrated into one segment at the highest scale, and the integrated segments well match to one segment in Sequence B at the lowest scale. Thus the set of the five segments in Sequence A and the one segment in Sequence B will be considered as a candidate for corresponding subsequences. While, another pair of segments will be matched at the lowest scale. In this way, matching is performed throughout all scales. The matching process can be fasten by implementing dynamic programming scheme [2].

After matching process is completed, we calculate total difference $d(A, B)$ of sequences A and B by summing up the remaining difference on each of the matched subsequences. Finally, we translate $d(A, B)$ to similarity of the sequences $s(A, B)$ as follows and use it as similarity measure in rough clustering.

$$s(A, B) = 1 - \frac{d(A, B)}{d_{max}},$$

where d_{max} denotes the maximum value of $d(A, B)$ over all pairs of A and B.

3.2 Rough Clustering

Generally, if similarity of objects is represented only as a relative similarity, it is not an easy task to construct interpretable clusters because some of important measures such as inter- and intra-cluster variances are hard to be defined. The rough-set based clustering method is a clustering method that clusters objects according to the indiscernibility of objects. It represents denseness of objects according to the *indiscernibility degree*, and produces interpretable clusters even for the objects mentioned above. Since similarity of sequences obtained through multiscale structure matching is relative, we use this clustering method to classify the sequences.

The clustering method lies its basis on the *indiscernibility* of objects, which forms basic property of knowledge in

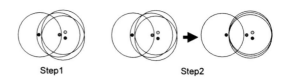

Figure 4. Rough clustering.

rough sets. Let us first introduce some fundamental definitions of rough sets related to our work. Let $U \neq \phi$ be a universe of discourse and X be a subset of U. An equivalence relation, R, classifies U into a set of subsets $U/R = \{X_1, X_2, ... X_m\}$ in which following conditions are satisfied:

$$
\begin{aligned}
&(1) X_i \subseteq U, X_i \neq \phi && \text{for any } i, \\
&(2) X_i \cap X_j = \phi && \text{for any } i, j, \\
&(3) \cup_{i=1,2,...n} X_i = U.
\end{aligned}
$$

Any subset X_i, called a category, represents an equivalence class of R. A category in R containing an object $x \in U$ is denoted by $[x]_R$. An indiscernibility relation $IND(R)$ is defined as follows.

$$x_i IND(R) x_j = \{(x_i, x_j) \in U^2 \mid (x_i, x_j) \in P, P \in U/R\}.$$

For a family of equivalence relations $\mathbf{P} \subseteq \mathbf{R}$, an indiscernibility relation over $\mathbf{P}$ is denoted by $IND(\mathbf{P})$ and defined as follows

$$IND(\mathbf{P}) = \bigcap_{R \in \mathbf{P}} IND(R).$$

The clustering method consists of two steps: (1)assignment of initial equivalence relations and (2)iterative refinement of initial equivalence relations. Figure 4 illustrates each step. In the first step, we assign an initial equivalence relation to every object. An initial equivalence relation classifies the objects into two sets: one is a set of objects similar to the corresponding objects and another is a set of dissimilar objects. Let $U = \{x_1, x_2, ..., x_n\}$ be the entire set of n objects. An initial equivalence relation R_i for object x_i is defined as

$$R_i = \{\{P_i\}, \{U - P_i\}\},$$

$$P_i = \{x_j \mid s(x_i, x_j) \geq S_i\}, \ \forall x_j \in U.$$

where P_i denotes a set of objects similar to x_i, that is, a set of objects whose similarity to x_i is larger than a threshold value. Similarity $s(x_i, x_j)$ is an output of multiscale structure matching where x_i and x_j correspond to A and B in the previous subsection respectively. Threshold value S_i is determined automatically at a place where s largely decreases. A set of indiscernible objects obtained using all sets of equivalence relations forms a cluster. In other words, a cluster corresponds to a category X_i of $U/IND(\mathbf{R})$.

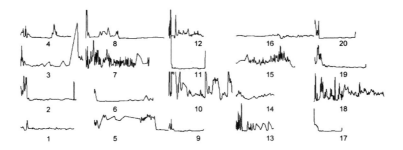

Figure 5. Test patterns.

Table 1. Similarity of the sequences

	1	2	3	4	5	6	7	8	9	10	11	12	13	14	15	16	17	18	19	20
1	1.00	0.70	0.68	0.78	0.00	0.63	0.48	0.71	0.72	0.61	0.73	0.66	0.64	0.72	0.50	0.00	0.53	0.00	0.74	0.45
2		1.00	0.61	0.73	0.00	0.68	0.22	0.46	0.68	0.67	0.72	0.73	0.72	0.68	0.68	0.00	0.68	0.00	0.77	0.41
3			1.00	0.75	0.45	0.51	0.68	0.47	0.71	0.70	0.69	0.73	0.71	0.81	0.68	0.00	0.62	0.00	0.72	0.55
4				1.00	0.00	0.60	0.52	0.47	0.75	0.71	0.64	0.79	0.75	0.82	0.47	0.00	0.60	0.00	0.75	0.48
5					1.00	0.23	0.62	0.49	0.33	0.53	0.44	0.45	0.50	0.44	0.56	0.01	0.00	0.26	0.53	0.30
6						1.00	0.00	0.00	0.59	0.00	0.58	0.39	0.61	0.65	0.00	0.00	0.47	0.00	0.47	0.48
7							1.00	0.49	0.54	0.80	0.57	0.73	0.73	0.59	0.76	0.00	0.00	0.44	0.62	0.39
8								1.00	0.53	0.47	0.57	0.56	0.51	0.49	0.54	0.00	0.00	0.00	0.66	0.51
9									1.00	0.00	0.68	0.00	0.00	0.00	0.00	0.00	0.82	0.00	0.00	0.00
10										1.00	0.59	0.83	0.76	0.75	0.81	0.00	0.47	0.11	0.59	0.37
11											1.00	0.76	0.54	0.68	0.00	0.00	0.74	0.00	0.76	0.00
12												1.00	0.81	0.78	0.67	0.00	0.70	0.00	0.63	0.40
13													1.00	0.75	0.00	0.00	0.64	0.00	0.67	0.35
14														1.00	0.00	0.00	0.66	0.00	0.71	0.00
15															1.00	0.00	0.43	0.20	0.55	0.39
16																1.00	0.00	0.00	0.43	0.19
17																	1.00	0.00	0.00	0.00
18																		1.00	0.39	0.03
19																			1.00	0.00
20																				1.00

In the second step, we refine the initial equivalence relations according to their global relationships. First, we define an indiscernibility degree, γ, which represents how many equivalence relations commonly regards two objects as indiscernible objects, as follows:

$$\gamma(x_i, x_j) = \frac{1}{|U|} \sum_{k=1}^{|U|} \delta_k(x_i, x_j),$$

$$\delta_k(x_i, x_j) = \begin{cases} 1, & \text{if } [x_k]_{R_k} \cap ([x_i]_{R_k} \cap [x_j]_{R_k}) \neq \phi \\ 0, & \text{otherwise.} \end{cases}$$

Objects with high indiscernibility degree can be interpreted as similar objects. Therefore, they should be classified into the same cluster. Thus we modify an equivalence relation if it has ability to discern objects with high γ as follows:

$$R'_i = \{\{P'_i\}, \{U - P'_i\}\},$$

$$P'_i = \{x_j | \gamma(x_i, x_j) \geq T_h\}, \quad \forall x_j \in U.$$

T_h is a threshold value that determines indiscernibility of objects. This prevents generation of small clusters formed due to the too fine classification knowledge. Given Th, refinement of equivalence relations is iterated until clusters become stable. Consequently, coarsely classified set of sequences are obtained as $U/IND(\mathbf{R}')$.

4 Experimental Results

We applied the proposed method to time-series GPT sequences in the hepatitis data set [18], which was used as a common dataset at ECML/PKDD Discovery Challenge 2002. The dataset contained long time-series data on laboratory examinations, which were collected at Chiba University Hospital in Japan. The subjects were 771 patients of hepatitis B and C who took examinations between 1982 and 2001. Here we remove 268 of them because biopsy information was not provided for them and thus their virus types were not clearly specified. Each sequence originally had different sampling intervals from one day to one year. From preliminary analysis we found that the most frequently appeared interval was one week; this means that most of the patients took examinations on a fixed day of a week. According to this observation, we determined resampling interval to seven days.

First, in order to evaluate applicability of multiscale matching to time-series data analysis, we applied the pro-

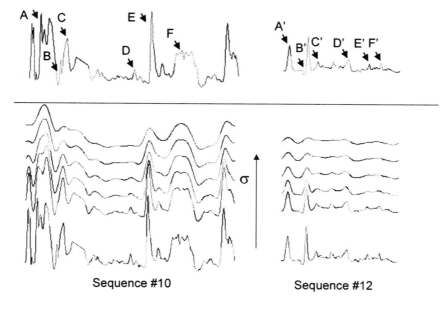

Sequence #10   Sequence #12

Figure 6. Matching result of sequences #10 and #12.

posed method to a small subset of sequences which was constructed by randomly selecting 20 sequences from the data set. Figure 5 shows all the pre-processed sequences. Table 1 shows normalized similarity of the sequences derived by multiscale matching. Since consistency of self-similarity ($s(A, B) = s(B, A)$) holds, the lower-left half of the matrix is omitted. We can observe that higher similarity was successfully assigned to intuitively similar pairs of sequences.

Based on this similarity, the rough clustering produced nine clusters:
$U/IND(\mathbf{R})$ = {{1,2,9,11,17,19}, {4,3,8}, {7,14,15}, {10,12,13}, {5}, {6}, {16}, {18}, {20}}. A parameter Th for rough clustering was set to $Th = 0.6$. Refinement was performed up to five times. It can be seen that similar sequences were clustered into the same cluster. Some sequences, for example #16, were clustered into independent clusters due to remarkably small similarity to other sequences. This is because multiscale matching could not find good pairs of subsequences.

Figure 6 shows the result of multiscale matching on sequences #10 and #12, that have high similarity. We changed σ from 1.0 to 13.5, with intervals of 2.5. At the bottom of the figure there are original two sequences at $\sigma = 1.0$. The next five sequences represent sequences at scales $\sigma = 3.5$, 6.0, 8.5, 11.0, and 13.5, respectively. Each of the colored line corresponds to a segment. The matching result is shown at the top of the figure. Here the lines with same color represent the matched segments, for example, segment A matches segment A' and segment B matches segment B'.

We can clearly observe that increase/decrease patterns of sequences are successfully captured; large increase (A and A'), small decrease with instant increase (B and B'), small increase (C and C') and so on. Segments $D - F$ and $D' - F'$ have similar patterns and the feature was also correctly captured. It can also be seen that the well-matched segments were obtained in the sequences with large time difference.

Next, we applied the proposed method to the full data set containing 503 GPT sequences. The resultant clusters were stratified according to the virus type and administration of the interferon (IFN) treatment. For clusters that had interesting compositions, we visually inspected common patterns in those clusters.

Clusters well reflected effectiveness of the interferon treatment. Table 4 shows a part of the clustering result. Two types of interesting patterns were found in the clustered sequences. The first pattern was found in cluster 4, which contained remarkably many cases of type C with IFN (B/C/C(IFN) = 6/3/25). In this cluster, GPT decreased after administration of IFN and then kept flattened at low level (figure 7). This pattern represented cases where interferon successfully suppressed activity of the type C hepatitis virus. The second pattern was found in clusters 1, 5 and 7. In these clusters, GPT had continuous vibrations (figure 7). Since this pattern was commonly observed regardless of virus type and administration of IFN, it implied ineffective cases of IFN treatment. Note that figures 7 and 8 represent matching results of the sequences grouped into the same cluster. The sequence number is shown as #xxx and the matched subsequences are painted in the same color.

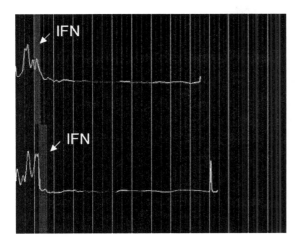

Figure 7. GPT cluster 4: #19(type C; IFN), #158(type C; IFN)

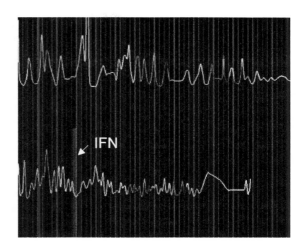

Figure 8. GPT cluster 1: #72(type C; IFN), #892(type B)

Table 2. Clusters of GPT sequences

cluster	IFN=N		IFN=Y	total
	B	C	C	
1	24	13	42	79
2	9		7	16
3	44	25	24	93
4	6	3	25	34
5	5	4	6	15
6	1		2	3
7	42	19	31	92
⋮				
44		1		1
total	206	100	197	503

5 Conclusions

In this paper, we have presented an analysis method of time-series medical databases based on the hybridization of phase-constraint multiscale structure matching and rough clustering. The method first obtained similarity of sequences by multiscale comparison of sequences in which connectivity of subsequences were preserved even if they were represented at different scales. Then rough clustering grouped up the sequences according to their relative similarity. This hybridization enabled us not only to cluster time-series sequence from both long- and short-term viewpoints but also to visualize correspondence of subsequences. In the experiments on the hepatitis data set, we showed that the sequences were successfully clustered into intuitively correct clusters, and that some interesting patterns were discovered by visualizing the clustered sequences. It remains as a future work to evaluate usefulness of the method in other databases.

Acknowledgment

This work was supported in part by the Grant-in-Aid for Scientific Research on Priority Area (B)(No.759) "Implementation of Active Mining in the Era of Information Flood" by the Ministry of Education, Culture, Science and Technology of Japan.

References

[1] H. Motoda (2001): Active Mining Project, Grant-in-Aid for Scientific Research on Priority Area, Interim Research Summary. URL: http://www.ar.sanken.osaka-u.ac.jp/activemining/2hearinge.html

[2] N. Ueda and S. Suzuki (1990): A Matching Algorithm of Deformed Planar Curves Using Multiscale Convex/Concave Structures. IEICE Transactions on Information and Systems, J73-D-II(7): 992–1000.

[3] S. Hirano and S. Tsumoto (2001): Indiscernibility Degrees of Objects for Evaluating Simplicity of Knowledge in the Clustering Procedure. Proceedings of the 2001 IEEE International Conference on Data Mining. 211–217.

[4] Z. Pawlak (1991): Rough Sets, Theoretical Aspects of Reasoning about Data. Kluwer Academic Publishers, Dordrecht.

[5] R Agrawal, C. Faloutsos, and A. N. Swami (1993): Efficient Similarity Search in Sequence Databases. Proceedings of the 4th International Conference on Foundations of Data Organization and Algorithms: 69–84.

[6] K. P. Chan and A. W. Fu (1999): Efficient Time Series Matching by Wavelets. Proceedings of the 15th IEEE International Conference on Data Engineering: 126–133.

[7] F. Korn, H. V. Jagadish, and C. Faloutsos (1997): Efficiently Supporting Ad Hoc Queries in Large Datasets of Time Sequences. Proceedings of ACM SIGMOD International Conference on Management of Data: 289–300.

[8] Y. Morinaka, M. Yoshikawa, T. Amagasa and S.Uemura (2001): The L-index: An Indexing Structure for Efficient Subsequence Matching in Time Sequence Databases. Proceedings of International Workshop on Mining Spatial and Temporal Data, PAKDD-2001: 51-60.

[9] E. J. Keogh, K. Chakrabarti, M. J. Pazzani, and S. Mehrotra (2001): "Dimensionality Reduction for Fast Similarity Search in Large Time Series Databases" Knowledge and Information Systems 3(3): 263-286.

[10] S. Z. Selim and M. A. Ismail (1984): K-means-type Algorithms: A Generalized Convergence Theorem and Characterization of Local Optimality. IEEE Transactions on Pattern Analysis and Machine Intelligence, 6(1): 81–87.

[11] J. C. Bezdek (1981): Pattern Recognition with Fuzzy Objective Function Algorithm. Plenum Press, New York.

[12] A. P. Dempster, N. M. Laird, and D. B. Rubin (1977): Maximum likelihood from incomplete data via the EM algorithm. J. of Royal Statistical Society Series B, 39: 1–38.

[13] R. Agrawal, J. Gehrke, D. Gunopulos, and P. Raghavan (1998): Automatic Subspace Clustering of High Dimensional Data for Data Mining Applications. Proceedings of ACM SIGMOD International Conference on Management of Data: 94–105.

[14] S. Guha, R. Rastogi, and K. Shim(1998): CURE: An Efficient Clustering Algorithm for Large Databases. Proceedings of ACM SIGMOD International Conference on Management of Data: 73–84.

[15] T. Zhang, R. Ramakrishnan, and M. Livny (1996): BIRCH: An Efficient Data Clustering Method for Very Large Databases. Proceedings of ACM SIGMOD International Conference on Management of Data: 103–114.

[16] M. R. Anderberg (1973): Cluster Analysis for Applications. Academic Press, New York.

[17] F. Mokhtarian and A. K. Mackworth (1986): Scale-based Description and Recognition of planar Curves and Two Dimensional Shapes. IEEE Transactions on Pattern Analysis and Machine Intelligence, PAMI-8(1): 24-43.

[18] URL: http://lisp.vse.cz/challenge/ecmlpkdd2002/

Mining Generalized Association Rules Using Pruning Techniques

Yin-Fu Huang and Chiech-Ming Wu
Institute of Electronics and Information Engineering
National Yunlin University of Science and Technology
Email: huangyf@el.yuntech.edu.tw

Abstract

The goal of the paper is to mine generalized association rules using pruning techniques. Given a large transaction database and a hierarchical taxonomy tree of the items, we try to find the association rules between the items at different levels in the taxonomy tree under the assumption that original frequent itemsets and association rules have already been generated beforehand. In the proposed algorithm GMAR, we use join methods and pruning techniques to generate new generalized association rules. Through several comprehensive experiments, we find that the GMAR algorithm is much better than BASIC and Cumulate algorithms.

1. Introduction

In recent ten years, with the developments of information and advances of Internet, vast data have been propagated and recorded in the databases of different applications. Currently data mining is arising to understand, analyze, and use these data. Data mining is designed for finding interesting samples in a large database, and thus it is also the knowledge exploration center part [3, 5]. One of the major tasks of data mining is to find association rules for helping retail industries to understand the consumers' behaviors [1, 2].

In data mining, the most well-known method is the Apriori algorithm [2]. Since the Apriori algorithm is costly to find candidate itemsets, many researches have been trying to improve it; i.e., reducing the size of candidate itemsets. For example, DHP algorithm is one using a hash-based skill to reduce the size of candidate itemsets [9]. Besides, someone used transaction reduction techniques, including partitioning proposed by Savasere et al. [10] and sampling proposed by Toivonen [14], to generate frequent itemsets quickly. What's more, a kind of data structure called FP-Tree (Frequent Pattern Tree) was proposed by Han et al. to directly produce frequent itemsets, not candidate itemsets [6].

The motivation of our research is initiated with two

situations. One is that although mining association rules has completed, but it did not consider the taxonomy tree at that time. Another is that although the taxonomy tree was considered, it may need to be adjusted as time goes by, and thus the generalized association rules mined before are not useful any more. Till now, all proposed researches can only mine all association rules from scratch. In the paper, our goal is to find generalized association rules without re-scanning the original database. Here the pre-knowledge including the taxonomy tree, the original frequent itemsets and association rules both generated beforehand, can be used to mine new generalized association rules. The data type used in the paper is a transactional data form [7]. At first, we create maximal itemsets [5, 13] from the original frequent itemsets. Next, given a hierarchical taxonomy tree [4, 12], we must calculate the supports of the non-leaf items in the taxonomy tree from the maximal itemsets or VTV table [5, 11]. Then, we use the original frequent itemsets L_1 and L_2, and non-leaf items with the supports $\geq$ the minimum support to create an association graph. In our paper different from those ones [8, 15], we assume the minimum supports of all the items are the same. Finally, in our algorithm GMAR (Generalized Mining Association Rules), we use join methods and pruning techniques to generate new generalized association rules. In the experiments, we find that the GMAR algorithm is much better than BASIC and Cumulate algorithms [12], since it generates fewer candidate itemsets, and furthermore prunes a large amount of irrelevant rules based on the minimum confidence.

The remainder of the paper is organized as follows. In Section 2, the mining problem for generalized association rules is defined. We propose the GMAR algorithm using the original frequent itemsets and association rules to find generalized association rules in Section 3. In Section 4, several experiments are undertaken and the results show the superiority of the GMAR algorithm over BASIC and Cumulate algorithms. Finally, we make a conclusion in Section 5.

2. Problem descriptions

The problem investigated here is to mine generalized association rules according to a large transaction database D and a hierarchical taxonomy tree H of the purchased items. Transaction database D is a set of transactions where each transaction T consists of a set of items, called an itemset, such that $T \subseteq I$. Here $I = \{i_1, i_2, i_3, ..., i_m\}$ is a set of the items purchased by all the transactions. Besides, hierarchical taxonomy tree H is a directed acyclic graph on the items where an edge in H represents an "is-a" relationship between items. For example, if there is an edge from p to c in H, we call p a parent of c and c a child of p. In other words, we can say p represents a generalization of c. Further, if there is a path from $\hat{e}$ to e in the transitive-closure of H, we call $\hat{e}$ an ancestor of e, and e a descendant of $\hat{e}$. Since H is acyclic, any item cannot be an ancestor of itself. Besides all the leaf items in H must come from I.

Recent researches are getting interested in finding the association rules spanning several different levels in the taxonomy tree, here called generalized association rules. A generalized association rule is an implication of the form $X \Rightarrow Y$, where $X \subseteq I$, $Y \subseteq I$, $X \cap Y = \varnothing$, and no item in Y is an ancestor of any item in X. If $c\%$ of the transactions in D that support X also support Y, we say that $X \Rightarrow Y$ holds in the transaction database D with confidence c. The definition of Support(X) is the number of transactions purchasing X, divided by the number of transactions in the database, as shown in formula (1). The definition of Conf($X \Rightarrow Y$) is the support of both antecedent and consequent divided by the support of antecedent in the rule, as shown in formula (2).

$$Support(X) = {X.count}\Big/{dbsize} \quad\text{.............................} (1)$$

$$Conf(X \Rightarrow Y) = {Support(X \cup Y)}\Big/{Support(X)} \quad\text{........} (2)$$

Definitely, we can find generalized association rules from scratch, given a large transaction database D and a hierarchical taxonomy tree H of the purchased items. However it is not avoidable to scan the original database once more, and this will be very inefficient. Thus an efficient mining algorithm proposed here is to make use of the original frequent itemsets and association rules that have already been generated beforehand, to produce new generalized association rules, rather than re-scanning the original database. Besides we also propose some pruning techniques to speed up the mining process.

3. Mining algorithms

3.1. Processing flow of mining algorithms

The processing flow of our mining algorithm for finding generalized association rules is shown in Figure 1. Supposed that the components shown inside the dotted

box, such as vertical-TID-vector table, frequent itemsets, and association rules, were generated before our mining algorithm is executed. Rather than scanning the original database, we make use of the vertical-TID-vector table transformed from the original database to mine generalized association rules. Since the bit storage is used in the vertical-TID-vector table, the memory space and processing time to get the database information will be saved. Besides the original frequent itemsets and association rules generated beforehand should not be thrown away, since we need them to produce generalized association rules.

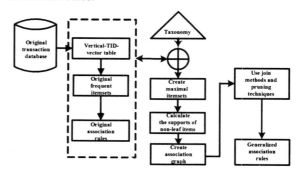

Figure 1. Processing flow of mining algorithms

At first, we create maximal itemsets from the original frequent itemsets, and then store them in an array to reduce disk space and speed up the mining operation. Although no subsets of a maximal itemset are stored, we can use a hash function to calculate the position of each subset in a maximal itemset and find its support. Next, given a hierarchical taxonomy tree, we must calculate the supports of the non-leaf items in the taxonomy tree from the maximal itemsets or VTV table. Basically, for a non-leaf item t being the ancestor of $\{i_1, i_2, ..., i_n\}$ where items $i_1, i_2, ...,$ and i_n are leaf-items, the support of item t can found in the array of maximal itemset I if $\{i_1, i_2, ..., i_n\}$ is a subset of maximal itemset I. Then, we use the original frequent itemsets L_1 and L_2, and non-leaf items with the supports $\geq$ the minimum support to create an association graph. It facilitates check whether k-itemsets ($k \geq 3$) involving non-leaf and leaf items are frequent or not. Finally, in our algorithm GMAR, we use join methods and pruning techniques to generate new generalized association rules. The join methods used in the GMAR algorithm can directly produce generalized association rules from the original association rules, and the pruning techniques are used to prune irrelevant rules, thereby speeding up the production of generalized association rules.

3.2. The vertical-TID-vector table

The vertical-TID-vector table was generated before the

228

mining algorithm is executed. It uses bit vectors to record the transaction information. Each item is represented with a bit vector where the length of the bit vector is the total number of transactions in the database. If an item appears in the jth transaction, the jth bit of the corresponding bit vector is set to 1; otherwise, the bit is set to 0. As shown in Figure 2 and 3, Since item i_3 appears in transactions 1, 8, 9, and 10, the bit vector for item i_3 can be expressed as [1000000111]. The bit vector facilitates the support computation of an itemset $\{i_1, i_2, i_3, ..., i_k\}$.

TID	Items
T1	i_3
T2	i_1, i_5
T3	i_2, i_5
T4	i_4
T5	i_4
T6	i_1, i_5
T7	i_2, i_5
T8	i_1, i_2, i_3, i_5
T9	i_1, i_2, i_3, i_5
T10	i_1, i_3, i_4, i_5

Figure 2. Transaction database

Items	T1	T2	T3	T4	T5	T6	T7	T8	T9	T10
i_1	0	1	0	0	0	1	0	1	1	1
i_2	0	0	1	0	0	0	1	1	1	0
i_3	1	0	0	0	0	0	0	1	1	1
i_4	0	0	0	1	1	0	0	0	0	1
i_5	0	1	1	0	0	1	1	1	1	1

Figure 3. Vertical-TID-vector table

3.3. Creating maximal itemsets

A maximal itemset is defined as a frequent itemset not contained in any other frequent itemset. For example, given a set of frequent itemsets $\{\{i_1\}, \{i_2\}, \{i_3\}, \{i_4\}, \{i_5\}, \{i_1, i_3\}, \{i_1, i_5\}, \{i_2, i_5\}, \{i_3, i_5\}, \{i_1, i_3, i_5\}\}$, the maximal itemsets are $\{i_4\}$, $\{i_2, i_5\}$ and $\{i_1, i_3, i_5\}$. As shown in Figure 1, the procedure to find the maximal itemsets from a set of frequent itemsets is described as follows:

Gen-Max-Itemset:
Step 1: Initialize all frequent itemsets unmarked.
Step 2: Set k the maximal length of frequent itemsets.
Step 3: For each unmarked frequent k-itemsets,
    Step 3.1: Generate all the proper subsets.
    Step 3.2: If any frequent h-itemset p (h < k) is one
        of the subsets, mark p.
Step 4: k=k-1 and then repeat from Step 3 until k=1.
Step 5: The maximal itemsets are those not marked so far.

An example, as shown in Figure 4, illustrates how to find the maximal itemsets from a set of frequent itemsets

where the unmarked itemsets are the maximal ones; i.e., $\{i_4\}$, $\{i_2, i_5\}$ and $\{i_1, i_3, i_5\}$.

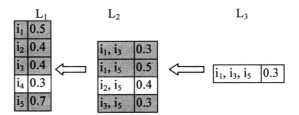

Figure 4. Finding maximal itemsets

Here we only need to store the maximal itemsets, as shown in Figure 5, to reduce disk space and speed up the mining operation. In the figure, the supports of all non-empty subsets of maximal itemset $\{i_1, i_3, i_5\}$ are 0.5 for $\{i_1\}$, 0.4 for $\{i_3\}$, 0.7 for $\{i_5\}$, 0.3 for $\{i_1, i_3\}$, 0.5 for $\{i_1, i_5\}$, 0.3 for $\{i_3, i_5\}$, and 0.3 for $\{i_1, i_3, i_5\}$, respectively. Instead of storing all non-empty subsets of a maximal itemset, we can use the hash function to calculate the position of any subset in a maximal itemset and find its support. For example, through the hash function, we can compute the value 5 for the position of $\{i_1, i_5\}$ in maximal itemset $\{i_1, i_3, i_5\}$, and find its support value 0.5. The hash function used here can be expressed as follows:

T: the length of a maximal itemset,
L: the length of a subset itemset
$X(i)$: the position in a maximal itemset for the ith item of a subset itemset, where $1 \leq i \leq L$ and $X(0)=0$
HF: the position of a subset item in a maximal itemset.

$$HF = \sum_{i=1}^{L-1} C_i^T + \sum_{i=0}^{L-1} \left(C_{L-i}^{T-X(i)} - C_{L-i}^{T-X(i+1)+1} \right) + 1$$

i_4	0.3						
i_2, i_5	0.4	0.7	0.4				
i_1, i_3, i_5	0.5	0.4	0.7	0.3	0.5	0.3	0.3

Figure 5. The maximal itemsets

3.4. Calculating the supports of non-leaf items

Given the original frequent itemsets and association rules already generated beforehand, and a hierarchical taxonomy tree, we can produce new generalized association rules, rather than re-scanning the original database. However the items, except those at the leaf level in the taxonomy tree, do not appear in the original frequent itemsets and association rules. Therefore we must calculate the supports of the non-leaf items in the taxonomy tree from the maximal itemsets or VTV table. For a non-leaf item t being the ancestor of $\{i_1, i_2, ..., i_n\}$ where items $i_1, i_2, ...,$ and i_n are leaf-items, the support of item *t* can be calculated as follows:

Support(t) = $I[HF(\{i_1, i_2, ..., i_n\})]$, if $\{i_1, i_2, ..., i_n\}$ is a subset of maximal itemset I
or
Support(t) = |vector(i_1) OR ... OR vector(i_n)|/no. of trans.

Here we take an example to illustrate how the supports of non-leaf items are calculated. Given the VTV table and the taxonomy tree as shown in Figure 3 and 6, we can calculate the supports of non-leaf items 1001, 1002, and 1003 as follows:

Support(1001) = |vector(1) OR vector(2)|/no. of trans.
= |[0110011111]|/10 = 0.7
Support(1002) = |vector(1) OR vector(2) OR vector(3)| /no. of trans.
= |[1110011111]|/10 = 0.8
Support(1003) = |vector(4) OR vector(5)|/no. of trans.
= |[0111111111]|/10 = 0.9

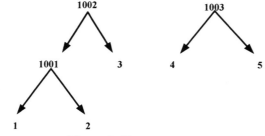

Figure 6. Taxonomy tree

3.5. Creating association graphs

In our mining algorithm, different from the Apriori algorithm, we only use the original frequent itemsets L_1 and L_2 to generate k-itemsets (k ≥ 3) involving non-leaf and leaf items and check whether they are frequent or not. Our method is based on a graph called association graph to search all these k-itemsets. The association graph is defined as follows:

A graph AG(V, E), called association graph, consists a set of vertices or items V and a set of edges E where
1) V = L_1 ∪ T where T = {v | v is a non-leaf item and support(v) ≥ the minimum support}, and
2) E = {u—v | {u, v} in L_2} ∪ {x—y | at least one item of {x, y} is in T, x and y are not in the ancestor-offspring relationship, and support({x, y}) ≥ the minimum support}

Given the VTV table and the taxonomy tree as shown in Figure 3 and 6, the minimum support 0.3, and the original frequent itemsets L_1 and L_2, we can obtain the

frequent itemsets T, and then create the association graph as shown in Figure 7.

L_1 = {1, 2, 3, 4, 5}, L_2 = {{1, 3}, {1, 5}, {2, 5}, {3, 5}},
T = {1001, 1002, 1003}

Support({1, 1003}) = 0.5, Support({2, 1003}) = 0.4
Support({3, 1001}) = 0.3, Support({3, 1003}) = 0.3
Support({4, 1001}) = 0.1, Support({4, 1002}) = 0.1
Support({5, 1001}) = 0.7, Support({5, 1002}) = 0.7
Support({1001, 1003}) = 0.7, Support({1002, 1003}) = 0.7

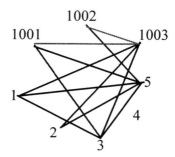

Figure 7. Association graph

3.6. Pruning techniques

In the GMAR algorithm to be discussed in the next section, we use pruning techniques to generate new generalized association rules since pruning irrelevant rules can speed up the production of generalized association rules. Here we have six pruning techniques described as follows:

PT 1: For a frequent itemset I where i_{min} is the item with the minimum support count within it, if support($\{i_{min}\}$)/support(subset(I)) is less than the minimum confidence, then we can prune any rule subset(I) ⇒ I − subset(I).

Rationale: For any rule subset(I) ⇒ I − subset(I), the confidence check is support(I)/support(subset(I)). Since support(I) must be less than or equal to support($\{i_{min}\}$), support(I)/support(subset(I)) is definitely less than the minimum confidence as long as support($\{i_{min}\}$)/support(subset(I)) is less than the minimum confidence. In other words, we can use support($\{i_{min}\}$) instead of support(I) in the confidence check.

PT 2: For a subset P in a frequent itemset I, if the rule P ⇒ I − P holds, then any rule whose antecedent containing P, such as superset(P) ⇒ I − superset(P), holds as well.

Rationale: If the rule P ⇒ I − P holds, it implies that

support(I)/support(P) is more than or equal to the minimum confidence. Nevertheless, since support(superset(P)) is less than or equal to support(P), support(I)/support(superset(P)) is definitely more than or equal to the minimum confidence, and thus the corresponding rule holds as well.

PT 3: For two rules with the same antecedent, if 1) the rule $P \Rightarrow Q_1$ holds and 2) the rule $P \Rightarrow Q_2$ does not hold due to support($P \cup Q_2$) < the minimum support, then all the rules corresponding to the itemset I (= $P \cup Q_1 \cup Q_2$) do not hold.

Rationale: If one of the rules corresponding to the itemset I holds, then I must be a frequent itemset and all the subsets are frequent itemsets as well. However we know $P \cup Q_2$ is not a frequent itemset since support($P \cup Q_2$) is less than the minimum support. Thus all these rules corresponding to the itemset I do not hold. For example, if 1) the rule $i_1 \Rightarrow i_2$ holds and 2) the rule $i_1 \Rightarrow i_3$ does not hold due to support($\{i_1, i_3\}$) < the minimum support, then all the rules, such as $i_1 \Rightarrow i_2 \wedge i_3$, $i_2 \Rightarrow i_1 \wedge i_3$, $i_3 \Rightarrow i_1 \wedge i_2$, $i_2 \wedge i_3 \Rightarrow i_1$, $i_1 \wedge i_3 \Rightarrow i_2$, and $i_1 \wedge i_2 \Rightarrow i_3$, do not hold.

PT 4: If the rule $P \Rightarrow Q_1$ holds, then the rule $P \Rightarrow Q_2$ always holds where Q_2 is derived from Q_1 by replacing some items in Q_1 with their ancestors.

Rationale: If the rule $P \Rightarrow Q_1$ holds, it implies that support($P \cup Q_1$)/support(P) is more than or equal to the minimum confidence. Since support(Q_2) is more than or equal to support(Q_1), support($P \cup Q_2$)/support(P) is definitely more than or equal to the minimum confidence and thus the rule $P \Rightarrow Q_2$ always holds.

PT 5: For two rules with the same antecedent, if 1) the rule $P \Rightarrow Q_1$ holds and 2) the rule $P \Rightarrow Q_2$ does not hold due to not satisfying the minimum confidence although it satisfies the minimum support, then the rule $P \Rightarrow Q_1 \cup Q_2$ does not hold.

Rationale: For the confidence check support($P \cup Q_2$)/support(P) < the minimum confidence, support($P \cup Q_1 \cup Q_2$)/support(P) is definitely less than the minimum confidence since support($P \cup Q_1 \cup Q_2$) is less than or equal to support($P \cup Q_2$). Thus the rule $P \Rightarrow Q_1 \cup Q_2$ does not hold.

PT 6: If any item in a frequent itemset I does not appear in association graph AG or all the items in I do not

form a complete connection in AG, then, for a subset P of I, the rule $P \Rightarrow I - P$ does not holds.

Rationale: If the rule $P \Rightarrow I - P$ holds, support(I)/support(P) is not only more than or equal to the minimum confidence, but also support(I) should be more than or equal to the minimum support. In other words, all the items in I would appear in AG and form a complete connection. This contradicts the assumption, and therefore the rule $P \Rightarrow I - P$ does not holds.

3.7. GMAR algorithm

The Apriori algorithm proposed by Agrawal and Srikant is a two-step process which consists of join and pruning actions to find frequent itemsets, and then uses the frequent itemsets to derive association rules. In the section, an algorithm GMAR (Generalized Mining Association Rules) is proposed, which generates generalized association rules not directly based on the raw data from the database, but based on the original frequent itemsets and association rules. Here an association rule is called weak when it satisfies the minimum support threshold, but not minimum confidence threshold. In the GMAR algorithm, we need both strong and weak association rules in the current level (*k-1*) to generate the generalized association rules for from the next level *k* to the next *2k-3* level, as shown in Figure 8. Therefore, the generation of the generalized association rules is not based on a step-by-step manner. The detailed algorithm is described as follows:

GMAR Algorithm:
Input: VTV table, original association rules (R_o), taxonomy tree, min_sup, min_conf
Output: new generalized association rules
Method:
Step 1: Generate new frequent 1-itemsets L_{n1} using VTV table and taxonomy tree;
Step 2: Create association graph AG using original frequent itemsets L_{o1} and L_{o2}, and new frequent 1-itemsets L_{n1};
Step 3: For each edge x—y in association graph AG where {x, y} is not in L_{o2}
  Add the rules "x $\Rightarrow$ y" and "y $\Rightarrow$ x" to R_{n2};
  If support({x, y})/support(x) $\geq$ min_conf
   Set the rule "x $\Rightarrow$ y" strong;
  If support({x, y})/support(y) $\geq$ min_conf
   Set the rule "y $\Rightarrow$ x" strong;
Step 4: For (k = 3; $R_{n(k-1)} \neq \varnothing$; k++)
  Generate weak (k-1)-association rules using the original frequent (k-1)-itemsets $L_{o(k-1)}$ and add them to $R_{o(k-1)}$;
  GMAR_Gen($R_{o(k-1)}$, $R_{n(k-1)}$);

GMAR_Gen($R_{n(k-1)}$, $R_{n(k-1)}$);
Step 5: $R_n = \cup_k \{r \mid r \in R_{nk}$ and r is a strong rule$\}$;

Procedure GMAR_Gen(R_1, R_2)
1. For each rule $r_1 \in R_1$
   For each rule $r_2 \in R_2$
      { /* Using PT 5 */
      If (r_1.antecedent = r_2.antecedent) and
         (r_1.consequent $\neq$ r_2.consequent) and
         (conf(r_1) $\geq$ min_conf) and
         (conf(r_2) $\geq$ min_conf)
      /* Using PT 3 and PT 6 */
         If all the items in $\{r_1$.antecedent$\}$ $\cup$
            $\{r_1$.consequent$\}$ $\cup$ $\{r_2$.consequent$\}$
            can form a complete connection in
            association graph AG
      /* Using PT 2 and PT 4 */
            r = "r_1.antecedent $\Rightarrow$ r_1.consequent
               $\wedge$ r_2.consequent ";
            i = length(r);
      /* Using PT 1 */
            Add the rule r to R_{ni};
            If conf(r) $\geq$ min_conf
               Set the rule r strong;
      If (r_1.antecedent $\neq$ r_2.antecedent) and
         (r_1.consequent = r_2.consequent)
      /* Using PT 3 and PT 6 */
         If all the items in $\{r_1$.antecedent$\}$ $\cup$
            $\{r_2$.antecedent$\}$ $\cup$ $\{r_1$.consequent$\}$
            can form a complete connection in
            association graph AG
      /* Using PT 2 and PT 4 */
            r = "r_1.antecedent $\wedge$ r_2. antecedent
               $\Rightarrow$ r_1.consequent";
            i = length(r);
      /* Using PT 1 */
            Add the rule r to R_{ni};
            If conf(r) $\geq$ min_conf
               Set the rule r strong;
      }

Figure 8. GMAR algorithm to generate new generalized association rules

Given the VTV table (as shown in Figure 3), the original frequent itemsets L_{o1} and L_{o2} (as shown in Figure 4), the original association rules R_o (including the strong rules in R_{o2} and R_{o3}), the taxonomy tree (as shown in Figure 6), the minimum support 0.3, and the minimum confidence 0.5, new generalized association rules R_n (including the strong rules in R_{n2} and R_{n3}) can be generated using the GMAR algorithm as follows. Among the rules, a rule is marked if it is a strong one.

R_{o2}

Rules	Confidence	Rules	Confidence
1$\Rightarrow$3	0.6	2$\Rightarrow$5	1
3$\Rightarrow$1	0.75	5$\Rightarrow$2	0.5714286
1$\Rightarrow$5	1	3$\Rightarrow$5	0.75
5$\Rightarrow$1	0.7142857	5$\Rightarrow$3	0.4285714

R_{n2}

Rules	Confidence	Rules	Confidence
1$\Rightarrow$1003	1	1002$\Rightarrow$5	0.875
1003$\Rightarrow$1	0.5555556	1001$\Rightarrow$1003	1
2$\Rightarrow$1003	1	1003$\Rightarrow$1001	0.7777778
3$\Rightarrow$1001	0.75	1002$\Rightarrow$1003	0.875
3$\Rightarrow$1003	0.75	1003$\Rightarrow$1002	0.7777778
5$\Rightarrow$1001	1	1003$\Rightarrow$2	0.4444444
1001$\Rightarrow$5	1	1001$\Rightarrow$3	0.4285714
5$\Rightarrow$1002	1	1003$\Rightarrow$3	0.3333333

R_{o3}

Rules	Confidence	Rules	Confidence
1$\Rightarrow$3,5	0.6	1,5$\Rightarrow$3	0.6
3$\Rightarrow$1,5	0.75	3,5$\Rightarrow$1	1
1,3$\Rightarrow$5	1	5$\Rightarrow$1,3	0.4285714

$R_{n3} = (R_{o2}$ join $R_{n2}) \cup (R_{n2}$ join $R_{n2})$

Rules	Confidence	Rules	Confidence
1$\Rightarrow$3,1003	0.6	3,1001$\Rightarrow$1003	1
3$\Rightarrow$1,1003	0.75	3,1003$\Rightarrow$1001	1
1,3$\Rightarrow$1003	1	1003$\Rightarrow$1,3	0.3333333
1,1003$\Rightarrow$3	0.6	1001$\Rightarrow$3,5	0.4285714
3,1003$\Rightarrow$1	1	5,1001$\Rightarrow$3	0.4285714
3$\Rightarrow$5,1001	0.75	5$\Rightarrow$3,1001	0.4285714
3,5$\Rightarrow$1001	1	1001,1003$\Rightarrow$3	0.4285714
3,1001$\Rightarrow$5	1	1001$\Rightarrow$3,1003	0.4285714
3$\Rightarrow$1001,1003	0.75	1003$\Rightarrow$3,1001	0.3333333

$R_{o4} = \emptyset$

$R_{n4} = \{r \mid r \in (R_{o3}$ join $R_{n3}) \cup (R_{n3}$ join $R_{n3})$ and length(r) = 4$\} = \emptyset$

4. Performance evaluations

4.1. Simulation model

In the section, we evaluate the performances of the three algorithms, including BASIC [12], Cumulate [12], and GMAR, on a DELL PowerEdge 4400 Server with Intel® Xeon Processor and 756MB main memory running Windows 2000 server. All the experimental data are generated randomly and stored on a local 30GB SCSI Disk (Ultra 160) with a RAID controller. The relative simulation parameters are shown in Table 1. To make our data representative, we generate two types of databases in the experiments; i.e., DENSE databases and SPARSE databases. Each item in the DENSE database is randomly generated from a pool P called potentially frequent itemsets with size 300, while each item in the SPARSE database is randomly generated from a pool N (i.e., the set of all the items) with size 1000. Since the items in the DENSE database are more clustered than those in the SPARSE database, larger frequent itemsets will probably be produced in the DENSE database for the same minimum support. Besides, we use the notations T for average number of items per transaction, I for average number of items in a frequent itemset, and D for number of transactions. For example, the experiment labeled with $T10.I3.D1K$ represents the simulation environment with 10 items on the average per transaction, 3 items on the average in a frequent itemset, and 1000 transactions in total.

Table 1. Simulation parameters with default values

D	Number of transactions	1000-500,000
T	Number of the items per transaction	5-15
P	Number of potentially frequent itemsets	300
I	Number of the items in a frequent itemset	2-5
N	Number of items	1000
R	Number of taxonomy trees	31-75
L	Number of levels in a taxonomy tree	3

4.2. Experimental results

Experiment 1:

In the experiment, we explore the execution time of BASIC, Cumulate, and GMAR algorithms for the environment $T10.I3.D1K$ under different minimum support and minimum confidence pairs, as shown in Figure 9. In the figure, we find that our algorithm GMAR is almost faster 2-16 times than BASIC, especially for larger minimum support and minimum confidence pairs, whereas Cumulate is only faster 1.3-1.5 times than BASIC, although R. Srikant and R. Agrawal claimed that Cumulate runs faster 2-5 times than BASIC [12]. In general, the larger the minimum support and minimum

confidence pair is, the faster the execution time of the three algorithms becomes. To be fair to all algorithms, we have added the extra time of generating original frequent itemsets and association rules for GMAR. However the time is below 1% of total execution time; thus we do not show it in the figure.

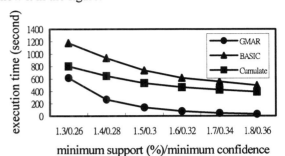

Figure 9. Execution time for different pairs

Experiment 2:

In the experiment, we extend Experiment 1 by fixing the minimum support 1.5%, and observe their variations. For the minimum support 1.5%, all the algorithms except GMAR are not sensitive to the changes of the minimum confidences, as shown in Figure 10. The reason is that larger minimum confidences will make GMAR prune more irrelevant rules. Nevertheless, GMAR is still in the first rank.

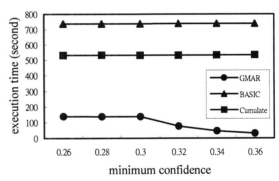

Figure 10. Execution time for different minimum confidences

Experiment 3:

In the experiment, we explore the execution time of the three algorithms for the environment $T10.I3.DxK$ (i.e., different numbers of transactions) generated in the SPARSE database and in the DENSE database, as shown in Figure 11.(a) and (b), respectively. Both cases have the same minimum confidence 0.3. However, to get comparable number of frequent itemsets, we set a smaller minimum support 1% in the SPARSE case, and a larger minimum support 2% in the DENSE case. As expected, GMAR is still the best one among them in the SPARSE and DENSE case, especially when there are a huge amount of transactions. From the both cases, we find that much more frequent itemsets are generated in the DENSE database than in SPARSE database, so that BASIC and Cumulate are not practicable candidates there.

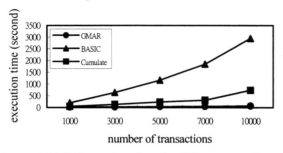

Figure 11.(a) Execution time for different numbers of transactions in the SPARSE database

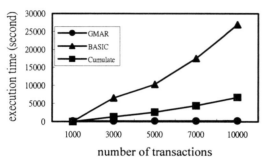

Figure 11.(b) Execution time for different numbers of transactions in the DENSE database

5. Conclusions

In the paper, we try to find the association rules between the items at different levels in the taxonomy tree under the assumption that original frequent itemsets and association rules have already been generated beforehand. The primary challenge is how to make use of the original frequent itemsets and association rules to directly generate new generalized association rules, rather than rescanning the database. In the proposed algorithm GMAR, we use join methods and pruning techniques to generate new generalized association rules. Through several comprehensive experiments, we find that the GMAR algorithm is much better than BASIC and Cumulate algorithms, since it generates fewer candidate itemsets, and furthermore prunes a large amount of irrelevant rules based on the minimum confidence.

6. Acknowledgments

This research was supported in part by the National Science Council, Taiwan, under contract NSC-90-2213-E-224-026.

7. References

[1] R. Agrawal, T. Imielinski, and A. Swami, "Mining Association Rules between Sets of Items in Large Databases," *Proc. ACM International Conference on Management of Data*, 1993, pp. 207-216.

[2] R. Agrawal and R. Srikant, "Fast Algorithms for Mining Association Rules," *Proc. 20th International Conference on Very Large Data Bases*, 1994, pp. 487-499.

[3] Yong-Jian Fu, "Data Mining," *IEEE Potentials, Vol. 16, No. 4*, 1997, pp. 18-20.

[4] Jia-Wei Han and Yong-Jian Fu, "Mining Multiple-level Association Rules in Large Databases," *IEEE Transactions on Knowledge and Data Engineering, Vol. 11, No. 5*, 1999, pp. 798-805.

[5] Jia-Wei Han and Micheline Kamber, *Data Mining: Concepts and Techniques*, Morgan Kaufmann Publishers, 2001.

[6] Jia-Wei Han, Jian Pei, and Yi-Wen Yin, "Mining Frequent Patterns without Candidate Generation," *Proc. ACM International Conference on Management of Data*, 2000, pp. 1-12.

[7] Mon-Fong Jiang, Shian-Shyong Tseng, and Shan-Yi Lia, "Data Types Generalization for Data Mining Algorithms," *Proc. IEEE International Conference on Systems, Man, and Cybernetics*, 1999, pp. 928-933.

[8] Bing Liu, Wynne Hsu, and Yi-Ming Ma, "Mining Association Rules with Multiple Minimum Supports," *Proc. 5th ACM International Conference on Knowledge Discovery and Data Mining*, 1999, pp. 337-341.

[9] J. S. Park, M. S. Chen, and P. S. Yu, "An Effective Hash-based Algorithm for Mining Association Rules," *Proc. ACM International Conference on Management of Data*, 1995, pp. 175-186.

[10] A. Savasere, E. Omiecinski, and S. Navathe, "An Efficient Algorithm for Mining Association Rules in Large Databases," *Proc. 21st International Conference on Very Large Data Bases*, 1995, pp. 432-443.

[11] Pradeep Shenoy, Jayant Haritsa, S. Sudarshan, Gaurav Bhalotia, Mayank Bawa, and Devavrat Shah, "Turbo-charging Vertical Mining of Large Databases," *Proc. ACM International Conference on Management of Data*, 2000, pp. 22-33.

[12] R. Srikant and R. Agrawal, "Mining Generalized Association Rules," *Proc. 21st International Conference on Very Large Data Bases*, 1995, pp. 407-419.

[13] S. Y. Sung, K. Wang, and L. Chua, "Data Mining in a Large Database Environment," *Proc. IEEE International Conference on Systems, Man, and Cybernetics*, 1996, pp. 988-993.

[14] H. Toivonen, "Sampling Large Databases for Association Rules," *Proc. 22nd International Conference on Very Large Data Bases*, 1996, pp. 134-145.

[15] Ming-Cheng Tseng, Wen-Yang Lin, and Been-Chian Chien, "Maintenance of Generalized + Association Rules with Multiple Minimum Supports," *Proc. 9th IFSA World Congress and 20th NAFIPS International Conference*, 2001, pp. 1294-1299.

A Formal Model for User Preference

Sung Young Jung
Machine Intelligence Group
LG Electronics Institute of Technology,
16 SeoCho-Gu WooMyeon-Dong, Seoul,
137-140, Korea, +82-2-16-245-2469,
chopinxenakis@hotmail.com
chopin@csone.kaist.ac.kr

Jeong-Hee Hong
Machine Intelligence Group
LG Electronics Institute of Technology,
16 SeoCho-Gu WooMyeon-Dong, Seoul,
137-140, Korea, +82-2-526-4128
jhhong@lge.com

Taek-Soo Kim
Machine Intelligence Group
LG Electronics Institute of Technology,
16 SeoCho-Gu WooMyeon-Dong, Seoul,
137-140, Korea, +82-2-526-4110
tskim@lge.com

Abstract

Personalization and recommendation systems require formalized model for user preference. This paper presents the formal model of preference including positive preference and negative preference. For rare events, we apply the probability of random occurrence in order to reduce noise effects caused by data sparseness. Pareto distribution is adopted for the random occurrence probability. We also present the method for combining information of joint feature variables in different sizes by dynamic weighting using random occurrence probability.

Keywords

User Preference, Recommendation, Personalization, Data Sparseness, Pareto Distribution, Random Occurrence Probability, Dynamic Weighting Model.

1. Introduction

User preference is an important concept to predict user behaviors and recommend preferred items in personalization systems. Many researches on personalization system [1] [2] [3] have adopted direct recommendation models which do not have formal preference model, so they have problems in dealing with intrinsic properties of preference, and interpreting intuitive meaning of preference from the results.

Preference is the concept to make relation between a person and a target item which contains several kinds of attributes. Usually preference of an item is indirectly related by preference of attributes contained in the item. So it can be said that preference deals with relation between attributes and the item. The concept of association [4] [5] [6] [7] is different from that of preference on the point that association deals with relation between two item sets although there are applied approaches to deal with general rule mining [8] [9] including profile building [10].

In personalization system of E-commerce area, each user has a behavior history such as purchasing, viewing, navigation, or explicit voting. An item may correspond to a product, a service, or a web page, which has contents such as categories, descriptions, costs, etc. Preference is computed by the user information composed by their behavior history, and the product information composed by contents. They share common attributes, in other words, features. For example, a user can have selection count for each category such as classic music, computer, stocks, etc., at the same time, each product can have corresponding category information, so that the category information can be a common feature.

It is necessary to find common features of a user and an item for preference modeling. More important thing is to combine the information of features to predict the preference value of the item containing them. Various features can contain redundant information since there can be superset joint features for a single feature variable. Long-sized joint feature provides more accurate information than short one, but they have *data sparseness problem* that the number of input variables grows exponentially whereas training data size is limited. It brings about severe noise because training data is insufficient to fulfill all the joint features practically. So a proper mechanism is necessary to combine various information sources which can contribute to degrade the data sparseness.

Many recommendation models such as association rule mining [4] [6], collaborative filtering [11] [12] [17], and Bayesian network [1] provide good methods to find meaningful information for recommendation, but they do not say how much the user prefers a given item or feature, and how much he dislikes it. It is necessary to make formal model of preference since the behavior of preference is different from the concept of probability or association, especially when the user dislikes given item, since information for dislike is very important in preference concept while not in association and collaborative filtering. This paper will describe the preference model for positive and negative cases derived by the formal definition of preference.

There are other researches related with the concept of preference. For example, many researches of decision theory uses preference values as given information [18], and it was applied to information retrieval researches which are aimed to estimate system accuracy by comparing system

235

output with explicit user ranking [19]. The researches oriented from decision theory are different from this paper in the point that they use preference as pre-given information and usually the data is given by explicit human rating, while the aim of this paper is to predict user preference of features and items from natural user behaviors.

This paper is organized as follows: The notations for this paper are listed in Table 1. The next section describes the preference model and the combining method for joint features considering random occurrence probability. And the next section describes how Pareto distribution is used for the random occurrence probability. And we present a feature preference model containing positive, and negative preference. Subsequently, we report on the experimental evaluation of proposed methods. Finally we summarize conclusions.

2. Preference Model

Preference is defined by the function representing how much a user likes a given *item*. The user has his behavior history V. Then *preference* for an item, Pref(x) is the function of item x and user history V. And it can be approximated by using user profile G.

$$\text{Pref}(x) = f(x,V)$$
$$\approx f(x,G) \qquad (1)$$

User history V is represented by the set of selected items like $V = \{x_1, x_2, \cdots, x_n\}$ which is collected by natural user behaviors such as purchasing, viewing, or voting. V can be considered as the user preferred item set. Each item x has the several attributes, and an attribute corresponds to a feature w. So an item x can be represented by the set of features $x = \{w_1, w_2, \cdots, w_m\}$. *User profile G* is defined by the preference value Pref(w) of each *feature w*, $G = \{\text{Pref}(w_1), \text{Pref}(w_2), \cdots\}$. *The feature preference* Pref(w) is computed from the user history.

Since user profile G and item x is not homogeneous information, they cannot be compared directly. They should be split into common features, Consequently, the preference function is defined by the common features which both of user profile G and item x have.

$$\text{Pref}(x) = f(x,G)$$
$$= \frac{1}{M(x)} \sum_{w_i \in x, \text{Pref}(w_i) \in G} \text{Pref}(w_i) \qquad (2)$$

where $M(x)$ is normalization term which is defined by the number of features appeared in item x. The preference for a given item is defined by the normalized summation of the feature preferences on the assumption that all the features are independent. We propose mutual information for the preference measure which makes equation (2) to be valid

and effective and gives intuitive interpretation of preference value.

$$\text{Pref}(w) = I(X(w); V) \qquad (3)$$

where $X(w) = \{x \mid w \in x\}$, $X(w)$ is the set of all items which contains the feature w, $I(X(w); V) = \log(P(X(w) \mid V) / P(X(w)))$, $I(X(w); V)$ is mutual information. $P(X(w))$ is called feature probability, and $P(X(w) \mid V)$ is feature probability given user history. The feature preference is defined by the mutual information between the item set containing the feature $X(w)$, and the preferred item set V. The preference value is larger when $X(w)$ is similar to V, and smaller when $X(w)$ and V are disjoint. It means that given feature w has a high preference value when user selected more items containing w, and it has a low preference value when user selected less items containing w. The preference value 0 means that it is neutral, and it happens when a user selected items containing the feature with the probability same to the feature probability, i.e. $P(X(w) \mid V) = P(X(w))$. So, the mid point which separates preference to be positive or negative is the feature probability value in the whole events.

Using mutual information for preference modeling gives intuitive interpretation of preference by the amount of information provided by user behavior. In other words, we can interpret the resulting preference value that a user prefers given item with additional bits of information compared with neutral situation.

2.1 Combining Information of Joint Features in Different Size

Preference for an item is acquired by normalized summation of feature preferences occurred in the item on the assumption that all features are independent variables. But in most problems, features are correlated, so that they are not independent. A *joint feature* w^k is the combination of k single features where the feature w is included as one of them.

$$w^k = w_{i_1} w_{i_2} \cdots w_{i_k} \qquad (4)$$

where $w^1 = w$, $w \in \{w_{i_1}, w_{i_2}, \cdots, w_{i_k}\}$, $\{w_{i_1}, w_{i_2}, \cdots, w_{i_k}\} \subseteq x$. A joint feature variable w^k provides more accurate information than a single feature variable w when sufficient data is observed in training data. k is *the size of joint feature*. Joint feature should be used in order to exploit more accurate information provided by correlated variables. We call w^{k+1}, or $w^{k+2}, \cdots$, or w^∞ *superset feature*, and w^{k-1}, or $w^{k-2}, \cdots$, or w^1 *subset feature* for given w^k.

As the size k grows, data sparseness problem arises, and joint feature suffers from severe noise. Training data cannot fulfill information of joint features since the required amount of training data explodes exponentially relative to k. In order to alleviate the data sparseness problem, subset features can be used and combined.

A joint feature always has redundant information with its subset features, for example, w^k has redundant information with all its subset features $w^{k-1}, w^{k-2}, \cdots, w^1$. When w^k has sufficiently observed data, its subset features should be ignored, but when it does not, subset features should not be disregarded since they provide useful information. We propose a method to combine superset and subset features by dynamic weighting depending on the reliability of the information source of its superset feature. The preference model is now deduced from equation (2) and (4) by combining subset feature information using dynamic weighting as follows.

$$\text{Pref}(x) = \frac{1}{M(x)} \sum_{w \in x} \sum_k \lambda_k(w) I(X(w^k); V) \qquad (5)$$

where $\lambda_k(w)$ is dynamic weight for the information source of joint feature w^k. $\lambda_k(w)$ has the value always between 0 and 1, $0 \leq \forall \lambda_k(w) \leq 1$. We will show details of dynamic weighting model in the next section.

2.2 Dynamic Weighting Model considering Random Occurrence Probability

The probability term for an event, estimated by observing training data, has sample probability, not true probability. Sample probability converges to true probability as the size of observed data grows to infinite. When the size of observed data is not sufficient, the sample probability becomes inaccurate because events appeared in sampled set follows a random distribution.

Random occurrence probability $P_{random}(w)$ represents the ratio of information provided by randomness of given event including sampling effects. We will describe details of this model in the next section.

We propose *dynamic weight model* $\lambda_k(w)$ using random occurrence probability. Here, the dynamic weight represents the randomness of all the superset features. It should have large value when all its superset features occurred randomly by lack of observed data. And it should have small value when one of its superset features has sufficiently observed data. We define the dynamic weight $\lambda_k(w)$ by the function of dynamic weight of k+1 superset feature $\lambda_{k+1}(w)$ multiplied by the random occurrence probability of k+1 superset feature $P_{random}(w^{k+1})$. The dynamic weight converges to 1 as the size of joint feature

grows to infinite $\lim_{k \to \infty} \lambda_k(w) = 1$ because the larger the size of joint feature, the more randomly it occurs in sampled set by lack of observed data.

$$\lambda_k(w) = \lambda_{k+1}(w) P_{random}(w^{k+1}) \qquad (6)$$

It means that the dynamic weight is the products of random occurrence probability of all the superset features.

$$\therefore \lambda_k(w) = \prod_{j=1}^{\infty} P_{random}(w^{k+j}) \qquad (7)$$

2.3 Random Occurrence Probability by Random Frequency Distribution

Let's think about random experiments such as uniform, exponential, or normal distribution, etc. An event occurred in the experiment has a specific frequency. And many events with the same frequency occupy specific portion among all the events. The number of events for each frequency has a probabilistic distribution for frequency domain. The probability density function for the frequency distribution is defined as equation (8).

$$P(freq(w)) = \frac{N(\{w' | freq(w') = freq(w)\})}{N(W')} \qquad (8)$$

where W' is the set of all events or that of all variables, (not simple events) occurred in the random experiment, $freq(w)$ is the frequency of the event w, and $N(W')$ is the number of events in the random experiment. The probability of a given frequency represents how many events with the frequency occur in the random experiment.

Random occurrence probability $P_{random}(w)$ of a given event w is the function of the frequency of w in a random experiment. $P_{random}(w)$ means the probability that events with the frequency same to w will be observed in the random experiment in the frequency domain. So it represents how many events with the frequency can occur in a random experiment.

$$P_{random}(w) = P(freq(w)) \qquad (9)$$

For the preference modeling, the random occurrence probability can be defined by the function of *random user history* V' which is composed through the random experiment. The frequency of feature w is defined by $N(X(w))$ which is the number of items containing the feature in the history.

$$P(freq(w)) = \frac{N(\{w' | N(X(w')) = N(X(w))\})}{N(W')} \qquad (10)$$

where $X(w), X(w') \subseteq V'$, W' is the set of all features occurred in the random experiment, $W' = \{w' | \exists x', (w' \in x') \wedge (x' \in V')\}$.

Fortunately, we do not have to do random experiments in order to make the random user history V' to get the random occurrence probability. Pareto distribution, which is one of the popular probability distribution for frequency, can be used for random occurrence probability instead of equation (10). We will explain it in the following section.

2.3.1 Pareto Distribution for Random Occurrence Distribution

It is well known that rank of words in randomly generated texts follows Zipf's distribution [13] which is used to alleviate noise of rare events in information retrieval area [14]. And it is also well known that a heavy-tailed distribution for the number of events given frequency follows Pareto distribution which is often used for modeling incomes in economics [15]. Both of them are a kind of power-laws distribution, and one of them can be directly transformed into the other since Zipf's distribution is for rank, and Pareto distribution is for frequency [16].

Any feature variables and joint features can be regarded as events in the random text generation experiments. A single feature can be regarded as a letter, and joint feature can be regarded as a word. The fact that randomly generated words follow Zipf's distribution means that any feature variables and their joint features also follow Zipf's distribution. Consequently, the number of features given frequency in the random experiments follows Pareto distribution.

Equation (11) shows the cumulative distribution function and probability distribution function of Pareto distribution. The probability random variable represents the frequency and the output value of the function represents the ratio of corresponding events with the frequency among all occurred events.

$$P[Z > z] = z^{-b}$$
$$P[Z = z] \approx z^{-(b+1)} = z^{-a} \qquad (11)$$

where a and b is constant. A training data set which is the collection of observed events, is assumed to be composed by random sampling from ideal population. Usually, events with small frequency occupy great deal of training data. For example, events with 1 frequency occupy the biggest part of events set. Events with small frequency bring about severe noise to cause significant problems because they occupy great portions. Pareto distribution can be used to measure the randomness of sample event based on frequency as equation (12).

$$P_{random}(w) = Pareto[Z = freq(w)]$$
$$= (freq(w))^{-a} \qquad (12)$$

where a is constant. The Pareto distribution represents the probability that events with the given frequency occurred in a random experiment. In other words, it represents how an event with the frequency is ubiquitous in a random experiment; for example, low frequency events have high Pareto probability value since there are many low frequency events in random experiments.

2.4 Feature Preference Model

We proposed the preference model using mutual information in equation (3). But we should consider the following two problems.

The one is data sparseness problem. Mutual information, which is computed from training data, may suffer from severe noise and data sparseness problem because of lack of observed data. We already showed that different information sources of subset features can be combined by using random occurrence probability. Similarly, the data sparseness problem of mutual information can be solved by random occurrence probability.

$$I(X(w);V) = (1 - P_{random}(w)) \cdot \tilde{I}(X(w);V) \qquad (13)$$

$$\tilde{I}(X(w);V) = \log \frac{\tilde{P}(X(w)\,|\,V)}{\tilde{P}(X(w))} \qquad (14)$$

where $\tilde{I}(X(w);V)$ is *observed mutual information* from training data, $I(X(w);V)$ is the *true mutual information* estimated, $\tilde{P}(\cdot)$ is *observed probability*. The observed mutual information can have noise, and the information caused by the noise will be removed by the random occurrence probability.

The other problem is the heterogeneous property of preference. The preferred items and the disliked items have different preference behavior. We call the former *positive preference*, and the latter *negative preference* respectively. Figure 1 shows an example where items containing feature w_1 are selected more frequently, and items containing feature w_2 are selected rarely or never by a user. We can regard a feature selected by a user much more as strongly positively preferred one. But it is dangerous to say that a feature selected much less is strongly negatively preferred one, because the fact that a user rarely selects an item usually means that he is indifferent to the item or he does not know that, for the lack of chance, not negatively preferred or disliked. In Figure 1, feature w_2 shows the case never selected by the user, but it is hard to be regarded as strongly disliked one definitely. Consequently, the absolute intensities of positive and negative case should be different for the cases.

Two kinds of preference model can be modeled by applying differential random occurrence probabilities in equation (13) since the disparity of positive and negative preference results from different reliability of events. We will show the positive and negative preference models in the following sections.

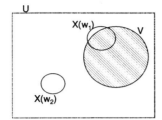

Figure 1. Positive and Negative Preference Examples

2.4.1 Positive Preference Model for a Feature

The mutual information for preference model uses the relative ratio of the *conditional probability* $\tilde{P}(X(w)|V)$ in comparison with *unconditional probability* $\tilde{P}(X(w))$ in equation (14). The mutual information may contain great noise when the size of observed data is small, so the random occurrence probability should remove the information created by noise. The random occurrence probability in positive preference is determined by the size of overlapped area between $X(w)$ and V as follows.

$$P_{random}(w) = Pareto[Z = N(X(w) \cap V)]$$
$$= N(X(w) \cap V)^{-a_1}$$
(15)

where a_1 is constant. One thing to be considered here is that if $N(X(w))$ is used for the random occurrence probability instead of the intersection with V, it may cause incorrect results when the whole item set U is sufficiently large. Figure 2 shows the example. Let's suppose the case that w_2 has positive preference where the whole item set U is relatively very large even though the overlapped set has small size. The set $X(w_2)$ itself contains rare noise because it has sufficient set size. But the overlapped area $X(w_2) \cap V$ has very small size, so that it can happen easily in random occasion and bring about great noise on mutual information since the overlapped area determine the actual mutual information. Consequently, the random occurrence probability should be the function of the intersection, $X(w) \cap V$. Figure 2 shows the case that $X(w_2)$ can overlap with V more randomly than $X(w_1)$ because the size of overlapped area is much smaller.

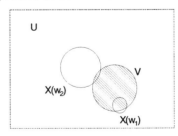

Figure 2. Examples of positive preference. The size of a universal set U is far larger than this picture shows.

2.4.2 Negative Preference Model for a Feature

When the mutual information is negative, the conditional probability $\tilde{P}(X(w)|V)$ has lower value than the unconditional probability $\tilde{P}(X(w))$. It means that a user selected the feature with probability less than unconditional probability of the feature. Figure 3 shows negative preference examples where w_1 is not selected at all, but it cannot be regarded as strongly negative preference, because it may happen in random occasion. Usually there are great many features with small frequency, and most of them are never selected by the user because he has not sufficient chance to select or notice them.

Only when a user did not select a feature even though it occurred frequently enough, the feature should be regarded to have strong negative preference. It can be assumed that the user avoided the feature because he probably had several chances to select, but did not choose it. w_2 in figure 3 shows the strong negative preference case.

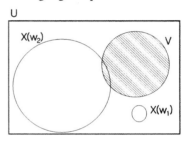

Figure 3. Examples of negative preference

The random occurrence probability for negative preference is defined by the unconditional probability of given feature $\tilde{P}(w)$.

$$P_{random}(w) = Pareto[Z = \left(1 + \frac{N(X(w))}{N(U)}\right)]$$
$$= (1 + \tilde{P}(X(w)))^{-a_2}$$
(16)

where a_2 is constant, U is a universal set of items. It means that the random occurrence probability is affected greatly only when the feature occurs frequently enough, and negative preference can have strong value only for the feature with high frequency.

2.4.3 Overall Feature Preference Model

As a concise summary for the preference model for a feature, equation (17) shows overall feature preference model.

$$\text{Pref}(w) = I(X(w);V)$$
$$= \tilde{I}(X(w);V) \times (1 - P_{random}(w))$$
$$\tilde{I}(X(w);V) = \log \frac{\tilde{P}(X(w)|V)}{\tilde{P}(X(w))} \qquad (17)$$

$$P_{random}(w) = \begin{cases} (X(w) \cap V)^{-a_1} & \text{when } \tilde{I}(X(w);V) > 0 \\ (1 + \tilde{P}(X(w)))^{-a_2} & \text{otherwise} \end{cases}$$

2.5 Approximation to Double Feature Model

In general, using long sized joint features suffers from data sparseness problem by lack of observed data. *Double feature,* which is joint feature in size two, can be one of good choices for many practical problems.

The preference model for an item, i.e. equation (5), can be deduced to maximum *K*-sized joint feature model by limiting upper bound of feature size to *K* as follows.

$$\text{Pref}(x) = \frac{1}{M(x)} \sum_{\forall w \in x} \sum_{k=1}^{K} \left(\left(\prod_{j=1}^{K-k} P_{random}(w^{k+j}) \right) \text{Pref}(w^k) \right) \quad (18)$$

Now, double feature preference model is derived by expanding summation terms by setting *K*=2, and applying equation (17) to equation (18).

$$\text{Pref}(x) \approx \frac{1}{M(x)} \sum_{w_1, w_2 \in x} (\text{Pref}(w_2 w_1) + P_{random}(w_2 w_1)\text{Pref}(w_1))$$

$$= \frac{1}{M(x)} \sum_{w_1, w_2 \in x} \left(\begin{matrix} (1 - P_{random}(w_2 w_1)) \log \dfrac{\tilde{P}(w_2 w_1 | V)}{\tilde{P}(w_2 w_1)} \\ + P_{random}(w_2 w_1)(1 - P_{random}(w_1)) \log \dfrac{\tilde{P}(w_1 | V)}{\tilde{P}(w_1)} \end{matrix} \right) \quad (19)$$

2.6 Scalability Issues

The models proposed here require only probability terms that can be calculated directly by occurrence frequency counted from training data. The time complexity for computing preference given an item is proportional to the number of feature variables used as input. For the single feature model (*K*=1), the time complexity is $O(M(x))$.

For general environment, i.e. the joint feature model (*K*>1), the time complexity becomes $O(_{M(x)}C_K)$, where $_nC_a$ is combination function. Since the number of available joint features explodes exponentially, it is computationally and practically infeasible unless additional restrictions are imposed. There are well known methods for selecting informative joint variables in association rule mining, where Apriori algorithm is practically proved to be nicely applied to reduce the number of joint variables in large data [4] [5] [6]. So, Apriori algorithm can be applied to select joint features in the preprocessing stage before preference computation. Consequently, it can be said that there are no significant problems related with scalability issues beyond what Apriori algorithm has.

For the case that only consecutive features are allowed for joint features, the time complexity becomes $O(M(x))$ equivalent to a single feature model, regardless of size of joint feature *K*.

Table 1. Notations for Preference Model

w	A feature
x	An item, $x = \{w_1, w_2, \cdots, w_m\}$
$\text{Pref}(x)$	Preference for an item x
V	User behavior history, $V = \{x_1, x_2, \cdots, x_n\}$
G	Profile, $G = \{\text{Pref}(w_1), \text{Pref}(w_2), \cdots\}$
$\text{Pref}(w)$	Feature preference
$M(x)$	Normalization term which is defined by the number of features appeared in item x
$X(w)$	The set of all items which contains the feature w, $X(w) = \{x \mid w \in x\}$
$P(X(w))$	Feature probability
$P(X(w)|V)$	Feature probability given user history.
w^k	A *joint feature* including w, $w^k = w_{i_1} w_{i_2} \cdots w_{i_k}$ $w \in \{w_{i_1}, w_{i_2}, \cdots, w_{i_k}\}$
$\lambda_k(w)$	Dynamic weight for joint feature w^k.
$freq(w)$	Frequency of the event (or feature) w
$N(A)$	The number of element in set A
$P_{random}(w)$	Random occurrence probability
$Pareto[.]$	Probability density function for Pareto distribution
$\tilde{I}(A;B)$	Observed mutual information from training data
$I(A;B)$	True mutual information
$\tilde{P}(\cdot)$	Observed probability from training data.
U	A universal set of items.
K	The limit of size of joint feature

3. Experimental Results

This preference model was created for Digital TV program recommendation system. We purchased TV watching history data from AC Nielsen Korea which is one of the authorized audience measurement company in Korea. The watching history data is collected by a monitoring device in a set-top box installed to every audience home sampled in balanced distribution considering location, sex, age, incomes, etc. The audience is recognized by login id which is assigned by the company, and the number of sampled users is 5700. The monitoring device collects all user behavior such as channel changing, login/logout, and power on/off in a minute precision unit. The connected data contains program data, and user history data etc. Program data consists of broadcasting time, channel, etc. It contains more than 2000 programs a day at 74 channels. User history data consist of user id, channel changing time, and corresponding channel id. We extracted three months data from June 15th, 2001 counting total 189,653 TV programs, and selected 100 users who switched channel more than 1500 times during the term for experimental data. Title and synopsis for each program were collected from TV program websites by webrobot, and joined to AC Nielsen program data. The data is segregated by two parts, the one is for training data excluding the last one week, the other is for test data composed by the last week only. Among the test data, the first day data is used for three experimental scenarios, and whole data is used only for the last scenario.

Preference for a TV program was modeled by regarding a TV program as an item x, and a word appeared in the TV program as a feature w. Only consecutive words are used as double feature w_2w_1 for equation (19). The words were extracted from title and synopsis by regular expression. All TV programs for each day were scored using the preference model, and preferred programs were recommended to the user.

We adopted precision as accuracy measure of this recommendation system. *Precision* is defined by the number of correct answers divided by the number of recommended candidates. We set $a_1=0.5$, $a_2=4$, parameters of Pareto distribution in equation (17).

A program series may consist of multiple program schedules that are broadcasted in different times with different episodes or subtitles. The recommendation engine predicts and selects preferring program schedules among all schedules in a given test day. A recommended program schedule is counted as correct one only if the user watched the exact program schedule at that time. So all program schedules, which are broadcasted in different time, channel, or with different subtopics, are regarded as different ones, although they are elements of a same program series. We created the additional experimental scenario called as 'title match' that regards a program with same title as correct one regardless of the broadcasting time and cannel, which is considered because many cable and local-area TV broadcast same programs.

Table 2 shows the results of four different recommendation scenarios. The first, variable candidates when the system recommends the same number of candidates to that of watched program in a day. The second, 10 candidates recommended. The third, title match which regards the candidate with the same title to any watched program as correct one since many channels broadcast a same program, even some channels broadcast a same program several times a day, but re-broadcasting program stated clearly in the title are regarded as different from the original one. The programs with a same title but different subtitles are regarded as different. All recommendation scenarios except the fourth one, measure for one day recommendation results, which is very strict testing

criterion for TV program environment. The fourth, test-extended-7-days regards the recommended program as correct one when it is watched in 7 days starting from the recommended date. It is more reasonable because a common TV audience does not watch his or her preferred program series all the times. We adopt the last scenario for the final accuracy comparison for each model.

Table 2. Accuracy results for each preference model.

Models ⟍ Evaluation Policy	Single Feature		Joint Feature	
	Sample Probability Eq. (2), (3)	Random Occurrence Probability Eq. (17)	Static weighting model	Dynamic weighting model Eq. (19)
Variable candidates	0.16796	0.18990	0.20537	0.23119
10 candidates	0.20505	0.22944	0.27594	0.30908
Title match, 10 candidates	0.28561	0.34900	0.35132	0.40429
7 day test extension, title match 10 candidates	0.59803	0.70994	0.69238	0.77734

Sample probability model represents the mutual information model which directly uses raw frequency from training data (equation (2), (3)). Single feature experimental results show that the random occurrence probability model (equation (17)) improved more than 10% precision in 7 days extension test. Static weighting model means the manner to set all of weight of joint features to equal constant. Joint feature experimental results show that the dynamic weighting model improved more than 10% precision from both of the static weighting model (0.598->0.692) and the single featured random occurrence probability model (0.709->0.777). Finally, the overall improvement of joint featured dynamic weighting model compared with the sample probability model is up to 30% precision (0.598->0.777). The improvement is 38% for variable candidates scenario (0.167->0.231).

It shows that mutual information model using random occurrence probability and dynamic weighting model using joint features are very effective for user preference.

4. Conclusions

We proposed a preference model using mutual information measure. Four additional ideas were proposed for the preference model. The first, the random occurrence probability was proposed in order to estimate true mutual information. The second, we showed that Pareto distribution can be used for random occurrence probability. We validated that this idea works well through experiments coping with noise caused by the lack of observed events and data sparseness problem. The third, we proposed the dynamic weighting model for combining subset and superset joint features. The dynamic weight is determined by the random occurrence probability. Experimental results showed that the dynamic weighting model has better accuracy than static weighting or single feature model. The fourth, positive and negative preference models were proposed, they were accomplished by adopting two different functions of random occurrence probability.

User preference is a relation of a user and an item. Usually it is represented by the set of features in order to predict the preference of new items, and the actual value is estimated from the user history. We showed that user preference can be effectively modeled by statistical method, Introducing the concept of random occurrence probability makes mutual information to be robust to the lack of observed data. It also realizes combining joint features by dynamic weighting, and concretizes positive and negative preference models. By using information measure, we are able to interpret the preference value intuitively as how much a user likes given item, which is a advantage of statistical model. We modeled also negative preference to say how much a user dislikes given item.

For the future work, the ideas presented in this paper can be applied to mining association rule. The measures of association rule mining such as confidence, conviction, chi-square, and lift (or dependency) have difficulties to be applied to recommendation since it is open problem to combine information of k-item sets for actual recommendation. Extending association rule extraction model to recommendation model will make it possible to compare the accuracy of such association measures. We will apply the mutual information to measure of association, and compare the accuracy of it with those of traditional models. Evaluation of mutual information measure with the random occurrence probability for association rule mining will be performed in the future work.

5. References

[1] Breese, J. S., D. Heckerman, and C. Kadie, "Empirical Analysis of Predictive Algorithms for Collaborative Filtering," in *Proc. of the 14th Conf. on Uncertainty in Artificial Intelligence*, July, 1998.

[2] Delgado, J., and N. Ishii, "Memory-Based Weighted-Majority Prediction for Recommender Systems," *ACM SIGIR'99 Workshop on Recommender Systems*, 1999.

[3] Goldman, S. A., M. K. Warmuth, "Learning Binary Relations Using Weighted Majority Voting", *ACM COLT* 1993, USA, pp453-462.

[4] Agrawal, R. T. Imielinski, A. Swami. "Mining association rules between sets of items in large databases", *Proc. of the ACM SIGMOD Int'l Conf. on the Management of Data*, 1993, pp. 207-216

[5] Agrawal, R., R. Srikant: "Fast Algorithms for Mining Association Rules", *Proc. of the 20th Int'l Conf. on Very Large Databases*, 1994.

[6] Brin, S., R., et al, "Beyond Market Baskets: Generalizing Association Rules to Correlations", *SIGMOD Conf.* pp. 265-276, 1997

[7] Silverstein, C., S. Brin, R. Motwani, "Beyond Market Baskets: Generalizing Association Rules to Dependence Rules." *Data Mining and Knowledge Discovery* 2(1), 1998

[8] Srikant, R., R. Agrawal, Mining Generalized Association Rules, *The VLDB Journal*, 1995

[9] Srikant, R., R. Agrawal, "Mining Quantitative Association Rules in Large Relational Tables", *Proc. of the ACM SIGMOD*, 1996.

[10] Adomavicius, G., A. Tuzhilin, "Using Data Mining Methods to Build Customer Profiles", *IEEE Computer*, 2001, pp74-82.

[11] Nakamura, A., Naoki Abe, "Collaborative Filtering using Weighted Majority Prediction Algorithms", *Proc. of Int'l Conf. of Machine Learning* 1998, pp. 395-403.

[12] Billsus, D., and M. J. Pazzani, "Learning Collaborative Information Filters", *Machine Learning Conf.*, 1998

[13] Li, Wentian, "Random Texts Exhibit Zipf's-Law-Like Word Frequency Distribution", *IEEE Transactions on Information Theory*, 38(6), 1842-1845, 1992

[14] Frakes, W. B., Baeza-Yates, R., "Information Retrieval: Data Structures & Algorithms", *Prentice-hall*, 1992.

[15] Reed, W. J., "The Pareto, Zipf and other power laws", *Economics Letters*, 2000

[16] Adamic, L. A., "Zipf, Power-laws, and Pareto – a ranking tutorial", Xerox Palo Alto Research Center, 2000, http://www.hpl.hp.com/shl/papers/ranking/ranking.html.

[17] Basu, C., H. Hirsh, W. Cohen, "Recommendation as Classification: Using Social and Content-Based Information in Recommendation", *Proc. of AAAI*, 1998

[18] Ha, Vu, P. Haddawy, "Toward Case-Based Preference Elicitation: Similarity Measures on Preference Structures" , *Proc. of the 14th Conf. on Uncertainty in Artificial Intelligence*, 1998

[19] Yao, Y. Y. "Measuring Retrieval Effectiveness Based on User Preference of Documents", *Journal of the American Society for Information Science* 46(2), 1995.

Convex Hull Ensemble Machine

Yongdai Kim
Department of Statistics
Ewha Womans University
Seoul, Korea
ydkim@mm.ewha.ac.kr

Abstract

We propose a new ensemble algorithm called "Convex Hull Ensemble Machine (CHEM)." CHEM in Hilbert space is developed first and it is modified to regression and classification problems. Empirical studies show that in classification problems CHEM has similar prediction accuracy as AdaBoost, but CHEM is much more robust to output noise. In regression problems, CHEM works competitively with other ensemble methods such as Gradient Boost and Bagging.

1. Introduction

Ensemble methods, which construct many classifiers (called "base learners") and combine them to make a final decision, have shown great success in statistics and machine learning areas for their significant improvements in classification accuracy. Examples of ensemble algorithms are Bagging (Breiman [2]), AdaBoost (Freund and Schapire [7], Schapire and Singer [18]), Arcing (Breiman [3]), Gradient Boost (Friedman [9]) and Random Forest (Breiman [4]). Among these, Bagging and AdaBoost are two most popular ensemble methods. Many comparison studies for Bagging and AdaBoost have been performed by Quinlan [14], Bauer and Kohavi [1], Opitz and Maclin [13] and Ditterich [6], to name just few. Their results indicate that even though AdaBoost is more accurate than Bagging in most cases, AdaBoost may overfit highly noisy data sets, thus decreasing its performance. Ridgeway [16] gives a simple example in which AdaBoost overfits the data seriously, and Breiman [4] demonstrates vulnerability of AdaBoost with output noise. Rätsch et al. [15] and Jiang [11] provide theoretical evidences of the possibility of overfitting of AdaBoost.

In this paper, we propose a new ensemble algorithm called "Convex Hull Ensemble Machine (CHEM)", which compromises advantages of Bagging and AdaBoost together. Classification accuracy of CHEM for low noise cases is competitive to that of AdaBoost, and at the same time CHEM is more robust to output noise.

This paper begins by investigating instability existing in decision trees. It is well known that decision trees are very unstable (Breiman [2]) and Bagging with decision trees yields large improvement in prediction accuracy. This is because Bagging is a device for reducing the variance. However, the sources of huge instability in decision trees are not clearly understood. We argue that huge instability of decision trees arises when many different models can explain the data similarly. In turn, the existence of many models similarly explaining the data is due to the fact that the true model does not locate inside the set of decision trees, but instead the true model locates inside the convex hull of the set of decision trees.

Once the geometry for instability is constructed, first we develop a hypothetical algorithm of CHEM in Hilbert space, which constructs a sequence of convex combinations of base learners converging to the optimal model inside the convex hull of the set of base learners. Even though it is hypothetical, CHEM in Hilbert space gives clear ideas about what is the object of CHEM and how CHEM accomplishments it in regression and classification problems.

After CHEM in Hilbert space is established, CHEM algorithms for regression and classification problems are developed. For regression problems, simply speaking, we develop an algorithm of CHEM by replacing the inner product used in CHEM in Hilbert space by its empirical counter part. For classification problems, we assume the symmetric logistic regression model, and embed the problem into a function estimation problem in Hilbert space. Then, we modify the algorithm of CHEM in Hilbert space accordingly as for regression problems.

CHEM unifies the regression and classification problems into the function estimation problem in Hilbert space, and thus performs well for the both problems. AdaBoost can also be interpreted as a way of estimating a function by use of the gradient descent method or Newton-like method (Schapire and Singer [18], Friedman et al. [10], Friedman

[9]). However, this interpretation results in overfitting in regression problems (Friedman [9] and Bühlman and Yu [5]).

The results of empirical studies show that CHEM has similar generalization errors as AdaBoost, CHEM is much more robust to output noise. In regression problems, CHEM works competitively with other ensemble methods such as Gradient Boost and Bagging.

This article is organized as follows. In section 2, instability of decision trees are studied, and the CHEM algorithm in Hilbert space is developed. The CHEM algorithm for regression models is given in section 3, and section 4 is devoted to the CHEM algorithm for classification. Results of empirical studies including simulation and real data analysis are presented in section 5. Discussions follow in section 6.

2   CHEM in Hilbert space

Let $\mathcal{F}$ be the family of functions (base learners), which is a non-convex subset of Hilbert space. CHEM assumes that the optimal function f^* locates inside the convex hull of $\mathcal{F}$. That is, f^* can be represented by

$$f^* = \sum_{i=1}^{\infty} w_i f_i / \sum_{i=1}^{\infty} w_i$$

for some sequences of base learners $f_1, f_2, \ldots$ and weights $w_1, w_2, \ldots$. Then, CHEM sequentially constructs the base learners and weights. Figure 1 describes this assumption.

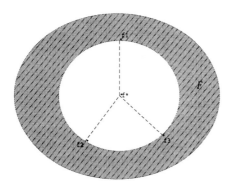

Figure 1. Assumed geometry

Any class of non-additive learners is non-convex. Examples are decision trees and neural networks. It is well known that ensemble methods work well with such learners, which are unstable. Figure 1 explains why non-additive learners are unstable and how CHEM improves them. "Instability" of learners means that small change of data results in large change of the final model constructed from the data. Suppose the data is $f^* + \epsilon$ where ϵ is noise and the distances

of f_1, f_2 and f_3 from f^* are equal in Figure 1. Then, the optimal model from the data,(i.e. the model closest from $f^* + \epsilon$) depends entirely on ϵ, and instability emerges. This instability can be removed by extending the class of learners from $\mathcal{F}$ to the convex hull of $\mathcal{F}$, which is what CHEM does. More explanations about the instability of decision trees, see Kim et al. [12].

Let $<, >$ be the inner product of the given Hilbert space. The norm of f in the Hilbert space is defined by $\|f\|^2 = <f, f>$. Then, the equivalent assumptions to the assumed geometry 1 are

A1. f^* locates inside the convex hull of $\mathcal{F}$;

A2. for any g in the convex hull of $\mathcal{F}$, $\mathcal{F}(g)$ is a non-empty set where

$$\mathcal{F}(g) = \{f :< g - f^*, f - f^* >= 0, f \in \mathcal{F}\};$$

A3. there exists a positive constant ρ such that $\inf \|f\| < \rho$ on $f \in \mathcal{F}(g)$ and for all g where $\|f\|^2 = <f, f>$.

Condition **A1** is a fundamental assumption. Condition **A2** means that the shaded area in Figure 1 (i.e $\mathcal{F}$) encompasses f^* completely. Condition **A3** implies that the distance from f^* to $\mathcal{F}$ at any angle is bounded by ρ. Hereafter, a model in $\mathcal{F}$ is called a "base learner" and any convex combination of finite base learners is called an "ensemble model".

Now, we explain how CHEM constructs a sequence of ensemble models in a given Hilbert space under the assumed geometry given in Figure 1. Suppose the mth ensemble model H_m is constructed. CHEM updates the ensemble model H_m to H_{m+1} as follows. First, CHEM finds the model f_{m+1} in $\mathcal{F}$ where

$$f_{m+1} = \operatorname{argmin}_{f \in \mathcal{F}(H_m)} \|f - f^*\|.$$

That is, f_{m+1} is the closest model from f^* satisfying $f - f^* \perp f - H_m$. After constructing f_{m+1}, CHEM updates the ensemble model by

$$H_{m+1} = \frac{u_m H_m + w_{m+1} f_{m+1}}{u_m + w_{m+1}}$$

where u_m and w_{m+1} are chosen so that $\|H_{m+1} - f^*\|$ is minimized.

The step-by-step description of CHEM is as follows. We construct the first base learner f_1 by

$$f_1 = \operatorname{argmin}_{f \in \mathcal{F}} \|f - f^*\|,$$

and we let $H_1 = f_1$. This procedure is depicted in Figure 2. There, $d_1 = \|f_1 - f^*\|$.

The second base learner is the closest one from f^* satisfying $f_2 - f^* \perp H_1 - f^*$. Then, the second ensemble model H_2 is given by

$$H_2 = \frac{u_1 H_1 + w_2 f_2}{u_1 + w_2},$$

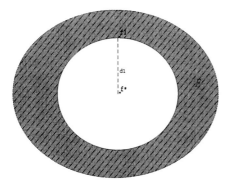

Figure 2. Construction of the first ensemble model

and choose u_1 and w_2 to minimize the distance between H_2 and f^*. Simple algebra yields that $u_1 = 1/d_1^1$ and $w_2 = 1/d_2^2$ where $d_2 = \|f_2 - f^*\|$. Hence, H_2 becomes

$$H_2 = \frac{w_1 f_1 + w_2 f_2}{w_1 + w_2}$$

where $w_i = 1/d_i^2$ for $i = 1, 2$. This procedure is summarized in Figure 3.

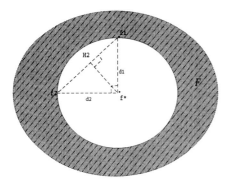

Figure 3. Construction of the second ensemble model

The third base learner can be constructed similarly, and direct calculation yields that the third ensemble model H_3 is given by

$$H_3 = \frac{w_1 f_1 + w_2 f_2 + w_3 f_3}{w_1 + w_2 + w_3}$$

where $w_i = 1/d_i^2$ for $i = 1, 2, 3$. This step is described in Figure 4.

By this way, we can keep constructing base learners $f_4, f_5, \ldots$ and ensemble models $H_4, H_5, \ldots$ by

$$H_m = \frac{\sum_{i=1}^{m} w_i f_i}{\sum_{i=1}^{m} w_i}$$

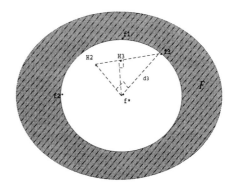

Figure 4. Construction of the third ensemble model

where $w_i = 1/d_i^2$ and $d_i = \|f_i - f^*\|$.

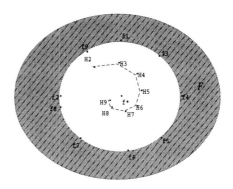

Figure 5. Construction of the sequence of ensemble models

The following theorem proves that the sequence of ensemble models constructed by CHEM in Hilbert space converges to f^* under the assumed geometry. The proof is in Kim et al. [12].

Theorem 1 *Under the assumptions **A1, A2** and **A3**,*

$$\|H_m - f^*\| \to 0$$

as $m \to \infty$.

3 CHEM for regression

In this section, we present the algorithm of CHEM for regression. Recall that the training data set consists of n input/output pairs $\{(\mathbf{x}_1, y_1), \ldots, (\mathbf{x}_n, y_n)\}$ which are a random sample of $(\mathbf{X}, Y)$ distributed according to an unknown joint distribution $P(x, y)$. Here, $\mathbf{X} \in R^p$ and $Y \in R$. We assume that

$$Y = f(\mathbf{X}) + \epsilon$$

where $\mathrm{E}(\epsilon) = 0$ and $\mathrm{Var}(\epsilon) = \sigma^2 > 0$. The objective of CHEM for regression is to estimate f based on the sample $\{(\mathbf{x}_1, y_1), \ldots, (\mathbf{x}_n, y_n)\}$.

To apply CHEM in Hilbert space to regression problem, we need two devices - (i) how to measure the distance of a given base learner to the true model (i.e. $\|f - f^*\|$ for a given $f \in \mathcal{F}$) and (ii) how to construct f_{n+1} for given H_n. Consider $L_2(P)$ space, that is $< f, g > = \int f(\mathbf{x}) g(\mathbf{x}) P(d\mathbf{x})$. For (i), for a given loss function $l(y, a)$, define the deviance of a base learner f by

$$d(f) = \sum_{i=1}^{n} l(y_i, f(\mathbf{x}_i))/n.$$

Then, we use $d(f)$ as a measurement of $\|f - f^*\|^2$. This is a reasonable choice, for with the square error loss (i.e. $l(y, a) = (y - a)^2$) $d(f)$ converges to $\|f - f^*\|^2 + \sigma^2$ under regularity conditions and σ^2 is relatively smaller than $\|f - f^*\|^2$ for unstable base learners. For (ii), we construct the model ϕ based on the residuals of H_n Then, $\phi - f^*$ and $H_n - f^*$ are expected to be nearly orthogonal since the residuals and H_n are orthogonal. Then, we construct f_{n+1} by

$$f_{n+1} = \mathrm{argmin}_{f \in \mathcal{F}_n} d(f)$$

where $\mathcal{F}_n = \{\eta\phi : \eta \in R\}$. That is, we first find the appropriate direction ϕ and construct the optimal model on that direction.

By use of these two devises, we construct a CHEM algorithm for regression problems as follows. Recall that $\mathcal{F}$ is a set of base learners.

Algorithm 1. CHEM algorithm for regression model

1. Initialization : Set $z_i = y_i$ for $i = 1, \ldots, n$.

2. Repeat $m = 1, \ldots, M$

    (a) Fit a regression model ϕ in $\mathcal{F}$ with output variables z_i and input variables $\mathbf{x}_i$.

    (b) Calculate the correction factor η by

    $$\eta = \mathrm{argmin}_\delta d(\delta\phi).$$

    (c) Set $f_m(\mathbf{x}) = \eta\phi(\mathbf{x})$.
    (d) Update the ensemble model

    $$H_m(\mathbf{x}) = \frac{\sum_{i=1}^{m} w_i f_i(\mathbf{x})}{\sum_{i=1}^{m} w_i}$$

    where $w_i = 1/d(f_i)$.

    (e) Update the new response $z_i = y_i - H_m(\mathbf{x}_i)$.

3. For a given new data with input $\mathbf{x}$, predict the output as $H_M(\mathbf{x})$.

4 CHEM for classification

We first consider a two class problem (i.e. $Y \in \{-1, 1\}$.). We assume the logistic model:

$$\Pr(Y = 1|\mathbf{X} = \mathbf{x}) = \frac{\exp(f(\mathbf{x}))}{\exp(-f(\mathbf{x})) + \exp(f(\mathbf{x}))},$$

and embed the classification problem into the function estimation problem (i.e. estimation of f). Under this set-up, CHEM for regression will be modified. First, we use the negative log-likelihood of the binomial distribution as a loss function instead of the squared error loss. Then, the deviance of a function f is

$$d(f) = \sum_{i=1}^{n} \log(1 + \exp(-2y_i f(\mathbf{x}_i)))/n.$$

Second, for residuals, we use the Pearson residual defined by

$$r_i = \frac{y_i^* - P_m(\mathbf{x}_i)}{\sqrt{P_m(\mathbf{x}_i)(1 - P_m(\mathbf{x}_i))}}$$

where $y_i^* = 2y_i - 1$, $P_m(\mathbf{x}) = \exp(H_m(\mathbf{x}))/(\exp(-H_m(\mathbf{x})) + \exp(H_m(\mathbf{x})))$ and $H_m(\mathbf{x})$ is the mth ensemble model. But, we do not use the residuals $\{r_i\}$ as a response variable. Instead, we use $|r_i|$ as a weight of the ith observation, and construct ϕ on a weighted bootstrap sample of the original sample $\{(\mathbf{x}_1, y_1), \ldots, (\mathbf{x}_n, y_n)\}$ with weights $\{|r_1|, \ldots, |r_n|\}$. In summary, the algorithm of CHEM for the two class problem is given below.

Algorithm 2. CHEM algorithm for two class classification problem

1. Initialization : let the weights $v_i = 1/n$ for $i = 1, \ldots, n$.

2. Repeat $m = 1, \ldots, M$

    (a) Make a bootstrap sample $\mathcal{L}^B$ with weights $\{v_i\}$.

(b) Estimate $p(\mathbf{x}) = \hat{P}(Y = 1 | \mathbf{X} = \mathbf{x})$ using $\mathcal{L}^B$ with a given class of base learners.

(c) Let $\phi(\mathbf{x}) = \frac{1}{2} \log(p(\mathbf{x})/(1 - p(\mathbf{x})))$.

(d) Calculate the correction factor η by

$$\eta = \mathrm{argmin}_\delta d(\delta \phi).$$

(e) Let $f_m(\mathbf{x}) = \eta f_m(\mathbf{x})$.

(f) Update the ensemble model $H_m(\mathbf{x}) = \sum_{i=1}^m w_i f_i(\mathbf{x})/\sum_{i=1}^m w_i$ where $w_i = 1/d(f_i)$.

(g) Update the weights $\{v_i\}$ by

$$v_i = \left| \frac{y_i^* - P_m(\mathbf{x}_i)}{\sqrt{P_m(\mathbf{x}_i)(1 - P_m(\mathbf{x}_i))}} \right|$$

where $P_m(\mathbf{x}) = \exp(H_m(\mathbf{x}))/(\exp(-H_m(\mathbf{x})) + \exp(H_m(\mathbf{x})))$.

3. For a new input $\mathbf{x}$, assign it to class 1 if $H_M(\mathbf{x}) > 0$ and to class -1 otherwise.

For multi-class problems (i.e. $Y \in \{1, \ldots, J\}, J > 2$), we assume the symmetric logistic model:

$$\mathrm{Pr}(Y = k | \mathbf{X} = \mathbf{x}) = \frac{\exp(f_k(\mathbf{x}))}{\sum_{j=1}^J \exp(f_j(\mathbf{x}))}.$$

For extension of CHEM to multi-class problems, we mimic the algorithm of the multi-class LogitBoost (Friedman et al. [10]). Consider J many two-class classification problems. The j-th base learner $f_j(\mathbf{x})$ constructed from the j-th two-class classification problem, in which new response variables $\{y_{ij}^* = I(y_i = j), i = 1, \ldots, n\}$ are used. Then, f_js are centered by

$$f_j(\mathbf{x}) = f_j(\mathbf{x}) - \sum_{k=1}^J f_k(\mathbf{x})/J. \qquad (1)$$

Then, the correction factor η is obtained by use of the negative log-likelihood of the multinomial distribution as a loss function, and $\underline{f} = (f_1, \ldots, f_J)$ is updated accordingly. In this set-up, the deviance of $\underline{f}$ is given by

$$d(\underline{f}) = -\sum_{i=1}^n \left[f_{y_i}(\mathbf{x}_i) - \log \left(\sum_{k=1}^J \exp(f_k(\mathbf{x}_i)) \right) \right].$$

Algorithm 3. CHEM algorithm for J class classification problem

---

1. Initialization

   (a) Set weights $\{v_{ij}\}$ by $v_{ij} = 1/n$ for $i = 1, \ldots, n$ and $j = 1, \ldots, J$.

   (b) Set $y_{ij}^* = I(y_i = j)$ for $i = 1, \ldots, n$ and $j = 1, \ldots, J$.

2. Repeat $m = 1, \ldots, M$

   (a) Repeat $j = 1, \ldots, J$

      i. Make a bootstrap sample $\mathcal{L}_j^B$ from $\{(y_{1j}^*, \mathbf{x}_1), \ldots, (y_{nj}^*, \mathbf{x}_n)\}$ with weights $\{v_{1j}, \ldots, v_{nj}\}$.

      ii. Estimate $p_j(\mathbf{x}) = \hat{P}(Y_j^* = 1 | \mathbf{X} = \mathbf{x})$ using $\mathcal{L}_j^B$ with a given class of base learners.

      iii. Set $\phi_j(\mathbf{x}) = \frac{1}{2} \log(p_j(\mathbf{x})/(1 - p_j(\mathbf{x})))$.

   (b) Set $\phi_j(\mathbf{x}) = \phi_j(\mathbf{x}) - \sum_{k=1}^J \phi_k(\mathbf{x})/J$ for $j = 1, \ldots, J$.

   (c) Calculate the correction factor η by

   $$\eta = \mathrm{argmin}_\delta d(\delta \underline{\phi})$$

   where $\underline{\phi} = (\phi_1, \ldots, \phi_J)$.

   (d) Let $\underline{f}_m(\mathbf{x}) = \eta \underline{\phi}(\mathbf{x})$.

   (e) Update the ensemble model $\underline{H}_m(\mathbf{x}) = \sum_{i=1}^m w_i \underline{f}_i(\mathbf{x})/\sum_{i=1}^m w_i$ where $w_i = 1/d(\underline{f}_i)$.

   (f) For $j = 1, \ldots, J$, update the weights $\{v_{ij}\}$ by

   $$v_{ij} = \left| \frac{y_{ij}^* - P_{mj}(\mathbf{x}_i)}{\sqrt{P_{mj}(\mathbf{x}_i)(1 - P_{mj}(\mathbf{x}_i))}} \right|$$

   where $P_{mj}(\mathbf{x}) = \exp(H_{mj}(\mathbf{x}))/(\sum_{k=1}^J \exp(H_{mk}(\mathbf{x})))$.

3. Assign a new data with input variable $\mathbf{x}$ to class $\mathrm{argmax}_j H_{Mj}(\mathbf{x})$.

Remark. Friedman et al. [10] proposed using

$$f_j(\mathbf{x}) = \frac{J-1}{J} \left(f_j(\mathbf{x}) - \sum_{k=1}^J f_k(\mathbf{x})/J \right)$$

instead of (1). Only the difference is the constant term $(J-1)/J$. In CHEM, this constant term is replaced by the correction factor.

5 Empirical studies

In this section, we present results of empirical studies for comparing various aspects of CHEM with AdaBoost and Bagging.

5.1 Set-up for classification

For base learners, unpruned trees (the largest one among the trees whose terminal nodes have no less than 5 instances) are used in CHEM and Bagging and best-first trees (Friedman et al. 2000) with 8 terminal nodes are used in AdaBoost. For the final ensemble model, 50 base learners are combined in Bagging and 500 base learners are combined in CHEM and AdaBoost. For data sets without test samples, the generalization errors (test set misclassification errors) are calculated by 10 repetitions of 10-fold cross validation.

5.2 Generalization error

Table 1 presents the generalization errors. The generalization errors of CHEM compare favorably with AdaBoost. On exactly half of the data sets (7 out of 14 data sets), CHEM has lower generalization errors than AdaBoost and vice versa. In comparison with Bagging, CHEM has lower generalization errors in most cases (10 out of 14 data sets).

ID	Data Set	CHEM	AdaBoost	Bagging
1	Breast Cancer	0.0333	0.0310	0.0315
2	Pima-Indian-Diabetes	0.2411	0.2764	0.2358
3	German	0.2299	0.2650	0.2361
4	Glass	0.2238	0.2104	0.2386
5	House-vote-84	0.0572	0.0649	0.0469
6	Image	0.0671	0.0881	0.0667
7	Ionosphere	0.0665	0.0662	0.0782
8	kr-vs-kp	0.0036	0.0050	0.0123
9	Letter	0.0485	0.0290	0.0975
10	Satimage	0.0880	0.0885	0.1075
11	Sonar	0.1515	0.1195	0.1798
12	Vehicle	0.2420	0.2194	0.2540
13	Vowel	0.4372	0.4805	0.5562
14	Waveform	0.1664	0.1592	0.1866

Table 1. Generalization errors

5.3 Robustness to output noise

Another important advantage of CHEM over boosting is that CHEM is much more robust to output noise than AdaBoost. To see this, the class labels of a random 10% of the training samples are changed at random and the three ensemble methods are compared. Table 2 presents the generalization errors. By comparing Tables 1 and 2, we can see that in most cases increases in error of AdaBoost due to noise are much larger than those of CHEM, and Bagging is least affected by noise. Vulnerability of AdaBoost to output noise has been noticed by many researchers, for example Breiman [4] and Rätsch et al. [15]. They explain that the main source of this vulnerability to output noise is the way how AdaBoost updates the weights. AdaBoost keeps increasing the weights on most frequently misclassified observations and instances having incorrect class labels tend to persist in being misclassified. Hence, AdaBoost concentrates the weights mistakenly on these noisy instances. In contrast, the weights of CHEM ($|r_i|$ in Algorithm 2) are not dominated by few larger ones. This is partly because the weights are adjusted by use of the normalized ensemble model (i.e. $\sum_{i=1}^{m} w_i f_i(\mathbf{x}) / \sum_{i=1}^{m} w_i$ in (f) of Algorithm 2).

ID	Data Set	CHEM	AdaBoost	Bagging
1	Breast Cancer	0.0438	0.0945	0.0373
2	Pima-Indian-Diabetes	0.2570	0.3135	0.2470
3	German	0.2452	0.3098	0.2479
4	Glass	0.2566	0.2542	0.2586
5	House-vote-84	0.0615	0.1236	0.0458
6	Image	0.0776	0.0900	0.0790
7	Ionosphere	0.0808	0.1034	0.0777
8	kr-vs-kp	0.0313	0.0808	0.0084
9	Letter	0.0830	0.1057	0.0947
10	Satimage	0.0960	0.1065	0.1110
11	Sonar	0.1820	0.1650	0.1851
12	Vehicle	0.2432	0.2338	0.2598
13	Vowel	0.4956	0.5303	0.5346
14	Waveform	0.1598	0.1650	0.1956

Table 2. Generalization errors with 10% output noise

5.4 Regression problems

In this section, the results of empirical studies on regression problems are presented. Two data sets from UC Irvine machine learning archive and three synthetic data sets are used. Detailed descriptions of the three synthetic data sets can be found in Friedman [8].

Three ensemble methods - CHEM, Gradient Boost (Friedman [9]) and Bagging are compared. For Gradient Boost, the squared error loss is used and the regularization through shrinkage with shrinkage parameter 0.1 is applied. Similarly to the classification problems, decision trees with 8 terminal nodes are used for base learners in Gradient Boost and unpruned tress are used in CHEM and Bagging. Also, the generalization errors (test sample mean squared errors) are calculated by the averages of 10 repetitions of 10-fold cross validation errors when test samples are not available.

Table 3 presents the generalization errors. Performance of the ensemble methods for regression problems is data-dependent. For the two real data sets and Friedman 1, CHEM as well as Gradient Boost improves Bagging while Bagging beats the other two

Data Set	CHEM	Gradient Boosting	Bagging
Boston Housing	6.1553	5.6529	7.5654
Servo	0.1801	0.1978	0.3788
Friedman 1	5.9930	4.3621	6.7511
Friedman 2	549.5285	546.3978	467.0340
Friedman 3	0.0414	0.0401	0.0411

Table 3. Mean-squared test set errors for regression problems

ensemble methods significantly for Friedman 2. Note that the regularization through shrinkage is used in Gradient Boost. The performance of CHEM would be improved further by similar regularization.

6 Discussions

In this paper, we proposed a new ensemble algorithm CHEM. CHEM has various advantages over Bagging and AdaBoost. CHEM has similar generalization errors as AdaBoost, and at the same time, is robust to output noise as Bagging. CHEM never overfits and has lower errors for regression problems too.

In CHEM, unpruned decision trees are used as base learners. Performance of CHEM with smaller trees tends to be degraded. This phenomenon can be partially explained as follows. CHEM constructs a sequence of ensemble models which converge to the true model inside the convex hull of the set of base learners. Hence, the size of the convex hull of the set of base learners is an important ingredient of the success of CHEM, and the convex hull of the set of unpruned decision trees is the largest.

The role of base learners in CHEM and AdaBoost is different. An explanation of the role of base learners in AdaBoost proposed by Friedman et al. [10] is that the complexity of base learners determines the level of dominant interaction of the final ensemble model. They argued that AdaBoost is an additive model, and only the final ensemble model has meaning of approximating the decision boundary and the complexity of base learners controls the level of dominant interactions. Hence, too complicated base learners may result in overfitting. The role of base learners in CHEM is different. In CHEM, each base learner is the best model (minimizing the deviance) for a given direction (based on residuals). This means that base learners in CHEM are not merely weak learners as in AdaBoost, but they are strong learners from various directions. Hence, each base learner has useful information about the data from a different angle and we can utilize this information for understanding the final decision. In this paper, we used unpruned decision trees. Better approach might let tree sizes of base learners vary.

Acknowledgement

This research was supported (in part) by US Air Force Research Grant F62562-02-P-0547.

References

[1] E. Bauer and R. Kohavi, "An empirical comparison of voting classification algorithms: Bagging, Boosting and Variants", *Machine Learning*, 1999, pp. 105-139.

[2] L. Breiman, "Bagging predictors", *Machine Learning*, 1996, pp. 123-140.

[3] L. Breiman, "Arcing classifiers", *Annals of Statistics*, 1998, pp. 801-846.

[4] L. Breiman, "Random forests", *Machine Learning*, 2001, pp. 5-32.

[5] P. Bühlmann and B. Yu, "Boosting with the L_2 loss: regression and classification", Technical Report, 2001.

[6] T.G. Dietterich, "An experimental comparison of three methods for constructing ensembles of decision trees: Bagging, Boosting and Randomization", *Machine Learning*, 2000, pp. 139-157.

[7] Y. Freund and R. Schapire, "A decision-theoretic generalization of on-line learning and an application to boosting", *Journal of Computer and System Sciences*, 1997, pp. 119-139.

[8] J.H. Friedman, "Multivariate adaptive regression splines (with discussion)", it Annals of Statistics, 1991, pp.1-141.

[9] J.H. Friedman, "Greedy function approximation : a gradient boosting machine", *Annals of Statistics*, 2001, pp/1189-1232.

[10] J.H. Friedman, T. Hastie and R. Tibshirani, "Additive logistic regression : a statistical view of boosting", *Annals of Statistics*, 2000, pp. 337-374.

[11] W. Jiang, "On weak base hypotheses and their implications for boosting regression classification", *Annals of Statistics*, 2002, pp.51-73.

[12] Y. Kim, J. Kim and W. Jeon, "Convex Hull Ensemble Machine", Unpublished manuscript at http://home.ewha.ac.kr/ ydkim, 2002.

[13] D. Opitz and R. Maclin, "Popular ensemble methods: An empirical study", *Journal of Artificial Intelligence Research*, 1999, pp. 169-198.

[14] J. Quinlan, "Boosting first-order learning", In S. Arikawa & Sharma Eds.), *LNAI, Vol. 1160: Proceedings of the 7th International Workshop on Algorithmic Learning Theory*, 143-155, Berlin : Springer.

[15] G. Räsch, T. Onoda and K.R. Müller, "Soft margins for AdaBoost", *Machine Learning*, 2001, pp. 287-320.

[16] G. Ridgeway, "Contribution to the discussion of paper by Friedman, Hastie and Tibshirani", *Ann. Statist.*, 2000, pp. 393-400.

[17] R. Schapire, Y. Freund, P. Bartlett and W. Lee, "Boosting the margin: a new explanation for the effectiveness of voting methods", *Ann. Statist.*, 1998, pp. 1651-1686.

[18] R. Schapire and Y. Singer, "Improved boosting algorithms using confidence-rated predictions", *Machine Learning*, 1999, pp. 297-336.

Recognition of Common Areas in a Web Page Using Visual Information: a possible application in a page classification

Miloš Kovacevic[1], Michelangelo Diligenti[2], Marco Gori[2], Veljko Milutinovic[3]

[1]School of Civil Engineering, University of Belgrade, Serbia
milos@grf.bg.ac.yu
[2]Dipartimento di Ingegneria dell'Informazione, University of Siena, Italy
{diligmic, maggini, marco}@dii.unisi.it
[3]School of Electrical Engineering, University of Belgrade, Serbia
vm@etf.bg.ac.yu

Abstract

Extracting and processing information from Web pages is an important task in many areas like constructing search engines, information retrieval, and data mining from the Web. Common approach in the extraction process is to represent a page as a "bag of words" and then to perform additional processing on such a flat representation. In this paper we propose a new, hierarchical representation that includes browser screen coordinates for every HTML object in a page. Using visual information one is able to define heuristics for the recognition of common page areas such as header, left and right menu, footer and center of a page. We show in initial experiments that using our heuristics defined objects are recognized properly in 73% of cases. Finally, we show that a Naive Bayes classifier, taking into account the proposed representation, clearly outperforms the same classifier using only information about the content of documents.

1. Introduction

Web pages are designed for humans! While previous sentence is more than obvious, still many machine learning and information retrieval techniques for processing Web pages do not utilize implicit visual information contained in the HTML source. By visual information we assume positions of HTML objects in the browser window. For example, one can say that certain image is on the top left corner of the screen or that the most informative paragraph is in the center of the page and it occupies the area of 100x200 pixels.

Where can this kind of information be useful? Consider the problem of feature selection to perform document classification. There are several methods to perform feature selection process like Information Gain [1] or TF-IDF (term frequency – inverse document frequency) [2]. In both cases we try to estimate what are the most relevant words that describe document D i.e. the best vector representation of D that will be used in

classification process. Assuming that Web pages are designed for visual sense, we can argue that some words represent noise (with respect to the task of assigning the page to its topic) if such words belong to menu, banner link or perhaps page footer. That noise can be misleading for classifiers. Also, we can suppose words that belong to the central part of the page (screen) carry more information than words from the down right corner. Hence there should be a way to weight differently words from different layout contexts. At present moment in classic algorithms, positions of words and their spanning areas are not considered at all!

Let us mention another problem – designing efficient crawling strategy for focused search engines. Given a specific topic T and starting set of pages S, it is necessary to find as more T on-topic pages as possible in a predefined number of steps. By step is meant visiting (and downloading and indexing) a page reachable from S following hyperlinks from pages in S. In other words it is important to estimate whether an outgoing link is promising or not. In [3,4,5] different techniques are described. In any case when a focus crawler decides to take into account page for link expansion, all links from the page are inserted into the crawl frontier (links that are to be visited). But many of them are not interesting at all (i.e. *"this page is designed by XYZ"*). Sometimes links that belong to menus or footer are also misleading. Can we measure the importance of the link according to link position in the page (on the browser screen)? Links in the center of the page are probably more important than links in the down left corner. Also, we can calculate link density in some area of the page (screen) and weight links taking into account that density factor. Links that are surrounded by "more" text are probably more important to topic than links positioned in groups, but groups of links can signify we are on the hub page that can also be important to our focused crawler. Can we learn positions of interesting links for some topics? In any case, we believe, information about position and belonging to a certain area can help to infer if a link is promising or not!

To note the final example, consider the problem of cheating search engines by inserting irrelevant keywords into an HTML source. This is widely used technique in order to raise the probability of indexing the page by search engine and representing it with higher rank among search results. While it is relatively easy to detect and reject false keywords where their foreground color is same as background color, there is no way to detect keywords of regular color but covered with images. If coordinates of objects in a page representation are known, then search engines could filter false keywords hidden by other objects and users would get better answers on their queries!

All the previously mentioned issues motivated us to define new representation of a page extracted from an HTML source, which include visual information, and to show how it can be utilized in recognition of common areas in a Web page. However, we were additionally encouraged to do this work when discovering the fact that users expect from Web designers to put certain objects at predefined areas on the browser screen [6].

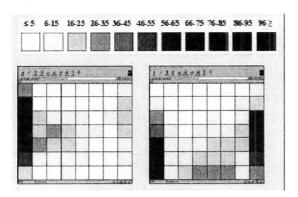

Figure 1: User expectance in percents concerning positions of internal (left) and external (right) links in the browser window [6].

Figure 1 shows the areas where users expect to find internal and external links. Dark regions correspond to page areas to which users looked when requested to locate internal/external links (such measurements where performed tracking users' eyes movements). This simple observations allowed us to define a set of heuristics for the recognition of specific page areas (menus, header, footer and "center" of a page).

The outline of the paper is as follows: In Section 2 we define the **M-Tree** format of a page used to render the page on the virtual screen, i.e. to obtain coordinates for every HTML object. Section 3 describes heuristics for recognition of header, footer, left and right menu, and "center" of the page. In Section 4, experimental results in a recognition process on a predefined dataset are shown. In section 5 we present some results concerning

Web page classification using previously extracted visual information. Finally, conclusion and remarks about the future work are given in Section 6.

2. Extracting visual information from an HTML source

We define a virtual screen (VS) that defines a coordinate system for specifying the positions of HTML objects (in further text - objects) inside Web pages (in further text - pages). The VS is a rectangle with a predefined width and an infinite height both measured in pixels. The VS is set to correspond to the page display area in a maximized browser window on a standard monitor with resolution of 1024x768 pixels. Of course one can set any desirable resolution. Width of the VS is set to be 1000 because when vertical scroll bars from browser are removed, that quantity is usually left for rendering the page. Obviously pages are of different length and so theoretically height can be infinite. Top left corner of the VS represents the origin of the VS coordinate system.

Now, the process of the visual information extraction will be described. Main operations applied in the extraction process are shown in Figure 2.

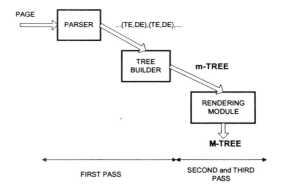

Figure 2: Constructing the **M-Tree** (main steps).

In the first step a page is parsed using an HTML parser that extracts two different types of elements – tags and data. Tag elements (**TE**) are delimited with <> while data elements (**DE**) are contained between two consecutive tags. Each **TE** includes name of the corresponding tag and a list of attribute-value pairs. **DE** is represented as a list of tokens, which taken all together form the data string between consecutive tags. Separators between tokens are white space characters and are omitted from the **DE** list of tokens. **DE** contains empty list if no token is placed between two consecutive tags (i.e. input stream is *...>W<...*, **W**-white space character or none). Parser skips *<SCRIPT>* and *<!--...>* tags.

In the second step, as soon as *<TE,DE>* pair is extracted from the input HTML stream, it is injected into the tree builder. Tree builder applies stack machine and a set of predefined rules to build the tree that represents the HTML structure of the page. The output of this component we named **m-Tree**. There are many papers that describe construction of the parsing tree of an HTML page [7,8]. In our approach a technique is adopted which constructs the tree in one single pass through the given page, i.e. parsing and building the **m-Tree** is done in a single pass. Rules are used to properly nest **TEs** into the hierarchy according to the HTML 4.01 specification [9]. Additional efforts were made to design tree builder that will be immune on bad HTML source.

Definition 1: a **m-Tree (mT)** is a directed n-ary tree defined with a set of nodes N and a set of edges E with following characteristics:

1. $N = N_{desc} \cup N_{cont} \cup N_{data}$

where:

- N_{desc} (description nodes) is a set of nodes, which correspond to **TEs** of the following HTML tags: {*<TITLE>, <META>*}

- N_{cont} (container nodes) is a set of nodes, which correspond to **TEs** of the following HTML tags: {*<TABLE>,<CAPTION>,<TH>,<TD>,<TR>,<P>, <CENTER>,<DIV>,<BLOCKQUOTE>,<ADDRESS> <PRE>,<H1>,<H2>,<H3>,<H4>,<H5>,<H6>, <OL>,<UL>,<LI>,<MENU>, <DIR>, <DL>, <DT>, <DD>, <A>, <IMG>,
,<HR>*}

- N_{data} (data nodes) is a set of nodes, which correspond to **DEs**.

Each $n \in N$ has following attributes: **name** equals the name of the corresponding tag except for N_{data} nodes where **name** = "*TEXT*", **attval** is a list of attribute-value pairs extracted from the corresponding tag and can be null (i.e. nodes from N_{data} have this attribute set to null). Additionally, each N_{data} node has four more attributes: **value, fsize, emph,** and **align**. First contains tokens from the corresponding **DE,** second describes font size of these tokens, third caries information whether tokens belong to the scope of validity of one or more of the following HTML tags: {*<B>,<I>,<U>, <STRONG>, <EM>, <SMALL>, <BIG>*}. The last one describes the alignment of the text (left, right or centered) In further text if n corresponds to tag X we write $n_{<X>}$ (n has attribute **name** = X).

2. Root of **mT**, $n_{ROOT} \in N_{cont}$ represents a page as a whole and its **name** is set to "*ROOT*" while **attval** contains only one pair (*URL : source url of the page itself*).

3. $E = \{(n_x, n_y) \mid n_x, n_y \in N\}$.

There can be only the following types of edges:

a) (n_{ROOT}, n_{desc}), $n_{desc} \in N_{desc}$
b) (n_{cont1}, n_{cont2}), $n_{cont1} \in N_{cont} \setminus \{n_{<IMG>}\}$, $n_{cont2} \in N_{cont} \setminus \{n_{ROOT}\}$ iff n_{cont2} belongs to the context of n_{cont1} according to the nesting rules of the HTML 4.01 specification
c) (n_{cont}, n_{data}), $n_{cont} \in N_{cont} \setminus \{n_{<IMG>}\}$, $n_{data} \in N_{data}$ iff n_{data} belongs to the context of n_{cont}

♦

From definition 1 it is clear that image and text nodes can be only leafs in an **mT**. Figure 3 shows a possible example of a simple page and its corresponding **mT**.

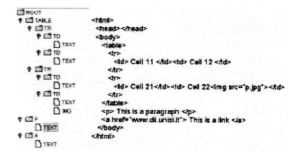

Figure 3: HTML source (right) and related **mT** (left)

The coordinates of every object of interest are computed by the rendering module using the **mT**. We followed some recommendations from W3C [10] and the visual behavior of one of the most popular browsers (Microsoft Internet Explorer) to design the renderer. In order to simplify and speed the rendering process, we assumed some simplifications which do not influence significantly the page representation for our specific task. The simplifications are the following:

1) Rendering module (RM) calculates only coordinates for nodes in **mT**, i.e. HTML tags out of definition 1 are skipped.
2) RM does not support layered HTML documents.
3) RM does not support frames.
4) RM does not support style sheets.

The Rendering module produces the final, desirable representation of a page – **M-Tree** (in further text **MT**). **MT** extends the concept of **mT** by incorporating coordinates for each $n \in N \setminus N_{desc}$.

Definition 2: A **MT** is the extension of a **mT** in which $\forall n \in N \setminus N_{desc}$ there are two additional attributes: X and Y. These are arrays which contain the x and y coordinates of the corresponding object polygon on the VS with following characteristics:

1. If $n \in N_{cont} \setminus \{n_{<A>}\}$ then it is assumed that the corresponding object occupies a rectangular area on the VS. Thus X and Y have dimension 4. The margins of the rectangle are:

- the bottom margin is equal to the top margin of the left sibling node if it exists. If n does not have a left sibling or $n = n_{<TD>}$, then the bottom margin is equal to the bottom margin of its parent node. If $n = n_{ROOT}$ then the bottom margin is the x-axes of the VS coordinate system.

   - the top margin is equal to the top margin of the rightmost leaf node of the sub-tree having n as the root node.

   - the left margin is equal to the left margin of the parent node of n, shifted to the right by a correction factor. This factor depends on the name of the node (e.g. if *name* = *"LI"* this factor is set to 5 times the current font width because of the indentation of list items). If $n = n_{<TD>}$ and n has a left sibling then the left margin is equal to right margin of the this left sibling. If $n = n_{ROOT}$ then the left margin is the y-axes of the VS coordinate system.

   - the right margin is equal to the right margin of the parent of node n. If $n = n_{<TABLE>}$ or $n = n_{<TD>}$ then the right margin is set to correspond to table/cell width.

3. If $n \in N_{data}$ or $n = n_{<A>}$ then X and Y can have dimensions from 4 to 8 depending on the area on the VS occupied by the corresponding text/link (see Figure 4). Coordinates are calculated considering the number of characters contained in the *value* attribute and the current font width. Text flow is restricted to the right margin of the parent node and then a new line is started. The height of the line is determined by current font height. ◆

The definition of M-Tree covers most aspects of the rendering process, but not all of them because of the complexity of the process. For example if the page contains tables then RM implements modified auto-layout algorithm [9] for calculating table/column/cell widths. So when $n_{<TABLE>}$ is encountered, RM makes one more pass from that node down the mT to calculate cell/column/table widths. Hence the first pass is dedicated to table width calculations, and in the second pass RM calculates final coordinates for nodes that belong to the observed sub tree. If there are other $n_{<TABLE>}$ nodes down on the path (nesting of tables in the page) the process of calculating widths is recursively performed, but with no additional passes. Before resolving a table, artificial cells (nodes) are inserted in order to simplify calculus in cases where cell spanning is present (*colspan* and *rowspan* attributes in a *<TD>*).

Let us consider the complexity of the MT extraction process. First and second step (extracting *<TE,DE>* pairs and building the mT) are performed in a single pass through the page. Hence the complexity so far is $O(s)$, where s represents the size of the file. In the third step RM transforms mT into MT while passing through mT and calculating coordinates for every non-descriptive

node. If mT does not contain nodes that represent table TEs (tables in a page) then one single pass in the third step is needed and complexity remains linear. If the page contains tables then in the worst case RM performs one pass more. Hence the complexity of the RM phase is $O(2s)$ and the resulting complexity of the MT extraction process is $O(3s)$ which is satisfactory for most applications.

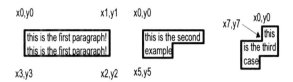

Figure 4: Some of the possible *TEXT* polygons

3. Defining heuristics for recognition of common areas of interest

Given the MT of a page and assuming the common Web design patterns, it is possible to define a set of heuristics for recognition of standard areas in a page such as menu or footer. First, areas of the interest are listed to be header *(H)*, footer *(F)*, left menu *(LM)*, right menu *(RM)*, and center of the page *(C)*. At present there are no exact definitions in the open literature for these page areas (one can think of these areas as groups of objects). Therefore we adopted intuitive definitions of these areas, which rely exclusively upon VS coordinates of logical groups of objects in a page. It is helpful to understand these groups of objects as frequently found areas in pages regardless of a page topic. They are tightly related to the presentational concept of a page. We employed some heuristics based on visual information to recognize area of interest.

After careful examination of many different pages on the Web, we restricted the areas in which H, F, LM, RM, and C can be found. We introduced a specific partition of a page into locations as it is shown in figure 5.

We set $W_1 = W_2$ to be 30% of the page width in pixels determined by the rightmost margin among nodes from MT. W_1 and W_2 define $\mathcal{LM}$ and $\mathcal{RM}$ respectively which are locations where LM and RM can be exclusively found. We set $H_1 = 200$ pixels and $H_2 = 150$ pixels. H_1 and H_2 define $\mathcal{H}$ and $\mathcal{F}$ which respectively are locations where H and F can be exclusively found. These values were found by a statistical analysis on a sample of Web pages. Components are recognized using the following heuristics:

Heuristic 1: H consists of all nodes from MT that satisfy one or more of the following conditions:

1. Subtree S of MT with its root r_S belongs to H iff r_S is of type $n_{<TABLE>}$ and $n_{<TABLE>}$ completely belongs to $\mathcal{H}$ (i.e. upper bound of a table is less than or equal to H_1).

2. Subtree S of MT with its root r_S belongs to H **iff** upper bound of r_S is less than or equal to m and r_S does not belong to sub trees found in **1.** Number m is the maximum upper bound of all $n_{<TABLE>}$ nodes found in **1.** ◆

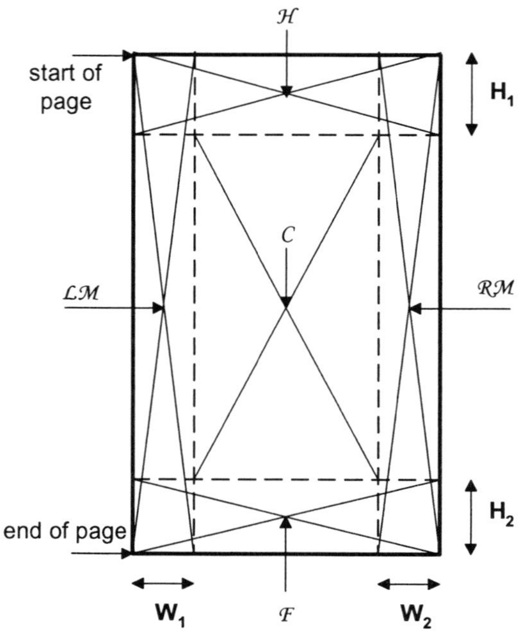

Figure 5: Position of areas of interest in a page

Heuristic 2: LM consists of all nodes from MT that are not contained in H and satisfy one or more of the following conditions:

1. Subtree S of MT with its root r_S belongs to LM iff r_S is of type $n_{<TABLE>}$ and $n_{<TABLE>}$ completely belongs to $\mathcal{LM}$ (i.e. right bound of a table is less than or equal to W_1).

2. Subtree S of MT with its root r_S belongs to LM iff r_S is of type $n_{<TD>}$, and $n_{<TD>}$ completely belongs to $\mathcal{LM}$, and $n_{<TABLE>}$ to which this $n_{<TD>}$ belongs has lower bound less than or equal to H_1, and upper bound greater then or equal to H_2. ◆

Heuristic 3: RM consists of all nodes from MT that are not contained in H, LM and satisfy one or more of the following conditions:

(Similar as heuristic 2 except $\mathcal{RM}$ and W_2 instead of $\mathcal{LM}$ and W_1) ◆

Heuristic 4: F consists of all nodes from MT that are not contained in H, LM, RM, and satisfy one or more of the following conditions:

1. Subtree S of MT with its root r_S belongs to F iff r_S is of type $n_{<TABLE>}$ and $n_{<TABLE>}$ completely belongs to $\mathcal{F}$ (i.e. down bound of a table is greater than or equal to H_2).

2. Subtree S of MT with its root r_S belongs to F iff lower bound of r_S is greater than or equal to m and r_S does not belong to sub trees found in **1.** Number m is the maximum lower bound of all $n_{<TABLE>}$ nodes found in **1.**

3. Let $n \in \{n_{
}, n_{<HR>}\}$ or n is in the scope of the central text alignment. Further, assume n is the lowest of all nodes in MT completely contained in $\mathcal{F}$. Sub tree S of MT with its root r_S belongs to F iff lower bound of r_S is greater than or equal to upper bound of n, and r_S does not belong to sub trees found in **1** and **2**. ◆

Heuristic 5: C consists of all nodes from MT that are not in H, LM, RM, and F. ◆

From previous definitions of heuristics one can realize the importance of the *<TABLE>* tag and its related tags *<TR>* and *<TD>*. These tags are commonly used ($\approx 88\%$) for purposes not originally intended by inventors of HTML [10]. Web designers usually organize layout of the page and alignment of objects by including a lot of tables in a page. Therefore every table cell often represents a smallest amount of logically grouped information, visually presented to the user in a browser window (in our case on the VS). The same stands for tables that often group menu objects, footers, search and input forms, and other common page objects. Realization of the previous heuristics is done in at most 2 additional passes through the given MT. Hence the resulting complexity of the whole recognition process is nearly $O(5s)$, and that allows us to apply it in different applications mentioned in Section 1.

4. Experimental results for object recognition

An experiment is performed to show how efficient can be recognition process using only visual information given through MT. The setup of the experiment was as follows:

Step 1: Construct a dataset D containing different pages from different sites.

Step 2: Walk through D manually and label areas that can be considered as H, F, LM, RM, and C.

Step **3**: Perform automatic extraction of *MT* for each page in *D*. Perform automatic recognition of areas of interest using defined heuristics on *MT*.

Step **4**: Estimate how well areas are recognized using a set of manually labeled areas of interest *D* as a reference point.

Step 1 is conducted by downloading nearly 16000 pages from the open source directory **www.dmoz.org** as a starting point for our crawler. We downloaded nearly 1000 files from the first level of each root category. *D* is constructed from the downloaded set by randomly choosing 515 files, uniformly distributed among categories and also in size. Two persons performed step 2 once. Second person was a kind of control and ultimate judge for labeling. Step 3 is performed using **Siena Tree** tool that includes *MT* builder and logic for applying recognition heuristics. **Siena Tree** is written in Java 1.3 and can be used to visualize objects of interest from a Web page. For example one can see in a scrolling window where are the paragraphs and line breaks placed (*<P>* and *
*). Also one can enter any sequence of HTML tags to obtain picture (visualization) of their positions. Again, two persons in step 4 make judgment of recognizer performance by entering into each labeled file and comparing automatic labels with hand made labels from step 2. After step 4 we got the results shown in Table 1.

In order to discuss results from Table 1, notions of *"bad"* or *"good"* in recognition process have to be clarified. If area *X* exists but it is not labeled at all, or if *X* does not exist but something is labeled as *X,* then mark *"not recognized"* is evidenced. If less than 50% of objects that belong to *X* are labeled, or if some objects out of *X* are labeled too, then mark *"bad"* is evidenced. Mark *"good"* is evidenced if more than 50% but less than 90% of objects from *X* are labeled and no objects out of *X* are labeled. Mark *"excellent"* is evidenced if more than 90% of objects from *X* and no objects out of *X* are labeled. We are also very aware that estimation of previously mentioned percentages is a subjective category due to lack of strict definitions for such objects (areas).

	Head.	Footer	Left M	Right M	Tot.
Not recognized	25	13	6	5	3
Bad	16	17	15	14	24
Good	10	15	3	2	50
Excellent	49	55	76	79	23

Table 1: Success in recognition process (in %).

We stress that mark *"bad"* is given in cases where something is wrongly recognized. That is because we intend to use **Siena Tree** to filter the noise for the text classification purposes. Therefore if some text from the center of the page is wrongly removed we could lose important information.

Also, recognition of *C* is, according to heuristic 5, complementary to recognition of other areas. So we did not include it in performance measurements. Results from column "overall" are obtained by introducing the total score *S* for the page *P* as a sum of all marks for recognition of all areas of interest. If $X \in \{H, F, LM, RM\}$ is *"not recognized"* then corresponding mark is 0. Marks *"bad"*, *"good"*, and *"excellent"* are mapped into 1, 2, and 3 respectively. Now, if *S=12* we assume recognition process for particular file (page) is *"excellent"*. Similar *"good"* stands for *8 ≤ S < 12, "bad"* stands for *4 ≤ S < 8*, and *"not recognized"* stands for *S < 4*. Analyzing pages that perform as *"bad"* or *"not recognized"* we found that in nearly 20% the *MT* was not quite correct but the *mT* was correct i.e. rendering process was not good enough. Typical error is that portions of a page are internally good rendered but they are scrambled as a whole. For the rest of 80% of *"not recognized"* and *"bad"* recognized pages we suppose defined heuristics are not sufficient enough. Finally we selected values for margins H_1, H_2, W_1, and W_2 according to statistics from [6]. In further research other values have to be considered as well.

5. Page classification using visual information

The rendering module provides an enhanced document representation, which can be used whenever the traditional bag-of-words representation cannot capture the complex structure of a Web page (i.e. page ranking, crawling, document clustering and classification). In particular, we have performed some document categorization experiments using the rich representation provided by the rendering module (*MT* representation).

At the time of writing, there is not a dataset of Web pages, which has been commonly accepted as a standard reference for classification tasks. Thus, we have decided to create our own. After extracting all the URLs provided by the first 5 levels of the DMOZ topic taxonomy, we selected 14 topics at the first level of the hierarchy (we rejected topic *"Regional"* which features many non-English documents). Each URL has been associated to the class (topic) from which it has been discovered. Finally, all classes have been randomly pruned, keeping only 1000 URLs for each class. Using a Web crawler, we downloaded all the documents associated to the URLs. Many links were broken (server down or pages not available anymore), thus only about 10.000 pages could be effectively retrieved (an average of 668 pages for each class). These pages have been used to create the dataset.

Such dataset[1] can be easily replicated, enlarged and updated (the continuous changing of Web format and styles does not allow to employ a frozen dataset since after few months it would be not representative of the real documents that can be found on the Internet).

5.1. Naive Bayes Classifier

The Naive Bayes classifier [11] is the simplest instance of a probabilistic classifier. The output $p(c/d)$ of a probabilistic classifier is the probability that the pattern d belongs to class c (posterior probability).

The Naive Bayes classifier assumes that text data comes from a set of parametric models (each single model is associated to a class). Training data are used to estimate the unknown model parameters. During the operative phase, the classifier computes (for each model) the probability $p(d/c)$ expressing the probability that the document is generated using the model. The Bayes theorem allows the inversion of the generative model and the computation of the posterior probabilities (probability that the model generated the pattern). The final classification is performed selecting the model yielding the maximum posterior probability.

In spite of its simplicity, the Naive Bayes classifier is almost as accurate as state-of-the-art learning algorithms for text categorization tasks [12]. The Naive Bayes classifier is the most used classifier in many different Web applications such as focus crawling, recommending systems, etc. For all these reasons, we have selected such classifier to measure the accuracy improvement provided by taking into account visual information.

5.2. Classification results

The dataset was split into training and a test set of equal size. First, a Naive Bayes classifier was trained on all the words in the documents. Such classifier is usually constructed when not considering visual information and it provides a baseline to validate the effectiveness of the proposed data representation.

In order to classify a page taking into account its visual appearance, each page from the training (test) set was processed, extracting the bag-of-words representation of its six basic constituents: header, footer, left menu, right menu, center and title and meta-tags (see Figure 6).

Then, we created six Naive Bayes classifiers where the i-th classifier was trained using the bag-of-words representations of the i-th constituents of the documents (i.e. the third classifier has been trained on the words belonging to the left menu of the documents).

When classifying a document, the i-th classifier assigns a score to the document equal to $p_i(c/d)$. Mixing the scores of each single classifier performs the final

decision. The mixture is performed assigning to the i-th classifier a weight w_i taking into account the expected relevance of the information stored into a specific part of the page:

$$p(c/d) = \Sigma_i \, w_i * p_i(c/d)$$

In particular, after some tuning we have assigned the following weights to each classifier: header 0.1, footer 0.01, left menu 0.05, right menu 0.04, center 0.5, title and meta-tags 0.3.

Table 2 shows the classification results of the proposed method. Taking into account the visual appearance of the page that is provided by MT, we achieved an improvement of more than 10% in the classification accuracy.

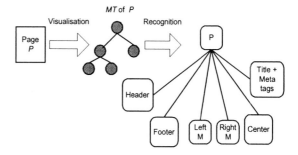

Figure 6: Page representation used as an input for six Naïve Bayes classifiers

	Correct (no visual)	Correct (visual)	Total
Arts	105	176	324
Business	123	224	316
Computers	129	182	319
Games	141	212	339
Health	271	284	380
Home	284	269	348
Kids & Teens	81	171	343
News	198	218	336
Recreation	161	161	338
Reference	232	180	320
Science	121	163	335
Shopping	126	203	304
Society	194	180	337
Sports	145	222	341
Total	2311 (49%)	2845 (61%)	4680 (100%)

Table 2. Comparison of the classification accuracy of a Naive Bayes classifier when taking into account a bag-of-words representation of the page versus a mixture of Naive Bayes classifiers taking into account the visual appearance of documents. Information carried by the visual appearance increases classification accuracy of more than 10%.

256

6. Conclusion

This paper describes a possible representation for a Web page in which objects are placed into well-defined tree hierarchy according to where they belong in an HTML structure of a page. We named this representation *M-Tree*. Further, each object (node from *M-Tree*) carries information about its position in a browser window. This visual information enables us to define heuristics for recognition of common areas such as header, footer, left and right menus, and center of the page. The crucial difficulty was to develop sufficiently good rendering algorithm i.e. to imitate behavior of popular user agents such as Internet Explorer.

We concluded from analyzed pages that HTML source was often far away from the proposed standard and it posed additional problems in rendering process. After applying some techniques for the error recovery in construction of the parsing tree and introducing some rendering simplifications (we do not deal with frames, layers and style sheets) we defined recognition heuristics based only on visual information. We could have included other types of information into recognition process, but we wanted to observe percentage of successfully recognized areas based only on page layout structure and common design patterns. The overall success in recognizing targeted areas yields 73%. From Table 1 one can see that menus are either recognized or not. On the other hand recognition of header and footer is more complex and heuristics other than just visual have to be considered. In further research we plan to improve rendering process and recognition heuristics.

Some preliminary results have shown that spatial information is important to classify Web documents. Classification accuracy of a Naive Bayes classifier was increased of more than 10%, when taking into account the visual information. In particular, we constructed a mixture of classifiers each one trained to recognize words appearing in a specific portion of the page. In the future, we plan to use Neural Networks to find the optimal weights of our mixture of classifiers. We hope our system will also improve focus crawling strategies [4] by estimating importance of the link based on its position and neighborhood. We believe that our visual page representation can find its application in many other areas related to search engines, information retrieval and data mining from the Web.

7. References

[1] Quinlan, J.R., "Induction of decision trees", *Machine Learning*, 1986, pp. 81-106.

[2] Salton, G., McGill, M.J., *An Introduction to Modern Information Retrieval*, McGraw-Hill, 1983.

[3] Chakrabarti S., van den Berg M., Dom B., "Focused crawling: A new approach to topic-specific Web resource discovery", *Proceedings of the 8th Int. World Wide Web Conference*, Toronto, Canada, 1999.

[4] Diligenti M., Coetzee F., Lawrence S., Giles C., Gori M., "Focused crawling using context graphs", *Proceedings of the 26th Int. Conf. On Very Large Databases*, Cairo, Egypt, 2000.

[5] Rennie J., McCallum A., "Using reinforcement learning to spider the Web efficiently", *Proceedings of the Int. Conf. On Machine Learning*, Bled, Slovenia, 1999.

[6] Bernard L.M., "Criteria for optimal Web design (designing for usability)", *http://psychology.wichita.edu/optimalweb/position.htm,* 2001

[7] Embley D.W., Jiang Y.S., Ng Y.K., "Record-Boundary Discovery in Web Documents", *Proceedings of SIGMOD,* Philadelphia, USA, 1999.

[8] Lim S. J., Ng Y. K., "Extracting Structures of HTML Documents Using a High-Level Stack Machine", Proceedings of the 12th *International Conference on Information Networking ICOIN*, Tokyo, Japan, 1998

[9] World Wide Web Consortium (**W3C**), "HTML 4.01 Specification", http://www.w3c.org/TR/html401/ , December 1999.

[10] James F., "Representing Structured Information in Audio Interfaces: A Framework for Selecting Audio Marking Techniques to Represent Document Structures", Ph.D. thesis, Stanford University, available online at http://www-pcd.stanford.edu/frankie/thesis/, 2001.

[11] Mitchell T., "Machine Learning", McGraw Hill, 1997.

[12] Sebastiani F., "Machine learning in automated text categorization", ACM Computing Surveys, 34(1), pp. 1-47

Discovering Frequent Geometric Subgraphs*

Michihiro Kuramochi and George Karypis

Department of Computer Science/Army HPC Research Center
University of Minnesota, MN 55455
{kuram, karypis}@cs.umn.edu

Abstract

As data mining techniques are being increasingly applied to non-traditional domains, existing approaches for finding frequent itemsets cannot be used as they cannot model the requirement of these domains. An alternate way of modeling the objects in these data sets, is to use a graph to model the database objects. Within that model, the problem of finding frequent patterns becomes that of discovering subgraphs that occur frequently over the entire set of graphs. In this paper we present a computationally efficient algorithm for finding frequent geometric subgraphs in a large collection of geometric graphs. Our algorithm is able to discover geometric subgraphs that can be rotation, scaling and translation invariant, and it can accommodate inherent errors on the coordinates of the vertices. Our experimental results show that our algorithms requires relatively little time, can accommodate low support values, and scales linearly on the number of transactions.

1 Introduction

Efficient algorithms for finding frequent itemsets—both sequential and non-sequential—in very large transaction databases have been one of the key success stories of data mining research [2, 1, 22, 8, 3, 20]. Nevertheless, as data mining techniques have been increasingly applied to non-traditional domains, such as scientific, spatial and relational datasets, situations tend to occur on which we can not apply existing itemset discovery algorithms, because these problems are difficult to be adequately and correctly modeled with the traditional market-basket transaction approaches.

Recently several approaches have been proposed for mining graphs in the context where the graphs are used to model relational, physical and scientific datasets [9, 19, 10, 12, 7, 11]. Modeling objects using graphs allows us to represent arbitrary relations among entities. The key advantage of graph modeling is that it allows us to solve problems that we could not solve previously. For instance, consider a problem of mining chemical compounds to find recurrent substructures. We can achieve that using a graph-based pattern discovery algorithm by creating a graph for each one of the compounds whose vertices correspond to different atoms, and whose edges correspond to bonds between them. We can assign to each vertex a label corresponding to the atom involved (and potentially its charge), and assign to each edge a label corresponding to the type of the bond (and potentially information about their relative three dimensional orientation). Once these graphs have been created, recurrent substructures across different compounds become frequently occurring subgraphs.

This paper focuses on the related problem of finding frequently occurring geometric patterns in geometric graphs—graphs whose vertices have two or three dimensional coordinates associated with them. These patterns correspond to geometric subgraphs that have a sufficiently large support. Datasets arising in many scientific domains often contain such geometric information, and any patterns discovered in them are of interest if they preserve both the topological and the geometric nature of the pattern. Moreover, being able to directly find geometric patterns (as opposed using a post-processing step on the topological patterns), holds the promise of leading to algorithms that are significantly more scalable than their topological counter-parts. Despite the importance of the problem, there has been limited work in developing generic algorithms to find such patterns. The notable exceptions are the work by Wang et al. proposed several algorithms for automated finding of interesting substructures in chemical or biomolecule domain [18, 17], and the work by Chew et al. that proposed an approach to find common substructures in protein sequences using root mean squared (RMS) distance minimization [4]. However, these approaches are either computationally too expensive,

*This work was supported by NSF CCR-9972519, EIA-9986042, ACI-9982274, ACI-0133464 by Army Research Office contract DA/DAAG55-98-1-0441, by the DOE ASCI program, and by Army High Performance Computing Research Center contract number DAAH04-95-C-0008. Access to computing facilities was provided by the Minnesota Supercomputing Institute.

or they find a restricted set of geometric subgraphs.

In this paper we present an algorithm called gFSG that is capable of finding frequently occurring geometric subgraphs in a large database of graph transactions. The key characteristic of gFSG is that it allows for the discovery of geometric subgraphs that can be rotation, scaling and translation invariant. Furthermore, to accommodate inherent errors on the coordinates of the vertices (either due to experimental measurements or floating point round-off errors), it allows for patterns in which the coordinates can match with some degree of tolerance. gFSG uses a pattern discovery framework that uses the level-by-level approach that was made popular by the Apriori [2] algorithm for finding frequent itemsets, and incorporate numerous computationally efficient algorithms for computing isomorphism between geometric subgraphs that are rotation, scaling and translation invariant, for candidate generation, and for frequency counting. Experimental results using a large database of over 20,000 real two dimensional chemical structures show that gFSG requires relatively little time, can accommodate low support values, and scales linearly on the number of transactions.

In the rest of the paper, we first defines basic notions and introduces notation. Then, we describe our problem setting of finding frequent geometric subgraphs, the outline and the details of the algorithm. Finally we experimentally evaluate our algorithm on a real dataset of chemical compounds and analyze the performance and the scalability of our algorithm.

2 Definitions And Notation

A **graph** $g = (V, E)$ is made of two sets, the set of vertices V and the set of edges E. Each vertex $v \in V$ has a label $l(v) \in L_V$, and each edge $e \in E$ is an unordered pair of vertices uv where $u, v \in V$. Each edge also a label $l(e) \in L_E$. L_E and L_V denote the sets of edge and vertex labels respectively. Those edge and vertex labels are not necessarily to be unique. If $|L_E| = |L_V| = 1$, then we call it an **unlabeled graph**. If each vertex $v \in V$ of the graph has coordinates associated with it, in either the two or three dimensional space, we call it a **geometric graph**. We will denote the coordinates of a vertex v by $c(v)$.

Two graphs $g_1 = (V_1, E_1)$ and $g_2 = (V_2, E_2)$ are **isomorphic**, denoted by $g_1 \sim g_2$, if they are topologically identical to each other, *i.e.*, there is a bijection $\phi : V_1 \mapsto V_2$ with $e = xy \in E_1 \leftrightarrow \phi(x)\phi(y) \in E_2$ for every edge $e \in E_1$ where $x, y \in V_1$. In the case of labeled graphs, this mapping must also preserve the labels on the vertices and edges, that means for every vertex $v \in V$, $l(v) = l(\phi(v))$ and for every edge $e = xy \in E$, $l(xy) = l(\phi(x)\phi(y))$. An **automorphism** of a graph $g = (V, E)$ is a bijection from the vertices in g to vertices in the same g. Given two graphs $g_1 = (V_1, E_1)$ and $g_2 = (V_2, E_2)$, the problem of *subgraph*

isomorphism is to find an isomorphism between g_2 and a subgraph of g_1, *i.e.*, to determine whether or not g_2 is included in g_1.

The notion of isomorphism and automorphism can be extended for the case of geometric graphs as well. A simple way of defining geometric isomorphism between two geometric graphs g_1 and g_2 is to require that there is an isomorphism ϕ that in addition to preserving the topology and the labels of the graph, to also preserve the coordinates of every vertex. However, since the coordinates of the vertices depend on the particular reference coordinate axes, the above definition is of limited interest. Instead, it is more natural to define geometric isomorphism that allows homogeneous transforms on those coordinates, prior to establishing a *match*. For the purpose of our work, we consider three basic types of geometric transformations: rotation, scaling and translation, as well as, their combination. In light of that, we define that two geometric graphs g_1 and g_2 are **geometrically isomorphic**, if there exists an isomorphism ϕ of g_1 and g_2 and a homogeneous transform $\mathcal{T}$, that preserves the coordinates of the corresponding vertices, *i.e.*, $\mathcal{T}(c(v)) = c(\phi(v))$ for every $v \in V$. In this case, ϕ is called a **geometric isomorphism** between g_1 and g_2. Geometric automorphism is defined in an analogous fashion. Figure 1(a) shows some examples illustrating this definition. There are four geometric graphs drawn in this two dimensional example, each of which is a rectangle. Edges are unlabeled and vertex labels are indicated by their colors. The graphs $r_1 \sim r_2$ if all of the rotation, scaling and translation are allowed, and $r_1 \sim r_3$ if both rotation and translation are allowed, and $r_1 \sim r_4$ if translation is allowed.

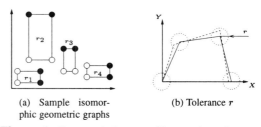

(a) Sample isomorphic geometric graphs

(b) Tolerance r

Figure 1. Geometric isomorphism and r-tolerance

One of the challenges in using the above definition of geometric graph isomorphism is that it requires an exact match of the coordinates of the various vertices. Unfortunately, geometric graphs derived from physical datasets may contain small amounts of error, and in many cases, we are interested in find geometric patterns that are similar to, but slightly different from each other. To accommodate these requirements, we allow a certain amount of tolerance r when we establish a match between coordinates. That is, if $\| \mathcal{T}(c(v)) - c(\phi(v)) \| \leq r$ for every $v \in V$, we regard ϕ as a valid geometric isomorphism. We will refer to the parameter r as the **coordinate matching tolerance**. A two dimensional example is shown in Figure 1(b). We can think of an imaginary circle or sphere of a radius r centered at each vertex. After aligning the local coordinate axes of the two geometric graphs with each other, if a corresponding vertex in another graph is inside this circle or sphere, we consider that the two vertices are located at the same position. We will refer to these isomorphisms as *r-tolerant geometric isomorphisms*, and will be the type of isomorphisms that will assume for the rest of this paper.

Finally, a graph is **connected** if there is a path between every pair of vertices in the graph. Given a graph $g = (V, E)$, a graph $g_s = (V_s, E_s)$ will be a **subgraph** of g if and only if $V_s \subseteq V$ and $E_s \subseteq E$. In a way similar to isomorphism, the notion of subgraph can be extended to *r-tolerant geometric subgraphs* in which the coordinates match after a particular homogeneous transform $\mathcal{T}$.

3 Problem Definition

The input for the frequent geometric subgraph discovery problem is a set of graphs D, each of which is an undirected labeled geometric graph, the minimum support σ such that $0 < \sigma \leq 1.0$, a set of allowed geometric transforms out of rotation, scaling and translation, and a coordinate matching tolerance r. The goal of the frequent geometric subgraph discovery is to find all connected undirected geometric graphs that have an r-tolerant geometric subgraph in at least $\sigma|D|$ graphs of the input dataset. We will refer to each of the graphs in D as a *geometric graph transaction* or simply a *transaction* when the context is clear, to D as the geometric graph transaction database, to σ as the *support* threshold, and each of the discovered patterns as the *r-tolerant frequent geometric subgraph*.

There are two key aspects in the above problem statement. First, we allow homogeneous transforms when we find instances of them in transactions. That is, a pattern can appear in a transaction in a shifted, scaled or rotated fashion. This greatly increases our ability to find interesting patterns. For instance in many chemical datasets, common substructures are at different orientation from each other, and the only way to identify them is to allow for translation and rotation invariant patterns. However, this added flexibility comes at a considerable increase in the complexity of discovering such patterns, as we need to consider all possible geometric configurations (a combination of rotation, scaling and translation) of a single pattern. For example, let us take a look at Figure 2 of a triangle. The triangle shown in Figure 2(a) has infinitely many geometric configurations, some of which are shown in Figure 2(b).

Second, we allow for some degree of tolerance when we try to establish a matching between the vertex-coordinates of the pattern and its supporting transaction. Even though this significantly improves our ability to find meaningful patterns and deal with measurement errors and errors due

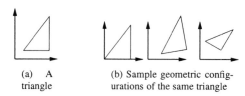

| (a)   A | (b) Sample geometric config- |
| triangle | urations of the same triangle |

Figure 2. A triangle and its geometric configurations under rotation and translation

to floating point operations (that are occurred by applying the various geometric transforms), it dramatically changes the nature of the problem for the following reason. In traditional pattern discovery problems such as finding frequent itemsets, sequential patterns, and/or frequent topological graphs there was a clear definition of what was the pattern given its set of supporting transactions. On the other hand, in the case of r-tolerant geometric subgraphs, there are many different geometric representations of the same pattern (all of which will be r-tolerant isomorphic to each other). The problem becomes not only that of finding a pattern and its support, but also finding the right representative of this pattern. Note that this representative can be either an actual instance, or a composite of many instances. The selection of the right representative can have a serious impact on correctly computing the support of the pattern. For example, given a set of subgraphs that are r-tolerant isomorphic to each other, the one that corresponds to an *outlier* will tend to have a lower support than the one corresponding to the *center*. Thus, the exact solution of the problem of discovering all r-tolerant geometric subgraphs involves a *pattern optimization* phase whose goal is to select the right representative for each pattern, such that it will lead to the largest number of frequent patterns.

4 gFSG—Frequent Geometric Subgraph Discovery Algorithm

To solve the problem of finding the frequently occurring r-tolerant geometric subgraphs, as defined in Section 3, we developed an algorithm called gFSG. gFSG represents a first attempt for addressing this problem, and due to the complexity imposed by allowing a tolerance on how the different coordinates are matched, gFSG is not guaranteed to find all such frequent r-tolerant geometric subgraphs. In particular, gFSG uses a simple approach that is based on the first occurrence in determining the representative for each pattern, that may lead to under-counting the frequency of certain patterns. However, gFSG can be easily extended to perform a shape optimization for these representative patterns, and those extensions are described in Section 6.

In addition to that, to improve the performance of gFSG, it imposes two additional conditions that must be satisfied by the input database. First, the closest distance between any pair of points in each graph is least $2r$; and second, the are no frequent subgraphs in the database that are $2r$-tolerant geometrically isomorphic to each other. Both of these conditions stem from the fact that we allow a tolerance to the mapping of the coordinates. The first condition allow as to efficiently compute geometric isomorphism between two graphs, whereas the second condition states that the frequent patterns in order to be distinguished as being different, they have to be reasonably far away from each other. If these conditions are not met, gFSG may fail to discover some patterns.

The gFSG algorithm follows the level-by-level structure of the Apriori algorithm used for finding frequent itemsets in market-basket datasets [2], and shares many characteristics with our previously developed frequent subgraph discovery algorithm for topological graphs [12]. The high level structure of our algorithm is shown in Algorithm 1. Edges in the algorithm correspond to items in traditional frequent itemset discovery. Our algorithm increases the size of frequent subgraphs by adding an edge one-by-one. gFSG initially enumerates all the frequent single, double and triple edge graphs. Then, based on the double and triple edge graphs, it starts the main computational loop. During each iteration it first generates candidate subgraphs whose size is greater than the previous frequent ones by one edge (Line 6) of Algorithm 1. Next, it counts the frequency for each of these candidates, and prunes subgraphs that do no satisfy the support constraint (Lines 8–12). Discovered frequent subgraphs satisfy the downward closure property of the support condition, which allows us to effectively prune the lattice of frequent subgraphs. The notation used in this algorithm and in the rest of this paper is explained in Table 1.

Algorithm 1 gfsg(D, s) (Frequent Geometric Subgraph)

1: $F^1 \leftarrow$ detect all frequent geometric 1-subgraphs in D
2: $F^2 \leftarrow$ detect all frequent geometric 2-subgraphs in D
3: $F^3 \leftarrow$ detect all frequent geometric 3-subgraphs in D
4: $k \leftarrow 4$
5: **while** $F^{k-1} \neq \emptyset$ **do**
6:     $C^k \leftarrow$ gfsg-gen(F^{k-1})
7:     **for each** candidate $g^k \in C^k$ **do**
8:         g^k.count $\leftarrow 0$
9:         **for each** transaction $t \in D$ **do**
10:             **if** candidate g^k is included in t **then**
11:                 g^k.count $\leftarrow g^k$.count $+ 1$
12:     $F^k \leftarrow \{g^k \in C^k \mid g^k$.count $\geq sD\}$
13:     $k \leftarrow k + 1$
14: **return** $F^1, F^2, \ldots, F^{k-2}$

In the rest of this section we outline the algorithms used by gFSG to compute geometric graph isomorphism, generate the candidate subgraphs, and compute their frequency. Additional details on some of these algorithms can be found in [13].

Table 1. Notation used throughout the paper

Notation	Description
D	A dataset of graph transactions
t	A graph transaction in D
k-(sub)graph	A (sub)graph with k edges
g^k	A k-subgraph
C^k	A set of candidates with k edges
F^k	A set of frequent k-subgraphs

4.1 Geometric Graph Isomorphism

One of the key computational kernels used by gFSG is that of determining whether or not two geometric graphs are geometrically isomorphic to each other. This operation is used extensively when computing the size one, two, three frequent subgraphs and during candidate generation to essentially establish whether two patterns are identical or not.

In gFSG, a geometric isomorphism between two graphs g_1 and g_2 is computed by first identifying the possible geometric transformations that will map the vertices of g_1 within an r distance of the vertices of g_2, and then check each one of them to see if it preserves the topology (and the vertex and edge labels) of the two graphs. The details of this algorithm and additional optimizations are described in the rest of this section. Note that our description will assume that we are interested in geometric isomorphism that include all three transformations: rotation, scaling and translation.

Each geometric graph has its own coordinate system, or a reference frame. When we check the geometric isomorphism between g_1 and g_2, both should be in the same coordinate system. Nevertheless, there are infinitely many possible local coordinate systems we can choose, especially when we consider rotation invariant isomorphisms. Our algorithm limits this number by using a subset of the edges of the graph to define the coordinate axes. In the two dimensional space, it suffices to choose an edge and its direction to determine a local coordinate system (*e.g.*, the edge uv in Figure 3(a) as the X axis), and in the three dimensional space, two connected non-collinear edges (edges uv and uw in Figure 3(b)) form the XY plane and set the reference frame. These reference frames allow us to find translation and rotation invariant isomorphisms. To accommodate isomorphisms that are scale invariant, we can uniformly scale the graph such that one of these edges (*e.g.*, the one defining the X-axis) is of unit length. We will refer to each one of the graphs obtained by using the edge-defined reference frames as a ***geometric configuration***.

The algorithm for computing the geometric isomorphism is shown in Algorithm 2. First we check to see if g_1 and g_2 are of the same size, and if not, then the algorithm returns "false" indicating that these graphs are not isomorphic to each other. Then, the algorithm chooses an arbitrary geometric configuration for g_2 and tries to find a bijection between that configuration of g_2 and all possible geometric

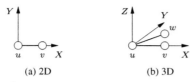

(a) 2D   (b) 3D

Figure 3. Edges for the basis of the local coordinate system

configurations of g_1. The bijection between a pair of geometric configurations is determined by iterating over each vertex of g_1 and pairing it with the closest vertex of g_2 with the same label that has not yet being paired. If at any given time, the pair of closest vertices are more than r-distance apart, the algorithm terminates the search for that configuration, as there is not an r-tolerant bijection between them. Once a bijection has been established, it is then checked to determine if it is a valid topological isomorphism (line 12–13).

The complexity of this algorithm is dependent on the size of the input geometric graphs. The number of possible geometric configuration is in $O(|V_1|^2)$ or $O(|V_1|^3)$ for the two or three dimensions respectively. Choosing the closest point out of $|V_2|$ vertices can be done in $O(|V_2|)$ time. It takes $O(|E_1|)$ steps to check the validity of a bijection ϕ. Therefore, the time complexity of geometric-isomorph is in $O(|V|^2|E|)$ for the two dimensions and $O(|V|^3|E|)$ for the three dimensions. Note that the expressions on the number of geometric configurations assume that g is dense. For most real-life problems, however, g will be sparse, dramatically reducing the overall complexity of this algorithm.

Algorithm 2 geometric-isomorph($g_1 = (V_1, E_1), g_2 = (V_2, E_2), r$) (Geometric Isomorphism)

1: **if** $|V_1| \neq |V_2|$ or $|E_1| \neq |E_2|$ **then**
2:     **return** false
3: choose one arbitrary geometric configuration of g_2.
4: **for each** geometric configuration of g_1 **do**
5:     change the coordinates of all the vertices in g_1 according to the chosen geometric configuration.
6:     {assume g_1 and g_2 now share the same coordinate system}
7:     **for each** vertex $v \in V_1$ **do**
8:         find the closest vertex $u \in V_2$ from v such that $l(u) = l(v)$
9:         **if** $\|c(v) - c(u)\| > r$ **then**
10:             **break**
11:         $\phi(v) \leftarrow u$
12:     **if** ϕ is a valid topological isomorphism between g_1 and g_2 **then**
13:         **return** true
14: **return** false

To further reduce the overall time spent in checking whether or not two graphs are geometrically isomorphic, gFSG employs both topological properties and geometric transform invariants. The key idea is to first check those properties and invariants, and proceed computing an isomorphism only if these properties and invariants match. We will collectively refer to those topological properties and ge-

ometric transform invariants as *simple keys*.

The topological properties used by gFSG is the distribution of vertex and edge labels since they are easy to compute and check. Geometric transform invariants are values computed from a geometric graph which remain the same no matter how we rotate, scale or translate the original geometric graph. Because it does not change by those transforms, we only need to calculate the invariant once for each geometric graph regardless of its geometric configuration. In gFSG we used the normalized sum of distances between the geometric center of the graph and its vertices. Because the normalized sum of distances has the same dimension as distances, we use the same coordinate matching tolerance r for checking the equality between two normalized sums.

4.2 Candidate Generation

In the candidate generation phase, we create a set of candidates of size $k + 1$, given frequent geometric k-subgraphs. Candidate geometric subgraphs of size $k + 1$ are generated by joining two frequent geometric k-subgraphs. In order for two such frequent k-subgraphs to be eligible for joining they must contain the same geometric $(k - 1)$-subgraph. We will refer to this common geometric $(k - 1)$-subgraph among two k-frequent subgraphs as their *core*. The joining algorithm is basically the same as the one used in our previous work for finding topological frequent subgraphs [12] and we will not describe the details, which can be found in [12, 13].

4.3 Frequency Counting

Once candidate subgraphs have been generated, gFSG computes their frequency. In the context of frequent itemset discovery by Apriori, the frequency counting is performed substantially faster by building a hash-tree of candidate itemsets and scanning each transaction to determine which of the itemsets in the hash-tree it supports. Developing such an algorithm for frequent subgraphs, however, is challenging because there is no natural way to build the hash-tree for graphs.

In gFSG frequency counting is performed using a scheme that performs geometric graph isomorphism (using effective topological and geometric invariants) combined with the use of TID lists to reduce the set of graph transactions for which these isomorphisms need to be computed. The resulting algorithm makes it possible to efficiently count the frequency of the patterns and achieve a scalable memory usage.

In order to determine if a graph transaction contains a particular pattern, we need to check each geometric configuration of the graph against a particular geometric configuration of the pattern. This can be achieved using an algorithm similar to that for geometric graph isomorphism.

To reduce the execution time, we first use some topological properties and geometric transform invariants to quickly identify most of the miss-matches (as it was done in the case of graph isomorphism). The geometric transform invariants that we use for detecting whether or not a particular pattern can exist in a graph is based on edge-angle lists.

Let $\angle e_i e_j$ denote the angle formed by two connected edges e_i and e_j. Then, an edge-angle list eal(g) of a geometric graph g is a multiset where eal(g) $=$ { $\angle e_i e_j$ | $\angle e_i e_j$, such that two distinct edges e_i, e_j share the same end point}. We create the edge-angle list for each of the transactions and candidate subgraphs. Because edge angles are invariant against rotation, scaling and translation, if a geometric subgraph g is included in a transaction t, then eal(g) $\subseteq$ eal(t). Equality of two angles is again determined with a certain threshold as the vertex coordinate matching. For example, the graph g in Figure 4 has the following edge-angle list; eal(g) $= \{\angle e_1 e_2, \angle e_2 e_3, \angle e_3 e_1\} = \{a_1, a_1, a_2\}$, where $a_1 = \angle e_1 e_2$ and $a_2 = \angle e_1 e_3$. Note this is because $\angle e_1 e_2 = \angle e_2 e_3$. By using the comparison on the edge angle

Figure 4. A star-shaped geometric graph with three edges

lists, we can easily detect cases where geometric subgraph isomorphism does not hold, without actually performing the subgraph isomorphism.

To limit the set of graph transactions that need to be checked while determining the frequency of a particular pattern, we use an approach motivated by the well-known technique of TID lists [6, 16, 23, 21, 22], but in a memory-efficient manner. We initially identify the set of frequent edge-angles over all graph transaction by exhaustive enumeration. Then, for each frequent edge angle, we create a list of transaction ID's that contain an instance of the edge-angle. Let tid(a) denote a list of transaction ID's that contain an instance of the edge-angle a. For example, if a transaction $t = (V, E)$ is included in tid(a), then there is a pair of edges e_i and $e_j \in E$ such that $\angle e_i e_j = a$.

Now, let g be a candidate geometric graph and let eal(g) $= \{a_1, a_2, \ldots, a_n\}$ be its edge-angle list. The frequency of g is computed by checking to see if g is contained only in the graph transactions that are in the set corresponding to the intersection of the various tid(a_i) lists. Of course, if the intersection of these TID-lists is smaller than the minimum support, then the exact frequency of g is not even computed, as it is not frequent.

5 Experimental Evaluation

We experimentally evaluated the performance of gFSG using a set of real geometric graphs representing chemical compounds. In particular, we used a dataset containing 223,644 chemical compounds with their two dimensional coordinates that is available from the Developmental Therapeutics Program (DTP) at National Cancer Institute (NCI) [5]. These compounds were converted to geometric graphs in which the vertices correspond to the various atoms with their two dimensional coordinates and the edges correspond to the bonds between the atoms. The various atom types were modeled as vertex labels and the various types of bonds were modeled as edge labels. Overall, there are a total of 104 distinct vertex labels (atom types) and three distinct edges labels (bond types).

Note that even though the gFSG algorithm can find frequent geometric subgraphs in both two and three dimensional datasets, at the time of writing of this paper, we had only finished and optimized the two dimensional version of the code. For this reason our evaluation will only include two dimensional geometric graphs.

All experiments were done on dual AMD Athlon MP 1800+ (1.53GHz) machines with 2GB main memory, running the Linux operating system. All the times reported are in seconds.

5.1 Scalability With Respect To The Database Size

Our first set of experiments were designed to evaluate the scalability of gFSG with respect to the number of input graph transactions. Toward this goal we created five datasets with different number of transactions varying from 1,000 to 20,000. Each graph transaction was randomly chosen from the original dataset of 223,644 compounds. This random dataset creation process resulted in datasets in which the average transaction size (the number of edges per transaction) was about 23.

Using these datasets we performed two types of experiments. In the first experiment we used gFSG to find all frequently occurring geometric subgraphs that are rotation and translation invariant; whereas in the second set of experiments we used gFSG to find subgraphs that are also scaling invariant. For both sets of experiments, we used different values of support ranging from 0.25% up to 3%, and set r to 0.05.

Table 2 show the results obtained for the first and second set of experiments, respectively. For each individual experiment, these tables show the amount of time required to find the frequent geometric subgraphs patterns, the size of the largest discovered frequent pattern, and the total number of geometric subgraphs that were discovered.

There are three main observations that can be made from these results. First, gFSG scales linearly with the database

Table 2. Running times in seconds for chemical compound data sets which are randomly chosen from the DTP dataset. The column "Support" shows the used minimum support (%), the column with t is the running time in seconds, the column with l shows the size of the largest frequent subgraph discovered, and the column with $\#f$ is the total number of discovered frequent patterns.

Scaling	Support %	Total Number of Transactions D														
		$D = 1000$			$D = 2000$			$D = 5000$			$D = 10000$			$D = 20000$		
		t[sec]	l	$\#f$	t[sec]	l	$\#f$	t[sec]	l	$\#f$	t[sec]	l	$\#f$	t[sec]	l	$\#f$
No	3.0	8	6	203	18	6	197	32	6	177	69	6	187	109	4	143
	2.0	14	6	371	38	6	356	62	6	321	128	6	321	216	5	269
	1.0	60	8	1124	134	7	1023	161	8	795	423	8	874	839	7	826
	0.5	263	8	3213	540	8	3009	622	9	2177	1514	9	2281	2465	7	2091
	0.25	790	10	10040	2051	10	10733	2224	10	6112	5351	9	6090	8590	10	5649
Yes	3.0	14	7	236	35	6	246	73	7	236	126	6	217	321	6	224
	2.0	26	7	415	72	7	430	124	7	404	205	7	352	522	7	359
	1.0	123	8	1393	315	8	1395	460	9	1189	1107	8	1295	1974	8	1019
	0.5	694	10	4960	1478	10	4623	2108	10	3593	4621	9	3869	9952	9	3354
	0.25	2043	13	14235	5674	12	15232	8972	12	11103	17421	9	10929	41895	11	11177

size. For most values of support, the amount of time required on the database with 20,000 transactions is 15–30 times larger than the amount of time required for 1,000 transactions. Second, as with any frequent pattern discovery algorithm, as we decrease the support the runtime increases and the number of frequent patterns increases. The overall increase in the amount of time tends to follow the increase in the number of patterns, indicating that the complexity of gFSG scales well with the number of frequent patterns. Third, comparing the scale invariant with the scale variant results, we can see that the latter is faster by almost a factor of two. This is because the number of discovered patterns is usually smaller, and each pattern has fewer supporting transactions, reducing the amount of time to compute their frequency.

5.2 Scalability With Respect To The Graph Size

Our second set of experiments was designed to evaluate the runtime of gFSG when the average size (*i.e.*, the number of edges) of each transaction increases. Again, using the whole set of chemical compounds, we created four different datasets by extracting 5,000 chemical compounds in the following way. First we sorted the original dataset based on the size of compounds. Then, we selected 5,000 compounds from four different locations of the sorted list, so that each dataset would have different transaction size. This resulted in four datasets whose average transaction size were 14, 19, 23 and 28. Because the chemical compounds are taken from the sorted order, almost all the transactions are in the same size as the average.

As with our earlier experiments, we used gFSG to find both scale invariant and scale variant patterns and we varied the minimum support from 3.0% to 0.25%. Tables 3 show the amount of time and the number of frequent patterns discovered in these two sets of experiments.

From these results we can see that as the average transac-

tion size increases, the time required to find the frequent geometric subgraphs increases, as well. In most cases, this increase is at a higher rate than the corresponding increase on the size of each transaction. In general, the running time for finding the patterns when the average transaction size is 28, is about ten times longer than the running time for the average transaction size 14. This non-linear relation between the time complexity and the size of the transaction is due to the fact that the algorithm needs to explore a much higher search space, and is consistent with the time increases for other pattern discovery algorithms, such as those for finding frequent itemsets [14] and sequential patterns [15]. Nevertheless, gFSG is able to mine the largest dataset with a support of 0.25 in less than two hours. Also, comparing the scale invariant with the scale variant experiments, we can see that as before, finding the scale variant patterns is faster by about a factor of two.

6 Conclusion

In this paper we presented an algorithm, gFSG, for finding frequently occurring geometric subgraphs in large graph databases, that can be used to discover recurrent patterns in scientific, spatial, and relational datasets. Our experimental evaluation shows that gFSG can scale reasonably well to very large graph databases provided that graphs contain a sufficiently many different labels of edges and vertices.

One of the limitations of the current implementation of gFSG is it does not perform any shape optimizations on the representation of each geometric pattern. However, some simple, and yet powerful optimizations can be performed by using an approach motivated by k-means clustering. In this approach, the frequency counting phase will be performed multiple times. During each iteration, the candidate pattern will be incrementally adjusted, as its supporting set is being identified, to represent the centroid consensus pattern of the supporting set of graph transactions. In principle the itera-

Table 3. Running times in seconds for the four chemical compound data sets. Each dataset has a different average transaction size, from 14 to 28. The column "Support" shows the used minimum support (%), the column with t is the running time in seconds, the column with l shows the size of the largest frequent subgraph discovered, and the column with $\#f$ is the total number of discovered frequent patterns.

Scaling	Support %	Average Transaction Size T											
		$T=14$			$T=19$			$T=23$			$T=28$		
		t[sec]	l	$\#f$	t[sec]	l	$\#f$	t[sec]	l	$\#f$	t[sec]	l	$\#f$
No	3.0	17	6	148	26	5	175	47	6	258	81	6	268
	2.0	27	7	270	49	5	324	81	7	418	288	6	792
	1.0	65	8	671	181	6	807	287	8	1164	1189	9	2975
	0.5	196	7	1613	610	7	2180	1002	9	3315	3454	11	8093
	0.25	497	9	3708	1726	9	5768	2622	12	8819	10172	12	24242
Yes	3.0	22	7	154	41	6	196	73	6	249	175	7	408
	2.0	36	7	264	81	6	325	142	7	420	543	8	993
	1.0	92	9	680	284	8	927	612	9	1385	2530	10	3936
	0.5	406	9	2072	1438	9	2859	3050	9	4620	9923	12	13178
	0.25	1226	10	5358	4997	10	8949	10824	12	15232	29686	14	38788

tive optimization on the shape of a pattern will stop, as soon as its support does not change in the course of an iteration. We are currently in the process of evaluating this algorithm and investigating efficient ways of implementing it.

References

[1] R. C. Agarwal, C. C. Aggarwal, V. V. V. Prasad, and V. Crestana. A tree projection algorithm for generation of large itemsets for association rules. IBM Research Report RC21341, 1998.

[2] R. Agrawal and R. Srikant. Fast algorithms for mining association rules. In *Proc. of the 20th VLDB*, 1994.

[3] R. Agrawal and R. Srikant. Mining sequential patterns. In *Proc. of the 11th ICDE*, 1995.

[4] L. P. Chew, D. Huttenlocher, K. Kedem, and J. Kleinberg. Fast detection of common geometric substructure in proteins. In *Proc. of the 3rd ACM RECOMB*, 1999.

[5] DTP/2D and 3D structural information. ftp:// dtpsearch.ncifcrf.gov/jan02_2d.bin.

[6] B. Dunkel and N. Soparkar. Data organizatinon and access for efficient data mining. In *Proc. of the 15th IEEE ICDE*, 1999.

[7] S. Ghazizadeh and S. Chawathe. Discovering freuqent structures using summaries. Technical Report CS-TR-4364, Dept. of Computer Science, University of Maryland, 2002.

[8] J. Han, J. Pei, and Y. Yin. Mining frequent patterns without candidate generation. In *Proc. of ACM SIGMOD*, 2000.

[9] L. Holder, D. Cook, and S. Djoko. Substructure discovery in the SUBDUE system. In *Proc. of the Workshop on Knowledge Discovery in Databases*, 1994.

[10] A. Inokuchi, T. Washio, and H. Motoda. An apriori-based algorithm for mining frequent substructures from graph data. In *Proc. of the 4th PKDD*, 2000.

[11] A. Inokuchi, T. Washio, K. Nishimura, and H. Motoda. A fast algorithm for mining frequent connected subgraphs. IBM Technical Report RT0448, 2002.

[12] M. Kuramochi and G. Karypis. Frequent subgraph discovery. In *Proc. of the 1st IEEE ICDM*, 2001.

[13] M. Kuramochi and G. Karypis. Discovering geometric frequent subgraphs. Technical Report 02-024, Dept. of Computer Science, University of Minnesota, 2002.

[14] M. Seno and G. Karypis. LPMiner: An algorithm for finding frequent itemsets using length decreasing support constraint. In *Proc. of the 1st IEEE ICDM*, 2001.

[15] M. Seno and G. Karypis. SLPMiner: An algorithm for finding frequent sequential patterns using length-decreasing support constraint. In *Proc. of the 2nd IEEE ICDM*, 2002.

[16] P. Shenoy, J. R. Haritsa, S. Sundarshan, G. Bhalotia, M. Bawa, and D. Shah. Turbo-charging vertical mining of large databases. In *Proc. of ACM SIGMOD*, 2000.

[17] J. T. L. Wang, Q. Ma, D. Shasha, and C. H. Wu. New techniques for extracting features from protein sequences. *IBM Systems Journal*, 40(2):426–441, 2001.

[18] X. Wang and J. T. L. Wang. Fast similarity search in three-dimensional structure databases. *Journal of Chemical Information and Computer Sciences*, 40(2):442–451, 2000.

[19] K. Yoshida and H. Motoda. CLIP: Concept learning from inference patterns. *Artificial Intelligence*, 75(1):63–92, 1995.

[20] M. J. Zaki. Fast mining of sequential patterns in very large databases. Technical Report 668, Dept. of Computer Science, Univeristy of Rochester, 1997.

[21] M. J. Zaki. Scalable algorithms for association mining. *IEEE TKDE*, 12(2):372–390, 2000.

[22] M. J. Zaki and K. Gouda. Fast vertical mining using diffsets. Technical Report 01-1, Dept. of Computer Science, Rensselaer Polytechnic Institute, 2001.

[23] M. J. Zaki and C.-J. Hsiao. CHARM: An efficient algorithm for closed association rule mining,. Technical Report 99-10, Dept. of Computer Science, Rensselaer Polytechnic Institute, October 1999.

Adapting classification rule induction to subgroup discovery

Nada Lavrač
Jožef Stefan Institute
Ljubljana, Slovenia
Nada.Lavrac@ijs.si

Peter Flach
University of Bristol
Bristol, UK
Peter.Flach@bristol.ac.uk

Branko Kavšek, Ljupčo Todorovski
Jožef Stefan Institute
Ljubljana, Slovenia
Branko.Kavsek@ijs.si
Ljupco.Todorovski@ijs.si

Abstract

Rule learning is typically used for solving classification and prediction tasks. However, learning of classification rules can be adapted also to subgroup discovery. This paper shows how this can be achieved by modifying the covering algorithm and the search heuristic, performing probabilistic classification of instances, and using an appropriate measure for evaluating the results of subgroup discovery. Experimental evaluation of the CN2-SD subgroup discovery algorithm on 17 UCI data sets demonstrates substantial reduction of the number of induced rules, increased rule coverage and rule significance, as well as slight improvements in terms of the area under the ROC curve.

1. Introduction

Classical rule learning algorithms were designed to construct classification and prediction rules [16, 4, 5]. In addition to this area of machine learning, referred to as *predictive induction*, developments in *descriptive induction* have recently gained much attention. These involve mining of association rules (e.g., the APRIORI association rule learning algorithm [1]), subgroup discovery (e.g., the MIDOS subgroup discovery systems [24]), and other approaches to non-classificatory induction.

The methodology presented in this paper can be applied to subgroup discovery. As in the MIDOS approach, a subgroup discovery task can be defined as follows: given a population of individuals and a property of those individuals we are interested in, find population subgroups that are statistically 'most interesting', e.g., are as large as possible and have the most unusual statistical (distributional) characteristics with respect to the property of interest.

This paper investigates how to adapt classical classification rule learning approaches to subgroup discovery, by appropriately modifying the heuristics and the covering algorithm for learning sets of rules. The proposed modifi-

cations of classification rule learners can, in principle, be used on top of any rule learner using the covering approach for rule set construction. In this work we show an upgrade of the well-known CN2 rule learning algorithm [4, 3]. Alternatively, we could have upgraded RL [15], RIPPER [5], SLIPPER [6] or other more sophisticated classification rule learners. The reason for upgrading CN2 is that other more sophisticated learners include modifications that make them more effective in classification tasks, improving their classification accuracy. Improved classification accuracy is, however, not of ultimate interest for subgroup discovery, whose main goal is to find interesting population subgroups.

We have implemented the new subgroup discovery algorithm CN2-SD in Java and incorporated it in the WEKA data mining environment [23]. The proposed approach performs subgroup discovery through the following modifications of the classical rule learning algorithm CN2: (a) incorporating example weights into the covering algorithm, (b) incorporating example weights into the weighted relative accuracy search heuristic, (c) probabilistic classification based on the class distribution of covered examples by individual rules, both in the case of unordered rule sets and ordered decision lists, and (d) area under the ROC curve rule set evaluation.

This paper presents the CN2-SD subgroup discovery algorithm, together with its experimental evaluation in selected domains of the UCI Repository of Machine Learning Databases [17]. The experimental comparison with CN2 demonstrates that the subgroup discovery algorithm CN2-SD produces substantially smaller rule sets, where individual rules have higher coverage and significance. These three factors are important for subgroup discovery: smaller size enables better understanding, higher coverage means larger support, and higher significance means that rules describe discovered subgroups that are significantly different from the entire population. The appropriateness for subgroup discovery is confirmed also by slight improvements in terms of the area under the ROC curve.

This paper is organized as follows. In Section 2 the

background for this work is explained: the standard CN2 rule induction algorithm, including the covering algorithm, the weighted relative accuracy heuristic, probabilistic classification and rule evaluation in the ROC space. Section 3 presents the modified CN2 algorithm, called CN2-SD, adapting CN2 for subgroup discovery. Section 4 presents the experimental evaluation on selected UCI domains. Some links to the related work are given in Section 5. Section 6 concludes by summarizing the results and presenting plans for further work.

2. Background

This section presents the backgrounds of our work: the classical CN2 rule induction algorithm, including the covering algorithm for rule set construction, the standard CN2 heuristics, the weighted relative accuracy heuristic, probabilistic classification and the basics of rule evaluation in ROC space.

2.1. The CN2 rule induction algorithm

CN2 is an algorithm for inducing propositional classification rules [4, 3]. Induced rules have the form if $Cond$ then $Class$, where $Cond$ is a conjunction of features (attribute values). In this paper we use the notation $Class \leftarrow Cond$.

CN2 consists of two main procedures: the search procedure that performs beam search in order to find a single rule and the control procedure that repeatedly executes the search. The search procedure performs beam search using classification accuracy of the rule as a heuristic function. The accuracy of the propositional classification rule $Class \leftarrow Cond$ is equal to the conditional probability of class $Class$, given that the condition $Cond$ is satisfied: $Acc(Class \leftarrow Cond) = p(Class|Cond)$. Different probability estimates, like the Laplace [3] or the m-estimate [2, 7], can be used in CN2 for estimating the above probability. The standard CN2 algorithm used in this work uses the Laplace estimate.

CN2 can apply a significance test to an induced rule. A rule is considered to be significant if it expresses a regularity unlikely to have occurred by chance. To test significance, CN2 uses the likelihood ratio statistic [4] that measures the difference between the class probability distribution in the set of examples covered by the rule and the class probability distribution in the set of all training examples. Empirical evaluation in [3] shows that applying a significance test reduces the number of induced rules (at a cost of slightly reduced predictive accuracy).

Two different control procedures are used in CN2: one for inducing an ordered list of rules and the other for the unordered case. In both procedures, a default rule (providing for majority class assignment) is added as the final rule in an induced rule set.

When inducing an ordered list of rules, the search procedure looks for the best rule, according to the heuristic measure, in the current set of training examples. The rule predicts the most frequent class in the set of examples, covered by the induced rule. Before starting another search iteration, all examples covered by the induced rule are removed. The control procedure invokes a new search, until all the examples are covered.

In the unordered case, the control procedure is iterated, inducing rules for each class in turn. For each induced rule, only covered examples belonging to that class are removed, instead of removing all covered examples, like in the ordered case. The negative training examples (i.e., examples that belong to other classes) remain and positives are removed in order to prevent CN2 finding the same rule again.

2.2. The weighted relative accuracy heuristic

Weighted relative accuracy is a variant of rule accuracy that can be meaningfully applied both in the descriptive and predictive induction framework; in this paper we apply this heuristic for subgroup discovery.

We use the following notation. Let $n(Cond)$ stand for the number of instances covered by a rule $Class \leftarrow Cond$, $n(Class)$ stand for the number of examples of class $Class$, and $n(Class.Cond)$ stand for the number of correctly classified examples (true positives). We use $p(Class.Cond)$ etc. for the corresponding probabilities. In our work, the Laplace estimate is used for probability estimation. Rule accuracy can be expressed as $Acc(Class \leftarrow Cond) = p(Class|Cond) = \frac{p(Class.Cond)}{p(Cond)}$. Weighted relative accuracy [14, 22], a reformulation of one of the heuristics used in EXPLORA [10] and MIDOS [24], is defined as follows.

$$WRAcc(Class \leftarrow Cond) =$$
$$p(Cond).(p(Class|Cond) - p(Class)). \quad (1)$$

Like most of the other heuristics used in subgroup discovery systems, weighted relative accuracy consists of two components, providing a tradeoff between rule generality (or the size of a group $p(Cond)$) and distributional unusualness (or relative accuracy, i.e., the difference between rule accuracy $p(Class|Cond)$ and default accuracy $p(Class)$). This difference can also be seen as the accuracy gain relative to the fixed rule $Class \leftarrow true$. The latter rule predicts all instances to satisfy $Class$; a rule is only interesting if it improves upon this 'default' accuracy. Another way of viewing relative accuracy is that it measures the utility of connecting rule body $Cond$ with a given rule head $Class$. However, it is easy to obtain high relative accuracy with highly specific rules, i.e., rules with low generality $p(Cond)$. To this end, generality is used as a 'weight', so that weighted relative accuracy trades off generality of the rule ($p(Cond)$, i.e., rule coverage) and relative accuracy ($p(Class|Cond) - p(Class)$).

In [10], these quantities are referred to as g (generality), p (rule accuracy) and p_0 (default accuracy), and the function $g(p - p_0)$ is investigated in the so-called 'p-g-space'. Klösgen also investigates other tradeoffs reducing the influence of generality, e.g. $\sqrt{g}(p - p_0)$ or $\sqrt{\frac{g}{1-g}}(p - p_0)$. Here we favor weighted relative accuracy because it has an intuitive interpretation in the ROC space (see Section 2.4).

2.3. Probabilistic classification

The induced rules can be ordered or unordered. Ordered rules are interpreted as a decision list [19] in a straightforward manner: when classifying a new example, the rules are sequentially tried and the first rule that covers the example is used for prediction.

In the case of unordered rule sets, the distribution of covered training examples among classes is attached to each rule. Rules of the form:

$$\texttt{if } Cond \texttt{ then } Class \, [ClassDistribution]$$

are induced, where numbers in the $ClassDistribution$ list denote, for each individual class, how many training examples of this class are covered by the rule. When classifying a new example, all rules are tried and those covering the example are collected. If a clash occurs (several rules with different class predictions cover the example), a voting mechanism is used to obtain the final prediction: the class distributions attached to the rules are summed to determine the most probable class. If no rule fires, a default rule is invoked which predicts the majority class of uncovered training instances.

2.4. ROC analysis for subgroup discovery

A point on the *ROC curve* (ROC: Receiver Operating Characteristic) [18] shows classifier performance in terms of false alarm or *false positive rate* $FPr = \frac{FP}{TN+FP}$ (plotted on the X-axis) that needs to be minimized, and sensitivity or *true positive rate* $TPr = \frac{TP}{TP+FN}$ (plotted on the Y-axis) that needs to be maximized. In the ROC space, an appropriate tradeoff, determined by the expert, can be achieved by applying different algorithms, as well as by different parameter settings of a selected data mining algorithm or by taking into the account different misclassification costs.

The ROC space is appropriate for measuring the success of subgroup discovery, since rules/subgroups whose TPr/FPr tradeoff is close to the diagonal can be discarded as insignificant. Conversely, significant rules/subgroups are those sufficiently distant from the diagonal.[1] The significant rules define the points in the ROC space from which a convex hull is constructed. The area under the ROC curve (AUC) can be used as a quality measure for comparing the success of different learners or subgroup miners.

Weighted relative accuracy is appropriate to measure the quality of a single subgroup, because it is proportional to the distance from the diagonal in the ROC space. To see this, note first that rule accuracy $p(Class|Cond)$ is proportional to the angle between the X-axis and the line connecting the origin with the point depicting the rule's TPr/FPr tradeoff. So, for instance, the X-axis has always rule accuracy 0 (these are purely negative subgroups), the Y-axis has always rule accuracy 1 (purely positive subgroups), and the diagonal represents subgroups with rule accuracy $p(Class)$, the prior probability of the positive class.

Relative accuracy re-normalizes this such that all points on the diagonal have relative accuracy 0, all points on the Y-axis have relative accuracy $1 - p(Class) = p(\overline{Class})$ (the prior probability of the negative class), and all points on the X-axis have relative accuracy $-p(Class)$. Notice that all points on the diagonal also have $WRAcc = 0$. In terms of subgroup discovery, the diagonal represents all subgroups with the same target distribution as the whole population; only the generality of these 'average' subgroups increases when moving from left to right along the diagonal. This interpretation is slightly different in classifier learning, where the diagonal represents random classifiers that can be constructed without any training.

More generally, one can show that points with the same $WRAcc$ value lie on straight lines parallel to the diagonal. In particular, a point on the line $TPr = FPr + a, -1 \leq a \leq 1$ has $WRAcc = ap(Class)p(\overline{Class})$. Thus, given a fixed class distribution, $WRAcc$ is proportional to the vertical (or horizontal) distance a between the line parallel to the diagonal on which the point lies, and the diagonal. In fact, the quantity $TPr - FPr$ would be an alternative quality measure for subgroups, with the additional advantage that we can use it to compare subgroups from populations with different class distributions. However, in this paper we are only concerned with comparing subgroups from the same population, and we prefer $WRAcc$ because it is a familiar measure in subgroup discovery.

3. The CN2-SD subgroup discovery algorithm

The main modifications of the CN2 algorithm, making it appropriate for subgroup discovery, involve the implementation of the weighted covering algorithm, incorporation of example weights into the weighted relative accuracy heuristic, probabilistic classification also in the case of the

---

[1]Any of those subgroups may be the 'best' according to some expert-defined operating conditions.

'ordered' induction algorithm, and the area under the ROC curve rule set evaluation.

3.1. Weighted covering algorithm

Subgroup discovery is, in general, aimed at discovering interesting properties of subgroups of the entire population. If used for subgroup discovery, the problem of standard rule learners like CN2 and RIPPER is in the use of the covering algorithm for rule set construction. The main deficiency of the covering algorithm is that only the first few induced rules may be of interest as subgroup descriptors with sufficient coverage and significance. Subsequently induced rules are induced from biased example subsets, i.e., subsets including only positive examples not covered by previously induced rules, which inappropriately biases the subgroup discovery process.

As a remedy to this problem we propose to use the weighted covering algorithm, in which the subsequently induced rules allow for discovering interesting subgroup properties of the entire population. The weighted covering algorithm modifies the classical covering algorithm in such a way that covered positive examples are not deleted from the current training set. Instead, in each run of the covering loop, the algorithm stores with each example a count that shows how many times (with how many rules induced so far) the example has been covered so far. Weights derived from these example counts then appear in the computation of WRAcc. Initial weights of all positive examples e_j equal $w(e_j, 0) = 1$. We have implemented two approaches:

(a) Multiplicative weights. In the first approach, weights decrease multiplicatively. For a given parameter $\gamma < 1$, weights of covered positive examples decrease as follows: $w(e_j, i) = \gamma^i$, where $w(e_j, i)$ is the weight of example e_j being covered i times. Note that the weighted covering algorithm with $\gamma = 1$ would result in finding the same rule over and over again, whereas with $\gamma = 0$ the algorithm would perform the same as the standard CN2 algorithm.

(b) Additive weights. In the second approach, weights of covered positive examples decrease according to the formula $w(e_j, i) = \frac{1}{i+1}$.

3.2. Modified WRAcc heuristic with example weights

The modification of CN2 reported in [22] affected only the heuristic function: weighted relative accuracy was used as search heuristic, instead of the accuracy heuristic of the original CN2, while everything else remained the same. In this work, the heuristic function was further modified to enable handling example weights, which provide the means to consider different parts of the instance space in each iteration of the weighted covering algorithm.

In the WRAcc computation (Equation 1) all probabilities are computed by relative frequencies. An example weight measures how important it is to cover this example in the next iteration. The initial example weight $w(e_j, 0) = 1$ means that the example hasn't been covered by any rule, meaning 'please cover this example, it hasn't been covered before', while lower weights mean 'don't try too hard on this example'. The modified WRAcc measure is then defined as follows.

$$WRAcc(Cl \leftarrow Cond) = \frac{n'(Cond)}{N'}(\frac{n'(Cl.Cond)}{n'(Cond)} - \frac{n'(Cl)}{N'}).$$
(2)

In this equation, N' is the sum of the weights of all examples, $n'(Cond)$ is the sum of the weights of all covered examples, and $n'(Cl.Cond)$ is the sum of the weights of all correctly covered examples.

To add a rule to the generated rule set, the rule with the maximum WRAcc measure is chosen out of those rules in the search space, which are not yet present in the rule set produced so far (all rules in the final rule set are thus distinct, without duplicates).

3.3. Probabilistic classification

Each CN2 rule returns a class distribution in terms of the numbers of examples covered, as distributed over classes. The CN2 algorithm uses class distribution in classifying unseen instances only in the case of unordered rule sets, where rules are induced separately for each class. In the case of ordered decision lists, the first rule that fires provides the classification. In our modified CN2-SD algorithm, also in the ordered case all applicable rules are taken into the account, hence the same probabilistic classification is used in both classifiers. This means that the terminology 'ordered' and 'unordered', which in CN2 distinguished between decision list and rule set induction, has a different meaning in our setting: the 'unordered' algorithm refers to learning classes one by one, while the 'ordered' algorithm refers to finding best rule conditions and assigning the majority class in the head.

3.4. Area under the ROC curve evaluation

In subgroup discovery there are two ways in which a rule learner can give rise to a ROC curve.

(a) AUC-Method-1. The first method treats each rule as a separate subgroup which is plotted in the ROC space with its true and false positive rates. We then calculate the convex hull of this set of points, selecting the subgroups which perform optimally under a particular range of operating characteristics. The area under this ROC convex hull (AUC) indicates the combined quality of the optimal subgroups, in the sense that it does evaluate whether a particular subgroup has anything to add in the context of all the other subgroups. However, the method does not take account of any overlap between subgroups, and subgroups not on the convex hull are simply ignored (the existence of many such subgroups may indicate overfitting, as we illustrate in Section 4).

Note that CN2-SD learns rules both for the positive and negative target class: rules for the positive target class represent subgroups with a higher proportion of positives than average, and rules for the negative target class represent subgroups with a lower than average proportion of positives. Consequently, this method constructs two convex hulls, one above the diagonal and one below (see Figure 1 in Section 4).

(b) AUC-Method-2. The second method employs the combined probabilistic classifications of all subgroups, as indicated below. If we always choose the most likely predicted class, this corresponds to setting a fixed threshold 0.5 on the positive probability: if the positive probability is larger than this threshold we predict positive, else negative. A ROC curve can be constructed by varying this threshold from 1 (all predictions negative, corresponding to (0,0) in the ROC space) to 0 (all predictions positive, corresponding to (1,1) in the ROC space). This results in $n + 1$ points in the ROC space, where n is the total number of classified examples. Equivalently, we can order all the examples by decreasing the predicted probability of being positive, and tracing the ROC curve by starting in (0,0), stepping up when the example is actually positive and stepping to the right when it is negative, until we reach (1,1).[2] The area under this ROC curve indicates the combined quality of all subgroups (i.e., the quality of the entire rules set). This method can be used with a test set or in cross-validation, but the resulting curve is not necessarily convex. A detailed description of this method applied to decision tree induction can be found in [11].

Which of the two methods is more appropriate for subgroup discovery is open for debate. The second method seems more appropriate if the discovered subgroups are also used for classification, while the first seems more appropriate for the selection and evaluation of a subset of potentially optimal individual subgroups. One advantage of the second method is that it is easier to apply cross-validation. A disadvantage of the first method is that it ignores redundant subgroups which may indicate overfitting. In the experimental evaluation in Section 4 we used AUC-Method-2, while the ROC convex hull obtained by AUC-Method-1 is only illustrated in one domain in Figure 1.

---

[2]In the case of ties, we make the appropriate number of steps up and to the right at once, drawing a diagonal line segment.

4. Experimental evaluation

For subgroup discovery, expert's evaluation of results is of ultimate interest. Nevertheless, before applying the proposed approach to a particular problem of interest, we wanted to verify our claims that the mechanisms implemented in the CN2-SD algorithm are indeed appropriate for subgroup discovery.

We experimentally evaluated our approach on 17 data sets from the UCI Repository of Machine Learning Databases [17]. In Table 1, the selected data sets are summarized in terms of the number of attributes, the number of examples, and the percentage of examples of the majority class. These data sets have been widely used in other comparative studies. Since currently our Java re-implementation of CN2 in WEKA does not support continuous attributes and can not handle missing values, all continuous attributes were discretized and data sets that contain no missing values were chosen. The discretization described in [8] was performed using the WEKA tool [23]. Moreover, in our experiments all of the data sets have two classes, either originally or by selecting one class as 'positive' and joining all the other in the 'negative' class (in Table 1, the selected positive class is indicated by {ClassName}); this was done for the purpose of enabling the area under the ROC curve evaluation.

Table 1. Data set characteristics.

	Data set	#Attr.	#Ex.	Maj. Class (%)
1	Anneal{3}	38	898	76.16
2	Australian	14	690	55.5
3	Balance{L}	4	625	46.08
4	Car{unacc}	6	1728	70.02
5	Credit-g	20	1000	70
6	Diabetes	8	768	65.1
7	Glass{build wind non-float}	9	214	35.51
8	Heart-stat	13	270	55.56
9	Ionosphere	34	351	64.1
10	Iris{Iris-setosa}	4	150	33.33
11	Lymph{metastases}	18	148	54.72
12	Segment{brickface}	19	2310	14.29
13	Sonar	60	208	53.36
14	Tic-tac-toe	9	958	65.34
15	Vehicle{bus}	18	846	25.77
16	Wine{2}	13	178	39.89
17	Zoo{mammal}	17	101	40.59

The comparison of CN2-SD with CN2 was performed in 17 UCI domains with AUC-Method-2 evaluation based on 10-fold stratified cross validation. Table 2 compares the CN2-SD subgroup discovery algorithm with the standard CN2 algorithm (*CN2-standard*, described in [3]) and the CN2 algorithm using *WRAcc* (*CN2-WRAcc*, described in [22]) in terms of area under the ROC curve (*AUC*). All these variants of the CN2 algorithm were first re-implemented in the WEKA data mining environment [23], because the use of the same system makes the comparisons more impartial. Due to space restrictions we only include the results of the unordered algorithms. The results of the CN2-SD algorithm were computed using both the multiplicative weights (with γ = 0.5, 0.7, 0.9) and the additive weights. Results with γ = 0.7 are not listed, as they are always between those of γ = 0.5 and γ = 0.9, as expected. All other parameters of the CN2 algorithm were set to their default values (beam-size = 5, significance-threshold = 99%).

Table 2. Area under the ROC curve with standard deviation ($AUC \pm sd$) for different variants of the unordered algorithm using 10-fold stratified cross-validation.

#	CN2 standard $AUC \pm sd$	CN2-SD WRAcc $AUC \pm sd$	CN2-SD ($\gamma = 0.5$) $AUC \pm sd$	CN2-SD ($\gamma = 0.9$) $AUC \pm sd$	CN2-SD (add. weight.) $AUC \pm sd$
1	99.41 ± 0.01	99.72 ± 0.00	99.24 ± 0.01	98.51 ± 0.01	98.17 ± 0.01
2	35.10 ± 0.11	87.83 ± 0.05	83.15 ± 0.05	84.32 ± 0.05	84.97 ± 0.04
3	86.22 ± 0.03	89.00 ± 0.03	93.89 ± 0.02	93.56 ± 0.02	91.82 ± 0.03
4	99.93 ± 0.00	96.55 ± 0.02	94.67 ± 0.02	93.00 ± 0.02	86.78 ± 0.02
5	70.10 ± 0.09	72.11 ± 0.06	71.38 ± 0.07	72.68 ± 0.07	70.12 ± 0.06
6	69.52 ± 0.08	78.93 ± 0.05	79.89 ± 0.04	80.14 ± 0.05	79.43 ± 0.05
7	68.23 ± 0.08	73.85 ± 0.12	70.71 ± 0.16	72.91 ± 0.15	72.67 ± 0.14
8	74.75 ± 0.09	74.56 ± 0.07	82.96 ± 0.08	86.16 ± 0.11	84.76 ± 0.09
9	93.81 ± 0.03	90.21 ± 0.06	90.66 ± 0.06	91.80 ± 0.06	91.36 ± 0.05
10	100.00 ± 0.00	100.00 ± 0.00	100.00 ± 0.00	100.00 ± 0.00	100.00 ± 0.00
11	94.34 ± 0.04	89.16 ± 0.08	88.15 ± 0.07	90.76 ± 0.06	88.53 ± 0.08
12	99.73 ± 0.01	99.79 ± 0.06	98.99 ± 0.01	98.19 ± 0.02	98.05 ± 0.02
13	65.32 ± 0.12	60.61 ± 0.10	69.35 ± 0.13	71.19 ± 0.16	65.10 ± 0.16
14	100.00 ± 0.00	81.00 ± 0.08	92.97 ± 0.03	91.96 ± 0.04	90.24 ± 0.04
15	97.27 ± 0.02	92.41 ± 0.03	94.38 ± 0.03	94.18 ± 0.02	93.43 ± 0.02
16	94.14 ± 0.05	96.30 ± 0.06	95.39 ± 0.05	95.53 ± 0.05	92.16 ± 0.09
17	100.00 ± 0.00	100.00 ± 0.00	100.00 ± 0.00	100.00 ± 0.00	100.00 ± 0.00
Avg	**85.17 ± 0.04**	**87.18 ± 0.05**	**88.58 ± 0.05**	**89.11 ± 0.05**	**87.51 ± 0.05**

We also compared the sizes of the rule sets, average rule coverage, and the likelihood ratio of rules, computed from the entire data sets (not using cross-validation). Table 3 compares *CN2-SD* with *CN2-standard* and *CN2-WRAcc* in terms of the size of the rule set (S is the number of rules in a rule set, including the default rule), average rule coverage (CVG is computed as the averaged percentage of covered positive and negative examples per rule), and likelihood ratio[3] per rule.

The experimental results show that *CN2-SD* achieves improvements across the board. In terms of AUC, the smallest improvement is achieved by additive weights and slightly better improvements of 3–4% are by multiplicative weights. On the other hand, additive weights result in about 2 times less rules on average than multiplicative weights, and 6.5 times less rules than *CN2-standard*. Average rule coverage is also optimal for additive weights, improving on the average the coverage of *CN2-standard* rules with a factor of

---

[3] The likelihood ratio is used in CN2 for testing the significance of the induced rule [4]. For two-class problems this statistic is distributed approximately as χ^2 with one degree of freedom.

3.5 and on *CN2-WRAcc* with a factor of 2. Note, however, that rules obtained with additive weights and multiplicative weights with high γ are highly overlapping, due to the relatively modest decrease of example weights.

In addition, there is also a substantial increase in the average likelihood ratio: while the ratios achieved by *CN2-standard* are already significant at the 99% level, this is further pushed up by *CN2-SD* with maximum values achieved by additive weights. An interesting question, to be verified with further experiments, is whether the weighted versions of the CN2 algorithm improve the significance of the induced subgroups also in the case when CN2 rules are induced without applying the significance test.

In summary, *CN2-SD* produces substantially smaller rule sets, where individual rules have higher coverage and significance.

Table 3. Average size (S), coverage (CVG) and likelihood ratio (LHR) of rules for different versions of the unordered algorithm induced from the entire data sets.

#	CN2 standard S	CVG	LHR	CN2 WRAcc S	CVG	LHR	CN2-SD ($\gamma = 0.5$) S	CVG	LHR	CN2-SD ($\gamma = 0.9$) S	CVG	LHR	CN2-SD (add. weight.) S	CVG	LHR
1	26	5.49	68.83	26	6.47	61.27	14	12.88	100.97	13	16.77	136.14	8	21.24	193.02
2	58	5.22	21.55	6	22.72	89.91	10	26.23	136.66	8	39.09	189.89	6	42.90	211.63
3	113	1.53	11.61	42	3.95	20.23	17	12.00	28.87	11	16.80	38.01	9	20.00	43.89
4	84	1.79	45.79	22	7.42	112.91	11	14.65	136.12	11	16.32	167.04	6	24.44	212.37
5	91	1.52	13.21	14	9.88	25.26	13	15.10	37.90	15	19.16	48.94	7	26.30	55.40
6	58	3.45	13.29	12	11.80	27.74	11	14.80	39.77	12	15.13	40.03	9	17.19	42.81
7	23	5.58	12.23	15	7.71	11.99	11	18.60	14.61	17	16.42	16.19	7	28.97	18.16
8	42	5.44	14.20	11	21.22	18.47	16	19.19	29.48	20	24.50	36.47	11	29.52	42.42
9	42	5.63	19.53	26	6.70	21.55	27	11.57	39.79	26	14.13	43.66	13	17.97	52.40
10	11	10.87	30.01	11	10.87	30.01	14	14.57	27.42	14	14.57	27.42	10	16.29	33.84
11	17	9.89	18.24	10	14.41	19.98	16	18.33	24.10	23	19.10	25.19	10	26.57	30.78
12	184	0.94	94.65	38	4.47	139.41	11	14.59	345.19	7	17.62	437.14	6	19.05	509.65
13	36	3.78	12.52	22	7.60	13.59	28	9.37	13.77	41	11.58	14.61	12	16.74	17.90
14	30	4.06	76.45	27	5.79	44.08	20	8.75	62.67	15	10.63	74.96	11	12.28	68.20
15	82	2.32	32.79	38	4.04	28.38	14	18.28	101.37	15	22.43	107.36	9	25.77	131.50
16	28	5.62	16.08	18	7.80	20.56	21	11.26	19.84	21	12.30	20.54	11	15.51	25.55
17	3	50.00	68.21	3	50.00	68.21	3	50.00	68.21	3	50.00	68.21	3	50.00	68.21
Avg	**54.6**	**7.24**	**33.48**	**20.0**	**11.93**	**44.33**	**15.1**	**17.07**	**72.16**	**16.0**	**19.80**	**87.75**	**8.7**	**24.16**	**103.40**

Finally, we illustrate our approach in the ROC space by means of the results on the Australian data set (Figure 1). The solid lines in this graph indicate the ROC curves obtained by *CN2-SD* and *CN2-standard*, evaluated with AUC-Method-2, i.e., probabilistic classification with overlapping rules: the top line (squares) for *CN2-SD* with additive weights, and the bottom line (triangles) for *CN2-standard*. *CN2-standard* finds many more rules than *CN2-SD*, which leads to overfitting as the ROC curve is mostly below the diagonal.

For illustrative purposes we also include positive and negative convex hulls constructed from individual subgroups using AUC-Method-1 (dotted lines). The points on the X and Y-axes close to the origin are all small, purely positive and negative subgroups found by *CN2-standard*, that do not contribute to the convex hull (presumably these are the rules that lead to poor performance using probabilistic classification). Using AUC-Method-1 we can remove those overly specific subgroups, leading to reasonable positive and negative convex hulls. Notice, however, that *CN2-SD* still improves on *CN2-standard* after removing redundant subgroups.

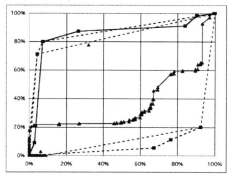

Figure 1. Example ROC curves on the Australian data set: solid curves for AUC-Method-2, and dotted positive and negative convex hulls for AUC-Method-1; squares for *CN2-SD* with additive weights, and triangles for *CN2-standard*.

5. Related work

Various rule evaluation measures and heuristics have been studied for subgroup discovery [10, 24], aimed at balancing the size of a group (referred to as factor g) with its distributional unusualness (referred to as factor p). The properties of functions that combine these two factors have been extensively studied (the so-called 'p-g-space', [10]). An alternative measure $q = \frac{TP}{FP+par}$ was proposed in [13], for expert-guided subgroup discovery in the TP/FP space, aimed at minimizing the number of false positives FP, and maximizing true positives TP, guided by generalization parameter par. Besides such 'objective' measures of interestingness, some 'subjective' measure of interestingness of a discovered pattern can be taken into the account, such as actionability ('a pattern is interesting if the user can do something with it to his or her advantage') and unexpectedness ('a pattern is interesting to the user if it is surprising to the user') [21].

Instance weights play an important role in boosting [12] and alternating decision trees [20]. Instance weights have been used also in variants of the covering algorithm implemented in rule learning approaches such as SLIPPER [6], RL [15] and DAIRY [9]. A variant of the weighted covering algorithm has been used also in the context of subgroup discovery for rule subset selection [13].

6. Conclusions

We have presented a novel approach to adapting standard classification rule learning to subgroup discovery. To this end we have appropriately adapted the covering algorithm, the search heuristics, the probabilistic classification and the performance measure. Experimental results on 17 UCI data sets demonstrate that *CN2-SD* produces substantially smaller rule sets, where individual rules have higher coverage and significance. These three factors are important for subgroup discovery: smaller size enables better understanding, higher coverage means larger support, and higher significance means that rules describe discovered subgroups that are significantly different from the entire population. We have evaluated the results of *CN2-SD* also in terms of AUC-Method-2 and shown insignificant increase in terms of the area under the ROC curve.

In further work we will evaluate the results also by using AUC-Method-1, where each subgroup establishes a separate point in the ROC space, and compare the results with the MIDOS subgroup discovery algorithm. We plan to investigate the behavior of *CN2-SD* also in multi-class problems. An interesting question, to be verified with further experiments, is whether the weighted versions of the CN2 algorithm improve the significance of the induced subgroups also in the case when CN2 rules are induced without applying the significance test. Finally, we plan to use the *CN2-SD* subgroup discovery algorithm for solving practical problems, in which expert evaluations of induced subgroup descriptions is of ultimate interest.

Acknowledgements

Thanks to Dragan Gamberger for joint work on the weighted covering algorithm, and José Hernández-Orallo and Cesar Ferri-Ramírez for joint work on AUC. The work reported in this paper was supported by the Slovenian Ministry of Education, Science and Sport, the IST-1999-11495 project Data Mining and Decision Support for Business Competitiveness: A European Virtual Enterprise, and the British Council project Partnership in Science PSP-18.

References

[1] R. Agrawal, H. Mannila, R. Srikant, H. Toivonen, and A.I. Verkamo. Fast discovery of association rules. In U.M. Fayyad, G. Piatetski-Shapiro, P. Smyth and R. Uthurusamy, editors, *Advances in Knowledge Discovery and Data Mining*, 307–328. AAAI Press, 1996.

[2] B. Cestnik. Estimating probabilities: A crucial task in machine learning. In L. Aiello, editor, *Proc. of the 9th European Conference on Artificial Intelligence*, 147–149. Pitman, 1990.

[3] P. Clark and R. Boswell. Rule induction with CN2: Some recent improvements. In Y. Kodratoff, editor, *Proc. of the 5th European Working Session on Learning*, 151–163. Springer, 1991.

[4] P. Clark and T. Niblett. The CN2 induction algorithm. *Machine Learning*, 3(4): 261–283, 1989.

[5] W.W. Cohen. (1995) Fast effective rule induction. In *Proc. of the 12th International Conference on Machine Learning*, 115–123. Morgan Kaufmann, 1995.

[6] W.W. Cohen and Y. Singer. A simple, fast, and effective rule learner. In *Proc. of AAAI/IAAI*, 335–342. American Association for Artificial Intelligence, 1999.

[7] S. Džeroski, B. Cestnik, and I. Petrovski. (1993) Using the m-estimate in rule induction. *Journal of Computing and Information Technology*, 1(1):37 – 46, 1993.

[8] U.M. Fayyad and K.B. Irani, K.B. Multi-interval discretisation of continuous-valued attributes for classification learning. In R. Bajcsy, editor, *Proc. of the 13th International Joint Conference on Artificial Intelligence*, 1022–1027. Morgan Kaufmann, 1993.

[9] D. Hsu, O. Etzioni and S. Soderland. A redundant covering algorithm applied to text classification. In *Proc. of the AAAI Workshop on Learning from Text Categorization*. American Association for Artificial Intelligence, 1998.

[10] W. Klösgen. Explora: A multipattern and multistrategy discovery assistant. In U.M. Fayyad, G. Piatetski-Shapiro, P. Smyth and R. Uthurusamy, editors, *Advances in Knowledge Discovery and Data Mining*, 249–271. MIT Press, 1996.

[11] C. Ferri-Ramírez, P.A. Flach, and J. Hernandez-Orallo. Learning decision trees using the area under the ROC curve. In *Proc. of the 19th International Conference on Machine Learning*, 139–146. Morgan Kaufmann, 2002.

[12] Y. Freund and R.E. Shapire. Experiments with a new boosting algorithm. In *Proc. of the 13th International Conference on Machine Learning*, 148–156. Morgan Kaufmann, 1996.

[13] D. Gamberger and N. Lavrač. Descriptive induction through subgroup discovery: A case study in a medical domain. In *Proc. of the 19th International Conference on Machine Learning*, 163–170. Morgan Kaufmann, 2002.

[14] N. Lavrač, P. Flach, and B. Zupan. Rule evaluation measures: A unifying view. In *Proc. of the 9th International Workshop on Inductive Logic Programming*, 74–185. Springer, 1999.

[15] Y. Lee, B.G. Buchanan, and J.M. Aronis. Knowledge-based learning in exploratory science: Learning rules to predict rodent carcinogenicity. *Machine Learning*, 30: 217–240, 1998.

[16] R.S. Michalski, I. Mozetič, J. Hong, and N. Lavrač. The multi-purpose incremental learning system AQ15 and its testing application on three medical domains. In *Proc. 5th National Conference on Artificial Intelligence*, 1041–1045. Morgan Kaufmann, 1986.

[17] P.M. Murphy and D.W. Aha. *UCI repository of machine learning databases* [http://www.ics.uci.edu/~mlearn/MLRepository.html]. Irvine, CA: University of California, Department of Information and Computer Science, 1994.

[18] F. Provost and T. Fawcett. Robust classification for imprecise environments. *Machine Learning*, 42(3): 203–231, 2001.

[19] R.L. Rivest. Learning decision lists. *Machine Learning*, 2(3): 229–246, 1987.

[20] R.E. Schapire and Y. Singer. Improved boosting algorithms using confidence-rated predictions. In *Proc. of the 11th Conference on Computational Learning Theory*, 80–91. ACM Press, 1998.

[21] A. Silberschatz and A. Tuzhilin. On subjective measures of interestingness in knowledge discovery. In *Proc. of the 1st International Conference on Knowledge Discovery and Data Mining*, 275–281, 1995.

[22] L. Todorovski, P. Flach, and N. Lavrač. Predictive performance of weighted relative accuracy. In D.A. Zighed, J. Komorowski, and J. Zytkow, editors, *Proc. of the 4th European Conference on Principles of Data Mining and Knowledge Discovery*, 255–264. Springer, 2000.

[23] I.H. Witten and E. Frank. *Data Mining: Practical Machine Learning Tools and Techniques with Java Implementations*. Morgan Kaufmann, 1999.

[24] S. Wrobel. An algorithm for multi-relational discovery of subgroups. In *Proc. of the 1st European Symposium on Principles of Data Mining and Knowledge Discovery*, 78–87. Springer, 1997.

Linear Causal Model Discovery Using the MML criterion

Gang Li   Honghua Dai   Yiqing Tu
School of Information Technology
Deakin University, Melbourne Campus
221 Burwood Highway, Vic 3125, Australia
{gangli, hdai, yiqingtu}@deakin.edu.au

Abstract

Determining the causal structure of a domain is a key task in the area of Data Mining and Knowledge Discovery. The algorithm proposed by Wallace et al. [15] has demonstrated its strong ability in discovering Linear Causal Models *from given data sets. However, some experiments showed that this algorithm experienced difficulty in discovering linear relations with small deviation, and it occasionally gives a negative message length, which should not be allowed. In this paper, a more efficient and precise MML encoding scheme is proposed to describe the model structure and the nodes in a* Linear Causal Model. *The estimation of different parameters is also derived. Empirical results show that the new algorithm outperformed the previous MML-based algorithm in terms of both speed and precision.*

1 Introduction

The rapid development of data collection methods, storage and processing technology has led the "Information Age" towards a new and exciting stage. Powerful database systems for collecting and managing data have been used in many companies for a long time. Researchers and practitioners from more diverse disciplines than ever before are attempting to use automated methods to analyze their data [1].

Graphical Model is a succinct and efficient way to represent relations among a set of variables [10]. Due to this, several applications have been carrying on in many fields such as diagnosis, expert systems, statistics, and control. However, the manual construction of *Graphical Model* is very time-consuming and subject to mistakes. Therefore, algorithms for automatic learning, that occasionally use the information provided by an expert, are very useful [8]. As *Graphical Model* can often be used for describing causal relations, the automatic construction of *Graphical Model* is usually referred as *Causal Discovery*.

In social sciences, there is a class of limited *Graphical Model*, usually referred as *Linear Causal Models*, including *Path Diagram* [16], and *Structural Equation Model* [2]. In *Linear Causal Models*, effect variables are strictly linear functions of exogenous variables. Although this is a significant limitation, its adoption allows for a comparatively easy environment in which to develop causal discovery algorithms. A substantial research project aimed at the automated learning of *Linear Causal Models* is by Clark Glymour and his group at the Carnegie Mellon University. This has lead to a successful delivery of a commercially available program TETRAD [12].

In parallel in 1996, Wallace *et al.* successfully introduced an information theoretic approach to the discovery of *Linear Causal Models* [15]. Their algorithm uses Wallace's *Minimum Message Length* (MML) criterion [13] to evaluate and guide the search of *Linear Causal Models*, and their experiments indicated that MML criterion is capable of recovering *Linear Causal Model* which is a quite accurate reflection of the original model [15]. In 1997, Dai *et al.* [4] further studied the learning reliability and robustness issues in causal discovery, they closely examined the relationships among the complexity of the causal model to be discovered, the strength of the causal links, the sample size of the given data set and the learning ability of individual causal learning approach.

However, some experiments showed that previous MML-based algorithms [15, 4, 5] had difficulty in discovering some linear relations with a small deviation, and in some cases, it turns out a negative message length for some related data set. In 2002, Li pointed out that previous MML-based algorithms implicitly implies an assumption that all measurement accuracy of regression residuals for each variables all equal to 1. This assumption is a bit strong in general case, and may not be satisfied by many data sets, especially for those generated from a linear function plus a *Gaussian* noise with small variation.

2 MML Discovery for Linear Causal Models

2.1 Basic Concepts

Let $U = \{V_1, V_2, \ldots, V_n\}$ be a set of random continuous variables. We will use lowercase letters such as v_1, $\ldots$, v_n denote specific values taken by those random variables. Formally, a *Linear Causal Model* is a tuple $LCM = \langle S, \Theta_S \rangle$, where

Structure S is a *Directed Acyclic Graph* (DAG) with the nodes[1] correspond to the variables in U, and whose edges represent dependencies between variables. For a node V_i, the set of nodes which have outgoing edge to V_i, is called *Parents* of node V_i, and represented by $Pa(V_i)$. A node without parent is called a *Root* node. For a *Linear Causal Model*, it is possible to have more than one *Root* nodes. In figure 1, nodes V_1 and V_2 are the parents of node V_4, and nodes V_1 and V_2 can be called *Root* nodes of the DAG.

Parameters Θ_S represents the set of parameters that quantifies the *Linear Causal Model* with a structure S. The relation between a node V_i and its parents $Pa(V_i)$ in a *Linear Causal Model* can be described by a linear function,

$$V_i = \sum_{k=1}^{K_i} \alpha_k Pa_k(V_i) + R_i \qquad (1)$$

Where K_i is the number of parents for node V_i, $\{\alpha_1, \ldots, \alpha_{K_i}\}$ are path coefficients, and R_i is assumed to be identically distributed following a *Gaussian* distribution with zero mean and a standard deviation σ_i that will also be treated as an adjustable parameters, that is $R_i \sim N(0, \sigma_i^2)$, so the set of local parameters for a node V_i with parents is $\{\sigma_i^2, \alpha_1, \ldots, \alpha_{K_i}\}$. On the other hand, a *Root* node V_i is assumed to be a random sample from a *Gaussian* distribution, $V_i \sim N(\mu_i, \sigma_i^2)$, where μ_i is the expect value of node V_i, and σ_i is the standard deviation, so the set of parameters for a root node V_i is $\{\mu_i, \sigma_i^2\}$.

An example of *Linear Causal Model* is given in Figure 1. The relation amongst 4 variables can be described by the following equations.

$$
\begin{aligned}
V_1 &\sim N(\mu_1, \sigma_1^2) \\
V_2 &\sim N(\mu_2, \sigma_2^2) \\
V_3 &= 0.3V_1 + R_3 \quad \text{with } R_3 \sim N(0, \sigma_3^2) \\
V_4 &= 0.6V_1 + 0.9V_2 + R_4 \quad \text{with } R_4 \sim N(0, \sigma_4^2)
\end{aligned}
$$

---

[1]In this paper, we will use *node* and *variable* intermediately.

Figure 1. A simple *Linear Causal Model.*

Once a *Linear Causal Model* is constructed, it can be used as an efficient tool in performing probabilistic inference. Nevertheless, some problem of building such a model remains. The next sub-section will describe the basic idea of evaluating a candidate model using *Minimum Message Length* criterion.

2.2 Minimum Message Length Criterion

Wallace and Freeman argue that statistical estimation and model selection can be done as a coding process. The basic idea of the minimum encoding methods was summarized by Wallace and Freeman as follows [14]:

> We may first estimate the parameters and then encode the data under the assumption that these are the true values. The encoded string must now, however, contain a specification of the estimated values. Any model is, therefore, only worth considering if the shortening of the encoded data string achieved by adopting it more than compensates for the lengthening caused by having to quote estimated parameter values. We thus naturally arrive at a very simple trade-off between the complexity of a model and its goodness of fit.

In the case of *Linear Causal Models* discovery, the whole message consists of 2 parts,

1. The message costed to describe the model. and this part can be further divided into 2 parts.

   (a) message encoding the model structure S.

   (b) message encoding parameters Θ_S, which includes a set of local parameters specifying the linear function at each node in the model.

2. message used to encode data set, under the assumption that the *Linear Causal Model* was the true model.

According to the MML criterion, the shorter the encoding message length is, the better the corresponding model

275

is. From *Information Theory*, the total message length can be approximated using the following formula 2 [2],

$$
\begin{aligned}
L &= L(S) + L(\Theta_S) + L(D|S, \Theta_S) \\
&= L(S) + \sum_{i=1}^{n} (L(\theta_i) + L(D_i|\theta_i)) \quad (2)
\end{aligned}
$$

Where n is the number of nodes, θ_i is the local parameters at node V_i, and D_i is the data set confined to node V_i.

2.3 Encoding the model structure

In [15], the model structure is encoded by specifying a total ordering (requiring $\log K!$ bits) and specifying which pairs of nodes are connected. Since in general more than one total ordering is consistent with the model structure, the encoding length of the structure is calculated by reducing the number of bits needed to select among those total orderings consistent with the model structure. However, the estimation of number of total orderings cost a lot of computational time [5]. In this paper, a different encoding schema is adopted.

The structure of a *Linear Causal Model* is a *Directed Acyclic Graph* (DAG), which can be described by specifying the parents set $Pa(V_i)$ for each node V_i of the DAG. This description consists of the number of parents, followed by the index of the set $Pa(V_i)$ in some enumeration of all sets of its cardinality. So the length for encoding the model structure can be calculated using the following formula:

$$
L(S) = \sum_{i=1}^{n} \left(\ln n + \ln \binom{n}{m_i} \right) \quad (3)
$$

Where n is the number of nodes, and m_i is the number of parents for node V_i. To avoid intensive computational time cost in calculating $\ln \binom{n}{m_i}$, we can use *Stirling's approximation* formula $x! = x^x e^{-x} \sqrt{2\pi x}$, so we get,

$$
\ln \binom{n}{m_i} \approx (n - m_i) \ln \left(\frac{n}{n - m_i} \right) + m_i \ln \left(\frac{n}{m_i} \right) \quad (4)
$$

Thus, the length of encoding the model structure can be approximated by,

$$
\begin{aligned}
& L(S) \\
& = \sum_{i=1}^{n} \left(\ln n + (n - m_i) \ln \left(\frac{n}{n - m_i} \right) + m_i \ln \left(\frac{n}{m_i} \right) \right) (5)
\end{aligned}
$$

2.4 Encoding data assuming the model

From formula 2, the length of encoding Θ_S and data set D can be calculated by summing the encoding length of local parameters θ_i and data D_i at each node. For different node types, we propose two different encoding schemes.

2.4.1 Encoding *Root* Nodes

Consider a *Root* node V_i, and suppose the data set $D_i = \{v_{i1}, v_{i2}, \ldots, v_{iT}\}$ drawn from a *Gaussian* distribution $N(\mu_i, \sigma_i^2)$, each data measurement is given to an accuracy of $\pm \frac{\epsilon_i}{2}$. Assuming that ϵ_i is small, the probability density function can be approximated as a constant over $[v_{it} - \frac{\epsilon_i}{2}, v_{it} + \frac{\epsilon_i}{2}]$. The message length for D_i is therefore:

$$
L(D_i|\mu_i, \sigma_i^2) \quad (6)
$$
$$
= -\ln(\prod_{t=1}^{T} \frac{1}{\sqrt{2\pi\sigma_i^2}} e^{-\frac{(v_{it} - \mu_i)^2}{2\sigma_i^2}} \epsilon_i)
$$
$$
= \frac{T}{2} \ln 2\pi + \frac{T}{2} \ln \sigma_i^2 + \sum_{t=1}^{T} \frac{(v_{it} - \mu_i)^2}{2\sigma_i^2} - T \ln \epsilon_i
$$

Where T is the sample size.

Assuming the prior for parameters $\theta_i = \{\mu_i, \sigma_i^2\}$ to be $h(\mu_i, \sigma_i^2) \sim \frac{1}{\sigma_i^2}$, following Wallace and Freeman [14], the message length for encoding parameters θ_i is

$$
L(\mu_i, \sigma_i^2)
$$
$$
= -\ln(\frac{h(\mu_i, \sigma_i^2)}{\sqrt{|F(\mu_i, \sigma_i^2)|}}) + \frac{2}{2} \ln \kappa_2 + \frac{2}{2}
$$
$$
= \frac{\ln |F(\mu_i, \sigma_i^2)|}{2} + \ln \sigma_i^2 + \ln \kappa_2 + 1 \quad (7)
$$

Where κ_2 is the 2-dimensional optimal quantizing lattice constant, with $\kappa_2 = \frac{1}{12}$, the value of κ_d can be found out in Table 2.3 of [3]. $F(\mu_i, \sigma_i^2)$ is the *expected Fisher Information* [3], for 1-dimensional *Gaussian* distribution, its determinant can be calculated by the following formula [7](Page 91),

$$
|F(\mu_i, \sigma_i^2)| = \frac{T^2}{2\sigma_i^6} \quad (8)
$$

So, the total length for parameters and confined data set can be calculated by,

$$
L(D_i, \mu_i, \sigma_i^2)
$$
$$
\begin{aligned}
= & \frac{1}{2} \ln(\frac{T^2}{2}) - \frac{1}{2} \ln \sigma_i^2 + \ln \kappa_2 + 1 + \frac{T}{2} \ln 2\pi \\
& + \frac{T}{2} \ln \sigma_i^2 + \sum_{t=1}^{T} \frac{(v_{it} - \mu_i)^2}{2\sigma_i^2} - T \ln \epsilon_i
\end{aligned}
$$
$$
\begin{aligned}
= & \frac{1}{2} \ln(\frac{T^2}{2}) + \ln \kappa_2 + 1 + \frac{T}{2} \ln 2\pi \\
& + \frac{T-1}{2} \ln \sigma_i^2 + \sum_{t=1}^{T} \frac{(v_{it} - \mu_i)^2}{2\sigma_i^2} - T \ln \epsilon_i \quad (9)
\end{aligned}
$$

---

[2]For convenience, we use natural logarithm through the paper, so calculate all message length in *nits*. If the logarithm is 2-based, the length will be calculated in *bits*.

[3]The *expected Fisher Information* in MML is the information integrated over all possible data values, and differs from the *Observed Fisher Information* [9].

To minimize the total encoding length, we examine its partial derivatives with respect to μ_i and σ_i^2, and obtain the estimate of them to be

$$\mu_i = \frac{\sum_{t=1}^{T} v_{it}}{T} \tag{10}$$

$$\sigma_i^2 = \frac{\sum_{t=1}^{T} (v_{it} - \mu_i)^2}{T - 1} \tag{11}$$

Since *Gaussian* distribution is continuous, measurement accuracy ϵ_i is important to turn the density function into a genuine probability. For the confined data set D_i, we take ϵ_i as the minimal positive difference between two data items.

2.4.2 Encoding Node with Parents

Now, we turn to the encoding for a node V_i with K parents. Suppose the relation between V_i and its K parents can be captured by the linear formula,

$$V_i = \sum_{k=1}^{K} \alpha_k Pa_k(V_i) + R_i \tag{12}$$

Where $Pa_k(V_i)$ is the k-th parent of node V_i, and R_i is the regression residuals for data set D_i. Assume R_i to be a random sample from a *Gaussian* distribution with zero mean and variation σ_i^2,

$$p(R_i|\theta_i) = \prod_{t=1}^{T} \frac{1}{\sqrt{2\pi\sigma_i^2}} e^{-\frac{(v_{it} - \sum_k \alpha_k Pa_k(v_{it}))^2}{2\sigma_i^2}} \tag{13}$$

Where $Pa_k(v_{it})$ represents the t-th observation of the k-th parent of node V_i.

Suppose the accuracy of measurement for regression residuals R_i to be ϵ_r, we can calculate the probability of regression residuals R_i using,

$$Prob(R_i|\theta_i) = \prod_{t=1}^{T} \frac{1}{\sqrt{2\pi\sigma_i^2}} e^{-\frac{(v_{it} - \sum_k \alpha_k Pa_k(v_{it}))^2}{2\sigma_i^2}} \epsilon_r \tag{14}$$

It should be noted that ϵ_r is not the measurement accuracy of data set D_y, but the measurement accuracy of regression residuals R_i.

If the parameters for 12 and R_i are known, we can calculate the value of D_i. So the encoding length for D_i can be calculated as the length of R_i given the local parameter $\theta_i = \{\sigma_i^2, \alpha_1, \ldots, \alpha_K\}$,

$$
\begin{aligned}
L(D_i|\theta_i) & \\
= \quad & L(R_i|\theta_i) \\
= \quad & -\ln Prob(R_i|\theta_i) \\
= \quad & \frac{T}{2}\ln 2\pi + \frac{T}{2}\ln\sigma_i^2 + \sum_{t=1}^{T}\frac{(v_{it} - \sum_k \alpha_k Pa_k(v_{it}))^2}{2\sigma_i^2} \\
& -T\ln\epsilon_r
\end{aligned} \tag{15}
$$

According to [7](page 96), the *Fisher Information* matrix for Gaussian regression models 12 is

$$F(\theta_i) = \begin{pmatrix} \frac{T}{2\sigma_i^4} & 0 \\ 0 & \frac{X'X}{\sigma_i^2} \end{pmatrix} \tag{16}$$

Where $\theta_i = \{\sigma_i^2, \alpha_1, \ldots, \alpha_K\}$, X is the $T \times K$ matrix consisting of T observations of K parents of node V_i, and we can use a $K \times K$ matrix A to represent $X'X$. So the determinant of $F(\theta)$ can be calculated by

$$|F(\theta_i)| = \frac{T}{2}|A|(\sigma_i^2)^{-(K+2)}$$

Assuming the prior probability of parameters to be $h(\theta_i) = \frac{1}{\sigma_i^2}$, following Wallace and Freeman [14], the encoding length for $\theta_i = \{\sigma_i^2, \alpha_1, \ldots, \alpha_K\}$ becomes

$$
\begin{aligned}
& L(\theta_i) \\
= \quad & -\ln\frac{h(\theta_i)}{\sqrt{|F(\theta_i)|}} + \frac{K+1}{2}\ln\kappa_{K+1} + \frac{K+1}{2} \\
= \quad & \frac{1}{2}\ln(\frac{T}{2}) + \frac{1}{2}\ln|A| - \frac{K}{2}\ln\sigma_i^2 \\
& + \frac{K+1}{2}\ln\kappa_{K+1} + \frac{K+1}{2}
\end{aligned} \tag{17}
$$

Where κ_{K+1} is the $(K+1)$-dimensional optimal quantizing lattice constant [3].

The combined message length for the parameters θ_i and the data set D_i is

$$
\begin{aligned}
& L(D_i, \sigma_i^2, \alpha_1, \ldots, \alpha_K) \\
= \quad & \frac{1}{2}\ln(\frac{T}{2}) + \frac{1}{2}\ln|A| - \frac{K}{2}\ln\sigma_i^2 \\
& + \frac{K+1}{2}\ln\kappa_{K+1} + \frac{K+1}{2} + \frac{T}{2}\ln 2\pi + \frac{T}{2}\ln\sigma_i^2 \\
& + \sum_{t=1}^{T}\frac{(v_{it} - \sum_k \alpha_k Pa_k(v_{it}))^2}{2\sigma_i^2} - T\ln\epsilon_r \\
= \quad & \frac{1}{2}\ln(\frac{T}{2}) + \frac{1}{2}\ln|A| + \frac{K+1}{2}\ln\kappa_{K+1} \\
& + \frac{K+1}{2} + \frac{T}{2}\ln 2\pi + \frac{T-K}{2}\ln\sigma_i^2 \\
& + \sum_{t=1}^{T}\frac{(v_{it} - \sum_k \alpha_k Pa_k(v_{it}))^2}{2\sigma_i^2} - T\ln\epsilon_r
\end{aligned} \tag{18}
$$

Given the uninformative priors for the coefficients, minimizing the combined message length involves minimizing $\sum_{t=1}^{T}(v_{it} - \sum_k \alpha_k Pa_k(v_{it}))^2$, which can be achieved by the least squares estimates. So the coefficients of the linear regression, $\{\alpha_1, \ldots, \alpha_K\}$ can be estimates by least squares estimation.

The partial derivative with respect to σ_i^2 is

$$
\begin{aligned}
& \frac{\partial L(D_i, \sigma_i^2, a_1, \ldots, a_K)}{\partial\sigma_i^2} \\
= \quad & \frac{T-K}{2\sigma_i^2} - \frac{\sum_{t=1}^{T}(v_{it} - \sum_k \alpha_k Pa_k(v_{it}))^2}{2\sigma_i^4}
\end{aligned}
$$

Solving for σ_i^2 gives us the following expression

$$\sigma_i^2 = \frac{\sum_{t=1}^{T}(v_{it} - \sum_k \alpha_k Pa_k(v_{it}))^2}{T - K}$$

The measurement accuracy ϵ_r is important to calculate the whole encoding length. The measurement accuracy of regression residuals ϵ_r is set to be the minimal positive difference between two data items.

3 Search Strategies

For a given sample data set, the number of possible model structures which may fit the data is exponential in the number of variables [4]. To find out the best model structure from this huge space, an efficient search strategy is highly demanded.

We have tested three greedy search strategies: (1) *Message Length Based Greedy search*, (2) *Best-first search* and (3) *Random Greedy search*. The experimental results show that the random search is not stable and the best-first does not do anything better than greedy search. On the other hand, although in theory, greedy search sometimes fails to find the global optima, previous empirical results indicated that at least for complete data set, *Message Length-based Greedy Search* converges faster than the more sophisticated search methods like *Genetic Algorithm*, or *Markov Chain Monte Carlo* method [6].

Start with a seed model, a directed acyclic graph provided by user or a null graph without any edge, *Message Length-based Greedy Search* runs through each pair of nodes attempting to add an edge if there is none or to delete or to reverse it if there already is one. Such adding, deleting or reversing is done only if such changes result in a decrease of the total message length of the new structure compared with the best we have found from the model space. If the new structure is better, it is kept and then try another change. This process continues until no better structure is found within a given number of search steps, or the search from the whole structure space is completed.

Algorithm 3.1 Message Length-based Greedy Search.
We denote the structure without a link from node i to node j as M_{noij}, the structure with a link from node i to node j as M_{ij} and the structure with a link from node j to node i as M_{ji}. In the following algorithm, $Cal(M)$ is a subroutine to calculate the message length of the structure M, and $Choose(M_1, M_2, M_3)$ is the subroutine to choose the structure with minimum message length among the given three structures M_1, M_2, M_3.

---

[4]The number of possible structure for a domain with n variables is given by the following recursive formula [11]:

$$f(n) = \sum_{i=1}^{n} (-1)^{i+1} \binom{n}{i} 2^{i(n-i)} f(n-i);$$
$$f(0) = f(1) = 1;$$

1. $isum \leftarrow 0$
2. $backsearch$: $iconl \leftarrow 0$
3. $istart$: $i \leftarrow 1$ $jstart$: $j \leftarrow i$
4. If $(i \neq j)$ **then**
5. $\quad total\_length \leftarrow Cal(M_{noij})$
6. $\quad If \neg \exists (i \rightarrow j)$ **then**
7. $\quad\quad le \leftarrow total\_length\ add(i \rightarrow j);$
8. $\quad\quad form\ M_{ij}\ l_{ij} \leftarrow Cal(M_{ij})$
9. $\quad\quad delete(i \rightarrow j);\ add(j \rightarrow i);$
10. $\quad\quad form\ M_{ji}\ l_{ji} \leftarrow Cal(M_{ji})$
11. $\quad\quad Choose(M_{noij}, M_{ij}, M_{ji})$
12. $\quad$ **else**
13. $\quad\quad total\text{-}length \leftarrow Cal(M_{ij})\ delete(i \rightarrow j);$
14. $\quad\quad form\ M_{noij}$
15. $\quad\quad le \leftarrow Cal(M_{noij})\ add(j \rightarrow i);$
16. $\quad\quad form\ M_{ji}$
17. $\quad\quad l_{ji} \leftarrow Cal(M_{ji})$
18. $\quad\quad Choose(M_{noij}, M_{ij}, M_{ji})$
19. $\quad If (j \leq K)$ *then*
20. $\quad\quad j \leftarrow j + 1;\ goto\ jstart;$
21. $\quad If (i \leq K)$ **then**
22. $\quad\quad i \leftarrow i + 1;\ goto\ istart;$
23. $\quad If (changes\ made)\ goto\ backsearch;$
24. $\quad isum \leftarrow isum + 1;$
25. $\quad If (isum < 2)$ **then** $goto\ backsearch;$
26. $\quad exit.$

Thus far this search strategy has worked adequately for modest sized problems. A comment on our *Message Length Based Greedy Search* algorithm is that

1. It does not search the complete model space, so it is an inexhaustive search;

2. the search is guided by message length, and we follow the MML theory and accept that the model with minimum message length is the best model;

3. this search algorithm itself has no mechanism to avoid the local minimum problem. In other words, this algorithm itself can not guarantee to achieve the global minimum.

4 Implementation and Results

In this section, we compare the new MML discovery algorithm proposed in this paper with the algorithm proposed in [15], and report the following results:

1. the experimental results of both the new and the old MML discovery algorithm on data sets reported in related literature [15, 5];

2. the time complexity comparison of between the new and the old MML discovery algorithm;

3. the experimental results an additional causal model where the linear relations have a small deviation.

Our technique is to take the model as reported, use it to stochastically generate the sample data, and use that data as input to both the new and the old MML discovery algorithms. Intuitively, if a causal discovery algorithm works perfectly, it should reproduce exactly the model used to generate the data. In practice, sampling errors will result in deviations from the original model, but algorithm which can reproduce a DAG structure similar to the original, and secondarily coefficient values similar to the original, must be considered to be performing better than those which do not.

4.1 Examination of the Induced Models

Six data sets reported in related literature [15, 5] are re-examined: *Fiji, Evans, Blau, case9, case10, case12*. The details of these data sets are described in Table 1.

Table 1. Information of Data Set

Data Set	Number of Nodes	Sample Size
Fiji	4	1000
Evans	5	1000
Blau	6	1000
Case9	9	1000
Case10	10	1000
Case12	12	1000

Figure 2 to 7 illustrated all the original models, and results derived from the new and the old algorithms. Both algorithms were tested under the same condition.

Table 2 gives the comparison of *the Minimum Number of Needed Manipulations*, which is the number of *adding, deleting, and reversing* needed to transform the recovered structure to the original model.

Since the MML discovery algorithm is derived from asymptotic approximations, minimizing MML doesn't coincide with the original model, especially for models with few variables (like *Fiji* or *Evans*).

Table 2. Number of Needed Manipulations

Data Set	New Algorithm	Old Algorithm
Fiji	2	3
Evans	3	4
Blau	2	2
Case9	0	0
Case10	0	0
Case12	0	0

(a) Original Model   (b) New Algorithm   (c) Old Algorithm

Figure 2. Comparison of Result on *Fiji*

From Table 2, we can see that the new algorithm can induce better results than the old algorithm for models with few variables, while keeping the precision of the old algorithm for other models. Specifically speaking, we can see that from Figure 2 the old algorithm missed the edge $X_2 \rightarrow X_4$, while the new algorithm can recover this edge. In figure 3, the old algorithm got a redundant edge $X_1 \rightarrow X_2$, while the new algorithm didn't has this problem. For the other testing models, both algorithms can find a structure similar to the original one.

4.2 Time Comparison of both Algorithms

Table 3 compares the time cost of the two algorithms in discovery causal models. From the Table, we can see that the new algorithm is faster than the old algorithm, especially for those testing data set with larger number of attributes.

This acceleration results from the time saving when encoding the model structures, in the old algorithm, large computational cost is needed, while in the new algorithm, *Stirling's Approximation* is adopted to simplify the calcula-

(a) Original Model   (b) New Algorithm   (c) Old Algorithm

Figure 3. Comparison of Result on *Evans*

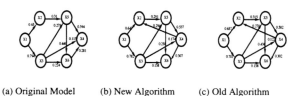

(a) Original Model   (b) New Algorithm   (c) Old Algorithm

Figure 4. Comparison of Result on *Blau*

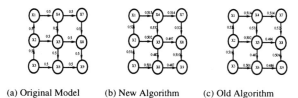

(a) Original Model   (b) New Algorithm   (c) Old Algorithm

Figure 5. Comparison of Result on *Case9*

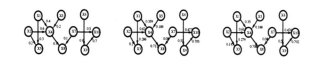

(a) Original Model   (b) New Algorithm   (c) Old Algorithm

Figure 6. Comparison of Result on *Case10*

(a) Original Model   (b) New Algorithm   (c) Old Algorithm

Figure 7. Comparison of Result on *Case12*

Table 3. Comparison of Time Complexity

Data Set	New Algorithm	Old Algorithm
Fiji	0.96 *seconds*	0.84 *seconds*
Evans	2.25 *seconds*	2.29 *seconds*
Blau	3.42 *seconds*	5.18 *seconds*
Case 9	16.32 *seconds*	19.23 *seconds*
Case 10	20.10 *seconds*	59.97 *seconds*
Case 12	36.20 *seconds*	126.20 *seconds*

Figure 8. Result for the example Model.

tion as described in equation 5.

4.3 Results on Data set with small Deviations

In this part, we generate a data set from the *Linear Causal Model* described in Figure 1. In the data generating step, we set the deviation related to each node as $\sigma_1^2 = 0.03, \sigma_2^2 = 0.03, \sigma_3^2 = 0.02, \sigma_4^2 = 0.01$, and 1000 samples were generated. The old causal discovery algorithm gave negative lengths for many directed acyclic graphs, whereas the new algorithm avoided the negative message length happening, and recover the original model as in Figure 8.

5 Conclusion and Future Work

This paper presented an new discovery algorithm for *Linear Causal Models* based on MML criterion. The experimental results reported in this paper show that

1. The new algorithm is capable of recovering what can be discovered by the previous discovery algorithm based on MML, but in terms of time complexity, the new algorithm is more efficient;

2. The new algorithm overcomes the negative message length problem in old algorithm, and can discover linear relations with very small deviation.

The results we presented in this paper further confirm that MML is a good model selection criterion in discovering *Linear Causal Models* [5]. The main contributes of this paper can be summarized as follows:

Time Complexity The advantages of our new algorithm arise from efficient encoding schemes for the data and the model. Especially in the calculation of encoding

---

[5]It should be noted that although both MML-based algorithm can discover accurate results from data, they have the same problem in deciding the edge direction.

length for model structure, *Stirling's Approximation* is adopted to reduce computation cost.

Negative Length The problem of negative message length is avoided by incorporating the measurement accuracy into the encoding scheme.

Refined Result The new algorithm can get more accurate results for models with few nodes, this comes from the terms κ_2 and κ_{K+1} as in formula 9 and 18, which are ignored in the old algorith [15].

We can enumerate several issues worth further work.

1. First, the *Linear Causal Model* need to be extended to deal with Categorial variables;

2. Second, the MML-based causal discovery algorithm need to be extended to deal with Missing values;

3. Third, both algorithms have difficulty in deciding the direction of edges, although in many cases, both algorithms could do well in this regard.

In addition to these, further work also promises to be of assistance to scientists wishing to use causal modelling techniques to understand their data and to assess their theories, which is important particularly in the social sciences; it also promises to shed light on the nature of the enterprise within artificial intelligence to model scientific discovery.

References

[1] Michael Berthold and David J. Hand, *Intelligent data analysis*, Springer-Verlag, Berlin Heidelberg, 1999.

[2] K.A. Bollen, *Structural equations with latent variables*, Wiley, New York, 1989.

[3] J.H. Conway and N.J.A. Sloane, *Sphere packings, lattices and groups*, Springer-Verlag, London, 1988.

[4] Honghua Dai, Kevin Korb, Chris Wallace, and Xindong Wu, *A study of causal discovery with small samples and weak links*, Proceedings of the 15th International Joint Conference On Artificial Intelligence **IJCAI'97**, Morgan Kaufmann Publishers, Inc., 1997, pp. 1304–1309.

[5] Honghua Dai and Gang Li, *An improved approach for the discovery of causal models via MML*, Proceedings of The 6th Pacific-Asia Conference on Knowledge Discovery and Data Mining (PAKDD-2002) (Taiwan), 2002, pp. 304–315.

[6] Honghua Dai, Gang Li, and Yiqing Tu, *An empirical study of encoding schemes and search strategies in discovering causal networks*, Proceedings of European Conference on Machine Learning (ECML/PKDD-2002) (Helsinki, Finland), 2002, to appear.

[7] A.C. Harvey, *The econometric analysis of time series*, 2 ed., The MIT Press, Cambridge, Massachusetts, 1990.

[8] Michael I. Jordan, *Learning in graphical models*, 1 ed., MIT Press, Cambridge, MA, 1998.

[9] Jonathan J. Oliver and Rohan A. Baxter, *MML and Bayesianism: Similarities and differences*, Technical Reports TR94/206, Department of Computer Science, Monash University, Clayton, Victoria 3168, Australia, 1994.

[10] Judea Pearl, *Probabilistic reasoning in intelligent systems*, revised second printing ed., Morgan Kauffmann Publishers, San Mateo, California, 1988.

[11] R.W. Robinson, *Counting unlabelled acyclic digraphs*, Lecture Notes in Mathematics 622, pp. 28–43, Springer-Verlag, 1977.

[12] Peter Spirtes, Clark Glymour, and Richard Scheines, *Causation,predication and search*, 2 ed., MIT Press, New York, 2000.

[13] Chris Wallace and David Boulton, *An information measure for classification*, Computer Journal **11** (1968), 185–194.

[14] Chris Wallace and P.R. Freeman, *Estimation and inference by compact coding*, Journal of the Royal Statistical Society **B,49** (1987), 240–252.

[15] Chris Wallace, Kevin B. Korb, and Honghua Dai, *Causal discovery via MML*, Proceedings of the 13th International Conference on Machine learning (ICML'96) (San Francisco), Morgan Kauffmann Publishers, 1996, pp. 516–524.

[16] Sewall Wright, *The method of path coefficients*, Annals of Mathematical Statistics **5** (1934), 161–215.

Attribute (Feature) Completion
– The Theory of Attributes from Data Mining Prospect

Tsay Young ('T. Y.') Lin
Department of Computer Science
San Jose State University
San Jose, CA 95192, USA
tylin@cs.sjsu.edu

Abstract

A "correct" selection of attributes (features) is vital in data mining. As a first step, this paper constructs all possible attributes of a given relation. The results are based on the observations that each relation is isomorphic to a unique abstract relation, called canonical model. The complete set of attributes of the canonical model is, then, constructed. Any attribute of a relation can be interpreted (via isomorphism) from such a complete set.

Keywords: attributes, feature, data mining, granular, data model

1. Introduction

Traditional data mining algorithms search for patterns only in the given set of attributes. Unfortunately, in a typical database environment, the attributes are selected primarily for record keepings, not for the understanding of real world. Hence, it is highly possible that there are no visible patterns in the given set of attributes; see Section 2. The fundamental question is: Is there a suitable set of attributes so that

- The "invisible" patterns can be mined?

Fortunately, the answer from this paper is yes. For this purpose, we examine the fundamental issues, such as what is the raw data, target patterns, and

- Build a mathematical model that captures exactly what data says

Based on such a model, we are able to develop a theory of attributes, and

- Construct the *complete* set of all attributes of a given relation

This is the main result of this paper. The paper is roughly organized into 3 parts. First is the motivational example (Section 2), followed by two sections of fundamental formulations(Section 3, refgdm), and conclude with the theory of attributes based on some foundational investigation of data mining

2 Motivation - Invisible Patterns

Let us consider a 3-column numerical relation, Table 1. The first column is the "independent variable," namely the universe of the entities (directed segments). It has three attributes, which consists of the beginning points, and "polar coordinates," the Length and the Degree. This table has

One association rule of length 2, that is, $(X_3, 2.0)$.

By switching to "Cartesian coordinate system," the table is transformed to Table 2; Interestingly,

The only association rule disappears.

A moment of reflection, one realize that since the association rule is a real world phenomenon (a geometric fact), the same information should be still carried in Table 2. The question

How can this "invisible" association rule be mined?

It is obvious that we need the derived attribute $Length$, which is a function of $Horizontal$ and $Vertical$. This phenomenon prompts us to consider the foundation of data mining, in particular

The foundation of attributes (features) from data mining prospect.

We would like to note that attribute (feature) theory from the prospect of database processing is very different this one.

Segment#	$Begin\_point$	Length	Direction
S_0	X_1	6.0	0
S_1	X_2	6.0	60
S_2	X_3	2.0	90
S_3	X_3	2.0	120
S_4	X_3	2.0	135
S_5	X_3	2.0	150
S_6	X_3	2.0	180
S_7	X_3	2.0	210
S_8	X_3	2.0	225
S_9	X_3	2.0	240

Table 1. Ten directed segments in polar coordinates

Segment#	Begin_Point	Horizontal	Vertical
S_0	X_1	6	0
S_1	X_2	$3\sqrt{3}$	3
S_2	X_3	0	2
S_3	X_3	-1	$\sqrt{3}$
S_4	X_3	$-\sqrt{2}$	$\sqrt{2}$
S_5	X_3	$-\sqrt{3}$	1
S_6	X_3	-2	0
S_7	X_3	$-\sqrt{3}$	-1
S_8	X_3	$-\sqrt{2}$	$-\sqrt{2}$
S_9	X_3	$-\sqrt{3}$	-1

Table 2. Ten directed segments in (X,Y)-coordinates

3 Basic Structures - the Data and Patterns

3.1 Raw Data - the Relations

The central objects of the study should be bag relations (we allow repeated tuples). However, without losing the essential idea, for simplicity, we focus on (set theoretical) relations, or more emphatically the relation instances. We will also assume

- All attributes are distinct (non-isomorphic); see Section 4.

Let V be the universe. Let $A = \{A^1, A^2, \ldots, A^n\}$ be a set of attributes, and their attribute domains be $C = \{C^1, C^2, \ldots, C^n\}$. Each C^j, often denoted by $Dom(A^j)$, is a set of elementary concepts (attribute values). Technically, they are the so-called semantics primitives in AI [6] or undefined primitive in mathematics. In other words, the semantics of these symbols are not part of the formal system.

The main raw data is a relation, which is a set (not a bag) of tuples. We will view a relation as a knowledge representation $V \longrightarrow Dom(A)$, where $Dom(A)$ is the Cartesian product of the $Dom(A^j)$'s. It is clear, we can view each A^j' as a map $V \longrightarrow Dom(A^j)$ (single column representation). Then, the relation, K, is a join of attribute maps; see [15, 17]. If one uses the information table (see below), the join is actual join of the relational algebra.

A map or function naturally induces a partition on its domain (the collection of all inverse images of the map), so each A^j induces a partition on V (and hence an equivalence relation); we use Q^j to denote both. We let Q be the collection of Q^j's.

In traditional database theory, the *image* of the *map K* (knowledge representation) is called the relation. The "independent variable V" plays no explicit role. However, in data mining, it is more convenient to have independent variables in the formulation. So in this paper, we may also use the *graph* $(v, K(v))$, called the information table. Throughout the whole paper K may mean the map, the image, or the graph, by abuse of notation. Since K is determined by A on V, we may use (V, A) for K.

3.2 Target - High Frequency Patterns

In association rule mining, two measures, called the support and confidence, are important. In this paper, we will be concerned the high frequency patterns, not necessarily in the form of rules. So only with the support will be considered.

Association rule mining is originated from on the market basket data [1]. However, in many software systems, the data mining tools are added to general DBMS. So we will be interested in data mining on general relations. For definitive, we have the following translations: an item is an attribute value, a q-itemset is a subtuple of length q, a large q-itemset is a high frequency q-pattern. In other words,

- A subtuple of length q is a high frequency q-patterns, or simply pattern, if its occurrences are greater than or equal to a given threshold.

4 What are we mining? - Isomorphic class

This paper focuses on database mining, more specifically, extracting high frequency patterns from a given relation (freeze at one database). In this section, we offer somewhat a surprised observation that the target patterns, such as

- association rules are the common patterns of whole isomorphic class, *NOT* an individual relation alone.

4.1 Isomorphic Relations and Patterns

Attributes A^i and A^j are isomorphic iff there is a one-to-one and onto map, $s : Dom(A^i) \longrightarrow Dom(A^j)$ such that $A^j(v) = s(A^i(v)) \; \forall \; v \; \in \; V$. The map s is called an isomorphism. Intuitively, two attributes (columns) are isomorphic iff one column turns into another one by properly renaming its attribute values.

Let $K = (V, A)$ and $H = (V, B)$ be two information tables, where $A = \{A^1, A^2, \ldots A^n\}$ and $B = \{B^1, B^2, \ldots B^m\}$. Then, K and H are said to be isomorphic if every A^i is isomorphic to some B^j, and vice versa. By our assumption (all attributes are distinct), K and H have the same degree (number of attributes), that is, $n = m$; See more general version in Section 11. The following theorem should be obvious.

Theorem 4.1. Isomorphic relations have isomorphic patterns.

The impacts of this simple theorem are rather far reaching. It essentially declares that patterns are syntactic in nature. They are patterns of the whole isomorphic class, yet many of isomorphic relations may have very different semantics; see Section ??.

- The "interesting-ness" (of association rules) may not be captured by the mere counting of the items (and hence the probability theory based on it).

Of course, something like unexpected-ness (which is probabilistic in nature) can be captured; the research on this topic will be reported in future.

5. Modeling what data says–Canonical Models

In classical data model, the (intension) functional dependency can never be expressed by the raw data, however, the data does express the extension functional dependency. So it is important to examine very fundamental question,

- What is the raw data (a given relation) really saying?

In this section, we construct the canonical models for each isomorphic class. In other words, the canonical model express *exactly* What raw data says about patterns.

Earlier, we have called them machine oriented models [15, 16], and have shown that it is very fast in computing the high frequency patterns [24].

5.1 Attributes and Equivalence Relations

We have observed that (Section 3.1) each A^j induces an equivalence relation Q^j on V. The set V/Q^j, which consists of all granules (equivalence classes), is called the quotient set. The map $P^j : V \longrightarrow V/Q^j : v \longrightarrow [v]$ is the natural projection, where [v] is the granule containing v. Next, we state an observation ([17], pp. 25):

Proposition 5.1. An attribute A^j, as a map, can be factored as $A^j = P^j \circ NAME^j$, where the naming map, $NAME^j : V/Q^j \longrightarrow C^j = Dom(A^j) : [v] \to NAME^j([v])$, is referred to as the interpretation.

1. The interpretation induces an isomorphism from V/Q^j to C^j; The interpretation assigns each granule an elementary concept (attribute value); we can regard it as a meaningful name of the granule. A^j is a meaningful name of Q^j;

2. The natural projection P^j is a map from V to V/Q^j. Formally, it can be regarded as an attribute. It is a single column representation of V into the quotient set.

3. The natural projection and the induced partition determine each other, we may use Q^j to denote the partition, the equivalence relation, including the natural projection.

5.2 Canonical Model and Granular Data Model

A relation K, as a map, can be factored through the natural projection $C_K : V \longrightarrow V/Q^1 \times \ldots \times V/Q^n$ and the naming map $NAME : V/Q^1 \times \ldots \times V/Q^n \longrightarrow C^1 \times \ldots \times C^n$. Note $NMAE$ is the product of $NAME^j$ and is often referred to as the interpretation. Table 3 illustrates how K is factored.

1. The natural projection C_K can be regarded as a knowledge representation of the universe V into quotient sets. It is called the canonical model of K.

2. The interpretation induces an isomorphism from V/Q to C (both are appropriate Cartesian products). The interpretation assigns a tuple of granules to a tuple of elementary concepts (attribute values). Each A^j can be regard as a meaningful name of Q^j, and an attribute value is a meaningful name of a granule(equivalence class).

3. Q^j is an attribute of C_K, called a canonical attribute (an uninterpreted attribute). $Dom(Q^j) = V/Q^j$ is called a canonical domain; a granule is a canonical attribute value [15].

Theorem 5.2.1. Patterns of the canonical model C_K is isomorphic (via interpretation) to the patterns of K.

This is a corollary of Theorem 4.1. To find all patterns of K, we only need to find the patterns on C_K (and vice versa).

		Canonical Model C_K				Relation K		
V		$(Q^0$	Q^2	$Q^3)$		$(S\#$	$STATUS$	$CITY)$
v_1		$(\{v_1\}$	$\{v_1, v_7\}$	$\{v_1\})$		$(S_1$	$TWENTY$	NY)
v_2		$(\{v_2\}$	$\{v_2, v_3, v_4, v_5, v_6\}$	$\{v_2, v_3, v_4, v_5, v_6\})$		$(S_2$	TEN	SJ)
v_3		$(\{v_3\}$	$\{v_2, v_3, v_4, v_5, v_6\}$	$\{v_2, v_3, v_4, v_5, v_6\})$	NAME	$(S_3$	TEN	SJ)
v_4	$\longrightarrow$	$(\{v_4\}$	$\{v_2, v_3, v_4, v_5, v_6\}$	$\{v_2, v_3, v_4, v_5, v_6\})$	$\longrightarrow$	$(S_4$	TEN	SJ)
v_5		$(\{v_5\}$	$\{v_2, v_3, v_4, v_5, v_6\}$	$\{v_2, v_3, v_4, v_5, v_6\})$		$(S_5$	TEN	SJ)
v_6		$(\{v_6\}$	$\{v_2, v_3, v_4, v_5, v_6\}$	$\{v_2, v_3, v_4, v_5, v_6\})$		$(S_6$	TEN	SJ)
v_7		$(\{v_7\}$	$\{v_1, v_7\}$	$\{v_7, v_8, v_9\})$		$(S_7$	$TWENTY$	LA)
v_8		$(\{v_8\}$	$\{v_8, v_9\}$	$\{v_7, v_8, v_9\})$		$(S_8$	$THIRTY$	LA)
v_9		$(\{v_9\}$	$\{v_8, v_9\}$	$\{v_7, v_8, v_9\})$		$(S_9$	$THIRTY$	LA)

Table 3. The canonical model C_K at left-hand-side is mapped to K at right-hand-side

The canonical model C_K is uniquely determined by its universe V, and the family Q of equivalence relations. In other words, the pair (V, Q) determines and is determined by C_K. From the pospect of first order logic, (V, Q) is a model of some rather simple kind of first order logic, where the only predicates are equivalence predicates (predicates that satisfy the reflexive, symmetric and transitive properties) [22].

1. One can regard the canonical model C_K as a table format of (V, Q).

2. We will call a granule of those original Q^j an *elementary granule*.

3. A q-tuple of C_K corresponds to an intersection, called a q-granule, of q elementary granules in (V, Q).

4. High frequency patterns of (V, Q) are q-granule whose cardinality is greater than the given threshold.

5. We have assume all attribute are distinct, to see more general version, we refer to [8].

Definition 5.2.2. The pair (V, Q) is called *granular data model*; it is a special case of granular structure [18].

(V, Q) is considered by both Pawlak and Lee. In his book, Pawlak call it knowledge base; implicitly Pawlak assumed all attributes are non-isomorphic [28], as we have done here. Since Knowledge base often has different meaning, we will not use it. Tony T. Lee considered the general case see Section 11.

Corollary 5.2.3. The patterns of (V, Q), C_K, and K are isomorphic.

6 Theory of derived Attributes (Features)

An attribute is also called a feature, especially in AI; they have been used interchangeably. In the classical data model, an attribute is a representation of property, characteristic, and etc.; see e.g., [26, 27]. In other words, it represents a human perception about the data (intensional view [5]). However, we should note that in a given relation instance (extensional view [5]), the data itself can*not* fully reflect such a human perception. As we have pointed out, the existence of an (extension) function dependency in a given table cannot imposes an (intension) function dependency on the data model. So in data mining, we should note that attributes are defined by the given instance of data (extension view), *not* what human perceived. Many very distinct attributes in intensional view (as human perceives) are actually isomorphic from the extensional view (as data says); see examples in [9, 8].

6.1 Attribute Transformations and Function Dependency

We will examine how a new attribute, that is transformed from the given ones, is related to the given them. Let B be a subset of A and let g be a function defined on $Dom(B) = Dom(B^1) \times \ldots \times Dom(B^k)$. We collect all function values in a set D. Using mapping notation, we have $g : Dom(B) \longrightarrow D$; it is called an attribute transformation. Since attributes can be regarded as maps, we have:

$$g \circ B : V \longrightarrow Dom(B) \longrightarrow D$$

The map $g \circ B : V \longrightarrow D$ is a new attribute. We write $Y = g \circ B = g(B^1, B^1, \ldots, B^k)$ and $D = Dom(Y)$. Y is called a derived attribute, and g an attribute transformation.

By joining K and Y, we have a new relation K': (joining in the sense of relational algebra on the information tables)

$$K' = K \wedge Y = A^1 \wedge \ldots \wedge A^n \wedge Y : V \longrightarrow Dom(A^1) \times \ldots \times Dom(A^n) \times Dom(Y)$$

Next we see how a new derived attribute Y is related the given attributes in the new relation K'.

Proposition 6.1. Y is a derived attribute of B iff Y is extension functionally depended (EFD) on B.

By definition, the occurrence of an (extension) functionally dependency (EFD) means there is an attribute transformation $f : Dom(B^1) \times \ldots Dom(B^k) \longrightarrow Dom(Y)$ such that $f(B(v)) = Y(v)$, $\forall\ v\ \in\ V$. By definition, $Y = f(B^1, B^1, \ldots, B^k)$; this completes our arguments. Table 4 illustrates the notion of EFD and attribute transformations.

B^1	B^2	$\ldots$	B^k	Y
b_1^1	b_1^2	$\ldots$	b_1^k	$y_1 = f(b_1^1, b_1^2, \ldots, b_1^k)$
b_2^1	b_2^2	$\ldots$	b_2^k	$y_2 = f(b_2^1, b_2^2, \ldots, b_2^k)$
b_3^1	b_3^2	$\ldots$	b_3^k	$y_3 = f(b_3^1, b_3^2, \ldots, b_3^k)$
		$\ldots$		$\ldots$
b_i^1	b_i^2		b_i^k	$y_i = f(b_i^1, b_i^2, \ldots, b_i^k)$
		$\ldots$		$\ldots$

Table 4. An Attribute Transformation in K

6.2 Feature Extractions and Constructions

Feature extractions and constructions in intensional view are much harder to describe formally since features represent human view, and their mathematical relations have to be set up for all possible instances *consistently*.

We will take extensional view, the view from data's prospect. Let us examine some assertions (in traditional view) from [25]: "All new constructed features are defined in terms of original features, .." and "Feature extraction is a process that extracts a set of new features from the original features through some functional mapping." By taking the data view, it is easy to see both assertions imply that the new constructed feature is a function (functional mapping) of old features. Note that

Let $A = \{A^1, \ldots A^n\}$ be the attributes *before* the extractions or constructions, and $A^{n+1} \ldots A^{n+m}$ be the *new* attributes. From the analysis above, the new attributes (features) are functions of old ones, we have

$$f : Dom(A^1) \times \ldots \times Dom(A^n)) \longrightarrow Dom(A^{n+k}).$$

From the analysis on Section 6.1, A^{n+k} is a derived attribute of A. We summarize the analysis in:

Proposition 6.2. The features constructed from classical feature extractions and constructions are derived attributes in extension view.

6.3 Derived Attributes in the Canonical Model

From Proposition 5.2.1, K is isomorphic to the canonical model C_K. So there is a corresponding Table 4 in the canonical model. In other words, there is a map,

$$V/B_E^1 \times \ldots \times V/B_E^k = V/(B_E^1 \cap \ldots \cap B_E^k) \longrightarrow V/Y_E$$

This map between quotient sets implies a refinements in the partitions; that is, Y_E is a coarsening of $B_E = B^1 \cap \ldots \cap B^k$. So we have the following:

Proposition 6.3. Y is a derived attribute of B, iff Y_E is a coarsening of $B_E = B^1 \cap \ldots B^k$, where $Y \in A$ and $B \subseteq A$

7 Granular Data Model of Relation Lattice

In this section, we modify Lee's work: At the beginning of Section 3.2, we have recalled the observation of [29, 7] that any subset of A induces a partition on V; the partition induced by A^j is denoted by Q^j. The power set 2^A is Boolean algebra and hence, a lattice, where meet and join operations are the union and intersection of the A respectively. Let $\Delta(V)$ be the set of all partitions on V (equivalence relations); $\Delta(V)$ forms a lattice, where meet is the intersection of equivalence relations and join is the "union," where the "union," denoted by $\cup_j Q^j$, is the smallest coarsening of all $Q^j, j = 1, 2, \ldots \Delta(V)$ is called the partition lattice.

Recall the convention, all attributes are non-isomorphic attributes. Hence all equivalence relations are distinct; see Section 3.1. Next proposition is due to Lee:

Proposition 7.1. There is a map

$$\theta : 2^A \longrightarrow \Delta(V),$$

that respects the meet, but not the join, operations. Lee called the image, $Im\theta$, the relation lattice and observe that

1. The join in $Im\theta$ is different from that of $\Delta(V)$.

2. So $Im\theta$ is a subset, but not a sublattice, of $\Delta(V)$.

Such an embedding is an unnatural one, but Lee focused his efforts on it; he established many connections between database concepts and lattice theory. However, we will, instead, take a natural embedding

Definition 7.2. The smallest lattice generated by $Im\theta$, by abuse of language, is called the (Lin's) relation lattice, denoted by L(Q).

This definition will not cause confusing, since we will not use Lee's notion at all. The difference between $L(Q)$ and $Im\theta$ is that former contains all the join of distinct attributes.

The pair $(V, L(Q))$ is the granular data model of the (Lin's) relation lattice. It should be clear

Definition 7.3. The high frequency q-patterns of (V, Q), $\forall$ q is the high frequency patterns of length one in $(V, Im\theta)$, and is a subset of the high frequency patterns of length one in $(V, L(Q))$.

8 Universal Model - Capture the invisibles

The smallest lattice, denoted by $L^*(Q)$, that consists of all coarsening of $L(Q)$ is called the *complete relation lattice*.

Main Theorem 8.1. $L^*(Q)$ is the set of all derived attributes of the canonical model.

Proof: (1) Let $P \in L^*(Q)$, that is, P is coarser than some $Q^{j_1} \cap ... \cap Q^{j_k}$. We will show it is a derived attribute. The coarsening implies a map on their respective quotient sets,

$$g : V/Q^{j_1} \times V/Q^{j_2}...V/Q^{j_k} = V/(Q^{j_1} \cap Q^{j_2}...Q^{j_k}) \longrightarrow V/P$$

In terms of relational notations, that is

$$g : Dom(Q^{j_1}) \times ... \times Dom(Q^{j_k}) \longrightarrow Dom(P)$$

Using the notations of functional dependency, we have (equivalence relations are attributes of the canonical model)

$$P = g(Q^{j_1}, Q^{j_2}..., Q^{j_k})$$

So g, as a map between attributes, is an attribute transformation. Hence P is a derived attribute.

(2) Let P be a derived attribute of C_K. That is, there is an attribute transformation

$$Dom(Q^{j_1}) \times ... \times Dom(Q^{j_k})) \longrightarrow Dom(P)$$

As C_K is the canonical model, it can be re-expressed in terms of quotient sets,

$$f : V/Q^{j_1} \times ... \times V/Q^{j_k} \longrightarrow V/P$$

Observe that $V/Q^{j_1} \times ... \times V/Q^{j_k} = V/(Q^{j_1} \cap ... \cap Q^{j_k})$, so the existence of f implies that P is coarser than $Q^{j_1} \cap ... \cap Q^{j_k}$. By definition P is an element in $L^*(Q)$. Q.E.D

Note that $L^*(Q)$ is finite, since $\Delta(V)$ is finite. The pair $(V, L^*(Q))$ is a granular data model, and its relation format

$$U_K : V \longrightarrow \prod_{P \in L^*(Q)} V/P.$$

is a knowledge representation. Its attributes are all the partitions in $L^*(Q)$, which contains all possible derived attributes of $K = (V, Q)$, by the theorem. We will not distinguish betweenthe granular data model and its realtiion format:

Definition 8.2. The pair $U_K = (V, L^*(Q))$ is the completion of $C_K = (V, Q)$ and is called the universal model of K.

9 Isomorphic Relations

V	K	($S\#$	Business Amount (in m.)	Birth Day	CITY)
v_1	$\longrightarrow$	(S_1	TWENTY	MAR	NY
v_2	$\longrightarrow$	(S_2	TEN	MAR	SJ
v_3	$\longrightarrow$	(S_3	TEN	FEB	NY
v_4	$\longrightarrow$	(S_4	TEN	FEB	LA
v_5	$\longrightarrow$	(S_5	TWENTY	MAR	SJ
v_6	$\longrightarrow$	(S_6	TWENTY	MAR	SJ
v_7	$\longrightarrow$	(S_7	TWENTY	APR	SJ
v_8	$\longrightarrow$	(S_8	THIRTY	JAN	LA
v_9	$\longrightarrow$	(S_9	THIRTY	JAN	LA

Table 5. An Information Table K

V	K	($S\#$	Weight	Part Name	Material
v_1	$\longrightarrow$	(P_1	20	SCREW	STEEL
v_2	$\longrightarrow$	(P_2	10	SCREW	BRASS
v_3	$\longrightarrow$	(P_3	10	NAIL	STEEL
v_4	$\longrightarrow$	(P_4	10	NAIL	ALLOY
v_5	$\longrightarrow$	(P_5	20	SCREW	BRASS
v_6	$\longrightarrow$	(P_6	20	SCREW	BRASS
v_7	$\longrightarrow$	(P_7	20	PIN	BRASS
v_8	$\longrightarrow$	(P_8	30	HAMMER	ALLOY
v_9	$\longrightarrow$	(P_9	30	HAMMER	ALLOY

Table 6. An Information Table K'

The two relations, Table 5, 6, are isomorphic, but their semantics are completely different, one table is about part, the other is about suppliers. These two relations have Isomorphic association rules;

1. Length one: TEN, TWENTY, March, SJ, LA in Table 5 and 10, 20, Screw, Brass, Alloy in Table 6

2. Length two: (TWENTY, MAR), (Mar, SJ), (TWENTY, SJ)in one Table 5, (20, Screw), (screw, Brass),(20, Brass), Table 6

However, they have non-isomorphic interesting rules:

1. Table 5: (TWENTY, SJ), that is, the business amount at San Jose is likely 20 millions; it is isomorphic to (20, Brass), which is not interesting.

2. Table 6: (SCREW, BRASS), that is, the screw is most likely made from Brass; it is isomorphic to (Mar, SJ), which is not interesting.

10 Conclusions

In this paper, we successfully enumerate all possible derived attributes of a given relation. The results seem striking; however, they are of theoretical nature. Even though $L*(Q)$ contains a complete list of all attributes, the number is insurmountably large; it is bounded by the Bell number B_n, where n is the cardinality of the smallest partiton in $L^*(Q)$. The exhaustive search of association rules on all those attributes are beyond the current reach. However, by combining the classical techniques of feature selections, we may reach new applications. Classical feature selection has focused on the original set of attributes, now with our new result, it seems suggest that the domain of feature selection should be extended to this complete universal set of derived attributes. We have tentatively called such a selection background knowledge. We will report such research in near future.

Next, we would like to remark that the simple observation that isomorphic relations have isomorphic patterns has a strong impact on the meaning of high frequency patterns. Isomorphism is a syntactic notion; it is highly probable that two isomorphic relations have totally different semantics. The patterns mined for one particular application may contain patterns for other applications. So relation with some additional structures need to be explored [23, 14, 15, 17, 20, 21, 11]. In particular, it implies that "interesting-ness" of association tuples may need extra semantics; the mere probability theory based on counting items may not be able to identify them; we only give a simple example (Section 9) more research will be reported in near future.

11 Elementary Operations

In this section, we do not assume the attributes are distinct. The isomorphism of relations is reflexive, symmetric, and transitive, so it classifies all relations into equivalence classes; we call them isomorphic classes.

Definition 11.1. H is a simplified information table of K, if H is isomorphic to K and only has non-isomorphic attributes.

Theorem 11.2. Let H be the simplified information table of K. Then the patterns (large itemsets) of K can be obtained from those of H by elementary operations that will be defined below.

To prove the Theorem, we will set up a lemma, in which we assume there are two isomorphic attributes B and B' in K, that is, degree K - degree H =1. Let $s : Dom(B) \longrightarrow Dom(B')$ be the isomorphism and $b' = s(b)$. Let H be the new table in which B' has been removed.

Lemma 11.3. The patterns of K can be generated from those of H by elementary operations, namely,

1. If b is a large itemset in H, then b' and (b, b') are large in K.

2. If (a. ., b, c. . .) is a large itemset in H, then (a. . , b', c. . .) and (a. . , b, b', c,. . .) are large in K.

3. These are the only large itemsets in K.

The validity of this lemma is rather straightforward; and it provides the critical inductive step for Theorem; we ill skip the proof.

References

[1] R. Agrawal, T. Imielinski, and A. Swami, "Mining Association Rules Between Sets of Items in Large Databases," in Proceeding of ACM-SIGMOD international Conference on Management of Data, pp. 207-216, Washington, DC, June, 1993

[2] G. Birkhoff and S. MacLane, A Survey of Modern Algebra, Macmillan, 1977

[3] Richard A. Brualdi, Introductory Combinatorics, Prentice Hall, 1992.

[4] Y.D. Cai, N. Cercone, and J. Han. Attribute-oriented induction in relational databases. In Knowledge Discovery in Databases, pages 213–228. AAAI/MIT Press, Cambridge, MA, 1991.

[5] C. J. Date, C. DATE, An Introduction to Database Systems, 7th ed., Addison-Wesley, 2000.

[6] A. Barr and E.A. Feigenbaum, The handbook of Artificial Intelligence, Willam Kaufmann 1981

[7] T. T. Lee, "Algebraic Theory of Relational Databases," The Bell System Technical Journal Vol 62, No 10, December, 1983, pp.3159-3204.

[8] T. Y. Lin, "Database Mining on Derived Attributes," to appear in the Spring-Verlag Lecture Notes on AI, 2002.

[9] T. Y. Lin, "Issues in Data Mining," in:the Proceeding of 26th IEEE Internaational Conference on Computer Software and Applications, Oxford, UK, Aug 26-29, 2002.

[10] T. Y. Lin "Feature Completion," Communication of IICM (Institute of Information and Computing Machinery, Taiwan) Vol 5, No. 2, May 2002, pp. 57-62. (the proceeding for the workshop "Toward the Foundation on Data Mining" in PAKDD2002, May 6, 2002.

[11] Ng, R., Lakshmanan, L.V.S., Han, J. and Pang, A. Exploratory mining and pruning optimizations of constrained associations rules, *Proceedings of 1998 ACM-SIGMOD Conference on Management of Data*, 13-24, 1998.

[12] T. Y. Lin "The Lattice Structure of Database and Mining Multiple Level Rules." Presented in COMPSAC 2001, Chicago, Oct 8-12, 2001; the exact copy appear "Feature Transformations and Structure of Attributes." In: Data Mining and Knowledge Discovery: Theory, Tools, and Technology IV, B. Dasarathy (ed), Proceeding of SPIE Vol 4730, Orlando,Fl, April 1-5, 2002

[13] T. Y. Lin and J. Tremba "Attribute Transformations for Data Mining II: Applications to Economic and Stock Market Data," International Journal of Intelligent Systems, to appear

[14] T. Y. Lin, " Association Rules in Semantically Rich Relations: Granular Computing Approach" JSAI International Workshop on Rough Set Theory and Granular Computing May 20-25, 2001. The Post Proceeding is in Lecture note in AI 2253, Springer-Verlag, 2001, pp. 380-384.

[15] T. Y. Lin, "Data Mining and Machine Oriented Modeling: A Granular Computing Approach," Journal of Applied Intelligence, Kluwer, Vol. 13, No 2, September/October,2000, pp.113-124.

[16] T. Y. Lin, "Attribute Transformations on Numerical Databases," Lecture Notes in Artificial Intelligence 1805, Terano, Liu, Chen (eds), PAKDD2000, Kyoto, Japan, April 18-20, 2000, 181-192.

[17] T. Y. Lin, "Data Mining: Granular Computing Approach." In: Methodologies for Knowledge Discovery and Data Mining, Lecture Notes in Artificial Intelligence 1574, Third Pacific-Asia Conference, Beijing, April 26-28, 1999, 24-33.

[18] T. Y. Lin, "Granular Computing on Binary Relations I: Data Mining and Neighborhood Systems." In: Rough Sets In Knowledge Discovery, A. Skoworn and L. Polkowski (eds), Springer-Verlag, 1998, 107-121.

[19] T. Y. Lin " Discovering Patterns in Numerical Sequences Using Rough set Theory," In: Proceeding of the Third World Multi-conferences on Systemics, Cybernatics, and Informatics, Vol 5, Computer Science and Engineering, Orlando, Florida, July 31-Aug 4, 1999

[20] T. Y. Lin, N. Zhong, J. Duong, S. Ohsuga, "Frameworks for Mining Binary Relations in Data." In: Rough sets and Current Trends in Computing, Lecture Notes on Artificial Intelligence 1424, A. Skoworn and L. Polkowski (eds), Springer-Verlag, 1998, 387-393.

[21] , T. Y. Lin and M. Hadjimichael, "Non-Classificatory Generalization in Data Mining," in Proceedings of the 4th Workshop on Rough Sets, Fuzzy Sets, and Machine Discovery, November 6-8, Tokyo, Japan, 1996, 404-411.

[22] T.Y. Lin, Eric Louie, "Modeling the Real World for Data Mining: Granular Computing Approach" Joint 9th IFSA World Congress and 20th NAFIPS Conference, July 25-28, Vancouver, Canada, 2001

[23] E. Louie,T. Y. Lin, "Semantics Oriented Association Rules," In: 2002 World Congress of Computational Intelligence, Honolulu, Hawaii, May 12-17, 2002, 956-961 (paper # 5702)

[24] E. Louie and T. Y. Lin, "Finding Association Rules using Fast Bit Computation: Machine-Oriented Modeling," in: Foundations of Intelligent Systems, Z. Ras and S. Ohsuga (eds), Lecture Notes in Artificial Intelligence 1932, Springer-Verlag, 2000, pp. 486- 494. (ISMIS00, Charlotte, NC, Oct 11-14, 2000)

[25] Hiroshi Motoda and Huan Liu "Feature Selection, Extraction and Construction," Communication of IICM (Institute of Information and Computing Machinery, Taiwan) Vol 5, No. 2, May 2002, pp. 67-72. (proceeding for the workshop "Toward the Foundation on Data Mining" in PAKDD2002, May 6, 2002.

[26] H. Liu and H. Motoda, "Feature Transformation and Subset Selection," IEEE Intelligent Systems, Vol. 13, No. 2, March/April, pp.26-28 (1998)

[27] H. Liu and H. Motoda (eds), Feature Extraction, Construction and Selection - A Data Mining Perspective, Kluwer Academic Publishers (1998).

[28] Z. Pawlak, Rough sets. Theoretical Aspects of Reasoning about Data, Kluwer Academic Publishers, 1991

[29] Z. Pawlak, Rough sets. International Journal of Information and Computer Science **11**, 1982, pp. 341-356.

[30] R. Ng, L. V. S. Lakshmanan, J. Han and A. Pang, " Exploratory Mining and Pruning Optimizations of Constrained Associations Rules", Proc. of 1998 ACM-SIGMOD Conf. on Management of Data, Seattle, Washington, June 1998, pp. 13-24.

O-Cluster: Scalable Clustering of Large High Dimensional Data Sets

Boriana L. Milenova & Marcos M. Campos
Oracle Data Mining Technologies
10 Van de Graaff Drive
Burlington, MA 1803, USA
{*boriana.milenova, marcos.m.campos*}*@oracle.com*

Abstract

Clustering large data sets of high dimensionality has always been a challenge for clustering algorithms. Many recently developed clustering algorithms have attempted to address either handling data sets with a very large number of records and/or with a very high number of dimensions. This paper provides a discussion of the advantages and limitations of existing algorithms when they operate on very large multidimensional data sets. To simultaneously overcome both the "curse of dimensionality" and the scalability problems associated with large amounts of data, we propose a new clustering algorithm called O-Cluster. O-Cluster combines a novel active sampling technique with an axis-parallel partitioning strategy to identify continuous areas of high density in the input space. The method operates on a limited memory buffer and requires at most a single scan through the data. We demonstrate the high quality of the obtained clustering solutions, their robustness to noise, and O-Cluster's excellent scalability.

1. Introduction

With an increasing number of new database applications dealing with very large high dimensional data sets, data mining on such data sets has emerged as an important research area. These applications include multimedia content-based retrieval, geographic and molecular biology data analysis, text mining, bioinformatics, medical applications, and time-series matching. For example, in multimedia retrieval, the objects (e.g., images) are represented by their features (e.g., color histograms, texture vectors, Fourier vectors, text descriptors, and shape descriptors), which define high dimensional feature spaces. In many such applications the data sets may consist of millions of records with thousands of dimensions.

There are a number of different clustering algorithms that are applicable to very large data sets, and a few that address high dimensional data. Clustering algorithms can be divided into partitioning, hierarchical, locality-based, and grid-based algorithms.

Given a data set with n records and $k < n$, the number of desired clusters, *partitioning algorithms* divide the data into k clusters. The clusters are formed to optimize an objective criterion such as distance. Each record is assigned to the closest cluster. Clusters are typically represented by either the mean of the records assigned to the cluster (k-means [14]) or by one representative record of the cluster (k-medoid [13]). CLARANS [16] is a partitioning clustering algorithm developed for large data sets, which uses a randomized and bounded search strategy to improve the scalability of the k-medoid approach. CLARANS enables the detection of outliers and its computational complexity is approximately $O(n^2)$.

Hierarchical clustering algorithms work by grouping data records into a hierarchy (e.g., a tree) of clusters. The hierarchy can be formed top-down (*divisive* hierarchical methods) or bottom-up (*agglomerative* hierarchical methods). Hierarchical methods rely on a distance function to measure the similarity between clusters. Their computational complexity is usually $O(n^2)$. Some newer methods such as BIRCH [21] and CURE [8] attempt to address the scalability problem and improve the quality of clustering results for hierarchical methods. BIRCH is an efficient divisive hierarchical algorithm. It has $O(n)$ computational complexity, can work with limited amount of memory, and has efficient I/O. It uses a special data structure CF-tree for storing summary information about subclusters of records. Due to the nature of the similarity measure it uses, BIRCH only performs well on data sets with spherical clusters. CURE is an $O(n^2)$ algorithm that produces high-quality clusters in the presence of outliers, and can identify clusters of complex shapes and different sizes. It employs a hierarchical clustering approach that uses a fixed number of representative points to define a cluster instead of a single centroid or record. CURE handles large data sets through a combination of random sampling and partitioning. Since CURE uses only a random sample of the data set, it manages to achieve good scalability for large data sets. CURE reports better times than BIRCH on the same benchmark data.

Locality-based clustering algorithms group data records based on conditions in a neighborhood. These algorithms allow clustering to be performed in one scan of the data set. DBSCAN [6] is a typical representative of this group of algorithms. It regards clusters as dense regions of records in the input space that are separated by regions of low density. DBSCAN's basic idea is that the density of points in a radius around each point in a cluster has to be above a certain threshold. It grows a cluster as long as, for each data point within this cluster, a neighborhood of a given radius contains at least a minimum number of points. DBSCAN has computational complexity $O(n^2)$. If a spatial index is used, the computational complexity is $O(n \log n)$. The clustering generated by DBSCAN is very sensitive to parameter choice. OPTICS is another locality-based clustering algorithm. It computes an augmented cluster ordering for automatic and iterative clustering analysis. OPTICS has the same computational complexity as DBSCAN.

In general, partitioning, hierarchical, and locality-based clustering algorithms do not scale well with the number of records in the data set. To improve efficiency, data summarization techniques integrated with the clustering process have been proposed. Besides the above-mentioned BIRCH and CURE algorithms, examples include: active data clustering [10], ScalableKM [4], and simple single pass k-means [7]. Active data clustering utilizes principles from sequential experimental design in order to interleave data generation and data analysis. It infers from the available data not only the grouping structure in the data, but also which data are most relevant for the clustering problem. The inferred relevance of the data is then used to control the re-sampling of the data set. ScalableKM requires at most one scan of the data set. The method identifies data points that can be effectively compressed, data points that must be maintained in memory, and data points that can be discarded. The algorithm operates within the confines of a limited memory buffer. Unfortunately, the compression schemes used by ScalableKM can introduce significant overhead. The simple single pass k-means algorithm is a simplification of ScalableKM. Like ScalableKM, it also uses a data buffer of fixed size. Experiments indicate that the simple single pass k-means algorithm is several times faster than standard k-means while producing clustering of comparable quality.

All the above-mentioned methods rely on near or nearest neighbor information and are not fully effective when clustering high dimensional data. In high dimensional spaces, it is very unlikely that data points are nearer to each other than the average distance between data points because of sparsely filled space. As a result, as the dimensionality of the space increases, the difference between the distance to the nearest and the farthest neighbors of a data record goes to zero [5, 9].

Grid-based clustering algorithms do not suffer from the nearest neighbor problem in high dimensional spaces. Examples include STING [20], CLIQUE [1], DENCLUE [11], WaveCluster [18], and MAFIA [15]. These methods divide the input space into hyper-rectangular cells, discard the low-density cells, and then combine adjacent high-density cells to form clusters. Grid-based methods are capable of discovering cluster of any shape and are also reasonably fast. However, none of these methods address how to efficiently cluster very large data sets that do not fit in memory. Furthermore, these methods work well only with input spaces with low to moderate numbers of dimensions. As the dimensionality increases, grid-based methods face serious problems. The number of cells grows exponentially and finding adjacent high-density cells to form clusters becomes very expensive [12].

In order to address the "curse of dimensionality" a couple of algorithms have focused on data projections in subspaces. Examples include PROCLUS [2], OptiGrid [12], and ORCLUS [3]. PROCLUS uses axis-parallel partitions to identify subspace clusters. ORCLUS uses generalized projections to identify subspace clusters.

OptiGrid is an especially interesting algorithm due to its simplicity and ability to find clusters in high dimensional spaces in the presence noise. OptiGrid constructs a grid-partitioning of the data by calculating partitioning hyperplanes using *contracting projections* of the data. OptiGrid looks for hyperplanes that satisfy two requirements: 1) separating hyperplanes should cut through regions of low density relative to the surrounding regions; and 2) separating hyperplanes should place individual clusters into different partitions. The first requirement aims at preventing oversplitting, that is, a cutting plane should not split a cluster. The second requirement attempts to achieve good cluster discrimination, that is, the cutting plane should contribute to finding the individual clusters. OptiGrid recursively constructs a multidimensional grid by partitioning the data using a set of cutting hyperplanes, each of which is orthogonal to at least one projection. At each step, the generation of the set of candidate hyperplanes is controlled by two threshold parameters. The implementation of OptiGrid described in the paper used axis-parallel partitioning hyperplanes. The authors show that the error introduced by axis-parallel partitioning decreases exponentially with the number of dimensions in the data space. This validates the use of axis-parallel projections as an effective approach for separating clusters in high dimensional spaces. Optigrid, however, has two main shortcomings. It is sensitive to parameter choice and it does not prescribe a strategy to efficiently handle data sets that do not fit in memory.

To overcome both the scalability problems associated with large amounts of data and a high dimensional data input space, this paper introduces a new clustering algorithm called O-Cluster (Orthogonal partitioning CLUSTERing). This new clustering method combines a novel active sampling technique with an axis-parallel partitioning strategy to identify continuous areas of high density in the input space. The method operates on a limited memory buffer and requires at most a single scan through the data.

2. The O-Cluster Algorithm

O-Cluster is a method that builds upon the contracting projection concept introduced by OptiGrid. Our algorithm makes two major contributions:

- It proposes the use of a statistical test to validate the quality of a cutting plane. This test proves crucial for identifying good splitting points along projections and enables automated selection of high quality separators.

- It can operate on a small buffer containing a random sample from the original data set. Active sampling ensures that partitions get additional data points if more information is needed to evaluate a cutting plane. Partitions that do not have ambiguities are 'frozen' and their data points are removed from the buffer.

O-Cluster operates recursively. It evaluates possible splitting points for all projections in a partition, selects the 'best' one, and splits the data into two new partitions. The algorithm proceeds by searching for good cutting planes inside the newly created partitions. Thus O-Cluster creates a hierarchical tree structure that tessellates the input space into rectangular regions. Figure 1 provides an outline of O-Cluster's algorithm. The main processing stages are:

1. **Load buffer**: If the entire data set does not fit in the buffer, a sample is used (the data records need to be in random order). O-Cluster assigns all points from the initial buffer to a single active root partition.

2. **Compute histograms for active partitions**: The goal is to determine a set of projections for the active partitions and compute histograms along these projections. Any partition that represents a leaf in the clustering hierarchy and is not explicitly marked ambiguous or 'frozen' is considered active. The process whereby an active partition becomes ambiguous or 'frozen' is explained in Step 4. O-Cluster computes a histogram for every projection within the active partition. It is essential to compute histograms that provide good resolution but also that have data artifacts smoothed out. A number of studies have addressed the problem of how many equi-width bins can be supported by a given

distribution [17,19]. Based on these studies, a reasonable, simple approach would be to make the number of equi-width bins inversely proportional to the standard deviation of the data along a given dimension and directly proportional to $N^{1/3}$, where N is the number of points inside a partition. Alternatively, one can use a global binning strategy and coarsen the histograms as the number of points inside the partitions decreases. O-Cluster is robust with respect to different binning strategies as long as the histograms do not significantly undersmooth or oversmooth the distribution density. Data sets with low number of records would require coarser binning and some resolution may potentially be lost.

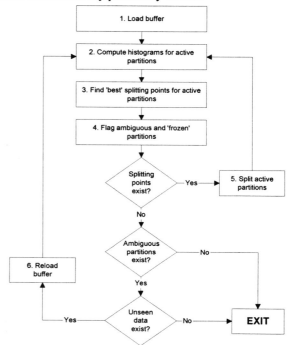

Figure 1. O-Cluster algorithm block diagram

3. **Find 'best' splitting points for active partitions**: For each histogram, O-Cluster attempts to find the 'best' valid cutting plane, if such exists. A valid cutting plane passes through a point of low density (a valley) in the histogram. Additionally, the point of low density should be surrounded on both sides by points of high density (peaks). O-Cluster attempts to find a pair of peaks with a valley between them where the difference between the peak and the valley histogram counts is statistically significant. Statistical significance is tested using a standard χ^2 test:

$$\chi^2 = 2\,(observed - expected)^2 \div expected \geq \chi^2_{\alpha,1},$$

where the observed value is equal to the histogram count of the valley and the expected value is the average of the histogram counts of the valley and the lower peak. The current implementation uses a 95% confidence level ($\chi^2_{0.05,1} = 3.843$). Since multiple splitting points can be found to be valid separators per partition according to this test, O-Cluster chooses the one where the valley has the lowest histogram count as the 'best' splitting point. Thus the cutting plane would go through the area with lowest density. In the case of a tie, it is possible to bias the algorithm towards favoring splitting points along dimensions with wide ranges or splitting points that would produce balanced partitions. The second approach is computationally more expensive.

4. **Flag ambiguous and 'frozen' partitions**: If no valid splitting points are found, O-Cluster checks whether the χ^2 test would have found a valid splitting point at a lower confidence level (e.g., 90% with $\chi^2_{0.1,1} = 2.706$). If that is the case, the current partition can be considered ambiguous. More data points are needed to establish the quality of the splitting point. If no splitting points were found and there is no ambiguity, the partition can be marked as 'frozen' and the records associated with it marked for deletion from the buffer.

5. **Split active partitions**: If a valid separator exists, the data points are split along the cutting plane and two new active partitions are created from the original partition. For each new partition the processing proceeds recursively from Step 2.

6. **Reload buffer**: This step can take place after all recursive partitioning on the current buffer has completed. If all existing partitions are marked as 'frozen' and/or there are no more data points available, the algorithm exits. Otherwise, if some partitions are marked as ambiguous and additional unseen data records exist, O-Cluster proceeds with reloading the data buffer. The new data replace records belonging to 'frozen' partitions. When new records are read in, only data points that fall inside ambiguous partitions are placed in the buffer. New records falling within a 'frozen' partition are not loaded into the buffer and discarded. If it is desirable to maintain statistics of the data points falling inside partitions (including the 'frozen' partitions), such statistics can be continuously updated with the reading of each new record. Loading of new records continues until either: 1) the buffer is filled again; 2) the end of the data set is reached; or 3) a reasonable number of records (e.g., equal to the buffer size) have been read, even if the buffer is not full and there are more data. The reason for the last condition is that if the buffer is relatively large and there are many points marked for deletion, it may take a long time to fill the entire buffer with data from the ambiguous regions. To avoid excessive reloading under these circumstances, the buffer reloading process is terminated after reading through a number of records equal to the data buffer size. Once the buffer reload is completed, the algorithm

proceeds from Step 2. The algorithm requires, at most, a single pass through the entire data set. In addition to the major differences from OptiGrid noted in the beginning of this section, there are two other important distinctions:

• OptiGrid's choice of a valid cutting plane depends on a pair of global parameters: noise level and maximal splitting density. Those two parameters act as thresholds for identifying valid splitting points. In OptiGrid, histogram peaks are required to be above the noise level parameter while histogram valleys need to have density lower than the maximum splitting density. The maximum splitting density should be set above the noise level threshold [personal communication with OptiGrid's authors]. Finding correct values for these parameters is critical for OptiGrid's performance. O-Cluster's χ^2 test for splitting points eliminates the need for preset thresholds – the algorithm can find valid cutting planes at any density level within a histogram. While not strictly necessary for O-Cluster's operation, it was found useful to introduce a third parameter called *sensitivity* (ρ). Analogous to OptiGrid's noise level, the role of this parameter is to suppress the creation of arbitrarily small clusters by setting a minimum count for O-Cluster's histogram peaks. The effect of ρ is discussed in Section 3.

• While OptiGrid attempts to find good cutting planes that optimally traverse the input space, it is prone to oversplitting. By design, OptiGrid can partition simultaneously along several cutting planes. This may result in the creation of clusters (with few points) that need to be subsequently removed. Additionally, OptiGrid works with histograms that undersmooth the distribution density [personal communication with OptiGrid's authors]. Undersmoothed histograms and the threshold-based mechanism of splitting point identification can lead to the creation of separators that cut through clusters.

These issues may not necessarily be a serious hindrance in OptiGrid's framework since the algorithm attempts to construct a multidimensional grid where the highly populated cells are interpreted as clusters. O-Cluster on the other hand, attempts to create a binary clustering tree where the leaves are regions with flat or unimodal density functions. Only a single cutting plane is applied at a time and the quality of the splitting point is statistically validated.

O-Cluster performs well on large-scale data sets with many records and high dimensionality. It is desirable to work with a sufficiently large buffer in order to calculate high quality histograms with good resolution. High dimensionality has been shown to significantly reduce the chance of cutting through data when using axis-parallel cutting planes [12]. There is no special handling for missing values – if a data record has missing values, this record does not contribute to the histogram counts along certain dimensions. However, if a missing value is needed to assign the record to a partition, the record is not assigned and it is marked for deletion from the buffer.

3. O-Cluster Analysis

This section illustrates the general behavior of O-Cluster and evaluates the correctness of its solutions. While a comparison to the original OptiGrid algorithm would have been very desirable, a publicly available code base does not exist and [12] does not offer sufficient implementation detail to enable an in-house version to provide a fair comparison.

The initial set of tests makes the assumption that the entire data set can fit in the buffer. In order to graphically illustrate O-Cluster's behavior, the first series of tests were carried out on a two-dimensional data set - DS3 [21]. This is a particularly challenging benchmark. The low number of dimensions makes the use of any axis-parallel partitioning algorithm problematic. Also, the data set consists of 100 spherical clusters that vary significantly in their size and density. The number of points per cluster is a random number in the range [0, 2000] drawn from a uniform distribution. The data range for each dimension is [0, 100] and the variance across dimensions for each cluster is a random number in the range [0, 2] drawn from a uniform distribution.

3.1. O-Cluster on DS3

Figure 2 depicts the partitions found by O-Cluster on the DS3 data set. The centers of the original clusters are marked with squares while the centroids of the points assigned to each partition are represented by stars.

Although O-Cluster does not function optimally when the dimensionality is low, it produces a good set of partitions. O-Cluster finds cutting planes at different levels of density and successfully identifies nested clusters. Axis-parallel splits in low dimensions can easily lead to the creation of artifacts where cutting planes have to cut through parts of a cluster and data points are assigned to incorrect partitions. Such artifacts can either result in centroid error or lead to further partitioning and creation of spurious clusters. For example, in Figure 2 O-Cluster creates 73 partitions. Of these, 71 contain the centroids of at least one of the original clusters. The remaining 2 partitions were produced due to artifacts created by splits going through clusters.

In general, there are two potential sources of imprecision in the algorithm: 1) O-Cluster may fail to create partitions for all original clusters; and/or 2) O-Cluster may create spurious partitions that do not correspond to any of the original clusters. To measure these two effects separately, we use two metrics borrowed from the information retrieval domain: *Recall* is defined as the percentage of the original clusters that were found and assigned to partitions; *Precision* is defined as the percentage of the found partitions that contain at least one original cluster centroid. That is, in Figure 2 O-Cluster found 71 out of 100 original clusters (resulting in recall of 71%), and 71 out of the 73 partitions created contained at least one centroid of the original clusters (a precision of 97%). The recall and precision measures reflect the trade-off between identifying as many as possible of the true clusters vs. creating spurious clusters due to excessive partitioning. The use of recall and precision is possible only when the correct number of clusters is available.

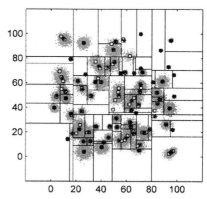

Figure 2. O-Cluster partitions on the DS3 data set: The grid depicts the splitting planes found by O-Cluster (recall = 71%, precision = 97%)

The effect of creating spurious clusters due to splitting artifacts can be alleviated by using O-Cluster's sensitivity (ρ) parameter. ρ is a parameter in the [0, 1] range that is inversely proportional to the minimum count required to find a histogram peak. A value of 0 requires the histogram peaks to surpass the count corresponding to a global uniform level per dimension. The global uniform level is defined as the average histogram count that would have been observed if the data points in the buffer were drawn from a uniform distribution. A value of 0.5 sets the minimum histogram count for a peak to 50% of the global uniform level. A value of 1 removes the restrictions on peak histogram counts and the splitting point identification relies solely on the χ^2 test. The results shown in Figure 2 were produced with ρ = 0.95.

Increasing ρ enables O-Cluster to grow the clustering hierarchy deeper and thus obtain improved recall performance. However, values of ρ that are too high may result in excessive splitting and poor precision. It should be noted that the effect of ρ is magnified by the particular characteristics of the DS3 data set. The 2D dimensionality leads to splitting artifacts that become the main reason for oversplitting. Additionally, the original clusters in the DS3 data set vary significantly in their number of records. Low ρ values can filter out some of the weaker clusters.

Higher dimensionality and more evenly represented clusters reduce O-Cluster's sensitivity to ρ.

It should be noted that ρ is the only algorithm parameter that could require tuning when O-Cluster is applied to a new data set where the number of clusters is unknown. The user has to determine whether it is desirable for small clusters to be treated as artifacts and therefore filtered out by increasing ρ. The χ^2 threshold parameters do not require data set specific adjustment.

In order to investigate the benefits of higher dimensionality, additional dimensions were added to the DS3 data set. O-Cluster's accuracy (both recall and precision) improves dramatically with increased dimensionality. For example, five dimensions produced recall of 99% and precision of 96%. Ten dimensions or more resulted in perfect recall and precision (100%). Increasing the number of dimensions allowed O-Cluster to achieve high accuracy on data sets with significantly higher cluster variance than the original DS3 problem. The main reason for the remarkably good performance is that higher dimensionality allows O-Cluster to find cutting planes that do not produce splitting artifacts.

3.2. The Effect of Uniform Noise

O-Cluster shares one remarkable feature with OptiGrid – it resistance to uniform noise. To test O-Cluster's robustness to uniform noise a synthetic data set consisting of 100,000 points was generated. The data range along each dimension was [0, 100]. There were 50 spherical clusters, with variance in the range [0, 2], each represented by 2,000 points. To introduce uniform noise to the data set, a certain percentage of the original records were replaced by records drawn from a uniform distribution on each dimension. O-Cluster was tested with 25%, 50%, 75%, and 90% noise. For example, when the percentage of noise was 90%, the original clusters were represented by 10,000 points (200 on average per cluster) and the remaining 90,000 points were uniform noise. All experiments were run with ρ = 0.8. Figure 3 illustrates O-Cluster's performance under noisy conditions. O-Cluster's accuracy degrades very gracefully with the increased percentage of background noise. Higher dimensionality provides a slight advantage when handling noise. In our experiments, increasing the number of dimensions beyond ten did not produce a noticeable advantage. Recall and precision were similar to those with ten dimensions.

It should also be noted that once background noise is introduced, the centroids of the partitions produced by O-Cluster are offset from the original cluster centroids. In order to identify the original centers, it is necessary to discount the background noise from the histograms and compute centroids on the remaining points. This can be accomplished by filtering out the histogram bins that would fall below a level corresponding to the average bin count for this partition.

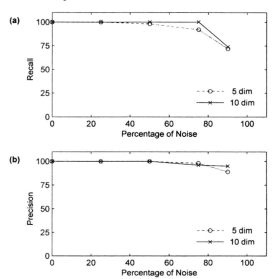

Figure 3. Effect of uniform noise: (a) recall and (b) precision for 5 and 10 dimensions

3.3. O-Cluster Complexity and Scalability

O-Cluster can use an arbitrary set of projections. Our current implementation is restricted to projections that are axis-parallel. The histogram computation step is of complexity $O(N \times d)$ where N is the number of data points in the buffer and d is the number of dimensions. The selection of best splitting point for a single dimension is $O(b)$ where b is the average number of histogram bins in a partition. Choosing the best splitting point over all dimensions is $O(d \times b)$. The assignment of data points to newly created partitions requires a comparison of an attribute value to the splitting point and the complexity has an upper bound of $O(N)$. Loading new records into the data buffer requires their insertion into the relevant partitions. The complexity associated with scoring a record depends on the depth of the binary clustering tree (s). The upper limit for filling the whole buffer is $O(N \times s)$. The depth of the tree s depends on the data set. In general, N and d are the dominating factors and the total complexity can be approximated as $O(N \times d)$.

The next series of tests addresses O-Cluster's scalability with increasing numbers of records and dimensions. All data sets used in the experiments consisted of 50 clusters. All 50 clusters were correctly identified in each test. When measuring scalability with increasing number of records, the number of dimensions was set to 10. When measuring scalability for increasing dimensionality, the number of records was set to 100,000. Figure 4 shows that there is a clear linear dependency of

O-Cluster's processing time on both the number of records and number of dimensions. These timing results can be improved significantly because the algorithm was implemented as a PL/SQL package in an ORACLE 9i database. There is an overhead associated with the fact that PL/SQL is an interpreted language.

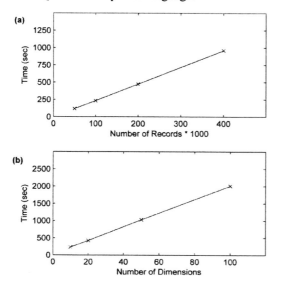

Figure 4. Scalability: (a) with number of records (10 dimensions); (b) with number of dimensions (100,000 records)

3.4. Working with a Limited Buffer Size

In all tests described so far, O-Cluster had a sufficiently large buffer to accommodate the entire data set. The next set of results illustrate O-Cluster's behavior when the algorithm is required to have a small memory footprint such that the buffer can contain only a fraction of the entire data set. This series of tests reuses the data set described in Section 3.3 (50 clusters, 2,000 point each, 10 dimensions). For all tests, ρ was set to 0.8. Figure 5 shows the timing and recall numbers for different buffer sizes (0.5%, 0.8%, 1%, 5%, and 10% of the entire data set). Very small buffer sizes may require multiple refills. For example, the described experiment showed that when the buffer size was 0.5%, O-Cluster needed to refill it 5 times; when the buffer size was 0.8% or 1%, O-Cluster had to refill it once. For larger buffer sizes, no refills were necessary. As a result, using 0.8% buffer proves to be slightly faster than using 0.5% buffer. If no buffer refills were required (buffer size greater than 1%), O-Cluster followed a linear scalability pattern, as shown in the previous section. Regarding O-Cluster's accuracy, buffer sizes under 1% proved to be too small for the algorithm to find all existing clusters. For buffer size of 0.5%, O-

Cluster found 41 out of 50 clusters (82% recall) and for buffer size of 0.8%, O-Cluster found 49 out of 50 clusters (98% recall). Larger buffer sizes allowed O-Cluster to correctly identify all original clusters (100% recall). For all buffer sizes (including buffer sizes smaller than 1%) precision was 100%. O-Cluster functions optimally when the order of data presentation is random. Residual dependencies within the subsets can result in premature termination of the algorithm and some of the statistically significant partitions may remain undiscovered.

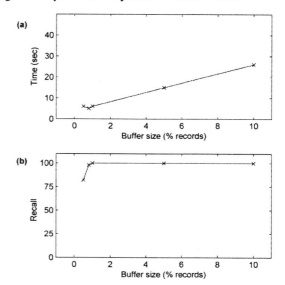

Figure 5. Buffer size: (a) time scalability; (b) recall

3.5. O-Cluster on Texture Data

The last series of tests illustrates O-Cluster's behavior on a real world data set. The VisTex image database (made available by the MIT Vision and Modeling Group) was combined with a database of proprietary texture images. The data set consisted of 850 images depicting homogeneous textures or multi-texture scenes. The image size was 250,000 pixels. The Oracle Intermedia group extracted 113 HSV global color and 5 global texture features. Subsequently, each feature was binned into 5 bins. O-Cluster discovered 14 clusters where images were grouped on the basis of their predominant color(s) and/or texture. Figure 6 shows examples of two groups of images with similar color scheme and texture pattern that were correctly assigned to two different clusters. To assess the quality of O-Cluster's results, the k-Means algorithm was run on the same data with the same number of clusters. Cluster compactness was measured as the average cluster mean square error (MSE) between the individual points and the corresponding cluster centroids. The average

MSE for O-Cluster was 14% smaller than that of *k*-Means. It should be emphasized that, unlike *k*-Means, O-Cluster does not explicitly attempt to optimize the average cluster MSE.

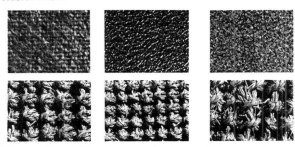

Figure 6. O-Cluster on texture data: each row shows examples of images in a different cluster

4. Conclusions

The majority of existing clustering algorithms encounter serious scalability and/or accuracy related problems when used on data sets with a large number of records and/or dimensions. We propose a new clustering algorithm, O-Cluster, capable of efficiently and effectively clustering large, high dimensional data sets. It relies on a novel active sampling approach and uses an axis-parallel partitioning scheme to identify hyper-rectangular regions of uni-modal density in the input feature space. O-Cluster has good accuracy and scalability, is robust to noise, and can successfully operate with limited memory resources.

Currently we are extending O-Cluster in a number of ways, including: parallel implementation, cluster representation through rules, probabilistic modeling and scoring with missing values, handling categorical and mixed (categorical and numerical) data sets. These extensions will be reported in a future paper.

References

[1] R. Agrawal, J. Gehrke, D. Gunopulos, and P. Raghavan, "Automatic Subspace Clustering of High Dimensional Data for Data Mining Applications", In *Proc. 1998 ACM-SIGMOD Int. Conf. Management of Data (SIGMOD'98)*, 1998, pp. 94–105.

[2] C. C. Aggarwal, C. Procopiuc, J. L. Wolf, P. S. Yu, and J. S. Park, "Fast Algorithms for Projected Clustering", In *Proc. 1999 ACM-SIGMOD Int. Conf. Management of Data (SIGMOD'99)*, 1999, pp. 61–72.

[3] C.C. Aggarwal and P.S. Yu, "Finding Generalized Projected Clusters in High Dimensional Spaces", In *Proc. 2000 ACM-SIGMOD Int. Conf. Management of Data (SIGMOD'00)*, 2000, pp. 70–81.

[4] P. Bradely, U. Fayyad, and C. Reina, "Scaling Clustering Algorithms to Large Databases", In *Proc. 1998 Int. Conf.*

Knowledge Discovery and Data Mining (KDD'98), 1998, pp. 8–15.

[5] K. Beyer, J. Goldstein, R. Ramakhrisnan, and U. Shaft, "When Is 'Nearest Neighbor' Meaningful?", In *Proc. 7th Int. Conf. on Database Theory (ICDT'99)*, 1999, pp. 217–235.

[6] M. Ester, H.-P. Kriegel, J. Sander, and X. Xu, "A Density-Based Algorithm for Discovering Clusters in Large Spatial Database", In *Proc. 1996 Int. Conf. Knowledge Discovery and Data Mining (KDD'96)*, 1996, pp. 226–231.

[7] F. Farnstrom, J. Lewis, and C. Elkan, "Scalability for Clustering Algorithms Revisited", *SIGKDD Explorations Vol. 2*, 2000, pp. 51–57.

[8] S. Guha, R. Rastogi, and K. Shim, "CURE: An Efficient Clustering Algorithm for Large Databases", In *Proc. 1998 ACM-SIGMOD Int. Conf. Management of Data (SIGMOD'98)*, 1998, pp. 73–84.

[9] A. Hinneburg, C. C. Aggarwal, D. A. Keim, "What Is the Nearest Neighbor in High Dimensional Spaces?", In *Proc. 26th Int. Conf. on Very Large Data Bases (VLDB'00)*, 2000, pp.. 506–515.

[10] T. Hofmann and J. Buhmann, "Active Data Clustering", In *Advances in Neural Information Processing Systems (NIPS'97)*, 1997, pp. 528–534.

[11] A. Hinneburg, and D. A. Keim, "An Efficient Approach to Clustering in Large Multimedia Databases with Noise", In *Proc. 1998 Int. Conf. Knowledge Discovery and Data Mining (KDD'98)*, 1998, pp. 58–65.

[12] A. Hinneburg, and D. A. Keim, "Optimal Grid-Clustering: Towards Breaking the Curse of Dimensionality in High-Dimensional Clustering", In *Proc. 25th Int. Conf. on Very Large Data Bases (VLDB'99)*, 1999, pp. 506–517.

[13] L. Kaufman, and P. J. Rousseeuw, *Finding Groups in Data: An Introduction to Cluster Analysis*, John Wiley & Sons, New York, 1990.

[14] J. MacQueen, "Some Methods for Classification and Analysis of Multivariate Observations", In *Proc. 5th Berkeley Symp. Math. Statist, Prob. Vol. 1*, 1967, pp. 281–297.

[15] H. Nagesh, S. Goil, and A. Choudhary, "MAFIA: Efficient and Scalable Subspace Clustering for Very Large Data Sets", *Technical Report 9906-010*, Northwestern University, 1999.

[16] R. Ng, and J. Han," Efficient and Effective Clustering Method for Spatial Data Mining", In *Proc. 1994 Int. Conf. on Very Large Data Bases (VLDB'94)*, 1994, pp. 144–155.

[17] D. W. Scott, *Multivariate Density Estimation*, John Wiley & Sons, New York, 1979.

[18] G. Sheikholeslami, S. Chatterjee, and A. Zhang, "WaveCluster: A Multi-Resolution Clustering Approach for Very Large Spatial Databases", In *Proc. 1998 Int. Conf. on Very Large Data Bases (VLDB'98)*, 1998, pp. 428–439.

[19] M. P. Wand, "Data-Based Choice of Histogram Bin Width", *The American Statistician Vol. 51*, 1996, pp. 59–64.

[20] W. Wang, J. Yang, M. Muntz, "STING: A Statistical Information Grid Approach to Spatial Data Mining", In *Proc. 1997 Int. Conf. on Very Large Data Bases (VLDB'97)*, 1997, pp. 186–195.

[21] T. Zhang, R. Ramakhrisnan, and M. Livny, "BIRCH: An efficient Data Clustering Method for Very Large Databases", In *Proc. 1996 ACM-SIGMOD Int. Conf. Management of Data (SIGMOD'96)*, 1996, pp. 103–114.

Employing Discrete Bayes Error rate for discretization and feature selection tasks

Ankush Mittal
Computer Science Dept.
National University of Singapore
Singapore 117543
Email: ankush@comp.nus.edu.sg

Loong-Fah Cheong
Electrical and Computer Engg. Dept.
National University of Singapore
Singapore 117576
Email: eleclf@nus.edu.sg

Abstract

The tasks of discretization and feature selection are frequently used to improve classification accuracy. In this paper, we use discrete approximation of Bayes error rate to perform discretization on the features. The discretization procedure targets minimization of Bayes error rate within each partition. A class-pair discriminatory measure can be defined on discretized partitions which forms the basis of feature selection algorithm. Small value of this measure for a class-pair indicates that the class-pair in consideration is confusing and the features which distinguish them well should be chosen first. A video classification problem on a large database is considered for showing the comparison of a classifier using our discretization and feature selection tasks with SVM, Neural network classifier, decision trees and K-Nearest neighbor classifier

1 Introduction

Many classification problems involve high-dimensional data because large feature vectors are generated to characterize the content. However, the amount of available data points could be limited in many practical situations. For a classifier the estimation of the class probability distributions in these sparsely sampled high-dimensional feature spaces is difficult task and it greatly affects the classification performance. To avoid these problems, discretization of feature space and dimensionality reduction are common sought solutions and can be considered as preprocessing of data (or " knowledge extraction") for the classification problem.

When descriptors have continuous values, the standard approach is to compute the conditional probability density by assuming that within each class, the values for a descriptor are normally distributed about some mean. However, Pazzani [10] showed that Gaussian assumption of numeric

data may lead to poor performance in many practical systems like electrical faults.

In order to maximize the utility of discretization and feature selection processes, we need to consider how they affect the performance of the Bayes classifier. Several popular approaches are not directly derived from Bayes error rate methodology, though they are indirectly related. In this paper, Discretely Approximated Bayes Error Rate (DABER) forms the explicit basis for the discretization algorithm and the dimensionality reduction process.

We chose to work on a video classification problem. Video classification is representative of a domain of tasks involving high dimensionality of the descriptor space and a large dissimilarity between the descriptors in their range and distribution. After providing an overview of the knowledge extraction process, Bayes Error rate is considered in section 3. The discretization algorithm is presented in section 4. Section 5 presents the dimensionality reduction algorithm. A simple probabilistic inference algorithm which is designed for comparison purpose is presented in section 6. Section 7 presents experiments and comparison results followed by conclusion in section 8.

2 Knowledge extraction

Figure 1 depicts the functionality of the knowledge extraction module during the two phases, the training phase and the querying phase. During the training phase, the descriptor vectors corresponding to all the classes are passed to the discretization algorithm (DABER) and the resulting partitions along with the corresponding probabilities of the classes form the input to the dimensionality reduction algorithm (CpDDR). By employing discretized partitions, CpDDR can make an effective decision in selecting the dimension set, $\mathcal{F}$, which can distinguish one class against another. During the querying phase in which the instantiation of the inference network and the subsequent evaluation have

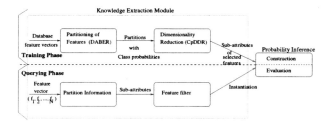

Figure 1. Knowledge extraction module

to take place, the partitions (i.e., attributes) corresponding to each of the selected dimensions, $s_f \in \mathcal{F}$, are passed to the inference module.

3 Bayes Error rate

Let π_i denote the *a priori* class probability of video class i, $1 \leq i \leq |V|$, and $p(\mathbf{s} \mid v_i)$ be the conditional probability density of $\mathbf{s}$, the descriptor vector for a video segment, given that it belongs to class i. $|V|$ is the number of video classes. $p(\mathbf{s})$, the probability distribution function of $\mathbf{s}$, is given by: $\sum_{i=1}^{|V|} p(\mathbf{s} \mid v_i)\pi_i$. The Bayes error which is associated with Bayes classifier is given by [6]:

$$E_{\mathbf{s}} = \int_R [\, 1 - \max_i p(v_i \mid \mathbf{s}) \,]\ p(\mathbf{s})d\mathbf{s} \qquad (1)$$

where R is the descriptor space and $p(v_i \mid \mathbf{s})$ is the *a posteriori* probability of class v_i, i = 1,2,3,...,$|V|$.

Evaluating the Bayes error, $E_{\mathbf{s}}$, might entail the complexity of evaluating the multi-dimensional integral of unknown multivariate functions and therefore, in practice the Bayes error can be computed directly only for a limited number of problems. Approximations and bounds on the Bayes error are instead commonly calculated. In [12], the outputs of various classifiers are used to calculate the upper and the lower bounds on the Bayes error rate.

In our approach, the partitioning process iterates on each dimension. Let at particular time instant, t, of the process, there be $N_p^j(t)$ partitions of dimension $s_j \in \mathbf{s}$. Consider any arbitrary partition l resulting from the discretization process. This partition might contain data points from more than one class. Let $m(l)$ be the total number of data points of all classes in the partition l and $m(i \mid l)$ be the total data points from class i in the partition l.

The Bayes error rate corresponding to dimension s_j alone is given by

$$E_{s_j} = \int_{R_j} [\, 1 - \max_i p(v_i \mid s_j) \,]\ p(s_j)ds_j \qquad (2)$$

where $p(v_i \mid s_j)$ is the *a posteriori* probability of class v_i and can be approximated to $m(i \mid l)/m(l)$ for l^{th} partition of dimension s_j. Using $ds_j \cong \triangle s_j$, the probability distribution

of dimension can be written as

$$p(s_j) \cong \frac{\mathrm{m}(l)}{[\sum_{l=1}^{N_p^j(t)} \mathrm{m}(l)] \times \triangle s_j} \qquad (3)$$

This assumes that in a partition, the feature points are uniformly distributed. In general, we could try to estimate the probability distribution within each partition using the mixture of Gaussian distributions. However, it is complicated and computationally expensive task. E_{s_j} can be, therefore, written as:

$$E_{s_j} \cong \sum_{l=1}^{N_p^j(t)} [1 - \max_i m(i \mid l)/m(l)] \times \frac{\mathrm{m}(l)\triangle s_j}{[\sum_{l=1}^{N_p^j(t)} \mathrm{m}(l)] \times \triangle s_j} \qquad (4)$$

This equation implies that the Bayes error would be less if the partition contains most of the sample points from one of the classes. The discrete approximated Bayes error $E_{s_j}^l$ for partition l alone can be written as:

$$E_{s_j}^l \cong \frac{1}{\sum_{k=1}^{N_p^j(t)} \mathrm{m}(k)}[m(l) - \max_i m(i \mid l)] = DABER_j^l \qquad (5)$$

4 Discretization Algorithm

The DABER algorithm is described below in detail.

DABER Algorithm

Formation Phase :
```
while (some-dimensions-left) {
  choose one of the unprocessed dimension s_j;
  sort_on_dimension(data,s_j);   /* Sort data on s_j */
    /* start forming a new partition l */
  while (Upper_limit(l) < maximum_value(s_j,data) {
    if (DABER_j^l > θ_err)   /* discriminability is poor */
    if (density(l) > ρ )
    { Pt_opt = Find-optimum-DABER-point(l);
      divide_the_partition(l, Pt_opt);
        /* Divide at optimum point */
      Set_Lower_limit(l) = Pt_opt; }
        /* Start growing from optimal point */
    Upper_limit(l) = Upper_limit(l) + step_increment; }
  If (number_of_partitions(s_j) > τ) discard_dimension(s_j) ;
      /* Case of irrelevant dimension */
}   /* Take another dimension */
Merging Phase :
  if combined_DABER(l1,l2) < ϑ   /*  ϑ > θ_err  */
    merge_partitions(l1,l2);
```

The DABER algorithm discretizes the data on each of the dimension s_j separately in two phases: Formation phase and merging phase. In formation phase, first the data is sorted on s_j. An expanding window that starts from minimum value of s_j is then considered. The window expands in direction of increasing value of dimension s_j in steps of *step_increment*. A partition is formed when DABER value falls below a threshold θ_{err} and the partition density is greater than ρ threshold. An optimal point for the partition is found iteratively on all the dimension value in the partition by minimizing the sum of the two partitions that would result from choosing that point. The partition is formed with the lower limit set to the least value of the expanding window and the upper value set to the optimal point. Expanding window then considers all points above optimum value for possibility of new partition and the process repeats till the maximum value points are considered. Large number of partitions could serve as an indication that there is a large overlap between the probability distributions of classes and therefore, the dimension is not useful. The merging phase serves to refine the partitions in second pass. Adjacent partitions are combined with the resulting partition has DABER value below threshold ϑ. Let $|s|$ be the number of features and t be the number of training samples, then it can be seen that DABER algorithm is $O(|s|\,[t\log(t) + t^2])$, i.e., $O(|s|\,t^2)$.

The DABER threshold, θ_{err}, and the density threshold, ρ, control the number of discretized dimensions (i.e., attributes). On increasing the value of θ_{err} or alternatively on decreasing ρ, the number of partitions can be increased. DABER algorithm constructs a set of hyperrectangular parallelepiped partitions such that the faces are perpendicular to the dimension axes and located at the maxima and minima of the samples in the partition.

Corresponding to the above algorithm, the probability distribution of the classes over the partitions of a chosen dimension of histogram descriptor is depicted in figure 2. The X-axis is marked by the partitions 1 to 10 while the classes (1 to 9) are marked on the Y-axis. Thus, a class distribution along the partitions can be determined by viewing parallel to the X-axis from the mark of the class. A significant number of partitions have only a few of the classes as the most dominant classes. For example, partition 1 has class 2 as the distinctly prominent class and similarly partition 10 has class 3 as the prominent class. Still there is ambiguity in making clear decision on the basis of one dimension.

5 Dimensionality reduction

Some of the well known feature selection algorithms have limitations in their application in the domain of video classification. FOCUS [1] is intractable in data mining applications with thousands or even hundreds of 'features' because it selects the minimal subset of 'features' by exhaustively examining all the subsets of 'features'. PRESET [8] works only in a noise-free domain. We devise a class-pair distinctive 'feature' selection which is efficient in compu-

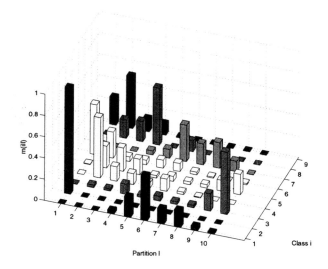

Figure 2. The probability distribution $m(i|l)$ of class i on a single dimension of histogram descriptor partition l using DABER algorithm. For example, for partition number 10, conditional probability of class 3 is around 0.6 and of class 4 is 0.2. The description of the descriptor and the set of classes is given in section 7

tation even for a large data and can work on noisy data as well.

5.1 Relationship of dimensionality reduction with Bayes error

Let us re-visit the basics of 'feature selection' process that is specifically employed to improve the classification accuracy. We would consider the "best" classifier (from the theoretical standpoint), the Bayesian classifier. If the cost of all types of correct classification is zero and the cost of all types of incorrect classification is one, the optimal Bayes decision rule assigns the sample to the class with the highest *a posteriori* probability. Thus, the Bayes risk associated with a given dimension set $\mathbf{s}$ reduces to the probability of error, $E_{\mathbf{s}}$, which was defined in equation (1). In order to minimize the classifier error rate, the most appealing function to evaluate the potency of a dimension to differentiate between the classes is the $E_{\mathbf{s}}$ function (see chapter 5 of [4]). A brute force method to select best the dimensions using $E_{\mathbf{s}}$ function would be to select combination with minimum classification error amongst $2^n - 1$ combinations of all dimensions. Therefore, the $E_{\mathbf{s}}$ function has not been used in practical applications because of its computational complexity; instead other measures for class separability were sought such as Bhattacharya distance, Matusita distance, Patrick-Fisher distance, and Shannon measure [2]. Note that all these measures are related to the E_s function as they provide an upper bound to the error probability. However, they are not ideal as they are not directly derived from the expression of classification error. Besides, the reliability of a separability measure depends on how tightly it bounds the error probability. Thus, we would like to employ a measure directly related from the E_s. Let us illustrate the strength and weakness of E_s function as a criteria for dimensionality reduction.

Consider a classification problem with four video classes $(v_1, ..., v_4)$ and five binary dimensions (or, in this case, attributes) $(s_1, ..., s_5)$ as presented in Table 1. The entries in the table represent the respective conditional probabilities for the presence of the attribute given the classes. If the prior probability of all the classes is equal to 0.25, the E_s values for all the attributes are given in Table 2 using equation (1) for discrete case (i.e., attribute value is 0/1). An attribute s_i is preferred to s_j if $E_{s_i} < E_{s_j}$. Thus, the attribute s_2 is preferred over all other attributes. Suppose, if s_2 is selected and it becomes active (i.e., $s_2 = 1$), then the approximate *a posteriori* probabilities for the four classes are: $P(v_1 \mid s_2) = 0.5$, $P(v_2 \mid s_2) = 0.25$, $P(v_3 \mid s_2) = 0.25$ and $P(v_4 \mid s_2) = 0.005$. In other words, the likelihood of class v_1 is doubled, while class v_4 is virtually eliminated. On the other hand, if s_4 is selected, the posterior probabilities of all the classes remain the same as the priors regardless of the results observed for s_4. Thus, the E_s rule is a good measure of how much a dimension contribute to differentiating amongst the classes.

Though the individual merit of a dimension can be assessed by the E_s rule, the selection of a group of dimensions for reducing the overall error is not straightforward. For example, if s_2 and s_3 are both selected, they both have almost the same discrimination characteristics (i.e., the ability to distinguish class v_1 against all other classes especially class v_4). It can be seen from this example that a good set of dimensions should discriminate every class from other classes or in other words, they should reduce the overlapping between the class probabilities.

5.2 The Algorithm

In the two-class case, the error rate in equation (1) can be expressed as:

$$E_s = \frac{1}{2}[1 - \int_R \mid p(s \mid v_1)\pi_1 - p(s \mid v_2)\pi_2 \mid ds] \quad (6)$$

where π_i is the prior probability of class v_i. The integral in the above equation is known as the Kolmogorov distance [11] which is theoretically a sound distance measure as compared to the other measures.

Classes \ Attribute (0/1)	s_1	s_2	s_3	s_4	s_5
v_1	0.75	0.90	0.92	0.40	0.10
v_2	0.10	0.45	0.52	0.40	0.90
v_3	0.80	0.45	0.60	0.40	0.75
v_4	0.85	0.01	0.05	0.40	0.80

Table 1. Classification problem to illustrate the working of E_s measure

Feature	s_2	s_3	s_5	s_1	s_4
E_{s_j}	0.52	0.53	0.55	0.56	0.75

Table 2. The ordering of the attributes using E_s function

To derive discriminatory measure, we consider Kolgomorov distance KD^{s_f} for a dimension s_f for discrete case (from equation (6) considering two-class (v_i, v_j) case):

$$KD^{s_f} = \sum_{l=1}^{N_p^f} \mid p(s_f^l \mid v_i)\pi_i - p(s_f^l \mid v_j)\pi_j \mid \quad (7)$$

where N_p^f is the number of partitions of the dimension s_f. The conditional probability density $p(s_f^l \mid v_i)$ for a partition l of a feature s_f is the probability of a sample belonging to class v_i in partition l and is given by

$$p(s_f^l \mid v_i) = \frac{m(i \mid l)}{\sum_{l=1}^{N_p^f} m(i \mid l)} \quad (8)$$

The discriminatory capacity $\mid P_{ij}^{s_f} \mid$ of a dimension s_f for the class pair (v_i, v_j) is simply KD^{s_f}. If the prior probabilities of all the classes are equal (i.e., there are equal training samples for the video classes), $\mid P_{ij}^{s_f} \mid$ can be written as:

$$\mid P_{ij}^{s_f} \mid = \sum_{l=1}^{N_p^f} \frac{\mid p(s_f^l \mid v_i) - p(s_f^l \mid v_j) \mid}{2} \quad (9)$$

Note that the discriminatory capacity $\mid P_{ij}^{s_f} \mid$ is a relative measure that lies between 0 and 1. A high value of $\mid P_{ij}^{s_f} \mid$ signifies that dimension s_f can distinguish well class v_i samples and class v_j samples.

Next, the Class-Pair Discrimination Measure $(CPDM_{ij})$ for each class pair (v_i, v_j) is evaluated by summing $\mid P_{ij}^f \mid$ over each dimension f, where f $\in$ s, as shown below:

$$CPDM_{ij} = \frac{1}{|\mathbf{s}|} \sum_{f=1}^{|\mathbf{s}|} |P_{ij}^{f}| \qquad (10)$$

A high value of $CPDM_{ij}$ indicates the relative ease of classifying the pair (v_i, v_j). Such a class pair is called a 'highly separable' class pair. All class pairs $(v_i, v_j), 1 \leq$ i,j $\leq |V|$, i $\neq$ j, are sorted according to the magnitude of $CPDM_{ij}$. The class pair (v_i, v_j) with minimum CPDM and those not yet covered are first examined to ensure that the dimensions which distinguish 'less-separable' class pair are first chosen. The α dimensions which have maximum discriminatory capacity $|P_{ij}^{sf}|$ in the class pair (v_i, v_j) are selected amongst the best γ $(\geq \alpha)$ dimensions.

CpDDR Algorithm
while (any-class_pair-unprocessed) {
    choose_class_pair(v_i, v_j) ; /* i $\neq$ j */
    $CPDM_{ij}$ = calculate_CPDM(v_i, v_j)
    /* Calculate using Eq. 10 */
    mark_class-pair_processed(v_i, v_j) }
/* Sort CPDM in non-descending order */
$CPDM_{sorted}$ = sort_order(CPDM);
    /* $CPDM_{sorted}$ is an array */
while (all_pairs_covered($CPDM_{sorted}$) ==FALSE)
    Take-the-next-uncovered-pair-in-order(v_i, v_j) {
/* Sort the dimensions index(f) on value of $|P_{ij}^{sf}|$ */
    SORTED_F_ARRAY = sort_dimension_index(i,j);
    /* Choose the α dimensions with highest $|P_{ij}^{sf}|$ */
    chosen_SET = chosen_SET $\cup$
        choose_α(SORTED_F_ARRAY)
    } /* Take another pair */
OUTPUT(chosen_SET)

The algorithm first computes the $CPDM_{ij}$ values for all class pairs. In each step, the least separable class pair (v_i, v_j) is chosen amongst the class pairs that are not yet considered. Next, all the dimensions are sorted based on their discriminatory capacity. Next step is to select α dimensions with highest discriminatory capacity (and include them in output set of features). These α dimensions best discriminate the least separable class pair (v_i, v_j). In our experiments with nine classes and 593 dimensions, the above algorithm selected 59 dimensions. For experimentation, when the number of dimensions were reduced to 59, the algorithm selected 29 dimensions.

Notice that even class separability measures like Bhattacharya, Mitusita etc. are for two-classes and an extension to multiple class requires separate formulation. A common strategy [4] is to calculate the overall discrimination power $D(\mathbf{s})$ of a dimension $\mathbf{s}$ by summing the distance $d_{ij}(\mathbf{s})$ be-

tween the two classes as follows:

$$D(\mathbf{s}) = \sum_i \sum_j \pi_i \pi_j d_{ij}(\mathbf{s}) \qquad (11)$$

However, the major disadvantage of this approach is that one large value of $d_{ij}(\mathbf{s})$ may dominate the value for $D(\mathbf{s})$ and impose a ranking that reflects only the distance between the most separable class pair.

Item	Value
Mean IACV of all features	0.21
Mean IACV of selected features (CpDDR)	0.26
Mean IACV of features selected by IACV algorithm	0.003
Number of features common in CpDDR and IACV algorithm	7 (12 %)
Number of CpDDR selected features which have IACV more than mean	43 (73 %)

Figure 3. CpDDR Vs. IACV Algorithm. The total number of dimension were 593. The threshold for IACV algorithm was kept such that it selected the same number of dimensions as CpDDR.

5.3 Comparison with two common approaches

Our approach to dimensionality reduction is superior to the standard statistical methods using measures like intra-class variation, inter-class variation or correlation etc. to differentiate how well the dimensions differentiate between the classes. Generally, the dimensions are rejected if their intra-class variation is above a given threshold or their inter-class variation is below a given threshold. Additionally, correlated dimensions can be eliminated from the selection set.

Figure 3 makes the comparison between the IACV algorithm with $\omega = 59$ (the number of dimensions selected by CpDDR) and CpDDR. It is interesting to note that the mean IACV of dimensions selected by CpDDR i.e. 0.26 is even higher than the mean IACV of all dimensions i.e. 0.21. Only 12% of the dimensions are common in the two algorithms. The difference in the functioning of the two algorithms can be explained as follows: the IACV algorithm is based on selecting the dimensions which have the

Item	Value
Mean IRCV of all features	42.42
Mean IRCV of selected features (CpDDR)	68.66
Mean IRCV of features selected by IRCV algorithm	83.6
Number of features common in CpDDR and IRCV algorithm	31 (53%)
Number of CpDDR selected features which have IRCV less than mean	7 (11%)

Figure 4. CpDDR Vs. IRCV Algorithm.

least scatter of data *around one cluster* within each class while CpDDR is based on selecting dimensions which have minimum overlap within the class pairs and thus highest discriminability. The distribution of data (see our previous work [7]) shows that although the data is distributed in the clusters for classes, each class might have several of such cliques. Secondly, IACV makes no reference to the distribution of data of another class.

Figure 4 presents the comparison between CpDDR and IRCV. We found that the mean of CpDDR selected dimensions i.e. 68.66 is significantly higher than the mean IRCV of all dimensions, i.e., 42.42. The number of common dimensions selected by both algorithms is 53%. This shows that the dimensions selected by CpDDR have high IRCV values, in general.

However, there are two significant advantages of the CpDDR over the IRCV algorithm: a) The set of dimensions selected by CpDDR necessarily has dimensions to distinguish every class-pair, which is not the case in IRCV. The IRCV algorithm may choose dimensions which may distinguish only a few class pairs. b) IRCV is based on the 'one cluster for one class' assumption. The CpDDR, on the other hand, is more generic for it can work with multi-modal distribution without making *a priori* assumption about the data.

Fisher's Discriminant Analysis (FDA) [4] approach is based on both maximizing the between-class scatter and minimizing the within-class scatter of the selected features. However, FDA does not have a direct relationship to the probability of error for the Bayes classifier, which is the optimum measure of feature effectiveness. Secondly, in case of higher dimension problems such as in CBR systems, use

of FDA is not suitable as regardless of the dimension of the original patterns, the FDA transforms a pattern vector onto a feature vector, whose dimension can be at most $|V| - 1$, where $|V|$ is the number of classes [5]. Besides, within-class scatter and between-class scatter are difficult to compute effectively when the class patterns are distributed in cliques.

6 Inference

Let the relation $C \subseteq V \times \mathbf{s}$ represent the pairwise causal associations between Video classes V and dimension values. Video class v_i giving rise to dimension value s_f corresponds to a link in the graph. A subset of $\mathbf{s}$, denoted $\mathbf{s}^+$, represents the set of all dimension values that are present, while $\mathbf{s}^- = \mathbf{s} - \mathbf{s}^+$ represents the set of dimension values assumed to be absent. Each causal link between a video class v_i and a dimension value s_f is associated with a number $c_{if} \in (0,1]$, called causal strength from v_i to s_f, representing how frequently v_i causes s_f. In other words, $c_{if} = P(v_i$ causes $s_f \mid v_i)$.

Let dimension s_f be partitioned into N_p^f sub-dimensions (or attributes), s_{f_k} for $1 < k < N_p^f$. After the execution of the DABER discretizing algorithm, each partition(s_{f_k}) of a dimension can be considered as a Boolean variable. At a particular instance, one and only one of the attributes, denoted by $s_{f_k}^\tau$, will have the status of being present (i.e. True). The link probabilities are also redefined as c_{if_k} denoting the causal strength from v_i to attribute s_{f_k}. Similarly, after partitioning, $\mathbf{s}^+{}_k$ refers to the set of all $s_{f_k}^\tau$ present and $\mathbf{s}^-{}_k$ refers to the set of other attributes (i.e. those which are not present).

If we let v_t, $v_t \in V$, be interpreted as the class that is present, a relative likelihood measure for a label v_t given $\mathbf{s}^+$ can be written as

$$L(v_t, \mathbf{s}^+) = \frac{\pi_t}{1 - \pi_t} \prod_{s_{f_k} \in \mathbf{s}^+} c_{tf_k} \prod_{s_{l_k} \in \mathbf{s}^-} (1 - c_{tl_k}) \quad (12)$$

The video segment is labeled by one of the video class v_{max} with the highest likelihood measure L_{max}.

7 Experiments and comparison

The descriptors which we use in our work are given in Table 3. The details of these descriptors can be found in MPEG-7 documentation [9]. The nine video classes considered were: basketball, educational, MTV, News, Soccer, swimming, tennis, table tennis and volleyball. The sequences were recorded from TV using VCR and grabbed in MPEG format. The size of the training database was 3600 sequences each with frame dimension 352×288. The size of the test database was 900 sequences comprising of an equal number of sequences for each class.

Descriptor	Dimension
Region shape	36
HomoTexture	62
GoF Color	96
Color Layout	12
Color structure	128
Edge Histogram	80
Average Color	3
Histogram Color	32*3
Motion	16
Intensity Variation	16*3
Feature Density	16
Total	**593**

Table 3. Set of descriptors used

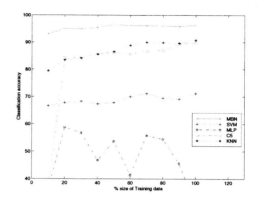

Figure 5. Performance with varying size of training data. The number of classes was 9 and the dimensions was fixed at 593.

Some of the most well known decision tree algorithms are C4.5 and its improved successor C5[1]. The application of SVM to a domain of more than two target classes is still in the development phase; however we use SVMTorch[2] C++ package [3] where $|V|$ SVM models are generated where V is the set of classes. In neural networks, a feedforward back-propagation network was used with two hidden layers consisting of 150 neurons and 100 neurons. The training function used was the resilient backpropagation ('trainrp'). It is one of the best learning functions for classification problems, is not sensitive to the fine settings of training parameters and converges faster than other functions.

For the purpose of comparing performance, two sets of experiment were done under these conditions: a) with varying size of the training data b) with varying number of dimensions. Type (a) experiment evaluates the generalization properties of the classification approach in relation to the non-linear input-output mapping while type (b) experiment demonstrates the effect of dimensionality on the performance.

Figure 5 illustrates the comparison of the percentage classification accuracy on type (a) experiment. The number of dimensions kept for this experiment set was 593 and the size of training data was varied by randomly selecting equal percentage of sequences for each class. Our approach is denoted as MBN and backpropogation networks as MLP. MBN has overall best performance, whereas KNN is the second best. It is interesting to note that the MBN performance is above 90% even with 10% of training samples, when the dimension space is relatively sparse. While in other methods, exact values are used, in MBN approach a partition is the basic unit of representation, which can provide good approximation when query point lies in the vicinity of the exact point. The second best performance of

KNN could be attributed to the strategy of working in local regions as opposed to estimating some parameters for the entire descriptor space. However, in KNN the boundaries are not so well defined as in MBN and therefore the boundary points are misclassified. Besides, in MBN, only meaningful dimensions are employed for inference.

Figure 6 shows the classification accuracy of the various tools for varying number of dimensions. The number of dimensions selected in MBN and its accuracy are also shown. The strategy in selecting dimensions were to select equal number of dimensions, as much as possible, from the descriptors in Table 3. With 10 dimensions only, the best performance was that of MBN and KNN (90%). It is noteworthy to observe that increasing the number of dimensions from 5 to 20 results in better performance by most of the tools and it appears that with a very few dimensions, information on distinction between the classes was less. The distinction achieved by a large number of dimensions shows the effectiveness of local feature extraction over the global one. On increasing the number of dimensions to more than 20, MBN gets sufficient meaningful dimensions and its performance is consistently more than 93%. A point to note in the experiment is that an optimization was performed for C5, SVM, ANN and KNN at 100% training data and 100% dimensions and thus we do not see the effect of 'curse of dimensionality'.

8 Conclusion

This paper presents an approach where Bayes error rate is directly used in discretization and feature selection tasks. Initial results with a simple probabilistic classifier using these two tasks as preprocesses gave good results as compared to some state-of-the-art classifiers. Theoretical is-

---

[1] http://www.rulequest.com/see5-unix.html

[2] http://www.idiap.ch/learning/SVMTorch.html

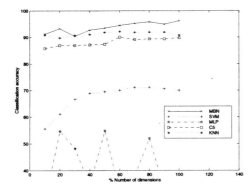

Figure 6. Performance with varying number of dimensions

sues with employing Bayes error in optimal manner (perhaps better than DABER algorithm and CpDDR algorithm), using/modifying DABER algorithm and CpDDR algorithm for other classification tools etc. are still open.

Acknowledgment

The first author is greatly indebted to his guide for reviving the inspiration to take this project seriously and dedicatedly.

References

[1] H. Almuallim and T. G. Dietterich. Learning boolean concepts in the presence of many irrelevant features. *Artificial Intelligence*, pages 279–305, vol.69, 1994.

[2] M. B. Bassat. Use of distance measures, information measures and error bounds in feature evaluation. *Handbook of Statistics, Krishnaiah and Kanal, eds.*, pages 773–791, 1982.

[3] R. Collobert and S. Bengio. SVMTorch: Support vector machines for large-scale regression problems. *Journal of machine learning research*, pages 143–160, vol. 1, 2001.

[4] P. J. Devijver and J. Kittler. Pattern recognition: A statistical approach. 1982.

[5] K. Fukunaga. Introduction to statistical pattern recognition. *Academic press*, 1990.

[6] F. Garber and A. Djouadi. Bounds on the Bayes classification error based on pairwise risk functions. *IEEE transactions on PAMI, vol. 10*, pages 281–288, 1988.

[7] A. Mittal and L.-F. Cheong. Techniques for designing a classifier for multimedia indexing. *SPIE Conference on storage and retrieval for multimedia databases*, pages 107–117, vol. 4315, 2001.

[8] M. Modrzejewski. Selection using rough sets theory. *European conference on Machine learning*, pages 213–226, 1993.

[9] I. J. C. of Moving pictures and audio. Overview of the MPEG-7 standard. *International organization for standarisation*, October 2000.

[10] M. Pazzani. An interative improvement approach for the discretization of numeric attributes in Bayesian classifiers. *KDD*, pages 228–233, 1995.

[11] V. I. Smirnov and A. M. Tikheyeva. The connection between the Bayesian risk and the Kolmogorov distance and a modification of it in recognition problems. *Engineering Cybernetics*, pages 147–150, vol. 15, 1977.

[12] K. Tumer and J. Ghosh. Estimating the Bayes error rate through classifier combining. *International Conference on Pattern recognition*, pages 695–699, 1996.

Feature Selection Algorithms: A Survey and Experimental Evaluation

Luis Carlos Molina, Lluís Belanche, Àngela Nebot
Universitat Politècnica de Catalunya
Departament de Llenguatges i Sistemes Informátics
Jordi Girona 1-3, C6, 08034, Barcelona, Spain.
{lcmolina,belanche,angela}@lsi.upc.es

Abstract

In view of the substantial number of existing feature selection algorithms, the need arises to count on criteria that enables to adequately decide which algorithm to use in certain situations. This work assesses the performance of several fundamental algorithms found in the literature in a controlled scenario. A scoring measure ranks the algorithms by taking into account the amount of relevance, irrelevance and redundance on sample data sets. This measure computes the degree of matching between the output given by the algorithm and the known optimal solution. Sample size effects are also studied.

1 Introduction

The feature selection problem in terms of supervised inductive learning is: given a set of candidate features select a subset defined by one of three approaches: a) the subset with a specified size that optimizes an evaluation measure, b) the subset of smaller size that satisfies a certain restriction on the evaluation measure and c) the subset with the best commitment among its size and the value of its evaluation measure (general case). The generic purpose pursued is the improvement of the inductive learner, either in terms of learning speed, generalization capacity or simplicity of the representation. It is then possible to understand better the results obtained by the inducer, diminish its volume of storage, reduce the noise generated by irrelevant or redundant features and eliminate useless knowledge.

A feature selection algorithm (FSA) is a computational solution that is motivated by a certain definition of *relevance*. However, the relevance of a feature –as seen from the inductive learning perspective– may have several definitions depending on the objective that is looked for. An irrelevant feature is not useful for induction, but not all relevant features are necessarily useful for induction[5].

In this research, several fundamental algorithms found in the literature are studied to assess their performance in

a controlled scenario. To this end, a measure to evaluate FSAs is proposed that takes into account the particularities of relevance, irrelevance and redundance on the sample data set. This measure computes the degree of matching between the output given by a FSA and the known optimal solution. Sample size effects are also studied. The results illustrate the strong dependence on the particular conditions of the FSA used and on the amount of irrelevance and redundance in the data set description, relative to the total number of features. This should prevent the use of a single algorithm specially when there is poor knowledge available about the structure of the solution.

2 Algorithms for Feature Selection

A FSA should be seen as a computational approach to a definition of relevance, although in many cases these definitions are followed in a somewhat loose sense. For a review of such definitions, see [16].

2.1 Feature Selection Definition

Let X be the original set of features, with cardinality $|X| = n$. The *continuous* feature selection problem refers to the assignment of weights w_i to each feature $x_i \in X$ in such a way that the order corresponding to its theoretical relevance is preserved. The *binary* feature selection problem refers to the assignment of binary weights. This can be carried out directly (like many FSAs in machine learning [4, 9]), or *filtering* the output of the continuous problem solution (see §4.1). These are quite different problems reflecting different design objectives. In the continuous case, one is interested in keeping all the features but in using them differentially in the learning process. On the contrary, in the binary case one is interested in keeping just a subset of the features and using them equally in the learning process.

The feature selection problem can be seen as a search in a hypothesis space (set of possible solutions). In the case of the binary problem, the number of potential subsets to evaluate is 2^n. In this case, a general definition is [13]:

306

Definition 1 (Feature Selection) *Let $J(X')$ be an evaluation measure to be optimized (say to maximize) defined as $J : X' \subseteq X \to \mathbb{R}$ The selection of a feature subset can be seen under three considerations:*

- *Set $|X'| = m < n$. Find $X' \subset X$, such that $J(X')$ is maximum.*
- *Set a value J_o, this is, the minimum J that is going to be tolerated. Find the $X' \subseteq X$ with smaller $|X'|$, such that $J(X') \geq J_o$.*
- *Find a compromise among minimizing $|X'|$ and maximizing $J(X')$ (general case).*

Notice that, with these definitions, an optimal subset of features is not necessarily unique.

2.2 Characterization of FSAs

There exist in the literature several considerations to characterize feature selection algorithms [3, 8, 14]. In view of them it is possible to describe this characterization as a search problem in the hypothesis space as follows:

- **Search Organization.** General strategy with which the space of hypothesis is explored. This strategy is in relation to the portion of hypothesis explored with respect to their total number.
- **Generation of Successors.** Mechanism by which possible variants (successor candidates) of the current hypothesis are proposed.
- **Evaluation Measure.** Function by which successor candidates are evaluated, allowing to *compare* different hypothesis to guide the search process.

2.2.1 Search Organization

A search algorithm is responsible for driving the feature selection process using a specific strategy. Each *state* in the search space specifies a *weighting* $w_1, \ldots, w_n$ of the possible features of X, with $|X| = n$. In the binary case, $w_i \in \{0, 1\}$, whereas in the continuous case $w_i \in [0, 1]$. Notice we are stating that relevance should be upper and lower bounded. Also in the binary case a partial order $\prec$ exists in the search space, with $S_1 \prec S_2$ if $S_1 \subset S_2$, whereas in the continuous case $S_1 \prec S_2$ if, for all i, $w_i(S_1) \leq w_i(S_2)$ holds. Being L a (labeled) list of weighed subsets of features (i.e. states), L maintains the (ordered) current list of solutions. The labels indicate the value of the evaluation measure. We consider three types of search: exponential, sequential and random. Most sequential algorithms are characterized by $|L| = 1$, whereas exponential and random ones typically use $|L| \geq 1$.

Exponential Search: It corresponds to algorithms that carry out searches whose cost is $O(2^n)$. The exhaustive search is an optimal search, in the sense that the best solution is guaranteed. An optimal search need not be exhaustive; for example, if an evaluation measure is *monotonic* a BRANCH AND BOUND[17] algorithm is optimal. A measure J is monotonic if for any two subsets S_1, S_2 and $S_1 \subseteq S_2$, then $J(S_1) \geq J(S_2)$. Another example would be an A^* search with an admissible heuristic[18].

Sequential Search: This sort of search selects one among all the successors to the current state. This is done in an iterative manner and once the state is selected it is not possible to go back. Although there is no explicit backtracking the number of such steps must be limited by $O(n)$ in order to qualify as a sequential search. The complexity is determined taking into account the number k of evaluated subsets in each state change. The cost of this search is therefore polynomial $O(n^{k+1})$. Consequently, these methods do not guarantee an optimal result, since the optimal solution could be in a region of the search space that is not visited.

Random Search: The idea underlying this type of search is to use its randomness to avoid the algorithm to stay on a local minimum and to allow temporarily moving to other states with worse solutions. These are *anytime* algorithms[14] and can give several optimal subsets as solution.

2.2.2 Generation of Successors

All of the operators act by modifying in some way the weights w_i of the features x_i, with $w_i \in \mathbb{R}$ (in the case of the *weighting* operator), or $w_i \in \{0, 1\}$ (for the rest).

Forward: Add features to the current solution X', among those that have not been selected yet. In each step, the feature that makes J be greater is added to the solution. Starting with $X' = \emptyset$, the *forward* step consists of:

$$X' := X' \cup \{x_i \in X \setminus X' \mid J(X' \cup \{x_i\}) \text{ is bigger}\} \quad (1)$$

The stopping criterion can be: $|X'| = n'$ (if n' has been fixed in advance), the value of J has not increased in the last j steps, or it surpasses a prefixed value J_0. The cost of the operator is $O(n)$. The main disadvantage is that it is not possible to have in consideration certain basic interactions among features. For example, if x_1, x_2 are such that $J(\{x_1, x_2\}) \gg J(\{x_1\}), J(\{x_2\})$, neither x_1 and x_2 could be selected, in spite of being very useful.

Backward: Remove features from the current solution X', among those that have not been removed yet. In each step, the feature that makes J be greater is removed from the solution. Starting with $X' = X$, the *backward* step is:

$$X' := X' \setminus \{x_i \in X' \mid J(X' \setminus \{x_i\}) \text{ is bigger}\} \quad (2)$$

The stopping criterion can be: $|X'| = n'$, the value of J has not increased in the last j steps, or it falls below a prefixed value J_0. This operator remedies some problems although there still will be many *hidden* interactions (in the sense of being unobtainable). The cost is $O(n)$, although in practice it demands more computation than *forward* [12].

Both operators (forward and backward) can be generalized selecting, at each step, subsets of k elements X'' and selecting the one making $J(X' \cup X'')$ or $J(X' \backslash X'')$ bigger, respectively. The cost of the operator is then $O(n^k)$.

Compound: Apply f consecutive forward steps *and* b consecutive backward ones. If $f > b$ the result is a forward operator, otherwise it is a backward one. An interesting approach is to perform the forward *or* the backward steps, depending on the respective values of J. This allows to discover new interactions among features. An interesting "backtracking mechanism" is obtained, although other stopping conditions should be established if $f = b$. For example, for $f = b = 1$, if x_i is added and x_j is removed, this could be undone in the following steps. A possible stopping criterion is $x_i = x_j$. In sequential FSA, $f \neq b$ assures a maximum of n steps, with a cost $O(n^{f+b+1})$.

Weighting: In the weighting operators, the search space is continuous, and all of the features are present in the solution to a certain degree. A successor state is a state with a different weighting. This is typically done by iteratively sampling the available set of instances.

Random: This group includes those operators that can potentially generate *any other* state in a single step. The rest of operators can also have random components, but they are restricted to some criterion of "advance" in the number of features or in improving the measure J at each step.

2.2.3 Evaluation Measures

Probability of error: Provided the ultimate goal is to build a classifier able of correctly labelling instances generated by the same probability distribution, minimizing the (bayesian) probability of error P_e of the classifier seems to be the most natural choice. Therefore, it is also a clear choice for J.

Let $\vec{x} \in \mathbb{R}^n$ represent the unlabeled instances, and $\Omega = \{\omega_1, \dots, \omega_m\}$ a set of labels (classes), so that $c : \mathbb{R}^n \to \Omega$. Such probability is defined as [7]:

$$P_e = \int [1 - \max_i P(\omega_i | \vec{x})] p(\vec{x}) d\vec{x} \quad (3)$$

where $p(\vec{x}) = \sum_{i=1}^m p(\vec{x}|\omega_i) P(\omega_i)$ is the (unconditional) probability distribution of the instances, and $P(\omega_i | \vec{x})$ is the *a posteriori* probability of ω_i being the class of $\vec{x}$.

Since the class-conditional densities are usually unknown, they can either be explicitly modeled (using parametric or non-parametric methods) or implicitly via the design of a classifier that builds the respective decision boundaries between the classes [7]. Some of these classifiers, like the one-nearest-neighbor rule, have a direct relation to the probability of error. This may require the use of more elaborate methods than a simple holdout procedure (cross validation, bootstrapping) in order to yield a more reliable value.

Divergence: These measures compute a probabilistic distance or *divergence* among the class-conditional probability densities $p(\vec{x}|\omega_i)$, using the general formula:

$$J = \int f[p(\vec{x}|\omega_1), p(\vec{x}|\omega_2)] d\vec{x} \quad (4)$$

To qualify as a valid measure, the function f must be such that the value of J satisfies the following conditions: (a) $J \geq 0$, (b) $J = 0$ only when the $p(\vec{x}|\omega_i)$ are equal and (c) J is maximum when they are non-overlapping. If the features used in a solution $X' \subset X$ are good ones, the divergence among the conditional probabilities will be significant. Poor features will result in very similar probabilities. Some classical choices are: Chernoff, Bhattacharyya, Kullback–Liebler, Kolmogorov and Matusita [7].

Dependence: These measures quantify how strongly two features are associated with one another, in the sense that knowing the value of one it is possible to predict the value of the other. In the context of feature selection, a feature is better evaluated the better it predicts the class.

Interclass distance: These measures are based on the assumption that instances of a different class are distant in the instance space. It is enough then to define a metric between classes and use it as measure:

$$D(\omega_i, \omega_j) = \frac{1}{N_i N_j} \sum_{k_1}^{N_i} \sum_{k_2 = k_1 + 1}^{N_j} d(x_{(i,k_1)}, x_{(j,k_2)}) \quad (5)$$

$$J = \sum_{i=1}^m P(\omega_i) \sum_{j=i+1}^m P(\omega_j) D(\omega_i, \omega_j) \quad (6)$$

being $x_{(i,j)}$ the instance j of class ω_i, and N_i the number of instances of the class ω_i. The most usual distances d belong to the Euclidean family. These measures do not require the modeling of any density function, but their relation to the probability of error can be very loose.

Information or Uncertainty: Similarly to the probabilistic dependence, we may observe $\vec{x}$ and compute the a posteriori probabilities $P(\omega_i | \vec{x})$ to determine how much information on the class of $\vec{x}$ has been gained, with respect to its prior probability. If all the classes become roughly equally probable, then the information gain is minimal and the uncertainty (entropy) is maximum.

Consistency: An *inconsistency* in X' and S is defined as two instances in S that are equal when considering only the features in X' and that belong to different classes. The aim is thus to find the *minimum* subset of features leading to zero inconsistencies [1]. The *inconsistency count* of an instance $A \in S$ is defined as [14]:

$$IC_{X'}(A) = X'(A) - \max_k X'_k(A) \quad (7)$$

where $X'(A)$ is the number of instances in S equal to A using only the features in X' and $X'_k(A)$ is the number of instances in S of class k equal to A using only the features in X'. The *inconsistency rate* of a feature subset in a sample S is then:

$$IR(X') = \frac{\sum_{A \in S} IC_{X'}(A)}{|S|} \quad (8)$$

This is a monotonic measure, in the sense

$$X_1 \subset X_2 \Rightarrow IR(X_1) \geq IR(X_2).$$

2.3 General Schemes for Feature Selection

The relationship between a FSA and the inducer chosen to evaluate the usefulness of the feature selection process can take three main forms: *embedded*, *filter* and *wrapper*.

Embedded Scheme: The inducer has its own FSA (either explicit or implicit). The methods to induce logical conjunctions[20] provide an example of this embedding. Other traditional machine learning tools like decision trees or artificial neural networks are included in this scheme[15].

Filter Scheme: If the feature selection process takes place before the induction step, the former can be seen as a filter of non-useful features prior to induction. In a general sense it can be seen as a particular case of the embedded scheme in which feature selection is used as a pre-processing. The filter schemes are independent of the induction algorithm.

Wrapper Scheme: In this scheme the relationship is taken the other way around: it is the FSA that uses the learning algorithm as a subroutine[11]. The general argument in favor of this scheme is to equal the bias of both the FSA and the learning algorithm that will be used later on to assess the goodness of the solution. The main disadvantage is the computational burden that comes from calling the induction algorithm to evaluate each subset of considered features.

2.4 General Algorithm for Feature Selection

An abstract algorithm that unifies the behavior of any FSA is depicted in Fig. 1. In particular, being L a (weighed) list of weighed subsets of features (i.e. states), L keeps the ordered set of solutions in course. Exponential algorithms are typically characterized by $|L| \geq 1$ (examples are BRANCH AND BOUND [17] or A^* [18]). The presence in the list is a function of the evaluation measure and defines the expansion order. Heuristic search algorithms also keep this list (of open nodes), and the weighting is the value of the heuristic. Random search methods as Evolutionary Algorithms [2] are characterized by $|L| \geq 1$ (the list is the population and the weighting is the fitness value of the individuals). Sequential algorithms maintain $|L| = 1$, though there are exceptions (e.g., a bidirectional algorithm [8] would use $|L| = 2$). The second weighting (on the features of each solution subset) allows to include the two types of FSA according to their outcome (see §2.1).

The initial list L is in general built out of the original set of features and the algorithm maintains the best solution at all times (*Solution*). At each step, a FSA with a given search organization manipulates the list in a specific way and calls its mechanism for the generation of successors which in turn uses J. The result is an updated list and the eventual update of the best solution found so far. Notice that the data sample S is considered global to the algorithm.

3 Empirical Evaluation of FSAs

The first question arising in relation to a feature selection experimental design is: what are the aspects that we would like to evaluate of a FSA solution in a given data set? In this study we decided to evaluate FSA performance with respect to four particularities: relevance, irrelevance, redundance and sample size. To this end, several fundamental FSAs are studied to assess their performance on synthetic data sets with known relevant features. Then sample data sets of different sizes are corrupted with irrelevant and/or redundant features. The experiments are designed to test the *endurance* of different FSAs (e.g., behaviour against the ratio number-of-irrelevant vs. number-of-relevant features).

3.1 Particularities to be evaluated

Relevance: Different families of problems are generated by varying the number of relevant features N_R. These are features that, by construction, have an influence on the output and whose role can not be assumed by the rest (i.e., there is no redundance).

Irrelevance: Irrelevant features are defined as those features not having any influence on the output, and whose values are generated at random for each example. For a problem with N_R relevant features, different numbers of irrelevant features N_I are added to the corresponding data sets (thus providing with several subproblems for each choice of N_R).

Redundance: In these experiments, a redundance exists whenever a feature can take the role of another (perhaps the simplest way to model redundance). This is obtained by choosing a relevant feature randomly and replicating it in the data set. For a problem with N_R relevant features, different numbers of redundant features $N_{R'}$ are added in a way analogous to the generation of irrelevant features.

```
Input:
    S  - data sample with features X, |X| = n
    J  - evaluation measure to be maximized
    GS - successor generation operator
Output:
    Solution - (weighed) feature subset

L := Start_Point(X);
Solution := { best of L according to J };
repeat
    L := Search_Strategy(L, GS(J), X);
    X' := { best of L according to J };
    if  J(X') ≥ J(Solution)  or  (J(X') = J(Solution)
            and  |X'| < |Solution|)
    then  Solution := X';
until  Stop(J, L)
```

Fig. 1. General Feature Selection Algorithm.

Sample Size: It refers to the number of instances $|S|$ of a data sample S. In these experiments, $|S|$ is defined as $|S| = \alpha k N_T c$, where α is a constant, k is a multiplying factor, N_T is the total number of features ($N_R + N_I + N_{R'}$) and c is the number of classes. Note this means that the sample size will depend linearly on the number of features.

3.2 Evaluation of Performance

The *score* criterion expresses the degree to which a solution obtained by a FSA matches the correct solution. This criterion behaves as a similarity $s(x, y) : X \times X \to [0, 1]$ in the classical sense [6], satisfying:

1. $s(x, y) = 1 \iff x = y$
2. $s(x, y) = s(y, x)$

where $s(x, y) > s(x, z)$ indicates that y is more similar to x than z. Let us denote by X the total set of features, partitioned in $X = X_R \cup X_I \cup X_{R'}$, being $X_R, X_I, X_{R'}$ the subsets of relevant, irrelevant and redundant features of X, respectively and call $X^* \subseteq X$ the ideal solution. Let us denote by $\mathcal{A}$ the feature subset selected by a FSA. The idea is to check how much $\mathcal{A}$ and X^* have in common. Let us define $\mathcal{A}_R = X_R \cap \mathcal{A}$, $\mathcal{A}_I = X_I \cap \mathcal{A}$ and $\mathcal{A}_{R'} = X_{R'} \cap \mathcal{A}$. In general, we have $\mathcal{A}_T = X_T \cap \mathcal{A}$ (hereafter T stands for a subindex in $\{R, I, R'\}$). Since necessarily $\mathcal{A} \subseteq X$, we have $\mathcal{A} = \mathcal{A}_R \cup \mathcal{A}_I \cup \mathcal{A}_{R'}$. The *score* $S_X(\mathcal{A}) : P(X) \to [0, 1]$ will fulfill the following conditions:

- $S_X(\mathcal{A}) = 0 \iff \mathcal{A} = X_I$
- $S_X(\mathcal{A}) = 1 \iff \mathcal{A} = X^*$
- $S_X(\mathcal{A}) > S_X(\mathcal{A}')$ indicates that $\mathcal{A}$ is more similar to X^* than $\mathcal{A}'$.

The score is defined in terms of the similarity in that for all $\mathcal{A} \subseteq X, S_X(\mathcal{A}) = s(\mathcal{A}, X^*)$. This scoring measure will also be parameterized, so that it can ponder each type of divergence (in relevance, irrelevance and redundance) to the optimal solution. The set of parameters is expressed as $\alpha = \{\alpha_R, \alpha_I, \alpha_{R'}\}$ with $\alpha_T \geq 0$ and $\sum \alpha_T = 1$.

Intuitive Description The criterion $S_X(\mathcal{A})$ penalizes three situations:

1. There are relevant features lacking in $\mathcal{A}$ (the solution is incomplete).
2. There are more than enough relevant features in $\mathcal{A}$ (the solution is redundant).
3. There are some irrelevant features in $\mathcal{A}$ (the solution is incorrect).

An order of importance and a weight will be assigned (via the α_T parameters), to each of these situations.

Formal Description

The precedent point (3.) is simple to model: if suffices to check whether $|\mathcal{A}_I| > 0$, being $\mathcal{A}$ the solution of the FSA. Relevance and redundance are strongly related given that, in this context, a feature is redundant or not depending on what other relevant features are present in $\mathcal{A}$.

Notice then that the optimal solution X^* is not unique, though all them should be equally valid for the *score*. To this end, the features are broken down in *equivalence classes*, where elements of the same class are redundant to each other (i.e., optimal solution must comprise only one feature of each equivalence class).

Being $\mathcal{A}$ a feature set, we define a binary relation between two features $x_i, x_j \in \mathcal{A}$ as: $x_i \sim x_j \iff x_i$ and x_j represent the same information. Clearly $\sim$ is an equivalence relation. Let $\mathcal{A}^\sim$ be the quotient set of $\mathcal{A}$ under $\sim$, $\mathcal{A}^\sim = \{[x] \mid x \in \mathcal{A}\}$, any optimal solution $\mathcal{A}^*$ will satisfy:

1. $|\mathcal{A}^*| = |X_R|$
2. $\forall [x_i] \in \mathcal{A}^\sim : \exists x_j \in [x_i] : x_j \in \mathcal{A}^*$

We denote by $\mathcal{A}^*$ *any* of these solutions.

Construction of the *score*

In the present case, the set to be split in equivalence classes is formed by all the relevant features (redundant or not) chosen by a FSA. We define then:

$$\mathcal{A}_{\tilde{R}} = (\mathcal{A}_R \cup \mathcal{A}_{R'})^\sim$$

(equivalence classes in which the relevant features chosen by a FSA are split)

$$X_{\tilde{R}} = (X_R \cup X_{R'})^\sim$$

(equivalence classes in which the original features are split)

Let $\mathcal{A}_{\tilde{R}} \uplus X_{\tilde{R}} = \{[x_i] \in X_{\tilde{R}} \mid \exists [x_j] \in \mathcal{A}_{\tilde{R}} : [x_j] \subseteq [x_i]\}$ and define, for Q quotient set:

$$F(Q) = \sum_{[x] \in Q} (|x| - 1)$$

The idea is to express the *quotient* between the number of redundant features chosen by the FSA and the number it could have chosen, given the relevant features present in its solution. In the precedent notation, this is written (provided the denominator is not null):

$$\frac{F(\mathcal{A}_{\tilde{R}})}{F(\mathcal{A}_{\tilde{R}} \uplus X_{\tilde{R}})}$$

Let us finally build the *score*, formed by three terms: relevance, irrelevance and redundance. Defining:

$$I = 1 - \frac{|\mathcal{A}_I|}{|X_I|}, \quad R = \frac{|\mathcal{A}_{\tilde{R}}|}{|X_R|}, \quad \text{with } \mathcal{A}_{\tilde{R}} = (\mathcal{A}_R \cup \mathcal{A}_{R'})^\sim$$

$$R' = \begin{cases} 0 & \text{if } F(\mathcal{A}_{\tilde{R}} \uplus X_{\tilde{R}}) = 0 \\ \frac{1}{|X_{R'}|} \left(1 - \frac{F(\mathcal{A}_{\tilde{R}})}{F(\mathcal{A}_{\tilde{R}} \uplus X_{\tilde{R}})}\right) & \text{otherwise.} \end{cases}$$

the score is $S_X(\mathcal{A}) = \alpha_R R + \alpha_{R'} R' + \alpha_I I, \mathcal{A} \subseteq X$.

Restrictions on the α_T

We can establish now the desired restrictions on the behavior of the score. From the more to the less severe: there are relevant features lacking, there are irrelevant features, and there is redundancy in the solution. This is reflected in the following conditions on the α_T:

1. Choosing an irrelevant feature is better than missing a relevant one: $\frac{\alpha_R}{|X_R|} > \frac{\alpha_I}{|X_I|}$

2. Choosing a redundant feature is better than choosing an irrelevant one: $\frac{\alpha_I}{|X_I|} > \frac{\alpha_{R'}}{|X_{R'}|}$

We also define $\alpha_T = 0$ if $|X_T| = 0$. Notice that the denominators are important for, as an example, expressing the fact that it is not the same choosing an irrelevant feature when there were only two that when there were three (in the latter case, there is an irrelevant feature that could have been chosen when it was not).

4 Experimental Evaluation

In this section we detail the experimental methodology and quantify the various parameters of the experiments. The basic idea consists on generating sample data sets with known particularities (synthetic functions f) and hand them over to the different FSAs to obtained a hypothesis H. The divergence between the defined function and the obtained hypothesis will be evaluated by the *score* criterion. This experimental design is illustrated in Fig. 2.

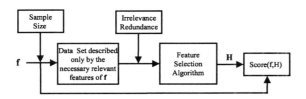

Figure 2. FlowChart of Experimental Design.

4.1 Description of the FSAs used

The ten FSAs used in the experiments were : E-SFG, QBB, LVF, LVI, C-SBG, RELIEF, SFBG, SFFG, W-SBG, and W-SFG (see Table 1). The algorithms E-SFG, W-SFG are versions of SFG using entropy and the accuracy of a C4.5 inducer, respectively. The algorithms C-SBG, W-SBG are versions of SBG using consistency and the accuracy of a C4.5 inducer, respectively. During the course of the experiments the algorithms FOCUS, B&B, ABB and LVW were put aside due to their unaffordable consumption of resources. For a review of all these algorithms, see [16].

Since RELIEF and E-SFG give as output an ordered list of features x_i according to their weight w_i, a filtering criterion is necessary to transform this solution to a subset of features. The procedure used here is simple: since the interest is in determining a good cut point, first those w_i further than two variances from the mean are discarded (that is to say, with very high or very low weights). Then define $s_i = w_i + w_{i-1}$ and $\sigma_j = \sum_{i=2}^{j} s_i$. The objective is to search for the feature x_j such that:

$$1 - \frac{\sigma_j}{\sigma_n}\frac{n-j}{n} \quad \text{is maximum.}$$

The cut point is then set between x_j and x_{j+1}.

Algorithm	Search Organization	Generation of Succesors	Evaluation Measure
LVF	Random	Random	Consistency
LVI	Random	Random	Consistency
QBB	Random/Expon.	Random/Backward	Consistency
RELIEF	Random	Weighting	Distance
C-SBG	Sequential	Backward	Consistency
E-SFG	Sequential	Forward	Entropy
SFBG	Exponential	Compound	Consistency
SFFG	Exponential	Compound	Consistency
W-SBG	Sequential	Backward	Accuracy(C4.5)
W-SFG	Sequential	Forward	Accuracy(C4.5)

Table 1. FSAs used in the experiments.

4.2 Implementations of Data Families

A total of twelve families of data sets were generated studying three different problems and four instances of each, by varying the number of relevant features N_R. Let $x_1, \ldots, x_n$ be the relevant features of a problem f.

Parity: This is the classic binary problem of parity n, where the output is $f(x_1, \cdots, x_n) = 1$ if the number of $x_i = 1$ is odd and $f(x_1, \cdots, x_n) = 0$ otherwise.

Disjunction: A disjunctive task, with $f(x_1, \cdots, x_n) = 1$ if $(x_1 \wedge \cdots \wedge x_{n'}) \vee (x_{n'+1} \wedge \cdots \wedge x_n)$, with $n' = n \, div \, 2$ if n is even and $n' = (n \, div \, 2) + 1$ if n is odd.

GMonks: This problem is a generalization of the classic *monks* problems [19]. In its original version, three independent problems were applied on sets of $n = 6$ features that take values of a discrete, finite and unordered set (nominal features). Here we have grouped the three problems in a single one computed on *each* segment of 6 features. Let n be multiple of 6, $k = n \, div \, 6$ and $b = 6(k' - 1) + 1$, for $1 \le k' \le k$. Let us denote for "1" the first value of a feature, for "2" the second, etc. The problems are the following:

1. $P1 : (x_b = x_{b+1}) \vee x_{b+4} = 1$
2. $P2 :$ two or more $x_i = 1$ in $x_b \cdots x_{b+5}$
3. $P3 : (x_{b+4} = 3 \wedge x_{b+3} = 1) \vee (x_{b+4} \neq 3 \wedge x_{b+1} \neq 2)$

For each segment, the boolean condition $P2 \wedge \neg(P1 \wedge P3)$ is checked. If this condition is satisfied for s or more segments with $s = n_s \, div \, 2$ (being n_s the number of segments) the function *GMonks* is 1; otherwise, it is 0.

4.3 Experimental Setup

The experiments were divided in three groups. The first group refers to the relationship between irrelevance vs. relevance. The second refers to the relationship between redundance vs. relevance. The last group refers to sample size. Each group uses three families of problems (*Parity, Disjunction* and *GMonks*) with four different instances for each problem, varying the number of relevant features N_R.

Relevance: The different numbers N_R vary for each problem, as follows: {4, 8, 16, 32} (for *Parity*), {5, 10, 15, 20} (for *Disjunction*) and {6, 12, 18, 24} (for *GMonks*).

Irrelevance: In these experiments, we have N_I running from 0 to 2 times the value of N_R, in intervals of 0.2 (that is, eleven different experiments of irrelevance for each N_R).

Redundance: Similarly to the generation of irrelevant features, we have $N_{R'}$ running from 0 to 2 times the value of N_R, in intervals of 0.2.

Sample Size: Given the formula $|S| = \alpha k N_T c$ (see §3.1), different problems were generated considering $k \in \{0.25, 0.5, 0.75, 1.0, 1.25, 1.75, 2.0\}$, $N_T = N_R + N_I + N_{R'}$, $c = 2$, $\alpha = 20$ and $N_I = N_{R'} = N_R \, div \, 2$.

4.4 Results

Due to space reasons, only a sample of the results are presented, in Figs. 3(a) and (b). Each point is the average of 10 independent runs with different random data samples. The horizontal axis represents the ratios between these particularities as explained above. The vertical axis represents the average results given by the score criterion.

In Fig. 3(a) the C-SBG algorithm shows at first a good performance but clearly as the irrelevance ratio increases, it falls dramatically (below the 0.5 level from $N_I = N_R$ on). Note that for $N_R = 4$ performance is always perfect (the plot is on top of the graphic). The plots in Fig. 3(b) show additional interesting results because we can appreciate the curse of dimensionality effect [10]. In this figure, W-SBG present an increasingly poor performance (see the figure from top to bottom) with the number of features provided the number of examples is increasing in a linear way. However, in general, as long as more examples are added performance is better (see the figure from left to right).

A summary of the results is displayed in Fig. 4 for the ten algorithms, allowing for a comparison across all the sample data sets with respect to each studied particularity. Specifically, Figs. 4(a), (b) and (c) show the average score of each algorithm for irrelevance, redundance and sample size, respectively. In each graphic there are two keys: the key to the left shows the algorithms ordered by *total* average performance, from top to bottom. The key to the right shows the algorithms ordered by average performance on the *last* abscissa value, also from top to bottom. In other words, the left list is topped by the algorithm that wins on average, while the right list is topped by the algorithm that ends on the lead. This is also useful to help reading the graphics.

Fig. 4(a) shows that RELIEF ends up on the lead of the irrelevance vs. relevance problems, while SFFG shows the best average performance. The algorithm W-SFG is also well positioned. Fig. 4(b) shows that the algorithms LVF and LVI together with C-SBG are the overall best. In fact, there is a bunch of algorithms that also includes the two *floating* and QBB showing a close performance. Note how RELIEF and the *wrappers* are very poor performers. Fig. 4(c) shows that the wrapper algorithms seem to be able to extract the most of the data when there is a shortage of it. Surprisingly,

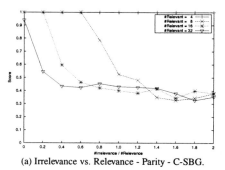

(a) Irrelevance vs. Relevance - Parity - C-SBG.

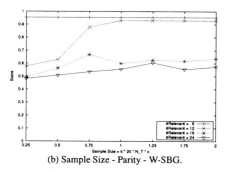

(b) Sample Size - Parity - W-SBG.

Figure 3. Some results to irrelevance, relevance and sample size.

the backward wrapper is just fairly positioned on average. The SFFG is again quite good on average, together with C-SBG. However, all of the algorithms are quite close and show the same kind of dependency to the data. Note the general poor performance of E-SFG, provided it is the only algorithm that computes its evaluation measure (entropy in this case) independently for each feature.

5 Conclusions

The task of a feature selection algorithm (FSA) is to provide with a computational solution to the feature selection problem motivated by a certain definition of *relevance*. This algorithm should be reliable and efficient. The many FSAs proposed in the literature are based on quite different principles (as the evaluation measure used, the precise way to explore the search space, etc) and loosely follow different definitions of relevance. In this work a way to evaluate FSAs was proposed in order to understand their general behaviour on the particularities of relevance, irrelevance, redundancy and sample size of synthetic data sets. To achieve this goal, a set of controlled experiments using artificially generated data sets were designed and carried out. The set of optimal solutions is then compared with the output given by the FSAs (the obtained hypotheses). To this end, a *scoring* measure was defined to express the degree of approximation of

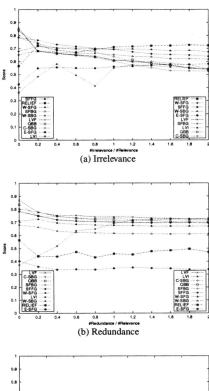

(a) Irrelevance

(b) Redundance

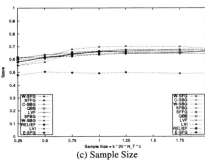

(c) Sample Size

Figure 4. Results ordered by total average performance on the data sets (left inset) and by end performance (right inset).

the FSA solution to the real solution. The final outcome of the experiments can be seen as an illustrative step towards gaining useful knowledge that enables to decide which algorithm to use in certain situations. The behaviour of the algorithms to different data particularities is shown and thus the danger in relying in a single algorithm. This points in the direction of using new hybrid algorithms or combinations thereof for a more reliable assessment of feature relevance.

Acknowledgements

This work is supported by the Spanish CICyT Project TAP99-0747 and by the Mexican Petroleum Institute.

References

[1] H. Almuallim and T. G. Dietterich. Learning Boolean Concepts in the Presence of Many Irrelevant Features. *Artificial Intelligence*, 69(1–2):279–305, 1994.

[2] T. Back. *Evolutionary Algorithms in Theory and Practice.* Oxford University Press, Oxford, 1996.

[3] A. L. Blum and P. Langley. Selection of Relevant Features and Examples in Machine Learning. In R. Greiner and D. Subramanian, editors, *Artificial Intelligence on Relevance*, volume 97, pp. 245–271. AI, 1997.

[4] R. A. Caruana and D. Freitag. Greedy Attribute Selection. In *Proc. of the 11th Int. Conf. on Machine Learning*, pp. 28–36, New Brunswick, NJ, 1994. Morgan Kaufmann.

[5] R. A. Caruana and D. Freitag. How Useful is Relevance? Technical report, AAAI Symposium on Relevance, 1994.

[6] S. Chandon and L. Pinson. *Analyse Typologique.* Masson, 1981.

[7] P. A. Devijver and J. Kittler. *Pattern Recognition – A Statistical Approach.* Prentice Hall, London, GB, 1982.

[8] J. Doak. An Evaluation of Feature Selection Methods and their Application to Computer Security. Technical Report CSE–92–18, Univ. of California, 1992.

[9] M. A. Hall. *Correlation–based Feature Selection for Machine Learning.* PhD thesis, University of Waikato, 1999.

[10] A. K. Jain and D. Zongker. Feature Selection: Evaluation, Application, and Small Sample Performance. *IEEE Transactions on Pattern Analysis and Machine Intelligence*, 19(2):153–158, 1997.

[11] G. H. John, R. Kohavi, and K. Pfleger. Irrelevant Features and the Subset Selection Problem. In *Proc. of the 11th Int. Conf. on Machine Learning*, pp. 121–129, New Brunswick, NJ, 1994. Morgan Kaufmann.

[12] D. Koller and M. Sahami. Toward Optimal Feature Selection. In *Proc. of the 13th Int. Conf. on Machine Learning*, pp. 284–292, Bari, IT, 1996. Morgan Kaufmann.

[13] M. Kudo and J. Sklansky. A Comparative Evaluation of medium and large–scale Feature Selectors for Pattern Classifiers. In *Proc. of the 1st Int. Workshop on Statistical Techniques in Pattern Recognition*, pp. 91–96, Prague, 1997.

[14] H. Liu and H. Motoda. *Feature Selection for Knowledge Discovery and Data Mining.* Kluwer Academic Publishers, London, GB, 1998.

[15] T. M. Mitchell. Generalization as Search. *Artificial Intelligence*, 18(2):203–226, 1982.

[16] L. C. Molina, L. Belanche, and A. Nebot. Feature Selection Algorithms: A Survey and Experimental Evaluation. Technical Report LSI-02-62-R, Universitat Politècnica de Catalunya, Barcelona, Spain, 2002.

[17] P. Narendra and K. Fukunaga. A Branch and Bound Algorithm for Feature Subset Selection. *IEEE Transactions on Computer*, C–26(9):917–922, 1977.

[18] J. Pearl. *Heuristics.* Addison Wesley, 1983.

[19] S. B. Thrun et al. The MONK's Problems: A Performance Comparison of Different Learning Algorithms. Technical Report CS-91-197, CMU, Pittsburgh, PA, 1991.

[20] P. H. Winston. Learning Structural Descriptions from Examples. In Winston, P. H., editor, *The Psychology of Computer Vision*, New York, NY, 1975. McGraw Hill.

Multivariate supervised discretization, a neighborhood graph approach

Fabrice Muhlenbach and Ricco Rakotomalala
ERIC Laboratory
Lumière University – Lyon II
5 avenue Pierre Mendès-France
F-69676 BRON Cedex – FRANCE
{fmuhlenb,rakotoma}@univ-lyon2.fr

Abstract

We present a new discretization method in the context of supervised learning. This method entitled HyperCluster Finder is characterized by its supervised and polythetic behavior. The method is based on the notion of clusters and processes in two steps. First, a neighborhood graph construction from the learning database allows discovering homogenous clusters. Second, the minimal and maximal values of each cluster are transferred to each dimension in order to define some boundaries to cut the continuous attribute in a set of intervals. The discretization abilities of this method are illustrated by some examples, in particular, processing the XOR problem.

1. Introduction

Supervised learning methods are very often required in the data mining domain. They try to find a functional link between a class attribute Y (label) –that is mostly categorical– and a set of predictive attributes $X_i, (i = 1, ..., p)$. Many methods developed in this context, issued from the artificial intelligence domain, can handle only categorical predictive attributes [11]. Then, before the learning process, it is necessary to re-encode each numerical predictive attribute in a categorical attribute constituted by a set of intervals. This process is known as *discretization* [4].

The discretization's subarea is often studied in the context of supervised machine learning [22] as a data pre-processing step [3]. The continuous attributes are replaced by their respective discretized equivalents to which the learning algorithms can be applied. Some authors think that it is better to discretize the continuous attributes even if the learning method is able to handle them directly [6]. Generally the direct use of continuous attributes requires some unrealistic hypothesis like a Gaussian distribution for the Naive Bayes or needs some time-consuming calculations when the learning process must sort the data more than once. Nevertheless the discretization is a step that must be attentively done. By modifying the nature of the data, the discretization process introduces an information loss that must be controlled: the performance of the predictive model will depend on the quality of the data partitioning [17].

Generally the discretization methods are distinguished with two criteria [8]: taking into account the class attribute Y (supervised) or not (unsupervised) while doing the cutting of the predictive attributes $X_1, ..., X_p$; doing the cutting of an individual attribute X_i (monothetic) or the whole predictive attributes taking into consideration the interactions between them (polythetic). In this paper we present a new supervised polythetic discretization method called *HyperCluster Finder*. The method is based on the notion of *clusters* and processes in two steps. First, with a neighborhood construction, we isolate the groups of individuals bearing the same label. Second, we proceed to the cutting of the predictive attributes by projecting the group extreme values on all axes of the representation space.

Unlike the unsupervised methods, this approach takes advantage of responding directly to the supervised learning problem because the cutting takes into consideration the values taken by the class attribute Y. Unlike the monothetic methods, *HyperCluster Finder* takes into consideration the possible interactions between the predictive attributes, this is why it can detect some hard-to-learn concepts like the "XOR" problem.

In the next section, we present the basic approach for the neighborhood graphs that we implemented for finding homogeneous groups. Then we use those notions in the following section to describe our supervised and polythetic discretization algorithm. In section 4, applications to some learning problems illustrate how the algorithm functions.

314

2. Neighborhood Graphs and Clusters

A neighborhood graph depicts how two examples are close or not in the representation space. Such graphs are the Relative Neighborhood Graph, the Gabriel Graph or the Minimum Spanning Tree [14]. For our work we have used the Relative Neighborhood Graph of Toussaint [20].

Definition: Let V be a set of points in a real space $\mathbb{R}^p$ (with p the number of predictive attributes). The Relative Neighborhood Graph (RNG) of V is a graph with vertices set V and the set of edges of the RNG graph of V which are exactly those pairs (a, b) of points for which $d(a, b) \leq Max\left(d(a, c), d(b, c)\right) \forall c, c \neq a, b$ where $d(u, v)$ denotes the distance between two points u and v in the real space $\mathbb{R}^p$.

This definition means that *lune* $L_{(u,v)}$ –corresponding to the intersection of hypercircles of radius $d(u, v)$ centered on u and v– is empty. For example, on 1(a), vertices 13 and 15 are connected because there is no vertex on the *lune* $L_{(13,15)}$.

Following Sebban [18] we introduce the concept of *cluster* to express that a set of close points belong to the same class. A cluster is a connected sub-graph of the neighborhood graph where all vertices belong to the same class. To construct all clusters, we proceed in two steps:

1. we generate the neighborhood graph (RNG) on the learning set;

2. we suppress the edges connecting two vertices belonging to different classes and thus we obtain connected sub-graphs where all vertices belong to the same class.

In our example on 1(b), we have two classes: the black and the white points. We have cut four edges to isolate three clusters.

For the cluster finding we have chosen the Relative Neighborhood Graph instead of the Minimum Spanning Tree (MST) or The Gabriel Graph (GG) because it is a good intermediary neighborhood graph: the MST produces too few edges and consequently too many clusters; the GG produces too many edges and too few clusters.

3. Description of *HyperCluster Finder*

3.1. Discretization Algorithm

HyperCluster Finder is a discretization method that works by the research of clusters –or more precisely *hyperclusters* because the points are in a space representation in p dimensions. It proceeds by:

1. generating the neighborhood graph (figures 2(a) and 2(b));

2. cutting the edges between two different classes to isolate the clusters (figure2(c));

3. selecting the most relevant clusters;

4. searching the minimal and maximal values of each cluster for each predictive continuous attribute;

5. using these minimal and maximal values to define the boundaries on each predictive attribute (figure 2(c));

6. replacing, for each attribute, the global minimum and maximum respectively by $-\infty$ and $+\infty$;

7. delimiting a set of intervals on each attribute with the values of these boundaries;

8. re-encoding the numerical values of the data by their corresponding interval.

3.2. Relevant Cluster Selection

To avoid creating clusters from isolated points, it is possible to drop small size clusters when constructing the intervals. To do this, many solutions exist for retaining only the clusters that have at least a given number of individuals: this number can be *a priori* fixed by the user, the number of individuals can be determined by the database's population size or by the number of instances for the most important cluster.

3.3. Computational Complexity

The computational complexity of the discretization method is $O(n^3)$ with n the number of instances due to the Relative Neighborhood Graph construction in $\mathbb{R}^p$ (with p the number of predictive attributes) [20]. Some improvements of this complexity exist when $p \leq 3$ [7] but not in the general case.

The other computations are $O(p \times n^2)$ (for the distance matrix calculation needed to construct the graph), $O(n \ln(n))$ (for finding the h hyperclusters) and $O(n \times p)$ to re-encode the continuous data.

3.4. After the Pre-processing

We pointed out that the discretization is well adapted to polythetic problems, ie, when there is an interaction between the predictive attributes. Therefore the data mining algorithm used after the discretization step must take into consideration these interactions during the learning process and be polythetic too.

Muhlenbach *et al.* [12] propose a new bottom-up rule induction method called *Data Squeezer* which is similar to AQ Learning [11]. These algorithms –known as *covering*

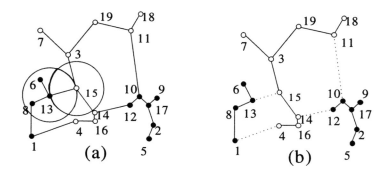

Figure 1. Relative Neighborhood Graph and Clusters with two classes

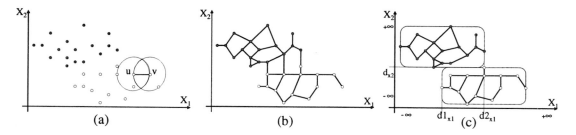

Figure 2. The different steps of the discretization process

algorithms– learn each single rule by repeatedly generalize the rule through removing conditions. In the *Data Squeezer* algorithm, all criteria are applied for having all possible groups of individuals and afterwards the data are squeezed. The squeezing process tries to gather such created groups together for the purpose of removing some criteria and obtaining a reasonable number of rules. Unlike decision trees and induction graphs that proceed by specialization (top-down), *Data Squeezer* method proceeds by generalization of the observed profiles (bottom-up).

4. Experiments

In the first part, we will illustrate the discretization process of *HyperCluster Finder* on three databases. In the second part, we will compare the performance obtained for different machine learning methods after two supervised discretizations. Then we will discuss the results obtained by the different methods of discretization and supervised learning.

4.1. Illustration

4.1.1 Pure XOR Database

Because *HyperCluster Finder* is a discretization method that is particulary adapted to detect the appropriate inter-

vals when there is an interaction between the predictive attributes, we illustrate how it processes on a *Pure XOR Database*. This database, presented on figure 3, contains 100 instances described by two continuous attributes X_1 and X_2. The class attribute Y is characterized by the following rule: an individual is *True* (in black) when only one predictive attribute is *True* (positive), else this individual is *False* (in white).

The different points are projected in the representation space (here in $\mathbb{R}^2$) and the neighborhood graph is constructed (figure 4).

The edges between points of different classes are cut for isolating the sub-graphs of the same class (the hyperclusters). On our example (figure 5), only 4 clusters are retained (two clusters of only one point are removed).

The minimal and maximal values are reported to the axis.
The intervals for X_1 are: $]-\infty; -0.3[$, $[-0.3; -0.1[$, $[-0.1; 0.1[$, $[0.1; 0.2[$, $[0.2; 4.7[$ and $[4.7; +\infty[$.

For the X_2 attribute, the intervals are: $]-\infty; -4.9[$, $[-4.9; -0.2[$, $[-0.2; 0.0[$, $[0.0; 0.2[$, $[0.2; 4.7[$ and $[4.7; +\infty[$.

This produces a paving of the representation space and all sub-spaces defined by the paving contain only the points of a unique class (figure 6).

The continuous values of the predictive attributes of the data are transformed in categorical values by using the dif-

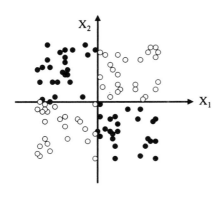

Figure 3. Pure XOR Database

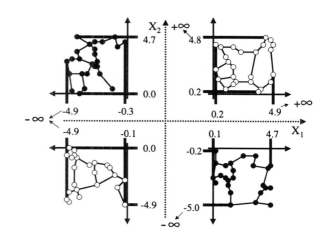

Figure 5. Selected Clusters and Interval Forming

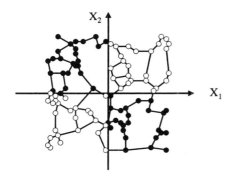

Figure 4. Neighborhood Graph on the Pure XOR Database

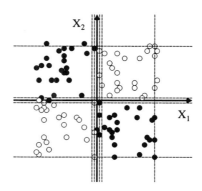

Figure 6. Space Paving with the Supervised Polythetic Discretization

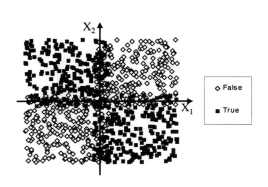

Figure 7. Mixed XOR Database

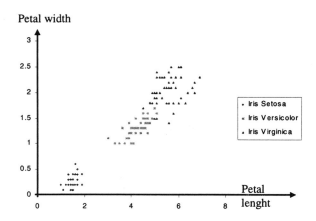

Figure 8. Iris Plants Database (by choosing the most discriminant attributes)

ferent generated intervals. The data can then be used by a supervised machine learning for extracting knowledge. With the *Data Squeezer* learning method, the different intervals are merged and 5 rules are produced (on the 4 expected rules describing the XOR function). The model can predict 99% of the data (only one error on a boundary point).

4.1.2 Mixed XOR Database

We have proceeded in a similar case but with 1,000 instances and with an overlapping of the class distributions (figure 7).

The cutting of the neighborhood graph between edges connecting different classes produces 127 clusters, nevertheless only 4 clusters are selected that define 7 intervals on each axis.

With this database, *Data Squeezer* can extract 13 rules. The model can predict 83.9% of the data (161 errors on 1,000 examples).

4.1.3 Iris Database

The Iris Plants Database is a well-known benchmark in the supervised machine learning domain: 4 continuous predictive attributes (sepal length, sepal width, petal length and petal width), 3 values for the class attribute (Iris Setosa, Iris Versicolour and Iris Virginica) and 150 instances (50 for each of 3 classes). The database is present on the Machine Learning Repository of the University of California at Irvine [2].

As shown in figure 8 by representing the class as a function of the petal length and the petal width, one class is linearly separable from the other two which are not linearly separable from each other.

The cut of the neighborhood graph edges produces 7 clusters but 4 of them are composed of only one individual. The 3 selected clusters define 5 intervals on each axis.

Data Squeezer extracts 9 predictive rules from the transformed database. The model can predict 97.3% of the data (4 errors that are the 4 isolated clusters detected during the discretization step).

4.2. Comparative Experiments

The performance of the *HyperCluster Finder* (*HCF*) discretization method has been analyzed in a comparative study. The other discretization method used in the tests is *Fusinter* [22], a state-of-the-art supervised and monothetic discretization method. The *Fusinter* method will show similar or better performances than the other monothetic supervised or non-supervised discretization methods presented in section 5.

For the three benchmarks presented in the previous section, we have randomly split the database in ten parts. The discretization and the learning processes were done on 9/10 of the database (training set) and the last tenth was used for the test (validation set). Table 4.2 displays the results of this 10-cross validation obtained with the following supervised learning method:

- *ID3* [15] and *C4.5* [16], two decision trees;

- *Sipina* [21], an induction graph method;

- *Data Squeezer* [12], a polythetic bottom-up method.

Table 1. Error rate on a 10-cross validation

Disc. method	Learning method	Pure XOR	Mixed XOR	Iris Plants
Fusinter	ID3	.609	.198	.046
Fusinter	C4.5	.616	.543	.054
Fusinter	Sipina	.225	.182	.057
Fusinter	D. Squeezer	.500	.500	.080
HCF	ID3	.608	.537	.061
HCF	C4.5	.117	.182	.053
HCF	Sipina	.608	.539	.307
HCF	D. Squeezer	.050	.194	.110

ID3 and *C4.5* are top-down induction methods. The former uses a pre-pruning process to determine the right size of the tree and for that reason it detects badly interactions between predictive attributes. The latter adopts a *hurdling* growing tree process (a split is accepted during the growing process even if the information gain is null) and determine the right size of the tree with post-pruning, it theoretically can better handle attribute interactions [16].

Sipina is a top-down induction graph method. It has similar properties than decision trees but it is more powerful, eg, it can easily represent disjunctive normal form [13].

4.3. Results and Discussion

The first result we can notice in table 4.2 is that *Data Squeezer + HyperCluster Finder* (HCF) is the best method to learn the classical (Pure) XOR problem (.05). *ID3* fails whatever the discretization may be but *C4.5*, with its *hurdling* growing tree process, takes advantage of the polythetic supervised discretization, at the contrary to *Sipina* that shows better results with *Fusinter* than with *HCF*. When there is some noise in the data (Mixed XOR), *C4.5*, like *Data Squeezer*, is better with the *HCF* discretization than with *Fusinter*. For the Iris database, the results are equivalent for the induction trees with the two discretization methods but the performance are lower with *HCF* for *Sipina*.

With the Pure or Mixed XOR database, *Data Squeezer* used after *Fusinter* fails to find a predictive model and produces only one rule that predicts a unique class value for all instances.

C4.5 seems to have a behavior similar to that of *Data Squeezer* and gains from a polythetic supervised discretization. By contrast, *Sipina* is well adapted to *Fusinter*. *ID3* plays an intermediary role, except for the Pure XOR with *Fusinter*, the results are close to those of *Sipina*. We can explain these results by the nature of the learning methods related to the discretization methods. *ID3* uses the most elementary strategy for induction tree construction. *C4.5* is based on *ID3* algorithm but is more elaborated by adding

some improvements like post-pruning and *hurdling* growing tree process, then it produces less complex models than *ID3*. *Sipina* is an induction graph that produces complex graph that can more or less handle the XOR problem with a monothetic supervised discretization. It produces a complex model and has bad performance with *HCF* which produces many intervals.

Therefore, we can conclude that *HCF* is well adapted for the learning methods that can handle attribute interactions such as polythetic supervised methods like *Data Squeezer*.

5. Related Work

Almost all studies on discretization have concluded that supervised discretization is more impressive than the unsupervised discretization (same size intervals, frequency equivalent intervals, etc.) in supervised learning problems [4].

These studies are principally based on empirical studies to evaluate the properties of these methods for cutting continuous attributes. Most of the recently published work pertains to the monothetic method, ie, the cutting of predictive attributes independently of each other. In this context, the discussion revolves mostly around the way to find the best cutting boundaries. The bottom-up approach [9] starts from the self-evident cutting where each interval contains only one instance and tries to merge the intervals having the same distribution. The top-down approach [5] starts from the whole set of instances and progressively adds boundaries to find the intervals that contain only individuals of a same class. However, experimentation shows that these methods perform at a similar level for supervised induction. What is worse, in spite of their being computation-intensive, optimal cutting methods are still not better in the sense of predictive quality of the ensuing classifier.

The polythetic discretization methods are rarely studied in the supervised learning domain. The major approaches have been developed in the context of the association rules when the unsupervised monothetic discretization methods do not yield satisfactory results. In these cases, each attribute is cut in relation to the other variables on the database and, unlike the supervised learning, no attribute plays a particular role.

Bay [1] suggests an approach that consists of doing a paving of the space representation by cutting each continuous attribute in some intervals, the initial number of intervals is a parameter settled by the user. The discretization process consists in merging the bordering intervals in which the data distribution is the same. Because of the merging test used is polythetic, the simultaneous role of all attributes is taken into consideration. In the context of the supervised learning, the author suggests to add the class attribute Y as a complementary attribute for the equivalency distribution test. Nevertheless, even if this strategy can introduce the class attribute in the discretization process, it can not give a particular role to the class attribute –other than the predictive attributes– and can induce the discretization to non-impressive results for the prediction.

In the same context of discretization for the association rule, Ludl and Widmer [10] propose a different approach that can be called multi-supervised. The cutting of an attribute X_i is based on $(p-1)$ monothetic supervised discretization where the attribute $X_{i'}$ ($i' \neq i$) plays the class attribute role. After that, the intervals deemed too small are merged. The most important weakness of this approach is the need of to proceed before a monothetic unsupervised discretization for each continuous attribute $X_{i'}$ that will play the role of class attribute in the cutting of attribute X_i, with the subjective choice of number of intervals to construct.

Compared with these methods, our approach, due to its supervised and polythetic properties, combines their respective advantages. Because it is a polythetic method, *Hyper-Cluster Finder* can take into account the interactions between the different predictive attributes X_i, it is the step of the graph construction. Because it is a supervised method, it gives a particular role for the class attribute Y and can automatically determine the appropriate number of discretization intervals, it is the step of cluster constitution and the extreme value projections of the clusters on each of the representation axis.

6. Conclusion and Future Work

HyperCluster Finder is a discretization method that processes in a supervised and polythetic way; it is very well adapted to databases that display interaction between the predictive attributes, as we have shown in our XOR database examples.

Even if our discretization method produces good results compared to other supervised method, we have identified 3 limitations and we plan to resolve them in our future work.

First, due to the neighborhood graph construction, the method of discretization works only when all predictive attributes of the database are numerical. But in many cases, a database contains numerical and categorical predictive attributes. *HyperCluster Finder* needs to construct a neighborhood graph with a distance matrix, then how can a categorical attribute play a role in this distance computation? We have found a solution by using the Stanfill-Waltz Value Difference Metric (VDM) [19]. The VDM takes into consideration the overall similarity of classification of all instances for each possible value of each feature, then a matrix distance defining the distance between all values of a feature is derived statistically, based on the training set. By using these distance matrices on each feature it is possible to construct the global distance matrix between each instances of the database.

Second, the construction of a Relative Neighborhood Graph of Toussaint is fairly time-consuming due to its $O(n^3)$ computational complexity. We have studied other less complex neighborhood graphs but the discretizations induced by the minimal spanning tree or the Gabriel graph are not as powerful as a discretization based on a RNG. We plan to find some algorithm heuristics to deliver more scalability to our discretization method. Another solution, when a $O(n^3)$ computation is inconceivable on the whole database, is to take a sample on which *HyperCluster Finder* can give the adapted intervals for the discretization. In this context, the true problem will be then to determine the size of a sample that will give the same cutpoints than using the whole dataset.

Third, the computational complexity of the discretization process is not so significant compared to the complexity of a bottom-up learning method. For example, *Data Squeezer*, that takes a great benefit of *HyperCluster Finder* discretization, is very time-consuming. Since we plan to make some predictive model on real applications where some amount of interaction among the predictive attributes exists, we intend to find some improvements of this polythetic supervised learning method to reduce the computational complexity. Moreover, we have seen in the comparative experiments that *C4.5*'s results are close to *Data Squeezer*'s, we plan to confirm this observation through supplemental theoretical studies.

Acknowledgements

We are very grateful to Mr Jean Dumais, Section Chief, Methodology Branch, Statistics Canada and guest lecturer at Université Lumière (Lyon II), for his careful proof reading of the manuscript and his suggestions.

References

[1] S. D. Bay. Multivariate discretization for set mining. *Knowledge and Information Systems*, 3(4):491–512, 2001.

[2] C. L. Blake and C. J. Merz. UCI repository of machine learning databases. Irvine, CA: University of California, Department of Information and Computer Science [http://www.ics.uci.edu/~mlearn/MLRepository.html], 1998.

[3] M. R. Chmielewski and J. W. Grzymala-Busse. Global discretization of continuous attributes as preprocessing for machine learning. In *Third International Workshop on Rough Sets and Soft Computing*, pages 294–301, 1994.

[4] J. Dougherty, R. Kohavi, and M. Sahami. Supervised and unsupervised discretization of continuous features. In *International Conference on Machine Learning (ICML95)*, pages 194–202, 1995.

[5] U. M. Fayyad and K. B. Irani. The attribute selection problem in decision tree generation. In *Proceedings of The 13th International Joint Conference on Artificial Intelligence*, pages 1022–1027, 1993.

[6] E. Frank and I. H. Witten. Making better use of global discretization. In *Proceedings of the 16th International Conference on Machine Learning*, pages 115–123. Morgan Kaufmann, San Francisco, CA, 1999.

[7] J. W. Jaromczyk and G. T. Toussaint. Relative neighborhood graphs and their relatives. *P-IEEE*, 80:1502–1517, 1992.

[8] R. Kohavi and M. Sahami. Error-based and entropy-based discretization of continuous features. In *Proceedings of the Second International Conference on Knowledge Discovery and Data Mining*, pages 114–119, 1996.

[9] H. Liu and R. Setiono. Chi2: Feature selection and discretization of numeric attributes. In *Proceedings of 7th IEEE International Conference on Tools with Artificial Intelligence*, 1995.

[10] M.-C. Ludl and G. Widmer. Relative unsupervised discretization for association rule mining. In *Proceedings of 4th European Conference for Principles of Data Mining and Knowledge Discovery (PKDD'2000)*, pages 148–158. Springer-Verlag, 2000.

[11] T. Mitchell. *Machine learning*. McGraw Hill, 1997.

[12] F. Muhlenbach, D. A. Zighed, and S. D'Hondt. Génération de règles par compression. *ECA*, 1(1–2):93–104, 2001.

[13] J. J. Oliver. Decision graphs - an extension of decision trees. In *Proceedings of the Fourth International Workshop on Artificial Intelligence and Statistics*, pages 343–350, 1993.

[14] F. P. Preparata and M. I. Shamos. *Computational Geometry, an introduction*. Springer-Verlag, New York, 2nd edition, 1988. First edition: 1985.

[15] J. R. Quinlan. Induction of decision trees. *Machine Learning*, 1:81–106, 1986.

[16] J. R. Quinlan. *C4.5: Programs for Machine Learning*. Morgan Kaufmann, San Mateo, CA, 1993.

[17] S. Rabaséda, M. Sebban, and R. Rakotomalala. A comparison of some contextual discretization methods. *Information Sciences: Intelligent Systems*, 92(1-4):137–157, 1996.

[18] M. Sebban and A. Lamole. String clustering and statistical validation of clusters. In R. E. Mercer and E. Neufeld, editors, *Proceedings of Advances in Artificial Intelligence (AI'98)*, pages 298–309. Springer Verlag, 1998.

[19] C. Stanfill and D. Waltz. Towards memory-based reasoning. *Communications of the ACM*, 29(12):1213–1228, 1986.

[20] G. Toussaint. The relative neighborhood graph of a finite planar set. *Pattern recognition*, 12:261–268, 1980.

[21] D. A. Zighed, J. P. Auray, and G. Duru. *SIPINA : Méthode et logiciel*. Lacassagne, 1992.

[22] D. A. Zighed, S. Rabaséda, and R. Rakotomalala. Fusinter: a method for discretization of continuous attributes for supervised learning. *International Journal of Uncertainty, Fuzziness and Knowledge-Based Systems*, 6(33):307–326, 1998.

Mining Association Rules from Stars

Eric Ka Ka Ng*, Ada Wai-Chee Fu*, Ke Wang+

*Chinese University of Hong Kong
Department of Computer Science and Engineering
{kkng1,adafu}@cse.cuhk.edu.hk

+Simon Fraser University
Department of Computer Science
wangk@cs.sfu.ca

Abstract

Association rule mining is an important data mining problem. It is found to be useful for conventional relational data. However, previous work has mostly targeted on mining a single table. In real life, a database is typically made up of multiple tables and one important case is where some of the tables form a star schema. The tables typically correspond to entity sets and joining the tables in a star schema gives relationships among entity sets which can be very interesting information. Hence mining on the join result is an important problem. Based on characteristics of the star schema we propose an efficient algorithm for mining association rules on the join result but without actually performing the join operation. We show that this approach can significantly out-perform the join-then-mine approach even when the latter adopts a fastest known mining algorithm.

1 Introduction

Association rules mining [AIS93, AS94] is identified as one of the important problems in data mining. Let us first define the problem for a database D containing a set of transactions, where each transaction contains a set of *items*. An **association rule** has the form of $X \Rightarrow Y$ where X and Y are sets of items. In such a rule, we require that the frequency of the set of items $X \cup Y$ is above a certain threshold called the *minsup*. The **frequency** (also known as **support**) of a set of items Z is the number of occurrences of Z in D, or the number of transactions in D that contain Z. The **confidence** of the rule should also be above a threshold. By confidence we mean the probability of Y given X.

The mining can be divided into two steps: first we find the sets of items that have frequencies above $minsup$, which we call the **frequent itemsets**. Second, from the sets of frequent itemsets we generate the association rules. The first step is more difficult and is shown to be NP-hard. In our subsequent discussion we shall focus on the first step.

The techniques in association rule mining has been extended to work on numerical data and categorical data in more conventional databases [SA96, RS98], some researchers have noted the importance of association rule mining in relation to relational databases [STA00]. Tools for association rule mining are now found in major products such as IBM's Intelligent Miner, and SPSS's Clementine.

In real databases, typically a number of tables will be defined. In this paper, we examine the problem of mining association rule from a set of relational tables. In particular we are interested in the case where the tables form a star structure [CD97] (see Figure 1). A star schema consists of a *fact table* (FT) in the center and multiple dimension tables. We aim to mine association rules on the join result of all the tables [JS00]. This is interesting because the join result typically tells us the relationship among different entities such as customers and products and to discover cross entities association can be of great value. The star schema can be considered as the building block for a snowflake schema and hence our proposed technique can be extended to the snowflake structure in a straightforward manner.

A (Student)

	address	age	GPA
a_1	Shatin	20-25	2.0-2.5
a_2	Taipo	25-30	2.5-3.0
a_3	Fotan	25-30	3.0-4.0

B (Course)

	subject	semester	credit
b_1	Maths	Fall 02	3
b_2	Phy	Spring 02	2
b_3	CS	Fall 02	3

FT

Tid(A)	Tid(B)	Tid(C)	o
a_1	b_1	c_1	o_1
a_1	b_1	c_1	o_1
a_2	b_3	c_3	o_2
a_3	b_2	c_2	o_2

C (Teacher)

	age	dept	office
c_1	30-39	CS	Rm 103
c_2	20-29	Phy	Rm 122
c_3	40-50	Mat	Rm 200

Figure 1. Star with 3 Dimensional Tables

At first glance it may seem easy to join the tables in a star schema and then do the mining process on the joined result. However, when multiple tables are joined, the resulting ta-

0-7695-1754-4/02 $17.00 © 2002 IEEE

ble will increase in size many folds. There are two major problems: Firstly, in large applications, often the join of all related tables cannot be realistically computed because of the many-to-many relationship blow up, large dimension tables, and the distributed nature of data.

Secondly, even if the join can be computed, the multi-fold increase in both size and dimensionality presents a hugh overhead to the already expensive frequent itemset mining step: (1) The number of columns will be close to the sum of the number of columns in the individual tables. As the performance of association rule mining is very sensitive to the number of columns (items) the mining on the resulting table can take much longer computation time compared to mining on the individual tables. (2) If the join result is stored on disk, the I/O cost will increase significantly for multiple scanning steps in data mining. (3) For mining frequent itemsets of small sizes, a large portion of the I/O cost is wasted on reading the full records containing irrelevant dimensions. (4) Each tuple in a dimension table will be read multiple times in one scan of the join result because of duplicates of the tuple in the join result.

We exploit the characteristics of tables in a star schema. Instead of "joining-then-mining", we can perform "mining-then-joining", in which the "joining" part is much less costly. Our strategy never produces the join result. In the first phase, we mine the frequent itemsets locally at each dimension table, using any existing algorithm. Only relevant information are scanned. In the second phase, we mine global frequent itemsets across two or more tables based on local frequent itemsets. Here, we exploit the following pruning strategy: if $X \cup Y$ is a frequent itemset, where X is from table A and Y is from table B, X must be a frequent itemset and Y must be a frequent itemset. Thus, the first phase provides all local frequent itemsets we need for the second phase. The difficulty lies in the second phase.

One major challenge in the second phase is how to keep track of the many-to-many relationship in the fact table without generating the join result. We make use of the feature that a foreign key for a dimension table A can appear many times in the join result, which allows us to introduce some structure to record the key once, together with a counter for the number of duplications. We also make use of the idea of semi-join in relational databases to facilitate the mining process. From these ideas we propose a set of algorithm and data structures for mining association rules on a star schema which does not involve a join step of the tables involved. Experiments show that the proposed method is efficient in many scenarios.

2 Problem Definition

Consider a relational database with a **star schema**. There are multiple **dimension tables**, which we would de-

note as A, B, C, ..., each of which contains only one primary key denoted by **transaction id (tid)** , some other attributes and no foreign keys. (Sometimes we simply refer to A, B, C, ..., as dimensions.) a_i, b_i, c_i denote the transaction id (*tid*) of dimension tables A, B, C, respectively. We assume that the attributes in the dimension tables are unique. (If initially two tables have some common attributes, renaming can make them different.) We assume that attributes take categorical values. (Numerical values can be partitioned into ranges, and hence be transformed to categorical values [RS98].) The set of values for an attribute is called the **domain** of the attribute.

Conceptually, we can view the dimension table in terms of a binary representation, where we have one binary attribute (or we call an "item") corresponding to one "attribute-value" pair in the original dimension table. We also refer to each tuple in A or the binary representation as a **transaction**. For example, consider Figure 2, v_1, v_2, v_3 are attribute names for dimension table A, and the value of attribute v_1 for transaction a_1 is R_2. In the conceptual binary representation in Figure 2, we have attributes for "$v_1 = R_0$", "$v_1 = R_1$" "$v_1 = R_2$", ... (we call them x_1, x_2, x_3, ..., respectively). For transaction a_1 in table A, the value of attribute x_3 is 1 ($v_1 = R_2$ is TRUE), and the values of x_1 and x_2 both equal to 0 (FALSE). In our remaining discussions, binary items (one item for each "attribute-value" pair) in the conceptual binary representation would be used. $x_{i_1}x_{i_2}x_{i_3}...$ denotes the itemset that is composed of items x_{i_1}, x_{i_2}, x_{i_3}, ... We assume an *ordering* of items which is adopted in any transaction and *itemset*. E.g. x_1 would always appear before x_2 if they exist together in some transaction or itemset. This ordering will facilitate our algorithm.

A (Student)					$v_1 = R_0$	$v_1 = R_1$	$v_1 = R_2$	$v_2 = R_0$	$v_2 = R_1$	$v_3 = R_0$	$v_3 = R_1$
	v_1	v_2	v_3		x_1	x_2	x_3	x_4	x_5	x_6	x_7
a_1	R_2	R_0	R_1	a_1	0	0	1	1	0	0	1
a_2	R_0	R_0	R_1	a_2	1	0	0	1	0	0	1
a_3	R_1	R_1	R_0	a_3	0	1	0	0	1	1	0

Figure 2. Dimension Table and its Binary Representation

There is one **fact table**, which we denote as FT. FT has attributes of $(tid(A), tid(B), tid(C), ...)$, where $tid(A)$ is the tid of table A. That is, FT stores the *tid*s from dimension tables $A, B, C, ...$ as foreign keys. (Later we shall discuss the more general case where FT also contains some other attributes.) In an ER model, typically, each dimension table corresponds to an entity set, and FT corresponds to the relationship among the entity sets. The relationships among entity sets can be of any form: many-to-many, many-to-one, one-to-many, or one-to-one.

We are interested to mine association rules from the star structure. In particular we shall examine the sub-problem of finding all **frequent itemsets** in the table T resulting from a natural join of all the given tables ($FT \bowtie A \bowtie B \bowtie C \ldots$). The join conditions are given by $FT.Tid(A) = A.tid$, $FT.Tid(B) = B.tid$, $FT.Tid(C) = C.tid$, ... In the following discussions, when we mention frequent itemset we always refer to the frequency of the itemset in the table T. We assume that a **frequency threshold** of $minsup$ is given for the frequent itemsets. A frequent item corresponds to a frequent itemset of size one.

In our mining process, the dimension tables will be kept in the form of the VTV (**Vertical Tid-Vector**) representation [SHS00] with counts. Specifically, suppose there are T_A, T_B, T_C transactions in tables A, B, C respectively. For each frequent item x in table A, we store a column of T_A bits, the ith bit is 1 if item x is contained in transaction i, and 0 otherwise. We also keep an array of T_A entries where the ith entry corresponds to the frequency of tid i in FT.

3 The Proposed Method

First we present a simple example to show the idea of discovering frequent itemsets across dimension tables without actually performing the join operation. We shall use a data type called tid_list in our algorithm. It is an ordered list of elements of the form $tid(count)$, where tid is a transaction ID, and **count** is a non-negative integer. Given two tid_lists L_1, L_2, the **union** $L_1 \cup L_2$ is the list of $tid(count)$, where tid appears in either L_1 or L_2, and the count is the sum of the counts of tid in L_1 and L_2. The **intersection** of two tid_lists L_1, L_2 is denoted by $L_1 \cap L_2$, which is a list of $tid(count)$, where tid appears in both L_1 and L_2 and the $count$ is the smaller of the counts of tid in L_1 and L_2. Suppose we have 2 dimension tables A, B, and a fact table FT. The following are some of the tid_lists we shall use.

• $tid_A(x_i)$: a tid_list for x_i, where x_i is an attribute (item) of table A. In each element of $tid(count)$ in the list, tid is the id of a transaction in A that contains x_i, and $count$ is the number of occurrences of the tid in FT. If the tid of a transaction that contains x_i does not appear in $tid_A(x_i)$, the count of it is 0 in FT.

E.g. $tid_A(x_3) = \{a_1(5), a_3(2)\}$ means that the tids of transactions in A that contain x_3 are a_1 and a_3; a_1 appears 5 times in FT, and a_3 appears 2 times.

• $tid_A(X)$ where X is an itemset with items from A, it is similar to $tid_A(x_i)$ except x_i is replaced by X. $tid_A(x_i x_j)$ can be obtained by $tid_A(x_i) \cap tid_A(x_j)$.

• $B\_key(a_n)$: Given a tid a_n from A, $B\_key(a_n)$ denotes a tid-list of $tid(count)$, where tid is a tid from B and $count$ is the number of occurrences of tid together with a_n in FT.

E.g. $B\_key(a_1) = \{b_3(4), b_5(2)\}$ means that $a_1 b_3$ occurs 4 times in FT, and $a_1 b_5$ occurs 2 times.

• $B\_tid(x_i)$: Given an item x_i in A, $B\_tid(x_i)$ denotes a tid-list, of $tid(count)$, where tid is a tid of B, and $count$ is the number of times tid appears together with any tid a_j of A such that transaction a_j contains x_i in A.

• $B\_tid(X)$: similar to $B\_tid(x_i)$ except item x_i is replaced by an itemset X from A.

Example 3.1 *Suppose we have a star schema for a number of dimension tables related by a fact table FT. The following figure shows 2 of the dimension tables A and B, and the projection of FT on the two columns that contains transaction ID's for A, B, but without removing duplicate tuples.*

A			Tid(A)	Tid(B)		B	
Tid	**Items**		a1	b5		**Tid**	**Items**
a1	x1,x3,x5		a1	b3		b1	y1,y3,y5
a2	x2,x3,x6		a1	b2		b2	y1,y3,y6
a3	x1,x3,x6		a3	b2		b3	y2,y4,y6
a4	x1,x4,x6		a3	b5		b4	y1,y4,y5
			a1	b5		b5	y1,y4,y6

FT

Some of the tids from the dimension tables may not appear in FT (e.g. a_2, b_1). Suppose minsup is set to 5. We first mine frequent itemsets from each of A and B. For example, x_1 and x_3 appear together in a_1, a_3, the total count of a_1, a_3 in FT is 6, hence $x_1 x_3$ is a frequent itemset. Next we check if a frequent itemset from A can be combined with a frequent itemset from B to form a frequent itemset of greater size. $y_1 y_6$ is a frequent itemset from B with frequency = 5. We want to see if $x_1 x_3$ can be combined with $y_1 y_6$ to form a frequent itemset, the steps are outlined as follows:

1. $tid_A(x_1) = \{a_1(4), a_3(2)\}, tid_A(x_3) = \{a_1(4), a_3(2)\},$
   $tid_A(x_1 x_3) = tid_A(x_1) \cap tid_A(x_3) = \{a_1(4), a_3(2)\},$
   $tid_B(y_1 y_6) = \{b_2(2), b_5(3)\}.$

2. $B\_key(a_1) = \{b_2(1), b_3(1), b_5(2)\},$
   $B\_key(a_3) = \{b_2(1), b_5(1)\}.$

3. $B\_tid(x_1 x_3) = B\_key(a_1) \cup B\_key(a_3)$
   $= \{b_2(2), b_3(1), b_5(3)\}.$

4. $B\_tid(x_1 x_3) \cap tid_B(y_1 y_6) = \{b_2(2), b_5(3)\}.$

5. *The combined frequency = total count in the list $\{b_2(2), b_5(3)\} = 5.$*

Hence the itemset $x_1 x_3 y_1 y_6$ is frequent. □

In general, to examine the frequency for an itemset X that contains items from two dimension tables A and B, we can do the following. We examine table A to find the set of transactions T_1 in A that contain the A items in X. Next we determine the transactions T_2 in B that appear with such transactions in FT. Note that this is similar to the derivation of an intermediate table in a **semi-join** strategy, where the result of joining a first table with the key of a second table are placed, the key of the second table is a

324

foreign key in this intermediate table. In the mean time, the set of transactions T_3 in B that contain the B items in X are identified. Finally T_2 and T_3 are intersected, and the resulting count is obtained.

The use of tid_list is a compressed form of recording the occurrences of tid's in the fact table. Multiple occurrences would be condensed as one single entry in a tid_list with the count associated.

Initial Step: In order to do the above, we need to have some initial information about $tid_A(x_i)$ for each item x_i in each dimension table A. One scan of a dimension table can give us the list of transactions for all items. In one scan of FT we can determine all the counts for all transactions in all the dimension tables. In the same scan, we can also determine $B\_key(a_i)$ for each tid a_i in each dimension table.

3.1 Overall Steps

For simplicity, let us first assume that there are 3 dimension tables A, B, C. The overall steps of our method are:

Step 1 : Preprocessing
Read the dimension tables, convert them into VTV (Vertical Tid-Vector) format with counts (see Section 2).

Step 2 : Local Mining
Perform local mining on each dimension table. This can be done with any known single table algorithm with a slight modification of refering to the counts of transactions in FT which has been collected in the initial step described in Section 2. The time taken for this step typcially is insignificant compared to the global mining steps.

Step 3 : Global Mining

Step 3.1 : Scan the Fact Table
Scan the Fact Table FT and record the information in some data structures.

We set an ordering for A, B, C. First we handle tables A and B with the following 2 steps:

Step 3.2 : Mining size-two itemsets
This step examines all pairs of frequent items x and y, which are from the two different dimension tables.

Step 3.3 : Mining the rest for A and B
Repeat the following for $k = 3, 4, 5.....$ Candidates are generated by the union of pairs of mined itemsets of size $k-1$ differing only in the last item. The technique of generation would be similar to FORC [SHS00]. Next count the frequencies of the candidates and determine the frequent itemsets.

After Steps 3.2 and 3.3, the results will be all frequent itemsets formed from items in tables A and/or B. This can be seen as the frequent itemset mined from a single dimension table AB. Similar steps as Steps 3.2 and 3.3 are then applied for the tables AB and C to obtain all frequent itemsets from the star schema.

3.2 Binding multiple Dimension Tables

We can easily generalize the overall steps above from 3 dimension tables to N dimension tables. Suppose there are totally N dimension tables and a fact table FT in the star schema. We start with two of the dimension tables, say A and B. We apply Steps 3.2 and 3.3 above to mine all frequent itemsets with items from A and/or B without joining the tables with FT. This set of itemsets is called F^{AB}. We call Steps 3.2 and 3.3 a **binding** step of A and B. After binding, we treat A and B as a single table AB and begin the process of binding AB with another table, this is repeated until all N dimensions are bound. Some notations we shall use are:

- F^A denotes the set of frequent itemsets with items from A, F^{AB} denotes the set of frequent itemsets with items from tables A and/or B. F^{AB_k} denotes the set of frequent itemsets of the form XY, where X is either empty set or an itemset from A, and Y is either an empty set or an itemset from B with size k. E.g. $F^{AB} = \{x_1, y_1, x_1 y_1\}$. E.g. $F^{AB_2} = \{y_1 y_2, y_2 y_3, x_1 y_1 y_2, x_1 y_2 y_3\}$.

- F^{A_k} denotes the set of frequent itemsets of size k from A. $F^{A_i B_j}$ denotes the set of frequent itemsets in which the subset of items from A has size i and subset of items from B has size j. E.g. suppose x_i's are items from table A, and y_j's are items from table B, we may have $F^{A_2 B_1} = \{x_1 x_2 y_1, x_3 x_4 y_2\}$.

After performing "binding", we can treat the items in the combined itemsets as coming from a single dimension table. For example, after "binding" A and B, we *virtually combine* A and B into a single dimension table AB, and all items in F^{AB} are from the new dimension table AB. We always "bind" 2 dimension tables at each step, and iterate for $N-1$ times if there are totally N dimension tables. At the end all frequent itemsets will be discovered.

Figure 3 shows a possible ordering of the "bind" operations on four dimension tables: A, B, C, D.

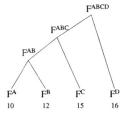

Figure 3. An example of "binding" order

We need to do two things to combine two dimension tables: (1) To assign each combination of tid from A and tid from B in FT a new tid, and (2) to set the tid in the tid_lists for items in AB to the corresponding new tid.

Consider an example in Figure 4, for a FT relating to

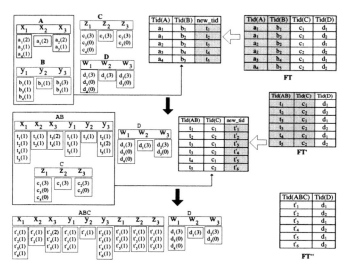

Figure 4. Concatenating tids after "binding"

4 dimensions A, B, C, D, after "binding" A and B, the columns storing tid(A) and tid(B) would be concatenated. Each combination of tid(A) and tid(B) would be assigned a new tid. A and B would be combined into AB. For example, before "binding", item x_1 appears in transactions a_1, a_3 and a_4. $tid_A(x_1) = \{a_1(2), a_3(1), a_4(1)\}$. After "binding", since a_1 corresponds to new tid t_1 and t_2, a_3 corresponds to new tid t_4, a_4 corresponds to new tid t_5. Therefore $tid_A(x_1)$ is updated to $tid_{AB}(x_1) = \{t_1(1), t_2(1), t_4(1), t_5(1)\}$.

Similarly, when F^{AB} is then "bound" with F^C, AB is combined with C and FT would be updated again. Note that in Figure 4, the tables with attribute new_tid and the multiple fact tables are not really constructed as tables, but instead stored in a structure which is a prefix tree.

We always bind a given dimension table with the result of the previous binding because the tid of the dimension table allows us to apply the technique of a foreign key as described in the previous section. The ordering can be based on the estimated result size of natural join of the tables involved, which can in turn be estimated by the dimension table sizes. A heuristic is to order the tables by increasing table sizes for binding.

3.3 Prefix Tree for FT

In Step 3.1 of the overall steps, the fact table FT is scanned once and the information is stored into a data structure which can facilitate the mining process. The data structure is in the form of a *prefix tree*. Each node in the prefix tree has a label (a tid) and also a counter. We need only scan FT once to insert each tuple into the prefix tree. Suppose we have 3 dimensions A, B, C, and a tuple is a_3, b_2, c_2, we

enter at the root node and go down a child with label a_3, from a_3 we go down to a child node with label b_2, from b_2 we go to a child node labeled c_2. Every time we visit a node, we increment the counter there by 1. If any child node is not found, it is created, with the counter initialized to 1. Hence level n of the prefix tree corresponds to tid's of the nth *dimension table* that would be "bound". When searching for a foreign tid_list, we can go down the path specified by the prefix. In this way, the *foreign key* and the global frequency in the ith iteration can be efficiently retrieved from the $i + 1^{th}$ level of the *prefix tree*. Figure 5 shows how a fact table is converted to a prefix tree.

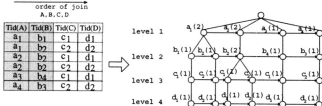

Figure 5. Prefix Tree structure representing FT

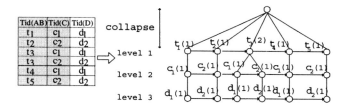

Figure 6. Collapsing the prefix tree

Use of the prefix tree – the foreign key: The prefix tree is a concise structuring of FT which can facilitate our mining step. When we want to "bind" F^A with F^B, we have to check whether an itemset (e.g. x_1) in F^A can be combined with an itemset in F^B (e.g. y_1). We need to obtain the information of a foreign key in the form of tid_list (e.g. $B\_tid(x_1)$). Let $tid_A(x_1) = \{a_1(2), a_2(1)\}$. We can find $B\_key(a_1)$ by searching the children of a_1 which are labeled $b_1(1)$, $b_2(1)$, similarly let $B\_key(a_2) = \{b_2(2)\}$. As a result, $B\_tid(x_1 y_1) = B\_key(a_1) \cup B\_key(a_2) = \{b_1(1), b_2(3)\}$.

Collapsing the prefix tree: Suppose A and B are bound, AB is the derived dimension. If B is not the last dimension to be bound, we can collapse the prefix tree by one level. A new root node is built, each node at the original second level becomes a child node of the new rootnode. The subtree under such a node is kept intact in the new tree. Figures 5 and 6 illustrate the collapse of one level in a prefix tree.

To facilitate the above, we create a horizontal pointer for each node in the same level so that the nodes form a linked list. A unique AB_tid is given to each of the nodes in the second level, which corresponds to the collapsed table AB. These unique tids at all the levels can be assigned when the prefix tree is first built.

Updating tid: We need to do the following with the collapse of the prefix tree. After binding two tables A and B, a "derived dimension" AB is formed. We update the tid_lists stored with the frequent itemsets and items that would be used in the following iteration, so that all of them are referencing to the same (derived) dimension table. For example, $tid_A(X)$ or $tid_B(Y)$ are updated to $tid_{AB}(X)$ or $tid_{AB}(Y)$.

3.4 Maintaining frequent itemsets in FI-trees

In both local mining and global mining (Steps 2 and 3), we need to keep frequent itemsets as they are found from which we can generate candidate itemsets of greater sizes. We keep all the discovered frequent itemsets of the *same size* in a tree structure which we call an **FI-tree** (FI stands for Frequent Itemset). Hence itemsets of $F^{A_3B_1}$ is mixed with itemsets of $F^{A_2B_2}$, the first one belongs to F^{AB_1}, the second belongs to F^{AB_2}.

4 Related Work

Some related work can be found in [JS00], where the joined table T is computed but without being materialized. When each row of the joined table is formed, it is processed and thereby storage cost for T is avoided. In the processing of each row in the table, an array that contains the frequencies for all candidate itemsets is updated. As pointed out by the authors, all itemsets are counted in one scan and there is no pruning from one pass to the next as in the apriori-gen algorithm in [AS94]. Therefore there can be many candidate itemsets and the approach is expensive in memory costs and computation costs. The empirical experiments in [JS00] compare their approach with a base case of applying the apriori algorithm on a materialized table for T. It is shown that the proposed method needs only 0.4 to 1 times the time compared to the base case. However, there are new algorithms in recent years such as [HPY00, SHS00] which are shown by experiment to often run many times faster than the apriori algorithm. Therefore, the approach in [JS00] may not be more efficient than such algorithms.

5 Experiments

We generate synthetic data sets in a similar way as [HPDW01]. First, we generate each dimension table individually, in which each record consists of a number of attribute values within the attribute domains, and model the existence of frequent itemsets. The parameters are listed in the following table:

D	number of dimensions
n	number of transactions in each dimension table
m	number of attributes in each dimension table
s	largest size of frequent itemsets
t	largest number of transactions with a common itemset
d	domain size of each attribute (same for all attributes)

The domain size d of an attribute is the number of different values for the attribute, which is the number of items derived from the attribute-value pairs for the attribute.

The value of n is set as 1000 in our experiment. After generating transactions for each dimension table, we generate FT based on parameters in the following table:

sup	target frequency of the association rules
$|L|$	number of maximal potentially frequent itemsets
N	number of noise transactions

In constructing FT, there can be correlations among two or more dimension tables so that some frequent itemsets contain items from multiple dimensions. For the case of two dimensions, we want the *tids* associated with the same group of transactions with common frequent itemsets from one dimension table to appear at least sup times together with another group of *tid* sharing common frequent itemsets from another dimension table. In doing so, frequent itemsets across dimensions from these 2 groups would appear with a frequency count greater than or equal to sup, after joining the two dimension tables and FT. We repeat this process for $|L|$ times, so that $|L|$ maximal potentially frequent itemsets would be formed (by **maximal**, we mean that no superset of the itemset is frequent).

In order to generate some random noise, transactions which do not contain frequent itemset are generated. N rows in FT are generated, in which each tid from the dimension tables is picked randomly.

We compare our proposed method with the approach of applying FP-tree algorithm [HPY00] on top of the joined table T. We assume T is kept on disk and hence requires I/O time for processing. FP-tree requires two scanning of T during the FP-tree mining. The I/O time required is up to 200 seconds in our experiments. It turns out that the table join time is not significant compared to the mining time.

All experiments are conducted on SUN Ultra-Enterprise Generic_106541-18 with SunOS 5.7 and 8192MB Main Memory. The average disk I/O rate is 8MB per second. Programs are written in C++. We calculate the total execution time of mining multiple tables as the sum of required

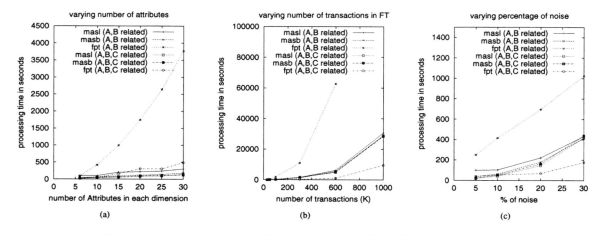

Figure 7. Running time for (A,B) related and (A,B,C) related datasets

CPU and I/O times, and that of mining a large joined table as the CPU and I/O times for joining and FP-tree mining.

For the local mining step in our approach, we use a vertical mining technique as in FORC [SHS00]: frequent itemsets of increasing sizes are discovered The tid_list of the itemsets are used to generate size $k + 1$ frequent itemsets from size k frequent itemsets, which is by intersecting the tid_lists of pairs of size k frequent itemsets with only one differing item. In the experiments, we compare the running time of **masl** (our proposed method, implementing tid_list as a linked list structure), **masb** (our proposed method, implementing tid_list as a fixed-size bitmap and an array of count), and **fpt** (the join-before-mine approach with FP-tree) with different data setting in 3 dimension tables A, B, C and a fact table FT. In most cases, $masb$ runs slightly faster than $masl$, but needs about 10 times more memory.

In the first dataset, we model the situation that items in A and B are strongly related, such that frequent itemsets contain items across A and B, while items in C are not involved. In such cases, transactions containing frequent itemsets from A and B can be related to Br transactions in C randomly. Br is set to 100 in all of our experiments reported here. (We have varied the value of Br and discovered little change in the performance.) The default values of other parameters used are :

number of transactions in the joined table	50K
number of attributes in each dimension table	10
size of each attribute domain	10
random noise	10%
max. size of potentially maximal frequent itemset	8

When we increase the number of items, the running time of fpt increases steeply, while that of both $masl$ and $masb$ would increase almost linearly. Running time of FP-tree

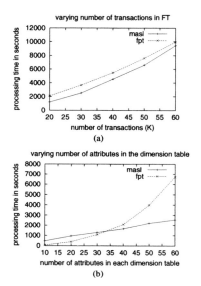

Figure 8. Running time for mixture datasets

grows exponentially with the depth of the tree, which is determined by the maximum number of items in a transaction. In this case, performance of our proposed method outperforms FP-tree, especially when the number of items in each transaction is large. (see Figure 7(a))

When the number of transactions in the joined table increases, running time of both methods would increase greatly. $masl$ and $masb$ are about 10 times faster than fpt (see Figure 7(b)). We also vary the percentage of random noise being included in the datasets, (see Figure 7(c)), both $masl$ and $masb$ are faster than fpt.

In the second dataset, we model the case that A, B, C are all strongly related, so that maximal frequent itemsets always contain items from all of A, B and C. Compared with the previous dataset, performance of our approach does not vary too much, while the running time of fpt is faster in some cases (Figures 7(b) and (c)). With the strong correlation, there would be less different patterns to be considered and the FP-tree will be smaller. However, we believe that in real life situation such a strong correlation will be rare.

In real life application, there are often mixtures of relationships across different dimension tables in the database. In the third group of dataset, we present data with such mixture. In particular, 10% of transactions contain frequent itemsets from only A, B, C, respectively, 15% contain frequent itemsets from AB, BC, AC respectively, 10% contain frequent itemsets from ABC, and 15% are random noise. We investigate how the running times of $masl$ and fpt vary against increasing number of items in each transaction, and increasing number of transactions in T.

In Figure 8(a), we vary the number of transactions from 20K to 60K, while keeping the number of attributes in each dimension table to be 30 In Figure 8(b), we vary the number of attributes in each dimension table from 10 to 60, and keep the number of transactions to be 30K. In this case, running time of fpt grows much faster than our approach. This demonstrates the advantage of applying our method, which would be more significant when we have more dimension tables so that the number of items in the T will be large.

6 Conclusion

We propose a new algorithm for mining association rules on a star schema without performing the natural join. We show by experiments that it can greatly outperform a method based on joining all tables even when the naive approach is equipped with a state-of-the-art efficient algorithm.

Our proposed method can be generalized to be applied to a **snowflake** structure, where there is a star structure with a fact table FT, but a dimension table can be replaced by another fact table FT' which is connected to a set of smaller dimension tables. We can consider mining across dimension tables related by FT' first. We then consider the result as a single derived dimension, and continue to process the star structure with FT. This means that we always mine from the "leaves" of the snowflake.

Our current experiments assume that the data structures we use can be kept in main memory. It will be of interest to study the case where disk memory is required for the intermediate steps. Since disk access is more expensive and our intermediate structure has been designed to be more compact than the fact table, we expect good performance to be found for the proposed approach in such cases. We have

not examined in our experiments the cases where the number of dimension tables is large. More study will be needed for these considerations.

In general, FT can contain attributes other than tid from dimension tables. In this case, we group all these attributes, put them in a separate new dimension table, and apply the same techniques to mine it as other dimension tables.

Acknowledgements This research is supported by the RGC (the Hong Kong Research Grants Council) grant UGC REF.CUHK 4179/01E. We thank Yin Ling Cheung for her help in the experiments and performance analysis.

References

[AIS93] R. Agrawal, T. Imilienski, and A. Swami. Mining association rules between sets of items in large datasets. Proceedings of the ACM SIGMOD International Conference on the Management of Data, pp 207-216, 1993.

[AS94] R. Agrawal and R. Srikant. Fast algorithm for mining association rules. Proceedings of the 20th VLDB Conference, pp 487-499, 1994.

[CD97] S. Chaudhuri and U. Dayal. An Overview of Data Warehousing and OLAP Technology. ACM SIGMOD Record, Vol. 26 No.1, pp 65-74, March 1997.

[HPDW01] J. Han, J. Pei, G. Dong, and K. Wang. Efficient computation of iceberg cubes with complex measures. Proceedings of the ACM SIGMOD International Conference on the Management of Data, pp 1-12, 2001.

[HPY00] J. Han and J. Pei and Y. Yin. Mining Frequent Patterns without Candidate Generation. Proceedings of the ACM SIGMOD International Conference on the Management of Data, pp 1-12, 2000.

[JS00] V.C. Jensen and N. Soparkar. Frequent Itemset Counting across Multiple Tables, Proceedings of Pacific-Asia Conference on Knowledge Discovery and Data Mining (PAKDD), pp 49-61, 2000.

[RS98] R. Rastogi and K. Shim, Mining Optimized Association Rules with Categorical and Numeric Attributes, Proc. of International Conference on Data Engineering (ICDE), pp 503-512, 1998.

[SHS00] P. Shenoy, J.R. Haritsa, S. Sudarshan. Turbo-charging vertical mining of large databases. Proceedings of the ACM SIGMOD International Conference on Management of Data, pp 22-33, 2000.

[SA96] Ramakrishnan Srikent, Rakesh Agrawal, Mining Quantitative Association Rules in Large Relational Tables, Proceedings of the ACM SIGMOD International Conference on Management of Data, pp 1-12, 1996.

[STA00] S.Sarawagi, S. Thomas, R. Agrawal Integrating association rule mining with relational database systems: Alternatives and implications. Data Mining and Knowledge Discovery, 4(2/3), 2000. (Also appeared in SIGMOD, pp 343-354, 1998.)

PERUSE: An Unsupervised Algorithm for Finding Recurring Patterns in Time Series

Tim Oates

Department of Computer Science and Electrical Engineering
University of Maryland Baltimore County
Baltimore, MD 21250
oates@cs.umbc.edu

Abstract

This paper describes PERUSE, *an unsupervised algorithm for finding recurring patterns in time series. It was initially developed and tested with sensor data from a mobile robot, i.e. noisy, real-valued, multivariate time series with variable intervals between observations. The pattern discovery problem is decomposed into two subproblems: (1) a supervised learning problem in which a teacher provides exemplars of patterns and labels time series according to whether they contain the patterns; (2) an unsupervised learning problem in which the time series are used to generate an approximation to the teacher. Experimental results show that* PERUSE *can discover patterns in audio data corresponding to recurring words in natural language utterances and patterns in the sensor data of a mobile robot corresponding to qualitatively distinct outcomes of taking actions.*

1. Introduction

We are interested in the unsupervised discovery of recurring patterns in noisy, real-valued, multivariate time series. Such time series can be produced, for example, by measuring indicators of the state of the economy, a patient in an intensive care unit, an industrial process, and so on. This paper describes the PERUSE algorithm (**P**attern **E**xtraction from **R**eal-valued sequences **US**ing **E**xpectation maximization), which was designed to address this problem. PERUSE was initially developed as a tool for discovering frequently recurring words in raw audio data, such as radio broadcasts. Because the algorithm is unsupervised and requires no domain knowledge, it solves a problem that is very similar to that faced by a child learning its first language - word discovery. This problem exhibits all of the difficulties that PERUSE was designed to handle, and will therefore be used as a motivating example.

Adults perceive spoken utterances as containing discrete words, sometimes leading to the false impression that word boundaries are somehow marked in the acoustic signal, much as word boundaries in written text are marked with spaces. It becomes clear that

this is not the case when listening to someone speak in an unfamiliar language. It is usually impossible to tell where one word leaves off and another begins. How do children discover sound patterns corresponding to words in their native language?

Consider the difficulties posed by the word discovery problem. The learner does not know how many distinct sound patterns (i.e. words) occur in the utterances, nor does it know whether or where a given pattern occurs in a given utterance. Different patterns have different temporal extents, e.g. the word "red" takes less time on average to utter than the word "conflagration", and different occurrences of the same pattern are never exactly the same, i.e. the audio waveforms corresponding to utterances of the same word by the same speaker are never identical. Some patterns are wholly contained in other patterns, e.g. "red" and "redolent". Finally, the learning problem is unsupervised. There is no teacher providing information beyond that contained in the utterances themselves.

The pattern discovery problem addressed by PERUSE can be conceptually decomposed into two subproblems. The first is a supervised learning problem in which a teacher provides exemplars of the patterns to be identified and labels time series according to whether they contain the patterns. Our solution to this problem is based on the Expectation Maximization (EM) algorithm and results in a representation of each pattern that can be used to determine the probability that a new time series contains a pattern and to localize the occurrence in time. The second subproblem is an unsupervised learning problem in which the time series are used to generate an approximation to the teacher. By composing the solutions to these two subproblems we obtain an unsupervised learning algorithm.

The remainder of the paper is organized as follows. Section 2 formally defines the pattern discovery problem. Sections 3 and 4 describe the two subproblems and their solutions. Section 5 describes experimental results showing that PERUSE can discover patterns in audio data corresponding to recurring words in natural language utterances (in English, German and Mandarin) and patterns in the sensor data of a mobile robot corresponding to qualitatively distinct outcomes of taking actions. Finally, section 6 summarizes, reviews related work, and points to future research directions.

2. Problem Description

We assume that a complete time series is generated by repeatedly selecting a pattern from a set of patterns according to some distribution and generating an exemplar. Some patterns may be chosen more frequently than others depending on this distribution. The goal of PERUSE is to discover the patterns used most frequently to generate segments of the time series data that it receives as input. This section makes precise the terms *time series* and *pattern*, and the next two sections describe how PERUSE identifies the latter in the former.

Let an *observation* be a pair of the form $(\mathbf{x}, t)$, where $\mathbf{x} \in \Re^n$ and $t \in \Re$. That is, $\mathbf{x}$ is a vector of length n whose elements are real numbers, and t is a real number that represents the time at which $\mathbf{x}$ was recorded. The vector $\mathbf{x}$ might contain the values produced by a set of n sensors attached to an ICU patient or the closing prices of a basket of n stocks.

A time series of length l is a set of l time-ordered observations:

$$\mathcal{S} = \{(\mathbf{x}_i, t_i) | 1 \le i \le l\}$$

The fact that the observations are time-ordered means that $t_i < t_j$ whenever $i < j$. Let $\mathbf{x}_i^k$ denote the value of the kth element in the vector observed at time t_i. A multivariate time series contains the following n univariate constituent time series:

$$\mathcal{S} = \{\{\{x_i^k, t_i\} | 1 \le i \le l\} | 1 \le k \le n\}$$

We define patterns in terms of a representation and a metric. The representation defines a space of possible patterns, and the metric makes it possible to identify "good" patterns in the data. Let a *pattern element* be a pair of the form $(\hat{\mathbf{x}}, \Delta t)$, where $\hat{\mathbf{x}} \in \{\Re^2 \cup \texttt{nil}\}^n$ and $\Delta t \in \Re^2$. Patterns occur in multivariate time series containing n constituent time series, so both observation vectors and pattern element vectors must contain n elements. A pattern of length l is represented as a totally-ordered set of l pattern elements:

$$\mathcal{P} = \{(\hat{\mathbf{x}}_j, \Delta t_j) | 1 \le j \le l\}$$

The above is a precise specification of pattern syntax. We now turn our attention to pattern semantics, i.e. the roles of $\hat{\mathbf{x}}$ and Δt.

Let $\hat{\mathbf{x}}^k$ be the kth element of pattern element vector $\hat{\mathbf{x}}$. When $\hat{\mathbf{x}}^k = \texttt{nil}$, the pattern element says nothing about the value in the kth constituent time series.

When $\hat{\mathbf{x}}^k \in \Re^2$, its value specifies the mean and standard deviation of a normal distribution to which the value in the kth constituent time series can be compared, i.e. $\hat{\mathbf{x}}^k = (\mu^k, \sigma^k)$. Let $\mu(\hat{\mathbf{x}}^k)$ and $\sigma(\hat{\mathbf{x}}^k)$ be the mean and standard deviation associated with $\hat{\mathbf{x}}^k$, respectively. Let $p(x|\mu, \sigma)$ be the value of the normal probability density function with parameters μ and σ at x. Given an observation vector, $\mathbf{x}$, and a pattern element vector, $\hat{\mathbf{x}}$, it is possible to compute the probability of $\mathbf{x}$ given $\hat{\mathbf{x}}$ as follows:

$$p(\mathbf{x}|\hat{\mathbf{x}}) = \prod_{k=1}^{n} \left\{ \begin{array}{ll} 1 & \text{if } \mathbf{x}^k = \texttt{nil} \\ p(\mathbf{x}^k|\mu(\hat{\mathbf{x}}^k), \sigma(\hat{\mathbf{x}}^k)) & \text{otherwise} \end{array} \right\}$$

Given a time series, $\mathcal{S}$, and a pattern, $\mathcal{P}$, it is natural to ask whether and where $\mathcal{P}$ occurs in $\mathcal{S}$. Let γ be a mapping from pattern elements in $\mathcal{P}$ to observations in $\mathcal{S}$. That is, if $\gamma(i) = j$, then the ith pattern element maps to the jth observation. γ specifies where $\mathcal{P}$ might occur in $\mathcal{S}$.

Given a mapping, it is possible to compute the time interval between two consecutive observations *in the mapping*, i.e. $t_{\gamma(i+1)} - t_{\gamma(i)}$. The two real numbers that comprise Δt_i are the mean and standard deviation of a normal distribution to which this time interval can be compared. When γ maps onto an actual occurrence of $\mathcal{P}$ in $\mathcal{S}$, it is assumed that the time between two observations in $\mathcal{S}$ that correspond to two consecutive pattern elements in $\mathcal{P}$ is normally distributed (or at least that the normal is a good approximation to the true distribution).

It is now possible to compute the probability that the observations in $\mathcal{S}$ onto which $\mathcal{P}$ is mapped represent an occurrence of the pattern as follows:

$$\begin{aligned} p(\mathcal{S}|\mathcal{P}, \gamma) &= p(\mathbf{x}_{\gamma(l)}|\hat{\mathbf{x}}_l) \prod_{i=1}^{l-1} p(\mathbf{x}_{\gamma(i)}|\hat{\mathbf{x}}_i) * \\ &\quad p(t_{\gamma(i+1)} - t_{\gamma(i)}|\mu(\Delta t_i), \sigma(\Delta t_i)) \quad (1) \end{aligned}$$

Equation 1 is simply the product of the probabilities of each observation vector given the corresponding pattern element vector and the probabilities of the time intervals between consecutive observations in the mapping given Δt for the corresponding pattern element. The probability $p(\mathbf{x}_l|\hat{\mathbf{x}}_{\gamma(l)})$ is outside of the product because $\mathbf{x}_l$ is the last observation in the mapping and there is thus no corresponding Δt_l.

Note that PERUSE must search over two spaces to find candidates with high scores - the space of candidate patterns and, for each candidate, the space of mappings from candidates onto time series (for the purpose of evaluating equation 1). The EM algorithm lies at the core of the search over candidate space, and dynamic programming is used to find optimal mappings (i.e. those that maximize equation 1) efficiently.

3. A Supervised Subproblem

Given a set of exemplars of a particular pattern, estimating the parameters of the pattern is trivial. Let $\mathcal{P}$ be a pattern and let $\mathcal{E} = \{S_1, S_2, \ldots, S_m\}$ be a set of m exemplars of $\mathcal{P}$. Each element of $\mathcal{E}$ contains a single pattern, i.e. $\mathcal{P}$. Let $\mathbf{x}_i(S)$ denote the ith observation vector in time series S, and let $\Delta t_i(S)$ be defined analogously. Let $\mu(\hat{\mathbf{x}}_i^k)$ denote the mean specified by the kth element of the ith vector in $\mathcal{P}$, and let $\sigma(\hat{\mathbf{x}}_i^k)$ be defined analogously. The maximum likelihood (ML) estimate of $\mu(\hat{\mathbf{x}}_i^k)$ is as follows:

$$\mu(\hat{\mathbf{x}}_i^k) = \frac{\sum_{S \in \mathcal{E}} \mathbf{x}_i^k(S)}{m}$$

That is, the ML estimate of $\mu(\hat{\mathbf{x}}_i^k)$ is simply the mean of the values generated from distribution $\hat{\mathbf{x}}_i^k$. One such value appears in position $\mathbf{x}_i^k$ in each of the exemplars. Likewise, the ML estimate of $\sigma(\hat{\mathbf{x}}_i^k)$ is as follows:

$$\sigma(\hat{\mathbf{x}}_i^k) = \left(\frac{\sum_{S \in \mathcal{E}} (\mathbf{x}_i^k(S) - \mu(\hat{\mathbf{x}}_i^k))^2}{m} \right)^{1/2} \quad (2)$$

The ML estimate of $\mu(\Delta t_i)$ is as follows:

$$\mu(\Delta t_i) = \frac{\sum_{S \in \mathcal{E}} (t_{i+1} - t_i)}{m} \quad (3)$$

That is, the ML estimate of $\mu(\Delta t_i)$ is simply the mean of the values generated from distribution Δt_i. One such value appears in each exemplar as the time interval between observation i and observation $i+1$. Finally, the ML estimate of $\sigma(\Delta t_i)$ is as follows:

$$\sigma(\Delta t_i) = \left(\frac{\sum_{S \in \mathcal{E}} ((t_{i+1} - t_i) - \mu(\Delta t_i))}{m} \right)^{1/2} \quad (4)$$

Given a set of exemplars generated from $\mathcal{P}$, estimating the parameters of $\mathcal{P}$ is straightforward.

Unfortunately, we do not have access to a set of clearly delineated exemplars of any patterns. In this section we assume that we have access to a single such exemplar and a set of time series that are labeled according to whether or not they contain an exemplar as well. Note that the time series that do contain an exemplar will in general contain additional unrelated data, perhaps generated by some other pattern or patterns.

It should be clear that given a set of time series containing exemplars of a pattern and the mappings for each of the time series, we can extract the exemplars and compute the maximum likelihood estimates of the

means and standard deviations of the pattern elements as described above. The resulting formula for $\mu(\hat{\mathbf{x}}_i^k)$, which applies the mapping function γ to translate positions in pattern elements to positions of exemplars in time series, is as follows:

$$\mu(\hat{\mathbf{x}}_i^k) = \frac{\sum_{S \in \mathcal{E}} \mathbf{x}_{\gamma_S(i)}^k(S)}{m}$$

The value generated by distribution $\hat{\mathbf{x}}_i^k$ is found at position $\mathbf{x}_{\gamma_S(i)}^k$ in the time series. The formulas for $\sigma(\hat{\mathbf{x}}_i^k)$, $\mu(\Delta t_i)$, and $\sigma(\Delta t_i)$ can be obtained in an analogous manner from equations 2, 3, and 4, respectively.

This is a classic example of a hidden data problem. Given the mappings, it is easy to compute the maximum likelihood estimates of $\mu(\hat{\mathbf{x}}_i^k)$, $\sigma(\hat{\mathbf{x}}_i^k)$, $\mu(\Delta t_i)$, and $\sigma(\Delta t_i)$. However, we are not given access to the mappings. This difficulty is overcome with the EM algorithm.

Suppose that all of the mappings are of the form $\gamma_S(i) = i + C_S$ for some constant C_S that differs for each time series S. Such mappings will be called consecutive mappings because consecutive pattern elements are mapped to consecutive observations in the time series. Let $z_{S,i}$ be an indicator variable defined for time series S. We will use the simpler notation z_i when the identity of S is clear. By definition, $z_i = 1$ if an an occurrence of the pattern ends at position i in S, otherwise $z_i = 0$. Under the assumption that all mappings are consecutive, knowledge of $z_{S,i}$ for all S and all i is sufficient to determine the maximum likelihood estimates of the pattern's parameters.

The E step involves computing the expected value of $z_{S,i}$ given the current estimate of $\mathcal{P}$. Recall that $z_{S,i} = 1$ if an exemplar of $\mathcal{P}$ ends at position i in time series S and it equals zero otherwise. Therefore, the expected value of $z_{S,i}$ is 0 times the probability that an exemplar of $\mathcal{P}$ does not end at position i in S plus 1 times the probability that an exemplar of $\mathcal{P}$ ends at position i in S, which is simply the latter probability (see equation 1).

In the M step, new parameter estimates are computed given the expected values of the hidden data. The formula for computing $\mu(\hat{\mathbf{x}}_i^k)$, which will be explained in detail shortly, is given below:

$$\mu(\hat{\mathbf{x}}_i^k) = \frac{\sum_{S \in \mathcal{E}} \sum_{j=|\mathcal{P}|}^{|S|} (z_{S,j} * \mathbf{x}_{j-|\mathcal{P}|+1+i}^k(S))}{\sum_{S \in \mathcal{E}} \sum_{j=|\mathcal{P}|}^{|S|} z_{S,j}} \quad (5)$$

Consider the numerator in the above expression. The outer sum is just a sum over all of the time series. For each time series, S, the inner sum is over all locations in S where a consecutive mapping of pattern $\mathcal{P}$ can end. Inside this double sum is a product of two quantities. The first is simply $z_{\mathcal{S},j}$, the probability that an exemplar of $\mathcal{P}$ ends at position j in $\mathcal{S}$. The second quantity is the value that would have been generated by $\mu(\hat{\mathbf{x}}_i^k)$ in that exemplar. If the exemplar ends at position j, then it begins at position $j - \texttt{length}(\mathcal{P}) + 1$, so $j - \texttt{length}(\mathcal{P}) + 1 + i$ is the index in $\mathcal{S}$ to which the ith element of $\mathcal{P}$ is mapped. The denominator is the same except the double sum is just over the values of $z_{\mathcal{S},j}$. The formula for computing $\sigma(\hat{\mathbf{x}}_i^k)$, which is similar to equation 5, is given below:

$$\sqrt{\frac{\sum_{\mathcal{S} \in \mathcal{E}} \sum_{j=|\mathcal{P}|}^{|\mathcal{S}|} (z_{\mathcal{S},j} * (\mathbf{x}_{j-|\mathcal{P}|+1+i}^k(\mathcal{S}) - \mu(\hat{\mathbf{x}}_i^k))^2)}{\sum_{\mathcal{S} \in \mathcal{E}} \sum_{j=|\mathcal{P}|}^{|\mathcal{S}|} z_{\mathcal{S},j}}}$$

The formula for $\mu(\Delta t_i)$ is an analogous extension to equation 3, and the formula for $\sigma(\Delta t_i)$ is an analogous extension to equation 4.

This section has assumed that we are given an exemplar of a particular pattern to be discovered, as well as a set of time series labeled according to whether or not they contain exemplars of the pattern. To ensure that EM identifies the parameters of the target pattern, rather than some other common pattern, our initial guess as to the parameters of $\mathcal{P}$ is guided by the exemplar. In particular, the means of the pattern are initialized to be the values in the exemplar, i.e. $\mu(\hat{\mathbf{x}}_i^k) = \mathbf{x}_i^k$, where $\mathbf{x}_i^k$ is the kth item in the ith element of the exemplar. The standard deviations are all initialized to be a small constant value. The goal is to start EM in an area in parameter space that is close to the set of parameters that we are seeking.

There is one last issue to contend with. All of the discussion to this point has assumed consecutive mappings. In general, such mappings will be inadequate. Given a time series $\mathcal{S}$, a pattern $\mathcal{P}$, and the constraint that mapping γ must end at location i is $\mathcal{S}$, it is possible to use dynamic programming to identify the mapping that maximizes $p(\mathcal{S}|\mathcal{P}, \gamma)$ in $O(|\mathcal{S}| * |\mathcal{P}|)$ time. When computing parameters in the M step, we use the mapping identified by dynamic programming that ends at a given position rather than the consecutive mapping that ends at that position.

4. Approximating the Teacher

Given an exemplar of pattern $\mathcal{P}$ and a set of time series labeled according to whether or not they contain exemplars, the preceding section described how the EM algorithm can be used to estimate the parameters of $\mathcal{P}$. This section describes how an approximation to this training information, i.e. exemplars and labels, can be obtained in an unsupervised manner from the data.

Recall that we assume a time series is generated by repeatedly selecting a pattern according to some distribution over patterns and then generating an exemplar of the chosen pattern. The time series is the concatenation of these exemplars. Time series generated in this manner have two useful properties. First, by definition, there are many exemplars in the data of frequently occurring patterns. We expect there to be one or more "good" exemplars of frequently occurring patterns. Second, pattern boundaries are characterized by a lack of predictability. Within a pattern there is regularity that can be used to predict future data. But when a pattern ends the next observation depends entirely on which pattern is chosen from the distribution over patterns.

PERUSE uses these observations to identify windows of data in the time series that fall within frequently occurring patterns. This is accomplished by passing a window that spans *window_size* time steps over each of the time series. *window_size* is a user-defined parameter that must be set appropriately for each problem domain. For each such window of data, a pattern $\mathcal{P}$ is created by initializing its parameters from the data inside the window as described in section 4. For each time series, $\mathcal{S}$, including the one from which the window of data was taken, dynamic programming is used to identify the mapping that yields the highest value of $p(\mathcal{S}|\mathcal{P}, \gamma_{\mathcal{S}})$ for that time series. That is, dynamic programming is used to find the mapping that is most likely to represent an exemplar of $\mathcal{P}$ in each of the time series. This mapping is called the *maximum probability mapping*.

Next, the *min_matches* time series whose maximum probability mappings yield the highest values of $p(\mathcal{S}|\mathcal{P}, \gamma_{\mathcal{S}})$ are identified. *min_matches* is a user-defined parameter, and typical values are small, such as three or four. Because these time series contain the best matches to the data in the window from which $\mathcal{P}$ was initialized, they are assumed to contain exemplars of $\mathcal{P}$. The window of data from which $\mathcal{P}$ was initialized is considered an exemplar, and this exemplar and the *min_matches* time series just identified are passed to the algorithm described in section 3 to obtain an ML estimate of the parameters of the underlying pattern.

When the parameters of $\mathcal{P}$ have been estimated, dynamic programming is once again used to identify the maximum probability mapping for each of the time series used in the estimation process. The sum of the logarithms of the probabilities associated with these mappings is recorded. This value is plotted as a function of window position for each of the time series.

The time series and window location that yield the highest value are identified. The data within this window are assumed to fall completely within a frequently occurring pattern (i.e. one that occurs more than *min_matches* times) because several "high quality" matches to the pattern occur in the data.

Let $\mathcal{E}$ be the set of *min_matches* time series used to estimate the parameters of the pattern underlying the data in the window, and let $\mathcal{P}$ be the result of the estimation process. Because the window spans a fixed time interval, the next step is to identify the true temporal extent of the underlying pattern. This is accomplished by extending the window used to initialize $\mathcal{P}$ by *grow_size* units of time. This new window of data and the time series in $\mathcal{E}$ are then handed to the algorithm described in section 4, resulting in a new pattern $\mathcal{P}'$.

Suppose $\mathcal{P}$ was initialized from time series data spanning time t_1 to time t_2. That means that $\mathcal{P}'$ spans t_1 to $t_2 + grow\_size$. If the quality of the maximum probability mappings for $\mathcal{P}'$ are higher for the portion of the pattern initialized from the data spanning time t_1 to t_2 are significantly higher than for the portion initialized from the data spanning time t_2 to $t_2 + grow\_size$, this is taken as an indication that growing the window resulted in a pattern boundary being crossed. The window is repeatedly extended by adding *grow_size* time steps to t_2 until a boundary crossing is detected, and then the window is extended in the other direction by subtracting *grow_size* time steps from t_1 until a boundary crossing is detected. The final values of t_1 and t_2 are taken to be the true temporal extent of the pattern underlying the original window of data.

How is it possible to determine when the quality of one portion of a maximum probability mapping is significantly higher than the quality of another portion? Recall that when $\gamma_S(i) = j$, it is the case that the ith pattern element maps to the jth observation in $\mathcal{S}$. That is, it is the case that $\hat{\mathbf{x}}_i$ maps to $\mathbf{x}_j$. The quality of this part of the total mapping is evaluated as follows (see equation 1):

$$q(\mathcal{P}, \mathcal{S}, i, j) = \log\left(p(\mathbf{x}_j | \hat{\mathbf{x}}_i) p(t_{j+1} - t_j | \Delta t_i)\right)$$

Let Q_{old} be the set of quality values associated with the portion of pattern $\mathcal{P}$ that was initialized from the data spanning time t_1 to t_2.

$$Q_{old} = \{q(\mathcal{P}, \mathcal{S}, i, \gamma_S(i)) | \mathcal{S} \in \mathcal{E}, t_1 \le t_i < t_2\}$$

Let Q_{new} be the set of quality values associated with the portion of pattern $\mathcal{P}$ that was initialized from the data spanning time t_2 to $t_2 + grow\_size$. To compare the quality of the matches due to these two portions of $\mathcal{P}$ we can compare the values in Q_{old} and Q_{new}. This comparison is made with a standard one-tailed t-test using a significance level of $\alpha_{temporal}$ which is specified by the user. If the result of the t-test is not significant at the specified level, then a pattern boundary

has not been crossed and the bounds of the window are extended again.

The next step is to determine whether and where the pattern occurs in the other time series. This is accomplished as follows. Dynamic programming is used to determine the maximum probability mapping for each of the time series. The *min_matches*+1 time series with the highest associated probabilities are identified. The pattern is then retrained on these time series. Then a large number of exemplars are generated from the pattern by sampling from the distributions in each $\hat{\mathbf{x}}$ and Δt and their probabilities given the pattern are calculated. The result is a distribution of such probabilities. Then the probability of the maximum likelihood mapping for each of the *min_matches* time series given the pattern is compared to this distribution. If any of these values is smaller than $100 * (1 - \alpha_{series})\%$ of the values in the distribution, then it is assumed that the corresponding data were not generated by the pattern. In this case, it is assumed that the original *min_matches* time series are the only ones that contain exemplars. Otherwise, the value of *min_matches* is increased by one and the procedure is repeated until either *min_matches* equals the total number of time series or the statistical test fails. The end result is the identification of which time series contain exemplars of the pattern and where they occur, as indicated by the maximum probability mappings.

5. Experiments

This section describes the results of two sets of experiments that show PERUSE can discover patterns in audio data corresponding to recurring words in natural language utterances and patterns in the sensor data of a mobile robot corresponding to qualitatively distinct outcomes of taking actions.

In the first experiment, four subjects were asked to create random configurations of styrofoam blocks of various sizes, shapes and colors. Fifty of these configurations were then shown to a native speaker of English, a native speaker of German, and a native speaker of Mandarin. They were asked to generate natural language utterances describing what they saw. The only restriction placed on the utterances was that they had to be truthful statements about the scenes. This, coupled with the limited number of colors, sizes and shapes exhibited by the blocks, ensured that some words would be used in multiple utterances. One of the configurations was described by the English speaker as follows: "The cone is on top of the rectangle and to the left of the red ball." This is typical of the kind of utterances that were recorded. The English speaker used 60 unique words in the 50 utterances and each utterance contained on average 11.06 words. These quantities are 89 and 11.46 for the German speaker, and 37 and 19.04 for the Mandarin speaker.

Utterances were recorded with a head-mounted, noise-canceling microphone at a sampling rate of 8000 Hz. The raw audio signals were pre-processed using the publicly available RASTA-PLP package to extract 20 coefficients every 80 samples (Hermansky et al., 1991).

All 50 utterances for a given language, appropriately pre-processed, were passed to the PERUSE algorithm to find recurring patterns, i.e. words. The algorithm requires the user to specify a number of parameters. These parameters were tuned on the English utterances and were used unchanged on the German and Mandarin utterances. The performance of the algorithm appeared to be robust with respect to the choice of parameters, with small changes in parameters leading to little or no effect on performance. The specific parameter values used were as follows: $window\_size = 2000$ samples, thereby spanning one-fourth of one second of speech; $min\_matches = 4$ time series; $grow\_size = 500$ samples and spans one-sixteenth of a second; $\alpha_{temporal} = 0.00001$; $\alpha_{series} = 0.00001$.

To understand the performance of PERUSE on this task, consider table 1. Of the 60 words used by the English speaker the table shows those words that occurred four or more times. Because PERUSE is designed to find frequently recurring patterns, it has no hope of finding words that occur only once or twice. Inflected variants of words are not shown. For the purpose of assessing the performance of PERUSE, the algorithm is considered to be successful if it discovers the base form of a word and identifies inflected variants as instances of the base form. For example, it is correct for the algorithm to say that the word "balls" represents an occurrence of the word "ball".

Table 1. The list of the words used frequently by the English speaker with those words that were discovered by PERUSE shown in bold.

A	Green	Small
Above	Is	**Square**
And	**Large**	**That's**
Balanced	**Little**	The
Ball	**Next to**	To
Below	Of	Top
Big	**On top of**	**Touching**
Blue	One	Two
Circle	**Rectangle**	**Yellow**
Cone	**Red**	

Those words identified by PERUSE are shown in bold. Intuitively, a word is said to be identified when a pattern is discovered that can be used with high accuracy both to determine whether an occurrence of the word occurs in an utterance and to localize such occurrences in time. More concretely, each pattern P discovered by PERUSE was used to determine whether and where it occurred in each of the input time series. An occurrence of pattern P is said to correspond to an occurrence of word W if the starting and ending points of the occurrence of P match the starting and ending points of the occurrence of W within a temporal window no greater than 5% of the total length of the occurrence of W. Given all of the locations in the time series where the pattern has been identified to occur, word W is said to be identified by pattern P if 90% or more of the occurrences of P correspond to occurrences of W and if no more than 10% of the occurrences of P do not correspond to occurrences of W. That is, the ratio of hits to misses must be at least 9-to-1 and the ratio of hits to false positives must be at least 9-to-1.

Several aspects of table 1 are noteworthy. First, PERUSE discovered more than 65% of the frequent words used by the English speaker. This is a remarkable feat given that the algorithm has access to a mere 50 utterances and that it does not make use of any knowledge about the English language. In particular, it has no knowledge of characteristics of human speech that indicate word boundaries and it has no knowledge of phonemes. Virtually all past work on word discovery with real utterances has assumed access to some knowledge of this type.

Second, both "next to" and "on top of" were discovered as single word units. On the face of it, this is an error. However, on close inspection of the transcripts of the English utterances, it is clear that the algorithm did exactly the right thing in these two cases. Every time the English speaker uttered the word "next" he said "next to", and every time he uttered the word "on" he said "on top of".

In virtually all cases, patterns discovered by PERUSE erred on the side of misses rather than false positives. That is, the patterns would more often fail to identify an occurrence of a word than say that a word occurred where it didn't. It is possible that raising the value of α_{series} can shift this balance in the other direction. Also, the patterns tended to match too much of the time series rather than too little. That is, the patterns would often match all of the data corresponding to an occurrence of the underlying word plus some amount of additional adjacent data.

The results for German and Mandarin were similar, with 72.9% of the German words that occurred four or more times being discovered and 78.4% of the mandarin words. Again, these results are impressive given the relatively small sample of training data and the total lack of any knowledge of language and linguistics on the part of the algorithm.

In the second experiment PERUSE was used to identify patterns in the sensor data of a mobile robot corresponding to qualitatively distinct outcomes of taking actions. The robot was given a controller parameterized by two real numbers that influenced how its movements would be affected by objects visible in the images returned by a CCD camera (Braitenberg, 1984). The robot explored its two-dimensional action space by stochastically selecting a pair of parameters for the controller and running it for a fixed amount of time. Prior to running the controller, a single object was placed in a random location in the robot's environment. Sensory information included the size of the object in pixels, the coordinates of its centroid in the visual field, its mean hue/saturation/intensity, the height and width of the bounding box around the object, and a wavelet-based representation of the shape of the object. Each of these values was recorded at a rate of approximately 10 Hz during invocations of the controller.

Data from a total of 50 invocations of the controller were gathered, and PERUSE was applied to the resulting time series in an effort to find patterns, i.e. possible effects of running the controller. Note that there were a total of 250 time series with one set of 50 time series for each of the five groups of sensors described above. PERUSE was applied to each of these five sets individually. The parameters used were as follows: $window\_size = 15$ samples, thereby spanning one and a half seconds; $min\_matches = 3$ time series; $grow\_size = 5$ samples, i.e. one half of a second; $\alpha_{temporal} = 0.001$; $\alpha_{series} = 0.001$.

Given the set of patterns discovered by PERUSE in the sensor data, each experience (i.e. controller invocation) was labeled according to the pattern that had the highest likelihood match on one of its constituent time series. This induced a partition of the robot's experiences. A human subject was shown video of the robot's experiences and asked to create their own partition. The similarity of these partitions was assessed as follows. Given two pairs of experiences, we can ask whether they were placed together or apart in the partition created by the human. We can also ask whether they were placed together or apart in the partition induced by PERUSE.

The human and PERUSE agreed on whether two experiences belonged together or apart 88.7% of the time. Accordance with respect to putting experiences together is 91.9% and accordance with respect to putting

them apart is 88.0%. The subsequences matched by patterns were on average one fifth the size of the full time series. Clearly, PERUSE discovered those portions of the time series that were central to the judgments made by the human in determining whether two experiences are qualitatively alike or not.

6. Discussion

The line of work that most directly influenced the development of PERUSE comes from the bioinformatics literature. Hertz *et al.* developed a greedy algorithm for discovering a single, fixed-width pattern shared by each member of a set of DNA sequences (Hertz et al., 1990). Lawerence and Reilly built on this work to develop an algorithm that solves the same problem using EM (Lawrence et al., 1993). All of this work served as the foundation for Bailey and Elkan's MEME algorithm (Bailey & Elkan, 1995), which uses data from the sequences to serve as seed patterns and uses a heuristic modification to EM that allows the number of occurrences of a pattern to be different than the total number of sequences.

PERUSE differs from MEME in a number of important ways. First, MEME is restricted to working with univariate, discrete data in which there is really no notion of time. Nucleotides simply follow one another spatially. PERUSE works with continuous, multivariate time series in which time is represented explicitly. This leads to very different considerations, and significant additional complexity, in determining how to represent patterns and apply EM. For example, PERUSE allows pattern elements to map to the same time step (i.e. insertions) or to skip over time steps (i.e. deletions) when being matched to the data. MEME does not allow either insertions or deletions. The patters discovered by PERUSE can have varying widths, compared to the fixed-width patterns discovered by MEME. Finally, to discover multiple patterns, the user of MEME must specify a parameter that tells the algorithm roughly how many patterns there are. PERUSE continues searching for patterns as long as the data support their existence.

The word discovery problem has been studied extensively, but virtually all existing approaches assume that utterances are represented as text with the spaces removed (Brent, 1999; de Marcken, 1996; Elman, 1990; Harris, 1954). Those algorithms that work with audio data typically incorporate knowledge of the target language, such as the phonemes that it contains (Roy, 1999). PERUSE does not require such knowledge and therefore moving from one language to another is trivial.

There has been a tremendous amount of work devoted to discovering patterns in time series, but in almost every case assumptions are made that are not made by PERUSE: that the data are categorical (Agrawal & Srikant, 1994; Das et al., 1998; Zaki, 2001); that patterns correspond to regions of time series generated by a single normal distribution rather than a complex sequence of different normal distributions; that the intervals between observations are fixed rather than variable (Oates & Cohen, 1996); that the time series are univariate rather than multivariate (Keogh, 1997); that patterns span entire time series rather than having multiple patterns in a single time series (Keogh & Pazzani, 1998).

Future work will involve creating an incremental version of the algorithm and applying it to additional problem domains.

Acknowledgments

The author would like to thank Paul R. Cohen for his support, both financial and intellectual, of the work described in this paper, which is based on the author's Ph.D. research. This research was supported by DARPA/USASMDC (Defense Advanced Research Projects Agency/U.S. Army Space and Missile Defense Command) under contract number DASG60-99-C-0074. The U.S. Government is authorized to reproduce and distribute reprints for governmental purposes notwithstanding any copyright notation hereon. The views and conclusions contained herein are those of the authors and should not be interpreted as necessarily representing the official policies or endorsements, either expressed or implied, of the DARPA/USASMDC or the U.S. Government.

References

Agrawal, R., & Srikant, R. (1994). Fast algorithms for mining association rules. *Proceedings of the 20th International Conference on Very Large Databases.*

Bailey, T. L., & Elkan, C. (1995). Unsupervised learning of multiple motifs in biopolymers using expectation maximization. *Machine Learning, 21,* 51–83.

Braitenberg, V. (1984). *Vehicles: Experiments in synthetic psychology.* The MIT Press.

Brent, M. R. (1999). An efficient and probabilistically sound algorithm for word discovery. *Machine Learning, 34,* 71–105.

Das, G., Lin, K.-I., Mannila, H., Renganathan, G., & Smyth, P. (1998). Rule discovery from time series. *Proceedings of the Fourth International Conference on Knowledge Discovery and Data Mining* (pp. 16–22).

de Marcken, C. (1996). *Unsupervised language acquisition.* Doctoral dissertation, MIT.

Elman, J. L. (1990). Finding structure in time. *Cognitive Science, 14,* 179–211.

Harris, Z. S. (1954). Distributional structure. *Word, 10,* 146–162.

Hermansky, H., Morgan, N., Bayya, A., & Kohn, P. (1991). *Rasta-plp speech analysis*Technical Report TR-91-069). International Computer Science Institute.

Hertz, G. Z., Hartzell, G. W., & Stormo, G. D. (1990). Identification of concensus patterns in un-aligned DNA sequences known to be functionally related. *Computer Applications in Biosciences, 6,* 81–92.

Keogh, E. (1997). Fast similarity search in the presence of longitudinal scaling in time series databases. *Proceedings of Ninth International Conference on Tools with Artificial Intelligence* (pp. 578–584).

Keogh, E., & Pazzani, M. J. (1998). An enhanced representation of time series which allows fast and accurate classification, clustering and relevance feedback. *Proceedings of the Fourth International Conference on Knowledge Discovery and Data Mining* (pp. 239–243).

Lawrence, C. E., Altschul, S. F., Boguski, M. S., Liu, J. S., Neuwald, A. F., & Wooton, J. C. (1993). Detecting subtle sequence signals: A gibbs sampling strategy for multiple alignment. *Science, 262,* 208–214.

Oates, T., & Cohen, P. R. (1996). Searching for structure in multiple streams of data. *Proceedings of the Thirteenth International Conference on Machine Learning* (pp. 346 – 354).

Roy, D. (1999). *Learning words from sights and sounds: a computational model.* Doctoral dissertation, MIT.

Zaki, M. J. (2001). SPADE: An efficient algorithm for mining frequent sequences. *Machine Learning, 42,* 31–60.

Adaptive and Resource-Aware Mining of Frequent Sets

S. Orlando[1], P. Palmerini[1,2], R. Perego[2], F. Silvestri[2,3]

[1]Dipartimento di Informatica, Università Ca' Foscari, Venezia, Italy
[2]Istituto ISTI, Consiglio Nazionale delle Ricerche (CNR), Pisa, Italy
[3]Dipartimento di Informatica, Università di Pisa, Italy

Abstract

The performance of an algorithm that mines frequent sets from transactional databases may severely depend on the specific features of the data being analyzed. Moreover, some architectural characteristics of the computational platform used – e.g. the available main memory – can dramatically change its runtime behavior. In this paper we present DCI *(Direct Count & Intersect), an efficient algorithm for discovering frequent sets from large databases. Due to the multiple heuristics strategies adopted,* DCI *can adapt its behavior not only to the features of the specific computing platform, but also to the features of the dataset being mined, so that it results very effective in mining both short and long patterns from sparse and dense datasets. Finally we also discuss the parallelization strategies adopted in the design of* ParDCI, *a distributed and multi-threaded implementation of* DCI.

1 Introduction

Association Rule Mining (ARM), one of the most popular topic in the KDD field, regards the extractions of association rules from a database of transactions $\mathcal{D}$. Each rule has the form $X \Rightarrow Y$, where X and Y are sets of items (*itemsets*), such that $(X \cap Y) = \emptyset$. A rule $X \Rightarrow Y$ holds in $\mathcal{D}$ with a minimum confidence c and a minimum support s, if at least the $c\%$ of all the transactions containing X also contains Y, and $X \cup Y$ is present in at least the $s\%$ of all the transactions of the database. In this paper we are interested in the most computationally expensive phase of ARM, i.e the Frequent Set Counting (*FSC*) one. During this phase, the set of all the *frequent* itemsets is built. An itemset of k items (k-itemset) is frequent if its support is greater than the fixed threshold s, i.e. the itemset occurs in at least $minsup$ transactions ($minsup = s/100 \cdot n$, where n is the number of transactions in $\mathcal{D}$).

The computational complexity of the FSC problem derives from the exponential size of its search space $\mathcal{P}(M)$, i.e. the power set of M, where M is the set of items contained in the various transactions of $\mathcal{D}$. A way to prune $\mathcal{P}(M)$ is to restrict the search to itemsets whose subsets are all frequent. The *Apriori* algorithm [5] exactly exploits this pruning technique, and visits breadth-first $\mathcal{P}(M)$ for counting itemset supports. At each iteration k, *Apriori* generates C_k, a set of candidate k-itemsets, and counts the occurrences of these candidates in the transactions. The candidates in C_k for which the the minimum support constraint holds are then inserted into F_k, i.e. the set of frequent k-itemsets, and the next iteration is started. Other algorithms adopt instead a depth-first visit of $\mathcal{P}(M)$ [8, 2]. In this case the goal is to discover long frequent itemsets first, thus saving the work needed for discovering frequent itemsets included in long ones. Unfortunately, while it is simple to derive all the frequent itemsets from the maximal ones, the same does not hold for their supports, which require a further counting step. In the last years several variations to the original *Apriori* algorithm, as well as many parallel implementations, have been proposed. We can recognize two main methods for determining the supports of the various itemsets present in $\mathcal{P}(M)$: a *counting*-based approach [3, 5, 10, 13, 8, 1, 7], and an *intersection*-based one [15, 9, 16]. The former one, also adopted in *Apriori*, exploits a *horizontal* dataset and *counts* how many times each candidate k-itemset occurs in every transaction. The latter method, on the other hand, exploits a *vertical* dataset, where a *tidlist*, i.e. a list of transaction identifiers (tids), is associated with items (or itemsets), and itemset supports are determined through tidlist intersections. The support of a k-itemset c can thus be computed either by a *k-way* intersection, i.e. by intersecting the k tidlists associated with the k items included in c, or by a *2-way* intersection, i.e. by intersecting the tidlists associated with a pair of frequent $(k - 1)$-itemsets whose union is equal to c. Recently another category of methods, i.e. the *pattern growth ones*, have been proposed [1, 11, 14]. FP-growth [11] is the best representant of this kind of algorithms. It is not based on candidate generation as *Apriori*, but builds in memory a compact representation of the dataset, where repeated patterns are represented once along with the associated repetition counters. FP-growth does not perform well on sparse datasets [17], so the same authors recently proposed a new pattern-growth algorithm, H-mine [14], based on an innovative hyper-structure that allows the in-core dataset to be recursively projected by selecting those transactions that include a given pattern prefix.

In this paper we discuss DCI (Direct Count & Intersect), a new algorithm to solve the FSC problem. We also introduce ParDCI, a parallel version of DCI, which explicitly targets clusters of SMPs. Several considerations concerning the features of real datasets to be mined and the characteristics of modern hw/sw system have motivated the design of DCI. On the one hand, transactional databases may have different peculiarities in terms of the correlations among items, so that they may result either dense or sparse. Hence, a desirable characteristic of a new algorithm should be the ability to adapt its behavior to these features. DCI, which supports this kind of adaptiveness, thus constitutes an innovation in the arena of previously proposed FSC algorithms, which often outperformed others only for specific datasets. On the other hand, modern hw/sw systems need high locality for effectively exploiting memory hierarchies and achieving high performances. Large dynamic data structures with pointers may lack in locality due to unstructured memory references. Other sources of performance limitations may be unpredictable branches. DCI tries to take advantages of modern systems by using simple array data structures, accessed by tight loops which exhibit high spatial and temporal locality. In particular, DCI exploits such techniques for intersecting tidlists, which are actually represented as bit-vectors that can be intersected very efficiently with primitive bitwise *and* instructions. Another issue regards I/O operations, which must be carefully optimized in order to allow DM algorithms to efficiently manage large databases. Even if the disk-stored datasets to be mined may be very large, DM algorithms usually access them sequentially with high spatial locality, so that suitable out-of-core techniques to access them can be adopted, also taking advantage of prefetching and caching features of modern OSs [6]. DCI adopts these out-of-core techniques to access large databases, prunes them as execution progresses, and starts using in-core strategies as soon as possible.

Once motivated the design requirements of DCI, we can now detail how it works. As *Apriori*, at each iteration DCI generates the set of candidates C_k, determines their supports, and produces the set F_k of the frequent k-itemsets. However, DCI adopts a hybrid approach to determine the support of the candidates. During its first iterations, DCI exploits a novel counting–based technique, accompanied by an effective pruning of the dataset, stored to disk in horizon-

tal form. During the following iterations, DCI adopts a very efficient intersection–based technique. DCI starts using this technique as soon as the pruned dataset fits into the main memory.

DCI deals with dataset peculiarities by dynamically choosing between distinct *heuristic strategies*. For example, when a dataset is dense, identical sections appearing in several bit-vectors are aggregated and clustered, in order to reduce the number of intersections actually performed. Conversely, when a dataset is sparse, the runs of zero bits in the bit-vectors to be intersected are promptly identified and skipped. We will show how the sequential implementation of DCI significantly outperforms previously proposed algorithms. In particular, under a number of different tests and independently of the dataset peculiarities, DCI results to be faster than *Apriori* and FP-growth. By comparing our experimental results with the published ones obtained on the same sparse dataset, we deduced that DCI is also faster than H-mine [14]. DCI performs very well on both synthetic and real-world datasets characterized by different density features, i.e. datasets from which, due to the different correlations among items, either short or long frequent patterns can be mined.

The rest of the paper is organized as follows. Section 2 describes the DCI algorithm and discusses the various adaptive heuristics adopted, while Section 3 sketches the solutions adopted to design ParDCI, the parallel version of DCI. In Section 4 we report our experimental results. Finally in Section 5 we present some concluding remarks.

2 The DCI algorithm

During its initial counting-based phase, DCI exploits an out-of-core, *horizontal* database with variable length records. DCI, by exploiting effective pruning techniques inspired by DHP [13], trims the transaction database as execution progresses. In particular, a pruned dataset $\mathcal{D}_{k+1}$ is written to disk at each iteration k, and employed at the next iteration. Let m_k and n_k be the number of items and transactions that are included in the pruned dataset $\mathcal{D}_k$, where $m_k \geq m_{k+1}$ and $n_k \geq n_{k+1}$. Pruning the dataset may entail a reduction in I/O activity as the algorithm progresses, but the main benefits come from the reduced computation required for subset counting at each iteration k, due to the reduced number and size of transactions. As soon as the pruned dataset becomes small enough to fit into the main memory, DCI adaptively changes its behavior, builds a *vertical* layout database in-core, and starts adopting an intersection-based approach to determine frequent sets. Note, however, that DCI continues to have a level-wise behavior. At each iteration, DCI generates the candidate set C_k by finding all the pairs of $(k-1)$-itemsets that are included in F_{k-1} and share a common $(k-2)$-

prefix. Since F_{k-1} is lexicographically ordered, the various pairs occur in close positions, and candidate generation is performed with high spatial and temporal locality. Only during the DCI counting-phase, C_k is further pruned by checking whether also all the other subsets of a candidate are included in F_{k-1}. Conversely, during the intersection-based phase, since our intersection method is able to quickly determine the support of a candidate itemset, we found much more profitable to avoid this further check. While during its counting-based phase DCI has to maintain C_k in main memory to search candidates and increment associated counters, this is no longer needed during the intersection-based phase. As soon as a candidate k-itemset is generated, DCI determines its support on-the-fly by intersecting the corresponding tidlists. This is an important improvement over other *Apriori*-like algorithms, which suffer from the possible huge memory requirements due to the explosion of the size of C_k [11].

DCI makes use of a large body of out-of-core techniques, so that it is able to adapt its behavior also to machines with limited main memory. Datasets are read/written in blocks, to take advantage of I/O prefetching and system pipelining [6]. The outputs of the algorithm, e.g. the various frequent sets F_k, are written to files that are mmap-ped into memory during the next iteration for candidate generation.

2.1 Counting-based phase

Since the counting-based approach is used only for few iterations, in the following we only sketch its main features. Further details about DCI counting technique can be found in [12], where we proposed an effective algorithm for mining short patterns. In the first iteration, similarly to all FSC algorithms, DCI exploits a vector of counters, which are directly addressed through item identifiers. For $k \geq 2$, instead of using complex data structures like hash-trees or prefix-trees, DCI uses a novel *Direct Count technique* that can be thought as a generalization of the technique used for $k = 1$. The technique uses a *prefix table*, PREFIX$_k$[ ], of size $\binom{m_k}{2}$. In particular, each entry of PREFIX$_k$[ ] is associated with a distinct *ordered prefix* of two items. For $k = 2$, PREFIX$_k$[ ] can directly contain the counters associated with the various candidate 2-itemsets, while, for $k > 2$, each entry of PREFIX$_k$[ ] contains the pointer to the contiguous section of ordered candidates in C_k sharing the same prefix. To permit the various entries of PREFIX$_k$[ ] to be directly accessed, we devised an order preserving, minimal perfect hash function. This prefix table is thus used to count the support of candidates in C_k as follows. For each transaction $t = \{t_1, \ldots, t_{|t|}\}$, we select all the possible 2-prefixes of all k-subsets included in t. We then exploit PREFIX$_k$[ ] to find the sections of C_k which must be visited in order to check set-inclusion of candidates in transaction t.

2.2 Intersection-based phase

Since the counting-based approach becomes less efficient as k increases [15], DCI starts its intersection-based phase as soon as possible. Unfortunately, the intersection-based method needs to maintain in memory the vertical representation of the pruned dataset. So, at iteration k, $k \geq 2$, DCI checks whether the pruned dataset $\mathcal{D}_k$ may fit into the main memory. When the dataset becomes small enough, its vertical in-core representation is built on the fly, while the transactions are read and counted against C_k. The intersection-based method thus starts at the next iteration.

The vertical layout of the dataset is based on fixed length records (tidlists), stored as *bit-vectors*. The whole vertical dataset can thus be seen as a bidimensional bit-array $\mathcal{VD}[\ ][\ ]$, whose rows correspond to the bit-vectors associated with non pruned items. Therefore, the amount of memory required to store $\mathcal{VD}[\ ][\ ]$ is $m_k \times n_k$ bits.

At each iteration of its intersection-based phase, DCI computes F_k as follows. For each candidate k-itemset c, we *and*-intersect the k bit-vectors associated with the items included in c (*k-way* intersection), and count the 1's present in the resulting bit-vector. If this number is greater or equal to *minsup*, we insert c into F_k. Consider that a bit-vector intersection can be carried out efficiently and with high spatial locality by using primitive bitwise *and* instructions with word operands. As previously stated, this method does not require C_k to be kept in memory: we can compute the support of each candidate c on-the-fly, as soon as it is generated.

The strategy above is, in principle, highly inefficient, because it always needs a *k-way* intersection to determine the support of each candidate c. Nevertheless, a caching policy could be exploited in order to save work and speed up our *k-way* intersection method. To this end, DCI uses a small "cache" buffer to store all the $k - 2$ intermediate intersections that have been computed for the last candidate evaluated. Since candidate itemsets are generated in lexicographic order, with high probability two consecutive candidates, e.g. c and c', share a common prefix. Suppose that c and c' share a prefix of length $h \geq 2$. When we process c', we can avoid performing the first $h - 1$ intersections since their result can be found in the cache.

To evaluate the effectiveness of our caching policy, we counted the actual number of intersections carried out by DCI on two different datasets: BMS, a real-world sparse dataset, and connect-4, a dense dataset (the characteristics of these two datasets are reported in Table 1). We compared this number with the best and the worst case. The best case corresponds to the adoption of a *2-way* intersection approach, which is only possible if we can fully cache the tidlists associated with all the frequent $(k - 1)$-itemsets in F_{k-1}. The worst case regards the adoption of a pure *k-way* intersection method, i.e. a method that does not exploit caching at all. Figure 1.(a) plots the results of this analysis on the sparse dataset for support threshold $s = 0.06\%$, while Figure 1.(b) regards the dense dataset mined with support threshold $s = 80\%$. In both the cases the caching policy of DCI turns out to be very effective, since the actual number of intersections performed results to be very close to the best case. Moreover, DCI requires orders of magnitude less memory than a pure *2-way* intersection approach, thus better exploiting memory hierarchies.

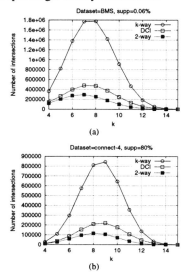

Figure 1. Evaluation of DCI intersection caching policy.

We have to consider that while caching reduces the number of tidlist intersections, we also need to reduce intersection cost. To this end, further heuristics, differentiated w.r.t. *sparse* or *dense* datasets, are adopted by DCI. In order to apply the right optimization, the vertical dataset is tested for checking its density as soon as it is built. In particular, we compare the bit-vectors associated with the *most frequent items*, i.e., the vectors which likely need to be intersected several times since the associated items occur in many candidates. If large sections of these bit-vectors turn out to be identical, we deduce that the items are highly correlated and that the dataset is dense. In this case we adopt a specific heuristics which exploits similarities between these vectors. Otherwise the technique for sparse datasets is adopted. In the following we illustrate the two heuristics in more detail.

Sparse datasets. Sparse or moderately dense datasets originate bit-vectors containing long runs of 0's. To speedup computation, while we compute the intersection of the bit-vectors relative to the first two items c_1 and c_2 of a generic candidate itemset $c = \{c_1, c_2, \ldots, c_k\} \in C_k$, we also identify and maintain information about the runs of 0's appearing in the resulting bit-vector stored in cache. The

further intersections that are needed to determine the support of c (as well as intersections needed to process other k-itemsets sharing the same 2-item prefix) will skip these runs of 0's, so that only vector segments which may contain 1's are actually intersected. Since information about the runs of 0's are computed once, and the same information is reused many times, this optimization results to be very effective.

Moreover, sparse and moderately dense datasets offer the possibility of further pruning vertical datasets as computation progresses. The benefits of pruning regard the reduction in the length of the bit-vectors and thus in the cost of intersections. Note that a transaction, i.e. a column of $\mathcal{VD}$, can be removed from the vertical dataset when it does not contain any of the itemsets included in F_k. This check can simply be done by *or*-ing the intersection bit-vectors computed for all the frequent k-itemsets. However, we observed that dataset pruning is expensive, since vectors must be compacted at the level of single bits. Hence DCI prunes the dataset only if turns out to be profitable, i.e. if we can obtain a large reduction in the vector length, and the number of vectors to be compacted is small with respect to the cardinality of C_k.

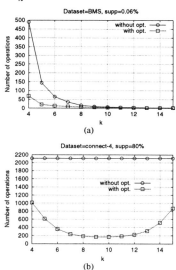

Figure 2. Evaluation of DCI optimization heuristics for sparse and dense datasets.

Dense datasets. If the dataset turns out to be dense, we expect to deal with a dataset characterized by strong correlations among the most frequent items. This not only means that the bit-vectors associated with the *most frequent items* contain long runs of 1's, but also that they turn out to be very similar. The heuristic technique adopted by DCI for dense dataset thus works as follows: A) we reorder the columns of the vertical dataset, in order to move identical segments of the bit-vectors associated with the most frequent items to the first consecutive positions; B) since each

Table 1. Datasets used in the experiments.

Dataset	Description
T25I10D10K	Synthetic dataset with 1K items and 10K transactions [11]. The average size of transactions is 25, and the average size of the maximal potentially frequent itemsets is 10.
T25I20D100K	Synthetic dataset with 10K items and 100K transactions [11]. The average size of transactions is 25, and the average size of the maximal potentially frequent itemsets is 20.
400k_t10_p8_m10k	10K items and 400K transactions. The average size of transactions is 10, and the average size of the maximal potentially frequent itemsets is 8. Synthetic dataset created with the IBM dataset generator [5].
400k_t30_p16_m1k	1K items and 400K transactions. The average size of transactions is 30, and the average size of the maximal potentially frequent itemsets is 16. Synthetic dataset created with the IBM dataset generator [5].
t20_p8_m1k	With this notation we identify a series of synthetic datasets characterized by 1K items. The average transaction size is 20, and the average size of maximal potentially frequent itemsets is 8. The number of transactions is varied for scaling measurements.
t50_p32_m1k	A series of three synthetic datasets with the same number of items (1K), average transaction size of 50, and average size of maximal potentially frequent itemsets equal to 32. We used three datasets of this series with 1000k, 2000k and 3000k transactions.
connect-4	Publicly available dense dataset with 130 items and about 60K transactions. The maximal transaction size is 45.
BMS	Publicly available sparse dataset also known as *Gazelle*. 497 items and 59K transactions containing click-stream data from an e-commerce web site gazelle.com.

candidate is likely to include several of these most frequent items, we avoid repeatedly intersecting the identical segments of the corresponding vectors. This technique may save a lot of work because (1) the intersection of identical vector segments is done once, (2) the identical segments are usually very large, and (3), long candidate itemsets presumably contains several of these most frequent items.

The plots reported in Figure 2 show the effectiveness of the heuristic optimizations discussed above in reducing the average number of bitwise *and* operations needed to intersect a pair of bit-vectors. In particular, Figure 2.(a) regards the *sparse* BMS dataset mined with support threshold $s = 0.06\%$, while Figure 2.(b) regards the *dense* dataset connect-4 mined with support threshold $s = 80\%$. In both cases, we plotted the per-iteration cost of each bit-vector intersection in terms of bitwise *and* operations when either our heuristic optimizations are adopted or not. The two plots show that our optimizations for both sparse and dense datasets have the effect of reducing the intersection cost up to an order of magnitude. Note that when no optimizations are employed, the curves exactly plot the bit-vector length (in words). Finally, from the plot reported in Figure 2.(a), we can also note the effect of the pruning technique used on sparse datasets. Pruning has the effect of reducing the length of the bit-vectors as execution progresses. On the other hand, when datasets are dense, the vertical dataset is not pruned, so that the length of bit-vectors remains the same for all the DCI iterations.

3 ParDCI

In the following we describe the different parallelization techniques exploited for the counting- and intersection-based phases of ParDCI, the parallel version of DCI. Since our target architecture is a cluster of SMP nodes, in both phases we distinguish between *intra-node* and *inter-node* levels of parallelism. At the inter-node level we used the message–passing paradigm through the MPI communication library, while at the intra-node level we exploited multithreading through the *Posix Thread* library. A *Count Distribution* approach is adopted to parallelize the counting-based phase, while the intersection-based phase exploits a very effective *Candidate Distribution* approach [4].

The counting-based phase. At the inter-node level, the dataset is statically split in a number of partitions equal to the number of SMP nodes available. The size of partitions depend on the relative powers of nodes. At each iteration k, an identical copy of C_k is independently generated by each node. Then each node p reads blocks of transactions from its own dataset partition $\mathcal{D}_{p,k}$, performs subset counting, and writes pruned transactions to $\mathcal{D}_{p,k+1}$. At the end of the iteration, an all-reduce operation is performed to update the counters associated to all candidates of C_k, and all the nodes produce an identical set F_k.

At the intra-node level each node uses a pool of threads, each holding a private set of counters associated with candidates. They have the task of checking in parallel candidate itemsets against chunks of transactions read from $\mathcal{D}_{p,k}$.

At the end of each iteration, a global reduction of counters take place, and a copy of F_k is produced on each node.

The intersection-based phase. During the intersection-based phase, a Candidate Distribution approach is adopted at both the inter- and intra-node levels. This parallelization schema makes the parallel nodes completely independent: inter-node communications are no longer needed for all the following iterations of ParDCI.

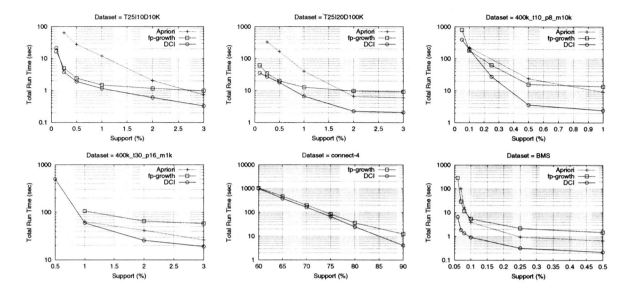

Figure 3. Total execution times for DCI, *Apriori*, **and** FP-growth **on various datasets as a function of the support threshold.**

Let us first consider the inter-node level, and suppose that the intersection-based phase is started at iteration $\overline{k}+1$. Therefore, at iteration $\overline{k}$ the various nodes build on-the-fly the bit-vectors representing their own in-core portions of the vertical dataset. Before starting the intersection-based phase, the partial vertical datasets are broadcast to obtain a complete replication of the whole vertical dataset on each node. The frequent set $F_{\overline{k}}$ (i.e., the set computed in the last counting-based iteration) is then partitioned on the basis of itemset prefixes. A disjoint partition $F_{p,\overline{k}}$ of $F_{\overline{k}}$ is thus assigned to each node p, where $\bigcup_p F_{p,\overline{k}} = F_{\overline{k}}$. It is worth remarking that this partitioning entails a Candidate Distribution schema for all the following iterations, according to which each node p will be able to generate a unique C_k^p ($k > \overline{k}$) independently of all the other nodes, where $C_k^p \cap C_k^{p'} = \emptyset$ if $p \neq p'$, and $\bigcup_p C_k^p = C_k$.

At the intra-node level, a similar Candidate Distribution approach is employed, but at a finer granularity by using dynamic scheduling to ensure load balancing.

4 Experimental Results

The DCI algorithm is currently available in two versions, a MS-Windows one, and a Linux one. ParDCI, which exploits the MPICH MPI and the *pthread* libraries, is currently available only for the Linux platform. We used the MS-Windows version of DCI to compare its performance with other FSC algorithms. For test comparisons we used the

FP-growth algorithm[1], and the Christian Borgelt's implementation of *Apriori*[2]. For the sequential tests we used a Windows-NT workstation equipped with a Pentium II 350 MHz processor, 256 MB of RAM memory and a SCSI-2 disk. For testing ParDCI performance, we employed a small cluster of three Pentium II 233MHz 2-way SMPs, for a total of six processors. Each SMP is equipped with 256 MBytes of main memory and a SCSI disk. For the tests, we used both synthetic and real datasets by varying the minimum support threshold s. The characteristics of the datasets used are reported in Table 1.

DCI performances and comparisons. Figure 3 reports the total execution times obtained running *Apriori*, FP-growth, and our sequential DCI algorithm on some datasets described in Table 1 as a function of the support threshold s. In all the tests conducted, DCI outperforms FP-growth with speedups up to 8. Of course, DCI also remarkably outperforms *Apriori*, in some cases for more than one order of magnitude. For connect-4, the dense dataset, the curve of *Apriori* is not shown, due to the relatively too long execution times. Note that, accordingly to [17], on the real-world sparse dataset BMS (also known as *Gazelle*), *Apriori* turned out to be faster than FP-growth. To overcome such bad performance results on sparse datasets, the same authors of FP-growth recently proposed a new pattern-growth algorithm, H-mine [14]. By comparing our experimental results with

---
[1]We acknowledge Prof. Jiawei Han for kindly providing us the latest, fully optimized, binary version of FP-growth.
[2]http://fuzzy.cs.uni-magdeburg.de/~borgelt

the published execution times on the BMS dataset, we deduced that DCI is also faster than H-mine. For $s = 0.06\%$, we obtained an execution time of about 7 sec., while H-mine completes in about 40 sec. on a faster machine.

The encouraging results obtained with DCI are due to both the efficiency of the counting method exploited during early iterations, and the effectiveness of the intersection-based approach used when the pruned vertical dataset fits into the main memory. For only a dataset, namely T25I10D10K, FP-growth turns out to be slightly faster than DCI for $s = 0.1\%$. The cause of this behavior is the size of C_3, which in this specific case results much larger than the final size of F_3. Hence, DCI has to carry out a lot of useless work to determine the support of many candidate itemsets, which will eventually result to be not frequent. In this case FP-growth is faster than DCI since it does not require candidate generation.

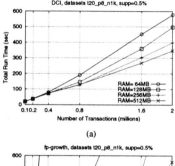

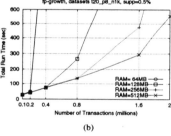

Figure 4. Total execution times of (a) DCI, and (b) FP-growth, on datasets in the series t20_p8_m1k ($s = 0.5\%$) on a PC equipped with different RAM sizes as a function of the number of transactions (ranging from $100K$ to $2M$).

We also tested the scale-up behavior of DCI when both the size of the dataset and the size of RAM installed in the PC vary. The datasets employed for these tests belong to the series t20_p8_m1k (see Table 1) mined with support threshold $s = 0.5\%$, while the available RAM was changed from 64MB to 512MB by physically plugging additional memory into the PC main board. Figure 4.(a) and 4.(b) plot several curves representing the execution times of DCI and FP-growth, respectively, as a function of the number of transactions contained in the dataset processed. Each curve plotted refers to a series of tests conducted with the same

PC equipped with a different amount of memory. As it can be seen from Figure 4.(a), DCI scales linearly also on machines with a few memory. Due to its adaptiveness and the use of efficient out-of-core techniques, it is able to modify its behavior in function of the features of the dataset mined and the computational resources available. For example, in the tests conducted with the largest dataset containing two millions of transactions, the in-core intersection-based phase was started at the sixth iteration when only 64MB of RAM were available, and at the third iteration when the available memory was 512MB. On the other hand the results reported in Figure 4.(b) show that FP-growth requires much more memory than DCI, and is not able to adapt itself to memory availability. For example, in the tests conducted with 64MB of RAM, FP-growth requires less than 30 seconds to mine the dataset with $200k$ transactions, but when we double the size of the dataset to $400k$ transactions, FP-growth execution time becomes 1303 seconds, more than 40 times higher, due to an heavy page swapping activity.

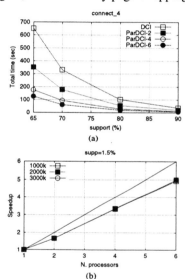

Figure 5. (a): Dense dataset `connect-4`: completion times of DCI and ParDCI varying the minimum support threshold. (b): Speedup for sparse datasets 1000K, 2000K and 3000K with $s = 1.5\%$

Performance evaluation of ParDCI. We evaluated ParDCI on both dense and sparse datasets. First we compared the performance of DCI and ParDCI on the dense dataset `connect-4`, for which we obtained very good speedups. Figure 5.(a) plots total execution times as functions of the support thresholds s. ParDCI-2 corresponds to the pure multithread version running on a single 2-way SMP, while ParDCI-4 and ParDCI-6 also exploit internode parallelism, and run, respectively, on two and three 2-way SMPs. For what regard sparse datasets, we used

344

the synthetic dataset series identified as $t50\_p32\_m1k$ in Table 1. We varied the total number of transactions from 1000k to 3000k. In the following we will identify the various synthetic datasets on the basis of their number of transactions, i.e. 1000k, 2000k, and 3000k. Figure 5.(b) plots the speedups obtained on the three synthetic datasets for a given support threshold ($s = 1.5\%$), as a function of the number of processors used. Consider that, since our cluster is composed of three 2-way SMPs, we mapped tasks on processors always using the minimum number of SPMP nodes (e.g., when we used 4 processors, we actually employed 2 SMP nodes). This implies that experiments performed on either 1 or 2 processors actually have identical memory and disk resources available, whereas the execution on 4 processors benefit from a double amount of such resources. According to the tests above, ParDCI showed a speedup that, in some cases, is close to the optimal one. Considering the results obtained with one or two processors, one can note that the slope of the speedup curve is relatively worse than its theoretical limit, due to resource sharing and thread implementation overheads at the inter-node level. Nevertheless, when additional SMPs are employed, the slope of the curve improves. The strategies adopted for partitioning dataset and candidates on our homogeneous cluster of SMPs sufficed for balancing the workload. In our tests we observed a very limited imbalance. The differences in the execution times of the first and last node to end execution were always below the 0.5%.

5 Conclusions

DCI uses different approaches for extracting frequent patterns: counting-based during the first iterations and intersection-based for the following ones. Adaptiveness and resource awareness are the main innovative features of the algorithm. On the basis of the characteristics of the dataset mined, DCI chooses at run–time which optimization to adopt for reducing the cost of mining. Dataset pruning and effective out-of-core techniques are exploited during the counting-based phase, while the intersection-based phase works in core, and is started only when the pruned dataset can fit into the main memory. As a result, our algorithm can manage efficiently, also on machines with limited physical memory, very large datasets from which, due to the different correlations among items, either short or long frequent patterns can be mined.

The experimental evaluations demonstrated that DCI significantly outperforms *Apriori* and FP-growth on both synthetic and real-world datasets. In many cases the performance improvements are impressive. Moreover, ParDCI, the parallel version of DCI, exhibits excellent scaleups and speedups on our homogeneous cluster of SMPs. The variety of datasets used and the large amount of tests con-

ducted permit us to state that the performances of DCI are not influenced by dataset characteristics, and that our optimizations are very effective and general. To share our efforts with the data mining community, we made the DCI binary code available for research purposes at `http://www.miles.cnuce.cnr.it/~palmeri/datam/DCI`.

References

[1] R. C. Agarwal, C. C. Aggarwal, and V.V.V. Prasad. A Tree Projection Algorithm for Generation of Frequent Itemsets. *JPDC*, 2000. Special Issue on High Performance Data Mining.

[2] R. C. Agarwal, C. C. Aggarwal, and V.V.V. Prasad. Depth first generation of long patterns. In *Proc. of the 6th ACM SIGKDD Int. Conf. on Knowledge Discovery and Data Mining*, pages 108–118, 2000.

[3] R. Agrawal, H. Mannila, R. Srikant, H. Toivonen, and A. Inkeri Verkamo. Fast Discovery of Association Rules in Large Databases. In *Advances in Knowledge Discovery and Data Mining*, pages 307–328. AAAI Press, 1996.

[4] R. Agrawal and J. C. Shafer. Parallel mining of association rules. *IEEE TKDE*, 8:962–969, 996.

[5] R. Agrawal and R. Srikant. Fast Algorithms for Mining Association Rules in Large Databases. In *Proc. of the 20th VLDB Conf.*, pages 487–499, 1994.

[6] R. Baraglia, D. Laforenza, S. Orlando, P. Palmerini, and R. Perego. Implementation issues in the design of I/O intensive data mining applications on clusters of workstations. In *Proc. of the 3rd HPDM Workshop, (IPDPS-2000), Cancun, Mexico*, pages 350–357. LNCS 1800 Spinger-Verlag, 2000.

[7] Y. Bastide, R. Taouil, N. Pasquier, G. Stumme, and L. Lakhal. Mining frequent patterns with counting inference. *ACM SIGKDD Explorations Newsletter*, 2(2):66–75, December 2000.

[8] R. J. Bayardo Jr. Efficiently Mining Long Patterns from Databases. In *Proc. of the ACM SIGMOD Int. Conf. on Management of Data*, pages 85–93, Seattle, Washington, USA, 1998.

[9] Brian Dunkel and Nandit Soparkar. Data organization and access for efficient data mining. In *Proc. of the 15th Int. Conf. on Data Engineering*, pages 522–529, Sydney, Australia, 1999. IEEE Computer Society.

[10] E. H. Han, G. Karypis, and Kumar V. Scalable Parallel Data Mining for Association Rules. *IEEE TKDE*, 12(3):337–352, May/June 2000.

[11] J. Han, J. Pei, and Y. Yin. Mining Frequent Patterns without Candidate Generation. In *Proc. of the ACM SIGMOD Int. Conf. on Management of Data*, pages 1–12, Dallas, Texas, USA, 2000.

[12] S. Orlando, P. Palmerini, and R. Perego. Enhancing the Apriori Algorithm for Frequent Set Counting. In *Proc. of the 3rd Int. Conf. on Data Warehousing and Knowledge Discovery, DaWaK 2001, LNCS 2114*, pages 71–82, Munich, Germany, 2001.

[13] J. S. Park, M.-S. Chen, and P. S. Yu. An Effective Hash Based Algorithm for Mining Association Rules. In *Proc. of the 1995 ACM SIGMOD Int. Conf. on Management of Data*, pages 175–186, 1995.

[14] J. Pei, J. Han, H. Lu, S. Nishio, and D. Tang, S. amd Yang. H-Mine: Hyper-Structure Mining of Frequent Patterns in Large Databases. In *Proc. of the 2001 IEEE ICDM Conf.*, San Jose, CA, USA, 2001.

[15] A. Savasere, E. Omiecinski, and S. B. Navathe. An Efficient Algorithm for Mining Association Rules in Large Databases. In *Proc. of the 21th VLDB Conf.*, pages 432–444, Zurich, Switzerland, 1995.

[16] M. J. Zaki. Scalable algorithms for association mining. *IEEE TKDE*, 12:372–390, May/June 2000.

[17] Z. Zheng, R. Kohavi, and L. Mason. Real World Performance of Association Rule Algorithms. In *Proc. of KDD-2001*, 2001.

A new implementation technique for fast Spectral based document retrieval systems

Laurence A. F. Park, Marimuthu Palaniswami and Kotagiri Ramamohanarao
ARC Special Research Centre for Ultra-Broadband Information Networks
Department of Electrical and Electronic Engineering,
The University of Melbourne, Victoria, Australia 3010.
{lapark,rao,swami}@ee.mu.oz.au

Abstract

The traditional methods of spectral text retrieval (FDS,CDS) create an index of spatial data and convert the data to its spectral form at query time. We present a new method of implementing and querying an index containing spectral data which will conserve the high precision performance of the spectral methods, reduce the time needed to resolve the query, and maintain an acceptable size for the index. This is done by taking advantage of the properties of the discrete cosine transform and by applying ideas from vector space document ranking methods.

1. Introduction

Due to the popularity of the World Wide Web and it's high textual content, the topic of text mining has become an important issue. While using the Web, we navigate with text based search engines to help us mine the gold nuggets of useful information from the vast range of documents. Our human nature compels us to want information at a faster rate, therefore quality of the results and the speed of Web search engines are important issues. Most search engines use traditional vector space methods [13, 5, 11, 12, 1] to classify and rank the text contained within a document. These methods provide fairly accurate results at a reasonable speed, but do not take into account the relative distance of the query terms in the documents.

Proximity searches [3] rank documents based on the relative positions of the query terms within the documents. To do this, they must either store all proximity data in the index, leading to a large index, or calculate the proximity information at query time, which slows the search. Proximity searches generally focus on one position of the document, so if the query terms appeared together in a document twice, it would be no more relevant than a document in which the query terms appeared together once.

Spectral based searches observe the frequency spectrum of the words through the document, rather than the position. We can easily determine the relevance of each term to a document by observing the magnitude of the spectral components, and we can determine the proximity of the terms by comparing the phase of the spectral components. A list of possible indexing methods to perform spectral based searches is shown in table 1. From this set, using no index and using a spectral index are infeasible because the former is too slow and the latter is too large. Our previous work on two spectral based search methods, Cosine Domain Scoring (CDS) [9] and Fourier Domain Scoring (FDS) [10], showed how these methods can perform well in terms of precision, but because we were using a spatial index[1] the query time was slow. For example, a simple four term query could take from one to three seconds when using the CDS method because the DCT must be performed for every word in every document at query time. Relative to current vector space methods, these methods are 100 times slower when using a spatial inverted index. To resolve this problem, we can perform the transforms before the query is given, which means we must store the spectral information from the transforms in an index rather than the spatial data. To make this method feasible, we must also compress the data further.

Our focus in this paper is to introduce the fourth index in table 1. We will observe the effects of storing spectral data in an index and incorporate the ideas on reducing latency and storage space developed for vector space methods to the CDS method. This will give us the usual high precision achieved in CDS, but also give us the compactness and speed of the vector space methods. The paper is organised as follows. Section 2 provides an explanation of the data set being used to test the developed techniques. Section 3 covers the CDS method and discusses problems with speed. Section 4 presents the compression techniques used in cre-

---

[1]an index which records the positions of the words in the documents

Table 1. Index types for Spectral based document retrieval systems.

Index Type	Precision	Index Size	Query speed
None	High	Zero	Very slow
Spatial index	High	Average	Slow
Spectral index	High	Very large	Fast
Spectral index with compression	High	Average	Fast

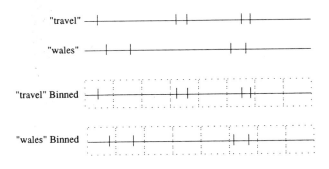

Figure 1. Example of word signal creation. The position of the word is found in the document, then the positions are grouped into bins so that each word signal is of a constant length.

ating the spectral index. Section 5 shows how we can adapt and apply the fast document ranking methods used in existing systems to the spectral index. We also provide extensive results. The results show that our method is very computationally competitive and at the same time provides high precision.

2. Evaluation Environment

To evaluate the performance of the CDS method with the spectral inverted index, we will be using the Associated Press document collection (AP2) found on disk two of the TREC data set [7], with queries 51 to 200. The document set contains 79919 documents and 143044 unique terms. To try to emulate the environment of a Web search engine, we will only use the titles of queries 51 to 200 as the query terms during our searches. Since we are trying to emulate the Web, our results will focus on the precision given after the first 10 documents have been retrieved. We will use the vector space measure BD-ACI-BCA as a relative performance judgment.

3. Cosine Domain Scoring

Cosine domain scoring (CDS) [9] and the closely related Fourier domain scoring (FDS) [10] are unique document ranking methods which analyse the spectrum of each document, rather than just obtain a word count for each document.

CDS uses a spatial inverted index to rank documents which is built by storing the spatial information of documents. The spatial information for each document comes in the form of a set of word signals, one for every unique word in the document. A word signal consists of a sequence of positive integers which describe where the word appears in the document. Our word signal had a set length (eight bins), each bin contained the count of the word in that fraction of the document (as shown in figure 1). For example if the

word *travel* appeared once in the first eighth of the document, the first bin would contain 1.

After the index is built, queries can be applied and the documents scored by the method shown in figure 3. The CDS method gives a certain degree of freedom when weights are applied. We can see in figure 3 that the preweighting (W_P) and query weighting functions (W_Q) have not been defined. When compared to the vector space methods, W_P is equivalent to the document weighting and W_Q is equivalent to the query weighting. We have used Term Bin Frequency weighting (TBF, a small variant of TF weighting):

$$W_P(f_{d,t,b}) = 1 + \log_e f_{d,t,b} \qquad (1)$$
$$W_Q(|\eta_{d,t,b}|) = f_{q,t}|\eta_{d,t,b}| \qquad (2)$$

where $f_{d,t,b}$ is the count of term t in bin b of document d, $\eta_{d,t,b}$ is the bth spectral component of term t in document d, and $f_{q,t}$ is the count of term t in query q.

The CDS method gives a higher precision than the vector space methods, but it is slow due to the processing that is to be performed (which includes numerous DCT's) during query time. To speed up this process, we will perform the preweighting and transform calculations during the index creation. We can store the spectral results in the index, leaving them ready to combine once the query terms are given. By creating the spectral inverted index, we now face a new problem of storage capacity. We deal with this in the following section via different coding schemes.

4. Compressing the Spectral Inverted Index

When storing a spectral index, we are faced with the problem of how to store it due to its excessive size. To reduce the size to an acceptable level we will use quantisation

1. For each query term $t \in T$
   (a) Retrieve inverted list I_t containing word signals $\{\hat{f}_{0,t}, \hat{f}_{1,t}, \ldots, \hat{f}_{D,t}\}$
   (b) Weight signals $\tilde{w}_{d,t} = W_P(\hat{f}_{d,t})$
   (c) Transform signals into spectra $\tilde{\eta}_{d,t} = \mathrm{DCT}(\tilde{w}_{d,t})$
   (d) For each spectral component $\eta_{d,t,b} \in \tilde{\eta}_{d,t}$
      i. Calculate signal component magnitudes $H_{d,t,b} = W_Q(|\eta_{d,t,b}|)$
      ii. Calculate signal component phase $\phi_{d,t,b} = \mathrm{sgn}\,(\eta_{d,t,b})$
2. For each document d in collection
   (a) For each component b in word signal spectra
      i. Calculate the selective phase precision $\bar{\Phi}_{d,b} = \left| \frac{\sum_{t \in T} \phi_{d,t,b}}{\#(T)} \right|$
      ii. Obtain component score $s_{d,b} = \Phi_{d,b} \sum_{t \in T} H_{d,t,b}$
   (b) Combine component scores to obtain document score $s_d = \sum_{b=0}^{B-1} s_{d,b}$

Figure 2. Cosine Domain Scoring

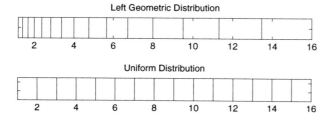

Figure 3. Distributions of the two quantisation methods.

when storing elements and a component cropping technique when storing vectors.

4.1. Quantisation

To successfully implement a spectral inverted index, we must consider quantisation. If we choose not to quantise the numerical data we will be left with an index of excessive size. For example, if we assume a floating point value to be 4 bytes and we were to store a document set which contained 80,000 document and 120,000 unique words, we would need an index of size $4 \times 80,000 \times 120,000 \times 0.01 = 384$ megabytes per bin (≈ 6 gigabytes for eight bins) assuming each word appears in 1% of the documents. Larger data structures also imply slower processing due to time being spent swapping data in and out of memory.

Anh *et al.* [2] used three separate quantisation methods,

two of which gave fairly precise results. These two methods were labeled *Left Geometric* and *Uniform*. The uniform distribution spreads the quantised values evenly over the entire range. The uniform quantised values are calculated using the following:

$$q_u(x) = \left\lfloor 2^b \frac{x - L}{U - L + \epsilon} \right\rfloor \quad (3)$$

where b is the number of bits allotted to store the quantised value, L is the smallest value in the set, U is the greatest value in the set, and ϵ is a small value. The term ϵ is introduced to limit the quantised range to $\{0, 1, \ldots, 2^b - 1\}$. The left geometric distribution places more quantised levels at the lower end of the value range. This way we obtain more precise quantised values (due to small quantisation error) at the lower end of the scale and less precise quantised values at the upper end of the scale. This can be seen in figure 3. The left geometric distribution is given by:

$$q_{lg}(x) = \left\lfloor 2^b \frac{\log x - \log L}{\log U - \log L + \epsilon} \right\rfloor \quad (4)$$

While Anh *et al.* used global quantisation for its simplicity, we prefer to use the alternative local version (local to each term) for the following reasons: 1) Before we can do any quantisation, we must find the upper and lower bound of the values to be quantised. The values to be quantised are the magnitude and phase of each frequency component of each word in each document. Since phase is a radial value, we know that it is bounded by $-\pi$ and π. All we know about the magnitude is that it is not less than zero. We could use zero as the lower bound, but since we do not record any zero values in the index, this would lead to a sub-optimal quantisation. Therefore we must perform preweighting and the transform, only then can we find the upper and lower bound of the magnitude parameter. If we were to do this globally, we would need to process the entire data set performing the preweighting and transform to obtain the bounds, then rescan data set (performing the same preweighting and transform) to obtain the quantised data. We chose to perform local quantisation because the data from each term (an inverted list) is small enough to perform the preweighting and transform and keep the calculated values in memory. Thus, we can find the upper and lower bound for that term and quantise the data immediately. 2) Each term will have a varying range, therefore we will achieve a smaller quantisation error with local quantisation. Local quantisation requires storage of the upper and lower bound for each term, where as with the global method, we need only store one upper and lower bound. For our case, the lexicon contained 143044 words, this added an extra 550 kilobytes to the index statistics file. This is a small price to pay for higher quality quantisation.

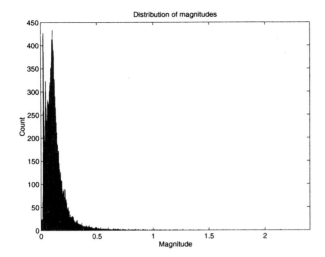

Figure 4. Distribution of the magnitude values of the word 'radio' from the data set AP2. Most of the magnitude values appear at the lower end of the scale.

The final decision is to choose how we are to quantise the magnitude and phase values. If we look at the distribution of the magnitude of each word (shown in figure 4) we can see that most of the values will appear at the lower end of the scale and only a few at the upper end. This makes sense because it implies that most documents will contain the word only a few times, while only a few documents will contain the larger magnitudes. Therefore when quantising, we need more quantum levels at the lower end of the scale and less at the upper end. It can be concluded that it is best to use the left geometric quantisation method with the magnitude of each spectral component.

The phase on the other hand is a radial value bound between $-\pi$ and π. It represents the shift in the signal represented by the spectral component. Since this is a relative value (the shift can only be compared relative to another signal), we expect the values to be evenly distributed across the range. In this case (using the cosine transform), the only values of phase that appear are 0 and π, therefore we will use the uniform distribution to represent phase and we will need only one bit to encode it.

Table 2 shows the results of an experiment displaying the effects of quantisation. We can see that the precision 10 and precision 20 remain close to the *float*[2] precision for all values except 1 and 2 bit quantisation. Choosing a quantisation bit size presents a trade off between index size and precision of results. We can see from table 3 that the spectral indexes range from three to seven times the size of the

---

[2]No quantisation, values are stored as floats.

Table 2. Results from running queries 51-200 on AP2 with varying magnitude quantisation bit size. Prec.10 and Prec.20 are the precision after 10 and 20 documents respectively.

Bits	Prec.10	Prec.20	Avg. Prec.	R-Prec.
1	0.2034	0.1770	0.1408	0.1737
2	0.3101	0.2747	0.2147	0.2539
3	0.3453	0.3030	0.2519	0.2905
4	0.3514	0.3108	0.2570	0.2960
5	0.3473	0.3132	0.2587	0.2956
6	0.3554	0.3122	0.2599	0.2981
7	0.3554	0.3132	0.2596	0.2975
8	0.3554	0.3128	0.2594	0.2969
9	0.3554	0.3125	0.2597	0.2969
10	0.3554	0.3118	0.2598	0.2970
float	0.3547	0.3108	0.2583	0.2971

Table 3. Size of inverted indexes relative to the document collection indexed.

Inverted index	AP2 %	Inverted index	AP2 %
Spatial	16.4		
Spectral			
$b_{MAG} = 1$	43.0	$b_{MAG} = 6$	71.1
$b_{MAG} = 2$	45.8	$b_{MAG} = 7$	80.3
$b_{MAG} = 3$	50.4	$b_{MAG} = 8$	90.9
$b_{MAG} = 4$	56.1	$b_{MAG} = 9$	103.5
$b_{MAG} = 5$	63.1	$b_{MAG} = 10$	118.3

Table 4. Size of inverted spectral indexes relative to the document collection indexed where the magnitude is quantised to 4 bits.

Inverted index	AP2 %
Spatial	16.4
Spectral, $b_{MAG} = 4$	
1 component	6.8
2 components	14.1
3 components	21.1
4 components	28.3
5 components	34.6
6 components	41.9
7 components	48.9
8 components	56.1

spatial index. This was expected due to the large amounts of information stored in the spectral index. In order to show why there is more data in the spectral domain, we can use the simple example of a word signal containing only one non-zero element. This represents the common case of a word appearing in a document once.

$$\begin{bmatrix} 0 & 0 & 1.4 & 0 \end{bmatrix} \xrightarrow{DCT} \begin{bmatrix} 0.49 & -0.26 & -0.49 & 0.64 \end{bmatrix}$$

We can see that the spatial data (before the DCT) can be represented by a single bin position and value, but the spectral data (after the DCT) requires at least eight values to be stored. Once quantisation has been applied, we can use Golomb coding [6] to compress the data further.

4.2. Component Cropping

To reduce the size of the spectral inverted index further, we can crop the number of components stored. In [9], we showed that we could take advantage of the relationship between the DCT and the Karhunen-Loève transform (KLT) when calculating the document scores, here we can do the same.

The KLT is a linear transform which converts a collection of vectors to a space such that the first n dimensions of each vector represents the n principal components of the vector set. By selecting the top n elements of the transformed vector, we are taking the least squares approximation of the vector in n dimensional space. Since the word signal components are independent of each other, the DCT of a word signal is considered to be a close approximation to the KLT for that signal.

Experiments in [9] showed that by using only the first two components we were able to maintain similar precision-recall results when compared to using all components, and we were able to achieve a 40% increase in precision when examining the first 20 documents using the short queries. Previously, the only advantage in this reduction of dimension was a few less calculations. The index contained spatial data, which is needed in its entirety to perform the DCT. Only after the DCT can the least significant components be ignored. Now that we have built a spectral inverted index, we are able to crop the data, which leads to significant reductions in index size. We can see in table 4 that the index size increases linearly with the number of components stored. If we take up to 3 components we have an inverted index of size comparable to that of the spatial inverted index.

4.3. Compression achieved

By combining the quantisation and cropping lossy compression methods, we are reducing the spectral index size by a large magnitude. Therefore we must examine the effect of this compression on the precision. Trials were run using quantisation values of 1 to 10 bits and by cropping 1 to 8 components. A plot of the results is shown in figure 5a. The plot also contains results for CDS using the slower spatial index and the BD-ACI-BCA vector space method. To aim for the most optimal method from the trials, we want to examine the trials which have the properties of high precision and small index size. To identify these trials we have taken a close up of this desired region of figure 5a in figure 5b. We can see that the best combination is quantising to 6 or 7 bits and cropping to one frequency component.

5. Fast Document Ranking

Once the spectral index has been created, documents can be ranked by extracting and combining certain elements relative to the query. Fast document ranking methods have been considered in vector space methods where the data is ordered in terms of importance. The ranking process will extract the elements and stop when it finds that *enough* data has been obtained. We will discuss how we can sort the data to give precise rankings and we will give a fast document ranking algorithm for spectral inverted indexes.

5.1. Sorting the Spectral data

The concept behind fast document ranking is to order the data in an index in such a way that the important information appears first. This way, each score can be quickly approximated and the the top d relevant documents can be selected. The scores can also be refined using the additional (less important) data appearing later in the index if desired. Therefore, when building an index, we must decide which information to treat as important and which to treat less important. Important data is information that will have a major effect on a document score. Every inverted index is arranged so that it is ordered into word groups called inverted lists, to allow fast word extraction when querying (this should not be modified). Each word contains data on which documents it appears in, which spectral components it appears in for every document, and the magnitude and phase of every spectral component of every document.

An early paper by Buckley and Lewit [4] shows how they sort the data according to query weight (w_t). This implies that query terms with high w_t values will contribute to the score, while those with low w_t will probably not. Anh *et al.* [2] showed us the effects of sorting each inverted list by weighted frequency, since it is the major influence to the document score. Experiments showed that it had little advantage in terms of precision over the term weight ordering from Buckley and Lewit, but was slightly faster. We found in [9] that the cosine transform orders its components by

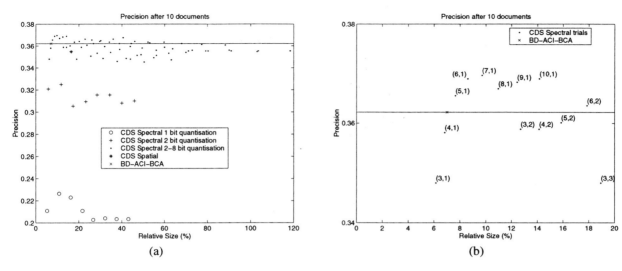

Figure 5. a) A comparison of the CDS method incorporating quantisation and cropping. Each point represents a different magnitude bits, components cropped combination. b) A close up of the trials with the greatest precision and smallest spectral index size from figure 5a. The points are labeled with their (Magnitude bits, components cropped) setting.

decreasing importance. Therefore it is intuitive to order the spectral components from each word by component number and then magnitude (as in equation 5).

$$\langle word, \langle bin, \langle magnitude, \langle document, phase \rangle \rangle \rangle \rangle \quad (5)$$

The document number and phase are stored together in order of appearance.

5.2. The Spectral Accumulator

The accumulator set found in the usual vector space searches is the set $\mathcal{A} = \{\mathcal{A}_{i_1}, \mathcal{A}_{i_2}, \ldots, \mathcal{A}_{i_K}\}$ where $\mathcal{A}_{i_n}$ is the progressive score (accumulator) of the i_nth document and K is the maximum number of documents wanted from the search. Accumulators are used to keep track of the document scores as the query progresses. Initially, the accumulator set is empty. As each element $w_{d,t}$ is taken from the inverted sorted index, the accumulator set is examined to see if accumulator $\mathcal{A}_d$ exists. If it does, the element is added to the accumulator ($\mathcal{A}_d \leftarrow \mathcal{A}_d + w_{d,t}$). If it does not, an accumulator is created and added to the set, so the weighted value can be assigned to it. Once we reach a predefined number of accumulators (K), we are left with the decision of what to do with the rest of the inverted index elements.

Since we are dealing with a spectral index, we need to make some adjustments to the accumulator set in order to gather the data. We do not combine the phase and magnitude information until we have gathered all of the docu-

ments, so we will need separate magnitude and phase accumulators. The magnitude and phase are combined according to the component value, so we will also need separate entries for each component. The accumulators used are of the form $\mathcal{A}_{d,b} = (H_{d,b}, \phi_{d,b})$. Once the score accumulation is over, the corresponding magnitude and phase values are multiplied and the results are added to obtain the document score.

5.3. Fast Query Processing

Fast query processing follows the ideology that if we want K documents, why should we have to calculate the scores of more than K. There have been a few strategies for fast query processing, we will briefly mention two of them. *Quit* and *Continue*, by Moffat and Zobel [8], both require that the query terms are ordered from highest to lowest weight (w_t). This ordering is done because it is assumed that the terms with the greatest weight (w_t) will have the most influence on the document score. The first strategy called *quit* fills the accumulators until K accumulators have been created. When this event occurs, the values in the accumulators are used to rank the documents. For example, if we take the inverted index shown in table 5 and we wanted to quit as soon as three accumulators were non zero, the process would proceed as follows. First, we set all accumulators to zero ($A_d = 0 \; \forall n$). Since the term *mariquita* has the greatest value of w_t, we will begin with it. The first (and only) non zero value we come to is for d_2, therefore we cre-

Table 5. Example inverted index sorted by w_t.

Query terms	w_t	d_1	d_2	d_3	d_4	d_5
mariquita	0.602	0	2	0	0	0
travel	0.301	0	1	0	0	2
wales	0.398	1	1	0	1	0

ate A_2 and assign $A_2 \leftarrow A_2 + w_{d,t} \cdot w_{q,t}$. Since there are no more non-zero values for the term *mariquita*, we move on to the term with the next greatest term weight (*wales*). The first value to appear comes from document 1 (d_1), therefore we create A_1 and assign $A_1 \leftarrow A_1 + w_{d,t} \cdot w_{q,t}$. The next nonzero value comes from document 2, then document 4. Once accumulator 4 is created, we find that we have three accumulators, which means we stop and return the results.

The second strategy called *continue* fills the accumulators until n are non-zero and then continues to fill only those accumulators, ignoring data that would normally be sent to other accumulators. For example, if we followed the continue strategy we would proceed as in the quit example until three accumulators were created. At this stage there are no values left to process in the term *wales* so we would move onto the term with the next greatest term weight (*travel*). The first value that appears is from document 2. Since accumulator 2 exists, we add this weighted value to it ($A_2 \leftarrow A_2 + w_{d,t} \cdot w_{q,t}$). The final value comes from document five and is ignored since accumulator five does not exist.

5.4. Fast Query Processing with Spectral Accumulators

If we try to apply the quit method to our spectral index, we will soon find that we will only be using the data from the first spectral component. This is due to the ordering of the index by component first. To make use of the data found in the other components, we have combined the quit and continue algorithms with the spectral accumulators to come up with the *quit-n* algorithm (figure 5.4). If we order the spectral data by component then by magnitude, we are able to perform the *Continue* method and quit when we reach a specific component number. By incorporating *Quit-n* into CDS and running the same trials as found in section 4.3, we obtain the plot in figure 7a. We can clearly see that the time per query of CDS using *Quit-n* is comparable to the query time of BD-ACI-BCA with *Continue*. The average time of a query using the spatial index is of the order of seconds, therefore by building a spectral index and using fast document raking, we have achieved a speedup by a factor of 100. Figure 7b gives a plot of the more precise trials and their average query times.

---

1. For each inverted list $I_t = \{\langle d, b, H_{d,t,b}, \phi_{d,t,b} \rangle | \forall d, \forall b \}$
    (a) Order elements by increasing bin value
    (b) For each bin set $\{\langle d, b, H_{d,t,b}, \phi_{d,t,b} \rangle | \forall d \}$
        i. Order elements by decreasing magnitude
2. Set $\mathcal{A} \leftarrow \emptyset$
3. For each query term $t \in T$, retrieve I_t
4. While $I_t \neq \emptyset \; \forall t \in T$
    (a) Select $\langle \delta, \beta, H_{\delta,t,\beta}, \phi_{\delta,t,\beta} \rangle \in \{I_t | \forall t \}$ where $\beta = \min(b)$ and $H_{\delta,t,\beta} = \max(H_{d,t,\beta})$
    (b) If $\beta < \hat{\beta}$ (stopping component)
        i. If $\mathcal{A}_{\delta,\beta} \notin \mathcal{A}$, $\mathcal{A} \leftarrow \mathcal{A} + \{\mathcal{A}_{\delta,\beta}\}$
        ii. Set $\mathcal{A}_{\delta,\beta} \leftarrow \mathcal{A}_{\delta,\beta} + (H_{\delta,t,\beta}, \phi_{\delta,t,\beta})$
        iii. Set $I_t \leftarrow I_t - \{\langle \delta, \beta, H_{\delta,t,\beta}, \phi_{\delta,t,\beta} \rangle\}$
        iv. If $|\mathcal{A}| > K$, goto step 5
5. While $\beta < \hat{\beta}$
    (a) Select $\langle \delta, \beta, H_{\delta,t,\beta}, \phi_{\delta,t,\beta} \rangle \in \{I_t | \forall t \}$ where $\beta = \min(b)$ and $H_{\delta,t,\beta} = \max(H_{d,t,\beta})$
    (b) If $\mathcal{A}_{\delta,\beta} \in \mathcal{A}$
        i. Set $\mathcal{A}_{\delta,\beta} \leftarrow \mathcal{A}_{\delta,\beta} + (H_{\delta,t,\beta}, \phi_{\delta,t,\beta})$
        ii. Set $I_t \leftarrow I_t - \{\langle \delta, \beta, H_{\delta,t,\beta}, \phi_{\delta,t,\beta} \rangle\}$
6. For each d such that $\mathcal{A}_{d,b} = (H_{d,b}, \Phi_{d,b}) \in \mathcal{A}$
    (a) Set $\bar{\Phi}_{d,b} \leftarrow |\Phi_{d,b}/|T||$
    (b) calculate $s_d = \sum_{b=0}^{\hat{\beta}} \bar{\Phi}_{d,b} H_{d,b}$
7. Identify the r highest values of s_d

Figure 6. Quit-n for CDS using K accumulators and $\hat{\beta}$ components.

If we perform the same trials as found in section 4.3, but this time use fast ranking, we will notice that the results are very similar (almost identical), but the BD-ACI-BCA method results in a lower precision. An explanation for the lack of change in the CDS trials would be due to the DCT. In these cases, the DCT is performing principal component analysis, which means it is shifting the important information from each word signal into the lower components. Therefore the document set relative to the query can be chosen based on the initial components.

6. Conclusion

It has been demonstrated that CDS is able to offer superior precision results, however there is a need for a spectral index due to its slow speed when using a spatial index. To build a spectral inverted index we considered the factors of precision, query speed and index size. In this paper, we have successfully shown how to build a spectral inverted index by employing techniques such as quantisation and cropping so that the index is compact. We have also shown how we can take advantage of the spectral index to perform fast docu-

352

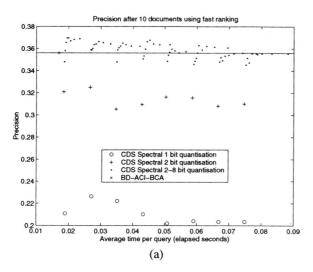
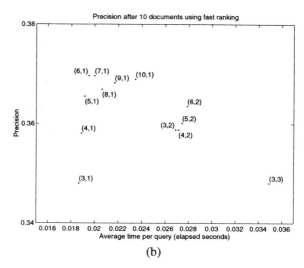

(a)   (b)

Figure 7. a) A comparison of the CDS method incorporating quantisation, cropping and fast document ranking. Each point represents a different magnitude bits, components cropped combination. b) A close up of the trials which have the fastest query time from figure 7a. Each point is accompanied with a (quantised magnitude bits, components cropped) label.

ment ranking, giving a query time speed up by a factor of 100 relative the the slower spatial index.

We have obtained a spectral index of comparable size to an index used by vector space methods and shown that the CDS method can retrieve documents at a comparable rate to the BD-ACI-BCA vector space method and still maintain its high precision and recall.

References

[1] J. Allan, J. Callan, F.-F. Feng, and D. Malin. Inquery and trec-8. In E. M. Voorhees and D. K. Harman, editors, *NIST Special Publication 500-246: The Eighth Text REtrieval Conference (TREC-8)*, pages 637–644, November 1999.

[2] V. N. Anh, O. de Kretser, and A. Moffat. Vector-space ranking with effective early termination. In *Proceedings of the 24th annual international ACM SIGIR conference on Research and development in information retrieval*, pages 35–42. ACM Press, 2001.

[3] W. G. Aref, D. Barbara, S. Johnson, and S. Mehrotra. Efficient processing of proximity queries for large databases. In *Proceedings of the Eleventh International Conference on Data Engineering*, pages 147–154, 1995.

[4] C. Buckley and A. F. Lewit. Optimisation of inverted vector searches. In *Proceedings of the ACM-SIGIR International Conference on Research and Development in Information Retrieval*, pages 97–110. ACM Press, New York, June 1985.

[5] C. Buckley and J. Walz. Smart in trec 8. In E. M. Voorhees and D. K. Harman, editors, *NIST Special Publication 500-246: The Eighth Text REtrieval Conference (TREC-8)*, pages 577–582, November 1999.

[6] S. W. Golomb. Run-length encodings. *IEEE Transactions on Information Theory*, 12:399–401, July 1966.

[7] D. Harman. Overview of the third text retrieval conference (trec-3). In *National Institute of Standards and Technology Special Publication 500-225*, Gaithersburg, Md. 20899.

[8] A. Moffat and J. Zobel. Self-indexing inverted files for fast text retrieval. *ACM Transactions on Information Systems (TOIS)*, 14(4):349–379, 1996.

[9] L. A. F. Park, M. Palaniswami, and K. Ramamohanarao. A novel web text mining method using the discrete cosine transform. In *6th European Conference on Principles of Data Mining and Knowledge Discovery*, August 2002.

[10] L. A. F. Park, K. Ramamohanarao, and M. Palaniswami. Fourier domain scoring : A novel document ranking method. *IEEE Transactions on Knowledge and Data Engineering*, Submitted February 2002. http://www.ee.mu.oz.au/pgrad/lapark/fds_compare3.pdf.

[11] S. E. Robertson and S. Walker. Okapi/keenbow at trec-8. In E. M. Voorhees and D. K. Harman, editors, *NIST Special Publication 500-246: The Eighth Text REtrieval Conference (TREC-8)*, pages 151–162, November 1999.

[12] K. Yang and K. Maglaughlin. Iris at trec-8. In E. M. Voorhees and D. K. Harman, editors, *NIST Special Publication 500-246: The Eighth Text REtrieval Conference (TREC-8)*, pages 645–656, November 1999.

[13] J. Zobel and A. Moffat. Exploring the similarity space. In *ACM SIGIR Forum*, volume 32, pages 18–34, Spring 1998.

Efficient Progressive Sampling for Association Rules *

Srinivasan Parthasarathy
Computer and Information Science
Ohio State University,
Columbus, OH 43235
srini@cis.ohio-state.edu

Abstract

In data mining, sampling has often been suggested as an effective tool to reduce the size of the dataset operated at some cost to accuracy. However, this loss to accuracy is often difficult to measure and characterize since the exact nature of the learning curve (accuracy vs. sample size) is parameter and data dependent, i.e., we do not know apriori what sample size is needed to achieve a desired accuracy on a particular dataset for a particular set of parameters. In this article we propose the use of progressive sampling to determine the required sample size for association rule mining. We first show that a naive application of progressive sampling is not very efficient for association rule mining. We then present a refinement based on equivalence classes, that seems to work extremely well in practice and is able to converge to the desired sample size very quickly and very accurately. An additional novelty of our approach is the definition of a support-sensitive, interactive measure of accuracy across progressive samples.

1 Introduction

As our ability to collect, store, and distribute huge amounts of data increases with advancing technology, discovering the knowledge hidden in these ever-growing databases has become a pressing problem. This problem referred to as data-mining, an effort to derive interesting conclusions from large bodies of data, is an interactive process. In fact, interactivity is often the key to facilitating effective data understanding and knowledge discovery. In such an environment response time is crucial. However, extracting knowledge from these massive databases is a compute and I/O intensive process which makes the task of guaranteeing quick response times difficult.

In order to to minimize the I/O traffic involved in such data-intensive applications researchers have evaluated the

viability of using sampling[6] to reduce the dataset size. While such methods have shown quite a lot of promise it has been observed by several researchers[14, 15, 20] that it is often very difficult to quantify, apriori, the quality of the results obtained for a given sample size. Recently, to address this problem some researchers have proposed and evaluated progressive sampling[14] for select data mining tasks. Progressive sampling starts with a small sample and uses progressively larger ones until model accuracy no longer improves beyond a user specified threshold. In this paper we study progressive sampling methods as they apply to association rule mining, a key data mining task. Realizing an efficient method to progressively sample a dataset for association rule mining poses several challenges.

First, and foremost, one needs to define a notion of model accuracy. In other words, for a particular dataset how does one define how good the sample is? This goodness criterion should be sensitive to relevant interaction parameters (e.g. support, confidence, important items[1] to the user) as well as the inherent properties of the dataset in question. A naive approach could be to compare the set of associations generated by the sample with the set of associations generated on the entire dataset. Obviously, this is self-defeating and does not take into account aspects of user interaction.

Second, while defining a notion of model accuracy is important, one must also be able to compute it efficiently. Zaki *et al*[20], have observed, that at low sample sizes, there is a tendency to detect a large number of false positives. This property can limit the effectiveness of progressive sampling.

Third, as noted by Provost and Kolluri [15] "most discussions on sampling assume that producing random samples efficiently from large datasets is not difficult. This is simply not true.". In fact most implementations require O(N) time where N represents the size of dataset and not the sample size (S). Naive implementations often may be much worse. Note, that one cannot afford to spend O(N) time to generate

---

*This work was partially supported by an Ameritech Faculty Fellowship.

[1]For example a user may be interested in associations pertaining to a specific item (say diapers).

each progressive sample.

We address these three problems in the context of progressively sampling for association rules. Specifically our contributions are:

- A novel measure of model accuracy for progressively sampling association rules. The measure is designed in such a way to be sensitive to user parameters and interactions while not requiring execution on the entire dataset.

- An efficient technique for identifying the optimal sample size. This key result is based on the identification and tracking of a representative set of frequent itemsets (a small subset of the entire set of frequent itemsets). Essentially the computational element (computing the associations for a given sample size) is reduced significantly enabling faster convergence to the optimal sample size. This technique also addresses the high false-positive problem for low support values.

- An efficient technique based on asynchronous I/O operations and a novel application of a well known sampling methodology to improve the efficiency of generating a random sample, as perceived by the processor.

The rest of this article is organized as follows. In Section 2 we provide some background on progressive sampling and association rules. In Section 3 we present our progressive sampling approach. We empirically evaluate the proposed approach on synthetic and real datasets in Section 4. Finally we conclude with directions for future work in section 5.

2 Background

Discovery of association rules is an important problem in database mining. The prototypical application is the analysis of sales or *basket* data [3] although more recently it has been adopted in the domains of scientific computing, bioinformatics and performance modeling. The problem can be formally stated as: Let $\mathcal{I} = \{i_1, i_2, \cdots, i_m\}$ be a set of m distinct attributes, also called *items*. Each transaction T in the database $\mathcal{D}$ of transactions, has a unique identifier, and *contains* a set of items, such that $T \subseteq \mathcal{I}$. An *association rule* is an expression $A \Rightarrow B$, where $A, B \subset \mathcal{I}$, are sets of items called *itemsets*, and $A \cap B = \emptyset$. Each itemset is said to have a *support* S if $S\%$ of the transactions in $\mathcal{D}$ contain the itemset. The association rule is said to have *confidence* C if $C\%$ of the transactions that contain A also contain B, i.e., $C = S(A \cup B)/S(A)$, i.e., the conditional probability that transactions contain the itemset B, given that they contain itemset A.

Data mining of association rules from such databases consists of finding the set of all rules which meet the user-specified minimum confidence and support values.

Database Layout: There are two possible layouts of the database for association mining. The *horizontal* layout consists of a list of transactions, where each transaction has an identifier followed by a list of items. The *vertical* layout consists of a list of items where each item contains a list of transactions that transacted on that particular item. Approaches based on the horizontal format include the popular Apriori algorithm[3] and its variants. The Apriori algorithm uses the downward closure property of itemset support to prune the itemset lattice - the property that all subsets of a frequent itemset must themselves be frequent. Thus the frequent k-itemsets are used to construct candidate (k+1)-itemsets. A pass over the data is made to identify which of the candidate (k+1)-itemsets are actually frequent. This process is repeated till there are no more frequent sets.

The vertical format has the advantage that the support for candidate k-itemset can be computed by simple tid-list intersections. The tid-lists cluster relevant transactions, and avoid scanning the whole databases to compute support, and the larger the itemset, the shorter the tid-lists, resulting in faster intersections[21]. An additional optimization of compressing the vertical lists results in additional gains due to lower memory and I/O traffic[4, 17]. Note that sampling in the vertical format will be inefficient. Essentially sampling in the vertical context will necessarily have to keep track of which transactions are in the sample and which are out and one would need to to scan through each tid-list and mark the transactions in the sample and those out of it. One can of course sample in the horizontal format and then convert to the vertical format on the fly.

Equivalence Class Partitioning: One way to improve the vertical approach is to use it in conjunction with equivalence class partitioning. Let the set of large two-itemsets, L_2, be {AB, AC, AD, AE, BC, BD, BE, CD, DE}. Equivalence class partitioning partitions these itemsets by their (k-1 length where k= 2 in the above example) prefixes resulting in the following four partitions: $S_A = [A] = \{AB, AC, AD, AE\}$, $S_B = [B] = \{BC, BD, BE\}$, $S_C = [C] = \{CD\}$, and $S_D = [D] = \{DE\}$. The same partitioning scheme can be recursively repeated to find all the associations. For instance, in the above example, partition **[B]** yields candidates {BCD,BCE,BDE}. Assuming that all of the candidates are deemed frequent then the level 3 partitions for **[B]** are S_{BC} = **[BC]** = {BCD,BCE}, and S_{BD} = **[BD]** = {BDE}. The advantage of this approach is that the algorithm can process an entire equivalence class partition before proceeding to the next partition. This improves memory locality and minimizes I/O traffic in the ECLAT algorithm[21], an approach based on the above equivalence class partitioning.

Note, that past work has not considered using the equivalence class idea within the context of sampling. For the present work it is important to define a notion of an equivalence superclass. Informally, an equivalence superclass is defined as the set of all frequent itemsets that can recursively be enumerated from a given partition. From the above example, the equivalence superclass from partition S_B, denoted as $ES_B = \{BC,BD,BE,BCD,BCE,BDE\}$.

Sampling for Associations: While several authors have proposed various strategies on the use of sampling for KDD[8, 14, 11] and database tasks[12], we limit the discussion in this section to those relevant to association mining. Toivonen [18] presents an association rule mining algorithm using sampling. The approach can be divided into two phases. During phase 1 a sample of the database is obtained and all associations in the sample are found. These results are then validated against the entire database. To maximize the effectiveness of the overall approach, the author makes use of lowered minimum support on the sample. Since the approach is probabilistic (i.e. dependent on the sample containing all the relevant associations) not all the rules may be found in this first pass. Those associations that were deemed not frequent in the sample but were actually frequent in the entire dataset are used to construct the complete set of associations in phase 2. A detailed theoretical analysis of sampling (using Chernoff bounds) for association rules was presented by Zaki *et al* [20]. Chernoff bounds provide information on how close is the actual occurrence of an itemset in the sample as compared to the expected count in the sample. Based on itemset frequencies, using Chernoff bounds one can obtain a sample size[20]. However, the sample size is independent of the original dataset size and can be quite large, sometimes larger than the original dataset! Empirical evidence in the same paper also showed that Chernoff bounds may be too pessimistic for association mining. It was also shown that sampling can be effective for association mining if the sample size were known apriori for the corresponding dataset and input parameters. However, determining the optimal sample size was left as an open problem. Note, that determining the optimal sample size efficiently can significantly improve on the overall performance of Toivenen's approach[18] since with a good estimate one could minimize the computational and I/O aspects of the second pass.

Progressive Sampling: In order to quickly estimate the optimal sample size, researchers have recently turned to progressive sampling. Before we detail this procedure we first define the notion of a learning curve. A learning curve is a mapping between sample size and model accuracy. Typically a learning curve is depicted with the vertical axis representing the accuracy of the model and the horizontal axis representing the sample size. Most learning curves typically have steeply sloping portion early in the curve, and a plateau late in the curve[14, 5]. The cost-performance tradeoff is best at the knee of the curve. Such curves exhibit the property that the slope of the curve is monotonically nonincreasing with n (excepting for small local variance). Most learning curves exhibit the above behavior but some curves can misbehave especially at small sample sizes[10].

The goal of progressive sampling is to start with small samples and progressively increase them as long as model accuracy improves sufficiently. Using such a technique one can identify the knee of the learning curve using basic slope characterization across recently evaluated samples. One problem in the association rule mining context is how does one quantify model accuracy? A simple metric would be to compare the set of associations found for a given sample size with the set of associations found for the entire dataset. However, to obtain the latter we would have to run the algorithm on the entire dataset!

The efficiency of progressive sampling is governed by the average case execution time performance of the algorithm, and by the sampling schedule. In the case of association rule mining algorithms while the worst case complexity is exponential the average case behavior typically tends to be linear, or in some cases quadratic. The issue of determining an optimal sampling schedule was addressed by Provost et al[14], where the authors show that a simple geometric sampling schedule is efficient in an asymptotic sense for most induction algorithms with a run time complexity of $O(n)$ or worse as long as the maximum sample size is $n/2$.

However, the above result is not useful if the desired accuracy is met only at a a sample size of 70% (for a linear time algorithm). This reduction (from 100%) may still result in significant performance benefits. Another problem with the above theoretical model is that sampling overheads are ignored. Efficiently obtaining a sample from a large dataset, is often ignored by most researchers as pointed out by Provost and Kolluri[15]. If one were to account for this the benefits of progressive sampling would decrease. Another overhead, induced within the context of association rules, is the avalanche effect of detecting false positives at very small sample sizes (see Zaki et al for details[20]). We address these issues in the next section.

3 Methodology

In this section we present our approach for efficient progressive sampling of association rules. We first describe our measure of model accuracy which is based on the notion of self-similarity of associations across progressive samples. A novelty of the proposed measure is that it is functionally dependent on user input parameters (support, constraints etc.). We then identify a representative subset of frequent itemsets such that the behavior of our measure of model accuracy on this representative subset mimics the behavior of our measure on the entire set of associations. The final problem we address relates to that of sampling overhead.

Model Accuracy: Absolute model accuracy, for a given sample is difficult to measure without running the algorithm on the entire dataset. Since this is not possible to do due to efficiency constraints we define a measure of accuracy that is based on the following key intuitions:

For progressive samples d_1 and d_2, where $size(d_2) > size(d_1)$, the self-similarity between the set of associations generated under the two samples is likely to be low during the growth phase and is likely to be much higher during the "plateau" phase. Therefore identification of the knee of the curve can be done by measuring the self-similarity between progressive samples.

We now define the our notion of interactive self-similarity: Let A and B respectively be a the set of frequent itemsets for a database sample d_1 and that for a database sample d_2. For an element $x \in A$ (respectively in B), let $\sup_{d_1}(x)$ (respectively $\sup_{d_2}(x)$) be the frequency of x in d_1 (respectively in d_2). Our metric is:

$$Sim(d_1, d_2) = \frac{\sum_{x \in A \cap B} \max\{0, 1 - \alpha | \sup_{d_1}(x) - \sup_{d_2}(x)|\}}{\|A \cup B\|}$$

where α is a scaling parameter. The parameter α has a default value of 1 and can be modified to reflect the significance the user attaches to variations in supports. For $\alpha = 0$ the similarity measure is identical to $\frac{\|A \cap B\|}{\|A \cup B\|}$, i.e., support variance carries no significance. Sim values are bounded and lie in $[0,1]$. Sim also has the property of *relative ordinality*, i.e., if $Sim(X, Y) > Sim(X, Z)$, then X is more similar to Y than it is to Z. Note, that while the above formulation does not explicitly consider correlations between itemsets (e.g. two itemsets (ABEK, AEFK) that have many items in common are not treated differently), they are accounted for implicitly as all itemsets that can be formed by the common items (A,E,K) are part of the summation.

An important point raised by Das, Manilla and Ronkainen[7], while evaluating the similarity between two attributes was that using a different set of external probes to measure similarity could potentially yield a different similarity measure. In our case the action of modifying the external probe set corresponds to modifying the association sets evaluated over different samples of the input database. This is achieved either by modifying the minimum support or by restricting the search for associations to those that satisfy certain conditions (Boolean properties over attributes) [2]. Note that the optimal sample size (the knee of the curve) can vary for a different set of parameter values.

Picking a Representative Set: The above metric suggests using the entire association set from consecutive samples to measure the self-similarity between progressive samples. However, as observed earlier, computing complete association sets for each sample may eventually defeat the purpose of sampling since evaluating each sample has various overheads associated with it. To overcome this problem what we need is a representative class of itemsets which has a behavior similar to the self-similarity curve of the original set of associations. Moreover, this representative

class of itemsets should satisfy the criterion that it should be efficient to compute. Given the above requirement, we evaluated three possible options for a representative set: a random sample of the set of frequent itemsets; a level-wise (horizontal–i.e., all k-itemsets for a given k) split of the frequent itemset lattice; an equivalence-superclass (vertical) split of the frequent itemset lattice.

The first option for a representative class is infeasible. A truly random sample of the set of frequent itemsets while ideal from a statistical perspective, is impossible to generate, *without first generating the set of frequent itemsets* and therefore self-defeating. The second option is impractical for higher order splits (the set of all k-itemsets where k is large) as again one has to compute pretty much all the frequent itemsets before reaching the higher order split in question. We found empirically that using lower order splits tends to result in an unreliable over-estimation (i.e. premature convergence) of the similarity between subsequent samples and was therefore not useful. Detailed analysis of these options was considered and the reader is refered to an extended version of this article for details[13].

Our proposed approach is to use equivalence super-classes (vertical splits) generated from the most frequent item(s) as representative sets. We considered using randomly selected equivalence superclasses as the representative class of itemsets but realized that these could suffer from the same problem as the horizontal split approaches. The key intuition behind using the most frequent item is that such an equivalence super-class in all likelihood most completely captures the entire set of frequent itemsets and the distribution of associated supports across all levels of frequent itemsets [13]. As we shall see from the empirical results in the next section this representative class based approach yields a very good predictor of the self similarity measure. The other nice feature of this representative class is that it can be quickly computed, with some straightforward modifications current-day vertical-set approaches[13].

Note, no changes are required to the self-similarity measure, we are just replacing the base association set with the representative set as determined by the first (few) equivalence class partition(s). However, the representative class selection is somewhat dependent on the similarity measure. For instance if the similarity metric, as discussed earlier, were restricted to those itemsets including a particular item (say A), then the best equivalence super-class to choose might be the equivalence super-class generated by that particular item (A). Also, while we have argued intuitively[13], that equivalence super-classes based on the most frequent item(s) are likely to be good representative sets in general, other splits, based on the constraints imposed on the similarity measure, may be better and are being investigated.

Efficient Sampling Methodology: Provost and Kolluri[15] point out that most sampling algorithms require O(N) or greater time to execute where N is the size of the database and that researchers rarely account for this overhead. For generating samples of the database we use the Method A algorithm presented by Vitter[19]. A simple algorithm for sampling generates an independent uniform random variate for each record to determine whether that record should be chosen for the sample. If m records have been chosen from the first t records then the next record will be chosen with probability (n-m)/N-t. This algorithm generates N random variates. Method A significantly speeds up the sampling process by efficiently determining the number of records to be skipped before the next one is chosen. It generates exactly n random variates. With appropriate support for database indexing the method A scheme allows the sampling procedure to take $O(n)$ time[2].

Note that even with direct indexing creating a sample still creates some level of overhead. This overhead can be split into two components computational overhead (determining which transactions are in the sample) and I/O overhead (reading in said transactions). The I/O component can be overcome with suitable systems support in the form of asynchronous I/O, a technique which allows I/O operations to overlap with useful computation. Essentially one can overlap the I/O required for the next progressive sample with the computation required for processing the current sample. In other words while we compute the association set for the current sample one can do the I/O for the next sample size (in the sampling schedule). With active disk-like approaches[1, 16], one can move the computational overhead associated with sampling off the critical path as well. This approach lends itself to accessing data over the network as well, since even that can be effectively overlapped with useful computation.

Algorithm Details: The basic steps to the progressive sampling approach are highlighted in Figure 1. We present two approaches, one based on estimating self-similarity between the current sample and the subsequent sample in the schedule (RC-SS), and the other based on estimating self-similarity between the current sample and the entire dataset using the first k equivalence super-classes (RC-S).

Step 0 for the RC-S algorithm computes the representative set on the entire dataset. Step 1 for the RC-SS algorithm computes the representative set on the lowest sample size in the schedule. Step 2 is an iterative for loop. Each iteration of this for loop first computes the next sample (Step3) in the schedule. Then the representative set for this sample is constructed (Step4). After this the self-similarity measure is computed. For the RC-SS algorithm we compute the self similarity between this representative set and the previous one. For the RC-S algorithm we compute the self similarity between this representative set and

---
[2]Note that if each transaction in the database is directly indexable proving this bound for the *worst-case* is trivial.

Step 0: Compute representative set
　　　　on entire dataset (RC-S only)
Step 1: Compute initial sample and
　　　　representative set on sample. (RC-SS only)
Step 2: For each sample size in the schedule:
Step 3: 　　Compute sample.
Step 4: 　　Compute representative set.
Step 5: 　　Is convergence criteria met?
Step 6: 　　If yes set effective sample
　　　　size (ESS) and break;
Step 7: 　　If no continue;
Step 8: Compute the rest of the entire set
　　　　of associations for the ESS.

Figure 1. Proposed Approach

the one pre-computed in Step 0. If the similarity metric is above a user-specified threshold, then convergence is achieved (Step 5). For RC-SS we modified the convergence criteria slightly after viewing empirical results. We found that the self-similarity curve for RC-SS is not always well behaved (is non-monotonic). For this algorithm we declared convergence only if the similarity metric is above the user-specified threshold for two consecutive iterations. This avoids premature convergence due to local variances and also protects against the possible misbehavior of self-similarity curves (found mainly at small sample sizes). If the convergence criteria is met we break out of the for loop (Step 6) else we continue (Step 7). In Step 8, we compute the overall association set for the determined sample size.

4 Experimental Methodology

In this section we empirically evaluate the proposed methodology on several synthetic and real datasets. We first describe the experimental setup (machine configuration, dataset properties etc.). We then evaluate the proposed measure of model accuracy: self similarity between consecutive samples; and the impact on this measure when using the first equivalence superclass as a representative set. We then quantify the performance gains from using this representative class (as opposed to the entire set of associations). At the end of this section we quantify the gains from our sampling methodology.

Experimental Setup: We used three synthetic datasets generated from the IBM dataset generator program[3]. These datasets mimic the transactions in a retailing environment. The properties of the synthetic datasets are inherent in the names. The number following the **T** refers to the average transaction length, the number following the **I** refers to the average maximal potentially frequent itemset size, the alpha-numeric-code following the **D** refers to the total number of transactions (1M means 1 Million). We also used two real datasets for our experiments. The first real dataset is the Gazelle dataset which formed a part of the KDD Cup 1999 competition. The properties of these three datasets are described in Table 2. The second real dataset is the VBook dataset which is a dataset from a prominent online bookstore retailer in South America.

Database	$numT$	Size
T10I4D5M	5000000	260MB
T8I5D25M	25000000	1.25GB
Gazelle	59602	1.35MB
Vbook	136809	4.3MB

Figure 2. Database properties

All experiments unless otherwise noted, were performed on a dual pentium node machine, 1GHz Pentium III, having 512 MB RAM and running Linux 2.4. For all the experiments we used a geometric sampling schedule up to 40% of the original dataset and an arithmetic progressive schedule from that point on, if required.

Impact of Representative Set on Self Similarity: The self similarity plots for all the datasets are described in Figure 3. In each graph the Y-axis corresponds to the self similarity and the X-axis corresponds to the sample size. In each graph there are four plots, the RC-S and RC-SS plots have already been explained in the previous section. The A-S plots (in bold) is the learning curve that we are trying to estimate. They represent the naive (impractical) approach of comparing the entire set of associations generated by the sample with the set of associations generated by the entire dataset. The A-SS plots mirror the procedure described for R-SS, the only difference being that the self-similarity measure is computed on the entire set of associations.

On viewing the plots for the real datasets (Figures 3a and 3b) one can observe that the plots for the representative set (prefix RC) closely follow the plots for the entire set of associations (prefix A) for the corresponding support values considered. For the gazelle dataset, note that if we required a self similarity cut off of 0.9, for 0.1% support we would never obtain this value (even if we went the distance), whereas at 0.25% support (not shown, see[13] for details) this could be achieved at a 50% sample size. This highlights the fact that the user-specified parameters has an important role to play in determining whether sampling is useful or not and if so at what level. Overall both plots follow the expected pattern of low self similarity at smaller samples, and higher self similarity at larger samples. The phase transition from lower self-similarities to higher self-similarities coincide with the knee of the learning curve.

The results for the synthetic datasets are better (see Figures 3c-d). The shape of the self similarity plots for the representative class almost exactly mirror the self similarity plots for the entire set of associations. Unlike the plots for the real datasets, the self similarities are quite high even at low sample sizes. This is mainly due to the fact that the synthetic datasets are much larger than the real datasets therefore the absolute number of transactions for a given sample size (expressed as percentage of the original) is much larger.

Overall the RC-S plots most closely mirrors A-S plots. Another interesting trend that is observed across both real and synthetic datasets is that there seems to be a relatively consistent overestimation or underestimation of the self-similarity across RC and A graphs. For example in Figure 3a the RC curves consistently underestimate their A-curve counterparts. This would seem to indicate that the curve we want to estimate (A-S) can be best estimated by using the RC-S curve and a translation factor that can be derived from the translations computed from the RC-SS and A-SS curves. This strategy is currently being evaluated.

Impact of Representative Set on Performance: In this section we highlight the performance gains from using the representative class of itemsets to compute self similarities over using the entire set of associations. Figure 4 plots the cumulative execution time for different sample sizes for the datasets under consideration. The cumulative execution time is the execution time of the algorithm (RC-S or RC-SS) when the convergence criteria is satisfied at the corresponding sample size. The *Baseline Execution Time* corresponds to the execution time of the association mining algorithm on the entire dataset. Essentially the break even point for progressive sampling, when computing on the entire set of associations (represented by the prefix A) at 0.5% support, is when the cumulative execution time intersects with this baseline. For the VBook dataset the break even point when using the entire set of associations is reached at a sample size of around 10% for this dataset at this value of support. The poor performance here can be traced to the fact that for this support value at low sample sizes the basic association mining algorithm detects a large number of false positives. However, for the representative class approach, after determining the effective sample size, the algorithm still has to be completely executed on that sample size (sans the representative class). For this dataset if the effective sample size determined was 50% (corresponding to a value of 0.9 in the RC-SS (RC-S) plot from Figure 3b) then the total execution time is equal to 1.1s (1.15s for RC-S) which is still below the baseline of 1.5s. This result is especially encouraging and shows that even for a small dataset the approach presented can be quite effective.

As can be observed from Figures 4b-c, the results on the synthetic datasets are even better. For T10I4D5M for a self similarity cut off of 0.95 or higher the optimal sample size is 50% (this can be seen from Figure 3c). The RC-SS approach required a total of 448 (496 for RC-S) seconds to compute the results (see Figure 4b). The approach using the entire association set requires 1037 seconds (which is above the baseline of 950s) to compute the same result. This results in a factor of improvment of 2.4 (2.1 over the baseline). For T8I5D25M (Figure 4c) for a self similarity cut off of 0.95 or higher the optimal sample size is 10% (from Figure 3d). The representative class approach requires a total

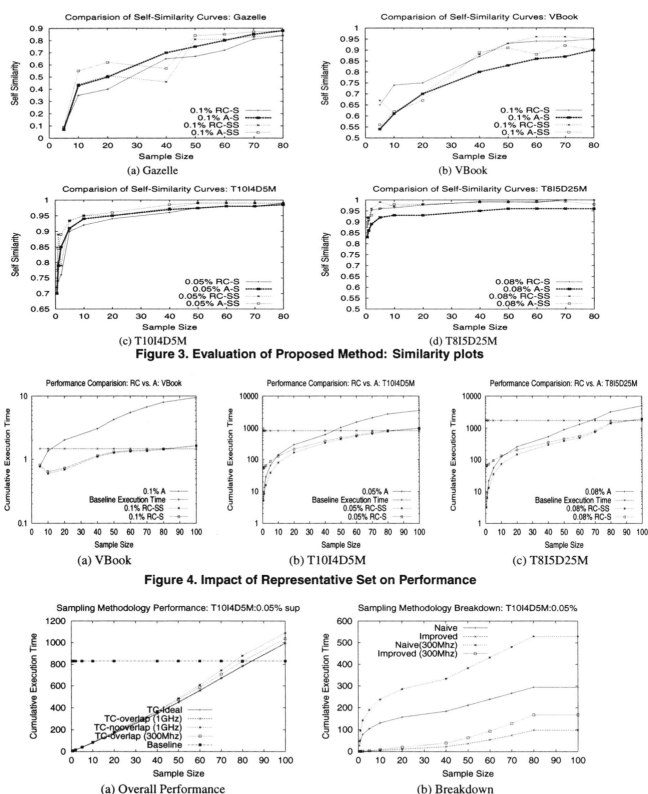

(a) Gazelle

(b) VBook

(c) T10I4D5M

(d) T8I5D25M

Figure 3. Evaluation of Proposed Method: Similarity plots

(a) VBook

(b) T10I4D5M

(c) T8I5D25M

Figure 4. Impact of Representative Set on Performance

(a) Overall Performance

(b) Breakdown

Figure 5. Sampling Methodology on Performance Breakdown

of 73.17 (125 for RC-SS) seconds to compute the results. The approach using the entire association set requires 140 seconds to compute the same result. When compared with the baseline execution time (1730s) the representative class approach's improvement factor is around 25.

Impact of Sampling Methodology: In Figure 5 we consider the performance of the sampling methodology presented in Section 3. Figure 5a compares the cumulative execution time performance of our the approach using the representative class to identify the ideal sample size while overlapping the sampling and I/O operations of the next stage with the computation of the current stage. In Figure 5a we compare the performance of ideal situation (where there is no sampling overhead: TC-ideal) with the actual performance with overlapping (TC-overlap) and without overlapping (TC-nooverlap). For the overlapping computation we used two scenarios, one where the processor handling the I/O and sampling was a 300Mhz Pentium II[3] (i.e. a more realistic scenario for active disks with a much slower processor than the compute processor) and the other where the I/O processor was 1GHz (ideal baseline).

On viewing the graphs it is clear that the TC-ideal graph and the TC-overlap (1GHz) are almost identical, reflecting the fact that almost all of the sampling overhead is overlapped with useful computation (computing the association set for the previous sample size). On relaxing the assumption and allowing for the fact that the processor doing the sampling and I/O is often much slower (300 Mhz) we observe a marginal drop in performance (slightly under 4%), so still most of the sampling overhead is overlapped with useful computation. Note that if we did not overlap the sampling overhead with computation then we perform 10-12% worse than the ideal (comparing the TC-Ideal and TC-noverlap graphs). This experiment assumes the best possible sampling algorithm (the Sample A algorithm). We further broke down the performance of the sampling overheads in Figure 5b for the two configurations (1GHz and 300Mhz). The performance of the naive algorithm (see Section 3) is much worse than the Sample A algorithm.

5 Conclusions and Future Work

We have presented an efficient method to progressively sample for association rules. Our approach relies on a novel measure of model accuracy (self-similarity of associations across progressive samples), the identification of a representative class of frequent itemsets that mimic (extremely accurately) the self-similarity values across the entire set of associations, and an efficient sampling methodology that hides

the overhead of obtaining progressive samples by overlapping it with useful computation. We evaluated the results on a set of real and synthetic datasets. We extensively benchmarked each aspect of our algorithm and obtained uniformly good performance (several factor-fold execution time improvements) across both real and synthetic datasets. In the current work we have considered each sample to be independent of the other. We would like to see if the proposed method can be improved by using adaptive sampling techniques[8]. Other directions of future work have been outlined already in the text.

References

[1] Anurag Acharya *et al*. Active disks: Programming model, algorithms and evaluation. In *ASPLOS*, 1998.

[2] C. Aggarwal and P. Yu. Online generation of association rules. In *ICDE*, 1998.

[3] R. Agrawal and R. Srikant. Fast algorithms for mining association rules. In *20th VLDB Conf.*, September 1994.

[4] Doug Burdick, Manuel Calimlim, and J. E. Gehrke. Mafia: A maximal frequent itemset algorithm for transactional databases. In *ICDE*, 2001.

[5] Jason Catlett. Megainduction: A test flight. In *Machine Learning*, pages 596–599, 1991.

[6] W. G. Cochran. *Sampling Techniques*. J. Wiley & Sons-1977.

[7] G. Das, H. Mannila, and P. Ronkainen. Similarity of attributes by external probes. In *KDD*, 1998.

[8] Carlos Domingo and Osamu Watanabe. Scaling up a boosting-based learner via adaptive sampling. In *PAKDD*, 2000.

[9] J. Han and J. Pei. Yiwen yin: Mining frequent patterns without candidate generation. In *SIGMOD*, 2000.

[10] Haussler, Kearns, Seung, and Tishby. Rigorous learning curve bounds from statistical mechanics. In *COLT*, 1994.

[11] George H. John and Pat Langley. Static versus dynamic sampling for data mining. In *KDD*, 1996.

[12] F. Olken and D. Rotem. Random sampling from database files - a survey. In *5th Intl. Conf. Statistical and Scientific Database Management*, April 1990.

[13] S. Parthasarathy. Efficient progressive sampling for association rules. OSU CIS Technical Report Number: TR-OSU-CISRC-5/02-TR13, November 2001, revised March 2002.

[14] Foster J. Provost, David Jensen, and Tim Oates. Efficient progressive sampling. In *KDD*, 1999.

[15] Foster J. Provost and Venkateswarlu Kolluri. A survey of methods for scaling up inductive algorithms. *Data Mining and Knowledge Discovery*, 3(2):131–169, 1999.

[16] E. Riedel, G. Gibson, and C. Faloutsos. Active storage for large-scale data mining and multimedia. In *VLDB*, 1998.

[17] Pradeep Shenoy *et al*. Turbo-charging vertical mining of large databases. In *SIGMOD*, pages 22–33, 2000.

[18] H. Toivonen. Sampling large databases for association rules. In *22nd VLDB Conf.*, 1996.

[19] J. S. Vitter. An efficient algorithm for sequential random sampling. In *ACM Trans. Mathematical Software*, volume 13(1), pages 58–67, March 87.

[20] M. J. Zaki, S. Parthasarathy *et al*. Evaluation of sampling for data mining of association rules. In *RIDE*, 1997.

[21] M. J. Zaki, S. Parthasarathy, *et al*. New algorithms for fast discovery of association rules. In *3rd Intl. Conf. on Knowledge Discovery and Data Mining*, August 1997.

---

[3]We did not have a dual processor system where one processor was fast and the other was slow. We timed the sampling overheads for each of the different sample sizes for this dataset on the slower machine, and we used these times (by precomputing the samples and busy waiting for the necessary amount of time) while evaluating the performance on this configuration.

Efficient Discovery of Common Substructures in Macromolecules *

Srinivasan Parthasarathy and Matt Coatney
Computer and Information Science, Ohio State University
{srini,coatney}@cis.ohio-state.edu

Abstract

Biological macromolecules play a fundamental role in disease; therefore, they are of great interest to fields such as pharmacology and chemical genomics. Yet due to macromolecules' complexity, development of effective techniques for elucidating structure-function macromolecular relationships has been ill explored. Previous techniques have either focused on sequence analysis, which only approximates structure-function relationships, or on small coordinate datasets, which does not scale to large datasets or handle noise. We present a novel scalable approach to efficiently discover macromolecule substructures based on three-dimensional coordinate data, without domain-specific knowledge. The approach combines structure-based frequent pattern discovery with search space reduction and coordinate noise handling. We analyze computational performance compared to traditional approaches, validate that our approach can discover meaningful substructures in noisy macromolecule data by automated discovery of primary and secondary protein structures, and show that our technique is superior to sequence-based approaches at determining structural, and thus functional, similarity between proteins.

1. Introduction

In recent years, data mining techniques have been extended beyond traditional domains such as business and marketing to apply to the physical science arena. Many of the hallmark characteristics of data mining, including detection of important patterns, handling of large search spaces, and coping with noisy datasets, are well-suited for the unique challenges presented by chemical domains. The substructure discovery sub-domain is a classic example of the need for powerful, efficient tools to discover unknown patterns. The motivation is that the structure of a molecule determines its biochemical function. This structure-function relationship is critical to understanding the mechanisms of drug activity, toxicity, and disease.

However, substructure mining is more difficult for macromolecules than for small chemicals. Macromolecules have large numbers of atoms, large interesting substructures, and a high amount of three-dimensional coordinate noise due to limitations of current coordinate retrieval techniques. Macromolecule size can produce an enormous search space; macromolecules can have thousands of atoms, each analogous to an object in a spatial database. Even smaller combinations of these atoms can lead to a computationally infeasible search space. For instance, a macromolecule containing 5000 atoms contains 12.5 million 2-atomsets and 20 billion 3-atomsets. The problem is exacerbated by the fact that interesting patterns in macromolecules often contain at least five atoms and perhaps twenty or more. This is because macromolecules are polymers, consisting of repeated similar subcomponents. Thus, interesting patterns are typically particular conformations and sequences of these subcomponents.

This paper presents a scalable method that combines traditional frequent pattern techniques with search space and noise-handling optimizations to efficiently identify *internal* substructures in *large* coordinate datasets. One of the key advantages of our approach is its relative independence from detailed chemical domain knowledge. While this algorithm was designed specifically to address issues related to macromolecules, it is capable of efficiently identifying substructures in any spatial coordinate data, without the need for in-depth scientific understanding of the dataset's properties. The search space is dramatically reduced by discarding atom pairs outside a specified range, an optimization that is possible because atom-atom interaction is inversely related to distance. This and other search space reductions allow efficient construction of larger substructures. Furthermore, we employ an approximate counting mechanism and distance binning to minimize coordinate data noise.

Experimental results on protein data show that this approach is capable of efficiently identifying the peptide backbone and secondary structures of several proteins. This serves as a validation that our technique can indeed find

---

*This work was partially supported by an Ameritech Faculty Fellowship.

meaningful substructures without protein-specific chemical knowledge. Finally, we show that the approach is more robust than traditional sequence-based approaches at determining structural similarity between proteins, including high structural similarity of Ribonuclease A from two evolutionarily diverse species.

The ideas presented in this paper form the first part of an exact structure- function macromolecular data mining process. Frequent substructures identified by this approach can then be fed into various data mining techniques, including classification [18], clustering [8], and sequence mining [17] algorithms to produce structure-derived macromolecule functional classes. This not only dramatically reduces the time to develop such classes, the technique also improves the quality of the classes, since they are formed directly from the three-dimensional structure and thus adhere to the structure-function principle.

2. Related Work

Many of the techniques recently developed for efficient data mining of frequent patterns are applicable to substructure discovery in molecules. The Apriori algorithm presented in [1] dramatically reduces the search space of a database through use of anti-monotone frequency constraints. The algorithm combines smaller patterns to produce only those candidate larger patterns that can possibly be frequent. Recent research has examined spatial data for such domains as cartography, network topography, and geographical information systems [12]. Sequence analysis and episodes have been analyzed as well by [2] [3] [14].

Application of data mining to discover frequent substructure patterns in three-dimensional graphs is not novel; however, previous research has primarily targeted small molecules and has not addressed issues of scalability and minimization of noise effects. The work of [20] detects substructures of three-dimensional graphs, but the algorithm does not consider atom type, which due to steric and electrostatic behavior is critical to the quality of discovered substructures. [5] more explicitly targets the chemical domain by considering atom and bond types as well as background biological information. However, this approach appears to have scalability issues for even small toxicological compounds let alone for macromolecules. [6] and [19] present more general and scalable approaches to substructure discovery, including using compression and interestingness heuristics as well as domain knowledge bias.

Recently, macromolecules such as proteins and nucleic acids have received increased attention in data mining [11] [15] [21]. Most macromolecular analysis has focused primarily on sequence analysis, which at best only approximates structure-function relationships. For example, [9] analyzes a small group of PDB protein data for substructure patterns through sequences of proximal amino acids. This

technique does consider some meta-structure information, but it still does not fully model structural aspects of the proteins. [10] presents a powerful method for obtaining useful meta-structural information when obtaining coordinate data from crystallography is infeasible. This approach complements the work presented here.

We extend the ideas presented in [13], providing a formal description of the algorithm, several performance optimizations, and quantified experimental results for the algorithm and optimizations. This paper also extends the analysis of secondary structures to include a β-sheet case study and includes using substructure fingerprints for finding similarity between proteins. A complete technical report is also available [16].

3. Algorithm

3.1. Substructure Representation

Molecules and their substructures are often described as three-dimensional coordinate graphs, where atoms are nodes and chemical bonds are edges. Examples include the MDL MOL format and the Protein Database PDB format. Substructures are subgraphs of overall coordinate graphs, normalized to account for varying orientations in space. Two substructures are considered equal if, after an arbitrary number of spatial translations on one substructure, both substructures are described by the same graph.

The type of connection between two atoms, known as the chemical bond type (single, double, or triple), can be ignored without loss of information, since the bond type can be inferred from the types of the two atoms and the distance between them. We consider all proximal atom relationships rather than just connections. This allows for detection of unconnected spatial interactions.

We define a new concept, the *atomset*, that captures all information of a three-dimensional graph in a form that facilitates quick comparison without the need for coordinate translation. We store three-dimensional information between a pair of atoms, A_i and A_j, in a *mining bond*. The mining bond $M(A_iA_j)$ is a 3-tuple of the form

$$M(A_iA_j) = \{A_itype, A_jtype, distance(A_iA_j)\}$$

A k-atomset X, which is a substructure containing k connected atoms, is then defined as a tuple of the form

$$X = \{\mathbf{S_X}, A_1, A_2, \ldots, A_k\},$$

where A_i is the ith atom and $\mathbf{S_X}$ is the set of mining bonds describing the atomset. By defining atom pair combinations with mining bonds, the three-dimensional graph is completely represented in a redundant form, such that two atomsets X and Y are considered to be the same chemical substructure if $\mathbf{S_X} = \mathbf{S_Y}$. While stereochemistry is not explicitly handled by this representation, it can be implicitly handled by appending a chirality label (e.g. L or R) to the atom type, such that different stereoisomers produce different, non-equivalent atomsets.

In a naive approach, $| \mathbf{S_X} |$ is equal to $\binom{k}{2}$, which represents all possible atomset permutations. We next introduce the concept of range pruning, which allows us to not only dramatically reduce the search space of the algorithm but also significantly reduce the number of mining bonds needed to describe a given atomset.

3.1.1 Range Pruning

An exhaustive analysis of possible atom combinations, even at lower levels, is computationally infeasible for large graphs such as macromolecules. Application of chemical domain knowledge through range pruning affords a great reduction in search space and allows us to fully describe the three-dimensional representation of a substructure with fewer mining bonds. Range is a user-specified constraint defined as the maximum allowable Euclidean distance between two atoms for them to be considered an atom pair.

The optimization relies on the fact that the associated energy between any two atoms in a molecule is inversely related to the inter-atom distance. Beyond a certain range, atom-atom interaction is negligible and the two atoms can be considered independent of one another. Thus, we can limit the space of atom pairs for candidate 2-atomset generation, ignoring atom combinations outside of the range.

The range of interaction differs depending on the atom types involved. For bio-molecules, the predominant atom by far is carbon, so we ensure that the range sufficiently describes possible carbon-carbon interactions. The typical carbon-carbon single bond has a bond length of 1.54 $\overset{\circ}{A}$, with double and triple bonds having shorter length. We have found that a range of 4.5 $\overset{\circ}{A}$, roughly three times a carbon-carbon single bond, is sufficient for encompassing all possible carbon-carbon interactions [13] and hydrogen bonding.

While we enforce the range restriction on initial atom pairs (2-atomsets), we relax this restriction when building up larger substructures such that two atoms may be included in an atomset even if they do not satisfy the range constraint, so long as they share common atoms that do meet the range constraint. For instance, if we have two atomsets X and Y with atoms (A_1, A_2, A_3) and (A_2, A_3, A_4) respectively, we allow the creation of a candidate atomset Z with atoms (A_1, A_2, A_3, A_4) even if distance(A_1, A_4) > range.

Without such a relaxation, higher range values would be needed to detect large substructures; this in turn would limit range pruning's ability to reduce the search space, which is a key optimization of this algorithm. Also, such a relaxation allows us to reduce the number of mining bonds needed to fully describe the atomset, since atoms not directly joined

by mining bonds are still indirectly associated through mining bonds with their shared atoms. This significantly improves both computational performance and memory efficiency.

3.2. Generating Incremental Atomsets

Our approach to generating incremental k-atomsets from two (k-1)-atomsets is similar in concept to frequent pattern discovery algorithms. However, our approach is distinctly different from traditional techniques in that removal of internal elements can cause the resulting substructures to become infrequent, based on the range constraint. We describe here a range-based anti-monotone frequency restriction for the chemical domain.

Definition 1 *Extremal atoms for a given k-atom structure are the two or more atoms that are furthest away from each other within the structure.*

Definition 2 *Extremal (k-1)-atom substructures for a given k-atom substructure are those substructures that contain at least one of the extremal atoms.*

By definitions 1 and 2, each structure has at least two extremal substructures. These definitions lead to the statement of Lemma 1, which will help prune the number of potentially frequent patterns (candidate atomsets) that will need to be evaluated.

Lemma 1 *Any frequently occurring k-atom structure has at least two (k-1)-atom substructures that are frequent and that satisfy the input range criteria (R)*

Corollary 1 *For any frequently occurring k-atom structure all of its extremal substructures are frequent and satisfy the input range criteria (R)*

3.2.1 Proof Sketch

It is trivial to show that all substructures of a given frequent substructure must be frequent. However not all of these substructures will satisfy the range criteria. A simple example that shows why this is so involves a line of points each separated by a distance corresponding to the range. If one takes out any of the points except the two end points, the resulting substructure will not satisfy the range criteria, because eliminating such a point breaks the linkage. The rest of the proof is based on the fact that eliminating either of the extremal points cannot possibly break the linkage.

Now assume we are given the set S of frequently occurring (k-1)-atomsets. By the above lemma and its corollary, the set C of potentially frequent k-atomsets is limited to those candidates whose extremal substructures are in S. In essence, if the extremal substructures are not in S then the potential candidate can never be frequent.

```
1. define set C    ; Incremented candidate atomsets
2. for all atomset_i in frequent k-atomsets
3.   for all atomset_j in frequent k-atomsets: j > i
4.     Set D = (atom_i ∉ atoms_j ∀atoms_i) ∪ (atom_j ∉ atoms_i ∀atoms_j)    ; Find atoms different
5.     if | D |= 2 and if ∀atom_x ∈ atomset_i ≠ D_i,
           distance(atom_x, D_j) ≤ distance (D_i, D_j)    ; if two extremal atoms are different
6.     candidateAtomset_ij = new atomset (S_i ∪ {M(A_i D_j) for A_i ∈ atomset_i
           | distance(A_i, D_j) < range} , A_1, ..., A_k, D_j)
7.     C = C ∪ {candidateAtomset_ij}    ; add to set of incremented atomsets
```

Figure 1. Candidate atomset generation algorithm

3.3. Algorithm Details

Candidate generation and pruning of (k+1)-atomsets from frequent k-atomsets requires special consideration. In a standard frequent pattern discovery approach, (k+1)-sets are constructed from k-sets without regard to the source from which the sets originated. Infrequent (k+1)-sets are then pruned by re-scanning the source and counting the number of occurrences for each (k+1)-set. This approach in a molecular context is computationally very expensive, due to a vast number of possible structural permutations. Rather, candidate generation and pruning are performed using only the available atomsets and do not re-scan the entire molecule.

(k+1)-atomsets are formed using only frequent k-atomsets; this approach is possible since atomset frequency is anti-monotone. Rather than simply generating incremented substructure *patterns*, which would then be used to query the molecule for frequency, *all* instances of (k+1)-atomsets are generated by combining the atoms of frequent k-atomsets. This is detailed in Figure 1.

Pruning is then accomplished simply by counting the number of atomsets that define, based on their mining bond sets, the same substructure, keeping those whose count is above a user-specified minimum support. This approach is faster than traditional approaches both because counting occurs without the need to go back to the entire molecule and because counting is done through pattern-pattern instead of pattern-dataset matching, which results in far fewer comparisons. Standard pruning is straightforward and can be accomplished simply by hashing atomsets into bins of substructures based on the set of mining bonds. More advanced approaches to pruning are needed when handling noisy data; this will be discussed in Section 4.

The complete algorithm is shown in Figure 2. This algorithm is general enough to handle substructure analysis for any type of molecule, and with additional optimizations is suitable for analyzing macromolecules.

```
1. Prune infrequent atoms (1-atomsets)
2. Generate candidate 2-atomsets
     from frequent atoms
3. Prune infrequent 2-atomsets
4. k = 3
5. while (| frequent k-atomsets |> 0)
6.   Generate candidate k-atomsets
       from frequent (k-1)-atomsets
7.   Prune infrequent k-atomsets
8.   k = k + 1
```

Figure 2. Substructure discovery algorithm

4. Optimizations

Distance Binning and Resolution for Noise Handling: Macromolecules are difficult to isolate, crystallize, and analyze; even with impressive advances in the field, the resulting data is still relatively noisy. One approach for handling this noise is discretization, a common data mining technique [7]. We discretize the raw Euclidean distance between two atoms by binning; a resolution value is chosen that divides the distance into equiwidth bins, represented efficiently as bits in the mining bond. Binning of the data not only simplifies calculations (thus improving performance), but it also handles *minor* fluctuations in distance. Initial studies on a PDB protein dataset suggest that algorithm resolutions between $0.04 \overset{\circ}{A}$ and $0.10 \overset{\circ}{A}$ best minimize noise effects while maintaining meaningful atom-atom relationships. Studies have also found that there is a direct relationship between crystallography resolutions and algorithm resolutions suitable for detecting meaningful substructures.

Recursive Fuzzy Hashing for Noise Handling: Due to the high level of noise inherent in current macromolecule structure deduction techniques, strict matching of patterns, even with binning, leads to poor results. What is needed is a pruning mechanism that relaxes the strict matching criteria such that two atomsets X and Y are considered to be

```
1. m = 1     ; Examine first mining bond
2. C = candidateAtomsets   ;
/*Start by examining all candidate atomsets*/
3. for all atomset_i in C
4.   hash(M_m, M_m + 1, M_m − 1 in atomset_i)
5. for all H_i in hash_bins
6.   remove H_i if | H_i | < minSupport
7. m = m + 1
8. while m <=| M |
9.   for all H_i as C
10.     goto step 3
11. frequentAtomsets = H_1 ∪ H_2 ... H_n
```

Figure 3. Recursive fuzzy hash pruning

the same chemical substructure if $S_X \approx S_Y$. One such approach is recursive fuzzy hashing (RFH), in which atomsets are analyzed one mining bond at a time and atomsets are hashed (using the current mining bond's integer value) both to the exact and neighboring locations.

This is significantly more computationally expensive than the standard approach; however, it is essential for effectively minimizing noise effects to allow for identification of larger substructures. This will be quantified in the next section; we present the technique in Figure 3.

RFH produces a top-down hash tree (see [4] for a thorough description of hash trees), with the root node representing the set of candidate atomsets for the particular k. We recursively split the nodes into child hash bins, based on the atomsets' mining bond for a particular tree level. We hash both to the exact hash location and $+/- 1$ resolution unit. Hash bins whose atomset count is less than a user-specified minimum support are pruned from further consideration. Once the tree is constructed, a new set of pruned atomsets is generated from the remaining leaf nodes.

Depth First Pruning for Performance: Hash trees produced by RFH are only as deep as the number of mining bonds used to represent the atomsets. The tree is significantly wider, however, due both to the large numbers (thousands or tens of thousands) of atomsets and the use of fuzzy-hashing, which can triple the width of the tree.

Breadth-first tree analysis must generate all hash bins for a particular depth before being able to prune away infrequent bins and free up memory. This can be quite memory intensive and does not scale well to deeper depths, where the tree width explodes. Depth-first analysis, on the other hand, only analyzes one branch of the tree at a time, which is a fraction of the tree's width. This results in a much smaller memory footprint.

As an example, let us consider a hash tree generated for hemoglobin. For a breadth-first analysis at level 7, the memory footprint includes 15000 bins, each including a group of atomset references. A depth-first analysis considers only 80 bins at any given time, requiring $\frac{1}{2}\%$ of the memory. In larger substructure analyses, this ratio will be even more pronounced. Clearly the depth-first approach is more memory efficient. Without further optimizations the bread-first approach leads to an explosion of the memory space at moderate ($k = 6$) levels, while depth-first analysis maintains a small memory footprint even at higher ($k \geq 9$) levels.

Dynamic Duplicate Screening for Performance: The RFH approach is not without its drawbacks. Its primary issue is redundant recursive calculations caused by overlapping hash bins. A naive approach to RFH prunes all duplicate substructure bins once the hash tree has been fully formed. However, this leads to a tremendous amount of redundant work.

We instead use a novel approach, dynamic duplicate screening (DDS), that handles duplicates *during* the run. At each level of the hashing algorithm, the set of substructure bins are analyzed, and duplicates are discarded from further consideration. While the analysis itself is expensive, significant time is saved in avoiding redundant calculations. In addition to speed improvements, this technique also has the benefit of significantly reducing the memory footprint needed for the hash tree by decreasing its width.

Analyzing Polymer Backbones for Performance: Often, we are primarily interested only in the global conformation and super-structures of macromolecules. When this is the case, we can further reduce the search space of a given macromolecule by only considering the polymer's backbone. Such an approach has the advantage of reducing the number of atoms and candidate atomsets through a pre-processing step. We applied this approach to the protein domain to analyze backbone conformations, and the results were promising. As an example, the backbone-only approach identified the same peptide substructures of lysozyme as the full-blown search and ran *five times faster*.

5. Experimental Results

All experiments were conducted under the Java 1.4 runtime environment on a 4 CPU Sun 420R workgroup server and were allocated 1 GB of memory. The program utilizes multi-threading to take advantage of an SMP architecture.

5.1. Performance

5.1.1 $k + k$ vs. $k + 2$ Candidate Generation

The initial algorithm presented in [13] utilized $k + 2$ candidate generation, in which k-atomsets were combined with 2-atomsets to produce (k+1)-atomsets. This approach was taken prior to full development of the range pruning theory presented in 3.2. With completion of this theory, we are now able to take full advantage of range pruning through $k + k$ candidate generation. $k + k$ combines k-atomsets

Table 1. Effect of range on search space

Range ($\mathring{A}$)	2-atomsets	3-atomsets	Exec Time (s)
4.5	9K	12K	4
6.0	20K	147K	25
9.0	54K	2.3M	536
∞	500K	N/A	N/A

Table 2. Effect of dynamic duplicate screening on redundant calculations

Level	DDS Duplicate Atomsets	Standard Duplicate Atomsets
2	18K	19K
3	64K	81K
4	49K	312K
5	19K	2.5M

with themselves for a more restricted superset of the frequent incremented (k+1)-atomsets than $k + 2$.

We compared the two approaches on the protein lysozyme. In terms of search space, the $k + k$ approach generates 13% of 4-atomsets produced by $k + 2$ and only 1% of 5-atomsets. The result is a 3-fold improvement in performance at $k = 4$ and a 4-fold improvement at $k = 5$. The benefit of using $k + k$ generation increases with larger substructure size; this is due to the larger number of possible combinations in the $k+2$ approach and the increased ability of $k + k$ to restrict atomset permutations. For the remaining experiments, we utilize only $k + k$ candidate generation.

5.1.2 Range Pruning

Range pruning, as mentioned before, has a dramatic impact on reduction of search space. Table 1 demonstrates this for the protein lysozyme for several different ranges. As expected, search space, and thus run time, decreases as the range becomes more restrictive. So long as the range incorporates all atom-atom interactions of interest, there is no loss of domain-relevant information. Traditional substructure discovery approaches do not consider range pruning and thus fail to scale for macromolecules.

5.1.3 Dynamic Duplicate Screening

The benefits of the DDS optimization are quite pronounced, particularly at higher levels, due to its ability to handle the exponential growth of redundant calculations. This is illustrated in Table 2. Clearly, DDS maintains a manageable number of duplicates even at higher levels. On the other hand, the standard approach, which screens duplicates only at the end of the run, suffers from an explosive exponential growth rate of duplicate calculations, as evidenced by over 2.5 million atomsets in duplicate substructures during level 5 of the run. For this same level, DDS produces only 19 thousand atomsets, a mere 1% of the standard approach.

At higher levels, the impressive gains of DDS become evident. For instance, a hemoglobin run to identify α-helices using 9-atomsets took 90 minutes without DDS. *With the optimization, the run took only 5 minutes, resulting in an eighteen-fold increase.*

5.1.4 Performance of Combined Optimizations

We combined all optimizations and compared the performance with traditional structure discovery techniques. The optimized run used $k + k$ candidate generation and depth-first RFH pruning with DDS. The standard run used $k + 2$ candidate generation with standard breadth-first RFH. The run analyzed the first subunit of hemoglobin (PDB ID: 1BZ0) with minimum support of 70, resolution of 0.06, and range of 4.5. Note that the runs located the same substructures; they merely differed in their approach to generating candidates and locating these substructures.

Table 3 shows the results for optimized and standard runs. The combined optimization approach is capable of efficiently detecting large substructures while maintaining a small memory footprint. On the other hand, the standard run exhibits an explosive search space; this leads to poor performance and memory use.

5.2. Substructure Discovery in Proteins

5.2.1 Discovery of the Peptide Backbone

We now turn to identifying relevant substructures in protein macromolecules as validation of our technique. We begin by analyzing the 128-amino-acid protein lysozyme (PDB ID: 193L) for 5-atomset peptide substructures. We configured the algorithm with a minimum support of 100 and range of 4.5 $\mathring{A}$. A resolution of 0.06 $\mathring{A}$ was settled on for RFH after attempting a series of values.

We also analyzed lysozyme without using RFH, and the strength of RFH for handling noise is evident; RFH was able to find 128 5-atomsets that describe the same peptide substructure. Thus, RFH is capable of fully defining lysozyme's peptide backbone. Even with significant optimizations to resolution, the standard approach found at most 125 atomsets. Above $k = 6$, the standard approach could not reliably detect any substructures. We therefore rely on RFH to identify interesting protein substructures.

The 5-atomsets found in lysozyme represent one substructure pattern, that of a peptide. This includes the backbone oxygen and carbon, the α-carbon of residue i and the backbone nitrogen and α-carbon of residue $i + 1$. Combining the atomsets, we can reconstruct the peptide backbone of lysozyme in its entirety.

Table 3. Comparison of combined optimizations and standard algorithm

Level	Combined Optimizations			Standard		
	Exec Time (s)	Memory (MB)	Atomsets	Exec Time (s)	Memory (MB)	Atomsets
2	2	8	9030	2	9	9030
3	24	221	89717	38	257	92524
4	98	152	68770	370	454	335677
5	121	153	10281	1100	1000	183141
6	165	295	1485	Out Of Memory		
7	183	297	147	Out Of Memory		

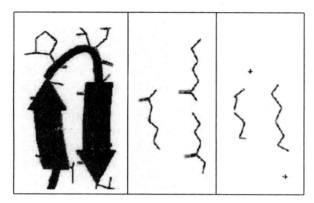

Figure 4. β-sheet (left) and reconstructed 8-atom strands (center, right) of Antibody 21D8

5.2.2 Discovery of β-Sheets

We now turn to the discovery of protein secondary structures. We previously discovered α-helices in hemoglobin, the details of which may be found in [13] [16]. We next set out to discover β-sheets. We examined Antibody 21D8 (PDB ID: 1C5C), a two-chain β-sheet rich protein. We considered the first 73 residues of the first chain; this portion contains 3 sheets composed of 11 β-strands.

Since β-sheet structures are formed primarily from peptide-peptide interactions, we employed the backbone optimization for pre-processing the protein. This reduced the search space by a factor of 2. A larger range of 6.5 $\overset{\circ}{A}$ was chosen to accommodate for the linear nature of these strands. We set the minimum support to 10 in an attempt to capture all 11 strands of interest. Lastly, we used a higher resolution, 0.1 $\overset{\circ}{A}$ due to poor coordinate resolution.

The algorithm located five classes of frequent 8-atomsets; each of these classes describe different portions of the same substructure. This substructure consists of three linear, connected peptides. These results are validated by biochemical data showing that β-strands have a linear structure and consist of at least 3 amino acids.

Figure 4 shows the first two β-strands of Antibody 21D8 along with two different atomset representations. The re-

sults when compared against the original antibody are impressive; between the five classes of atomsets, all β-strands can be fully reconstructed. Furthermore, a smaller portion (15%) of atomsets describe the ends of *beta*-strands and are distinct from central *beta*-strand atomsets. This shows the power of the algorithm for detecting subtle yet important differences in three-dimensional structure.

5.2.3 Structural Similarity of Proteins

Last, we demonstrate how structural features, represented by substructure fingerprints, provide better insight into structure-function relationships than traditional sequence analysis. A substructure fingerprint is a vector representation of a set of interesting substructures. Elements contained in that molecule are marked either with a 1 for a bit vector or with the occurrence count for a frequency vector. Elements not in the molecule are marked with a 0.

We consider the protein Ribonuclease A from two disparate species: bovine (PDB ID: 1JVT) and rat (PDB ID: 1RRA), as well as a similar protein from a related protein kinase class (PDB ID: 1BDY) and a significantly different protein, the ρ transcription terminator (PDB ID: 1A8V). The coordinate sets all have comparable resolution (between 2.0 and 2.5 $\overset{\circ}{A}$) and chain lengths (between 120 and 125 residues).

We ran our algorithm using the following parameters: 0.12 $\overset{\circ}{A}$ resolution, 6.5 $\overset{\circ}{A}$ range, minimum support of 20, and the backbone optimization. From the run, we collected all substructure motifs with five or more atoms and generated bit vector substructure fingerprints. We then analyzed fingerprints and sequences using the common Tanimoto similarity coefficient, defined as

$$Tanimoto(A, B) = \frac{|A \cap B|}{|A| + |B| - |A \cap B|}$$

The traditional sequence-based approach using the primary amino acid sequence gave only moderate similarity between the two Ribonuclease A proteins (Tanimoto coefficient of 0.50); this is a sign of evolutionary divergence and demonstrates the main limitation of sequence analysis. However, when comparing the Ribonuclease A substructure-based bit vector fingerprints, we obtain a Tanimoto similarity coefficient of *0.75*, which is a significant improvement over the sequence-based approach. This is to be expected, since functional structures are evolutionarily conserved despite innocuous sequence mutations.

Furthermore, sequence analysis of the two Ribonuclease A proteins with the kinase (functionally related) and transcription factor (functionally unrelated) proteins give Tanimoto coefficients of only 0.03, suggesting no relationship. Yet our approach detects substantial structural similarity between Ribonuclease A and the related kinase (coefficient 0.35-0.45), which is consistent with the similar function of the proteins' classes. Furthermore, our approach detects little structural similarity (coefficient of 0.17) between the Ribonuclease A and transcription factor, a result consistent with the disparity in function.

While preliminary, these results support the commonly held belief that a structure-based technique such as ours is capable of more robust macromolecule classification than traditional sequence-based approaches.

6. Conclusion

This paper presents a novel approach and several key optimizations for mining frequent substructures in complex, noisy spatial data such as macromolecules. The approach differs from previous substructure mining techniques in that it locates frequent substructures *within a single large molecule* and is designed specifically to address scalability and noise issues chronic to the macromolecule domain. Furthermore, it operates on exact structures instead of sequences or meta-structural information. Through a series of experiments, the algorithm is validated both for good performance when compared to standard techniques and for good frequent substructure identification as evidenced by its ability to detect meaningful substructures in proteins as well as common structural features between similar proteins from different species.

Performance is always an issue when dealing with such large molecules, and as such research is in progress for further optimizing analysis based on both domain knowledge and computer science principles. One domain-centered approach for proteins is consideration of peptide ϕ and ψ angles in reduction of search space. More efficient approximate pruning, such as use of a three-dimensional sliding box, and graph compression techniques using substructures [6] are under consideration.

With a framework in place for efficient analysis of substructures in macromolecules, we are now able to conduct further research in this area in a timely manner. Future work includes the analysis of higher-order substructures in an attempt to discover novel secondary structures and the development of functionally significant classification models for proteins based on discovered substructures. In addition, we

hope to extend this approach to other types of biologically significant macromolecules such as DNA and the various forms of RNA. Eventually, this algorithm will be combined with other data mining techniques to provide a robust structural analysis framework for spatial datasets.

References

[1] R. Agrawal and R. Srikant. Fast algorithms for mining association rules. In *VLDB Conference*, 1994.

[2] R. Agrawal and R. Srikant. Mining sequential patterns. In *ICDE*, 1995.

[3] R. Agrawal and R. Srikant. Mining sequential patterns: Generalizations and performance improvements. In *EDBT*, 1996.

[4] E. G. Coffman and J. Eve. File structures using hashing functions. *Comm. Assoc. Comp. Mach.*, 1970.

[5] L. Dehaspe, H. Toivonen, and R. King. Finding frequent substructures in chemical compounds. In *KDD*, 1998.

[6] S. Djoko et al. Analyzing the benefits of domain knowledge in substructure discovery. In *KDD*, 1995.

[7] J. Dougherty, R. Kohavi, and M. Sahami. Supervised and unsupervised discretization of continuous features. In *ICML*, 1995.

[8] A. Jain and R. Dubes. *Algorithms for Clustering Data*. Prentice Hall, 1988.

[9] I. Jonassen et al. Structure motif discovery and mining the pdb. In *German Conference on Bioinformatics*, 2000.

[10] J. Kim et al. Identification of novel multi-transmembrane proteins from genomic databases using quasi-periodic structural properties. In *Bioinformatics*, 2002.

[11] R. King et al. Genome scale prediction of protein functional class from sequence using data mining. In *KDD*, 2000.

[12] K. Koperski, J. Han, and N. Stefanovic. An efficient two-step method for classification of spatial data. In *Proceedings of the Intl. Symposium on Spatial Data Handling*, 1998.

[13] H. Li and S. Parthasarathy. Automatically deriving multi-level protein structures through data mining. In *HiPC Conference Workshop on Bioinformatics and Computational Biology*, Hyderabad, India, 2001.

[14] H. Mannila and H. Toivonen. Discovering generalized episodes using minimal occurrences. In *KDD*, 1996.

[15] W. Pan, J. Lin, and C. Le. Model-based cluster analysis of microarray gene-expression data. *Genome Biology*, 2002.

[16] S. Parthasarathy and M. Coatney. Efficient discovery of common substructures in macromolecules. Technical Report OSU-CISRC-8/02-TR20, Ohio State University, 2002.

[17] S. Parthasarathy et al. Incremental and interactive sequence mining. In *ACM CIKM*, 1999.

[18] J. Quinlan. Induction of decision trees. *Machine Learning*, 5(1):71–100, 1996.

[19] L. D. Raedt and S. Kramer. The level-wise version space algorithm and its application to molecular fragment finding. In *IJCAI*, 2001.

[20] X. Wang et al. Automated discovery of active motifs in three dimensional molecules. In *KDD*, 1997.

[21] X. Zheng and T. Chan. Chemical genomics: A systematic approach in biological research and drug discovery. *Current Issues in Molecular Biology*, 2002.

Mining Motifs in Massive Time Series Databases

Pranav Patel   Eamonn Keogh   Jessica Lin   Stefano Lonardi
University of California - Riverside
Computer Science & Engineering Department
Riverside, CA 92521, USA
{prpatel, eamonn, jessica, stelo}@cs.ucr.edu

Abstract

The problem of efficiently locating previously known patterns in a time series database (i.e., query by content) has received much attention and may now largely be regarded as a solved problem. However, from a knowledge discovery viewpoint, a more interesting problem is the enumeration of previously unknown, frequently occurring patterns. We call such patterns "motifs", because of their close analogy to their discrete counterparts in computation biology. An efficient motif discovery algorithm for time series would be useful as a tool for summarizing and visualizing massive time series databases. In addition it could be used as a subroutine in various other data mining tasks, including the discovery of association rules, clustering and classification.

In this work we carefully motivate, then introduce, a non-trivial definition of time series motifs. We propose an efficient algorithm to discover them, and we demonstrate the utility and efficiency of our approach on several real world datasets.

1. Introduction

The problem of efficiently locating previously defined patterns in a time series database (i.e., query by content) has received much attention and may now be essentially regarded as a solved problem [1, 8, 13, 21, 22, 23, 35, 40]. However, from a knowledge discovery viewpoint, a more interesting problem is the detection of previously unknown, frequently occurring patterns. We call such patterns *motifs*, because of their close analogy to their discrete counterparts in computation biology [11, 16, 30, 34, 36]. Figure 1 illustrates an example of a motif discovered in an astronomical database. An efficient motif discovery algorithm for time series would be useful as a tool for summarizing and visualizing massive time series databases. In addition, it could be used as subroutine in various other data mining tasks, for instance:

- The discovery of association rules in time series first requires the discovery of motifs (referred to as "*primitive shapes*" in [9] and "*frequent patterns*" in [18]). However the current solution to finding the motifs is either high quality and very expensive, or low quality but cheap [9].

- Several researchers have advocated K-means clustering of time series databases [14], without adequately addressing the question of how to seed the initial points, or how to choose K. Motifs could potentially be used to address both problems. In addition, seeding the algorithm with motifs rather than random points could speed up

convergence [12].

- Several time series classification algorithms work by constructing typical prototypes of each class [24]. While this approach works for small datasets, the construction of the prototypes (which we see as motifs) requires quadratic time, as is thus unable to scale to massive datasets.

In this work we carefully motivate, then introduce a non-trivial definition of time series motifs. We further introduce an efficient algorithm to discover them.

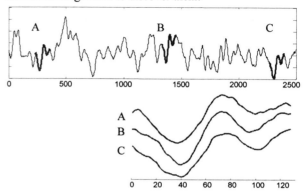

Figure 1: An astronomical time series (above) contains 3 near identical subsequences. A "zoom-in" (below) reveals just how similar to each other the 3 subsequences are.

The rest of this paper is organized as follows. In Section 2 we formally define the problem at hand and consider related work. In Section 3 we introduce a novel low-dimensional discrete representation of time series, and prove that it can be used to obtain a lower bound on the true Euclidean distance. Section 4 introduces our motif-finding algorithm, which we experimentally evaluate in Section 5. In Section 6 we consider related work, and finally in Section 7 we draw some conclusions and highlight directions for future work.

2. Background and Related Work

The following section is rather dense on terminology and definitions. These are necessary to concretely define the problem at hand, and to explain our proposed solution. We begin with a definition of our data type of interest, time series:

Definition 1. *Time Series*: A time series $T = t_1, ..., t_m$ is an ordered set of m real-valued variables.

Time series can be very long, sometimes containing billions of observations [15]. We are typically not interested in any of the global properties of a time series; rather, data miners confine their interest to subsections of the time series [1, 20, 23], which are called subsequences.

Definition 2. *Subsequence*: Given a time series T of length m, a subsequence C of T is a sampling of length $n < m$ of contiguous position from T, that is, $C = t_p, ..., t_{p+n-1}$ for $1 \leq p \leq m - n + 1$.

A task associated with subsequences is to determine if a given subsequence is similar to other subsequences [1, 2, 3, 8, 13, 19, 21, 22, 23, 24, 25, 27, 29, 35, 40]. This idea is formalized in the definition of a match.

Definition 3. *Match*: Given a positive real number R (called *range*) and a time series T containing a subsequence C beginning at position p and a subsequence M beginning at q, if $D(C, M) \leq R$, then M is called a *matching* subsequence of C.

The first three definitions are summarized in Figure 2, illustrating a time series of length 500, and two subsequences of length 128.

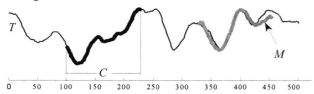

Figure 2: A visual intuition of a time series T (light line), a subsequence C (bold line) and a match M (bold gray line)

For the time being we will ignore the question of what distance function to use to determine whether two subsequences match. We will address this in Section 3.3.

The definition of a match is rather obvious and intuitive; but it is needed for the definition of a *trivial match*. One can observe that the best matches to a subsequence (apart from itself) tend to be the subsequences that begin just one or two points to the left or the right of the subsequence in question. Figure 3 illustrates the idea.

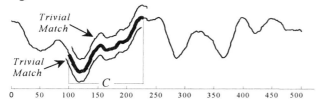

Figure 3: For almost any subsequence C in a time series, the best matches are the trivial subsequences immediately to the left and right of C

Intuitively, any definition of motif should exclude the possibility of over-counting these trivial matches, which we define more concretely below.

Definition 4. *Trivial Match*: Given a time series T, containing a subsequence C beginning at position p and a matching subsequence M beginning at q, we say that M is a *trivial match* to C if either $p = q$ or there does not exist a subsequence M' beginning at q' such that $D(C, M') > R$, and either $q < q' < p$ or $p < q' < q$.

We can now define the problem of enumerating the K most significant motifs in a time series.

Definition 5. *K-Motifs*: Given a time series T, a subsequence length n and a range R, the most significant motif in T (called thereafter *1-Motif*) is the subsequence C_1 that has the highest count of non-trivial matches (ties are broken by choosing the motif whose matches have the lower variance). The Kth most significant motif in T (called thereafter *K-Motif*) is the subsequence C_K that has the highest count of non-trivial matches, and satisfies $D(C_K, C_i) > 2R$, for all $1 \leq i < K$.

Note that this definition forces the set of subsequences in each motif to be mutually exclusive. This is important because otherwise two motifs might share the majority of their elements, and thus be essentially the same.

Having carefully defined the necessary terminology, we now introduce a brute force algorithm to locate 1-motif. The generalization of this algorithm to finding K-motifs is obvious and omitted for brevity.

```
Algorithm Find-1-Motif-Brute-Force(T,n,R)
1.   best_motif_count_so_far = 0;
2.   best_motif_location_so_far = null;
3.   for i = 1 to length(T)- n + 1
4.     count    = 0;
5.     pointers = null;
6.     for j = 1 to length(T)- n + 1
7.       if non_trivial_match(T[i:i+n-1],T[j:j+n-1],R)
8.         count = count + 1;
9.         pointers = append(pointers,j);
10.      end;
11.    end;
12.    if count > best_motif_count_so_far
13.      best_motif_count_so_far = count;
14.      best_motif_location_so_far = i;
15.      motif_matches = pointers;
16.    end;
17.  end;
```

Table 1: The Find-1-Motif-Brute-Force algorithm

The algorithm requires $O(m^2)$ calls to the distance function. Since the Euclidean distance is symmetric [22], one could theoretically cut in half the CPU time by storing $D(A,B)$ and re-using the value when it is necessary to find $D(B,A)$, however, this would require storing $m(m-1)/2$ values, which is clearly untenable for even moderately sized datasets.

We will introduce our sub-quadratic algorithm for finding motifs in Section 4. Our method requires a discrete representation of the time series that is reduced in dimensionality and upon which a lower bounding distance measure can be defined. Since no representation in the literature fulfills all these criteria, we will introduce such a representation in the next section.

3. Dimensionality Reduction and Discretization

Our discretization technique allows a time series of arbitrary length n to be reduced to a string of arbitrary length w, ($w < n$, typically $w \ll n$). The alphabet size is also an arbitrary integer a, where $a > 2$.

As an intermediate step between the original time series and our discrete representation of it, we must create a dimensionality-reduced version of the data. We will utilize the Piecewise Aggregate Approximation (PAA) [22, 40], which we review in the next section.

3.1 Dimensionality Reduction

A time series C of length n can be represented in a w-dimensional space by a vector $\overline{C} = \overline{c}_1, \ldots, \overline{c}_w$. The ith element of $\overline{C}$ is calculated by the following equation:

$$\overline{c}_i = \frac{w}{n} \sum_{j=\frac{n}{w}(i-1)+1}^{\frac{n}{w}i} c_j \qquad (1)$$

Simply stated, to reduce the time series from n dimensions to w dimensions, the data is divided into w equal sized "frames". The mean value of the data falling within a frame is calculated and a vector of these values becomes the data-reduced representation. The representation can be visualized as an attempt to approximate the original time series with a linear combination of box basis functions as shown in Figure 4.

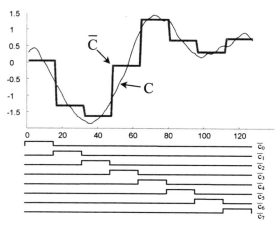

Figure 4: The PAA representation can be readily visualized as an attempt to model a sequence with a linear combination of box basis functions. In this case, a sequence of length 128 is reduced to 8 dimensions

The PAA dimensionality reduction is intuitive and simple, yet has been shown to rival more sophisticated dimensionality reduction techniques like Fourier transforms and wavelets [8, 22, 40]. In addition it has several advantages over its rivals, including being much faster to compute, and being able to support many different distance functions, including weighted distance functions [24], arbitrary Minkowski norms [40], and dynamic time warping [13].

3.2 Discretization

Having transformed a time series database into the PAA we can apply a further transformation to obtain a discrete representation. For reasons that will become apparent in Section 4, we require a discretization technique that will produce symbols with equiprobability. This is easily achieved since normalized time series have a Gaussian distribution. To illustrate this, we extracted subsequences of length 128 from 8 different time series and plotted a normal probability plot of the data as shown in Figure 5.

Given that the normalized time series have highly Gaussian distribution, we can simply determine the "breakpoints" that will produce a equal-sized areas under Gaussian curve.

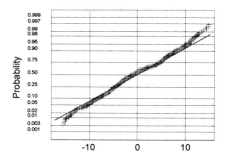

Figure 5: A normal probability plot of the distribution of values from subsequences of length 128 from 8 different datasets. The highly linear nature of the plot strongly suggests that the data came from a Gaussian distribution.

Definition 6. *Breakpoints*: breakpoints are a sorted list of numbers $B = \beta_1, \ldots, \beta_{a-1}$ such that the area under a $N(0,1)$ Gaussian curve from β_i to $\beta_{i+1} = 1/a$ (β_0 and β_a are defined as $-\infty$ and ∞, respectively).

These breakpoints may be determined by looking them up in a statistical table. For example Table 2 gives the breakpoints for values of a from 3 to 10.

a \ β_i	3	4	5	6	7	8	9	10
β_1	-0.43	-0.67	-0.84	-0.97	-1.07	-1.15	-1.22	-1.28
β_2	0.43	0	-0.25	-0.43	-0.57	-0.67	-0.76	-0.84
β_3		0.67	0.25	0	-0.18	-0.32	-0.43	-0.52
β_4			0.84	0.43	0.18	0	-0.14	-0.25
β_5				0.97	0.57	0.32	0.14	0
β_6					1.07	0.67	0.43	0.25
β_7						1.15	0.76	0.52
β_8							1.22	0.84
β_9								1.28

Table 2: A lookup table that contains the breakpoints that divide a Gaussian distribution in an arbitrary number (from 3 to 10) of equiprobable regions

Once the breakpoints have been obtained we can discretize a time series in the following manner. We first obtain a PAA of the time series. All PAA coefficients that are below the smallest breakpoint are mapped to the symbol "**a**", all coefficients greater than or equal to the smallest breakpoint and less than the second smallest breakpoint are mapped to the symbol "**b**", etc. Figure 6 illustrates the idea.

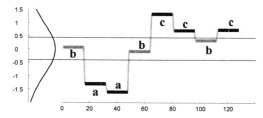

Figure 6: A time series is discretized by first obtaining a PAA approximation and then using predetermined breakpoints to map the PAA coefficients into symbols. In the example above, with $n = 128$, $w = 8$ and $a = 3$, the time series is mapped to the word **baabccbc**

Note that in this example the 3 symbols, "a", "b" and "c" are approximately equiprobable as we desired. We call the concatenation of symbols that represent a subsequence a *word*.

Definition 7. *Word*: A subsequence C of length n can be represented as a *word* $\hat{C}=\hat{c}_1,\ldots,\hat{c}_w$ as follows. Let $alpha_i$ denote the ith element of the alphabet, i.e., $alpha_1 = \mathbf{a}$ and $alpha_2 = \mathbf{b}$. Then the mapping from a PAA approximation $\overline{C}$ to a word $\hat{C}$ is obtained as follows:

$$\hat{c}_i = alpha_j, \quad iif \quad \beta_{j-1} < \overline{c}_i \leq \beta_j \quad (2)$$

We have now defined the two representations required for our motif search algorithm (the PAA representation is merely an intermediate step required to obtain the symbolic representation).

3.3 Distance Measures

Having considered various representations of time series data, we can now define distance measures on them. By far the most common distance measure for time series is the Euclidean distance [8, 22, 23, 32, 40]. Given two time series Q and C of the same length n, Eq. 3 defines their Euclidean distance, and Figure 7.A illustrates a visual intuition of the measure.

$$D(Q,C) \equiv \sqrt{\sum_{i=1}^{n}(q_i - c_i)^2} \quad (3)$$

If we transform the original subsequences into PAA representations, $\overline{Q}$ and $\overline{C}$, using Eq. 1, we can then obtain a lower bounding approximation of the Euclidean distance between the original subsequences by:

$$DR(\overline{Q},\overline{C}) \equiv \sqrt{\tfrac{n}{w}}\sqrt{\sum_{i=1}^{w}(\overline{q}_i - \overline{c}_i)^2} \quad (4)$$

This measure is illustrated in Figure 7.B. A proof that $DR(\overline{Q},\overline{C})$ lower bounds the true Euclidean distance appears in [22] (an alternative proof appears in [40]).

If we further transform the data into the symbolic representation, we can define a MINDIST function that returns the minimum distance between the original time series of two words:

$$MINDIST(\hat{Q},\hat{C}) \equiv \sqrt{\tfrac{n}{w}}\sqrt{\sum_{i=1}^{w}\left(dist(\hat{q}_i,\hat{c}_i)\right)^2} \quad (5)$$

The function resembles Eq. 4 except for the fact that the distance between the two PAA coefficients has been replaced with the sub-function *dist*(). The *dist*() function can be implemented using a table lookup as illustrated in Table 3.

	a	b	c
a	0	0	0.86
b	0	0	0
c	0.86	0	0

Table 3: A lookup table used by the MINDIST function. This table is for an alphabet of cardinality, i.e. $a = 3$. The distance between two symbols can be read off by examining the corresponding row and column. For example $dist(\mathbf{a},\mathbf{b}) = 0$ and $dist(\mathbf{a},\mathbf{c}) = 0.86$.

The value in cell (r,c) for any lookup table of can be calculated by the following expression.

$$cell_{r,c} = \begin{cases} 0, & if\ |r-c| \leq 1 \\ \beta_{\max(r,c)-1} - \beta_{\min(r,c)}, & otherwise \end{cases} \quad (6)$$

For a given value of the alphabet size a, the table need only be calculated once, then stored for fast lookup. The MINDIST function can be visualized is Figure 7.C.

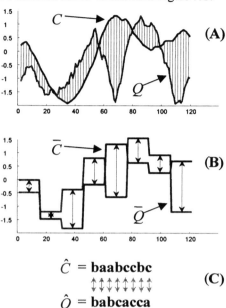

$$\hat{C} = \mathbf{baabccbc}$$
$$\hat{Q} = \mathbf{babcacca}$$

(C)

Figure 7: A visual intuition of the three representations discussed in this work, and the distance measures defined on them. A) The Euclidean distance between two time series can be visualized as the square root of the sum of the squared differences of each pair of corresponding points. B) The distance measure defined for the PAA approximation can be seen as the square root of the sum of the squared differences between each pair of corresponding PAA coefficients, multiplied by the square root of the compression rate. C) The distance between two symbolic representations of a time series requires looking up the distances between each pair of symbols, squaring them, summing them, taking the square root and finally multiplying by the square root of the compression rate.

4. Efficient Motif Discovery

Recall that the brute force motif discovery algorithm introduced Table 1 requires $O(m^2)$ calculations of the distance function. As previously mentioned, the symmetric property of the Euclidean distance measure could be used to half the number of calculations by storing $D(Q,C)$ and re-using the value when it is necessary to find $D(C,Q)$. In fact, further optimizations would be possible under this scenario. We now give an example of such optimization.

Suppose we are in the innermost loop of the algorithm, attempting to enumerate all possible matches within $R = 1$, to a particular subsequence Q. Further suppose that in previous iterations we had already discovered that $D(C_a,C_b) = 2$. As we go through the innermost loop we first calculate the distance $D(Q,C_a)$ and discover it to be 7. At this point we should continue on to measure $D(Q,C_b)$, but in fact we don't have to do this calculation! We can use the triangular inequality to discover that $D(Q,C_b)$ could not be a match to Q. The triangular inequality requires that [2, 22, 33]:

$$D(Q,C_a) \leq D(Q,C_b) + D(C_a,C_b) \qquad (7)$$

Filling in the known values give us

$$7 \leq D(Q,C_b) + 2 \qquad (8)$$

Rearranging the terms gives us

$$5 \leq D(Q,C_b) \qquad (9)$$

But since we are only interested in subsequences that are a distance less than 1 unit away, there is no point in determining the exact value of $D(Q,C_b)$, which we now know to be at least 5 units away.

The first formalization of this idea for fast searching of nearest neighbors in matrices is generally credited to Burkhard and Keller [5]. More efficient implementations are possible; for example, Shasha and Wang [33] introduced the Approximation Distance Map (ADM) algorithm that pre-computes an arbitrary set of distances instead of using just one randomly chosen reference point.

For the problem at hand, however, the techniques discussed above seem of little utility, since as previously noted, we are unlikely to have $O(m^2)$ space in which to store the entire matrix. We propose to use just such a technique as a subroutine in our motif discovery algorithm. Our idea is to create only a small portion of the matrix at a time, and exploit the techniques above to search it. Our contribution comes from the method we use to construct the small matrix. As we will demonstrate, we can use our MINDIST function to create a matrix, much smaller than $O(m^2)$, which is *guaranteed* to contain all the subsequences which are within R of a promising candidate for a motif.

In addition to all the matching sequences to a promising candidate, the small matrix will generally contain some non-matching subsequences, or "false hits". We use Shasha and Wang's ADM algorithm to efficiently separate the true matches to the false hits.

There is a possibility that a promising candidate for a motif will pan out. That is, after searching the small matrix we will discover that most or all of the subsequences don't match. In this case we will have to construct a new small matrix and continue the search with the next most promising motif. If the new small matrix has any overlap with the previous matrix, we reuse the calculated values rather than recalculating them.

Constructing these small matrices would be of limited utility if their total size added up to $O(m^2)$. While this is possible in pathological cases, we can generally search a space much smaller in total size, and still guarantee that we have returned the true best K-Motifs.

This, in essence, is the intuition behind our motif discovery algorithm. We will achieve speed up by:

- Searching a set of smaller matrices, whose total size is much less than the naïve $O(m^2)$ matrix.
- Within the smaller matrices, using ADM to prune away a large fraction of the search space.

We will concretely define our algorithm, which we call EMMA (Enumeration of Motifs through Matrix Approximation), in the next section.

4.1 The EMMA Algorithm

As before, we only discuss the algorithm for finding the 1-Motif. The generalization of the algorithm to finding K-motifs is obvious and omitted for brevity and clarity of presentation. The pseudocode for the algorithm is introduced in Table 4. The line numbers in the table are used in the discussion of the algorithm that follows.

The algorithm begins by sliding a moving window of length n across the time series (line 4). The hash function $h()$ (line 5), normalizes the time series, converts it to the symbolic representation and computes an address:

$$h(C,w,a) = 1 + \sum_{i=1}^{w} (ord(\hat{c}_i) - 1) \times a^{i-1} \qquad (10)$$

Where $ord(\hat{c}_i)$ is the ordinal value of $\hat{c}_i$, i.e., $ord(\mathbf{a}) = 1$, $ord(\mathbf{b}) = 2$, and so on. The hash function computes an integer in the range 1 to w^a, and a pointer to the subsequence is placed in the corresponding bucket (line 6).

Algorithm Find-1-Motif-Index(T,n,R,w,a)	
1.	best_motif_count = 0;
2.	best_motif_location = null;
3.	finished = **FALSE**;
4.	**for** i = 1 to length(T) - n + 1 // Hash pointers
5.	hash_val = h($T_{[i:i+n-1]}$,w,a); // to subsequences
6.	append(bucket(hash_val).pointers, i);
7.	**end**;
8.	MPC = address(largest(bucket)); // Find MPC
9.	neighborhood = bucket(MPC).pointers;
10.	**while not**(finished)
11.	**for** i = 1 to w^a // Build neighborhood
12.	**if** MINDIST(MPC, bucket(i)) < R // around
13.	temp = bucket(i).pointers; // the MPC
14.	neighborhood = append(neighborhood,temp)
15.	**end**;
16.	**end**; // Search neighborhood for motifs
17.	[motif_cntr,count] = ADM(T,neighborhood,R);
18.	**if** count > largest_unexplored_neighborhood
19.	best_motif_location = motif_cntr;
20.	best_motif_count = count;
21.	finished = **TRUE**;
22.	**else** // Create the next neighborhood to search
23.	MPC = address(largest_unexplored(bucket));
24.	neighborhood = bucket(MPC).pointers;
25.	**end**;
26.	**end**;

Table 4: The Find-1-Motif-Index algorithm

At this point we have simply rearranged the data into a hash table with w^a addresses, and a total of size $O(m)$. This arrangement of the data has the advantage of approximately grouping similar subsequences (more accurately, pointers to similar subsequences) together. We can use this information as a heuristic for motif search, since if there is a truly over-represented pattern in the time series, we should expect that most, if not all, copies of it hashed to the same location. We call the address with the most hits the Most Promising Candidate (MPC) (line 8). We can build a list of all subsequences that mapped to this address (line 9), but it is possible that some subsequences that hashed to different addresses are also within R of the subsequences contained in MPC. We can use the MINDIST function that we defined in Section 3.3 to determine which addresses could possibly contain such subsequences (line 12). All such subsequences are added to the list of subsequences that need to be examined in our small matrix (line 14). We call the contents of a promising address, together with the contents of all the addresses within a MINDIST of R to it, a *neighborhood*.

At this point we can pass the list of similar subsequences into the ADM subroutine (line 17). We will elucidate this algorithm later, in Section 4.2. For the moment we just note that the algorithm will return the best motif from the original MPC subset, with a count of the number of matching subsequences.

If we wish to implement the algorithm as an online algorithm, then at this point we can report the current motif as a tentative answer, before continuing the search. Such "anytime" behavior is very desirable in a data-mining algorithm [7].

Next, a simple test is performed. If the number of matches to the current best-so-far motif is greater than the largest unexplored neighborhood (line 18), we are done. We can record the best so far motif as the true best match (line 19), note the number of matching subsequences (line 20), and then abandon the search (line 21).

If the test fails, however, we must set the most promising candidate to be the next largest bucket (line 23), initialize the new neighborhood with the contents of the bucket (line 24), and loop back to line 11, where the full neighborhood is discovered (lines 13 and 14) and the search continues.

For simplicity the pseudocode for the algorithm ignores the following possible optimization, it is possible (in fact, likely), that the neighborhood in one interaction will overlap with the neighborhood in the next. In this case, we can reuse the subset of calculated values from iteration to iteration.

4.2 The ADM Algorithm

The algorithm we use for searching the small neighborhood matrix is a minor modification of the Shasha and Wang's ADM algorithm [33]. The algorithm begins by pre-computing an arbitrary set of distances. A matrix ADM is maintained, of which each entry [i,j] is either the exact distance between objects i and j (i.e. those that are pre-computed), or the lower bound for the distance between i and j. The algorithm utilizes the property of triangle inequality to find the lower-bound distances. Details on how to construct the matrix ADM can be found in [33].

After the matrix ADM is constructed, we scan the matrix and compute the actual distance between i and j if ADM[i,j] is a lower bound that is smaller than R (because the true distance might be greater than R), and omit it if it's greater than R. For each object, we keep track of the number of items smaller than R. Finally, the algorithm returns the best-matching motif (i.e. one with the most items within R), with a count of number of matching subsequences.

5. Experimental Evaluation

We begin by showing some motifs discovered in a variety of time series. We deliberately consider time series with very different properties of noise, autocorrelation, stationarity etc. Figure 8 shows the 1-Motif discovered in various datasets, together with a much larger subsequence of the time series to give context. Although the subsequences are normalized [22] before testing to see if they match, we show the unnormalized subsequences for clarity.

We next turn our attention to evaluating the efficiency of the proposed algorithm. For simplicity we have only considered the problem of speeding up motif search when

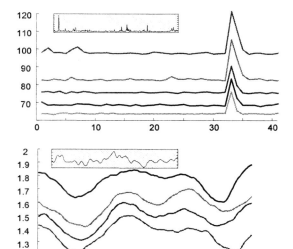

Figure 8: The 1-Motif discovered in various publicly available datasets. From top to bottom, "Network" and "Burst". Details about the datasets are available from the UCR time series data mining archive. The small inset boxes show a subsequence of length 500 to give context to the motif

the whole time series fits in main memory (we intend to address efficient disk-based algorithms in future work). So we can evaluate the efficiency of the proposed algorithm by simply considering the ratio of how many times the Euclidean distance function must be evaluated by EMMA, over the number of times it must be evaluated by the brute force algorithm described in Table 1.

$$efficiency = \frac{number\ of\ times\ EMMA\ calls\ Euclidean\ dist}{number\ of\ times\ brute-force\ calls\ Euclidean\ dist} \quad (11)$$

This measure ignores the cost of building the hash table, but this needs be done only once (even if the user wishes to try several values of R), and is in any case linear in m.

The efficiency depends on the value of R used in the experiments. In the pathological case of $R = \infty$, only one "small" matrix would be created, but it would be $O(m^2)$, even if we could fit such a large matrix in main memory, the only speed-up would come from ADM algorithm. The other pathological case of $R = 0$ would make our algorithm behave very well, because only a few very small matrices would be created, and the triangular inequality pruning of ADM algorithm would be maximally efficient. Of course, neither of these scenarios is meaningful, the former would result in a Motif with every (non-trivial) subsequence in the time series included, and the latter case would almost certainly result in no motif being found (since we are dealing with real numbers).

In order to test with realistic values of R we will consider the efficiency achieved when using the values used to create the results shown in Figure 8. The results are shown in Table 5.

Dataset	Network	Burst
efficiency	0.0018	0.0192

Table 5: The efficiency of the EMMA algorithm on various datasets

These results indicate a one to two order of magnitude speedup over the brute force algorithm.

6. Related work

To the best of our knowledge, the problem of finding repeated patterns in time series has not been addressed (or even formulated) in the literature.

Several researchers in data mining have addressed the discovery of reoccurring patterns in event streams [39], although such data sources are often referred to as time series [38]. The critical difference is that event streams are sequentially ordered variables that are nominal (have no natural ordering) and thus these researchers are concerned with similar subsets, not similar subsequences. Research by Indyk et. al. [20], has addressed the problem of finding representative trends in time series, this work is more similar in spirit to our work. However, they only consider trends, not more general patterns, and they only consider locally representative trends, not globally occurring motifs as in our approach.

While there has been enormous interest in efficiently locating *previously known* patterns in time series [1, 2, 3, 8, 13, 19, 22, 23, 24, 27, 29, 32, 35, 40], our focus on the discovery of previously unknown patterns is more similar to (and was inspired by) work in computational biology, which we briefly review below.

In the context of computational biology, "pattern discovery'" refers to the automatic identification of biologically significant patterns (or *motifs*) by statistical methods. The underlying assumption is that biologically significant words show distinctive distribution patterns within the genomes of various organisms, and therefore they can be distinguished from the others. During the evolutionary process, living organisms have accumulated certain biases toward or against some specific motifs in their genomes. For instance, highly recurring oligonucleotides are often found in correspondence to regulatory regions or protein binding sites of genes. Vice versa, rare oligonucleotide motifs may be discriminated against due to structural constraints of genomes or specific reservations for global transcription controls.

Pattern discovery in computational biology originated with the work of Rodger Staten [34]. Along this research line, a multitude of patterns have been variously characterized, and criteria, algorithms and software have been developed in correspondence. We mention a few representatives of this large family of methods, without claiming to be exhaustive: CONSENSUS [16], GIBBS SAMPLER [26], WINNOWER [30], PROJECTION [36], VERBUMCULUS [4, 28] These methods have been studied from a rigorous statistical viewpoint (see, e.g., [31] for a review) and also employed successfully in practice (see, e.g., [17] and references therein).

While there are literally hundreds of papers on discretizing (symbolizing, tokenizing) time series [2, 3, 9, 13, 19, 25, 27] (see [10] for an extensive survey), and dozens of distance measures defined on these representations, none of the techniques allows a distance measure which lower bounds a distance measure defined on the original time series.

7. Conclusions

We have formalized the problem of finding repeated patterns in time series, and introduced an algorithm to efficiently locate them[1]. In addition, a minor contribution of this paper is to introduce the first discrete representation of time series that allows a lower bounding approximation of the Euclidean distance. This representation may be of independent interest to researchers who use symbolic representations for similarity search [3, 19, 25, 27, 29], change point detection [13], and extracting rules from time series [9, 18].

There are several directions in which we intend to extend this work.

- As previously noted, we only considered the problem of speeding up main memory search. Techniques for dealing with large disk resident data are highly desirable [6].
- On large datasets, the number of returned motifs may be intimidating; we plan to investigate tools for visualizing and navigating the results of a motif search.
- Our motif search algorithm utilizes the Euclidean metric, and can be trivially modified to use any Minkowski metric [40]. However, recent work by several authors has suggested that the Euclidean may be inappropriate in some domains [21, 29]. We hope to generalize our results to work with other more robust distance measures, such as Dynamic Time Warping [29].
- It may be possible to extend our work to multi-dimensional time series (i.e., trajectories) [37].

8. References

[1] Agrawal, R., Faloutsos, C. & Swami, A. (1993). Efficient similarity search in sequence databases. In *proceedings of the 4th Int'l Conference on Foundations of Data Organization and Algorithms*. Chicago, IL, Oct 13-15. pp 69-84.

[2] Agrawal, R., Psaila, G., Wimmers, E. L. & Zait, M. (1995). Querying shapes of histories. In *proceedings of the 21st Int'l Conference on Very Large Databases*. Zurich, Switzerland, Sept 11-15. pp 502-514.

[3] André-Jönsson, H. & Badal. D. (1997). Using signature files for querying time-series data. In *proceedings of Principles of Data Mining and Knowledge Discovery*, 1st European Symposium. Trondheim, Norway, Jun 24-27. pp 211-220.

[4] Apostolico, A., Bock, M. E. & Lonardi, S. (2002). Monotony of surprise and large-scale quest for unusual words (extended abstract). Myers, G., Hannenhalli, S., Istrail, S., Pevzner, P. & Waterman, M. editors. In *proceedings of the 6th Int'l Conference on Research in Computational Molecular Biology*. Washington, DC, April 18-21. pp 22-31.

[5] Burkhard, W. A. & Keller, R. M. (1973). Some approaches to best-match file searching. *Commun. ACM*, April. Vol. 16(4), pp 230-236.

[6] Böhm, C., Braunmüller, B., Krebs, F. & Kriegel, H. P. (2002). Epsilon grid order: An algorithm for the similarity join on massive high-dimensional data. In *proceedings of ACM SIGMOD Int. Conf. on Management of Data*, Santa Barbara.

[7] Bradley, P. S., Fayyad, U. M. & Reina, C. A. (1998). Scaling clustering algorithms to large databases. In *proceedings of the 4th Int'l Conference on Knowledge Discovery and Data Mining*. New York, NY, Aug 27-31. pp 9-15.

[8] Chan, K. & Fu, A. W. (1999). Efficient time series matching by wavelets. In *proceedings of the 15th IEEE Int'l Conference*

---

[1] A slightly expanded version of this paper is available by emailing the authors.

on Data Engineering. Sydney, Australia, Mar 23-26. pp 126-133.

[9] Das, G., Lin, K., Mannila, H., Renganathan, G. & Smyth, P. (1998). Rule discovery from time series. In *proceedings of the 4th Int'l Conference on Knowledge Discovery and Data Mining*. New York, NY, Aug 27-31. pp 16-22.

[10] Daw, C. S., Finney, C. E. A. & Tracy, E. R. (2001). Symbolic analysis of experimental data. *Review of Scientific Instruments*. To appear.

[11] Durbin, R., Eddy, S., Krogh, A. & Mitchison, G. (1998). Biological sequence analysis: probabilistic models of proteins and nucleic acids. Cambridge University Press.

[12] Fayyad, U., Reina, C. &. Bradley. P (1998). Initialization of iterative refinement clustering algorithms. In *Proceedings of the 4th International Conference on Knowledge Discovery and Data Mining*. New York, NY, Aug 27-31. pp 194-198.

[13] Ge, X. & Smyth, P. (2000). Deformable Markov model templates for time-series pattern matching. In *proceedings of the 6th ACM SIGKDD International Conference on Knowledge Discovery and Data Mining*. Boston, MA, Aug 20-23. pp 81-90.

[14] Goutte, C. Toft, P., Rostrup, E.,. Nielsen F.Å & Hansen L.K. (1999). On clustering fMRI time series, NeuroImage, 9(3): pp 298-310.

[15] Hegland, M., Clarke, W. & Kahn, M. (2002). Mining the MACHO dataset, *Computer Physics Communications*, Vol 142(1-3), December 15. pp. 22-28.

[16] Hertz, G. & Stormo, G. (1999). Identifying DNA and protein patterns with statistically significant alignments of multiple sequences. *Bioinformatics*, Vol. 15, pp 563-577.

[17] van Helden, J., Andre, B., & Collado-Vides, J. (1998) Extracting regulatory sites from the upstream region of the yeast genes by computational analysis of oligonucleotides. *J. Mol. Biol.*, Vol. 281, pp 827-842.

[18] Höppner, F. (2001). Discovery of temporal patterns -- learning rules about the qualitative behavior of time series. In *Proceedings of the 5th European Conference on Principles and Practice of Knowledge Discovery in Databases*. Freiburg, Germany, pp 192-203.

[19] Huang, Y. & Yu, P. S. (1999). Adaptive query processing for time-series data. In *proceedings of the 5th Int'l Conference on Knowledge Discovery and Data Mining*. San Diego, CA, Aug 15-18. pp 282-286.

[20] Indyk, P., Koudas, N. & Muthukrishnan, S. (2000). Identifying representative trends in massive time series data sets using sketches. In *proceedings of the 26th Int'l Conference on Very Large Data Bases*. Cairo, Egypt, Sept 10-14. pp 363-372.

[21] Kalpakis, K., Gada, D. & Puttagunta, V. (2001). Distance measures for effective clustering of ARIMA time-series. In *proceedings of the 2001 IEEE International Conference on Data Mining*, San Jose, CA, Nov 29-Dec 2. pp 273-280.

[22] Keogh, E,. Chakrabarti, K,. Pazzani, M. & Mehrotra (2000). Dimensionality reduction for fast similarity search in large time series databases. *Journal of Knowledge and Information Systems*. pp 263-286.

[23] Keogh, E., Chakrabarti, K., Pazzani, M. & Mehrotra, S. (2001). Locally adaptive dimensionality reduction for indexing large time series databases. In *proceedings of ACM SIGMOD Conference on Management of Data*. Santa Barbara, CA, May 21-24. pp 151-162.

[24] Keogh, E. & Pazzani, M. (1998). An enhanced representation of time series which allows fast and accurate classification, clustering and relevance feedback. In *proceedings of the 4th*

[25] Koski, A., Juhola, M. & Meriste, M. (1995). Syntactic recognition of ECG signals by attributed finite automata. *Pattern Recognition*, 28 (12), pp. 1927-1940.

[26] Lawrence, C.E., Altschul, S. F., Boguski, M. S., Liu, J. S., Neuwald, A. F. & Wootton, J. C. (1993). Detecting subtle sequence signals: A Gibbs sampling strategy for multiple alignment. *Science*, Oct. Vol. 262, pp 208-214.

[27] Li, C., Yu, P. S. & Castelli, V. (1998). MALM: a framework for mining sequence database at multiple abstraction levels. In *proceedings of the 7th ACM CIKM International Conference on Information and Knowledge Management*. Bethesda, MD. pp 267-272.

[28] Lonardi, S. (2001). Global Detectors of Unusual Words: Design, Implementation, and Applications to Pattern Discovery in Biosequences. PhD thesis, Department of Computer Sciences, Purdue University, August, 2001.

[29] Perng, C., Wang, H., Zhang, S., & Parker, S. (2000). Landmarks: a new model for similarity-based pattern querying in time series databases. In *proceedings of 16th International Conference on Data Engineering*.

[30] Pevzner, P. A. & Sze, S. H. (2000). Combinatorial approaches to finding subtle signals in DNA sequences. In *proceedings of the 8th International Conference on Intelligent Systems for Molecular Biology*. La Jolla, CA, Aug 19-23. pp 269-278.

[31] Reinert, G., Schbath, S. & Waterman, M. S. (2000). Probabilistic and statistical properties of words: An overview. J. Comput. Bio., Vol. 7, pp 1-46.

[32] Roddick, J. F., Hornsby, K. & Spiliopoulou, M. (2001). An Updated Bibliography of Temporal, Spatial and Spatio-Temporal Data Mining Research. In *Post-Workshop Proceedings of the International Workshop on Temporal, Spatial and Spatio-Temporal Data Mining*. Berlin, Springer. Lecture Notes in Artificial Intelligence. 2007. Roddick, J. F. and Hornsby, K., Eds. 147-163.

[33] Shasha, D. & Wang, T. (1990). New techniques for best-match retrieval. *ACM Trans. on Information Systems*, Vol. 8(2). pp 140-158.

[34] Staden, R. (1989). Methods for discovering novel motifs in nucleic acid sequences. *Comput. Appl. Biosci.*, Vol. 5(5). pp 293-298.

[35] Struzik, Z. R. & Siebes, A. (1999). Measuring time series similarity through large singular features revealed with wavelet transformation. In *proceedings of the 10th International Workshop on Database & Expert Systems Applications*. pp 162-166.

[36] Tompa, M. & Buhler, J. (2001). Finding motifs using random projections. In *proceedings of the 5th Int'l Conference on Computational Molecular Biology*. Montreal, Canada, Apr 22-25. pp 67-74.

[37] Vlachos, M., Kollios, G. & Gunopulos, G. (2002). Discovering similar multidimensional trajectories. In *proceedings 18th International Conference on Data Engineering*. pp 673-684.

[38] Wang. W., Yang, J. and Yu., P. (2001). Meta-patterns: revealing hidden periodical patterns. In *Proceedings of the 1st IEEE International Conference on Data Mining*. pp. 550-557.

[39] Yang, J., Yu, P., Wang, W. and Han. J. (2002). Mining long sequential patterns in a noisy environment. In *proceedings SIGMOD International. Conference on Management of Data*. Madison, WI.

[40] Yi, B, K., & Faloutsos, C. (2000). Fast time sequence indexing for arbitrary Lp norms. In *proceedings of the 26st Intl Conference on Very Large Databases*. pp 385-394.

On Computing Condensed Frequent Pattern Bases

Jian Pei
State Univ. of New York at Buffalo
jianpei@cse.buffalo.edu

Guozhu Dong
Wright State Univ.
gdong@cs.wright.edu

Wei Zou
Jiangxi Normal Univ.
zouwei@jxnu.edu.cn

Jiawei Han
Univ. of Illinois
hanj@cs.uiuc.edu

Abstract

Frequent pattern mining has been studied extensively. However, the effectiveness and efficiency of this mining is often limited, since the number of frequent patterns generated is often too large. In many applications it is sufficient to generate and examine only frequent patterns with support frequency in close-enough approximation instead of in full precision. Such a compact but close-enough frequent pattern base is called a **condensed frequent patterns-base**.

In this paper, we propose and examine several alternatives at the design, representation, and implementation of such condensed frequent pattern-bases. A few algorithms for computing such pattern-bases are proposed. Their effectiveness at pattern compression and their efficient computation methods are investigated. A systematic performance study is conducted on different kinds of databases, which demonstrates the effectiveness and efficiency of our approach at handling frequent pattern mining in large databases.

1 Introduction

It has been well recognized that frequent pattern mining plays an essential role in many important data mining tasks (e.g., mining association [2]). However, it has also been widely recognized that frequent pattern mining often produces a huge number of patterns [15], which reduces not only the efficiency but also the effectiveness of mining, since it is unrealistic to store and comprehend so many patterns. Recently, efforts have been devoted to address this problem. In general, interesting proposals can be classified into two categories. First, concise representations of frequent patterns have been explored, such as *frequent closed patterns* [12, 15, 14], that can be used to remove sub-patterns which have the same support as some of their super-patterns. Studies like [15] have shown that, by doing so, the total number of patterns and rules can be reduced substantially, especially in dense data sets. Second, constraints can be used to capture users' focus, and effective strategies have been developed to push various constraints deep into the mining process [11, 9, 13].

Even though these approaches are useful, they may not be powerful enough in many cases. The compression by the closed-pattern approach may not be so effective since there often exist slightly different counts between super- and sub- patterns. Constraint-based mining, though useful, can hardly be used for pre-computation since different users may likely have different constraints.

Although it seems to be inherent that a large database may contain numerous frequent patterns, it is easy to observe a simple fact in practice: "*Most applications will not need* **precise** *support information of frequent patterns, a* **good approximation** *on support count could be more than adequate.*" Here, by "*good approximation*", we mean that the frequency of every frequent pattern can be estimated with a *guaranteed maximal error bound*. For example, for a frequent pattern {diaper, beer}, instead of giving the exact support count (e.g., 10000), a range, e.g., $10000 \pm 1\%$, may be good enough; the range is a user-specified *error bound*.

"*Why is a condensed frequent pattern base acceptable and often more preferable?*" First, *when mining large database, a small deviation often has a very minor effect on analysis.* For an analyst, the exact information "*diaper and beer have been bought together* $10,050$ *times out of the* 10 *million transactions*" and an approximation "*diaper and beer have been bought together* $10,050 \pm 50$ *times*" may not have any essential difference. Analysis often has to deal with approximation sooner or later, by truncation or rounding. What an analyst is really concerned is that a specified error bound is guaranteed.

Second, *condensing frequent pattern base leads to more effective frequent pattern mining.* By computing a condensed pattern base, the number of patterns can be reduced dramatically, but the general information about frequent patterns still retain. A much smaller base of patterns certainly helps users comprehend the mining results.

Third, *computing a condensed frequent pattern base may lead to more efficient frequent pattern mining.* A condensed frequent pattern base could be much smaller than the complete frequent pattern base. Thus, one may need to compute and access a much smaller pattern base, which leads to better efficiency.

In summary, mining a condensed frequent pattern base may make frequent pattern mining more realistic in real-life applications. In this paper, we introduce the concept of *condensed frequent pattern-base with guaranteed maximal error bound* and study the *efficient computation of such a condensed pattern-base*, with the following contributions. First, we introduce the concept *condensed frequent pattern-base* and devise systematic representations of such frequent pattern-bases. We show that such representations achieve satisfactory approximation with a guaranteed maximal error bound on the support. Second, we develop efficient algorithms for computing condensed pattern bases from transaction databases directly. Our algorithms facili-

378

tate the relaxation of counting requirement and prune many patterns in the mining. Third, we present a systematic performance study to verify the effectiveness and efficiency of condensed frequent pattern bases. Our results show that computing condensed frequent pattern base is promising. Previously, the ideas of approximating frequent patterns have been probed in some related studies. For example, [10] shows that approximative association rules are interesting and useful. In [4], the notion of free-sets is proposed and can lead to an error-bound approximation of frequencies. However, none of the previous studies systematically explores the problem of designing and mining condensed frequent pattern-based with guaranteed maximal error bound.

The remaining of this paper is organized as follows. The problem of computing a condensed frequent pattern base is introduced in Section 2. A level-by-level frequent pattern base construction method is presented in Section 3. In Section 4, we develop an effective and efficient method for frequent pattern-base construction using max-patterns at various layers. Section 5 presents a comprehensive performance study to demonstrate the effectiveness and efficiency of our approach. Section 6 concludes the study.

2 Problem Definition

We first review some standard terminology for frequent pattern mining. Let $I = \{i_1, \ldots, i_n\}$ be a set of literals, called *items*. An *itemset* (or *pattern*) X, denoted as $X = i_{j_1} \cdots i_{j_l}$ (i.e., by omitting set brackets), is a subset of items in I. An itemset with l items is called an *l-itemset*. For two patterns X and Y such that $X \subseteq Y$, Y is called a *super-pattern* of X, and X a *sub-pattern* of Y.

A *transaction* $T = (tid, X)$ is a tuple where tid is a *transaction-id* and X is an itemset. A transaction $T = (tid, X)$ is said to *contain* itemset Y if $Y \subseteq X$. A *transaction database* TDB is a set of transactions. The *support* of an itemset X in TDB, denoted as $sup(X)$, is the number of transactions in TDB containing X, i.e., $sup(X) = |\{(tid, Y)|((tid, Y) \in TDB) \wedge (X \subseteq Y)\}|$.

Given a transaction database TDB and a *support threshold* min_sup, an itemset X is called a *frequent itemset* or a *frequent pattern* if $sup(X) \geq min\_sup$. The problem of frequent pattern mining is to find the complete set of frequent patterns from TDB w.r.t. a user-specified support threshold min_sup. The set of all frequent patterns is called a *frequent pattern base*, or *FP-base* in short.

It is often expensive to find the complete set of frequent patterns, since an FP-base may contain a huge number of frequent patterns. In this paper, we propose to overcome the difficulty caused by "huge amount of frequent patterns" as follows: we compute a smaller set of frequent patterns, i.e., a "condensed FP-base", and then use it to approximate the supports of arbitrary frequent patterns.

Problem statement. Given a transaction database, a support threshold, and a user-specified *error bound* k, the *problem of computing a condensed FP-base* is to find a subset of frequent patterns $\mathcal{B}$ and a function $f_{\mathcal{B}}$ such that the following holds for each pattern X:

$$
f_{\mathcal{B}}(X) = \begin{cases} 0 & \text{if } X \text{ is infrequent} \\ [sup_{lb}, sup_{ub}] \text{ s.t. } (sup_{lb} \leq sup(X) \leq sup_{ub}) \\ \quad \text{and } (sup_{ub} - sup_{lb}) \leq k & \text{if } X \text{ is frequent} \end{cases}
$$

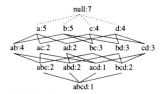

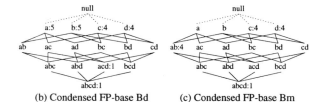

(b) Condensed FP-base Bd (c) Condensed FP-base Bm

Figure 1. Lattice of frequent patterns for Example 1.

The function $f_{\mathcal{B}}$ is called a *(support) approximation function*, and the set $\mathcal{B}$ a *condensed FP-base* w.r.t. $f_{\mathcal{B}}$.[1] ■

Example 1 Consider the transaction database shown in Table 1. Let the support threshold be $min\_sup = 1$ and the error bound be $k = 2$. The lattice of totally 15 frequent patterns is shown in Figure 1(a).

Transaction-id	Itemset
10	a
20	ab
30	abc
40	$abcd$
50	cd
60	abd
70	bcd

Table 1. A transaction database with seven transactions.

The set $\mathcal{B}_d = \{a : 5, b : 5, c : 4, d : 4, acd : 1, abcd : 1\}$ is a *condensed FP-base*. Patterns in $\mathcal{B}_d$ are those labelled with supports in Figure 1(b). For each pattern X, the function $f_{\mathcal{B}_d}$ is defined as follows:

$$
f_{\mathcal{B}_d}(X) = \begin{cases} 0 & \text{if there exists no } X' \in \mathcal{B}_d \text{ s.t. } X \subseteq X' \\ [sup(X), sup(X)] & \text{if } X \in \mathcal{B}_d \\ [sup(X_0) - 2, sup(X_0)], \text{ where } (X_0 \subset X \text{ and} \\ \quad sup(X_0) = \min(sup(X'')) \text{ for } X'' \subset X \\ \quad \text{and } X'' \in \mathcal{B}_d), \quad \text{otherwise} \end{cases}
$$

For example, $f_{\mathcal{B}_d}(abcde) = 0$ for the infrequent pattern $abcde$, since there is no $X' \in \mathcal{B}_d$ s.t. $abcde \subseteq X'$; $f_{\mathcal{B}_d}(ac) = [4-2, 4] = [2, 4]$, since c is a sub-pattern of ac in $\mathcal{B}_d$ with the smallest support count (of 4). Here, we used the well known "*Apriori*" property that $supp(X) \geq supp(Y)$ if $X \subseteq Y$. One can verify that, $f_{\mathcal{B}_d}$ can approximate the support count of each frequent pattern as required by the definition given above. For example, $sup(ab)$ is approximated by $[3, 5]$ and $sup(abc)$ is by $[2, 4]$.

---

[1]Instead of an absolute error bound k, a relative, percentage-based error bound $k\%$ can also be used to compute a condensed FP-base. In this case, $\frac{sup_{ub} - sup_{lb}}{sup_{lb}} \leq k\%$ should be satisfied for frequent patterns.

Moreover, $\mathcal{B}_m = \{c : 4, d : 4, ab : 4, abcd : 1\}$ is another condensed FP-base, as plotted in Figure 1(c). The corresponding approximation function $f_{\mathcal{B}_m}$ is defined (for each pattern X) as follows:

$$f_{\mathcal{B}_m}(X) = \begin{cases} 0 & \text{if there exists no } X' \in \mathcal{B}_m \text{ s.t. } X \subseteq X' \\ [sup(X), sup(X)] & \text{if } X \in \mathcal{B}_m \\ [sup(X_0), sup(X_0) + 2] & \text{where } (X_0 \supset X \\ & \text{and } sup(X_0) = \max\{sup(X'') \mid \\ & X'' \supset X, X'' \in \mathcal{B}_m\}), \quad \text{otherwise} \end{cases}$$

Condensed FP-bases and approximation functions are not unique. A superset of a condensed FP-base is also a base w.r.t. the identical approximation function. A condensed FP-base is *minimal* (w.r.t. an approximation function f) if it does not contain a proper subset which is also a condensed FP-base w.r.t. f. Interestingly, even minimal condensed FP-bases are not unique. For Example 1, both $\mathcal{B}_d$ and $\mathcal{B}_m$ are *minimal* condensed FP-bases.

Among possible approximation bases, we prefer those requiring as little space as possible. Such condensed FP-bases offer significant compression effect, which can be measured by *compression ratio* δ, defined as

$$\delta = \frac{\text{\# of patterns in the condensed FP-base}}{\text{total \# of frequent patterns}} \quad (1)$$

Clearly, the smaller the compression ratio, the better the compression effect. We observe from Example 1 that condensed FP-bases can produce considerable space savings even with a small error bound. For example, $\mathcal{B}_d$ achieves a compression ratio of 40%, whereas $\mathcal{B}_m$ achieves 26.7%. $\mathcal{B}_m$ achieves better compression than $\mathcal{B}_d$.

Previous research also considered computing reduced sets of frequent patterns, including reduction based on frequent closed itemsets [12] and containment based reduction [3, 6]. An itemset X is called a *closed pattern* if there exists no proper superset X' of X such that $sup(X) = sup(X')$, while X is called a *max-pattern* if there exists no superset X' of X such that X' is also frequent. Interestingly, it can be shown that the complete set of frequent closed patterns is a minimal condensed FP-base with error bound 0, while the complete set of max-patterns is a minimal condensed FP-base with error bound $(|TDB| - min\_sup)$, where min_sup is the support threshold. However, none of these considers approximating supports of frequent patterns with a user-specified error bound as we do here.

How can we construct condensed FP-bases effectively and efficiently? This is the topic of the following sections.

3 Constructing a Condensed FP-Base Level-by-level

We now consider an approach that constructs a condensed FP-base by examining all frequent patterns level-by-level: A frequent pattern is added into the condensed FP-base only if it cannot be approximated by its sub-patterns in the base. The method is illustrated next.

Example 2 A condensed FP-base $\mathcal{B}_d$ for the transaction database TDB in Table 1, for the support threshold of 1 and the error bound of 2 is constructed as follows (as shown

in Figure 1(b)), where the approximation function $f_{\mathcal{B}_d}$ is defined in Example 1.

For each pattern X, let $X.ub$ denote $\min\{sup(X') \mid X' \in \mathcal{B}, \text{ and } X' \subseteq X\}$, i.e., $X.ub$ is the minimum of supports of all sub-patterns of X currently in $\mathcal{B}_d$.

Step 1. We initialize $\mathcal{B}_d = \emptyset$ and mine length-1 and length-2 frequent patterns. Since length-1 frequent patterns are the "*most frequent-end borders*" of frequent patterns and none of their sub-patterns is in the base, we insert all of them (i.e. a, b, c, and d) into $\mathcal{B}_d$.

For each length-1 frequent pattern x, $x.ub = sup(x)$.

Step 2. For the next level, i.e., length-2 frequent patterns, we have $xy.ub = \min(x.ub, y.ub)$ for each length-2 frequent pattern xy.

We do two types of insertions into $\mathcal{B}_d$.

(i) A length-2 frequent pattern X is added into $\mathcal{B}_d$ if $X.ub - sup(X)$ is over the error bound (i.e., if its support cannot be approximated by its sub-patterns in the base $\mathcal{B}_d$). In this example, since all length-2 frequent patterns can be approximated properly by their length-1 sub-patterns, no length-2 frequent pattern is inserted into $\mathcal{B}_d$.

(ii) If a length-2 frequent pattern has no frequent length-3 super-pattern, i.e., it is a max-pattern, then it is inserted into $\mathcal{B}_d$. Max-patterns are needed in $\mathcal{B}_d$ since they are used to determine whether a pattern is frequent. In this example, no such length-2 frequent pattern exists.

Step 3. For the length-3 level, since $acd.ub - sup(acd) = 4 - 1 > 2$, pattern acd is inserted into $\mathcal{B}_d$. Here, $abc.ub = \min(ab.ub, ac.ub, bc.ub)$. After the insertion, we set $abc.ub = sup(abc) = 1$. We then mine length-4 frequent patterns and see that there is no length-3 max-pattern.

Step 4. The length-4 frequent pattern $abcd$ is a max-pattern (since there is no length-5 frequent pattern), and it is inserted into $\mathcal{B}_d$.

At the end, the base $\mathcal{B}_d$ contains 6 patterns: a, b, c, d, acd, and $abcd$. Since the search is downward from length-1 patterns, we call the resulting base as a *downward condensed FP-base*. ∎

Let us generalize the level-by-level condensed FP-base construction method. We first define the approximation function ϑ as follows.

Definition 1 Given a condensed FP-base $\mathcal{B}$, an error bound k and a pattern X.

$$\vartheta(X) = \begin{cases} 0 & \text{if there exists no } X' \in \mathcal{B} \\ & \text{s.t. } X' \supseteq X \\ [sup(X), sup(X)] & \text{if } X \in \mathcal{B} \\ [m - k, m] & \text{if } X \notin \mathcal{B}, \text{ where } m = \\ & \min\{sup(X') \mid X' \in \mathcal{B}, \\ & X' \subset X\} \end{cases}$$

∎

The following algorithm computes a condensed FP-base with respect to approximation function ϑ.

Algorithm 1 (*CFP-D: a Level-by-level downward search method*)

Input: transaction database TDB, support threshold min_sup, and error bound k;

Output: a condensed FP-base $\mathcal{B}$ w.r.t. ϑ;

Method:

1. let $\mathcal{B} = \emptyset$;

2. find length-1 frequent patterns and insert them into $\mathcal{B}$; for each length-1 frequent pattern X, let $X.ub = sup(X)$;

3. let $i = 2$;

4. generate the set $\mathcal{F}_i$ of length-i frequent patterns; for each length-i frequent pattern X, let $X.ub = \min(X'.ub)$, where X' ranges over length-$(i-1)$ sub-patterns of X;
   /* the calculation of $X.ub$ can be done as a byproduct of candidate-generation */

5. if $(X.ub - sup(X)) > k$, then insert X into $\mathcal{B}$ and set $X.ub = sup(X)$;

6. for each length-$(i-1)$ frequent pattern X s.t. X has no super-pattern in $\mathcal{F}_i$, insert X into $\mathcal{B}$;
   /* rationale: X is a max-pattern */

7. if $\mathcal{F}_i \neq \emptyset$ then let $i = i + 1$ and goto Step 4;

8. return $\mathcal{B}$. ∎

One advantage of the method shown in Example 2 is that it is intuitive and can be easily integrated into the Apriori algorithm. The correctness and effectiveness of the algorithm are obvious. Limited by space, we omit the proof here.

What kind of patterns are included in $\mathcal{B}$ computed by Algorithm 1? A frequent pattern X is called a *seed pattern* if for each proper sub-pattern $X' \subset X$, $sup(X') > sup(X)$. Interestingly, it is easy to show that *every pattern in $\mathcal{B}$ computed by Algorithm 1 is either a seed pattern or a max-pattern.*

4 Constructing a Condensed FP-base Using Max-patterns

While Algorithm 1 is intuitive and correct, it has to check every frequent pattern. When there are many frequent patterns, the mining cost is non-trivial. *Can we avoid checking every frequent pattern when constructing a condensed FP-base?* In this section we will answer this question positively by providing a type of condensed FP-base and efficient mining techniques to find such a base.

Intuitively, we are going to construct a condensed FP-base consisting of maximal frequent patterns for a series of support thresholds. More specifically, given a support threshold min_sup and error bound k, we divide the set of frequent patterns into a number of disjoint subsets: (1) the set of patterns with support in the range $[min\_sup, min\_sup+k]$, (2) those with support in the range $[min\_sup + k + 1, min\_sup + 2k + 1]$, etc. The i-th subset contains those patterns with support in the range

$$[min\_sup + (i-1)(k+1), min\_sup + ik + i - 1] \text{ where}$$
$(1 \leq i \leq \frac{|TDB|+1-min\_sup}{k+1})$.

Given a frequent pattern, we can approximate its support with maximal error of k, by determining which subset the pattern belongs to. To determine which subset a pattern belongs to, we only need to record the max-patterns at various layers w.r.t. the lower bounds of supports of the ranges. The idea is illustrated in the following example.

Example 3 Given the transaction database TDB in Table 1, support threshold of 1 and error bound of 2, a condensed FP-base $\mathcal{B}_m$ can be constructed as follows.

Since the support threshold is 1 and the total number of transactions in the database is 7, we consider three ranges of supports: $[1, 3]$, $[4, 6]$, and $[7, 7]$. We mine max-patterns w.r.t. support threshold 1, 4, and 7, respectively. The only max-pattern w.r.t. support threshold 1 is $abcd$, the max-patterns w.r.t. support threshold 4 are ab, c and d, while there is no max-pattern w.r.t. support threshold 7. These four patterns form a condensed FP-base $\mathcal{B}_m$.

The base $\mathcal{B}_m$ is shown in Figure 1(c). The approximation function is $f_{\mathcal{B}_m}$, as defined in Example 1. In essence, for each given pattern X we find the super-pattern Y of X in $\mathcal{B}_m$ having the largest support, and use the range of the support for Y as the estimate of the support of X. ∎

We now generalize the ideas by providing the definition of a condensed FP-base.

Definition 2 Given a transaction database TDB, support threshold min_sup and error bound k, let the *number of levels* be

$$n\_level = \lfloor \frac{|TDB| + 1 - min\_sup}{k + 1} \rfloor$$

Define

$$min\_sup_1 = min\_sup$$
$$min\_sup_2 = min\_sup + k + 1$$
$$\cdots$$
$$min\_sup_i = min\_sup + (i-1)(k+1) \text{ for } (1 \leq i \leq n\_level)$$

Then, $\mathcal{B} = \bigcup_{i=0}^{i<n\_level} \mathcal{M}_i$ is called an *M-base*, w.r.t. the approximation function ζ defined below. Here $\mathcal{M}_i$ is the set of max-patterns w.r.t. support threshold min_sup_i.

The name *M-base* is used because the base is based on max-patterns.

Definition 3 Given an error bound k, an M-base $\mathcal{B}$, and a pattern X, let

$$\zeta(X) = \begin{cases} 0 & \text{if there exists no } X' \in \mathcal{B} \\ & \text{s.t. } X' \supseteq X \\ [sup(X), sup(X)] & \text{if } X \in \mathcal{B} \\ [m, m + k] & \text{if } X \notin \mathcal{B}, \text{ where } m = \\ & \max\{sup(X') \mid X' \in \mathcal{B}, \\ & X' \supset X\} \end{cases}$$

It can be shown that each M-base is not only a proper condensed FP-base w.r.t. function ζ but also a minimal one. Limited by space, we omit the formal result here.

The remaining problem is *how to find the max-patterns efficiently in the condensed FP-base $\mathcal{B}_m$.*

There are many methods for mining max-patterns, such as MaxMiner [3], Depth-first Search [1], MAFIA [5], and GenMax[7]. A naïve method to compute $\mathcal{B}_m$ is to call a max-pattern mining algorithm multiple times, once for each lower bound of the ranges as a support threshold.

How do we mine the patterns of M-bases more efficiently than the naïve method? Roughly speaking, we will propose an algorithm to mine the database only once, for all the max-patterns w.r.t. the series of support thresholds. The algorithm proceeds in a depth-first manner. Moreover, our algorithm also uses additional pruning techniques. We will demonstrate the spirit of our algorithm with the following example.

Example 4 Consider the mining of max-patterns w.r.t. support thresholds of 1 and 4 in the M-base $\mathcal{B}_m$ for the transaction database TDB of Table 1.

By scanning the transaction database TDB once, all frequent items, namely $a : 5$, $b : 5$, $c : 4$, and $d : 4$, are found. These items are sorted in support descending order, producing the list $F\text{-}list = a - b - c - d$.

$F\text{-}list$ can be used to divide all max-patterns into four disjoint subsets: (1) the set of max-patterns containing item a; (2) those containing item b but no a; (3) those containing item c but no a nor b; and (4) those containing item d, i.e., the pattern d itself, if it is a max-pattern. We mine these four subsets of max-patterns one by one.

1. To find max-patterns containing item a, we form the *a-projected database* TDB_a by collecting all transactions containing item a, namely b, bc, bcd, and bd.

Items b, c, and d are local frequent items in TDB_a. A list $F\text{-}list_a = b - c - d$ is formed by sorting these local frequent items in local support descending order. Based on $F\text{-}list_a$, all max-patterns containing item a can be further divided into four disjoint subsets: (1) pattern a itself, if it is a max-pattern; (2) those containing ab; (3) those containing item ac but no b; and (4) pattern ad if it is a max-pattern. We mine them one by one recursively.

1(a). The support of b in TDB_a is 4, denoted as $sup_{TDB_a}(b) = 4$. Since $sup(ab) = sup_{TDB_a}(b) = 4$, pattern a is not a max-pattern w.r.t. support threshold 4.

1(b). To find max-patterns containing ab, we form the *ab-projected database* TDB_{ab}, which contains c, cd, and d. Items a and b are omitted in TDB_{ab}, since they appear in every transaction in the ab-projected database. There is no item having support 4 or over in TDB_{ab}. Thus, ab is a max-pattern w.r.t. support threshold 4 (the lower bound of the second range of supports).

Items c and d are frequent in TDB_{ab}. We recursively mine max-patterns by forming projected databases. It can be checked that $abcd$ is a max-pattern w.r.t. support threshold 1. Thus, the max-patterns containing ab are $ab : 4$ itself and $abcd : 1$.

1(c). To find max-patterns containing ac but not b, we form ac-projected database TDB_{ac}, which contains d. Here, items a, b and c are omitted since ac appears in every transaction and b occurs before c in F-list. The only frequent item in TDB_{ac} is d. However, $ac \subset abcd$ and $4 > sup(ac) > sup(abcd) = 1$. That means there exists no max-pattern containing ac but no b.

1(d). Since $4 > sup(ad) > sup(abcd) = 1$, ad is not a max-pattern.

Therefore, the max-patterns containing a are ab and $abcd$.

2. To find all max-patterns containing b but not a, we form

the b-projected database, which contains c, cd, d, and cd. The local frequent items in TDB_b are c and d, and $F\text{-}list_b = c - d$. The max-patterns containing b but not a can be divided into three subsets: (1) pattern b itself, if it is a max-pattern; (2) those containing bc; and (3) pattern bd, if it is a max-pattern. Let us mine them one by one.

Since $b \subset ab$ and ab is a max-pattern, b is not a max-pattern;

Since $sup(bc) = sup_{TDB_b}(c) = 2$, we have $4 > sup(bc) \geq sup(bcd) > sup(abcd)$. It follows that there are no max-pattern containing bc but not a.

Similarly, we can check that bd is not a max-pattern.

Thus, there are no max-patterns containing b but not a.

3. To mine max-patterns containing c but not a nor b, we can form the c-projected database and mine it recursively. It can be verified that c is the only such max-pattern.

4. similarly, it can be verified that d is a max-pattern.

Thus the complete set of max-patterns for condensed FP-base $\mathcal{B}_m = \{ab : 4, abcd : 1, c : 4, d : 4\}$. ∎

As shown in the example, the general framework is the depth-first search. A list of frequent items in support descending order, called $F\text{-}list$, is used to divide the data as well as the mining task. In general, given $F\text{-}list = x_1 \cdots x_n$, the set of max-patterns can be divided into n disjoint subsets: the i-th subset contains max-pattern having item x_i but none of x_j ($0 < j < i$).

To mine max-patterns containing $X = x_{i_1} \cdots x_{i_m}$ (items in X are listed according to $F\text{-}list$), an X-projected database TDB_X is formed: every transaction $t = (tid, Y) \in TDB$ such that $X \subset Y$ is projected to TDB_X as (tid, Y'), only items after x_{i_m} in the $F\text{-}list$ are in Y'. In Example 4, $F\text{-}list = a - b - c - d$. Thus, the ac-projected database TDB_{ac} contains only one transaction d (see Step 2). Here, the transaction-id is omitted.

The pruning techniques used in the mining are verified as follows.

First, *how can we determine whether a frequent pattern X is a local max-pattern?* We have the following lemma, while the proof is skipped due to lack of space.

Lemma 4.1 *Let X be a frequent pattern and $i_X = \max\{i \mid sup(X) \geq min\_sup_i\}$. Then, X is a max-pattern w.r.t. $min\_sup_{i_X}$ if and only if X is not a sub-pattern of any max-pattern w.r.t. $min\_sup_{i_X}$ and $sup_{TDB_X}(x) < min\_sup_{i_X}$ for each item x in TDB_X.*

In Step 1.b of Example 4, pattern ab is determined as a max-pattern w.r.t. support threshold 4 according to Lemma 4.1.

Second, *can we prune some unpromising patterns as early as possible?* We have the following lemma.

Lemma 4.2 *Let X be a frequent pattern and $F\text{-}list_X = y_1 - \ldots - y_m$ be the F-list of local frequent items in TDB_X. For an item y_i in $F\text{-}list_X$, if there exists a max-pattern Z and i ($1 \leq i \leq n\_level$) such that $(X \cup y_i \cdots y_m) \subseteq Z$ and*

$$min\_sup_i \leq sup(Z) \leq sup_{TDB_X}(y_i) < min\_sup_{i+1}$$

then for $Y \subseteq y_i \cdots y_m$, $X \cup Y$ *cannot be a max-pattern, and thus* $(X \cup y_i)$-, ..., $(X \cup y_m)$-*projected databases can be pruned.*

Proof. We only need to notice the following two facts: (1) for X and y_i as stated in the lemma, $X \cup y_i \cdots y_m \subseteq Z$ is not a max-pattern, which follows Lemma 4.1, and (2) from X and $y_i \cdots y_m$, we cannot derive any max-pattern which is a super-pattern of Z, since $X \cup y_i \cdots y_m \subseteq Z$. Thus, we have the lemma. ∎

In Step 2 of Example 4, we do not need to form and mine bc-projected database since (1) the frequent items in b-projected database are c and d with support less than 4; and (2) bcd is not a max-pattern w.r.t. support threshold 1. Thus, Lemma 4.2 is applied here.

Based on the above analysis, we summarize the algorithm for constructing an M-base as follows.

Algorithm 2 *(CFP-M: a method for mining max-patterns at various layers)*

Input: transaction database TDB, support threshold min_sup, and error bound $k\%$;

Output: an M-base $\mathcal{B}$ w.r.t. ζ;

Method: Let I be the set of all items; call $mine(TDB, \emptyset, I)$.

Function $mine(DB_X, X, I_X)$

// DB_X: a projected database, X: a frequent pattern, I_X: a set of items to be processed

1. scan DB_X once to find all frequent items within I_X;

2. let F_e be the set of items appearing in every transaction in DB_X, i.e., $F_e = \{x \mid x \in I_X, sup(x) = |DB_X|\}$; let $F_r = F_X - F_e$;

3. let $i = \max\{j \mid |DB_X| \geq min\_sup_j\}$;
   if $min\_sup_i > sup(y)$ for each item $y \in F_r$, and $X \cup F_e$ is not contained in any max-pattern w.r.t. support threshold min_sup_i, then output $X \cup F_e$;
   // $X \cup F_e$ is a max-pattern w.r.t. min_sup_i. This step is based on Lemma 4.1.

4. let F-$list_X$ be the list of items in F_r in support descending order;
   for each item $x \in F$-$list_X$ (processed in the order) do

   (a) if the pruning criteria of Lemma 4.2 is satisfied for X, x (as y_i), and F_r (as F-$list_X$), then return;

   (b) otherwise, let $DB_{Xx} \subset DB$ be the subset of transactions containing x;
   let $I_{Xx} \subset F_r$ be the set of frequent items after x in F_X;
   call $mine(DB_{Xx}, F_e \cup \{x\}, I_{Xx})$;

5. return;

Analysis. The correctness of the algorithm follows the lemmas having shown before. In this algorithm, we do not check every frequent pattern. Instead, we only check frequent patterns without a proper super-pattern having exact same support count. Furthermore, by using Lemma 4.2, we prune patterns approximately contained by other max-patterns. ∎

The implementation of Algorithm 2 involves projected databases and containment tests of frequent patterns. Accordingly, we propose the following two implementation optimizations.

First, we use FP-tree [8] to compress database and projected databases. An FP-tree is a prefix tree storing transactions. Only frequent items in transactions are stored. From FP-trees, projected databases can be derived efficiently.

Second, one critical implementation issue of Algorithm 2 is that we need to identify max-patterns containing a given pattern and staying in the same support range. In our implementation, we index max-patterns of the condensed FP-base by support level i (i.e., the pattern is w.r.t. min_sup_i) and length. Moreover, to facilitate the search, we organize all max-patterns using a prefix tree, while all nodes with same item label are linked together.

5 Empirical Evaluation

To evaluate the effectiveness and efficiency of condensed FP-bases, we conducted a comprehensive set of experiments. In this section, we report a summary of our results. All experiments are conducted on a PC with Pentium III-750 CPU and 188Mb main memory. All the programs are coded using Microsoft Visual C++6.0. We use both synthetic datasets and real datasets in the experiments. The results are consistent. Due to lack of space, we only report results on three datasets as follows.

To report results on effectiveness and efficiency of FP-bases, we use two dense datasets, *Mushroom* and *Connect-4*, from the UC-Irvine Machine Learning Database Repository. A dataset is dense if it contains many long patterns even though the support threshold is relatively high. The *Mushroom* dataset contains 8124 transactions, while the average length of transaction is 23. The *Connect-4* dataset has 67557 transactions and each transaction has 43 items. Both of them are typical dense datasets. Mining frequent patterns from dense databases is very challenging.

To test the scalability of FP-bases, we also use a synthetic dataset $T10I4D100 - 1000k$. This dataset is generated using the well-known IBM synthetic data generator [2]. It is a sparse dataset simulating the market basket data. The number of transactions in this dataset is up to 1 million.

In our experiments, we compare the following three algorithms for mining condensed FP-bases.

CFP-D: the level-by-level method for constructing condensed FP-base $\mathcal{B}_d$, i.e., Algorithm 1.

CFP-CLOSET: we adapt the CLOSET algorithm [14] to *CFP-CLOSET* for mining condensed FP-base $\mathcal{B}_m$ as follows. CFP-CLOSET finds frequent closed patterns and checks whether a frequent closed pattern is in $\mathcal{B}_m$ according to Lemma 4.1. It outputs only frequent closed patterns.

CFP-M: it is Algorithm 2, which finds condensed FP-base $\mathcal{B}_m$ with all pruning and optimization.

Effect of Compression

The compression effects of condensed FP-bases can be measured by compression ratio defined in Equation 1. Please note that the smaller the compression ratio, the better the compression effect.

First, we fix the support threshold and test the compression ratio with respect to various error bounds. The results on datasets *Mushroom* and *Connect-4* are shown in Figure 2 and Figure 3, respectively.

Here, the error bound is set as a percentage of the total number of transactions in the dataset. If there are 1000 transactions in the dataset, then an error bound of 0.1% means that the absolute error bound is 1.

It is clearly shown that condensed FP-base B_m can achieve much better compression ratio than B_d. For example, in dataset *Mushroom*, when the support threshold is set to 14%, there are in total $103,845$ frequent patterns, and $2,591$ frequent closed patterns. As shown in Figure 2, B_m is much smaller than B_d. For both condensed FP-bases, the larger the error bound, the better the compression ratio.

Note when error bound is 0%, B_m is exactly the set of frequent closed patterns. As can be seen, frequent closed itemsets can achieve a good compression ratio. Condensed FP-base B_m can carry the benefit and take the advantage of error bound to do an even better compression.

Since condensed FP-base B_m performs better than B_d, we now focus on the compression effect of B_m with respect to support threshold. The results are shown in Figure 4 and 5, respectively.

To help verify the compression effect, we also plot the compression ratio of condensed FP-base using frequent closed patterns. A condensed FP-base using frequent closed patterns is with an error bound 0. As clearly shown in the two figures, the larger the error bound, the better the compression. The results also confirm that, even with some small error bound, condensed FP-base B_m can be much smaller than the condensed FP-base of frequent closed patterns.

The compression ratio also is sensitive to the distribution of frequent patterns with respect to a specific support threshold. Fortunately, the general trend is that the lower the support threshold, the better the compression. When the support threshold is low, there are many frequent patterns with similar support counts. Thus, one pattern in a condensed FP-base may be a "representative" of many patterns.

Similar trends can be observed for the compression effect of B_d, but the compression ratio of B_d is larger than that of B_m in the same setting, i.e., the compression power of B_d is weaker.

Efficiency of computing condensed FP-bases

We compare the runtime of *CFP-D*, *CFP-CLOSET* and *CFP-M* with respect to various error bounds in Figure 6. The support threshold is set to 93%. From the figure, we can see that the trends are as follows. The runtime of both *CFP-D* and *CFP-CLOSET* are insensitive to the error bound. The two methods find the complete set of frequent patterns and frequent closed patterns, respectively, which are their dominant costs. We note that the cost of computing $X.ub$ for pattern X in *CFP-D* and that of the super-pattern checking in *CFP-CLOSET* are very minor comparing to the expensive pattern mining in these two algorithms.

CFP-D fully utilize the error bound to prune the search space. The larger the bound, the faster the execution. Thus, it is faster than the other two algorithms when the error

bound is not very small.

We observe a similar trend on dataset *Mushroom*. Limited by space, we omit the details here. Moreover, since *CFP-D* is dramatically slower than *CFP-CLOSET* and *CFP-M*, in the remainder of this subsection, our discussion focuses on *CFP-CLOSET* and *CFP-M*.

In Figure 7, we compare the runtime of *CFP-CLOSET* and *CFP-M* with respect to support threshold. The error bound is set to 0.1% of the total number of transactions in the dataset. When the support threshold is high, the runtime of both methods are close. However, when the support threshold is low, the runtime of *CFP-CLOSET* increases dramatically, since it has to mine and check the complete set of frequent closed patterns. The runtime of *CFP-M* increases moderately even when the support threshold is low, since the pruning techniques help confine the search in a small subset of frequent closed patterns.

Again, the similar trends are observed in experiments on other datasets. We omit the details here.

Scaling-up Test

We also test the scalability of condensed FP-bases as well as related algorithms.

First, we test the scalability of compression ratio of condensed FP-bases. (If the curve is flatter, we say that the curve is more scalable, since the compression ratio is not sensible to the database size.) In Figure 8, we show the results on dataset *Connect-4*. We fix the support threshold as 90% of the number of transactions in the tests, and vary the number of transactions from 10% to 100% of that in the original dataset. In the figure, we compare the compression ratio of an FP-base using frequent closed patterns and B_m. Interestingly, as the number of transactions increases, the compression ratio also increases. The reason is that, when there are more transactions, there are more patterns with various support. Thus, the compression effect is not as good as that in the databases with small numbers of transactions. Fortunately, both the number of frequent closed patterns and that of patterns in B_m do not increase dramatically. Moreover, B_m is more scalable, since its compression ratio increases in a more moderate way.

Second, we use the synthetic dataset $T10I4D100 - 1000k$ to show the scalability of Algorithm *CFP-M*. To make a comparison to the traditional frequent pattern mining, we include the runtime of CLOSET in the figure. CLOSET computes the set of frequent closed patterns. The results are shown in Figure 9. In this test, the error bound for *CFP-M* is set to 0.1%. From the figure, we can see that both methods are scalable with respect to the number of transactions in the datasets. Their runtime are also close. CLOSET is faster when the database is large, since it does not need to check against the error bound. *CFP-M* has a scalability comparable to CLOSET and, at the same time, achieves non-trivial compression.

In summary, from the experimental results, we can draw the following conclusions. First, condensed FP-bases can achieve non-trivial compression for frequent patterns. B_m often performs considerably better than B_d, and thus is more preferable. Second, the larger the error bound, the more we compress. Error bound can help to make the condensed FP-bases more compact. Third, *CFP-M* is an effi-

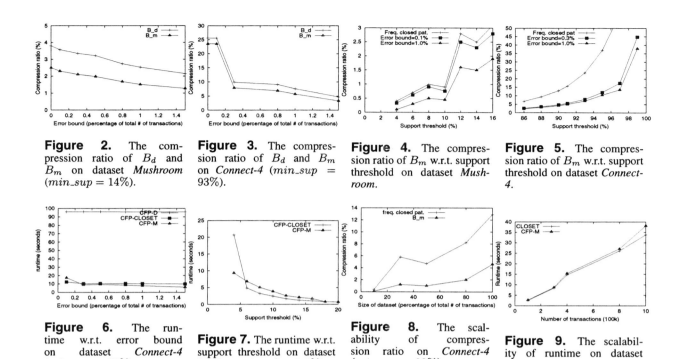

Figure 2. The compression ratio of B_d and B_m on dataset *Mushroom* ($min\_sup = 14\%$).

Figure 3. The compression ratio of B_d and B_m on *Connect-4* ($min\_sup = 93\%$).

Figure 4. The compression ratio of B_m w.r.t. support threshold on dataset *Mushroom*.

Figure 5. The compression ratio of B_m w.r.t. support threshold on dataset *Connect-4*.

Figure 6. The runtime w.r.t. error bound on dataset *Connect-4* ($min\_sup = 93\%$).

Figure 7. The runtime w.r.t. support threshold on dataset *Mushroom* ($err\_b = 0.1\%$).

Figure 8. The scalability of compression ratio on *Connect-4* ($min\_sup = 90\%$).

Figure 9. The scalability of runtime on dataset $T10I4D100 - 1000k$.

cient and scalable algorithm for computing condensed FP-base B_m. It is comparable to CLOSET in terms of runtime and scalability, and B_m achieves better compression effect than the set of all frequent closed patterns. The optimization and pruning techniques help make *CFP-M* efficient and scalable. Overall, B_m and *CFP-M* are the clear winners for frequent pattern base compression and corresponding computation.

6 Conclusions

In this paper, we introduced and considered the problem of mining a condensed frequent pattern base. The notion of condensed FP-base is introduced to significantly reduce the set of patterns that need to be mined, stored, and analyzed, while providing guaranteed error bound for frequencies of patterns not in the bases. We considered two types of condensed FP-bases: the downward condensed FP-base B_d and the max-pattern based condensed FP-base B_m. Interesting algorithms and several novel optimization techniques are developed to mine condensed FP-bases. Experimental results show that we can achieve substantial compression ratio of condensation using the condensed FP-bases, and our algorithms are efficient and scalable. We also discussed some interesting extensions of our methods. As future work, it would be interesting to explore other effective condensed FP-bases and efficient mining methods.

Acknowledgements. The work was supported in part by U.S. NSF IIS-02-09199, Microsoft Research, University of Illinois, and NSERC and NCE/IRIS of Canada. The authors would like to thank the anonymous reviewers' comments which help improve the quality of the paper.

References

[1] R.C. Agarwal, C.C. Aggarwal, V. V. V. Prasad. Depth first generation of long patterns. In *KDD'00*.

[2] R. Agrawal and R. Srikant. Fast algorithms for mining association rules. In *VLDB'94*.

[3] R. J. Bayardo. Efficiently mining long patterns from databases. In *SIGMOD'98*.

[4] J.-F. Boulicaut, A. Bykowski, C. Rigotti. Approximation of frequency queris by means of free-sets. In *PKDD'00*.

[5] D. Burdick, M. Calimlim, J. Gehrke. Mafia: A maximal frequent itemset algorithm for transactional databases. In *ICDE'01*.

[6] G. Dong and J. Li. Efficient mining of emerging patterns: Discovering trends and differences. In *Proc. KDD'99*.

[7] K. Gouda and M.J. Zaki. Efficiently mining maximal frequent itemsets. In *ICDM'01*.

[8] J. Han, J. Pei, and Y. Yin. Mining frequent patterns without candidate generation. In *SIGMOD'00*.

[9] L. V. S. Lakshmanan, R. Ng, J. Han, and A. Pang. Optimization of constrained frequent set queries with 2-variable constraints. In *SIGMOD'99*.

[10] H. Mannila and H. Toivonen. Multiple uses of frequent sets and condensed representations. In *KDD'96*.

[11] R. Ng, L. V. S. Lakshmanan, J. Han, A. Pang. Exploratory mining and pruning optimizations of constrained associations rules. In *SIGMOD'98*.

[12] N. Pasquier, Y. Bastide, R. Taouil, L. Lakhal. Discovering frequent closed itemsets for association rules. In *ICDT'99*.

[13] J. Pei, J. Han, L. V. S. Lakshmanan. Mining frequent itemsets with convertible constraints. In *ICDE'01*.

[14] J. Pei, J. Han, R. Mao. CLOSET: An efficient algorithm for mining frequent closed itemsets. In *DMKD'00*.

[15] M. Zaki. Generating non-redundant association rules. In *KDD'00*.

Automatic Web Page Classification in a Dynamic and Hierarchical Way

XIAOGANG PENG   &   BEN CHOI
Computer Science, College of Engineering and Science
Louisiana Tech University, Ruston, LA 71272, USA
pro@BenChoi.org

Abstract

Automatic classification of web pages is an effective way to deal with the difficulty of retrieving information from the Internet. Although there are many automatic classification algorithms and systems that have been proposed, most of them ignore the conflict between the fixed number of categories and the growing number of web pages going into the system. They also require searching through all existing categories to make any classification. We propose a dynamic and hierarchical classification system that is capable of adding new categories as required, organizing the web pages into a tree structure, and classifying web pages by searching through only one path of the tree structure. Our test results show that our proposed single-path search technique reduces the search complexity and increases the accuracy by 6% comparing to related algorithms. Our dynamic-category expansion technique also achieves satisfying results on adding new categories into our system as required.

1. Introduction

The World Wide Web is growing at a great speed but the documents in the Web do not form a logical organization and inevitably making the manipulation and retrieval difficult. The need for mechanisms to assist in locating relevant information becomes more and more urgent. One of the solutions to assist in retrieving documents on the Web is provided by classified directories [5]. However, current systems, such as Yahoo [30] still require human labor in doing the classification. Whether manual classification is able to keep up with the growth of the Web remains a question. First, manual classification is slow and costly since it relies on skilled manpower. Second, the consistency of categorization is hard to maintain since different human experiences are involved. Finally, the task of defining the categories is difficult and subjective since new categories emerge continuously from many domains. Considering all these problems, the need of automatic classification becomes more and more important.

In this paper we present an automatic web page classification algorithm. The algorithm, unlike others, stresses the dynamic growing issue. It considers the hierarchical structure information for improving the classification accuracy. The core of the algorithm is a hierarchical classification technique that assigns a web page to a category. The number of web pages on the Web increases continuously in great speed and thus it is impossible for a fixed category set to provide accurate classification. To address this problem, we propose and implement a dynamic expanding technique.

1.1 Related Research

This paper relates to text learning and document classification. Text learning is a machine learning method on textual data that combines information retrieval techniques and is used as a tool to extract the content of textual data. A simple, yet limited, document representation (DR) is the "bag-of-words" text DR [12] [14]. Many experiments have been done to improve the performance of the DR. For example, Mladenic [18] extends the "bag-of-words" to the "bag-of-phrases" representation. Chan [4] also suggested that using phases is a better choice than using single words. The goal of using phrases as features is to attempt to preserve the information left out by the "bag of words" methods. A document representation called "feature vector representation" uses a feature vector to capture the characteristics of the document by an "N-gram" feature

This research was supported in part by Center for Entrepreneurship and Information Technology (CEnIT), Louisiana Tech University, Grant iCSe 200123.

selection. An N-gram feature could be a word or a sequence of N words. A vector consists of a feature along with the occurrences of that feature within the document. Experiments show that N ranging from two to three is sufficient in most classification systems.

In information retrieval, TFIDF (Term Frequency–Inverse Document Frequency) classification algorithm is well studied [25]. Based on the document vector model, the distance between vectors is calculated by the cosine of the angle between them for the purpose of classification. Joachims [11] analyzed the TFIDF classifier in a probabilistic way based on the implicit assumption that the TFIDF classifier is as explicit as the Naïve Bayes classifier. By combining the probabilistic technique from statistic pattern recognition into the simple TFIDF classifier, Joachims proposed the PrTFIDF classifier with the formula:

$$P(d \mid c_j) = \sum_{w \in (d \cap c_j)} \frac{P(w \mid c_j) * P(c_j)}{\sum_{c \in C} P(w \mid c) * P(c)} * P(w \mid d)$$

(1.1).

Where c and c_j are categories taken from a category set C, $P(d|c_j)$ is the probability for a document d given a category c_j, and $P(w|d)$ is the probability of a feature w given the document d.

The PrTFIDF classifier optimizes the parameter selection in TFIDF and reduces the error rate in five out of six reported experiments by 40%. Other more sophisticated classification algorithms and models were proposed including: multivariate regression models [8][26], nearest neighbor classifiers [31], Bayesian classifiers [15], decision tree [15], Support Vector Machines [7][10], voted classification [28]. Tree structures appear with all of these systems. Some proposed systems focus on classification algorithms to improve the accuracy of assigning testing documents to related catalogs [11], while others go even further by taking the classifier structure into account [12].

1.1 Organization

This paper is organized into the following sections: Section 2 describes our hierarchical classification module. Section 3 describes our dynamic expansion module. In Section 4 we use Yahoo structure as a test base and conduct several experiments to evaluate our system. Finally, in Section 5 we draw conclusions and provide future research.

2. Our Proposed Hierarchical Classification

In this section, we propose a new classification algorithm on a hierarchical structure. We first provide an overview of the algorithm then detail follows. The algorithm consists following stages: (1) generating category information tree, (2) hierarchical feature propagation, (3) feature selection on category information, and (4) single path traversal.

2.1 Generating Category Information Tree

For a web page classification system, the first step is to define the concept hierarchy using domain knowledge and to collect text data that corresponds to the concept hierarchy. The data is collected into an appropriate format for classification by a text-learning algorithm. The characteristics of each category are represented as a "bag of words" or a feature list based on the "well-grained text-learning method" [24]. Categories are arranged in a hierarchical tree structure. Each tree node represents one category. A child note of any given node represents a subcategory under the given node.

2.2 Hierarchical Feature Propagation

Many existing category structures are unbalanced hierarchical structures. In order to ensure the actual containment relation, the feature information of a category is propagated upward from leaf nodes to the root node of our classification tree. For example, Mladenic [22] studied Yahoo unbalanced structure and proposed an algorithm for featuring propagation. The algorithm takes care of the structure of the tree hierarchy. As proposed in [22], with a tree T rooted at node N having k sub-trees (SubTi $_{(i=1...k)}$), we can calculate the probability for a feature w belonging to a category after propagation as follows:

$$P(w \mid T) =$$
$$\sum_{i=1}^{k} P(w \mid SubTi) * P(SubTi \mid T) + P(w \mid N) * P(N \mid T)$$

(2.1)

Where $P(w|T)$ is the propagated feature probability given tree T and $P(w|N)$ is the probability of the feature w in the node N before the propagation, which can be calculated by dividing the particular term frequency by the total term frequency. $P(SubTi|T)$ and $P(N|T)$ are the weight factor of the sub-tree $SubTi$ given tree T and the probability of current node given tree T.

In the generated classification tree (from stage 1), each node represents a category by a feature list. The propagated feature list is generated by adding the original feature list of the current node and all the propagated feature lists of the sub-categories and by assigning different weights. By propagating in this way, the feature list captures the characteristics of a sub-tree rooted in the current node rather than in an isolated category set.

2.3   Feature Selection on Category Information

It is clear that what really contributed in distinguish between categories are those unique features belonging to the categories. Because of the feature propagation, these unique features will be weighted and propagated upwards and become the features of the parent category. In this case, by tracing these unique features it is easy to locate the correct category. Due to the uniqueness of the features, there is only one path in the tree for reaching the features. This phenomenon provides a foundation for our single path classification algorithm.

Mladenic and Grobelnic [20] conducted similar experiments in feature selection on Yahoo category tree and proposed Odd Ratio measurement, but they used the complement of a note from the entire tree as negative examples to calculate the Odd Ratios.

The goal of our feature selection is to compare the features in a node to its sibling nodes and try to distinguish the unique features. In order to do this, we take advantage of the feature propagation and use the features of the parent node as negative examples to determine a ranking. After propagation, each propagated feature probability is actually the weighted sum of the same feature probability from the sub-trees and the current node itself. We proposed the following formula for determining the uniqueness ranking $R_c(w)$ of a feature w of a category c.

$$R_c\left(w\right) = \frac{P(w \mid c) * P(SubT_C \mid T)}{P(w \mid parent)}$$

(2.3)

Where c is the current node and *parent* is the parent node of c. *P(SubT_c|T)* is the weight factor that assigned to node *c* when it is propagated to the parent. If a feature is unique in one node, it is the only source that can propagate to the parent feature list. In this case, we get the maximum value of the formula, which is 1. The unique features will be considered as key features that differentiate the node from its siblings and forms the basis for our single path traversal algorithm.

2.4   Single Path Traversal

The concept of text classification requires the use of a classifier to assign values to a document and to each catalog. Matching a document feature values to a category feature values, the catalog with a global maximum value is considered the correct place to hold the document. Most automatic classification researches concentrated on the global search algorithm. They treat all categories in a flat structure when trying to find the maximum. It follows that in order to find the category with the greatest value, it is necessary to compare all the categories.

In the tree structure that we have configured, we claim that traveling one path is sufficient to achieve this goal. If there are N categories in the tree, the complexity of searching all categories is θ(N), but by our single path algorithm it is merely θ(log (N)).

The idea of the single path traversal is to eliminate the impact of other branch in the tree. After feature propagation, the propagated feature list of the parent node is a scaled summation of the propagated feature lists of its children. Thus, by checking the parent node we can know the information of its descendents. In our tree structure, all the features are propagated upwards with the ranking function of formula 2.3, so each category has unique features of its own to differentiate from its siblings. These two steps make the single path traversal possible.

The first step of the single path traversal is to discriminate sibling nodes in each level and find a correct path for the incoming web page. In order to determine the discriminating probability for each node, we only consider the nodes at each level and apply the PrTFIDF formula 1.1 on the features with a ranking of 1, which indicate a unique feature. At each level, we chose the node with the maximum discriminating probability as the starting point for the next iteration. Recursively applying this rule creates a path from the root of the tree to one of the leaf nodes.

Then following this path we apply the PrTFIDF classifier again using all the features of the nodes belonging to the path, to get the actual probability for the page with categories within this path. By picking the node along the classification path with maximum actual probability value, we determine the candidate category for the page.

3.   Dynamic Expansion and Updating

In this section, we describe our proposed new dynamic tree expansion algorithm. As more and more documents being put into a catalog set, the diversities of the documents make the existing catalogs unable to guarantee classification accuracies. The problem of how to dynamically generate more sub-catalogs for the existing catalog set becomes evident. The highlight of our approach is as follow; details are provided in following subsections. Based on statistical results, we determine a set of criteria and check whether the criteria have been met for putting a page under the current category. If the criteria have not been met, we will create a new node for the page. As the results, the tree will be expanded by adding a new category. An updating algorithm is also introduced to incorporate the expansion information into the existing catalog set.

3.1 Dynamic Expansion

As the number of pages that need to be classified grows larger and because of their diversity, the original number of categories does not always fit the true content of the incoming pages. It is necessary for expending the category tree to accommodate all the pages in order to yield accurate results. The criteria for creating new categories must be established. There are two types of expansion, deeper and wider, and two thresholds will be used to determine the criteria.

The two thresholds B and D are obtained in the following ways. We take a set of sample pages from a category and calculate the probability of these pages relating to its category. We denote the resulting values for each category as S_i for i from 1 to the number of all categories n. Then, we compute the normal distribution of all sample S_i for i = 1 to n, and obtain the mean μ and the standard deviation d. We set B = μ - d and D = 2d.

We define the relation between a document and the category it should be placed as the "belongs to" relation. It is a basic assumption that the probability of a page given a category having the "belongs to" relation will have a maximum value. In expansion, we set a lower bound for this relation, threshold B will be used to ensure the maximum characteristic of the relation.

A deeper expansion happens when the maximum actual probability value (obtained from single-path search described in the last subsection) is smaller than threshold B. That is although the value is the maximum found, its corresponding category is not considered to be sufficiently suitable for the new page. A new sub-category under the category is then created to hold the new page.

A wider expansion occurs in the following situation: the probability of the page comparing to that the candidate category (the one with the maximum actual

probability value) is much bigger than the probability of the page and that the candidate's children categories. The difference of probability represents the distinction between the page and the candidate's children nodes. Ignoring this distinction will cause the inconsistency of the "belongs to" relation between parent and children. When updating the category information after a page is put into a category, those features, which contribute to the difference, will also be incorporated into the category. This makes the relation between the category and the existing children more and more distinct. By creating the new category, we put the distinction to the siblings other than making the relation between parent and children far apart. Thus, the newly added features will only heavily affect the new created category. When propagating the new features to the candidate category, the weight factor is used to reduce the effect of the new feature. This reduces the inconsistent effect.

Based on these two cases, the threshold B ("belongs to" threshold) and the threshold D (difference threshold) are used as criteria to determine when expansion is needed. For deeper expansion, the probability for the new page (document d) given the candidate node is less than B, that is P(d|c)< B. In this case, we will create a new category. For wider expansion, the candidate note is not a leaf node of the tree. We need to check the probability of the page given each sub-categories of the candidate category P(d|Sub$_i$). If the difference of P(d|c) and the maximum number of the P(d|Sub$_i$) is out of the range of threshold D, that is P(d|c) - Max(P(d|Sub$_i$)) > D, then the new page is considered to be substantially different from any of its sub-categories. In this case, we will create a new category.

3.2 Updating Category Information

When a page is assigned to a category, whether a page is just created or an existing one, the feature vector of the page will be contributed to the category information. It is necessary to update the category information feature list to maintain the concordance and the hierarchical structure and expansion of the vocabulary will inevitably change the characteristic of some of the categories.

After the page has been put into a category, the page is considered to be one part of the category, so it will contribute its own characteristics to the category. Both the page and category information are represented as feature vectors. Merging the page vectors into the category vectors is a solution for updating the category information. Since the page features are selected by a "well-grained text-learning method" [24] with those low frequency patterns removed, we assume that the extracted

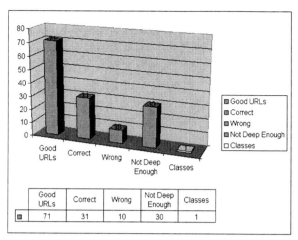

	Good URLs	Correct	Wrong	Not Deep Enough	Classes
▣	71	31	10	30	1

Figure 4.1 Results for accuracy of deeper expansion

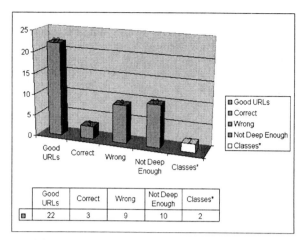

	Good URLs	Correct	Wrong	Not Deep Enough	Classes*
▣	22	3	9	10	2

Figure 4.2 Experiment results of wider expansion

features are considered to be relevant to represent the page. We use the following formula for updating:

$$P'(w \mid N) = \frac{|V| * P(w \mid N) + |Vpage| * P(w \mid Page)}{|V| + |Vpage|}$$

(3.1)

Where |V| represents the size of the category vector and the |Vpage| is the page vector size.

After merging page vectors, the category information is changed, so the ranking and propagated feature probability should be recalculated. Since those changes happen just along the classification path, the updating takes place only along the single path.

4. Experiments and Results

We design experiments to test two aspects of our system: accuracy in dynamic expansion and performances of the single path traversal. The root of our experiment is set to Yahoo /Science/Engineering/, one of the sub-categories of Yahoo's classification tree. We also chose the categories that are strictly following the levels of this root category; that is, we eliminated those categories that either go to another root category or do not follow the level structure. As we have noticed, many of the outgoing URLs in Yahoo are not accessible. We chose the Science/Engineering as the root because it is newly generated and covers 4068 outgoing URLs as advertised. Our expectation is that it will somewhat reduce the number of outdated outgoing URLs and provide enough testing examples for our system.

4.1 Machine Learning Setting

Considering processing time for testing purposes, we direct our program in getting the category information of three levels in the Yahoo "Science/Engineering" sub-tree. Labrou and Finin [13] compared several different ways in describing the category information and the web page information. By their experiments, they pointed out that, the best way of describing category was entry summaries and entry titles; correspondingly the best choice of web page description (called entry in their paper) was the entry summaries. Because of this, when generating the category information, we use summaries that are generated by man power and already there in Yahoo website, instead of using the actually website contents to generate the category information tree.

The testing examples of our system are actual website contents whose URLs are taken from three levels of the Yahoo sub-tree rooted in "Science/ Engineering." Some non-text format paged associated with the URLs cannot yet be classified, for example, jpeg, swf, and gif files. We only use the URLs whose pages having more than 70 features after our well grain 3-gram feature extraction, and these URLs are called "good" URLs.

The two global variables (thresholds) are generated at the machine-learning step using the statistic of the page-category probability. All the categories at the second and the third levels of "Science/ Engineering", except the "Science/ Engineering/organizations" category, are defined as existing categories. One third of the URLs that belong to those categories are taken to calculate the two thresholds based on the ways that we have described in section 3.1.

Table 4.1 Results of comparing two algorithms

Same classification results		
Correct results	Wrong results	
333	6	
Different classification results		
Correct results by Single path algorithm	Correct results by thorough search algorithm	Wrong results by both algorithm
58	30	37

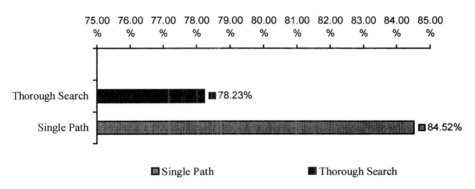

Figure 4.3 Correct rates of both algorithms

4.2 Expansion Tests

Our expansion experiments are designed to test two kinds of accuracies: deeper test – testing the accuracy for deeper expansions, (see results in Figure 4.1), and wider test – testing the accuracy for wider expansions, (see results in Figure 4.2).

All of the URLs that have the "belong to" relation to the category "Science/Engineering/organization" are considered to be a "new" group and used to test the wider expansion. In this experiment, the number in "correct" column means how many pages are classified to an expanded category that is under the selected "Science/ Engineering/organization". If the page is classified to a category that contains the category where this page comes from, it is called "Not Deep Enough." The column "Classes" keeps the number of the newly expanded category. Since all the URLs are taken from a same category, we are expecting the number to be 1. In deeper test, the testing URLs come from "Science/ Engineering/ Civil _Engineering /Institutes/." Similar for wider test, we

have same settings for the experiment results. Experiment results are provided on figure 4.1 and 4.2.

4.3 Testing our Single Path Algorithm

In order to test the accuracy of single path algorithm, we compare the actual classification results of the single path algorithm to the one that searches all categories. Using 33% of all the web pages in Yahoo "Science/Engineering" tree as testing web pages, we compare the two algorithms by the accuracy and the effectiveness, and the result is shown in Table 4.1 and Figure 4.3.

By the results, we can see that the two algorithms have the same result is more than 73% of all testing cases. Surprisingly, even when we have ignored most of the branches of the tree, the single path classification still has an accuracy of 84.26%, which even outperforms by more than 6% the accuracy that was achieved by the thorough search algorithm. From these results, we can see the advantage of our single-path search algorithms.

5. Conclusion

In this paper, we describe an approach that utilizes class hierarchies for improving text classification. Our single path classification algorithm, in the hierarchical classification module, reduces the computational expense compared to the thorough search algorithm that is used by most of the existing classification algorithms. By distinguishing the siblings, the algorithm recognizes a correct path containing the destination category. The algorithm is successful not only in saving computational resources but even improving the correct hits to a higher percentage. Our experiment also shows that because of the diversity of contents of the pages, the thorough search algorithm sometimes cannot tell the key information from the common information since it treats all the information equally. The single path algorithm avoids this problem by only considering unique features in discriminating siblings. Our experiments support that the single path algorithm is more competent both in time and in accuracy.

The expansion and updating modules emphasize the developing of a dynamic system. The expansion algorithm creates a new category when it detects that the page is not similar enough for the current node or might affect the containment relation between current node and its children. The updating algorithm keeps the tree database in a valid state. With expansion and updating, our database grows more diverse in order to proficiently categorize more incoming web pages.

Finally, since the Internet is growing in great speed but the arrangement of the web pages do not have a logical or semantic organization, to find a structured semantic Internet, we should find a standard organization for all Internet data. Since Internet resources can be considered as different kinds of information units, for grouping proposes, classification is perhaps the most appropriated way to organize them. Our system provides a starting point. Hierarchical structure and dynamic growing mechanism can be considered as bases of a structured Internet. We expect that in the near future, when all Internet resources can be classified, the whole Internet will be converted to a well-structured system based on certain classification standard. To achieve this goal much future research remains to be done.

References

[1]   AltaVista, http://altavista.digital.com

[2]   A. Berker and V. Mittal, "OCELOT: a system for summarizing web pages", In Proceedings of SIGIR, 144-151, 2000

[3]   M. CatePazzani and D. Billsus, "Learning and Revising User Profiles: The Identification of Interesting Web Sites", Machine Learning 27, 313-331, 1997

[4]   Philip K. Chan, "A non-invasive learning approach to building web user profiles", KDD-99 Workshop on Web Usage Analysis and User Profiling, 1999

[5]   Chandra Chekuri, Michael H. Goldwasser, Prabhakar Raghavan and Eli Upfal, "WebSearch Using Automatic Classification", In Proceedings of the Sixth International World Wide Web Conference, 1997

[6]   P. Dominggos and M. Pazzani, "On the optimality of the simple Baysian classifier under zero-one loss ", Machine learning 29, 103-130, 1997

[7]   Susan Dumais, Hao Chen, "Hierarchical Classification of Web Content". Proceedings of SIGIR-00, 23rd ACM International Conference on Research and Development in Information Retrieval, 2000

[8]   N. Fuhr, S. Hartmanna, G. Lustig, M. Schwantner, and K. Tzeras, "A rule-based multi-stage indexing system for large subject fields", Proceedings of RIAO'91, 06-623, 1991

[9]   HotBot, http://www.hotbot.com

[10]   Thorsten Joachims, "Text categorization with support vector machines: Learning with many relevant features", Proc. 10th European Conference on Machine Learning (ECML), Springer Verlag, 1998

[11]   Thorsten Joachims. "A probabilistic analysis of the Rocchio algorithm with TFIDF for text categorization", In International Conference on Machine Learning (ICML), 1997

[12]   D. Koller and M. Sahami, "Hierarchically classifying documents using very few words", Proceedings of the 14th international Conference on Machine Learning ECML98, 1998

[13]   Yannis Labrou and Tim Finin, "Yahoo! as an ontology – using Yahoo! Categories to Describe Document" In CIKM '99. Proceedings of the Eighth International Conference on Knowledge and Information Management, 180-187, ACM, 1999

[14]   K. Lang, "Newsweeder: Learning to filter news", In Proceedings of the 12th International Conference on Machine Learning, 331--339, 1995

[15]   D.D. Lewis, and M. Ringuette, "A comparison of two learning algorithms for text categorization", Third Annual Symposium on Document Analysis and Information Retrieval (SDAIR'94), 81-93, 1994

[16]   Lycos, http://www.lycos.com

[17] Daniel Marcu. "From Discourse Structures to Text Summaries", Proceedings of the ACL/EACL-97 Workshop on Intelligent Scalable Text Summarization, 1997

[18] Dunja Mladenic and Marko Grobelnik, "Word sequences as features in text-learning", In Proceedings of ERK-98, the Seventh Electro-technical and Computer Science Conference, 145--148, 1998

[19] Dunja Mladenic, "Feature subset selection in text-learning", In Proceedings of the 10th European Conference on Machine Learning ECML98, 1998

[20] Dunja Mladenic and Marko Grobelnik, "Feature selection for classification based on text hierarchy", Working Notes of Learning from Text and the Web, Conference on Automated Learning and Discovery, 1998

[21] Dunja Mladenic, "Turning Yahoo! into an Automatic Web-Page Classifier", Proceedings of the 13th European Conference on Artificial Intelligence ECAI'98, 473- 474, 1998

[22] Dunja Mladenic, "Machine Learning on non-homogeneous, distributed text data", PhD thesis, University of Ljubljana, Slovenia, 1998

[23] C. D. Paice, "Constructing Literature Abstracts by Computer: Techniques and Prospects", In Information Processing & Management, 26(1), 171--186, 1990.

[24] Xiaogang Peng, "Automatic Web Page Classification in a Dynamic and Hierarchical Way", MS Thesis, Louisiana Tech University, 2002

[25] G. Salton, and C, Buckley, "Term Weighting Approaches in Automatic Text Retrieval", Technical Report, COR-87-881, Department of Computer Science, Cornell University,November

[26] H. Schutze, D. Hull, and O.J. Pedersen, "A comparison of classifiers and document representations for the routing problem", Proceedings of the 18th Annual International ACM SIGIR Conference on Research and Development in Information Retrieval, 229-237, 1995

[27] C.J. van Rijbbergen, D.J. Harper, and M.F. Porter, "The selection of good search terms", Information Processing & Management, 17, 77-91, 1981

[28] S.M. Weiss, C. Apte, F. Damerau, D.E. Johnson, F.J. Oles, T. Goets, and T. Hampp, "Maximizing text-mining performance", IEEE Intelligent Systems, 14(4), 63--69, 1999

[29] Michael J. Witbrock and Vibhu O. Mittal, "Ultra-Summarization: A Statistical Approach to Generating Highly Condensed Non-Extractive Summaries", 1999

[30] Yahoo! http://www.Yahoo.com

[31] Y. Yang and O.J. Pedersen, "A comparative Study o Feature Selection in Text Categorization", Proc. of the fifth International Conference on Machine Learning ICML97, 412-420, 1997

User-directed Exploration of Mining Space with Multiple Attributes

Chang-Shing Perng   Haixun Wang   Sheng Ma   Joseph L. Hellerstein
{perng,haixun,shengma,hellers}@us.ibm.com
IBM Thomas J. Watson Research Center
Hawthorne, NY 10532

Abstract

There has been a growing interest in mining frequent itemsets in relational data with multiple attributes. A key step in this approach is to select a set of attributes that group data into transactions and a separate set of attributes that labels data into items. Unsupervised and unrestricted mining, however, is stymied by the combinatorial complexity and the quantity of patterns as the number of attributes grows. In this paper, we focus on leveraging the semantics of the underlying data for mining frequent itemsets. For instance, there are usually taxonomies in the data schema and functional dependencies among the attributes. Domain knowledge and user preferences often have the potential to significantly reduce the exponentially growing mining space. These observations motivate the design of a user-directed data mining framework that allows such domain knowledge to guide the mining process and control the mining strategy. We show examples of tremendous reduction in computation by using domain knowledge in mining relational data with multiple attributes.

1 Introduction

Mining for frequent itemsets has been studied extensively because of the potential for actionable insights. Typically, before mining is done, a preprocessing step uses data attributes to group records into transactions and to define the items used in mining. For example in supermarket data, the MarketBasket attribute might be used to group data into transactions and the ProductType attribute (with values such as domestic beer) to specify items. We refer to this as **fixed attribute mining** in that mining does not change which attributes are used to determine transactions and items. Unfortunately, fixed attribute mining imposes severe limitations on the patterns that can be discovered in that the analyst must specify in advance the attributes used to designate items (e.g., Imported/Domestic

and Product Class) and how to group them for the purposes of pattern discovery (e.g., Transaction or CustomerName + TimeOfDay). To this end, a framework for mining multi-attribute data, *FARM*[14], proposes an approach to mining multi-attribute data in which itemizing and grouping attributes are selected in the course of the mining operation itself. While this greatly expands the range of patterns that can be discovered, it also creates another level of combinatorial complexity. This paper proposes a framework for specifying constraints on the itemizing and grouping attributes. Not only does this reduce computational complexity, it can also result in patterns of more interest to the analyst.

We have observed that fixing the attributes used to define transactions and items can severely constrain the patterns that are discovered. To go beyond the limits of fixed attribute mining, **multiple-attribute mining** applies the notion of mining spaces to discover frequent patterns for transactions and items that are defined in terms of data attributes. A **transaction** is a general term for a group of records. This approach does not require pre-specified taxonomies, although it exploits such information if it is available. Further, because of various downward closure properties, multiple-attribute mining is considerably faster than simply employing apriori-like algorithms on each choice of attributes for defining transactions and items.

To illustrate the foregoing and to better motivate the problem we address, consider the domain of event management of complex networks. Events are messages that are generated when special conditions arise. The relationship between events often provides actionable insights into the cause of current network problems as well as advanced warnings of future problem occurrences. Figure 1 illustrates a portion of event data we obtained from a production network at a large financial institution. We initially focus on the attributes Date, Time, Intrvl5 (five minute interval), EventType, Host from which the event originated, and Severity. The column labeled Rec is only present to aid in making references to the data. The full data set evidenced the following patterns:

Rec	Date	Time	AM/PM	Intrvl5	Intrvl30	EventType	Host	Site	Source	Subsource	Severity	Maint
(1)	8/21	2:12:23	AM	2:10	2:00	TcpCls	prtsvr3	haw	infoprint	prtdaemon	harmless	No
(2)	8/21	2:13:41	AM	2:10	2:00	IntrfcDwn	netsvr38	ykt	netagt	cat5-agt	severe	No
(3)	8/21	2:14:11	AM	2:10	2:00	IntrfcDwn	netsvr22	haw	netagt	cdl-agt	severe	No
(4)	8/21	2:14:37	AM	2:10	2:00	IntrfcDwn	netsvr5	haw	netagt	ibm-agt	severe	No
(5)	8/21	2:15:02	AM	2:15	2:00	IntrfcDwn	netsevr24	haw	netagt	ibm-agt	severe	No
(6)	8/21	2:16:09	AM	2:15	2:00	CiscoLnkUp	router16	haw	cisco-agt	cat5-agt	severe	Yes
(7)	8/21	2:38:48	AM	2:35	2:30	NetMgrUp	netview16	ykt	netview	ibm-nev	harmless	No
(8)	8/21	2:48:23	AM	2:45	2:30	RtrLnkUp	router16	haw	cisco-agt	cat5-agt	harmless	No
(9)	8/21	3:13:12	AM	3:10	3:00	IntrfcDwn	netsrv45	ykt	netagt	tvl-agt	severe	No

Figure 1. Distributed System Management Events

1. Host `netsvr38` generated a large number of `IntrfcDwn` events on 8/21 and may indicate a problem.

2. When host `netsvr22` generates an `IntrfcDwn` event, host `router16` generates a `CiscoLnkUp` (failure recovery) event within the same five minute interval. Thus, an `IntrfcDwn` on `netsvr22` may provide a way to anticipate the failure of `router16`.

More detailed discussion about the example can be found in [14].

While *FARM* discovers a more complete set of patterns, it creates challenges as well. First, analysts may be overwhelmed by dealing with the abundance of patterns discovered. Second, even though the *FARM* approach exploits downward closure properties to provide computational efficiencies, the time required for pattern discovery can be substantial. For example, we show later in the paper that mining data with 20 attributes is equivalent to performing $3,485,735,825$ (or $3^{20} - 2^{20}$) rounds of market-basket style mining on the same data set if all different combinations of itemizing and groupings are to be explored. Thus, it is clear that such unsupervised approach is not feasible.

The foregoing motivates us to constrain the selection of grouping and itemizing attributes so as to make *FARM* more computationally efficient and its results more meaningful. To this end, we develop attribute predicates that constrain the ways in which grouping and itemizing occur, and we show how these predicates can be incorporated into *FARM*. Figure 1 provides examples of such predicates, especially if we also consider the attributes AM/PM (twelve-hour period), `Intrvl30` (thirty-minute intervals), `Site` (location of the host), and `Maint`.

1. `Time` is in a twelve hour format. Thus, if the grouping attributes include `Time`, they should also include AM/PM. The same argument applies to `Intrvl5` and `Intrvl30`.

2. The reason for a perceived host failure may be that it is recovering after a normal maintenance operation. In-

deed, in Figure 1 we see that the failure of `router16` at `2:16:09` occurs within the maintenance window for that host. Thus, if `EventType` is an itemizing attribute, we should also include `Maint`.

3. Certain logical dependencies exist in the data that can reduce the attribute combinations. For example, if we use `Intrvl5`, we know `Intrvl30` (i.e., there is a functional dependency). Similarly, if we know the `Host`, then we know the `Site`.

Exploiting these relationships between attributes can result in a substantial reduction in the number of patterns reported. Indeed, in our studies, reductions of several orders of magnitude are achieved.

1.1 Problem Statement and Scope

We have two goals in this study. The first is to design a small and comprehensible set of directives that allow users to specify constraints based on attributes intuitively. The specification language should be expressive enough to incorporate common knowledge without operational instructions. For example, users should be able to indicate relationships (such as functional dependencies) among attributes, in which way should these attributes be used in itemizing or grouping, and whether some attributes should be included in mining at all.

The second goal is to design an inference system that can translate the constraints to operational instructions that guide the frequent itemset mining algorithms to avoid unnecessary computation.

To realize these goals, we organize the search space into novel architecture that is conducive to attribute-based pruning. Our approach is based on the FARM framework [14], where each mining template directly corresponds to a unique attribute mapping, and connects to other mining templates through a rich set of downward closure relationships. It is through these relationships that user-directed pruning of the search space takes place. In this paper, we omit issues such as candidate generation, aggregating functions, and instance counting. Interested readers can find the details in [14].

1.2 Related Work

Agrawal et.al. [2, 3] identified the association rule problem and developed the level-wise search algorithm. Since then, many algorithms have been proposed to make mining more efficient (e.g. [1, 4, 9, 11] and [5] for a review).

Mining data with multiple attributes has been recognized as an important task. Srikant et.al. [16] and Han et.al. [8] consider multi-level association rules based on item taxonomies and hierarchies. More recently, Grahne et.al. [6] proposed the dual mining for mining situations of a frequent pattern. Our previous work [14] developed a framework and algorithm for mining multi-attribute data called FARM that extends a tranditional mining task to a more general setting.

Considerable work has been done in characterizing pattern interestingness and constraints [15, 13, 10] and item constraints [12, 17, 10]. Such interestingness and constraints are defined based on items. A framework has been developed for describing either interestingness or constraints on items (e.g. city A and B can not be in the same pattern. Here, city A and B are two items of attribute city) and for efficient mining by pushing the constraints to the level-wise search in reducing the number of candidates generated at each level. In contrast, this paper discusses how to express knowledge at the attribute level(e.g. attributes {event, type, name} can not used as itemizing attributes at the same time), which is on a higher level than the previous item-based approach. We demonstrate that such knowledge (or constraints) about attributes (or variables) helps us drastically reduce the mining space. Further, we describe a language that can be used to describe common constraints and develop algorithms to construct optimal mining paths.

Our FARM work also relates to attribute-oriented mining [7]. Our focus is on frequent patterns mining and exploring the relationship among mining camps and constraints at the attribute level.

1.3 Paper Organization

We first review the *FARM* framework in Section 2. In Section 3, we describe the Attribute Specification Language (ASL), which enables users to specify attribute-level domain knowledge. The section also shows how the system interprets the specifications in ASL and infer meta-properties from the basic semantic definition of predicates. In Section 4, we demonstrate how to express domain knowledge in ASL and how the inference system can greatly reduce the mining space. Section 5 concludes the paper.

2 The FARM Framework

We use the term **mining camp** to provide the context in which patterns are discovered. The context includes the length of the pattern (as in existing approaches), the grouping attributes, and the itemizing attributes.

Definition 1 *A **mining camp** is a triple (n, G, S) where n is number of records in a pattern, G is a set of grouping attributes, S is a set of itemizing attributes, and $G \bigcap S = \emptyset$, $S \neq \emptyset$.*

Next, we formalize the notion of a pattern. There are several parts to this. First, note that two records occur in the same grouping if their G attributes have the same value. Let $r \in D$. We use the notation $\pi_G(r)$ to indicate the values of r that correspond to the attributes of G.

Definition 2 *Given a mining camp (n, G, S) where $S = \{S_1, \cdots, S_m\}$. A **pattern component** or **item** is a sequence of attribute values $sv = \langle s_1, \cdots, s_m \rangle$ where $s_i \in S_i$ for $1 \leq i \leq m$. We call $p = \{sv_1, \cdots, sv_n\}$ a **pattern** for this mining camp if each sv_i is a pattern component for S.*

An instance of a pattern is a set of records whose values of grouping attributes agree and whose itemizing attributes match those in the pattern.

Definition 3 *Let $p = \{sv_1, \cdots, sv_n\}$ be a pattern in mining camp (n, G, S) and let D be a set of records. An **instance** of pattern p is a set of n records $R = \{r_1, \cdots, r_n\}$ such that $r_i \in D$ and $\pi_S(r_i) = sv_i$ for $1 \leq i \leq n$, and r_i and r_j are G-equivalent for all $r_i, r_j \in R$.*

Note that if G and S are fixed, then we have the traditional fixed attribute data mining problem. Here, downward closure of the pattern length is used to look for those patterns in $(n + 1, G, S)$ for which there is sufficient support in (n, G, S).

FARM defines a rich set of interrelationships among different mining camps. Consider a mining camp (n, G, S), and attribute $A_i \notin S$. Let p be a pattern in (n, G, S). Now consider $(n + 1, G, S \bigcup \{A_i\})$. If p is a sub-pattern of p' in this second mining camp, then every occurrence of p' in this camp is also an occurrence of p in the first camp.

The foregoing suggests that mining camps can be ordered in a way that relates to the downward closure property.

Definition 4 *Given a mining camp $C = (n, G, S)$ and an attribute $A_i \notin G \cup S$ then*

1. *$(n + 1, G, S)$ is the **type-1** successor of C.*

2. *$(n, G \cup \{A_i\}, S)$ is a **type-2** successor of C.*

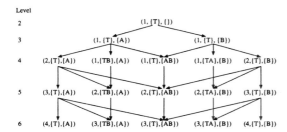

Level

Figure 2. Search Space $MS(1, \{T\}, \{\})$ **for attribute set** $\{T, A, B\}$

3. $(n, G, S \cup \{A_i\})$ *is a **type-3** successor of C.*

We use $succ(C_p, C_s)$ *to denote* C_s *is a successor of* C_p.

Figure 2 depicts the predecessor and successor relationships present among different mining camps. The root precedes all other mining camps. (In this case, it is not a real camp since $S = \emptyset$.)

3 Attribute Specification Language

In this section, we present the Attribute Specification Language (ASL) designed to express domain knowledge for the underlying relational data in mining. The language is small and easy to comprehend, at the same time it allows most types of domain knowledge to be specified easily. It is also a high level specification which hides the inference mechanism behind it. The ASL is essentially a set of predicates that specify the properties of the attributes. An attribute specification is a set of ground atoms (well-formed formulae without connectives).

A mining camp essentially specifies a way to partition all attributes to three sets: G: the grouping attributes, S: the itemizing attributes, and O: the rest. The main focus of the ASL is to specify whether a partition conforms to users' interest hence the corresponding mining camps should be mined.

3.1 Defining Predicates

The building blocks of the ASL are predicates. A definition of a predicate containing the following two parts.

1. Its basic semantics; or *allowed range*.

2. Its meta-properties.

We will discuss the basic semantics in this subsection and meta-properties in Section 3.3.

In ASL, the built-in ASL predicates (predefined popular predicates) and user-defined predicates are defined in exactly the same way. Now we show how to define the semantics of a predicate. First, we define the *signature function*.

Definition 5 *Assume* (G, S, O) *is a partition of all attributes,* A *is an arbitrary attribute set. The signature function* sig *is defined as:*

$$
sig(A) = \begin{cases}
g & \text{if } A \subseteq G \\
s & \text{if } A \subseteq S \\
o & \text{if } A \subseteq O \\
gs & \text{if } A \subseteq G \cup S,\ A \cap G \neq \emptyset \text{ and } A \cap S \neq \emptyset \\
go & \text{if } A \subseteq G \cup O,\ A \cap G \neq \emptyset \text{ and } A \cap O \neq \emptyset \\
so & \text{if } A \subseteq S \cup O,\ A \cap S \neq \emptyset \text{ and } A \cap O \neq \emptyset \\
gso & \text{if } A \cap G \neq \emptyset,\ A \cap S \neq \emptyset \text{ and } A \cap O \neq \emptyset
\end{cases}
$$

When there is no constraint, the signature of an attribute set can be any of the 7 values. A specification is a restriction on the image of the signature function. The predicates of ASL is defined by their allowed range.

Definition 6 *Let* $T = \{g, s, o, gs, go, so, gso\}$. *The allowed range of an n-arity predicate is a proper subset of the product set* T^n.

For example, the allowed range of a unary predicate is a proper subset of T; the allowed range of a binary predicate is a proper subset of $T \times T$.

Built-in uniary predicates includes the following:

- $ignore(A) \equiv sig(A) \in \{o\}$ means attribute set A has very little significance in analysis and should be completely left out. For example, attributes with unique values (*Rec* in Figure 1), and other numerical attributes that are not appropriate for frequent itemset mining can be ignored.

- $together(A) \equiv sig(A) \in \{g, s, o\}$ means no subset of attribute set A can be used independently. In other words, all attributes in A together forms an atomic semantic unit.

- $item\_only(A) \equiv sig(A) \in \{s, o, so\}$ specifies that attributes in A, when used, should only be used as itemizing attributes.

- $group\_only(A) \equiv sig(A) \in \{g, o, go\}$ specifies that attributes in A, when used, should only be used as grouping attributes.

- $always\_group(A) \equiv sig(A) \in \{g\}$ means A should always be included as grouping attributes.

- $always\_item(A) \equiv sig(A) \in \{s\}$ means A should always be included as grouping attributes.

	g	s	o	gs	go	so	gso
ignore			•				
together	•	•	•				
item_only		•	•		•		
group_only	•		•			•	
always_group	•						
always_item		•					

Figure 3. Allowed ranges of built-in unary predicates

Users can choose any of the $2^7 - 1$ (excluding the empty set) subset of T to define new predicates.

Unary predicates can be defined in a truth-table-like manner. Figure 3 shows the graphical definition of ASL built-in unary predicates. The • symbol indicates the allowed values.

An atomic formula $p(A)$ conforms to a partition (G, S, O) is denoted as $(G, S, O) \models p(A)$.

Example 1 Assume $(G, S, O) = (\{a, b\}, \{c, d\}, \{e, f\})$ and $A = \{c, d\}$, then $sig(A) = s$. Looking at the s-column of Figure 3, we conclude that $together(A)$, $item\_only(A)$, and $always\_item(A)$ hold but $ignore(A)$, $group\_only(A)$, and $always\_group(A)$ do not hold.

Binary predicates are defined similarly. The built-in binary predicates includes the following:

1. $decide(A_1, A_2)$ specifies functional dependency: the value of attribute set A_1 uniquely determines the value of attribute set A_2. If $A_1 \subset S$ and $a_i \in S \cap A_2$, then the value of a_i can be inferred by the functional dependency, hence the result of a corresponding mining camp can be derived from the mining camp that has identical configuration except a_i is removed from S. If $A_1 \subseteq G$, then no member of A_2 can be in G because it would be redundant; also, no member of A_2 can be in S either because when $a_i \in S \cap A_2$, the value of a_i is different in each transaction hence the support can not exceed 1.

2. $follow(A_1, A_2)$ specifies those attributes that by themselves are insufficient to form an independent semantic unit, and thus must be combined with other attributes. For example, attribute `City` alone does not provide sufficient information for the location. There are six *Orange* counties/cities and 24 *Springfield* cities in the U.S. To avoid this ambiguity, users can simply specify $follow(\{City\}, \{State\})$. With this, `State` can be used freely but whenever `City` is used, `State` must be used as well.

3. $repel(A_1, A_2)$ means if $A_1 \subset G$, then $A_2 \cap G = \emptyset$ and if $A_1 \subset S$, the $A_2 \cap S = \emptyset$. The typical use of *repel* is when A_2 overshadow A_1. For example, in Figure 1, `Intrvl5` is a finer division of time than `Intrvl30`, hence it is wise to specify $repel(\{Intrvl30\}, \{Intrvl5\})$.

Binary predicates can also be defined by the truth-table-like notation as shown in Figure 4.

3.2 Infering Downward Closure Property

To find and utilize the downward closure property, a.k.a *a priori property*, is a focal topic of frequent itemset mining study. In short, the question is that when a mining camp violates the specified constraints and the system decides to skip it, whether all its successors should be skipped as well.

Definition 7 *Let (G', S', O') be the partition of a mining camp that is a successor of a mining camp with (G, S, O) partition. An atomic specification $p(\vec{A})$ is downward closed if for any partition $(G, S, O) \not\models p(\vec{A}) \implies (G', S', O') \not\models p(\vec{A})$.*

Note the downward closeness is defined on the negative side of specifications. To infer the downward closure property, we have to start from predicting the sigature of an attribute set in successor mining camps.

Definition 8 *Given an attribute set A, the immediate successor function $succ : T \longrightarrow 2^T$ maps the signature of A in a mining camp to all possible signatures of A in the successor mining camps.*

Recall that the only possible change in (G, S, O) division from a mining camp to its successors is to move one element in O to either G or S, so we have the following.

$$
\begin{aligned}
succ(o) &= \{g, s, o, go, so\} \\
succ(g) &= \{g\} \\
succ(s) &= \{s\} \\
succ(go) &= \{g, go, gs, gso\} \\
succ(so) &= \{s, gs, so, gso\} \\
succ(gs) &= \{gs\} \\
succ(gso) &= \{gs, gso\}
\end{aligned}
$$

The graphical representation of the *succ* function is shown in Figure 5. With this, we can define the transitive closure function $succ^*$ of the immediate successor function.

$$
\begin{aligned}
succ^*(o) &= \{o, go, so, g, s, gso, gs\} \\
succ^*(g) &= \{g\} \\
succ^*(s) &= \{s\}
\end{aligned}
$$

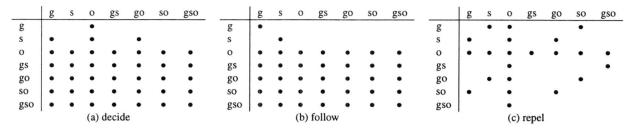

Figure 4. Binary predicates

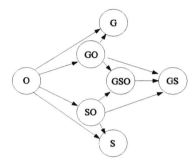

Figure 5. Signature Transition

$$succ^*(go) = \{gso, go, g, gs\}$$
$$succ^*(so) = \{so, gso, s, gs\}$$
$$succ^*(gs) = \{gs\}$$
$$succ^*(gso) = \{gso, gs\}$$

From the above definitions, now we are ready to approach the main theorem of this study. To make it easier to understand, we start from unary predicates.

Lemma 1 *A unary predicate p defined as $p(A) \equiv sig(A) \in D$ is downward closed if for every $d \in \bar{D}$, where $\bar{D}$ is the complement set of D, $succ^*(d) \subseteq \bar{D}$.*

Or more intuitively, a unary predicate is downward closed if and only if once the signature of an attribute set falls out of its allowed range in a partition, it will remain so in the successor partition.

Example 2 *1. item_only is a downward closed property. By definition, $item\_only(A) \equiv sig(A) \in \{s, o, so\} = D$, then $\bar{D} = \{g, gs, go, gso\}$. So*

$$\bigcup \{succ^*(d)|d \in \bar{D}\} = \{g, gs, gso, go\}\} \subseteq \bar{D}.$$

2. always_item is not a downward closed property. By definition, $always\_item(A) \equiv sig(A) \in \{s\} = D$, then $\bar{D} = \{g, o, gs, go, so, gso\}$. So

$$\bigcup \{succ^*(d)|d \in \bar{D}\} = \{g, s, o, gs, go, so, gso\}\} \not\subseteq \bar{D}.$$

The lemma can be extended to predicates of any arity and hence the following main theorem of this work holds.

Theorem 1 *An n-ary predicate p defined as $p(\vec{A}) \equiv (sig(A_1), \cdots, sig(A_n)) \in D \subset T^n$ is downward closed if for every $d = (d_1, \cdots, d_n) \in \bar{D}$ and any $d' \in succ^*(d_1) \times \cdots \times succ^*(d_n)$, $d' \in \bar{D}$.*

3.3 Meta-predicates

For each predicate, beside the basic semantics defined its allowed range, other logic rules can be defined to extend the scope of the predicate. For example, given $decide(A_1, A_2)$, $decide(A_3, A_4)$, and $A_3 \subset A_2$, we would like to deduce $decide(A_1, A_4)$. In this subsection, we show this deduction can partially done automatically, e.g. inferring $decide(A_1, A_3)$, and partially relies on users to define the properties for the predicate.

Assume $\vec{A} = \{A_1, \cdots, A_n\}$ and $1 \leq k \leq n$. Let $sub(\vec{A}, k, A'_k)$ be the result of replacing $\vec{A}$'s k-th element with A'_k. Some common meta-properties include:

1. **transitivity** $TR(p) \equiv p(A_1, A_2) \wedge p(A_2, A_3) \rightarrow p(A1, A3)$.

2. **Symmetry** $SY(p) \equiv p(A_1, A_2) \rightarrow p(A_2, A_1)$.

3. **Ascending Closeness** $AC_k(p) \equiv p(\vec{A}) \rightarrow p(sub(\vec{A}, k, A_k \cup X))$ for any attribute set X.

4. **Descending Closeness** $DC_k(p) \equiv p(\vec{A}) \rightarrow p(sub(\vec{A}, k, A_k \setminus X))$ for any attribute set X.

The system can infer some of the properties. A predicate is symmetric if its truth-table-like representation remains the same under transposition. Ascending and descending closeness can be inferred as well. We illustrate the inference on unary predicates. Similar process can be applied to n-ary predicates.

Figure 6 shows when given the signature of A, what might be the signature of $A \cup \{a_k\}$ and $A \setminus \{a_k\}$. The signature of $A \cup \{a_k\}$ is either the same or another value pointed by an upward link. The signature of $A \setminus \{a_k\}$ is either the

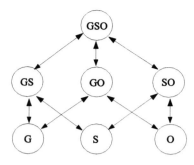

Figure 6. Signature changes in inclusion and exclusion

$ignore(\{Rec\})$
$ignore(\{Time\})$
$together(\{EventType, Maint\})$
$follow(\{Date\}, \{AM/PM\})$
$follow(\{Intrvl5, Intrvl30\}, \{AM/PM\})$
$group\_only(\{Date, Intrvl5, Intrvl30, AM/PM\})$
$item\_only(\{EventType, Source, Subsource, Severity\})$
$decide(\{EventType\}, \{Subsource\})$
$decide(\{Subsource\}, \{Source\})$
$decide(\{EventType\}, \{Severity\})$
$decide(\{Host\}, \{Site\})$
$repel(\{Intrvl30\}, \{Intrvl5\})$

Figure 7. Specification System Management Events

same or another value pointed by an downward link. If the allowed range of a predicate is upward-complete, i.e. any value pointed by a upward link from a value in the allowed range is also in the allowed range, then the predicate has the ascending closeness property. If the allowed range of a predicate is downward-complete, i.e. any value pointed by a downward link from a value in the allowed range is also in the allowed range, then the predicate has the descending closeness property.

However, transitivity can not be inferred automatically. So such properties, e.g. $TR(decide)$, have to be specified while defining the predicate. Meta-properties are translated to first order formulae. Then common inference methods can infer the *semantic closure* of a set of constraints. In the example discussed in the beginning of this subsection, $DC_2(decide)$ can be proven automatically hence $decide(A_1, A_3)$ can be deduced from $decide(A_1, A_2)$. With $TR(decide)$ and $decide(A_3, A_4)$, $decide(A_1, A_4)$ can be proven. We call the set of all constraints deducible from users' specification, such as $decide(A_1, A_4)$ in this case, the semantic closure of users' specification.

With all the definitions and theorems introduced so far, to decide a mining camp is now obvious. *If a mining camp violates any constraint in the semantic closure of users' specification, skip this mining camp. If the violated predicate is downward closed, then skip all its successor as well.*

4 Case Study

In this section, we demonstrate how the problem size of the example in Section 1 can be greatly reduced. The data set in the example contains 13 attributes. If no constraint is applied, there are $1,586,131(= 3^{13} - 2^{13})$ possible mappings. Exhausted mining is obvious not a feasible option. However, manually selecting mappings is not a good option either because it is tedious and prone to miss some inter-

esting mappings. With ASL, domain experts can state the constraints in Figure 7

As stated before, domain experts can specify their knowledge in a casual way without thinking too much about the implication. The inference system will find the semantic closure of the specification as true intention of the domain experts. So many different specifications may have the same intention. For example, $follow(\{Intrvl5, Intrvl30\}, \{AM/PM\})$ can be broken up to two clauses or merge with $follow(\{Date\}, \{AM/PM\})$ and become $follow(\{Date, Intrvl5, Intrvl30\}, \{AM/PM\})$. With $group\_only(\{Date, Intrvl5, Intrvl30, AM/PM\})$ already specified, $repel(\{Intrvl5, Intrvl30\})$ has the same effect as $decide(\{Intrvl5, Intrvl30\})$.

The reduction of mining space is shown in Figure 8. The data set has 13 attributes so levels above 14 all have the same number of mining camps. The table shows the numbers of mining camps for the cases of exhausting all mining camps, ignoring 2 attributes, ignoring 3 attributes, and applying the specification in Figure 7.

With the help of domain knowledge, the maximal number of mining camps of a level is reduced from $527,345$ to 321. The problem becomes solvable and the resulting patterns have better chance to be interpreted and responded to. The inference system can be used alone without actually mining data; it can list all the remaining mining camps in the mining space for user to specify more domain knowledge for further reduction.

5 Conclusion

Advances in association rule mining has come the point to deal with common relational data with multiple attributes. However, the enormity of attribute mappings posts a severe challenge to multi-attribute mining on both the

Level	2	3	4	5	6	7	8	9	10	11	12	13	14
exhaust	12	210	1750	9175	33727	91939	192523	318748	431168	498686	523250	527345	1586131
ignore 2	10	145	985	4135	11947	25177	40417	51892	57002	58025	58025	58025	58025
ignore 3	9	117	705	2595	6501	11793	16365	18660	19171	19171	19171	19171	19171
user-directed	6	32	86	177	269	313	321	321	321	321	321	321	321

Figure 8. Number of Mining Camps of each level

computational complexity and usability of the results. However, minimal domain knowledge of the attributes can provide tremendous reduction on the problem size while not losing any interesting patterns.

We presented a multi-attribute data mining framework with the capability of utilizing domain knowledge about attributes to in association rule discovery. The framework includes two parts. The first part is an attribute specification language, ASL, that allows users to specify what and how attributes should be used. ASL consists a set of predicates with simple and comprehensible semantics. The second part is an inference system that is responsible for determining whether a mapping of attributes to itemizing and grouping attributes may produce any interesting results. We presented a case study on system management event mining. With domain knowledge, we can transform the multi-attribute mining problem from being virtually impossible to solve to a reasonable problem size; and the results are more meaningful.

References

[1] R. Aggarwal, C. Aggarwal, and V. Parsad. Depth first generation of long patterns. In *Int'l Conf. on Knowledge Discovery and Data Mining (SIGKDD)*, 2000.

[2] R. Agrawal, T. Imielinski, and A. Swami. Mining association rules between sets of items in large databases. In *Proc. of Very Large Database (VLDB)*, pages 207–216, 1993.

[3] R. Agrawal and R. Srikant. Fast algorithms for mining association rules. In *Proc. of Very Large Database (VLDB)*, 1994.

[4] R. Bayardo. Efficiently mining long patterns from database. In *Int. Conf. Management of Data (SIGMOD)*, pages 85–93, 1998.

[5] J. Deogun, V. Raghavan, A. Sarkar, and H. Sever. Data mining: Research trends, challenges, and applications, 1997.

[6] G. Grahne, L. Lakshmanan, X. Wang, and M. Xie. On dual mining: From patterns to circumstances, and back. In *Int. Conf. Data Engineering (ICDE)*, pages 195–204, 2001.

[7] J. Han, Y. Cai, and N. Cercone. Knowledge discovery in databases: An attribute-oriented approach. In L.-Y. Yuan, editor, *Proceedings of the 18th International Conference on Very Large Databases*, pages 547–559, San Francisco, U.S.A., 1992. Morgan Kaufmann Publishers.

[8] J. Han and Y. Fu. Discovery of multiple-level association rules from large databases. In *Proc. of Very Large Database (VLDB)*, 1995.

[9] J. Han, J. Pei, and Y. Yin. Mining frequent patterns without candidate generation. In *Int. Conf. Management of Data (SIGMOD)*, 2000.

[10] R. Hilderman and H. Hamilton. Knowledge discovery and interestingness measures: A survey, 1999.

[11] J. Hipp, A. Myka, R. Wirth, and U. Guntzer. A new algorithm for faster mining of generalized association rules. In *Proc. 2nd PKKD*, 1998.

[12] R. Ng, L. Lakshmanan, J. Han, and A. Pang. Exploratory mining and pruning optimizations of constrained associations rules. In *Int. Conf. Management of Data (SIGMOD)*, pages 13–24, 1998.

[13] B. Padmanabhan and A. Tuzhilin. Unexpectedness as a measure of interestingness in knowledge discovery, 1999.

[14] C.-S. Perng, H. Wang, S. Ma, and J. L. Hellerstein. Farm: A framework for exploring mining spaces with multiple attributes. In *IEEE Int. Conf. on Data Mining(ICDM)*, 2001.

[15] A. Silberschatz and A. Tuzhilin. What makes patterns interesting in knowledge discovery systems. *IEEE Trans. On Knowledge And Data Engineering*, 8:970–974, 1996.

[16] R. Srikant and R. Agrawal. Mining generalized association rules. In *Proc. of Very Large Database (VLDB)*, pages 407–419, 1995.

[17] R. Srikant, Q. Vu, and R. Agrawal. Mining association rules with item constraints. In *Int'l Conf. on Knowledge Discovery and Data Mining (SIGKDD)*, pages 67–93, 1997.

Mining Significant Associations in Large Scale Text Corpora

Prabhakar Raghavan
Verity Inc.
pragh@verity.com

Panayiotis Tsaparas*
Department of Computer Science
University of Toronto
tsap@cs.toronto.edu

Abstract

Mining large-scale text corpora is an essential step in extracting the key themes in a corpus. We motivate a quantitative measure for significant associations through the distributions of pairs and triplets of co-occurring words. We consider the algorithmic problem of efficiently enumerating such significant associations and present pruning algorithms for these problems, with theoretical as well as empirical analyses. Our algorithms make use of two novel mining methods: (1) matrix mining, and (2) shortened documents. We present evidence from a diverse set of documents that our measure does in fact elicit interesting co-occurrences.

1 Overview

In this paper we (1) motivate and formulate a fundamental problem in text mining; (2) use empirical results on the statistical distributions of term associations to derive concrete measures of "interesting associations"; (3) develop fast algorithms for mining such text associations using new pruning methods; (4) analyze these algorithms, invoking the distributions we observe empirically; and (5) study the performance of these algorithms experimentally.

Motivation: A major goal of text analysis is to extract, group, and organize the concepts that recur in the corpus. Mining significant associations from the corpus is a key step in this process. In the automatic classification of text documents each document is a vector in a high-dimensional "feature space", with each axis (feature) representing a term in the lexicon. Which terms from the lexicon should be used as features in such classifiers? This "feature selection" problem is the focus of substantial research. The use of significant associations as features can improve the quality of automatic text classification [18]. Clustering significant terms and associations (as opposed to *all* terms) is shown [8, 14] to yield clusters that are purer in the concepts they yield.

---

*This work was conducted while the author was visiting Verity Inc.

Text as a domain: Large-scale text corpora are intrinsically different from structured databases. First, it is known [15, 22] that terms in text have skewed distributions. How can we exploit these distributional phenomena? Second, as shown by our experiments, *co-occurrences* of terms themselves have interesting distributions; how can one exploit these to mine the associations quickly? Third, many statistically significant text associations are intrinsically uninteresting, because they mirror well-known syntactic rules (e.g., the frequent co-occurrence of the words "of" and "the"); one of our contributions is to distill relatively significant associations.

2 Background and contributions

2.1 Related previous work

Database mining: Mining association rules in databases was studied by Agrawal et al. [1, 2]. These papers introduced the support/confidence framework as well as the *a priori* pruning paradigm that is the basis of many subsequent mining algorithms. Since then it has been applied to a number of different settings, such as mining of sequential patterns and events. Brin, Motwani and Silverstein [6] generalize the a priori framework by establishing and exploiting closure properties for the χ^2 statistic. We show in Section 3.2 that the χ^2 test does not work well for our domain. Brin et al. [5] extend the basic association paradigm in two ways: they provide performance improvements based on a new method of enumerating large itemsets and additionally propose the notion of *implication rules* as an alternative to association rules, introducing the notion of *conviction*. Bayardo et al. [4] and Webb [20] propose branch and bound algorithms for searching the space of possible associations. Their algorithms apply pruning rules that do not rely solely on support (as in the case of a priori algorithms). Cohen et al. [7] propose an algorithm for fast mining of associations with high confidence without support pruning. In the case of text data, their algorithm favors pairs of low support. Furthermore, it is not clear how to extend it to associations of more than two terms.

Extending database mining: Ahonen et al. [3] build on the paradigm of *episode mining* (see [16] and references therein) to define a text sequence mining problem. Where we develop a new measure that directly mines semantically useful associations, their approach is to first use a "generic" episode mining algorithm (from [16]) then post-filter to eliminate uninteresting associations. They do not report any performance/scaling figures (their reported experiments are on 14 documents), which is an area we emphasize. Their work is inspired by the similar work of Lent et al. [13]. Feldman *et al.* describe the KDT system [10, 12] and Document Explorer [11]. Their approach, however, requires prior labeling (through some combination of manual and automated methods) using keywords from a given ontology, and cannot directly be used on general text. DuMouchel and Predigibon [9] propose a statistically motivated metric, and apply empirical Bayes methodology for mining associations in text. Their work has similar motivation to ours. The authors do not report on efficiency and scalability issues.

Statistical natural language processing: The problem of finding associations between words (often referred to as *collocations*) has been studied extensively in the field of Statistical Natural Language Processing (SNLP) [17]. We briefly review some of this literature here, but expand in Section 3.1 on why these measures fail to address our needs.

Frequency is often used as a measure of interestingness, together with a part-of-speech filter to discard syntactic collocations like "of the". Another standard practice is to apply some statistical test that, given a pair of words, evaluates the null hypothesis that this pair is generated by picking two words independently at random. The interestingness of the pair is measured by the deviation from the null hypothesis. The t test and the χ^2 test are statistical tests frequently used in SNLP. There is a qualitative difference between collocations and the associations that we are interested in. Collocations include patterns of words that tend to appear together (e.g. phrasal verbs – "make up", or common expressions like "strong tea"), while we are mostly interested in associations that convey some latent concept (e.g. "chapters indigo" – this pertains to the recent acquisition of Chapters, then Canada's largest bookstore, by the Indigo corporation).

2.2 Main contributions and guided tour

1. We develop a notion of semantic as opposed to syntactic text associations, together with a statistical measure that mines such associations (Section 3.3). We point out that simple statistical frequency measures such as the χ^2 test and mutual information (as well as variants) will not suffice (Section 3.2).

2. Our measure for associations lacks the monotonicity and closure properties exploited by prior work in association mining. We therefore require novel pruning

techniques to achieve scalable mining. To this end we propose two new techniques: (i) matrix mining (Section 4.2) and (ii) shortened documents (Section 4.3).

3. We analyze the pruning resulting from these techniques. A novel aspect of this analysis: to our knowledge, it is the first time that the Zipfian distribution of terms and pairs is used in the *analysis* of mining algorithms. We combine these pruning techniques into two algorithms (Section 4 and Theorem 1).

4. We give results of experiments on three test corpora for the pruning achieved in practice. These results suggest that the pruning is more efficient than our (conservative) analytical prediction and that our methods should scale well to larger corpora (Section 4.4).

We report results on three test corpora taken from news agencies: the CBC corpus, the CNN corpus and the Reuters corpus. More statistics on the corpora are given in Section 4.4.

3 Statistical basis for associations

In this section we develop our measure for significant associations. We begin (Section 3.1) by discussing qualitatively the desiderata for significant text associations. Next, we give a detailed study of pair occurrences in our test corpora (Section 3.2). Finally, we bring these ideas together in Section 3.3 to present our new measure for interesting associations.

3.1 Desiderata for significant text associations

We first experimented with naive support measures such as document pair frequency, sentence pair frequency and the product of the individual sentence term frequencies. We omit the detailed results here due to space constraints. As expected, the highest ranking associations are mostly *syntactic* ones, such as (of,the) and (in,the), conveying little information about the dominant concepts. Furthermore, it is clear that the document level is too granular to mine useful associations – two terms could co-occur in many documents for template (rather than semantic) reasons; for example, associations such as (business, weather), and (corporate, entertainment) in the CBC corpus.

We also experimented with well known measures from SNLP such as the χ^2 test and mutual information as well as the *conviction* measure, a variation of the well known confidence measure defined in [6]. We modified the measure slightly so that it is symmetric. Table 1 shows the top associations for the CNN corpus for these measures. The number next to each pair indicates the number of sentences in

rank	χ^2		conviction		mutual information		weighted MI	
1	afghani libyan	:2	afghani libyan	:2	allowances child-care	:1	of the	:40073
2	antillian escudo	:2	antillian escudo	:2	alanis morissette	:1	the to	:41504
3	algerian angolan	:2	algerian angolan	:2	americanas marisa	:1	in the	:34750
4	allowances child-care	:1	allowances child-care	:1	charming long-stem	:1	click here	:13594
5	alanis morissette	:1	alanis morissette	:1	cane stalks	:1	and the	:30397
6	arterial vascular	:2	arterial vascular	:2	hk$116.50 hk$53.50	:1	a the	:32088
7	americanas marisa	:1	americanas marisa	:1	ill.,-based pyrex	:1	a to	:28211
8	balboa rouble	:2	balboa rouble	:2	boston.it grmn	:1	call market	:11061
9	bolivian lesotho	:2	bolivian lesotho	:2	barbed inventive	:1	latest news	:11740
10	birr nicaraguana	:2	birr nicaraguan	:2	160kpns telias	:1	a of	:23362

Table 1. Top associations from the CNN corpus under different measures.

which this pair appears. Although these measures avoid syntactic associations, they emphasize on pairs of words with very low sentence frequency. If two words t and q appear only a few times but they always appear in the same sentence, then the pair $\{t, q\}$ scores highly for all of these measures, since it deviates significantly from the independence assumption. This is especially true for the mutual information measure [17]. We also experimented with a weighted version of the mutual information measure [17], where we weight the mutual information of a pair by the sentence frequency of the pair. However, in this case the weight of the sentence pair frequency dominates the measure. As a result, the highly ranked associations are syntactic ones.

It appears that any statistical test that compares against the independence hypothesis (such as the χ^2 test, the t test, or mutual information) falls prey of the same problem: it favors associations of low support. One might try to address this problem by applying a pruning step before computing the various measures: eliminate all pairs that have sentence pair frequency below a predefined threshold. However, this approach just masks the problem. The support threshold directly determines the pairs that will be ranked higher.

3.2 Statistics of term and pair occurrences

We made three measurements for each of our corpora: the distributions of *corpus term frequencies* (the fraction of all words in the corpus that are term t), *sentence term frequencies* (fraction of sentences containing term t) and *document term frequencies* (fraction of documents containing term t). We also computed the distribution of the *sentence pair frequencies* (fraction of sentences that contain a pair of terms). We observed that the Zipfian distribution essentially holds, not only for corpus frequencies but also for document and sentence frequencies, as well as for sentence pair frequencies. Figure 1 presents the sentence term frequencies and the sentence pair frequencies for the CNN corpus. We use these observations for the analysis of the pruning algorithms in Section 4. The plots for the other test corpora are essentially the same as those for CNN.

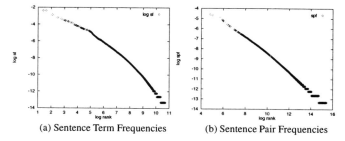

(a) Sentence Term Frequencies   (b) Sentence Pair Frequencies

Figure 1. Statistics for the CNN corpus

3.3 The new measure

Intuitively we seek pairs of terms that co-occur frequently in sentences, while eliminating pairs resulting from very frequent terms. This bears a strong analogy to the concept of weighting term frequencies by *inverse document frequency* (*idf*) in text indexing.

Notation: Given a corpus of documents C, let N_d denote the number of documents in C, let N_s denote the number of sentences in C and let N_t denote the the number of distinct terms in C. For a set of terms $T = \{t_1, t_2, \ldots, t_k\}$, for $k \geq 1$, let $n_d(t_1, t_2 \ldots, t_k)$ denote the number of documents in C that contain all terms in T and let $n_s(t_1, t_2, \ldots, t_k)$ denote the number of sentences in C that contain all terms in T. We define the *document frequency* of T as $df(t_1, t_2, \ldots, t_k) = n_d(t_1, t_2 \ldots, t_k)/N_d$, and the *sentence frequency* of the set T as $sf(t_1, t_2, \ldots, t_k) = n_s(t_1, t_2, \ldots, t_k)/N_s$. If $k = 2$, we will sometimes use *dpf* and *spf* to denote the document and sentence pair frequencies. For a single term t, we define the inverse document frequency of t, $idf(t) = \log(N_d/n_d(t))$ and the inverse sentence frequency $isf(t) = \log(N_s/n_s(t))$. In typical applications the base of the logarithm is immaterial since it is the relative values of the *idf* that matter. The particular formula for *idf* owes its intuitive justification to the underlying Zipf distribution on terms; the reader is referred to [17, 21] for details.

Based on the preceding observations, the following idea

rank	$spf \times idf \times idf$	$spf \times isf \times isf$	$dpf \times idf \times idf$	$\log(spf) \times idf \times idf$
1	deutsche telekom	click here	danmark espaol	conde nast
2	hong kong	of the	espaol svenska	mph trains
3	chevron texaco	the to	danmark svenska	allegheny lukens
4	department justice	in the	espaol travelcenter	allegheny teledyne
5	mci worldcom	and the	danmark travelcenter	newell rubbermaid
6	aol warner	a the	svenska travelcenter	hummer winblad
7	aiff wav	call market	espaol norge	hauspie lernout
8	goldman sachs	latest news	danmark norge	bethlehem lukens
9	lynch merrill	a to	norge svenska	globalstar loral
10	cents share	a of	norge travelcenter	donuts dunkin

Table 2. Top associations for variants of our measure for the CNN corpus.

suggests itself: weight the frequency of a pair by the (product of the) idf's of the constituent terms. The generalization beyond pairs to k-tuples is obvious. We state below the formal definition of our new measure for arbitrary k.

Definition 1 *For terms $t_1, t_2, \ldots, t_k$, the measure for the association $\{t_1, t_2, \ldots, t_k\}$ is*

$$m_k(t_1, t_2, \ldots, t_k) = sf(t_1, t_2, \ldots, t_k) \times \prod_{j=1}^{k} idf(t_j) .$$

Variants of the measure: We experimented with several variants of our measure and settled on using idf rather than isf, and spf rather than dpf. Table 2 gives a brief summary from the CNN corpus to give the reader a qualitative idea. Replacing idf with isf introduces more syntactical associations. This is due to the fact that the sentence frequency of words like "the" and "of" is lower than their document frequency, so the impact of the isf as a dampening factor is reduced. This allows the sentence frequency to take over. A similar phenomenon occurs when we replace spf with dpf. The impact of dpf is too strong, causing uninteresting associations to appear. We also experimented with $\log(spf)$, an idea that we plan to investigate further in the future.

Figure 2 shows two plots of our new measure. The first is a scatter plot of our measure (which weights the spf's by idf's) versus the underlying spf values[1]. The line $y = x$ is shown for reference. We also indicate the horizontal line at threshold 0.002 for our measure; points below this line are the ones that "succeed". Several intuitive phenomena are captured here. (1) Many frequent sentence pairs are attenuated (moved upwards in the plot) under our measure, so they fail to exceed the threshold line. (2) The pairs that do succeed are "middling" under the raw pair frequency. The plot on the right shows the distribution of our measure, in a log-log plot, suggesting that it in itself is roughly Zipfian; this requires further investigation. If this is indeed the case then we can apply the theoretical analysis of Section 4.1 to the case of higher order associations.

---

[1] The axes are scaled and labeled negative logarithmically, so that the largest values are to the bottom left and the smallest to the top and right.

Non-monotonicity: A major obstacle in our new measure: weighting by idf can increase the weight of a pair with low sentence pair frequency. Thus, our new measure does not enjoy the *monotonicity property* of the support measure exploited by the *a priori* algorithms. Let I be some measure of interestingness that assigns a value $I(T)$ to every possible set of of terms T. We say that I is monotone if the following holds: if $T' \subseteq T$, then $I(T') \geq I(T)$. This property allows for pruning, since if for some $T' \subseteq T$, $I(T') \leq \theta$, then $I(T) \leq \theta$. That is, all interesting sets must be the union of interesting subsets. Our measure does not enjoy this property. For some pair of terms $\{t_1, t_2\}$, it may be the case that $m_2(t_1, t_2) > \theta$, while $m_1(t_1) \leq \theta$, or $m_1(t_2) \leq \theta$.

Formal problem statement: Given a corpus and a threshold θ, find (for $k = 2, 3, \ldots$) all k-tuples for which our measure exceeds θ.

4 Fast extraction of associations

We now present two novel techniques for efficiently mining associations deemed significant by our measure: *matrix mining* and *shortened documents*. Following this, we analyze the efficiencies yielded by these techniques and give experiments corroborating the analysis. We first describe how to find all pairs of terms $\{x, y\}$ such that the measure $m(x, y) = spf(x, y) idf(x) idf(y)$ exceeds a prescribed threshold θ. We also show how our techniques generalize for arbitrary k-tuples.

4.1 Pruning

Although our measure is not monotone we can still explore some monotonicity properties to apply pruning. We observe that

$$m(x, y) = spf(x, y) idf(x) idf(y) \leq sf(x) idf(x) idf(y) . \tag{1}$$

Let $q(x) = sf(x) idf(x)$ and $f(y) = idf(y)$. The value of $f(y)$ cannot exceed $\log N_d$. Therefore, $m(x, y) \leq$

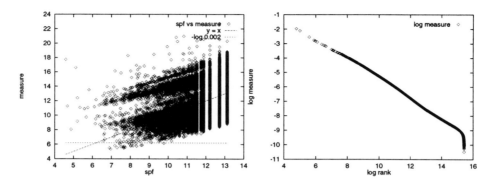

Figure 2. The new measure

$q(x)f(y) \le q(x)\log N_d$. Thus, we can safely eliminate any term x for which $q(x) \le \theta/\log N_d$. We observe experimentally that this results in eliminating a large number of terms that appear in just a few sentences. We will refer to this pruning step as *low end pruning* since it eliminates terms of low frequency.

Equation 1 implies that if $m(x,y) > \theta$, then $q(x)f(y) > \theta$. Therefore, we can safely eliminate all terms y such that $f(y) \le \theta/\max_x q(x)$. We refer to this pruning step as *high end pruning* since it eliminates terms of high frequency. Although this step eliminates only a small number of terms, it eliminates a large portion of the text.

We now invoke additional information from our studies of sentence term frequency distributions in Section 3.2 to estimate the number of terms that survive low end pruning.

Theorem 1 *Low end pruning under a power law distribution for term frequencies eliminates all but $O(\log^2 N_d)$ terms.*

Proof: The *sf* values are distributed as a power law: the ith-largest frequency is proportional to $1/i^\alpha$. If t_i denotes the ith most frequent term, $sf(t_i) = A/i^\alpha$ for a constant A. Since no *idf* value exceeds $\log N_d$, we have $q(t_i) = sf(t_i)idf(t_i) \le A\log N_d/i^\alpha$. If $q(t_i) > \theta/\log N_d$, then $\theta < A\log^2 N_d/i^\alpha$. Therefore, $i < (A/\theta)^{1/\alpha}\log^{2/\alpha} N_d$. Let $c = (A/\theta)^{1/\alpha}$ and $\beta = 2/\alpha$. If $B = c\log^\beta N_d$, then only $O(B)$ terms can generate candidate pairs. Since $\alpha \ge 1$, $O(B) = O(\log^2 N_d)$. ∎

Pruning extends naturally to k-tuples. A k-tuple can be thought as a pair consisting of a single term and a $(k-1)$-tuple. Since $m_k(t_1,\ldots,t_k) \le m_{k-1}(t_1,\ldots,t_{k-1})idf(t_k)$, we can safely prune all $(k-1)$-tuples such that $m_{k-1}(t_1,\ldots,t_{k-1}) \le \theta/\log N_d$. Proceeding recursively we can compute the pruning threshold for i-tuples and apply pruning in a bottom up fashion (terms, pairs, and so on). We define $\theta_i = \theta/\log^{k-i} N_d$ to be the threshold for i-tuples for all $1 \le i \le k$.

4.2 Matrix mining

Given the terms that survive pruning we now want to minimize the number of pairs for which we compute the $spf(x,y)$ value. Let N_t' denote the number of (distinct) terms that survive pruning. The key observation is best visualized in terms of the matrix depicted in Figure 3(left). It has N_t' rows and N_t' columns, one for each term. The columns of the matrix are arranged left-to-right in non-increasing order of the values $q(x)$ and the rows bottom-up in non-increasing order of the values $f(x)$. Let q_i denote the ith largest value of $q(x)$ and f_j denote the jth largest value of $f(x)$. Imagine that matrix cell (i,j) is filled with the product q_if_j (we do not actually *compute* all of these values).

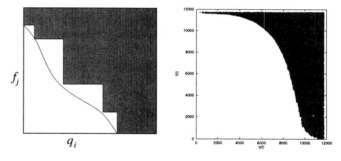

Figure 3. Matrix mining

The next crucial observation: by Equation 1 the pair (i,j) is eliminated from further consideration if the entry in cell (i,j) is less than θ. This elimination can be done especially efficiently by noting a particular structure in the matrix: entries are non-increasing along each row and up each column. This means that once we have found an entry that is below the threshold θ, we can immediately eliminate all entries above and to its right, and not bother computing those entries (Figure 3). We have such a "upper-right" rectangle in each column, giving rise to a frontier (the curved line in the left

```
MATRIX-WAM(θ)

(1) Collect Term Statistics
(2) T ← Apply pruning; n ← |T|
(3) X ← sort T by sf × idf in decreasing order
(4) Y ← sort T by idf in decreasing order
(5) For y = Y[0] to Y[n]
(6)     For x = X[0] to X[n]
(7)         if x has not been considered already
(8)             if sf(x) × idf(x) × idf(y) > θ
(9)                 Compute spf(x, y)
(10)                if spf(x, y) × idf(x) × idf(y) > θ
(11)                    Add {x, y} to answer set A
(12)                else discard all terms right of x; break
(13) return A
```

Figure 4. The MATRIX-WAM algorithm

```
SHORT-WAM(k,θ)

Collect Term Statistics.
H₁ ← Prune Terms; C₁ ← Corpus
For i = 2 to k
    For each sentence s in C_{i-1}
        I_s = (i − 1)-tuples in s that are in H_{i-1}
        s' = i-tuples generated by joining I_s with itself
        Add tuples in s' to H_i
        if s' ≠ ∅ Add s' to C_i
    H_i ← apply pruning on H_i.
```

Figure 5. The SHORT-WAM algorithm

figure) between the eliminated pairs and those remaining in contention. For cells remaining in contention, we proceed to the task of computing their *spf* values, computing $m(x, y)$, and comparing with θ. Applying Theorem 1 we observe that there are at most $O(log^4 N_d)$ candidate pairs. In practice our algorithm computes the *spf* values for only a fraction of the $\binom{N'_t}{2}$ candidate pairs. Figure 3 (right) illustrates the frontier line for the CNN corpus.

We now introduce the first Word Associations Mining (WAM) algorithm. The MATRIX-WAM algorithm shown in Figure 4.2 implements matrix mining. The first step makes a pass over the corpus and collects term statistics. The pruning step performs both high and low end pruning, as described in Section 4.1. For each term we store an *occurrence list* keeping all sentences the term appears in. For a pair $\{x, y\}$ we can compute the $spf(x, y)$ by going through the occurrence lists of the two terms. Lines (8)-(12) check the column frontier and determine the pairs to be stored.

For higher order associations, the algorithm performs multiple matrix mining passes. In the ith pass, one axis of the matrix holds the *idf* values as before, and the other axis the m_{i-1} values of the $(i − 1)$-tuples that survived the previous pass. We use threshold θ_i for the ith pass

4.3 Shortened documents

While matrix mining reduces the computation significantly, there are still many pairs for which we compute the *spf* value. Furthermore, for most of these pairs the *spf* value is actually zero, so we end up examining many more pairs than the ones that actually appear in the corpus. We invoke a different approach, similar to the AprioriTID algorithm described by Agrawal and Srikant [2]. Let H_1 denote the set of terms that survive the pruning steps described in Section 4.1 – we call these the *interesting* terms. Given H_1 we make a second pass over the corpus, keeping a counter for each pair of *interesting* terms that appear together in a sentence.

That is, we replaced each document by a *shortened document* consisting only of the terms deemed interesting.

The shortened documents algorithm extends naturally for higher order associations (Figure 4.3). The algorithm performs multiple passes over the data. The input to the ith pass is a corpus C_{i-1} that consists of sentences that are sets of $(i-1)$-tuples and a hash table H_{i-1} that stores all interesting $(i-1)$-tuples. An i-tuple t is interesting if $m_i(t) > \theta_i$. During the ith pass the algorithm generates candidate i-tuples by joining interesting $(i − 1)$-tuples that appear together in a sentence. The join operation between $(i − 1)$-tuples is performed as in the case of the a priori algorithms [2]. The candidates are stored in a hash H_i and each sentence is replaced by the candidates it generates. At the end of the pass, the algorithm outputs a corpus C_i that consists of sentences that are collections of i-tuples. Furthermore, we apply low end pruning to the hash table H_i using threshold θ_i. At the end of the pass H_i contains the interesting i-tuples.

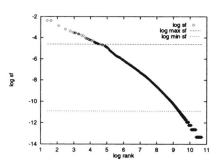

Figure 6. Pruned Terms for CNN corpus

4.4 Empirical study of WAM algorithms

We ran our two algorithms on our three corpora, applying both high and low end pruning. Figure 6 shows a plot of how the thresholds are applied. The terms that survive pruning correspond to the area between the two lines in the plot. The top line in the figure was determined by high end pruning,

		CBC	CNN	Reuters
Corpus Statistics				
1	distinct terms	16.5K	44.7K	37.1K
2	corpus terms	471K	3.6M	1.3M
3	distinct sp's	1.2M	5M	3.7M
4	corpus sp's	3.9M	28.8M	16.3M
Pruning Statistics				
5	threshold	0.002	0.001	0.015
6	pruned	9.6K (58%)	33.2K (74%)	31.4K (84%)
7	high pruned	20	57	0
8	collected	2,798	3,006	2,699
MATRIX-WAM Statistics				
9	naive pairs	23.8M	66.2M	16.2M
10	computed spf's	19.1M (80%)	47M (70%)	9.2M (57%)
11	zero spf	22.5M	60.6M	13.6M
SHORT-WAM Statistics (w/o high pruning)				
12	pruned corpus terms	45K (10%)	0.2M (5%)	0.1M (7%)
13	gen sp's	3.5M (91%)	26.6M (92%)	14.1M (86%)
14	distinct sp's	963K (77%)	3.6M (72%)	2.1M (57%)
SHORT-WAM Statistics (with high pruning)				
15	pruned corpus terms	134K (29%)	1.2M (32%)	0.1M (7%)
16	gen sp's	2.4M (60%)	16.3M (56%)	14.1M (86%)
17	distinct sp's	898K (72%)	3.3M (67%)	2.1M (57%)

Table 3. Statistics for the WAM algorithms

while the bottom line was determined by low end pruning.

Table 3 shows the statistics for the two algorithms when mining for pairs for all three corpora. In the table sp stands for sentence pair and corpus sp's is the total number of sentence pairs in the corpus. We count the appearance of a term in a sentence only once. In all cases we selected the threshold so that around 3,000 associations are collected (line 8). Pruning eliminates at least 58% of the terms and as much as 84% for the Reuters corpus (line 6). Most terms are pruned from the low end of the distribution; high end pruning removes just 20 terms for the CBC corpus, 57 for the CNN corpus and none for the Reuters corpus (line 7). The above observations indicate that our theoretical estimates for pruning may be too conservative. To study how pruning varies with corpus size we performed the following experiment. We sub-sampled the CNN and Reuters corpora, creating synthetic collections with sizes $N_d = 2^8, 2^9, 2^{10}, 2^{11}, 2^{12}, 2^{13}$. For each run, we selected the threshold so that the percentage of pairs above the threshold (over all distinct pairs in the corpus) is approximately the same for all runs. The results are shown in Figure 7. The x axis is the log of the corpus size, while the y axis is the fraction of terms that were pruned.

Matrix mining improves the performance significantly: compared to the naive algorithm that computes the spf values for all $\binom{N_t'}{2}$ pairs of the terms that survive pruning (line 9), the MATRIX-WAM algorithm computes only a fraction of these (maximum 80%, minimum 57%, line 10). Note however that most of the spf's are actually zero (line 11).

The SHORT-WAM algorithm considers only (a fraction of) pairs that actually appear in the corpus. To study the im-

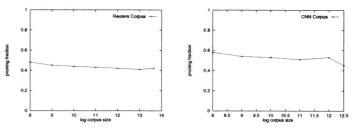

Figure 7. Pruning for Reuters and CNN corpus

portance of high end pruning we implemented two versions of SHORT-WAM, one that applies high end pruning and one that does not. In the table, lines 12 and 15 show the percentage of the corpus terms that are pruned, with and without high end pruning. Obviously, high end pruning is responsible for most of the removed corpus. For the CNN corpus, the 57 terms removed due to high end pruning cause 28% of the corpus to be removed.

The decrease is even more impressive when we consider the pairs generated by SHORT-WAM (lines 13, 16). For the CNN corpus, the algorithm generates only 56% of all possible corpus sp's (ratio of lines 4 and 16). This decrease becomes more important when we mine higher order tuples, since the generated pairs will be given as input to the next iteration. Again high end pruning is responsible for most of the pruning of the corpus sp's. Finally, our algorithm generates at most 72% of all possible *distinct* sentence pairs (line 17). These pairs are stored in the hash table and they reside in main memory while performing the data pass: it is important to keep their number low. Note that AprioriTID generates all pairwise combinations of the terms that survived pruning (line 9).

	CBC	CNN	Reuters
threshold	0.006	0.003	0.03
pruned terms	39%	53%	56%
computed spf's	50.4M	212M	129M
generated sp's	13,757	17,547	64,513
computed stf's	79.3M	203M	659M
collected	2,970	3,213	3,258

Table 4. MATRIX-WAM for triples

We also implemented the algorithms for higher order tuples. Table 4 shows the statistics for MATRIX-WAM, for triples. Clearly we still obtain significant pruning. Furthermore, the volume of sentence pairs generated is not large, keeping the computation in control.

We implemented SHORT-WAM for k-tuples, for arbitrarily large k. In Figure 8 we plot, as a function of the iteration number i, the size of the corpus C_i (figure on the left), as well as the number of candidate tuples and the number of these tuples that survived each pruning phase (figure on the right). The threshold is set to 0.07 and we mine 8,335 5-tuples. Although the sizes initially grow significantly, they fall fast at subsequent iterations. This is consistent with the observations in [2].

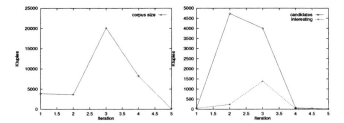

Figure 8. Statistics for SHORT-WAM

4.5 Sample associations

At http://www.cs.toronto.edu/~tsap/TextMining/ there is a full list of the associations. Table 5 shows a sample of associations from all three corpora that attracted our interest.

Pairs
deutsche telekom, hong kong, chevron texaco, department justice, mci worldcom, aol warner, france telecom, greenspan tax, oats quaker, chapters indigo, nestle purina, oil opec, books indigo, leaf maple, states united, germany west, arabia saudi, gas oil, exxon jury, capriati hingis

Triples
chateau empress frontenac, indigo reisman schwartz, del monte sun-rype, cirque du soleil, bribery economics scandal, fuel spills tanker, escapes hijack yemen, al hall mcguire, baker james secretary, chancellor lawson nigel, community ec european, arabia opec saudi, chief executive officer, child fathering jesse, ncaa seth tournament, eurobond issuing priced, falun gong self-immolation, doughnuts kreme krispy, laser lasik vision, leaf maple schneider

Table 5. Sample associations

5 Conclusions

In this paper, we introduced a new measure of interestingness for mining word associations in text, and we proposed new algorithms for pruning and mining under this (non-monotone) measure. We provided theoretical and empirical analyses of the algorithms. The experimental evaluation demonstrates that our measure produces interesting associations, and our algorithms perform well in practice. We are currently investigating applications of our pruning techniques to other non-monotone cases. Furthermore, we are interested in examining if the analysis in Section 4.1 can be applied to other settings.

References

[1] R. Agrawal, T. Imielinski, A. N. Swami. Mining Association Rules between Sets of Items in Large Databases. SIGMOD 1993.

[2] R. Agrawal, R. Srikant. Fast Algorithms for Mining Association Rules in Large Databases. VLDB 1994.

[3] H. Ahonen, O. Heinonen, M. Klemettinen, A. Inkeri Verkamo. Applying Data Mining Techniques for Descriptive Phrase Extraction in Digital Document Collections. ADL 1998.

[4] R. Bayardo, R. Agrawal, D. Gunopulos, Constraint-based rule mining in large, dense databases. ICDE, 1999.

[5] S. Brin, R. Motwani, J. D. Ullman, S. Tsur. Dynamic Itemset Counting and Implication Rules for Market Basket Data. SIGMOD 1997.

[6] S. Brin, R. Motwani, C. Silverstein. Beyond Market Baskets: Generalizing Association Rules to Correlations. SIGMOD 1997.

[7] E. Cohen, M. Datar, S. Fujiwara, A. Gionis, P. Indyk, R. Motwani, J. Ullman, C. Yang, Finding Interesting Associations without Support Pruning, ICDE 2000.

[8] D.R. Cutting, D. Karger, J. Pedersen and J.W. Tukey. Scatter/Gather: A cluster-based approach to browsing large document collections. 15th ACM SIGIR, 1992.

[9] W. DuMouchel and D. Pregibon, Empirical Bayes Screening for Multi-Item Associations, KDD 2001.

[10] R. Feldman, I. Dagan and W. Klosgen. Efficient algorithms for mining and manipulating associations in texts. *13th European meeting on Cybernetics and Systems Research*, 1996.

[11] R. Feldman, W. Klosgen and A. Zilberstein. Document explorer: Discovering knowledge in document collections. *10th International Symposium on Methodologies for Intelligent Systems*, Springer-Verlag LNCS 1325, 1997.

[12] R. Feldman, I. Dagan, H. Hirsh. Mining text using keyword distributions. *Journal of Intelligent Information Systems* 10, 1998.

[13] B. Lent, R. Agrawal and R. Srikant. Discovering trends in text databases. KDD, 1997.

[14] D.D. Lewis and K. Sparck Jones. Natural language processing for information retrieval. *Communications of the ACM* 39(1), 1996, 92–101.

[15] A. J. Lotka. The frequency distribution of scientific productivity. *J. of the Washington Acad. of Sci.*, 16:317, 1926.

[16] H. Mannila and H. Toivonen. Discovering generalized episodes using minimal occurrences. KDD, 1996.

[17] C. Manning and H. Schütze. *Foundations of Statistical Natural Language Processing*, 1999. The MIT Press, Cambridge, MA.

[18] E. Riloff. Little words can make a big difference for text classification. 18th ACM SIGIR, 1995.

[19] F. Smadja. Retrieving collocations from text: Xtract. *Computational Linguistics* 19(1), 1993, 143–177.

[20] G. Webb, Efficient Search for association rules, KDD, 2000.

[21] I. Witten, A.Moffat and T. Bell. *Managing Gigabytes*. Morgan Kaufman, 1999.

[22] G. K. Zipf. Human behavior and the principle of least effort. *New York: Hafner*, 1949.

On a Capacity Control Using Boolean Kernels for the Learning of Boolean Functions

Ken Sadohara

National Institute of Advanced Industrial Science and Technology (AIST)
AIST Tsukuba Central 2, 1-1-1 Umezono, Tsukuba-shi, Ibaraki, Japan
ken.sadohara@aist.go.jp

Abstract

This paper concerns the classification task in discrete attribute spaces, but consider the task in a more fundamental framework: the learning of Boolean functions. The purpose of this paper is to present a new learning algorithm for Boolean functions called Boolean Kernel Classifier (BKC) employing capacity control using Boolean kernels. BKC uses Support Vector Machines (SVMs) as learning engines and Boolean kernels are primarily used for running SVMs in feature spaces spanned by conjunctions of Boolean literals. However, another important role of Boolean kernels is to appropriately control the size of its hypothesis space to avoid overfitting. After applying a SVM to learn a classifier f in a feature space H induced by a Boolean kernel, BKC uses another Boolean kernel to compute the projections f^k of f onto a subspace H_k of H spanned by conjunctions with length at most k. By evaluating the accuracy of f^k on training data for any k, BKC can determine the smallest k such that f^k is as accurate as f and learn another f' in H_k expected to have lower error for unseen data. By an empirical study on learning of randomly generated Boolean functions, it is shown that the capacity control is effective, and BKC outperforms C4.5 and naive Bayes classifiers.

1. Introduction

This paper concerns the classification task in discrete attribute spaces. Classification, which is a primary data mining task, is learning a function that maps data into one of several predefined classes. Especially, numerous studies have been made in a specific framework where data are described by a fixed set of attributes and their discrete values. Among classification algorithms in the framework, C4.5 [11] is one of the most widely used learning algorithms. However, it has been pointed out several problems causing poor accuracy. For instance, in the literature [10],

it is shown that C4.5 produces poor accuracy when there exists strong dependency between attributes. Also, in the literature [4, 5], it is demonstrated that C4.5 has higher risk of overfitting than simple learning machines such as Naive Bayes Classifiers (NBCs). The purpose of this paper is to present a new learning algorithm more accurate than the existing algorithms even when there exists strong dependency between attributes, or when there exists high risk of overfitting.

In this paper, the classification task is considered in a more fundamental framework: the learning of Boolean functions. Because the classification task in discrete attribute spaces can be reduced to the learning of Boolean functions as follows. Firstly, an n-class classification task is reduced to n 2-class classification tasks of discriminating each class from the other classes. Secondly, by assigning a Boolean variable x_{ik} to the proposition $A_i = v_{ik}$ for each value v_{ik} of any attribute A_i ($1 \leq k \leq \ell_i$), each 2-class classification task can be reduced to the learning of Boolean functions $f : \{0,1\}^d \rightarrow \{0,1\}$, where $d = \sum_i \ell_i$.

The learning of Boolean functions has been studied extensively [14, 6, 8, 1]. These studies have shown that learnability or nonlearnability of various classes of Boolean functions. For example, for the class of k-DNF formulae, i.e. Disjunctive Normal Form (DNF) formulae consisting of conjunctions with length at most k, a polynomial time algorithm is known [14] although it is not practical one. On the other hand, for the most general class of Boolean functions, i.e. the class of DNF formulae, it is still one of the main open problems in the learning theory whether there exists an efficient learning algorithm. However, many researchers believe that the class of DNF formulae is not efficiently learnable. If this conjecture is true, the best we can do is to find a good heuristics to obtain an appropriate k and apply an efficient learning algorithm to the class of k-DNF formulae. This paper presents a learning algorithm employing a procedure for choosing an appropriate length k of conjunctions.

The algorithm uses Support Vector Machines (SVMs) [3,

15] as learning engines. A remarkable advantage of SMVs is efficient learning in a feature space consisting of a large number of features derived from attributes. Instead of learning in a given attribute space, SVMs perform learning in a high dimensional feature space. For the learning of Boolean functions, it is reasonable to use the feature space whose features are all possible conjunctions of negated or non-negated Boolean variables. This is because any Boolean function can be written in DNF and thus the function can be represented as a weighted linear sum of the features [12].

Although it seems to be computationally infeasible to learn the linear function in the high dimensional feature space, e.g. $3^d - 1$ for a d-variable Boolean function, SVMs can perform efficient learning with the help of kernel functions. A kernel function computes the inner product of a feature space and the use of it allows SVMs to deal with an alternative representation of the linear function that does not depend on the dimension of the feature space. Several kernel functions called Boolean kernels are known [12, 7] for the learning of Boolean functions. Especially, the DNF-kernel computes the inner product of the feature space consisting of all possible conjunctions, and thus it is applicable to the learning of the most general class of Boolean functions.

However, the accuracy of a SVM using the DNF kernel degrades rapidly when d becomes large. This is because the size of its hypothesis space grows exponentially as d increases, and thus the learning machine overfits to training data with high probability. To overcome the difficulty, this paper presents a procedure for capacity control that appropriately limits the length of conjunctions in the feature space.

This procedure uses another kernel function called the k-DNF kernel which is a kernel function of the feature space H_k spanned by conjunctions with length at most k. For a learned classifier f in a given feature space H and any k, this kernel function can be used to effectively compute the projection f^k of f onto a subspace H_k of H. By evaluating f^k on training data for any k, learning machines can determine an appropriate k and learn more accurate classifiers in H_k. In the final learning stage, the k-DNF kernel is again used for running SVMs in H_k.

Employing the procedure for capacity control, a learning algorithm for Boolean functions, which is named Boolean Kernel Classifier (BKC), is devised. As described above, BKC uses Boolean kernels for two different purposes: one is for running SVMs in the Boolean domain, and the other one is for capacity control.

In order to see capabilities of BKC under controlled conditions by varying several parameters such as the number of Boolean variables, experiments on learning of randomly generated Boolean functions are performed. These experiments show that the capacity control using the k-DNF ker-

nel is effective, and BKC outperforms C4.5 and NBC under various conditions.

2. Support Vector Machines

This section serves as a brief introduction to the learning principle of SVMs. For a more complete introduction, consult the literature [15, 3, 13].

Given positive and negative data in a data space, SVMs produce non-linear decision surfaces in the data space that discriminate between the positives and the negatives. These non-linear decision surfaces are obtained by learning hyperplanes in a high dimensional feature space derived from the data space. The feature space is derived by a *feature mapping* ϕ that maps points in the data space X into the feature space Z. Suppose that a set of class labels is $Y = \{-1, 1\}$, a training data is $S = \{(x_i, y_i)\}_{i=1}^{n} \subseteq X \times Y$, and $\phi(x_i) = z_i \in Z$. Then, SVMs learn a hyperplane $f(z) = \langle w \cdot z \rangle + b = 0$ that discriminates between the positive data $\{z_i \mid y_i = 1\}$ and the negative ones $\{z_i \mid y_i = -1\}$ as shown in Figure 1. For any hy-

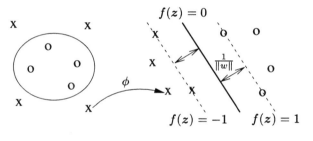

X: Data Space Z: Feature Space

Figure 1. A hyperplane in a feature space

perplane $f(z) = \langle w \cdot z \rangle + b = 0$, the Euclidean distance of the closest point $z^* \in \{z_1, \ldots, z_n\}$ is called the *margin* of the hyperplane. If we normalize hyperplanes so that $|f(z^*)| = 1$, then the margin of the hyperplane is $\frac{1}{\|w\|}$. Among normalized hyperplanes, SVMs find the *maximal margin hyperplane* that has the maximal margin and discriminates between positive data and negative ones. Thus, the learning task of SVMs can be stated as the following convex quadratic programming problem:

$$\begin{aligned} &\text{minimize} &&\|w\|^2, \\ &\text{subject to} &&y_i f(z_i) \geq 1 \quad (1 \leq i \leq n). \end{aligned}$$

The choice of the maximal margin hyperplane is justified by a theorem saying that maximizing the margin minimizes a statistical bound of *generalization error* [3]. Generalization error $\text{err}_\mathcal{D}$ is the expected misclassification rate under an unknown distribution $\mathcal{D}$ over a data space, i.e. it means misclassification rate for unseen data. On the other hand, the average misclassification rate for a training set S is said to be *training set error* err_S.

Unfortunately, the problem specification described above is not applicable to real-world problems. Because there exists a case that data are not linearly separable. Especially, if data are noisy, there will be in general no linear separation. To cope with non separable cases, we need slack variables that allow violation of the margin constraints as follows:

$$\text{subject to} \quad y_i f(z_i) \geq 1 - \xi_i \quad (1 \leq i \leq n)$$
$$\xi_i \geq 0 \quad (1 \leq i \leq n).$$

It is known that, under this condition, minimizing $\|w\|^2 + C \sum_{i=1}^n \xi_i$ amounts to approximately minimizing a bound of generalization error for a suitable positive constant C [13].

According to the optimization theory, the above convex quadratic programming problem is transformed into the following dual problem:

$$\text{maximize} \quad \sum_{i=1}^n \alpha_i - \frac{1}{2} \sum_{i=1}^n \sum_{j=1}^n \alpha_i \alpha_j y_i y_j \langle z_i \cdot z_j \rangle,$$

$$\text{subject to} \quad 0 \leq \alpha_i \leq C \quad (1 \leq i \leq n), \sum_{i=1}^n \alpha_i y_i = 0.$$

It is known that the above convex quadratic programming can be solved efficiently [2, 9]. For a solution $\alpha_1^*, \ldots, \alpha_n^*$, the maximal margin hyperplane $f^*(z) = 0$ can be expressed in the dual representation in terms of these parameters:

$$f^*(z) = \sum_{i=1}^n \alpha_i^* y_i \langle z_i \cdot z \rangle + b^*$$

$$b^* = y_s - \sum_{i=1}^n \alpha_i^* y_i \langle z_i \cdot z_s \rangle \text{ for some } \alpha_s^* \neq 0$$

An advantage of the use of the dual representation is that we can side-step evaluation of the feature mapping ϕ, which is infeasible when the dimension of the feature space is very high. Notice that, in the dual representation, the feature mapping ϕ appears only in the form of inner products

$$\langle z_i \cdot z_j \rangle \stackrel{\text{def}}{=} \langle \phi(x_i) \cdot \phi(x_j) \rangle.$$

Therefore, if we have a way of computing the inner product directly from the input points, i.e. if we know a function K defined in the data space such that

$$K(x_i, x_j) = \langle \phi(x_i) \cdot \phi(x_j) \rangle,$$

then we can side-step the computational problem inherent in evaluating the feature mapping. Such functions K are called *kernel functions*. The use of kernel functions makes it possible to map the data implicitly into a high dimensional feature space and to find the optimal hyperplane in the feature space.

The next section considers feature spaces and kernel functions appropriate for the learning of Boolean functions.

3 Boolean Kernels

For the learning of Boolean functions, several kernel functions have been devised in the literatures [12, 7]. Theses kernel functions appropriate for the Boolean domain are referred to as *Boolean kernels*.

One of the most general Boolean kernels is the DNF kernel [12], which induces the feature space spanned by all possible conjunctions. More specifically, in a case of the learning of 2-variable Boolean functions, it implicitly uses the following 9-dimensional feature space whose coordinate axes are x_1, x_2, $1 - x_1$, $1 - x_2$, $x_1 x_2$, $x_1(1 - x_2)$, $(1 - x_1)x_2$, $(1 - x_1)(1 - x_2)$. The DNF kernel is the most general in the sense that every Boolean function can be represented as a hyperplane in this feature space [12] because any Boolean functions can be written in the DNF formulae. For example, $x_1 \vee \overline{x_2}$ can be represented as a hyperplane $f(x_1, x_2) = x_1 + (1 - x_1)(1 - x_2) - (1 - x_1)x_2 = 0$ although its margin is not maximal.

The DNF kernel is formally defined as follows.

Definition 1 (the DNF kernel)

$$K(u, v) \stackrel{\text{def}}{=} -1 + 2^{s(u,v)},$$

where $s(u, v)$ *denotes the number of bits that have the same value in* u *and* v *for any* $u, v \in \{0, 1\}^d$.

The following theorem says that the DNF kernel is really a kernel function of the feature space.

Theorem 1 (Sadohara [12]) *Let* ϕ *be the feature mapping that maps data into the feature space consisting of all possible conjunctions. Then, the following holds.*

$$K(u, v) = \langle \phi(u) \cdot \phi(v) \rangle$$

We easily see that the DNF kernel computes inner products of the $3^d - 1$ dimensional feature space in time complexity $O(d)$. Therefore it enables efficient learning in the high dimensional feature space.

Although the DNF kernel has enough expressive power to learn any Boolean functions, we can limit its expressive power if need arises. For example, if we know in advance that a target function belongs to a certain class of Boolean functions, then the use of a feature space restricted for the class is expected to produce higher accuracy. Applying SVMs to the restricted feature space needs another kernel function that computes inner product of the subspace. It has been proposed several kernel functions for different subspaces, such as the monotone DNF kernel [12] for the feature space consisting of all possible conjunctions without negation. In this paper, we consider another kernel function for the feature space consisting of conjunctions with length at most k, which is proposed in the literature [7].

Definition 2 (k-DNF kernel)

$$K^k(u, v) \stackrel{\text{def}}{=} \sum_{i=1}^{k} \binom{\text{s}(u, v)}{i}$$

Theorem 2 (Khardon et al. [7])

$$K^k(u, v) = \langle \phi^k(u) \cdot \phi^k(v) \rangle,$$

where ϕ^k denotes the feature mapping into the feature space spanned by conjunctions with length at most k.

We see that the DNF kernel is the particular k-DNF kernel when $k = d$ since $\sum_{i=0}^{s} \binom{s}{i} = 2^s$. However time complexity of k-DNF kernel is slightly larger.

Proposition 1 *Time complexity of K^k is $O(dk)$.*

Proof Assume that $C(k, m)$ denotes $\sum_{i=1}^{k} \binom{m}{i}$ and s denotes $\text{s}(u, v)$.

Because $\binom{m}{i} = \binom{m-1}{i} + \binom{m-1}{i-1}$,

$$
\begin{aligned}
& C(k, s) \\
&= \sum_{i=1}^{k} \left(\binom{s-1}{i} + \binom{s-1}{i-1} \right) \\
&= \sum_{i=1}^{k} \binom{s-1}{i} + \binom{s-1}{0} + \sum_{i=1}^{k-1} \binom{s-1}{i} \\
&= C(k, s-1) + C(k-1, s-1) + 1.
\end{aligned}
$$

Therefore, time complexity of $C(k, s)$ is $O(dk)$. Since computation of s requires time linear in d, time complexity of K^k is $O(dk)$. $\square$

The proposition shows that the k-DNF kernel enables efficient learning in the subspace spanned by conjunctions with length at most k, whose dimension is $O(d^k)$. In addition to the use of the k-DNF kernel for learning, next section considers another use of the k-DNF kernel for capacity control.

4 Capacity Control

The k-DNF kernel described in the previous section yields a nested sequence of hypothesis spaces

$$H_1 \subseteq \cdots \subseteq H_k \subseteq \cdots \subseteq H_d,$$

where H_k denotes the set of hyperplanes defined in the feature space spanned by the conjunctions with length at most k.

Choosing an appropriate size of the hypothesis space is known as *capacity control* and is quite important for learning machines to produce low generalization error. If a hypothesis space is too small then learning machines cannot approximate a target function and produce high generalization error. On the other hand, too large hypothesis space also yields high generalization error because the larger the capacity, the higher the risk of *overfitting*. Overfitting is a phenomenon that learning machines overly fit to noises, outliers or random fluctuation of the training data, and thus capture underlying model poorly. As a result, learning machines produce high generalization error although they produce low training-set error. In fact, an experiment described later in this paper demonstrates that the performance of a learning machine without capacity control degrades rapidly when d becomes large.

The importance of capacity control is also suggested by the following theorem, which is a slightly modified version of the Theorem 4.6 in [3].

Theorem 3 *Let H be the set of linear functions on $\mathcal{R}^D$. For any probability distribution $\mathcal{D}$ on $X \times \{-1, 1\}$, with probability $1 - \delta$ over n random examples S, any hypothesis $f \in H$ has error no more than*

$$\text{err}_{\mathcal{D}}(f) \leq 2\text{err}_S(f) + \frac{4}{n}\left((D+1)\log\frac{2en}{D+1} + \log\frac{4}{\delta}\right),$$

provided $D + 1 \leq n$.

For any H_k, let f_k be a hypothesis that has minimum training set error. If two hypothesis $f_k \in H_k$ and $f_j \in H_j$ have the same training set error and the dimension of H_k is smaller than that of H_j, then the theorem says that the above bound of generalization error for f_k is smaller than that for f_j. Therefore f_k is expected to have lower generalization error.

According to this observation, this paper considers the following strategy of capacity control. First, in a given hypothesis space, a learning machine finds f that has minimum training set error R. Then, it finds a smaller hypothesis space H_k that contains a hypothesis f_k with training set error R. In order to find H_k, the learning machine computes the projection f^k of f onto H_k and test whether f^k is as accurate as f on the training data. The following theorem says that the projection can be computed efficiently by using the k-DNF kernel.

Theorem 4 *Assume that $f(x) = \sum_{j=1}^{n} y_j \alpha_j K^m(x_j, x)$ and let $f^k(x)$ be the projection of f onto the feature space spanned by the conjunctions with length at most k, where $k \leq m \leq d$. Then $f^k(x) = \sum_{j=1}^{n} y_j \alpha_j K^k(x_j, x)$ holds.*

Proof From the definition, $f(x)$ and $f^k(x)$ can be written as follows, where $\phi^m(x_j) = z_j = (z_1^j, \ldots, z_{\ell_m}^j)$ and ℓ_m (resp., ℓ_k) denotes the number of conjunctions with length at most m (resp., k).

$$
\begin{aligned}
f(x) &= \sum_{j=1}^{n} y_j \alpha_j K^m(x_j, x) \\
&= \sum_{j=1}^{n} y_j \alpha_j \langle \phi^m(x_j) \cdot \phi^m(x) \rangle \\
&= \sum_{j=1}^{n} y_j \alpha_j \left(z_1^j z_1 + \cdots + z_{\ell_k}^j z_{\ell_k} + \cdots + z_{\ell_m}^j z_{\ell_m} \right) \\
f^k(x) &= \sum_{j=1}^{n} y_j \alpha_j \left(z_1^j z_1 + \cdots + z_{\ell_k}^j z_{\ell_k} \right)
\end{aligned}
$$

Therefore,

$$
\begin{aligned}
f^k(x) &= \sum_{j=1}^{n} y_j \alpha_j \langle \phi^k(x_j) \cdot \phi^k(x) \rangle \\
&= \sum_{j=1}^{n} y_j \alpha_j K^k(x_j, x).
\end{aligned}
$$

$\square$

As described above, the k-DNF kernel can be used as a low-pass filter that effectively filters out useless and long conjunctions. Hence the filter reduces the dimension of a given feature space and yields a smaller feature space in which the learning machine is expected to produce lower generalization error.

Employing the strategy of capacity control, the following learning algorithm for Boolean functions called Boolean Kernel Classifier (BKC) is devised.

Boolean Kernel Classifier (BKC)

1. Given a set of training data and a positive integer k ($1 \leq k \leq d$), where d is the number of Boolean variables.

2. Learn a hyperplane f using SVM with the k-DNF kernel.

3. For each i ($1 \leq i \leq k$), compute f^i using the i-DNF kernel and evaluate f^i on the training data.

4. Find the minimum i such that f^i is as accurate as f.

5. Stop if $i = k$, otherwise let k be i and return to 2.

As described so far, BKC uses the k-DNF kernel for two different purposes. One is for learning to run SVM in the feature space spanned by the conjunctions with length at most k. The other one is for capacity control to compute projections of the learned classifiers onto subspaces spanned by shorter conjunctions.

5 Experiments

To explore capabilities of BKC under controlled condition by varying various parameters, the author conducted experiments on learning of randomly generated Boolean functions. In the experiments described below, the following parameters are varied: the number d of Boolean variables, the number n of training data, the rate η of class noise and the complexity of target Boolean functions determined by the length ℓ of conjunctions.

In a certain parameter setting, 200 different Boolean functions and data of the functions are generated as follows. The random d-variable Boolean functions are generated in DNF. Each variable is included in a disjunct with probability $\frac{\ell}{d}$ and negated with probability $\frac{1}{2}$. Therefore, the average length of disjuncts is ℓ. The number of disjuncts is set to $2^{\ell-2}$ so as to produce approximately equal numbers of positive and negative examples. For each Boolean function, n training data and 2000 test data were independently drawn from the uniform distribution. For the training data, class noise is added with the probability η, i.e. the class label of each datum are inverted with the probability η. From the training data, a classifier is learned, and the misclassification rate of the classifier is measured on the test data. The misclassification rate is averaged across 200 different Boolean functions. Each experiment below measures misclassification rates of classifiers learned by the following four learning algorithms: NBC, C4.5, a SVM with the DNF kernel (denoted by SVM) and BKC.

Figure 2 describes a result of an experiment varying n when $d = 32$, $\ell = 8$ and $\eta = 0$.

The result shows that BKC achieves the highest performance and requires the smallest training data to attain a certain level of accuracy. Another interesting observation is that NBC is superior to C4.5 and SVM at small sample sizes. This result agrees with observations of other researchers that the strong bias can be canceled by weak overfitting and simple classifiers can outperform more elaborated classifiers. However notice that even at the small sample size, BKC is superior to NBC although it has larger

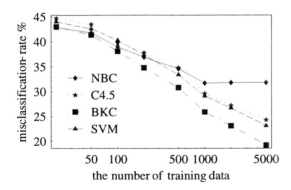

Figure 2. Error rates vs. n.

capacity and has higher risk of overfitting. This means that the capacity control of BKC is effective.

Figure 3 describes a result of an experiment varying ℓ when $d = 32$, $n = 2000$ and $\eta = 0$. The result shows that BKC again achieves the highest performance. It also shows that NBC and C4.5 produce higher error than SVM and BKC do.

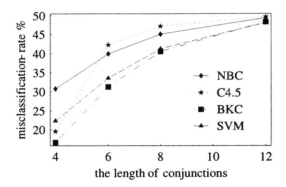

Figure 3. Error rates vs. ℓ.

One reason for the poor accuracy of NBC and C4.5 might be dependency between attributes. Strong dependence between attributes possibly causes NBC and C4.5 poor performance because NBC assumes independence of attributes and C4.5 adopts univariate node-splits strategy. During construction of a decision tree, C4.5 splits nodes by a single attribute most relevant to class membership. This strategy has a problem that an attribute does not necessarily have large information gain even when the attribute, together with other attributes, has high relevancy to class membership [10]. That is, both NBC and C4.5 learn classifiers not by measuring relevancy of sets of attributes but by measuring relevancy of each attribute. This contrasts with

the SVM with the DNF kernel and BKC; both of them measure relevancy of conjunctions of attributes.

Another reason for notably rapid increase of the misclassification rate of C4.5 might be its overfitting avoidance mechanism. C4.5 avoids overfitting by pruning of decision trees, that is, given two trees with the same training-set error, it prefers simpler one based on the assumption that overfitting is caused by overly complex trees. This way of overfitting avoidance is known as Occam's razor and is widely used. However, this empirical wisdom is not supported theoretically, and is shown not to be always effective as a practical heuristic [4, 5]. Several empirical studies show that the smallest consistent trees are not the most accurate ones in many cases. Accordingly, in the above experiment, the preference of C4.5 for simpler trees increases discrepancy between learned classifiers and target ones as the complexity of the target Boolean functions increases. On the other hand, SVM and BKC adopt a more principled way of overfitting avoidance: minimizing a statistical bound of generalization error. The misclassification rates of SVM and BKC seem to increase smoothly as the sample complexity increases.

Figure 4 describes a result of an experiment varying d when $\ell = 8$, $n = 2000$ and $\eta = 0$.

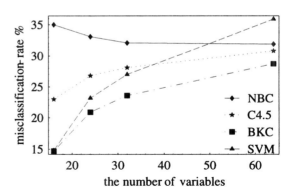

Figure 4. Error rates vs. d.

This result dramatically shows the effectiveness of the capacity control using the k-DNF kernel. As the curve of SVM shows, without the capacity control, misclassification rate increases rapidly as the size of the hypothesis space grows. On the other hand, BKC with the capacity control using the k-DNF kernel achieves the best performance among four algorithms even when the number of variables becomes large.

Figure 5, Figure 6 and Figure 7 describe results of experiments with 10% class noise. More precisely, Figure 5 describes a result of an experiment varying n when $d = 32$, $\ell = 8$ and $\eta = 0.1$. Figure 6 describes a result of an ex-

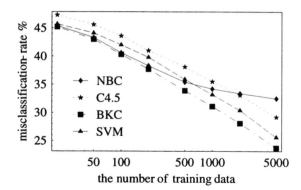

Figure 5. Error rates vs. n ($\eta = 0.1$).

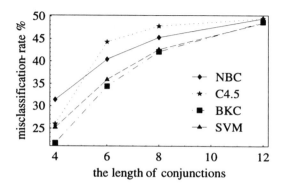

Figure 6. Error rates vs. ℓ ($\eta = 0.1$).

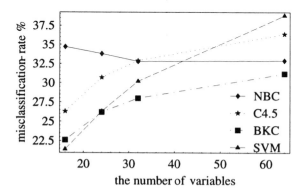

Figure 7. Error rates vs. d ($\eta = 0.1$).

periment varying ℓ when $d = 32$, $n = 2000$ and $\eta = 0.1$. Figure 7 describes a result of an experiment varying d when $\ell = 8$, $n = 2000$ and $\eta = 0.1$. In all experiments above, C is set to 1. As these results show, BKC does not overfit to the noise extremely. However, it is reasonable to consider that this phenomenon comes from the capacity control of SVMs, not from the capacity control using k-DNF kernel, since the SVM with the DNF kernel also exhibits weak overfitting to the noise.

6   Concluding Remarks

This paper considered an inductive learning algorithm for Boolean functions that uses SVMs and Boolean kernels. Boolean kernels are used for two different purposes. One is to run SVMs in feature spaces appropriate for the learning of Boolean functions. The other one is to control the size of hypothesis spaces to avoid overfitting. Boolean kernels enable to effectively compute projections of learned classifiers onto subspaces of a given hypothesis space. By evaluating the projections, the learning algorithm can determine an appropriate subspace of its hypothesis space and learn more accurate classifiers in the subspace. The resulting algorithm BKC was tested in experiments on learning of randomly generated Boolean functions under various conditions. The results of the experiments show that BKC outperforms C4.5 and naive Bayes classifiers in all parameter settings. The results also show that the capacity control using the k-DNF kernel employed in BKC is effective.

The k-DNF kernel considered in this paper enables learning and capacity control in feature spaces whose features are conjunctions of negated or non-negated Boolean variables. However, the literatures [12, 7] propose other kernel functions for feature spaces spanned by negation-free conjunctions. Fortunately, the arguments about BKC in this paper are valid if we replace the k-DNF kernel with its negation free version. An advantage of the negation free kernel is that their computation is easier than the k-DNF kernel; instead of counting bits having the same value, it is sufficient to count bits that take value 1 at the same position. Therefore, these kernel are especially suitable for applications where the total number of attributes are very large, possibly infinite, but in any one datum, only a small number of attributes are active, e.g. text classification where documents are represented by word vectors. It is an interesting feature research to apply BKC with the negation free DNF kernel to such application domains.

Another interesting research direction concerns comprehensibility of learned classifiers. In the context of knowledge discovery, explanation for decision made by learned classifiers is important as well as accuracy of the classifiers. To obtain the explanation, features induced by Boolean kernels might be helpful because a coefficient of hyperplanes quantifies importance of the corresponding conjunction. Therefore, by extracting important conjunctions, comprehensible explanation for output of classifiers might be obtainable.

Acknowledgment

This work is partially supported by Grant-in-Aid for Young Scientists (B) (No. 14780315) from the Ministry of Education, Culture, Sports, Science and Technology (MEXT).

References

[1] D. Angluin. Queries and concept learning. *Machine Learning*, 2:319–342, 1988.

[2] M. Bellare and P. Rogaway. The complexity of approximating a nonlinear program. In *Complexity of Numerical Optimization*, pages 16–32. World Scientific, 1993.

[3] N. Cristianini and J. Shawe-Taylor. *An Introduction to Support Vector Machines*. Cambridge Press, 2000.

[4] P. Domingos. On the optimality of the simple Bayesian classifier under zero-one loss. *Machine Learning*, 29:103–130, 1997.

[5] P. Domingos. The role of Occam's razor in knowledge discovery. *Data Mining and Knowledge Discovery*, 3:409–425, 1999.

[6] M. Kearns, M. Li, L. Pitt, and L. Valiant. On the learnability of Boolean formulae. In *Proceedings of ACM Symposium on Theory of Computing*, pages 285–295, 1987.

[7] R. Khardon, D. Roth, and R. Servedio. Efficiency versus convergence of Boolean kernels for on-line learning algorithms. Technical Report UIUCDCS-R-2001-2233, Department of Computer Science, University of Illinois at Urbana-Champaign, 2001.

[8] L. Pitt and L. Valiant. Computational limitations on learning from examples. *Journal of the Association for Computing Machinery*, 35(4):965–984, 1988.

[9] J. Platt. Fast training of support vector machines using sequential minimal optimization. In *Advances in Kernel Methods – Support Vector Learning*, pages 185–208. MIT Press, 1998.

[10] J. Quinlan. An empirical comparison of genetic and decision-tree classifiers. In *Proceedings of International Conference on Machine Learning*, pages 135–141, 1988.

[11] J. Quinlan. *C4.5: Programs for Machine Learning*. Morgan Kaufmann, 1993.

[12] K. Sadohara. Learning of Boolean functions using support vector machines. In *Proceedings of International Conference on Algorithmic Learning Theory*, LNAI 2225, pages 106–118. Springer, 2001.

[13] B. Schölkopf and A.J. Smola. *Learning with kernels*. MIT Press, 2002.

[14] L. Valiant. A theory of the learnable. *Communications of the ACM*, 27(11):1134–1142, 1984.

[15] V. Vapnik. *The Nature of Statistical Learning Theory*. Springer-Verlag, 1995.

SLPMiner: An Algorithm for Finding Frequent Sequential Patterns Using Length-Decreasing Support Constraint[*]

Masakazu Seno and George Karypis
Computer Science Department, University of Minnesota, Minneapolis, MN 55455
{seno, karypis}@cs.umn.edu

Abstract

Over the years, a variety of algorithms for finding frequent sequential patterns in very large sequential databases have been developed. The key feature in most of these algorithms is that they use a constant support constraint to control the inherently exponential complexity of the problem. In general, patterns that contain only a few items will tend to be interesting if they have a high support, whereas long patterns can still be interesting even if their support is relatively small. Ideally, we desire to have an algorithm that finds all the frequent patterns whose support decreases as a function of their length. In this paper we present an algorithm called SLPMiner, that finds all sequential patterns that satisfy a length-decreasing support constraint. Our experimental evaluation shows that SLPMiner achieves up to two orders of magnitude of speedup by effectively exploiting the length-decreasing support constraint, and that its runtime increases gradually as the average length of the sequences (and the discovered frequent patterns) increases.

1 Introduction

Data mining research during the last years has led to the development of a variety of algorithms for finding frequent sequential patterns in very large sequential databases [7, 9, 5]. These patterns can be used to find sequential association rules or extract prevalent patterns that exist in the sequences, and have been effectively used in many different domains and applications.

The key feature in most of these algorithms is that they control the inherently exponential complexity of the problem by finding only the patterns that occur in a sufficiently large fraction of the sequences, called the *support*. A limita-

tion of this paradigm for generating frequent patterns is that it uses a constant support value, irrespective of the length of the discovered patterns. In general, patterns that contain only a few items will tend to be interesting if they have a high support, whereas long patterns can still be interesting even if their support is relatively small. Unfortunately, if constant-support-based frequent pattern discovery algorithms are used to find some of the longer but infrequent patterns, they will end up generating an exponentially large number of short patterns. Ideally, we desire to have an algorithm that finds all the frequent patterns whose support decreases as a function of their length. Developing such an algorithm is particularly challenging because the downward closure property of the constant support constraint cannot be used to prune short infrequent patterns.

Recently [6], we introduced the problem of finding frequent itemsets whose support satisfies a non-increasing function of their length. An itemset is frequent only if its support is greater than or equal to the minimum support value determined by the length of the itemset. We found a property that an itemset must have in order to support longer itemsets given a length-decreasing support constraint. This property, that we call the *smallest valid extension* or *SVE* for short, enabled us to prune many short itemsets that are irrelevant to finding longer itemsets. We developed an algorithm called LPMiner that efficiently finds frequent itemsets given a length-decreasing support constraint by pruning large portion of search space.

In this paper, we extend the problem of finding patterns that satisfy a length-decreasing support constraint to the much more challenging problem of finding sequential patterns. We developed an algorithm called SLPMiner that finds all frequent sequential patterns that satisfy a length-decreasing support constraint. SLPMiner follows the database-projection-based approach for frequent pattern generation, that was shown to lead to efficient algorithms, and serves as a platform to evaluate our new three pruning methods based on the SVE property. These pruning methods exploit different aspects of the sequential pattern discovery process and prune either entire sequences, items

---

[*]This work was supported by NSF CCR-9972519, EIA-9986042, ACI-9982274, ACI-0133464 by Army Research Office contract DA/DAAG55-98-1-0441, by the DOE ASCI program, and by Army High Performance Computing Research Center contract number DAAH04-95-C-0008.

within certain sequences, or entire projected databases. Our experimental evaluation shows that SLPMiner achieves up to two orders of magnitude of speedup by effectively exploiting the SVE property, and that its runtime increases gradually as the average length of the sequences (and the discovered patterns) increases.

The rest of this paper is organized as follows. Section 2 provides some background information. Section 3 describes the basic pattern discovery algorithm of SLPMiner and how the length-decreasing support constraint can be exploited to prune the search space of frequent patterns. The experimental results of our algorithm are shown in Section 4, followed by a conclusion in Section 5.

2 Background

2.1 Sequence Model and Notation

The basic sequence model that we will use was introduced by Srikant et al [7] and is defined as follows. Let $I = \{i_1, i_2, \ldots, i_n\}$ be the set of all items. An *itemset* is a subset of items. A *sequence* $s = \langle t_1, t_2, \ldots, t_l \rangle$ is an ordered list of itemsets, where $t_j \subseteq I$ for $1 \leq j \leq l$. A sequential database D is a set of sequences. The length of a sequence s is defined to be the number of items in s and denoted as $|s|$. Similarly, given an itemset t, let $|t|$ denote the number of items in t. Given a sequential database D, $|D|$ denotes the number of sequences in D. This model can describe a wide range of real data. For example, at a retail shop, customer transactions can be modeled by this sequence model such that an itemset represents a set of goods (or items) purchased by a customer at a visit and a sequence represents an ordered purchased itemsets history of a customer.

Sequence $s = \langle t_1, t_2, \ldots, t_l \rangle$ is called a *sub-sequence* of sequence $s' = \langle t'_1, t'_2, \ldots, t'_m \rangle$ $(l \leq m)$ if there exist l integers $i_1, i_2, \ldots i_l$ such that $1 \leq i_1 < i_2 < \ldots < i_l \leq m$ and $t_j \subseteq t'_{i_j}$ $(j = 1, 2, \ldots, l)$. If s is a sub-sequence of s', then we write $s \subseteq s'$ and say sequence s' *supports* s. The *support* of a sequence s in a sequential database D, denoted as $\sigma_D(s)$, is defined to be $|D_s|/|D|$, where $D_s = \{s_i | s \subseteq s_i \land s_i \in D\}$. From the definition, it always holds that $0 \leq \sigma_D(s) \leq 1$. We use the term *sequential pattern* to refer to a sequence when we want to emphasize that the sequence is supported by many sequences in a sequential database.

We assume that we can give a lexicographic ordering on the items in I. Although an itemset is just a set of items without the notion of ordering, it is essential to be able to define an ordering among the items for our algorithm. When we represent the items in an itemset, we order the items according to the lexicographic ordering and put those ordered items within matched parentheses (). When we represent the items in a sequence, we represent each itemset in this way and arrange these itemsets according to the ordering in the sequence within matched angled parentheses $\langle \rangle$.

2.2 Sequential Pattern Mining with Constant Support

The problem of finding frequent sequential patterns given a constant minimum support constraint [7] is formally defined as follows:

Definition 1 (Sequential Pattern Mining with Constant Support) *Given a sequential database D and a minimum support σ ($0 \leq \sigma \leq 1$), find all sequences each of which is supported by at least $\lceil \sigma |D| \rceil$ sequences in D.*

Efficient algorithms for finding frequent itemsets or sequences [2, 8, 1, 4, 3, 5, 10] in very large itemset or sequence databases have been one of the key success stories of data mining research. The key feature in these algorithms is that they control the inherently exponential complexity of the problem by using the downward closure property [7]. This property states that in order for a pattern of length l to be frequent, all of its sub-sequences must be frequent as well. As a result, once we find that a sequence of length l is infrequent, we know that any longer sequences that include this particular sequence cannot be frequent, and thus eliminate such sequences from further consideration.

2.3 Finding Patterns with Length-Decreasing Support

Recently, we introduced the idea of length-decreasing support constraint [6] that helps us to find long itemsets with low support as well as short itemsets with high support. A length-decreasing support constraint is given as a function of the itemset length $f(l)$ such that $f(l_a) \geq f(l_b)$ for any l_a, l_b satisfying $l_a < l_b$. The idea of introducing this kind of support constraint is that by using a support function that decreases as the length of the itemset increases, we may be able to find long itemsets that may be of interest without generating an exponentially large number of shorter itemsets. We can naturally extend this idea to the sequence model by using the length of the sequence instead of the length of the itemset. Figure 1 shows a typical length-decreasing support constraint. In this example, the support constraint decreases linearly to the minimum value and then stays the same for sequential patterns of longer length. Formally, the problem of finding this type of patterns is stated as follows:

Definition 2 (Sequential Pattern Mining with Length-Decreasing Support) *Given a sequential database D and a length-decreasing support constraint $f(l)$, where $f(l)$ is a non-increasing function defined over all the positive integers and always $0 \leq f(l) \leq 1$, find all the sequential patterns each s of which satisfies $\sigma_D(s) \geq f(|s|)$.*

Finding the complete set of frequent sequential patterns that satisfy a length-decreasing support constraint is particularly challenging since we cannot rely solely on the

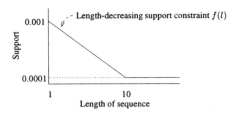

Figure 1. An example of typical length-decreasing support constraint

downward closure property of the constant support pattern mining. Notice that, under a length-decreasing support constraint, a sequence can be frequent even if its subsequences are infrequent since the minimum support value decreases as the length of a sequence increases. We must use $\min_{l \geq 1} f(l)$ as the minimum support value to apply the downward closure property, which will result in finding an exponentially large number of uninteresting infrequent short patterns.

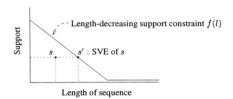

Figure 2. Smallest valid extension (SVE)

A key property regarding sequences whose support decreases as a function of their length is the following. Given a sequential database D and a particular sequence $s \in D$, if the sequence s is currently infrequent ($\sigma_D(s) < f(|s|)$), then $f^{-1}(\sigma_D(s)) = \min(\{l | f(l) \leq \sigma_D(s)\})$ is the minimum length that a sequence s' such that $s' \supset s$ must have before it can potentially become frequent. Figure 2 illustrates this relation graphically. The length of s' is nothing more than the point at which a line parallel to the x-axis at $y = \sigma_D(s)$ intersects the support curve; here, we essentially assume that the best case in which s' exists and it is supported by the same set of sequences as its sub-sequence s. This property is called the *smallest valid extension* property or *SVE* property for short and was initially introduced for the problem of finding itemsets that satisfy a length-decreasing support constraint [6].

3 SLPMiner Algorithm

We developed an algorithm called SLPMiner that finds all the frequent sequential patterns that satisfy a given length-decreasing support constraint. SLPMiner serves as a platform to develop and evaluate pruning methods for reducing the complexity of finding this type of patterns. Our design goals for SLPMiner was to make it generic enough so

that any conclusions drawn from our experiments can carry through other database-projection-based sequential pattern mining algorithms [3, 5].

This section consists of two main parts. First, we will explain how SLPMiner finds frequent sequential patterns. Second, we will explain how SLPMiner prunes unnecessary data by using three different pruning methods that exploit the SVE property.

3.1 Sequential Database-Projection-based Algorithm

SLPMiner finds frequent sequential patterns using the database-projection-based approach. First, we describe the general idea of the the database-projection-based approach and then discuss about details specific to SLPMiner. The description of the database-projection-based approach is based on [3].

SLPMiner grows sequential patterns by adding an item at a time. It uses a prefix tree that determines which items are to be added to grow each pattern. Each node in the tree represents a frequent sequential pattern with one item added to the end of the sequential pattern that its parent node represents. As a result, if a node represents a sequential pattern p, its parent node represents the length-$(|p| - 1)$ prefix of p. For example, if a node represents a pattern $\langle (1), (2, 3) \rangle$, its parent node represents $\langle (1), (2) \rangle$.

SLPMiner starts from the root node that represents the null sequence to find all the frequent items in the input database and expands the root node into the child nodes corresponding to the frequent items. Then it recursively moves to each child node and expands it into child nodes that represent frequent sequential patterns.

SLPMiner grows each pattern in two different ways, namely, *itemset extension* and *sequence extension*. Itemset extension grows a pattern by adding an item to the last itemset of the pattern, where the added item must be larger than any item in the last itemset of the original pattern. For example, $\langle (1), (2) \rangle$ is extended to $\langle (1), (2, 3) \rangle$ by itemset extension, but cannot be extended to $\langle (1), (2, 1) \rangle$ or $\langle (1), (2, 2) \rangle$. Sequence extension grows a pattern by adding an item as a new itemset next to the last itemset of the pattern. For example, $\langle (1), (2) \rangle$ is extended to $\langle (1), (2), (2) \rangle$ by sequence extension.

Figure 3 shows a sequential database D and its prefix tree that contains all the frequent sequential patterns given minimum support 0.5. Since D contains a total of four sequences, a pattern is frequent if and only if at least two sequences in D support the pattern. The root of the tree represents the null sequence. At each node of the tree in the figure, its pattern and its supporting sequences in D are depicted together with symbol SE or IE on each edge representing itemset extension or sequence extension respectively.

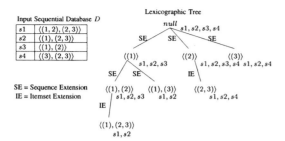

Figure 3. The prefix tree of a sequential database

At each node we need to know the support of each possible extension to see whether it is frequent or not. In principle, we can count the number of supporting sequences at each node by scanning the input sequential database D. However, if only a small number of sequences in D support the pattern, scanning the whole database costs too much for a pattern. We can avoid this overhead by scanning a database called *projected database*, which is generally much smaller than the original sequential database D. The projected database of a sequential pattern p has only those sequences in D that support p. For example, at the node $\langle (2,3) \rangle$ in Figure 3, its projected database needs to contain only $s1, s2, s4$ since $s3$ does not support this pattern. Furthermore, we can eliminate preceding items in each sequence that will never be used to extend the current pattern. For example, at the node $\langle (2) \rangle$ in Figure 3, we can store sequence $s1' = \langle (2,3) \rangle$ instead of $s1$ itself in its projected database. Overall, database projection reduces the amount of sequences that need to be processed at each node and enhances efficient pattern discovery.

There are various database-projection-based algorithms for both finding frequent itemsets and finding frequent sequential patterns [1, 3, 4, 5]. SLPMiner builds the tree in depth first order and generates a projected database at every node explicitly to maximize opportunities for applying the various pruning methods. As a result, its overall approach is similar to that used by PrefixSpan [5]. However, the main difference between them is that SLPMiner generates several projected databases at a time before exploring those generated child nodes, whereas PrefixSpan generates and explores one projected database at a time.

3.2 Performance Optimizations

Expanding each node of the tree, SLPMiner performs the following two steps. First, it calculates the support of each item that can be used for itemset extension and each item that can be used for sequence extension by scanning the projected database D' once. Second, SLPMiner projects D' into a projected database for each frequent extension found in the previous step.

Since we want SLPMiner to be able to run against large input sequential databases, the access to the input database

and all projected databases is disk-based. To facilitate this, SLPMiner uses two kinds of buffers: a read-buffer and a write-buffer. The read-buffer is used to load a projected database from disk. If the size of a projected database does not fit in the read-buffer, SLPMiner reads part of the database from disk several times. The write-buffer is used to temporally store several projected databases that are generated at a node by scanning the current projected database once using the read-buffer. There are two conflicting requirements concerning how many projected databases we should generate at a time. In order to reduce the number of database scans, we want to generate as many projected databases as possible in one scan. On the other hand, if we keep small buffers for many projected databases simultaneously within the write-buffer, it will reduce the size of the buffer assigned to each projected database, leading to expensive frequent I/O between the write-buffer and disk. In order to balance these two conflicting requirements, SLPMiner calculates the size of each projected database when calculating the support of every item in the current projected database before it actually generates new projected databases. Then SLPMiner generates projected databases as many as they fit in the write-buffer by one database scan, writes those projected databases on the write-buffer to the disk, and traverses only those generated child nodes in depth first order. This method also facilitates storing each projected database in a chunk rather than fragmented small pieces, which improves and stabilizes disk I/O efficiency dramatically.

Even though the disk I/O of SLPMiner is quite efficient, it is still a bottle-neck of the total performance. In order to reduce the size of projected database, SLPMiner prunes all items from a projected database if the support is less than $\min_{l \geq 1} f(l)$ since such items will never contribute to any frequent sequential patterns.

3.3 Pruning Methods

Given a length-decreasing support constraint, SLPMiner follows the sequential database-projection-based approach explained so far using $\min_{l \geq 1} f(l)$ as the constant minimum support constraint. Then SLPMiner outputs sequential patterns if their support satisfies the given length-decreasing support constraint. But this algorithm itself does not reduce the number of discovered patterns and will be very inefficient as our experimental results will show. In this subsection, we introduce three pruning methods that exploit the length-decreasing support constraint using the SVE property.

3.3.1 Sequence Pruning, SP

The first pruning method is used to eliminate certain sequences from the projected databases. Recall from Section 3 that SLPMiner generates a projected database at every node. Let us assume that we have a projected database D' at a node N that represents a sequential pattern p. Each sequence in D' has p as its prefix. If p is infrequent, we know from the SVE property that in order for this pattern to grow to something indeed frequent, it must have a length of at least $f^{-1}(\sigma_D(p))$. Now consider a sequence s that is in the projected database at node N, i.e., $s \in D'$. The largest sequential pattern that s can support is of length $|s| + |p|$. Now if $|s| + |p| \leq f^{-1}(\sigma_D(p))$, then s is too short to support any frequent patterns that have p as prefix. Consequently, s does not need to be considered any further and can be pruned. We will refer to this pruning method as the *sequence pruning* method or *SP* for short, which is formally defined as follows:

Definition 3 (Sequence Pruning) *Given a length-decreasing support constraint $f(l)$ and a projected database D' at a node representing a sequential pattern p, a sequence $s \in D'$ can be pruned from D' if $f(|s| + |p|) > \sigma_D(p)$.*

SLPMiner checks if a sequence can be pruned before inserting it onto the write-buffer. We evaluated the complexity of this method in comparison with the complexity of inserting a sequence to a projected database. There are three parameters required to prune a sequence: $|s|$, $|p|$, and $\sigma_D(p)$. As the length of each sequence is part of sequence data structure in SLPMiner, it takes a constant time to calculate $|s|$ and $|p|$. As for $\sigma_D(p)$, we know this value when we generated the projected database for the pattern p. Evaluating function f takes a constant time because SLPMiner has a lookup table that contains all possible $(l, f(l))$ pairs. Thus, the complexity of this method is just a constant time per inserting a sequence.

3.3.2 Item Pruning, IP

The second pruning method eliminates some items of each sequence in projected databases. Let us assume that we have a projected database D' at a node N that represents sequential pattern p and consider an item i in a sequence $s \in D'$. From the SVE property we know that the item i will contribute to a valid frequent sequential pattern only if

$$|s| + |p| \geq f^{-1}(\sigma_{D'}(i)) \tag{1}$$

where $\sigma_{D'}(i)$ is the support of item i in D'. This is because of the following. The longest sequential pattern that s can participate in is $|s| + |p|$, and we know that, in the subtree rooted at N, sequential patterns that extend p with item i have support at most $\sigma_{D'}(i)$. Now, from the SVE property, such sequential patterns must have length at least $f^{-1}(\sigma_{D'}(i))$ in order to be frequent. As a result, if equation (1) does not hold, item i can be pruned from the sequence s. Once item i is pruned, then $\sigma_{D'}(i)$ and $|s|$ decrease, possibly allowing further pruning. Essentially, this pruning

method eliminates some of the infrequent items from the short sequences. We will refer to this method as the *item pruning* method, or *IP* for short, which is formally defined as follows:

Definition 4 (Item Pruning) *Given a length-decreasing support constraint $f(l)$ and a projected database D' at a node representing a sequential pattern p, an item i in a sequence $s \in D'$ can be pruned from s if $|s| + |p| < f^{-1}(\sigma_{D'}(i))$.*

We can implement this pruning method simply as follows: for each projected database D', repeat scanning D' to collect support values of items and scanning D' again to prune items from each sequence until no more items can be pruned. Then, we can project the database into a projected database for each frequent item in the pruned projected database. This algorithm, however, requires multiple scans of the projected database and hence will be too costly.

Instead, we can scan a projected database once to collect support values and use those support values for pruning items as well as for projecting each sequence. Notice that we are using approximate support values that might be higher than the real values since the support values of some items might decrease during the pruning process. SLPMiner applies IP before generating a projected sequence s' of s as well as after generating s' just before inserting s' onto the write-buffer. By applying IP before projecting sequences, we can reduce the computation of projecting sequences. By applying IP once again for projected sequence s', we can exploit the reduction of length $|s| - |s'|$ to prune items in s' furthermore. Pruning items from each sequence is repeated until no more item can be pruned or the sequence becomes short enough to be pruned by SP.

IP can potentially prune larger portion of projected database than SP since it always holds that $\sigma_D(p) \geq \sigma_{D'}(i)$ and hence $f^{-1}(\sigma_D(p)) \leq f^{-1}(\sigma_{D'}(i))$. However, the pruning overhead of IP is much larger than that of SP. Let us consider the complexity of pruning items from a sequence s. The worst case is that only one item is pruned in every iteration over the items in s. Since this can be repeated as many as the number of items in the sequence, the worst case complexity for one sequence is $O(n^2)$ where n is the number of items in the sequence.

3.3.3 Structure-based Pruning

Given two sequences s_1, s_2 of the same length k, these two sequences are treated equally under SP and IP. In fact, the two sequences can be quite different from each other. For example, $\langle(1, 2, 3, 4)\rangle$ and $\langle(1), (2), (3), (4)\rangle$ support the same 1-sequence $\langle(1)\rangle$, $\langle(2)\rangle$, $\langle(3)\rangle$, and $\langle(4)\rangle$ but never support the same k-sequences for $k \geq 2$. From this observation, we considered ways to split a projected database into smaller equivalent classes. By having smaller databases instead of one large database, we may be able to reduce the depth of a certain path from the root to a leaf node of the tree.

As a structure-based pruning, we developed the min-max pruning method. The basic idea of the min-max pruning is to split a projected database D' into two D'_1, D'_2 such that D'_1 and D'_2 contribute to two disjoint sets of frequent sequential patterns. In order to separate D' into such D'_1 and D'_2, we consider the following two values for each sequence $s \in D'$:

1. $a(s)$ = the minimum number of itemsets in frequent sequential patterns that s supports

2. $b(s)$ = the maximum number of itemsets in frequent sequential patterns that s supports

These two values define an interval $[a(s), b(s)]$, that we call the min-max interval of sequence s. If two sequences $s, s' \in D'$ satisfy $[a(s), b(s)] \cap [a(s'), b(s')] = \emptyset$, then s and s' cannot support any common sequential pattern since their min-max intervals are disjoint.

If we have D'_1 and D'_2 satisfy $\cup_{s \in D'_1}[a(s), b(s)] \cap \cup_{s \in D'_2}[a(s), b(s)] = \emptyset$, then D'_1 and D'_2 support distinct sets of frequent sequential patterns. However, this is not possible in general. Instead, D' will be split into three sets A, B, C of sequences as shown in Figure 4. More precisely, these three sets are defined for some positive integer k as follows.

$$
\begin{aligned}
A(k) &= \{s | s \in D' \wedge b(s) < k\} \\
B(k) &= \{s | s \in D' \wedge a(s) \geq k\} \\
C(k) &= D' - (A \cup B)
\end{aligned}
$$

$A(k)$ and $B(k)$ support distinct sets of frequent sequential patterns, whereas $A(k)$ and $C(k)$ as well as $B(k)$ and $C(k)$ support overlapping sets of frequent sequential patterns. From these three sets, we form $D'_1 = A(k) \cup C(k)$ and $D'_2 = B(k) \cup C(k)$. If we mine frequent sequential patterns of length up to $k - 1$ from D'_1 and patterns of length no less than k from D'_2, we can gain the same patterns as we would from original D'.

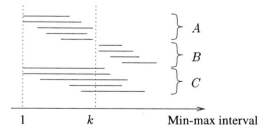

Figure 4. Min-max intervals of a set of sequences

Through our experiments, we observed $|C|$ is so close to $|D'|$ that mining D'_1 and D'_2 defined above will cost more than mining the original database D'. However, we can prune entire D' if both $|D'_1|$ and $|D'_2|$ are smaller than the $\min_{l \geq 1} f(l)$. Furthermore, we can increase this minimum support by the fact that any sequential patterns that the current pattern p can extend to is of length at most $\max_{s \in D'}(|s|) + |p|$. Now, from the SVE property, we know that if both $|D'_1|$ and $|D'_2|$ are smaller than $f^{-1}(\max_{s \in D'}(|s|) + |p|)$, then we can eliminate entire D'. Essentially, this means that if we can split a projected database into two subsets each of which is too small to be able to support any frequent sequential pattern, then we can eliminate the entire original projected database. We call this pruning method the *min-max pruning* or *MP* for short, which is formally defined as follows:

Definition 5 (Min-Max Pruning) *Given a length-decreasing support constraint $f(l)$ and a projected database D' at a node representing a sequential pattern p, entire D' can be pruned if there exists a positive integer k such that*

$$
\begin{aligned}
|D'_1| &= |A(k)| + |C(k)| < f(\max_{s \in D'}(|s|) + |p|)|D|, \text{ and} \\
|D'_2| &= |B(k)| + |C(k)| < f(\max_{s \in D'}(|s|) + |p|)|D|. \quad (2)
\end{aligned}
$$

We apply MP just after a new projected database D' is generated if the entire sequences in D' is still kept on the write-buffer and if $|D'| \leq 1.2f(\max_{s \in D'}(|s|))|D|$. The first condition is necessary to avoid costly disk I/O and the second condition is necessary to increase the probability of successfully eliminating the projected database. The algorithm of MP consists of two parts: the first part to calculate the distribution of the number of sequences over possible min-max intervals and the second part to find k that satisfies condition (2). The first part requires scanning D' on memory once and finding the min-max interval for each sequence. For each sequence s, SLPMiner generates a histogram of itemset size and calculates $a(s)$ by summing up itemset sizes from the largest one. The other value $b(s)$ is simply the number of itemsets in s. This part requires $O(m)$ where m is the total number of itemsets in D'. The second part uses an $n \times n$ upper triangular matrix $Q = (q_{ij})$ where $q_{ij} = |\{s | a(s) = i \wedge b(s) = j \wedge s \in D'\}|$ and n is the maximum number of itemsets in a sequence in D'. Matrix Q is generated during the database scan of the first part. Given matrix Q, we have

$$
\begin{aligned}
|A(k)| + |C(k)| &= \sum_{i=1}^{k-1} \sum_{j=i}^{n} q_{ij} \\
|B(k)| + |C(k)| &= \sum_{j=k}^{n} \sum_{i=1}^{j} q_{ij}
\end{aligned}
$$

423

parameter	DS1	DS2
$\lvert D \rvert$	25000	25000
$\lvert C \rvert$	$x = 10, 12, \cdots, 30$	3 to 10
$\lvert T \rvert$	2.5	$x = 2.5, 3.0, \cdots, 7.0$
N	10000	10000
$\lvert S \rvert$	$x/2$	5
$\lvert I \rvert$	1.25	$x/2$

Table 1. Parameters for datasets used in our tests

Using relations

$$(\lvert A(k+1) \rvert + \lvert C(k+1) \rvert) - (\lvert A(k) \rvert + \lvert C(k) \rvert) = \sum_{j=k}^{n} q_{kj}$$

$$(\lvert B(k+1) \rvert + \lvert C(k+1) \rvert) - (\lvert B(k) \rvert + \lvert C(k) \rvert) = -\sum_{i=1}^{k} q_{ik}$$

we can calculate $\lvert A(k) \rvert + \lvert C(k) \rvert$ and $\lvert B(k) \rvert + \lvert C(k) \rvert$ incrementally for all k in $O(n^2)$. So the total complexity of the min-max pruning for one projected database is $O(m + n^2)$. This complexity may be much larger than the runtime reduction by eliminating projected databases. However, our experimental results show that the min-max pruning method generally reduces the total runtime substantially when other pruning methods are not used together.

4 Experimental Results

We experimentally evaluated the performance of SLPMiner using a variety of datasets generated by the synthetic sequence generator that is provided by the IBM Quest group and was used in evaluating the AprioriAll algorithm [7]. All of our experiments were performed on Linux workstations with AMD Athlon at 1.5GHz and 2GB of main memory. All the reported runtime values are in seconds.

We used two classes of datasets DS1 and DS2, each of which contained 25K sequences. For each class we generated different problem instances as follows. For DS1, we varied the average number of itemsets in a sequence from 10 to 30 by interval 2, obtaining a total of 11 datasets, DS1-10, DS1-12, $\cdots$, DS1-30. For DS2, we varied the average number of items in an itemset from 2.5 to 7.0 by interval 0.5, obtaining a total of 10 datasets, DS2-2.5, DS2-3.0, $\cdots$, DS2-7.0. For DS1-x, we set the average size of maximal potentially frequent sequences to be $x/2$. For DS2-x, we set the average size of maximal potentially frequent itemsets to be $x/2$. Thus, the dataset contains longer frequent patterns as x increases. The characteristics of these datasets are summarized in Table 1, where $\lvert D \rvert$ is the number of sequences, $\lvert C \rvert$ is the average number of itemsets per sequence, $\lvert T \rvert$ is the average number of items per itemset, N is the number of items, $\lvert S \rvert$ is the average size of maximal potentially frequent sequences, and $\lvert T \rvert$ is the average size of maximal potentially frequent itemsets.

In all of our experiments, we used a minimum support

constraint that decreases linearly with the length of the frequent sequential pattern. In particular, the initial value of support was set to 0.001 and it was decreased linearly down to 0.0001 for sequences of up to length $\lfloor \lvert C \rvert \lvert T \rvert / 2 \rfloor$.

We ran SPADE [9] to compare runtime values with SLPMiner. When running SPADE, we used the depth first search option, which leads to better performance than the breadth first search option on our datasets. We set the minimum support value to be $\min_{l \geq 1} f(l)$.

4.1 Results

Tables 2 and 3 show the experimental results that we obtained for the DS1 and DS2 datasets respectively. Each row of the tables shows the results obtained for a different DS1-x or DS2-x dataset, specified on the first column. The column labeled "SPADE" shows the amount of time taken by SPADE, which includes the runtime of preprocessing to transform the input sequential database into the vertical format [9]. The column labeled "None" shows the amount of time taken by SLPMiner using a constant support constraint that corresponds to the smallest support of the support curve, that is 0.0001 for all datasets. The other columns show the amount of time required by SLPMiner that uses the length-decreasing support constraint and a total of five different varieties of pruning methods and their combinations. For example, the column label "SP" corresponds to the pruning scheme that uses only sequence pruning, whereas the column labeled "SP+IP+MP" corresponds to the scheme that uses all the three pruning methods. Note that values with a "–" correspond to experiments that were aborted because they were taking too long time.

A number of interesting observations can be made from the results in these tables. First, even though SLPMiner without any pruning method is slower than SPADE, the ratio of runtime values is stable ranging from 1.9 to 2.7 with average 2.3. This shows that the performance of SLPMiner is comparable to SPADE and good enough as a platform to evaluate our pruning methods.

Second, either one of pruning methods performs better than SLPMiner without any pruning method. In particular, SP, IP, SP+IP, and SP+IP+MP have almost the same speedup. For DS1, the speedup by SP is about 1.76 times faster for DS1-10, 7.61 times faster for DS1-16, and 141.16 times faster for DS1-22. Similar trends can be observed for DS2, in which the performance of SLPMiner with SP is 1.76 times faster for DS2-2.5, 8.78 times faster for DS2-3.5, and 296.59 times faster for DS2-5.0.

Third, SP pruning alone can achieve almost the best performance among all the other tested combinations. This was counter-intuitive for us since we expected SP+IP would be much better than SP or IP alone. On the other hand, this result shows that many other sequential pattern mining algorithms can exploit the SVE property by using SP since it

424

Dataset	SPADE	SLPMiner					
		None	SP	IP	MP	SP+IP	SP+IP+MP
DS1-10	10.562	20.219	11.514	11.570	12.641	12.006	11.839
DS1-12	18.245	41.420	15.316	15.430	17.804	15.358	15.935
DS1-14	46.216	98.359	21.290	21.583	24.453	21.429	21.297
DS1-16	87.289	208.187	27.342	26.635	31.230	26.186	27.383
DS1-18	273.325	592.886	39.228	39.030	43.490	38.790	40.172
DS1-20	594.777	1438.932	46.147	48.440	54.727	47.864	47.723
DS1-22	4702.697	8942.943	63.351	65.123	74.905	65.232	65.907
DS1-24	–	–	82.756	85.622	94.640	82.377	83.148
DS1-26	–	–	106.986	112.180	126.647	111.699	106.567
DS1-28	–	–	139.369	142.760	162.062	137.955	138.411
DS1-30	–	–	180.715	189.029	212.848	185.601	184.105

Table 2. Comparison of pruning methods using DS1

Dataset	SPADE	SLPMiner					
		None	SP	IP	MP	SP+IP	SP+IP+MP
DS2-2.5	10.562	20.219	11.514	11.570	12.641	12.006	11.839
DS2-3.0	21.159	45.887	16.627	16.940	18.719	15.871	15.902
DS2-3.5	117.486	279.617	31.851	35.319	43.267	31.445	31.696
DS2-4.0	333.786	899.025	32.783	32.488	39.805	31.940	32.107
DS2-4.5	731.402	1784.572	35.871	37.955	43.138	38.030	36.539
DS2-5.0	6460.641	17106.370	57.677	61.654	77.835	59.115	59.096
DS2-5.5	–	–	59.500	62.617	73.759	61.187	61.798
DS2-6.0	–	–	77.752	78.684	96.951	77.925	75.186
DS2-6.5	–	–	98.061	105.475	144.387	101.213	102.184
DS2-7.0	–	–	116.986	119.907	136.513	113.443	117.602

Table 3. Comparison of pruning methods using DS2

is easy to implement. For example, it is straight-forward to implement SP in PrefixSpan [5], for both its disk-based projection and pseudo-projection. Even SPADE [9], which has no explicit sequence representation during pattern mining, can use SP by adding the length of sequence to each record in the vertical database representation.

Fourth, among the three pruning methods, SP leads to the largest runtime reduction, IP leads to the second largest runtime reduction, and MP achieves the smallest reduction. The problem with MP is the overhead of splitting a database into two subsets. Even so, it seems surprising to gain such a great speedup by MP alone. This shows a large part of the runtime of SLPMiner with no pruning method is accounted for by many small projected databases that never contribute to any frequent patterns. As for SP and IP, SP is slightly better than IP because IP and SP prune almost the same amount of projected databases for those datasets but IP has much larger overhead than SP.

Fifth, the runtime with three pruning methods increases gradually as the average length of the sequences (and the discovered patterns) increases, whereas the runtime of SLP-Miner without any pruning increases exponentially.

5   Conclusion

In this paper we presented an efficient algorithm for finding all frequent sequential patterns that satisfy a length-decreasing support constraint. The key insight that enabled us to achieve high performance was the smallest valid extension property of the length-decreasing support con-

straint.

References

[1] R. Agarwal, C. Aggarwal, V. Prasad, and V. Crestana. A tree projection algorithm for generation of large itemsets for association rules. *IBM Research Report*, RC21341, November 1998.

[2] R. Agrawal and R. Srikant. Fast algorithms for mining association rules. In *Proc. of the 20th Int'l Conference on Very Large Databases*, Santiago, Chile, September 1994.

[3] V. Guralnik, N. Garg, and G. Karypis. Parallel tree projection algorithm for sequence mining. In *European Conference on Parallel Processing*, pages 310–320, 2001.

[4] J. Han, J. Pei, and Y. Yin. Mining frequent patterns without candidate generation. In *Proc. 2000 ACM-SIGMOD Int. Conf. Management of Data (SIGMOD'00)*, pages 1–12, Dallas, TX, May 2000.

[5] J. Pei, J. Han, B. Mortazavi-Asl, H. Pinto, Q. Chen, U. Dayal, and M. Hsu. Prefixspan: Mining sequential patterns by prefix-projected growth. In *ICDE*, pages 215–224, 2001.

[6] M. Seno and G. Karypis. Lpminer: An algorithm for finding frequent itemsets using length-decreasing support constraint. In *1st IEEE Conference on Data Mining*, 2001.

[7] R. Srikant and R. Agrawal. Mining sequential patterns. In *11th Int. Conf. Data Engineering*, 1995.

[8] R. Srikant and R. Agrawal. Mining sequential patterns: Generalizations and performance improvements. In *5th Int. Conf. Extending Database Technology*, 1996.

[9] M. J. Zaki. Fast mining of sequential patterns in very large databases. Technical Report TR668, 1997.

[10] M. J. Zaki and K. Gouda. Fast vertical mining using diffsets. Technical Report 01-1, RPI, 2001.

Objective-Oriented Utility-Based Association Mining

Yi-Dong Shen
Laboratory of Computer Science
Institute of Software, Chinese Academy of Sciences
Beijing 100080, P. R. China
ydshen@ios.ac.cn

Zhong Zhang
School of Computing Science
Simon Fraser University
Burnaby, BC, Canada V5A 1S6
zzhang@cs.sfu.ca

Qiang Yang
Department of Computer Science
Hong Kong University of Science and Technology
Clearwater Bay, Kowloon Hong Kong
qyang@cs.ust.hk

Abstract

The necessity to develop methods for discovering association patterns to increase business utility of an enterprise has long been recognized in data mining community. This requires modeling specific association patterns that are both statistically (based on support and confidence) and semantically (based on objective utility) relating to a given objective that a user wants to achieve or is interested in. However, we notice that no such a general model has been reported in the literature. Traditional association mining focuses on deriving correlations among a set of items and their association rules like diaper → beer only tell us that a pattern like {diaper} is statistically related to an item like beer. In this paper, we present a new approach, called Objective-Oriented utility-based Association (OOA) mining, to modeling such association patterns that are explicitly relating to a user's objective and its utility. Due to its focus on a user's objective and the use of objective utility as key semantic information to measure the usefulness of association patterns, OOA mining differs significantly from existing approaches such as the existing constraint-based association mining. We formally define OOA mining and develop an algorithm for mining OOA rules. The algorithm is an enhancement to Apriori with specific mechanisms for handling objective utility. We prove that the utility constraint is neither monotone nor anti-monotone nor succinct nor convertible and present a novel pruning strategy based on the utility constraint to improve the efficiency of OOA mining.

1 Introduction

Association mining is an important problem in data mining. Briefly, given a historical dataset of an application, we derive frequent patterns and association rules from the dataset by using some thresholds, such as a minimum support and a minimum confidence. Since Agrawal's pioneer work [1], a lot of research has been conducted on association mining. Major achievements include approaches to improving the efficiency of computing the frequent patterns from large datasets [2, 5], approaches to applying constraints to find more interesting patterns [3, 11, 15], and approaches to eliminating irrelevant association rules by making use of some interestingness measures [9, 14].

Observe that most existing approaches to association mining are itemset-correlation-oriented in the sense that they aim to find out how a set of items are statistically correlated by mining association rules of the form

$$I_1, ..., I_m \rightarrow I_{m+1}(s\%, c\%) \qquad (1)$$

where $s\%$, the *support* of the rule, is the probability of all items $I_1, ..., I_{m+1}$ occurring together, and $c\%$, the *confidence* of the rule, is the conditional probability of I_{m+1} given the itemset $\{I_1, ..., I_m\}$. Both $s\%$ and $c\%$ are obtained simply by counting the frequency of the respective itemsets in a given dataset, and are greater than or equal to the user-specified minimum support and minimum confidence, respectively.

Although finding correlations of itemsets like *diaper* → *beer* is very important, in many situations people may be more interested in finding out how a set of items support a specific objective *Obj* that they want to achieve by discovering association rules of the form

$$I_1, ..., I_m \rightarrow Obj(s\%, c\%, u) \qquad (2)$$

where $s\%$ is the probability that all items $I_1, ..., I_m$ together with Obj hold, $c\%$ is the conditional probability of Obj given the itemset $\{I_1, ..., I_m\}$, and u is the *utility* of the rule, showing to what degree the pattern $\{I_1, ..., I_m\}$ semantically supports Obj. Due to its focus on an objective and the use of objective utility as key semantic information to measure the usefulness of association patterns, we refer to this new type of association mining as *Objective-Oriented utility-based Association (OOA)* mining, as opposed to traditional *Itemset-Correlation-Oriented Association (ICOA)* mining.

OOA mining derives patterns that both statistically and semantically support a given objective Obj. Informally, $I = \{I_1, ..., I_m\}$ is said to *statistically support Obj* if the support $s\%$ and confidence $c\%$ of the rule (2) are not below a user-specified minimum support $ms\%$ and a user-specified minimum confidence $mc\%$, respectively. And I is said to *semantically support Obj* if the utility u of the rule (2) is not below a user-specified minimum utility mu. As a result, all patterns derived in OOA mining must be interesting to an enterprise since when employed, they would increase the (expected) utility of the enterprise above the user-specified minimum level ($u \geq mu$). Therefore, OOA mining has wide applications in many areas where people are looking for objective-centered statistical solutions to achieve their goals. For a typical example, in business situations a manager may use OOA mining to discover the best business strategies by specifying his/her objective as "high profit and low risk of loss." Another example is in medical field. A doctor may use OOA mining to find the best treatments for a disease by specifying an objective "high effectiveness and low side-effects."

The term *utility* is commonly used to mean "the quality of being useful" and utilities are widely used in decision making processes to express user's preferences over decision objects towards decision objectives [6, 13]. In decision theory, we have the well-known equation "Decision = probability + utility," which says that a decision object is chosen based on its probability and utility. Since association mining can be viewed as a special decision problem where decision objects are patterns, we may well have, correspondingly, an equation "Interestingness (of a pattern) = probability + utility." This equation further justifies the necessity and significance of enhancing traditional probability (support and confidence) based association mining with objective related utilities.

Since utilities are subjective, they can be acquired from domain experts/users. We would point out, however, that this does not mean we need to acquire a utility for each single item in a dataset. As we will see in Section 3, it suffices

to obtain utilities only for those items in a dataset which are directly related to the given objective. The population of such *objective items* would be quite small in practical applications.

In this paper, we systematically study OOA mining. In Section 3, we formally define the concepts of objective, support, confidence, and utility under the frame of OOA mining. In Section 4, we develop an algorithm for mining OOA frequent patterns and rules. The algorithm is based on Apriori, with an enhancement that handles objective utility. Traditional association mining is NP-hard, but OOA mining does not seem to be easier. To improve the efficiency of OOA mining, we will present a novel strategy for pruning itemsets based on the support and utility constraints. In Section 5, we present some experimental results.

2 Related Work

The necessity to develop methods for finding specific patterns which can be used to increase business utility has long been recognized by several researchers [7, 10, 14]. To the best of our knowledge, however, no work on association mining has been reported in the literature which formally models such patterns that are explicitly relating to a user's objective and its utility.

Our work is related to but different from existing constrained association mining. Existing constrained association mining, typically represented by the work of Bayardo, Agrawal, and Gounopolos [3], Han, Lakshmanan, Ng, Pang and Pei [11, 12], and Srikant, Agrawal and Vu [15], takes the form $\{(S \rightarrow T)|C\}$ where S and T are sets of items and C is a set of constraints on the selection of S and T. When T is not empty, such kind of association mining belongs to ICOA mining because no matter what constraints C is, it always derives asociation rules of the form $I_1, ..., I_m \rightarrow J_1, ..., J_n$ where both itemsets $\{I_1, ..., I_m\}$ and $\{J_1, ..., J_n\}$ satisfy C. Certainly, OOA mining can use constraints, too. Constrained OOA mining takes the form $\{(S \rightarrow Obj)|C_{obj}\}$ where C_{obj} is a set of constraints on the selection of S in terms of the objective Obj. Constrained OOA mining always derives OOA rules.

Another significant difference between existing constrained association mining and OOA mining is that most exisitng work focuses on SQL-style constraints including item selection, pattern length, set relations ($\subseteq$, $\supseteq$, etc.), $max(S)\theta v$, $min(S)\theta v$, $sum(S)\theta v$, $count(S)\theta v$ and $avg(S)\theta v$, where S is an itemset, v is a real number, and θ is $\leq$ or $\geq$ (see [12] for a summary of types of constraints discussed in the literature). These constraints fall into one of the following four well-defined categories: monotone, antimonotone, succinct or convertible. In OOA mining, however, we introduce objective utility as a key constraint. On the one hand, an (arbitrary) objective and its utility are difficult, if not impossible, to be formulated using SQL-style constraints. On the other hand, the utility constraint is neither monotone nor anti-monotone nor succinct nor convertible. Therefore, no existing constrained association mining methods are applicable to it. In this work we push the utility constraint deep into OOApriori (a variant of Apriori) to prune candidate patterns in order to efficiently derive all OOA rules.

We would point out that although business objectives, such as "high profit and low risk of loss," can be viewed as constraints, such constraints seem to be at a meta-level w.r.t. the above mentioned SQL-style constraints. Therefore, specific mechanisms are required to represent and handle them. The proposed OOA mining may then be the first such mechanism.

Most recently, Wang, Zhou and Han [16] and Lin, Yao and Louie [8] suggested adding values to association rules. The former takes into account the price and quantity of supermaket sales during association mining, while the latter tries to attach a value to every item in a dataset and use the added values to rank association rules. There are three major differences between their approaches and ours. First, we do general objective centered mining by explicitly declaring a user's objective and formulating it in a simple, uniform way (see Section 3). As a result, utilities are assigned only to those items which directly contribute to the objective. Second, we handle both positive and negative utilities, whereas they only consider positive values. Negative utility represents punishment/loss, and it is with negative values that our utility constraints become neither monotone nor anti-monotone nor succinct nor convertible. Third, we push the utility constraints into Apriori and use them to prune candidate itemsets. Neither of the above two approaches addressed this.

Finally, our work is different from existing research on "interestingness" [9, 14], which focuses on finding "interesting patterns" by matching them against a given set of user's beliefs. Informally, a derived association rule is considered "interesting" if it conforms to or conflicts with the user's beliefs. In contrast, in OOA mining we measure the interestingness of OOA rules in terms of their probabilities as well as their utilities in supporting the user's objective.

3 Objective, Support, Confidence, and Utility

We assume that readers are familiar with traditional association rule mining, especially with the widely used Apriori algorithm [2]. A *data base* or *dataset DB* is associated with a finite set DB_{att} of attributes. Each attribute A_i has a finite domain V_i (continuous attributes can be discretized using methods such as that in [4]). For each $v \in V_i$, $A_i = v$ is called an *item*. An *itemset* or a *pattern* is a set of items. A *k-itemset* is an itemset with k items. DB consists of a fi-

nite set of records/transactions built from DB_{att}, with each *record* being a set $\{A_1 = v_1, ..., A_m = v_m\}$ of items where $A_i \neq A_j$ for any $i \neq j$. We use $|DB|$ to denote the total number of records in DB. Finally, for any itemset I the function $count(I, DB)$ returns the number of records in DB that are supersets of I.

An objective describes anything that we want to achieve or we are interested in. In order to discover patterns in a dataset DB that support our objective Obj, we need first to formulate Obj in terms of items of DB. This can be done by first partitioning DB_{att} into two disjoint subsets: $DB_{att} = DB_{att}^{Obj} \cup DB_{att}^{nObj}$ where each attribute $A \in DB_{att}^{Obj}$ obviously contributes to Obj, whereas each $A \in DB_{att}^{nObj}$ does not. For convenience, we refer to attributes in DB_{att}^{Obj} as *objective attributes*.

Let A be an objective attribute and V its domain. For each $v \in V$, $A = v$ is called an *objective item* or a *class* of A. We use $class(A)$ to denote all classes of A. Let $\Re$ be a relation symbol such as $=, >, <$, etc. For each $v \in V$, $A\Re v$ is called an *objective relation*. An objective can then be represented by a logic formula over objective relations using the connectives $\wedge$, $\vee$ or $\neg$. Formally, we have

Definition 1 An objective Obj over a dataset DB is a disjunctive normal form $C_1 \vee ... \vee C_m$ $(m \geq 1)$ where each C_i is a conjunction $D_1 \wedge ... \wedge D_n$ $(n \geq 1)$ with each D_j being an objective relation or the negation of an objective relation.

With an objective Obj as formulated above, we can then evaluate against a dataset how a pattern $I = \{I_1, ..., I_m\}$ statistically and semantically supports Obj by defining the support, confidence and utility of the corresponding rule $I_1, ..., I_m \rightarrow Obj$. In OOA mining, we say an objective Obj *holds* in a record r in DB (or we say r *supports Obj*) if Obj is true given r. Furthermore, for any itemset $I = \{I_1, ..., I_m\}$ we say $I \cup \{Obj\} = \{I_1, ..., I_m, Obj\}$ holds in r if both Obj and all I_is are true in r. We then extend the function $count(I, DB)$ to $count(I \cup \{Obj\}, DB)$ that returns the number of records in DB in which $I \cup \{Obj\}$ holds.

Definition 2 Let $I_1, ..., I_m \rightarrow Obj$ $(s\%, c\%, u)$ be an association rule in OOA mining. Then the support and confidence of the rule are respectively given by

$$s\% = \frac{count(\{I_1, ..., I_m, Obj\}, DB)}{|DB|} * 100\%, \quad (3)$$

$$c\% = \frac{count(\{I_1, ..., I_m, Obj\}, DB)}{count(\{I_1, ..., I_m\}, DB)} * 100\%. \quad (4)$$

Let Obj be an objective and A an objective attribute. Based on Obj, the classes of A can be subjectively classified into three disjoint groups: $class(A) = class^+(A) \cup class^-(A) \cup class^o(A)$ where $class^+(A)$ consists of all classes of A that show positive support for Obj, $class^-(A)$ of all classes of A that show negative support for Obj, and $class^o(A)$ of all classes of A that show neither positive nor negative support for Obj. Therefore, classes in $class^+(A)$ will bring Obj positive utilities, whereas classes in $class^-(A)$ bring negative utilities. We then associate each class $A = v$ in $class^+(A)$ or $class^-(A)$ with a utility $u_{A=v}$ (a real number). Since any class in $class^o(A)$ can be considered as a special positive class with a utility 0, we can merge $class^o(A)$ into the positive group. Therefore, in the sequel we always assume that any class $A = v$ belongs to either $class^+(A)$ or $class^-(A)$. The groups of positively and negatively supporting classes of a dataset DB for Obj are then respectively defined as follows: $class^+(DB) = \{A = v \ (u_{A=v})|A \in DB_{att}^{Obj}$ and $A = v \in class^+(A)\}$ and $class^-(DB) = \{A = v \ (u_{A=v})|A \in DB_{att}^{Obj}$ and $A = v \in class^-(A)\}$.

An *OOA itemset* (or *OOA pattern*) is a set $\{A_1 = v_1, ..., A_m = v_m\}$ of items with $A_i \in DB_{att}^{nObj}$ and $A_i \neq A_j$ for any $i \neq j$. Let I be an OOA itemset and r a record in DB with $I \subseteq r$. Let C_r be the set of classes in r. The *positive utility* $u_r^+(I)$ (resp. *negative utility* $u_r^-(I)$) of r for I is the sum of the utilities of all positively (resp. negatively) supporting classes in C_r, given by

$$u_r^+(I) = \sum_{A=v \in C_r \wedge A=v(u_{A=v}) \in class^+(DB)} u_{A=v}, \quad (5)$$

$$u_r^-(I) = \sum_{A=v \in C_r \wedge A=v(u_{A=v}) \in class^-(DB)} u_{A=v}, \quad (6)$$

The *positive* and *negative utility* of DB for I are then

$$u_{DB}^+(I) = \sum_{r \in DB \wedge I \subseteq r} u_r^+(I), \quad (7)$$

$$u_{DB}^-(I) = \sum_{r \in DB \wedge I \subseteq r} u_r^-(I). \quad (8)$$

Definition 3 Let $I_1, ..., I_m \rightarrow Obj$ $(s\%, c\%, u)$ be an association rule with $I = \{I_1, ..., I_m\}$ an OOA itemset. Let $u_{DB}(I) = u_{DB}^+(I) - u_{DB}^-(I)$. The utility of the rule (or the itemset I) is given by

$$u = \frac{u_{DB}(I)}{count(I, DB)} \quad (9)$$

Example 1 Let us consider a simplified dataset DB_1 about medical treatments for a certain disease as shown in Table 1, where treatment, effectiveness and side-effect are attributes with domains $\{1, 2, ..., 5\}$, $\{1, 2, ..., 5\}$ and $\{1, 2, 3, 4\}$, respectively. $R\#$ is not an attribute of DB_1. It is used to identify records by assigning a unique number to each record. Table 2 shows the degrees of the effectiveness and

side-effects which are assigned by experienced domain experts. The doctor then wants to discover from DB_1 the best treatments with high effectiveness and low side-effects. Apparently, this is a typical objective-oriented utility-based mining problem.

Table 1. A medical dataset DB_1.

$R\#$	treatment	effectiveness	side-effect
1	1	2	4
2	2	4	2
3	2	4	2
4	2	2	3
5	2	1	3
6	3	4	2
7	3	4	2
8	3	1	4
9	4	5	2
10	4	4	2
11	4	4	2
12	4	3	1
13	5	4	1
14	5	4	1
15	5	4	1
16	5	3	1

Table 2. Degrees of the effectiveness and side-effects.

	effectiveness		side-effect
5	getting much better	4	very serious
4	getting better	3	serious yet tolerable
3	no obvious effect	2	a little
2	getting worse	1	normal
1	getting much worse		

The objective Obj is "high effectiveness with low side-effects," which divides the set of attributes DB_{1att} into DB_{1att}^{Obj} ={effectiveness, side-effect} and DB_{1att}^{nObj} ={treatment}. Based on the measurement of the effectiveness and side-effects (Table 2), Obj may be formulated by the formula: (effectiveness>3) $\wedge$ (side-effect<3). Assume we are given the following groups of positively and negatively supporting classes (*eff* stands for effectiveness and *sid* for side-effect):

$class^+(DB_1) = \{eff = 5(1), eff = 4(0.8),$
$\qquad eff = 3(0), sid = 1(0.6), sid = 2(0)\},$
$class^-(DB_1) = \{eff = 1(1), eff = 2(0.8),$
$\qquad sid = 4(0.8), sid = 3(0.4)\}.$

Table 3 shows the supports, confidences and utilities for all rules of the form "treatment=$k \rightarrow Obj$" where k is a treatment number, which are composed from the dataset DB_1.

Table 3. Supports, confidences and utilities.

Obj : (effectiveness>3) $\wedge$ (side-effect<3)			
rules	$s\%$	$c\%$	u
treatment=1$\rightarrow Obj$	0	0	-1.6
treatment=2$\rightarrow Obj$	12.5%	50%	-1
treatment=3$\rightarrow Obj$	12.5%	66%	-0.2
treatment=4$\rightarrow Obj$	18.75%	75%	0.8
treatment=5$\rightarrow Obj$	18.75%	75%	1.2

Note that the last two rules have quite different utilities for the objective, although their support and confidence are the same. Therefore, "treatment=5" should be the best because it has the highest utility in supporting the objective.

4 Mining OOA Rules

4.1 Objective-Oriented Apriori

Definition 4 Let DB be a dataset and Obj an objective. Let $ms\%$, $mc\%$ and mu be a user-specified minimum support, minimum confidence and minimum utility, respectively. Let $I = \{I_1, ..., I_m\}$ be an OOA itemset. I is an *OOA frequent pattern/itemset* in DB if $s\% \geq ms\%$. Let I be an OOA frequent pattern. $I_1, ..., I_m \rightarrow Obj$ $(s\%, c\%, u)$ is an *OOA association rule (OOA rule)* if $c\% \geq mc\%$ and $u \geq mu$. Here $s\%$, $c\%$ and u are as defined in Equations (3), (4) and (9), respectively.

OOA mining is then to derive all OOA rules from DB. We extend Apriori [2] to generating OOA frequent patterns and rules by enhancing it with mechanisms for handling objectives and utilities. For convenience, we refer to the extended algorithm as *Objective-Oriented Apriori (OOApriori)*.

For the data structure, we associate each OOA itemset with some necessary data fields to record data like counts and utilities. This is done by organizing an itemset into a structure using pseudo C^{++} language. That is, each OOA itemset $I = \{I_1, ..., I_m\}$ is internally an instance of the data type ITEMSET defined as follows:

```
typedef struct {
    set      pattern; //store the pattern {I_1, ..., I_m}
    int      count_1; //store count(I, DB)
    int      count_2; //store count(I ∪ {Obj}, DB)
    float    u^+; //store u^+_DB(I) (see the formula (7))
    float    u^-; //store u^-_DB(I) (see the formula (8))
} ITEMSET;
```

We use $I.D$ to refer to the field D of I. $I.count_1$, $I.count_2$, $I.u^+$ and $I.u^-$ are all initialized to 0 when I is

created. Moreover, when no confusion would occur, by I we refer to its pattern $I.pattern = \{I_1, ..., I_m\}$.

Algorithm 1: Objective-Oriented Apriori.
Input: $ms\%$, $mc\%$, mu, Obj and DB.
Output: FP, the set of OOA frequent itemsets, and
$\qquad\quad AR$, the set of OOA rules.
function $OOApriori(ms\%, mc\%, mu, Obj, DB)$
1) $\quad AR = FP = \emptyset;$
2) $\quad k = 1;$
3) $\quad C_k = \{I \mid I$ is an OOA 1-itemset in $DB\};$
$\qquad$ //Part 1: Collect counts and utilities of k-itemsets
4) $\quad$ **for** each record r in DB
5) $\qquad$ **for** each k-itemset $I \in C_k$
6) $\qquad\quad$ **if** $I \subseteq r$ **then begin**
7) $\qquad\qquad I.count_1$++;
8) $\qquad\qquad I.u^+ = I.u^+ + u_r^+(I);$
9) $\qquad\qquad I.u^- = I.u^- + u_r^-(I);$
10) $\qquad\qquad$ **if** Obj holds in r **then**
11) $\qquad\qquad\quad I.count_2$++
12) $\qquad$ **end**
$\qquad$ //Part 2: Check for frequent patterns (L_k) and rules (AR)
13) $\quad L_k = \emptyset;$
14) $\quad$ **for** each $I = \{I_1, ..., I_k\} \in C_k$
15) $\qquad$ **if** $s\% = \frac{I.count_2}{|DB|} \geq ms\%$ **then begin**
16) $\qquad\quad L_k = L_k \cup \{I\};$
17) $\qquad\quad c\% = \frac{I.count_2}{I.count_1};$
18) $\qquad\quad u = \frac{I.u^+ - I.u^-}{I.count_1};$
19) $\qquad\quad$ **if** $c\% \geq mc\%$ and $u \geq mu$ **then**
20) $\qquad\qquad AR = AR \cup \{I_1, ..., I_k \rightarrow Obj(s\%, c\%, u)\}$
21) $\qquad$ **end**
$\qquad$ //Part 3: Generate (k+1)-itemsets
22) $\quad$ **if** $L_k \neq \emptyset$ **then begin**
23) $\qquad k$++;
24) $\qquad C_k = aprioriGen(L_{k-1});$ //New candidate itemsets
25) $\qquad$ **goto** 4)
26) $\quad$ **end**
27) $\quad$ **return** $FP = \bigcup_i L_i$ and AR
end

In Algorithm 1, for each $k \geq 1$ C_k is used to store candidate frequent OOA k-itemsets, L_k to store frequent OOA k-itemsets, and AR to store all OOA rules. OOApriori consists of three major parts. The first part (lines 4-12) scans the dataset DB and applies each record in DB to counting the frequency and computing the positive and negative utilities of each candidate itemset in C_k. At lines 8 and 9, $u_r^+(I)$ and $u_r^-(I)$ are as defined in Equations (5) and (6). The second part (lines 13-21) checks the support, confidence and utility of each candidate itemset $I = \{I_1, ..., I_k\}$ in C_k against the three user-specified minimums $ms\%$, $mc\%$ and mu to see if I is an OOA frequent pattern and $I_1, ..., I_k \rightarrow Obj$ is an OOA rule. After all OOA frequent k-itemsets and rules have been generated, the third part (lines 22-26) of OOApriori generates new candidate $(k+1)$-itemsets based on L_k by calling the following function $aprioriGen()$. This function is borrowed from Apriori [2].

function $aprioriGen(L_k)$
1) $C_{k+1} = \emptyset$;
2) **for** each pair of itemsets in L_k of the form
3) $\quad \{I_1, ..., I_{k-1}, I_k\}$ and $\{I_1, ..., I_{k-1}, I_{k+1}\}$
4) $\quad C_{k+1} = C_{k+1} \cup \{\{I_1, ..., I_{k+1}\}\}$;
  //Prune itemsets
5) **for** each $I \in C_{k+1}$
6) $\quad$ **if** some k-sub-itemset of I is not in L_k **then**
7) $\quad\quad C_{k+1} = C_{k+1} - \{I\}$; //Remove I from C_{k+1}
8) **return** C_{k+1}
end

After the set C_{k+1} of new candidate itemsets has been generated, the process goes to the next cycle (line 25) for deriving OOA frequent $(k+1)$-itemsets and rules. OOApriori will continue this way until no new OOA frequent itemsets can be generated (line 22).

Theorem 1 *If $I = \{I_1, ..., I_m\}$ is an OOA frequent pattern and $J \subset I$ with $J \neq \emptyset$, then J is an OOA frequent pattern.*

Theorem 2 *OOApriori is sound and complete in the sense that I is an OOA frequent itemset if and only if $I \in FP$ and that $I_1, ..., I_m \to Obj(s\%, c\%, u)$ is an OOA rule if and only if it is in AR.*

4.2 A Pruning Strategy for Mining OOA Rules

Theorem 2 shows the correctness of applying OOApriori to computing OOA frequent itemsets and rules. In this section we develop a pruning strategy to improve its efficiency. Here and throughout, when we say that an OOA itemset $I = \{I_1, ..., I_m\}$ passes/violates the confidence or the utility constraint, we mean that the OOA rule $I_1, ..., I_m \to Obj$ passes/violates the constraint.

Four types of constraints for association mining have been identified in the literature [11, 12]. Let C be a constraint and S_1 and S_2 be two arbitrary itemsets. For $S_1 \subset S_2$, C is *anti-monotone* if S_1 violating C implies S_2 violates C, and C is *monotone* if S_1 satisfying C implies S_2 satisfies C. If C is *succinct* then S_1 and S_2 satisfying C implies $S_1 \cup S_2$ satisfies C. C is *convertible* if there exists an order R on items such that for any itemset S satisfying C, every prefix of S w.r.t. R satisfies C.

Theorem 1 assures us that the support constraint for OOA frequent patterns is anti-monotone. Therefore, in OOApriori we can safely delete an itemset I from L_k when its support is below the minimum support (see line 15) because no frequent patterns will be built from I. It turns out, however, that neither the confidence nor the utility constraint for OOA rules is anti-monotone.

Theorem 3 *The utility constraint for OOA rules is neither monotone nor anti-monotone nor succinct nor convertible.*

The pruning problem is then described as follows: For any itemset I in L_k (see the OOApriori algorithm) that has passed the support constraint but violates either the confidence or the utility constraint, can we delete I from L_k without missing any OOA rules? Without any pruning mechanism, OOApriori will generate all OOA frequent items, many of which may produce no OOA rules because of the violation of the confidence or the utility constraint. Look at the function $aprioriGen(L_k)$ again. Since all $(k+1)$-itemsets are composed from the k-itemsets in L_k, we need to keep L_k as small as possible by removing some OOA frequent itemsets from which no OOA rules would be possibly built.

We present a pruning strategy using the support and utility constraints. To describe the pruning strategy, we add two more data fields to the internal structure of an OOA itemset I as shown below:

```
typedef struct {
    set      pattern; //store the pattern {I_1, ..., I_m}
    int      count_1; //store count(I, DB)
    int      count_2; //store count(I ∪ {Obj}, DB)
    float    u^+; //store u_DB^+(I)
    float    u^-; //store u_DB^-(I)
    int      count_2^+; //store |S^+|
    float    lnu; //store the least negative utility
} ITEMSET;
```

Here, let S be the set of records in DB in which $I \cup \{Obj\}$ holds and S^+ be the set of records in S which contain no negative class (i.e., all classes of these records are in $class^+(DB)$), then the first new field $count_2^+$ is used to store $|S^+|$ (note that the field $count_2$ stores $|S|$) and the second new field lnu is used to store the least negative utility of a record in $S - S^+$, i.e. $lnu \leq u_r^-(I)$ for any r in $S - S^+$.

Strategy 1 Remove any OOA itemset $I = \{I_1, ..., I_k\}$ from L_k if $I.count_2^+ < ms\% * |DB|$ and $\frac{I.u^+ - LB^-}{ms\% * |DB|} < mu$, where $LB^- = (ms\% * |DB| - I.count_2^+) * I.lnu$.

Since I is a frequent OOA itemset, there are at least $ms\% * |DB|$ records in $|DB|$ in which $I \cup \{Obj\}$ holds. When $I.count_2^+ < ms\% * |DB|$, there are at least $(ms\% * |DB| - I.count_2^+)$ records in DB in which $I \cup \{Obj\}$ holds that contain negative classes. Therefore, $LB^- > 0$ is the least negative utility of DB for I and thus is the lower bound of $I.u^-$. As a result, $I.u^+ - LB^-$ is the upper bound of the utility of DB for I. To sum up, this strategy says that an OOA frequent itemset I is removable if the upper bound of its expected utility is below the minimum utility. The following theorem shows that applying this strategy will not miss any OOA rules.

Theorem 4 *Let* $I = \{I_1, ..., I_k\}$ *be an OOA frequent itemset. If* $I.count_2^+ < ms\% * |DB|$ *and* $\frac{I.u^+ - LB^-}{ms\%*|DB|} < mu$ *then there is no OOA itemset* $J = \{J_1, ..., J_n\} \supseteq I$ *such that* $J_1, ..., J_n \rightarrow Obj$ *is an OOA rule.*

It is easy to push Strategy 1 into the OOApriori algorithm. This is done by replacing lines 14-21 of Algorithm 1 with the following lines:

14) **for** each $I = \{I_1, ..., I_k\} \in C_k$
15)   **if** $s\% = \frac{I.count_2}{|DB|} \geq ms\%$ **then begin**
16) $L_k = L_k \cup \{I\}$;
17) $c\% = \frac{I.count_2}{I.count_1}$;
18) $u = \frac{I.u^+ - I.u^-}{I.count_1}$;
19)   **if** $c\% \geq mc\%$ and $u \geq mu$ **then**
20) $AR = AR \cup \{I_1, ..., I_k \rightarrow Obj(s\%, c\%, u)\}$;
20-1)   **else begin**
20-2) $LB^- = (ms\% * |DB| - I.count_2^+) * I.lnu$;
20-3)   **if** $I.count_2^+ < ms\% * |DB|$ and $\frac{I.u^+ - LB^-}{ms\%*|DB|}$
20-4) $< mu$ **then** $L_k = L_k - \{I\}$ //by Strategy 1
20-5)   **end**
21)   **end**

The above procedure works as follows: For each candidate k-itemset in C_k, if it passes the support constraint then it is added to L_k (lines 15 and 16). If it also passes both the confidence and the utility constraint, an OOA rule built from I is added to AR (lines 17-20). Otherwise, when I passes the support constraint but violates either the confidence or the utility constraint, our pruning strategy is applied (lines 20-1 to 20-5) to remove some OOA frequent itemsets from L_k from which no OOA rules will be produced. The correctness of the OOApriori algorithm enhanced with the pruning strategy follows immediately from Theorems 2 and 4. That is, $I_1, ..., I_m \rightarrow Obj(s\%, c\%, u)$ is an OOA rule if and only if it is in AR.

5 Experimental Evaluation

We show the effect of applying our pruning strategy by empirical experiments. We choose the widely used *German Credit* dataset from the UCI Machine Learning Archive (ftp://ftp.ics.uci.edu/pub /machine-learning-databases/statlog/german/). This dataset consists of 1000 records (each record represents a customer) with 21 attributes such as *Status, Duration, Credit-history, Purpose, Employment*, etc. The last attribute *Conclusion* classifies a customer as *good* or *bad* in terms of his/her credits. The reason we use this dataset in our experiment is that its attributes are semantically easy to understand so that we can flexibly create different objectives from them to test our approach.

We build four datasets with different sizes from the 1000 records. DS_1 consists of 600 records, DS_2 of 700 records, ..., and DS_4 of 900 records. The objective attributes are *Liable-people, Foreign* and *Conclusion*, and the objective *Obj* is defined as (Conclusion=good) $\wedge$ (Liable-people=2 $\vee$ Foreign=no). That is, suppose we are interested in customers whose credit is good and who either are not foreign workers or have more than one person being liable to provide maintenance for the credit account. All the remaining eighteen attributes are treated as non-objective attributes. The utilities of the major classes of the objective are defined in Table 4 where we normalize the utilities into [0, 100].

Table 4. Class utilities.

	Conclusion	Foreign	Liable-people
$class^+(DB)$	*good* (70)	*no* (10)	2 (20)
$class^-(DB)$	*bad* (70)	*yes* (10)	1 (20)

Let N_1 and N_2 be the sizes of the two sets of OOA candidate itemsets generated by OOApriori with and without applying Strategy 1, respectively. We evaluate the effect of applying Strategy 1 to pruning OOA itemsets by demonstrating its *itemset reduction rate* defined by $\frac{N_2 - N_1}{N_2}$. Figure 1 shows our experimental results on the itemset reduction rates where we use different minimum utilities while keeping the minimum support and minimum confidence unchanged. The results strongly demonstrate that applying our pruning strategy can greatly improve the efficiency of the OOApriori algorithm. On average, they pruned $8\% - 9\%$ of the candidate itemsets during the mining process. Figure 2 further demonstrates the effectiveness of the pruning strategy, where we use the same minimum confidence and minimum utility while letting the minimum support vary.

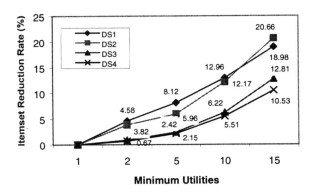

Figure 1. The itemset reduction rates against minimum utilities.

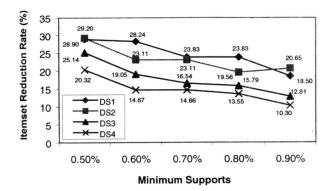

Figure 2. The itemset reduction rates against minimum supports.

6 Conclusions

We have developed a new approach to modeling association patterns. OOA mining discovers patterns that are explicitly relating to a given objective that a user wants to achieve or is interested in and its utility. As a result, all OOA rules derived from a dataset by OOA mining are useful because applying them would increase business utility of an enterprise. This shows a significant difference from traditional association mining.

We developed an algorithm for mining OOA frequent patterns and rules. The algorithm is an enhancement to Apriori with specific mechanisms for handling objective utility. Since the utility constraint is neither anti-monotone nor monotone nor succinct nor convertible, finding effective pruning strategies is of great significance. We developed a novel pruning strategy for mining OOA rules by combining the support and utility constraints. As far as we can determine, no similar work has been reported in the literature.

Acknowledgement

Yi-Dong Shen is supported in part by Chinese National Natural Science Foundation, Trans-Century Training Program Foundation for the Talents by the Chinese Ministry of Education, and Foundations from Chinese Academy of Sciences. Qiang Yang thanks NSERC and IRIS-III program for their support.

References

[1] R. Agrawal, T. Imilienski, and A. Swami. Mining association rules between sets of items in large datasets. In *SIGMOD*, pages 207–216, 1993.

[2] R. Agrawal and R. Srikant. Fast algorithm for mining association rules. In *VLDB*, pages 487–499, 1994.

[3] R. Bayardo, R. Agrawal, and D. Gounopolos. Constraint-based rule mining in large, dense databases. In *ICDE*, pages 188–197, 1999.

[4] J. Dougherty, R. Kohavi and M. Sahami. Supervised and unsupervised discretization of continuous features. *ICML*, 1995.

[5] J. Han, J. Pei, and Y. Yin. Mining frequent patterns without candidate generation. In *SIGMOD*, pages 1–12, 2000.

[6] R. Howard. Risk preference. In R. Howard and J. Matheson, eds. *Readings in Decision Analysis*, pages 429–465, 1977.

[7] J. Kleinberg, C. Papadimitriou, and P. Raghavan. A microeconomic view of data mining. *Journal of Data Mining and Knowledge Discovery*, 6(1):83–105, 1998.

[8] T. Lin, Y. Yao, and E. Louie. Value added association rules. In *PAKDD*, pages 328–333, 2002.

[9] B. Liu, W. Hsu, S. Chen, and Y. Ma. Analyzing the subjective interestingness of association rules. *IEEE Intellgent Systems*, 15:47–55, 2000.

[10] B. Masand and G. Piatetsky-Shapiro. A comparison of approaches for maximizing business payoff of prediction models. In *KDD*, pages 195–201, 1996.

[11] R. Ng, L. Lakshmanan, J. Han, and A. Pang. Exploratory mining and pruning optimizations of constrained association rules. In *SIGMOD*, pages 13–24, 1998.

[12] J. Pei and J. Han. Constrained frequent pattern mining: a pattern-growth view. *ACM SIGKDD Explorations* (Special Issue on Constrained Data Mining) 2(2), 2002.

[13] S. Russell and P. Norvig. *Artificial Intelligence: A Modern Approach*. Englewood Cliffs, NJ: Prentice Hall, 1994.

[14] A. Silberschatz and A. Tuzhilin. What makes patterns interesting in knowledge discovery system. *IEEE Trans. on Knowledge and Data Engineering*, 8:970–974, 1996.

[15] R. Srikant, Q. Vu, and R. Agrawal. Mining association rules with item constraints. In *KDD*, pages 67–73, 1997.

[16] K. Wang, S. Zhou and J. Han. Profit mining: from patterns to actions. In *EDBT*, pages 70-87, 2002.

A Self-Organizing Map with Expanding Force for Data Clustering and Visualization

Wing-Ho Shum, Hui-Dong Jin, Kwong-Sak Leung
Department of Computer Science and Engineering
The Chinese University of Hong Kong
Hong Kong
{whshum, hdjin, ksleung}@cse.cuhk.edu.hk

Man-Leung Wong
Department of Information Systems
Lingnan University
Hong Kong
mlwong@ln.edu.hk

Abstract

The Self-Organizing Map (SOM) is a powerful tool in the exploratory phase of data mining. However, due to the dimensional conflict, the neighborhood preservation cannot always lead to perfect topology preservation. In this paper, we establish an Expanding SOM (ESOM) to detect and preserve better topology correspondence between the two spaces. Our experiment results demonstrate that the ESOM constructs better mappings than the classic SOM in terms of both the topological and the quantization errors. Furthermore, clustering results generated by the ESOM are more accurate than those by the SOM.

1   Introduction

The Self-Organizing Map (SOM) has been proven to be useful as visualization and data exploratory analysis tools [6]. It maps high-dimensional data items onto a low-dimensional grid of neurons. The regular grid can be used as a convenient visualization surface for showing different features of data [9, 12]. SOMs have been successfully applied in various areas such as full-text and image analysis, and travelling salesman problem [3, 4, 7].

However, because a SOM maps the data from a high-dimensional space to a low-dimensional space which is usually 2-dimensional, a dimensional conflict may occur and a perfect topology preserving mapping may not be generated [1, 5]. For example, consider the two trained SOMs depicted in Fig.1, although they preserve good neighborhood relationships, the SOM depicted in Fig.1(b) folds the neuron string onto data irregularly and loses much topology information in comparison with the SOM shown in Fig.1(a).

There are many research efforts to enhance SOMs for visualization and cluster analysis. Most of them focus on how to visualize neurons clearly and classify data [2, 10, 12].

Figure 1. Two SOMs from 2-dimensional space to 1-dimension. The connected dots indicate a string of neurons, and other dots indicate data.

Some work has concentrated on better topology preservation. Kirk and Zurada [5] trained their SOM to minimize the quantization error in the first phase and then minimize the topological error in the second phase.

In this paper, we propose a new learning rule to enhance the topology preservation and overcome the irregularity problem. The paper is organized as follows. We introduce our ESOM in Section 2, followed by its theoretic analysis.. The visualization and clustering results of the ESOM are presented and compared with the SOM in Section 3. A conclusion is given in the last section.

2   Expanding SOM

Besides the neighborhood relationship in the SOM, another topology relationship can be detected and preserved during the learning process to achieve a better topology preserving mapping for data visualization. This is a linear ordering relationship based on the distance between data and their center. A neural network can detect and preserve this ordering relationship. If the distance between a data item and the center of all data items is larger, the distance between the corresponding output neuron and the center is

434

also larger.

Our Expanding SOM (ESOM) can construct a mapping that preserves both the neighborhood and the ordering relationships. Since this mapping preserves more topology information of the input data, better performance in visualization can be achieved.

We introduce a new learning rule to learn the linear ordering relationship. Different from the SOM, the learning rule of the ESOM has an additional factor, the expanding coefficient $c_j(t)$, which is used to push neurons away from the center of all data items during the learning process. In other words, the flexible neuron network is expanding gradually in our ESOM algorithm. Moreover, the expanding force is specified according to the ordering of the data items. In general, the larger the distance between the corresponding data item and the center, the larger the expanding coefficient $c_j(t)$. Consequently, the associated output neuron is pushed away from the center and the ordering of data items is thus preserved in the output neurons. In the following sub-sections, the ESOM algorithm will be discussed first. Theoretical analysis of the ESOM algorithm will then be described.

2.1 The ESOM algorithm

The ESOM algorithm consists of 6 steps.

1. Linearly transform the coordinates $\vec{x}_i' = [x_{1i}', x_{2i}', \cdots, x_{Di}']^T$ ($i = 1, \cdots, N$) of all given data items so that they lie within a sphere S_R centered at the origin with radius R (< 1). Here N is the number of data items, D is the dimensionality of the data set. Hereafter, $[x_{1i}, x_{2i}, \cdots, x_{Di}]^T$ denotes the new coordinate of $\vec{x}_i$. Let the center of all data items be $\vec{x}_C' = \frac{1}{N} \sum_{i=1}^{N} \vec{x}_i'$ and the maximum distance of data from the data center be D_{max}, then

$$\vec{x}_i = \frac{R}{D_{max}} \left(\vec{x}_i' - \vec{x}_C' \right) \text{ for all } i. \quad (1)$$

2. Set $t = 0$, and the initialize weight vectors $\vec{w}_j(0)$ ($j = 1, \cdots, M$) with random values within the above sphere S_R where M is the number of output neurons.

3. Select a data item at random, say $\vec{x}_k(t) = [x_{1k}, x_{2k}, \cdots, x_{Dk}]^T$, and feed it to the input neurons.

4. Find the winning output neuron, say $m(t)$, nearest to $\vec{x}_k(t)$ according to the Euclidean metric:

$$m(t) = \arg \min_j \|\vec{x}_k(t) - \vec{w}_j(t)\|. \quad (2)$$

5. Train neuron $m(t)$ and its neighbors by using the following formula:

$$\begin{aligned} \vec{w}_j(t+1) &= c_j(t)\vec{w}_j'(t+1) \stackrel{\triangle}{=} c_j(t)\{\vec{w}_j(t) \\ &+ \alpha_j(t)\left[\vec{x}_k(t) - \vec{w}_j(t)\right]\} \end{aligned} \quad (3)$$

The parameters include:

- *the interim neuron* $\vec{w}_j'(t+1)$, which indicates the position of the excited neuron $\vec{w}_j(t)$ after moving towards the input data item $\vec{x}_k(t)$;

- *the learning parameter* $\alpha_j(t)(\in [0,1])$, which is specified by a learning rate $\epsilon(t)$ and a neighborhood function $h_{j,m(t)}(\sigma(t))$:

$$\alpha_j(t) = \epsilon(t) \times h_{j,m(t)}(\sigma(t)); \quad (4)$$

- *the expanding coefficient* $c_j(t)$, which is specified according to

$$c_j(t) = \left[1 - 2\alpha_j(t)\left(1 - \alpha_j(t)\right)\kappa_j(t)\right]^{-\frac{1}{2}}, \quad (5)$$

where $\kappa_j(t)$ is specified by

$$\begin{aligned} \kappa_j(t) &= 1 - \langle \vec{x}_k(t), \vec{w}_j(t) \rangle - \\ &\sqrt{(1 - \|\vec{x}_k(t)\|^2)(1 - \|\vec{w}_j(t)\|^2)} \end{aligned} \quad (6)$$

6. Update the neighbor width parameter $\sigma(t)$ and the learning parameters $\epsilon(t)$ with predetermined decreasing schemes. If the learning loop does not reach a predetermined number, go to Step 3 with $t := t + 1$.

The first step facilitates the realization of the expanding coefficient $c_j(t)$. After the transformation, we can use the norm of a data item $\|\vec{x}_k(t)\|$ to represent its distance from the center of the transformed data items since the center is the origin. Thus, the norm $\|\vec{x}_k(t)\|$ can indicate the ordering topology in the data space. This ordering will be detected and preserved in $\|\vec{w}_j(t)\|$ through the expanding process.

The learning rule defined in Eq.(3) is the key point of the proposed ESOM algorithm. Different from the SOM learning rule, it has an additional multiplication factor — the expanding coefficient $c_j(t)$. It is worth pointing out that, although the expanding coefficient $c_j(t)$ is relevant to all data items, the calculation of $c_j(t)$ only depends on $\alpha_j(t)$, $\vec{x}_k(t)$ and $\vec{w}_j(t)$. If $c_j(t)$ is a constant 1.0, the ESOM is simplified to a conventional SOM. Since $c_j(t)$ is always greater than or equal to 1.0, the expanding force pushes the excited neuron away from the center. In other words, the inequality $\|\vec{w}_j(t+1)\| \geq \left\|\vec{w}_j'(t+1)\right\|$ is always true. Fig.2(b) illustrates the expanding functionality. After moving the excited neuron $\vec{w}_j(t)$ towards the input data $\vec{x}_k(t)$, as indicated by

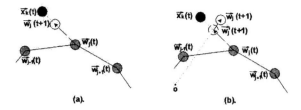

(a).   (b).

Figure 2. A schematic view of two different learning rules. (a). The learning rule for the SOM; (b). The learning rule for the ESOM. A black disc indicates a data item; a gray disc indicates a neuron; a solid line indicates the neighbor relationship on the grid; a circle indicates the new position of a neuron; a dashed circle indicates a neuron's temporary position; a dashed arrow indicates a movement direction; and 'o' indicates the the center of data.

$\vec{w}'_j(t+1)$, the neuron is then pushed away from the center. So, during the learning process, the flexible neuron net is expanding in the data space. More interestingly, as the expanding force is specified according to the ordering relationships, distant data items are likely to be mapped to the distant neurons, while data items near the center are likely to be mapped to the neurons in the center of map, therefore, $c_j(t)$ can help us to detect and preserve the ordering relationship.

Researchers have introduced several measures to evaluate the quality of a mapping [1, 13]. In this paper, we employ both the quantization error E_Q and the topological error E_T used in [5, 11] to evaluate the mapping obtained by our ESOM. E_T is defined as the proportion of the data items whose closest and second-closest neurons are not adjacent on the grid. The quantization error evaluates how well the weight vectors represent the data set [5, 12]. It is specified as follows:

$$E_Q = \frac{1}{N} \sum_{k=1}^{N} \|\vec{x}_k(t) - \vec{w}_{m_k}(t)\| \quad (7)$$

where m_k is the winner for the data item $\vec{x}_k(t)$. These two criteria usually conflict with each other in the SOM.

2.2 Theoretical analysis

To show the feasibility of the ESOM, we should verify that the ESOM does generate a map that preserve both the good neighborhood relationship and the ordering relationship. In this paper, we only give a theorem on a one-step

trend to support the feasibility of the ESOM because it is very difficult to prove the convergence of the SOM-like networks in high dimensional cases. In fact, it is still one of the long-standing open research problems in neural networks [8]. We will perform a more rigorous convergence analysis in our future research work. In the following theorem, we assume that all input data items are located within the sphere S_R and their center coincides with the origin because the preprocessing procedure in Step 1 has been executed.

Theorem 1 *Let S_R be the closed sphere with radius R (< 1) centered at the origin, $\{\vec{x}_k(t) \in S_R\}$ (for $k = 1, \cdots, N$) be the input data and $\{\vec{w}_j(t)\}$ (for $j = 1, \cdots, M$) be the weight vectors of the ESOM at time t. Then, for any $t \geq 0$,*

(i). for $j \in \{1, 2, \cdots, M\}$,

$$1 \leq c_j(t) \leq \frac{1}{\sqrt{1 - R^2}}; \quad (8)$$

and $\vec{w}_j(t) \in S_R$, that is,

$$\|\vec{w}_j(t)\| \leq R. \quad (9)$$

(ii). the expanding coefficient $c_j(t)$ increases with $\|\vec{x}_k(t)\|$ when $\|\vec{x}_k(t)\| \geq \|\vec{w}_j(t)\|$.

Proof. (i). We prove Eqs.(8) and (9) together by induction. This is trivially true for $t = 0$ according to Step 2 of the ESOM algorithm. If we assume that both equations hold for certain $t(\geq 0)$, then we find

$$\begin{aligned}
1 - \kappa_j(t) &= \langle \vec{x}_k(t), \vec{w}_j(t) \rangle + \sqrt{(1 - \|\vec{x}_k(t)\|^2)} \\
&\quad \times \sqrt{(1 - \|\vec{w}_j(t)\|^2)} \\
&\leq \left(\sum_{d=1}^{D} x_{dk}^2(t) + \left(\sqrt{(1 - \|\vec{x}_k(t)\|^2)} \right)^2 \right) \\
&\quad \times \left(\sum_{d=1}^{D} w_{dj}^2(t) + \left(\sqrt{(1 - \|\vec{w}_j(t)\|^2)} \right)^2 \right) \\
&= 1.
\end{aligned}$$

Similarly,

$$\begin{aligned}
1 - \kappa_j(t) &= \langle \vec{x}_k(t), \vec{w}_j(t) \rangle + \sqrt{(1 - \|\vec{x}_k(t)\|^2)} \\
&\quad \times \sqrt{(1 - \|\vec{w}_j(t)\|^2)} \\
&\geq -\frac{1}{2}(\|\vec{x}_k(t)\|^2 + \|\vec{w}_j(t)\|^2) + \sqrt{(1 - R^2)} \\
&\quad \times \sqrt{(1 - R^2)} \\
&\geq 1 - 2R^2.
\end{aligned}$$

Thus,

$$0 \leq \kappa_j(t) \leq 2R^2$$

On the other hand, for any learning parameter $\alpha_j(t) \in [0, 1]$, the following inequality is true,

$$0 \le \alpha_j(t)(1 - \alpha_j(t)) \le 0.25.$$

According to Eq.(5), we get $1 \le c_j(t) \le \frac{1}{\sqrt{1-R^2}}$. According to the ESOM learning rule, we have

$$1 - \|\vec{w}_j(t+1)\|^2 = \left[\begin{array}{c} [c_j(t)]^{-2} \\ -\|\vec{w}_j(t) + \alpha_j(t)(\vec{x}_k(t) - \vec{w}_j(t))\|^2 \end{array} \right]$$
$$\times (c_j(t))^2 \qquad (10)$$
$$= \frac{1}{(c_j(t))^{-2}} \times$$
$$\left[\begin{array}{c} (1 - \alpha_j(t))\sqrt{1 - \|\vec{w}_j(t)\|^2} \\ +\alpha_j(t)\sqrt{1 - \|\vec{x}_k(t)\|^2} \end{array} \right]^2$$
$$\ge \left[\begin{array}{c} (1 - \alpha_j(t))\sqrt{1 - R^2} \\ +\alpha_j(t)\sqrt{1 - R^2} \end{array} \right]^2$$
$$= 1 - R^2.$$

This implies that $\|\vec{w}_j(t+1)\| \le R$ for any $j = 1, \cdots, M$. Thus, by induction, $\vec{w}_j(t) \in S_R$ for any j and t.

(ii). We rewrite $\vec{x}_k(t)$ and $\vec{w}_j(t)$ as follows,

$$\vec{x}_k(t) = \rho \times \vec{e}_{x_k}, \quad \vec{w}_j(t) = r \times \vec{e}_{w_j}$$

Here $\vec{e}_{x_k}$ and $\vec{e}_{w_j}$ are two unit vectors, and $\rho = \|\vec{x}_k(t)\|$ and $r = \|\vec{w}_j(t)\|$. According to the assumption that $\rho \ge r$ holds. Let

$$F(\rho) = \langle \vec{w}_j(t), \vec{x}_k(t) \rangle$$
$$+ \sqrt{(1 - \|\vec{w}_j(t)\|^2)(1 - \|\vec{x}_k(t)\|^2)} \qquad (11)$$
$$= \rho \cdot r \cdot \langle \vec{e}_{w_j}, \vec{e}_{x_k} \rangle + \sqrt{(1 - \rho^2)(1 - r^2)}.$$

According to Eq.(5), it is obvious that $F(\rho) = 1 - \frac{1 - c_j^{-2}(t)}{2\alpha_j(t)(1 - \alpha_j(t))}$. $F(\rho)$ decreases with the expanding coefficient $c_j(t)$. So, to justify the increasing property of $c_j(t)$, it is sufficient to show that $F(\rho)$ decreases with ρ whenever $\rho \ge r$. A direct calculation shows

$$\frac{\partial F(\rho)}{\partial \rho} = r \cdot \langle \vec{e}_{w_j}, \vec{e}_{x_k} \rangle - \frac{\rho}{\sqrt{1 - \rho^2}} \sqrt{1 - r^2} \quad (12)$$
$$\le r - \rho \le 0. \qquad (13)$$

This implies the decreasing property of $F(\rho)$ on ρ when $\rho \ge r$. ∎

Theorem 1 (i) says that the expanding coefficient $c_j(t)$ is always larger than or equal to 1.0. In other words, it always pushes neurons away from the origin. Thus, during learning, the neuron net is expanding. Furthermore, though the expanding force is always greater than or equal to 1.0, it will never push the output neurons to infinite locations. In fact, it is restricted by sphere S_R in which the data items are located. This point is substantiated by Eq.(9). This supports the feasibility of our ESOM.

Theorem 1 (ii) gives a theoretic support that the ESOM aims to detect and preserve the ordering relationship among the training data items. It points out that the expanding coefficient $c_j(t)$, or the expanding force, is different for various data items. The larger the distance between a data item and the center of all data items is, the stronger the expanding force will be on the associated output neuron. Consequently, the neuron will be pushed away from the center.

We now briefly discuss another interesting trend based on the proof procedure. If $\vec{w}_j(t)$ is far away from $\vec{x}_k(t)$[1], $\langle \vec{e}_{w_j}, \vec{e}_{x_k} \rangle$ will be very small or even less than 0. From Eq.(12), $\frac{\partial F(\rho)}{\partial \rho} \approx -\frac{\rho}{\sqrt{1-\rho^2}}\sqrt{1 - r^2} \le 0$. In other words, the expanding coefficient $c_j(t)$ increases with ρ which is the distance of the input data item $\vec{x}_k(t)$ from the center. So, the ordering of $\|\vec{x}_k(t)\|$ is reflected by the expanding coefficient $c_j(t)$ and then is learned by $\vec{w}_j(t)$. This also explains why the topological error of the ESOM decreases more quickly than that of the SOM at the beginning of learning. A typical example can be found in Fig.4 in Section 3.

3 Experimental results

3.1 Experimental setting

We examined the ESOM on 3 synthetic data sets and 1 real-life data set. All experimental results are compared with those of the SOM in terms of both the quantization and the topological errors. All data sets were preprocessed using the same linear transformation as in Eq.(1) in order to compare results fairly. All experiments were done with the same set of parameters. The initial values of the learning rate ϵ, the neighbor width parameter σ, and the radius R were 0.5, 0.9 and 0.999 respectively. Both the learning rate α and the neighbor width parameter σ were decreased by factor of 0.998 per iteration. Except for the last data set, we used a rectangular grid with 20*20 neurons. All experiments were run for 2000 iterations in total.

The three synthetic data sets are quite interesting in both their special cluster shapes and locations as illustrated in Fig.3. The conventional clustering algorithms such as K-means and Expectation-Maximization (EM) are unable to identify the clusters. The first data set has 3,000 data items in 2-dimensional space with 3 clusters. The most inside cluster looks like a triangle which is surrounded by two strip-like clusters. This data set is designed to demonstrate the topology preservation capacity of SOMs, because we

---

[1] the case is common at the beginning of learning since the weight vector $\vec{w}_j(t)$ is randomly initialized.

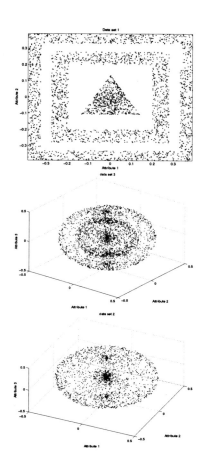

Figure 3. Illustration of Data set 1 (Upper), Data set 2 (Middle) and Data set 3 (Lower)

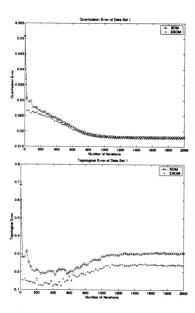

Figure 4. The quantization error (Upper) and the topological error (Lower) during the learning of the ESOM and the SOM.

can compare the resultant mapping with the original data set directly. The second data set contains 2,000 data items in 3-dimensional space with 2 clusters (the middle one in Fig.3). The third data set has 3,000 3-dimensional data items (the lower one in Fig.3). The last data set, Iris, is a benchmark problem and is downloadable from UCI Machine Learning Repository (www.ics.ucs.edu/umlearn/ULSummary.html). It has 150 data items in 4-dimensional space with 3 classes. As there are not many data items in the last data set, we use an output grid with 10 * 10 neurons for both algorithms.

3.2 Results for the first data set

First, we check how good the mappings the two algorithms can generate in terms of the two criteria given in Subsection 2.1. Fig.4 illustrates the quantization and the topological errors during a typical run of both algorithms. It is clearly seen that the quantization error decreases gradually as the learning process continues. The quantization error of

the trained ESOM is 0.017 which is a bit smaller than that of the trained SOM, 0.018. During learning, the topological error curve clearly has three stages: decreasing, increasing and convergence. At the very beginning of the training process, the neuron's weights are fairly dislike, while some of them even contain remnants of random initial values, thus higher topological errors are got. After several iterations, the topological error decreases dramatically. Because the learning rate ϵ is large and the neighborhood function is also large then, the neurons adjacent on the grid may move much closer the input data item together. At this stage, the ESOM can learn the ordering topology of data items very quickly. As shown in Fig.4, the topological error of the ESOM is much smaller than that of the SOM. Though the topological errors of both algorithms increase later, the ESOM keeps the gain and always has smaller topological error than the SOM. Finally, the topological errors of the ESOM and the SOM are 0.238 and 0.304 respectively. ESOM makes about 20% improvement on the topological error in comparison with the SOM, and the ESOM gets slightly smaller quantization error than the SOM. Thus, the ESOM can generate better topology preserving maps than the SOM.

Now let us see how well the trained ESOM identifies the clusters in the first data set. Fig.5 illustrates the trained ESOM and SOM in the form of U-matrix. The x-axis and y-axis of the U-matrix indicate a neuron's position on the grid, and the z-axis is the average Euclidean distance of

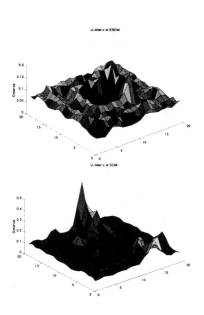

Figure 5. U-Matrix of the trained ESOM (Upper) and the trained SOM (Lower).

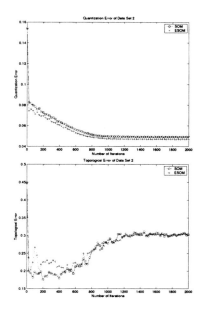

Figure 7. The quantization error (Upper) and the topological error (Lower) in the learning of the ESOM and the SOM.

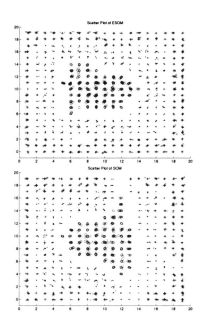

Figure 6. Scatter plot the trained ESOM (Upper) and the trained SOM (Lower).

neurons from its adjacent ones [2]. A sequence of consecutive peaks can be regarded as a boundary among clusters, while the basins beside are regarded as clusters. There are clearly two sequences of peaks in the ESOM's U-matrix, which indicate three clusters in the first data set. The layer structure in the data set has been clearly illustrated. In contrast, The boundaries in the SOM's U-matrix is not so clear because some high peaks blur the boundaries. The scatter plots shown in Fig.6 illustrate data clusters on the grid. In the scatter plot, each marker represents a mapping of a data item and the shape of the marker indicates its cluster label. The marker is placed on the winning neuron of the data item. To avoid overlapping, the marker has plotted with a small offset which is specified according to the data item's Euclidean distance from the winning neurons. The ESOM maps data items in well-organized layers. We can easily find the three clusters in its scatter plot which is quite similar with the original data set as shown in Fig.3. However, as we can see from Fig.6, the SOM cannot map data very well. The outer cluster in Fig.3 is even separated into three subclusters (indicated by '+').

3.3 Results for the second data set

Fig.7 shows the quantization and the topological errors during a typical run of both algorithms for the second data set. Though the topological errors of both the ESOM and

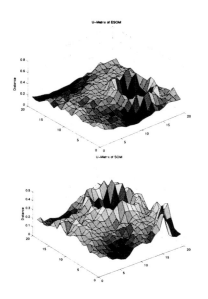

Figure 8. U-Matrix of the trained ESOM (Upper) and the trained SOM (Lower).

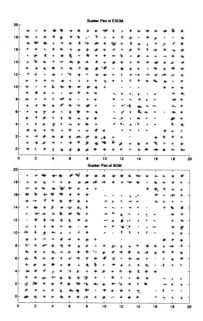

Figure 9. Scatter plot the trained ESOM (Upper) and the trained SOM (Lower).

the SOM are very close, the ESOM has smaller quantization error than the SOM. Observed from Fig.8, the U-matrix of the ESOM clearly shows two clusters as one cluster is separated by a sequence of peaks. However, the U-matrix of the SOM indicates three clusters. An extra cluster has been added at the bottom-right corner. This results is further confirmed by the scatter plots of the two maps as illustrated in Fig.9. The SOM separates one of the clusters in the original data set into two clusters(represented by '.'). In contrast, the scatter plot of the ESOM clearly shows two clusters where one cluster surrounds the other as in the original data set depicted in Fig.3.

Table 1. Average Quantization Errors based on 10 independent runs.

Data Set Name	ESOM	SOM	Improvement (%)
Data Set 1	0.01767	0.01800	1.80060
Data Set 2	0.04753	0.04832	1.64508
Data Set 3	0.05991	0.06042	0.83417
Data Set 4	0.02907	0.02774	-4.81993

Table 2. Average Topological Errors based on 10 independent runs.

Data Set Name	ESOM	SOM	Improvement (%)
Data Set 1	0.24088	0.26039	7.49154
Data Set 2	0.30215	0.30555	1.11241
Data Set 3	0.33132	0.34763	4.69203
Data Set 4	0.33200	0.33667	1.38624

Table 3. Average Execution Times based on 10 independent runs.

Data Set Name	ESOM	SOM	Difference (%)
Data Set 1	2371.6	2283.2	3.87176
Data Set 2	2068.9	2051.2	0.86291
Data Set 3	2904.7	2872.1	1.13506
Data Set 4	28.8	28.5	1.05263

Tables 1, 2 and 3 show the average quantization errors, topological errors and execution time for all the four data sets, based on 10 independent runs, respectively. We can see that the ESOM has better capability in topology preservation, while the execution times are comparable with those of SOM. However, the ESOM have not much improvement on quantization error yet, because topological error and quantization error are in conflict and it is difficult to optimize both of them at the same time.

4 Conclusion

In this paper, we have proposed an Expanding Self-Organizing Map (ESOM) to detect and preserve better topology correspondence between the input data space and the output grid. During the learning process of our ESOM, the flexible neuron net is expanding and the neuron corresponding to a distant data item gets large expanding force. Besides the neighborhood relationship as in the SOM (Self-Organizing Map), the ESOM can detect and preserve an linear ordering relationship as well. Our experiment results have substantiated that the ESOM constructs better visualization results than the classic SOM in terms of both the topological and the quantization errors. Furthermore, clustering results generated by the ESOM are more accurate than those obtained by the SOM on both synthetic and real-life data sets.

In our future work, we will study different methods to scale-up the ESOM algorithm for large data sets and investigate various techniques for visualizing large data sets efficiently, and compare the performance of the ESOM with other extensions of SOM.

Acknowledgement

This research was supported by RGC Earmarked Grant for Research CUHK 4212/01E of Hong Kong.

References

[1] H. U. Bauer, M. Herrmann, and T. Villmann. Neural maps and topographic vector quantization. *Neural Networks*, 12:659–676, 1999.

[2] J.A.F. Costa and M.L. de Andrade Netto. A new tree-structured self-organizing map for data analysis. In *Proceedings of International Joint Conference on Neural Networks*, volume 3, pages 1931–1936, 2001.

[3] Huidong Jin, Kwong-Sak Leung, and Man-Leung Wong. An integrated self-organizing map for the traveling salesman problem. In Nikos Mastorakis, editor, *Advances in Neural Networks and Applications*, pages 235–240, World Scientific and Engineering Society Press, Feb. 2001.

[4] Huidong JIN, Kwong-Sak Leung, Man-Leung Wong, and Zongben Xu. An efficient self-organizing map designed by genetic algorithms for the traveling salesman problem. Accepted by IEEE Trans. SMC Part B., May 2002.

[5] J. S. Kirk and J. M. Zurada. A two-stage algorithm for improved topography preservation in self-organizing maps. In *2000 IEEE International Conference on Systems, Man, and Cybernetics*, volume 4, pages 2527–2532. IEEE Service Center, 2000.

[6] Teuvo Kohonen. *Self-Organizing Maps*. Springer-Verlag, New York, 1997.

[7] Teuvo Kohonen, Samuel Kaski, Krista Lagus, Jarkko SalojAvi, Vesa Paatero, and Antti Saarela. Organization of a massive document collection. *IEEE Transactions on Neural Networks, Special Issue on Neural Networks for Data Mining and Knowledge Discovery*, 11(3):574–585, May 2000.

[8] Siming Lin and Jennie Si. Weight-value convergence of the SOM algorithm for discrete input. *Neural Computation*, 10(4):807–814, 1998.

[9] Mu-Chun Su and Hsiao-Te Chang. A new model of self-organizing neural networks and its application in data projection. *IEEE Transactions on Neural Networks*, 12(1):153 –158, Jan. 2001.

[10] Juha Vesanto. SOM-based data visualization methods. *Intelligent Data Analysis*, 3:111–26, 1999.

[11] Juha Vesanto. Neural network tool for data mining: SOM toolbox. In *Proceedings of Symposium on Tool Environments and Development Methods for Intelligent Systems (TOOLMET2000)*, pages 184–196, Oulu, Finland, 2000.

[12] Juha Vesanto and Esa Alhoniemi. Clustering of the self-organizing map. *IEEE Transactions on Neural Networks*, 11(3):586–600, May 2000.

[13] Thomas Villmann, Ralf Der, Michael Herrmann, and Thomas M. Martinetz. Topology preservation in self-organizing feature maps: exact definition and measurement. *IEEE Transactions on Neural Networks*, 8(2):256 –266, March 1997.

On the Mining of Substitution Rules for Statistically Dependent Items

Wei-Guang Teng, Ming-Jyh Hsieh and Ming-Syan Chen
Department of Electrical Engineering
National Taiwan University
Taipei, Taiwan, ROC
E-mail: {eev, mintz}@arbor.ee.ntu.edu.tw, mschen@cc.ee.ntu.edu.tw

Abstract

In this paper, a new mining capability, called mining of substitution rules, is explored. A substitution refers to the choice made by a customer to replace the purchase of some items with that of others. The process of mining substitution rules can be decomposed into two procedures. The first procedure is to identify concrete itemsets among a large number of frequent itemsets, where a concrete itemset is a frequent itemset whose items are statistically dependent. The second procedure is then on the substitution rule generation. Two concrete itemsets X and Y form a substitution rule, denoted by $X \triangleright Y$ to mean that X is a substitute for Y, if and only if (1) X and Y are negatively correlated and (2) the negative association rule $X \rightarrow \overline{Y}$ exists. In this paper, we derive theoretical properties for the model of substitution rule mining. Then, in light of these properties, algorithm SRM (standing for substitution rule mining) is designed and implemented to discover the substitution rules efficiently while attaining good statistical significance. Empirical studies are performed to evaluate the performance of algorithm SRM proposed. It is shown that algorithm SRM produces substitution rules of very high quality.

1. Introduction

Various data mining capabilities have been explored in the literature [5, 7, 14]. Among them, the one receiving a significant amount of research attention is on mining association rules [2]. Given a database of sales transactions, the goal of mining an association rule is to discover the relationship that the presence of some items in a transaction will imply the presence of other items in the same transaction. Note that in addition to the association rules, the data in a transaction database also possesses some other consumer purchase behaviors. Specifically, it is important to understand the choice made by consumers, which, corresponding to the purchase of some items instead of that of others, is termed *substitution* in this paper. For example, in a grocery

store, the purchase of apples may be substituted for that of pears. Intuitively, the substitutes are of analogous properties and therefore are often possible choices for customers. However, in some cases, the substitutes could be formed due to purchasing purposes. For example, the purchase of roses may be substituted for that of a Teddy bear and a box of chocolates. The mining of substitution rules in a transaction database, same as that of association rules, will lead to very valuable knowledge in various aspects, including market prediction, user behavior analysis and decision support, to name a few. Despite of its importance, the mining of substitution rules, unlike that of association rules, has been little explored in the literature.

Mining negative association rules of the form $X \rightarrow \overline{Y}$, where $\overline{Y}$ means the absence of itemset Y, is useful for the mining of substitutive itemsets, since in a negative association rule, the presence of the antecedent itemset implies the absence of the positive counterpart of the consequent itemset, meaning that X could be a substitute for Y. It is noted that some efforts were elaborated upon the mining of negative association rules. In [15], the taxonomy of items is introduced and a heuristic of using similarity among items in the same category is utilized to facilitate the mining of negative association rules. On the other hand, a constraint-based approach is adopted in [3]. Notice, however, that in the negative association rule mining, the dependency of items in an itemset is not considered since the itemset frequency is the only measurement when generating frequent itemsets. In contrast, to discover substitution rules, one should first determine possible itemsets which could be choices for customers. The purchasing frequency, i.e., support of an itemset, is not adequate to identify these possible substitutes. The dependency of items has to be examined to identify concrete sets of items which are really purchased together by customers. Specifically, a frequent itemset whose items are statistically dependent is called a *concrete* itemset in this paper. Note that if a frequent itemset is not concrete, that itemset is likely to consist of frequent items which, though appearing together frequently due to their high individual occurrence counts, do not possess adequate dependency among themselves and are thus of little practical implication to be used as a whole in *either* the antecedent *or* the consequent of a substitution rule. In addition, the negative correlation of two itemsets should be verified if these two itemsets are considered to be substitutes for each other. Without considering these aspects, the mining of negative association rules is not applicable to the mining of substitution rules.

Consequently, we develop in this paper a new model of mining substitution rules. The process of mining substitution rules can be decomposed into two procedures. The first procedure is to identify concrete itemsets among a large number of frequent itemsets. The second procedure is on the substitution rule generation. Two concrete itemsets X and Y form a substitution rule, denoted by X▷Y to mean that X is a substitute for Y, if and only if (1) X and Y are negatively correlated and (2) the negative association rule X→ $\overline{Y}$ exists. Without loss of generality, the chi-square test [8] is employed to identify concrete itemsets by statistically evaluating the dependency among items in individual itemsets. Moreover, the Pearson product moment correlation coefficient [8, 11] is utilized to measure the correlation between two itemsets. Explicitly, we derive theoretical properties for the model of mining substitution rules. Then, in light of these properties, algorithm SRM (standing for substitution rule mining) is designed and implemented to discover the substitution rules efficiently while attaining good statistical significance. For comparison purposes, a companion method which is extended from algorithm Apriori, called algorithm Apriori-Dual, is also implemented.

Extensive experimental studies have been conducted to provide many insights into algorithm SRM proposed. The quality of substitution rules in terms of statistical measurements is also evaluated. It is shown by experiments that algorithm SRM significantly outperforms algorithm Apriori-Dual. It is noted that algorithm SRM produces substitution rules of very high quality as measured by the correlation and the violation ratio [1]. The advantage of SRM is even more prominent when the transaction database is sparser.

The rest of the paper is organized as follows. The framework of mining negative association rules is explored and the model of substitution rule mining is presented in Section 2. Algorithm SRM and an illustrative example are described in details in Section 3. Several experiments are conducted in Section 4. This paper concludes with Section 5.

2. Model of Substitution Rule Mining

To facilitate our discussion, we shall first review the framework of negative association rules mining in Section 2.1. The model of substitution rule mining is then presented in Section 2.2.

2.1. Mining of Negative Association Rules

Same as in most prior work on mining association rules [2, 5], an itemset is a set containing one or many items. The support of an itemset X, denoted by S_X, is the fraction of transactions containing X in the whole dataset. The itemsets which meet the minimum support constraint are called frequent itemsets or large itemsets [5]. An association rule is an implication of the form X→Y with X∩Y=∅, where X and Y are both frequent itemsets. The support of the rule X→Y, i.e., Sup(X→Y), is $S_{X\cup Y}$, and the confidence of the rule X→Y, i.e., Conf(X→Y), is $\frac{S_{X\cup Y}}{S_X}$. Given a large database of transactions, the goal of mining association rules is to generate all rules that satisfy the user-specified constraints of minimum support and the minimum confidence, i.e., Sup(X→Y)≥MinSup and Conf(X→Y)≥MinConf.

Definition 1: An itemset X is *positive* if and only if it contains no complement items, i.e., X={$i_1, i_2, ..., i_k$} where i_j is an item for $1 \leq j \leq k$. On the other hand, the *negative* itemset is an itemset containing one or more complement items. If a negative itemset is composed by complement items only, i.e., {$\overline{i_1}, \overline{i_2}, ..., \overline{i_k}$}, then this itemset is *pure negative* and can be denoted by $\overline{X}$.

A negative association rule refers to an association rule of which either the antecedent itemset, the consequent itemset, or both are negative. An example of mining negative itemsets through a naive approach is given below for illustrative purposes.

Example 1: Consider the transaction database in Table 1(a). We first append the complement items to each transaction as shown in Table 1(b). For example, the transaction with TID=1, i.e., {a, c, d} in Table 1(a), becomes {a, $\overline{b}$, c, d, $\overline{e}$, $\overline{f}$} in Table 1(b). The resulting database in Table 1(b) is the input to the itemset generation algorithm.

Table 1. (a) The original transaction database; (b) After complement items are added

TID	Items		TID	Items
1	a, c, d		1	a, $\overline{b}$, c, d, $\overline{e}$, $\overline{f}$
2	b, c		2	$\overline{a}$, b, c, $\overline{d}$, $\overline{e}$, $\overline{f}$
3	c		3	$\overline{a}$, $\overline{b}$, c, $\overline{d}$, $\overline{e}$, $\overline{f}$
4	a, b, f		4	a, b, $\overline{c}$, $\overline{d}$, $\overline{e}$, f
5	a, c, d	⟹	5	a, $\overline{b}$, c, d, $\overline{e}$, $\overline{f}$
6	e		6	$\overline{a}$, $\overline{b}$, $\overline{c}$, $\overline{d}$, e, $\overline{f}$
7	b, f		7	$\overline{a}$, b, $\overline{c}$, $\overline{d}$, $\overline{e}$, f
8	b, c, f		8	$\overline{a}$, b, c, $\overline{d}$, $\overline{e}$, f
9	a, b, e		9	a, b, $\overline{c}$, $\overline{d}$, e, $\overline{f}$
10	a, d		10	a, $\overline{b}$, $\overline{c}$, d, $\overline{e}$, $\overline{f}$
(a)			(b)	

Given that MinSup=0.3, all the frequent itemsets can then be discovered from Table 1(b) as summarized in Table 2. Note that we are only interested in those complement items whose positive counterparts are frequent for market basket analysis. As a result, the complement item $\overline{e}$ is not shown in Table 2, since the item e is not frequent.

Table 2. Frequent itemsets generated from the database in Table 1(b) (MinSup=0.3)

I_1	S_I	I_2	S_I	I_2	S_I	I_3	S_I
a	0.5	a, d	0.3	d, f	0.3	a, d, $\bar{b}$	0.3
b	0.5	a, $\bar{b}$	0.3	f, $\bar{d}$	0.3	a, d, f	0.3
c	0.5	a, $\bar{c}$	0.3	$\bar{a}$, d	0.5	a, $\bar{b}$, f	0.3
d	0.3	a, f	0.4	$\bar{a}$, f	0.3	b, f, $\bar{d}$	0.3
f	0.3	b, f	0.3	$\bar{b}$, f	0.5	b, $\bar{a}$, $\bar{d}$	0.3
$\bar{a}$	0.5	b, $\bar{a}$	0.3	$\bar{c}$, d	0.4	b, $\bar{c}$, $\bar{d}$	0.3
$\bar{b}$	0.5	b, $\bar{c}$	0.3	$\bar{c}$, f	0.3	c, $\bar{a}$, $\bar{d}$	0.3
$\bar{c}$	0.5	b, $\bar{d}$	0.3	$\bar{d}$, f	0.4	c, $\bar{b}$, $\bar{f}$	0.3
$\bar{d}$	0.7	c, $\bar{a}$	0.3			d, $\bar{b}$, $\bar{f}$	0.3
$\bar{f}$	0.7	c, $\bar{b}$	0.3			$\bar{a}$, d, f	0.3
		c, $\bar{d}$	0.3				
		c, f	0.4			I_4	S_I
		d, $\bar{b}$	0.3			a, d, $\bar{b}$, $\bar{f}$	0.3

Clearly, with this straightforward addition of complement items into the database, the mining of negative association rules can be performed by directly using methods devised for mining conventional association rules. However, this benefit may not be able to justify several drawbacks of this naive approach in practice. First, excessive storage space is required to store complement items and also the additional itemsets resulted. Next, many of the frequent itemsets generated are composed of complement items only. These itemsets are usually of little use in real applications. Finally, extra database scans are needed for the mining process. In real applications, this naive approach will suffer a prolonged execution time and make mining of negative association rules an infeasible task.

Once the negative itemsets are generated, one can discover all negative association rules in a straightforward manner. For two itemsets X and Y where Y⊂X, the rule Y→(X-Y) is output if the required MinConf is satisfied. However, for our purpose of discovering substitution rules, two positive itemsets are required to form a substitute pair. Thus, the algorithm Apriori-Dual, i.e., a companion method extended from algorithm Apriori, is proposed to generate only rules whose antecedent is positive and consequent is pure negative, i.e., $X \rightarrow \bar{Y}$ where X and Y are positive itemsets.

Algorithm Apriori-Dual
// Input: MinSup and MinConf
// Procedure of generating all frequent itemsets, including
// the negative ones
1. append the complement items whose positive counterpart is not original present to each transaction;
2. generate the set of frequent (positive and negative) items, i.e., L_1;
3. remove the negative items whose positive counterpart is not frequent from L_1;
4. **for** k ≥ 2 **do**{
5.   generate the candidate set of k-itemsets from L_{k-1}, i.e., $C_k = L_{k-1} \bowtie L_{k-1}$;
6.   **if** (C_k is empty) **then break**;
7.   scan the transactions to calculate supports of all candi-

date k-itemsets;
8. $L_k = \{ c \in C_k \mid S_c \geq MinSup \}$;
9. }
// Procedure of negative association rule generation
10. **foreach** negative itemset X in L_ks **do**{
11.   let $\bar{Y}$ be the largest pure negative itemset that $\bar{Y} \subset X$;
12.   **if** (X-$\bar{Y}$) is not an empty set   *// (X-$\bar{Y}$) is positive*
13.   **if** ($Conf((X-\bar{Y}) \rightarrow \bar{Y}) \geq MinConf$)
14.   output the rule $(X-\bar{Y}) \rightarrow \bar{Y}$;
15. }

As pointed out before, the problem formulation of the negative association rule mining is different from that of the substitution rule mining. In addition, since complement items are appended to the original transaction database, the computation cost of algorithm Apriori-Dual is, as conformed by our experimental results, very high. These drawbacks reduce the practicability of using algorithm Apriori-Dual for identifying substitute itemsets. Consequently, a new algorithm for mining substitution rules is proposed and will be described in later sections.

2.2. Mining of Substitution Rules

As mentioned before, the process of mining substitution rules can be decomposed into two procedures. The first one is to identify concrete itemsets among large amounts of itemsets. The second one is on the substitution rule generation. The chi-square test [8] is employed to identify concrete itemsets by statistically evaluating the dependency among items in individual itemsets. Also, the Pearson product moment correlation coefficient [8, 11] is utilized to measure the correlation between two itemsets.

2.2.1. Identification of Concrete Itemsets. Concrete itemsets are those possible itemsets which could be choices for customers with some purchasing purposes. To qualify an itemset as a concrete one, not only the purchasing frequency, i.e., support of an itemset, but also the dependency of items has to be examined to declare that these items are *purposely* purchased together by customers. One common approach is to evaluate the dependence among items in an itemset by the chi-square test [4, 10, 13]. Specifically, the chi-square value for an itemset can be derived in terms of supports and expected supports of its corresponding itemsets, as stated in Theorem 1 below.

Theorem 1: Let $X=\{x_1, x_2, ..., x_k\}$ be a positive k-itemset, the chi-square value for X is computed as

$$Chi(X) = n \times \left[\left(\sum_{I \in \{Y \mid Y^+=X\}} \frac{S_I^2}{E_I} \right) - 1 \right],$$

where n is the number of total transactions, Y^+ denotes the positive itemset where all complement items in itemset Y are replaced by their positive counterparts, e.g., $\{a,\bar{b},\bar{c}\}^+=\{a,b,c\}$ where a, b and c are positive items, and $E_I = \prod_{i \in I} S_i$ is the expected support of I.

Proof: Since the itemset X is of size k and the presence of an item in each transaction is 0-1 valued, a corresponding $2 \times 2 \times \cdots \times 2$ k-dimensional contingency table can be constructed. Each dimension of this contigency table corresponds to the presence of an item, i.e., $x_i \in X$, in each transaction. The values of these 2^k cells are exactly the supports of itemsets $\{\overline{x_1}, \overline{x_2}, ..., \overline{x_k}\}$, $\{\overline{x_1}, \overline{x_2}, ..., x_k\}$, ..., $\{x_1, x_2, ..., x_k\}$ and the summation of these values is n, i.e., the number of transactions. Also, the corresponding itemsets above can be formulated as $\{Y \mid Y^+=X\}$. The chi-square value is then computed by

$$Chi(X) = \sum_{c \in cells} \frac{(O_c - E_c)^2}{E_c},$$

where O_c is the observed value and E_c is the expected value of cell c in the contingency table. For any itemset I and its corresponding cell c that $I^+=X$, we have

$$O_c = n \times S_I \text{ and } E_c = n \times \prod_{i \in I} S_i.$$

With some algebraic manipulations, we have

$$
\begin{aligned}
Chi(X) &= \sum_{c \in cells} \frac{O_c^2 - 2O_c E_c + E_c^2}{E_c} \\
&= \sum_{c \in cells} \frac{O_c^2}{E_c} - 2 \sum_{c \in cells} O_c + \sum_{c \in cells} E_c \\
&= \left(\sum_{c \in cells} \frac{O_c^2}{E_c} \right) - n \quad \left(\because \sum_{c \in cells} O_c = \sum_{c \in cells} E_c = n \right) \\
&= \left(\sum_{I \in \{Y \mid Y^+=X\}} \frac{n^2 \times S_I^2}{n \times \prod_{i \in I} S_i} \right) - n \\
&= n \times \left[\left(\sum_{I \in \{Y \mid Y^+=X\}} \frac{S_I^2}{E_I} \right) - 1 \right]. \quad \textbf{Q.E.D.}
\end{aligned}
$$

To utilize the chi-square test to verify whether the occurrences of given items are dependent, two contradictive hypotheses are made

$\begin{cases} H_0: \text{The occurrences of all items}(x_1 \sim x_k) \text{ are independent,} \\ H_1: H_0 \text{ is rejected.} \end{cases}$

With Theorem 1, to declare the dependency among items in an itemset X, or to support hypothesis H_1, the chi-square value for X is required to be no less than a threshold, i.e., $Chi(X) \geq \chi^2_{df(X),\alpha}$.

In addition, it follows from advanced statistics and information theory [9] that corresponding degree of freedom for this test can be denoted by

$$df(X) = \prod_i c(v_i) - \sum_i [c(v_i) - 1] - 1 = 2^k - k - 1$$

where $c(v_i)$ is the number of categories in dimension i, i.e., $c(v_i)=2$ for all dimensions since the presence of an item in each transaction is 0-1 valued.

We comment that the results derived in Theorem 1 are essential for our mining of substitution rules and are not subsumed by the work in [4]. In [4], it was stated that "if S is correlated with significance level α, any superset of S is also correlated with significance level α." From Theorem 1 in [4], one may mistakenly assume that the chi-square test for itemsets at a given significance level is upward closed (as stated in Theorem 1 in [4].) However, as also noted in [6], this upward closure property is not fully correct. Explicitly, the first statement of the proof of Theorem 1 in [4] "The key observation in proving this is that not matter what k is, the chi-squared statistic has only one degree of freedom" which its subsequent proof is based upon is not true, thereby leading to incorrect conclusions. A counterexample of Theorem 1 in [4] is given in the Appendix for interested readers. Specifically, as opposed to what Theorem 1 in [4] suggests, all correlated itemsets, rather than only *minimally* correlated ones, should be discovered. This in turn justifies the necessity of our development of the process to identify concrete itemsets in this paper.

Without loss of generality, a *concrete* itemset is thus defined to be a frequent itemset which is positively correlated given a significance level α (usually $\alpha = 0.05$), if it contains more than one item. Note that the significance level of a concrete itemset is expected to be at least no less than that of its subsets. For example, if the itemset {flashlight, battery} has a quite high chi-quare value, then its superset, e.g., {flashlight, battery, pencil), could still have a high chi-square value ($> \chi^2_{df(X),\alpha}$) even though pencil is not so correlated with the other items.

Definition 2: A positive frequent itemset $X=\{x_1, x_2, ..., x_k\}$ is called a *concrete* itemset, if and only if
(1) k=1, or
(2) $k \geq 2$,

$$S_X > \prod_{x_i \in X} S_{x_i} \text{ and } Chi(X) \geq \chi^2_{df(X),\alpha},$$

where $\prod_{x_i \in X} S_{x_i}$ corresponds to the *expected* support for itemset X, and $\chi^2_{df(X),\alpha}$ is the value of chi-square distribution with degree of freedom $df(X)$ at probability α. Note that $S_X > \prod_{x_i \in X} S_{x_i}$ is required to ensure that all $x_i \in X$ are positively correlated.

The value of $\chi^2_{df(X),\alpha}$ can be obtained by the table lookup. As mentioned earlier, the usual value $\alpha = 0.05$ is used in this study for statistical significance. Considering itemset {a, d} in Table 2 for example, $S_{ad} = 0.3 > S_a \times S_d = 0.6 \times 0.3$. Also, the chi-square value for {a, d} is

$$
\begin{aligned}
Chi(\{a,d\}) &= n \times \left[\left(\frac{S_{\overline{a}\overline{d}}^2}{E_{\overline{a}\overline{d}}} + \frac{S_{\overline{a}d}^2}{E_{\overline{a}d}} + \frac{S_{a\overline{d}}^2}{E_{a\overline{d}}} + \frac{S_{ad}^2}{E_{ad}} \right) - 1 \right] \\
&= 10 \times \left(\frac{0.5^2}{0.5 \times 0.7} + 0 + \frac{0.2^2}{0.5 \times 0.7} + \frac{0.3^2}{0.5 \times 0.3} - 1 \right) \\
&= 4.29 > \chi^2_{1,0.05} = 3.84.
\end{aligned}
$$

Thus, {a, d} is a concrete itemset.

2.2.2. Testing of Negative Correlation.
To evaluate the correlation between two *concrete* itemsets, we adopt the measurement of Pearson product moment correlation coefficient [8]. Theorem 2 states that the correlation coefficient of two itemsets can be determined by their supports.

Theorem 2: Let X and Y be two itemsets with $X \cap Y = \emptyset$. The correlation coefficient of X and Y can be formulated in terms of their supports. Explicitly,

$$\rho(X,Y) = \frac{Cov(X,Y)}{\sqrt{Var(X) \cdot Var(Y)}} = \frac{S_{XY} - S_X \cdot S_Y}{\sqrt{S_X(1-S_X)S_Y(1-S_Y)}}.$$

Proof: Since variables corresponding to occurrence of items in a transaction database are all 0-1 valued, it follows that

$$EX = EX^2 = S_X, \; EY = EY^2 = S_Y \text{ and } E(XY) = S_{XY}$$

where E stands for the expected value. According to the definition of correlation coefficient, we have

$$\rho(X,Y) = \frac{Cov(X,Y)}{\sqrt{Var(X) \cdot Var(Y)}}$$
$$= \frac{E[(X-EX)(Y-EY)]}{\sqrt{E[(X-EX)^2] \cdot E[(Y-EY)^2]}}$$
$$= \frac{E(XY) - (EX)(EY)}{\sqrt{[EX^2 - (EX)^2] \cdot [EY^2 - (EY)^2]}}$$
$$= \frac{S_{XY} - S_X \cdot S_Y}{\sqrt{[S_X - (S_X)^2][S_Y - (S_Y)^2]}}$$
$$= \frac{S_{XY} - S_X \cdot S_Y}{\sqrt{S_X(1-S_X)S_Y(1-S_Y)}} \qquad \textbf{Q.E.D.}$$

Note that when both variables to be correlated are binary as in this case, we may use the phi coefficient of correlation as stated in [11, 12] instead of $\rho(X,Y)$ in Theorem 2. However, the phi coefficient of correlation and the Pearson product moment correlation coefficient are in fact algebraically equivalent and give identical numerical results. Therefore, for notational simplicity, we employ $\rho(X,Y)$ to express the results of Theorem 2.

Consequently, a substitution rule can be defined as below.

Definition 3: Given two itemsets X and Y and $X \cap Y = \emptyset$, X is a substitute for Y, denoted by $X \triangleright Y$, if and only if
(1) both X and Y are concrete,
(2) X and Y are negatively correlated, i.e., $\rho(X,Y) < -\rho_{min} \leq 0$ (usually $\rho_{min} = 0$ for simplicity), and
(3) the negative association rule $X \rightarrow \overline{Y}$ is valid, i.e.,
   $Sup(X \rightarrow \overline{Y}) \geq MinSup$ and $Conf(X \rightarrow \overline{Y}) \geq MinConf$.

3. SRM: Substitution Rule Mining

Given the definitions of concrete itemsets and substitution rules, a detailed description of algorithm SRM for mining substitution rules is given.

Algorithm SRM
// Input: MinSup, MinConf, and ρ_{min}
// Procedure of identifying concrete itemsets
1. generate the set of all frequent (positive) items, i.e., L_1, and assign L_1 to the set of concrete itemsets;
2. **for** $k \geq 2$ **do**{
3. generate the candidate set of k-itemsets from L_{k-1}, i.e., $C_k = L_{k-1} \bowtie L_{k-1}$;
4. **if** (C_k is empty) **then break**;
5. scan the transactions to calculate supports of all candidate k-itemsets;
6. $L_k = \{ c \in C_k \mid S_c \geq MinSup \}$;
7. **foreach** frequent itemset X in L_k **do**{
8.   **if** $(S_X > \prod_{x_i \in X} S_{x_i})$ **&&** $(Chi(X) \geq \chi^2_{df(X),\alpha})$
9.   add X to the set of concrete itemsets;
10. }
11. }
// Procedure of substitution rule generation
12. **foreach** pair of concrete itemsets X, Y **do**{
13. **if** $(\rho(X,Y) < -\rho_{min})$
14.   **if** $(Sup(X \rightarrow \overline{Y}) \geq MinSup)$ **&&** $(Conf(X \rightarrow \overline{Y}) \geq MinConf)$ // $X \rightarrow \overline{Y}$ is valid
15.   output the substitution rule $X \triangleright Y$;
16. }

The execution of algorithm SRM can be best understood by the example below.

Example 2: Consider the transaction database in Table 1(a). Algorithm SRM first performs the procedure of identifying concrete itemsets, i.e., operations from line 1 to line 11 in algorithm SRM. Given MinSup=0.2 and MinConf=0.7, the frequent itemsets can be first obtained as in Table 3.

The dependency among items in these frequent itemsets is then evaluated. By Definition 2, chi-square tests of concreteness are performed on each k-itemset for $k \geq 2$. The chi-square values of these frequent itemsets are also shown in Table 3 where only two frequent 2-itemsets are found concrete. Note that {a, c, d} fails to pass the test since $df(\{a, c, d\}) = 2^3 - 3 - 1 = 4$ and $Chi(\{a,c,d\}) = 6.38 < \chi^2_{4,0.05} = 9.49$.

Table 3: Frequent (positive) itemsets, their supports and chi-square values generated from Table 1(a) (concrete itemsets are in italics)

I_1	S_I	I_2	S_I	$Chi(I)$
a	0.5	a, b	0.2	0.4
b	0.5	a, c	0.2	0.4
c	0.5	*a, d*	*0.3*	*4.29*
d	0.3	b, c	0.2	0.4
e	0.2	*b, f*	*0.3*	*4.29*
f	0.3	c, d	0.2	0.48

I_3	S_I	$Chi(I)$
a, c, d	0.2	6.38

Next, in the procedure of substitution rule generation, i.e., operations from line 12 to line 16 in algorithm SRM, the candidate substitution pairs can then be generated by

446

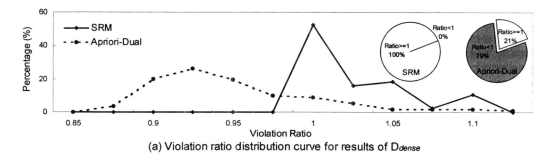

(a) Violation ratio distribution curve for results of D$_{dense}$

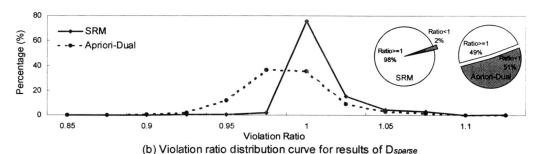

(b) Violation ratio distribution curve for results of D$_{sparse}$

Figure 1. Violation ratio distribution curves

joining on these concrete itemsets. By examining the support, confidence and correlation of these candidate pairs, substitution rules can be generated as in Table 4.

Table 4: Substitution rules discovered with MinSup=0.2, MinConf=0.7, and ρ_{min}=-0.5

Rule(X▷Y)	Sup	Conf	Correlation(X, Y)
{b}▷{d}	0.5	1	-0.65
{d}▷{b}	0.3	1	-0.65
{a, d}▷{b}	0.3	1	-0.65

4. Experimental Results

The simulation model of our experimental studies is described in Section 4.1. The quality of substitution rules generated is evaluated in Section 4.2.

4.1. Simulation Model

As mentioned in Section 2.1, mining negative association rules by appending complement items to the original transaction database incur both an excessive storage space and a huge computational cost. Without the process of generating rules with the required form as adopted by Apriori-Dual, the computation time of the naive approach for generating negative association rules is shown by our experiments to be longer, in several orders, than those of both the algorithms Apriori-Dual and SRM. Therefore, only the

algorithms Apriori-Dual and SRM are being compared in following experiments.

We use two synthetic datasets, i.e., D$_{dense}$ and D$_{sparse}$, generated by a randomized transaction generation algorithm in [16]. The values of parameters used to generate the datasets are summarized in Table 5, where both the dense and the sparse dataset distributions are considered.

Table 5. Parameter settings of the synthetic datasets

	D$_{dense}$	D$_{sparse}$	Meaning
T	10	5	Average size of transactions
I	50	100	Number of items
D	10,000	10,000	Number of transactions

4.2. Evaluation of Rule Quality

To evaluate the quality of a substitution rule, we may count the number of transactions which contain only one of the substitutive itemsets in the rule, i.e., the antecedent or the consequent. Hence, the violation ratio proposed in [1] is adopted. Specifically, a pair of substitutive itemsets is said to be in violation if exactly only one of them is present in a transaction. The violation ratio is defined as the ratio of the number of real violations to the expected number of violations. Thus, the larger the value of the violation ratio of a rule, the more likely its antecedent and consequent itemsets are substitutes for each other. Note that the violation ratio of an interesting substitution rule should be lager than one.

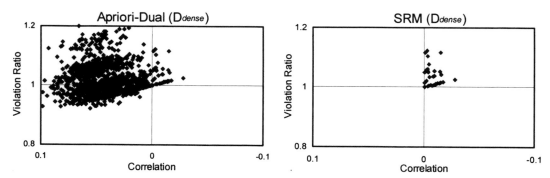

Figure 2. Quality matrix in the dense dataset

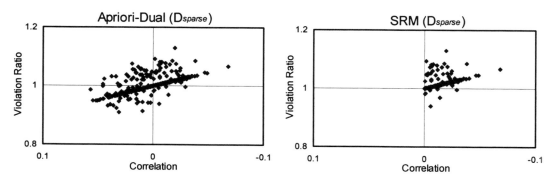

Figure 3. Quality matrix in the sparse dataset

Experiments on the two datasets are conducted with MinSup=15% (D_{dense}), MinSup=10% (D_{sparse}) and Min-Conf=50%. The distribution curves for results of both sparse and dense datasets are depicted in Figure 1. Note that the percentage of population rather than the actual number of rules is used as the measurement for vertical axes in both charts. Also, to provide a remarkable index for evaluating the quality of rules, proportions of interesting rules, i.e., whose violation ratios are larger than 1, to uninteresting ones are also presented as pie charts in Figure 1. Note that more than half of rules generated by algorithm Apriori-Dual in both datasets have a violation ratio less than one. In contrast, more than 98% of rules generated by algorithm SRM are interesting for both datasets. Also note that algorithm Apriori-Dual favors dense databases while algorithm SRM performs well in each dataset, showing that algorithm SRM is more adaptive and robust.

The resulting rules by Apriori-Dual and SRM for both datasets are plotted in Figure 2 and Figure 3, where each point corresponds to a rule produced. The y-axis indicates the violation ratio and the x-axis shows the correlation of the antecedent and the consequent itemsets of the rule. Each figure is divided into four areas. *In the upper right area,*

the rules are the most interesting ones among those in all areas due to the negative correlation of the antecedent and the consequent of each rule and high violation ratios.

Note that rules generated by algorithm Apriori-Dual and algorithm SRM are subsets of negative association rules. It can be seen from Figure 2 and Figure 3 that algorithm SRM can generate the most appropriate ones on the basis of negative association rules.

5. Conclusions

In this paper, a new mining capability, called mining of substitution rules, is explored. The notion of evaluating the dependency among items in a concrete itemset proposed in this paper offers another dimension for itemset selection (in addition to the one of using the support threshold), thereby being able to lead to more interesting results in the subsequent rule derivation based on these itemsets. We have derived theoretical properties for the model of substitution rule mining and devised a technique on the induction of positive itemset supports to improve the efficiency of support counting for negative itemsets. In light of these properties, algorithm SRM is proposed to discover the substitution rules efficiently while attaining good statistical significance. It is shown by empirical studies that algorithm SRM not only has very good execution efficiency but also produces substitution rules of very high quality.

Acknowledgement

The authors are supported in part by the National Science Council, Project No. NSC 91-2213-E-002-034 and NSC 91-2213-E-002-045, Taiwan, Republic of China.

References

[1] C. C. Aggarwal and P. S. Yu. A New Framework for Itemset Generation. *Proceedings of the 17th ACM SIGACT-SIGMOD-SIGART Symposium on Principles of Database Systems*, pages 18–24, June 1998.

[2] R. Agrawal, T. Imielinski, and A. Swami. Mining Association Rules between Sets of Items in Large Databases. *Proceedings of the 1993 ACM SIGMOD International Conference on Management of Data*, pages 207–216, May 1993.

[3] J.-F. Boulicaut, A. Bykowski, and B. Jeudy. Towards the Tractable Discovery of Association Rules with Negations. *Proceedings of the 4th International Conference on Flexible Query Answering Systems*, pages 425–434, October 2000.

[4] S. Brin, R. Motwani, and C. Silverstein. Beyond Market Baskets: Generalizing Association Rules to Correlations. *Proceedings of the 1997 ACM SIGMOD International Conference on the Management of Data*, pages 265–276, May 1997.

[5] M.-S. Chen, J. Han, and P. S. Yu. Data Mining: An Overview from Database Perspective. *IEEE Transactions on Knowledge and Data Engineering*, 8(6):866–883, December 1996.

[6] W. DuMouchel and D. Pregibon. Empirical Bayes Screening for Multi-Item Associations. *Proceedings of the 7th ACM SIGKDD International Conference on Knowledge Discovery and Data Mining*, pages 67–76, August 2001.

[7] J. Han and M. Kamber. *Data Mining: Concepts and Techniques*. Morgan Kaufmann Publishers, 2000.

[8] R. V. Hogg and E. A. Tanis. *Probability and Statistical Inference, 6/e*. Prentice-Hall International, Inc., 2001.

[9] J. C. Hosseini, R. R. Harmon, and M. Zwick. An Information Theoretic Framework for Exploratory Multivariate Market Segmentation Research. *Decision Sciences*, 22:663–677, 1991.

[10] C. Jermaine. The Computational Complexity of High-Dimensional Correlation Search. *Proceedings of the 1st IEEE International Conference on Data Mining*, pages 249–256, November 2001.

[11] R. A. Johnson and D. W. Wichern. *Applied Multivariate Statistical Analysis, 5/e*. Prentice-Hall International, Inc., 2002.

[12] M. G. Kendall and G. U. Yule. *Journal of Royal Statistical Society 115*, pages 156–161, 1952.

[13] B. Liu, W. Hsu, and Y. Ma. Identifying Non-Actionable Association Rules. *Proceedings of the 7th ACM SIGKDD International Conference on Knowledge Discovery and Data Mining*, pages 329–334, August 2001.

[14] S. Ma and J. L. Hellerstein. Mining Mutually Dependent Patterns. *Proceedings of the 1st IEEE International Conference on Data Mining*, November 2001.

[15] A. Savasere, E. Omiecinski, and S. Navathe. Mining for Strong Negative Associations in a Large Database of Customer Transactions. *Proceeding of the 14th International Conference on Data Engineering*, pages 494–502, February 1998.

[16] R. Srikant and R. Agrawal. Mining Generalized Association Rules. *Proceedings of the 21th International Conference on Very Large Data Bases*, pages 407–419, September 1995.

Appendix: A Counterexample to Theorem 1 in [4]

Theorem 1 in [4]: In the binomial case, the chi-square statistic is upward closed.

This theorem means that "if S is correlated with significance level α, any superset of S is also correlated with significance level α." Consider a contingency table which is slightly modified from the one provided in [4].

Table 6. An example contingency table of market basket data for coffee (c), tea (t), and doughnuts (d)

d	c	$\bar{c}$	Σ row		d	c	$\bar{c}$	Σ row
t	8	2	10		t	10	2	12
$\bar{t}$	40	2	42		$\bar{t}$	34	2	36
Σ col	48	4	52		Σ col	44	4	48

From Theorem 1 in this paper, we have

$$Chi(\{c,t\}) = \frac{(8+10)^2}{(100)\frac{(48+44)}{100}\frac{(10+12)}{100}} + \frac{(40+34)^2}{(100)\frac{(48+44)}{100}\frac{(42+36)}{100}}$$
$$+ \frac{(2+2)^2}{(100)\frac{(4+4)}{100}\frac{(10+12)}{100}} + \frac{(2+2)^2}{(100)\frac{(4+4)}{100}\frac{(42+36)}{100}} - 100$$
$$= 3.98, \text{ and}$$

$$Chi(\{d,c,t\}) = \frac{8^2}{(100)\frac{52}{100}\frac{(48+44)}{100}\frac{(10+12)}{100}} + \frac{40^2}{(100)\frac{52}{100}\frac{(48+44)}{100}\frac{(42+36)}{100}}$$
$$+ \frac{2^2}{(100)\frac{52}{100}\frac{(4+4)}{100}\frac{(10+12)}{100}} + \frac{2^2}{(100)\frac{52}{100}\frac{(4+4)}{100}\frac{(42+36)}{100}}$$
$$+ \frac{10^2}{(100)\frac{48}{100}\frac{(48+44)}{100}\frac{(10+12)}{100}} + \frac{34^2}{(100)\frac{48}{100}\frac{(48+44)}{100}\frac{(42+36)}{100}}$$
$$+ \frac{2^2}{(100)\frac{48}{100}\frac{(4+4)}{100}\frac{(10+12)}{100}} + \frac{2^2}{(100)\frac{48}{100}\frac{(4+4)}{100}\frac{(42+36)}{100}} - 100$$
$$= 4.49.$$

As mentioned in Section 2.2, the corresponding degrees of freedom should increase with k, i.e., df($\{c, t\}$)=1 and df($\{d, c, t\}$)=4, respectively. Given a significance level α=0.05, it can be verified that Chi($\{c, t\}$) = 3.98 > $\chi^2_{1,0.05}$ = 3.84 and Chi($\{d, c, t\}$) = 4.49 < $\chi^2_{4,0.05}$ = 9.49. Note that $\{c, t\}$ passed the chi-square test and $\{d, c, t\}$ did not, meaning that the chi-square test is not upward closed. This leads to a counterexample to Theorem 1 in [4].

TreeFinder: a First Step towards XML Data Mining

Alexandre Termier, Marie-Christine Rousset, Michèle Sebag
{termier, mcr, sebag}@lri.fr
LRI - CNRS UMR 8623, Université Paris-Sud, 91405 Orsay

Abstract

In this paper, we consider the problem of searching frequent trees from a collection of tree-structured data modeling XML data. The $TreeFinder$ algorithm aims at finding trees, such that their exact or perturbed copies are frequent in a collection of labelled trees.

To cope with complexity issues, $TreeFinder$ is correct but not complete: it finds a subset of the actually frequent trees. The default of completeness is experimentally investigated on artificial medium size datasets; it is shown that $TreeFinder$ reaches completeness or falls short to it for a range of experimental settings.

1 Introduction

In this paper, we consider the problem of searching *frequent trees* from a collection of tree-structured data modeling XML data. We present a method that automatically extracts from a collection of labelled trees a set of frequent trees occurring as common (exact or approximate) trees embedded in a sufficient number of trees of the collection. By construction, this method provides (i) a clustering of the input trees, and (ii) a characterization of each cluster by a set of frequent trees. The important point is that we are not looking for an exact embedding but for trees that may be approximately embedded in several input trees. An *approximate tree inclusion* preserves the ancestor relation but not necessarily the parent relation. This point distinguishes our work from existing work on DTD inference [16]. This choice is motivated by the need for robustness regarding the possible variations in the label nesting of XML documents which we still want to be recognized as having a similar tree structure.

The main motivating application of this work is the construction of a tree-based *mediated schema* for integrating multiple and heterogeneous sources of XML data. A data integration system enables users to pose queries through a mediated schema, thus freeing them from having to interrogate each source separately, and to deal with the heterogeneity of their schema. For example, Xyleme [23, 24, 3] is a huge warehouse integrating XML data of the Web.

In Xyleme, the mediated schema is a set of labelled trees (called *abstract trees*). Each abstract tree is related to a given domain (e.g., culture, tourism), and is an abstract merger of the *concrete trees* modeling the tree-structure of the actual XML documents relative to that domain. The abstract trees are the support of a visual query interface tool, based on forms, intended to be used by end-users. Today, the abstract trees in the mediated schema in Xyleme are built manually. To scale up to the Web, the challenge is to build them as automatically as possible.

The paper is organized as follows. In Section 2, we start with a motivating example. In section 3, we describe the formal background of our approach. In Section 4, we describe our two-step method for discovering frequent trees, which has been implemented in the $TreeFinder$ system. In Section 5, we report preliminary experimental results on medium-size artificial data. Finally, in Section 6 we compare our approach with related work and we draw some conclusions and perspectives in Section 7.

2 Motivating example

Fig. 1 is an illustration of heterogeneous XML data structures with various nesting of the labels.

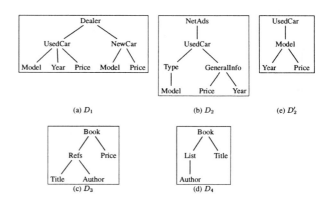

Figure 1. Various tree-structures

The nesting of the *Title* node differs in trees D_3 and D_4. Similarly, the node labelled with *Model* is the direct son of the node labelled with *UsedCar* in D_1, while there is a node in between the corresponding nodes in D_2.

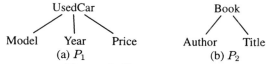

(a) P_1 (b) P_2

Figure 2. Frequent trees

Despite the variation in the structure, we want to group together:

- D_1, D_2 and D_2', because the same tree P_1 (Fig. 2 (a)) is (exactly or approximately) included in D_1, D_2 and D_2',

- D_3 and D_4, because they have in common the tree P_2 (Fig. 2 (b)), even if the embedding in D_3 and D_4 is approximate.

The two trees P_1 and P_2 of Fig. 2 are the frequent trees corresponding to the input trees of Fig. 1: they are common to several different trees in the input collection.

3 Formal background

In this section, we introduce an elementary tree model for XML data structure. We further introduce the formal definitions of tree inclusion, (maximal) common trees and frequent trees.

3.1 Modeling XML Data Structure

We model an XML data structure (e.g., a DTD) as a labelled tree. We ignore ID-references and hyperlinks. Each node d has a label, written as $label(d)$. We do not distinguish between elements and attributes. They are all mapped to nodes using the element or the attribute name as label. We assume that all labels and real-world concepts are in a one-to-one correspondance (neither synonymy nor polysemy are accounted for).

Definition 1 (Labelled trees) *A **labelled tree** is a pair $\langle t, label \rangle$ where (i) t is a finite **tree** whose nodes are in $\mathcal{N}$, (ii) label is a **labeling function** that assigns a label to each node in t.*

The labels play the role of the begin-end tag in XML data models. We use the current terminology about trees: root, children, descendant, leaf, subtree, etc. We also use some functional notations such as: $root(t)$ returns the root node of the tree t, $children(u)$ (resp. $desc(u)$, $anc(u)$) returns the set of nodes that are children (resp. descendants, ancestors) of node u, and $label(t)$ returns the set of labels of the nodes of the tree t.

Note that within a given tree, two different nodes may have the same label.

We consider that we are given a collection of labelled trees that constitute the input set of trees to which our method applies for discovering frequent trees.

3.2 Tree inclusion

We consider a weak inclusion relation between trees, termed *tree subsumption*.

Definition 2 (Inclusion by tree subsumption) *Let t and t' be two labelled trees. We say that t is **included according***

T_i	$Rel(T_i)$	$Rel^+(T_i)$
U_1/a / \ U_2/b U_3/a | U_4/c | U_5/d	$ab(U_1, U_2)$ $aa(U_1, U_3)$ $ac(U_3, U_4)$ $cd(U_4, U_5)$	$a*b(U_1, U_2)$ $a*a(U_1, U_3)$ $a*c(U_1, U_4)$ $a*d(U_1, U_5)$ $a*c(U_3, U_4)$ $a*d(U_3, U_5)$ $c*d(U_4, U_5)$
U_1'/a / \ U_2'/f U_3'/c | / \ U_4'/b U_5'/d U_6'/e	$af(U_1', U_2')$ $ac(U_1', U_3')$ $fb(U_2', U_4')$ $cd(U_3', U_5')$ $ce(U_3', U_6')$	$a*f(U_1', U_2')$ $a*c(U_1', U_3')$ $a*b(U_1', U_4')$ $a*d(U_1', U_5')$ $a*e(U_1', U_5')$ $f*b(U_2', U_4')$ $c*d(U_3', U_5')$ $c*e(U_3', U_6')$

Figure 3. Two example trees T_1 and T_2, and their relational encoding

to tree subsumption (or included when no confusion is possible) in t' if there exists a mapping f from the nodes of t into the set of nodes of t' such that f preserves the ancestor relation:

$$\forall \ u \ in \ t, \ label(u) \ = \ label(f(u)) \ and$$
$$\forall u, v \ in \ t, \ anc(u, v) \Longrightarrow anc(f(u), f(v))$$

The advantage of the above definition is the following: if we choose to represent labelled trees as relational formulas ([12]), then tree subsumption is equivalent to the θ-subsumption relation defined by ([17]). Let us first describe how labelled trees can be put in relational form.

Definition 3 (Relational description of labelled trees)
Let t be a labelled tree. $Rel(t)$ is the conjunction of all atoms $ab(u, v)$, such that u and v are nodes in t, with $label(u) = a$, $label(v) = b$ and u is the parent node of v. $Rel^+(t)$ is the conjunction of atoms $a*b(u, v)$, such that u and v are nodes in t, with $label(u) = a$, $label(v) = b$ and u is an ancestor node of v.

Fig. 3 illustrates the two encoding functions Rel and Rel^+ for two labelled trees.

The following proposition states the equivalence between inclusion by tree subsumption (Definition 2) and θ-subsumption.

Proposition 1 *Let t and t' be two labelled trees. Then:*
t is included by tree subsumption in t' iff $Rel^*(t)$ θ-subsumes $Rel^*(t')$

The advantage of this relational representation is that, though θ-subsumption test is NP complete, efficient implementations have been proposed [13].

3.3 Common trees and frequent trees.

Let us formally define the notion of maximal common tree (with respect to tree subsumption) for a set of trees.

Definition 4 (Maximal common tree) *Let* $t, t_1, ..., t_n$ *be labelled trees. We say that* t *is a **maximal common tree** of* $t_1, ..., t_n$ *iff :*

- $\forall i \in [1..n]$ t **is included in** t_i
- t *is maximal for the previous property, i.e. if there is a labelled tree* t' *such as* t **is included in** t' *and* $\forall i \in [1..n]$ t' **is included in** t_i *then* t' *is identical to* t.

For instance, tree P_1 (Fig. 2) is a maximal common tree of D_1, D_2 and D'_2 (Fig. 1).

Let us now define the notion of *frequent tree*.

Definition 5 (Frequent tree) *Let* T *be a set of labelled trees, and let* t *be a labelled tree. Let* ε *be a real number in* $[0, 1]$.

We say that t *is a* ε-***frequent tree** of* T *iff:*

- *there exists* l *trees* $\{t_1, ..., t_l\}$ *in* T *such that* t *is maximal common tree of* $\{t_1, ..., t_l\}$.
- l *is greater or equal to* $\varepsilon \times |T|$.

*The **support set** of* t *in* T *is the set of all trees* t_i *such that* t *is included in* t_i.

For instance according to Definition 2, the two trees P_1 and P_2 (Fig. 2) are the 0.4-frequent trees w.r.t. the set of the trees D_1, D_2, D'_2, D_3 and D_4 (Fig. 1).

Let F_ε denote the set of all ε-frequent trees w.r.t. a set of trees T; due to monotonicity : $\varepsilon > \varepsilon' \Longrightarrow F_\varepsilon \subseteq F_{\varepsilon'}$.

Maximal ε-frequent trees are defined as the maximal elements (for tree inclusion) in F_ε.

4 Overview of the TreeFinder system

Let $T = \{t_1, t_2, ..., t_n\}$ be a set of labelled trees, let ε be a frequency threshold. The $TreeFinder$ method for discovering ε-frequent trees in T is a two-step algorithm. The first step is described in Section 4.1. It is a clustering step that groups input trees in which same pairs of labels occur together frequently enough in the ancestor relation. The second step is described in Section 4.2. It is a tree construction step based on the computation of maximal trees that are common to all the trees of each cluster. In Section 4.3, the trees that are returned as output of this two-step algorithm are formally characterized w.r.t. to its input.

4.1 Clustering guided by co-occurence of labels pairs

Input: An abstraction of the input $T = \{t_1, ..., t_n\}$, where each t_i is viewed as a transaction made of all the items $l*m$ such that l is the label of an ancestor of a node labelled by m in t_i. Each item $l*m$ has a unique identifier. Let $\mathcal{I}$ be the set of those identifiers.
For example, the input transaction corresponding to tree D_1 of Fig. 1 is:

$D_1 = \{$ Dealer*UsedCar, Dealer*NewCar,
UsedCar*Model, UsedCar*Year, UsedCar*Price,
NewCar*Model, NewCar*Price, Dealer*Model,
Dealer*Year, Dealer*Price $\}$

This splitting of the trees in separate items corresponding to pairs of labels breaks the tree structure but makes possible

the use of a standard frequent item sets algorithm [1] for discovering frequent label pairs in the input trees. The co-occurrence of same pairs of labels is considered as semantically significant if it occurs frequently in the input data.

Clustering method: Many algorithms have been developed to compute frequent item sets. Our current implementation involves the well-known $Apriori$ algorithm [1]. We apply the $Apriori$ algorithm to the set of transactions T over the items $\mathcal{I}$ identifying the pairs of labels, with the frequency threshold (a.k.a minimum support) set to ε.

Output: the *support sets* of the *largest frequent item sets* returned by the $Apriori$ algorithm. The support set of an item set $s \subseteq \mathcal{I}$, denoted $support(s)$, is the subset of T made of all the transactions including s. A frequent item set is a subset of $\mathcal{I}$ which is supported by more than $\varepsilon \times |T|$ transactions.

For instance, the largest frequent item sets returned by the $Apriori$ algorithm applied with the frequency threshold 0.4 to the set of transactions $\{D_1, D_2, D'_2, D_3, D_4\}$, given previously and abstracting the trees of Fig. 1 are:

$s_1 = \{$UsedCar*Model, UsedCar*Year, UsedCar*Price$\}$
$s_2 = \{$Book*Price, Book*Title, Book*Author$\}$

The corresponding support sets, that are thus returned as output clusters, are:

$support(s_1) = \{D_1, D_2, D'_2\}$
$support(s_2) = \{D_3, D_4\}$.

4.2 Computation of maximal common trees

Input: This step takes as input the output of the previous clustering step, and computes for each cluster the maximal trees that are common to (i.e. included in) *all* the trees of the cluster

Method: For each cluster $\{t_{i_1}, t_{i_2}, ..., t_{i_n}\}$, we compute the *least general generalization* [17] $LGG(Rel^+(t_1), ..., Rel^+(t_n))$ of the relational formulas encoding the trees.

The *least general generalization* of two relational formulas $Rel(f_1)$ and $Rel(f_2)$ is the most specific formula which θ-subsumes $Rel(f_1)$ and $Rel(f_2)$. From [17] it is shown that the least general generalization of two conjunctive formulas with no function symbol is unique (up to variable renaming).

In the example of Fig. 3 :
$LGG(Rel^+(T_1), Rel^+(T_2)) = a*b(U_1, U_2) \wedge a*c(U_1, U_3) \wedge$
$a*d(U_1, U_4) \wedge c*d(U_3, U_4)$.

Output: the set of trees resulting from the tree decoding of the least general generalizers of the relational formulas encoding the trees for each cluster.

The subtle point is that from $LGG(Rel^+(t_1), ..., Rel^+(t_n))$, which is a conjunction of atoms of the form $l*m(U_i, U_j)$, modeling the ancestor relation, we can reconstruct the atoms defining the underlying parent relation. This results from the fact that, because of the tree structure of the inputs $t_1, ..., t_n$, the implicit parent relation p whose transitive closure leads

LGG	$star^{-1}$
$a*b(U_1, U_2)$ $a*c(U_1, U_3)$ $a*d(U_1, U_4)$ $c*d(U_3, U_4)$	$ab(U_1, U_2)$ $ac(U_1, U_3)$ $cd(U_3, U_4)$
$Rel^{-1}(star^{-1}(LGG(Rel^+(T_1), Rel^+(T_2))))$	

$$U_1/a$$
$$U_2/b \qquad U_3/c$$
$$U_4/d$$

Figure 4. Relational LGG and its tree decoding

to $LGG(Rel^+(t_1), ..., Rel^+(t_n))$ has necessarily a forest structure, and the corresponding explicit ancestor relation has a dag structure. It is the application of a traversal of that dag structure in a topological order that makes possible to reconstruct the parent relation from the ancestor relation which is stated in $LGG(Rel^+(t_1), ..., Rel^+(t_n))$. Let $star^{-1}(LGG(Rel^+(t_1), ..., Rel^+(t_n)))$ be the resulting conjunction of atoms of the form $lm(U_i, U_j)$.

In the example of Fig. 3 :
$star^{-1}(LGG(Rel^*(T_1), Rel^*(T_2))) = ab(U_1, U_2) \wedge ac(U_1, U_3) \wedge cd(U_3, U_4)$.

Fig. 4 illustrates the relational least general generalizer corresponding to our example and its tree decoding.

4.3 Formal characterization of the TreeFinder results

The following proposition states that the results produced by $TreeFinder$ are correct. We also provide a sufficient condition for these results to be complete, i.e. to include *all* the maximal frequent trees present in the input trees.

Proposition 2 *Let T be a set of labelled trees, let ε be a frequency threshold, let $ft_1, ft_2, \ldots, ft_n$ be the trees obtained as output of the two-step $TreeFinder$ method applied to T:*
- ***correctness:*** *$ft_1, ft_2, \ldots, ft_n$ are ε-frequent trees for T.*
- ***sufficient condition for completeness:*** *If T is such that the trees in the support of each maximal ε-frequent trees have no label pair in common with trees out of the support, then $ft_1, ft_2, \ldots, ft_n$ are exactly the maximal ε-frequent trees of T.*

The following example shows that $TreeFinder$ is not guaranteed to find the maximal ε-frequent trees in the general case.

Fig. 5 illustrates a case where $TreeFinder$ applied with a frequency threshold of 0.5 would find a single big cluster made of all the input trees (corresponding to the maximal item set $\{a*b, a*c\}$, which appears in fact in all the transactions). The result returned by $TreeFinder$ would then be the two trees ft_1, ft_2 reduced to one edge each,

which are common to all the input trees: they are 1.0-frequent trees and thus a fortiori 0.5-frequent trees. However, $TreeFinder$ does not find the unique 0.5-frequent tree whose root is labelled by a and has two children labelled by b and c respectively.

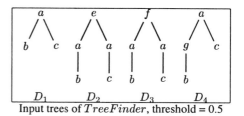
Input trees of $TreeFinder$, threshold = 0.5

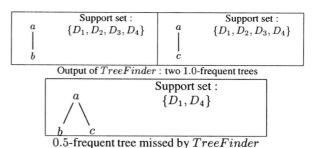
0.5-frequent tree missed by $TreeFinder$

Figure 5. When $TreeFinder$ misses frequent trees

This example is illustrative of the fact that $TreeFinder$ can fail to find all the ε-frequent trees in the data. We estimate this loss of completeness by comparison with the ideal algorithm, which we will refer to as $AprioriTree$. $AprioriTree$ is an extension of the levelwise algorithm $Apriori$ to tree structures:

- Find the trees of size 1 (trees with one edge) that are common to more than $\varepsilon \times$ (number of input trees) input trees.
- $i := 1$
- While there exists frequent trees of size i:
  - **generate** candidate frequent trees of size $i + 1$ from the frequent trees of size i and those of size 1,
  - **test** the inclusion of those candidate frequent trees in the input trees in order to select those candidate frequent trees that are actually frequent.
- $i := i + 1$

$AprioriTree$ is a naive method which is not tractable in practice because clearly, it hardly scales up: first of all, the test step intensively relies on tree subsumption, which is NP complete. Furthermore, the number of candidate trees constructed from a frequent i-edge tree grows like $i \times e$, where e is the number of frequent edges; in contrast, the number of candidates constructed from a frequent i-item set is $e - i$, where e is the number of frequent items.

We have implemented $TreeFinder$ in C++, and its experimental validation is detailed in the next section.

5 Experimental results

This section first details the experiment goals and the experimental setting used for the empirical validation of *TreeFinder*. The results obtained are then reported and discussed with regard to computational cost (section 5.3) and frequent tree quality (section 5.4).

5.1 Experiment goals

A key criterion for data mining algorithms concerns their robustness and scalability w.r.t. the characteristics of input data [1]. Therefore, the computational cost of *TreeFinder* w.r.t. the number and size of input trees will be investigated in section 5.3.

Another criterion regards the quality of the results provided by *TreeFinder*. Let us consider as baseline algorithm *AprioriTree*.

Proposition 2 has given sufficient conditions for *TreeFinder* to find exactly the same frequent trees as *AprioriTree*. In the general case however, *TreeFinder* will miss some frequent trees as illustrated in Fig. 5.

The second experiment goal will thus be to estimate the percentage of frequent frequent trees missed by *TreeFinder*, compared to the baseline algorithm. This percentage, termed loss factor, will be investigated experimentally in section 5.4.

All experiments consider artificial medium-size datasets, according to the following experimental setting.

5.2 Experimental setting

As mentioned in the introduction, the mining of XML data raises two major difficulties. The first one, not considered in the present paper, regards the potential synonymy and polysemy of tags. The second difficulty, tackled in the paper, concerns the tree-structure of the XML data.

As a preliminary investigation, we thus consider artificial XML data, generated from known target frequent trees using a randomized tree-structure generator. This generator[1] proceeds as follows:

• A set of target frequent trees $\mathcal{P} = \{P_1, \dots P_K\}$ is given by the user.

• A set of external labels $\mathcal{L}$ is defined, disjoint (unless otherwise specified) from the labels involved in the target frequent trees. The size L of $\mathcal{L}$ is a user-supplied parameter of the generator.

• Each tree-document is recursively generated. Let u be the top node in the node list (initialized at the root node). Two options are considered: with probability p, a (perturbed) copy of one target frequent tree is inserted at node u (see below the target frequent tree insertion). Otherwise (with probability $1 - p$), the number of son nodes for the current

---

[1] The generator is available at :
`http://www.lri.fr/~termier/generator.tgz`.

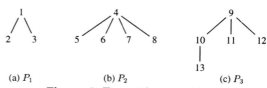

Figure 6. Target frequent trees

node u is uniformly selected in $[0..B]$, where B is the maximum branching factor; the label for the current node u is selected with uniform probability in $\mathcal{L}$; u is removed from the node list, and its son nodes are added to the node list.

• The insertion of a target frequent tree P, uniformly selected in $\mathcal{P}$, proceeds by copying at node u a perturbed copy of P. A number m of additional nodes is randomly selected in $[0, \delta]$, where δ is the perturbation parameter. These nodes are randomly inserted in the target frequent tree, and their labels are randomly selected in $\mathcal{L}$.

The parameters of the artificial tree generator are summarized in Table 1.

K	number of target frequent trees
L	number of external labels
p	probability of including a target frequent tree in each node
δ	maximal number of nodes added to perturbate a target frequent tree
B	maximal branching factor
D	maximal tree depth

Table 1. Parameters of the artificial tree-structure generator

Due to the stochastic generation of the datasets, the reported results are obtained by averaging the results obtained for ten independent runs (launched with same parameter values and distinct random seeds).

5.3 Empirical study of computational cost

Various experiments consider up to 10,000 artificial tree-structured documents, generated with the following parameters:

• The set of target frequent trees is displayed in Fig. 6.

• The total number of labels is set to 100. With no loss of generality, labels 1 to 13 denote the labels involved in the target frequent trees, and $\mathcal{L}$ is made of all labels $14 \dots 100$. In these tests, the labels of the target frequent trees are not disjoint from the external labels, so $L = 100$.

• The probability p of including a target frequent tree at each node is set to 0.2

• The maximal number δ of perturbations is set to 25.

• The maximal branching factor is set to 5.

• The maximal tree depth is set to 3

A first series of results, obtained with the frequency threshold 0.05 is displayed on Fig. 7.

The average computational complexity (Fig. 7 a) is dominated by the least general generalization (LGG) computational complexity. The LGG thus is the limiting factor; no results could be obtained for a number of trees greater than

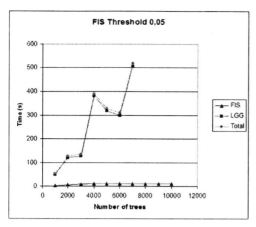

a) Varying tree number, random tree size

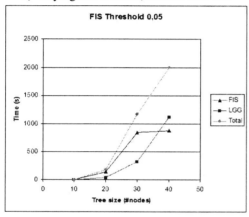

b) Varying tree size, 1000 trees

Figure 7. Scalability tests results

8,000 due to memory saturation.

Similar results are obtained by varying the average tree size. For these tests parameter p was set to 1.0, so trees were just perturbed target frequent trees, and we varied the value of δ. Actually, the FIS step only depends on the number of edges in the target frequent trees. But the supports of frequent edge sets are large, which implies that LGG considers many trees (Fig. 7 b).

Again, it can be seen that the limiting complexity factor is the LGG step.

5.4 Empirical study of $TreeFinder$ loss factor

The study empirically investigates the loss factor, measuring the percentage of "true" frequent trees missed by $TreeFinder$.

As noted earlier (Proposition 2), the loss factor is zero when the target frequent trees do not overlap. The empirical study therefore considers five sets of target frequent trees, with increasingly overlapping edges. Practically, five series of experiments are launched, corresponding to the five sets of four target frequent trees displayed in Fig. 8.

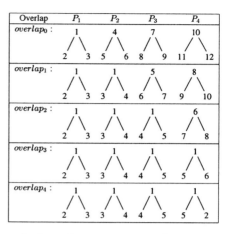

Figure 8. Set of target trees with increasing overlap

The other generator parameters are set as follows:
• The number L of external labels is set to 50.
• The probability p of including a target frequent tree at each node is set to 0.4.

$TreeFinder$ is run with frequency threshold ε varying in 0.2, 0.1, 0.05.

Fig. 9 displays the loss factor for each frequency threshold ε and for each collection of target frequent trees.

The loss factor has been computed as follows. Ideally, it measures the percentage of frequent trees that would return $AprioriTree$, which are missed by $TreeFinder$. However, because of the inherent complexity of $AprioriTree$, the frequent trees occuring in the actual tree datasets cannot be extracted with reasonable complexity. The number of such frequent trees is therefore approximated during the generation step.

Practically, for a tree t, let $\mathcal{Q}(t)$ be the set of target frequent trees P_i such that t includes (at least) one occurence of P_i; $\mathcal{Q}(t)$ can easily be determined since no destructive perturbations of target frequent trees are considered in the generator.

For each such set of target frequent trees $\mathcal{Q}$ (with $\mathcal{Q}$ included in the set of target frequent trees $overlap_i$ at hand), one might thus determine its support in the generated input trees; if its support includes more than $100 \times \varepsilon\%$ of the input data, $\mathcal{Q}$ is a frequent tree.

The number of such frequent trees is taken as a lower bound on the number of actually frequent trees. For each frequency threshold ε and set of frequent trees $overlap_i$, the loss factor is defined as:

$Loss(\varepsilon, overlap_i) = 1 - TF(\varepsilon, overlap_i)/AT(\varepsilon, overlap_i)$

where $TF(\varepsilon, overlap_i)$ denotes the (median) number of frequent trees actually produced by $TreeFinder$ over 10 datasets independently generated according to the target frequent tree set $overlap_i$, and $AT(\varepsilon, overlap_i)$ likewise is

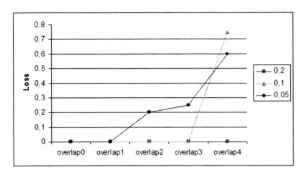

Figure 9. Sensitivity analysis: $TreeFinder$ **Loss factor for** $\varepsilon = 0.05$, 0.1 **and** 0.2 **depending on the overlapping rate between target frequent trees**

the lower bound on the number of actually frequent trees, defined as above. The loss factor so-computed thus corresponds to a pessimistic estimate.

As expected from Proposition 2, the loss factor is zero for non-overlapping target frequent trees (Fig. 9). Two types of behavior are observed depending on the frequency threshold.

For a small frequency threshold ($\varepsilon = 0.05$), the loss factor degrades gracefully as the overlapping rate increases from small to moderate; the loss is around 20% for an overlapping rate of 75%.

For a larger frequency threshold ($\varepsilon = 0.1$), the loss factor remains zero until the overlapping rate becomes actually heavy (all target frequent trees share one edge with another target frequent tree); then the loss factor abruptly rises up to almost 80%. One interpretation for this fact is the following. As the overlapping rate increases from $overlap_3$ to $overlap_4$, a discontinuity occurs: all edges become equally frequent; this entails that the edge sets can no longer be filtered out based on the frequency threshold ($TF(\varepsilon = 0.1, overlap_4) \approx TF(\varepsilon = 0.05, overlap_3)$). In the meanwhile, the number of frequent trees decreases as ε increases due to monotonicity ($AT(\varepsilon = 0.1, overlap_4) < AT(\varepsilon = 0.05, overlap_4)$), which explains why the loss factor is worse for $\varepsilon = 0.1$ than for $\varepsilon = 0.05$ in the case of $overlap_4$.

This effect can be likened to the example case illustrated on Fig. 5: the more overlap between the target frequent trees, the larger the support of any set of frequent edges, the more general the frequent trees extracted through LGG from their support, and the more likely specific trees are missed by $TreeFinder$.

It must be noted that for an even larger frequency threshold ($\varepsilon = 0.2$) the loss factor remains 0 in all the experiments.

6 Related Work

The extraction of frequent patterns from structured or semi-structured data has attracted much interest recently, as more and more application domains involve structured (e.g. bio-informatics, chemistry [7]) or semi-structured (text, Web pages [15]) data. The earliest work aiming at complex frequent patterns to our best knowledge is [6], which gradually abstracts frequent substructures from graphs using an MDL criterion. The major difference with our approach is twofold. On the one hand, $TreeFinder$ takes advantage of the tree structure being simpler than that of graphs; typically, $TreeFinder$ would not extend to handle graph data, for the transitive closure of graphs will only deliver coarse information (connex components) in the general case. On the other hand, [6] can only consider frequent substructures in the graph which are made of edges; if it were applied on trees (trees being a particular case of graphs) it could only discover frequent trees in the sense of exact ordered tree inclusion. Same remarks apply for more recent works concerned with graph mining, AGM (Apriori-based Graph Mining) [10] and FREQT (Frequent Trees) [5].

Another work aiming at frequent structured patterns is WARMR [7], tackling First Order Logic expressions. Again the main difference is that WARMR is designed for full-fleshed First Order Logic data, while $TreeFinder$ takes advantage of the comparative simplicity of trees. Admittedly, $TreeFinder$ as well as WARMR cannot scale up beyond certain limits; but the computational explosion should be delayed in $TreeFinder$ compared to WARMR, for the test step (the θ-subsumption cost) is less expensive.

The closest work to ours is presented by [25], which proposes two algorithms, $TreeMinerH$ and $TreeMinerV$, for mining frequent trees in a forest (set of trees). Similarly to our work, they consider an approximate tree embedding based on ancestor relationship instead of parent relationship. The major difference is that they consider *ordered trees*. This characteristic is exploited to propose a smart tree representation based on string encoding, which facilitates the candidate checking (subsumption test) step. Another difference is that $TreeFinder$ computes an approximation of the result to ensure better scalability. The approximated result is a set of frequent trees guaranteed to subsume the actual frequent trees of the input.

Note that the discovery of common tree structures has been tackled from another perspective, that of DTD inference. For instance, [16] studies the automatic inference of a unique DTD (tree grammar) from a set of XML data (labelled trees). The problem considered in this work is different from ours since the expected output tree structures must satisfy a subtree inclusion and no approximation is allowed.

Likewise, approximate tree matching has been considered in the perspective of answering XML queries (e.g.,[19, 8, 4]). [19] is based on tree embedding, the others use relaxation operators, some of which (e.g. node deletion) correspond to tree embedding, some others (e.g. node unfolding [8]) do not.

7 Discussion and Perspectives

Extending a previous work [21], this paper presents the *TreeFinder* algorithm, concerned with the discovery of frequent trees w.r.t. a set of trees. Contrasting with [5], *TreeFinder* uses a relaxed inclusion test which allows for detecting trees which are not present *verbatim* in the data. Therefore, *TreeFinder* achieves a more flexible and robust tree-mining and can detect trees that could not be discovered using a strict subtree inclusion.

The main limitation of *TreeFinder* is to be an approximate miner; in the general case, it is only guaranteed to find a subset of the actual frequent trees. Its performances were empirically validated on artificial medium-size data, demonstrating that it reaches completeness (or falls short to it) in a range of problems.

The distinctive feature of *TreeFinder* is to involve a preliminary process based on a flat boolean representation of the trees, coding the presence or absence of all possible label pairs (ancestor relations) in each tree. This way, standard FIS algorithms can be applied to determine the frequent label pairs sets (FLPS). Each FLPS is thereafter exploited in order to actually construct frequent trees, through a least general generalization of the FLPS support trees. Indeed, the LGG step is computationally expensive; however, it is done only once for each FLPS. As a counterpart, this saves the subsumption tests undergone in the candidate test step, the number and complexity of which are exponential in the size of the frequent trees.

Ongoing work is concerned with investigating in more depth the loss factor of *TreeFinder*, using WARMR to emulate *AprioriTree*. Further research will investigate how the postprocessing of the frequent label pairs sets can be used to refine their support sets, and further decrease the chance of missing frequent trees.

Acknowledgements

The authors wish to thank Jérôme Azé and Jérôme Maloberti, LRI, who kindly gave respectively their implementation of Apriori, and of least general generalisation.

References

[1] R. Agrawal and R. Srikant. Fast algorithms for mining association rules. In *Proceedings of the 20th VLDB Conference*, Santiago, Chile, 1994.

[2] R. Agrawal and R. Srikant. Mining sequential patterns. In *Proc. of Eleventh International Conference on Data Engineering*, pages 3–14, 1995.

[3] V. Aguiléra, S. Cluet, P. Veltri, D. Vodislav, and F. Wattez. Querying the XML Documents on the Web. In *Proc. of the ACMSIGIR Workshop on XML and I. R., Athens*, July 28, 2000.

[4] S. Amer-Yahia, S. Cho, and D. Srivastava. Tree pattern relaxation. In *Proc. of the EDBT 2002 Conference*, 2002.

[5] T. Asai, K. Abe, S. Kawasoe, H. Arimura, H. Sakamoto, and S. Arikawa. Efficient substructure discovery from large semi-structured data. In *Proc. Second SIAM International Conference on Data Mining*, pages 158–174, 2002.

[6] D. J. Cook and L. B. Holder. Substructure discovery using minimum description length and background knowledge. *Journal of Artificial Intelligence Research*, 1:231–255, 1994.

[7] L. Dehaspe and H. T. Toivonen. *Relational Data Mining*, chapter Discovery of Relational Association Rules, pages 189–212. Springer-Verlag, 2001.

[8] C. Delobel and M.-C. Rousset. A uniform approach for querying large tree-structured data through a mediated schema. In *Proc. of the 2001 Int. Workshop on Foundations of Models for Information Integration*, September 2001.

[9] J. Hipp, U. Güntzer, and G. Nakhaeizadeh. Algorithms for association rule mining – a general survey and comparison. *SIGKDD Explorations*, 2(1):58–64, July 2000.

[10] A. Inokuchi, T. Washio, and H. Motoda. An apriori-based algorithm for mining frequent substructures from graph data. In *Principles of Data Mining and Knowledge Discovery*, pages 13–23, 2000.

[11] P. Kilpeläinen. *Tree Matching Problemas with Applications to Structured Text Databases*. PhD thesis, University of Helsinki, 1992.

[12] J. Lloyd. *Foundations of logic programming*. Springer-Verlag, 2nd edition, 1987.

[13] J. Maloberti and M. Sebag. Theta-subsumption in a constraint satisfaction perspective. In *Proc. of the ILP'01 Conference*, pages 164–178, 2001.

[14] H. Mannila, H.Toivonen, and A. Verkamo. Discovery of frequent episodes in event sequences. *Data Mining and Knowledge Discovery*, 1(3):259–289, 1997.

[15] T. Miyahara, T. Shoudai, T. Uchida, K. Takahashi, and H. Ueda. Discovery of frequent tree structured patterns in semistructured web documents. In Springer-Verlag, editor, *Proc. 5th PACKDD*, pages 47–52, 2001.

[16] Y. Papakonstantinou and V. Vianu. DTD inference for views of XML data. In *Symposium on Principles of Database Systems*, pages 35–46, 2000.

[17] G. Plotkin. A note on inductive generalisation. *Machine Intelligence*, 5:153–163, 1970.

[18] R. Ramesh and L. Ramakrishnan. Nonlinear pattern matching in trees. *Journal of the ACM*, 39(2):295–316, April 1992.

[19] T. Schlieder and F. Naumann. Approximate tree embedding for querying XML data. In *ACM Sigir Workshop on Information Retrieval*, July 2000.

[20] R. Srikant and R. Agrawal. Mining sequential patterns: Generalizations and performance improvements. In *Proc. of 5th International Conference on Extending Database Technology*, pages 3–17, 1996.

[21] A. Termier, M.-C. Rousset, and M. Sebag. Mining XML data with frequent trees. In *DBFusion'02 Workshop*, 2002.

[22] H. Toivonen. Sampling large databases for association rules. In T. M. Vijayaraman, A. P. Buchmann, C. Mohan, and N. L. Sarda, editors, *In Proc. 1996 Int. Conf. VLDB*, pages 134–145. Morgan Kaufman, 09 1996.

[23] Xyleme. : http://www.xyleme.com.

[24] L. Xyleme. A dynamic warehouse for XML data of the web. *IEEE Data Engineering Bulletin*, 2001.

[25] M. Zaki. Efficiently mining frequent trees in a forest. Technical Report 01-7, Renselaer Polytechnic Institute, 2001.

Computing Frequent Graph Patterns from Semistructured Data

N. Vanetik, E. Gudes, S. E. Shimony

Department of Computer Science, Ben Gurion University, P.O. Box 653 Beer-Sheva, 84105 Israel
{orlovn, ehud, shimony}@cs.bgu.ac.il

Abstract

Whereas data mining in structured data focuses on frequent data values, in semi-structured and graph data the emphasis is on frequent labels and common topologies. Here, the structure of the data is just as important as its content. We study the problem of discovering typical patterns of graph data. The discovered patterns can be useful for many applications, including: compact representation of source information and a road-map for browsing and querying information sources. Difficulties arise in the discovery task from the complexity of some of the required sub-tasks, such as sub-graph isomorphism. This paper proposes a new algorithm for mining graph data, based on a novel definition of support. Empirical evidence shows practical, as well as theoretical, advantages of our approach.

1. Introduction

Due to increasing amounts of data collected by various companies and institutes, the importance of data mining has grown significantly over the last several years. Traditional data mining is applied mainly to structured data and flat files. Lately, there has been growing interest in mining semi-structured data, such as web data, XML data, large object databases, etc. {[3],[10],[19]}. Discovery and understanding of patterns that statistically represent a sufficiently large part of the database can be helpful in the following areas: improving database design [5], efficient indexing [7], user preference based applications [6], user behavior predictions, database storage and archival [4].

In structured data-mining, frequent data *values* and their common appearances are of interest. For mining semi-structured and graph data, the focus is on frequent *labels* and common appearances of sub-sets of such labels (in terms of XML [2], one looks for frequent occurrences of structures of elements or attributes - see section 6.1.) Most of the work done so far has dealt with either single path patterns [3] or tree-like patterns [10],[19]. However, much of the data on the web is graph-like, both *acyclic* and *cyclic*. We found only one graph mining paper, [9], but its constructing algorithm and support definitions are too simple to handle the general case. In this paper we present an algorithm for mining frequent patterns in semi-structured data, where the data is modeled as a labeled graph - either di-

rected or undirected, depending on the mining goals. In our scheme, unlike related work, topology of permissible patterns is not restricted. Frequent patterns may or may not be labeled (or partially labeled). Unlabeled patterns can be handled as a special case of our approach.

In any data-mining algorithm which uses an analog of Apriori [1] (our algorithm belongs to this general category), two issues arise: (1) the basic building block from which frequent patterns are composed; (2) making sure that at each step of the algorithm all frequent patterns for that step are found. As long as correctness is maintained, it is beneficial to make the building blocks as large as possible, in order to minimize the number of candidate patterns. Our idea is to use *edge-disjoint paths* as building blocks. A major issue in this work was proving that our edge-disjoint based algorithm is complete. This is the first major contribution of this paper.

In attempting to find frequently occurring subgraph patterns within a graph, computing the frequency of occurrence of the pattern in the larger graph (the database), also called *support computation*, is a major issue. Even for simple cases, such as association rules, it is desirable to minimize the number of candidates, as support computation is expensive (see section 6.1.) For graph patterns, minimizing the number of candidates is even more critical - as we show that in the worst case computing support of a graph pattern is NP-hard! In order to decrease the number of extremely expensive support computations, we must discard, as early as possible, as many candidate patterns as possible.

As the Apriori algorithm does a good job of dismissing unlikely candidates by avoiding their creation entirely, we believe its adaptation to graph patterns should be extremely useful, even if it entails considerable overhead over the naive methods of generating and testing patterns.

Despite the fact that several algorithms for finding tree-like frequent patterns in semi-structured data were proposed during the last years ([10],[19]), no general definition of support for frequent pattern in a semi-structured database exists. A second contribution of the paper is our approach to support measures for frequent graph patterns in a graph database, and the refined definition of support.

To prove the feasibility of our scheme we implemented the proposed algorithms, tested them on some XML databases and synthetic graphs, and compared them to the naive approach for counting graphs patterns.

The rest of this paper is organized as follows. Section 2 reviews formal definitions of data mining and graph-theoretic terms and introduces new definitions used in specifying the algorithm. Section 3 discusses the issue of support. Section 4 describes the graph mining algorithm. Experimental results appear in Section 5. An evaluation of our scheme and its comparison to other work is discussed in section 6.

2. Background

This section reviews terms from prior work, including graph theory, and data mining literature.

An *Apriori-based* algorithm is an algorithm that finds frequent item sets in a database using the following principles: (1) frequent single items are found by scanning the database, and storing them in the set called the 1st item set; (2) the $i + 1$st item set is constructed from pairs of items from the ith item set; (3) after the ith set has been constructed, all non-frequent items are removed.

2.1. Graph facts

A *labeled graph* is a graph that has a label associated with each node v, denoted by $label(v)$. Given two graphs $G' = (V', E')$ and $G'' = (V'', E'')$, a *labeled isomorphism* $G' \simeq_\phi G''$ between them is any isomorphism $\phi : V' \to V''$ such that for any $i \in V'$ $label(i) = label(\phi(i))$. P is a *graph pattern* in graph G if it is isomorphic to a connected subgraph of G. The *set of instances* of pattern P in graph G is the set of all subgraphs of G that are isomorphic (if G is not labeled) or label isomorphic (if G is labeled) to P.

A *path number* $p(G)$ of a graph G is the minimal number of edge-disjoint paths into which G can be decomposed. A set of $p(G)$ edge-disjoint paths covering all edges of G exactly once is called a *minimal path cover* of G. *Removing path P from graph G*, denoted by $G \setminus P$, consists of removing all edges of P from G and later removing all stand-alone nodes. For computation of a path number we rely on well-known graph-theoretic facts:

1. A connected undirected graph $G = (V, E)$ is *Eulerian* (can be covered by a single cyclic path) iff for every $v \in V$, $d(v)$ is even. A connected digraph $G = (V, E)$ is *Eulerian* (can be covered by a single directed cyclic path) iff for every $v \in V$, $d^+(v) = d^-(v)$.

2. For any connected undirected graph $G = (V, E)$ the size of its minimal path cover is 1 if G is Eulerian and $|\{v \mid v \in V, d(v) \; is \; odd\}|/2$ otherwise. For any connected directed graph $G = (V, E)$, $p(G) = 1$ if G is Eulerian and $p(G) = (\sum_{v \in V} |d^+(v) - d^-(v)|)/2$ otherwise.

The path number of a graph can be computed in linear time since only node degrees are required. In our data mining

algorithm iteration, we keep in the kth frequent item set only graphs with path number k. We produce members of the $(k + 1)$th frequent item set from the kth item set. We need to show that the above is always feasible:

Theorem 2.1 If G is a connected graph and its minimal path cover $P = \{P_1, ..., P_k\}$ has size k, then $G' = G \setminus P_i$ has a minimal path cover of size $k - 1$ for all $i \in [1, k]$.

We show that a graph with k paths can be constructed by our scheme from two smaller graphs.

Theorem 2.2 Let $G = (V, E)$ be a connected graph with $p(G) = n, n \geq 2$ and $P_1, ..., P_n$ its minimal path decomposition. Then there exist $j, k \in [1, n], j \neq k$ such that graphs $G \setminus P_j$ and $G \setminus P_k$ are connected.

These two theorems together are needed to assure that using path number as an item set parameter is correct (see Section 4.) The proofs can be found in [18].

2.2. Lexicographical ordering

In most Apriori-based algorithms $(k - 1)$−itemsets are combined into k−itemsets in a lexicographical order which assures completeness. A similar method is applied here in combining graphs. For this purpose, we use a canonical representation of paths and path sequences. We thus define a lexicographical ordering (see [18] for details) over path pairs, using node labels and degrees of nodes within paths. Based on the above ordering, an ordering between path sequences is defined and sub-sequentially a notion of minimality, called *P-minimal* is defined over paths sequences. This minimum is not necessarily unique.

2.3. Graph merger

During the "merge" phase we need to combine graphs, each composed of paths. The next set of definitions describes composition of graphs and operations necessary for removing a path from a graph, joining two graphs with common paths, and adding additional "intersections" (common nodes) to a pair of paths within a graph.

We define a new structure, called a ***composition relation***, for the purpose of representing a graph as a union of edge-disjoint paths. This structure is a table (a two-dimensional array) with graph nodes as rows and paths as columns. A cell in row i and column j contains a non-null value if and only if the j-th path contains the i-th node of a graph. Nodes of the paths can be named/enumerated differently from the nodes of a graph. Figure 1 shows a graph consisting of 3 paths: P_1, P_2, P_3 and Table 1 presents a corresponding composition relation ($\perp$ symbolizes a null value). A composition relation on paths $P_1, ..., P_n$ is denoted by $C(P_1, ..., P_n)$ or, C if paths are known unambiguously. The order of rows in a relation is insignificant, i.e. two composition relations are considered to be equal ($=$) if their tables contain the same rows, regardless of their order.

Given a proper composition relation C on n paths, one can construct a corresponding graph in a unique way by treating rows of the table as graph nodes and defining edges

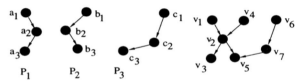

Figure 1: **Graph consisting of 3 edge-disjoint paths**

Table 1: **Composition relation** $C(P_1, P_2, P_3)$

Node	P_1	P_2	P_3
v_1	a_1	$\perp$	$\perp$
v_2	a_2	b_2	$\perp$
v_3	a_3	$\perp$	$\perp$
v_4	$\perp$	b_1	$\perp$
v_5	$\perp$	b_3	c_3
v_6	$\perp$	$\perp$	c_1
v_7	$\perp$	$\perp$	c_2

(i, j) when two nodes of the same path P appearing in rows i and j, have an edge between them. This operation is called a **graph realization** on composition relation and is denoted by $\Omega(P_1, ..., P_n, C)$ or $\Omega(C)$ for short.

An operation of **subtraction** of a path P_i from composition relation consists of eliminating the i-th column from a composition relation table followed by subsequent removal of all rows that contained only null values. This operation is denoted by $C(P_1, ..., P_n) \backslash P_i$ or, shorthand, $C \backslash i$. If several paths P_i, $i \in I$ are to be subtracted, we write $C \backslash I$ or $C \mid_{\{j \mid j \notin I\}}$ (a **projection** of C onto paths P_j, $j \notin I$).

Next we describe operations of "joining" two k-path graphs that have $k - 1$ paths in common and adding nodes common to two paths within the graph. Let C_1 and C_2 be composition relations, and let I_1 and I_2 be sets of indices such that $C_1 \mid_{I_1} = C_2 \mid_{I_2}$. A **bijective sum** $BS(C_1, C_2, I_1, I_2)$ is a composition relation that is obtained from the table of C_1 by adding columns for all the paths that are in C_2 but not in C_1 (taking into account a possibly different order of rows in $C_1 \mid_{I_1}$ and $C_2 \mid_{I_2}$). Tables 2 demonstrates a bijective sum $C_3 = BS(C_1, C_2, \{1, 2\}, \{1, 2\})$ of two composition relations $C_1(P_1, P_2, P_3)$ and $C_2(P_1, P_2, P_4)$ and Figure 2 shows graph realizations $G_1 = \Omega(C_1)$, $G_2 = \Omega(C_2)$ and $G_3 = \Omega(C_3)$. Null values were omitted from the tables.

A **splice** $\oplus_{i,j}$ of two composition relations $C_1(P_1, ..., P_n)$ and $C_2(P_i, P_j)$, $1 \leq i, j \leq n$, is a composition relation that turns every node common to P_i and P_j in C_2, into the node common to P_i and P_j in C_1 as well. A splice is a merger of two nodes belonging to two different paths in a graph into a single node. It is achieved by copying the table of C_1 and merging the rows of $v \in P_i$, $u \in P_j$ in C_1, for every v, u appearing in a single row of C_2. Table 3 describes composition relations $C_1(P_1, P_2, P_3)$, $C_2(P_2, P_3)$ and $C_3 = C_1 \oplus_{2,3} C_2$. Figure

Table 2: **Bijective sum**

	C_1				C_2			
Node	P_1	P_2	P_3	Node	P_1	P_2	P_4	
v_1	a_1			v_1	a_1			
v_2	a_2	b_2		v_2	a_2	b_2		
v_3	a_3			v_3	a_3			
v_4		b_1		v_4		b_1	d_1	
v_5		b_3	c_3	v_5		b_3		
v_6			c_1	v_6			d_2	
v_7			c_2	v_7			d_3	

	C_3			
Node	P_1	P_2	P_3	P_4
v_1	a_1			
v_2	a_2	b_2		
v_3	a_3			
v_4		b_1		d_1
v_5		b_3	c_3	
v_6			c_1	
v_7			c_2	
v_8				d_2
v_9				d_3

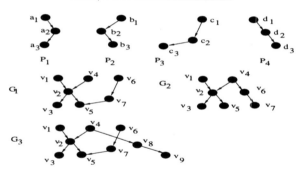

Figure 2: **Graph realization of a bijective sum**

3 shows corresponding graph realizations $G_1 = \Omega(C_1)$, $G_2 = \Omega(C_2)$ and $G_3 = \Omega(C_3)$.

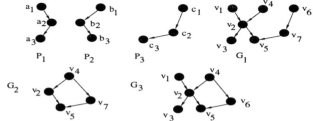

Figure 3: **Graph realization of a splice**

Bijective sum and splice operations are used in our mining algorithm to construct larger graphs from smaller ones.

3. Support measures

The standard measure of support in the literature is as follows. Let $0 \leq \sigma \leq 1$ and let D be a set of transactions. An item set $I = <i_1, ..., i_k>$ is called *frequent* if $S(I) =$

Table 3: **Splice**

C_1				C_2		
Node	P_1	P_2	P_3	Node	P_2	P_3
v_1	a_1			v_2	b_1	c_1
v_2	a_2	b_2		v_4	b_2	
v_3	a_3			v_5	b_3	c_3
v_4		b_1		v_7		c_2
v_5		b_3	c_3			
v_6			c_1			
v_7			c_2			

C_3			
Node	P_1	P_2	P_3
v_1	a_1		
v_2	a_2	b_2	
v_3	a_3		
v_4		b_1	c_1
v_5		b_3	c_3
v_6			c_2

$\frac{|t \mid t \in D, <i_1,...,i_k> \in t|}{|D|} \geq \sigma$. Here, S is called the support of item set I.

This definition of support does not suit structured databases very well. When trying to define support in terms of fraction of the information represented by all instances of a pattern in the database, the following issues arise: (1) a "frequent" pattern should obviously appear more than once in the database - otherwise, the database graph itself would be considered a frequent pattern; (2) instances of a frequent pattern that have common edges should have less "weight" in a support measure than instances that are disjoint. (See Figure 4); (3) the number of pattern instances can be greater than the database size, the standard support measure may result in a support greater than 1, which is undesirable.

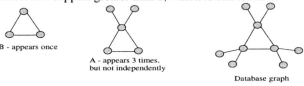

B - appears once

A - appears 3 times, but not independently

Database graph

Figure 4: **Graph pattern support**

Support of pattern P in graph G is a measure of frequency of instances of P in G. A *support measure* is a function that, for each pattern P in graph G, returns a number in range $[0,1]$. A pattern P is called *frequent* if its support measure $S(P)$ is higher than a support threshold TS. Our support measure uses the following constraint.

Definition 3.1 A support measure S is *admissible* if for every P, $S(P) \geq 0$ and for all P_1, P_2 such that $P_1 \subseteq P_2$ we have $S(P_1) \geq S(P_2)$.

Let D be a (not necessarily connected) database graph. Let $G = (V, E)$ be the pattern for which we compute support. Let $A_1, ..., A_m$ be all instances of G in database D

(i.e. subgraphs of D that are label isomorphic to G). This set of instances is denoted by A_G. Two instances A_i, A_j are said to be intersecting, $A_i \wedge A_j$, if they have a common edge. The instance graph I_G is an undirected graph whose nodes are instances from A_G and edges are all pairs (A_i, A_j) where $A_i \wedge A_j$.

We use here an operation of *clique contraction*, which is a replacement of a clique G_1 in a graph G_2 by a single new node v_{new} and (optionally) adding some of the edges (u, v_{new}) where $u \in G_1 \setminus G_2$ such that $\forall v \in G_1$, $(u,v) \in E(G)$. We also use an opposite operation of *node expansion*, which is a replacement of a node v in graph G_1 by a new graph G_2 (disjoint from G_1) and a replacement some of the edges (u, v), $u \in V(G_1)$ by a set of edges $\{(u, v') \mid v' \in V(G_2)\}$. An operation of *node addition*, which is defined as adding a new node v to a graph, where v may or may not be connected by edges to any of the previously existing nodes, is also used here. Using these operations we can characterize all admissible support measures using the following theorem:

Theorem 3.2 A positive valued function on I_G is an admissible support measure if it is a non-decreasing under the following operations on I_G: clique contraction, node addition, edge removal, and node expansion.

Due to space limitations the proof is given in [18]. It can be shown that the maximum independent set computed over the instance graph is an admissible support measure according to this theorem, since all the above operations do not reduce the size of a maximum independent set of an instance graph. This measure is in fact the **maximal number of edge-disjoint instances** of a graph pattern in the database. We denote by $size(D)$ the number of edges in the database graph D and define support of pattern G as $S(G) = \frac{MIS(I_G)}{size(D)}$ where MIS denotes the maximum independent set size of a graph. This measure reduces to the standard support measure for transaction databases.

4. Frequent graph-pattern algorithm

This section presents algorithm pseudocode for mining frequent graph patterns, which works for both directed and undirected graphs. We use following notation: (a) Π denotes a path sequence $P_1, ..., P_k$; (b) $\Pi\backslash_i$ denotes a path sequence $P_1, ..., P_{i-1}, P_{i+1}, ..., P_k$; (c) $\bar{k} - \{i, j\}$ denotes the sequence $1, .., i-1, i+1, .., j-1, j+1, .., k$; (c) L_i is a set containing frequent i-path graph patterns, C_i is a corresponding candidate set.

4.1. The intuition behind the algorithm

In a preprocessing phase, we find all frequent edge-disjoint paths (including paths with cycles), starting with frequent edges. In phase 1 we find all frequent single path graphs. In phase 2, we find all graphs composed of two paths, i.e. all possible intersections between pairs of paths from phase 1. In phase 3 we try to merge all pairs of graphs with $n - 1$ paths in an attempt to produce graphs with n paths. We assume that some admissible support measure is used, for example the one described in section 3.

Phase 1 constructs the frequent paths by adding one edge at a time. **Phase 2** constructs the frequent graphs with path number 2. It does it by uniting one-path graphs. The non-trivial steps are steps 2, 3 and 4, where in step 2 *all* possible compositions of the two paths are considered, and in step 3 both the path number and the support measure are calculated; step 4 removes all non-minimal isomorphic graphs.

Phase 3 constructs the frequent graphs with path number k from graphs with path number $k - 1$. The non-trivial step is step 3. In case 3(a) the graph is constructed by finding the common $k - 1$ subgraph structure in a pair of frequent k-path graphs and joining them, using the bijective sum operation, into a single $(k + 1)$-path pattern. In case 3(b), L_2 is scanned and for *any* combination of P_i and P_j which is frequent, the nodes common to P_i and P_j in this combination are set to be common in the candidate graph as well. Since joining two patterns directly (using BS) may overlook several common vertices of P_i and P_j, we need to "add" missing common vertices to the candidate pattern using splice. Again, steps 4 and 5 are the isomorphic graph removal and support computation as in phases 1 and 2. The final step of the algorithm (not shown here) is removing all frequent sub-graphs which are not maximal, i.e. contained in larger frequent graphs (this step must be done last to avoid overlooking the larger frequent graphs.) The proof of correctness (given in [18]) of this algorithm shows that each of the 3 phases above is sound and complete.

Algorithm 1 Frequent paths - Phase #1 (textual description)

---

1. Scan the database and find all frequent labeled edges. Store them in the first frequent set.

2. Build the k-th candidate set in the following manner: try adding frequent edges to every frequent path of length $(k - 1)$ (stored in $(k - 1)$-th frequent set) in such a way that a path is obtained. Add this path to the candidate set. Once the candidate set is constructed, evaluate support for every pattern, and store frequent ones in the k-th frequent set.

3. If the k-th frequent set is empty, output the set L_1 of all frequent paths obtained so far and stop.

---

5. Experimental results

An empirical evaluation of our algorithm, compared to two "naive" algorithms, is provided below. Two types of databases were used: synthetic, where we can control both the topology and labeling of graphs, and a real-life XML "movies" database [15].

5.1. Experimental setting

The experimental environment is a Sun Ultra-30 workstation running at 247 MHz and 128 MB of main memory.

Algorithm 2 Frequent path pairs - Phase #2

---

1. Compute frequent paths using algorithm 1, and store these paths in the set L_1. Let $C_2 = \emptyset$, $L_2 = \emptyset$.

2. For every pair of frequent paths $P_1, P_2 \in L_1$ and every possible label preserving edge-disjoint composition relation C on $V(P_1), V(P_2)$ add tuple $< P_1, P_2, C >$ to C_2.

3. For every tuple $< P, Q, C > \in C_1$, if $G = \Omega(P, Q, C)$ has path number 2 and is frequent, add $\{< P, Q, C >\}$ to L_2.

4. Remove all non P-minimal tuples from L_2.

5. Output $\{\Omega(P, Q, C) \mid < P, Q, C > \in L_2\}$.

We use two software products: (1) for graph isomorphism computations we use [8]; (2) for maximal independent set size, we use *wcclique* (see [11]) on a a reverse of graph is built to obtain maximum independent set size. We use graph generation schemes described in [12] in order to produce all non-isomorphic graphs of a certain size.

The real XML file we used is a portion of the "movies" database. XML elements are treated as nodes, and inheritance relationships and references - as edges. The detailed procedure can be found in [18].

5.2. The implemented algorithms

We implemented our mining algorithm for fully labeled graphs described in section 4, as well as the two types of "naive" algorithms discussed below. The latter were used in order to compare run-time and number of generated candidate patterns with our algorithm, due to lack of competing algorithms for general pattern-mining algorithms in the literature. The same admissible support measure (a maximum independent set of an instance graph) was used for all algorithms. Tests were conducted multiple times and time averages were taken to eliminate factors of system load.

The first naive algorithm is based on generation of all non-isomorphic graphs of a certain size. The main idea is to produce connected graphs one by one, find all possible legal labelings for it and compute the support of all resulting graphs until no frequent graph of size K can be found. However, after a graph size exceeds 10 the number of graphs generated is very large, which made using this algorithm on large graphs somewhat unrealistic. The second algorithm is based on finding all frequent graphs with K edges and later extending them to graphs with $K + 1$ edges by either adding a new node and an edge to a frequent graph or by adding an edge between two existing nodes of the frequent graph with K edges. This algorithm is more efficient than exhaustive generation, but can produce many isomor-

Algorithm 3 Frequent graphs - Phase #3

1. Set $k = 3$.

2. Set $C_k = \emptyset, L_k = \emptyset, I_k = \emptyset$.

3. For every sequence of k paths Π such that
$< \Pi\backslash_i, C_1 >, < \Pi\backslash_j, C_2 > \in L_{k-1}$, then if
$C_1 \mid_{\overline{k}-\{i,j\}} = C_2 \mid_{\overline{k}-\{i,j\}}$ (subtracting P_j from C_1
and P_i from C_2), do:
(a) Let $C_{BS} = BS(C_1, C_2, \overline{k} - \{i, j\}, \overline{k} - \{i, j\})$.
If $G = \Omega(\Pi, C_{BS})$ has path number k, add
$t = < \Pi, C_{BS} >$ to C_k.
(b) For every $< P_i, P_j, C > \in L_2$, if
$G = \Omega(\Pi, (C_{BS} \oplus_{i,j} C)$ has path number k, add
$t = < \Pi, C_{BS} \oplus_{i,j} C >$ to C_k.

4. Remove non P-minimal tuples from C_k.

5. For every $t \in C_k$ add t to L_k if $\Omega(t)$ is frequent.

6. If $L_k = \emptyset$, output $\bigcup_{i=2}^{k-1} \{\Omega(t) \mid t \in L_i\} \bigcup L_1$.
Otherwise, set $k := k + 1$ and go to step 3.

---

phic copies of each graph.

5.3. Experimental results

We investigated behavior of the algorithms using the following performance parameters: (1) *number of candidate patterns* produced by an algorithm during data mining; (2) *number of isomorphism computations* during data mining, and overall number of support computations; (3) *total time* spend on data mining (**not** a CPU time) and on support computations.

Table 5 presents results of testing on trees and Table 6 on sparse graphs. The notation used in all three tables are explained in Table 4. For our algorithm the number of candidate patterns can sometimes be less than the number of frequent patterns since frequent nodes and edges are computed directly without generating candidate patterns.

Table 4: **Notations**

N, E, L	# of nodes, edges and labels in the database
S	support threshold in %
C, FP	# of candidate and frequent patterns
I, SC	# of isomorphism and support computations
TT	total time (seconds) spent on data mining
ST	time in sec. of support computations
N#2	naive edge addition algorithm
A	our algorithm
#	serial number of a database graph

Since the run time of all algorithms depends mainly on support computations, and the support computation time of a single pattern G in its turn depends on the number of subgraphs in a database graph that are of the same size as G,

the time spent on support computation increases drastically as the database graph becomes dense.

Since our implementation needs to generate all appropriate subgraphs of a database graph, find among them all subgraphs that are isomorphic to the pattern in question, build an instance graph and find its maximum independent size, testing our algorithm on dense graphs seems to be extremely time consuming. An additional consideration was the fact that most real-life databases represent sparse graphs rather than dense ones. Therefore, we decided to limit our tests to trees and sparse graphs and to choose a support threshold that, on the one hand, will not limit the output to trivial graphs (nodes and edges) and on the other hand, will not turn every connected subgraph of a database to frequent.

Table 5: **Experimental results for trees**

#	N, L, S, FP	Alg	C, I, SC	ST	TT
1	40 4 7% 15	N#2	100 24 92	41	44
		A	52 47 52	12	20
2	50 4 7% 16	N#2	110 41 102	676	682
		A	45 45 42	22	29
3	50 6 3% 37	N#2	470 82 458	326	340
		A	202 239 205	68	106
4	50 8 3% 27	N#2	306 62 290	280	290
		A	119 91 111	12	39
5	60 4 5% 15	N#2	100 24 92	220	224
		A	52 47 52	56	63
6	60 6 5% 44	N#2	728 203 716	3493	3537
		A	175 868 276	238	376
7	60 8 5% 14	N#2	103 18 87	19	22
		A	41 29 26	4	9

Table 6: **Experimental results for sparse graphs**

#	N, E, L, S, FP	Alg	C, I, SC	ST	TT
1	40 50 4 7% 14	N#2	60 33 52	19	24
		A	49 55 42	14	23
2	40 50 6 5% 17	N#2	84 48 76	33	40
		A	59 70 54	15	26
3	50 60 6 5% 28	N#2	355 74 343	314	326
		A	117 185 143	41	70
4	60 80 4 4% 16	N#2	101 31 93	609	614
		A	56 58 56	123	132
5	60 80 6 3% 27	N#2	265 86 253	842	857
		A	120 102 110	41	57
6	70 90 8 3% 27	N#2	252 77 236	44	57
		A	126 98 110	21	37
7	80 100 8 3% 32	N#2	403 74 387	160	172
		A	149 127 141	41	60

From Tables 5 and 6 we conclude that our algorithm runs faster even though it conducts more isomorphism checks than naive edge addition algorithm. It happens because our algorithm produces fewer candidate patterns, and thus less time is wasted on support computation.

Table 7 contains the number of frequent patterns found in six different subsets of movie database with different support values. It shows that the structure of the database (a tree as in set #6 or a sparse graph) has more impact on the number of frequent patterns than the support value.

Table 7: **Movie DB: support vs frequent patterns**

Data set	Properties
#1	12656 nodes, 13878 edges, 112 labels
#2	8337 nodes, 9416 edges, 25 labels
#3	7027 nodes, 7851 edges, 22 labels
#4	4730 nodes, 4813 edges, 90 labels
#5	2757 nodes, 2794 edges, 76 labels
#6	1293 nodes, 1292 edges, 91 labels

Support	#1	#2	#3	#4	#5	#6
90%	3	3	3	3	2	4
80%	3	3	3	3	2	5
70%	4	3	3	4	2	5
60%	4	3	3	4	2	9
50%	5	3	3	5	2	21
40%	6	4	4	5	2	32
30%	7	5	4	8	5	34
20%	8	6	5	9	6	46
10%	15	12	10	11	7	79
9%	16	12	10	11	7	79
8%	16	12	10	12	8	84
7%	18	12	10	12	9	84
6%	21	13	11	12	10	86
5%	22	14	11	16	11	86

As seen from Table 7, for the same values of support, the number of frequent patterns is smaller, and thus the execution time is *much smaller* in the movie database than in the synthetic one. This indicates the feasibility of our algorithm in real-life cases. As the graph becomes larger, the number of frequent patterns for the same support value decreases since a larger amount of edge-disjoint instances is required for each pattern in order to pass the support threshold. Finally, Figure 5 shows some of the frequent patterns we found in the movies database. Note that the patterns do not contain titles of movies or names of directors, since these are present only as *attributes* and not as *tags* in the XML database. Related research [13] attempts to treat attributes and values of an XML database as well.

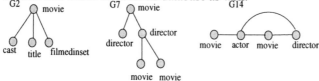

Figure 5: **Pattern examples**

6. Discussion and related work

6.1. Evaluation

In most semi-structured data, there is no distinction between values and labels. Usually, the 'label' of a leaf node is its value, using our approach. In XML, one can have attribute values in internal nodes. One can then either include values as a separate two-node branch (attribute, value) and apply our approach, or filter out attributes with non-interesting values (e.g. identifiers) [13]. Another approach is to find the structures first, and then build a separate table containing attribute values as in [13].

Another issue is complexity. The complexity of our algorithm is exponential in the size of the pattern. This complexity is inherent to apriori-like algorithms. The complexity of Apriori is due to the fact that the *number* of frequent patterns can be exponential, and the complexity of any graph mining algorithm is bounded by the need to find all subgraphs of a database isomorphic to a given pattern in order to evaluate its support. Therefore isomorphism computations done by our algorithm do not affect the complexity, as the graph isomorphism problem is at worst exponential on a size of a pattern, not the database size. The main goal of a mining algorithm should thus be to decrease the number of candidate patterns, and by doing so decrease the number of support computations. Our approach is feasible, because the number of patterns remaining from one phase to the next is reduced considerably, according to our experiments.

6.2. Related work

As mentioned in the introduction, there is little related work on mining frequent sub-graphs in a graph database. Since we assume the reader is familiar with the basic algorithms for mining association rules, e.g. Apriori [1], we only review here the most relevant papers, [3],[10],[19],[9].

[3] presents two algorithms for mining frequent directed simple path patterns in a web environment. Both algorithms are based on an algorithm called MF, that finds all maximal forward references in a set of traversal sequences contained in the database. The MF algorithm is a DFS algorithm which eliminates backward references, and outputs a set of linear paths. The goal of the two mining algorithms is to find frequent sequences in these paths. The support measure here is equivalent to the one used for association rule support ([1]) and equals the number of maximal forward references containing some pattern, divided by a total number of maximal forward references in the database. The main differences between the algorithm of [3] and ours is that the former handles only linear paths, making its support measure computationally trivial.

Paper [10] also discusses the problem in the context of a web environment - finding frequent patterns in logs of web accesses. Rather than dealing with linear paths, it examines tree-like structures. Furthermore, the number of times a user visits a web page within a single navigation path is ignored. One important restriction in this paper is that only *rooted* trees are considered, i.e. trees whose root is the same as the root of the entire web database! Naturally, this limits the complexity of the problem and the algorithm.

The problem is discussed in a wider context in [19].

That paper describes an algorithm for finding maximal frequent tree-like patterns in semi-structured documents, represented in the standard OEM model. Although this algorithm searches only for tree-like patterns, it can also handle patterns containing cycles by transforming them into trees.

The differences between [19] and our work are: (1) frequent patterns produced by [19] must contain the document's root whereas our algorithm finds arbitrary patterns; (2) our support denotes the fraction of the database represented by a certain pattern, and not simply the number of its instances; (3) with arbitrary patterns, replacing a cycle-causing edge by an edge to a leaf node will not work.

Finally, algorithm [9], as in our paper, finds frequent graph patterns but uses edges as building blocks. Our approach, for real-world databases, generally provides faster convergence of the algorithm. Additionally, [9] handles transaction databases only, thus avoiding the problem of support measure definition addressed in our work.

In summary, the ideas presented in the above papers, have influenced our work considerably. However, the extensions of these ideas to general graphs are not obvious and are the major contributions of this paper.

7. Summary

An apriori-like algorithm for retrieving frequent graph patterns from a given set of graphs is the central issue in this paper. In contrast with most existing work, the pattern can be either a directed or an undirected graph, and may contain cycles. The added functionality can support data mining on the increasing fraction of on-line documents, which consist of blocks connected by references. Knowledge about typical structure of documents is helpful in analyzing complex repositories of semistructured data (e.g. XML databases, the web), and is potentially useful for querying data, indexing it and storing it efficiently.

In a general topology, the issue of support becomes non-trivial - meeting intuitive desiderata such as monotonicity of the support measure, while being consistent with support measures defined for existing data-mining schemes, is important. We defined a notion of support-measure admissibility, and presented one such measure, based on independence of pattern instances.

In searching for frequent patterns, candidates are constructed using frequent paths. The scheme is evaluated empirically and is promising, as it shows a decided advantage over competing algorithms.

The scheme proposed here can be extended in several ways: (a) using more complex building blocks; (b) adapting extend the algorithm to the dynamic database model; (c) treating similar patterns equivalent, for example, by using bisimulation [14] as a criterion of pattern resemblance; (d) exploring additional admissible support measures.

References

[1] R. Agrawal and R. Srikant, Fast Algorithms for Mining Association Rules, *Proc. of the 20th Int'l Conf. on VLDB*, Santiago, Chile, September 1994.

[2] Editors: T. Bray, J. Paoli, and C. Sperberg-McQueen, Extensible markup language (XML) 1.0, February 1998, http://www.w3.org/XML/#9802xml10.

[3] M.S. Chen, J. S. Park, P. S. Yu, Efficient Data Mining for Path Traversal Patterns, *IEEE Transactions on Knowledge and Data Engineering*, 10(2), 1998: 209-221.

[4] A. Deutsch , M. Fernandez , D. Florescu , A. Levy , D. Maier , D. Suciu, Querying XML data, *IEEE Data Engineering Bulletin* 22(3), 1999: 27-34.

[5] A. Deutsch, M. F. Fernandez, D. Suciu, Storing Semistructured Data with STORED, *Proceedings of SIGMOD Conference* 1999: 431-442.

[6] C. Domshlak, R. Brafman and S.E. Shimony, Preference-based Configuration of Web Page Content, *Proceedings of IJCAI*, August 2001.

[7] R. Goldman and J. Widom, DataGuides: Enabling Query Formulation and Optimization in Semistructured Databases, *Proc. of 23rd VLDB Conf.*, Athens, Greece, 1997.

[8] VFLib Graph Matching Library, http://amalfi.dis.unina.it/graph/db/vflib-2.0/doc/vflib.html.

[9] M. Kuramochi and G. Karypis, Frequent Subgraph Discovery, *Proceedings of IEEE ICDM*, 2001.

[10] X.Lin, Ch.Liu, Y.Zhang and X.Zhou, Efficiently Computing Frequent Tree-Like Topology Patterns in a Web Environment, *Proceedings of 31st Int. Conf. on Tech. of Object-Oriented Language and Systems*, 1998.

[11] Maximum weight clique program, http://www.tcs.hut.fi/~pat/wclique.html.

[12] B. D. McKay, *I*somorph-free exhaustive generation, *Journal of Algorithms*, vol. 26, 1998: 306-324.

[13] A. Meisels, M. Orlov, T. Maor, Discovering associations in XML data, *BGU Technical report*, 2001.

[14] R. Milner, Calculi for synchrony and asynchrony, *Proceedings of TCS 25*, 1983: 267-310.

[15] *Movie database*, http://us.imdb.com.

[16] P. R. J. Ostergard, A new algorithm for the maximum-weight clique problem, Helsinki University of Technology, internal report, 2001.

[17] D.M.R. Park, Concurrency and automata on infinite sequences, *Proceedings of 5th GI Conference (P.Deussen, ed.), LNCS 104, Springer-Verlag,* 1981: 167-183.

[18] N.Vanetik, Discovery of frequent patterns in semi-structured data, *M.Sc. thesis, Dept. of Computer Science, Ben Gurion University, 2002.*

[19] K. Wang, H. Liu, Discovering Typical Structures of Documents: A Road Map Approach, *Proceedings of SIGIR 1998*: 146-154.

Estimating the number of segments in time series data using permutation tests

Kari T. Vasko & Hannu T.T. Toivonen*
University of Helsinki
Department of Computer Science
PO Box 26, FIN-00014, Finland
{Kari.Vasko,Hannu.Toivonen}@cs.helsinki.fi

Abstract

Segmentation is a popular technique for discovering structure in time series data. We address the largely open problem of estimating the number of segments that can be reliably discovered. We introduce a novel method for the problem, called Pete. Pete is based on permutation testing.

The problem is an instance of model (dimension) selection. The proposed method analyzes the possible overfit of a model to the available data rather than uses a term for penalizing model complexity. In this respect the approach is more similar to cross-validation than regularization based techniques (e.g., AIC, BIC, MDL, MML). Further, the method produces a p value for each increase in the number of segments. This gives the user an overview of the statistical significance of the segmentations. We evaluate the performance of the proposed method using both synthetic and real time series data. The experiments show that permutation testing gives realistic results about the number of reliably identifiable segments and that it compares favorably with the Monte Carlo cross-validation (MCCV) and commonly used BIC criteria.

1. Introduction

Time series segmentation is an instance of clustering analysis. It addresses the following data mining problem: given a time series T, find a partitioning of T to segments that are internally homogeneous. Depending on the application, the goal could be to locate stable periods of time, to identify change points, or to simply compress the original time series into a more compact presentation. In this paper, we are concerned with the discovery of interesting features in data rather than with compression as such. For an overview to methods and approaches to time series segmentation see, e.g., [7, 8, 13, 5, 6].

As an example application, consider the analysis of biostratigraphic data collected from microfossils accumulated and preserved in lake sediments [4, 11]. Paleoecologists obtain deep cores of sediment and analyse them layer by layer. Deeper layers correspond to distant points in time and the topmost layers are the most recent ones. Typically such data spans a period from hundreds to thousands of years. In each layer (time point), the species composition of some suitable organisms is analysed. The abundances of these species in the different sediment layers form a multidimensional time series, where homogeneous segments correspond to environmentally relatively stable periods and segment boundaries to more significant changes in the environment.

We introduce a novel method, *Pete*, for estimating the number of segments that can be reliably found in a given time series. The method is based on permutation tests on the available data. Instead of defining a data independent measure for model complexity, like penalized likelihood based approaches, it only measures the dataset specific overfit resulting from increased model complexity, and is in this respect similar to cross-validation techniques.

Another recent application for time series segmentation is in context sensitivity of mobile devices. Being able to measure and sense the environment is not enough: a problem that remains is how to recognize different contexts from the measurements. An approach proposed recently is to segment the measurement time series and, in the spirit of unsupervised learning, to identify different contexts with the discovered homogeneous segments [6]. Again, the number of segments to be discovered has a significant effect on the results.

In a nutshell, the Pete algorithm can be described as follows. The given time series is segmented in steps to $m = 1, 2, \ldots$ segments. The segmentation can be done with any segmentation algorithm; all that Pete needs from each segmentation is the amount of error that remains (or the goodness of fit). Pete recognizes overfitting by analyzing at each segmentation step m the reduction of error. The relative reduction is contrasted to the respective reduction

---

*Also at Nokia Research Center

in the case there no segment structure in the data. If the reduction is not significantly better in the observed data then segmentation is stopped.

2. Background and definitions

2.1. Time series and segmentations

A time series $T = (x(t)|1 \leq t \leq n)$ is a finite set of n samples labeled by time points $1, 2, \ldots, n$. A segment of T is a set of consecutive time points $S_T(a, b) = (t|a \leq t \leq b)$. An m-segmentation S_T^m ($m \leq n$) of time series T is a partition of T to m non-overlapping segments

$$S_T^m = \{S_T(a_i, b_i)|1 \leq i \leq m\}$$

such that $a_1 = 1, b_m = n$, and $a_i = b_{i-1}+1$ for $1 < i \leq m$. In other words, an m-segmentation splits T to m disjoint time intervals. For simplicity, the segments are denoted by $S_1, \ldots, S_m$.

Usually the goal is to find homogeneous segments from a given time series. For instance, in paleoecological studies an objective is to find periods of time where the species composition and thus also the climate has been relatively stable. In such a case the segmentation problem can be described as constrained clustering: data points should be grouped by their similarity, but with the constraint that all points in a cluster must come from successive time points.

We assume that the segmentation is based on fitting a (simple) function within each segment, and on searching for a segmentation that results in a good overall fit. Usually the function is a constant or linear function, or a polynomial of a higher but limited degree, fitted to approximate the values within the segment.

2.2. The error of a segmentation

A good segmentation fits the data well and has a small error. The estimation error is usually defined as a positive function of the distances between the actual values in the time series and the values given by the functions within segments.

Let T be a time series of length n and $S_T^m = \{S_1, \ldots, S_m\} \in \mathcal{S}_m$ an m-segmentation, where $\mathcal{S}_m$ denotes the set of all possible m-segmentations of T. Let θ_i denote the vector of parameters for the function in segment S_i. (For a constant function there obviously is only one parameter and for a non-continuous linear function there are two parameters per segment.)

The error

$$e(S_T^m) = e(S_T^m, \theta_1, \theta_2, \ldots, \theta_m) \qquad (1)$$

of a segmentation describes how far the model, i.e., the function consisting of the local functions in the segments,

is from the data. The error function is usually the sum of squared errors or a function of the (log) likelihood in probabilistic settings. Since different approaches base the segmentation on different error measures, we do not assume any particular segmentation algorithm or error function. We do assume that the modeling error $e(S_T^1), e(S_T^2), \ldots$ for a given segment T is a positive non-increasing function of the number of segments.

2.3. Finding good segmentations

Suppose that finding the parameter values $\theta = (\theta_1, \ldots, \theta_m)$ that (approximately) minimize the error function for a given segmentation S_T^m is a tractable task, e.g., computation of the least squares line. Given that θ is easily available the question remains how to explore the set $\mathcal{S}_m$ for good solutions: the search space is exponential in n, the length of the time series.

The optimal m-segmentation can be characterized in a recursive way so that dynamic programming can be used to find it (e.g. [6]). Unfortunately, dynamic programming is computationally intractable for many real data sets. Consequently, heuristic optimization techniques such as greedy top-down or bottom-up techniques are frequently used to find good but suboptimal m-segmentations [6, 7].

In this paper, we do not address the problem of how to find good segmentations. We simply assume one of the many available methods is used.

2.4. Relative reduction of error

Recall that $e(S_T^m)$ is the error of segmentation S_T^m. Then

$$RR(m|T) = \frac{e(S_T^{m-1}) - e(S_T^m)}{e(S_T^{m-1})} \qquad (2)$$

is the relative reduction of error when m segments are used instead of $m - 1$ segments. The Pete method will analyze the relative reduction of error as the number of segments is increased and stop segmentation when statistically significant reductions are not achieved any more.

The assumptions we make about the underlying segmentation algorithm and the error function can be summarized as follows. For a fixed time series T and a given segmentation algorithm, the error $e(S_T^1), e(S_T^2), \ldots$ is a positive non-increasing function of the number of segments. This follows naturally if the power of the local functions is constant, as is usually the case. Obviously then $RR(m|T)$ is in $[0, 1]$ for all $m > 1$.

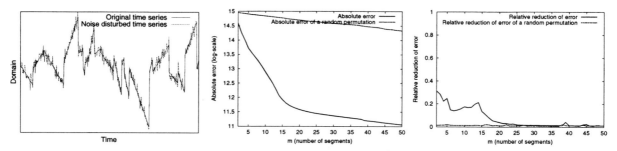

Figure 1. A noisy piece-wise linear time series (left). Absolute error (middle) and relative reduction of error (right) as a function of the number of segments.

3. Estimating the number of segments

3.1. The method

We now introduce the Pete algorithm for determining an appropriate number of segments in a given time series. The idea is perhaps best conveyed by a simple example. We will justify the use of permutation tests more formally in the following subsection.

Imagine a piecewise linear time series consisting of, say, around 20 segments, with some noise in the data (Figure 1, left). Segmenting the time series into $m = 2, 3, \ldots, 20$ segments keeps improving the fit and decreasing the error, as more and more of the true segments of the data are matched (solid line in the middle panel of Figure 1). With $m = 21, 22, \ldots$ segments the error keeps decreasing as well, but the reduction of error is due to noise in the data. We devise a method that tests if the reduction of error is likely to be due to noise or due to some structure in the data.

So how to tell if the reduction of error is due to noise? Let T be the given time series of length n, and let $\mathcal{T}$ be a similar random time series consisting of noise only and of no non-random structure. What we want to do is to test the alternative hypothesis $h_1 : RR(m|T) > RR(m|\mathcal{T})$ against the null hypothesis $h_0 : RR(m|T) = RR(m|\mathcal{T})$. If we can test the null hypothesis and the observed reduction of error is very unlikely to result from noise, then (at least) m segments can be considered justified.

Where to obtain random time series $\mathcal{T}$ that are somehow representative of the properties of the original time series T, without making any assumptions about T? The short answer is to use permutations of T: randomly permute the order of the datapoints, and the result is a random time series with value distribution identical to T. Figure 1 shows the absolute errors (middle) and their relative reductions (right) for the time series (left) and for one randomly permuted time series. For the random time series with no temporal structure the error decreases constantly — but remarkably

slowly. The original and the permuted time series do not have similar reductions of error until about 22 segments.

The null hypothesis can be tested by generating a number of random timeseries $\mathcal{T}$ having the same value distribution as T and counting how often $RR(m|\mathcal{T}) \geq RR(m|T)$. This (approximated) probability of getting reduction $RR(m|T)$ by chance is the p value of the data under the null hypothesis. If it is low, e.g. below 0.05, then $RR(m|T)$ is unlikely to result from noise and m segments are justified.

Table 1 gives the Pete algorithm. To sum it up: we propose to generate random permutations of the given time series and to compare the reduction of error in the original data to that of permuted data sets, and to stop segmentation when a relatively large fraction (say, 0.05) of the permuted data sets has at least as good reduction of error as the original data set. Throughout this paper we use a cutoff value of 0.05 for the p value.

3.2. Statistical justification for the method

We next go through the approach more formally. Denote by M_T the set of all time series of length n whose value distribution is identical with the given time series T of length n. Further, let $\mathcal{T}$ be a uniformly distributed random time series in M_T.

Let $I_T(\mathcal{T}, m)$ be an indicator (a Bernoulli random variable) for whether $\mathcal{T}$ results in no smaller reduction of error than T when segmented to m segments:

$$I_T(\mathcal{T}, m) = \begin{cases} 1 & \text{if } RR(m|\mathcal{T}) \geq RR(m|T) \\ 0 & \text{otherwise.} \end{cases} \quad (3)$$

Let us denote by $p_T(m)$ the probability of $RR(m|\mathcal{T}) \geq RR(m|T)$, i.e., of $I_T(\mathcal{T}, m) = 1$.

The p value of the m-segmentation of T, denoted $p_T(m)$, can be estimated as follows. First, we have

$$p_T(m) = \frac{\sum_{\mathcal{T}_i \in M_T} I_T(\mathcal{T}_i, m)}{|M_T|}. \quad (4)$$

468

Algorithm Pete

Input: time series T, segmentation algorithm A, error
function e, number of permutations N, cutoff value
p' for p value

Output: number of reliably identifiable segments

Method:

1. Generate N random permutations $\mathcal{T}_i$ of T
2. Use segmentation algorithm A to compute $e(S_T^1)$
   and each $e(S_{\mathcal{T}_i}^1)$, i.e., errors with one segment
3. For $m := 2, \ldots, n$ (where n is the length of T):
   - 3.1. Use A to segment T and each $\mathcal{T}_i$ to m segments
   - 3.2. Let $r := |\{\mathcal{T}_i : RR(m|\mathcal{T}_i) \geq RR(m|T)\}|/N$ be
     the fraction of permutations where the reduction
     of error was at least as good as with T
   - 3.3. If $r > p'$ then return $m - 1$
4. Return n

Table 1. Pete permutation procedure for estimating the number of segments

Second, permutations can be used to approximate the right hand side of Equation 4: instead of summing over all $\mathcal{T}_i \in M_T$, we sum over a random sample from M_T, obtained using random permutations of the original time series T.

Permutation testing is a special case of Monte Carlo integration: the p value is estimated with N random points as

$$\hat{p}_T^N(m) = \frac{1}{N}\sum_{i=1}^{N} I_T(\mathcal{T}_i, m) \approx \mathbf{E}(I_T(\mathcal{T}, m)) = p_T(m) \quad (5)$$

where $\mathcal{T}_1, \mathcal{T}_2, \ldots, \mathcal{T}_N$ are uniform random samples from M_T. Random sampling from M_T can be carried out efficiently by simply generating random permutations of T, since the set M_T is exactly the same as the set of all permutations of time series T.

Figure 2 illustrates the Monte Carlo estimated distribution of $RR(m|\mathcal{T})$ ($m = 2, \ldots, 50$) as well as the relative reduction of the observed time series (Figure 1) obtained in 1000 random permutations. The region where $p \leq 0.05$, i.e., where the relative reduction is statistically significant, is drawn with stronger lines.

We emphasize that the p value $p_T(m)$ is used only as a tool to decide when to stop segmentation. It should not be thought of as a statement about the probability of any exact number of segments. Also, we obviously do not expect the data to actually consist of any constant or linear segments, even when evidence for several segments is discovered. Segmentation itself is a tool for discovering useful structure in the data, and constant and linear segments are suitable classes of concepts to be used in such an analysis.

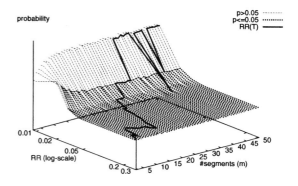

Figure 2. Monte Carlo approximated probabilities $p[RR(m|\mathcal{T}) = x|T]$**of the relative reduction (RR) given the time series T of Figure 1 (left) and the number of segments.**

3.3. Related work

The problem of determining an appropriate number of segments is a special case of estimating the number of dimensions of a model. The question is about overfitting: how to avoid too complex models that fit noise in addition to the 'true signal'.

There are several approaches for determining the dimension of a model. They can be roughly divided into two groups: (1) some measure model complexity without regard to the data, as well how well a model fits the data, (2) some only analyze the fit to the data.

(1) *Penalized likelihood*, e.g., MDL, MML, BIC, AIC, SIC and structural risk minimization [1, 12, 3, 16, 17], and generally all regularization based approaches to estimate an unknown target function, specify a cost for the model complexity and then minimize the sum of the model complexity and error. In the *pure Bayesian approach* the full probability model for all variables of the application domain, including model dimension m, is defined, including (data independent) prior distributions. The Bayesian approach can be considered as an instance of the penalized likelihood without asymptotically derived complexity term.

(2) *Cross-validation* is is a general and well-understood technique for addressing overfitting. In particular, *Monte Carlo cross-validation*, a variant of the standard v-fold cross-validation, has been successfully applied to model dimension selection [14, 15]. *The generalized likelihood ratio test* [2] is an example of a test on the increase in the model likelihood, compared to an assumed underlying distribution. There are techniques that try to locate a knee in the error or likelihood curve (cf. Figure 1, middle). The

broken stick model [10] is widely used by paleoecologists in the zonation problem. The broken stick model gives the expected amount of variance (error) accounted for by a segment, under the assumption that those variances follow the broken stick distribution. It is primarily applicable in top-down segmentation, where splits are added incrementally to an existing segmentation.

The permutation test method Pete differs significantly from methods in the first category since it does not assign any data-independent cost to model complexity. It does have an analogy to the generalized likelihood ratio test [2] when the error function is the log-likelihood function. However, the biggest difference to most methods in the second category is that Pete does not assume any particular distribution for the data or the error function. Cross-validation is clearly the closest match to Pete in these respects.

4. Experiments

We evaluated Pete against BIC and MCCV using both synthetic and real data. Since the real data has no "right" answers, we focus here on the synthetic cases.

4.1. Generation of synthetic data

We generated simulated data in order to assess the performance of Pete in controlled settings. The data was generated using random piecewise constant models. The performance was evaluated with respect to signal to noise ratio (SNR).

For the piecewise constant time series, the constants were generated from the normal distribution $N(0, \sigma_{loc})$, and noise was added from the normal distribution $N(0, \sigma)$. The change points were drawn from a uniform distribution. In data generation, σ was a constant and the signal to noise ratio $SNR = \frac{\sigma_{loc}}{\sigma}$ was adjusted by varying the variance σ_{loc} of the signal (Figure 3). The synthetic data sets consisted of 100 data points each.

4.2. Evaluation methodology

The true number of statistically identifiable segments is not known for the data sets with noise, so we do not have any right answers to the number of segments, except for the extreme cases. Without any noise (SNR $\to \infty$) exactly the original number of (noiseless) segments should ideally be identified; and with noise alone (SNR $\to 0$), only one segment should be discovered. Sensitivity to the original, noiseless segments was used as the basis for the numerical results, despite these shortcomings.

The following parameters were used in estimating the number of segments. Segmentations to piecewise constant functions were done with the greedy top-down method, and

the error function was the sum of squared errors (which is proportional to log-likelihood function with normal noise). A cutoff value $p \leq 0.05$ was used to decide whether to continue segmentation. 2500 permutations were used to estimate the p values. Finally, all results with the synthetic data sets were averaged over 100 similarly generated random data sets.

The prediction accuracy obtained by Pete was evaluated against the penalized likelihood-based BIC-score [12] and Monte Carlo cross-validation [14, 15].

We evaluated the performance of BIC in two ways: (i) in a realistic setting, in which the variance of noise was estimated from the residuals (maximum likelihood), and (ii) in an unrealistic setting in which the true variance of noise was given as a parameter (we call this "oracle BIC" to reflect the fact that the variance is not known for real data sets). The first setting gives a practical benchmark for the performance of the method, and the second setting gives an (unfair) upper limit for the performance of BIC. For the permutation tests there obviously is no need to estimate the variance of noise.

Monte Carlo cross-validation (MCCV) or 'repeated-learning testing' was carried out as follows. Given a time series T, randomly selected 50% of time points in T are assigned to the test set, and the remaining 50% constitute the training set. This procedure is repeated M times, giving M paired test sets T_i^{test} and training sets T_i^{train} ($1 \leq i \leq M$). For each number of segments $m = 1, 2, \ldots$, the training set T_i^{test} is used for segmentation and the segmentation error is then computed in the corresponding test set T_i^{train}. In the MCCV procedure we choose the number m of segments that minimizes the average of test errors. The average is taken over several random splits M to reduce variance in the estimates.

Recent experiments indicate that MCCV might give more reliable results than v-fold cross-validation in terms of choosing the correct number of cluster components [14, 15]. We adopted in our experiments split fraction 50% since it is reasonably robust across a variety of problems [14]. The number of splits was chosen to be $M = 100$.

4.3. Results

Figure 4 gives a summary of the experimental comparisons between Pete, BIC, Monte Carlo Cross-validation and the imaginary "oracle BIC". SNR decreases and the amount of noise increases from top to bottom. The left and right columns differ only in the number of segments. Except in the very noisy bottom row, Pete and "oracle BIC" quite consistently peak at the actual number of segments and have the highest density region roughly around it. BIC, instead, tends to position its estimations systematically to smaller values, and so does MCCV. MCCV tends to make "flat"

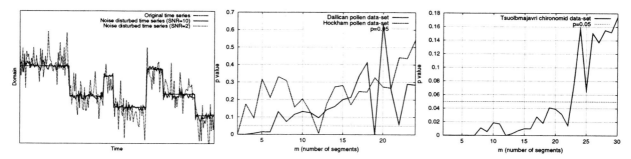

Figure 3. Two example time series consisting of 7 piecewise constant segments and two different levels of noise (SNR=2 and 10) (left panel). P **values for segmentations of paleoecological data sets (middle and right panel)**

predictions, i.e., the variance is large. The expected number of segments is however closer to the original number than in the results from BIC. All methods — quite expectedly — find less and less segments as the amount of noise is increased.

Based on the results, Pete is a most competitive approach. It outperforms BIC and MCCV almost constantly. Pete compares well even with the non-existing "oracle BIC" or the "BIC upper limit".

An interesting phenomena is that Pete sometimes gives very small estimates for the number of segments, even with large SNR (little noise). This is probably due to the permutation test being conservative and predicting a small number of segments if evidence for more segments is not very strong. It is also possible that a single p value above the cutoff value stops segmentation prematurely. Overall, the cutoff value obviously has a direct effect on the number of segments. We do no not believe, however, that increasing the value from 0.05 to get more segments would give better results. On the contrary: it is likely that spurious segments would then be discovered. Analysis of this is a topic for future research.

4.4. Real data

We applied Pete to three real-world data sets from the field of paleoecology. Paleoecological analysis of the first data set is presented in [9] and the two other data sets have been discussed in [4].

The first data set (Tsuolbmajavri) consists of chironomid assemblages collected from a lake sediment in northern Lappland. It is composed of 51 chironomids in 148 sediment layers [9]. The other two data sets (Dallican and Hockham)[1] are sediment cores consisting of pollen data [4]. Dallican data set consists of 23 pollen taxa in 80 time points, and Hockham data set consists of 132 pollen taxa in 163 time points. The high dimensionality with respect to the

length of the time series makes segmentation of these data sets very challenging. (Obviously, dimensionality reduction techniques could be useful here, but they are outside the scope of this paper.)

Middle and right panels of Figure 3 shows the p value curves obtained for Tsuolbmajavri, Dallican and Hockham data sets, respectively (top-down algorithm, sum of variances within segments as error function, 10000 permutations). With a cutoff value $p \leq 0.05$, the p value curves can be interpreted to indicate that the Dallican data set consists of 6 segments, and that there are only two reliably identifiable segments in the Hockham data set. For the chironomid data set of Tsuolbmajavri it seems, in turn, that it is possible to identify 23 segments.

5. Conclusions and future work

We have introduced a new method, called Pete, for estimating the number of segments in time series data. Pete compares the quality of segmentations of the given data to the quality of segmentations of its random permutations.

We evaluated the performance of Pete against BIC and MCCV using synthetic time series. Experimental results show that Pete is very competitive: it was able to give very realistic estimations about the number of segments, and clearly and consistently seems to outperform BIC and MCCV in this task. However, permutations are computationally heavy and not necessarily suitable for time critical systems.

BIC was used here as a representative of a family of methods that use a model complexity term for model selection. Unlike many methods based on Occam's Razor, the proposed method does not use such a term. This is achieved by examining the derivative of the error function (relative

1. We acknowledge Keith D. Bennett and European Pollen Database for permission to use Hockham and Dallican data sets and Atte Korhola and Heikki Olander for permission to use Tsuolbmajavri data-set

reduction of error), e.g., the likelihood function, with respect to the derivates of the errors in a control group, as the model complexity is increased.

Cross-validation is the closest match to Pete in an important respect: the available data alone is used to select the model. No model complexity term nor assumptions about the data are needed. The subtle difference is that cross-validation holds out a part of the available data as a test set to estimate how well a model learned from the rest of the data actually generalizes. The permutation procedure in turn uses the full data set and its permutations to estimate the probability of obtaining a good model (in the sense of a small training error) just by chance. One reason for the inferior performace of cross-validation in our experimental results might be due to the size of the data set used to build the model: permutation tests use all of the available data whereas cross-validation holds back a fraction (50% in our experiments, selected based on results in [14]).

Possible future research issues include the following topics.

(i) The effect of different segmentation algorithms and error functions. For instance, consider greedy top-down segmentation that adds one segment boundary at a time without moving the existing ones. Instead of permuting the whole time series we could permute each segment separately, just like the top-down method tests the effect of a split in each existing segments, to obtain a p value that more closely matches the selected induction principle.

(ii) The approach we presented here is based on using a random sample from a data-dependent control group in model selection. Which kind of problems could this approach be generalized to?

(iii) Multidimensional data sets. Our current artificial data sets are one dimensional (in addition to time) but many of the interesting applications, such as the paleoecological data, are multidimensional. More tests are needed in this front.

(iv) An analysis of the p values. The longer the time series, the more p values are generated, and the more likely it is that some seem to indicate significant results, just by chance. For instance, what can be said of isolated small p values, such as the ones in two of our ecological data sets (Figure 3, middle)? Do they indicate a larger number of segments, or are they just random effects? Currently we bend towards the latter assumption.

References

[1] H. Akaike. A new look at the statistical model identification. *IEEE Transactions on Automatic Control*, 19(6):716 – 723, 1974.

[2] F. Arnold. *Mathematical Statistics*. Prentice-Hall, New Jersey, 1990.

[3] A. Barron, J. Rissanen, and B. Yu. The minimum description length principle in coding and modeling. *IEEE Transactions on Information Theory*, 44(6):2743–2760, 1998.

[4] K. Bennett. Determination of the number of zones in a biostratigraphical sequence. *New Phytol.*, 132:155–170, 1996.

[5] X. Ge and P. Smyth. Segmental Semi-Markov models for endpoint detection in plasma etching. Technical Report 00-08, UCI-ICS, 2000.

[6] J. Himberg, K. Korpiaho, H. Mannila, J. Tikanmäki, and H. T. Toivonen. Time series segmentation for context recognition in mobile devices. In *The 2001 IEEE International Conference on Data Mining (ICDM'01)*, pages 203 – 210, San Jose, California, November–December 2001.

[7] E. Keogh, S. Chu, D. Hart, and M. Pazzani. An online algorithm for segmenting time series. In *IEEE International Conference on Data Mining*, pages 289–296, 2001.

[8] E. Keogh and P. Smyth. A probabilistic approach to fast pattern matching in time series databases. In *Proceedings of the Third International Conference on Knowledge Discovery and Data Mining (KDD'97)*, pages 20–24. AAAI Press, 1997.

[9] A. Korhola, K. Vasko, H. Toivonen, and H. Olander. Holocene temperature changes in northern Fennoscandia reconstructed from chironomids using Bayesian modelling. *Quaternary Science Review*, 21:1841–1860, 2002.

[10] R. MacArthur. On the relative abundance of bird species. *Proceedings of the National Academy of Science*, 43:293 – 295, 1957.

[11] H. Mannila, H. Toivonen, A. Korhola, and H. Olander. Learning, mining, or modeling? A case study in paleoecology. In *Discovery Science, First International Conference*, Lecture Notes in Artificial Intelligence 1532, pages 12 – 24, Fukuoka, Japan, 1998. Springer-Verlag.

[12] G. Schwarz. Estimating the dimension of a model. *The Annals of Statistics*, 7(2):461 – 464, 1978.

[13] H. Shatkay and S. B. Zdonik. Approximate queries and representations for large data sequences. In *Proceedings of the 12th International Conference on Data Engineering*, pages 536–545, Washington - Brussels - Tokyo, Feb. 1996. IEEE Computer Society.

[14] P. Smyth. Clustering using Monte Carlo cross-validation. In *Second International Conference on Knowledge Discovery and Data Mining*, pages 126–133, Portland, Oregon, USA, 1996.

[15] P. Smyth. Model selection for probabilistic clustering using cross-validated likelihood. Technical Report UCI-ICS 98-09, Information and Computer Science, University of California, Irvine, CA, 1998.

[16] M. Sugiyama and H. Ogawa. Subspace information criterion for model selection. *Neural Computation*, 13(8):1863 – 1889, 2001.

[17] V. Vapnik. *The Nature of Statistical Learning Theory*. Springer-Verlag, N.Y., 1995.

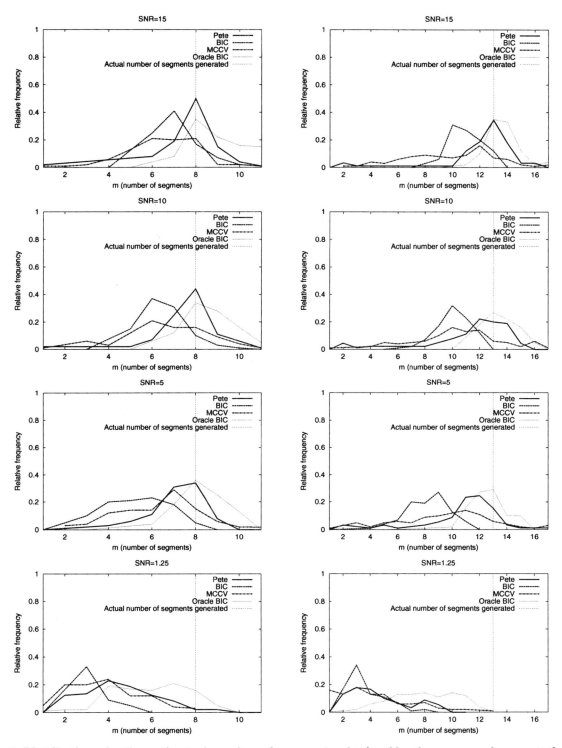

Figure 4. Distributions for the estimated number of segments obtained by the proposed permutation test (Pete), BIC, Monte Carlo cross-validation (MCCV) and "oracle BIC". The true number of segments is 8 (left column) or 13 (right column). Each graph is obtained using 100 random data sets.

Predicting Rare Events In Temporal Domains

Ricardo Vilalta
Department of Computer Science
University of Houston
Houston TX, 77204-3010, USA
vilalta@cs.uh.edu

Sheng Ma
IBM T.J. Watson Center
19 Skyline Dr.
Hawthorne N.Y., 10532, USA
shengma@us.ibm.com

Abstract

Temporal data mining aims at finding patterns in historical data. Our work proposes an approach to extract temporal patterns from data to predict the occurrence of target events, such as computer attacks on host networks, or fraudulent transactions in financial institutions. Our problem formulation exhibits two major challenges: 1) we assume events being characterized by categorical features and displaying uneven inter-arrival times; such an assumption falls outside the scope of classical time-series analysis, 2) we assume target events are highly infrequent; predictive techniques must deal with the class-imbalance problem. We propose an efficient algorithm that tackles the challenges above by transforming the event prediction problem into a search for all frequent eventsets preceding target events. The class imbalance problem is overcome by a search for patterns on the minority class exclusively; the discrimination power of patterns is then validated against other classes. Patterns are then combined into a rule-based model for prediction. Our experimental analysis indicates the types of event sequences where target events can be accurately predicted.

1 INTRODUCTION

Learning to predict infrequent but highly correlated subsequences of events, such as an attack in a computer network, or a fraudulent transaction in a financial institution, is a difficult problem. The difficulty in learning to recognize rare events may stem from several sources: few examples support the target class; events are described by categorical features that display uneven inter-arrival times; and time recordings only approximate the true arrival times, such as occurs in computer-network logs, transaction logs, speech signals, etc.

In this paper we describe an approach to predict rare events, called *target events*, in event sequences with categorical features, uneven inter-arrival times, and noisy sig-

nals. Our approach differs from previous work in the learning strategy. Most learning algorithms assume even class distributions and adopt a discriminant-description strategy: they search for a separator that best discriminates examples of different class. Under skewed distributions, however, separating away the under-represented class is difficult. We show that a better approach is to adopt a characteristic-description strategy: we specify common properties of examples of the same class before validating those properties against other classes. The new strategy helps improve efficiency, accuracy, and interpretability.

Our prediction strategy divides into the following steps:

1. We characterize target events by finding the types of events frequently preceding target events within a fixed time window.

2. We validate that these event types uniquely characterize target events, and do not occur often far from the time arrival of target events.

3. We combine validated event types to build a rule-based system for prediction.

Since our final rules are obtained by combining association rule mining and classification techniques, they receive the name of associative classification rules [8, 12, 7, 5]. Most previous work has focused on exploring this type of integration without any concern for the time dimension. We show how the same integration on event sequences requires special consideration.

We test our approach in the domain of service problems in computer networks, where predicting rare events brings multiple benefits. First, detecting system failures on a few servers can prevent widespread dissemination of those failures over the entire network. For example, low response time on a server may gradually escalate to technical difficulties on all nodes attempting to communicate with that server. Second, prediction can be used to ensure continuous provision of network services through the automatic implementation of corrective actions. For example, prediction of high CPU demand on a server can initiate a process to balance the CPU load by re-routing new demands to a back-up server.

Using both artificial and real production-network data, we conduct an empirical evaluation of our rule-based model. Our results show low error rates when the probability of a pattern occurring by chance is low, and when the size of the time window preceding target events is sufficiently large (Section 6).

The paper organization is described next. Section 2 introduces background information and our problem statement. Section 3 presents the logic to find all frequent and accurate eventsets preceding target events. Section 4 describes how to combine the frequent and accurate set of eventsets into a rule-based model. Section 5 analyzes the computational efficiency of our approach. Section 6 reports an empirical assessment of our approach. Section 7 reviews related work. Finally, Section 8 states our summary and conclusions.

2 THE EVENT PREDICTION PROBLEM

In our problem formulation the fundamental unit of study is an **event**. Events belong to sequences, and can be identified by their time of occurrence and type [9].

Definition 1. A sequence of events is an ordered collection of events $D = < d_1, d_2, \cdots, d_n >$, where each event d_i is a pair $d_i = (e_i, t_i)$. The first element of the pair, e_i, indicates the event type. The second element of the pair, t_i, indicates its occurrence time.

We assume the possible number of event types is finite, and that all events are ordered along time. For example, events obtained when monitoring a computer network can be classified based on severity level (e.g., normal, critical, fatal), or by the kind of disruption (e.g., node-down, link-failed, printer-failed, etc.). In a sequence of events, ((node-down, t_1), (link-failed, t_2), etc)), each t_i specifies date and time. If multiple attributes are necessary to describe an event, one may think of event type e_i as an attribute vector.

We are interested in predicting certain kinds of events that occur in sequence D. We refer to this subset of events, $D_{\text{target}} \subset D$, as *target events*. We assume the proportion of target events with respect to all events in sequence D is low; target events do not represent a *global* property of D, such as periodicity or constant trend, but rather a *local* property of D, such as a computer attack on a host network.

We assume the user specifies a target event type e_{target}, that characterizes D_{target} as,

$$D_{\text{target}} = \{d_i \in D | e_i = e_{\text{target}}\} \qquad (1)$$

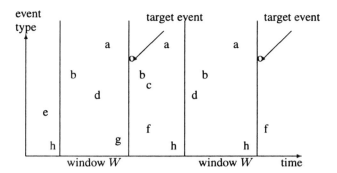

Figure 1. A plot of different event types vs. time. A time window before each target event enables us to identify frequent sets of event-types acting as precursors.

For example, if severity level defines the type of event, target events could be all events sharing one kind of severity level (e.g., all fatal events). The definition of target events, however, can be made more general. We can use an arbitrary function over the features characterizing each event (e.g., all events occurring in the time interval $[t_1, t_2]$).

Our framework assumes a dataset D of size n, containing a sequence of events (Definition 1). Event types take on categorical values. We also assume we have identified a set of events, $D_{\text{target}} \subset D$, of size m, $m \ll n$, as our set of target events.

In this paper we describe an approach to capture patterns characterizing the conditions preceding each target event. We wish to know what types of events frequently precede a target event for the purpose of prediction. In particular we look at those events occurring within a time window of fixed size W before a target event, as illustrated in Figure 1. We are interested in finding sets of event types, called *eventsets*, which occur frequently before a target event within a window of size W.

Definition 2. An eventset Z is a set of event types $\{e_i\}$. Eventset Z matches the set of events in window W, if every event type $e_i \in Z$ is found in W.

For example, in Figure 1, eventset $\{a, b, d\}$ matches the sets of events within the two time windows preceding the target events.

Definition 3. Eventset Z has *support* s in D if $s\%$ of all windows of size W preceding target events are matched by Z. Eventset Z is *frequent* if s is above a minimum user-defined threshold.

Definition 4. Eventset Z has *confidence* c in D if $c\%$ of all time windows of size W matched by Z precede a target event. Eventset Z is *accurate* if c is above a minimum user-

Algorithm 1: Finding Frequent Eventsets
Input: event sequence D, window size W,
minimum support $s\%$, target-event type e^*
Output: frequent eventsets $\mathcal{F}$
FREQUENTEVENTSETS(D,W,s,e^*)
(1) $B = \emptyset; T = \emptyset$
(2)   **foreach** event $d_i = (e_i, t_i) \in D$
(3)   currentTime $= t_i$
(4)   **foreach** event $d_j = (e_j, t_j) \in T$
(5)   **if** (currentTime $- t_j$) $> W$
(6)   Remove d_j from T
(7)   **end**
(8)   **if** d_i is a target event (i.e., $e_i = e^*$)
(9) $B = B \cup \{e_j \mid (e_j, \cdot) \in T\}$
(10) $T = T \cup d_i$
(11)   **end**
(12)   Use A-priori over B to find all frequent
(13)   eventsets with minimum support $s\%$.
(14)   Let $\mathcal{F}$ be the set of all frequent eventsets.
(15)   **return** $\mathcal{F}$

Figure 2. Logic to find all frequent eventsets.

defined threshold.

Notice our definition of support is not simply an extension of that used in non-temporal domains: it is restricted to eventsets preceding target events. A periodic eventset in D may not qualify as frequent if it fails to appear before target events. In Figure 1, for example, eventset $\{a, b, d\}$ has support 100%, since it always appears before a target event; its confidence is also 100%. Eventset $\{a, b\}$, on the other hand, has support 100%, but since it also appears within a time window of size W that does not precede a target event, its confidence is 67%.

Our goals can now be enumerated as follows: 1) to find all frequent and accurate eventsets, and 2) to combine eventsets into a rule-based model for prediction. We describe each step in turn.

3 SEARCHING FOR EVENTSETS

This section presents the logic to find all frequent and accurate eventsets from input sequence D, given a set of target events D_{target}. We proceed by first finding all frequent eventsets.

3.1 FREQUENT EVENTSETS

Figure 2 (Algorithm 1) illustrates the logic to find all frequent eventsets. The general idea is to maintain in memory

all events within a sliding window of size W. On every occurrence of a target event, all event types within the sliding window are simply stored as a new transaction. Once all events have been analyzed, it is straightforward to apply the A-priori algorithm to find all eventsets above a minimum user-defined support.

Specifically, our algorithm makes one pass through the sequence of events in D (lines 2-11), which we assume to be in increasing order along time. With each new event, the current time is updated (line 3); the algorithm keeps in memory only those events within a time window of size W from the current time (lines 5-6). If the current event is a target event, the set of event types contained in the most recent time window become a new transaction in database B (lines 8-9). Finally, we invoke the A-priori algorithm to find all eventsets above a minimum user-defined support over B (lines 12-14).

As an example, the result of applying Algorithm 1 over the data shown in Figure 1 yields the following database of event types: $B = \{\{a, b, d, g\}, \{a, b, d, h\}\}$. Although not shown in Figure 1, it is admissible for consecutive target events to generate time windows that overlap. If the minimum support is 1.0, then eventset $\{a, b, d\}$ is the only frequent eventset.

Note that both the ordering of events and the inter-arrival times between events within each time window are not relevant. This is useful when an eventset occurs under different permutations, and when inter-arrival times exhibit high variation (i.e., signals are noisy). These characteristics are present in many domains, including the real production network used for our experiments. For example, we observed a printer-network problem may generate a set of events under different permutations, and with inter-arrival-time variation in the order of seconds. Our approach to overcome these uncertainties is to collect all event types falling inside the time windows preceding target events, which can then be simply treated as database transactions.

3.2 ACCURATE EVENTSETS

Once the set of frequent eventsets is available, we proceed to filter out those eventsets below a minimum degree of confidence. Figure 3 (Algorithm 2), illustrates the filtering mechanism. The general idea is to look at the number of times each of the frequent eventsets occurs outside the time windows preceding target events. Such information enables us to compute the confidence of each frequent eventset and to eliminate those below a minimum threshold.

Specifically, the first part of the algorithm (lines 1-9) assumes as input a set of intervals corresponding to all time windows of size W that do not overlap with the time windows preceding target events. These are the true nega-

Algorithm 2: Finding Confident Eventsets
Input: event sequence D, minimum confidence $c\%$, time intervals I, frequent eventsets $\mathcal{F}$, database eventsets B
Output: confident eventsets $\mathcal{F}'$
CONFIDENTEVENTSETS($D,c,I,\mathcal{F},B$)
(1) $T = \emptyset$; $[a,b]$ = next interval from I
(2)   **foreach** $d_i = (e_i, t_i) \in D$
(3)   **if** $t_i \in [a,b]$
(4) $T = T \cup d_i$
(5)   **if** $t_i > b$
(6) $B' = B' \cup \{e_j \mid (e_j, \cdot) \in T\}$
(7) $T = \emptyset$; $[a,b]$ = next interval from I
(8)   Add d_i to D
(9)   **end**
(10) $\mathcal{F}' = \emptyset$
(11)   **foreach** eventset Z in $\mathcal{F}$
(12)   **if** confidence(Z,B,B')$> c$ AND
(13) $P(Z|B) > P(Z|B')$
(14) $\mathcal{F}' = \mathcal{F}' \cup Z$
(15)   **end**
(16)   **return** $\mathcal{F}'$

Figure 3. Logic to find all confident eventsets.

tive time windows[1]. We proceed to capture all event types within each window (line 6) to construct a new database of eventsets, B'. This database contains all eventsets not preceding target events. The second part of the algorithm uses our two eventset databases, B and B', to compute the confidence of each frequent eventset Z (lines 10-16). Let x_1 and x_2 be the number of transactions in B and B' respectively matched by eventset Z. Then the confidence of Z is defined as follows:

$$\text{confidence}(Z, B, B') = x_1/(x_1 + x_2) \qquad (2)$$

Confidence is an estimation of the conditional probability of Z belonging to a time window that precedes a target event, given that Z matches the event types in that same time window.

Our filtering mechanism performs one more test to validate an eventset (line 13). The reason is that confidence alone is not sufficient to guarantee that the probability of finding an eventset Z within database B is significantly higher than the corresponding probability in B'; confidence does not check for negative correlations [4]. Thus, we add a validation step described as follows.

Let $P(Z|B)$ denote the probability of Z occurring within database B, and $P(Z|B')$ the corresponding probability within B'. Eventset Z is validated if we can reject the null hypothesis:

---

[1]These intervals can be easily obtained as a side output from Algorithm 1.

$$H_0 : P(Z|B) \leq P(Z|B') \qquad (3)$$

with high confidence. If the number of events is large, one can assume a Gaussian distribution and reject the null hypothesis in favor of the alternative hypothesis:

$$H_1 : P(Z|B) > P(Z|B') \qquad (4)$$

if, for a given confidence level α, the difference between the two probabilities (normalized to obtain a standard normal variate) is significant. In such case we reject H_0. The probability of this happening when H_0 is actually true is α. By choosing a small α we can be almost certain that Z is related to the occurrence of target events.

In summary, our validation phase ensures that the probability of an eventset Z appearing before a target event is significantly larger than the probability of Z not appearing before target events. The validation phase discards any negative correlation between Z and the occurrence of target events. In addition, this phase serves as a filtering step to reduce the number of candidate patterns used to build a rule-based model for prediction.

Together, Algorithms 1 and 2 enable us to attain our goal of finding the set of all frequent and accurate eventsets. We now turn to our goal of finding a model for prediction.

4 BUILDING A RULE-BASED MODEL

In this section we describe how to combine the frequent and accurate set of eventsets into a rule-based model. Before describing our algorithm we provide definitions that are common in the construction of associative classification rules [8].

Definition 5. Eventset Z_i is said to be more specific than eventset Z_j, if $Z_j \subset Z_i$.

For example, eventset $\{a, b, c\}$ is more specific than eventset $\{a, b\}$.

Definition 6. Eventset Z_i is said to have higher rank over eventset Z_j, represented as $Z_i \succ Z_j$, if any of the following conditions is true:

1. The confidence of Z_i is greater than that of Z_j.

2. The confidence of Z_i equals that of Z_j, but the support of Z_i is greater than the support of Z_j

3. The confidence and support of Z_i equal that of Z_j, but Z_i is more specific than Z_j.

Definition 6 imposes a partial ordering over the space of eventsets. Note condition 3 favors eventsets that represent maximal characteristic descriptions of the target class (i..e, specific descriptions). Most approaches prefer minimal discriminant descriptions (i.e., general descriptions). The difference stems from our approach to classification: instead of discriminating among classes, we first characterize the target class, and then validate our descriptions. This is convenient when the a priori probability of the target class is small. Otherwise we must face the class imbalance problem in classification [6].

The rationale behind our rule-based system is to find the most accurate and specific rules first [11]. Our assumption of having a large number of available eventsets and few positive examples obviates ensuring each example is covered by a rule. Specifically, let $\mathcal{F}'$ be the set of large and validated eventsets. Figure 4 (Algorithm 3) illustrates our approach. The first step (line 2) sorts all eventsets according to definition 6. In general other metrics can be used to replace confidence, such as information gain, gini, or χ^2 [17]. In the next step (lines 4-6), our algorithm selects the next best eventset Z_i and removes all other eventsets Z_j in $\mathcal{F}'$ more general than Z_i. This step eliminates eventsets that refer to the same pattern as Z_i but are overly general. The resulting rule is of the form $Z_i \rightarrow \text{targetevent}$. The search then continues for all eventsets capturing different patterns preceding the occurrence of target events. The final rule-based system $\mathcal{R}$ can be used for prediction by checking for the occurrence of any of the eventsets in $\mathcal{R}$ along the event sequence used for testing. The model predicts finding a target event within a time window of size W after any such eventset is detected. Section 7 compares our approach with other rule-based methods.

5 COMPUTATIONAL EFFICIENCY

We now analyze the efficiency of our approach. Finding all eventsets preceding target events requires a single pass over D. Looking for all frequent eventsets is in the worst case exponential in the number of event types. Since the number of target events is much lower than the total number of events, $m \ll n$, we are able to keep in memory the database B of eventsets preceding target events. As a result, finding all frequent eventsets is inexpensive in both memory and time.

Filtering out frequent eventsets below a minimum confidence requires a single pass over D. Algorithms 1 and 2 obviate keeping the whole event sequence in memory; we keep in memory only those events within a time window of size W.

The algorithm to build a rule-based model for prediction (Figure 4) runs in (worst-case) time that is exponential in the number of validated and frequent eventsets. We find the running time to be within a few seconds for large enough minimum support values (Figure 5), which shows our ap-

Algorithm 3: Building Rule-Based Model
Input: eventsets $\mathcal{F}'$
Output: Set of rules $\mathcal{R}$
RULE-BASED-EVENTSETS($\mathcal{F}'$)
(1) $\mathcal{R} = \emptyset$
(2)   Sort $\mathcal{F}'$ in decreasing order by rank
(3)   **while** $\mathcal{F}'$ is not empty
(4)   Let Z_i be the first eventset in $\mathcal{F}'$
(5)   if $Z_j \subset Z_i, i \neq j$, remove Z_j from $\mathcal{F}'$
(6)   Make a new rule $r : Z_i \rightarrow \text{targetevent}$
(7) $\mathcal{R} = \mathcal{R} \cup r$
(8)   Remove Z_i from $\mathcal{F}'$
(9)   **end**
(10)   **return** $\mathcal{R}$

Figure 4. Logic describing the process to build a rule-based system from eventsets.

proach makes efficient use of memory and disk space.

6 EXPERIMENTS

We now describe an empirical assessment of our approach. We use both artificial and real production data to evaluate the performance of our method.

6.1 ARTIFICIAL DATA

To assess the performance of our algorithm we first use artificial domains. Our data generator outputs a sequence of events uniformly distributed over a fixed time interval. By default we use a time interval of 1 week; the total number of event types is set to $k = 50$; we use a time window of size $W = 5$ minutes to capture patterns preceding target events; the number of target events is set to 50; the minimum-support level while searching for large eventsets is set to $s = 0.1$; the significance level for hypothesis testing while validating eventsets is set to $\alpha = 0.01$.

For each event sequence, the first 50% events serve for training and the other 50% serve for testing. Each point in the graphs is the average over 30 runs (i.e., 30 different input sequences) using 95% confidence intervals. Runs were performed on a RISC/6000 IBM model 7043-140.

Error is computed on the testing set only as follows. Starting at the beginning of the sequence, non-overlapping time windows of size W that do not intersect the set of time windows preceding target events are considered negative examples; all time windows preceding target events are considered positive examples. Error is defined as the fraction of examples incorrectly classified by the rule-based model.

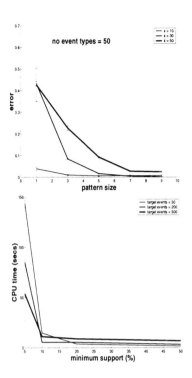

Figure 5. Artificial Data. (top) Error rate vs pattern size when the number of event types k is set to 50; (bottom) CPU time vs minimum support.

ASSESSING ERROR

Our first experiment measures the error of the rule-based model vs. the size of the pattern. Figure 5 (top) shows our results. Since we guarantee that the pattern will always occur within 5-minutes preceding a target event, any form of error stems from the pattern occurring by chance outside the 5-minute window intervals (i.e., errors are false positives). The number of events per time takes values in the set $\{10, 30, 50\}$. Figure 5 (top) shows results when the number of event types is set to 50. The results agree with the fact that the probability of a pattern occurring by chance decreases as the size of the pattern increases. The different lines show how the probability decreases when fewer events populate each time window.

ASSESSING CPU TIME

Our next experiment compares CPU time vs different levels of minimum support f. Figure 5 (bottom) shows our results. CPU time rarely exceeds 20 seconds when $f > 0.10$, but it grows considerably higher when $f < 0.05$. The value of f imposes a trade-off between computational cost and performance. Setting the value of f too high increases the chances of missing relevant eventsets, while setting the value too low increases the computational cost. In our experiments, a value of $f = 0.10$ appears to provide a good balance between both factors.

6.2   REAL PRODUCTION DATA

We now report results obtained from a production computer network. Data was obtained by monitoring systems active during one month on a network having 750 hosts. One month of continuous monitoring generated over 26,000 events, with 165 different types of events. Our analysis concentrates on two types of target events labelled as *critical* by domain experts. The first type, EPP Event, indicates that end-to-end response time to a host generated by a probing mechanism is above a critical threshold. The second type, URL Time-Out, indicates a web site is unaccessible. Detecting the cause of these event types and providing a mechanism to predict their occurrence is important to guarantee continuous network operation and compliance with service level agreements.

In our production computer network an event is characterized by three features: time, event type, and host. We merge event-type and host into a single feature to identify the nature of the event. A target event is, therefore, the combination of type (EPP Event or URL Time-Out) and a particular host of interest. Our parameters take the same default values as with synthetic data.

VARYING TIME WINDOW

We investigate the effect of varying the time window preceding target events on the error of the rule-based model. In all our experiments, the error corresponding to false positives is small (< 0.1) and does not vary significantly while increasing the time windows. We focus on the false negative error rate defined as the proportion of times the rule-based model fails to predict a true target event. Figure 6 (top) shows our results when the target event corresponds to URL Time-Out on a particular host. With a time window of 300 seconds, the error is 0.39 (9/23). But as the time window increases, the error decreases significantly. Evidently, larger time windows enable us to capture more information preceding target events. The number of false positives (false alarms) is close to 35/800.

We also investigate the effect of having a *safe-window* before each target event in case the rule-based model were used in a real-time scenario with a need for corrective actions to take place. In this case, the algorithm does not capture any events within the safe-window while characterizing the conditions preceding target events. Figure 6 (top) shows our results for a safe-window of 60 seconds. Our results show a degradation of performance when the safe-window is incorporated, albeit to a small degree.

Figure 6 (bottom) shows our results with a different target event: EPP Event on a particular host. With a time window of 300 seconds the error is as high as 0.83 (9/62). Increasing the window to 2000 seconds brings the error rate down to 0.16. Our results highlight the importance of the size of the time window preceding target events: a low value may fail to capture relevant patterns. In this case adding a safe-window causes no degradation of performance.

Not all our experiments show positive results. In some cases the false negative error rate is as high as 95%; increasing the time window does not reduce the error beyond 80%. An inspection of the data reveals no pattern (i.e., sets of event types) preceding target events. Thus, the success of our algorithm is contingent on the existence of patterns preceding target events.

In terms of the significance of the discovered rules, our findings reveal interesting patterns. In the production-network data, for example, a URL Time-Out on a particular host, set as the target event, reveals the frequent presence of a URL Time-Out on a remote host within a 15-minute interval. Such information helps establish a correlation between the two hosts, and may prove crucial in finding the nature of the underlying problem.

7 RELATED WORK

Our approach is different from other methods for classification. Traditional classification methods like C4.5 [13] recursively split the instance space until each region is class uniform (i.e., they follow a discriminant-description strategy). Our approach differs not only in the temporal nature of the data but in the prediction strategy. Since in our case target events are highly infrequent, we first characterize the positive class and then validate those descriptions against the negative class (i.e., we follow a characteristic-description strategy).

Other studies have been performed attempting to integrate classification and association-rule mining [2, 3, 10, 12, 7, 5, 8]. Associative classification methods like CBA [8] find all frequent and accurate rules for each class, whereas we only concentrate on the positive class. CBA selects the rule with highest confidence for each example while ensuring all examples are covered, as opposed to other methods that vote among several rules [7]. We also select the highest confidence rule; our assumption of having a large number of available eventsets and few positive examples obviates ensuring each example is covered by a rule. Compared to methods like CBA, our strategy of mining the positive class only enables us to keep the transaction database of positive examples in memory, which allows for efficient mining of frequent and accurate eventsets (Section 3).

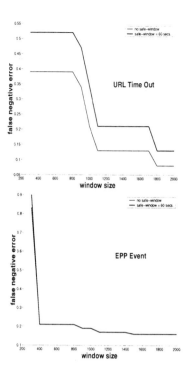

Figure 6. Real Production Data. Error vs window size with and without a safe window. (top) target events is URL Time Out; (bottom) target event is EPP Event (note that the curves with and without safe window are identical).

Our work has the same goal as that of others [16, 15], namely to predict the occurrence of target events along an event sequence. In previous work, however, a classification technique is employed to distinguish between time windows preceding target events and time windows not preceding target events; mining for eventsets is not done. As mentioned above, mining for frequent and accurate eventsets on the positive class provides an advantage under skewed class distributions, and enables us make efficient use of memory.

Finally, our work is also related to the area of sequential mining [1, 9, 14, 18], in which traditional data mining is extended to search for frequent sub-sequences. Our work is different in that we first detect those events preceding a target event within a (fixed) time window. A data mining step is then applied without any further consideration of the temporal distribution of events within the time window.

8 CONCLUSIONS

This paper describes an approach to detect patterns in event sequences. In particular, we assume the existence of specific kinds of events of interest along the sequence, called *target events*. We describe a method to find patterns frequently occurring before target events using association-rule mining techniques. Patterns are then combined into a rule-based model for prediction.

Results on artificial domains show patterns are easier to discern as the size of the pattern increases, as the number of event types increases, and as the density of events (per time window) decreases. Our results also show how setting the level of minimum support high enough decreases the amount of CPU time.

Results on a real-world production network show how the size of the time window preceding target events is crucial to the effectiveness of our approach. Experiments on two different combinations of event-type and host of interest show how the false negative error rate decreases significantly as the time window increases. Our approach, however, is not universally applicable. Clearly the method proposed is contingent on sets of events frequently occurring before target events.

Future work will consider alternative ways to formulate the classification model. A rule-based approach has the advantage of providing output amenable to interpretation. Our main goal, however, is to find highly accurate models. We believe a promising research avenue is to adapt the predictive model according to the characteristics of the sequence under analysis. The problem is related to the field of meta-learning: we want to learn to match the right bias for each different event sequence.

ACKNOWLEDGMENTS

This work was funded by IBM T.J. Watson Research Center.

References

[1] R. Agrawal and R. Srikant. Mining sequential patterns. *Proc. 11th Int. Conf. Data Engineering, ICDE*, pages 3–14, 1995.

[2] K. Ali, S. Manganaris, and R. Sikant. Partial classification using association rules. *ACM SIGMOD Management of Data*, pages 115–118, 1997.

[3] R. Bayardo. Brute-force mining of high confidence classification rules. *Proceedings of the Third International Conference on Knowledge Discovery and Data Mining (KDD-97)*, pages 123–126, 1997.

[4] S. Brin, R. Motwani, and C. Silverstein. Beyond market baskets: generalizing association rules to correlations. *Proceedings of the Third International Conference on Knowledge Discovery and Data Mining (KDD-97)*, pages 265–276, 1997.

[5] G. Dong, X. Zhang, L. Wong, and J. Li. Caep: Classification by aggregating emerging patterns. *Proceedings of the International Conference on Discovery Science*, 1999.

[6] N. Japkowicz. The class imbalance problem: Significance and strategies. *Proceedings of the International Conference on Artificial Intelligence*, pages 111–117, 2000.

[7] W. Li, J. Han, and J. Pei. Cmar: Accurate and efficient classification based on multiple class-association rules. *IEEE International Conference on Data Mining*, pages 369–376, 2001.

[8] B. Liu, W. Hsu, and Y. Ma. Integrating classification and association rule mining. *Proceedings of the Fourth International Conference on Knowledge Discovery and Data Mining (KDD-98)*, pages 80–86, 1998.

[9] H. Mannila, H. Toivonen, and A. I. Verkamo. Discovering frequent episodes in sequences. *Proceedings of the International Conference on Knowledge Discovery and Data Mining (KDD-95)*, 1995.

[10] D. Meretakis and B. Wuthrich. Classification as mining and use of labeled itemsets. *ACM SIGMOD Workshop on Research Issues in Data Mining and Knowledge Discovery (DMKD-99)*, 1999.

[11] R. S. Michalski. A theory and methodology of inductive learning. *Machine Learning: An Artificial Intelligence Approach*, pages 83–134, 1983.

[12] W. Pijls and R. Potharst. Classification and target group selection based upon frequent patterns. *Proceedings of the Twelfth Belgium-Netherlands Artificial Intelligence Conference (BNAIC 00)*, pages 125–132, 2000.

[13] J. R. Quinlan. *C4.5: Programs for Machine Learning*. Mogan Kaufmann, 1994.

[14] R. Srikant and R. Agrawal. Mining sequential patterns: Generalizations and performance improvements. *Proceedings of the 5th International Conference Extending Database Technology, EDBT*, 1057:3–17, 1996.

[15] R. Vilalta, S. Ma, and J. Hellerstein. Rule induction of computer events. *Proceedings of the 12th IFIP/IEEE International Workshop on Distributed Systems: Operations & Management*, 2001.

[16] G. Weiss and H. Hirsh. Learning to predict rare events in event sequences. *Knowledge Discovery and Data Mining*, pages 359–363, 1998.

[17] A. White and W. Liu. Bias in information-based measures in decision tree induction. *Machine Learning*, 15:321–329, 1994.

[18] M. J. Zaki. Sequence mining in categorical domains. *Sequence Learning: Paradigms, Algorithms, and Applications*, pages 162–187, 2001.

Mining Associations by Pattern Structure in Large Relational Tables

Haixun Wang   Chang-Shing Perng   Sheng Ma   Philip S. Yu
IBM T. J. Watson Research Center
Yorktown Heights, NY 10598
{haixun, perng, shengma, psyu}@us.ibm.com

Abstract

Association rule mining aims at discovering patterns whose support is beyond a given threshold. Mining patterns composed of items described by an arbitrary subset of attributes in a large relational table represents a new challenge and has various practical applications, including the event management systems that motivated this work. The attribute combinations that define the items in a pattern provide the structural information of the pattern. Current association algorithms do not make full use of the structural information of the patterns: the information is either lost after it is encoded with attribute values, or is constrained by a given hierarchy or taxonomy. Pattern structures convey important knowledge about the patterns. In this paper, we present a novel architecture that organizes the mining space based on pattern structures. By exploiting the interrelationships among pattern structures, execution times for mining can be reduced significantly. This advantage is demonstrated by our experiments using both synthetic and real-life datasets.

1   Introduction

The problem of mining frequent itemsets in a set of transactions wherein each transaction is a set of items was first introduced by Agrawal et al [1]. There is a pressing need for algorithms to support relational data mining [4], as a majority of datasets in the real world are stored in the relational form, or generated on the fly by other query tools (e.g. OLAP tools) in the relational form. An item can be described by a set of attributes [5, 10]. For instance, a system event can be described by attributes such as EVENTTYPE, CATEGORY, SOURCE, APPLICATION, HOST, and SEVERITY. The dataset shown in Figure 1 contains five events that *occurred together* (occurred during the same time interval according to their TIDs). One association rule or pattern supported by the dataset is "TCPConnectionClose (EVENT) from Vesuvio (HOST) occurs together with Security (CATEGORY) problems during Authorization (APPLICATION)". Interesting rules or patterns often relate to items each described by a *subset* of these attributes. We call such items **structured-items**.

Rules or patterns composed of structured-items are often more interesting and informative because their varied composition enables them to represent concepts at all possible granularity levels. The structures of the items in a pattern combine to form the **pattern structure**. Pattern structure conveys important knowledge about the patterns. Our work in mining such patterns in event data brings forth some interesting issues and challenges.

EXPONENTIAL SEARCH SPACE. Multi-attribute items incur a huge search space. The item in R_1 is defined by two attributes: EVENTTYPE, and HOST. Indeed, any subset of attributes can be used to define a structured-item. This introduces a combinatorial challenge: in a dataset with N attributes, items can be defined in as many as $2^N - 1$ different ways, in other words, they have as many as $2^N - 1$ different structures. Furthermore, they can be combined differently to form different patterns. This introduces another combinatorial challenge: patterns containing k items can have as many as $\binom{2^N + k - 2}{k}$ different pattern structures (Lemma 1).

RELATIONAL SENSITIVE. The patterns embedded in the event data, unlike supermarket purchasing patterns that are more or less stable over the time, are constantly evolving as old problems in the system being solved, and new types of problems being generated. The mining algorithms should focus on newly generated data instead of the entire history archive. Furthermore, we often need to mine data streams generated on the fly by other query tools, such as OLAP, which requires our mining algorithms to be relational sensitive [4], as it is often inefficient and unnecessary to first convert the data to a mining format, then discover all frequent itemsets among them, and finally filter out the answers to the queries. The dynamic nature of the data prevents us from running a mining algorithm once and for all, and saving the results for future analysis.

(Rec)	TID	EVENTTYPE	CATEGORY	SOURCE	APPLICATION	HOST	SEVERITY
(1)	1001	TCPConnectionClose	Network	IO	System	Vesuvio	Low
(2)	1001	CiscoDCDLinkUp	Network	DHCP	Routing	Etna	Low
(3)	1001	AuditFailure	Security	Software	Authorization	Magna	High
(4)	1001	CoreDump	Memory	Exception	Kernel 2.4	Stromboli	High
(5)	1001	IRQConflict	Device	PCI Bus	System	Vulcano	High

Figure 1. Event Database (the 5 records form one transaction, according to their TIDs)

USER PREFERENCES. Traditional association rule algorithms return *all* frequent itemsets. However, the user may only be interested in some specific pattern structures according to his domain knowledge and the current focus of study for a given dataset. For instance, a user wants to mine all patterns where EVENTTYPE and SOURCE are involved in describing the patterns. At the same time, he wants to ignore patterns which contain elements described by both the SOURCE and CATEGORY attributes. Note that such *user preferences can not be enforced by preprocessing the data to exclude certain attributes or values*, as these attributes and values may combine in different ways to form patterns that are interesting to the user. Thus, we need a mechanism that is conducive to incorporate user preferences into the mining process. Although user preferences and mining constraints are beyond the scope of this paper, the framework proposed in this work makes such incorporation possible [11].

2 Related Works

Agrawal and Srikant [3, 8] led the pioneering work of mining sequential patterns. Each item in a pattern is represented by a set of literals, and patterns on level k (patterns with a total number of k literals) are generated by joining patterns on level $k-1$. To map our problem into that of mining sequential patterns, we convert each structured-item to a set of literals by encoding its attribute information (for instance, for each value a of attribute A, we create an item A_a). However, the pattern structure is lost through such encoding: patterns on the same level take part in candidate generation and pruning as a whole, regardless of their pattern structure, i.e., what combination of attributes are used in describing each item in the patterns. As a result, user preferences can not be incorporated in the mining process. The algorithm mines (unnecessarily) all frequent patterns before the answers conformed to user's mining targets can be filtered out during the final step. It will apparently slow down the mining process when the dataset is large and high-dimensional, and it also creates difficulty in understanding the mining results since patterns are all mixed together instead of partitioned by their pattern structures.

Srikant et al [7] and Han et al [5] consider multi-level association rules based on item taxonomy and hierarchy.

These approaches are further extended [6, 9] to handle more general constraints. In Table 1, we compare them with HIFI. With a pre-specified hierarchy or taxonomy, the mining space is severely restricted. The ability to discover patterns $(R_1, \cdots, R_5$, e.g.) totally depends on whether their pattern structures happen to fit into the given taxonomy or hierarchy. In contrast, our framework enables us to mine patterns without a pre-specified item hierarchy. HIFI offers the maximum flexibility in defining patterns: patterns containing k items can have $\binom{2^N + k - 2}{k}$ different pattern structures. The search space of hierarchy and taxonomy is much smaller and their discoveries are limited by the taxonomy or the fixed hierarchy they use.

3 Definitions and Notations

Let $\mathcal{D}$ be a set of transactions, where each transaction contains a set of records, and each record is defined by a set of attributes $\mathcal{A}$. Our task is to find frequent k-itemsets, however, the fundamental concept of *item* is defined differently.

Definition 1. *Let* $\mathcal{T} = \{t_1, ..., t_k\}$ *be a subset of* $\mathcal{A}$. *A* **structured-item** I *is a set of attribute-value pairs* $\{t_1 = v_1, ..., t_k = v_k\}$, *where* v_i *is a value in the domain of attribute* t_i. *We call* $\mathcal{T}$ *the* **item structure** *of* I.

Based on the event data in Figure 1, an example of a structured-item is {CATEGORY=Security, SEVERITY=High}, and its item structure is {CATEGORY, SEVERITY}. We also use ⟨security, high⟩ to denote the structured-item when no confusion arises.

Definition 2. *A record R is an* **instance** *of a structured-item* $I : \{t_1 = v_1, ..., t_k = v_k\}$, *if* $R.t_i = v_i, \forall t_i \in \{t_1, ..., t_k\}$.

Obviously, if R is an instance of structured-item I, then $\forall I' \subseteq I$, R is an instance of I'.

Definition 3. *A* **pattern** *is a set of structured-items. A k-itemset pattern is a pattern containing k structured-items.*

Let i_1 and i_2 be two structured-items. Pattern $\{i_1, i_2\}$ is different from pattern $\{i_1 \cup i_2\}$, the former being a 2-itemset pattern, the latter a 1-itemset pattern.

	# of different item structures	# of different pattern structures	discovers				
			R_1	R_2	R_3	R_4	R_5
taxonomy	limited by taxonomy	limited by taxonomy	?	?	?	?	no
hierarchy	N	N	?	?	no	?	no
HIFI	$2^N - 1$	$\binom{2^N+k-2}{k}$	yes	yes	yes	yes	yes

Table 1. A comparison of the three approaches. N **is the number of attributes of the dataset. '?' means the discovery of corresponding rules depends on the particular taxonomy or hierarchy in use.**

Definition 4. *A transaction S* **supports** *pattern X, if each structured-item $I \in X$ maps to a unique record $R \in S$ such that R is an instance of I. Pattern X has* **support** *s in dataset D if $s\%$ of the transactions in D support X.*

We continue our example in Figure 1. Record (2) is an instance of structured-item i_1: {SOURCE=DHCP}, and an instance of i_2: {HOST=Etna}, which makes it an instance of $i_3 = i_1 \cup i_2$: {SOURCE=DHCP, HOST=Etna} as well. Also, we can see that record (3) is an instance of i_4: {HOST=Magna}. Thus, we derive some of the 2-itemset patterns supported by transaction 1001 (the first 5 records): $\{i_1, i_4\}$, $\{i_2, i_4\}$, and $\{i_3, i_4\}$.

However, transaction 1001 does not support 2-itemset pattern $\{i_1, i_2\}$. This is because i_1 and i_2 are supported by one record and one record only in transaction 1001. According to the definition, in order to support $\{i_1, i_2\}$, the transaction needs to have at least two records that are instances of i_1 and i_2 respectively.

Definition 5. *We define* **pattern structure** *as a multi-set, $c = \{T_1, ..., T_k\}$, where each T_i is a non-empty set of attributes. A pattern of structure c has the form $p = \{I_1, ..., I_k\}$, where the item structure of I_i is T_i.*

For presentation simplicity, we use parenthesis to separate each T_i in a pattern structure. For instance, assuming A, B and C are 3 of the attributes in a dataset, we use $(A)(AB)(C)$ to represent pattern structure $c = \{T_1, T_2, T_3\}$, where $T_1 = \{A\}$, $T_2 = \{A, B\}$, $T_3 = \{C\}$. This notation is used in Figure 2, for example.

4 The HIFI Framework

If there is only one attribute, then all pattern structures are of the form $(A)(A)...(A)$, and the problem degenerates to traditional association rule mining. However, as shown by Lemma 1, the mining space grows exponentially when the number of attributes increases.

Proposition 1. *Given a dataset with N different attributes, there are a total of $\binom{2^N+k-2}{k}$ different pattern structures for k-itemset patterns.*

Proof. An equivalent problem is: how many different outcomes are there after a throw of k dice, each having m sides? The answer is $\binom{m+k-1}{k}$. In our case, we have k items, each can be defined in $m = 2^N - 1$ ways. Thus, there are a total of $\binom{2^N+k-2}{k}$ different pattern structures for k-itemset patterns. $\square$

To handle such a huge mining space, we need to explore the relationships among different pattern structures. For instance, pattern structure (AB) is a specification of structure (A) and structure (B). The HIFI framework explore these links by defining the successor/predecessor relationships.

Definition 6. *Given a pattern structure $c = \{T_1, ..., T_m\}$, and an attribute $t \in A$, c's immediate successors are in one of the following forms:*

1. *$\{T_1, ..., T_m, T_{m+1}\}$, where $T_{m+1} = \{t\}$*

2. *$\{T_1, ..., T_j \cup \{t\}, ..., T_m\}$, $t \notin T_j$*

Figure 2 depicts a graph of pattern structures tightly coupled by the predecessor/successor relationships for two attributes A and B. Note that a pattern structure $c = \{T_1, ..., T_m\}$ on level L has no more than L predecessors, where level L is defined as $L = \sum_{i=1}^{m} |T_i|$, the total number of attributes that appear in the relevant attributes of c.

The benefits of structuring the search space in the level-wise, tightly coupled form are the following:

- The framework reveals all the relationships among pattern structures. These relationships are essential for candidate generation and pruning.

- Instead of joining the patterns on level K to derive candidate patterns on level $K + 1$ and then using the patterns on level K again for pruning, we can *localize* the candidate generation and pruning procedure to each pattern structure. For instance, in order to find frequent patterns of structure $(A)(A)(B)$ and $(A)(B)(B)$, only 4 nodes (their predecessors) in Figure 2 need to be explored. The improvement in performance is most significant in mining high dimensional data since the search space grows exponentially as the number of attributes increases.

484

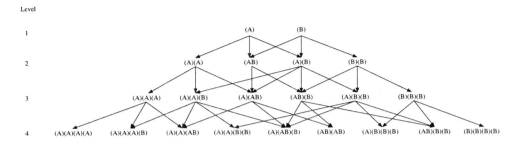

Figure 2. Mining space of the HIFI framework: a graph of tightly coupled pattern structures

- The framework requires no data encoding. Each structure represents a mining target and more importantly, the generated patterns are structured in the same form. Following the links among the pattern structures, users can choose to have a more general or a more specific view of the patterns. It helps users to overcome the difficulty in interpreting and analyzing the results.

4.1 Downward Closure Properties

The extended *Downward Closure Property*, which holds between each pair of parent and child pattern structures, enables us to eliminate candidate patterns.

Proposition 2. *(Downward Closure Property) Let* $p = \{I_1, ..., I_k\}$ *be a pattern of structure c, and the support of p is less than* min_sup*, then*

1. *the support of pattern* $p_a = \{I_1, ..., I_k, I_a\}$*, where* I_a *is an arbitrary structured-item, is less than* min_sup*;*

2. *the support of pattern* $p_b = \{I_1, ..., I_{k-1}, I_b\}$*, where* $I_b \supset I_k$*, is less than* min_sup*.*

Proof. Similar to the Apriori property [2]. □

The organization of the search space in Figure 2 is justified by Lemma 2. The level-wise Apriori property has been broken down to a much finer granularity, i.e., to the pattern structure level. It enables us to localize candidate generation and pruning for specific pattern structures.

4.2 Join Properties

In this section, we explore the most efficient way of pattern generation. First, we show that the patterns of a pattern structure can be generated by joining the patterns of *any two* of its predecessor structures. However, although any pair of predecessors can be used, the computational cost can be very different. We hence identify a specific type of join, referred to as *simple join*, which can be implemented efficiently if the patterns are sorted in certain order. Finally,

we present the conditions that lead to simple joins without pre-sorting.

Unique Representation of Items and Pattern Structures

To facilitate further discussions, we assume that there exists an order (e.g., alphabetical order) among the attributes in $\mathcal{A}$. Given a set of attributes $\mathcal{T} \subseteq \mathcal{A}$, we use $\vec{\mathcal{T}}$ to denote the ordered sequence of the same attributes. Assuming $\vec{\mathcal{T}_1}$ and $\vec{\mathcal{T}_2}$ are two such sequences, we say $\vec{\mathcal{T}_1} \preceq \vec{\mathcal{T}_2}$ if $\vec{\mathcal{T}_1}$ holds lexicographical precedence over $\vec{\mathcal{T}_2}$. Thus, we can uniquely represent a structure c by its ordered version $\vec{c} = \langle \vec{\mathcal{T}_1}, ..., \vec{\mathcal{T}_k} \rangle$, where $\vec{\mathcal{T}_1} \preceq, ..., \preceq \vec{\mathcal{T}_k}$. Figure 2 shows each pattern structure using the ordered representation, assuming alphabetical order among the attributes, i.e., $A \prec B$.

Now, given a pattern structure $\vec{c}$ on level L, $\vec{c} = \langle \vec{\mathcal{T}_1}, ..., \vec{\mathcal{T}_k} \rangle$, the patterns of c can be represented by a table with L columns: $\langle t_{11}, ..., t_{21}, ..., t_{k1}, ... \rangle$, where $\langle t_{i1}, ... \rangle$ is the (ordered) attributes of $\vec{\mathcal{T}_i}$. We use $\vec{c}.t_{ij}$ to denote the column defined by the j-th attribute of $\vec{\mathcal{T}_i}$, and *we use c_k to denote a parent structure of c resulted from taking out the k-th column from $\vec{c}$.* For instance, the patterns of structure $c = (A)(BC)$ are represented by a table of three columns as shown in Figure 3(a), while the patterns of its three parent structures are represented by tables of two columns.

The Join Operation

We show how patterns of parent structures can be joined to produce patterns of child structures. To generate the candidate patterns of structure $(A)(BC)$, we can join the patterns of its parents c_3 and c_1 as follows:

Example 1. *Join* $c_3 = (A)(B)$ *and* $c_1 = (BC)$ *to derive* $c = (A)(BC)$

```
SELECT c_3.t_{11}, c_3.t_{21}, c_1.t_{12}
FROM   c_3, c_1
WHERE  c_3.t_{21} = c_1.t_{11}
```

However, not all join operations can be expressed as succinctly. For example, to generate all possible patterns of

$\mathcal{T}_1$	$\mathcal{T}_2$	
$t_{11} : A$	$t_{21} : B$	$t_{22} : C$

(a) $c = (A)(BC)$

$\mathcal{T}_1$	$\mathcal{T}_2$
$t_{11} : A$	$t_{21} : B$

(b) $c_3 = (A)(B)$

$\mathcal{T}_1$	$\mathcal{T}_2$
$t_{11} : A$	$t_{21} : C$

(c) $c_2 = (A)(C)$

$\mathcal{T}_1$	
$t_{11} : B$	$t_{12} : C$

(d) $c_1 = (BC)$

Figure 3. Representing patterns using relational schema. Notation: $c.t_{ij}$ is the column defined by the j-th attribute of $\mathcal{T}_i$, and c_k is a parent structure of c resulted from taking out the k-th column of c.

$(A)(AC)$ by joining $c_3 = (A)(A)$ and $c_1 = (AC)$, we will have to use the following SQL:

Example 2. *Join $c_3 = (A)(A)$ and $c_1 = (AC)$ to derive $c = (A)(AC)$*

```
SELECT   CASE WHEN c1.t11 = c3.t11
         THEN c3.t21 ELSE c3.t11 END CASE,
         c1.t11,
         c1.t12
FROM     c1, c3
WHERE    c1.t11 = c3.t11 OR c1.t11 = c3.t21
```

The reason of the complexity is because of the following: if $p = \langle a_0 \rangle \langle a_1 \rangle$ is a pattern of $(A)(A)$, then patterns derived from p for $(A)(AC)$ can have two alternative forms: $\langle a_0 \rangle \langle a_1, * \rangle$ and $\langle a_1 \rangle \langle a_0, * \rangle$. Thus, in the join condition we need to compare attribute A of c_1 to both attributes of c_3. We show later that such join operations can be avoided.

The Completeness of the Join Operation

We show that the above join operations are *complete*, meaning that the result of the join contains all the patterns that have a support greater than min_sup.

Proposition 3. *(Join Property I) Given a pattern structure c on level L, $L \geq 2$, the candidate patterns derived by joining the patterns of any of its two predecessor structures contain all the frequent patterns of c.*

Proof. Let p be a pattern of structure c, and let c_i and c_j be any two parents of c. Removing the i-th column and then the j-th column of p, we get two subpatterns, p_i and p_j. Since p is a pattern of c, according to the anti-monotonicity property, p_i and p_j must be patterns of c_i and c_j respectively. Thus, pattern p can be derived by joining p_i and p_j on their common columns. $\square$

Join Property I also implies that joining the patterns of a structure's immediate predecessors generates fewer candidates than joining its ancestors. This is because the patterns of its predecessors are a subset of the join results of the predecessors' predecessors.

According to *Join Property I*, for any pattern structure on level L, $L \geq 2$, we can generate its candidate patterns by joining the patterns of any of its 2 predecessors. Other

predecessors can be used to further prune the candidate patterns according to the anti-monotonicity property.

Joins in the Simple Form

Our goal is to generate candidates efficiently through a join operation such as Example 1, without indexing or sorting. We denote join operations in Example 1 as joins in the **simple form**, while join operations in Example 2 with a disjunctive WHERE condition in the **non-simple form**. Joins in the simple form can be implemented efficiently if the patterns are stored in a certain order. For instance, Example 1 can be implemented efficiently if patterns in c_3 and c_1 are ordered by attribute B.

It is harder to implement the join operation in Example 2 effciently because *two* indices on table c_3 are required: one on column t_{11}, the other on t_{21}; otherwise we have to do a linear scan on table c_3. Since patterns are generated on the fly, maintaining extra index is expensive.

Given a pattern structure c and any of its two parents c_i and c_j, it is easy to check if patterns of c can be derived by joining c_i with c_j in the simple form. Assume $c = \{\mathcal{T}_1, ..., \mathcal{T}_k, ..., \mathcal{T}_n\}$ and parent $c_i = \{\mathcal{T}_1, ..., \mathcal{T}_k', ..., \mathcal{T}_n\}$, where $\mathcal{T}_k = \mathcal{T}_k' \cup \{A\}$. We call c_i a *simple parent* of c, if $\mathcal{T}_i \neq \mathcal{T}_k', \forall \mathcal{T}_i \in c$.

Proposition 4. *Patterns of structure c can be derived by joining c_i and c_j in the simple form, if both c_i and c_j are simple parents of c.*

Proof. Omitted for lack of space. $\square$

Proposition 5. *(Join Property II) Given a pattern structure c on level L, there exist at least two predecessor structures, c_i and c_j, that can be joined in the simple form to generate patterns for c.*

Proof. Let $\vec{c} = \langle \vec{\mathcal{T}}_1, ..., \vec{\mathcal{T}}_k \rangle$, $|\mathcal{T}_1| = m$, and $|\mathcal{T}_k| = n$. We show that c_m and c_{L-n+1} can be joined in the simple form. c_m is the parent structure of c after removal of the last attribute of $\vec{\mathcal{T}}_1$. Assuming the removal of the last attribute of $\vec{\mathcal{T}}_1$ results in a new sequence of attributes, $\mathcal{T}'$, we have either $\mathcal{T}' = \emptyset$, or $\vec{\mathcal{T}}' \prec \vec{\mathcal{T}}_1 \preceq, ..., \preceq \vec{\mathcal{T}}_k$, which means there can be no $\mathcal{T}_i \in c$ such that $\mathcal{T}' = \mathcal{T}_i$. Similar reasoning applies to c_{L-n+1}, which is the parent structure of c after removing of the first attribute of $\vec{T}_k$. Since $m + n \leq L$, we know $m \neq L - n + 1$, according to Lemma 4, c_m and c_{L-n+1} can be joined in the simple form. $\square$

Efficient Candidate Generation: Merge-Join without Pre-sorting

Let's assume patterns of the parent structures are ordered by their attribute values (i.e., patterns of $(AB)(CD)$ are ordered by their values of A, then B, C, and D). Then, candidate patterns (of a child structure) derived by merge-joining the ordered patterns of its parent structures maintain the order. Thus, the new patterns can be used to merge-join with other patterns to derive patterns on the next level, which still maintain the order. We can repeat this process to generate patterns on all levels through merge-joining without re-sorting the data.

For instance, say we want to derive the candidate patterns for structure $(AB)(CD)(EF)$ on level 6. These can be generated by joining the patterns of $c_6 = (AB)(CD)(E)$ and $c_5 = (AB)(CD)(F)$. We can merge-join c_6 and c_5 because they share the same prefix: $(AB)(CD)$ of length 4. Furthermore, the results of the join are still ordered by the attributes, which makes them ready to generate patterns on the next level without sorting. The question is, can patterns of every structure be derived by merge-joining two of its parents using their existing order?

Apparently, the parents that can be merge-joined to produce the patterns of c must have the same first $(L - 2)$ attributes. Thus, the only two parents that can qualify are c_L and c_{L-1}, the two structures resulted by the removal of the last and the next-to-last column of c respectively. However, sometimes c_L and c_{L-1} do not have the same first $L - 2$ attributes. Take $\vec{c} = (AB)(AB)$ on level $L = 4$ for example. Parent structure $\vec{c}_4$ does not exist in the form of $(AB)(A)$, but rather $(A)(AB)$ since $(A) \prec (AB)$. Thus, patterns of $\vec{c}_4$ are not ordered by the same first $L - 2 = 2$ attributes as $\vec{c}_3 = (AB)(B)$. On the other hand, even if c_L and c_{L-1} do share the first $L - 2$ attributes, they are not merge-joinable, if they can not even be joined in the simple form. An example of such a case is $(A)(AB)$.

Proposition 6. *(Join Property III) The candidate patterns of a structure c on level $L \geq 3$ can be derived by merge-joining the patterns of c_L and c_{L-1}, if the following are satisfied: i) c_L and c_{L-1} can be joined in the simple form; and ii) c_L and c_{L-1} share the same first $L - 2$ attributes.*

Proof. i) guarantees only a single ordering of the patterns is required, and ii) guarantees they can be merge-joined. $\square$

For instance, candidate patterns of 5 out of the 6 pattern structures on level 3 in Figure 2 can be derived by merge-joining the patterns of their parents without re-sorting.

Overall, around 80% of the structures can be derived by merge-join.

5 Algorithm

The main procedure for mining the HIFI framework is outlined in Algorithm 1. We start by generating frequent itemsets on the first level, where each pattern structure has one attribute. The resulted frequent patterns are paired to generate candidate patterns on the second level. Then, on line 6 we scan the dataset to count the occurrences of each pattern on the current level, and on 7, we eliminate infrequent patterns. Next, we generate all possible pattern structures for the next level (Algorithm 2) and populate each pattern structure by candidate patterns by the method described in the previous section (Algorithm 3). We repeat the process until no more patterns can be generated.

Algorithm 1 HIFI(SetOfAttributes: A, Dataset: D, Min-Support: min_sup)

1: generate frequent patterns of structures on the 1st level;
2: $L \leftarrow 2$;
3: $Structure_L \leftarrow$ structures on the 2nd level;
4: $Cand_L \leftarrow$ join patterns on the 1st level to generate candidate patterns on the 2nd level;
5: **while** $Cand_L \neq \emptyset$ **do**
6:      countSupport($D, Cand_L$);
7:      eliminate candidates whose support are lower than min_sup;
8:      $L \leftarrow L + 1$;
9:      $Structure_L \leftarrow StructureGen(Structure_{L-1}, A)$;
10:      CandidateGen($Structure_L$);
11: **end while**
12: **return** $\{t.patterns | t \in Structure_L\}$;

Algorithm 2 StructureGen(SetOfStructures: *parents*)

1: $S \leftarrow \emptyset$;
2: **for each** $p \in parents$ **do**
3:      **for each** child structure c of p **do**
4:          $S \leftarrow S \cup \{c\}$ if all of c's parent structures exist and have non-empty pattern set;
5:      **end for**
6: **end for**
7: **return** S;

Given all candidate patterns on a certain level, the countSupport procedure scans the dataset once to count the occurrences of each pattern. The counting itself is not a trivial problem, especially when "exclusive" concepts are to be supported. Efficient access to all valid items are essential for this purpose. In HIFI, we build an *item tree* for this task.

Algorithm 3 CandidateGen(SetOfStructures: $Structures$)

1: **for each** $c \in Structures$ **do**
2:     Let c_i and c_j be parents of c with fewest patterns;
3:     **if** joining c_L and c_{L-1} is less costly **then**
4:         $c.patterns \leftarrow$ mergeJoin(c_L, c_{L-1});
5:     **else**
6:         sort the patterns in c_i and c_j;
7:         $c.patterns \leftarrow$ mergeJoin(c_i, c_j);
8:         sort the patterns in $c.patterns$;
9:     **end if**
10:     **for each** parent c_k of c, and c_k does not take part in the join operation **do**
11:         **for each** pattern $p \in c.patterns$ **do**
12:             remove p from $c.patterns$ if the sub-pattern of p with regard to c_k does not exists in $c_k.patterns$;
13:         **end for**
14:     **end for**
15: **end for**

The details of countSupport and the item tree structure can be found in [11].

Based on the structures on the previous level, a naive way of generating all the current structures is shown in Algorithm 2. A child structure is to be generated only if all of its parents exist and have non-empty patterns. Algorithm 2 is not optimal since each structure can have multiple successors, and they are generated and tested multiple times. The implementation of HIFI uses an efficient algorithm. Based on a parent structure $\vec{p} = \langle \vec{T}_1, ..., \vec{T}_k \rangle$, we create a subset of its child structures using the following methods: i) adding a single attribute item $\vec{T}_{k+1}$ to $\vec{p}$ such that $\vec{T}_k \preceq \vec{T}_{k+1}$; ii) adding a new attribute to an existing item $\vec{T}_i$ to create a new item T' such that $\vec{T}_k \preceq T'$. We prove that each structure on the new level is generated once and only once [11].

The core of HIFI is the candidate generation procedure shown in Algorithm 3. The rationale and the correctness are discussed in the previous section.

6 Experimental Results

Experiments on both synthetic datasets and real life datasets were carried out on a Pentium III machine running Linux OS 2.2.1 with a 766 MHz CPU, 256M memory. We implemented two other approaches: *Hierarchy* and *Taxonomy*. Hierarchy is based on the ML_T* algorithms [5]. Given a dataset with N attributes, *Hierarchy* enumerates all $N!$ possible hierarchies of N levels, and for each hierarchy, we use ML_T* to find frequent itemsets. Furthermore, we also find "cross-level" patterns by combining frequent itemsets on different hierarchy levels [5]. *Taxonomy* is based on EstMerge [10]. A record with N attributes are encoded into $2^N - 1$ items, such that a transaction with k records contains as many as $k(2^N - 1)$ items. *Taxonomy* then performs an Apriori search in the extended transactions.

The synthetic data generator is parameterized by D number of records, A number of attributes, I average records per transaction, N average number of distinct values for each attribute, and P number of maximum patterns. Both I and N are Poisson distribution parameters. The number of items in a maximum pattern is decided by the Poisson distribution with $\lambda = I/2$, and the number of attributes in an item is decided by the Poisson distribution with $\lambda = A/2$. We set $N = 30$ and $P = 100$. We use $D?.A?.I?$ as a name template, for instance, D100K.A5.I8 is the dataset generated by setting $D = 100K$, $A = 5$ and $I = 8$.

Figure 4 shows the scalability of the HIFI Algorithm. Figure 4(a) shows the execution time increases linearly with the size of the dataset. Figure 4(b), however, shows that the performance is heavily dependent on the number of attributes, since more attributes brings a combinatorial growth of the number of structures. Shown in Figure 4(c), the execution time also increases significantly as we increase I, the average number of records in a transaction. This is because when I becomes larger, patterns will contain more items and require more passes of data scans to discover. In Figure 4(d,e,f), we compared the performance of HIFI against the other two approaches, namely *Hierarchy* and *Taxonomy*. Despite the fact that these two approaches only discover a subset of the patterns discovered by HIFI, HIFI is much more efficient because a large amount of candidate itemsets are pruned by taking advantage of the anti-monotonic relationships in the tightly coupled mining space.

We also applied the HIFI algorithm on a real life dataset, NETVIEW, which is generated by a production network at a financial service company. Events in the dataset are grouped into transactions by their timestamps based on a 30-second interval, and on average each transaction contains about 10 events. Each event has multiple attributes, which include Event, Host, Severity, and Category. Overall, there are 241 event types, 2526 hosts, 6 severity levels, and 17 event categories. The patterns discovered by HIFI offers valuable insights into the understanding of the operational environment.

7 Conclusion

We present the search space of frequent patterns in a novel architecture, where pattern structures are tightly coupled in the anti-monotonic relationships. Using such relationships, and an efficient candidate generation algorithm based on merge-join, our approach is able to prune away a large amount of candidate patterns, thus greatly improves the mining performance.

Unlike the level-wise mining algorithms used in Apriori

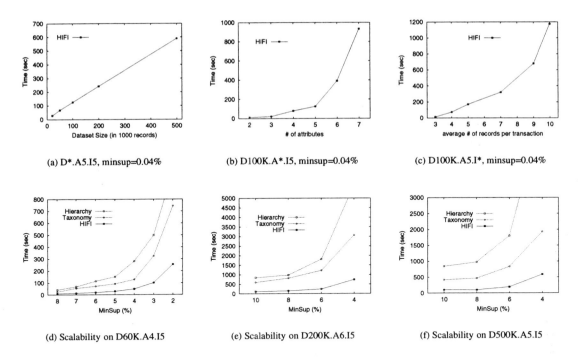

(a) D*.A5.I5, minsup=0.04%   (b) D100K.A*.I5, minsup=0.04%   (c) D100K.A5.I*, minsup=0.04%

(d) Scalability on D60K.A4.I5   (e) Scalability on D200K.A6.I5   (f) Scalability on D500K.A5.I5

Figure 4. Execution Time

and its extensions [3, 8], our algorithm localizes the candidate generation and pruning procedure to each pattern structure. Given a set of query structures, we are able to find their frequent itemsets by exploring a much smaller search space than the other approaches. Furthermore, our algorithm is relational and attribute sensitive in that we do not encode the attribute information of a relational table into items. The organization of the search space is also conducive to the interpretation and analysis of the resulting patterns.

References

[1] R. Agrawal, T. Imielinski, and A. Swami. Mining association rules between sets of items in large databases. In *VLDB*, pages 207–216, 1993.

[2] R. Agrawal and R. Srikant. Fast algorithms for mining association rules. In *VLDB*, 1994.

[3] R. Agrawal and R. Srikant. Mining sequential patterns. In *ICDE*, 1995.

[4] Surajit Chaudhuri. Data mining and database systems: Where is the intersection? In *Bulletin of the IEEE Computer Society Technical Committee on Data Engineering*, 1998.

[5] J. Han and Y. Fu. Discovery of multiple-level association rules from large databases. In *VLDB*, 1995.

[6] R. Ng, L. Lakshmanan, J. Han, and A. Pang. Exploratory mining and pruning optimizations of constrained associations rules. In *SIGMOD*, pages 13–24, 1998.

[7] R. Srikant and R. Agrawal. Mining generalized association rules. In *VLDB*, pages 407–419, 1995.

[8] R. Srikant and R. Agrawal. Mining sequential patterns: generalization and performance improvements. In *EDBT*, 1996.

[9] R. Srikant, Q. Vu, and R. Agrawal. Mining association rules with item constraints. In *SIGKDD*, pages 67–93, 1997.

[10] Ramakrishnan Srikant and Rakesh Agrawal. Mining generalized association rules. In *VLDB*, Zurich, Switzerland, September 1995.

[11] Haixun Wang, Chang-Shing Perng, Sheng Ma, and Philip S. Yu. Mining associations by pattern structure in large relational tables. Technical report, IBM T. J. Watson, 2002.

Comparison of Lazy Bayesian Rule and Tree-Augmented Bayesian Learning

Zhihai Wang
School of Information Technology,
Deakin University, 3125, Australia
zhw@deakin.edu.au

Geoffrey I. Webb
School of CSSE, Monash University,
Victoria, 3800, Australia
webb@csse.monash.edu.au

Abstract

The naive Bayes classifier is widely used in interactive applications due to its computational efficiency, direct theoretical base, and competitive accuracy. However, its attribute independence assumption can result in sub-optimal accuracy. A number of techniques have explored simple relaxations of the attribute independence assumption in order to increase accuracy. Among these, the lazy Bayesian rule (LBR) and the tree-augmented naive Bayes (TAN) have demonstrated strong prediction accuracy. However, their relative performance has never been evaluated. This paper compares and contrasts these two techniques, finding that they have comparable accuracy and hence should be selected according to computational profile. LBR is desirable when small numbers of objects are to be classified while TAN is desirable when large numbers of objects are to be classified.

1. Introduction

The Naive Bayesian classifier is one of the most computationally efficient algorithms for machine learning and data mining. It has been shown in many domains to be surprisingly accurate compared to alternatives including decision tree learning, rule learning, neural networks, and instance-based learning [10], [11], [4], [8], [5], [12]. It is based on Bayes' theorem and an assumption that all attributes are mutually independent within each class.

Assume X is a finite set of instances, and $A = \{A_1, A_2, \cdots, A_n\}$ is a finite set of n attributes. An instance $x \in X$ is described by a vector $< a_1, a_2, \cdots, a_n >$, where a_i is a value of attribute A_i. C is called the class attribute. Prediction accuracy will be maximized if the predicted class $L(< a_1, a_2, \cdots, a_n >) = argmax_c(P(c| < a_1, a_2, \cdots, a_n >)$. Unfortunately, unless $< a_1, a_2, \cdots, a_n >$ occurs many times within X, it will not be possible to directly estimate $P(c| < a_1, a_2, \cdots, a_n >)$ from the frequency with which each class $c \in C$ co-

occurs with $< a_1, a_2, \cdots, a_n >$ within X. Bayes' theorem provides an equality that might be used to help estimate $P(c_i|x)$ in such a circumstance:

$$P(c_i|x) = \frac{P(c_i)P(< a_1, a_2, \cdots, a_n > |c_i)}{P(< a_1, a_2, \cdots, a_n >)}. \quad (1)$$

If the n attributes are mutually independent within each class value, then the probability is directly proportional to:

$$P(c_i| < a_1, a_2, \cdots, a_n >) \propto P(c_i) \prod_{k=1}^{n} P(a_k|c_i). \quad (2)$$

Classification selecting the most probable class as estimated using formulas 1 and 2 is the well-known naive Bayesian classifier.

2. Approaches of improving naive Bayesian method

The attribute independence assumption makes the application of Bayes' theorem to classification practical in many domains, but this assumption rarely holds in real world problems. Notwithstanding Domingos and Pazzani's (1996) analysis that demonstrates that some violations of the independence assumption are not harmful to classification accuracy [4], previous research has shown that semi-naive techniques [10] and Bayesian networks [5] that explicitly adjust the naive strategy to allow for violations of the independence assumption, can improve upon the prediction accuracy of the naive Bayesian classifier in many domains.

One approach is to select attribute subsets. The selective Bayesian classifier [11] is a variant of the naive method that uses only a subset of the given attributes in making predictions. Kohavi and John (1997) use best-first search, based on accuracy estimates, to find a subset of attributes [9]. Their algorithm can wrap around any classifiers, including either the decision tree classifiers or the naive Bayesian classifiers. Another of the most important research approaches is directly to relax the independence assumptions.

Kononenko (1991) proposed a semi-naive Bayesian classifier [10], which partitioned the attributes into disjoint groups and assumed independence only between attributes of different groups. Pazzani (1996) proposed an algorithm based on the wrapper model for the construction of Cartesian product attributes to improve the naive Bayesian classifier [13].

Friedman, Geiger and Goldszmidt (1997) compared the naive Bayesian method and Bayesian network, and showed that using unrestricted Bayesian networks did not generally lead to improvements in accuracy and even reduced accuracy in some domains [5]. They presented a compromise representation, called tree-augmented naive Bayes (TAN), in which the class node directly points to all attributes nodes and an attribute node can have only at most one additional parent to the class node. Based on this presentation, they utilized the concept of mutual information to efficiently find the best tree-augmented naive Bayesian classifier. Keogh and Pazzani (1999) took a different approach to constructing tree-augmented Bayesian networks [7]. They use the same representation, but use leave-one-out cross validation to estimate the classification accuracy of the network when an arc is to add. The two methods mainly differ in the criterion of attribute selection used to select dependence relations among the attributes while building a tree-augmented Bayesian network.

Zheng and Webb (2000) proposed the lazy Bayesian rule (LBR) learning technique [17]. LBR can be thought of as applying lazy learning techniques to naive Bayesian rule induction. At classification time, for each test example, it builds a most appropriate rule with a conjunction of conditions as its antecedent and a local naive Bayesian classifier as its consequent. LBR has been compared experimentally with a naive Bayesian classifier, a decision tree classifier, a Bayesian tree learning algorithm, a constructive Bayesian classifier, a selective naive Bayesian classifier, and a lazy decision tree algorithm in a wide variety of natural domains. In their extensive experiments, LBR obtained lower error than all the alternative algorithms.

Both LBR and TAN can be viewed as variants of naive Bayes that relax the attribute independence assumption. TAN relaxes this assumption by allowing each attribute to depend upon at most one other attribute in addition to the class. LBR allows an attribute to depend upon many other attributes, but all attributes depend upon the same set of other attributes. These two different approaches to relaxing the attribute independence assumption have not previously been compared. This paper compares the two techniques, focusing primarily on prediction accuracy but also investigating the significance of the use of lazy learning in LBR in comparison to the use of eager learning in TAN, and the criteria used for attribute selection.

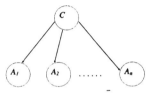

Figure 1. The Bayesian network structure of the naive Bayesian classier

3. The representation of dependencies

Bayesian networks have been a popular medium for graphically representing and manipulating attribute inter-dependencies. Bayesian networks are directed acyclic graphs (DAG) that allow for efficient and effective representation of joint probability distributions over a set of random variables. Each vertex in the graph represents a random variable, and each edge represents direct correlations between the variables. Each variable is independent of its non-descendants given its parents in the graph.

3.1. Basic Bayesian network

We now more formally introduce some notation for Bayesian networks. Let $A = \{A_1, A_2, \cdots, A_n\}$ be a finite set of discrete random variables where each variable A_i may take on values from a finite domain. A Bayesian network is an annotated directed acyclic graph that encodes a joint probability distribution over A. It can be formally defined as follows.

Definition 1. A Bayesian network is defined as a pair:

$$\mathbf{B} = <\mathbf{G}, \Theta> \qquad (3)$$

where $\mathbf{G} = <\mathbf{N}, \mathbf{E}>$ is a directed acyclic graph where each node $A \in \mathbf{N}$, corresponds to a random variable (an attribute in standard naive Bayesian terminology) and where each arc $E \in \mathbf{E}$ represents a direct dependence between variables. Θ is the set of parameters that quantifies the Bayesian network, in which each $\theta \in \Theta$ represents a conditional probability distribution for the corresponding node.

Bayesian networks provide a kind of direct and clear representation for the dependencies among the variables or attributes. These dependencies can be exploited to calculate the posterior probability $P(<a_1, a_2, \cdots, a_n> | c_i)$ in formula 1. A Bayesian network for the naive Bayesian classifier is the simple structure depicted in Figure 1, which has the class node as the parent node of all other nodes. No

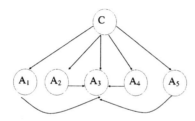

Figure 2. A Bayesian network for TAN

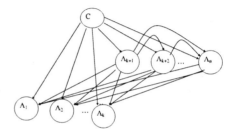

Figure 3. A Bayesian network for LBR

other arcs are allowed in its structure. That means every attribute is independent from the rest of the attributes given the state of the class variable. The naive Bayesian classifier has surprisingly outperformed many sophisticated classifiers over a large number of data sets, especially where the attributes are not strongly correlated. However, when the attribute independence assumption is violated, which appears to be very common, the performance of the naive Bayesian classifier might be poor.

3.2. Tree-augmented Bayesian networks

From the viewpoint of the representation of dependencies, we can think of the structure of the naive Bayesian network as being the most restrictive case of the attribute dependencies, in that it strictly allows no dependencies between attributes given the class variable. In order to improve the performance of the naive Bayesian classifier and reduce the negative impact of the independence assumption, many efforts have been made to extend the structure of the naive Bayesian classifier to account for dependence between attributes [14, 5, 7, 2, 3, 16]. Both of the algorithms of Friedman et al (1997) and Keogh et al (1999) are based on tree-augmented Bayesian networks, which can be viewed as a compromise between the restrictive naive Bayesian network and an unrestricted Bayesian network.

Definition 2. A tree-augmented Bayesian network is defined by the following conditions:

- Each attribute has the class attribute as a parent;

- Attributes may have one other attribute as a parent.

Figure 2 shows an example of an augmented Bayesian network. There are two reasons for this restriction [7]. First, it reduces the search space of classifiers that must be considered. Secondly, the probability estimates for a node become more unreliable as additional parents are added, because the size of the conditional probability tables increases exponentially with the number of parents. In a tree-augmented Bayesian network, a node without any parent,

other than the class node, is called an orphan. Given a tree-augmented Bayesian network, if we extend arcs from node A_k to every orphan node A_i, then node A_k is said to be a super parent. Assume that $Parents(v)$ is the set of all parents of node v, and $Parents$ is the set of $Parents(v)$ for all nodes in a tree-augmented Bayesian network, i.e., $Parents = \{Parents(v) : \forall v \in V\}$. Actually, here $Parents$ just represents a tree-augmented Bayesian network. If v is an orphan, then $Parents(v) = \emptyset$.

3.3. Lazy Bayesian Rule Learning

Lazy learning algorithms exhibit three characteristics that distinguish them from other learning algorithms [1]. First, they defer processing of their inputs until they receive requests for information; they simply store their inputs for future use. Next, they reply to information requests by combining their stored data. Finally, they discard the constructed answer and any intermediate results. This provides another approach to alleviating the small disjunct problem of decision tree learning, and further improving the performance of naive Bayesian classification.

In general, any lazy learning approach to building a Bayesian network will build a new network based on each given test instance. For a given test instance and training instances, the network is initialised to a naive Bayesian network, which means all nodes in the network are orphans and $Parents = \emptyset$. For any training instance, each attribute only has two values to be used in the network. One is equal to the value of the test instance, and another value is not equal to the value of the test instance on this attribute. We don't need to differentiate any different value that is not equal to the value on the test instance.

3.4. The Bayesian network for a lazy Bayesian rule

The lazy Bayesian rule (LBR) learning technique [18, 17] can be thought of as applying lazy learning techniques to Bayesian rule induction. LBR is similar to $LazyDT$ (Lazy Decision Tree learning algorithms) [6], which can be considered to generate decision rules at classification time.

For each instance to be classified, $LazyDT$ builds one rule that is most appropriate to the instance by using an entropy measurement. The antecedent of the rule is a conjunction of conditions in the form of attribute-value pairs. The consequent of the rule is the class to be predicted, being the majority class of the training instances that satisfy the antecedent of the rule. LBR can be considered as a combination of the two techniques $NBTree$ and $LazyDT$. Before classifying a test instance, it generates a Bayesian rule that is most appropriate to the test instance. Alternatively, LBR can be viewed as a lazy approach to classification using the following variant of Bayes theorem,

$$P(C_i|V_1 \wedge V_2) = P(C_i|V_2)P(V_1|C_i \wedge V_2)/P(V_1|V_2) \quad (4)$$

Here, V_1 and V_2 are any two conjunctions of attribute values such that each a_i from belongs to exactly one of V_1 or V_2. The structure of a Bayesian network for a lazy Bayesian rule is shown in Figure 3, here $V_1 = \{A_1, A_2, \cdots, A_k\}$ and $V_2 = \{A_{k+1}, A_{k+2}, \cdots, A_n\}$. At classification time, for each instance to be classified, the attribute values in V are allocated to V_1 and V_2 in a manner that is expected to minimize estimation error. The antecedent of a Bayesian rule is the conjunction of attribute-value pairs from the set V_2, and the consequent of a Bayesian rule is a local naive Bayesian classifier created from those training instances that satisfy the antecedent of the rule, which only uses those attributes that belong to the set V_1. That is to say, we have known there are some dependencies among the attributes in V_2, but we don't need to clarify what they are. And a weaker assumption that all the attributes in V_1 are mutual independent given class value and V_2 is hold. During the generation of a Bayesian rule, the test instance to be classified is used to guide the selection of attributes for creating attribute-value pairs. The values in the attribute-value pairs are always the same as the corresponding attribute values of the test instance. The objective is to grow the antecedent of a Bayesian rule that ultimately decreases the errors of the local naive Bayesian classifier in the consequent of the rule.

4. Classification using Bayesian networks

On In this section, we will discuss some issues to be related to our Bayesian learning framework. In general speaking, a Bayesian network allows for modeling of arbitrarily complex dependencies between attributes. Sahami (1996) makes use of the notion of k-dependence Bayesian classifiers to illustrate the relationship of the naive Bayesian classifier and a full unrestricted Bayesian classifier [14].

Definition 3. A k-dependence Bayesian classifier is a Bayesian network which contains the structure of the naive Bayesian classifier and allows each attribute to have

a maximum of k attribute nodes as its parents.

The naive Bayesian classifier is a 0-dependence Bayesian classifier. The full unrestricted Bayesian Network classifier is a $(n-1)$-dependence Bayesian classifier, where n is the number of domain attributes. Thus, Bayesian networks have much representational power at the cost of computationally expensive learning and inference. Restricting the number of parents to two could mitigate problems in estimating probabilities from the training data while allowing some amount of dependencies among attributes to be represented.

Finding the best Bayesian network is an intractable problem. What is the best Bayesian network for the training data? In building a Bayesian network, how to evaluate a new Bayesian network when an arc is added? Friedman, Geiger and Goldszmidt (1997) described the problem of learning a Bayesian network from training data as follows [5].

Statement 1. Given a training data set $X = \{x_1, x_2, \cdots, x_m\}$ of instances of $A^* = \{A_1, A_2, \cdots, A_n, C\}$, find a Bayesian network B that best matches the training set X.

However, the use of such criteria runs the risk of overfitting. Cerquides (1999) presented an alternative statement as follows [2].

Statement 2. Given a training data set $X = \{x_1, x_2, \cdots, x_m\}$ of a probability distribution P^*, find the Bayesian network B that best matches P^*.

In practice, this statement is still not operative with respect to building a Bayesian network. In order to efficiently express the classification purpose, we prefer the following statement.

Statement 3. Given a training data set $X = \{x_1, x_2, \cdots, x_m\}$ of instances of $A^* = \{A_1, A_2, \cdots, A_n, C\}$, find a Bayesian network B that has the best classification accuracy.

The algorithm of Friedman, Geiger and Goldszmidt (1997) builds a tree structure over the training data using the concept of mutual information tests conditioned on class variable [5]. Cerquides' (1999) algorithm uses a variant of mutual information ($loglikelihood$) to evaluate a network [2]. Neither algorithm directly reflects classification accuracy. Keogh and Pazzani (1999) take a different approach to evaluating a tree-augmented Bayesian network [7]. They used leave-one-out cross validation to estimate the accuracy of the network with that arc added.

LBR [17] also uses leave-one-out cross validation and a significance test to manage the trade-off between the degree to which the attribute independence assumption of the naive Bayesian classifier is violated and the number of training instances available for training the local naive Bayesian classifier.

5. Lazy tree-augmented Bayesian network learning

LBR and TAN differ in two respects. The first is the types of inter-dependencies that they allow. TAN allows every node to have different parents, but each node may have at most one parent. LBR requires all nodes to have the same parents, but places no restriction on the number of parents. The primary reason for each of these restrictions is to restrict the space of alternative networks that is explored, both to reduce computation and also to reduce variance.

The second respect in which they differ is that LBR uses lazy learning while TAN uses eager learning. In consequence, LBR may create a different network for each case to be classified while TAN will apply the same network to all cases classified. To evaluate the effect of this latter difference, we implement a lazy version of TAN ($LazyTAN$). For a lazy learning method, the Bayesian classifier is only based on specific attribute values of the test instance to be classified.

Now, we further give some notations and functions to be used in the following lazy learning algorithm for building tree-augmented Bayesian classifiers, which is used mainly to explain the differences between the lazy Bayesian rule learning technique and the tree-augmented Bayesian network learning technique. We will then explain some special issues for our implementations. We also discuss criteria for attribute selection while building a Bayesian network to predict the class of an unseen instance.

5.1. Basic functions description

Assume e is a conjunction of some attributes values, then X_e is the subset of X that satisfies the conjunction of attributes values e. And $Parents(v)$ is the set of all parents of node v, and $Parents$ is the set of $Parents(v)$ for all nodes in a Bayesian network, i.e., $Parents = \{Parents(v) : \forall v \in V\}$. If v is an orphan, then $Parents(v) = \emptyset$. When an arc is to added into the current Bayesian network, we use the following functions to check whether the new Bayesian network is still a tree-augmented Bayesian network.

- $Ancestor(b,a)$ is a Boolean function, its value is true if ($b \in Parenst(a)$) or ($\exists v \in Parents(a) : Ancester(v,b)$).

Table 1. The Description of LazyTAN

ALGORITHM: LazyTAN (X, V, C, s)
INPUT: 1) X is the set of training instances,
        2) V is the set of attribute values of the test,
        3) C is the set of class values,
OUTPUT: Estimated values of the probabilities
        $P(a_1 \wedge a_2 \wedge \cdots \wedge a_n | c_i)$.
FOR all $v \in V$, $Parents(v) = \emptyset$
/* Initialize the parents of each value */
$MiniErrors = Estimate(X, \mathbf{Parents})$
DO
     $BestSuperParent = Argmin_{v \in V}$
         $Estimate(X, InsertAll(\mathbf{Parents}, v))$
     /* This is the value for which making that value a parent of all qualified values will have the greatest effect.*/
     IF $Eestimate(X, InsertAll(Parents, a)) >$
         $MiniErrors$ THEN BREAK
     $b = Argmin_{\{v:Qualified(a,v)\}}$
         $Estimate(X, Insert(Parents(v), a, v))$
     /* This selects the value which is most desirable to add to a.*/
     IF $Estimate(X, Insert(Parents(b), a, b)) >$
         $MiniErrors$ THEN BREAK
     $Parents = Insert(Parents(b), a, b)$
RETURN
the class probability estimates for V and $Parents$.

- $Qualified(b,a)$ is a Boolean function to check whether an arc, which is from node a to node b, can be added. Its value is true if $\neg ancestor(b,a)$ and $Parents(b) = \emptyset$.

The first condition $\neg ancestor(b,a)$ ensures the network is still acyclic if the arc is added. The second condition $Parents(b) = \emptyset$ guarantees node a is a unique parent for node b. The function $Insert(Parents(b), a, b)$ add nodes a into $Parents(b)$. That is, it adds an arc from node a to node b into the current Bayesian network. The function $InsertAll(\mathbf{Parents}, b)$ is the result of adding b to each node a of $\mathbf{Parents}$ such that $qualified(b,a)$. Given a tree-augmented network $\mathbf{B}$, if we extend an arc from node A_k to each orphan in turn, and test the effect on predictive accuracy, the node pointed to by the best arc is said to be the favourite child of node A_k.

The evaluation of classification accuracy is done by $Estimate(X, \mathbf{Parents})$, which is an integer function, its value is the number of instances which are classified incorrectly using leave-one-out cross validation estimate on the training data set X of a tree-augmented Bayesian network with $\mathbf{Parents}$.

5.2. *LazyTAN* algorithm

A lazy TAN algorithm is described in Table 1. The main loop is a straight-forward translation to lazy learning of Keogh and Pazzani's (1999) variant of the TAN algorithm [7]. First, it makes each node a super parent and the classification accuracy of the corresponding network is evaluated using leave-one-out cross validation. It then finds the best super parent. Next it tries to find the favourite child, by assessing the effect of adding a single arc from the best super parent to each orphan. For one test instance, the complexity of selecting the best super parent is $O(n)$, because there are at the most n Bayesian networks to be evaluated, and the complexity of selecting the favourite child is also $O(n)$, because there are at the most n arcs to be tested.

Each tree-augmented Bayesian network in our lazy algorithm is based on a single given test instance. Thus, an attribute only has two values to be used in the network. One is equal to the value of the test instance, and the other value is not equal to the value of the test instance on this attribute. We don't need to differentiate different values that are not equal to the value on the test instance. This kind of Bayesian network does not reflect the joint probability distributions for all attributes, but reflects the specific dependencies between the attribute values of the current test instance.

6. Experiments on Weka system

We compare the classification performance of four learning algorithms. We use the naive Bayes classifier implemented in the Weka system, simply called Naive. We implemented in Weka a lazy Bayesian rule (LBR) learning algorithm [17], a tree-augmented Bayesian network (TAN) learning algorithm [7], and a lazy tree-augmented Bayesian network learning algorithm (called $LazyTAN$). All the experiments were performed in the Weka system [15], which provides a workbench that includes full and working implementations of many popular learning schemes that can be used for practical data mining or for research.

Thirty-two natural domains are used in the experiments shown in Table 2. Twenty-eight of these are drawn from twenty-nine data sets used in previous research in the area [7, 17]. Splice-junction had to be discarded as computations could not be completed in reasonable time. The original corpus of data sets is dominated by small data sets. As LBR and TAN are directed at larger data sets, the remaining twenty-seven data sets were augmented by a selection of four larger data sets (vehicle, mfeat-mor, sign, segment).

In Table 2, 3, "$S\sharp$" means the number of instances in a data set. "$C\sharp$" means the number of values of a class attribute. "$A\sharp$" means the number of attributes, not including the class attribute. The classification accuracy

Table 2. Descriptions of Data

	Domain	S♯	C♯	A♯
1	Annealing Processes	898	6	38
2	Audiology	226	24	69
3	Breast Cancer(Wisconsin)	699	2	9
4	Chess (King-rook-vs-king-pawn)	3196	2	36
5	Credit Screening(Australia)	690	2	15
6	Echocardiogram	74	2	6
7	Glass Identification	214	7	10
8	Heart Disease(Cleveland)	303	2	13
9	Hepatitis Prognosis	155	2	19
10	Horse Colic	368	2	22
11	House Votes 84	435	2	16
12	Hypothyroid Diagnosis	3163	2	25
13	Iris Classification	150	3	4
14	Labor Negotiations	57	2	16
15	LED 24(noise level=10%)	1000	10	24
16	Liver Disorders(bupa)	345	2	6
17	Lung Cancer	32	3	56
18	Lymphography	148	4	18
19	Mfeat-mor	2000	10	6
20	Pima Indians Diabetes	768	2	8
21	Post-Operative Patient	90	3	8
22	Primary Tumor	339	22	17
23	Promoter Gene Sequences	106	2	57
24	Segment	2310	7	19
25	Sign	12546	3	8
26	Solar Flare	1389	2	9
27	Sonar Classification	208	2	60
28	Soybean Large	683	19	35
29	Tic-Tac-Toe End Game	958	2	9
30	Vehicle	846	4	18
31	Wine Recognition	178	3	13
32	Zoology	101	7	16

of each classifier on each domain is obtained by running 10-fold cross validation, and the random seed for 10-fold cross validation takes on the default value in Weka system. We also use the default discretization method "weka.filters.DiscretizeFilter" as the discretization method for continuous values, which is offered by the Weka system. All experimental results for classification accuracies of the algorithms are shown in Table 3.

Tables 4, 5 and 6, present the WIN/LOSS/DRAW records for LBR, TAN and $LazyTAN$, respectively. This is a record of the number of data sets for which the nominated algorithm achieves lower, higher, and equal error to the comparison algorithm, measured to two decimal places. The tables also include the outcome of a two-tailed binomial sign test. This indicates the probability that the observed outcome or more extreme should occur by chance if wins and losses were equiprobable. LBR and TAN demonstrate comparable levels of error rate.

LBR has a lower error rate than the naive Bayes classifier in fourteen out of the twenty-seven data sets, and a higher error rate in only three data sets. This outcome is statistically significant at the 0.05 level. LBR and TAN demonstrate comparable levels of error rate. LBR has a higher error rate than TAN classifier in thirteen data sets, and lower error rate in ten. $LazyTAN$ also has similar error performance to LBR and TAN, but the $LazyTAN$ algorithm is not so efficient as LBR classifier.

In the thirty-two databases, there are fifteen databases which TAN has higher classification accuracy than Naive Bayes, and eight for which it has lower classification accuracy. On these data sets TAN has failed to improve upon the error of naive Bayes with significant frequency. It is remarkable that the pattern of the databases for which each of TAN and LBR outperforms naive Bayes differs substantially. It is clear that they find different Bayesian networks topologies.

There are nineteen databases which $LazyTAN$ has higher classification accuracy than the naive Bayes classifier, and nine for which it has lower classification accuracy. This result approaches but does not achieve statistical significance at the 0.05 level (although if one-tailed tests were applied, as it could be argued is appropriate in this case as we expected $LazyTAN$ to outperform naive Bayes, then the result would be significant - 0.044). $LazyTAN$ has lower error than TAN for fourteen data sets and higher for eleven. This difference is not statistically significant. $LazyTAN$ has similar error performance to the LBR classifier. These results give some suggestion that directly using lazy learning techniques to build a tree-augmented Bayesian network for a given test instance benefit classification accuracy.

The mean accuracy over all data sets for each algorithm is given in Table 7. Due to the incommensurability of accuracy scores across different data sets this is a gross measure to which it is not wise to pay too much attention. Nonetheless, it might be indicative that LBR achieves the highest mean accuracy.

To further compare LBR and TAN we calculate the geometric mean accuracy ratio. For each data set the accuracy of TAN is divided by the accuracy of LBR. The geometric mean of these values is 0.994. A value above 1.0 favors TAN while a value below 1.0 favours LBR. A value of 0.994 indicates a very slight advantage toward LBR for the data sets studied.

Table 3. Average Error Rate for Each Dataset

	Domain	$Naive$	LBR	TAN	$LTAN$
1	Annealing	5.46	5.46	4.01	3.45
2	Audiology	29.20	29.20	29.20	28.32
3	B Cancer	2.58	2.58	2.58	2.58
4	Chess	12.36	3.57	5.07	5.07
5	Australia	15.07	14.64	14.35	14.64
6	Echocardiogram	27.48	27.48	28.24	28.24
7	Glass	11.68	9.81	6.07	9.81
8	Cleveland	16.50	16.50	16.50	18.48
9	Hepatitis	16.13	16.13	16.13	14.84
10	Horse Colic	20.11	19.29	18.48	18.48
11	House Votes	9.89	7.13	6.90	9.66
12	Hypothyroid	2.94	2.78	2.88	2.66
13	Iris	6.67	6.67	6.00	4.67
14	Labor	3.51	3.51	3.51	3.51
15	LED	24.50	24.70	24.50	24.60
16	Bupa	36.81	36.81	40.29	37.39
17	L Cancer	46.88	43.75	50.00	46.88
18	Lymphography	14.19	14.19	15.54	12.84
19	Mfeat-mor	30.65	29.95	30.10	29.95
20	PID	25.00	24.87	25.39	26.56
21	Post-Operative	28.89	28.89	30.00	34.44
22	PT	48.97	49.85	49.85	49.85
23	Promoter	8.49	8.49	8.49	9.43
24	Segment	11.08	6.41	6.28	6.54
25	Sign	38.58	20.93	26.85	28.71
26	Solar Flare	18.57	15.69	16.85	15.48
27	Sonar	25.48	25.96	23.56	23.08
28	Soybean	7.17	7.17	7.03	7.32
29	TTT	29.54	14.61	28.81	25.57
30	Vehicle	39.48	31.44	31.68	30.61
31	Wine	3.37	3.37	3.37	2.81
32	Zoology	5.94	5.94	5.94	5.94

Table 4. Comparison of LBR to others

	WIN	$LOSS$	$DRAW$	P
$Naive$	14	3	15	0.013
TAN	13	10	9	0.678
$LazyTAN$	13	13	6	1.000

Table 5. Comparison of TAN to others

	WIN	LOSS	DRAW	P
Naive	15	8	9	0.210
LBR	10	13	9	0.678
LazyTAN	11	14	7	0.690

Table 6. Comparison of $LazyTAN$ to others

	WIN	LOSS	DRAW	P
Naive	19	9	4	0.087
LBR	14	11	7	0.690
TAN	13	13	6	1.000

Table 7. The Mean Error Rate

	Naive	TAN	LBR	LazyTAN
Error Rate	19.47	18.26	17.43	18.13

7. Conclusion

Lazy Bayesian Rules and tree-augmented Bayesian networks are two extensions to naive Bayes that have previously independently been shown to substantially reduce its error. We have presented the first comparative evaluation of these two approaches. Our evaluation suggests that the two algorithms are most effective on quite different data sets. Neither exhibits a general advantage over the other. To evaluate the impact of the lazy/eager differentiation between the two algorithms we also implemented a lazy version of TAN. The comparison indicated that $LazyTAN$ enjoyed at best a modest improvement upon TAN. These outcomes suggest that the most important difference between LBR and TAN is the difference in the topologies of the networks that they construct. Due to its lazy approach, LBR enjoys greater computational efficiency than TAN when few objects are to be classified from a single training set and TAN enjoys a computational advantage when many objects are to be classified.

References

[1] D. W. Aha. Lazy learning: special issue editorial. *Artificial Intelligence Review*, pages 7–10, 11 1997.

[2] J. Cerquides. Applying general Bayesian techniques to improve TAN induction. In *Proceedings of the International Conference on Knowledge Discovery and Data Mining - KDD'1999*, pages 292–296, 1999.

[3] J. Cheng and R. Greiner. Comparing Bayesian network classifiers. In *Proceedings of the Fifteenth Conference on Uncertainty in Artificial Intelligence (UAI-99)*, Sweden, 1999.

[4] P. Domingos and M. Pazzani. Beyond independence: conditions for the optimality of the simple Bayesian classifier. In *Proceedings of the Thirteenth International Conference on Machine Learning*, pages 105–112, San Francisco, CA, 1996. Morgan Kaufmann Publishers, Inc.

[5] N. Friedman, D. Geiger, and M. Goldszmidt. Bayesian network classifiers. *Machine Learning*, 29:131–163, 1997.

[6] N. Friedman, R. Kohavi, and Y. Yun. Lazy decision tree. In *Proceedings of the Thirteenth National Conference on Artificial Intelligence*, pages 717–724, Menlo Park, CA, 1996. The AAAI PressMorgan Kaufmann Publishers, Inc.

[7] E. J. Keogh and M. J. Pazzani. Learning augmented Bayesian classifiers: a comparison of distribution-based and classification-based approaches. In *Proceedings of the Seventh International Workshop on Artificial Intelligence and Statistics*, pages 225–230, 1999.

[8] R. Kohavi. Scaling up the accuracy of naive-Bayes classifiers: a decision-tree hybird. In E. Simoudis, J. W. Han, and U. M. Fayyad, editors, *Proceedings of the Second International Conference on Knowledge Discovery and Data Mining*, pages 202–207, Menlo Park, CA, 1996. The AAAI Press.

[9] R. Kohavi and G. H. John. Wrappers for feature subset selection. *Artificial Intelligence*, pages 273–324, 1997.

[10] I. Kononenko. Semi-nave Bayesian classifier. In *Proceedings of European Conference on Artificial Intelligence*, pages 206–219, 1991.

[11] P. Langley and S. Sage. Induction of selective Bayesian classifiers. In *Proceedings of the Tenth Conference on Uncertainty in Artificial Intelligence*, pages 339–406, Seattle, WA, 1994. Morgan Kaufmann Publishers.

[12] T. M. Mitchell. *Machine Learning*. The McGraw-Hill Companies, Inc., New York, 1997.

[13] M. Pazzani. Constructive induction of Cartesian product attributes. In *Proceedings of Information, Statistics and Induction in Science*, Melbourne, Australia, 1996.

[14] M. Sahami. *Learning limited dependence Bayesian classifiers*, pages 335–338. AAAI Press, Portland, OR, 1996.

[15] I. H. Witten and E. Frank. *Data Mining: Practical Machine Learning Tools and Techniques with Java Implementations*. Morgan Kaufmann Publishers, Seattle, WA, 2000.

[16] H. Zhang and X. Ling. Learnability of augmented naive Bayes in nominal domains. In *Proceedings of the Eighteenth International Conference on Machine Learning (ICML-2001)*, Williams College, 2001.

[17] Z. Zheng and G. I. Webb. Lazy learning of Bayesian rules. *Machine Learning*, 41(1):53–84, 2000.

[18] Z. Zheng, G. I. Webb, and K. M. Ting. Lazy Bayesian Rules: A lazy semi-naive Bayesian learning technique competitive to boosting decision trees. In *Proceedings of the Sixteenth International Conference on Machine Learning (ICML-99)*, pages 493–502, Bled, Slovenia, 1999. Morgan Kaufmann.

A Hybrid Approach to Discover Bayesian Networks From Databases Using Evolutionary Programming

Man Leung Wong
Department of Information Systems
Lingnan University
Tuen Mun, Hong Kong
mlwong@ln.edu.hk

Shing Yan Lee
Department of Computer Science
and Engineering, CUHK,
Shatin, Hong Kong
sylee@cse.cuhk.edu.hk

Kwong Sak Leung
Department of Computer Science
and Engineering, CUHK,
Shatin, Hong Kong
ksleung@cse.cuhk.edu.hk

Abstract

This paper describes a novel data mining approach that employs evolutionary programming to discover knowledge represented in Bayesian networks. There are two different approaches to the network learning problem. The first one uses dependency analysis, while the second one searches good network structures according to a metric. Unfortunately, both approaches have their own drawbacks. Thus, we propose a novel hybrid algorithm of the two approaches, which consists of two phases, namely, the Conditional Independence (CI) test and the search phases. A new operator is introduced to further enhance the search efficiency. We conduct a number of experiments and compare the hybrid algorithm with our previous algorithm, MDLEP [18], which uses EP for network learning. The empirical results illustrate that the new approach has better performance. We apply the approach to a data sets of direct marketing and compare the performance of the evolved Bayesian networks obtained by the new algorithm with the models generated by other methods. In the comparison, the induced Bayesian networks produced by the new algorithm outperform the other models.

1 Introduction

Conventional business research is a process in which data are analyzed manually to explore the relationships among various factors defined by the researcher. Even with powerful computers and versatile statistical software, many hidden and potentially useful relationships may not be recognized by the analyst. Nowadays, such problems are more acute as many businesses are capable of generating and collecting a huge amount of data in a relatively short period. The explosive growth of data requires a more efficient way

to extract useful knowledge. Thus, business research is a major area for applying data mining that aims at discovering novel, interesting, and useful knowledge from databases [4]. Through data mining, researchers can discover complex relationships among various factors and extract meaningful knowledge to improve the efficiency and quality of managerial decision making. In this paper, we propose a novel data mining approach that employs Evolutionary Programming (EP) to discover knowledge represented in Bayesian networks and apply the approach to handle the business problem of finding response models from direct marketing data.

A Bayesian network is a graphical representation that depicts conditional independence among random variables in the domain and encodes the joint probability distribution [13]. With a network at hand, probabilistic inference can be performed to predict the outcome of some variables based on the observations of others. Therefore, Bayesian networks are often used in diagnostic systems [8].

Typically, a Bayesian network is constructed by eliciting knowledge from domain experts. To reduce imprecision due to subjective judgments, researchers start to be interested in constructing a Bayesian network from collected data or past observations in the domain. In the literature, there are two main approaches to this network learning problem [3]. The first one is the dependency analysis approach [3, 17]. Since a Bayesian network describes conditional independence, we could make use of dependency test results to construct a Bayesian network that conforms to our findings. The second one, called the score-and-search approach [7, 6, 10], uses a metric to evaluate a candidate network structure. With the metric, a search algorithm is employed to find a network structure which has the best score. Thus, the learning problem becomes a search problem. Unfortunately, the two approaches both have their own drawbacks. For the former approach, an exponential number of dependency tests have to be performed. Moreover,

498

some test results may be inaccurate [17]. For the latter approach, since the search space is huge, some Bayesian network learning algorithms [7] adopt greedy search heuristics which may easily make the algorithms get stuck in a local optimum [6].

In this work, a hybrid approach is developed for the network learning problem. Simply put, dependency analysis results are used to reduce the search space of the score-and-search process. With such reduction, the search process would take less time for finding the optimal solution. Together with the introduction of a new operator and some modifications of our previous work, MDLEP [18], we call our new approach HEP (hybrid EP). HEP is found to have the best results in a real-life application of direct marketing amongst similar state-of-the-art approaches.

This paper is organized as follows. In section 2, we present the backgrounds of Bayesian networks, the MDL metric, and MDLEP. In section 3, we describe our algorithm in detail. In sections 4 and 5, we report our experimental findings. We conclude the paper in section 6.

2 Learning BAYESIAN networks from data

2.1 Bayesian networks

A Bayesian network, G, has a directed acyclic graph (DAG) structure. Each node in the graph corresponds to a discrete random variable in the domain. An edge, $X \leftarrow Y$, on the graph, describes a parent and child relation in which X is the child and Y is the parent. All parents of X constitute the parent set of X which is denoted by Π_X. In addition to the graph, each node has a conditional probability tables (CPT) specifying the probability of each possible state of the node given each possible combination of states of its parent. If a node contains no parent, the table gives the marginal probabilities of the node [13].

Since Bayesian networks are founded on the idea of conditional independence, it is necessary to give a brief description here. Let U be the set of variables in the domain and let P be the joint probability distribution of U. Following Pearl's notation, a conditional independence (CI) relation is denoted by $I(X, Z, Y)$ where X, Y, and Z are disjoint subsets of variables in U. Such notation says that X and Y are conditionally independent given the *conditioning set*, Z. Formally, a CI relation is defined with:

$$P(x, y \mid z) = P(x \mid z) \quad \text{whenever} \quad P(y, z) > 0 \quad (1)$$

where x, y, and z are any value assignments to the set of variables X, Y, and Z respectively. A CI relation is characterized by its *order*, which is the number of variables in the conditioning set Z.

As mentioned before, researchers treat the network learning problem in two very different ways. The first approach tries to construct a Bayesian network using dependency information obtained from the data. By assuming that P is faithful to a Bayesian network G [17], we could add or remove edges from G according to the discovered conditional independence relations. Given the sets of variables, X, Y, and Z, we could check the validity of $I(X, Z, Y)$ by performing statistical test, called CI test. The major problem of this approach is that it is difficult to know if two nodes are conditionally independent [17]. Furthermore, when a high-order CI relation is tested in a small data set, the test result may be unreliable [17]. The second approach makes use of a metric which evaluates the quality of a Bayesian network with respect to the given data. Such metric may be derived from information theory, Bayesian statistics, or Minimum Description Length principle (MDL). With the metric, the network learning problem becomes a search problem. Unfortunately, since the search space is huge, the search problem is difficult [6].

2.2 The MDL metric

The MDL metric [10] is derived from information theory and incorporates the Minimum Description Length principle. With the composition of the description length for network structure and the description length for data, the MDL metric tries to balance between model accuracy and model complexity. Hence, the best network needs to be both accurate and simple. Using the metric, a better network would have a smaller score. Similar to other metrics, the MDL score for a Bayesian network, G, is *decomposable* [6] and could be written as in equation 2. Let $U = \{N_1, \ldots, N_n\}$ be the set of nodes and let Π_{N_i} denotes the parent set of node N_i. The MDL score of the network is simply the summation of the MDL score of Π_{N_i} of every node N_i in the network.

$$\text{MDL}(G) = \sum_{N_i \in U} \text{MDL}(N_i, \Pi_{N_i}) \quad (2)$$

2.3 MDLEP

Our previous work [18], called MDLEP, belongs to the score-and-search approach in which we use the MDL metric together with evolutionary programming (EP) for searching a good network structure. An individual in the search population is a candidate network structure. MDLEP uses simple, reversion, move, and knowledge-guided mutations to generate new individuals. When comparing MDLEP against another approach using GA [12], it is found that MDLEP generally outperforms its opponent.

3   Hybrid EP (HEP)

Although MDLEP outperforms its GA opponent, its efficiency can be enhanced by employing a number of strategies. First, a hybrid approach is introduced so that the knowledge from dependency tests is exploited during searching. Second, previous search results are reused through a new merge operator. Third, in contrast to MDLEP where repairing is needed, the formation of cycle is avoided altogether when producing new individuals.

Since a hybrid approach is adopted in Bayesian network learning, this approach is called HEP (hybrid EP). In the following subsections, the ideas will be discussed in detail.

3.1   A hybrid approach

In dependency analysis approach, CI test is typically used to check the validity of a conditional independence assertion $I(X, Z, Y)$ of any given two nodes X, Y and a conditioning set Z. Assume that the χ^2 test is employed, the assertion is modeled as the null hypothesis. A χ^2 test generates a p-value, ranges between 0 and 1, which shows the least level of significance for which the given data leads to the rejection of the null hypothesis. In effect, if the p-value is less than a predefined cutoff value, α, the hypothesis $I(X, Z, Y)$ is rejected. Otherwise, if the p-value is greater than or equal to α, the hypothesis could not be rejected and $I(X, Z, Y)$ is assumed to be valid. Consequently, this implies that the two nodes, X and Y, cannot have a direct edge between them. In other words, the edges $X \leftarrow Y$ and $X \rightarrow Y$ cannot exist in the resultant network.

With such observation, a hybrid framework for learning Bayesian networks is formulated which consists of two phases. In the first phase, low-order CI tests are conducted so that some edges could be removed. Only low-order CI tests are performed because their results are more reliable than higher order tests and the time complexity is bounded. In the second phase, a score-and-search approach is used together with the knowledge obtained previously. In particular, the search space is limited by excluding networks that contain the edges $X \leftarrow Y$ or $Y \rightarrow X$ for which $I(X, Z, Y)$ is assumed to be valid. Since the search space is reduced, the learning problem becomes easier and less time will be needed for finding the best network.

This idea could be applied readily in MDLEP. After obtaining the test results, all candidate networks having invalid edges are prevented from being generated.

Although such formulation can work fine, it must be emphasized that the choice of α has a critical impact. If improper α is used, in the worst case, either all edges are pruned away or all edges are retained. Hence, although it is possible to impose the restrictions from CI tests as *global* constraints, there is the risk of assuming our choice of α is

appropriate.

As an alternative, a novel realization of the hybrid framework is developed in which a different α is used for each individual in the population. Thus, each individual has, besides the network structure, a cutoff value α which is also subjected to be evolved. As the evolutionary search proceeds, individual having an improper value of α will eventually be eliminated. In general, small value of α implies more constraints (less likely to reject an hypothesis) and results in a more restricted search space. Hence, if the value of α of an individual is too small which excludes some *important* edges, the individual will have a greater chance of being eliminated. On the other hand, if the value of α of an individual is too large, it is less likely to find the *right* edge (because there are many *wrong* alternatives) for its offspring. Consequently, the individual will also have a higher chance of being eliminated.

This idea is implemented in the first phase by storing the largest p-value returned by the CI tests for every possible conditioning set, Z (restricted to order-0 and all order-1 tests) in a matrix, Pv. In the second phase, for a given individual G_i in the population with associated cutoff value α_i, an edge $X \leftarrow Y$ cannot be added if Pv_{XY} is greater than α_i (i.e. $I(X, Z, Y)$ is assumed to be valid). The value of each α_i is randomly initialized in the beginning. In subsequent generations, an offspring will inherit the cutoff value from its parent with a possible increment or decrement by Δ_α.

3.2   The merge operator

In addition to the four mutation operators, a new operator called merge is introduced. Taking a parent network G_a and another network G_b as input, the merge operator attempts to produce a better network structure (in terms of MDL score) by modifying G_a with G_b. If no modification can be done, G_a is returned.

Let M_i^x denotes the MDL score of the parent set $\Pi_{N_i}^x$ of node $N_i \in U$ in the network G_x. Recalling that the MDL score is decomposable and a network is an agglomeration of Π_{N_i} (for $i = 1, \dots, n$). Thus, given two input networks G_a and G_b, a better network, G_c, could be generated by selecting $\Pi_{N_i}^c$ from $\Pi_{N_i}^a$ or $\Pi_{N_i}^b$ so that (1) there is no cycle in G_c and (2) the sum $\sum_{N_i \in U} M_i^c$ is less than $\sum_{N_i \in U} M_i^a$. With such observation, the merge operator is devised and is the heuristics for finding a subset of nodes, $W \subset U$, with which $\Pi_{N_j}^a$ are replaced with $\Pi_{N_j}^b$ in G_a for every $N_j \in W$. Meanwhile, the replacement would not create cycles and has a MDL score smaller than that of G_a. The pseudo-code for the merge operator is presented in Table 1.

For the two input networks G_a and G_b, the merge procedure produces a node ordering by sorting $\delta_i = M_i^a - M_i^b$ in descending order. Since positive δ_i means that $\Pi_{N_i}^b$ is better

Procedure merge(G_a, G_b)

1. Find $\delta_i = M_i^a - M_i^b$ for every node $N_i \in U$.
2. Produce a node ordering L by sorting δ_i in descending order.
3. Set $W = \phi$.
4. While there are still nodes in L left unconsidered,
   - Get the next node, N_i, from L which is unconsidered.
   - Set $W' = \phi$.
   - Invoke the procedure `findSubset`(N_i, W') which returns W' on completion.
   - Calculate the sum of δ_j for every node $N_j \in (W' - W)$.
   - If the sum is greater than zero
     - Mark every node $N_j \in W'$ in L as considered.
     - Replace $\Pi_{N_j}^a$ with $\Pi_{N_j}^b$ for every node $N_j \in (W' - W)$.
     - Set $W = W \cup W'$.

Table 1. Pseudo-code for the merge operator.

than $\Pi_{N_i}^a$, the procedure follows the ordering in considering the replacement of $\Pi_{N_i}^a$ with $\Pi_{N_i}^b$. Beginning with the first node, N_i, in the ordering, the merge procedure invokes the procedure `findSubset`(N_i) to find a subset of nodes W' such that by replacing $\Pi_{N_j}^a$ with $\Pi_{N_j}^b$ for every $N_j \in W'$ in G_a, the resultant graph is still acyclic.

After obtaining W', the merge procedure calculates the sum $\sum_{N_j \in (W'-W)} \delta_j$. If the sum is greater than zero, it replaces $\Pi_{N_j}^a$ with $\Pi_{N_j}^b$ in G_a for every $N_j \in (W' - W)$, removes W' from the ordering and then inserts W' into W. The procedure repeatedly examines the next node in the ordering until all nodes are considered.

Essentially, the merge operator increases the efficiency in several ways. Since the score of the composite network can be readily calculated, it is not necessary to invoke the procedure for MDL score evaluation which is time-consuming. Thus, the merge operator offers an economical way to create new structures. Furthermore, the operator improves the search efficiency by creating more good individuals in each generation. In our current implementation, the operator merges networks at the current population with dumped networks from the last generation. Thus, it reuses the search results obtained in previous generations.

3.3 Prevention of cycle formation

Since MDLEP consumes much time in repairing networks that contain cycles, HEP prevents cycle formation in all candidate networks to handle this problem. HEP main-

tains the *connectivity matrix* containing the count of directed paths between every pair of nodes. If $X \rightarrow \cdots \rightarrow Y$ exists in a network, HEP forbids adding the edge $X \leftarrow Y$ to the network. The matrix is updated when an edge is added or removed.

The algorithm of HEP is summarized in Table 2.

4 Comparing HEP with MDLEP

In our experiments, we compare HEP against MDLEP on a number of data sets generated from the ALARM Bayesian network, which appears in [18]. The data sets have respectively 1,000, 2,000, 5,000, and 10,000 cases. Since both algorithms are stochastic in nature, we have conducted 40 trials for each experiment. The programs are executed on the same Sun Ultra-5 workstation. For HEP, we set Δ_α to be 0.02. For both algorithms, the population size is 50 and the tournament size (q) is 7. We use 5000 generations as the common termination criterion and the maximum size of parent set is set to be 5. We compare the performance under five different aspects:

- average MDL score obtained, the smaller the better (AFS),

- average score of the first generation solution (AIS),

- average running time in seconds (AET),

- average generation that the best-so-far is found (ANG),

- average number of edges added, omitted, or reversed in compared to the original structure (ASD).

Table 3 provides a summary of the performance comparison between the two algorithms. The figures are average values of 40 trials. Numbers in parentheses are the standard deviations. The structural differences between the networks obtained by Bayesian Network Power Constructor (BNPC) [3] and the original networks are also presented. It can be observed that HEP performs better than BNPC, because the ASD values of HEP are smaller than those of BNPC in all data sets.

For all data sets, HEP could always find better or equally good network structures in terms of both MDL score (AFS) and structural difference (ASD). The difference is statistically significant at 0.05 level for all data sets. If we compare the ANG statistics, it is found that HEP uses much less generations to obtain the final solution (statistically significant at 0.05 level using a one-tailed t-test). Given that HEP and MDLEP essentially use the same formulation in searching, the experimental results readily suggest that HEP is more efficient as it uses fewer generations to obtain similar, or better, solutions. From the AET statistics, HEP uses much

CI Test Phase

1. For every pair of nodes (X, Y),
   - Perform order-0 and all order-1 CI tests.
   - Store the highest p-value in the matrix Pv.

Evolutionary Programming Search Phase

1. Set t, the generation count, to 0.
2. Initialize the value of m, the population size.
3. For each individual in the population Pop(t),
   - initialize the α value randomly.
   - refine the search space by checking the α value against the Pv matrix.
   - Inside the reduced search space, create a DAG randomly.
4. Each DAG in the population is evaluated using the MDL metric.
5. While t is less than the maximum number of generations,
   - select $m/2$ individuals from Pop(t), the rest are marked "NS" (not selected)
   - For each of the selected ones,
     - merge with a random pick from the dumped half in Pop$'(t-1)$.
     - If merge does not produce a new structure, mark the individual with "NS"
     - otherwise, regard the new structure as an offspring.
   - For each individual marked "NS",
     - produce an offspring by cloning.
     - alter the α value of the offspring by a possible increment or decrement of Δ_α.
     - refine the search space by checking the α value against the Pv matrix.
     - change the structure by performing a number of mutation operations. Note that cycle formation is prohibited.
   - The DAGs in Pop(t) and all new offspring are stored in the intermediate population Pop$'(t)$. The size of Pop$'(t)$ is 2*m.
   - Conduct a number of pairwise competitions over all DAGs in Pop$'(t)$. For each DAG G_i in the population, q other individuals are selected. The fitness of G_i is compared against the q individuals. The score of G_i is the number of individuals (out of q) that are worse than G_i.
   - Select the m highest score individuals from Pop$'(t)$ with ties broken randomly. The individuals are stored in Pop($t + 1$).
   - increment t by 1
6. Return the individual that has the lowest MDL metric in any generation of a run as the output of the algorithm.

Table 2. Algorithm of HEP.

Size		AFS	AIS	AET	ANG	ASD
1000	HEP	17,880.56 (31.9)	24,323.5 (1,186.6)	204.75 (3.9)	817.6 (1,163.0)	11.15 (2.3)
	MDLEP	17,990.5 (73.1)	30,831.0 (795.6)	1,003.9 (70.8)	4,301.2 (654.3)	19.4 (4.2)
	BNPC	–	–	–	–	20
2000	HEP	33,777.8 (62.9)	44,199.45 (1,324.9)	225.63 (10.0)	1,410.78 (1,540.2)	9.05 (1.4)
	MDLEP	33,932.6 (215.8)	56,896.6 (1,259.5)	1,307.8 (125.1)	4,046.6 (634.1)	12.9 (4.9)
	BNPC	–	–	–	–	15
5000	HEP	81,004 (0.0)	102,310.02 (2,352.0)	290.3 (11.9)	448.57 (796.0)	6.05 (0.5)
	MDLEP	81,287.6 (419.9)	134,487.2 (1,836.0)	1,843.2 (359.0)	3,946.3 (651.2)	10.7 (4.9)
	BNPC	–	–	–	–	10
10000	HEP	158,498.5 (298.5)	199,210.75 (5,082.8)	384.77 (27.5)	970.42 (879.4)	4.53 (2.8)
	MDLEP	158,704.4 (513.1)	256,946.2 (3,843.7)	2,435.1 (350.1)	3,596.7 (720.0)	8.7 (5.1)
	BNPC	–	–	–	–	10

Table 3. Performance comparison between HEP and MDLEP

less time to finish than MDLEP under the same termination criterion.

If we compare the AIS statistics, it is clear that HEP could often have a better starting point than MDLEP. Apparently, this is also the benefit of the hybrid approach as we take CI test results into consideration rather than to initialize the population randomly.

5 Application in direct marketing

In this section, we investigate the feasibility of applying Bayesian networks on a real world data mining problem. The problem relates with direct marketing in which the objective is to predict buyers from a list of customers. Advertising campaign, which includes mailing of catalogs or brochure, is then targeted on the most promising prospects. Hence, if the prediction is accurate, it can help to enhance the *response rate* of the advertising campaign and increase the return of investment (ROI). The direct marketing problem requires ranking the customer list by the likelihood of purchase [19, 1]. Given that Bayesian networks estimate the posterior probability of an instance (a customer) belonging to a particular class (active or inactive respondents), they are particularly suitable for handling the direct marketing problem.

5.1 The direct marketing problem

Direct marketing concerns communication with prospects, so as to elicit response from them. In contrast to the mass marketing approach, direct marketing is targeted on a group of individuals that are potential buyers and are likely to respond. In retrospect, direct marketing emerged because of the prevalence of mail ordering in the nineteenth century [14]. As technology advances, marketing is no longer restricted to mailing but includes a variety of media. Nevertheless, the most important issue in the business remains to be the maximization of the profitability, or ROI, of a marketing campaign.

In a typical scenario, we often have a huge list of customers. This list could be records of existing customers or data bought from *list brokers*. But among the huge list, there are usually few real buyers which amount to a few percents [2]. Since the budget of a campaign is limited, it is important to focus the effort on the most promising prospects so that the response rate could be improved.

Before computers became widely used, direct marketers often used simple heuristics to enhance the response rate. One straightforward approach is to use common sense to make the decision. In particular, we could match prospects by examining the demographics of the customers in the list. For example, in the life insurance industry, it is natural to target the advertising at those who are rich and aging. Another common approach to enhance the response rate is to conduct list testing by evaluating the response of samplings from the list. If a certain group of customers gives a high response rate, the actual campaign may be targeted on the customers similar to this group. A more systematic approach, which was developed in 1920s but is still being used today, is to differentiate potential buyers from non-buyers using the recency-frequency-monetary model (RFM) [14]. In essence, the profitability of a customer is estimated by three factors including the recency of buying, the frequency of buying, and the amount of money spent. Hence, only individuals that are profitable will be the targets of the campaign.

With the advancement of computing and database technology, people seek for computational approaches to assist in decision making. From the data set that contains demographic details of customers, the objective is to develop a *response model* and use the model to predict promising prospects. In certain sense, response models are similar to classifiers in the classification problem. However, unlike the classifier which makes a dichotomous decision (i.e. active or inactive respondents), the response model needs to score each customer in the data set with the likelihood of purchase. The customers are then ranked according to the score. A ranked list is desired because it allows decision makers to select the portion of customer list to roll out [19]. For instance, out of the 200,000 customers on the list, we might wish to send out catalogs or brochures to the most promising 30% of customers so that the advertising campaign is cost-effective (the 30% of the best customers to be mailed is referred to as the *depth-of-file*) [1]. Hence, one way to evaluate the response model is to look at its performance at different depth-of-file.

5.2 Experiment

Because Bayesian networks can estimate the probability of an object belonging to certain class(es), they are suitable to handle the direct marketing problem. By assuming the estimated probability to be equal to the likelihood of purchase, a Bayesian network is readily applicable to the direct marketing problem. Thus, it is interesting to evaluate the empirical performance of Bayesian network response models. Specifically, we compare the performance of the evolved Bayesian network models obtained by HEP and MDLEP, the logistic regression models, the naïve Bayesian classifier (NB) [5, 11], and the tree-augmented naïve Bayesian network classifier (TAN) [5]. NB simplifies the estimation of the joint probability distribution by assuming that each attribute is conditionally independent of others given the class variable. Although the assumption behind the naïve Bayesian classifier seems unrealistic [5], the classifier often exhibits surprisingly good and robust performance in many real-life problems [11]. TAN contains augmented edges which form a spanning tree. It is regarded as the state-of-the-art Bayesian network classifier [9].

For both HEP and MDLEP, the population size is 50, the maximum number of generations is 5000, and the tournament size (q) is 7. The maximum size of parent set is 5. For HEP, Δ_α is set to 0.02.

5.2.1 Experimental methodology

The response models are evaluated on a real-life direct marketing data set. It contains records of customers of a specialty catalog company, which mails catalogs to good customers on a regular basis. There is a total of 106,284 customers in the data set and each entry is described by 361 attributes. The response rate is 5.4%.

Typically in any data mining process, it is necessary to reduce the dimension of the data set by selecting the attributes that are considered relevant and necessary. Towards this feature selection process, there are many possible options. For instance, we could use either a *wrapper* or a *filter* selection process [16]. In a wrapper selection process, different combinations are iteratively tried and evaluated by building an actual model out of the selected attributes. In a filter selection process, a certain evaluation function, which is based on information theory or statistics, is defined to score a particular combination of attributes. Then, the final combination is obtained in a search process. In this experiment, we use a manual selection procedure. We have selected nine attributes, which are relevant to the prediction, out of the 361 attributes.

To compare the performance of different response models, we use decile analysis which estimates the enhancements of the response rates for marketing at different depth-of-file. Essentially, the ranked list is equally divided into ten deciles. Customers in the first decile are the top ranked customers that are most likely to give response. On the other hand, customers in the tenth decile are ranked lowest. Then, a *gains table* is constructed to describe the performance of the response model. In a gains table, we collect various statistics at each decile, including [15]:

Percentage of Active: It is the percentage of active respondents in the decile.

Lift: It is calculated by dividing the percentage of active respondents by the response rate of the file. Intuitively, it estimates the enhancement by the response model in discriminating active respondents over a random approach for the current decile.

Cumulative Lift: It is calculated by dividing the cumulative percentage of active respondents by the response rate of the file. Intuitively, this evaluates how good the response model is for a given depth-of-file over a random approach. The measure provides an important estimate of the performance of the model.

5.2.2 Cross-validation results

To make a comparison concerning the robustness of the response models, we adopt a cross-validation approach for performance estimation. Specifically, we employ a 10-fold cross-validation where the ten folds are partitioned randomly. In Table 4, the experimental results for the Bayesian networks evolved by HEP (HEP models) are shown. We tabulate the statistics at each decile averaged over the ten runs. Numbers after the "$\pm$" sign are the standard deviations. Table 4 shows that the HEP models have cumulative lifts of 392.40, 287.30, and 226.70 in the first three deciles respectively, suggesting that by mailing to the top three deciles alone, the HEP models generate over twice as many respondents as a random mailing without a model.

To facilitate direct comparison, the cumulative lifts of different models are summarized in Table 5. In this table, the highest cumulative lift in each decile is highlighted in bold. The superscript + represents the cumulative life of the HEP models is significant higher at 0.05 level than that of the corresponding models. The superscript − represents the cumulative life of the HEP models is significant lower at 0.05 level than that of the corresponding models. Table 5 indicates that the logistic regression models have cumulative lifts of 342.27, 249.20, and 210.40 in the first three deciles respectively. The cumulative lifts of the HEP models are significantly higher than those of the logistic regression models at 0.05 level (*p*-values are 0.00002, 0.0, and 0.00002 respectively).

Table 5 shows that the Bayesian networks generated by MDLEP (MDLEP models) have cumulative lifts of 377.20, 287.40, and 220.40 in the first three deciles respectively. The cumulative lifts of the HEP models in the first and the third deciles are significantly higher than those of the MDLEP models at 0.05 level (*p*-values are 0.01189 and 0.00377 respectively). The TAN classifiers have cumulative lifts of 385.20, 278.00, and 220.00 in the first three deciles respectively. The cumulative lifts of the HEP models in the second and the third deciles are significantly higher than those of the TAN classifiers at 0.05 level (*p*-values are 0.00063 and 0.00008 respectively). The NB classifiers have cumulative lifts of 378.10, 274.40, and 222.20 in the first three deciles respectively. The cumulative lifts of the HEP models in the first three deciles are significantly higher than those of the NB classifiers at 0.05 level (*p*-values are 0.00301, 0.00089, and 0.02793 respectively). Overall, the HEP models perform significantly better than the other models in predicting consumer response to direct mailing promotions.

Decile	Percent Actives	Lift	Cum. Lift
1	21.21% ± 1.34%	392.4 ± 19.36	392.4 ± 19.36
2	9.88% ± 0.87%	182.3 ± 12.48	287.3 ± 6.18
3	5.69% ± 0.64%	105.1 ± 12.60	226.7 ± 6.15
4	4.84% ± 0.63%	89.3 ± 13.37	192.2 ± 3.94
5	3.47% ± 0.78%	63.8 ± 13.80	166.6 ± 3.17
6	2.96% ± 0.72%	54.1 ± 12.91	147.7 ± 1.34
7	2.07% ± 0.51%	37.8 ± 8.69	132.2 ± 0.92
8	1.58% ± 0.27%	28.6 ± 4.65	119.2 ± 1.03
9	1.38% ± 0.36%	25.0 ± 7.06	108.8 ± 0.42
10	0.92% ± 0.28%	16.6 ± 5.13	100.0 ± 0.00

Table 4. Results of the HEP models.

Decile	HEP	Logistic regression	MDLEP	TAN	NB
0	**392.4** (19.36)	342.7+ (12.82)	377.2+ (20.04)	385.2 (18.73)	378.1+ (14.18)
1	287.3 (6.18)	249.2+ (7.96)	**287.4** (6.90)	278.0+ (8.89)	274.4+ (8.91)
2	**226.7** (6.15)	210.4+ (5.10)	220.4+ (2.84)	220.0+ (4.81)	222.2+ (4.37)
3	192.2 (3.94)	186.7+ (2.58)	**200.0−** (4.57)	187.4+ (3.78)	187.6+ (3.53)
4	**166.6** (3.17)	163.1+ (1.45)	160.6+ (3.37)	164.0+ (2.91)	162.5+ (1.90)
5	147.7 (1.34)	144.9+ (1.52)	**150.1−** (2.47)	145.1+ (2.02)	145.3+ (1.64)
6	**132.2** (0.92)	130.7+ (1.49)	128.7+ (2.11)	130.9+ (0.88)	130.5+ (1.18)
7	**119.2** (1.03)	118.4 (1.35)	118.7 (0.95)	118.4+ (0.97)	118.9 (1.10)
8	108.8 (0.42)	108.2+ (0.42)	**110.9−** (0.32)	108.1+ (0.74)	108.1+ (0.57)
9	100.0 (0.00)	100.0 (0.00)	100.0 (0.00)	100.0 (0.00)	100.0 (0.00)

Table 5. Cumulative lifts of different models.

The average execution time and the corresponding standard deviations for different methods are summarized in

Table 6. Although HEP is slower than logistic regression, TAN, and NB, it is much faster than MDLEP. Moreover, HEP is able to learn Bayesian networks from a large database in one minute. Thus, it can be used in real-life data mining applications.

	HEP	Logistic regression	MDLEP	TAN	NB
Average (sec.)	54.676	6.355	1999.04	20.101	19.598
Std.	3.838	0.5035	324.695	1.1503	0.9727

Table 6. The execution time for different methods.

Since an advertising campaign often involves huge investment, a response model which can categorize more prospects into the target list is valuable as it will enhance the response rate. From the experimental results, it seems that the HEP models are more desirable than the other models.

6 Conclusion

In this paper, we have described a new algorithm, HEP, for learning Bayesian networks efficiently. We have applied HEP to a data set of direct marketing and compared the Bayesian networks obtained by HEP and the models generated by other methods. From the experimental results, the HEP models predict more accurately than the other models. This study shows that HEP can potentially become a powerful and efficient data mining tool for direct marketing problems.

In our current implementation, we change the cutoff value of an offspring by arbitrarily increasing or decreasing a fixed value of Δ_α from the parent's value. However, it is also possible to use an adaptive mutation strategy such that the Δ_α will become smaller as time proceeds. In effect, the search space is gradually stabilized which may lead to a further speed up. In future, we will explore this and other alternatives that are worth investigating.

Acknowledgments

This research was partially supported by the RGC Earmarked Grant LU 3012/01E.

References

[1] S. Bhattacharyya. Direct marketing response models using genetic algorithms. In *Proceedings of the Fourth International Conference on Knowledge Discovery and Data Mining*, pages 144–148, 1998.

[2] P. Cabena, P. Hadjinian, R. Stadler, J. Verhees, and A. Zansi. *Discovering Data Mining: From Concept to Implementation.* Prentice-Hall Inc., 1997.

[3] J. Cheng, R. Greiner, J. Kelly, D. Bell, and W. Liu. Learning Bayesian network from data: An information-theory based approached. *Artificial Intelligence*, 137:43–90, 2002.

[4] U. M. Fayyad, G. Piatetsky-Shapiro, P. Smyth, and R. Uthurusamy, editors. *Advances in Knowledge Discovery and Data Mining.* AAAI Press, 1996.

[5] N. Friedman, D. Geiger, and M. Goldszmidt. Bayesian network classifiers. *Machine Learning*, 29:131–163, 1997.

[6] D. Heckerman. A tutorial on learning Bayesian networks. Technical report, Microsoft Research, Advanced Technology Division, March 1995.

[7] E. Herskovits and G. Cooper. A Bayesian method for the induction of probabilistic networks from data. *Machine Learning*, 9(4):309–347, 1992.

[8] F. V. Jensen. *An Introduction to Bayesian Network.* University of College London Press, 1996.

[9] E. J. Keogh and M. J. Pazzani. Learning augmented Bayesian classifiers: A comparison of distribution-based and classification-based approaches. In D. Heckerman and J. Whittaker, editors, *Proceedings of the Seventh International Workshop on AI and Statistics*, pages 225–230, Fort Lauderdale, Florida, January 1999. Morgan Kaufmann.

[10] W. Lam and F. Bacchus. Learning Bayesian belief networks-an approach based on the MDL principle. *Computational Intelligence*, 10(4):269–293, 1994.

[11] P. Langley and S. Sage. Induction of selective Bayesian classifier. In R. L. de Mantaras and D. Poole, editors, *Proceedings of the Tenth Conference on Uncertainty in Artificial Intelligence*, Seattle, Washington, July 1994. Morgan Kaufmann.

[12] P. Larrañaga, M. Poza, Y. Yurramendi, R. Murga, and C. Kuijpers. Structural learning of Bayesian network by genetic algorithms: A performance analysis of control parameters. *IEEE Transactions on Pattern Analysis and Machine Intelligence*, 18(9):912–926, September 1996.

[13] J. Pearl. *Probabilistic Reasoning in Intelligent Systems: Networks of Plausible Inference.* Morgan Kaufmann, 1988.

[14] L. A. Petrison, R. C. Blattberg, and P. Wang. Database marketing: Past present, and future. *Journal of Direct Marketing*, 11(4):109–125, 1997.

[15] O. P. Rud. *Data Mining Cookbook: modeling data for marketing, risk and customer relationship management.* Wiley, New York, 2001.

[16] M. Singh. *Learning Bayesian Networks for Solving Real-World Problems.* PhD thesis, University of Pennsylvania, 1998.

[17] P. Spirtes, C. Glymour, and R. Scheines. *Causation, Prediction, and Search.* MIT Press, MA, second edition, 2000.

[18] M. L. Wong, W. Lam, and K. S. Leung. Using evolutionary programming and minimum description length principle for data mining of Bayesian networks. *IEEE Transactions on Pattern Analysis and Machine Intelligence*, 21(2):174–178, February 1999.

[19] J. Zahavi and N. Levin. Issues and problems in applying neural computing to target marketing. *Journal of Direct Marketing*, 11(4):63–75, 1997.

Adapting Information Extraction Knowledge For Unseen Web Sites*

Tak-Lam Wong and Wai Lam
Department of Systems Engineering and Engineering Management
The Chinese University of Hong Kong
Hong Kong
{wongtl,wlam}@se.cuhk.edu.hk

Abstract

We propose a wrapper adaptation framework which aims at adapting a learned wrapper to an unseen Web site. It significantly reduces human effort in constructing wrappers. Our framework makes use of extraction rules previously discovered from a particular site to seek potential training example candidates for an unseen site. Rule generalization and text categorization are employed for finding suitable example candidates. Another feature of our approach is that it makes use of the previously discovered lexicon to classify good training examples automatically for the new site. We conducted extensive experiments to evaluate the quality of the extraction performance and the adaptability of our approach.

1 Introduction

World-Wide Web has been growing rapidly providing a large amount of information electronically in a wide spectrum of areas. Human browsing and keyword searching are two common approaches for retrieving useful information from the Web. The lack of automation and large quantity of irrelevant data returned raise the need of a system that can automatically extract useful information precisely. Information Extraction (IE) aims at identifying useful text fragments from textual documents such as newswire articles or Web pages [3]. IE systems are concerned with transforming unstructured or semi-structured documents into structured data. The data extracted can then be stored in a database or used for other intelligent processing exemplified by online comparison-shopping agents [5].

Various IE techniques have been proposed to deal with different kinds of textual documents ranging from highly structured texts to free texts [7]. Some IE systems are designed to extract information from natural language texts. For example, in the "Latin American terrorism" domain in the Message Understanding Conferences (MUCs) [4], IE systems for this problem try to extract the perpetrator names, victim names, instruments, and location of attacks from a collection of newswire articles on Latin American terrorism. Another example is the Question-Answering track in the Text REtrieval Conference (TREC) [17]. It aims at finding a short phrase or sentence that precisely answers a user's question from a text collection. Natural language processing (NLP) techniques are usually required for IE systems to deal with free texts. Other IE systems are designed to handle texts organized in a rigid and highly-structured format. These systems usually make use of uniform syntactic rules such as labels and mark-up tags which delimit the text fragment to be extracted [1].

Unlike free texts and structured texts, Web documents are a kind of semi-structured texts. Semi-structured texts are characterized by the fact that they are not grammatical and not organized in a structured format. NLP techniques and uniform syntactic rules for structured text cannot apply well to semi-structured texts directly. This makes information extraction from semi-structured texts a challenging task.

Various IE techniques for Web documents have been proposed. Many of these techniques make use of wrappers. A wrapper usually contains extraction rules or patterns which can identify attribute items in a HTML document. Wrappers are constructed manually in the past [9]. Heavy involvement of human work makes wrapper construction become error-prone, tedious, costly, and time-consuming. They also require high-level of expertise. This raises the need of automatic wrapper construction by using machine learning techniques.

A number of wrapper learning techniques [8, 10, 12, 15, 16] have been proposed. Wrapper learning systems generate extraction rules based on attribute item annotations pre-

---

*The work described in this paper was partially supported by grants from the Research Grant Council of the Hong Kong Special Administrative Region, China (Project Nos.: CUHK 4385/99E and CUHK 4187/01E).

pared by users. The annotations are treated as training examples during the learning process. However, the wrappers discovered by these existing techniques can only handle Web documents coming from the same information source. The wrapper learned from one information source cannot apply to other information sources. In principle, a separate effort for attribute item annotations is required for each information source. Wrapper adaptation can help solve this problem.

Maintenance of wrappers is another problem for existing wrapper learning techniques. The layout of Web pages changes from time to time. Wrapper constructed previously may become obsolete when the layout has changed.

A system called RAPTURE [11] is developed for the wrapper verification problem by regression approach. Another system called WebCQ [14] is designed for detecting the changes in Web documents. Both of them can only partially solve the the wrapper maintenance problem. A system called $(LP)^2$ [2] is an adaptive algorithm for information extraction from Web documents. It makes use of shallow natural language processing and bottom-up generalization in the extraction rule learning. Recently, a neural-network based approach has been proposed to refine information extraction knowledge [6]. However, the extraction knowledge needs to be provided by users manually in advance. All of the above approaches focus on extraction of information from the same source and cannot adapt a learned wrapper to a new source.

In order to tackle the above problems and reduce the effort users involved, we develop a novel approach, known as WrapMA (Wrapper Mining and Adaptation for Web Sites). WrapMA consists of two major components, namely, the wrapper mining component and the wrapper adaptation component. The wrapper mining component is based on our previous approach on hierarchical extraction rule learning algorithm [13]. By providing user annotated training examples, the wrapper mining component can learn the hierarchical record structure and extraction rules tailored to an information source automatically. It can handle both missing attribute items and multi-valued attribute items. The attribute items can also appear in different orders. Most of the existing wrapper induction techniques only consider the surrounding texts of the attribute item. Instead, our wrapper mining component also considers the content of the attribute item itself to enrich the expressiveness of the extraction rules.

The wrapper adaptation component aims at adapting a learned wrapper to an unseen information source. To achieve this goal, we make use of extraction rules previously discovered from a particular site to seek potential candidates of training examples for an unseen site. Rule generalization and text categorization are employed for finding suitable example candidates. The rationale of rule generalization is to relax the constraint of exact matching of previously learned extraction rules. The text categorization model attempts to capture the knowledge of identifying the characteristics of training examples. Another feature of our approach is that it makes use of the previously discovered lexicon to classify good training examples automatically. The overall degree of confidence of these potential candidates being "good" positive training examples for the unseen Web site can then be predicted via the evidence combination algorithm. Hence the training examples in the target Web site can be automatically annotated. Based on the automatically annotated training examples, a new wrapper for this unseen Web site can then be discovered. We present encouraging experimental results on wrapper adaptation for real-world Web sites.

2 Overview of WrapMA

WrapMA consists of two core components, namely, the wrapper mining component and the wrapper adaptation component. The purpose of the wrapper mining component is to learn the wrapper for a particular Web site. The goal of the wrapper adaptation component is to adapt a learned wrapper to an unseen Web site.

Figure 1 shows an example of a Web page containing information about electronic appliance catalog. The attribute items of interest are model number, descriptions, list price, final price, and availability. In this example, the first product has a model number "Kenwood DVD Home Theater System HTB404DV", a list of descriptions "100 Watts x 6", "5 Voice-Matched Satellites", "8" Passive Subwoofer" and "DV505 DVD/CD Changer", a list price "750.00", a final price "649.95", and an availability "In Stock". A user can simply provide samples of attribute items on a Web page via a graphical user interface. After WrapMA collects some samples, it invokes the wrapper mining component to discover the extraction rules of the wrapper. The learned wrapper is able to automatically extract precise information from different Web pages in the same site.

Our previous work has presented the design of the wrapper mining component [13]. We make use of a hierarchical record structure to model the relationship among the attribute items in a record. The hierarchical record structure for the above Web site is shown in Figure 2. A hierarchical record structure is a tree-like structure. The root node represents a record which consists of one or more attribute items. An internal node represents a certain fragment of its parent node. An internal node can be a repetition, which may consist of another sub-tree or a leaf node. The child of the repetition node may appear repeatedly. A leaf node represents an attribute item of interest. The hierarchical record structure may contain one or more levels. There is no fixed ordering among the nodes in the same level. It also allows

507

Figure 1. An example of Web page about electronic appliance catalog

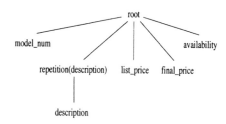

Figure 2. Hierarchical record structure for the electronic appliance information shown in Figure 1

missing items. These features can model both missing and multi-valued attribute items within a record.

There is a set of extraction rules associated with each node in the hierarchical record structure. The extraction rule of the root node is to identify each record inside the document. The extraction rule of the internal nodes will be applied to their parents to extract the appropriate fragments. For a repetition node, the extraction rules will be applied iteratively to extract multiple elements from its parent. The attribute items extracted are then grouped together according to the hierarchical record structure.

An extraction rule consists of three parts: the left pattern component, the right pattern component, and the target component. The following is one of the extraction rules for the final price for the Web document in Figure 1:

Left pattern component	Target component	Right pattern component
Scan_Until("Your"), *Scan_Until("Price"),* *Scan_Until(":"),* *Scan_Until("$").*	*Contain(<NUMBER>).*	*Scan_Until("</b>"),* *Scan_Until("<font class='n'>"),* *Scan_Until("Availability"),* *Scan_Until(":").*

Both of the left and right pattern components make use of a token scanning instruction, *Scan_Until()*, to identify the left and right boundaries of the attribute item. The token scanning instruction instructs the wrapper to scan and consume any token until a particular token matching is found. The argument of the instruction can be a token or a semantic class. For the target component, it makes use of an instruction, *Contain()*, to represent the context of the attribute item. An extraction rule learning algorithm is developed

based on a covering-based learning algorithm. The details of the wrapper mining component can be found in [13].

Our next goal is to adapt a learned wrapper from one Web site to an unseen Web site of the same domain. This can reduce the human effort of providing samples for unseen Web sites. This capability is also useful for wrapper maintenance when the layout of the Web site has been changed and the old wrapper can no longer be used correctly.

We develop the wrapper adaptation framework in WrapMA. It aims at discovering new training examples of an unseen information source. There are two major stages. The first stage is to seek the potential candidates of training examples from the target Web site. To achieve this task, we make use of extraction rules previously learned from a particular site. The second stage is to classify the potential candidates. Rule generalization, text categorization, and lexicon approximate matching are used to score the potential candidate and identify "good" training examples. The rationale of rule generalization is to relax the constraint of exact matching of previously learned extraction rules. The text categorization model attempts to capture the knowledge of identifying the characteristics of training examples. In addition, we make use of the previously discovered lexicon to classify good training examples automatically. The overall degree of confidence of being "good" positive training examples for the unseen Web site can then be predicted via the evidence combination algorithm.

3 Seeking Potential Training Example Candidates

As mentioned before, the first stage of wrapper adaptation is to make use of extraction rules previously learned from a particular site to seek potential training example candidates for the unseen site. Recall that a Web document can be regarded as a sequence of text tokens. A token can be a word, number, punctuation, date, HTML tag, specific ASCII character, or domain specific contents like *price* and *product feature*. We define a *segment* to be a sequence of continuous tokens in a Web page not containing any HTML tags. For each attribute item of interest, our method will first try to locate potential candidates using the target component of the previously learned extraction rules. The initial candidate is the segment containing the pattern of the target component. Next, we try to produce a set of potential candidates by extending this segment forward and backward. A parameter T is used to control the seeking window size.

We define *Pre-Candidate* and *After-Candidate* for identifying the position of the beginning and the ending element of a potential candidate. For a candidate c, *Pre-Candidate* is defined as the position of the first element of the segment immediately before the segment of the candidate c. A set of {*Pre-Candidate*} is generated by extending the initial candidate c_0 backward for a seeking window size T. Similarly, *After-Candidate* is defined as the position of the last element of the segment immediately after the segment of the candidate c. A set of {*After-Candidate*} is generated by extending the initial candidate c_0 forward for a seeking window size T.

After the positions are identified, all the combinations of {*Pre-Candidate*} and {*After-Candidate*} constitute the potential candidates for the attribute item of interest. For example, if {*Pre-Candidate*} $= \{s_1, s_2, s_3\}$ and {*After-Candidate*} $= \{e_1, e_2, e_3\}$, a set of potential candidates is generated as follows:

$$\{(s_1, e_1), (s_1, e_2), (s_1, e_3), (s_2, e_1), (s_2, e_2),$$
$$(s_2, e_3), (s_3, e_1), (s_3, e_2), (s_3, e_3)\}$$

where (s_i, e_j) denotes a candidate with starting position at s_i and ending position at e_j.

Once the potential candidates for an attribute item of interest are identified, they are further considered to determine the confidence of being correct training samples.

4 Classifying Good Candidates

4.1 Rule Generalization

The objective of rule generalization is to relax the requirement of exact matching of the extraction rules. It allows the process for generalizing a specific token into a more generalized form by relaxing some constraints. For example, "*<IMG SRC="./a.html">*" can be matched with "*<IMG SRC="./b.html">*" because both of them represent the image object in HTML documents, namely, "*HTML_IMAGE*". Moreover, "*HTML_IMAGE*" and other HTML tags, say "*<a>*", can also be matched because they are HTML tags. We organize the tokens and semantic classes as a hierarchical structure. For example, Figure 3 depicts the semantic classes appeared in the following fragment of a HTML document:

Now Sell : $ < B > 265.95 < /B >< BR >

Let f_1 be the score reflecting the degree of matching of a candidate with a particular rule. An exact match of the token scanning elements with the candidate text will give the full matching score, i.e.: $f_1 = 1$. Suppose a rule is not matched with the candidate. Each token scanning element of the left (or right) pattern component will relax its constraint by moving one level upper in the semantic class hierarchy. For each relaxation of the token scanning element, a penalty p will be introduced to calculate the matching score, where $0 < p < 1$. Then

$$f_1 = \sum_{i=1}^{n} \frac{(1-p)^{q_i}}{n}$$

where q_i is the number of relaxation for the i-th token scanning element, and n is the number of of token scanning element in the rule. For example, a token scanning element *Scan_Until("<FONT SIZE = "+1">")* of a left (or right) pattern component will match with the left (or

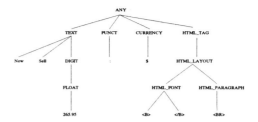

Figure 3. Examples of semantic classes

right) token of a candidate, "*<FONT SIZE = "+1">*", with a matching score $f_1 = 1$. *Scan_Until("<FONT SIZE = "+1">")* will match with "*<FONT SIZE = "+2">*" with $f_1 = (1 - p)$ because the token scanning element need to move one level upper in the semantic class hierarchy to the "*<FONT>*" level in order to match with the candidate. *Scan_Until("<FONT SIZE = "+1">")* will match with "*
" with $f_1 = (1 - p)^2$ because the token scanning element need to move one more level upper to the "<HTML_LAYOUT>*" level. This relaxation process terminates when the relaxed rule matches with the candidates. Then the matching score of the candidate with a particular rule can be computed. Recall that there may be more than one rule in the rule set for a particular attribute item. Hence the final f_1 of the candidate will be obtained by selecting the maximum matching score among all the scores calculated based on the rules in the rule set. This relaxation makes the extraction rules learned from one information source possible for finding training examples automatically from a new information source.

4.2 Text Categorization Model

We identify a set of features for characterizing the content of an attribute item. A text categorization model can be generated based on the training data in the source Web site. Then the degree of confidence of a potential candidate being "good" training example can be predicted by the model. We identify a set of features to represent the characteristics of the content of an attribute item. The features are:

1. **length:** number of characters in the content

2. **token count:** number of tokens in the content

3. **mean token length:** average number of characters in each token in the content

4. **digit density:** proportion of digits in the content

5. **letter density:** proportion of alphabetic characters in the content

6. **uppercase density:** proportion of uppercase characters in the content

7. **lowercase density:** proportion of lowercase characters in the content

8. **punctuation density:** proportion of punctuation symbols in the content

9. **HTML density:** proportion of HTML tags in the content

The positive examples are prepared based on the training examples in the source site. The negative examples are prepared by selecting text fragments near the positive examples within a windows size. Suppose a positive example exists starting at the i-th token and ending at the j-th token, We construct the negative examples by taking the text fragments which start at $(i - r_1)$-th (or $(i + r_1)$-th) token and ends at the $(j - r_2)$-th (or $(j + r_2)$-th) token, where r_1 and r_2 are two randomly generated number. All feature values of an example are normalized by using the cosine normalization. After collecting the examples, a text categorization model can be learned. To learn the model, we employ Support Vector Machines (SVM) [18], a machine learning technique.

After a SVM model has been learned, it will be used during the process of classification of candidates. Each potential candidate is represented by the same set of features. Then a score f_2 can be computed by this SVM model to predict the degree of confidence of a potential candidate being "good" training examples.

4.3 Lexicon Approximate Matching

For each attribute item in the same domain, we maintain a lexicon by storing the items automatically collected from different sites. For example, there is a lexicon containing description entries for the description attribute in the electronic appliance domain. This previously discovered lexicon can help determine good training examples for an unseen site. Precisely, the content of a lexicon can be taken into consideration for classifying the potential candidates. Both of the lexicon and potential candidates need to be pre-processed in advance. Firstly, stop words, such as *is, am, are, etc.*, are removed. Secondly, each word in different morphological forms should be reduced to its word stem. For example, "computes" and "computing" should be reduced to the word stem "comput". We employ a technique called *stemming* to achieve this task.

Suppose a potential candidate is represented by a vector $d = [d_1 d_2 ... d_q]$ where $d_i = 1$ if the candidate consists of the token T_i; otherwise, $d_i = 0$. Let the previously discovered lexicon contains $L_1, L_2, ..., L_r$ where each L_i is represented by a vector $l_i = [l_{i1} l_{i2} ... l_{iq}]$ where $l_{ij} = 1$ if L_i consists of the token T_j; otherwise, $l_{ij} = 0$. Then the score, f_3, of a potential candidate is computed by the following two steps. The first step is to calculate the cosine similarity between the candidate and each of the entry in the lexicon. The second step is to take the maximum value from all the similarity values. Therefore, f_3 is given as follows:

$$f_3 = \max_i \{ \frac{\sum_j d_j l_{ij}}{\sqrt{(\sum_j d_j^2)(\sum_j l_{ij}^2)}} \}$$

4.4 Evidence Combination

An overall score will be calculated for each candidate to reflecting goodness of the candidate being a positive example for the new site. Recall that f_1, f_2, and f_3 are the scores computed in rule generalization, text categorization model, and lexicon approximate matching respectively. For each candidate, the overall score is calculated by combining evidences using a weighted scoring scheme as:

$$Cscore = \sum_k \alpha_k f_k \quad \text{and} \quad \sum_k \alpha_k = 1$$

where $Cscore$ is the overall score of a candidate; α_k is the weight for f_k; $0 \leq \alpha_k \leq 1$; and $k = 1, 2, 3$.

We define node n_{ij} to be the j-th node on the i-th level in the hierarchical record structure. The root node is at level 0. For a particular node in the hierarchical record structure, $Pscore$ of this node is defined as the maximum of the $Cscore$ among all of its candidates. Assume that there are m candidates for the node n_{ij} in the hierarchical record structure, $Pscore$ of this node is defined as:

$$Pscore(n_{ij}) = \max\{Cscore_1, \cdots, Cscore_m\}$$

Based on the hierarchical record structure, a final score will be determined for a record candidate to represent the similarity between all attribute items of that record and the corresponding extraction rules. The final score for a particular record candidate is calculated by propagating the individual similarity score for each node in the hierarchical record structure in a bottom up fashion.

$$Score(n_{ij}) = \begin{cases} Pscore(n_{ij}) \text{ if } n_{ij} \text{ is a leaf node} \\ \beta Pscore(n_{ij}) + \frac{1-\beta}{c_{ij}}[Score(n_{(i+1)1}) \\ \quad + \cdots + Score(n_{(i+1)(c_{ij})})] \text{ otherwise} \end{cases}$$

where $Score(n_{ij})$ is the finalized score of node n_{ij} in the structure for a record candidate; c_{ij} is the number of children of n_{ij} in the structure; and β is a parameter controlling the weighting of the parent score to its children score.

The score of a particular node in the structure is dependent on the scores of its children. For a leaf node in the structure, its score remains unchanged. For an internal node in the structure, its score is a weighted score of its own score and the scores of its children.

Those record candidates with finalized score exceeding a pre-defined threshold δ are regarded as good training records. The candidates within these records are treated as training examples of attribute items of interest. In a training record, there may be many candidates for a particular attribute item of interest. We select the one with highest $Cscore$ as the training example. We design a method to annotate training examples for attribute items. For a particular attribute item of interest, we first select the candidate with the highest $Cscore$ and mark this score as $MAXCscore$. Then, we use another pre-defined threshold γ, which is a small number. For those candidates with $(Cscore - \gamma)$ exceeding δ are treated as training examples of that particular attribute item of interest. We adopt this strategy because we want to select those candidates with "near-maximum"

	Web site	URL	Total number of Records
S1	AAAprice.com	http://www.aaaprice.com	174
S2	CircuitCity.com	http://www.circutcity.com	337
S3	Overstock.com	http://www.overstock.com	203
S4	1-888Camcorder.com	http://www.1888camcorder.com	200
S5	Etronics.com	http://www.etronics.com	169
S6	SimplyCheap.com	http://www.SimplyCheap.com	190
S7	4till9.com	http://www.4till9.com	210
S8	Micro Warehouse Inc.	http://www2.warehouse.com	120
S9	World Trade Electronics	http://www.worldtradeelectronics.com	216
S10	Zones.com	http://www.zones.com	366

Table 1. Electronic appliance Web site

Figure 4. Layout of S1 (AAAprice.com)

Cscore as the output. Optionally the automatic annotated training examples can then be further verified and revised manually to produce better training examples for the target Web site.

Once the training examples are prepared, a hierarchical record structure and the extraction rules for the target document can be learned by the wrapper mining component of WrapMA. By preparing only one set of training examples from one information source manually, WrapMA can extract information from other Web sites of the same domain.

5 Case Studies and Experiments for Electronic Appliance Domain

In order to evaluate the performance of WrapMA, we conducted experiments from several electronic appliance Web sites. Table 1 shows the information of these electronic appliance Web sites. For each record in the Web sites, the attribute items of interest are model number, price, and description. We manually extracted all items of interest from each site. Some items will be used for training and mining purpose. The remaining ones are reserved for evaluation purpose. To evaluate the extraction performance, we use two commonly used metrics, namely, *recall* and *precision*. The definition of *recall* is defined as the number of attribute instances correctly extracted divided by the total number of actual attribute instances. The definition of *precision* is defined as number of attribute instances correctly extracted divided by the total number of extracted attribute instances.

We first present a case study on wrapper mining. Next, we present a case study on wrapper adaptation. Finally, we

```
<TD ALIGN=right VALIGN=top> < IMG SRC=/img/trans_1x1.gif BORDER=0 WIDTH=1
HEIGHT=5> <BR> </TD>
<TD COLSPAN=2> <FONT SIZE=3> <A
HREF="http://store.yahoo.com/aaaprice/govideodvr4000.html"> <b> Go Video DVR-4000 </b> </A> </TD>
<TD ALIGN=right> <FONT SIZE=2 > <B>   $219.00 </TD> </TR>
<TR> <TD> </TD> <TD> < A HREF="http://store.yahoo.com/aaaprice/govideodvr4000.html"> <img
width=70 height=70 src="http://store2.yimg.com/I/aaaprice_1691_1759076" border=0> </A> </TD>
<TD> <FONT SIZE=2> DVR4000   GO VIDEO DVR4000 <font color=red> DVD </font> /VCR Combo
Unit The Go-Video DVR4000 combines a state-of-the-art <font color=red> DVD </font> player for digital quality
audio and video with a highly advanced 4 ... for movie lovers It s space-saving and easy to use One remote controls
<font color=red> DVD </font> and VCR with one-touch A/V switching between TV VCR and <font
color=red> DVD </font> deck One easy connection to your TV with Composite S-Video and ...
</FONT> </TD> <TD>
</TD> </TR>
<TR> <TD> </TD> <TD> </TD> <TD> </TD> <TD> </TD> </TR>
```

Figure 5. Fragment of the HTML code of the Web page shown in Figure 4

Attribute	Sample
model number:	Go Video DVR-4000
price:	219.00
description:	DVR4000 GO VIDEO DVR4000 <font color=red> DVD </font> /VCR Combo Unit The Go-Video DVR4000 combines a state-of-the-art <font color=red> DVD </font> player for digital quality audio and video with a highly advanced 4 ... for movie lovers It s space-saving and easy to use One remote controls <font color=red> DVD </font> and VCR with one-touch A/V switching between TV VCR and <font color=red> DVD </font> deck One easy connection to your TV with Composite S-Video and ...

Table 2. Example of a sample record for S1

discuss the experimental results of all the Web sites shown in Table 1.

5.1 Case Study on Wrapper Mining

We present a case study on wrapper mining of WrapMA in one of the Web sites, S1. Figures 4 and 5 show the layout and a fragment of the HTML code of one of the Web pages in S1. In order to learn the wrapper for S1, we make use of some manually extracted records as training examples. An example of a sample record is shown in Table 2.

The wrapper mining component is invoked to learn a wrapper using the training samples for S1. A hierarchical record structure and a set of extraction rules are discovered for the wrapper. Figure 6 shows the hierarchical record structure. Table 3 shows one of the extraction rules for the node *model_number* of the hierarchical record structure. We used the learned wrapper to extract the records in other Web pages within S1.

We obtained encouraging results; the recall and precision for the model number are 100.0% and 100.0% respectively; the recall and precision for the price are 100.0% and 100.0% respectively; the recall and precision for the description are 97.0% and 94.8%.

Figure 6. Hierarchical record structure for the Web page shown in Figure 4

Left pattern component	Target component	Right pattern component
Scan_Until("<TD COLSPAN=2>").	Contain(<WORD>)	Scan_Until("").
Scan_Until("<FONT SIZE=3>").		Scan_Until("</A>").
Scan_Until("<A>").		Scan_Until("</TD>").
Scan_Until("").		Scan_Until("<TD ALIGN=right>").

Table 3. One extraction rule for the *model_number* of the hierarchical record structure shown in Figure 6

Figure 7. Layout of S2 (CircuitCity.com)

5.2 Case Study on Wrapper Adaptation

We present a case study on adapting the learned wrapper of S1 to another Web site, S2. Figure 7 shows the layout of one of the Web pages in S2. We first used the wrapper learned from S1 to automatically annotate the training examples of S2 via the wrapper adaptation component in WrapMA.

The automatically annotated training samples can be optionally reviewed by users. We manually scrutinized the auto-annotations and mainly performed deletion for those extra text fragments in some auto-annotations. The remaining auto-annotations were used as training examples to learn the wrapper for S2 in the same manner using WrapMA. We then used the newly learned wrapper to extract the records in S2. We obtained a very satisfactory result. The recall and precision of model number are 76.7% and 98.8% respectively. The recall and precision of price are 84.5% and 100.0% respectively. The recall and precision of description are 59.6% and 77.8% respectively. On contrary, by directly applying the wrapper learned in S1 without adaptation, none of the record can be extracted in S2. It demonstrates the effectiveness of the wrapper adaptation of WrapMA.

5.3 Experimental Results for All Electronic Web Sites

We conducted extensive experiments for the wrapping mining component of WrapMA on all the Web sites listed in Table 1. Table 4 depicts the experimental results showing that the wrapping mining component has good extraction performance. The learned wrapper generally can ex-

Source	Model Number		Price		Description	
	Average Recall	Average Precision	Average Recall	Average Precision	Average Recall	Average Precision
S1	1.000	1.000	1.000	1.000	0.970	0.948
S2	0.789	0.989	0.889	0.863	0.629	0.797
S3	1.000	1.000	1.000	1.000	0.990	0.990
S4	1.000	1.000	1.000	1.000	1.000	1.000
S5	1.000	0.994	0.982	0.976	0.978	0.791
S6	0.989	0.989	1.000	1.000	0.984	0.934
S7	1.000	1.000	1.000	1.000	1.000	1.000
S8	1.000	1.000	1.000	1.000	1.000	1.000
S9	0.917	1.000	0.917	1.000	0.917	1.000
S10	0.964	0.931	0.962	0.926	0.964	0.923
Average	0.966	0.990	0.975	0.977	0.943	0.938

Table 4. Average extraction performance for applying a learned wrapper for a Web site to extract records from the same Web site in the electronic appliance domain

tract records with both average recall and average precision higher than 90%.

We also conducted extensive experiments for the wrapper adaptation component of WrapMA. We used the learned wrapper from one particular Web site and adapted to the other nine Web sites. Table 5 shows the experimental results. For instance, the row labeled with S1 refers to adapting the learned wrapper of S1 to all sites from S2 to S10. The columns labeled with "Without Adaptation" represent the extraction performance when using the wrapper directly without adaptation to extract records in other Web sites. The columns labeled with "With Adaptation" represent the extraction performance when using the wrapper adaptation component to learn a new wrapper for the unseen Web sites. The results show that the wrapper learned from a particular Web site normally cannot apply well to others. There are exceptions for S1, S4, and S6 because their layouts and the format regularities are quite close. The extraction performance with adaptation is much better than that without adaptation. The extraction performance of price attribute is good. It is due to the fact that the price often appears in a regular format. For example, the price often has one token of floating point, and appears after currency literals such as "$". The extraction of performances of model number and description are fair. The reason is that both of them may appear in different format in different Web sites. However, it demonstrates that wrapper adaptation can significantly improve the extraction performance when our adaptation framework is used.

6 Conclusions and Future Work

We have developed a wrapper mining technique which can learn information extraction rules tailored to a Web site based on sample item attribute annotations provided by users. It significantly reduces human effort in constructing wrappers. We have also investigated the problem of adapting a learned wrapper to an unseen Web site. To achieve this goal, we propose a wrapper adaptation framework which

	Model Number				Price				Description			
	Without Adaptation		With Adaptation		Without Adaptation		With Adaptation		Without Adaptation		With Adaptation	
	Ave. Rec.	Ave. Pre.	Ave. Rec.	Ave. Pre.	Ave. Rec.	Ave. Pre.	Ave. Rec.	Ave. Pre.	Ave. Rec.	Ave. Pre.	Ave. Rec.	Ave. Pre.
S1	0.221	0.221	0.625	0.610	0.222	0.222	0.865	0.853	0.219	0.220	0.879	0.859
S2	0.000	0.000	0.333	0.333	0.000	0.000	0.978	0.981	0.000	0.000	0.570	0.572
S3	0.000	0.000	0.460	0.536	0.000	0.000	0.870	0.806	0.000	0.000	0.404	0.365
S4	0.215	0.221	0.527	0.518	0.218	0.222	0.817	0.858	0.206	0.215	0.885	0.830
S5	0.000	0.000	0.658	0.653	0.000	0.000	0.880	0.878	0.000	0.000	0.000	0.000
S6	0.222	0.222	0.556	0.544	0.222	0.222	0.871	0.800	0.213	0.219	0.883	0.808
S7	0.000	0.000	0.221	0.197	0.000	0.000	0.863	0.877	0.000	0.000	0.507	0.483
S8	0.000	0.000	0.546	0.540	0.000	0.000	0.981	0.980	0.000	0.000	0.042	0.100
S9	0.000	0.000	0.653	0.652	0.000	0.000	0.982	0.982	0.000	0.000	0.270	0.277
S10	0.000	0.000	0.372	0.428	0.000	0.000	0.768	0.774	0.000	0.000	0.333	0.302
Ave.	0.066	0.066	0.495	0.501	0.066	0.067	0.888	0.879	0.064	0.065	0.477	0.460

Table 5. Average extraction performance on adapting a learned wrapper to other Web sites in the electronic appliance domain for the case with and without using the wrapper adaptation component of WrapMA. (Ave. Rec. and Ave. Pre. denote the average recall and average precision respectively.)

can automatically identifying good training examples for the target unseen Web site. We develop a candidate seeking technique to seek potential training examples in the target unseen Web site using extraction rules previously learned. Rule generalization and text categorization are employed to classify potential candidates for good training examples automatically. The text categorization model involves feature design which captures the characteristics of the content of the attribute items. Another feature of our approach is that it makes use of the previously discovered lexicon during the candidate classification process. We have conducted several case studies and extensive experiments. The results demonstrate that our wrapper adaptation framework achieves a very satisfactory results. We conducted another set of extensive experiments from several sites in the book store domain. Due to space limit, we cannot report the details of the results. However, the results demonstrate that wrapper adaptation can deal with unseen sites effectively.

Further research can be explored to improve the effectiveness. One direction is to make use of some natural language processing (NLP) techniques for the free text portion of a Web page. For example, part-of-speech tagging and lexical semantic tagging may be useful.

Another direction is to incorporate background knowledge. Very often, users may already have some background information or knowledge about the domain. We hope to develop a mechanism that can consider such information in the process of mining and adaptation. The ultimate goal is to improve the extraction quality and widen the applicability of WrapMA.

References

[1] S. Chawathe, H. Garcia-Molina, J. Hammer, K. Ireland, Y. Papakonstantinou, J. Ullman, and J.Widom. The TSIMMIS project: integration of heterogeneous information sources. *Proceedings of the Information Processing Society of Japan,* pages 7-18, 1994.

[2] F. Ciravegna. $(LP)^2$ An adaptive algorithm for information extraction from Web-related Texts. *Proceedings of the Seventeenth International Joint Conference on Artifical Intelligence,* pages 1251-1256, 2001.

[3] J. Cowie and W. Lehnert. Information Extraction. *Communications of the ACM,* 39(1):80-91, 1996.

[4] Defense Advanced Research Projects Agency. *Proceedings of the Seventh Message Understanding Conference (MUC-7).* Morgan Kaufmann Publisher, Inc., 1998.

[5] R. B. Doorenbos, O. Etzioni, and D. S. Weld. A scalable comparison-shopping agent for the World-Wide Web. *Proceedings of the First International Conference on Autonomous Agents,* pages 39-48, 1997.

[6] T. Eliassi-Rad and J. Shavlik. A theory-Refinement Approach to Information Extraction. *Proceedings of the Eighteenth International Conference on Machine Learning,* pages 130-137, 2001.

[7] R. Feldman, Y. Aumann, Y. Libetzon, K. Ankori, J. Schler and B. Rosenfeld. A domain independent environment for creating information extraction modules. *Proceedings of the Tenth International Conference on Information and Knowledge Management CIKM,* pages 586-588, November 2001.

[8] D. Freitag and A. McCallum. Information extraction with HMMs and shrinkage. *AAAI-99 Workshop on Machine Learning for Information Extraction,* July 1999.

[9] J. Hammer, H. Garcia-Molina, J. Cho, R. Aranha, and A. Crespo. Extracting semistructured information from the Web. *Workshop on Management of Semistructrued Data,* May 1997.

[10] C. Hsu and M. Dung. Generating finite-state transducers for semi-structured data extraction from the Web. *Journal of Information Systems, Special Issue on Semistructured Data,* 23(8):521-528, November 1998.

[11] N. Kushmerick. Regression testing for wrapper maintenance. *Proceedings of the Sixteenth National Conference on Artificial Intelligence,* pages 74-79, July 1999.

[12] N. Kushmerick. Wrapper induction: Efficiency and expressiveness. *Artificial Intelligence,* 118(1-2):15-68, April 2000.

[13] W. Y. Lin and W. Lam. Learning to extract hierarchical information from semi-structured documents. *Proceedings of the Ninth International Conference on Information and Knowledge Management CIKM,* pages 250-257, November 2000.

[14] L. Liu, C. Pu and W. Tang. WebCQ - Detecting and delivering information changes on the Web *Proceedings of the Ninth International Conference on Information and Knowledge Management CIKM,* pages 512-519, November 2000.

[15] I. Muslea, S. Minton, and C. Knoblock. Hierarchical wrapper induction for semistructured information sources. *Journal of Autonomous Agents and Multi-Agent Systems,* 4(1-2):93-114, March 2001.

[16] S. Soderland. Learning information extraction rules for semistructured and free text. *Machine Learning,* 34(1-3):233-272, February 1999.

[17] R. Srihari and W. Li. Question Answering supported by information extraction. *The Eighth Text REtrieval Conferenc (TREC-8),* page185-196, 1999.

[18] V. N. Vapnik. *The Nature of Statistical Learning Theory.* Springer, 1995.

From Path Tree To Frequent Patterns:
A Framework for Mining Frequent Patterns

Yabo Xu,   Jeffrey Xu Yu
Chinese University of Hong Kong
Hong Kong, China
{ybxu,yu}@se.cuhk.edu.hk

Guimei Liu,   Hongjun Lu
The Hong Kong University of Science and Technology
Hong Kong, China
{cslgm,luhj}@cs.ust.hk

Abstract

In this paper, we propose a new framework for mining frequent patterns from large transactional databases. The core of the framework is of a novel coded prefix-path tree with two representations, namely, a memory-based prefix-path tree and a disk-based prefix-path tree. The disk-based prefix-path tree is simple in its data structure yet rich in information contained, and is small in size. The memory-based prefix-path tree is simple and compact. Upon the memory-based prefix-path tree, a new depth-first frequent pattern discovery algorithm, called PP-Mine, is proposed in this paper that outperforms FP-growth significantly. The memory-based prefix-path tree can be stored on disk using a disk-based prefix-path tree with assistance of the new coding scheme. We present efficient loading algorithms to load the minimal required disk-based prefix-path tree into main memory. Our technique is to push constraints into the loading process, which has not been well studied yet.

1. Introduction

Recent studies show pattern-growth method is one of the most effective methods for frequent pattern mining [1, 2, 4, 5, 8, 7, 9]. As a divide-and-conquer method, this method partitions (projects) the database into partitions recursively, but does not generate candidate sets. This method also makes use of Apriori property [3]: if any length k pattern is not frequent in the database, its length $(k + 1)$ super-patterns can never be frequent. It *counts* frequent patterns in order to decide whether it can assemble longer patterns. Most of the algorithms use a tree as the basic data structure to mine frequent patterns, such as the lexicographic tree [1, 2, 4, 5] and the FP-tree [8]. Different strategies were extensively studied such as depth-first [2, 1], breath-first [2, 4], top-down [11] and bottom-up [8]. Coding techniques are also used. In [1], bit-patterns are used for efficient counting. In [5], a vertical tid-vector is used, in which a bit of

1 and 0 represent the presence and absence, respectively, of the items in the set of transactions. Other data layout such as vertical tid-list, horizontal item-vector, horizontal item-list were also studied [10, 6, 12].

In this paper, we study a general framework for a multi-user environment where a large number of users might issue different mining queries from time to time. In brief, the main tasks in our general framework are listed below.

§1. Constructing an initial tree in memory for a transactional database.

§2. Mining using the tree constructed in main memory.

§3. Converting the in-memory tree to a disk-based tree.

§4. Loading a portion of the tree on disk into main memory for mining. (Note the mining is the same as §2.)

We observe that the existing algorithms become deficient in such an environment, due to the fact that all of the algorithms aim at mining a single task in a one-by-one manner. In other words, the existing algorithms repeat the first two tasks, §1 and §2, for every mining query, even though the mining queries are the same. In order to efficiently process mining queries in a multi-user environment, it is highly desirable to i) have an even *faster* algorithm when mining in main memory (task §1 and §2), and ii) reduce the cost of reconstructing a tree (task §3 and §4). Both motivate us to study new mining algorithms and new data structures which differentiate from the existing FP-growth algorithm and its data structure, FP-tree, because the complex node-links cross the FP-tree in a unpredictable manner, and the bottom-up FP-growth algorithm makes FP-tree difficult to be efficiently implemented on disk.

The main contribution of our work is given below. We propose a novel *coded* prefix-path tree, *PP*-tree, as the core of our framework. This prefix-path tree has two representations, a disk-based representation and a memory-based representation. Both are node-link-free. It is worth noting that the memory-based representation and the disk-based representation are designed for different purposes. The former is for fast mining and the latter is for efficiently loading a portion of the tree into main memory. The novel coding scheme assists conversion between memory-representation and disk-representation of the prefix-path tree, and assists loading the minimum subtree from disk into memory. For task §2, we propose a novel mining algorithm, called *PP*-Mine, which does not generate any conditional FP-tree, and outperforms FP-growth significantly. A collection of novel loading algorithms are also proposed by which constraints can be further pushed into the loading process (task §4). We will address task §1 and §3, which are straightforward, and report our finding in our experimental studies later in this paper.

2. Frequent Pattern Mining

Let $I = \{x_1, x_2, \cdots, x_n\}$ be a set of items. An itemset X is a subset of items I, $X \subseteq I$. A transaction $T_X = (tid, X)$ is a pair, where X is an itemset and *tid* is its unique identifier. A transaction $T_X = (tid, X)$ is said to contain $T_Y = (tid, Y)$ if and only if $Y \subseteq X$. A transaction database TDB is a set of transactions. The number of transactions in TDB that contains X is called the support of X, denoted as $sup(X)$. An itemset X is a frequent pattern, if and only if $sup(X) \geq \tau$, where τ is a threshold called a minimum support. The frequent pattern mining problem is to find the complete set of frequent patterns in a given transaction database with respect to a given support threshold, τ.

Example 1 *Let the first two columns of Table 1 be our running transaction database TDB. Let the minimum support threshold be $\tau = 2$. The frequent items are shown in the third column of Table 1.*

Trans ID	Items	Frequent items
100	c,d,e,f,g,i	c,d,e,g
200	a,c,d,e,m	a,c,d,e
300	a,b,d,g,k	a,d,e,g
400	a,c,h	a,c

Table 1. The transaction database TDB

Given a threshold τ and a non-empty itemset V. In this paper, we consider three primary types of mining queries.

- **Frequent Itemsets Mining**: mining frequent patterns whose support is greater than or equal to τ.
- **Frequent Superitemsets Mining**: mining frequent patterns that include all items in V, and have a support that is greater than or equal to τ. Examples include how to find causes of a certain rule, for example, $* \rightarrow X$, where $*$ indicates any sets.

- **Frequent Subitemsets Mining**: mining frequent patterns that are included in V, and have a support that is greater than or equal to τ. Examples include mining rules for a limited set of products, for example, daily products.

For conducting the three frequent itemsets mining, we propose a new novel coded prefix-path tree, *PP*-tree. which has two representations: a memory-based representation (PP_M-tree) and a disk-based representation (PP_D-tree). In our framework, a PP_D-tree, with a threshold τ_m, called a materialization threshold, is possibly maintained on disk for the database TDB. The PP_D-tree is built on disk by i) constructing a PP_M-tree with τ_m in memory (task §1), and ii) converting PP_M-tree to PP_D-tree (task §3). The materialization threshold, τ_m, is selected as the minimum threshold to support most mining tasks. With $\tau_m = 1$, the whole database can be materialized.

There are two main cases when processing one of the three types of mining queries with a threshold τ and a possible itemset V.

- When PP_D is not available or PP_D is available but $\tau < \tau_m$, the mining is conducted as constructing an initial PP_M-tree from the raw TDB (task §1) and mining the PP_M-tree in memory (task §2). We propose a novel mining algorithm, *PP*-Mine, that mines PP_M-tree efficiently in memory. *PP*-Mine outperforms both FP-growth [8] and H-Mine [9], as shown in our experimental studies later in this paper.
- When PP_D is available and $\tau \geq \tau_m$, the mining is conducted in two steps: loading (task §4) and mining (task §2).

  - In the loading phase, a minimum subtree of PP_D-tree is loaded from disk, and a PP_M-tree is constructed in memory. The given τ and V are pushed into the loading phase. We propose three primary loading algorithms: PP_τ-load, $PP_\supseteq$-load and $PP_\subseteq$-load. The PP_τ-load algorithm supports loading for frequent itemsets mining. The integration of $PP_\supseteq$-load with PP_τ-load supports loading for frequent superitemsets mining. The integration of $PP_\subseteq$-load with PP_τ-load supports loading for frequent subitemsets mining.
  - In the mining phase, as above, *PP*-Mine mines the PP_M-tree efficiently in memory. It is important to know that, because $\subseteq$ ($\supseteq$) is pushed into the loading phase, here, *PP*-Mine does not need to check $\subseteq$ ($\supseteq$) in the mining phase.

In the following, we concentrate on the coded prefix-path tree, the mining algorithm, *PP*-Mine, and the three loading algorithms.

3. A Coded Prefix-Path Tree

Definition 1 *A Prefix-Path tree (or PP-tree in short) is an order tree. Let F be a set of frequent items (1-itemsets) in a total order ($\preceq$).[1] A node in the tree is labelled for a frequent item in F. The root of the tree represents "null" item. The children of a node are listed following the order. A path of length l from the root to a node in the tree represents a l-itemset. The rank of a PP-tree is the number of frequent 1-itemsets.*

Definition 2 *A complete prefix-path tree of rank N is a prefix-path tree with 2^N nodes, denoted as $\overline{PP}$-tree. Each node is encoded with a number (of the* pre-order *of traversal of the tree). The number associated with a node is called the* code *of that node. The code for the root is 0.*

Definition 3 *A PP-tree is coded using the code of the corresponding node in the complete $\overline{PP}$-tree with the same rank.*

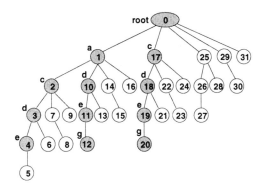

Figure 1. The $\overline{PP}$-tree for Example 1

In the following, a PP-tree is a coded prefix-path tree, unless otherwise specified. The PP-tree for the frequent items in the third column of Table 1 is shown as the shaded subtree in Figure 1. The rank of this PP-tree is 5, because five frequent items, a, c, d, e and g, are represented in frequency order – their support is greater than or equal to the minimum support ($\tau = 2$). Its complete prefix-path tree, $\overline{PP}$-tree has 32 ($= 2^5$) nodes in total. The root is numbered 0 and its five children, a, c, d, e and g, are numbered 1, 17, 25, 29 and 31, respectively. The first subtree of the root, a, has four children, c, d, e and g, and are numbered 2, 10, 14 and 16. A code in a PP-tree uniquely represents a path from the root and therefore an itemset. The code 3 represents a path (a frequent itemset) acd, and 19 represents cde.

Given a PP-tree of rank N where F is a set of frequent 1-itemsets kept in the P-tree. Some observations can be made below.

[1]The order can be any order like frequency order, lexicographic order.

- A PP-tree of rank N is built for a database with a given minimum support, τ_m, called materialization threshold, where N is the number of frequent 1-itemsets. When $\tau_m = 1$, the whole database is maintained as the PP-tree.
- The PP-tree can be used to mine the database with a minimum support $\tau \geq \tau_m$.
- It has N subtrees and the size of the k-th subtree is 2^{N-k} ($1 \leq k < N$).
- A function $kth(N, n_i)$ is defined, which indicates that code n_i, $1 \leq n_i < 2^N$, is in the k-th subtree. $kth(N, n_i) = N - k_r$ where k_r is the maximum number satisfying $2^N - n_i - (2^{k_r} - 1) \geq 0$. Recall 0 is the code of the root.
- The code of its k-th child, $1 \leq k < N$, can be calculated with a function $code(N, k) = 1 + \sum_{i=1}^{k-1} 2^{N-i} = 1 + 2^N - 2^{(N-k+1)}$. The function code can be easily calculated using bit shift operator.
- The item that the k-th child represents, $1 \leq k < N$, is the k-th item in F.
- All codes in the k-th subtree are ranged between code (N, k) and $code(N, k + 1)$ for $k < N - 1$. The last subtree has no children.

It is important to know that, given a PP-tree of rank N, the codes/itemsets along the path from the root to a node, n, can be computed from the code of the node, $\overline{n}$. For example, as shown in Figure 1, code 19 represents an itemset, {c, d, e}.

In our framework, we use the notion of complete prefix-path tree to code nodes. In practice, a PP-tree of rank N is much smaller than the corresponding complete prefix-path tree. We only deal with prefix-path trees.

3.1 PP-tree Representations and Its Construction

A prefix-path tree has its memory-based and disk-based representations. The in-memory representation of PP-tree, denoted PP_M-tree, is of a tree. Despite the pointers to the children nodes, a node in PP_M-tree consists of item-name, count, and a node-link. The count registers the number of transactions represented by the portion of the path reaching from the root to this node. The disk representation of PP-tree of rank N, denoted PP_D-tree, is represented as (T, F, I, τ_m). Here, T is a heap for the tree structure in which an element consists of a code and its count. F stores N frequent 1-itemsets with their counts in order. I is an index indicating the ranges of codes in disk-pages. τ_m is the minimum support used to build PP_D-tree on disk. This PP_D-tree can be used for mining frequent itemsets with a minimum $\tau \geq \tau_m$.

The PP_M-tree and PP_D-tree for Example 1 ($\tau = 2$) are shown in Figure 2 (a) and (b), respectively. Recall, when

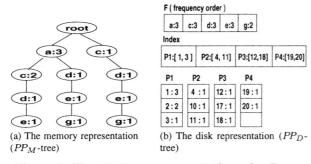

F (frequency order)				
a:3	c:3	d:3	e:3	g:2

Index

P1:[1, 3]	P2:[4, 11]	P3:[12,18]	P4:[19,20]

P1	P2	P3	P4
1 : 3	4 : 1	12 : 1	19 : 1
2 : 2	10 : 1	17 : 1	20 : 1
3 : 1	11 : 1	18 : 1	

(a) The memory representation (PP_M-tree)

(b) The disk representation (PP_D-tree)

Figure 2. The PP-tree representations for Example 1

$\tau = 2$, the frequent items are shown in the third column of Table 1, and are represented as shaded nodes in Figure 1. In the PP_M-tree, $\mathtt{i:s}$ represents item:count. All node-links in the PP_M-tree are initialized as null. Those node-links are used when mining. In the PP_D-tree, T is stored in four pages, where $\mathtt{c:s}$ represents code:count. In F, $\mathtt{i:s}$ represents item:count. As mentioned above, we can simply compute the item(s) a code represents. Therefore, we do not necessarily store items in T. The index I indicates that code 1-3 are stored in page P_1, and so on so forth. The minimum support τ_m to build this tree is 2.

Given a transactional database TDB and a minimum support (τ_m), an initial PP_M-tree can be constructed as follows. First, we scan the database to find all the frequent items, then, we scan the database again to construct PP_M-tree in memory. For each transaction, the infrequent items are removed. The remaining frequent items are sorted in a total order, and are inserted into PP_M-tree. The constructing time for PP_M-tree is slightly less than FP-Tree, because it does not need to build node-links in the tree initially. PP_M-tree can be converted to PP_D-tree and maintained on disk continuously using our coding scheme. We omit the details here.

4. PP-Mine: Mining In-Memory

In this section, we propose a novel mining algorithm, called PP-Mine, using a PP_M-tree. For simplicity, we use a prefix-path to identify a subtree. Here, the prefix-path is expressed as a dot-notation to concatenate items. For example, in Figure 3, a-prefix identifies the leftmost subtree containing a, and $a.c$-prefix identifies the second subtree rooted at a-prefix. In the following, we use i_j and i_k for a single item prefix-path, and use α, β and γ for a prefix-path in general which are possible empty.

The PP-Mine algorithm is based on two properties. The first property states the Apriori property as below.

Property 1 *Given a PP_M-tree of rank N for a set of frequent itemsets $I = (i_1, i_2, \cdots, i_N)$, where a total order ($\preceq$) is defined on I. A pattern represented by $\alpha.i_j.i_k$-prefix can be frequent if the pattern represented by $\alpha.i_j$-prefix is frequent, where $i_j \preceq i_k$.*

The second property specifies subtrees that need to be mined for a pattern. The second property is given on top of two concepts: containment and coverage. We describe them below. Given a PP_M-tree of rank N for a set of frequent itemsets $I = (i_1, i_2, \cdots, i_N)$, where a total order ($\preceq$) is defined on I. We say a prefix-path (representing a subtree), $i_k.\alpha$-prefix, is contained in $i_j.\alpha$-prefix, denoted $i_k.\alpha$-prefix $\subseteq i_j.\alpha$-prefix, if $i_j \preceq i_k$. In addition, α-prefix $\subseteq \gamma$-prefix, if α-prefix $\subseteq \beta$-prefix and β-prefix $\subseteq \gamma$-prefix. A *coverage* of a prefix-prefix α-prefix is defined as all the β-prefixes that contain α-prefix (including α-prefix itself).

Property 2 *Given a PP_M-tree of rank N for a set of frequent itemsets $I = (i_1, i_2, \cdots, i_N)$, where a total order ($\preceq$) is defined on I. Mining a pattern represented by a path-prefix α-prefix is to mine the coverage of α-prefix.*

For example, Figure 3 shows a PP-tree with four items $\{a, b, c, d\}$. Assume they are in lexicographic order. The coverage of $b.c.d$-prefix includes $b.c.d$-prefix and $a.b.c.d$-prefix. It implies that we only need to check these two subtrees, in order to determine whether the pattern, $\{b, c, d\}$, is frequent. Also, the coverage of $c.d$-prefix includes $c.d$-prefix, $b.c.d$-prefix, $a.c.d$-prefix and $a.b.c.d$-prefix. It implies that we only need to check these four subtrees, in order to determine whether the pattern, $\{c, d\}$, is frequent.

Based on the above two properties, we derive three main features including two pushing operations and a no-counting strategy below.

- **Push-down**: Processing at a node in a PP_M-tree is to check an itemset represented by the path-prefix from the root to the node in question. Pushing-down to one of its children is to check the itemset with one more item. Property 1 states the Apriori heuristic. We implement it as a depth-first traversal with building a sub header-table.

- **Push-right**: Mining an itemset requires to identify a minimal coverage in PP_M-tree to mine. Property 2 specifies such a minimal coverage for any path-prefix. Pushing-right is a technique that helps to identify the coverage transitively, based on Property 2. In other words, the push-right strategy is to push the child to its corresponding sibling. We implement it as a dynamic link-justification. It is the best to illustrate it using an example. In Figure 3, after we have mined all the patterns in the leftmost subtree (a-prefix), we push-right $a.b$-prefix to the subtree b-prefix, push-right $a.c$-prefix to the subtree c-prefix, and push-right $a.d$-prefix to the subtree d-prefix. After mining the subtree (*b*-prefix), *b.c*-prefix is pushed to *c*, as well as *a.b.c*-prefix transitively. It is worth noting that the subtree *a.c*-prefix does not need to be pushed into the subtree *b.c*-prefix, because the former is to check the itemset $\{a, c, d\}$ excluding $\{b\}$, whereas the latter is to check the item $\{b, c, d\}$ excluding $\{a\}$.

- **No-counting**: Counting is done as a side-effort of pushing-right (dynamic link-justification) in an accumulated manner. For example, after we push-right *a.b*-prefix to the subtree *b*-prefix, all the prefix-paths and their support counts for *b*-prefix are collected by dynamic link-justification automatically. Therefore, all the counting cost is minimized. No extra counting is needed.

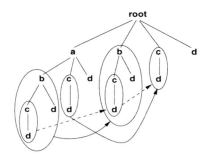

Figure 3. A PP_M-tree with four items

The PP-Mine algorithm is illustrated in Algorithm 1. The procedure is to check all the items in the header table H passed (line 1-10). In line 2-3, we check if the corresponding count (num) for a_i is greater than or equal to the minimum support, τ. Recall that counts are accumulated through pushing-right. If num for a_i is greater than or equal to τ, we output the pattern as represented by the path. Then, at line 4, a sub header table is created by removing all the entries before a_i (including a_i). Pushing-down a_i (line 5) is outlined below. Because the coverage of a_i-prefix has already linked through the link field in the header-table H (by the previous push-rights), all a_i's j-th children on the link are pushed-down (chained) into the corresponding j-th entry in the sub header table ($H_{\alpha.a_i}$). Line 6 calls PP-Mine recursively to check (k+1)-itemset if the length of the path is k. After returning, the sub header table will be deleted. Irrelevant with the minimum support, pushing-right a_i (line 9) is described below: a) the coverage of a_i's left siblings are pushed-right from a_i to its right siblings, b) all a_i's j-th children on the link are pushed-right (chained) into the corresponding entry in the header table H.

Consider the mining process using the constructed PP_M-tree (Figure 2(a)). Here, the initial header table H includes all single items in PP_M-tree. Only the children of the root are linked from the header-table, and their counts are copied into the corresponding num fields in the header-table. Other

Algorithm 1 PP-Mine(α, H)

Input: A constructed PP_M-tree identified by the prefix-path, α, and the header table H.

1: **for all** a_i in the header table H **do**
2:    **if** a_i's support $\geq \tau$ **then**
3:       output $\alpha.a_i$ and a_i's support;
4:       generate a header-table, $H_{\alpha.a_i}$, for the subtree rooted at $\alpha.a_i$, based on H;
5:       push-down(a_i);
6:       PP-Mine($\alpha.a_i$, $H_{\alpha.a_i}$);
7:       delete $H_{\alpha.a_i}$;
8:    **end if**
9:    push-right(a_i);
10: **end for**

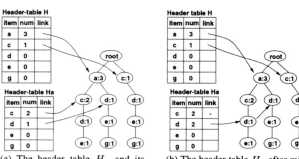

(a) The header table H_a and its PP_M-tree rooted at *a*-prefix

(b) The header table H_a after mining the PP_M-subtree rooted at *a.c*-prefix

Figure 4. An Example

links/nums in the header-table are initialized as null and zero. (The initial header H is shown in Figure 4 (a).)

1. Call PP-Mine(root, H). Item *a* is first to be processed, as the first entry in H. The support of *a* is 3. It is the exact total support for the item *a*, because *a* does not have any left siblings. Next, the subtree *a*-prefix is to be mined.

   The second header table, H_a, consists of all items in H except for *a*. Only the children nodes of *a* are pushed-down into H_a (Figure 4 (a)). In H_a, *c* and *d* counts are copied from the node *a.c* and *a.d*, in the PP_M-tree. Their values are 2 and 1.

2. Call PP-Mine(*a*-prefix, H_a). Item *c* is picked up as the first entry in H_a. Because *c*'s count (num) is 2 (frequent), we output *a.c*. Next, the subtree *a.c*-prefix is to be mined.

   The third header-table is constructed for the subtree of *a.c*-prefix, denoted as H_{ac}, in which *d*'s num is 1 and *d*'s link points to the node *a.c.d*. Other fields for *e* and *g* are set as zero/null.

3. Call PP-Mine($a.c$-prefix, H_{ac}). Item d is picked up. Because d's num is 1 (infrequent), return.

4. Backtrack to the subtree a-prefix. Here, the header-table H_a is reset (Figure 4 (b)). First, the entry c in H_a becomes null (done). Second, $a.c$'s child, d, is pushed-right into d's entry in the header-table H_a. In other words, the link of the entry d in H_a is linked to the node $a.d$ through the node $a.c.d$. The d's count (num) in H_a is accumulated to 2, which indicates $\{a, d\}$ occurs 2 times.

The correctness of PP-Mine can be showed as follows in brief. A PP_M-tree of rank N has N subtrees. First, we mine patterns in a subtree following a depth-first traversal order. All patterns in a subtree will be mined (vertically). Second, the k-th subtree is mined by linking all required subtrees in its left siblings (horizontally). Linking to those subtrees will be completed at the time when the k-subtree is to be mined. Third, the above holds for any subtrees in the PP_M-tree of rank N (recursively).

5. Efficient Loading

In this section, we assume that a PP_D-tree is available on disk with τ_m, and discuss how to process any of the three primary types of mining queries (frequent itemsets mining, frequent superitemsets mining and frequent subitemsets mining) with a threshold τ and an itemset V. We emphasize on two things: a) loading a sub PP_D-tree from disk, and b) constructing a *minimum PP_M-tree* in memory. Here, the minimum PP_M-tree is a PP_M-tree such that it cannot process the mining query correctly if any node in the tree is removed. It is important to note that, here, a) is to reduce I/O costs for loading, and b) is for further reducing CPU costs for mining in memory.

We studied three primary loading algorithms: PP_τ-load, $PP_\supseteq$-load and $PP_\subseteq$-load. These algorithms load subtrees of a PP_D-tree from disk and construct a PP_M-tree in memory. The PP_τ-load algorithm supports loading for frequent itemsets mining. The integration of $PP_\supseteq$-load with PP_τ-load supports loading for frequent superitemsets mining. The integration of $PP_\subseteq$-load with PP_τ-load supports loading for frequent subitemsets mining. Due to space limit, we only present our PP_τ-load algorithm in this paper.

The loading algorithm, PP_τ-load, is outlined in Algorithm 2. Four parameters will be passed, the code of a root node p of a prefix-path tree of rank N, the reading position d, and a new rank M. The new rank is computed by the given τ as follows. Suppose the prefix-path tree on disk is based on frequency order. M is the total number of frequent 1-itemsets stored that are greater than τ. If a given threshold τ is larger, the computed M will be smaller. Therefore, the PP-tree to loaded into memory will be smaller. The newly computed M reduce the number of page accesses.

Initially, when loading, we call PP_τ-load(0, M, N, 0), where the first zero is the code of the root of the PP-tree of rank N, and the second zero is the reading position of the PP_D-tree on disk. Algorithm 2 is a recursive algorithm. The PP_D-tree, represented by p, to be loaded has N children at most. Line 1-3 reads the page where d exists, if d has not been read-in. Line 4-5 calculate the code of children nodes. Here, c_i is the code in terms of the PP_D-tree, passed by the parameter p, and a_i is the code in terms of the whole PP_D-tree on disk. Line 7-12 attempt to jump to a page and find the next page to read if the code in the reading position is less than the i-th child (a_i). The readPage function will use the index to load a page in which at least a d exists whose code is greater than or equal to a_i. If the code of d matches a_i (line 13), a new child node is constructed in memory, and PP_τ-load will be recursively called. Note, d is called by-reference. The coding scheme and the index allows us to reduce the I/O cost to minimum.

Algorithm 2 PP_τ-load(p, M, N, d)

Input: the code of root (p), the required rank (M), the rank of the PP_D-tree (N), and the current reading position on disk (d) (call by reference).

Output: a PP_M-tree.

```
1:  if page(d) does not exist in memory then
2:      readPage(d) using the index;
3:  end if
4:  let c_i be the code of the i-th child of p (of rank N);
5:  a_i ← c_i + p;
6:  while i < M do
7:      if code(d) < a_i then
8:          d ← readPage(a_i);
9:          while code(d) < a_i do
10:             d++;
11:         end while
12:     end if
13:     if a_i = code(d) then
14:         build the new child node for d in memory as the
            child of p;
15:         d++;
16:         PP_τ-load(a_i, M − i, N − i, d);
17:     end if
18: end while
```

---

6. Performance Study

We conducted performance studies to analyze the efficiency of PP-Mine in comparison of FP-tree [8] and H-Mine [9]. We did not compare PP-Mine with TreeProjection [2], because, as reported in [8], FP-growth outperforms TreeProjection.

All the three algorithms were implemented using Visual C++ 6.0. The synthetic data sets were generated using the procedure described in [3]. All our experimental studies were conducted on a 900MHz Pentium PC, with 128MB main memory and a 20GB hard disk, running Microsoft Windows/NT.

Given a database TDB. We reemphasize the differences between PP-Mine and FP-tree/H-Mine for the mining task with a minimum support τ below.

- In our framework, A PP_D-tree is possibly stored on disk with a materialized threshold τ_m. For a mining task with a minimum support $\tau \geq \tau_m$ with/without ($\subseteq V$, $\supseteq V$), a loading algorithm loads a subtree from disk and constructs a PP_M-tree in memory. The conditions (τ, $\supseteq$, $\subseteq$) are pushed into the loading. Upon the prefix-path tree is constructed in memory, PP-Mine further mines PP_M-tree using τ only. Otherwise, when PP_D-tree is not available or $\tau < \tau_m$, a PP_M-tree is constructed from the transactional database in memory to be mined.

- Both FP-growth and H-Mine consists of two phases, *constructing* and *mining*. In the constructing phase, they scan TDB and construct a FP-tree/H-struct in memory using a minimum support τ. In the mining-phase, they conduct the mining task further using the minimum support τ.

6.1 PP-Mine, FP-growth, H-Mine

In this section, we focus on the mining task with a minimum support only. We assume that no PP_D-tree exist on disk. For a given minimum support τ, we assume that we have to construct PP_M-tree, FP-tree and H-struct in memory from scratch. The constructing time for both H-struct and PP_M-tree is marginally better than FP-tree construction. To give a fair view on this three algorithms, here we only compare the mining-phase of the three algorithms.

We have conducted experimental studies using the same datasets as reported in [8]. We report our results using one of them, T25.I20.D100K with 10K items, as representative. In this dataset, the average transaction size and average maximal potentially frequent itemset size are set to be 25 and 20, respectively, while the number of transactions in the dataset is 100K. There are exponentially numerous frequent itemsets in this dataset, when the minimum support is small. The frequent patterns include long frequent itemsets as well as a large number of short frequent itemsets.

The scalability of the three algorithms, PP-Mine, FP-tree and H-Mine, is shown in Figure 5 (a). While the support threshold decreases, the number as well as the length of frequent itemsets increases. High overhead incurs for handling projected transactions. FP-growth needs to construct

conditional FP-trees using extra memory space repeatedly. H-Mine needs to count every projected transactions. PP-Mine does not need to construct conditional trees and uses accumulation technique, which avoids unnecessary counting. From Figure 5 (a), we can see PP-Mine significantly outperforms FP-growth and H-Mine. PP-Mine scales much better than both FP-tree and H-Mine.

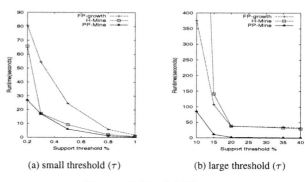

(a) small threshold (τ)   (b) large threshold (τ)

Figure 5. Scalability

We also compared the mining phase of the three algorithms using a very dense dataset. The dataset was generated with 101 distinct items and 1K transactions. The average transaction size and average maximal potentially frequent itemset size are set to 40 and 10. When the minimum support is 40%, the number of frequent patterns is 65,540. When the minimum support becomes 10%, the number of frequent patterns is up to 3,453,240. As shown in Figure 5 (b), PP-Mine outperforms both FP-growth and H-Mine significantly. PP-Mine has the best scalability while the threshold decreases.

For sparse datasets and small datasets, PP-Mine marginally outperforms H-Mine, because both use the similar dynamic link adjusting technique. The effectiveness of PP-Mine's accumulation (or non-counting) techniques becomes weaker. Both PP-Mine and H-Mine outperform FP-growth.

6.2 PP-Mine Analysis

In this section, we further analyze the effectiveness of PP-Mine (and PP-tree) in terms of loading/constructing/mining, using a very large tree. Such a large tree was generated using T40I10D100K. Its average transaction size and average maximal potentially frequent itemset size are 40 and 10, respectively. The number of distinct items generated was 59. We chose a minimum support (50%) to build a PP_D-tree on disk for this dataset. The minimum support was chosen, because the resulting number of frequent patterns is large enough for our testing purposes, 138,272,944. The PP_D-tree we built on disk has 51,982 nodes, which is considerably small.

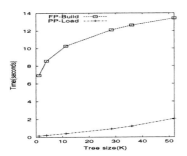

Figure 6. Scalability with the tree size

Figure 6 compares the cost for FP-growth to construct a FP-tree in memory with the cost for PP_T-load to load a sub PP_D-tree and construct a rather small PP_M-tree. The intension of the figure is to show the necessity of PP_D-tree. In Figure 6, we use tree size rather than threshold, because a threshold does not precisely indicate the tree size. Different thresholds may end up the same tree size. The tree sizes and the corresponding thresholds used in this figure are listed below, as a pair of tree size and threshold, $(1, 100, 90\%)$, $(3, 943, 80\%)$, $(11, 281, 77\%)$, $(28, 474, 76\%)$, $(36, 038, 75\%)$, $(51, 982, 50\%)$. The tree sizes are the same for the threshold in the range of 75-50%. Note: a smaller threshold results in a larger tree.

As shown in Figure 6, PP_T-loading time is much smaller than FP-growth constructing time (constructing an initial FP-tree in memory), as expected. Saving PP_D-tree on disk can significantly reduce both the time to construct a tree in memory and the memory space. It is worth noting that the loading time for a tree is proportional to the size of the PP_D-tree size. That suggests that, if we only need a small portion of the data, with the help of PP_D-tree, we do not need to load the whole dataset.

7. Conclusion

In this paper, we propose a new framework for mining frequent patterns from large transactional databases in a multiuser environment. With this framework, we propose a novel coded prefix-path tree with two representations, a memory-based prefix-path tree and a disk-based prefix-path tree. The coding scheme is based on a depth-first traversal order. Its unique features include easy identifying of the location in a prefix-path tree, and easy identifying of the itemsets. The loading scheme makes the disk-based prefix-path tree node-link-free. With help of a simple index, several new loading algorithms are proposed which can further push constraints into the loading process, and, therefore, reduce both I/O cost and CPU cost, because the prefix-path tree constructed in memory becomes smaller. In terms of mining in memory, PP-Mine algorithm outperforms FP-

tree significantly, because PP-Mine does not need to construct any conditional FP-trees for handling projected databases. Instead, dynamic link adjusting are used. Both PP-Mine and H-Mine adopt dynamic link adjusting technique. In addition, PP-Mine further minimizes counting cost. Accumulation technique is used, and therefore, unnecessary counting is avoided. PP-Mine outperforms H-Mine significantly when dataset is dense, and outperforms H-Mine marginally when dataset is sparse and is small.

Acknowledgment: The work described in this paper was supported by grants from the Research Grants Council of the Hong Kong Special Administrative Region, China (CUHK4229/01E, DAG01/02.EG14).

References

[1] R. C. Agarwal, C. C. Aggarwal, and V. V. V. Prasad. Depth first generation of long patterns. In *Proc. 6th ACM SIGKDD Int. Conf. on Knowledge discovery and data mining*, pages 108–118. ACM Press, 2001.

[2] R. C. Agarwal, C. C. Aggarwal, and V. V. V. Prasad. A tree projection algorithm for generation of frequent item sets. *Journal of Parallel and Distributed Computing*, 61:350–371, 2001.

[3] R. Agrawal and R. Srikant. Fast algorithms for mining association rules. In J. B. Bocca, M. Jarke, and C. Zaniolo, editors, *Proc. 20th Int. Conf. Very Large Data Bases, VLDB*, pages 487–499. Morgan Kaufmann, 12–15 1994.

[4] R. J. Bayardo. Efficiently mining long patterns from databases. In *1998 ACM SIGMOD Intl. Conference on Management of Data*, pages 85–93. ACM Press, 05 1998.

[5] D. Burdick, M. Calimlim, and J. Gehrke. MAFIA: A maximal frequent itemset algorithm for transactional databases. In *2001 Intl. Conference on Data Engineering, ICDE*, pages 443–452, 04 2001.

[6] B. Dunkel and N. Soparkar. Data organization and access for efficient data mining. In *Proc. of 15th IEEE Intl. Conf. on Data Engineering*, pages 522–529, 03 1999.

[7] J. Han and J. Pei. Mining frequent patterns by pattern-growth: Methodology and implications. In *ACM SIGKDD Explorations*. ACM Press, 12 2001.

[8] J. Han, J. Pei, and Y. Yin. Mining frequent patterns without candidate generation. In W. Chen, J. Naughton, and P. A. Bernstein, editors, *2000 ACM SIGMOD Intl. Conference on Management of Data*, pages 1–12. ACM Press, 05 2000.

[9] J. Pei, J. Han, H. Lu, S. Nishio, and D. Y. S hiwei Tang. H-mine:hyper-structure mining of frequent patterns in large databases. In *2001 IEEE Conference on Data Mining*. IEEE, 11 2001.

[10] P. Shenoy, J. R. Haritsa, S. Sudarshan, G. Bhalotia, M. Bawa, and D. Shah. Turbo-charging vertical mining of large databases. In *2000 ACM SIGMOD Intl. Conference on Management of Data*, pages 22–33. ACM Press, 05 2000.

[11] K. Wang, L. Tang, J. Han, and J. Liu. Top down fp-growth for association rule mining. In *Proc. of 6th Pacific-Asia conference on Knowledge Discovery and Data Mining*, 2002.

[12] M. J. Zaki. Scalable algorithms for association mining. *Knowledge and Data Engineering*, 12(2):372–390, 2000.

Mining Case Bases for Action Recommendation

Qiang Yang and Hong Cheng
Department of Computer Science
Hong Kong University of Science and Technology
Clearwater Bay, Kowloon, Hong Kong, China
(qyang, csch)@cs.ust.hk

Abstract

Corporations and institutions are often interested in deriving marketing strategies from corporate data and providing informed advice for their customers or employees. For example, a financial institution may derive marketing strategies for turning their reluctant customers into active ones and a telecommunications company may plan actions to stop their valuable customers from leaving. In data mining terms, these advice and action plans are aimed at converting individuals from an undesirable class to a desirable one, or to help devising a direct-marketing plan in order to increase the profit for the institution. In this paper, we present an approach to use 'role models' for generating such advice and plans. These role models are typical cases that form a case base and can be used for customer advice generation. For each new customer seeking advice, a nearest-neighbor algorithm is used to find a cost-effective and highly probable plan for switching a customer to the most desirable role models. In this paper, we explore the tradeoff among time, space and quality of computation in this case-based reasoning framework. We demonstrate the effectiveness of the methods through empirical results.

Keywords: case base mining, AI contributions to data mining (case-based reasoning), actionable data mining, financial applications of data mining.

1. Introduction

Data mining has traditionally focused on studying how to build statistical models from large databases. These models can be used to classify a given customer into a most probable class. Using these models, managers in corporations and institutions can decide whether to accept or reject a customer into a certain class membership. In this work, we take one step further: we not only use statistical models to make decisions on new customers, we also produce advice for the failed customers in the form of actions or plans. For example, a cell-phone company may decide to reduce the monthly fee for a subgroup of its customers who are both highly valuable and likely to leave the company for its competitors. Likewise, in a university scenario, instead of rejecting a graduate-school applicant with only a "no" answer, it helps to suggest steps that might be taken by the applicant in the future to increase his/her chance of being admitted the next time around. Similarly, these plans can be used to give advice to the customers who fall short of a loan application and to corporate managers on the strategies in marketing campaigns.

As an example, consider a customer-loan database on customer information and past loan in Table 1. Suppose that we are interested in providing advice for Steve (the last row) who failed to apply for a bank loan. Obviously, there are many candidate actions that one can advise Steve to take in order to succeed in his next loan application. These actions are designed based on other successful applicants who serve as positive examples in the same database. In this example, we have two such positive cases: John and Mary. For Steve, we can advise him to find another job with a salary close to 80K and increase his car number from one to three; this will make him look more like John. Alternatively, we can advise Steve to take up a mortgage from the bank worth at least 300K. This will make Steve look more like Mary. In either situation, Steve might have a higher chance of succeeding than before, but the actions come with different costs. The prescribed actions for Steve are shown in Table 2.

This example also introduced a number of interesting aspects for the problem. First, for each advisee such as Steve, there are potentially many possible actions that we can provide. Each action comes with an inherent cost associated with it. For example, it may be more costly for Steve to buy two more cars. Thus, the action for buying cars may be so prohibitive that the advice should not be given to Steve. Second, not all attributes can be acted on; some attributes cannot be changed.

Table 1. An example customer database. The last attribute is the class attribute.

Customer	Salary	Cars	Mortgage	Loan Approved?
John	80K	3	None	Y
Mary	40K	1	300K	Y
...	...	...	...	...
Steve	40K	1	None	N

Table 2. Prescribed alternative actions for Steve.

Advice for Steve	Salary	Cars	Mortgage
Plan 1	40K→80K	1→3	
Plan 2			0→300K

These correspond to *non-actionable attributes*. For example, it would be impossible to change the salary of Steve to that of John by taking a simple action, or to change the gender of a person. This impossibility can be modeled through prohibited high cost measures. Third, some attributes may not be relevant to the problem at hand. For example, the *address* attribute (not shown in the table) may be such an irrelevant attribute. Finally, the actions are not guaranteed to succeed 100% of the time; some actions may have higher probability of success than others. Our task is to choose high-utility actions that increase the probability of success while reducing costs.

We formulate the above problem as a case-based reasoning problem [13], where the key issue is to look for actionable plans on a case-by-case basis. Our approach is to first identify typical positive cases to form a small and highly representative case base, and then use the case base as "role models" to formulate the marketing actions that adapt each incoming problem to its nearest neighbor in the case base. Our focus in this paper is to identify the case bases automatically; we leave the planning issues in our future work.

More specifically, we first classify the training data into two classes: the "good" or "positive" data set contains data that belong to customers who have already been accepted into the good class and the "bad" or "negative" set for those who have not. Given this labeled dataset, our second step is to perform an analysis on the positive data to find out a number of representative cases of customers that can be "role models" for the rest. Finally, the negative cases are converted to positive ones by formulating marketing actions. Figure 1 (a) and (b) illustrate two distributions of the positive and negative classes in a two-attribute dataset. We will study the effect of the data distributions on our case-mining algorithms.

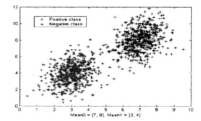

Figure 1(a). A demonstration of well-separated positive class and negative class distributions.

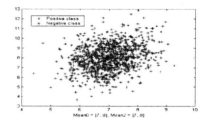

Figure 1(b). A demonstration of mixed positive class and negative class distributions.

Typically, real customer data are highly unbalanced and quite large. For example, the 1998 KDDCUP dataset [4] contains only 5% positive data and 95% negative data. Given such a dataset, a naïve application of classification such as decision tree would result in no useful information. In dealing with the unbalanced data problem, our case-mining algorithm will focus on the positive cases in the selection of role models, thus avoiding overwhelming the data distribution by negative cases. We consider three case-mining approaches. The most naïve one is to simply use the original database as the case base. While this model allows the creation of optimal actions from the past data, this approach is highly inefficient. The second approach constructs clusters from the database, and takes the centroids of the clusters as the potential cases for the case base. This approach can be very efficient, but the quality of the cases is still not optimized. This is because in creating role models for the positive class, it is more desirable to find cases that are "close" to the majority of the negative instances. These cases are often located near the "boundary" of the distributions of these classes. In order to find these boundary cases, our third approach is to apply a support-vector-machine (SVM) learning algorithm for extracting the support vectors as cases. These cases can give rise to more cost-effective plans.

In data mining area, researchers are interested in building statistical models of the database for classification and data analysis [2, 5, 17]. A typical statistical model partitions the test data into different classes according the trained model learned from the training data. Some recent work has specifically targeted the issue of marketing strategies in data mining [14, 8]. A major difference between our work and the majority of data mining work is that we do not stop at classification of the data into different classes; instead, we propose actions to switch customers to more desirable classes. Another related area is case based reasoning, in particular case-base maintenance [6, 18] and case-transformation [12, 13]. In this area, a new problem is solved by consulting a case base of past solutions. The new solution is formed by deriving the difference between a past solution and the new problem. In this area, the problem of identifying concise, high-quality case bases remains an open question.

2. Mining Case Bases

We formulate the problem formally. Given a database of customer records, we assume that each customer record is labeled as either a positive or negative class. Multiple class generalization is possible but will be considered separately in future work. In this section, we discuss three progressive more sophisticated solutions, each having its own computational advantages. The three methods are, respectively, instance-based, cluster-based and support-vector-based.

2.1. Instance-based Case-Base Mining

A first method to construct the case base is to use the entire positive population of data as the case base. Then for each negative instance we need to identify its nearest neighbor among the positive data instances. Thus the collection of all positive instances is taken as the case base. This method is purely memory based, and the learning is delayed until model application time. For this reason, it is also known as lazy evaluation or instance-based learning [1]. An advantage of this method is that for any given negative instance, it is guaranteed to find its nearest positive neighbor in terms of either the cost measure or utility. Thus, we also call this algorithm the *optimal* algorithm, because the customer-switching plan found will have optimal quality. However, the instance-based approach may suffer from computational inefficiency.

2.2. Cluster Centroid-based Case-Base Mining

A second idea is to compute clusters of positive instances and extract the centroids. The case-base mining algorithm thus constructed is described in Table 3. After feature selection, we divide the database

Table 3. Algorithm *Centroids-CBMine* (database DB, int *K*)

Steps	Begin
1	*casebase*= emptyset;
2	DB = *FeatureSelection*(DB);
3	Separate the DB into DB+ and DB-;
4	Clusters+ = *ApplyKMedoids*(DB+, *K*);
5	**for each** *cluster* in Clusters+, **do**
6	C = *findCentroid*(cluster);
7	*Insert*(C, *casebase*);
8	**end for**;
9	Return *casebase*;
	End

into a positive class database DB+ and a negative class database DB-. The training database consists of the positive instances of the original database, whereas the testing data are the negative instances.

In the algorithm *Centroids-CBMine* in Table 3, the input database is DB. There are two classes in this database, where the positive class corresponds to population of desired cases and the negative class the unconverted cases.

Step 2 of the algorithm performs feature extraction by applying a feature filter to the database to remove all attributes that are considered low in information content or in classification power. In our implementation, subroutine *FeatureSelection* filters each attribute using an extended *OddLogRatio* algorithm [15] as the criterion for feature selection. *OddLogRatio* is designed for dataset with a highly unbalanced class distribution and asymmetric misclassification costs, which are exactly the characteristics of realistic dataset such as the KDDCUP'98 dataset. Using this criterion for feature selection on the KDDCUP'98 dataset, for example, we can reduce the number of attributes from 481 to 25. Subsequently, our case mining and planning activities is done on the selected subset of attributes. Using feature selection, we can avoid unnecessary changes on the "irrelevant" attributes, thus reducing overall customer switching costs.

Step 3 of the algorithm separates the training database into two partitions, a positive-class subset and a negative-class subset. Step 4 of the algorithm performs the *K*-medoids clustering on the positive-class sub-database [10]. Other good clustering algorithms can also be used here in place of *K*-medoids. For example, the density-based learning algorithm has been successfully applied to clustering on very large and complex data [9]. Step 6 of the algorithm finds centroids of the K clusters found in the previous step. These centroids are the bases of the case base constructed thus far, and are returned to the user. Finally, Step 9 returns the case base as the output.

Once the case base is built, it can then be applied to set of testing negative-class cases to see what the total cost would be for converting all the negative cases to positive ones. For each negative class case C1 in the test data set, a one-nearest neighbor algorithm is applied to the case base to find the most similar case C2. The difference between C1 and C2 are used to generate the switch plan.

Our notion of distance is based on a notion of cost of switching an attribute from one value to the next. For each attribute A and values v1 and v2 of A, there is a cost function: *cost(A, v1, v2)* which is a real value denoting the cost of changing from v1 to v2 on attribute A. In practice, such knowledge is not available in the dataset, but comes from domain expert. In our subsequent experiments, we set those values manually according to the semantic of attribute. For each nominal attribute, we have a cost matrix, each element of which denotes the cost changing from one value to the other. For each numeric attribute, we define a math function.

Consider the following example of the cost matrix. Suppose we have a nominal attribute which has three distinct values. We use 0, 1 and 2 to denote these three values. The cost matrix C is:

$$\begin{bmatrix} 0 & \infty & \infty \\ 200 & 0 & \infty \\ 500 & 300 & 0 \end{bmatrix}$$

In the cost matrix C, the value of C[1][0] is $200. That means the cost of changing from value 1 to value 0 is $200. All the elements in the diagonal are zero, which means that the cost of changing a value to itself is zero. The value of C[0][2] is infinite, which means that changing value 0 to value 2 is impossible or too prohibitive.

Finally, the cost of the model on an entire population of test data is the sum of all costs for all actions on each datum in the testing set. Assuming that the jth attribute for an ith customer is A_{ij}, Equation (1) shows the cost formula.

$$Cost = \sum_{i=1}^{|DB|} \sum_{j=1}^{l} \cos t(A_{ij}, v_1, v_2) \quad (1)$$

2.3. SVM-based Case-Base Mining

The centroid-based case-mining method extracts cases from the positive-class cluster centroids and takes into account only the positive class distribution. By considering the distribution of both the positive and negative class clusters, we can do better. This idea is as follows. Suppose C1 is the centroid of a positive-class cluster, while C2 is the centroid of a negative-class cluster. According to the *Centroids-CBMine* algorithm, C1 can be chosen as the

corresponding positive case for the negative cases in the C2-cluster. However, if a positive case C3 that lies on the boundary of C1 cluster is nearer to the C2-cluster cases and we take C3 as the case instead of C1, the total cost of switching plans would be less. This is the intuition behind the SVM-based case mining.

The key issue then is to identify the positive cases on the *boundary* between the positive and negative cases, and select those cases as the final ones for the switching-plan generation. The cases along the boundary hyper-plane correspond to the support vectors found by an SVM classifier [16, 7]. These cases are the instances that are closest to the maximum margin hyper-plane in a hyperspace after an SVM system has discovered the classifier.

By exploiting the above idea, we have a different case-mining algorithm, *SVM-CBMine*. In the first step, we perform SVM learning on the database to locate the support vectors. Then we find the support vectors and insert them into the case base. This algorithm is illustrated in Table 4.

Compared with the *Centroids-CBMine* algorithm, the *SVM-CBMine* algorithm has several advantages. First, because the cases are the support vectors themselves, there is no need to specify the input parameter K as in the *Centroids-CBMine* algorithm; the parameter K is used to determine the number of clusters to be generated in K-medoids. Second, because the cases are themselves the boundary cases, they are naturally better examples for the entire negative-class members to switch to; the costs would be lower.

Table 4. Algorithm *SVM-CBMine* (Database *DB*, int *K*)

Steps	Begin
1	*casebase* = Emptyset;
2	*Vectors* = SVM(DB);
3	**for each** positive support vector C in *Vectors* **do**
4	Insert(C, *casebase*);
5	**end for**
6	Return casebase;
	End

3. Switching Plan Generation

A straightforward plan-generation solution is to use a nearest neighbor approach. The plan used to advise a customer is one that is associated with the least cost. In our subsequent experiments, we call this the *MinCost* approach. While this approach is guaranteed to generate a cost effective plan, it is not guaranteed to generate a plan that will achieve its intended target all the time. In reality, the positive and negative cases are often distributed in a mixed manner. When executing a customer-switching plan, it is likely that the customer following the plan will land on a wrong target; it is wrong because it corresponds to an "unreliable" positive case whose neighborhood is dominated by negative instances, rendering the switching low probability of success. A more sensible method will consider not only the cost of switching, but also the probability of success of each switching. Together we have a notion of the utility of a plan, both in terms of success probability and costs [3, 11].

We can estimate the probability of success of switching to a certain target to be the probability density of positive instances around a target. More formally, let $p(+|t)$ be the probability density of an instance t, $cost(x, t)$ be the cost of switch from x to target case t, and $maxCost$ be the maximum value among the different costs of switching from x to every possible case y in the case base. The utility function we use for ranking cases in a case base is defined in Equation (2) below. The target case t with the maximum rank is chosen as the role model for switching-plan generation for customer x.

$$rank(x,t) = p(+|t) - \frac{Cost(x,t)}{maxCost} \qquad (2)$$

The algorithm for choosing the maximum utility plan for negative instances is called *MaxRank* algorithm. Once the role-model case is identified, the difference between the negative and positive cases can be taken and their differences are taken as recommended actions for the negative cases.

4. Experimental Results

In this section, we present the experimental results to test and compare the different algorithms we have proposed. Our experiments are aimed at finding out the tradeoff among the system execution time, which is the model-building time plus the model-application time on test cases, the size of the model (the number of cases) and the total cost and utility of switching plans for converting all negative examples into positive ones.

4.1. Artificial Dataset

Our first test uses an artificial dataset generated on a two-dimensional space *(x, y)*, using a Gaussian distribution with different means and co-variance matrix for the positive (+) and the negative (−) classes. Our purpose is to demonstrate the effect of data distribution and case base size on the switching-plan quality and case mining efficiency. When the means of

the two distributions are separated, we expect the class boundaries are easy to identify by the SVM-based method (see Figure 1 (a)). When the distributions are very close to each other, there will not be an easy-to-find boundary between the positive and negative classes; in this case the centroid-based method will perform better. The cost of switching a negative case to a positive one is defined as in this test as the Euclidean distance on the *(x, y)* plane. In the experiments with the artificial dataset, the cost matrix has a uniform cost value.

The mean for the positive class distribution is fixed to be *mean0*=(7, 8), with a co-variance matrix [(0.6, 0.3), (0.3, 1.8)]. For the negative class, the location of the mean moves from being far away from the *mean0* to being close to it to explore the effect of data distribution. In Artificial Data I, the mean for negative class *mean1*=(3, 4). The co-variance matrix for the negative class is defined as [(0.8, -0.5) (-0.5, 3.2)]. Figure 2 and Figure 3 show the test results comparing the case bases of different sizes and the resulting cost of switching plans. In Figure 2, we show the relative cost, as compared to the optimal cost, of switching all negative instances to positive cases for the corresponding case base size, using the minimal cost algorithm. In Figure 3, we show the same data for the MaxRank algorithm, which selects plans for each negative instance based on the utility formula (2). In both figures, SVM stands for the *SVM-CBMine* result. For example, SV=3 indicates that three support vectors were found to populate the case base. Parameter *K* indicates the number of clusters generated by *K*-medoids algorithm for the *Centroids-CBMine* system. "Optimal" indicates the cost for building and using the model using all positive examples in the original training data as the cases in the case base. As can be seen, the relative cost of switching from negative to positive cases decreases with the size of the case base. This is because as the case-base size increases, the choice in possible role models also increases.

To study the effect of different distribution of data, a second distribution is generated for the situation when the centers for the negative distribution are moved closer to that of the positive distributions (see Figure 1(b)). The result shown in Figures 4 and 5 – Artificial Data II with *mean2*=(7, 8), corresponds to the situation when there is no clear boundary between the two distributions.

As can be seen from the progression of the data distribution, as the two classes are distributed farther apart from each other (Figures 2, 3), the SVM-based method is a clear winner. This is because it uses far less time than the optimal method, and yet its total cost is nearly the same as that of the optimal method. As can be seen from the *K-medoids* based method, as the number *K* of clusters increases, the cost of switching plans also decreases. However, the time it takes to build and execute the model also increases with K (Figure 6). On the other hand, as the two distributions move close to each other such that there are no clear boundaries, as in the case of Figure 4, the SVM-based method selects nearly all the positive examples as cases in the case base, rendering it useless. Thus, its time expense is also very high (Figure 6). In this case, the *K-medoids-based* method is preferred.

Figures 7 and 8 show the success probability P(+|t) as a function of case base size. The *MaxRank* method for case retrieval obtains cases with higher costs, but much higher probability of success. For example, when K=100, there are 100 cases in the case base, the *MaxRank* method incurs a cost of 1583.5 as compared to the cost of 1243 for *MinCost,* but has a probability of success at 0.9 as compared to 0.3 for *MinCost.* It is also interesting to note that the as K increases from 10 to 100, the average probability of success decreases for *MinCost*, but not for *MaxRank* (Figure 7). This is because when the number of cases is large, it is more likely that the low probability cases will be selected as target cases for the plan generation, as compared with smaller case bases. However, as can also be seen from the figure, the *MaxRank* method for plan generation suffers less from this drawback, since in target-case selection, both the cost information and the probability information are taken into consideration.

4.2. KDDCUP Datasets

Besides the above results, we also carried out experiments on some more realistic datasets, since real world dataset often has much more unbalanced distribution than the artificial data. The attributes in real data have their own semantics. Therefore, in the subsequent experiments, we define the cost matrix and functions for each attribute in the dataset. In the tests, we still use the case-base mining algorithm to provide advice for each failed customer. However, if a customer consulted all the role models in the case base and cannot find a finite-cost switching plan, we consider the customer a failed one. Only those advices with finite costs are considered successful. We define a *SwitchingRate* measure to be the proportion of negative instances in test data for which there exists a finite-cost role-model case in the case base. When the case-base size is small, this *SwitchingRate* will be low as well, since the majority of negative cases cannot be switched to a positive one. The switching rate should be the highest for the optimal case when the entire set of positive instances serve as the case base.

Figures 9 – 12 show the test result of the algorithms on the KDDCUP'98 dataset. The training dataset consists of over 90,000 records for persons who were approached to make donations to a certain charity. The characteristic of this dataset is that it is highly unbalanced and has 481 attributes. For this dataset, we first performed the *OddLogRatio* feature-selection algorithm on the attributes. This resulted in a total of 25 remaining attributes, for which we constructed a cost matrix. The test result on this dataset is shown in Figures 9 to 12.

For the KDDCUP'98 data, the SVM based method returned over one half of the entire positive instances as the case base (SV=2645). Thus it does not really save any time in the case base mining. In contrast, the *Centroid*-based method performed very well, resulting in decreasing costs when K increases. As can be seen from Figure 11, when the number of cases reaches 100, the success rate for switching the negative cases reaches nearly 80%. Thus, the cases selected are quite representative of the positive instances, and the probability of success for the case base is comparable to that of the optimal case base.

5. Conclusions and Future Work

In this paper, we described solutions for mining case bases for customer action recommendation. The central issue of the problem lies in the discovery of high-quality case bases from a large data set, a case-mining problem. We proposed two solutions for the problem. For the data distribution where the two classes are clearly separated, the SVM-CBMine algorithm, which is an SVM-based method, should be used. When the data distributions are not separated well by a boundary, the cluster-centroids based method is recommended. Furthermore, we compared the solutions where plan generation is done based on cost alone and the solution where the probability of success is also taken into account. It was shown that the solution with utility consideration is superior. In addition, the centroid-based method is shown to scale much better than the SVM-based method, demonstrating a quality-speed tradeoff.

In the future, we will continue to explore the planning aspect of the problem, and apply the approach to more business databases.

References

[1] Aha, D. W., Kibler, D., & Albert, M. K. (1991). Instance-based learning algorithms. *Machine Learning, 6,* 37-66.

[2] R. Agrawal and R. Srikant. 1994. *Fast algorithm for mining association rules.* Proceedings of the Twentieth International Conference on Very Large Databases. pp 487-499

[3] F. Bacchus and A. Grove. 1995. *Graphical Models for Preference and Utility*, Proceedings of the Uncertainties in AI.

[4] C. L. Blake, C.J. Merz. 1998. *UCI Repository of machine learning databases* Irvine, CA: University of California, Department of Information and Computer Science. http://www.ics.uci.edu/~mlearn/MLRepository.html

[5] P. S. Bradley and U. M. Fayyad. 1998. *Refining initial points for k-means clustering*. In Proceedings of the Fifteenth International Conference on Machine Learning (ICML '98), pages 91--99, San Francisco, CA. Morgan Kaufmann Publishers.

[6] *Computational Intelligence Journal, Special Issue on Case-base Maintenance*. 2001. Blackwell Publishers, Boston MA UK. Vol. 17, No. 2, May 2001. Editors: D. Leake, B. Smyth, D. Wilson and Q. Yang.

[7] G. C. Cowley. 2000. *MATLAB Support Vector Machine Toolbox. v0.54B* University of East Anglia, School of Information Systems, Norwich, Norfolk, U.K. NR4 7TJ, 2000. http://theoval.sys.uea.ac.uk/~gcc/svm/toolbox

[8] P. Domingos and M. Richardson. 2001. *Mining the Network Value of Customers*. Proceedings of the Seventh ACM SIGKDD International Conference on Knowledge Discovery and Data Mining. August 2001. ACM. N.Y. N.Y. USA

[9] M. Ester, H.P. Kriegal, J. Sander and X. Xu (1996). A Denity-Based Algorithm for Discovering Clusters in Large Spatial Databases with Noise. In KDD 96 – Proceedings of 2nd International Conference on Knowledge Discovery and Data Mining. 1996

[10] L. Kaufman and P.J. Rousseeuw. 1990. *Finding Groups in Data: An Introduction to Cluster Analysis*. New York: John Wiley & Sons.

[11] R. L. Keeney and H. Raiffa. 1976. Decisions with Multiple Objectives: Preferences and Value Trade-offs, Wiley, New York.

[12] J.L. Kolodner. 1993. *Case-based Reasoning*. Morgan Kauffman Publishers. San Mateo, CA, USA

[13] D. Leake. 1996. *Case-based Reasoning -- Experiences*, Lessons and Future Directions. AAAI Press/ The MIT Press.
[14] C. X. Ling and C. Li. 1998. *Data mining for direct marketing: Problems and solutions*. In Proceedings 4th International Conference on Knowledge Discovery in Databases (KDD-98), New York.

[15] Mlademnic, D., Grobelnik, M. 1999 *Feature selection for unbalanced class distribution and Naïve Bayes*. Machine Learning: Proceedings of the Sixteenth International Conference, pp.258-267.

[16] J. C. Platt. 1999. *Fast training of support vector machines using sequential minimal optimization*, in Advances in Kernel Methods - Support Vector Learning, (Eds) B. Scholkopf, C. Burges, and A. J. Smola, MIT Press, Cambridge, Massachusetts, chapter 12, pp 185-208.

[17] J. R. Quinlan. 1993. C4.5: *Programs for Machine Learning*. Morgan Kaufmann Publishers, Inc., San Mateo, CA.

[18] B. Smyth and M. T. Keane. 1995. *Remembering to forget: A competence--preserving deletion policy for case--based reasoning systems*. In Proceedings of the 14th International Joint Conference on Artificial Intelligence, pp 377—382.

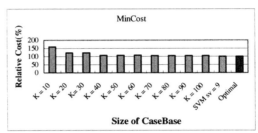

Figure 2. Relative cost vs. size of CB in *MinCost*. (Artificial data I, Mean 1 = [3, 4].)

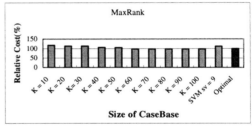

Figure 3. Relative cost vs. size of CB in MaxRank. (Artificial data I, Mean 1 = [3, 4].)

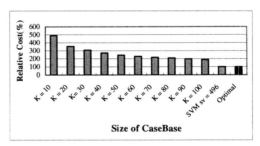

Figure 4. Relative cost vs. size of CB in MinCost. (Artificial data II, Mean 2 = [7, 8].)

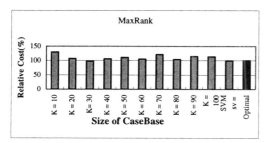

Figure 5. Relative cost vs. size of CB in MaxRank. (Artificial data II, Mean 2 = [7, 8].)

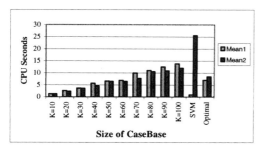

Figure 6. Comparison of CPU time for case-base mining for two different distributions Mean1 and Mean2 in the artificial dataset tests

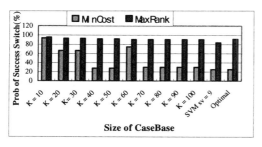

Figure 7. Success Prob P(+|t) vs. size of the CB. (Artificial data I, Mean 1 = [3, 4].)

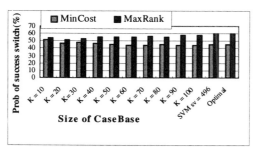

Figure 8.Success Probability P(+|t) vs. size of CB. (Artificial data II, Mean 2 = [7, 8].)

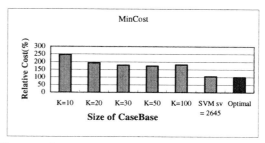

Figure 9 Relative cost vs. size of CB in MinCost. (KDD Cup98 data.)

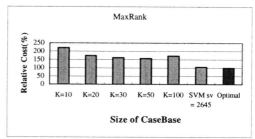

Figure 10. Relative cost vs. size of CB in MaxRank. (KDD Cup98 data.)

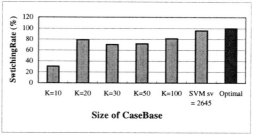

Figure 11. *SwitchingRate* vs. Size of CB for KDD Cup98 data.

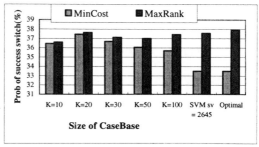

Figure 12. Success Prob P(+|t) vs. size of CB for KDD Cup98 data.

529

Adaptive Ripple Down Rules Method based on Minimum Description Length Principle

Tetsuya Yoshida
I.S.I.R., Osaka University
8-1 Mihogaoka, Ibaraki, 560-0047, Japan
yoshida@ar.sanken.osaka-u.ac.jp

Takuya Wada
R&D Laboratories, Nippon Organon K.K.
1-5-90 Tomobuchi, Miyakojima, 534-0016, Japan
Takuya.Wada@organon.jp

Hiroshi Motoda
I.S.I.R., Osaka University
8-1 Mihogaoka, Ibaraki, 560-0047, Japan
motoda@ar.sanken.osaka-u.ac.jp

Takashi Washio
I.S.I.R., Osaka University
8-1 Mihogaoka, Ibaraki, 560-0047, Japan
washio@ar.sanken.osaka-u.ac.jp

Abstract

When class distribution changes, some pieces of knowledge previously acquired become worthless, and the existence of such knowledge may hinder acquisition of new knowledge. This paper proposes an adaptive Ripple Down Rules (RDR) method based on the Minimum Description Length Principle aiming at knowledge acquisition in a dynamically changing enviromnent. To cope with the change of class distribution, knowledge deletion is carried out as well as knowledge acquisition so that useless knowledge is properly discarded. To cope with the change of the source of knowledge, RDR knowledge based systems can be constructed adaptively by acquiring knowledge from both domain experts and data. By incorporating inductive learning methods, knowledge acquision can be carried out even when only either data or experts are available by switching the source of knowledge from domain experts to data and vice versa at any time of knowledge acquisition. Since experts need not be available all the time, it contributes to reducing the cost of personnel expenses. Experiments were conducted by simulating the change of the source of knowledge and the change of class distribution using the datasets in UCI repository. The results are encouraging.

1. Introduction

With the recent development of computer network, huge amount of information in various forms is communicated through the network. To exploit the network infrastructure it is required to provide a methodology to construct a reliable and adaptive Knowledge Based System (KBS), which is ac-cessible to both experts and users over the network. However, receiving up-to-date information can induce changes on the domain from which knowledge is acquired. In such a changing environment it is necessary not only to incorporate new knowledge into a KBS but also to discard obsolete knowledge from the KBS so that the KBS can adapt to the changing environment dynamically.

When huge amount of data is available, it is difficult for human experts and knowledge engineers to process data manually. Utilizing machine learning methods is one promising approach to discover new knowledge from data automatically. However, human experts are capable of capturing the precious knowledge intuitively, which is difficult for machines. Thus, it is important to provide a methodology for the construction of a KBS which can exploit the information processing capability of both human experts and machines. For example, at the initial phase of the construction of a KBS there is not enough data available, and a human expert is the sole source of knowledge. However, at a later stage we can switch the source of knowledge to accumuated data without rebuilding the KBS from scratch. Being able not to rely on a human expert at all times during the construction of a KBS will contirubute to reducing the cost of personnel expenses.

As one promising methodology, we have been conducting research on "Ripple Down Rules [2] (RDR)" method, which is a knowledge acquision (KA) method from human experts. This paper proposes an adaptive RDR method based on the Minimum Description Length Principle (MDLP) [7, 4] aiming at knowledge acquisition in a dynamically changing enviromnent. As for the change of class distribution, knowledge deletion is carried out as well as knowledge acquisition so that useless knowledge is discarded to ensure efficient knowledge acquisition. In addition, a KBS can be constructed adaptively by acquiring knowledge from both domain experts and data so that the source of knowledge can be switched adaptively from domain experts to data and vice versa at any time during the construction of a KBS. Thus, in our apporoach, it is possible that an expert is involved only at the initial stage of the construction of a KBS and later the source of knowledge is switched to data so that the KBS is constructed inductively only from data afterward.

The proposed adaptive RDR method is evaluated through experiments on the synthesized data and the results are encouraging.

2. Ripple Down Rules

The basis of this method is the maintenance and retrieval of cases. When a case is incorrectly retrieved by an RDR system, the KA (maintenance) process requires the expert to identify how a case stored in a KBS differs from the present case. The structure of an RDR knowledge base is shown in Figure 1(a). Each node in the binary tree is a rule with a desired conclusion (If-Then rule). Each node has a "cornerstone case (CS-case)" associated with it, that is, the case that prompted the inclusion of the rule. An inference process for an incoming case starts from the root node of the binary tree. Then the process moves to the YES branch of the present node if the case satisfies the condition part of the node, and if it doesn't, the process moves to the NO branch. This process continues until there is no branch to move on. The conclusion for the incoming case is given by the conclusion part of the node in the inference path for the case whose condition part is lastly satisfied. Note that this node which has induced the conclusion for the case is called "last satisfied node (LSN)".

If the conclusion is different from that judged by an expert, knowledge (new rule) is acquired from him/her and added to the existing binary tree. The KA process in RDR is illustrated in Figure 1(b). When the expert wants to add a new rule, there must be a case that is misclassified by a rule in RDR. The system asks him/her to select conditions for the new rule from the "difference list (D-list)" between two cases: the misclassified case and the CS-case. Then, the misclassified one is stored as the refinement case (new CS-case) with the new rule whose condition part distinguishes these two cases. Depending on whether the LSN is the same as the end node (the last node in the inference path), the new rule and its CS-case are added at the end of YES or NO branch of the end node. Knowledge is never removed or changed, simply modified by adding exception rules.

3. Minimum Description Length Principle in RDR

"Description length (DL)" can measure the complexity of a hypothesis. When a hypothesis is a classifier of some representation (decision tree [6] or neural network [4]), given some appropriate encoding method, the value can be the sum of (1) a DL for encoding the hypothesis itself and (2) a DL for encoding the misclassified cases by the hypothesis. According to the MDLP, the model with the smallest total DL should be selected.

One of the differences between the proposed adaptive RDR and the standard one is that each node in the proposed binary tree of RDR keeps not only the CS-case but also the cases whose LSN is assigned to that node. Let P be a set consisting of m cases that has passed a node α in the inference process, and let O be a subset of P ($O \subseteq P$), consisting of r cases for which the node α is the LSN. In our encoding the DL of the tree is calculated first and then the one for the misclassified cases is calculated. The DL of the tree is calculated based on the pairs of an attribute and its value in P for the knowledge base. On the other hand, the one for the misclassified cases is based on the class information in O. Calculation of DL is illustrated using the cases and the binary tree in Figure 2.

No.	Swim	Breath	Legs	Class
1	can	lung	2legs	Dog
2	can	lung	4legs	Penguin
3	can	skin	2legs	Monkey
4	can	skin	4legs	Dog
5	can_not	lung	2legs	Dog
6	can_not	lung	4legs	Monkey
7	can_not	gill	2legs	Penguin
8	can_not	gill	4legs	Dog
9	can_not	skin	2legs	Dog
10	can_not	skin	4legs	Monkey

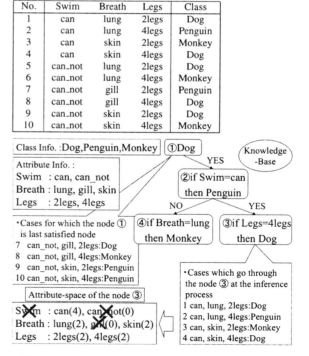

Figure 2. An example knowledge base and cases to calculate the DL.

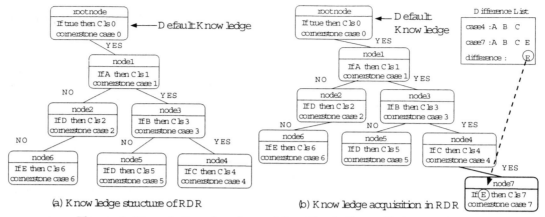

(a) Knowledge structure of RDR   (b) Knowledge acquisition in RDR

Figure 1. Knowledge structure of the Ripple Down Rules method

3.1. The DL of a Binary Tree

First, inference is made for all the cases which remain in the constructed binary tree to obtain the attribute-space of each node in the binary tree. From m cases that have passed through a node α, the frequency distribution of each attribute-value is used to obtain the attribute-space of the node α. The corresponding attribute-space consists of a set of attributes each having at least 2 attribute-values with its frequency of at least 1 case. The attribute-space of node No.3 in Figure 2 is {Breath:lung,skin, Legs:2legs,4legs}, which is depicted in the lower left-hand side of Figure 2.

Two kinds of information need to be encoded for the node α: one for the branches below the node and the other for an If-Then rule that is stored as knowledge in the node. The branch-information of the node No.3 is {YES-branch:<u>no</u> NO-branch:<u>no</u>} (there is no branch below the node No.3) and the rule-information of the node is {If Legs=4legs then Dog}. There are four branch-combinations for all nodes except for the root node, that is, the number of candidates is 4. Therefore, $\log_2 {}_4C_1$ bits are necessary to encode this information for the node α. The information needed to describe the If-Then rule consists of 4 components, **(1)** {the number of attributes used in the condition part}, **(2)** {attributes used in the condition part}, **(3)** {the attribute value for each used attribute} and **(4)** {the class used in the conclusion part}. $\log_2 {}_nC_1$ bits are necessary to encode the information of **(1)** because there are n candidates, {1,2,...,n}. Let the number of attributes used in the condition part be t. The information of **(2)** can be encoded by $\log_2 {}_nC_t$ bits because the number of combinations of having t 1's and n-t 0's is given by ${}_nC_t$. Next, $\log_2 {}_{m_i}C_1 + \log_2 {}_2C_1$ bits are necessary for each used attribute to encode the information of **(3)**. Here, m_i is the number of values for each attribute. The second term is the DL necessary to specify whether it is negated or not. Finally $\log_2 {}_{class\_num-1}C_1$ bits are necessary to encode the information of **(4)** because

the number of classes that are possible to use as the conclusion in each node except for the root node is $class\_num - 1$. Here, $class\_num$ is the number of classes in the problem domain.

For a numerical attribute A_i, the condition can be $\{? < A_i\}$, $\{A_i \leq ?\}$ or $\{? < A_i \leq ?\}$. Thus, $\log_2 {}_3C_1$ bits are necessary to identify which one to use for the DL of **(3)**. Suppose that m_i is the number of candidates for a cut-off value for the attribute A_i. When the condition is $\{? < A_i\}$ or $\{A_i \leq ?\}$, another $\log_2 {}_{m_i}C_1$ bits are necessary. On the other hand, when it is $\{? < A_i \leq ?\}$, $\log_2 {}_2C_1$ bits are needed to indicate which is encoded first lower bound or upper bound. In the former case, the upper one is encoded with $\log_2 {}_{m_i-k_i}C_1$ bits after the lower one is done with $\log_2 {}_{m_i}C_1$ bits. In the latter, the lower one is encoded with $\log_2 {}_{m_i-l_i}C_1$ bits after the upper one is encoded with $\log_2 {}_{m_i}C_1$ bits. Here, k_i (l_i) means that the lower (upper) cut-off value is the k_i-th (l_i-th) one from the left edge (right edge).

The sum of DLs to encode **(1)**, **(2)**, **(3)** and **(4)** is the DL necessary to encode the If-Then rule information for the node α. In the case of node No.3, it is $\log_2 {}_4C_1 + \log_2 {}_2C_1 + \log_2 {}_2C_1 + \log_2 {}_2C_1 + \log_2 {}_2C_1 + \log_2 {}_2C_1 = 5\log_2 {}_2C_1 + \log_2 {}_4C_1$ bits. The sum of the DL for the branch-information and the one for the rule-information is the DL for the node α. The whole knowledge base can be encoded by encoding every node in the tree from the root node downward.

3.2. The DL for Class Labels of Misclassified Cases

Suppose that k cases in O has the same class label with the consequence part of the rule in the node α. First, $\log_2 {}_rC_1$ bits are necessary to express that $r - k$ cases have different classes from the consequence part. If $k = r$, there is no misclassified case and no further encoding is required. If $k < r$, it is necessary to represent which class the remaining $r - k$ cases have. Suppose that the number of classes which are different from that for the CS-case is s and the number of cases for each class is $p_i (i = 1, 2, ..., s)$. The class labels are sorted in descending order with p_i, i.e., $p_s \geq p_{s-1} \geq ... \geq p_2 \geq p_1$. The DL for misclassified cases is calculated using the algorithm shown in Table 1. The function **ceil()** in the table returns the least greatest integer for the argument.

The DL for the i-th different class is calculated at the line "$DL = DL + \log_2(j) + ...$". The first term is for specifying which class label the case has, the second one is for the number of cases p_i with the class, and the last one is to encode the locations for p_i cases. With this encoding it is possible to identify the true class labels for $r - k$ cases if the encoded bits are decoded. Encoding the entire binary tree in top-down produces the bit string for the class labels which are attached to each misclassified case in the tree.

Table 1. Algorithm for DL to specify true classes of misclassified cases

initialize DL **to** 0,   : reset
    all_num **to** r,   : the # of O
    $right\_num$ **to** k,   : the # of right cases
    j **to** $class\_num - 1$,   : the # of class candidates
    i **to** s, **and**   : the # of different classes
    max_i **to** ∞.
repeat while $(all\_num \neq right\_num)$
  if $all\_num - right\_num < max_i$,
    then $candi = all\_num - right\_num$,
    else $candi = max_i$,
  if $all\_num - right\_num > j$
    then $candi = $
         $candi - \mathbf{ceil}((all\_num - right\_num) \div j)$.
  $DL = DL + \log_2(j) + \log_2(candi) + \log_2(_{all\_num}C_{p_i})$.
  $all\_num = all\_num - p_i$.
  $max_i = p_i$.
  decrement j **and** i.

3.3. The MDLP for the RDR method

Based on the MDLP, the binary tree with the smallest total DL should be most accurate for prediction. However, it is empirically known that most encoding methods tend to overestimate the DL for the knowledge base compared with the one for the class labels for the misclassified cases [5]. Thus, generally the following weighted sum is used to estimate the total DL:

$$Total\ DL = W \times (DL\ of\ Subsection\ 3.1) + (DL\ of\ Subsection\ 3.2) \qquad (1)$$

W is a weight and usually set to less than 1. In our approach W is set to 0.3 based on our experience [8].

4. Adaptive Ripple Down Rules Method

In addition to knowledge acquisition from human experts, we have incorporated various functions into RDR based on MDLP to enable efficient knowledge acquisition in a dynamically changing environment.

4.1. Knowledge Acquisition from Experts and Data

There are multiple candidates for the condition in D-list which distinguishes between the misclassified case and the CS-case. In our approach the element is selected which minimizes the total Description Length (DL) through greedy search based on the already encountered cases.

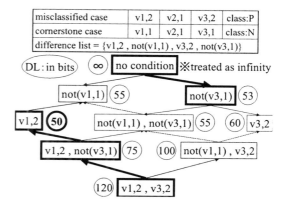

Figure 3. Greedy search for smaller DL.

Figure 3 is an example in which an input case misclassified by the so far grown RDR tree has the attributes values $\{v_{1,2}, v_{2,1}, v_{3,2}\}$ and a CS-case whose node has derived the false conclusion has the values $\{v_{1,1}, v_{2,1}, v_{3,1}\}$. The greedy search is carried out both from the most specialized condition to the misclassified case and from the most general condition to it. Thus, the search starts with a condition $\{v_{1,2} \& v_{3,2}\}$ which is most specialized to the input case, and it finds a condition $\{v_{1,2}\}$ that falls in a local minimum total DL. The search restarts with a condition $\{no\ condition\}$ which is most general for the input case, and it finds another condition $\{not(v_{3,1})\}$ that falls in a local minimum total DL. The condition $\{v_{1,2}\}$ found by the search from the most specialized condition has a smaller total DL than the condition $\{not(v_{3,1})\}$ by the search from the most general condition. The condition $\{v_{1,2}\}$ is selected as the condition part of a new node for the incoming case.

When a human expert is available as the source of knowledge, the set of elements which are selected by him/her is used to initiate search for finding out the condition with smaller DL in the above process. This can lead to finding a better condition from the viewpoint of MDLP, compared with the one selected by the expert. Experiments showed that incorporating the judgement (i.e., the selected set of conditions) from the human expert during the inductive construction of a KBS statistically improves its accuracy.

4.2. Knowledge Deletion for Changes of Class Distribution

Part of knowledge acquired previously may become worthless when class distribution or the noise rate on the domain changes over time. Moreover, such invalid knowledge may hinder efficient acquisition of new pieces of knowledge. When class distribution changes, the D-list may have no element even if the input case is misclassified by the current KBS. Even if the list is not empty, it does not make sense to add a node when no element in the list is judged as important by the expert. A naive way to cope with this issue is to discard the constructed KB completely when such a change is detected and to re-construct a new KB under new environment. However, when the change is slow, it is difficult to detect. Moreover, since some knowledge might be still valid for new environment, it would be reasonable to reuse such knowledge as much as possible.

The proposed criterion is based on the assumption that a new node is not to be added even if the input case is misclassified, when adding the node does not decrease the DL. First, tentatively delete the node which induces the wrong conclusion. The cases of the same class as the conclusion part of the deleted node are also deleted. Other cases of different classes, which were in the deleted node, are restored and redistributed in the tree to their new LSNs. If the normalized [1] total DL for the knowledge base after deletion is smaller than that of the current one, accept the deletion. Otherwise, recover the current knowledge base by retracting the deletion process.

A method for deleting a node is illustrated in Figure 4. Suppose that node No.2 is judged as contradictory. First, the node is deleted from the tree. Then, node No.4, which is the child node of the Yes branch, is connected to the Yes branch of node No.1. At the same time, the condition "a", which is the premise of the If-Then rule in node No.2, is added to node No.4. Next, the subtree below node No.3 is connected to the No branch of node No.7. Finally, the condition "a" is added to node No.7.

---

[1] Because the DL monotonically increases in proportion to the number of cases, comparing the total DLs for knowledge bases with different number of cases makes no sense. Since the number of cases stored in the knowledge base is different before and after the deletion, the total DL in comparison is normalized as DL_α/DL_α' and DL_β/DL_β'. Here, DL' denotes the DL for encoding the true class information for the whole cases in the current RDR tree without using the tree information, i.e. using the root node information alone.

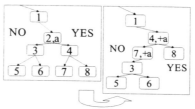

Delete node No.2 and reorganize the remaining RDR binary tree. "a" represents the condition of If-Then rule in node No.2. The condition "a" is attached to the nodes in the reorganized tree.

Figure 4. Deletion Algorithm

It is easy to confirm that no consistency arises for the stored CS-cases by this reconstruction of the tree. The illustrated process achieves the deletion of the CS-cases in a KBS and the cases which support the If-Then rule attached to the case simultaneously.

4.3. Pruning in RDR

In the context of inductive construction of a KBS, it is important to construct a model which avoids overfitting to training data so that it has high prediction accuracy for future data. C4.5, which is one of the machine learning methods for constructing a model in a batch, utilizes pruning to generalize the classifier which is constructed for the training data. Following this approach, pruning is also incorporated into the proposed RDR method for the incremental construction of a KBS.

Pruning is carried out as follows. First, tentatively prune (delete) a node from the RDR tree and calculate the total DL for the remaining KBS. If DL gets smaller, then adopt pruning since smaller DL means better prediction accuracy on future data from the viewpoint of MDLP. The major difference from knowledge deletion by data is that all the cases which are stored in the pruned node are stored in other nodes in the pruned KBS. Thus, what is removed from the KBS is only the piece of knowledge which is represented as the If-Then rule on the pruned node, not the cases themselves. This function is effective even for the static environment in which class distribution does not change. It plays the role of avoiding overfitting to the incoming data (i.e., training data), as in C4.5.

5. Evaluations and Discussions

Experiments were carried out using 15 datasets from University of California Irvine Data Repository [1]. Two types of experiment are reported. Knowledge deletion in Subsection 4.2 was examined in the first experiment to investigate the effect of the change of class distribution. Based on the promising result in the first experiment, the influence of the change of the source of knowledge (i.e., from an expert to data and vice versa) was examined in the second experiment. Synthesized cases were created and used in the experiments and the results were evaluated with respect to the prediction accuracy and the ratio of DL of the constructed KBS. Note that it was assumed that the expert could immediately change his/her internal model or expertise for the domain according to the change of class distribution. Said differently, the label of incoming data is always assumed to be correct, reflecting the eivironment.

[Generation of Datasets with different Class Distribution] A set of cases X_{chg} with different class distribution from the original dataset X_{org} were generated. First, all the cases in X_{org} are sorted with respect to values in lexical order for nominal attributes and in ascending order for numerical attributes. Then, they are sorted in lexical order for class label. Finally, the labels for (#of all cases $\div$ #of classes $\div$ ($100 \div x$)) cases are changed by shifting them so that the class label for about $x\%$ of cases in X_{org} is changed to the neighboring class label.

[Training Data and Test Data] Each dataset was divided into the 75% training data (e.g., $X_{org}^{train}, X_{chg}^{train}$) and the 25% test data (e.g., $X_{org}^{test}, X_{chg}^{test}$).

[Accuracy of Knowledge Base] The error rate of misclassified case for the test data was examined using the knowledge base at prespecified time points for each datasets. Note that we use $X_{org}^{test}, X_{chg}^{test}$ as the test data when the population is $X_{org}^{train}, X_{chg}^{train}$, respectively. Since a different ordering of input cases results in a different knowledge base of RDR [8], we repeated the simulation 10 times, changing the parameter of random sampling for the input case from the population at each simulation and the error rate was calculated as the average.

5.1. Experiment on the Change of Class Distribution

On each dataset the class distribution of the problem domain was changed abruptly twice during the simulation for the RDR system to acquire knowledge from the data. A set of cases X_α, X_β with different class distribution from the original dataset X_{org} were generated. The class labels for about 10% of cases in X_{org} were modified in X_α and those of about 20% of cases in X_{org} were modified in X_β. First, by treating X_β as the original population, input cases which are selected randomly from X_β^{train} (with replacement as many times as required) are passed to the RDR system. When the total number of cases passed to the system becomes equal to three times large as that of the original population, the population is changed to X_α. After that the system receives the cases drawn from the X_α^{train}. When

Table 2. Summary of experimental results.

Data Set	RDR				C4.5 (%)	C4.5 with whole cases(%)
	X_β (%)	X_α (%)	X_{org} (%)	% of cases		
Car	8.4	10.1	9.2	92.6	9.6	11.6
Nursery	2.7	4.4	6.3	93.5	5.7	8.7
Mush rooms	0.1	2.1	5.7	92.2	5.2	12.2
Krvkp	3.9	4.5	6.3	87.9	6.1	10.9
Voting Record	12.0	10.9	9.8	85.6	6.1	7.3
Breast Cancer	6.6	6.2	5.3	89.9	4.6	9.1
Splice	14.3	9.9	11.3	88.3	9.3	17.4
Image	11.5	9.1	5.0	90.3	4.8	14.0
Page Blocks	3.2	6.3	6.3	81.1	6.3	9.4
Pen Digits	9.5	6.8	5.6	90.1	5.2	14.2
Yeast	60.6	47.8	47.0	50.3	42.9	17.8
Pima Indians	39.6	33.2	29.1	43.8	26.1	16.7
German Credit	26.6	23.0	20.1	75.3	16.4	13.0
Cmc	52.4	53.7	47.2	41.4	42.4	23.3
Ann Thyroid	1.5	3.8	3.4	86.2	3.8	10.3

*cases which exist in the knowledge base eventually

the total number of cases drawn from X_α^{train} becomes three times large as that of the population, it is changed to X_{org}.

Table 2 summarizes the results at the end of each simulation when the RDR system received all the cases. The columns for **% of cases** represent the ratio of cases which were kept inside the knowledge base with respect to the whole cases. The ones for **RDR**, namely, for X_β, X_α, X_{org}, represent the error rate of the knowledge base for the respective test data at the end of each interval. The decision trees were constructed by C4.5 using the cases held in the knowledge bases at the end of simulation. The column for **C4.5** represents the error rate of such decision trees. Moreover, the column for **C4.5 with whole cases** shows the error rate of decision trees using all input cases.

From the results knowledge deletion is effective for the change of class distribution since the column for X_{org} shows lower error rate than that for **C4.5 with whole cases** in 10 datasets out of 15. However, with knowledge deletion the number of cases used to construct a KB of RDR becomes different from that for **C4.5 with whole cases**. Comparison of the column for X_{org} and that for **C4.5** shows the difference in error rate for the same number of cases. Although C4.5 showed lower error rate in many datasets, C4.5 constructs a classifier in batch, contrary to the incremental approach in RDR. If C4.5 were modified to construct a decision tree incrementaly, the error rate of the constructed decision tree would increase. Moreover, for the dataset "AnnThyroid", more accurate knowledge bases were constructed for **RDR** compared with **C4.5**. This result also suggests that the deletion algorithm works well, and can delete the worthless knowledge. Other dataset where such a tendency is shown is "Car".

Unfortunately, the error rate for **RDR** was high for some datasets with relatively small number of cases (e.g., "Cmc" and "Yeast") compared with **C4.5 with whole cases**. Since the construction of a KBS is based on the MDLP, if only small amount of cases are available, it is difficult to construct a KB with high prediction accuracy. Our current conjecture is that the deletion algorithm tends to delete too many cases, especially when the size of the original datasets is relatively small. For instance, only 41.4% of the original cases were held in the KB for "Cmc" with deletion.

5.2. Experiment on the Change of the Souce of Knowledge

The second experiment was carried out to investigate the effect of turning on and off the proposed functions in RDR during the consecutive course of knowledge acquistion in more detail. The dataset "nursery" with 12960 cases, 5 classes, and 8 attributes [2] was used and a set of cases X_α were generated so that the class label for about 10% in X_{org} was changed. First, by treating X_{org} as the original population, cases which were selected randomly from X_{org}^{train} were passed to the RDR system. When the total number of cases passed to the system becomed 3000, the population was changed to X_α. After that the system received 6000 cases drawn from X_α^{train}. Thus, the change of class distribution occured at the 3001st case and the RDR system received 9000 cases in total.

Simulated Expert [3] (SE) is usually used instead of a human expert for the reproduction of experiments and consistent performance estimation in the RDR research community. Note that when $X_{org}^{train}(X_{chg}^{train})$ is the population, we make an If-Then rule set derived from a decision tree constructed by the standard C4.5 [5] using $X_{org}(X_{chg})$ to be the SE. A set of elements selected from the D-list by the SE is defined as the intersection between the list and the condition part of the If-Then rule in the SE which predicts correctly the case misclassified by the RDR system at the KA stage. For a numeric attribute, if there is an element in the D-list that satisfies the inequality condition of the SE rule, this inequality is interpreted as an element in the intersection. Thus, the condition which is nearest to the set selected by SE out of the candidates in the lattice space illustrated in Figure 3 is the starting condition for the search.

Five methods which selectively utilized the proposed functions in RDR for the predifined period were examined in the experiment. As in the first experiment, C4.5 was also

---

[2] All the attributes are discrete.

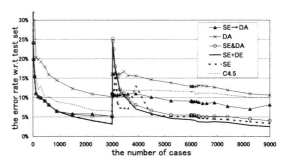

Figure 5. The number of misclassified cases.

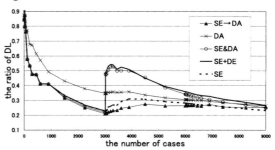

Figure 6. The ratio of DL.

examined for comparison. The characteristics of five methods and C4.5 are shown in Table 3. Note that since C4.5 is not an incremental method, every time a new case was drawn from the population, the already constructed decision tree was discarded and a new tree was constructed. For instance, the decision tree for the 6000 cases was constructed by treating the cases as the training set.

The result is illustrated in Figure 5 and 6, which show the change of error rate with respect to the test data and the change of the ratio of DL, respectively. In "SE→DA" the SE was used as the source of knowledge at the initial phase of the construction of a KBS and only data were utilized after 1000 cases for constructing the KBS. Compared with "DA" in which only data is used for constructiong a KBS, the speed of KA seems faster in "SE→DA". Even after the change of class distribution at the 3000th case, the error rate was kept low. "SE+DA" is the same with "SE→DA" except that the SE was also utilized from the 3000th case to the 4500th one. Compared with "SE→DA" and "DA", "SE→DA" showed even faster KA after the change of class distribution.

"SE&DE" , in which the SE was utilized as the source of knowledge all the time, showed the immidiate adaptation to the change and the error rate for future data was the lowest. Note that the error rate in "SE+DA" was equivalent with that in "SE&DE". This result indicates that even if the expert is not available all the time, it would be possible to construct an equivalent KBS if KA from the expert is carried out at an appropriate timing.

Compared with C4.5, the methods except "DA" showed lower error rate. Since learning is carried out incrementally

536

Table 3. Five methods and C4.5 in simulation.

method	the number of cases				
	1~1000	1000~2500	2500~3000	3000~4500	4500~9000
SE→DA	KA with SE	KA,PR,DE with DA	KA,PR,DE with DA	KA,PR,DE with DA	KA,PR,DE with DA
DA	KA,PR,DE with DA	KA,PR,DE with DA	KA,PR,DE with DA	KA,PR,DE with DA	KA,PR,DE with DA
SE+DA	KA with SE	KA with DA	KA,PR,DE with DA	KA,PR with SE	KA,PR,DE with DA
SE&DE	KA with SE	KA with SE	KA with SE	KA,DE with SE	KA,DE with SE
SE	KA with SE	KA with SE	KA with SE	KA with SE	KA with SE
C4.5	C4.5	C4.5	C4.5	C4.5	C4.5

SE: Simulated Expert！$DA: Data！$KA: Knowledge Acquision！$PR: PRuning！$DE: DEletion of Knowledge

and inductively only from data in "DA", it seems reasonable that the error rate in that method is higher than that in C4.5, which carries out learning in a batch. However, the difference in the error rate between "DA", and C4.5 becomes small after the change of class distribution in Figure 5. This can be attributed to the deletion of useless pieces of knowledge in "DA", as in "SE→DA" and "SE+DA", which enables it to follow the change of class distribution adaptively.

In Figure 6 the ratio of DL suddenly increases in "SE+DA" and "SE&DE" at the 3001st case when class distribution changed. However, it rapidly decreases compared with "SE→DA" and "DA". This rapid decrease is attributed to the deletion of useless piece of knowledge by the SE, which enables the RDR method to acquire new pieces of knowledge into a KBS. "SE" is the same with "SE&DE" except that deletion by the expert is not utilized. Figure 5 shows that the error rate in "SE" is equivalent to that in "SE&DE" from the 6000th to 9000th case. However, the change of the ratio of DL differs in these methods.

The ratio of DL is small in "DA", which does not rely on the SE, and in "SE→DA", which uses the SE only at the initial phase in the construction of a KBS. However, the error rate of these methods are greater than that of the ones in which the SE is more heavily used, namely, "SE+DA", "SE&DE" and "SE". In our approach DL is calculated based on the already encounterd data (cases) and the remaining training cases are not used even if they are expected to be passed to RDR for constructing the KBS. Thus, there is some limitation for constructing effective RDR incrementally solely based on the MDLP with respect to the prediction accuracy for unseen future data.

6. Conclusion

This paper has proposed an adaptive Ripple Down Rules method based on the Minimum Description Length Principle aiming at knowledge acquisition in a dynamically changing enviromnent. To cope with the change of class distribution, knowledge deletion is carried out as well as knowledge acquisition so that useless knowledge is discarded to facilitate efficient knowledge acquisition. In addi-

tion, a KBS can be constructed adaptively by switching the source of knowledge from domain experts to data and vice versa at any time depending on their availablility. The proposed method is evaluated through experiments on the synthesized datasets and the results show the possibility of constructing knowledge base systems adaptively without fully relying on domain experts in a dynamically changing environment.

Acknowledgements

This work was partially supported by the grant-in-aid for scientific research 1) on priority area "Active Mining" (No. 13131101, No. 13131206) and 2) No. 13558034 funded by the Japanese Ministry of Education, Culture, Sport, Science and Technology.

References

[1] C. Blake and C. Merz. UCI repository of machine learning databases, 1998. http://www.ics.uci.edu/~mlearn/MLRepository.html.

[2] P. Compton, G. Edwards, G. Srinivasan, et al. Ripple down rules: Turning knowledge acquisition into knowledge maintenance. *Artificial Intelligence in Medicine*, pages 47–59, 1992.

[3] P. Compton, P. Preston, and B. Kang. The use of simulated experts in evaluating knowledge acquisition. In *Proc. of the 9th Knowledge Acquisition for Knowledge Based Systems Workshop*, Banff, Canada, University of Calgary, 1995. SRDG Publications.

[4] D. Gary and J. Trevor. Optimal network construction by minimum description length. *Neural Computation*, pages 210–212, 1993.

[5] J. Quinlan, editor. *C4.5: Programs for Machine Learning*. Morgan Kaufmann, 1993.

[6] J. Quinlan and R. Rivest. Inferring decision trees using the minimum description length principle. *Information and Computation*, pages 227–248, 1989.

[7] J. Rissanen. Modeling by shortest data description. *Automatica*, pages 465–471, 1978.

[8] T. Wada, H. Motoda, and T. Washio. Knowledge acquisition from both human expert and data. In *Proc. of the Fifth Pacific-Asia Conference on Knowledge Discovery and Data Mining*, pages 550–561, 2001.

Heterogeneous Learner for Web Page Classification

Hwanjo Yu, Kevin Chen-Chuan Chang, Jiawei Han
University of Illinois at Urbana-Champaign
Department of Computer Science
University of Illinois, Urbana-Champaign, IL, USA
{hwanjoyu, kcchang, hanj}@uiuc.edu

Abstract

Classification of an interesting class of Web pages (e.g., personal homepages, resume pages) has been an interesting problem. Typical machine learning algorithms for this problem require two classes of data for training: positive and negative training examples. However, in application to Web page classification, gathering an unbiased sample of negative examples appears to be difficult. We propose a heterogeneous learning framework for classifying Web pages, which (1) eliminates the need for negative training data, and (2) increases classification accuracy by using two heterogeneous learners. Our framework uses two heterogeneous learners – a decision list and a linear separator which complement each other – to eliminate the need for negative training data in the training phase and to increase the accuracy in the testing phase. Our results show that our heterogeneous framework achieves high accuracy without requiring negative training data; it enhances the accuracy of linear separators by reducing the errors on "low-margin data". That is, it classifies more accurately while requiring less human efforts in training.

1. Introduction

Automatic categorization or classification of Web pages has been studied extensively, and most of those classification techniques are usually based on similarity between documents' contents or their hyperlink structures. However, the categories generated by those techniques do not always fit end-users' search purposes since they cannot consider each user's specific interest. Let's think about a query "Find XML experts" on a common search engine. We may want to hit the keyword "XML" or "experts" on any search engine, and try to refine the search results repeatedly until we collect a fair amount of XML expert pages. However, if we are able to specify a search class or domain into "resume" or "personal homepage," we could simply apply a search term

"XML" within the classes of resume or personal homepage to collect XML expert pages.

Automatic classification of specific types of documents such as newspaper articles, patent documents, calls for papers, and personal homepage have been proposed for this problem[7, 15]. However, these solutions have some limitations: they are quite dependent on specific classes, and they require laborious work to create a new classifier of interest. In particular, they require collecting positive training data and unbiased negative training data that uniformly represents the negative class. Finally, they show relatively poor performance particularly on classifying *low-margin data*. *Low-margin data* is the data that is relatively close to the separator, thus is often misclassified by linear separators. For example, if a personal homepage has not much personal information, it may be close to the separator of personal homepage class, and thus becomes a *low-margin data*. This problem is a well-known drawback of linear separators such as Winnow, Perceptron, and Perceptron-like algorithms [14, 18, 4, 6, 19, 12].

We present here a new machine learning framework that exactly matches these problems of Web page classification. Our framework uses two heterogeneous learners – a decision list and a linear separator which complement each other – in both training and testing phases. There have been many attempts to use multiple homogeneous learners to increase classification accuracy. However, combination of homogeneous learners generally does not overcome the genuine weaknesss of each learner. The purpose of the decision list in training phase is to eliminate the need for negative training data in constructing a linear separator. The decision list in testing phase enhances the accuracy of the linear separator especially for low-margin data. As a result, our heterogeneous framework (1) makes easier to create a classifier for a new concept by reducing the work to collect training documents, and also (2) increases the final classification accuracy by complementing the weakness of linear separators for low-margin data.

The contributions of our framework are the following.

- Our heterogeneous framework enables *pre-filtering* stage in training phase to induce negative training data from universe and positive training data. Previous machine learning schemes need to classify large number of pages manually to prepare *unbiased* positive and negative training documents. The pre-filtering stage makes possible to construct a classifier without requiring negative training data, which speeds up the process of creating a classifier for a new class, but also opens a possible way to support type-specific queries on the Internet from sample pages.

- We propose a new *early-inclusion* stage for correctly classifying low-margin data. Linear separators such as Winnow, Perceptron, and SVMs have been studied extensively and have proved their outstanding performances when the environment has high dimensions, the number of active features is small, and the instance spaces are sparse. Consequently, the linear separators are the most widely used algorithms for Web page classification problems since Web page classification has the same properties as environment these linear separators work well. However, they have showed weakness in classification of low-margin data [14, 18, 4, 6, 19, 12]. Our *early-inclusion* stage complements this weakness and achieves higher accuracy for low-margin data without sacrificing any performance on other data.

The rest of the paper is organized as follows. Section 2 describes the problem and our approach in detail. Section 3 presents the algorithm of each stage in the framework. In Section 4, we describe the experiment environment and results, and we evaluate the experiment results. Section 5 describes the related work. The conclusions and future works are discussed in Section 6.

2 Problem Description and Heterogeneous Framework

A typical algorithm for learning linear separators consists of two phases: training phase and testing phase (Figure 1). In training phase, the algorithm reads positive and negative training data to construct a linear separator (LS). The testing phase classifies testing documents by the LS constructed in the training phase. The typical learning framework suffers from the need of negative training data and the inherent inaccuracy for classifying low-margin data as we briefly mentioned in Section 1. To address these problems, we propose a heterogeneous framework built upon a linear separator (LS). Specifically, we introduce two stages: To eliminate the need for collecting class-specific negative data, our heterogeneous framework uses a *pre-filtering*

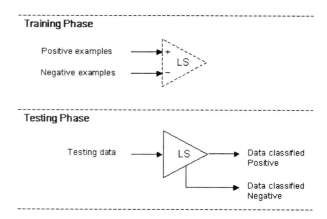

Figure 1. The typical learning framework

stage in the training phase. To improve classification accuracy on the low-margin data, the testing phase adopts an *early-inclusion* stage. The two stages use a decision list (DL) having different threshold parameter values. Figure 2 shows the linear separator (LS) and the decision list (DL) of the pre-filtering and early-inclusion stages in each phase of the framework. The DL of the pre-filtering and early-inclusion stages is constructed in the training phase I, and the LS is trained using pre-filtering DL in the training phase II. The early-inclusion DL and LS classify the testing data in the testing phase. In the following, we describe the problems and the approaches of each stage in details.

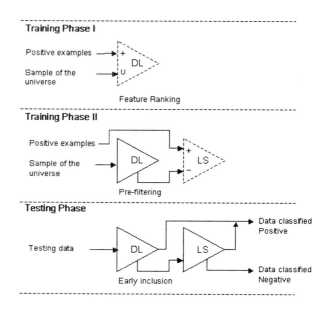

Figure 2. Our heterogeneous framework

2.1 Pre-filtering: Inducing Negative Training Data

An important issue to make a good linear separator is to prepare a good set of training documents that uniformly represent the concept without any bias. Since we are dealing with binary classification that separates a class of interest from the others, users would need to collect two sets of training data, the sample of class C and its complement $\neg C$. The portion of the class C in the universe ($P(C)$) is usually much smaller than the portion of its complement ($P(\neg C)$). For instance, "college admission pages" take very small percentages of the Internet. $P(C)$ may be less than 0.1%, and $P(\neg C)$ more than 99.9% in this case. Collecting negative training data $\neg C$ requires significant amount of manual classifications because the sample of negative data must represent the entire universe while excluding the instances of C.

One might argue that using a sample of universal set itself as a substitute for negative training data is valid since $P(C)$ is usually much smaller than $P(\neg C)$. However, a small number of false positives in the training data can impair the classification performance of linear separators, as our experiments show in Section 4.

Our heterogeneous framework does not require collecting $\neg C$ to construct a classifier. Instead, it uses a uniform sample of the universe, which can be collected automatically from a repository such as DMOZ[1]. Once the uniform sample is collected, it is reused for any classes, and thus making the training of a new classifier much easier. In our experiments, we used a random sampler to collect a uniform sample of the universe from DMOZ automatically. The pre-filtering stage in the training phase constructs an unbiased sample of negative training data from the sample of the universe and the positive training data. The unbiased negative training data is used then with the positive training data in order to learn a linear classifier. Our results show that the pre-filtering stage helps to achieve high accuracy without requiring negative training data.

2.2 Early-inclusion: Identifying Low-margin Data

The performance of linear separator such as Winnow, Perceptron, and Perceptron-like algorithms is dependent on the distance between the separator and example, usually referred to as "margin" [6]. In other words, most classification errors of those linear separators come from low-margin data, the data near the separator. The distance D between an example and the separator is formulated as

$$D = \frac{w \cdot h(d)}{||w|| ||h(d)||},\qquad(1)$$

where w is a weight vector of the linear function (i.e. $< w_1, w_2, w_3, ..., w_n >$), and $h(d)$ is a feature vector of an example d (i.e. $< h_1(d), h_2(d), h_3(d), ..., h_n(d) >$).

In order to identify the relationship between the distance D and the classification performance on real Web data, we randomly chose three common classes – "computer shopping," "sports shopping," and "stocks and bonds" – from DMOZ, and classified the pages of the classes using one of those linear separators (i.e. the Winnow algorithm). Figure 3 shows the distribution of examples at each distance from the separator in the feature space. For this figure, we used randomly selected 200 pages of each class to train each class, and used another 200 pages for testing. The figure shows that each class has fairly many pages near the separator and that most of false negatives come from examples near the separator. This observation shows that the inaccuracy of classifying low-margin data is a major problem for Web page classification.

The distance of an example from the separator is determined by the weight (w) of every active feature ($h_i(d)$) of the example as shown in the formula of D. The linear separators such as Winnow, Perceptron, or Perceptron-like algorithms determine the weight of each feature according to its likelihood to appear in the training data. Therefore, an example would be located near the separator if the example has a small number of *discriminative* positive features that may not occur frequently in the positive class, and if the example also has many non-positive features. For instance, if a personal homepage has the title "personal homepage", it is a personal homepage even if it does not have any personal information in it. That is, "personal homepage" in title is a discriminative feature for the personal homepage class although it does not occur frequently in the class.

Our early-inclusion stage helps to identify those misclassified low-margin data. As a result, this stage reduces the total classification error rate. The early-inclusion stage identifies the small number of discriminative positive features from positive training data and the sample of the universe, and uses these features to label obvious positive pages before sending the documents to the next stage of linear separator function as Figure 2 shows.

Our results show that the accuracy of classification increases for all test classes we considered (i.e. personal homepages, resume pages, and college admission pages) by adding the early-inclusion stage, which implies the early-inclusion stage actually identifies the discriminative features that may not get weights high enough to be classified correctly by the linear separators.

3 Algorithms

This section explains the algorithms of each stage in the framework. First, we discuss the linear separator algorithms

---

[1] http://dmoz.org

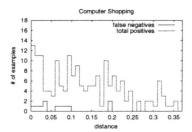
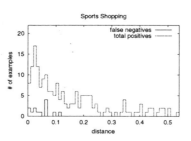
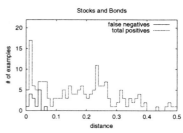

Figure 3. The distribution of misclassified examples according to their distance from the separator (The distribution of false positives is also similar, but we only show false negatives because the *early-inclusion* deals with only false negatives. See Section 4 for details)

that can be plugged into this framework. After that, we describe the feature ranking algorithm that we use for the pre-filtering and early-inclusion stages, and explain how each stage uses this feature ranking algorithm.

3.1 Linear separators

Different kinds of linear separators can be used in our framework. In comparison, Winnow performs better than Perceptron when the number of relevant features is small. Perceptron performs better than Winnow when the instance spaces are sparse [11]. We use Winnow [14] and SVM (Support Vector Machine) [4] in our experiments because both algorithms have shown good performance for Web page classification and are among the most widely used for this purpose.

3.2 Feature ranking

Both the pre-filtering and early-inclusion stages use a feature ranking algorithm that ranks only positive features according to their frequencies of occurrence in the positive example and the universe. We call *positive features* the features that are active in positive examples. Among such features we distinguish *strong positive features* that are very likely to appear in a positive example. We call *strong positive* the examples that have one or more active strong positive features. In the following we will develop a quantitative model describing these concepts.

We would like to measure the strength of a positive feature. For this purpose, we use weights that capture the relative frequencies of the corresponding feature in the sample of a particular class s: $f_s(x) = n_s(x)/N_s$, where $n_s(x)$ is the number of pages in the sample having feature x and N_s is the total number of pages in the sample. We calculate the weight of feature x as follows:

$$w(x) = \frac{f_+(x)}{f_U(x)} * (f_+(x) - f_U(x)), \qquad (2)$$

where $f_+(x)$: the relative frequency of feature x in the sample of positive class, and $f_U(x)$: the relative frequency of feature x in the sample of the universe.

Note we do not use entropy loss to rank features because it is hard to estimate the probabilities of positive and negative examples, or P_+ and P_- respectively. In this case, a small error in estimating the probability of each class can make a large difference in ranking result when P_+ is extremely small compared to P_- (as we discussed in the previous section).

Our weighting formula considers the rate $(\frac{f_+}{f_U})$ and difference $(f_+ - f_U)$ of each feature's frequency in the positive class and the universe. This formula has shown advantages among several other weighting formulas that were explored in our experiments (including TFIDF weights).

We will use this weighting function in constructing the pre-filtering algorithm which uses strong features to approximate negative training data.

3.3 Pre-filtering

The pre-filtering stage uses strong positive features to filter out strong positive data from the sample of the universe, and thus induces a good approximation of the negative training data. Figure 4 shows the pre-filtering algorithm.

We first extract positive features from T_+ and T_U, and rank them by the weighting formula in Equation (2). (Steps 1 through 3 of the algorithm in Figure 4). We take out a chunk of top ranked features by applying the following threshold function θ onto the list (set) of positive features (Steps 4 and 5 of the algorithm in Figure 4).

$$\theta = max_{x \in t}(\gamma(x)), \qquad (3)$$

where $t = \{ x \mid x \text{ is the strongest positive feature in some document } d, \forall d \in T_+ \}$.

The threshold θ is the worst ranking among the strongest positive features in each document. For example, say that we have only three positive documents d_1, d_2, and d_3, and

Input: T_+ a sample of the positive class, T_U a sample of the universe
Output: T_- a sample of the negative class needed for training the linear separator stage
Notation: A document d denotes a set of its active features. ($x \in d$ means a feature x is present in document d. $x \in T_+$ implies $x \in d, \forall d \in T_+$)
Algorithm:

1. Extract all positive features R from T_+ ($R = \cup_{x \in T_+} x$)

2. Rank the features in R based on the weighting function $w(x)$ ($w(x) = \frac{f_+(x)}{f_U(x)} * (f_+(x) - f_U(x))$)

3. Let $\gamma(x)$ returns the ranking of feature x (a smaller number indicates higher ranking.)

4. Compute a threshold θ with the following formula
$\theta = max_{x \in t}(\gamma(x))$,
$t = \{ x \mid x \text{ is the strongest positive feature in some document } d, \forall d \in T_+ \}$.

5. Extract strong positive features S by applying θ to R ($S = \{ x \in R \mid \gamma(x) < \theta \}$)

6. Extract negative documents T_- ($T_- = \{ d \in T_U \mid d \cap S = \emptyset \}$)

Figure 4. The pre-filtering algorithm

the global rankings $\gamma(x)$ of the strongest positive feature in each document are 11, 14, and 7 respectively. (That is, feature x with $\gamma(x) = 11$ is the strongest positive feature in document d_1.) Then we set the threshold θ to 14, which is the lowest ranking of them. This heuristic for the threshold θ fairly reasonably approximates negative training examples which does not significantly impact classification performance.

The negative training data T_- is constructed by excluding the documents having any of those strong features S from the sample of the universe T_U. We assume that the document d is positive if the intersection $d \cap S$ not empty. We exclude such documents from T_U to obtain an induced sample of the negative class.

3.4 Early-inclusion

In early-inclusion stage, we scan test documents to see if they have any discriminative features. If they have, we label them as positives, and exclude them from the next stage. We will call a feature x as discriminative if $\gamma(x) < \theta'$ (i.e. the feature x is ranked higher than θ') for some threshold γ'.

We apply a linear function computed in the training phase only to the rest of the test documents which are not labeled in the early-inclusion stage. We induce the discriminative positive feature set by applying another smaller threshold θ' to the same feature ranking function γ. Note that θ' is smaller than θ because the discriminative positive feature set needs stronger requirement of positivity.

Thus, the set of discriminative positive features S' is

$$S' = \{ x \in R \mid \gamma(x) < \theta' \} \quad (4)$$

Documents from the testing set T having at least one of active features from S' are labeled positive such that

$$T_+' = \{ d \in T \mid d \cap S' \neq \emptyset \} \quad (5)$$

The documents that are not labeled in the early-inclusion stage are routed into the linear separator.

The threshold θ' can be adjusted through a validation process, such that it is set as high as possible under the condition that the early-inclusion (T_+') does not introduce false positive. Our experiment (Table 1 in Section 4) shows that the early-inclusion stage does not increases the number of false positives while it does decrease the number of false negatives.

This two-stage classification can be viewed as a serial connection of a simple decision list and a linear separator because the early-inclusion is essentially a decision list using discriminative features. Our experiments described in Section 4 show that this combination of two classifiers complements the weakness of each other.

4 Experiments

4.1 Experimental Methodology

To test our framework, we chose three classes: personal homepages, college admission pages, and resume pages. For each class, we collected 233, 97, and 100 positive training documents respectively. We randomly selected 2514 pages from DMOZ to construct a uniform sample of the universe. For each class, we tested around 600 pages that are not duplicated with the training data. In reality, personal homepages are extremely diverse, so we confined the personal homepage class to pages having personal information. Pages having only images or extremely small amount of text were removed from the experiments.

We extracted features from different parts of a page—URL, title, headings, link, anchor-text, normal text, and meta tags. Each feature is a predicate indicating whether each term or special character appears in each part, e.g., '~' in URL, or a word 'homepage' in title. We did not use stemming or a stoplist because it could hurt performance in

Web page classification. For example, a common stopword, "I" or "my", is a good indicator of a student homepage.

As we mentioned in previous section, we performed the experiments using two different linear separators, Winnow [14] and SVM (Support Vector Machine) with linear kernel function [4]. We use SNOW (Sparse Network Of Winnow) [2] for Winnow implementation, and SVM LIGHT [9] for SVM implementation.

4.2 Results

We first show the performance comparison on the three classes between the typical framework and our heterogeneous framework. After that, we discuss the concrete impacts of early-inclusion stage on performance.

4.2.1 Performance comparison

Table 1 shows the classification error rates of Winnow and SVM respectively on the three classes "resume", "college admission", and "personal homepage." Typical learning framework that uses positive training data and samples of universe as negative training data shows high rates of false negatives. This problem is the consequence of placing too deep in the positive class. Using pre-filtering stage, the false negatives decrease substantially without much sacrificing the performance on negative testing documents. The early-inclusion stage decreases even more the classification errors on the positive examples while keeping the classification errors on the negative examples from increasing (Table 1).

4.2.2 Impact of the early-inclusion stage on performance and data margin

The early-inclusion stage uses a decision list. Figure 5 shows the performance gain by serializing the early-inclusion stage and the linear classification stage for personal homepage classification. The first graph in Figure 5 shows the number of false negatives at each distance when using only a linear separator (i.e. Winnow using the SNOW [2]). In this graph, most errors of the linear separator come from low-margin data. The second graph in the figure shows the classification errors when using only a decision list of the early-inclusion stage. The classification errors of the second graph are fairly spread over every distance compared to the linear separator graph. The last graph of the figure 5 shows the reduced classification errors using the two stages connected serially. In this case, the decision list of early-inclusion stage complements the linear separator's shortcoming by reducing the errors on low-margin data, which results in higher overall accuracy. Figures 6 and 7 show the same results when classifying resume pages and college admission pages respectively.

4.3 Discussion

When we classify Web pages manually, we may consider many factors such as title, text, url, and so on as the typical machine learning algorithms do. However, a small number of discriminative positive features could determine the class of a page regardless of the other factors. (e.g. if we see "personal homepage" on title, it is likely to be a personal homepage no matter what content it has.) A learning algorithm such as linear separators (i.e. Winnow, Perceptron, or Perceptron-like algorithms) may not weigh the discriminative features high enough. This problem can occur if the features occur infrequently. In this case, the linear separator can misclassify a page if the page has much non-relevant information. Usually, the distance of those pages are close to the separator as we discussed in Section 2.

Our framework identifies discriminative features using the feature ranking algorithm we explained in Section 3. The early-inclusion stage uses discriminative features to include low-margin positive data in the positive class, preventing misclassification of this data by a linear separator. Thus, the final classification accuracy increases.

5 Related Work

The research community has been extensively working on text classification problems, and there have been many attempts to extend this work to Web page classification [5, 17, 1, 3]. Most of those classification techniques are usually based on similarity of documents or their hyperlink structures. They usually require pre-defined categories that cover the entire target domain and that each class is assumed to be mutually exclusive.

Matsuda and Fukushima identified Web page type classification problem, and tried to solve it by human description of structural characteristics of a type [16]. Yi and Sundaresan used Naive bayes method with structured vector model [21]. It performs well on structured or tightly formatted semi-structured documents such as US Patent data (XML sharing same DTD) or Resumes (tightly formatted documents), but those structured vector model is not likely to perform well for classification of normal HTML documents having various formats. Glover et al. classified "personal homepage" and "call-for-paper." [7] They classified manually a large amount of documents to collect negative training data and used SVM with fixed set of features. Similar methods were used for classification of newspaper articles [8] and patent documents [15]. Most of these works are quite dependent on specific classes, and they require much efforts to create a new classifier for a new class of interest.

There are some recent papers on multistage classification [10, 20, 13] that use the arrangement of homogeneous classifying elements to achieve better quality of classification.

	Winnow						SVM					
	T		T+P		T+P+E		T		T+P		T+P+E	
	f-	f+	f-	f+	f-	f+	f-	f+	f-	f+	f-	f+
Resume	6.38	2.06	4.26	0.19	1.06	0.19	3.19	0.56	3.19	0.56	1.06	0.56
Admission	8.25	0.00	2.06	0.89	1.03	0.89	3.09	0.00	3.09	0.89	2.06	0.89
Homepage	27.67	0.22	6.29	3.56	3.50	3.56	13.29	0.45	6.99	2.67	5.60	2.67

T: typical learning framework using positive training data and the universe as a substitute for the negative training data. T+P: typical learning framework + pre-filtering stage. T+P+E: typical learning framework + pre-filtering stage + early-inclusion stage. f-: % of false negatives. f+: % of false positives.

Table 1. Error rate (%) comparison of each framework using Winnow and SVM

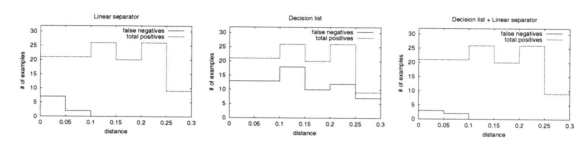

Figure 5. Advantage of the two heterogeneous stages for personal homepage classification

However, like typical learning algorithms, they also require the positive and negative training sets.

H. Yu et al. [22] also propose a scheme to remove the requirement of negative training pages in Web page classification. The algorithm uses a rule-based algorithm in the first stage to map an initial boundary from positive and unlabeled data. After that, it iterates SVMs to induce an accurate class boundary from the initial boundary. The marginal property of SVM guarantees the convergence of the boundary.

Our framework also uses heterogeneous stages. However, we identify another intrinsic problem of Web page classification – high error on low-margin data. By using the two heterogeneous learners in both training and testing phases, we obviate the need for negative training data, while at the same time reduce the errors on low-margin data.

6 Conclusions

In this paper, we propose a heterogeneous learning framework for classifying Web pages, which (1) eliminates the need for negative training data, and (2) increases classification accuracy by using two heterogeneous learners. Our framework uses two heterogeneous learners – a decision list and a linear separator which complement each other – to eliminate the need for negative training data in the training

phase and to increase the accuracy in the testing phase. Our results show that our heterogeneous framework achieves high accuracy without requiring negative training data; it enhances the accuracy of linear separators by reducing the errors on "low-margin data". That is, it classifies more accurately while requiring less human efforts in training.

References

[1] D. Boley, M. Gini, R. Gross, E.-H. S. Han, K. Hastings, G. Karypis, V. Kumar, B. Mobasher, and J. Moore. Partitioning-based clustering for web document categorization. *Decision Support Systems*, 1999.

[2] A. J. Carlson, C. M. Cumby, J. L. Rosen, and D. Roth. *SNoW User Guide*. Cognitive Computation Group, Computer Science Department, University of Illinois at Urbana-Champaign, August 1999.

[3] H. Chen, C. Schuffels, and R. Orwig. Internet categorization and search: A self-organizing approach. *Journal of Visual Communication and Image Representation*, 7(1):88–102, 1996.

[4] C. Cortes and V. Vapnik. Support vector networks. *Machine Learning*, (20):273–297, 1995.

[5] M. Craven and S. Slattery. Relational learning with statistical predicate invention: Better models for hypertext. *Machine Learning*, 43(1/2):97–119, 2001.

[6] Y. Freund and R. E. Schapire. A short introduction to boosting. *Journal of Japanese Society for Artificial Intelligence*, 5(14):771–780, 1999.

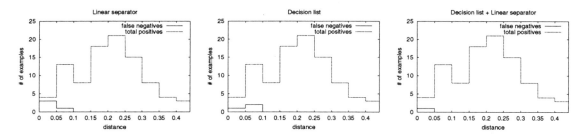

Figure 6. Advantage of the two heterogeneous stages for resume page classification

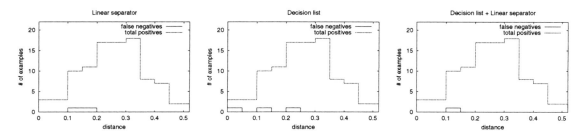

Figure 7. Advantage of the two heterogeneous stage for college admission page classification

[7] E. J. Glover, G. W. F. S. Lawrence, W. P. Birmingham, A. Kruger, C. L. Giles, and D. M. Pennock. Improving category specific web search by learning query modifications. In *Symposium on Applications and the Internet, SAINT 2001*, San Diego, California, January 8-12, January 8-12 2001.

[8] J. Hayes and W. S. P. A system for content-based indexing of a database of news stories. In *Proceedings of Second Annual Conference on Innovatative Applications of Artificial Intelligence*, pages 1–5, 1990.

[9] T. Joachims. Making large-scale svm learning practical. In B. Scholkopf, C. Burges, and A. Smola, editors, *Advances in Kernel Methods - Support Vector Learning*. MIT-Press, 1999.

[10] C. Kaynak and E. Alpaydin. Multistage cascading of multiple classifiers: One man's noise is another man's data. In *ICML*, 2000.

[11] J. Kivinen, M. K. Warmuth, and P. Auer. The Perceptron algorithm vs. Winnow: linear vs. logarithmic mistake bound when few input variables are relevant. *Artificial Intelligence*, 1-2:325–343, 1997.

[12] A. R. Klivans and R. A. Servedio. Learning dnf in time $2^{O(n^{1/3})}$. citeseer.nj.nec.com/329971.html.

[13] A. Kosorukoff. Genetic synthesis of cascade structures for particle classification. In D. Whitley, editor, *Late Breaking Papers at the 2000 Genetic and Evolutionary Computation Conference*, pages 170–174, Las Vegas, Nevada, USA, 8 2000.

[14] N. Littlestone. Learning quickly when irrelevant attributes abound. a new linear-threshold algorithm. *Machine Learning*, (2):285–318, 1988.

[15] H. Mase, H. Tsuji, H. Kinukawa, Y. Hosoya, K. Koutani, and K. Kiyota. Experimental simulation for automatic patent categorization. In *Proceedings of Advances in Production Management Systems*, pages 377–382, 1996.

[16] K. Matsuda and T. Fukushima. Task-oriented world wide web retrieval by document type classification. In *CIKM '99*, Kansas City, Mo, USA.

[17] H.-J. Oh, S. H. Myaeng, and M.-H. Lee. A practical hypertext categorization method using links and incrementally available class information. In *SIGIR 2000*, Athens, Greece, 2000.

[18] F. Rosenblatt. The perceptron: A probabilistic for information storage and organization in the brain. *Psychological Review*, (65):386–407, 1958. Reprinted in Neurocomputing (MIT Press, 1988).

[19] R. A. Servedio. On pac learning using winnow, perceptron, and a perceptron-like algorithm. citeseer.nj.nec.com/329971.html.

[20] J. Smith and S. Chang. Multi-stage classification of images from features and related text. In *EDLOS Workshop*, San Miniato, Italy, 1997.

[21] J. Yi and N. Sundaresan. A classifier for semi-structured documents. In *KDD 2000*, Boston, MA USA, 2000.

[22] H. Yu, J. Han, and K. C.-C. Chang. Pebl: Positive-example based learning for web page classification using svm. In *KDD*, Edmonton, Alberta, Canada, 2002.

Using Category-Based Adherence to Cluster Market-Basket Data

Ching-Huang Yun, Kun-Ta Chuang+ and Ming-Syan Chen
Department of Electrical Engineering
Graduate Institute of Communication Engineering+
National Taiwan University
Taipei, Taiwan, ROC
E-mail: chyun@arbor.ee.ntu.edu.tw, doug@arbor.ee.ntu.edu.tw, mschen@cc.ee.ntu.edu.tw

Abstract

In this paper, we devise an efficient algorithm for clustering market-basket data. Different from those of the traditional data, the features of market-basket data are known to be of high dimensionality, sparsity, and with massive outliers. Without explicitly considering the presence of the taxonomy, most prior efforts on clustering market-basket data can be viewed as dealing with items in the leaf level of the taxonomy tree. Clustering transactions across different levels of the taxonomy is of great importance for marketing strategies as well as for the result representation of the clustering techniques for market-basket data. In view of the features of market-basket data, we devise in this paper a novel measurement, called the category-based adherence, *and utilize this measurement to perform the clustering. The distance of an item to a given cluster is defined as the number of links between this item and its nearest large node in the taxonomy tree where a large node is an item (i.e., leaf) or a category (i.e., internal) node whose occurrence count exceeds a given threshold. The category-based adherence of a transaction to a cluster is then defined as the average distance of the items in this transaction to that cluster. With this category-based adherence measurement, we develop an efficient clustering algorithm, called algorithm* CBA *(standing for Category-Based Adherence), for market-basket data with the objective to minimize the category-based adherence. A validation model based on* Information Gain *(IG) is also devised to assess the quality of clustering for market-basket data. As validated by both real and synthetic datasets, it is shown by our experimental results, with the taxonomy information, algorithm CBA devised in this paper significantly outperforms the prior works in both the execution efficiency and the clustering quality for market-basket data.*

1 Introduction

Data clustering is an important technique for exploratory data analysis [16]. Explicitly, data clustering is a well-known capability studied in information retrieval [6], data mining [7], machine learning [9], and statistical pattern recognition [15]. In essence, clustering is meant to divide a set of data items into some proper groups in such a way that items in the same group are as similar to one another as possible. Most clustering techniques utilize a pairwise similarity for measuring the distance of two data points. Recently, there has been a growing emphasis on clustering very large datasets to discover useful patterns and/or correlations among attributes [3][4][10][23]. Note that clustering is an application dependent issue and certain applications may call for their own specific requirements.

Market-basket data (also called transaction data) has been well studied in mining association rules for discovering the set of frequently purchased items [5][13][18]. Different from the traditional data, the features of market-basket data are known to be of high dimensionality, sparsity, and with massive outliers. ROCK is an agglomerative hierarchical clustering algorithm by treating market-basket data as categorical data and using the links between the data points to cluster categorical data [11]. The authors in [17] proposed an EM-based algorithm by using the maximum likelihood estimation method for clustering transaction data. OPOSSUM is a graph-partitioning approach based on a similarity matrix to cluster transaction data [19]. The work in [20] proposed a K-Mean-based algorithm by using large items as the similarity measurement to divide the transactions into clusters such that transactions with similar large items are grouped into the same clusters. OAK in [21] combined hierarchical and partitional clustering techniques. STC in [22] utilized a fixed small to large item ratio to perform the clustering of market-basket data. In market-basket data, the taxonomy of items defines the generalization relationships for the concepts in different ab-

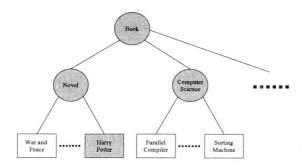

Figure 1. An example taxonomy tree for books.

straction levels. Item taxonomy (i.e., *is-a* hierarchy) is well addressed with respect to its impact to mining association rules of market-basket database [13][18] and can be represented as a tree, called *taxonomy tree*.

In view of the features of market-basket data, we devise in this paper a novel measurement, called the *category-based adherence*, and utilize this measurement to perform the clustering. The *distance* of an item to a given cluster is defined as the number of links between this item and its nearest large node in the taxonomy tree. In the taxonomy tree, the leaf nodes are called the item nodes and the internal nodes are called the category nodes. For the example shown in Figure 1, "War and Peace" is an item node and "Novel" is a category node. As formally defined in Section 2, a *large item (category)* is basically an item (category) with its occurrence count in transactions exceeding a given threshold. If an item (or category) is large, its corresponding node in the taxonomy tree is called a *large node*. For the example shown in Figure 1, nodes marked gray are assumed to large nodes. The *category-based adherence* of a transaction to a cluster is then defined as the average distance of the items in this transaction to that cluster. With this category-based adherence measurement, we develop an efficient clustering algorithm, called algorithm *CBA* (standing for *Category-Based Adherence*), for market-basket data. Explicitly, CBA employs the category-based adherence as the similarity measurement between transactions and clusters, and allocates each transaction to the cluster with the minimum category-based adherence. To the best of our knowledge, without explicitly considering the presence of the taxonomy, previous efforts on clustering market-basket data. [11][17][19][20][21] unavoidably restricted themselves to deal with the items in the leaf level (also called item level) of the taxonomy tree. However, clustering transactions across different levels of the taxonomy is of great importance for marketing strategies as well as for the result representation of the clustering techniques

for market-basket data. Note that in the real market-basket data, there are volume of transactions containing only single items, and many items are purchased infrequently. Hence, without considering the taxonomy tree, one may inappropriately treat a transaction (such as the one containing "parallel compiler" in Figure 1) as an outlier. However, as indicated in Figure 1, purchasing "parallel compiler" is in fact instrumental for the category node "computer science" to become a large node. In contrast, by employing category-based adherence measurement for clustering, many transactions will not be mistakenly treated as outliers if we take categorical relationships of items in the taxonomy tree into consideration, thus leading to better marketing strategies. The details of CBA will be described in Section 3. A validation model based on *Information Gain* (*IG*) is also devised in this paper for clustering market-basket data. As validated by real and synthetic datasets, it is shown by our experimental results, with the taxonomy information, algorithm CBA devised in this paper significantly outperforms the prior works [14][20] in both the execution efficiency and the clustering quality for market-basket data.

This paper is organized as follows. Preliminaries are given in Section 2. In Section 3, algorithm CBA is devised for clustering market-basket data. Experimental studies are conducted in Section 4. This paper concludes with Section 5.

2 Preliminary

The problem description will be presented in Section 2.1. In Section 2.2, we describe a new validation model, *IG* validation model, for the assessment to the quality of different clustering algorithms.

2.1 Problem Description

In this paper, the market-basket data is represented by a set of transactions. A database of transactions is denoted by $D = \{t_1, t_2, ..., t_h\}$, where each transaction t_j is represented by a set of items $\{i_1, i_2, ..., i_h\}$. A example database for clustering market-basket data is described in Table 1 where there are twelve transactions, each of which has a transaction identification (abbreviated as TID) and a set of purchased items. For example, transaction ID 40 has items h and item z. A clustering $U =< C_1, C_2, ..., C_k >$ is a partition of transactions into k clusters, where C_j is a cluster consisting of a set of transactions.

Items in the transactions can be generalized to multiple concept level of the taxonomy. An example taxonomy tree is shown in Figure 2. In the taxonomy tree, the leaf nodes are called the *item nodes* and the internal nodes are called the *category nodes*. The root node in the highest level is a virtual concept of the generalization of all categories. In

TID	10	20	30	40	50	60
Items	g, x	m, y	y, z	h, z	g, x, y	g, n
TID	70	80	90	100	110	120
Items	k, m, n	y	g, k, n	m, n	y, z	g, h, n

Table 1. An example database D.

this taxonomy structure, item g *is-a* category B, category B *is-a* category A, and item h *is-a* category B, etc. In this paper, we use the measurement of the occurrence count to determine which items or categories are major features of each cluster.

Definition 1: The count of an item i_k in a cluster C_j, denoted by $Count(i_k, C_j)$, is defined as the number of transactions in cluster C_j that contain this item i_k. An item i_k in a cluster C_j is called a *large item* if $Count(i_k, C_j)$ exceeds a predetermined threshold.

Definition 2: The count of a category c_k in a cluster C_j, denoted by $Count(c_k, C_j)$, is defined as the number of transactions containing items under this category c_k in cluster C_j. A category c_k in a cluster C_j is called a *large category* if $Count(c_k, C_j)$ exceeds a predetermined threshold.

Note that one transaction may include more than one item from the same category, in which case the count contributed by this transaction to that category is still one. In this paper, the minimum support percentage S_p is a given parameter for determining the large nodes of the taxonomy tree in the cluster. For a cluster C_j, the minimum support count $S_c(C_j)$ is defined as follows.

Definition 3: For cluster C_j, the minimum support count $S_c(C_j)$ is defined as:

$$S_c(C_j) = S_p * |C_j|.$$

where $|C_j|$ denotes the number of transactions in cluster C_j.

Consider the example database in Table 1 as an initial cluster C_0 with the corresponding taxonomy tree recording the counts of the items/categories shown in Figure 2. Then, $Count(g, C_0) = 5$ and $Count(E, C_0) = 7$. With $S_p = 50\%$, we have $S_c(C_0) = 6$. In this example, all categories are large but all items are not.

2.2 Information Gain Validation Model

To evaluate the quality of clustering results, some experimental models were proposed [8][12]. In general, *square*

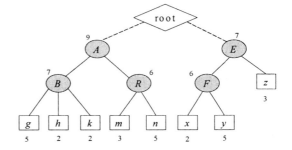

Figure 2. An illustrative taxonomy example whose transactions are shown in Table 2 ($S_p = 0.5$).

error criterion is widely employed in evaluating the efficiency of numerical data clustering algorithms [8]. Note that the nature feature of numeric data is quantitative (e.g., weight or length), whereas that of categorical data is qualitative (e.g., color or gender) [16]. Thus, validation schemes using the concept of variance are thus not applicable to assessing the clustering result of categorical data. To remedy this problem, some real data with good classified labels, e.g., mushroom data, congressional votes data, soybean disease [2] and Reuters news collection [1], were taken as the experimental data for categorical clustering algorithms [11][20][21]. In view of the feature of market-basket data, we propose in this paper a validation model based on Information Gain (IG) to assess the qualities of the clustering results.

The definitions required for deriving the information gain of a clustering result are given below.

Definition 4: The entropy of an attribute J_a in the database D is defined as:

$$I(J_a, D) = -\sum_{i=1}^{n} \frac{|J_a^i|}{|D|} * log_2 \frac{|J_a^i|}{|D|}.$$

where $|D|$ is the number of transactions in the database D and $|J_a^i|$ denotes the number of the transactions whose attribute J_a is classified as the value J_a^i in the database D.

Definition 5: The entropy of an attribute J_a in a cluster C_j is defined as:

$$I(J_a, C_j) = -\sum_{i=1}^{n} \frac{|J_{a,c_j}^i|}{|C_j|} * log_2 \frac{|J_{a,c_j}^i|}{|C_j|}.$$

where $|C_j|$ is the number of transactions in cluster C_j, and $|J_{a,c_j}^i|$ denotes the number of the transactions whose attribute J_a is classified as the value J_a^i in C_j.

Definition 6: Let a clustering U contain C_1, C_2, ..., C_m clusters. Thus, the entropy of an attribute J_a in the clustering U is defined as:

$$E(J_a, U) = \sum_{C_j \in U} \frac{|C_j|}{|D|} I(J_a, C_j).$$

Definition 7: The information gain obtained by separating J_a into the clusters of the clustering U is defined as:

$$Gain(J_a, U) = I(J_a, D) - E(J_a, U).$$

Definition 8: The information gain of the clustering U is defined as:

$$IG(U) = \sum_{J_a \in I} Gain(J_a, U).$$

where I is the data set of the total items purchased in the whole market-basket data records.

A complete numerical example on the use of these definitions will be given in Section 3.3. For clustering market-basket data, the larger an IG value, the better the clustering quality is. In market-basket data, with the taxonomy tree structure, there are three kinds of IG values, i.e., $IG_{item}(U)$, $IG_{cat}(U)$, and $IG_{total}(U)$, for representing the quality of a clustering result. Specifically, $IG_{item}(U)$ is the information gain obtained on items and $IG_{cat}(U)$ is the information gain obtained on categories. $IG_{total}(U)$ is the total information gain, i.e., $IG_{total}(U) = IG_{item}(U) + IG_{cat}(U)$. In general, market-basket data set is typically represented by a 2-dimensional table, in which each entry is either 1 or 0 to denote purchased or non-purchased items, respectively. In IG validation model, we treat each item in market-basket data as an attribute J_a with two classified label, 1 or 0.

3 Design of Algorithm CBA

The similarity measurement of CBA, called category-based adherence, will be described in Section 3.1. The procedure of CBA is devised in Section 3.2 and an illustrative example is given in Section 3.3.

3.1 Similarity Measurement: Category-Based Adherence

The similarity measurement employed by algorithm CBA, called category-based adherence, is defined as follows. In the taxonomy tree, the *nearest large node* of an item i_k is itself if i_k is large and is its nearest large ancestor node otherwise. Then, the distance of an item to a cluster is defined below.

Definition 9: (Distance of an item to a cluster): For an item i_k of a transaction, the *distance* of i_k to a given cluster C_j, denoted by $d(i_k, C_j)$, is defined as the number of links between i_k and the nearest large nodes of i_k. If i_k is a large node in cluster C_j, then $d(i_k, C_j) = 0$. Otherwise, the nearest large node is the category node which is the lowest generalized concept level node among all large ancestors of item i_k. Note that if an item or category node is identified as large node, all its high level category nodes will also be large nodes.

Definition 10: (Adherence of a transaction to a cluster): For a transaction $t = \{i_1, i_2, ..., i_p\}$, the adherence of t to a given cluster C_j, denoted by $H(t, C_j)$, is defined as the average distance of the items in t to C_j and shown below.

$$H(t, C_j) = \frac{1}{p} \sum_{k=1}^{p} d(i_k, C_j).$$

where $d(i_k, C_j)$ is the distance of i_k in cluster C_j.

3.2 Procedure of Algorithm CBA

The overall procedure of algorithm CBA is outlined as follows.

Procedure of Algorithm CBA

Step 1. Randomly select k transactions as the seed transactions of the k clusters from the database D.

Step 2. Read each transaction sequentially and allocates it to the cluster with the minimum category-based adherence. For each moved transaction, the counts of items and their ancestors are increased by one.

Step 3. Repeat Step 2 until no transaction is moved between clusters.

Step 4. Output the taxonomy tree for each cluster as the visual representation of the clustering result.

In Step 1, algorithm CBA randomly selects k transactions as the seed transactions of the k clusters from the database D. For each cluster, the items of the seed transaction are counted once in the taxonomy tree. In each cluster, the items and their ancestors are all large in the very beginning because their count is one (which means 100% in the only seed transaction), larger than the minimum support threshold. For each cluster, these large nodes represent the hot sale topics in this cluster. In Step 2, algorithm CBA reads each transaction sequentially and allocates it to the cluster with the minimum category-based adherence. After one transaction is inserted into a cluster C_j, the counts of the items and

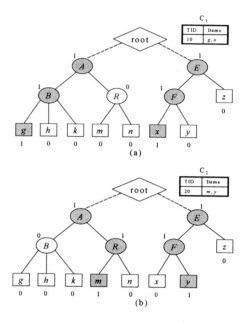

Figure 3. In Step 1, algorithm CBA randomly chooses the seed transaction for each cluster.

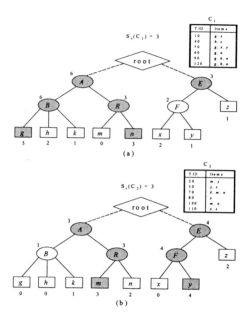

Figure 4. In Step 2, algorithm CBA reads each transaction sequentially and allocates it to the cluster with the minimum category-based adherence.

their ancestors are increased by one in the corresponding nodes in the taxonomy tree of C_j. In addition, the minimum support count of C_j is updated. In Step 3, algorithm CBA repeats Step 2 until no transaction is moved between clusters. In Step 4, algorithm CBA outputs the taxonomy tree of the final clustering result for each cluster, where the items, categories, and their corresponding counts are presented.

3.3 An Illustrative Example

For the example database D shown in Table 1, we set $k = 2$ and $S_p = 50\%$. In Step 1, algorithm CBA randomly chooses TID 10 and TID 20 as the seed transaction of the cluster C_1 and C_2, respectively. Then, for cluster C_1 shown in Figure 3(a), nodes marked gray are the purchased items of TID 10 and the corresponding categories in the taxonomy tree, and they are identified as large nodes. Similarly, for cluster C_1, shown in Figure 3(b), nodes marked gray are large. In Figure 3, the count of each node is illustrated nearby. For example, $Count(g, C_1)$ is 1 and $Count(g, C_2)$ is 0. In Step 2, algorithm CBA first allocates TID 30 to cluster C_2 because $H(30, C_2) = \frac{1}{2}(1 + 0) = \frac{1}{2}$ (i.e., the link number of item y to category F plus the link number of item z to category E) is smaller than $H(30, C_1) = \frac{1}{2}(1+1) = 1$. Similarly, TIDs 40, 50, 60, 90, and 120 are allocated to clus-

ter C_1 which is shown in Figure 4(a). TIDs 30, 70, 80, 100, and 110 are allocated to cluster C_2 which is shown in Figure 4(b). Then, algorithm CBA derives $S_c(C_1) = 3$ and $S_c(C_2) = 3$ by $S_p * |C_1| = 0.5 * 6 = 3$ and $S_p * |C_2| = 0.5*6 = 3$, respectively. Because $Count(g, C_1) > S_c(C_1)$, category A is identified as a large node in cluster C_1 and marked gray. In Step 3, algorithm CBA proceeds to iteration 2. In iteration 2, two transactions, TID 50 and TID 70 are moved. TID 50 is moved from cluster C_1 to cluster C_2 because $H(50, C_1) = \frac{1}{3}(0 + 2 + 2) = \frac{4}{3} > H(50, C_2) = \frac{1}{3}(2 + 1 + 0) = 1$, and TID 70 is moved from cluster C_2 to cluster C_1 due the $H(70, C_1) = \frac{1}{3}(1 + 1 + 0) = \frac{2}{3} < H(70, C_2) = \frac{1}{3}(2+0+1) = 1$. Then, algorithm CBA identifies the large nodes again. In iteration 3, only one transaction TID 100 is moved from cluster C_2 to cluster C_1. In iteration 4, there is no movement and thus algorithm CBA proceeds to Step 4. The final feature trees for the clusters are shown in Figure 5.

Note that a transaction at item level may not be similar to any cluster. For example, TID 10 $\{g, x\}$ and TID 40 $\{h, z\}$ have no common items, but item g and item h have common category B and item x and item z have common category E. Thus, TID 10 is similar to TID 40 in the high level concept. By taking category-based adherence mea-

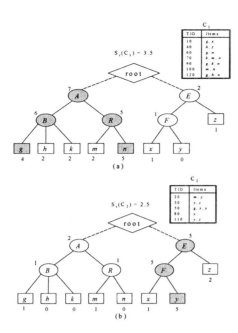

$S_i(C_1) = 3.5$

C_1

TID	Items
1 0	g , x
4 0	h , z
6 0	g , n
7 0	k , m , n
9 0	g , k , n
100	m , n
120	g , h , n

(a)

$S_i(C_2) = 2.5$

C_2

TID	Items
2 0	m , y
3 0	y , z
5 0	g , x , y
8 0	y
110	y , z

(b)

Figure 5. In Step 4, algorithm CBA generates the clustering U_1.

surement, many transactions may not be taken as outliers if we take categorical relationships of items into consideration. In addition, transactions at the item level may have the same similarities in different clusters. However, by summarizing the similarities of every item across their category levels, algorithm CBA allocates each transaction to a proper cluster. For example, TID 50 has three items: g, x, and y. Item g is large in cluster C_1 and item y is large in cluster C_2. Thus, TID 50 has the same similarities in both C_1 and C_2. However, item x is a category F which is a large node in C_2. Thus, TID 50 is allocated to C_2.

To provide more insight into the quality of CBA, we calculate the IG values of the clustering U_1 shown in Figure 5. Note that for an item i_k, $I_{i_k}^{Yes}, I_{i_k}^{No}$ are the two classified labels of item i_k for representing purchased and non-purchased values. For item g, the information gain $Gain(g, U_1) = I(g, D) - E(g, U_1) = (-\frac{5}{12}log_2\frac{5}{12} - \frac{7}{12}log_2\frac{7}{12}) - [\frac{7}{12}(-\frac{4}{7}log_2\frac{4}{7} - \frac{3}{7}log_2\frac{3}{7}) + \frac{5}{12}(-\frac{1}{5}log_2\frac{1}{5} - \frac{4}{5}log_2\frac{4}{5})] = 0.10$. Similarly, IG values of other items are $Gain(h, U_1) = 0.15$, $Gain(k, U_1) = 0.48$, $Gain(m, U_1) = 0.31$, $Gain(n, U_1) = 0.48$, $Gain(x, U_1) = 0$, $Gain(y, U_1) = 0.98$, and $Gain(z, U_1) = 0.39$. Hence, $IG_{item}(U_1) = \sum_{J_a \subset I} Gain(J_a, U_1) = 2.89$, where I is the set of items $\{g, h, k, m, n, x, y, z\}$. Similarly, $Gain(B, U_1) = $

0.33, $Gain(R, U_1) = 0.2$, $Gain(A, U_1) = 0.41$, $Gain(F, U_1) = 0.65$, $Gain(E, U_1) = 0.48$, and $IG_{cat}(U_1) = \sum_{J_a \subset C} Gain(J_a, U_1) = 2.07$, where C is the set of categories $\{A, B, E, F, R\}$. Then, $IG_{total}(U_1) = IG_{item}(U_1) + IG_{cat}(U_1) = 4.96$.

4 Experimental Results

To assess the efficiency of CBA, we conducted experiments to compare CBA with a traditional hierarchical clustering algorithm, called *CL* (standing for *Complete Link*) [14] and another algorithm proposed in [20] (for the convenience, the algorithm is named as *Basic* in this paper). By extending both previous approaches with taxonomy consideration in market-basket data, we also implement algorithm *CLT* (standing for *Completed Link with Taxonomy*) and algorithm *BasicT* (standing for *Basic with Taxonomy*) for comparison purposes. The details of data generation are described in Section 4.1. The experimental results are shown in Section 4.2

4.1 Data Generation

We take the real market-basket data from a large bookstore company for performance study. In this real data set, there are $|D| = 100K$ transactions and $N^I = 21807$ items. Note that in this real data, there are volume of transactions containing only single items, and many items are purchased infrequently. In addition, the number of the taxonomy level in this real data set is 3. In addition, to provide more insight into this study, we use a well-known market-basket synthetic data generated by the IBM Quest Synthetic Data Generation Code [5], as the synthetic data for performance evaluation. This code will generate volumes of transaction data over a large range of data characteristics. These transactions mimic the transactions in the real world retailing environment. This generation code also assumes that people will tend to buy sets of items together, and each such set is potentially a maximal large itemset. The average size of the transactions is denoted by $|T|$. The average size of the maximal potentially large itemsets is denoted by $|I|$. The number of maximal potential large itemsets is denoted by $|L|$. The number of items in database is denoted by N^I. The number of roots is denoted by N^R and the number of the taxonomy level is denoted by N^L.

4.2 Performance Study

We conduct two experiments in this section for performance study and the clustering quality is evaluated by the IG values. For algorithms CBA, Basic, and BasicT, the minimum support percentage S_p is set to 0.5%. Recall that

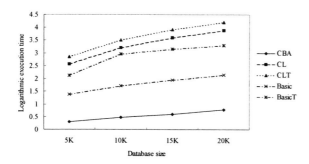

Figure 6. Execution time in logarithm for CBA, CL, CLT, Basic, and BasicT when the database size $|D|$ varies.

there are three kinds of IG values, i.e., IG_{item}, IG_{cat}, and IG_{total}, for evaluating the quality of the clustering result. IG_{item} is the information gain obtained on items and IG_{cat} is the information gain obtained on categories. $IG_{total} = IG_{item} + IG_{cat}$.

4.2.1 Experiment One: When the database size $|D|$ varies

In this experiment, the scalability of CBA is evaluated by both the real data. By varying the real database size $|D|$ from $5K$ to $20K$, it is shown in Figure 6 that CBA significantly outperforms other algorithms in execution efficiency. Note that the logarithmic scale with base 10 is used in the y-axis of Figure 6 since the execution time of CBA is significantly shorter than those of other algorithms and the execution times of CBA increase linearly as the database size increases, indicating the good scale-up feature of algorithm CBA.

4.2.2 Experiment Two: When the number of taxonomy levels N^L varies in synthetic data

In the synthetic data experiment shown in Figure 7, we set $|D| = 100K$, $|T| = 5$, $|I| = 2$, $|L| = 2000$, $N^I = 5000$, $N^R = 100$, and N^L varies from 3 to 5. When the number of taxonomy levels increases, the number of internal (i.e., category) nodes also increases. Thus, the IG_{cat} increases so that CBA can obtain more information gain on categories than on items, indicating the advantage of CBA by employing the category-based adherence as the measurement.

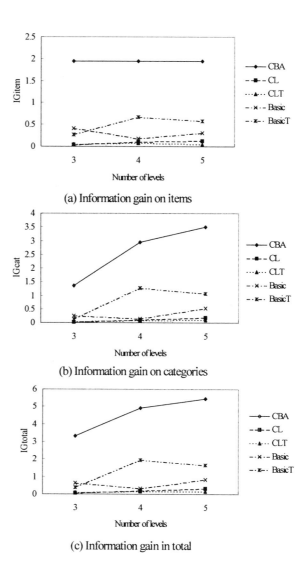

(a) Information gain on items

(b) Information gain on categories

(c) Information gain in total

Figure 7. The IG values when the number of taxonomy levels N^L varies.

5 Conclusion

In view of the features of market-basket data, we devised in this paper a novel measurement, called the category-based adherence, and utilize this measurement to perform the clustering. With this category-based adherence measurement, we developed algorithm CBA for market-basket data with the objective to minimize the category-based adherence. A validation model based on Information Gain (IG) was also devised in this paper to assess the quality of clustering for market-basket data. As validated by both real and synthetic datasets, it was shown by our experimental results, with the taxonomy information, algorithm CBA devised in this paper significantly outperforms the prior works in both the execution efficiency and the clustering quality for market-basket data.

Acknowledgement

The authors are supported in part by the National Science Council, Project No. NSC 91-2213-E-002-034 and NSC 91-2213-E-002-045, Taiwan, Republic of China.

References

[1] Reuters-21578 news collection, http://www.research.att.com/ lewis/reuters21578.html.

[2] UCI Machine Learning Repository. *http://www.ics.uci.edu/~mlearn/MLRepository.html.*

[3] C. C. Aggarwal, C. M. Procopiuc, J. L. Wolf, P. S. Yu, and J.-S. Park. Fast Algorithms for Projected Clustering. *ACM SIGMOD International Conference on Management of Data*, pages 61–72, June 1999.

[4] R. Agrawal, J. Gehrke, D. Gunopulos, and P. Raghavan. Automatic Subspace Clustering of High Dimensional Data for Data Mining Applications. *ACM SIGMOD International Conference on Management of Data*, 27(2):94–105, June 1998.

[5] R. Agrawal and R. Srikant. Fast Algorithms for Mining Association Rules in Large Databases. *Proceedings of the 20th International Conference on Very Large Data Bases*, pages 478–499, September 1994.

[6] M. Charikar, C. Chekuri, T. Feder, and R. Motwani. Incremental Clustering and Dynamic Information Retrieval. *Proceedings of the 29th ACM Symposium on Theory of Computing*, 1997.

[7] M.-S. Chen, J. Han, and P. S. Yu. Data Mining: An Overview from a Database Perspective. *IEEE Transactions on Knowledge and Data Engineering*, 8(6):866–833, 1996.

[8] R. Duda and P. Hart. Pattern Classification and Scene Analysis. *Wiley, New York*, 1973.

[9] D. H. Fisher. Knowledge Acquisition via Incremental Conceptual Clustering. *Machine Learning*, 1987.

[10] S. Guha, R. Rastogi, and K. Shim. CURE: An Efficient Clustering Algorithm for Large Databases. *ACM SIGMOD International Conference on Management of Data*, 27(2):73–84, June 1998.

[11] S. Guha, R. Rastogi, and K. Shim. ROCK: A Robust Clustering Algorithm for Categorical Attributes. *Proceedings of the 15th International Conference on Data Engineering*, 1999.

[12] M. Halkidi, Y. Batistakis, and M. Vazirgiannis. On Clustering Validation Techniques. *Journal of Intelligent Information Systems*, 2001.

[13] J. Han and Y. Fu. Discovery of Multiple-Level Association Rules from Large Databases. *Proceedings of the 21th International Conference on Very Large Data Bases*, pages 420–431, September 1995.

[14] A. K. Jain and R. C. Dubes. Algorithms for Clustering Data. *Prentice Hall*, 1988.

[15] A. K. Jain, R. P. Duin, and J. Mao. Statistical Pattern Recognition: A Review. *IEEE Transaction on Pattern Analysis and Machine Intelligence*, pages 4–37, Jan. 2000.

[16] A. K. Jain, M. N. Murty, and P. J. Flynn. Data Clustering: A Review. *ACM Computer Surveys*, 31(3), Sept. 1999.

[17] C. Ordonez and E. Omiecinski. A Fast Algorithm to Cluster High Dimensional Basket Data. *Proceedings of the 1st IEEE International Conference on Data Mining (ICDM 2001)*, Nov./Dec. 2001.

[18] R. Srikant and R. Agrawal. Mining Generalized Association Rules. *Proceedings of the 21th International Conference on Very Large Data Bases*, pages 407–419, September 1995.

[19] A. Strehl and J. Ghosh. A Scalable Approach to Balanced, High-dimensional Clustering of Market-baskets. *Proceedings of the 7th International Conference on High Performance Computing*, December 2000.

[20] K. Wang, C. Xu, and B. Liu. Clustering Transactions Using Large Items. *Proceedings of ACM CIKM International Conference on Information and Knowledge Management*, 1999.

[21] Y. Xiao and M. H. Dunham. Interactive Clustering for Transaction Data. *Proceedings of the 3rd International Conference on Data Warehousing and Knowledge Discovery (DaWaK 2001)*, Sept. 2001.

[22] C.-H. Yun, K.-T. Chuang, and M.-S. Chen. Self-Tuning Clustering: An Adaptive Clustering Method for Transaction Data. *Proc. of the 4th International Conference on Data Warehousing and Knowledge Discovery (DaWaK 2002)*, Sep. 2002.

[23] T. Zhang, R. Ramakrishnan, and M. Livny. BIRCH: An Efficient Data Clustering Method for Very Large Databases. *ACM SIGMOD International Conference on Management of Data*, 25(2):103–114, June 1996.

A Comparison Study on Algorithms for Incremental Update of Frequent Sequences *

Minghua Zhang   Ben Kao   Chi-Lap Yip

Department of Computer Science and Information Systems,
The University of Hong Kong, Hong Kong.
{mhzhang, kao, clyip}@csis.hku.hk

Abstract

The problem of mining frequent sequences is to extract frequently occurring subsequences in a sequence database. Algorithms on this mining problem include GSP, MFS, and SPADE. The problem of incremental update of frequent sequences is to keep track of the set of frequent sequences as the underlying database changes. Previous studies have extended the traditional algorithms to efficiently solve the update problem. These incremental algorithms include ISM, GSP+ and MFS+. Each incremental algorithm has its own characteristics and they have been studied and evaluated separately under different scenarios. This paper presents a comprehensive study on the relative performance of the incremental algorithms as well as their non-incremental counterparts. Our goal is to provide guidelines on the choice of an algorithm for solving the incremental update problem given the various characteristics of a sequence database.

keyword: sequence, incremental update, data mining

1. Introduction

One of the many data mining problems is mining frequent sequences from transactional databases. The goal is to discover frequent sequences of events. The problem was first introduced by Agrawal and Srikant [1]. In their model, a database is a collection of transactions. Each transaction is a set of items (or an itemset) and is associated with a customer ID and a time ID. If one groups the transactions by their customer IDs, and then sorts the transactions of each group by their time IDs in increasing value, the database is transformed into a number of customer sequences. Each customer sequence shows the order of transactions a cus-

tomer has conducted. Roughly speaking, the problem of mining frequent sequences is to discover "subsequences" (of itemsets) that occur frequently enough among all the customer sequences.

Sequence mining finds its application in many different areas. A few efficient algorithms for mining frequent sequences have been proposed, notably, AprioriAll [1], GSP [6], SPADE [7], MFS [9] and PrefixSpan [4].

We note that in a typical data mining process, data is rarely fully collected in one attempt. In many cases, data collection is carried out in phases. Consequently, the content of the underlying database changes over time. To keep track of the frequent sequences, sequence mining algorithms have to be executed whenever the underlying database changes. We refer to this problem the incremental update of frequent sequences.

A simple approach to the update problem is to mine the new database from scratch, using a sequence mining algorithm mentioned previously. This approach, however, fails to take advantage of the valuable information obtained from the mining results of a previous exercise. To utilize the previous mining results to efficiently mine the updated database, several incremental versions of the basic sequence mining algorithms have been proposed, including GSP+ [8], MFS+ [8] and ISM[3]. The above three incremental algorithms are based on GSP, MFS and SPADE, respectively.

With the different algorithms for (incremental) sequence mining available, an interesting question is which one to choose given a particular application with a specific dataset characteristic and a particular computing environment. We note that the incremental algorithms we just mentioned, namely, GSP+, MFS+, and ISM, have different requirements and assumptions. They were also studied and evaluated separately under different scenarios.

Our goal in this paper is to conduct a comprehensive study on the relative performance of the algorithms. We evaluate the three incremental algorithms (GSP+, MFS+, and ISM) as well as their non-incremental counterparts

*This research was supported by Hong Kong Research Grants Council under grant number HKU 7040/02E.

554

(GSP, MFS, and SPADE). This comparison study allows us to:

- identify the various factors (such as database update model, data characteristics, and memory availability) that affect the algorithms' performance;
- understand when and how an incremental algorithm outperforms its non-increment version; and
- provide guidelines on how to choose the most efficient algorithm.

The rest of this paper is organized as follows. In Section 2 we give a formal definition of the problem. We also states the two models of database update, namely, the sequence model and the transaction model. In Section 3 we briefly describe the six algorithms: GSP, MFS, SPADE, GSP+, MFS+, and ISM. Section 4 presents an extensive performance study. Finally, we conclude the paper in Section 5.

2. Problem definition and model

In this section, we give a formal definition of the problem of mining frequent sequences. Also, we describe two update models of the incremental update problem.

2.1. Mining frequent sequences

Let $I = \{i_1, i_2, \ldots, i_m\}$ be a set of literals called items. An itemset X of the universe I is a set of items. A sequence $s = \langle t_1, t_2, \ldots, t_n \rangle$ is an ordered set of transactions, where each transaction t_i ($i = 1, 2, \ldots, n$) is an itemset.

The length of a sequence s is defined as the number of items contained in s. If an item occurs several times in different itemsets of a sequence, the item is counted for each occurrence. We use $|s|$ to represent the length of s.

Given two sequences $s_1 = \langle a_1, a_2, \ldots, a_n \rangle$ and $s_2 = \langle b_1, b_2, \ldots, b_l \rangle$, we say s_1 contains s_2 (or equivalently s_2 is a subsequence of s_1) if there exist integers $j_1, j_2, \ldots, j_l$, such that $1 \leq j_1 < j_2 < \ldots < j_l \leq n$ and $b_1 \subseteq a_{j_1}, b_2 \subseteq a_{j_2}, \ldots, b_l \subseteq a_{j_l}$. We represent this relationship by $s_2 \sqsubseteq s_1$.

In a sequence set V, a sequence $s \in V$ is *maximal* if s is not a subsequence of any other sequence in V.

Given a database D of sequences, the *support count* of a sequence s, denoted by δ_D^s, is defined as the number of sequences in D that contain s. The *fraction* of sequences in D that contain s is called the *support* of s. If we use the symbol $|D|$ to denote the number of sequences in D (or the size of D), then support of $s = \delta_D^s / |D|$.

If the support of s is not less than a user specified support threshold, ρ_s, s is a frequent sequence. The problem of mining frequent sequences is to find all *maximal* frequent sequences in a database D.

2.2. Update model

A sequence database can be updated in two ways, depending on whether a sequence or a transaction is the unit of update. In this subsection, we describe the two update models.

Sequence Model. In the sequence model, the database is updated by adding and/or removing whole sequences.

Formally, in the sequence model, we assume that a previous mining exercise has been executed on a sequence database D to obtain the support counts of its frequent sequences. The database D is then updated by deleting a set of sequences Δ^- followed by inserting a set of sequences Δ^+. Let us denote the updated database by D'. Note that $D' = (D - \Delta^-) \cup \Delta^+$. We denote the set of unchanged sequences by $D^- = D - \Delta^- = D' - \Delta^+$.

For the incremental update problem, the objective is to find all maximal frequent sequences in the database D' given Δ^-, D^-, Δ^+, and the mining result of D.

We note that in [8], algorithms GSP+ and MFS+ are evaluated under the sequence model.

Transaction Model. In the transaction model of the update problem, individual sequences in the database can be updated by appending new transactions.

Given a sequence database D and its mining result, and a set of transactions ΔT, the incremental update problem under the transaction model is to determine the set of maximal frequent sequences in D with the transactions in ΔT appended to the sequences in D. In [3], algorithm ISM is evaluated under the transaction model.

Before we end this section, we remark that technically the two update models can model each other. For example, if transactions are appended to a sequence s to form a new sequence s', we can consider this update as a removal of s from the database followed by an insertion of s'. Also, if a sequence s is inserted into a database, we can consider this update as appending all the transactions in s to an initially empty sequence.[1] In fact, the studies on the three incremental algorithms claim that the algorithms are applicable under both update models by the above mentioned mapping. One of the goals of this paper is to determine the effectiveness of these algorithms under the different update models.

3. Algorithms

In this section, we review three sequence mining algorithms, namely, GSP, MFS, SPADE, and their incremental versions, namely, GSP+, MFS+, and ISM.

---

[1]The transaction model cannot model sequence deletion unless we consider transaction removal as well. We do not consider this modification in this paper.

3.1. GSP

Algorithm GSP was proposed by Srikant and Agrawal [6]. Similar to the structure of the Apriori algorithm [5] for mining association rules, GSP starts by finding all frequent length-1 sequences from the database. A set of candidate length-2 sequences is then generated. The support counts of the candidate sequences are then counted by scanning the database once. Those frequent length-2 sequences are then used to generate candidate sequences of length 3, and so on. In general, GSP uses a function GGen to generate candidate sequences of length $k + 1$ given the set of all frequent length-k sequences. The algorithm terminates when no more frequent sequences are discovered during a database scan. For the details of the candidate generation function GGen, please refer to [6].

GSP is an efficient algorithm. However, the number of database scans it requires is determined by the length of the longest frequent sequences. Consequently, if there are very long frequent sequences and if the database is huge, the I/O cost of GSP could be substantial.

3.2. MFS

To improve the I/O efficiency of GSP, the algorithm MFS was proposed [9]. Similar to GSP, MFS is an iterative algorithm. MFS first requires an initial estimate, S_{est}, of the set of frequent sequences of the database be available. The set S_{est} can be obtained by mining a small sample of the database, and using the frequent sequences of the sample as S_{est}. For the incremental update problem, MFS can use the frequent sequences in the old database as S_{est}.

In the first iteration of MFS, the database is scanned to obtain the support counts of all length-1 sequences as well as those of the sequences in the estimated set, S_{est}. Sequences that are found frequent are collected into a set *MFSS*. Essentially, *MFSS* captures the set of frequent sequences that MFS has known so far. Typically, the set *MFSS* contains frequent sequences of various lengths. MFS then applies a candidate generation function MGen on *MFSS* to obtain a set of candidate sequences. The database is then scanned to determine which candidate sequences are frequent. Those that are frequent are added to the set *MFSS*. MFS then again applies the generation function MGen on the *refined MFSS* to obtain a new set of candidate sequences, whose supports are then counted by scanning the database, and so on. MFS executes this candidate-generation-verification-refinement iteration until the set *MFSS* cannot be refined further.

The heart of MFS is the candidate generation function MGen. MGen can be considered as a generalization of GGen (used in GSP) in that MGen takes as input a set of frequent sequences of various lengths and generates a set of candi-

date sequences of various lengths. For the details of the MGen function, please refer to [9].

It shows that if the set S_{est} is a reasonably good estimate of the true set of frequent sequences, then MFS will generate long candidate sequences early (compared with GSP). As a result, in many cases, MFS requires fewer database scans and less data processing than GSP does. This reduces both CPU and I/O costs.

3.3. GSP+ and MFS+

Based on GSP and MFS, two incremental algorithms GSP+ and MFS+ were proposed in [8]. In the study, the sequence model of database update is assumed.

The structures of GSP+ and MFS+ follow those of GSP and MFS. The major difference is that during each iteration, after a set of candidate sequences is generated, the incremental algorithms first deduce whether a candidate sequence s can be frequent by considering the mining result of the old database, and in some cases, s's support count w.r.t. Δ^+ and/or Δ^- (the updated portion of the database). If the candidate sequence s cannot be frequent, it is pruned from the candidate set.

Two lemmas are proposed in [8] to help GSP+ and MFS+ make the pruning decision. In the lemmas, the symbol b_X^s refers to an upper bound of the support count of a sequence s in a dataset X, and is calculated by $b_X^s = \min_{s'} \delta_X^{s'}$, where $(s' \sqsubseteq s) \wedge (|s'| = |s| - 1)$.

Lemma 1 *If a sequence s is frequent in D', then $\delta_D^s + b_{\Delta^+}^s \geq \delta_D^s + b_{\Delta^+}^s - \delta_{\Delta^-}^s \geq |D'| \times \rho_s$.*

Lemma 2 *If a sequence s is frequent in D' but not in D, then $b_{\Delta^+}^s \geq b_{\Delta^+}^s - \delta_{\Delta^-}^s \geq \delta_{\Delta^+}^s - \delta_{\Delta^-}^s > (|\Delta^+| - |\Delta^-|) \times \rho_s$.*

Lemma 1 applies to a candidate sequence s that is frequent w.r.t. the old database D, and Lemma 2 applies to candidates that are infrequent in D. For a candidate sequence s that cannot be pruned, its support count w.r.t. the new database is then calculated. For further details, please refer to [8].

GSP+ and MFS+ gain efficiency by avoiding processing D^- (the unchanged part of the database). If the database does not change greatly across an update, then D^- is relatively large compared with Δ^+ and Δ^-. The performance gain would then be substantial.

3.4. SPADE

The algorithms we have reviewed so far, namely, GSP, MFS, GSP+ and MFS+ assume a *horizontal database representation*. In this representation, each row in the database table represents a transaction. Each transaction is associated with a customer ID, a transaction timestamp, and an

Table 1. Horizontal database

Customer ID	Transaction timestamp	Itemset
1	110	A
1	120	B C
2	210	A
2	220	C D

Table 2. Vertical database

Item	Customer ID	Transaction timestamp
A	1	110
	2	210
B	1	120
C	1	120
	2	220
D	2	220

Table 3. ID-list of $\langle \{A\}, \{C\} \rangle$

Customer ID	Transaction timestamp
1	110
2	210

Table 4. Horizontal database generated for computing L_2

Customer ID	(item, transaction timestamp) pairs
1	(A 110) (C 120)
2	(A 210) (C 220)

itemset. Table 1 shows an example of a database in the horizontal representation.

In [7], it is observed that a *vertical* representation of the database may be better suited for sequence mining. In the vertical representation, every item in the database is associated with an id-list. For an item a, its id-list is a list of (customer ID, transaction timestamp) pairs. Each such pair identifies a unique transaction that contains a. A vertical database is composed of the id-lists of all items. Table 2 shows the vertical representation of the database shown in Table 1.

In [7], the algorithm SPADE is proposed that uses a vertical database to mine frequent sequences. To understand SPADE, let us first define two terms: *generating subsequences* and *sequence id-list*.

Generating subsequences. For a sequence s such that $|s| \geq 2$, the two generating subsequences of s are obtained by removing the first or the second item of s.

Sequence id-list. Similar to the id-list of an item, we can also associate an id-list with a sequence. The id-list of a sequence s is a list of (Customer ID, transaction timestamp) pairs. If the pair (C, t) is in the id-list of a sequence s, then s is contained in the sequence of Customer C, and that the first item of s occurs in the transaction of Customer C at timestamp t. Table 3 shows the id-list of $\langle \{A\}, \{C\} \rangle$.

We note that if id-lists are available, counting the supports of sequences is trivial. In particular, the support count of a length-1 sequence can be obtained by inspecting the vertical database. In general, the support count of a sequence s is given by the number of distinct customer id's in s's id-list. The problem of support counting is thus reduced to the problem of sequence id-list computation.

With the vertical database, only the id-lists of length-1 sequences can be readily obtained. The id-lists of longer sequences have to be computed. It is shown in [7] that the id-list of a sequence s can be computed easily by *intersecting* the id-lists of the two generating subsequences of s.

Here, we summarize the key steps of SPADE.

1. Find frequent length-1 sequences. This is done by scanning the id-lists of the items from the vertical database.

2. Find frequent length-2 sequences. Suppose there are M frequent items, then the number of candidate frequent length-2 sequences is $O(M^2)$. If the support counts of these length-2 sequences are obtained by first computing their id-lists using the intersection procedure, we have to access id-lists from the vertical database $O(M^2)$ times.[2] This could be very expensive.

Instead, SPADE solves the problem by building a horizontal database on the fly that involves only frequent items. In the horizontal database, every customer is associated with a list of (item, transaction timestamp) pairs. For each frequent item found in Step 1, SPADE reads its id-list from disk and the horizontal database is updated accordingly. For example, if the frequent items of our example database (Table 2) are A, C, then the constructed horizontal database is shown in Table 4. After obtaining the horizontal database, the supports of all candidate length-2 sequences are computed from it.

We remark that maintaining the horizontal database might require a lot of memory. This is especially true if the number of frequent items and the vertical database are large.

3. Find long frequent sequences. In step 3, SPADE generates the id-lists of long candidate sequences (those of length ≥ 3) by the intersection procedure. SPADE carefully controls the order at which candidate sequences (and their id-lists) are generated to keep the memory requirement at a minimum. For details, readers are referred to [7].

3.5. ISM

ISM is an incremental update algorithm based on SPADE. With ISM, the transaction model of database up-

---

[2]This is because computing the id-list of a length-2 sequence requires accessing the 2 id-lists of the 2 items involved.

date is assumed, although it also handles sequence insertion.

Similar to SPADE, ISM requires the availability of the vertical database. Besides that, it needs a lattice structure called *increment sequence lattice*, or ISL w.r.t. the old database D. A node in ISL represents either a frequent sequence, or a sequence in the negative border (In ISM, a sequence is called in the negative border if it is infrequent, and either its length is 1 or both of its two generating subsequences are frequent). The node also contains the support count of the sequence w.r.t. D. Edges in the ISL connect a sequence with its generating subsequences. ISM assumes that the ISL of the old database is available before the incremental update.

There are three key steps of ISM.

In the first step, ISM checks whether there are new sequences added to the old database D in the update. If there are, ISM computes the new support count threshold and adjusts ISL accordingly. In the adjustment, frequent sequences may remain frequent, be moved to the negative border, or be deleted from ISL. Also, sequences in the negative border may stay in the negative border or be removed.

In the second step, ISM updates support counts of the sequences in ISL. And the third step of ISM is to capture sequences that were not originally in ISL. Similar to the first step, both the second step and the third step need to process ISL. For further details, please refer to [3].

4. Experiment results and analysis

We performed a number of experiments comparing the performance of the three incremental algorithms GSP+, MFS+, ISM and their non-incremental counterparts GSP, MFS and SPADE. The non-incremental algorithms were executed directly on the updated database. For MFS, GSP+, MFS+, and ISM, we assume that the set of frequent sequences w.r.t the old database and their support counts are available. For MFS and MFS+, this set of frequent sequences is used as the estimated set S_{est} (see Section 3). Furthermore, for SPADE and ISM, the database is stored in the vertical representation. Also, for ISM, we assume that ISL w.r.t. the old database is available. The experiments were done under the two database update models. In this section we present some representative results.

The experiments were performed on synthetic databases generated by the sequence generator of the IBM Quest data mining project [2]. The generator takes a number of parameters as input. In our experiment, we let $N_s = 5,000$, $N_i = 25,000$, and use $C10T2.5S4I1.25$ settings. For the details of the parameters, please refer to [1].

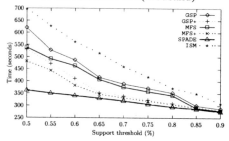

N5000 D1000+100(thousand)

Figure 1. Execution time vs. support threshold (sequence model)

4.1. Sequence model

In the first set of experiments, the database is updated under the sequence model. We first generate a database D of 1,000,000 sequences. After that, another 100,000 sequences are generated and are inserted into the database to form a new database D'. In this experiment, the number of items, N, is set to 5,000. We execute SPADE on D to obtain the necessary information for the incremental algorithms. The six algorithms GSP, MFS, SPADE, GSP+, MFS+ and ISM are then executed to mine D'. The experiments were performed on a 700MHz PIII Xeon machine with 4GB of main memory running Solaris 8. The execution times of the six algorithms under different support thresholds ($0.5\% \leq \rho_s \leq 0.9\%$) are shown in Figure 1.

From the figure, we see that as the support threshold increases, the running times of all six algorithms decrease. This is because a larger ρ_s means fewer and shorter frequent sequences. Therefore, fewer iterations and less support countings are needed. Also, the performance difference among the algorithms is more substantial when the support threshold is small.

We observe that the two pruning algorithms, GSP+ and MFS+, perform much better than their non-incremental counterparts, GSP and MFS. As we have discussed, the savings mostly come from pruning candidate sequences. With fewer candidate sequences to consider, less amount of subsequence testing and support counting is done, which leads to performance gains. In general, MFS+ has a slight edge over GSP+ (and so does MFS over GSP). Recall that MFS+ (and also MFS) uses the set of frequent sequences w.r.t. the old database as an initial estimate (S_{est}). MFS+ is able to generate and count long sequences early, potentially reducing the I/O cost and the processing time.

Another interesting observation we can make from Figure 1 is that the incremental algorithm ISM performs worse than its non-incremental version, SPADE. This shows that ISM may not be a good choice under the sequence model of database update.

Recall that there are three key steps of ISM, all have to do with maintaining the increment sequence lattice (ISL). Moreover, before ISM terminates, it has to output ISL for the next incremental update.

We note that under the sequence model of database update, ISM needs to work harder in maintaining ISL compared with the case under the transaction model. First, under the transaction model of update, a sequence that is frequent w.r.t the old database must also be frequent w.r.t. the updated one; while it is not true under the sequence model. Also, the first step of ISM can be omitted under the transaction model, while this step of ISL adjustment is needed under the sequence model, since by inserting new sequences, the support count requirement is changed. So the changes made to ISL could thus be more drastic under the sequence model than it is under the transaction model. This explains why in our experiment, ISM performs worse than the other algorithms that do not handle ISL.

Finally, we see that SPADE is the most efficient algorithm. This shows that the vertical database representation allows very efficient support counting using the idea of id-lists. A potential disadvantage of SPADE is that it requires much memory in the construction of a horizontal database (see Step 2 of the description of SPADE, Section 3.4). Since the machine on which we ran the experiment has 4GB of memory, the large memory requirement of SPADE is not a factor. We will study the impact of memory availability on SPADE later in this section.

The above discussion suggests that the performance of ISM is affected greatly by the size of ISL, which is in turn, dependent on a number of factors. One of these factors is the support threshold ρ_s. A larger ρ_s gives fewer frequent sequences, and a smaller negative border. Hence, ISL is smaller.

Another factor is the number of items, N, in the database. A large value of N is both a blessing and a curse. First, note that all length-1 sequences are in ISL Since each item derives one length-1 sequence, a large N gives a very fat (and large) ISL. On the other hand, if there are many items, transactions will have more variety. Given the same database parameters, there will be fewer frequent sequences. This factor makes ISL smaller. Figure 2 shows the performance of the algorithms under different values of N. Since GSP and MFS are outperformed by their incremental versions (i.e., GSP+ and MFS+), their curves are omitted to make the graph more readable. In this experiment, the support threshold is set to 0.7%. The number of items N is varied from 1,000 to 10,000.

From Figure 2, we see that, in general, when the number of items increases, the execution times of GSP+, MFS+ and SPADE decrease. This is because using the same values for the other parameters of the database generator, a larger

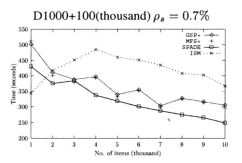

Figure 2. Execution time vs. N (sequence model)

number of items means each item has a smaller probability of appearing in a transaction. This leads to smaller support counts and thus fewer frequent sequences to discover. As a result, the three algorithms take less time to complete. For ISM, we see the opposing effects we mentioned earlier. When N is small, increasing N causes a dramatic increase in ISL's size, which outweights the effect of a reduction in the number of frequent sequences. The result is an increase in ISM's execution time. When N is large (say, $> 4,000$), the weightings of the two factors shift. This results in a decrease in execution time.

From the figure, we notice that even under the sequence model, ISM can be the best algorithm. This happens when the number of items is very small. In this case, ISM maintains a small ISL, leading to a very efficient algorithm.

From Figures 1 and 2, we see that with a memory-abundant system (4GB in our experiment), SPADE is a very efficient algorithm. To study the effect of memory availability on the algorithms, we re-ran the experiment on an 866MHz PC with 512MB memory running Solaris 8. In the experiment, ρ_s is set to 0.7% and N is set to 5,000. We vary the size of D from 200,000 sequences to 2,000,000 sequences. For each case, the updated database D' is 10% larger than D. Figure 3 shows the result.

Figure 3 shows that while GSP+ and MFS+ scale linearly with the database size, SPADE and ISM perform poorly when the database is relatively large. The reason for the performance degradation is that SPADE requires a lot of memory to transform the vertical database to the horizontal one in order to find frequent length-2 sequences. When the database size is large compared with the amount of physical memory available, expensive memory paging occurs. Since ISM is based on SPADE, it suffers a similar performance degradation.

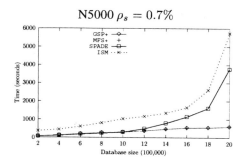

Figure 3. Effect of database size (sequence model)

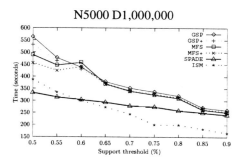

Figure 4. Execution time vs. support threshold (transaction model)

4.2. Transaction model

In the second set of experiments, we study the algorithms' performance under the transaction model of database update. In the experiments, we first generate a database of 1,000,000 sequences. We regard this database as the *updated* one, D'. We then randomly select 1% of the sequences from the database and delete the last two transactions from the selected sequences. We regard the resulting database as the old database, D. Hence, the update is equivalent to adding two transactions to 1% of the sequences in D. For GSP+ and MFS+, this update is modeled by sequence deletion followed by sequence insertion. We note that, in this case, $|\Delta^-| = |\Delta^+|$.

After the data generation, we run SPADE on the old database to obtain the necessary information for incremental algorithms. Figure 4 shows the performance of the six algorithms executed on a 700MHz Xeon machine with 4GB memory. In this experiment, the number of items, N, is set to 5,000, and the support threshold, ρ_s, is varied from 0.5% to 0.9%.

Similar to the sequence model, from Figure 4, we see that as ρ_s increases, in general, the execution times of the algorithms decrease. Again, this is because a larger ρ_s means

fewer sequences to discover.

Unlike the sequence model case, under the transaction model, ISM performs better than the other algorithms (unless ρ_s is very small). This is because, under the transaction model of database update, there is much less change to ISL. For example, the first step of ISM is not needed. Moreover, ISM outperforms the other algorithms by a large margin when ρ_s is large. This is because ISL is small under a large ρ_s, hence its maintenance cost is small. On the other hand, when ρ_s is small, the set of frequent sequences as well as the negative border are large. In this case, ISM is not as efficient as SPADE, since it has to maintain a fairly large ISL.

From Figure 4, we also observe that under the transaction model, the two pruning algorithms (GSP+ and MFS+) are not very effective. They achieve very little performance gain over their non-incremental versions. Recall that the main idea of the pruning algorithms is to deduce which candidate sequences cannot be frequent without resorting to support counting. To make that deduction, the pruning algorithms consider two cases:

Case 1: a candidate sequence s is frequent w.r.t D. Under the transaction model, we note that a sequence that is frequent w.r.t D must also be frequent w.r.t D'. Hence, no sequences in this case can be pruned.

Case 2: a candidate sequence s is not frequent w.r.t. D. In this case, we check if the inequality $\delta^s_{\Delta+} - \delta^s_{\Delta-} > (|\Delta^+| - |\Delta^-|) \times \rho_s$ is true (see Lemma 2, Section 3.3). If not, s can be pruned. However, under the transaction model, $|\Delta^+| = |\Delta^-|$. Hence the right hand side of the inequality is always 0. The inequality is false only if $\delta^s_{\Delta+}$ exactly equals $\delta^s_{\Delta-}$, which is unlikely. Therefore, very few candidate sequences can be pruned.

With ineffective pruning, not much advantage is obtained from the pruning algorithms.

Finally, we remark that, with plenty of memory (4GB), SPADE performs consistently well over the range of ρ_s.

In another experiment, we study how the extent of database update affects the algorithms' performance. Again, we generate a database D' of 1,000,000 sequences. We then randomly select $x\%$ ($1 \leq x \leq 10$) of the sequences in D' from each of which the last two transactions are removed. The resulting database is used as D. Figure 5 shows the experiment result. For readability, we omit the curves for GSP and MFS, since their performance is very similar to that of GSP+ and MFS+.

From the figure, we see that GSP+ and MFS+ are relatively unaffected by the percentage change. The curve for SPADE stays flat since it is applied directly on the the updated database, and in the experiment D' stays the same. For ISM, its execution time increases linearly with the percentage change. This is because more update made to the database leads to more changes to ISL. ISM, therefore, has

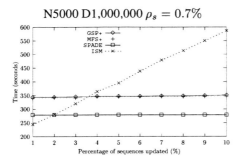

N5000 D1,000,000 $\rho_s = 0.7\%$

Figure 5. Execution time vs. percentage of sequences being updated (transaction model)

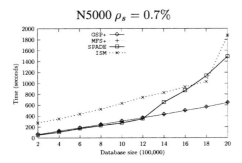

N5000 $\rho_s = 0.7\%$

Figure 6. Execution time vs. database size (transaction model)

to spend more effort in updating the lattice. We see that for small database update (say, 1%), ISM gives the best performance. On the other hand, if the database is changed substantially, SPADE is the best choice.

Our last experiment studies the performance of the algorithms under the transaction model when memory is limited. We performed the experiment on an 866MHz PC with 512MB of memory. We varied the size of D' from 200,000 sequences to 2,000,000 sequences. In each run, 5% of the sequences in D' were selected to have their last two transactions removed to form D. Figure 6 shows the result. Again, we omit the curves of GSP and MFS for readability.

From the figure, we see that when the database is large, SPADE and ISM perform poorly. This is again because of their relatively large memory requirements.

5. Conclusions

In this paper we studied the problem of incremental update of frequent sequences. We compared the performance of three incremental algorithms, namely, GSP+, MFS+, ISM, and their non-incremental counterparts GSP, MFS and SPADE. We studied two database update models, namely,

the sequence model and the transaction model. We discussed the various characteristics of the algorithms and showed their performance under various situations. Based on the experiment results, we derive the following guidelines on choosing the most efficient algorithm:

Under the sequence model of database update
- If the amount of main memory is relatively large compared with the database size and the number of items is small, ISM is the most efficient.
- If the amount of main memory is relatively large compared with the database size and the number of items is large, SPADE is the best choice.
- If memory is limited, GSP+ or MFS+ should be considered.

Under the transaction model of database update
- If memory is abundant and only a small portion of the database is updated, ISM is the best choice.
- If memory is abundant and a significant portion of the database is changed, SPADE is the most efficient.
- If the database is large compared with the amount of memory available, pick anyone of GSP, MFS, GSP+, or MFS+.

References

[1] R. Agrawal and R. Srikant. Mining sequential patterns. In *Proc. of the 11th Int'l Conference on Data Engineering*, Taipei, Taiwan, March 1995.
[2] http://www.almaden.ibm.com/cs/quest/.
[3] S. Parthasarathy, M. J. Zaki, M. Ogihara, and S. Dwarkadas. Incremental and interactive sequence mining. In *Proceedings of the 1999 ACM 8th International Conference on Information and Knowledge Management (CIKM'99)*, Kansas City, MO USA, November 1999.
[4] J. Pei, J. Han, B. Mortazavi-Asl, H. Pinto, Q. Chen, U. Dayal, and M.-C. Hsu. Prefixspan: Mining sequential patterns by prefix-projected growth. In *Proc. 17th IEEE International Conference on Data Engineering (ICDE)*, Heidelberg, Germany, April 2001.
[5] T. I. R. Agrawal and A. Swami. Mining association rules between sets of items in large databases. In *Proc. ACM SIGMOD International Conference on Management of Data*, page 207, Washington, D.C., May 1993.
[6] R. Srikant and R. Agrawal. Mining sequential patterns: Generalizations and performance improvements. In *Proc. of the 5th Conference on Extending Database Technology (EDBT)*, Avignion, France, March 1996.
[7] M. J. Zaki. Efficient enumeration of frequent sequences. In *Proceedings of the 1998 ACM 7th International Conference on Information and Knowledge Management(CIKM'98)*, Washington, United States, November 1998.
[8] M. Zhang, B. Kao, D. Cheung, and C.-L. Yip. Efficient algorithms for incremental update of frequent sequences. In *Proc. of the sixth Pacific-Asia Conference on Knowledge Discovery and Data Mining (PAKDD)*, Taiwan, May 2002.
[9] M. Zhang, B. Kao, C. Yip, and D. Cheung. A GSP-based efficient algorithm for mining frequent sequences. In *Proc. of IC-AI'2001*, Las Vegas, Nevada, USA, June 2001.

On Active Learning for Data Acquisition

Zhiqiang Zheng and Balaji Padmanabhan
Operations and Information Management,
The Wharton School, University of Pennsylvania
{zhengzhi, balaji}@wharton.upenn.edu

Abstract

Many applications are characterized by having naturally incomplete data on customers – where data on only some fixed set of local variables is gathered. However, having a more complete picture can help build better models. The naïve solution to this problem – acquiring complete data for all customers – is often impractical due to the costs of doing so. A possible alternative is to acquire complete data for "some" customers and to use this to improve the models built. The data acquisition problem is determining how many, and which, customers to acquire additional data from. In this paper we suggest using active learning based approaches for the data acquisition problem. In particular, we present initial methods for data acquisition and evaluate these methods experimentally on web usage data and UCI datasets. Results show that the methods perform well and indicate that active learning based methods for data acquisition can be a promising area for data mining research.

1. Introduction

Many data mining applications are characterized by the collection of naturally incomplete data in which the application only has data on some fixed set of "local" variables due to reasons such as data ownership, business issues and technological issues. Credit card companies have data on customer transactions with their cards, but do not have data on customer transactions with other cards. There are examples in the online world too where the inherent incompleteness of collected data shows up. For example, consider two users who browse the web for air tickets. Assume that the first user's session is as follows $Cheaptickets_1$, $Cheaptickets_2$, $Travelocity_1$, $Travelocity_2$, $Expedia_1$, $Expedia_2$, $Travelocity_3$, $Travelocity_4$, $Expedia_3$, $Cheaptickets_3$ where X_i represents some page i, at website X and in this session assume that the user purchases a ticket at Cheaptickets. Assume that the second user's session is $Expedia_1$, $Expedia_2$, $Expedia_3$, $Expedia_4$ and that this user purchases a ticket at Expedia (in the booking page $Expedia_4$, in particular). Expedia's local data would include the following:

User1: $Expedia_1$, $Expedia_2$, $Expedia_3$
User2: $Expedia_1$, $Expedia_2$, $Expedia_3$,, $Expedia_4$

In one case (user 2) the first three pages result in the user booking a ticket at the next page. In the other case (user 1), the first three pages result in no booking. Expedia sees the "same" initial browsing behavior, but with opposite results – one which resulted in a booking and one which did not. In [15] we showed that models built on such incomplete snapshots of web browsing data can result in significantly worse models, and sometimes even in erroneous conclusions.

Generalizing from these, there are many data mining applications characterized by the following features:

1. There is some "local" data available. For example, for Expedia, this local data could be variables constructed from its clickstream (logfile) data. For credit card companies, all customer transactions conducted with their card create local data. Essentially, by local data we mean readily available data that is collected automatically.

2. There is also a specific objective and the target variable (e.g. "purchase prediction", "customer value") related to this is also readily available and is known for all the data records. Expedia needs to understand purchase behavior of customers and Expedia clearly knows which user sessions resulted in purchases and which did not. Credit card companies know which of their customers are profitable for them and which are not. Online media companies know who clicked on an advertisement and who did not.

3. There is additional information representing useful variables that are not usually available, but it is known *what* these variables are. For example, Expedia does not know customer information representing browsing behavior across sites, online media companies know that there are customer characteristics that affect what advertisement is likely to be clicked on but this information is not readily available, credit card companies know that customers transact with other cards but have no information on features of such transactions. In all these cases, even though the data collected is only a snapshot of the true picture, it is easy to identify what the relevant unknown (not collected) variables are.

562

Note that the first two conditions hold for any data mining application - these indicate the availability of data and a target variable being modeled. The third condition is particularly relevant for the ideas presented in this paper. Note that it can be empirically tested if the 'additional' data is useful. Indeed for personalization, in prior work [15], we show that the magnitudes of the gains obtained from complete data are striking. For example, with complete user browsing behavior, the purchase prediction accuracies in many cases increase by more than 100%.

What can be done in such situations? If it is not possible to acquire this additional data by any means, then there is no fix. In reality for most situations additional data *can* be acquired, but at a cost. Given that it may be possible to acquire additional data, the naïve solution to this problem – acquiring complete data for *all* customers – is impractical in many cases due to the costs of doing so. It may just not be feasible to acquire all the unknown data from all customers (for all the data records). In this paper, we investigate an alternative – whether, and if so how, to acquire complete data for 'some' customers and to use this to improve the models built. We use the term *active data acquisition strategies* to refer to such methods.

Data acquisition by itself is a well-studied problem. Literature in survey sampling [5], experimental design [2, 4] and active learning [6,9,11,13,17] have developed extensive methods that are applicable for different problems. The main goal in survey sampling and experimental design is to have a sample such that inferences from the sample will be applicable to the entire population. Given constraints, non-random sampling strategies can be useful in order to obtain points in parts of the search space that are currently not present in the sample. There are two characteristics here that are different from the data acquisition scenario considered in this paper. First, these problems normally do not know the target values for the points that they acquire and indeed, the main reason for acquiring the points in the first place is to determine what the target value for that point is. Second, the strategies are not goal-directed. They do not acquire points with the specific goal of improving the performance of a *model* – the process of data acquisition and model building are usually independent.

Active learning [7,11,13], on the other hand, represents goal-directed data acquisition. The usual scenario considered in active learning is that all explanatory variables are known, a current model of the target exists but the *target* values are often unknown and expensive to acquire. The problem is to determine which points to acquire this target value from with the specific goal of improving model performance at manageable cost. It is important to note that for the data acquisition scenario considered in this paper, it is *not* the target variables that are unknown, but rather some explanatory variables which are not known and traditional active learning approaches,

therefore, cannot be directly applied. However the goal-oriented ideas of active learning could be effective for this problem, though research is needed to study how this can be done. In this paper we present initial approaches and show that active learning ideas can be applied for data acquisition strategies of the type considered in this paper.

We present two active learning based algorithms for data acquisition. The algorithms are based on two different active learning heuristics and show that using active learning ideas for data acquisition can be effective. We present results and discussion based on extensive experimentation using real web usage data as well as UCI datasets [3]. The results demonstrate that the methods perform well and indicate that active learning based methods for data acquisition can be effective and suggest that this may be a promising area for data mining research.

2. Preliminaries

Assume that in the domain, there exists a specific target variable, Y, that is being modeled. For example, Y could be whether or not a user transacts at a web site during a visit. Let N be the number of total data points. Let $X_1, X_2, ..., X_M, Y$ be attributes whose values are known initially for all points. We use the term "local data" to refer to data records consisting of $X_1, X_2, ..., X_M, Y$. Let $X_{M+1}, ..., X_P$ be the attributes whose values are all unknown initially. We use the term "global data" to refer to the complete data $X_1, X_2, ..., X_P, Y$.

In this paper we assume that initially only local data is available for all N records and subsequently global data is acquired for K of these records where K < N. As currently structured, the problem of deciding which K points to acquire global data for is still under-specified.

The choice clearly depends on the modeling method used. After acquiring these additional data, there are three scenarios involving how to model Y that can be visualized as shown in Figure 1. In Scenario 1 a local model is built involving the local variables only. This is the default model that exists before any additional data is acquired. In Scenario 2 a global model is built using global data for the K data points. The tradeoff between scenarios 1 and 2 is that the model built in scenario 2 uses more global information but less local information. In Scenario 3, Y is modeled using all available data, but this scenario involves dealing with some complete and some incomplete data in the process of modeling Y. The choice of which K points to acquire complete data from clearly depends on how the final model is built – whether as scenario 2 or 3. In this paper we focus on scenario 2, i.e. when K points are acquired based on active learning, we build a global model using the K points and compare that to the default local model (scenario 1). In order to make this comparison we essentially test the performance of the models on out of sample data where all the variables are known.

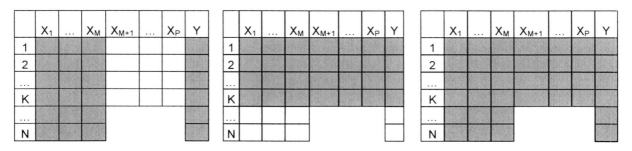

Scenario1: Local   Scenario 2: Global   Scenario 3: Combined

Figure 1. Three scenarios of model building

3. Algorithms for Active Data Acquisition

Let D_L denote the set of all known local data. Each record in D_L therefore consists of ID, X_1, X_2,..., X_M, Y where ID is an index ranging from 1 to N and $| D_L | = N$. D_L remains constant throughout the procedure. D_G is the set of all known global data. Each record in D_G therefore consists of ID, X_1, X_2, ..., X_M, X_{M+1},..., X_P, Y. $| D_G | = 0$ initially and $| D_G | = K$ at the end of the data acquisition process. There are two active data acquisition strategies that we present in this section, both based on applying ideas from traditional active learning.

3.1 Algorithm AVID

In this section we present AVID (Acquisition based on Variance of Imputed Data), an algorithm for choosing K data points to acquire global data about. The heuristic used here is determining how useful global data may be based on trying to estimate it from known local data. For instance, for any candidate point, if the global information *can be guessed* from the local information, then global data about this point is less likely to be informative. The literature on missing data [1,12,18] provides several methods for data imputation that can be used for this purpose. The problem here is determining how good the imputation model is for a candidate point, when the true global values for this point are not known. AVID uses an approach which is based on estimating the uncertainties in imputation by using several bootstrap samples to build different imputation models and determining the variance of the imputed values. Points for which the imputed global data has higher variances are points for which the global data can be guessed with less certainty from the local data. Hence these may be good candidates from whom true global data can be acquired.

The idea of estimating variance of an unknown value based on multiple bootstrap samples has been developed independently in both the missing data and the traditional

active learning literature. The multiple imputation mechanism proposed in [12,18] works as follows. Each missing value is replaced with a set of plausible values that represent the uncertainty about the right value to impute. Statistical procedures can be applied to each data set and the results are combined according to methods proposed in [12,18]. Bootstrapping is also proposed as a method to generate the set of plausible values [18, 20]. In the active learning literature, [17] proposes a method that determines the variances of class probability estimates empirically based on using several bootstrap samples.

AVID is presented in Figure 2. In addition to the local data, the inputs to AVID are an imputation model, a desirable number of points to be acquired K, a minimum step size (representing the number of points for which global data is acquired at each acquisition stage) and the number of bootstrap samples B.

The set I_G incrementally maintains the list of indexes in the local data for which global data is acquired. Initially this set consists of *sz* (the step size) random points for which global data is acquired (steps 1-10). Once an initial set of global data is acquired, step 12 builds several (*B*) imputation models based on bootstrap samples from the known global data. Steps 14 through 18 applies the imputation models to all the unknown global data in order to determine the points for which the imputation uncertainty is the most. The actual uncertainty score is computed in step 17 and this represents a measure of the variance of the imputed values for all the unknown variables. Step 19 selects the next best *sz* points to acquire. This entire process is continued until the desired number of points, K, are acquired.

Note that AVID does not depend on the classifier and also does not take the actual target values for Y into account in the data acquisition strategy. In this sense, it is a naïve approach for data acquisition. In the next section we present GODA, a *goal-oriented data acquisition* approach, which depends on the classifier and the target values during the course of data acquisition.

```
Input: Local data D_L, Desired number of points to be acquired K, Step size sz, Imputation Method IM,
Number of bootstrap samples B

Output: K points for which global data is acquired

    1   N = |D_L|
    2   I_L={ 1, 2, .., N}      /* index of all points in D_L */
    3   D_G = {}                /* known global data, initially empty */
    4   I_G = {}                /* index of all points in D_G */
    5   S ← randomly select sz integers from I_L-I_G
    6   do {
    7        Forall (j ∈ S) {
    8              Acquire d_G = { ID, X_1,..,X_P, Y} for the element in D_L where ID=j
    9              D_G = D_G U d_G      /* add-in this newly acquired global data point */
   10              I_G = I_G U { j}
   11        }
   12        Build B imputation models IM_1, IM_2, ... IM_B by applying IM to B bootstrap samples of D_G
   13        UID = I_L-I_G /* current set of IDs for which global data is unknown */
   14        U_G = { t | t ∈ D_L and t.ID ∈UID}
   15        Forall (t ∈ U_G) {
   16        x_ij ← the imputed value for variable i of record t using imputation
                  model IM_j (M+1≤ i ≤ P,  1≤ j≤ B).
```

$$17 \quad Score(t) = \sum_{i=M+1}^{P} \sum_{j=1}^{B} \sqrt{(x_{ij} - \mu_i)^2 / B} \text{ where } \mu_i = \left(\sum_{j=1}^{B} x_{ij} \right) / B$$

```
   18        }
   19        S ← select min(sz, K-|I_G|) IDs in U_G with the highest scores
              /* alternately, one can sample according to the distribution implied by the scores */
   20   }
   21   while ( |S| ≤ K)
   22   Output: D_G
```

Figure 2. Algorithm AVID (Data Acquisition based on Variance of Imputed Data)

3.2 Algorithm GODA

GODA (goal-oriented data acquisition) chooses K data points to maximize the performance of the model of the target using a given classifier. Assume that at some point in the process, GODA has a subset of known global data. The idea is to choose the next point to maximize the expected improvement of the model built on the global data. The heuristic used here is that for each candidate point, GODA guesses its global data first and then adds this record to the known global data, builds a model based on all available global data and then considers the goodness of the model. GODA chooses the candidate point to acquire additional data from based on the one with the most expected improvement. This is a greedy heuristic.

Rather than fixing what model goodness criterion to use, in GODA we allow various measures by treating this as an input. A number of measures have been proposed in literature [6,17] including prediction accuracy, MSE, lift curve and AIC. In particular we use AIC (Akaike Information Criteria) in our implementation of GODA. AIC measures model performance in terms of the likelihood and complexity of the model. The common AIC is in the form of AIC = -2 $L(\theta)$ + 2$|\theta|$, where θ is the

set of the parameters of the classifier and $|\theta|$ is the number of parameters, and $L(\theta)$ is the likelihood of the classifier. AIC can be easily computed for probabilistic classifiers such as Logit model as implemented in our experiments.

Algorithm GODA is presented in Figure 3. The inputs are the local data, a classifier, an imputation model, a desirable number of points to be acquired K and a minimum step size.

The initial steps (1-10) are similar to that of AVID – a random sz points are acquired to begin. Once an initial set of global data is acquired, step 12 builds an imputation model from the known global data. Steps 13 and 14 compute the set of all transactions for which global data is unknown (U_G). For each of the records in U_G, the unknown values are imputed (step 16) and a model is built by adding this imputed point to the current known global data (step 17 and 18) and the goodness of this model is computed in Step 19. Step 22 selects the next best sz points to acquire. This entire process is continued until the desired number of points, K, are acquired.

In this section we presented AVID and GODA, two algorithms for active data acquisition. In the next section we present experimental results by applying the two algorithms to 15 datasets.

```
Input: Local data D_L, Desired number of points to be acquired K, Step size sz, Classifier C, Goodness
Criterion GC, Imputation Method IM
Output: K points for which global data is acquired

1    N = |D_L|
2    I_L={ 1, 2, .., N}        /* index of all points in D_L */
3    D_G = {}                  /* known global data, initially empty */
4    I_G = {}                  /* index of all points in D_G */
5    S ← randomly select sz integers from I_L-I_G
6    do {
7      Forall (j ∈ S) {
8              Get d_G = { ID, X_1,..,X_P, Y} for the element in D_L where ID=j
9              D_G = D_G U d_G
10             I_G = I_G U { j}
11     }
12     Build an imputation model IM_1 from D_G
13     UID = I_L-I_Gs /* current set of IDs for which global data is unknown */
14     U_G = { t | t ∈ D_L and t.ID ∈UID}
15     Forall (t ∈ U_G) {
16             d_g = IM_1 (record t)   /* impute record t using IM_1 to get d_g */
17             D_G = D_G U d_g
18             M_G ← Apply classifier C on D_G to get model M_G
19             Score(t) ← Compute goodness score of M_G using GC /*e.g. MSE, AIC*/
20             D_G = D_G - d_g  /* reset D_G */
21     }
22     S ← select min(sz, K-|I_G|) IDs in U_G with the best scores
23     } /* end do */
24   while ( |S| ≤ K)
25   Output: D_G
```

Figure 3: Algorithm GODA (Goal Oriented Data Acquisition)

4. Experiments

We test our results on 15 datasets each of which has a binary target variable. Five of these datasets are UCI datasets [3] and the remaining ten datasets are real user-centric browsing data (described in [15]) for ten popular web sites. For the real datasets the selection of global versus local data is natural – the data captured by individual web sites about user browsing behavior at that site is "local" information. The additional information about the users' activities across sites during a browsing session is "global" information. In our prior work [15] we describe how this data is generated from a panel of users whose browsing behavior is tracked. In each of these datasets, 15 of the 40 explanatory variables are local variables. Each UCI dataset as a whole is treated as the global data and the local data is generated by randomly 'hiding' 50% of the variables. The number of total variables in the 5 UCI datasets considered ranges from 4 to 16 (and half are local for each as explained above).

For each dataset, we apply data acquisition algorithms AVID and GODA to acquire global data and subsequently build models on the acquired data. In the absence of data acquisition, the only available data are all the local variables for the entire datasets (scenario 1 in figure 1). Based on this local data, we build local models and treat this as the benchmark against which global models (built from the data points selected by AVID and GODA) are compared. In addition, we also consider random data acquisition as a naïve alternative and use this as an additional benchmark to compare the local and global

models. We use mean square error on a random 50% out of sample data to make the comparisons.

For each data acquisition procedure, a final global model is built based on only the data points acquired from the learning sample. This global model's performance is then tested on out of sample data, in which we assume the data points are points for which we know all the global variables. In essence what is being tested here is theoretical model performance, i.e. how good the data acquisition procedures are with respect to building a good final model.

The classifier we use is the Logit model [10] since it is commonly used for binary classification and moreover is relatively fast as compared to other classifiers. The imputation method used in the algorithms use multiple imputation as implemented by the *Proc MI* procedure in SAS 8.2.

4.1 Sample Graphs

We vary the desirable size of global data (K) from 0% to 100% of the training data in order to observe the performance of each method over the entire range. Due to space constraints, we do not present plots for all the 15 datasets. Figure 4 and 5 present two examples. The x-axis represents the percentage of acquired global training data and the y-axis represents the MSE (mean square error) of the models on the out of sample data. Each learning curve shows how MSE decreases as more global data are acquired for training. As mentioned before, the benchmark Local model is built using the local variables in the entire training data and thus represents a straight line in this graph. Note that the converging point (when all methods acquire 100% of the global data) represents the MSE of a global model built using global variables in the entire training data.

Consider the performance on the Penndigits data (Figure 4). Observe that in general, GODA > AVID > RANDOM. We use the term *critical mass* to refer to the percentage of data at which a model based on acquiring additional global variables beats the performance of the local model. Observe that from just 14% of acquired data based on GODA, a better model can be built than from using the entire local data. It hence represents the point at which additional local data can be traded off for more complete data.

For some other datasets, the results are not as striking. For example, performance on the Amazon.com dataset is shown in Figure 5. The benefit of using GODA and AVID over random acquisition is lower. In this case the critical mass is closer to 20% for all the three methods. To make more general conclusions we studied the performance over a range of datasets and present the results below.

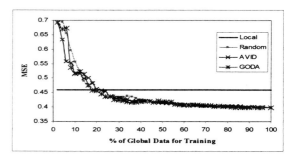

Figure 5. Performance on Amazon dataset

4.2 Comparative Results

In order to draw more general conclusions, we compared metrics across several datasets. From each chart (dataset) we construct the following metrics for each of the three methods (random, AVID, GODA):

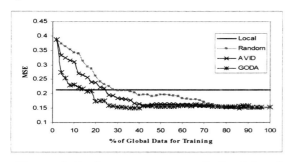

Figure 4. Performance on pendigits dataset

Table 1: Experimental results summary

	Global	Random			AVID			GODA		
DataSet	Gain % over local	Critical Mass %	Avg gain %	Avg gain after CM	Critical Mass	Avg gain %	Avg gain after CM	Crit.Mass (CM)	Avg gain %	Avg gain after CM
Amazon	13.3	20.0	3.1	11.1	18.0	4.1	11.6	20.0	5.3	11.6
B&N	10.5	30.0	-1.8	7.1	34.0	2.0	8.3	12.0	6.0	8.0
CDNow	6.5	50.0	-11.0	11.4	60.0	-11.0	10.4	54.0	-6.7	12.8
Expedia	30.2	22.0	19.1	25.8	18.0	18.9	24.4	12.0	19.9	26.8
Travelocity	10.2	32.0	-3.3	8.2	40.0	-3.0	9.0	22.0	1.9	9.6
BMG	3.0	30.0	-4.4	6.2	32.0	-2.0	6.0	46.0	-5.0	6.6
Buy	6.1	28.0	-4.7	2.9	30.0	-2.0	1.3	38.0	-2.8	4.3
QVC	12.2	32.0	-2.9	8.6	32.0	0.0	9.0	24.0	2.5	9.8
Priceline	25.3	28.0	4.4	17.1	24.0	9.3	9.5	8.0	19.3	20.2
Etoys	12.4	44.0	-12.5	7.7	12.0	6.1	9.6	22.0	0.6	11.1
Iris	38.0	16.0	34.3	33.8	8.0	33.0	34.7	8.0	33.0	34.0
Cancer	13.9	62.0	-10.4	9.9	34.0	-4.3	8.7	24.0	-0.5	8.8
Liver	9.0	24.0	2.5	5.8	16.0	4.1	6.2	16.0	6.6	7.8
Pima	10.2	22.0	2.2	8.8	18.0	4.7	7.8	10.0	7.8	9.2
Pendigits	28.6	30.0	1.4	17.6	26.0	10.0	24.0	14.0	17.2	23.7
Average	**15.3**	**31.3**	**1.1**	**12.1**	**26.8**	**4.7**	**12.0**	**22.0**	**7.0**	**13.6**
Avg_web	13.0	31.6	-1.4	10.6	30.0	2.2	9.9	25.8	4.1	12.1
Avg_uci	19.94	30.8	6	15.18	20.4	9.5	16.28	14.4	12.8	16.7

1. Critical Mass - percentage of data to be acquired to outperform the local model
2. Average gain in MSE over the local model computed as average of percentage gains across the entire training data range (0-100%). This value can be highly affected by the initial points when very little acquired data is significantly worse than the local model, hence we also compute the next metric.
3. Average gain in MSE over the local model *after* the critical mass.

For each metric, we seek to get a better handle on the following questions:

- On average, what are the values for these metrics for the methods?
- Is the metric for GODA/AVID significantly better than that for random?

Table 1 summarizes results from each dataset for each method. As a reference, we also report the gain of the global model over the local model (column 2) as the upper bound that each method can attain.

In terms of critical mass, the above results show that a relatively small portion of global data is needed to outperform local models. The average critical masses, across the 15 datasets considered, are 31.3%, 26.8%, and 22% for Random, AVID and GODA respectively. For the 5 UCI datasets selected, GODA only needs 14.4% of global data to beat local models. In terms of average gain and critical mass, GODA > AVID > RANDOM and the pairwise differences are significant.

These results indicate that the methods work well and that active learning based approaches can be useful approaches for data acquisition strategies. There is much opportunity for future research work and better heuristics. Some of the opportunities arise from the various different fields that have studied related questions and in the next section we briefly review them. Subsequently in a discussion in Section 6 below, we go beyond the initial approaches presented thus far and raise several issues that need to be addressed in future research.

5. Related Work

As mentioned in Section 1, data acquisition methods have been considered in survey sampling, experimental design and active learning but in different contexts.

In survey sampling [5], the focus is on drawing inferences about the population through interview, email, telephone, questionnaires, etc. Survey sampling primarily uses simple random sampling. When the population forms into homogeneous groups, the *stratified sampling* or *cluster sampling* [5] method is often used where the population is divided into subgroups and then each group

is randomly sampled. The missing data problem encountered in survey sampling is when there is non-response from some of those surveyed [17]. Note that survey sampling is usually goal-independent - the sampling procedure does not depend on how the data is to be used in model building.

Experimental design deals with acquiring data through experiments when the data is not available in natural settings [4]. In order to observe unbiased effect of treatment, randomization is key [4]. When subjects fall into homogenous groups, randomized block design is often used. *Optimal experimental design* (OED) aims to generate a smaller sample in experimental design than regular randomized experimental design [2,8]. OED proposes an incremental method during the course of acquiring data. At each phase, OED decides which subject to be experimented, rather than randomly select from the pool. In doing so, OED uses optimization techniques to decide which subject to go after. A variety of optimization techniques have been developed and further reviews could be found in [2,8].

Active learning is a relatively more recent approach where learning models have control on what data to feed into the model for training [7] and a good summary of active learning is provided in [11,17]. Active learning assumes that the utility of a data point to the model could be discerned by some measure during the course of learning. By selecting only those data with high utility to the model, active learning aims to minimize the number of data needed for training without compromising model performance. Ideas in active learning have similarities with those in optimal experimental design. Active learning methods broadly fall into two categories: heuristic based and optimization based approaches [11].

Query by committee (QBC) [9] is a well-known heuristic-based approach. QBC employs several committee members (each of them is a model) and each member makes its own predictions on unseen data. The data points chosen are those in which there is maximum disagreement among the committee. The rationale here is that those data points that the committee mostly disagrees with are most uncertain to the principle model and thus they are more informative. Another type of heuristic was proposed in [11,13] that is similar to boosting -- selecting those data points that the model misclassifies.

Optimization approaches employ an objective function and those data points that optimize this objective function are selected. Some well-known objective functions are variance-based objective functions and those based on some measure of information gain [13,19]. In [6] data points are selected to minimize the overall prediction variance of a model and [17] selects those data according to the variance of bootstrap predictions of class probability estimates. As mentioned in Section 1, for the data acquisition scenario considered in this paper, it is not the target variables that are missing, but rather explanatory variables and traditional active learning approaches cannot be directly applied.

The methods proposed in this paper use data imputation as a component. Some commonly used missing data approaches are mean substitution, nearest neighbor substitution, imputation using regression, EM [14], and multiple imputation [12,18]. A good review of these approaches are presented in [1].

6. Discussion

In Section 2, we suggested that data acquisition strategies could depend on how the final model from the acquired data is built. In Figure 1 we presented three scenarios and in this paper only compared scenarios 1 and 2. The third scenario has the potential of doing even better since all the available data will be used. In this scenario, local and global models can be weighted and combined. In future work this will need to be studied.

Less obvious is the fact that good data acquisition strategies could also depend on how the model is *applied* in practice (i.e. how it is used after all the points are acquired and a final model is built). Assume that we have acquired K points and have built a final model which will be used to make predictions for new customers. Now, there are three types of customers (data points) that may be encountered in practice. First, there are *friends*, customers for whom $X_1, X_2,..., X_P$ are all known and the task is to predict Y as well as possible. This is the scenario used in the experiments in this paper where we assumed that in the out of sample data, all the global variables are known. Second, there are *strangers*, customers for whom only local data $(X_1, X_2,...,X_M)$ will be available. In this case, predicting Y better may involve making good guesses on $X_{M+1},..., X_P$ and it would help if the acquired points help in making good guesses. Finally there are *mercenaries*, customers from whom the additional data does not have to be guessed, but can be acquired at a cost.

These represent several opportunities for new data acquisition strategies. In this paper we focused on one such situation - building good global models by data acquisition and show experimentally how the methods perform for friends. In future work we plan to develop data acquisition procedures geared towards strangers and mercenaries and to also develop approaches to combine local and global models as laid out in Figure 1.

In this paper we introduced the idea of using active learning based procedures for data acquisition, presented initial approaches and results from extensive experimentation using proprietary as well as UCI datasets. The initial results indicate that the methods perform well and that data acquisition strategies can be a promising application of active-learning based approaches.

References

[1] Acock, A.C. (1997). Working with missing data. Family Science Review. 10(1):76-102

[2] Atkinson, A. and Donev A., 1992, Optimum Experimental Designs, Oxford Science Publications.

[3] Blake, C.L. & Merz, C.J.,1998, UCI Repository of machine learning databases Irvine, CA: University of California, Department of Information and Computer Science.

[4] Box, G E P, Hunter, W G , and Hunter, J S ,1978, *Statistics for Experimenters*, John Wiley & Sons.

[5] Chaudhuri, Arijit and Stenger, Horst, 1992, Survey Sampling: Theory and Methods, Marcel Dekker, INC.

[6] Cohn, D., Ghahramani, Z., & Jordan, M. (1996). Active learning with statistical models. Journal of Artificial Intelligence Research, 4, 129.

[7] Cohn, D., Minimizing Statistical Bias with Queries, 1995, CBCL Proceedings.

[8] Cohn, D. (1996) , Neural network exploration using optimal experiment design, Journal of Econometrics, 37, 87--114.

[9] Freund, Y., Seung, H., Shamir, E., Tishby, N., 1997, Selective Sampling Using Query by Committee Algorithm, Machine Learning, 28, 133-168.

[10] Friedman J. , H., Hastie, T. and Tibshirani, R. ,1998, Additive Logistic Regression: A statistical view of Boosting. Dept. of Statistics, Stanford University Tech. Report.

[11] Hasenjäger,M.; H. Ritter, Active Learning in Neural Networks, working paper in the university of Bielefeld, 1999, available at http://citeseer.nj.nec.com/404108.html

[12] Little, R. J. A. and D. B. Rubin. 1987, Statistical Analysis with Missing Data., New York: John Wiley & Sons.

[13] MacKay, D. J. C. 1992, Information-based objective functions for active data selection,. Neural Computation, vol. 4 (4), pp. 590-604.

[14] McLachlan G., and Krishnan, T., 1997, The EM Algorithms and Extensions, John Wiley & Sons, Inc.

[15] Padmanabhan, B.; Zheng Z. and Kimbrough, S., 2001, Personalization from Incomplete Data: What You Don't Know Can Hurt, In Proceeding of the Seventh ACM SIGKDD International Conference on Knowledge Discovery and Data Mining, KDD01.

[16] Plutowski, M., & White, H. (1993). Selecting concise training sets from clean data. IEEE Transactions on Neural Networks, 4, 305-318.

[17] Saar-Tsechansky Maytal; Foster J. Provost, 2001, Active Learning for Class Probability Estimation and Ranking, IJCAI 2001.

[18] Schafer, M. K., J. L. & Olsen. (1998). Multiple imputation for multivariate missing-data problems: A data analysts perspective. Multivariate Behavioral Research , 33 (4), pp. 545-571.

[19] Tong, S., Koller, D., 2001, Active Learning for Structure in Bayesian Networks, In Proceedings of the International Joint Conference on Artificial Intelligence 2001.

[20] Yuan, Y., 2000, Multiple Imputation for Missing Data: Concepts and New Developments, SAS Institute Inc. http://www.sas.com/rnd/app/papers/multipleimputation.pdf.

SmartMiner: A Depth First Algorithm Guided by Tail Information for Mining Maximal Frequent Itemsets

Qinghua Zou
Computer Science Department
University of California-LA
zou@cs.ucla.edu

Wesley W. Chu
Computer Science Department
University of California-LA
wwc@cs.ucla.edu

Baojing Lu
Computer Science Department
North Dakota State University
baojing.lu@ndsu.nodak.edu

Abstract

Maximal frequent itemsets (MFI) are crucial to many tasks in data mining. Since the MaxMiner algorithm first introduced enumeration trees for mining MFI in 1998, several methods have been proposed to use depth first search to improve performance. To further improve the performance of mining MFI, we proposed a technique that takes advantage of the information gathered from previous steps to discover new MFI. More specifically, our algorithm called SmartMiner gathers and passes tail information and uses a heuristic select function which uses the tail information to select the next node to explore. Compared with Mafia and GenMax, SmartMiner generates a smaller search tree, requires a smaller number of support counting, and does not require superset checking. Using the datasets Mushroom and Connect, our experimental study reveals that SmartMiner generates the same MFI as Mafia and GenMax, but yields an order of magnitude improvement in speed.

1. Introduction

Mining frequent itemsets in large datasets is an important problem since it enables essential data mining tasks such as discovering association rules, data correlations, sequential patterns, etc.

Let I be a set of items and D be a set of transactions, where a transaction is an itemset. The support of an itemset is the number of transactions containing the itemset. An itemset is frequent if its support is at least a user specified minimum support value, minSup. Let FI denote the set of all frequent itemsets. An itemset is closed if there is no superset that has the same support. Let FCI be the set of all frequent closed itemsets. A frequent itemset is called maximal if it is not a subset of any other frequent itemset. We denote MFI as the set of all maximal frequent itemsets. Any maximal frequent itemset X is a frequent closed itemset since no nontrivial superset of X is frequent. Thus we have MFI$\subseteq$FCI$\subseteq$FI.

There are three different approaches for generating FI. First, the candidate set generate-and-test approach [1,11,14,8,12,7]: most previous algorithms belong to this group. The basic idea is to generate and then test the candidate set. This process is repeated in a bottom up fashion until no candidate set can be formed. Second, the sampling approach [7]: it selects samples of a dataset to form the candidate set. The candidate set is tested in the entire dataset to identify frequent itemsets. Sampling reduces computation complexity but yields incomplete result. Third, data transformation approach [6,16,17]: it transforms a dataset for efficient mining. For example, the FP-tree [6] builds up a compressed data representation called FP-tree from a dataset and then mines *FI* directly from the FP-tree. Another example is the pattern decomposition algorithm (PDA) [16,17] which decomposes transactions and shrinks the dataset in each pass.

When the frequent patterns are long, mining FI is infeasible because of the exponential number of frequent patterns. Thus, algorithms mining FCI [9,15,10] are proposed since FCI is enough to generate association rules. However, FCI could also be as large as the FI. As a result, researchers now turn to find MFI. Given the set of MFI, it is easy to analyze many interesting properties of the dataset, such as the longest pattern, the overlap of the MFI, etc. Moreover, we can focus on part of the MFI via supervised data mining.

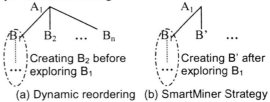

Figure 1: SmartMiner takes advantages of the information from previous steps.

The current MFI mining uses depth first search with dynamic reordering as in DepthProject[2], Mafia[4], and GenMax[5]. Those methods are significantly faster than previous approaches. However, they do not use the information from previous steps for exploring next nodes and requires the traverse of a larger search space than necessary. As shown in Figure 1, the dynamic reordering technique creates a set of sub nodes B_1~B_n before exploring B_1. In contrast, SmartMiner takes full advantage of the information from previous steps and explores B_1 before selecting the node B'.

Using tail information has many benefits: it does not require superset checking, reduces the computation for counting support, and yields a small search tree.

In this paper, we first discussed the limitations of current MFI algorithms, then introduced the partition and pruning properties used in the SmartMiner. The SmartMiner strategy and implementation are then presented. Finally, the experimental performance comparison of SmartMiner with Mafia and GenMax are included.

1.1 Related works

We first introduce an enumeration tree for an itemset I. Assume there is a total ordering over I which can be used to enumerate the search space. Each node has a head and a tail representing a state. The head is a candidate while the tail contains items to form new heads. For example, Figure 2 shows a complete enumeration tree over five items $abcde$ with the ordering a,b,c,d,e. Each node is written as $head:tail$. For an item a_i in the tail of a node $X:Y$, a sub-node is created with Xa_i as its head and the items after a_i in Y as its tail. For instance, the head of $:abcde$ is empty and its tail is $abcde$.

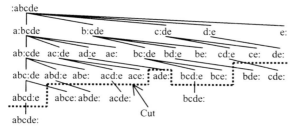

Figure 2: An enumeration tree for *abcde* for the given order of *a, b, c, d, e*.

The problem of mining frequent itemsets is to find a cut through this lattice such that all itemsets above the cut are frequent, and those below the cut are infrequent (see Figure 2) [14].

Using the enumeration tree as shown in Figure 2, we can describe recent approaches to the problem of mining MFI. MaxMiner [3] uses a breadth-first search and performs look-ahead pruning which prunes a whole tree if the head and tail together is frequent. MaxMiner also first uses dynamic reordering which reorder the tail items in the increasing order of their supports. In general, however, superset pruning works better with a depth-first approach [2] since many long frequent itemsets may already have been discovered. But MaxMiner uses a breadth-first approach to limit the number of passes over the database.

Since large main memory size is available in Gigabytes, current MFI mining uses depth first search to improve performance to find long patterns.

DepthProject[2] uses depth first search on a lexicographic tree of itemsets to find MFI, and projects transactions database on the current node to speed up the

counting for support. DepthProject also uses look-ahead pruning and dynamic reordering. With dynamic reordering, infrequent items at the current node can be deleted from the tail so that the size of the search space can be greatly reduced.

Mafia [4] proposes parent equivalence pruning (PEP) and differentiates superset pruning into two classes FHUT and HUTMFI. For a given node $X:aY$, the idea of PEP is that if $sup(X)=sup(Xa)$, i.e., every transaction containing X also contains the item a, then the node can simply be replaced by $Xa:Y$. The FHUT is to use the leftmost tree to prune its sister; if the entire tree with root $Xa:Y$ is frequent, then we do not need to explore the sisters of the node $Xa:Y$. The HUTMFI is to use the known MFI set to prune a node. That is if an itemset of XaY is subsumed by some itemset in the MFI set, the node $Xa:Y$ can be pruned. Mafia also uses dynamic reordering. The results show that PEP has the largest effect of the above pruning methods (PEP, FHUT, and HUTMFI) and dynamically reordering also has significant savings in computation.

Both DepthProject and Mafia mine a superset of the MFI, and require a post-pruning to eliminate non-maximal patterns [5]. GenMax [5] integrates pruning with mining and returns the exact. First, just like the transaction database is projected on the current node, the known MFI can also be projected on the node and thus yields fast superset checking. Second, GenMax uses Diffset propagation to perform fast frequency computation. Experimental results show that GenMax has comparable performance with Mafia.

1.2 Limitations of previous approaches

The algorithms discussed above do not take full advantage of previous searching. Let us use Mafia as an example to illustrate that limitations exist in previous approaches. For the example in Figure 2, Mafia will generate a search tree as in Figure 3, assuming that frequent itemsets have different support and the nodes are already sorted in the order of increasing support. In the figure, the shaded nodes will be removed by superset pruning. The node $abcde:$ in the dotted box is not in the search. The nodes with crossing lines are tested and found to be infrequent.

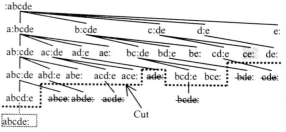

Figure 3: The search tree for Mifia.

First, the size of the tree is too large and can be reduced. Although the shaded nodes can be pruned away, a more efficient strategy is not to generate those nodes in the search tree. As shown in Figure 3, Mafia traverses 31 nodes. SmartMiner uses such a strategy and traverses only 9 nodes (see section 3.2) for the same example.

Second, there is too much counting for determining the frequency of tail items. Figure 4 shows the counting tree for Figure 2. Let X be an itemset and $T(X)$ be the set of transactions that contains X. For the root node at the top level, the transaction set is $T(\phi)$ since the head of the node is empty ϕ. For the node, the supports of a,b,c,d,e are counted and found to be above *minsup*. In the transaction set $T(a)$, we found b,c,d,e frequent. Likewise, items c,d,e are frequent in $T(ab)$, and item d is frequent and e infrequent in $T(abc)$. Mafia requires a total of 30 frequency tests. Using tail information and a heuristic select function, SmartMiner needs only 23 such tests.

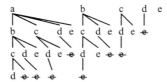

Figure 4: The Mafia counting tree.

Finally, all previous approaches require superset checking for two purposes: pruning nodes and removing non-maximal itemsets in MFI. If the set of MFI is large, as in most real datasets, superset checking can be very expensive. In the above example, Mafia performs 30 superset checks. As will be discussed later, SmartMiner does not require any superset checking.

2. Partition and Pruning Properties

2.1 Partitioning a search space

Let $N=X:Y$ be a node where X is the head of N and Y is the tail of N. The power set of Y is the set of all possible subsets of Y, denoted by $P(Y)$.

Definition 1 For a node $N=X:Y$, the set of all itemsets obtained by concatenating X with the members in $P(Y)$ is called the **search space** of N, denoted as $\{X:Y\}$. That is
$$\{X:Y\} = \{ X \cup Y \mid V \in P(Y)\}.$$

For example, the search space $\{b:cd\}$ includes four itemsets b, bc, bd, and bcd. Likewise, the search space $\{:abcde\}$ includes all subsets of $abcde$.

By definition 1, we have $\{X:Y\}=\{X:Z\}$ where $Z=Y-X$. Thus we will assume the X and Y share no item when $\{X:Y\}$ is used in this paper.

Definition 2 Let S, S_1, and S_2 be search spaces. The set $\{S_1, S_2\}$ is a *partition* of S if and only if $S= S_1 \cup S_2$ and $S_1 \cap S_2 = \phi$. The relationship is denoted by $S=S_1+S_2$ or $S_1= S-S_2$ or $S_2= S-S_1$. We say S is partitioned into S_1 and S_2. Similarly, a set $\{S_1, S_2, ..., S_k\}$ is a partition of S if and only if $S= S_1 \cup S_2 \cup ... \cup S_k$ and $S_i \cap S_j = \phi$ for $i,j \in [1..k]$ and $i \neq j$. We denote it as $S=S_1+S_2+...+S_k$.

Let a be an item, then aX is an itemset by adding a to X.

Theorem 1 For $a \notin X,Y$, the search space of $\{X:aY\}$ can be partitioned into $\{Xa:Y\}$ and $\{X:Y\}$ by item a, that is, $\{X:aY\}=\{Xa:Y\}+\{X:Y\}$.

Proof: It follows from the fact that each itemset of $\{X:aY\}$ either contains a or does not contain a.

For example, we have $\{b:ad\}=\{ba:d\}+\{b:d\}$.

In general, $a_1,a_2,...,a_k$ can be distinct items and $a_1a_2...a_kY$ form an itemset.

Theorem 2 *Partition search space*: the search space of $\{X: a_1a_2...a_kY\}$ can be partitioned into

$$\sum_{i=1}^{k}\{Xa_i : a_{i+1}...a_kY\}+\{X : Y\}, \text{ where } a_i \notin X,Y.$$

Proof: It follows by partitioning the search space via items $a_1,a_2,...,a_k$ sequentially as in theorem 1.

For example, we have $\{b:cd\}=\{bc:d\}+\{bd:\}+\{b:\}$ and $\{a:bcde\}= \{ab:cde\} +\{ac:de\}+\{a:de\}$.

Let $\{X:Y\}$ be a search space and Z be a known frequent itemset. Since Z is frequent, all subsets of Z will be frequent, i.e. every itemset of $\{:Z\}$ is frequent.

Theorem 3 *Pruning search space*: if Z does not contain the head X, the space $\{X:Y\}$ can not be pruned by Z, i.e., $\{X:Y\}-\{:Z\}=\{X:Y\}$. Otherwise, the space can be pruned as

$$\{X:Y\}-\{:Z\} = \sum_{i=1}^{k}\{Xa_i : a_{i+1}...a_k(Y \cap Z)\}, a_1a_2...a_k=Y-Z.$$

Proof: If Z does not contain X, no itemset in $\{X:Y\}$ is subsumed by Z. Therefore, knowing Z is frequent can not prune away any part of the search space $\{X:Y\}$. Otherwise, X is a subset of Z. Thus we have

$$\{X:Y\}= \sum_{i=1}^{k}\{Xa_i : a_{i+1}...a_kV\}+ X : V, \text{where } V=Y \cap Z.$$

The head in the first part is Xa_i. Since Z does not contain a_i, the first part can not be pruned. For the second part, we have $\{X:V\}-\{:Z\}=\{X:V\}-\{X:(Z-X)\}$. Since $X \cap Y=\phi$, we have $V \subseteq Z-X$. Therefore $\{X:V\}$ can be pruned away entirely.

For example, we have $\{:bcde\}-\{:abcd\}=\{:bcde\}-\{:bcd\}= \{e:bcd\}$. Likewise, $\{e:bcd\}-\{:abe\}=\{e:bcd\}-\{:be\}= \{e:bcd\}-\{e:b\} = \{ec:bd\}+\{ed:b\}$.

2.2 Evaluating Tail Information

Definition 3 Let M be the known frequent itemsets and $N=X:Y$ be a node. The **tail information** of M for N, $TInf(N/M)$, is the tail parts of the frequent itemsets in $\{X:Y\}$ that can be obtained from M, i.e.,

$$TInf(N \mid M) = \{Y \cap Z \mid \forall Z \in M, X \subseteq Z\}$$

For example, $TInf(e:bcd/\{abcd,abe,ace\})=\{b,c\}$, which means that eb and ec are frequent given $\{abcd,abe, ace\}$ is frequent. Likewise, $Inf(e:bcd/\{abcd,abe,ace,bce\})$ = $\{b,c,bc\}$. For simplicity, we refer to tail information as information.

Definition 4 Let W be tail information and Z be a member of W. The value of tail information W is the union of the power set of Z. That is,

$$VTI = \cup P(Z), Z \in W$$

For example, $VTI(\{b,c,bc\}) = \{\phi, b, c, bc\} = VTI(\{bc\})$. Notice that removing non-maximal itemsets from tail information does not decrease its value. Therefore, a non-maximal itemset in the information set can be deleted.

3. The SmartMiner

3.1 Information guided depth-first search

Since the tail of a node contains many infrequent items, pure depth-first search is inefficient. Hence, current approache uses dynamic reordering to prune away infrequent items from the tail of a node before exploring its sub nodes.

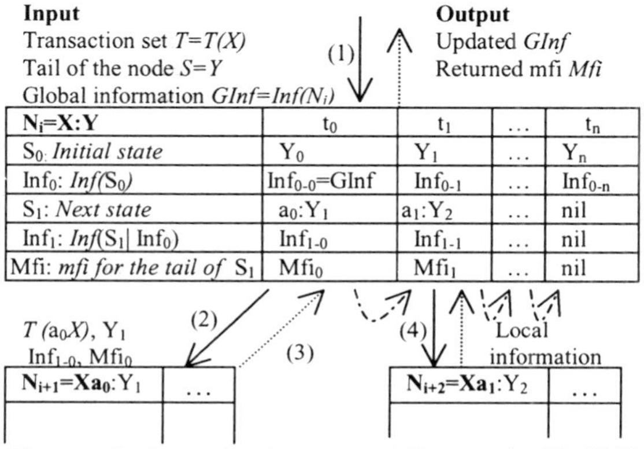

Figure 5: Search strategy at the node $N_i = X{:}Y$

In contrast, SmartMiner uses tail information to guide depth-first search to improve search efficiency. We illustrate the strategy for a given node $N_i = X{:}Y$ as shown in Figure 5. The purpose of the node $N_i = X{:}Y$ is to compute maximal frequent itemsets in the transaction set $T(X)$. The input for node $N_i = X{:}Y$ is transaction set $T(X)$, the tail Y, and the tail information for N_i known so far, $Ginf$, is called global tail information for node N_i. The output of the node is the updated $GInf$ and discovered maximal frequent itemsets Mfi. Upon calling the node N_i, we count the supports for the items in the tail Y. Y_0 is obtained by removing infrequent items from Y.

The time sequence at node N_i in Figure 5 is $t_0, t_1, ..., t_n$. At the moment t_0, item a_0 is selected from Y_0 to be the head of next state S_1 and $Y_1 = Y_0 - a_0$ is the tail of S_1. The tail information Inf_{1-0} is computed by $Inf(a_0{:}Y_1 | GInf)$. We then create node $N_{i+1} = Xa_1{:}Y_1$. The call for node N_{i+1} returns Mfi_0 and updated Inf_{1-0} in which the members survive in the node N_{i+1} are returned, i.e. those subsumed by Mfi_0 are deleted (no superset checking). At t_1, we calculate the tail information Inf_{0-1} for Y_1 from Inf_{0-0}, Inf_{10}, and Mfi_0. The information from Inf_{0-0} and Inf_{1-0} is updated global information. The information from Mfi_0 is local

information. Using information Inf_{0-1}, item a_1 is selected from Y_1 to be the head of the next state S_1 and $Y_2 = Y_1 - a_1$ is the tail of S_1. Then node $N_{i+2} = Xa_2{:}Y_2$ is created and called to compute maximal frequent itemsets in transaction sets $t(Xa_2)$. This process continues untill t_n where no item can be selected as head of S_1. The returned maximal frequent itemsets $Mfi = \cup a_i Mfi_i$, $i \in [0..n-1]$; the updated $GInf$ are these itemsets in the original $GInf$ which have not been marked as deleted.

SmartMiner uses tail information to guide the depth-first search which is different from dynamic reordering depth-first strategies (DFS). First, SmartMiner defers creating a node untill its preceding nodes are visited, while DFS creates nodes for each item in the tail of a node in the increasing order of their supports. DFS creates as many sub trees as the number of frequent items in the tail. Second, SmartMiner uses a heuristic select function with consideration of the tail information and the frequency about each item (see section 4.3). Using this heuristic, SmartMiner creates far fewer sub trees than dynamic reordering. Finally, by passing tail information, SmartMiner does not require the time for superset checking that is required for DFS.

3.2 An example

We now use an example to illustrate how SmartMiner finds the same MFI for the example in Figure 3. As shown in Figure 6, there are nine nodes $N_0, N_1, ..., N_8$ in the search tree. For a given node, the columns $t_0, t_1, ..., t_m$ represent sequential time points. The row S_0 represents the initial state and the Inf_0 is the tail information for S_0. The row S_1 is the next state to explore and the relevant information is on the row Inf_1. Note here Inf_1 also called the global information as input for the next state and will be updated. The row Mfi is the returned mfi after exploring the state S_1. On top of each node, we give the transaction set for the node. For example, the transaction set for N_0 is the entire dataset $T(\phi)$; the transaction set for N_1 is $T(a)$ which represents all the transactions containing item a.

SmartMiner begins at the node N_0 at t_0, $N_0(t_0)$, where $S_0 = :abcde$ and Inf_0 is empty. At this point, item a is selected and thus the next state $S_1 = a{:}bcde$. Here Inf_1 is empty since Inf_0 is empty. Next SmartMiner creates the node N_1 for the state $S_1 = a{:}bcde$ by setting its transaction set $T(a)$ and its initial set $S_0 = :bcde$. When SmartMiner calls the new node N_1, each item in the tail $S_0 = :bcde$ will be sorted in the increasing order of their support in $T(a)$ and the infrequent items will be dropped. The process continues to $N_2(t_0)$, and then to $N_3(t_0)$ where $S_0 = :de$ and e is dropped since it is infrequent in $T(abc)$. This yields $S_0 = :d$; SmartMiner returns d as mfi to $N_2(t_0)$ which will be added into Inf_0 at $N_2(t_1)$. Thus at $N_2(t_0)$, $Inf_0 = d$. SmartMiner then selects $S_1 = e{:}d$ for the next node, $N_4(t_0)$.

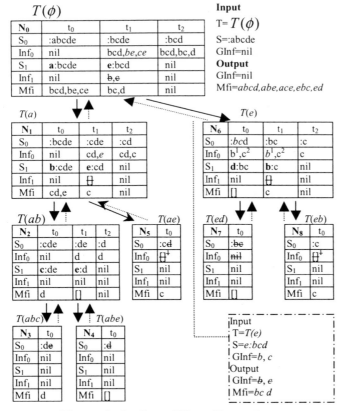

$T(\phi)$

N_0	t_0	t_1	t_2
S_0	:abcde	:bcde	:bcd
Inf_0	nil	bcd,*be,ce*	bcd,bc,d
S_1	**a**:bcde	**e**:bcd	nil
Inf_1	nil	~~b,e~~	nil
Mfi	bcd,be,ce	bc,d	nil

Input
T= $T(\phi)$
S=:abcde
GInf=nil
Output
GInf=nil
Mfi=*abcd,abe,ace,ebc,ed*

$T(a)$

N_1	t_0	t_1	t_2
S_0	:bcde	:cde	:cd
Inf_0	nil	cd,*e*	cd,c
S_1	**b**:cde	**e**:cd	nil
Inf_1	nil	~~[]~~	nil
Mfi	cd,e	c	nil

$T(e)$

N_6	t_0	t_1	t_2
S_0	:bcd	:bc	:c
Inf_0	b^1,c^2	b^1,c^2	c
S_1	**d**:bc	**b**:c	nil
Inf_1	nil	~~[]~~	nil
Mfi	[]	c	nil

$T(ab)$

N_2	t_0	t_1	t_2
S_0	:cde	:de	:d
Inf_0	nil	d	d
S_1	**c**:de	**e**:d	nil
Inf_1	nil	nil	nil
Mfi	d	[]	nil

$T(ae)$

N_5	t_0
S_0	:~~cd~~
Inf_0	~~[]~~$^+$
S_1	nil
Inf_1	nil
Mfi	c

$T(ed)$

N_7	t_0
S_0	:~~bc~~
Inf_0	~~nil~~
S_1	nil
Inf_1	nil
Mfi	[]

$T(eb)$

N_8	t_0
S_0	:c
Inf_0	~~[]~~$^+$
S_1	nil
Inf_1	nil
Mfi	c

$T(abc)$

N_3	t_0
S_0	:de
Inf_0	nil
S_1	nil
Inf_1	nil
Mfi	d

$T(abe)$

N_4	t_0
S_0	:~~d~~
Inf_0	nil
S_1	nil
Inf_1	nil
Mfi	[]

Input
T=*T(e)*
S=*e:bcd*
GInf=*b, c*
Output
GInf=*b, e*
Mfi=*bc d*

Figure 6: An SmartMiner Example.

The entire search route will be $N_0(t_0)$, $N_1(t_0)$, $N_2(t_0)$, $N_3(t_0)$, $N_2(t_1)$, $N_4(t_0)$, $N_2(t_2)$, $N_1(t_1)$, $N_5(t_0)$, $N_1(t_2)$, $N_0(t_1)$, $N_6(t_0)$, $N_7(t_0)$, $N_6(t_1)$, $N_8(t_0)$, $N_6(t_2)$, and $N_0(t_2)$. As shown in the figure 6, at $N_0(t_1)$, Inf_0=bcd,be,ce, S_1=e:bcd, and the two itemsets *be,ce* contain *e*. By removing *e* from *be,ce*, we get Inf_1=b,c. When calling N_6, global information Ginf=b,c is passed from $N_0(t_1)$ to $N_6(t_0)$. Upon completing exploring the node N_6, bc,d are found to be *mfi* and Ginf=b,c will be updated to be empty since they are dropped respectively at $N_8(t_0)$ to $N_6(t_1)$ and at $N_6(t_1)$ to $N_6(t_2)$. When it returns from N_6, the Inf_1 at $N_0(t_1)$ will be empty. By collecting *Mfi*, Inf_1, and unselected Inf_0 at $N_0(t_1)$, we have Inf_0=bcd,bc,d at $N_0(t_2)$. The search terminates at $N_0(t_2)$ since the tail of S_0=:bcd is in the Inf_0.

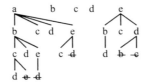

Figure 7: The counting tree for SmartMiner.

Figure 7 shows the tree for counting support using *SmartMiner*. At node N_0, *SmartMiner* counts the supports for *a,b,c,d,e* and finds they are frequent. At node N_1, items *b,c,d,e* are found to be frequent in *T(a)*. It is shown that there are a total of 23 times to count for support.

4. Implementation of SmartMiner

4.1 Object model design

Our data mining system is implemented in Java rather than C++ because Java has better portability. Figure 8 shows the three classes in our system whose data types are specified using Java language. The class *VData* is the vertical data model for a transaction dataset. It loads data from a given *fileName* and builds up a *BitSet* for each frequent item. The *TInf* class manages the tail information for a given node. The *Miner* class uses the proposed tail information based on depth-first search to recursively discover all *MFI*. An instance of *Miner* has exactly one object of *VData* and will dynamically create one object of *TInf* for a node when the mining starts. More details are given in the following sections.

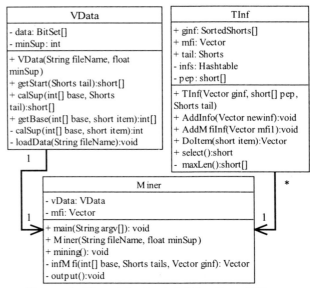

Figure 8: The object model for SmartMiner

4.2 Vertical data class: VData

We chose to use a vertical *BitSet* representation for the database. A vertical *BitSet* corresponds to one frequent item. In a *BitSet*, there is one bit for each transaction in the database. If item *i* appears in transaction *j*, then bit *j* of the *BitSet data[i]* is set to one; otherwise, the bit is set to zero. The constructor *VData(String filename, float minSup)* calls the private function *Load(String filename)* to load data from the file into the variable *data*. It also calculates the *minSup* by multiplying the float *minSup* with the number of transactions. The variable *int[] base* in methods *calSup* and *getBase* is an array of transaction IDs. The base of a node represents the transaction set *T(X)* where *X* is the head of the node. The private method *calSup(int[] base, short item):int* is to calculate the support of the *item* in the given *base*.

The *VData* provides three methods for data mining. First, the method *getStart(Shorts tail):short[]* returns the set of items that occur in every transaction. It also passes other items by *Shorts tail* in the order of increasing support. The *getStart* is called at a root node. Second, the public method *calSup(int[] base, Shorts tail):short[]* is similar to the *getStart*. It returns the set of items in every transaction of the *base* and passes other frequent items at the *base* in the order of increasing support. Finally, the method *getBase(int[] base, short item):int[]* simply returns a new base which is the subset of the *base* whose corresponding transactions contain the *item*.

Note that when calculating support of an item in a *base*, the *VData* needs to test as many bits as the size of the *base*. It is slower than the *Bitmap* model where supports can be calculated a byte (8 bits) at a time. Our *VData* model is also slower than the *diffset* model of *GenMax*[] . However, the *VData* keeps only one copy of data and thus needs less memory than the other two models. In other words, both *Mafia* and *GenMax* need to build up new datasets for the mining of sub nodes. Moreover, the *VData* is easy to implement and is fair to use as a common data model to compare different search strategies of *SmartMiner*, *Mafia*, and *GenMax*.

4.3 Tail information class: TInf

For a given node, an instance of the *TInf* class is created to manage the tail information. The *ginf* is passed from its parent node and the *mfi* is the local maximal frequent itemsets for the node. The itemsets to be explored is stored in the *tail* whose information is stored in the hash table *infs*. The *pep* is the set of items occurring in every transaction of the node.

The constructor method accepts *ginf*, *pep*, and *tail* to create a new instance. The public methods *AddInfo* and *AddMfiInf* calculate relevant information of the *newinf* and the *mfi1* on *tail* respectively and then hash them into the hash table *infs*. The method *DoItem* separates the members in the *infs* into two groups: one mentions the item; another does not. The first group will be removed from the hash table and returned as a vector after dropping the item from every itemset. The second group remains in the table. The method also removes the item from the tail. For every item in the tail, the private method *maxLen* is to find the maximal length of itemsets in *infs* that contains the item. Note that, in our experiment, we use a simplified *maxLen* that returns an array of value either 0 or the maximal length. More specifically, the maxLen first finds the longest itemset *V* in the infs and then set the lengths of items in *V* to |*V*| and the lengths of others to 0.

```
/**
 * Select an item to build a sub node.
 * @return  >=0 if success, -1 if no next items.
 */
public short select()
1 if(tail.size()<=1)
2    if tail in infs then mfi=null else mfi=tail;
3    return -1;
4 short[] len = maxLen();
5 find the min, max position minp, maxp in len;
6 if(len[maxp]==tail.size())
7    update the ginf info;
8    return -1;
9 return tail.get(minp);
```

Figure 9: The selection method: a heuristic to select an item for partitioning the search space.

Figure 9 describes the heuristic method to select an item to partition the search space. In dynamic reordering, the item of the least support is chosen to explore first. Such heuristic has been shown to be effective. Our heuristic select function considers both tail information and the supports. The observation is that, if an item contained by an itemset of size k in the *infs*, there are 2^k itemsets that are known to be frequent and can be pruned away from the search space. Therefore our heuristic chooses an item of the smallest known space. If the size of current tail is less than 2, the search space is immediately solvable as shown in line 1~3. Line 4 calls the method *maxLen*. Line 5 is to find the positions of the minimal and maximal values in *len*. Note that, if several items have the minimal value, we will choose the one having the least support. If an itemset in the *infs* has the size of the *tail*, this means the whole search space of the *tail* is frequent and thus there is no need to build a sub node as shown in lines 6-8; other itemsets in the *infs* are non-maximal and those originated from *ginf* will be deleted. Note that no superset checking is used to eliminate non-maximal itemsets. Line 9 returns the selected item.

4.4 Data mining class: Miner

The *Miner* class has two attributes and five methods as shown in Figure 8. The *vData* stores transaction data in vertical format. The *mfi* is a vector of maximal frequent itemsets. The *main* reads *filename* and *minSup* from command line and calls *Miner*, *mining*, and *output* sequentially. The *Miner* initializes *vData* and the *output* stores the *mfi* into a file. The *mining* method is to mine the *vData*.

Now we present the information guided depth first algorithm which returns local MFI as in Figure 10. The parameter *base* is the transaction set for the node head. The globe information *ginf* will be updated upon return. Line 1 calls *vData.calSup* to get the *pep* and an updated *tails* sorted in the increasing order of supports. Line 2 creates an instance of the *Information* class for this node.

Lines 3-9 loop selects an item for the next node and solve it. More specifically, it selects an item *itm* for next node as show in line 3. If there is no node selected, it goes to line 10. Otherwise, it enters the loop body. A new base is calculated at line 4, the *inf.DoItem* method is called and the new_tail is set. Then line 7 solves the sub node. Upon returning from the sub node, it adds the updated *new_ginf* into the *inf* at line 8 and also saves the *new_mfi* by method *AddMfiInf* at line 9. It returns the *mfi* of the node at line 10.

```
/**
 * Recursively find mfi.
 * @param base The tidSet for current head.
 * @param tail The possible extension of the head.
 * @param ginf The global information.
 * @return  The local maximal frequent itemsets.
 */
private Vector infMfi(int[] base, Shorts tails,
                      Vector ginf)
1 short[] pep = vData.calSup(base,tails);
2 TInf inf = new TInf(ginf, pep, tails);
3 while((itm=inf.select())>=0)
4    int[] newbase = vData.getBase(base,itm);
5    Vector newginf=inf.DoItem(itm);
6    Shorts newtail=new Shorts(inf.tail);
7    Vector newmfi=infMfi(newbase,newtail,newginf);
8    inf.AddInfo(newginf);
9    inf.AddMfiInf(newmfi);
10 return inf.mfi;
```

Figure 10: The infMfi method

For the node at the level 0, the local *new_mfi* is actually maximal frequent itemsets and can output directly into a file. Since its information for future searching is saved by the method *inf.AddMfiInf* in line 9, there is no need to keep the *new_mfi* and the memory of *new_mfi* can be released.

5. Experimental Results

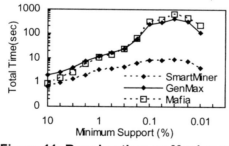

Figure 11: Running time on Mushroom.

We compare SmartMiner with Mafia and GenMax. All of them are implemented in Java JDK1.3. For fair comparison, the three methods use the same vertical data model VData. As we discussed before, there are many ways to implement the vertical data model. In this paper, our purpose is to study the efficiency of different search strategies. We choose VData because it takes less memory and is easy to implement. The experiment was done on a 1Ghz Celeron with 512 MB of memory. A detailed comparison of SmartMiner with Mafia and GenMax was conducted on two datasets: Connect-4 and Mushroom.

Figure 11 shows the performance comparison of the three methods on Mushroom. All three methods use the PEP pruning technique. Our running time does not include the input time but does include the output time. The horizontal axis shows minimum support in percentage. The vertical axis is the running time in seconds. In general, SmartMiner is one order of magnitude faster than both Mafia and Genmax. When minimal support is high, Mafia is faster than Genmax. Low minimal support increase the number of MFI, then Genmax performs better than Mafia.

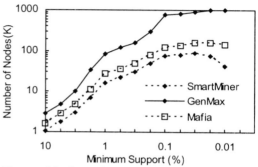

Figure 12: Search tree size on Mushroom.

Figure 12 compares the sizes (number of nodes in a tree) of the search trees for the three methods. From the figure, we noticed that Genmax generates 10 times more nodes than SmartMiner and also much more than Mafia. This indicates that the static ordering in GenMax is not as efficient as the dynamic reordering used by both SmartMiner and Mafia. Moreover, we noticed that SmartMiner generates less nodes than Mafia, which is due to the heuristic select function used the SmarMiner.

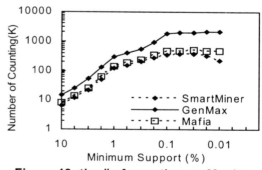

Figure 13: the # of counting on Mushroom.

Figure 13 compares the number of support counting which shows the number of times that the private method calSup(int[] base, short item) in VData is called. As shown in Figure 13, Genmax calls the calSup methods significantly more than both SmartMiner and Mafia.

Further, SmartMiner needs less number of support counting than Mafia.

Since GenMax introduces a fast superset checking algorithm, the performance gain of dynamic reordering of Mafia is mitigated by the increasing time for superset checking when the set of MFI becomes large. This is the reason we see in Figure 10 and Figure 13 that Mafia is better than Genmax when minimal support is high and the reverse when minimal support is low.

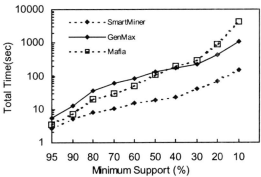

Figure 14: Running time on Connect.

Figure 14 shows the performance comparison of the three methods for the Connect dataset. Again, we noticed the significant performance improvements of SmartMiner than Mafia and GenMax.

6. Conclusion

In this paper, we propose the SmartMiner algorithm to find exact maximal frequent itemsets for large datasets. The SmartMiner algorithm is able to take advantage of the information gathered from previous steps to search for MFI. First, it gathers global and local tail information and uses an heuristic select function to reduce the search tree. Second, the passing of tail information eliminates the need of known MFI for superset checking. Smartminer does not require superset checking which can be very expensive. Finally, SmartMiner also reduces the number of support counting for determining the frequency of tail items and thus greatly saves counting time. Our experiments reveal that the SmartMiner algorithm yields an order of magnitude improvement over Mafia and GenMax in generating the MFI on the two datasets.

Acknowledgements

The authors wish to thank Professor Mohammed J. Zaki for stimulating discussion in the performance study.

References

[1] R. Agrawal and R. Srikant. Fast algorithms for mining association rules. In Proceedings of the 20th VLDB Conference, Santiago, Chile, 1994.

[2] R. Agarwal, C. Aggarwal and V. Prasad. A tree projection algorithm for generation of frequent itemsets. Journal of Parallel and Distributed Computing, 2001.

[3] Roberto Bayardo. Efficiently mining long patterns from databases. In ACM SIGMOD Conference, 1998.

[4] D. Burdick, M. Calimlim, and J. Gehrke. MAFIA: a maximal frequent itemset algorithm for transactional databases. In Intl. Conf. on Data Engineering, Apr. 2001.

[5] K. Gouda and M. J. Zaki. Efficiently Mining Maximal Frequent Itemsets. Proc. of the IEEE Int. Conference on Data Mining, San Jose, 2001.

[6] J. Han, J. Pei, and Y. Yin. Mining Frequent Patterns without Candidate Generation, Proc. 2000 ACM-SIGMOD Int. Conf. on Management of Data (SIGMOD'00), Dallas, TX, May 2000.

[7] Heikki Mannila, Hannu Toivonen, and A. Inkeri Verkamo. Efficient algorithms for discovering association rules. In KDD-94: AAAI Workshop on Knowledge Discovery in Databases, pages 181-192, Seattle, Washington, July 1994

[8] J. S. Park, M. Chen, and P. S. Yu. An effective hash based algorithm for mining association rules. In Proc. ACM SIGMOD Intl. Conf. Management of Data, May 1995.

[9] N. Pasquier, Y. Bastide, R. Taouil, and L. Lakhal. Discovering frequent closed itemsets for association rules. In 7th Intl. Conf. on Database Theory, January 1999.

[10] J. Pei, J. Han, and R. Mao. Closet: An efficient algorithm for mining frequent closed itemsets. In SIGMOD Int'l Workshop on Data Mining and Knowledge Discovery, May 2000.

[11] Brin, S.; Motwani, R.; Ullman, J.; and Tsur, S. 1997. Dynamic Itemset Counting and Implication Rules for Market Basket Data. In Proc. of the 1997 ACM-SIGMOD Conf. On Management of Data, 255-264.

[12] Ashok Sarasere, Edward Omiecinsky, and Shamkant Navathe. An efficient algorithm for mining association rules in large databases. In 21st Int'l Conf. on Very Large Databases (VLDB), ZTrich, Switzerland, Sept. 1995.

[13] Hannu Toivonen. Sampling large databases for association rules. In Proc. of the VLDB Conference, Bombay, India, September 1996.

[14] M. J. Zaki, S. Parthasarathy, M. Ogihara, and W. Li. New algorithms for fast discovery of association rules. In 3rd Intl. Conf. on Knowledge Discovery and Data Mining., August 1997.

[15] M. J. Zaki and C. Hsiao. Charm: An efficient algorithm for closed association rule mining. In Technical Report 99-10, Computer Science, Rensselaer Polytechnic Institute, 1999.

[16] Q. Zou, W. Chu, D. Johnson and H. Chiu. A Pattern Decomposition (PD) Algorithm for Finding All Frequent Patterns in Large Datasets. Proc. of the IEEE Int. Conference on Data Mining, San Jose, 2001.

[17] Q. Zou, W. Chu, D. Johnson and H. Chiu. Pattern Decomposition Algorithm for Data Mining of Frequent Patterns. Journal of Knowledge and Information System, Volume 4, page 466-482, 2002.

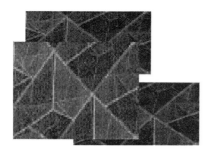 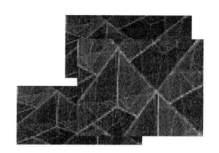

Main-Track Short Papers

Neighborgram Clustering
Interactive Exploration of Cluster Neighborhoods

Michael R. Berthold, Bernd Wiswedel, and David E. Patterson
Data Analysis Research Lab, Tripos Inc.
601 Gateway Blvd., Suite 720; South San Francisco, CA 94080; USA
email: {berthold,bwiswede,pat}@tripos.com

Abstract

We describe an interactive way to generate a set of clusters for a given data set. The clustering is done by constructing local histograms, which can then be used to visualize, select, and fine-tune potential cluster candidates. The accompanying algorithm can also generate clusters automatically, allowing for an automatic or semi-automatic clustering process where the user only occasionally interacts with the algorithm. We illustrate the ability to automatically identify and visualize clusters using NCI's AIDS Antiviral Screen data set.

1. Introduction

The analysis of large data sets usually results in the extraction of models that describe some aspect of the process that originally generated the data. In many real world applications, users are often willing to accept models with not-optimal generalization performance if they can explore the underlying decision process and, preferably, are able to influence the construction of the model interactively throughout the training process. A summary of methods for interactive visualization can be found in [7].

This paper presents an interactive visualization technique for a clustering algorithm, which provides such an interactive model-construction method. The presented method visualizes cluster neighborhoods in detail by displaying each example in the clusters' neighborhood individually and is accompanied by a clustering algorithm, which finds close-to-optimal cluster centers for certain classes of interest. The visualization component allows the user to interact with the clustering algorithm, thus inserting domain knowledge into the cluster formation process. In addition, the clustering process is not limited to low dimensional feature space, in fact we have successfully used the presented approach in feature spaces with thousands of features.

The algorithm described here belongs to the category of clustering techniques which pick representative examples from the training data (similar to the algorithm described in [3]) rather than represent prototypes by weighted averages of several training points (such as for example fuzzy c-means [5]). Instead of relying on the usual heuristics or greedy algorithms to select example patterns as cluster representatives, the presented method analyses the neighborhood of each cluster candidate and picks the optimal cluster representative directly. This neighborhood can additionally be visualized to give the user insights into the patterns each cluster candidate represents. Such a complete and hence computationally expensive approach obviously only works for all classes of a medium sized data set or - in case of very large data sets - to model a minority class of interest. In many real world applications this scenario is the one that matters, however. Especially in bioinformatics applications it is often more important to extract detailed knowledge about few, rare classes within the larger context.

2. Neighborgram Clustering

In the following we assume a feature space in which M training instances $\vec{x}_i$ are given ($i = 1 \ldots M$) along with a function $d(\cdot)$, which computes distances between training instances. Each example $\vec{x}_i$ is also assigned to one of C classes, indicated by the class index k_i ($k_i = 1 \ldots C$).

2.1. Neighborgrams

The basic algorithm operates on all training examples in parallel and computes a so-called Neighborgram for each example of the class(es) of interest. A Neighborgram records the patterns and associated classes of the immediate neighbors for the corresponding center $\vec{x}_i$ in an ordered list:

$$\text{NG}_i = [(l_1, k_1), \ldots, (l_r, k_r), \ldots, (l_R, k_R)]$$

where $l_r = 1 \ldots M$ indicates the index of a training example and $k_r = 1 \ldots C$ is the corresponding class index. The list is

581

sorted according to the distance of pattern $\vec{x}_{l_r}$ to the center vector $\vec{x}_i$:

$$\forall r \ : \ 2 \le r \le R \wedge d(\vec{x}_i, \vec{x}_{l_{(r-1)}}) \le d(\vec{x}_i, \vec{x}_{l_r}).$$

Note that $l_1 = i$, because $d(\vec{x}_i, \vec{x}_i) = 0$ for all i, that is, each pattern is closest to itself. The overall length of this list is determined by parameter R, where $R \ll M$ for large data sets. Hence a Neighborgram simply lists all neighbors of a particular pattern in order of their distance, up to a certain depth of the list.

Obviously in case of large data sets the computation of Neighborgrams for each training pattern is excessively time and memory consuming. As noted earlier, however, the main target of the algorithm discussed here are problems where one (or several) minority class(es) are of prime interest. The computation of Neighborgrams for all these patterns is then of complexity $O(M \cdot M') \cdot O(d(\cdot))$, where $O(d(\cdot))$ depends linearly on the dimension of the feature space for most distance functions and M' indicates the number of examples of the minority class(es), i.e. $M' \ll M$ in case of large data sets.

2.2. The Basic Clustering Algorithm

The main idea behind the clustering algorithm based on Neighborgrams can be summarized as follows: determine cluster-candidates from each Neighborgram, then find the "best" Cluster, and remove all patterns it "covers". Now find the next "best" Cluster, remove all patterns that are covered and so on. Obviously the notions of "best" and "covers" need to be clarified, and we need to explain how a suitable cluster candidate can be derived from each Neighborgram. In order to do this, we first introduce a number of measures:

- *Purity*: The purity of a Cluster is computed based on the Neighborgram i it stems from. Purity basically determines how many patterns of the correct class are contained within a certain neighborhood of depth r with respect to patterns of all classes inside this area:

$$\text{Purity}_i(r) = \frac{|\{(l_{r'}, k_{r'}) \in \text{NG}_i \mid 1 \le r' \le r \wedge k_{r'} = k_i\}|}{|\{(l_{r'}, k_{r'}) \in \text{NG}_i \mid 1 \le r' \le r\}|}$$

- *OptDepth*: is the optimal depth for which a certain Purity $= p_{\min}$ is guaranteed, that is,

$$\text{OptDepth}_i(p_{\min}) = \max \arg_r \{$$
$$\text{Purity}_i(r) \ge p_{\min} \wedge \text{Purity}_i(r+1) < p_{\min}\}$$

- *Coverage*: The default coverage of a cluster with a certain depth r determines how many positive patterns it

"explains", that is, fall within its radius:

$$\text{Coverage}_i(r) =$$
$$|\{(l_{r'}, k_{r'}) \in \text{NG}_i \mid 1 \le r' \le r \wedge k_i = k_{r'}\}|$$

We can now specify clearer what we mean by "best" cluster and "covers". Starting from a user-defined value for parameter *Purity* we can compute values for parameters *OptDepth* and *Coverage* for each Cluster. The best cluster is then the one with the highest *Coverage*. This cluster "covers" all patterns that are within its radius.

The only remaining parameter is a limit on the overall amount of coverage desired: *MaxCoverage*. Once the sum of all covered patterns exceeds this threshold, the algorithm terminates. The following pseudo code summarizes the resulting algorithm:

1) $\forall \vec{x}_i$: k_i is minority class $\Rightarrow$ compute NG_i
2) $\forall \text{NG}_i$: compute OptDepth_i
3) $\forall \text{NG}_i$: compute Coverage_i
4) while MaxCoverage not reached:
5) $i_{\text{best}} = \max \arg_i \{\text{Coverage}_i(\text{OptDepth}_i)\}$
6)   add $(i_{\text{best}}, \text{OptDepth}_{i_{\text{best}}})$ to list of clusters
7)   determine list of covered patterns
8)   remove them from all Neighborgrams NG_i
9) $\forall \text{NG}_i$: recompute Coverage_i
10) end while

3. Experimental Results and Visual Clustering

In the following we will focus on the main contribution of the presented method, the ability to visually investigate cluster candidates. Obviously the presented algorithm could also be used as a stand-alone clustering method. The resulting classification performance is comparable to state-of-the-art classification methods and performs on par with the method presented in [3].

3.1. Neighborgram Visualization

Visualizing a Neighborgram requires only one dimension, since we are interested in the distance to the center point only. In addition, we are usually only interested in a small neighborhood (i.e. Neighborgrams with a small depth R) and can invest some screen area for each individual neighbor. Figure 1 shows an example of a visualization of one Neighborgram built for a pattern of class Iris-Setosa (x_{l_1}). In case that two or more patterns are too close to each other so that they would overlap we decided to stack them on top of each other. The vertical axes therefore has no geometrical meaning, it is simply used to avoid overlaps[1].

---

[1] Obviously many other ways to depict one-dimensional spaces can be used, dense-pixel displays [6] come to mind if the neighborhood to be displayed contains several thousands or more patterns.

Figure 1. A Neighborgram for the Iris data.

Note how in this case, all 50 patterns of class Iris-Setosa are in a close neighborhood of x_{l_1}, and the two other classes are clumped together further apart. In this case the depth was chosen to be $R = 150$, i.e. the last pattern shown is $x_{l_{150}}$. This particular example shows a good cluster candidate, which is also the one returned first by the algorithm explained above.

As a test case we used a well-known data set from the National Cancer Institute, the DTP AIDS Antiviral Screen data set [8]. We have used the class assignment provided with the data, that is, compounds that provided at least 50% protection on retest were listed as moderately active (**CM**), compounds that reproducibly provided 100% protection were listed as confirmed active (**CA**), and compounds not meeting these criteria were listed as confirmed inactive (**CI**). Available online [1] are screening results and chemical structural data on compounds. We have generated Unity Fingerprint descriptors [4], which represent each compound through a 990-dimensional bit string. Unity fingerprints represent a collection of pre-defined chemical substructures of interest. The used distance metric was the usual Tanimoto distance, which computes the number of bits that are different between two vectors normalized over the number of bits that are turned on in one or both vectors.

We next generated Neighborgrams for classes **CA** and **CM**. The first and biggest cluster covered quite a large number of patterns of class **CA**. At first we were surprised to see that none of the compounds contained in this cluster fall in any of the classes of active compounds listed on NIH's website [1]. As it turns out when looking at the corresponding structures, this cluster covers m-acylaminobenzamides which probably all inhibit folic acid synthesis, but are likely too toxic and hence not very interesting as active compounds to fight HIV. This is therefore a nice example of a cluster that a chemist might discard as "useful but not very interesting for the current task at hand". The clustering algorithm has no insights other than numerical cluster measures and therefore would rank this first without any expert interaction. Subsequent clusters reveal groupings very much in line with the known classes of compounds, one particular example is shown in Figure 2. Here the group of Azido Pyrimidines is rediscovered, probably one of the best-known class of active compounds for HIV.

Experiments with this (and other similar) data sets showed nicely how the interactive clustering using Neigh-

borgrams helps to include domain knowledge in the clustering process and how Neighborgrams help to quickly display cluster candidates. Without the additional display of chemical structure this would not have worked as convincingly. It is important to display the discovered knowledge in a "language" the expert understands.

4 Extensions

A couple of issues that we do not have space to discuss in detail, but that are worth being mentioned are listed in the following:

Partial Coverage and Fuzzy Clusters: It is obvious that the basic algorithm sketched in the previous section is very strict - a pattern will be completely removed from any further consideration as soon as it falls within the optimal radius for just one single cluster. This effect might be desirable for patterns lying close to the center of the new cluster but it will reduce accuracy in areas further away from the cluster center. We therefore introduced the notion of *Partial Coverage* using fuzzy membership functions [9], which allow us to model a degree of membership of a particular pattern to a cluster.

Binning Neighborgrams: Obviously for only few hundreds of patterns in each Neighborgram it is possible to plot all patterns individually. For larger neighborhoods it is preferable to bin the neighborhood and just display how many patterns of each class are encountered in each bin. We have experimented with this type of display as well but for all our applications smaller neighborhoods have shown to be sufficient to find good clusters.

Fuzzy Class Membership: In many pharmaceutical applications class information is not as exact as the example above seems to suggest. Here fuzzifying the class information as well could allow to build better clusters. The purity of a cluster candidate would then be computed based on the degree of membership to the correct vs. conflicting class.

Minimum Cluster Size: Computing Purity as described above has the disadvantage that for noisy data sets many clusters will not extend as far as they could because an early encountering of a pattern of wrong class will set *OptDepth* very close to the cluster's center. To avoid this, we have introduced a parameter *minSize*, which allows to specify a minimum number of patterns in a neighborhood before *Purity* and *OptDepth* are determined. Early experiments with noisy data sets have shown a decrease in number of clusters and better generalization ability.

Parallel Universes: The algorithm described above does not require that the clusters reside in the same feature space. Besides the fact that a chosen cluster removes covered patterns from consideration there is no obvious need for two clusters to be based on the same distance function or the same features. Hence we can find clusters in different fea-

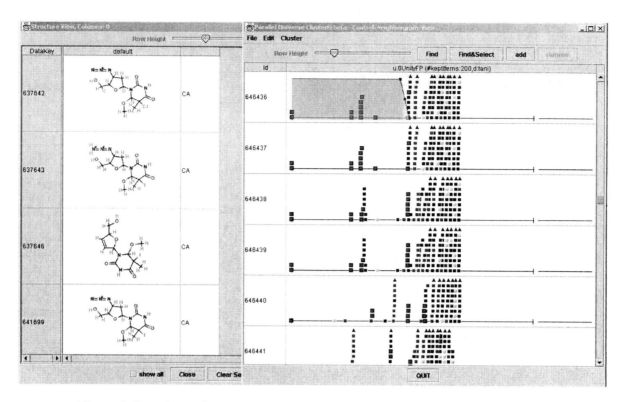

Figure 2. One cluster for the NIH-Aids data (top row) covering Azido Pyrimidines.

ture spaces in parallel. Covered patterns will then be removed from all universes and the result is a set of clusters, spread out over different descriptor spaces.

Detecting Outliers and Mislabeled Training Instances: A problem that often occurs when collecting large amounts of biological data is the reliability of the labels. The presented approach offers an interesting option to discover at least some of these wrong labels. By letting the user investigate "bad" Neighborgrams (i.e. Neighborgrams that have a high density of wrong patterns surrounding a center of different class), we can point out potential false positives.

5. Conclusions

We have presented a method to build clusters based on Neighborgrams, which model the local distribution of patterns for each potential cluster candidate. The proposed visualization of Neighborgrams allows the user to explore the proposed cluster selection and enables experts to inject domain knowledge into the clustering process by selecting, discarding, or fine-tuning cluster candidates. Analysis of chemical data has shown the usefulness of the provided visualization. By displaying cluster candidates it is possible to naturally incorporate expert knowledge through interactive feedback.

References

[1] http://dtp.nci.nih.gov/docs/aids/aids_data.html.

[2] M. Berthold and D. J. Hand, editors. *Intelligent Data Analysis: An Introduction.* Springer Verlag, second edition, 2002.

[3] M. R. Berthold and J. Diamond. Constructive training of probabilistic neural networks. *Neurocomputing*, 19:167–183, 1998.

[4] R. D. Clark. Relative and absolute diversity analysis of combinatorial libraries. In *Combinatorial Library Design and Evaluation*, pages 337–362. Marcel Dekker, New York, 2001.

[5] R. Davé and R. Krishnapuram. Robust clustering methods: A unified view. *IEEE Transactions on Fuzzy Systems*, 5(2):270–293, May 1997.

[6] D. A. Keim and H.-P. Kriegel. Visualization techniques for mining large databases. *IEEE Transactions on Knowledge and Data Engineering*, 8(6):923–938, 1996.

[7] D. A. Keim and M. Ward. Visualization. In *[2, Chapter 11]*.

[8] O. Weislow, R. Kiser, D. Fine, J. Bader, R. Shoemaker, and M. Boyd. New soluble formazan assay for HIV-1 cytopathic effects: application to high flux screening of synthetic and natural products for AIDS antiviral activity. *Journal National Cancer Institute*, 81:577–586, 1989.

[9] L. A. Zadeh. Fuzzy sets. *Information and Control*, 8:338–353, 1965.

A New Algorithm for Learning Parameters of a Bayesian Network from Distributed Data

R. Chen and K. Sivakumar

School of EECS, Washington State University Pullman WA 99164-2752, USA (siva@wsu.edu)

Abstract

We present a novel approach for learning parameters of a Bayesian network from distributed heterogeneous dataset. In this case, the whole dataset is distributed in several sites and each site contains observations for a different subset of features. The new method uses the collective learning approach proposed in our earlier work and substantially reduces the computational and transmission overhead. Theoretical analysis is given and experimental results are provided to illustrate the accuracy and efficiency of our method.

1 Introduction

A Bayesian Network (BN) is a probabilistic model based on a directed acyclic graph. In order to use a Bayesian network for inference or decision making, it must first be constructed using prior knowledge from experts and/or observed data. Most of the work reported in the literature assume that all the observed data are available at a single site. However, there are many scientific and non-scientific applications, where the observed data is distributed among different sites. Cost of data communication between the distributed databases is a significant factor in an increasingly mobile and connected world with a large number of distributed data sources. In this paper, we consider a distributed heterogenous data scenario, where each site has observations corresponding to a subset of the attributes. We assume that there exists a "key" that can link the observations across sites. A naive approach to learn a BN from distributed heterogenous data is to transmit all local datasets to a central site, and then learn a BN from the resulting merged dataset (centralized learning). Howover, limited network bandwidth and/or data security might render this approach infeasible.

In our earlier work [1], we proposed an approach to learn a BN from distributed heterogenous data. In the sequel, we will refer to the collective method proposed in [1] as Collective Method 1 (CM1). It was shown in [1] that the CM1 produces an accurate BN with only a small fraction of samples transmitted. However, CM1 required considerable computations (to identify the subset of observations to be transmitted) at each of the local sites. For real time or online learning applications, we need to considerably reduce the amount of computation at the local sites. Towards that end, we propose a new collective learning method called CM2 for learning the parameters of a BN (CM2 assumes that the structure of the BN is known). Using the parameter modularity property, CM2 provides a new data selection method, which dramatically reduces the local computation time and whose performance is almost identical to that of CM1.

The remainder of this paper is structured as follows. Section 2 provides an overview of BN and discusses related literature. Section 3 discusses the proposed CM2 algorithm. Experimental results comparing the performance of CM1, CM2, and a random sample selection method is presented in Section 4. We conclude with some discussions in Section 5.

2 Background and Related Work

A BN is a probabilistic graph model that can be defined as a pair $B=(\mathcal{G}, \theta)$. Here, $\mathcal{G} = (\mathcal{V}, \mathcal{E})$ is a directed acyclic graph (DAG) that represents the structure of the BN. $\mathcal{V}$ is the node set and a node $X \in \mathcal{V}$ represents a variable in the problem domain. The edge set $\mathcal{E}$ denotes probabilistic relationships among the variables. For a node $X \in \mathcal{V}$, a parent of X is a node from which there exists a directed link to X. The set of parents of X is denoted by $pa(X)$. Figure 1 is a BN called ASIA model. From figure 1, $pa(E) = \{T, L\}$.

In this paper, we consider a BN over N discrete variables X_i $(1 \leq i \leq N)$. Let V_i denote the set of possible values of node X_i. Conditional probability $\theta_{ijk} = P(X_i = k \mid pa(X_i) = j)$ is the probability of variable X_i in state k when $pa(X_i)$ is in state j. If

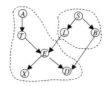

Figure 1. ASIA Model

a variable X_i has no parents (root node), then θ_{ijk} corresponds to the marginal probability of node X_i. We will denote by θ_{ij} the distribution of a variable X_i with a fixed parent state and by θ_i the Conditional Probability Table (CPT) of node X_i. We will denote by θ the set of all θ_{ijk}, called the parameter set or parameters of a BN.

Learning a BN involves learning the structure of the network ($\mathcal{G}$) and obtaining the conditional probabilities (parameters θ). With a fixed (or known) structure $\mathcal{G}$, learning θ from data is called parameter learning. Two widely used parameter learning methods are maximum likelihood (ML) and maximum a posteriori (MAP) methods. Let N_{ijk} be the number of samples in which $X_i = k$ and $pa(X_i) = j$. The ML estimate of θ is

$$\hat{\theta}_{ijk}^{ML} = \frac{N_{ijk}}{N_{ij}}. \qquad (1)$$

where $N_{ij} = \sum_{k=1}^{r_i} N_{ijk}$ and r_i is the number of possible values for X_i.

3 A New Collective Method (CM2)

We introduced a collective method (CM1) for distributed BN learning in [1, 2]. CM1 can be used for both parameter and structure learning. The main steps in CM1 are as follows: (1) Learn local BN (local model) involving the variables observed at each site based on local data set. (2) At each site, based on the local BN, identify the samples that are most likely to be evidence of coupling between local and non-local variables. (3) Transmit the index of low likelihood samples from each local site to the central site. At the central site, compute the intersection of these index sets and obtain samples corresponding to this intersection set from all the local sites. (4) At the global site, a limited number of observations of all the variables is now available. Using this dataset, learn the structure and parameters of links across different sites. (5) Combine the local models with the parameters of cross links to obtain a collective BN B_{coll}. The key issue in CM1 is to correctly identify the coupling between variables that belong to two (or more) sites. The samples at local site A with high likelihoods are evidence of "local relationships"

between site A variables, whereas those with low likelihoods are possible evidence of "cross relationships" between variables across sites. Therefore, samples with low likelihoods (at all local sites) are transmitted to the central site to identify cross links.

Let B_{cntr} denote the BN obtained by a centralized learning approach (simply aggregating all data at one site, followed by traditional single site learning). We compare the BN B_{coll} learnt from the collective method with B_{cntr} to evaluate the performance of our algorithm. Our experiments illustrate that the performance of CM1 is close to that of obtained by a centralized approch with modest data transmission [1]. One drawback of CM1 is that the likelihood computation in local site is not a trivial job and introduces some computational overhead. This may not be acceptable for real-time applications like online monitoring of stock market data.

Cross Set

In order to discuss the new collective method (CM2), we first introduce the notion of a cross set. At each local site, we split the set of variables into a local set and a cross set. This would help in the identification of samples to be transmitted to the central site in CM2.

If we use maximum likelihood (ML) to estimate parameters (see equation (1)), the estimate of θ_{ijk} is entirely determined by N_{ijk}. Then we have the following property:

Parameter modularity [3]: Given two BNs B_1 and B_2, if a variable X_i has same set of parents $pa(X_i)$, then CPT θ_i is the same in these two BNs.

In [3], the authors describe this property as an assumption for MAP learning. That is, if we assume the prior has the parameter modularity property, then the parameters learnt by MAP also have this property. For ML learning, parameter modularity can be derived from equation (1).

If a variable X_i and its parents are all in the same site, then X_i is called a local variable. Otherwise X_i is called a cross variable (CV) (some of its parents are in a different site). Then define cross set (CS) of a site S_i as the set of variable in that site that is a CV or the parent of a CV in this site. That is

$$CS(S_i) = \{X \in S_i \mid X \in CV(S_i) \text{ or } X \in pa(CV(S_i))\}. \qquad (2)$$

A variable that is not in the CS of site S_i is said to be in the local set (LS) of that site. The global cross set is defined as the union of all cross sets in different sites and global local set is defined as the union of all local sets. For example, in the ASIA model, the local variables in site 1 is A, T, X, local set is $\{A, X\}$ and cross set is $\{T, E, D\}$. In our collective learning method (CM1 and CM2), we first learn a local BN in-

586

volving the variables observed at each site based on local data set. Let B_{local}^i denote local BN at site i. From parameter modularity, we can conclude that: (1) CPT of local variable in B_{local}^i is same as that in B_{cntr}. This guarantees that local learning can achieve the same accuracy as the centralized learning approach for for local variables. (2) Only variables in cross set $(CS(S_i))$ are useful for the parameter learning of cross variables.

Since after local learning the job of collective learning is only to learn parameters for cross variables, we can transmit only the columns corresponding to variables in cross set to the central site (i.e., drop those variables that is in the local set). For the ASIA model, only columns for $\{T, E, D\}$ (3/5 of all columns) in site 1 need to be transmitted. For a large BN with many variables in local set in each site, the reduction of transmission overhead can be significant.

Overview of CM2 Algorithm
The main steps in CM2 are similar to that of CM1 and are as follows: (1) Learn local BN (local model) involving the variables observed at each site based on local data set. (2) At each site S_i, based on the local BN, compute the joint distribution for variables in cross set $CS(S_i)$. Based on the joint distribution of cross set, select a subset of samples. Let I_{coll}^i denote the set of indices of these samples. (3) Transmit the index set I_{coll}^i from each local site to the central site. At the central site, compute the intersection set I_{coll} of these index sets. From each local site S_i, obtain the values of variables in the cross set $CS(S_i)$ corresponding to samples in the index set I_{coll}. (4) At the global site, a limited number of observations of all the variables is now available. Using this dataset, learn the parameters of cross variables. (5) Combine the local models with the parameters of cross variables to obtain a collective BN.

The main steps in CM1 and CM2 are similar. CM2 is different from CM1 in two main respects (Steps 2 and 3): (a) In CM2, only the observations of variables in the cross set $CS(S_i)$ at site S_i is transmitted. Clearly, this reduces the data transmission overhead. (b) In CM2, the selection of samples to be transmitted is based on the joint distribution of the cross set variables (not the joint distribution of all site variables). As we shall discuss in the following subsection, this results in significant computational savings.

Data selection in CM2
We now discuss details of steps 2 and 3 in the CM2 algorithm. As noted earlier, in CM2, the selection of samples to be transmitted is based on the joint distribution of the cross set variables (not the joint distribution of all site variables). We shall first discuss why this is justified. Later, we will describe the actual details of the data selection process.

Most of local computation in CM1 can be attributed to the likelihood computation step. This involved computing the joint distribution of all local variables after the local BN is constructed and is computationally intensive. Consider a local site A with cross set variables CS and local set variables LS. The joint distribution of all variables in site A can be denoted as $p(CS, LS)$. Consider the marginal distribution of $P(CS)$: $p(CS) = \sum_{LS} p(CS, LS)$. Therefore, if a sample configuration for CS variables has low likelihood value under $p(CS)$, then there is at least one configuration of LS variables such that the corresponding joint configuration (CS, LS) has low likelihood value under $p(CS, LS)$. So the samples with low likelihood in $p(CS)$ is a subset of those with low likelihood in $p(CS, LS)$. Therefore, the identification of samples for transmission can be based on the likelihood under $p(CS)$ instead of $p(CS, LS)$. In general, the cardinality of CS is much smaller than the total number of variables at the local site, which results in faster computation.

Moreover, the total number of configurations (CS, LS) is usually prohibitively large, so that we cannot save all the $p(CS, LS)$ values and create a lookup table — the likelihoods have to be computed sample by sample in this case. However, the total number of configurations (CS) is relatively small and a table lookup method is feasible.

As observed in CM1, those samples with low likelihood under $p(CS, LS)$ are possible evidence of "cross relationships" between variables across sites. In CM1, we set a threshold for each local site and choose the samples whose likelihood is smaller than this threshold (data subset D_2). In CM2, we consider the set of samples with low likelihood under $p(CS)$ (data subset D_3). As discussed earlier, $D_3 \subseteq D_2$. Some of samples with low likelihood under $p(CS, LS)$ are in D_2 but not in D_3. Therefore, we introduce a random sampling for the samples not in D_3. That is, if a sample has likelihood (under $p(CS)$) larger than the local threshold, we select it with some probability α. For example, if $\alpha = 0.1$, 10% of samples not in D_3 will be selected (along with the set D_3) for transmission.

The main steps in the sample selection process can now be described as follows: (a) At each local site, identify the cross set CS and local set LS. Based on the local BN, compute joint distribution $p(CS)$ of variables in cross set. (b) Based on $p(CS)$ and local threshold, identify set D_3 of samples with low likelihood. (c) Select all samples in D_3 and a fraction α of the samples (uniform random sampling) in D_3^c. Get the index set of selected samples and transmit it to the central site.

4 Experimental Results

In order to compare the performance of two different methods, a metric called Conditional KL (CKL) distance is used. It measures the error in estimating the conditional probabilities of the cross variables and is defined as follows: $D_{CKL}(i, B_1, B_2) = \sum_j p_1(j) \times D_{KL}(p_1^{ij}, p_2^{ij})$. Here, $D_{CKL}(i, B_1, B_2)$ is the distance between two conditional probability tables (CPT) corresponding to the BNs B_1 and B_2 at node X_i. In our experiments, we always compare the performance of a collective method (CM1 or CM2 or random) with that of the centralized approach. In other words, we fix B_1 to be B_{cntr}. Also, $D_{KL}(p_1^{ij}, p_2^{ij})$ is the KL distance between conditional probabilities of variable X_i, the two conditional probabilities being computed using two different methods — say CM1 and CM2, with a fixed parent configuration j. KL distance $D_{KL}(p, q)$ between two discrete probabilities, $\{p_i\}$, $\{q_i\}$, $i = 1, 2, \ldots, N$ is defined as $D_{KL}(p, q) = \sum_{i=1}^{N} p_i \ln(\frac{p_i}{q_i})$, where N is the number of possible outcomes.

We now provide experimental results, based on the ASIA model, to illustrate the accuracy and efficiency of the proposed CM2 algorithm. Simialar results were obtained for larger BNs like the ALARM network but have not been presented here due to space constraints. There are two sites and variables E, D are the cross variables. We generated a dataset that has 6000 samples. By changing the threshold of high vs. low likelihood samples in the sample selecting step, we can change the size of set D_{coll}, which is the subset of data transmitted to central site.

Since we use a random sampling method in CM2 for samples in D_3^c, the CKL distances would depend on the specific run. Therefore, we repeated each experiment 20 times and computed the average CKL distance. Algorithm CM1 was applied to the same dataset and the result of CM1 is used for comparison. The CKL distances for nodes E, D for the BNs B_{CM1} and B_{CM2} was computed (both with respect to B_{cntr}). Figure 2 depicts the results graphically as a function of the fraction $|D_{coll}|/|D|$ of data transmitted. For our experiment $|D| = 6000$. It is clear from Figure 2 that the performance of CM2 is almost identical to that of CM1. The local computation times for the two sites are depicted in Table 1. Clearly, CM2 achieves a significant computational savings (speedup factor in excess of 400) over CM1 for almost identical performance.

5 Conclusion

We have presented a new collective method (CM2) for learning the parameters of a BN from distributed

Table 1. Comparison of local computation time (in second) for CM1 and CM2

Site #	CM1	CM2	Speedup factor: CM1/CM2
Site 1	5.7	0.012	475
Site 2	3.9	0.0094	415

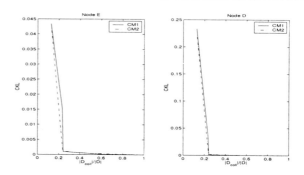

Figure 2. ASIA Model: CKL distance for cross variables

heterogenous data. This is based on our earlier work (CM1) for learning the structure and parameters of a BN. Both CM1 and CM2 are based on a collective learning strategy, where a local model is obtained at each site and the global parameters are determined by a selective transmission of data to a central site. Using knowledge of the BN structure, CM2 proposes a computationally simpler approach to selecting samples for learning parameters of cross variables in a BN. The performance of CM2 is comparable to that of CM1. However, CM2 requires much fewer local computations as compared to CM1, with speedup factors of 500-1000 in our experiments. It is therefore suitable for real-time applications.

Acknowledgements: This work was supported by NASA under Cooperative agreement NCC 2-1252.

References

[1] R. Chen, K. Sivakumar, and H. Kargupta. Distributed web mining using Bayesian networks from multiple data streams. In *Proceedings of the IEEE Conference on Data Mining*, pages 75–82, 2001.

[2] R. Chen, K. Sivakumar, and H. Kargupta. Collective mining of bayesian networks from distributed heterogeneous data. *Knowledge and Information Systems*, (accepted) 2002.

[3] D. Heckerman, D. Geiger, and D. M. Chickering. Learning Bayesian networks: The combination of knowledge and statistical data. *Machine Learning*, 20:197–243, 1995.

Optimal Projections of High Dimensional Data

Emilio Corchado[1] and Colin Fyfe[2]

[1]*Departamento de Ingeniería Civil*
Universidad de Burgos. Spain
Tel. +34 94725 8989
escorchado@ubu.es
[2]*Applied Computational Intelligence Research Unit*
The University of Paisley. Scotland
Tel:+44 141 848 3305
colin.fyfe@paisley.ac.uk

Abstract

In this paper, we compare two artificial neural network algorithms for performing Exploratory Projection Pursuit, a statistical technique for investigating data by projecting it onto lower dimensional manifolds. The neural networks are extensions of a network which performs Principal Component Analysis. We illustrate the technique on artificial data before applying it to real data.

1. Introduction

In this paper, we investigate ways of extracting information from high dimensional data sets by projecting the data sets onto low dimensional (typically 2 dimensional) subspaces. We derive two artificial neural network methods of performing Exploratory Projection Pursuit which is a statistical method for deriving the optimal projections of a data set which reveal its structure. Both artificial neural network methods are extensions of a network which has been shown to perform Principal Component Analysis.

Principal Component Analysis (PCA) is a standard statistical technique for compressing data; it can be shown to give the best linear compression of the data in terms of least mean square error. There are several artificial neural networks which have been shown to perform PCA e.g. [12]; [13]. We shall be most interested in a negative feedback implementation [3].

The basic PCA network [3] is described by equations (1)-(3). Let us have an N-dimensional input vector at time t, $\mathbf{x}(t)$, and an M-dimensional output vector, $\mathbf{y}$, with W_{ij} being the weight linking input j to output i. η is a learning rate. Then the activation passing and learning is described by

(1) Feedforward: $y_i = \sum_{j=1}^{N} W_{ij} x_j , \forall i$

(2) Feedback: $e_j = x_j - \sum_{i=1}^{M} W_{ij} y_i$

(3) Change weights: $\Delta W_{ij} = \eta e_j y_i$

We can readily show that this algorithm is equivalent to Oja's Subspace Algorithm [12]:

(4) $\Delta W_{ij} = \eta e_j y_i = \eta (x_j - \sum_k W_{kj} y_k) y_i$

and so this network not only causes convergence of the weights but causes the weights to converge to span the subspace of the Principal Components of the input data. We might ask then why we should be interested in the negative feedback formulation rather than the formulation (4) in which the weight change directly uses negative feedback. The answer, as we shall see in the next section, is that the explicit formation of residuals (2) allows us to consider probability density functions of the residuals in a way which would not be brought to mind if we use (4).

Exploratory Projection Pursuit (EPP) is a more recent statistical method aimed at solving the difficult problem of identifying structure in high dimensional data. It does this by projecting the data onto a low dimensional subspace in which we search for its structure by eye. However not all projections will reveal the data's structure equally well. We therefore define an index that measures how "interesting" a given projection is, and then represent the data in terms of projections that maximise that index.

The first step in our exploratory projection pursuit is to define which indices represent interesting directions. Now "interesting" structure is usually defined with respect to the fact that most projections of high-dimensional data onto arbitrary lines through most multi-dimensional data give almost Gaussian distributions [2]. Therefore if we wish to identify "interesting" features in data, we should look for those directions onto which the data-projections are as far from the Gaussian as possible.

We have previously implemented EPP using an artificial neural network [4]; the method is essentially a non-linear modification of the negative
feedback network. The network can be described by the following set of equations where x_j is the sphered activation of the jth input neuron, s_i is the activation of the ith output neuron, W_{ij} is the weight between these two and r_i is the value of the function f() on the ith output neuron.

$$(5) \qquad s_i = \sum_{j=1}^{N} W_{ij} x_j$$

$$(6) \qquad e_j = x_j - \sum_{k=1}^{M} W_{kj} s_k$$

$$(7) \qquad r_i = f(s_i)$$

$$(8) \qquad \Delta W_{ij} = \eta r_i e_j$$

It was shown in [9] that the use of a (non-linear) function f() in equation (7) creates an algorithm to find those values of W which maximise that function whose derivative is f() under the constraint that W is an orthonormal matrix. This was applied in [4] to the above network in the context of the network performing an Exploratory Projection Pursuit. Thus if we wish to find a direction which maximises the kurtosis of the distribution which is measured by s^4, we will use a function $f(s) \approx s^3$ in the algorithm. If we wish to find that direction with maximum skewness, we use a function $f(s) \approx s^2$ in the algorithm.

2. ε-Insensitive Hebbian Learning

It has been shown [15] that the nonlinear PCA rule

$$(9) \quad \Delta W_{ij} = \eta \left(x_j f(y_i) - f(y_i) \sum_k W_{kj} f(y_k) \right)$$

can be derived as an approximation to the best non-linear compression of the data.
Thus we may start with a cost function

$$(10) \quad J(W) = 1^T E\left\{ \left(\mathbf{x} - W f(W^T \mathbf{x}) \right)^2 \right\}$$

which we minimise to get the rule(9). [11] used the residual in the linear version of (10) to define a cost function of the residual

$$(11) \quad J = f_1(\mathbf{e}) = f_1(\mathbf{x} - W\mathbf{y})$$

where $f_1 = \|\cdot\|^2$ is the (squared) Euclidean norm in the standard linear or nonlinear PCA rule. With this choice of $f_1(\ )$, the cost function is minimized with respect to any set of samples from the data set on the assumption that the residuals are chosen independently and identically distributed from a standard Gaussian distribution [1].
We may show that the minimization of J is equivalent to minimizing the negative log probability of the residual, $\mathbf{e}$. , if $\mathbf{e}$ is Gaussian.

$$(12) \qquad \text{Let } p(\mathbf{e}) = \frac{1}{Z} \exp(-\mathbf{e}^2)$$

Then we can denote a general cost function associated with this network as

$$(13) \qquad J = -\log p(\mathbf{e}) = (\mathbf{e})^2 + K$$

where K is a constant. Therefore performing gradient descent on J we have

$$(14) \qquad \Delta W \propto -\frac{\partial J}{\partial W} = -\frac{\partial J}{\partial \mathbf{e}} \frac{\partial \mathbf{e}}{\partial W} \approx \mathbf{y}(2\mathbf{e})^T$$

where we have discarded a less important term (see [9] for details).
In general [14] , the minimisation of such a cost function may be thought to make the probability of the residuals greater dependent on the pdf of the residuals. Thus if the probability density function of the residuals is known, this knowledge could be used to determine the optimal cost function.

[11] investigated this with the (one dimensional) function:

$$(15) \quad p(\mathbf{e}) = \frac{1}{2+\varepsilon} \exp\left(-|\mathbf{e}|_\varepsilon\right)$$

where

$$(16) \quad |e|_\varepsilon = \begin{cases} 0 & \forall |\mathbf{e}| < \varepsilon \\ |e| - \varepsilon & \text{otherwise} \end{cases}$$

with ε being a small scalar ≥ 0 .

[11] described this in terms of noise in the data set. However we feel that it is more appropriate to state that, with this model of the pdf of the residual, the optimal $f_1(\ )$ function is the ε-insensitive cost function:

$$(17) \quad f_1(\mathbf{e}) = |\mathbf{e}|_\varepsilon$$

In the case of the negative feedback network, the learning rule is

$$(18) \quad \Delta W \propto -\frac{\partial J}{\partial W} = -\frac{\partial f_1(\mathbf{e})}{\partial \mathbf{e}} \frac{\partial \mathbf{e}}{\partial W}$$

which gives:

(19)

$$\Delta W_{ij} = \begin{cases} 0 & \text{if } |e_j| < \varepsilon \\ \eta y(sign(\mathbf{e})) & \text{otherwise} \end{cases}$$

The difference with the common Hebb learning rule is that the sign of the residual is used instead the value of the residual. Because this learning rule is insensitive to the magnitude of the input vectors $\mathbf{x}$, the rule is less sensitive to outliers than the usual rule based on mean squared error.

This change from viewing the difference after feedback as simply a residual rather than an error permits us to consider a family of cost functions each member of which is optimal for a particular probability density function associated with the residual.

3. Maximum Likelihood Hebbian Learning

Now the ε-insensitive learning rule is clearly only one of a possible family of learning rules which are suggested by the family of exponential distributions[1]. Let the residual after feedback have probability density function

$$(20) \quad p(\mathbf{e}) = \frac{1}{Z} \exp(-|\mathbf{e}|^p) .$$

Then we can denote a general cost function associated with this network as

$$(21) \quad J = E(-\log p(\mathbf{e})) = E(|\mathbf{e}|^p + K)$$

where K is a constant independent of W and the expectation is taken over the input data set. Therefore performing gradient descent on J we have
(22)

$$\Delta W \propto \frac{\partial J}{\partial W}\Big|_{W(t-1)} = -\frac{\partial J}{\partial \mathbf{e}} \frac{\partial \mathbf{e}}{\partial W}\Big|_{W(t-1)} \approx E\{\mathbf{y}(p|\mathbf{e}|^{p-1} sig(\mathbf{e}))^T |_{W(t-1)}\}$$

where T denotes the transpose of a vector and the operation of taking powers of the norm of $\mathbf{e}$ is on an

---

[1] This family was called an exponential family in (Hyvärinen et al, 2002) though statisticians use this term for a somewhat different family.

elementwise basis as it is derived from a derivative of a scalar with respect to a vector.

Computing the mean of a function of a data set (or even the sample averages) can be tedious, and we also wish to cater for the situation in which samples keep arriving as we investigate the data set and so we derive an online learning algorithm. If the conditions of stochastic approximation [10] are satisfied, we may approximate this with a difference equation. The function to be approximated is clearly sufficiently smooth and the learning rate can be made to satisfy $\eta_k \geq 0, \sum_k \eta_k = \infty, \sum_k \eta_k^2 < \infty$ and so we have the rule:

$$(23) \quad \Delta W_{ij} = \eta.y_i.sign(e_j)| e_j |^p$$

We would expect that for leptokurtotic residuals (more kurtotic than a Gaussian distribution), values of p<2 would be appropriate, while for platykurtotic residuals (less kurtotic than a Gaussian), values of p>2 would be appropriate. Researchers from the community investigating Independent Component Analysis ([7], [8]) have shown that it is less important to get exactly the correct distribution when searching for a specific source than it is to get an approximately correct distribution i.e. all supergaussian signals can be retrieved using a generic leptokurtotic distribution and all subgaussian signals can be retrieved using a generic platykutotic distribution. Our experiments will tend to support this to some extent but we often find accuracy and speed of convergence are improved when we are accurate in our choice of p.

Therefore the network operation is:

$$(24) \quad \text{Feedforward: } y_i = \sum_{j=1}^{N} W_{ij} x_j , \forall_i$$

$$(25) \quad \text{Feedback: } e_j = x_j - \sum_{i=1}^{M} W_{ij} y_i$$

$$(26) \quad \text{Weight change: } \Delta W_{ij} = \eta.y_i.sign(e_j)| e_j |^p$$

[6] described their rule as performing a type of PCA, but this is not strictly true since only the original (Oja) ordinary Hebbian rule actually performs PCA. It might be more appropriate to link this family of learning rules to Principal Factor Analysis since PFA makes an assumption about the noise in a data set and then removes the assumed noise from the covariance structure of the data before performing a PCA. We are doing something similar here in that we are basing our PCA-type rule on the assumed distribution of the residual. By maximising the likelihood of the residual with respect to the actual

distribution, we are matching the learning rule to the pdf of the residual.

More importantly, we may also link the method to the standard statistical method of Exploratory Projection Pursuit: now the nature and quantification of the interestingness is in terms of how likely the residuals are under a particular model of the pdf of the residuals. In the results reported later, we also sphere the data before applying the learning method to the sphered data and show that with this method we may also find interesting structure in the data.

5. Experimental Results

To illustrate our method, we follow [4] in creating artificial data sets, each of 10 dimensions. All results reported are based on a set of 10 simulations each with different initial conditions. It is our general finding that sphering is necessary to get the most accurate results presented below.

5.1. Artificial data set 1

In this data set, we have 9 independent leptokurtotic dimensions and one gaussian dimension; this is almost the opposite of the standard EPP data sets described in [5] and is rather far from being a typical data set in that most projections onto its natural basis are interesting. However, since we wish to investigate our new models, it is a good test set since we can easily see the results of our method. We wish to identify the single Gaussian dimension and ignore the leptokurtotic dimensions. The leptokurtotic dimensions may be characterised as having long tails; if a residual can be created by removing the Gaussian direction from the data set, the residual will automatically be leptokurtotic. Thus we consider maximising the likelihood of the residual using the model

$$(27) \quad p(\mathbf{e}) = \frac{1}{Z}\exp(-|\mathbf{e}|^p) \text{ with } p<2;$$

We have experimented with a number of values of p and report on simulations with p=1.5. A typical result is shown in Figure 1; the Gaussian direction is clearly identified.

Figure 1: The Gaussian direction was the third among 9 leptokurtotic dimensions. It has clearly been identified in this Hinton map of the weights.

We have similar results with a data set containing 9 platykurtotic dimensions and one Gaussian dimension. We use the same learning rules as before but with a value of p=3.

5.2. Artificial data set 2

In this data set, we have 9 Gaussian dimensions and 1 kutotic dimension. The kurtotic dimension are actually samples from a Cauchy distribution which is a distribution which is often used to model noise in spiking neurons. To identify this distribution in the Gaussian mixture, we create our model to maximise the likelihood that the residuals come from a platykurtotic distribution such as

$$(31) \quad p(\mathbf{e}) = \frac{1}{Z}\exp(-|\mathbf{e}|^p) \text{ with } p>2;$$

Now all the distributions which comprise the independent sources underlying this data set are wrong (in that they do not match the model) but the Cauchy distribution is most wrong (it is a highly leptokurtotic distribution). The mean converged weights over 10 simulations are shown in Table 1 for which we used p=3; in each case the first dimension was the Cauchy distribution and the other 9 were Gaussians. These results were taken after 20 iterations through the data set of 30000 samples though typically over 90 percent convergence occurred after 2 iterations.

Dim	1	2	3	4	5
Weight	0.959	0.006	0.004	0.008	0.005

Dim	6	7	8	9	10
Weight	0.006	0.003	0.005	0.005	0.009

Table 1. The mean converged weights over 10 simulations in which the first dimension was the Cauchy distribution and the other 9 were Gaussians.

We may equally consider a data set with 9 platykurtotic dimensions and one Gaussian and identify the single Gaussian. We note that this is not a typical data set but it does suggest that this method could usefully be used for denoising. In this case we would use a learing rule with p<2.

6. Epsilon insensitivity

Now the learning rule described in [6] used an ε-insensitive region. This may be described as a region where the probability density function does not change. This was originally motivated by the fact that there is innate noise in the bars data set caused by the fact that each vertical bar intersects each horizontal bar. The net effect on our learning rules is to create a region of the space of residuals which does not affect learning: if the residual is sufficiently close to 0, no learning takes place in the network. We have an even stronger need for such a region: in some of our learning rules (see below) there is the possibility of dividing by the residual which is an extremely dangerous thing to do when the residual is approximately 0.

The learning rules become

$$(32) \quad \Delta W \propto -\frac{\partial J}{\partial W} = -\frac{\partial J}{\partial \mathbf{e}} \frac{\partial \mathbf{e}}{\partial W} \approx \mathbf{y}(p\mid \mathbf{e}\mid^{p-1} sign(\mathbf{e}))^T$$

if $|\mathbf{e}| < \varepsilon$ and is 0 otherwise.

This has been found to be particularly appropriate for use with values of p less than 1. For example, if p=0.5, then the learning rule is

$$(33) \quad \Delta W \propto -\frac{\partial J}{\partial W} = -\frac{\partial J}{\partial \mathbf{e}} \frac{\partial \mathbf{e}}{\partial W} \approx y(\mid \mathbf{e}\mid^{-0.5} sign(\mathbf{e}))^T$$

if $|\mathbf{e}| < \varepsilon$ and is 0 otherwise.

Without the ε-insensitive region, there is an inherent instability to this rule since we are dividing by a value which can be arbitrarily close to 0. This has resulted in huge weight values on occasion. We have also experimented with values of p less than 0.

For example, p=-0.5 gives a distribution whose shape is shown in Figure 2.

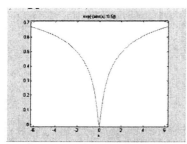

Figure 2: An improper but useful probability density function. $p(x) = e^{-|x|^{0.5}}$.

This is clearly an improper pdf (it cannot be integrated to 1 if its support is infinite) but since we are using a finite sample of data drawn from any distribution, the support is in fact finite and the above function can be made proper by using an appropriate normalising factor. This distribution has actually been found to be useful in modelling kurtotic distributions.

An example of the use of ε-insensitivity is shown in Figure 3. We used a value of p=0.5 and ε=0.05. Our data set contains one platykurtotic dimension (the furthest to the left) and nine Gaussian dimensions. The platykurtotic

dimension was identified each of 10 times but with a great deal of noise.

Figure 3. The platykurtotic dimension is the furthest to the left. It has been identified but the weight vector contains a great deal of noise.

This is typical of our experiments with ε-insensitivity: the method finds the interesting directions consistently but perhaps somewhat less accurately than without this region. This is particularly true when we search for leptokurtosis: such distributions will often have a peak near the origin which is often removed when we use ε-insensitivity.

7. Minimum Likelihood Hebbian Learning

It is well known that the standard PCA rule:
$$\Delta W_{ij} = \eta y_i (x_j - \sum_k W_{kj} y_k)$$
finds the first principal component (that with greatest eigenvalue) of a data set while $\Delta W_{ij} = -\eta y_i (x_j - \sum_k W_{kj} y_k)$ finds the first minor component (that with least eigenvalue) of a data set. Therefore just as the Hebbian learning rule has an opposite known as the anti-Hebbian rule, we may change our rules so that

$$(34) \quad \Delta W \propto \frac{\partial J}{\partial W} = \frac{\partial J}{\partial \mathbf{e}} \frac{\partial \mathbf{e}}{\partial W} \approx -\mathbf{y}(p\mid \mathbf{e}\mid^{p-1} sign(\mathbf{e}))^T$$

Now we may argue that, in doing so, we are aiming to minimise the likelihood of the residual given the current model. In detail, if the residual has probability density function

$$(35) \quad p(\mathbf{e}) = \frac{1}{Z} \exp(-\mid \mathbf{e}\mid^p).$$

and we denote the general cost function associated with this network as

$$(36) \quad J = E(-\log p(\mathbf{e})) = E(\mid \mathbf{e}\mid^p + K)$$

where K is a constant, we may perform gradient ascent on J to get

$$(37) \quad \begin{aligned} \Delta W \propto \frac{\partial J}{\partial W}\mid_{W(t-1)} &= \frac{\partial J}{\partial \mathbf{e}} \frac{\partial \mathbf{e}}{\partial W}\mid_{W(t-1)} \approx \\ &\approx E(-\mathbf{y}(p\mid \mathbf{e}\mid^{p-1} sign(\mathbf{e}))^T\mid_{W(t-1)}) \end{aligned}$$

We are thus using our learning rules to make the residuals as unlikely as possible under the current model assumptions (determined by the p parameter). This is therefore particularly useful for data sets in which our previous results were less accurate. For example, when we have 9 Gaussian dimensions and 1 platykurtotic dimension (a data set on which we had rather inaccurate results previously) we get results as in Figure 4 (with p=3 in our minimum likelihood rule). By identifying and removing the platykurtotic dimension we are leaving a residual which has 0 kurtosis.

Figure 4: The platykurtotic dimension has been identified among the gaussian dimensions.

Note that with Minimum Likelihood Hebbian learning we are using the correct model for the distribution that we are seeking but minimising the probability of the residual being taken from this distribution. Thus we find and extract this distribution.

8. Application to Different Real data sets

To show the power of the family of learning rules that we have derived we applied them to different data sets.

8.1. Bank data

To compare the new method of EPP with our previous neural implementation of the technique, we apply both methods on a small database of bank customers consisting of 1000 records each having 12 fields. Information held includes an unique identifier, age, sex, salary, type of area in which they live, whether married or not, number of children and then several fields of financial information such as type of bank account, whether they own a Personal Equity Plan etc.

Figure 5 shows the projection of this data set on the filters found by the previous EPP network, equagtions (5)-(8), when a cosine nonlinearity searching for clusters was used.

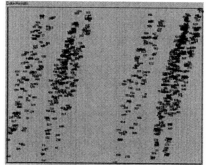

Figure 5: A two dimensional projection of the bank customer dataset clearly illustrating four clusters in the data set.

The network has clearly identified 4 clusters in the data set. Notice that neither of the one dimensional projections would have been sufficient to clearly identify four clusters (though one would have identified two clusters). Manual investigation of the clusters readily reveals that the clusters are forming on the place of residence field – each cluster is specific to one of RURAL, TOWN, INNER_CITY and URBAN sites. We should emphasise at this stage that this is far from the most interesting projection of the data set revealed by EPP but is being used for illustrative purposes.

Now we compare with the new EPP method; results are shown in Figure 6.

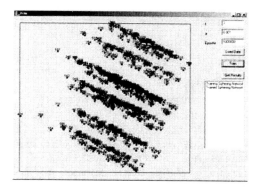

Figure 6. A two dimensional projection found by Maximum Likelihood Hebbian learning with p=0.

We see far more structure in the projection from the Maximum Likelihood Hebbian rule than we had previously: not only are six main clusters found but also within each of these clusters we see distinct subgroups. This is a more interesting projection than that provide by the previous implementation of EPP which simple projects on AREA and SEX in the first axis and SALARY on the second. The ML method has separated each main cluster on AREA, CAR with the main sub-cluster of each diagonal separating on SEX. But we can see that the ML method has also many more well defined sub-clusters in its projections; these highlight groups of individuals whose profiles are slightly different from the main cluster. This shows the power of the ML rule as the number of sub-clusters identify far more texture in the projection than that identified by the previous implementation of EPP.

8.2. Algae data

Our next data set is from a scientific study of various forms of algae some of which have been manually identified. Each sample is recorded as a 18 dimensional vector representing the magnitudes of various pigments.

Some algae have been identified as belonging to specific classes which are numbered 1 to 9. Others are as yet unclassified and these are labelled 0. Figure 7 shows a projection of this data set onto the first two Principal Components. We can see that some separation of the classes has been achieved. However Figure 8 shows a projection of the same data set onto the filters found using Minimum Likelihood Hebbian learning with p=1; a rather better separation of the individual classes has been found.

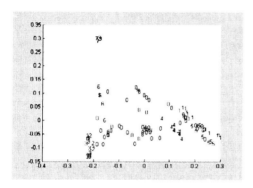

Figure 7. Projection of the algae data set onto the first two principal components.

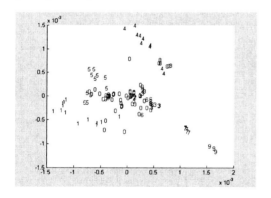

Figure 8. Projection of the algae data set onto the first two filters found using Minimum Likelihood Hebbian Learning with p=1.

9. Comparing the two EPP methods

We now compare the effectiveness of these two algorithms on both artificial and real data sets. The artificial data is used to determine the speed of convergence of the algorithms in identifying interest in a data set since we know, in advance, exactly what sort of interesting structure is in the data set and can measure the progress of the algorithm towards identifying the structure. We will call the original algorithm the Higher Moments Algorithm.

9.1. Rate of Convergence

In this section, we create a 10 dimensional data set in which 9 dimensions are drawn from a Gaussian distribution and one dimension from a uniform distribution. The uniform distribution is platykurtotic (has less kurtosis than the Gaussians) and so the higher moments algorithm can use y^3 or more stably tanh(); the maximum likelihood method will use p<2. The rate of convergence of the algorithms is shown in Figure 9: the left figure shows the dot product of the weights with the ideal solution when the higher moments EPP algorithm with a tanh() nonlinearity is used while the right shows the convergence of the Maximum Likelihood EPP algorithm with p=1. We see that the latter has extremely fast convergence but does not achieve an accuracy of more than 0.9 while the former, though it takes a little longer to get to the optimum, is much more accurate. This suggests that an algorithm which uses both rules might gain by having the best attributes of both and this is in fact the case.

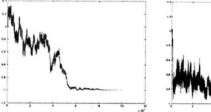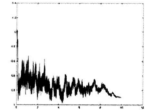

Figure 9. The left figure shows the convergence of the higher moments EPP algorithm while the right one shows the convergence of the Maximum Likelihood EPP algorithm in terms of the dot product to the ideal solution.

Figure 11 shows the convergence of an algorithm which uses a combination of these two rules i.e.

(38)   Feedforward: $y_i = \sum_{j=1}^{N} W_{ij} x_j, \ \forall_i$

(39)   Feedback: $e_j = x_j - \sum_{i=1}^{M} W_{ij} y_i$

(40)   Weightchange: $\Delta W_{ij} = \eta . f(y_i) . sign(e_j) | e_j |^p$

where f() is the tanh() function in the experiment whose results are shown in Figure 10. We seem to be getting the best of both worlds with this combined method though it must be conceded that the combination is somewhat ad hoc.

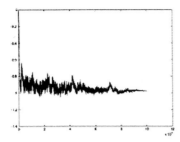

Figure 10. Convergence of the algorithm using the combined learning rule.

10. Conclusion

In this paper, we have shown how two artificial neural network algorithms for performing Exploratory Projection Pursuit. Both algorithms find low dimensional projections of a data set; we may then investigate by eye these low dimensional projections. Often we find that the two algorithms give similar projections but note that, since this is an exploratory method, we are quite content when they do not: the more different structures found in the data set, the more we learn about the data set. We have discussed an algorithm which attempts to get the best of both worlds by using an element from each method but have not used this in this paper since it is not as rigorously derived as the two basic methods. We suspect, however, that the mixed method may be attractive in a practical setting in which unveiling data structure is the sole criterion for effectiveness.

These are powerful new tools for the data mining community and should take their place along with existing exploratory methods.

Acknowledgements. Colin Fyfe was Visiting Professor at the University of Burgos when this work was prepared and would like to gratefully acknowledge the financial assistance of the University of Burgos.

11. References

[1] C.M. Bishop. Neural Networks for Pattern Recognition, Oxford, 1995.

[2] P. Diaconis, and D. Freedman. Asymptotics of Graphical Projections. The Annals of Statistics. 12(3): 793-815. 1984.

[3] Fyfe, C. "PCA Properties of Interneurons", From Neurobiology to Real World Computing, Proceedings of International Conference on Artificial on Artificial Neural Networks, ICAAN 93, pages 183-188, 1993.

[4] C. Fyfe, and R. Baddeley, Non-linear data structure extraction using simple Hebbian networks, Biological Cybernetics 72(6), p533-541. 1995.

[5] C. Fyfe, Negative Feedback as an Organising Principle for Artificial Neural Networks, PhD Thesis, Strathclyde University. 1995.

[6] C. Fyfe and D. MacDonald, ε-Insensitive Hebbian learning, Neuro Computing. 2001.

[7] A.Hyvärinen, Complexity Pursuit: Separating interesting components from time series. Neural Computation, 13: 883-898. 2001.

[8] A, Hyvärinen, J. Karhunen, and E. Oja, Independent Component Analysis, Wiley, ISBN 0-471-40540-X. 2002.

[9] J. Karhunen, and J. Joutsensalo, Representation and Separation of Signals Using Non-linear PCA Type Learning, Neural Networks, 7:113-127, 1994.

[10] R.L Kashyap, C.C. Blaydon, and K. S. Fu, Stochastic Approximation. in A Prelude to Neural Networks: Adaptive and Learning Systems, Ed Jerry M. Mendel, Prentice Hall, ISBN 0-13-147448-0. 1994.

[11] P.L. Lai, D. Charles, and C. Fyfe, Seeking Independence using Biologically Inspired Artificial Neural Networks, in Developments in Artificial Neural Network Theory : Independent Component Analysis and Blind Source Separation, Editor M. A. Girolami, Springer Verlag. 2000.

[12] E. Oja, Neural Networks, Principal Components and Subspaces, International Journal of Neural Systems, 1:61-68. 1989.

[13] E. Oja, H. Ogawa, and J. Wangviwattana,. Principal Components Analysis by Homogeneous Neural Networks, part 1, The Weighted Subspace Criterion, IEICE Transaction on Information and Systems, E75D: 366-375. 1992.

[14] A.J. Smola, and. Scholkopf, B. A Tutorial on Support Vector Regression. Technical Report NC2-TR-1998-030, NeuroCOLT2 Technical Report Series. 1998.

[15] L. Xu, Least Mean Square Error Reconstruction for Self-Organizing Nets", Neural Networks, Vol. 6, pp. 627-648. 1993.

Generating an informative cover for association rules

Laurentiu Cristofor
University of Massachusetts at Boston,
Department of Computer Science,
Boston, Massachusetts 02125, USA
laur@cs.umb.edu

Dan Simovici
University of Massachusetts at Boston,
Department of Computer Science,
Boston, Massachusetts 02125, USA
dsim@cs.umb.edu

Abstract

Mining association rules may generate a large numbers of rules making the results hard to analyze manually. Pasquier et al. have discussed the generation of Guigues-Duquenne–Luxenburger basis (GD-L basis). Using a similar approach, we introduce a new rule of inference and define the notion of association rules cover as a minimal set of rules that are non-redundant with respect to this new rule of inference. Our experimental results (obtained using both synthetic and real data sets) show that our covers are smaller than the GD-L basis and they are computed in time that is comparable to the classic Apriori algorithm for generating rules.

1 Introduction

The number of association rules generated by data mining algorithms can easily overwhelm a human analyst. To address this problem several methods were proposed. Our paper continues the line of research from [7] by introducing a new rule of inference for association rules and by defining the concept of a cover of the association rules as a minimal set of rules that are non-redundant with respect to this new inference rule.

We use the terminology and notations of [9]. Let $\tau = (T, H, \rho)$ be a table, where T is the name of the table, $H = A_1 \ldots A_n$ is the heading of the table, and $\rho \subseteq \{0, 1\}^n$. We assume that each attribute have $\{0, 1\}$ as its domain. The projection of a tuple on a set $L \subseteq H$ is denoted by $t[L]$. The tuple over I that consists of 1s is denoted by $\mathbf{1}_I$. An *itemset* I is a set of items $I \subseteq H$. The *support* of I, denoted by $\mathrm{supp}(I)$, is given by $\mathrm{supp}(I) = \frac{|\{t \in \rho | t[I] = \mathbf{1}_I\}|}{|\rho|}$. In addition, $\mathrm{supp}(\emptyset)$ is defined to be 1. The *closure* of an itemset I is $\mathrm{cl}(I) = \{A_i \in H | \text{if } t[I] = \mathbf{1}_I \text{ then } t[A_i] = 1\}$. An itemset is called *closed* if it is equal to its closure.

An *association rule* $X \to Y$ consists of two disjoint non-empty itemsets X and Y, called *antecedent* and *consequent* and denoted by $\mathtt{antc}(r)$ and $\mathtt{cons}(r)$, respectively. We refer to the items of a rule r by $\mathtt{items}(r) = \mathtt{antc}(r) \cup \mathtt{cons}(r)$. The *support* of the association rule is the support of $\mathtt{items}(r)$. The *confidence* of the association rule is the ratio:

$$\mathtt{conf}(r) = \frac{\mathrm{supp}(\mathtt{items}(r))}{\mathrm{supp}(\mathtt{antc}(r))}.$$

If $\mathtt{conf}(r) = 1$, then r is called an *exact* association rule and denoted by $X \Rightarrow Y$; otherwise, r is called an *approximative* association rule (see [7]). Given a table τ, a minimum support value $\mathtt{minsupp}$, and a minimum confidence value $\mathtt{minconf}$, we seek to generate all *valid association rules* (cf. [8]), that is, all rules with support greater or equal to $\mathtt{minsupp}$ and confidence greater or equal to $\mathtt{minconf}$.

To deal with the usual large number of association rules it is preferable to generate only the association rules that cannot be inferred from other rules by using rules of inference. A minimal set of such association rules was called *basis* in [7]. To avoid confusion, we mention here that the single word "rule" will only be used in the sense of an association rule and will never be used to denote an inference rule. The *Guigues-Duquenne basis* for exact rules and the *Luxenburger basis* for approximative rules are introduced in [7]; together they form a basis for the valid rules.

The Guigues-Duquenne basis is a minimal set of exact rules from which the complete set of exact rules can be deduced using as following two inference rules: $X \Rightarrow Y, W \Rightarrow Z \vdash XW \Rightarrow YZ$, and $X \Rightarrow Y, Y \Rightarrow Z \vdash X \Rightarrow Z$. The Guigues-Duquenne basis does not allow us to infer the support of the rules and in fact, by ignoring the support values, the first inference rule can lead to rules that have inferior support compared to the rules used in its generation.

The Luxenburger basis is a minimal set of approximative rules from which the complete set of approximative rules can be deduced using the two properties introduced in [6]: (1) the association rule $X \to Y$ has the same support and confidence as the rule $\mathrm{cl}(X) \to \mathrm{cl}(Y)$, and (2) for any three closed itemsets X, Y, and Z, such that $X \subseteq Y \subseteq Z$,

597

the confidence of the rule $X \rightarrow Z$ is equal to the product of the confidences of the rules $X \rightarrow Y$ and $Y \rightarrow Z$, and its support is equal to the support of the rule $Y \rightarrow Z$ Both these properties can be regarded as new inference rules and they permit the inference of both the support and confidence of the resulting rules. Together, the Guigues-Duquenne basis and the Luxenburger basis, provide a minimal basis for rules, which we will denote as the GD-L basis.

Next, we introduce a new rule of inference for rules.

Theorem 1.1 *Let r, r' be two rules such that $items(r') \subseteq items(r)$ and $supp(antc(r')) \leq supp(antc(r))$. Then, $supp(r') \geq supp(r)$ and $conf(r') \geq conf(r)$.*

This justifies the introduction of the inference rule:

$$\frac{r, items(r') \subseteq items(r), \quad supp(antc(r')) \leq supp(antc(r))}{r'}.$$

Definition 1.2 If for two rules, r_1 and r_2, it is possible to infer r_2 from r_1 using Theorem 1.1, then we say that rule r_2 is *covered* by rule r_1 (and that r_1 *covers* r_2), and we write $r_1 \prec r_2$. The *coverage relation* $\prec$ consists of all ordered pairs of rules (r_1, r_2), such that $r_1 \prec r_2$. If $r_1 \prec r_2$ and $r_2 \prec r_1$, then r_1, r_2 are said to be *equipotent*. □

Because of Definition 1.2, we will also refer to the property of Theorem 1.1 as the *coverage rule*.

Theorem 1.3 *The rules r_1 and r_2 are equipotent if and only if $items(r_1) = items(r_2)$ and $supp(antc(r_1)) = supp(antc(r_2))$.*

Equipotent rules are interchangeable from the point of view of the coverage relation, that is, if r_1 and r_2 are equipotent and $r_1 \prec r_3$ for some r_3, then $r_2 \prec r_3$.

2 Covers for association rules

Theorem 1.1 suggests the following definition:

Definition 2.1 Let $\mathcal{R}$ be the set of all valid rules extracted from a table τ. A *cover of* $\mathcal{R}$ is a minimal set $\mathcal{C} \subseteq \mathcal{R}$, such that any rule from $\mathcal{R} - \mathcal{C}$ is covered by a rule in $\mathcal{C}$. A rule belonging to $\mathcal{C}$ is called a $\mathcal{C}$-*cover rule*. □

Theorem 2.2 *Let $\mathcal{C}$ be a cover of a set of rules $\mathcal{R}$ extracted from a table τ. If r is a $\mathcal{C}$-cover rule, then for any $r' \in \mathcal{R}$ such that $items(r) = items(r')$, we have $supp(r) \leq supp(r')$ and $conf(r) \leq conf(r')$ and there is no $r_1 \in \mathcal{R}$ such that $antc(r) = antc(r_1)$ and $cons(r) \subset cons(r_1)$. Further, if $r_1, r_2 \in \mathcal{C}$, then $items(r_1) \neq items(r_2)$.*

Definition 2.3 An *informative cover* is a cover where for each cover rule r there is no equipotent rule r' such that $antc(r') \subset antc(r)$. □

Theorem 2.4 *Let $\mathcal{C}$ be an informative cover of a set of rules $\mathcal{R}$ extracted from a table τ. If r is a $\mathcal{C}$-cover rule, then there is no valid rule r' such that $items(r') = items(r)$ and $antc(r') \subset antc(r)$.*

Note that it is possible to have an informative cover rule r and a valid rule r', such that $items(r) = items(r')$ and $|antc(r)| > |antc(r')|$, as the next example shows.

A cover summarizes the set of valid rules in a similar way in which the large itemsets summarize the set of frequent itemsets [2]. A cover can also be used to simplify the presentation of rules to users: initially, only cover rules could be shown to a user, then the user could select a cover rule r and retrieve a subset of all rules covered by r, and then the process could be repeated. In this manner, the user could guide his search for rules without being overwhelmed by their number. A similar type of rule exploration has been proposed in [5], in the context of the so called *direction setting rules*.

The following pseudocode describes an algorithm for generating an informative cover for the set of valid rules.

Algorithm 2.5 (The CoverRules Algorithm) Let R be a queue that will contain frequent itemsets and let C be the set of rules in which we will place the cover rules.

1 Initialize R by enqueuing into it all maximal frequent itemsets, in decreasing order of their size. C is $\emptyset$.

2 If R is empty, then output C and exit; else extract an itemset I from R.

3 For all strict non-empty subsets I_i of I, with $i = 1 \ldots 2^{|I|} - 2$, sorted primarily by their support values (decreasingly) and secondarily by their cardinality (increasingly), do:

    3.1 If the rule $I_i \rightarrow I - I_i$ is valid, then add it to C if it is not covered by a rule already in C. Go to step 2.

    3.2 If $i = 1$ and $|I| > 2$, then add to R each subset of I that has size $|I| - 1$ and that is not already included in an itemset from R. Continue step 3.

Algorithm **CoverRules** starts from the set of maximal frequent itemsets and examines them in decreasing order of their cardinalities (steps 1–2). For each such itemset I, we search for a subset S having maximum support, such that $S \rightarrow I - S$ is a valid association rule (step 3). Such a rule is a candidate cover rule and, once found, the search stops and the rule is added to the set of cover rules C if it is not covered by one of the rules of C (step 3.1). During the examination of each subset S of I, we may encounter some subsets such that they cannot be used as an antecedent of a rule based on the items of I. For these subsets, we will have to verify whether they can be antecedents of rules based on subsets of I. This is why, in step 3.2 of the algorithm, we add to R all the subsets of I. Those subsets that are already included in an itemset of R, however, do not need to be added. Step 3.2 needs to be performed only once, so we perform it if the first subset examined in step 3 cannot be used as an antecedent. The collection R is a queue because we want to examine the maximal frequent itemsets in decreasing order of their size before we examine their subsets (added in step 3.2). We examine these itemsets in decreasing order of their size because a rule whose set of items is larger cannot be covered by a rule whose set of items is smaller. This ensures that a cover rule added to C cannot be covered by another cover rule that we may discover later. Each time that we intend to add a rule to C, however, we still need to check whether that rule can be covered by one of the rules already in C.

The strategy of examining first the maximal frequent itemsets and then their subsets, in decreasing order of their size, guarantees that the set of rules that we generate is minimal. Step 3.2 guarantees that all valid rules can be inferred from the rules in set C. Together, these ensure that the resulting set C is a minimal set of rules from which all valid rules can be inferred, and thus, C is a cover. The cover is informative because, in step 3, for subsets with same support, we examine first those with smaller cardinality.

3 Experimental results

The optimized version of **CoverRules** implemented in Java is available in ARtool [4]. We tested **CoverRules** on several databases. In a first experiment, presented in Table 1, we executed the algorithm on the Mushroom database from the UCI Repository of Machine Learning Databases [3]. Note that the UCI repository contains two versions of the Mushroom database. We have used the version containing fewer rows, which was used in the experiments of [7].

Mushroom database (minsupp = 30%)			
minconf	Valid rules	Cover	GD-L Basis
90%	20399	238	382
70%	45147	176	453
50%	64179	159	479
30%	78888	78	493

Table 1. Results for Mushroom database

The cover contains fewer rules than the GD-L basis and its size decreases as minconf is lowered (see also Fig. 1).

This may seem surprising at first, but is due to the fact that, as minconf is lowered, more valid rules exist, the re-

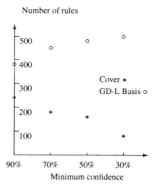

Figure 1. Comparative Results on Mushroom Database

dundancy of these rules is greater, and thus they can be summarized better. In fact, for minconf = 30%, the size of the cover is identical to the number of maximal frequent itemsets existing in the mushroom database (for minsupp = 30% there are 78 such maximal frequent itemsets), and this happens because all rules that can be generated using subsets of a maximal frequent itemset are valid. In this case, the cover size is one order of magnitude smaller than the size of the GD-L basis, and three orders of magnitude smaller than the total number of valid rules.

For minconf = 30%, all cover rules have the item veil-type = partial as antecedent. Interestingly, this item is common to all the mushrooms described in the database, so its support value is 1 — the maximum possible support value. By looking at a cover rule separately, the fact that the rule has the most frequent item as antecedent might make us think that the rule is trivial. Knowing that this is a cover rule, however, its antecedent being the most frequent item takes new meaning because it implies that any rule that we can build from the items of the cover rule will be a valid association rule. Usually, the most frequent items are known to the users of the database, so a cover rule having such an item as antecedent can be easily interpreted, even without the help of the computer.

In the case of the Mushroom database, the **CoverRules** algorithm is about as fast as the Apriori **ap-genrules** procedure for generating all valid rules, which was described in [1]. Both algorithms finished their processing in a couple of seconds, so we do not include their detailed time results here.

To test the on synthetic data we generated database SPARSE with 100,000 transactions of average size 10, having 100 items, and containing 300 patterns of average size 5. We mined SPARSE for minsupp = 5% and discovered 207 maximal frequent itemsets. For all our experiments on this database, the times taken by **CoverRules** and **ap-genrules** were well below 1 second so we omit them again. The number of rules discovered and the corresponding cover size are presented in Table 2.

SPARSE database (minsupp = 5%)		
minconf	Valid rules	Cover
90%	3	2
80%	19	13
70%	42	25
60%	87	55
50%	186	124
40%	321	196
30%	455	240
20%	658	257
10%	880	194
5%	880	194
1%	880	194

Table 2. Results for SPARSE database

Note that the cover size increases initially as minconf decreases. This happens because the database is sparse, so the redundancy is poor and rules that are discovered when the confidence threshold is lowered do not necessarily allow the inference of rules with higher confidence. For minconf = 10%, we obtain all valid rules and lowering the confidence threshold further does not bring any new rules. In fact, the 194 cover rules correspond to the maximal large itemsets that have cardinality greater than one, since there are 13 such maximal frequent itemsets of size one.

For our final experiment, we generated a dense synthetic database, which we will call DENSE, with 100,000 transactions of average size 15, having 100 items, and containing 100 patterns of average size 10. Our strategy for obtaining dense synthetic databases consists of choosing fewer and longer patterns. We mined this database for minsupp = 5% and we obtained 3,182 maximal frequent itemsets. For this experiment, the times taken by the **CoverRules** and **ap-genrules** algorithms became noticeable and we include them in Table 3.

Again, for this dense database, the cover size generally tends to decrease as we lower the confidence threshold. All valid rules are discovered for confidence 5%, so lowering

minconf further does not result in more rules. There is only one maximum frequent itemset of size one, which accounts for the difference between the number of maximal frequent itemsets and the cover size obtained in this case. The time taken by the rule generation algorithms is more significative and allows us to notice that **CoverRules**'s performance tends to improve with the lowering of the confidence threshold, while **ap-genrules** tends to take more time as minconf is decreased. **ap-genrules** runs initially faster than **CoverRules**, which performs better for lower values of minconf. These results, however, do not include the time necessary to output the generated rules. The space requirements of **ap-genrules** are more significant than those of **CoverRules**, and in some experiments we had to increase the memory available to the Java Virtual Machine so that **ap-genrules** would not run out of memory.

As expected, the performance of **CoverRules**, as well as that of **ap-genrules**, slows down when the databases are denser, and when the number of maximal frequent itemsets increases. The performance of the algorithms varies differently with the change of minconf. For dense databases, the size of the cover is one–two orders of magnitude smaller than the number of valid rules and shows the tendency of getting smaller as the redundancy in the generated rules increases.

References

[1] R. Agrawal and R. Srikant. Fast algorithms for mining association rules. RJ 9839, IBM Almaden Research Center, Almaden, California, 1994.

[2] R. J. Bayardo. Efficiently mining long patterns from databases. In *Proceedings of ACM-SIGMOD International Conference on Management of Data*, pages 85–93, 1998.

[3] C. L. Blake and C. J. Merz. University of California, Irvine: Repository of machine learning databases, 1998. http://www.ics.uci.edu/~mlearn/MLRepository.html.

[4] L. Cristofor. ARtool: Association rule mining algorithms and tools, 2002. http://www.cs.umb.edu/~laur/ARtool/.

[5] B. Liu, W. Hsu, and Y. Ma. Pruning and summarizing the discovered associations. In *Proceedings of the 5th ACM SIGKDD International Conference on Knowledge Discovery and Data Mining*, pages 125–134, 1999.

[6] M. Luxenburger. Implications partielles dans un contexte. *Mathématiques, Informatique et Sciences Humaines*, 29(113):35–55, 1991.

[7] N. Pasquier, Y. Bastide, R. Taouil, and L. Lakhal. Closed set based discovery of small covers for association rules. In *Proceedings of the 15th Conference on Advanced Databases*, pages 361–381, 1999.

[8] N. Pasquier, Y. Bastide, R. Taouil, and L. Lakhal. Efficient mining of association rules using closed itemset lattices. *Information Systems*, 24(1):25–46, 1999.

[9] D. A. Simovici and R. L. Tenney. *Relational Database Systems*. Academic Press, New York, 1995.

DENSE database (minsupp = 5%)				
minconf	Valid rules	ap-genrules Time(seconds)	Cover	CoverRules Time(seconds)
90%	87722	9	8875	215
80%	344001	30	9375	236
70%	511191	46	9020	220
60%	574554	49	7878	178
50%	603861	50	6483	130
40%	630706	52	6506	133
30%	656724	51	5496	104
20%	682076	53	5674	99
10%	703373	52	3416	41
5%	703924	52	3181	37
1%	703924	52	3181	37

Table 3. Results for DENSE database

Extraction Techniques for Mining Services from Web Sources

Hasan Davulcu, Saikat Mukherjee, I.V. Ramakrishnan

Dept. of Computer Science
SUNY Stony Brook
Stony Brook, NY 11794, USA
{davulcu,saikat,ram}@cs.sunysb.edu

Abstract

The Web has established itself as the dominant medium for doing electronic commerce. Consequently the number of service providers, both large and small, advertising their services on the web continues to proliferate. In this paper we describe new extraction algorithms for mining service directories from web pages. We develop a novel propagation technique for identifying and accumulating all of the attributes related to a service entity in a web page. We provide experimental results of the effectiveness of our extraction techniques by mining a database of veterinarian service providers from web sources.

1. Introduction

A number of service providers operate their own web sites promoting their services at length while others are merely listed in a referral site. Aggregating all of the providers into a queriable service directory makes it easy for customers to locate the best suited servicies for their needs. An attractive solution is to create the service directory by mining the web for service providers. Such a solution has several merits. Firstly, it does not need any explicit participation by the service provider and hence is scalable. Secondly, since the process is automated and repeatable the content can always be kept current. Finally, the same process can be readily adapted to different domains. We characterize services by an on-

tology consisting of a taxonomy of service concepts, their associated attributes (such as names and addresses) and type descriptions for the attributes. In addition the ontology also associates an attribute identifier function with each attribute. Applying the function to a web page will locate all the occurrences of the attribute in that page. Each web page is parsed into a DOM (Document Object Model) tree and the identifier functions, specified in the ontology for locating occurrences of the attributes in the page, are applied. The problem is to group all the attributes corresponding to each service provider. In this paper we describe a novel ontology-directed propagation technique for identifying and accumulating all of the attributes related to each service entity in a web page. By using a concept of *scoring* and *conflict resolution* to prevent erroneous associations, our algorithm groups the attributes related to each service provider in a web document.

2. Ontology Directed Mining

A service ontology is characterized by a set of service concepts C, the IS-A relationship between concepts, a set of single-valued attributes A_s, a set of multi-valued attributes A_m, a function A that associates a set of attributes with a concept, and the extraction function $Attr\_id$ associoated with an attribute. Each entity is *uniquely* identified by a set of single-valued attributes. We call any such set as a *key*. e.g. for service providers two possible keys are $\{street, city\}$ and $\{street, zip\}$. Let T be the DOM tree of a page. $Parent(n)$ denotes the parent of node n and $children(n)$ denotes all its children. We are interested in identifying subtrees in T in which no single-valued attribute occurs more than once. We use the notion of a *mark* for doing so. Whenever *mark(n)* is ϕ it means that there exists more than one occurrence of a single valued attribute in its subtree. Specifically, the subtrees rooted at a node can be merged as long as no single-valued attribute occurs in more than one subtree. A maximally marked node n is an internal node such that $mark(Parent(n))$ is ϕ. Let $\sigma(n)$ denote the concatenation of the text strings associated with the leaf nodes of the subtree rooted at n; $Attr$ be the set of attributes of the concept c; $\{k_1, ..., k_n\}$ be the attributes that constitute the key of c; $R(a_1, ..., a_n)$ denote the tuple of attributes associated with an entity. We will extract one tuple from a home page and several such tuples from a referral page. We use $score(n)$ to denote $|mark(n)|$. Algorithm Extract takes as input the tree of the page and the set of attributes names of the concept c. It outputs either a single tuple containing the values of the attributes if it is a home page or a set of tuples if it is a referral page. Extract_Home_Page takes as input the set of attribute names whose values are to be extracted and the set of maximally marked nodes in the document tree. The intuition behind this algorithm is that the maximally marked node contains the key attributes associated with the service entity and any node in the document tree might contain occurrences of the multi-valued attributes. For referral pages we have to extract the attributes of several entities. The main problem here is associating the extracted attributes with their corresponding entities. We use the notion of a *conflicting* set that will be used in making such an association. Let Γ be as defined in Algorithm Extract. Observe that Γ is an ordered set of nodes. Let $< m_1, m_2, ..., m_q >$ denote the nodes in this ordered sequence. We say that Γ is *conflict-free* whenever $\exists i, m_i, m_{i+1} \in \Gamma$ such that $mark(m_i) \cup mark(m_{i+1})$ is consistent. Γ is not conflict-free if all pairs of consecutive nodes are mutually incon-

sistent. Observe that whenever Γ is not conflict-free then any maximally marked node represents a single entity. All we need to do is simply pick the attributes in it and create the tuple for that entity. If this is not the case then attributes of an entity may be distributed across neighboring nodes. In that case we will have to detect the boundaries separating each entity. In addition even if Γ is conflict-free the leaf nodes in it will have conflicts and we will have to detect boundaries separating the attributes of entities in the text string at the leaf node.

Algorithm Extract $(T, Attr)$
begin
1. **for**all nodes $n \in T$ **do**
2. $mark(n)$
3. **end**
4. Let Γ = { maximally marked nodes } $\cup$ { leaf nodes marked ϕ }
5. **if** $\exists m_i, m_j \in \Gamma \wedge \{Attr\_id(k_1)(\sigma(m_i)), ..., Attr\_id(k_n)(\sigma(m_i))\}$
    $\neq \{Attr\_id(k_1)(\sigma(m_j)), ..., Attr\_id(k_n)(\sigma(m_j))\}$ **then**
6. T is a referral page
7. **else**
8. T is a home page
9. **endif**
10. **if** T is a home page **then**
11. R = Extract_Home_Page($Attr, \Gamma$)
12. **elseif** T is a referral page **then**
13. $\{R_1, ..., R_n\}$ = Extract_Referral_Page($Attr, \Gamma$)
14. **end**
end

Algorithm Extract_Home_Page $(Attr, \Gamma)$
begin
1. pick the node n in Γ with the maximum *score*
2. **for**all $a_i \in Attr \wedge a_i \in A_s$ **do**
3. $R[a_i] = Attr\_id(a_i)(\sigma(n))$
4. **end**
5. **for**all $a_i \in Attr \wedge a_i \in A_m$ **do**
6. $R[a_i] = \bigcup_{m_i \in \Gamma} Attr\_id(a_i)(\sigma(m_i))$
7. **end**
8. **return** R
end

3. Service Directory Mining System Implementation

The system consists of three main components: an *acquisition* component, a *classification* component and an *extraction* component. The acquisition component retrieves HTML pages from the web that are likely to be relevant for the intended domain of services. This is done by doing a keyword search for the service with a web search engine. The search engine returns a number of urls pointing to pages that match the keywords. All of these web pages are fetched by the acquisition component.

Algorithm Extract_Referral_Page (*Attr*, Γ)
begin
1.   **if** Γ is not conflict-free **then**
2.   **for**all $m_i \in \Gamma$ **do**
3.   **if** m_i is a leaf $\wedge mark(m_i) = \phi$ **then**
4. $\{R_1, ..., R_n\}$ = Boundary_Detection(*Attr*, m_i)
5.   **else**
6.   **for**all $a_j \in Attr$ **do**
7. $R_i[a_j] = Attr\_id(a_i)(\sigma(m_i))$
8.   **end**
9.   **end**
10.   **end**
11. **else**
12. $\{R_1, ..., R_n\}$ = Boundary_Detection(*Attr*, Γ)
13. **end**
14. return $\{R_1, ..., R_n\}$
end

The classification component filters the retrieved pages into a set of web pages that the classifier has judged to be actually relevant for the intended service. For training the classifer one hand picks examples of web pages that are relevant to the intended domain of service. These serve as the positive examples. One must also choose pages unrelated to the service as the negative examples. The extraction component, driven by the service ontology, does unsupervised extraction of attribute values from classified pages and builds the services direcxtory. The mining system described above was used to create a service directory of veterinarians. For veterinarian service providers, we built an ontology consisting of two concepts: the *Service Provider* concept at the root, and the concept *Veterinarian*. The *Service Provider* concept consists of the attributes *service provider name, street, city, state, zip, phone, email, url*. The concept *Veterinarian* consists of the attribute *vet's name*. In addition, *Veterinarian* inherits all the attributes of *Service Provider*. The attributes *phone, email* and *vet's name* are multi-valued while the other attributes are single-valued. Regular expressions were used to identify *phone number, email, state* and *zip* in a page. Rules were used to identify *street, vet's name* and *service provider name*. We trained the classifier by picking 371 veterinarian home/referral and 303 non-veterinarian web pages. The web search yielded 13,691 distinct pages. The trained classifier was used to select the relevant pages from them. Classification identified 3400 pages as positive or relevant to the veterinarian domain. The extraction algorithm was run on all of the 3400 pages. We provide experimental results of this case study below. From these 3400 positively classified pages, 950 were identified as home pages of veterinarian service providers while 1900 were identified as referral pages by the extraction algorithm. The $< city, state, zip >$ triple was used as the key. There were about 550 pages with missing zips that were discarded. Table 1 shows the statistics of different attribute values collected for these 2850 pages.

Attribute	Number of Records	
	Home Pages	Referral Pages
City	950	12300
State	950	12300
Zip	950	12300
Street	950	12300
Phone	806	10930
Email	938	780
Doctor Name	711	3930
Hospital Name	856	12300
URL	950	-

Table 1. Number of records extracted for each attribute for home and referral pages

For comparison we retrieved a total of 650 email addresses and 990 urls of veterinarian service providers listed in http://vetquest.com, http://vetworld.com and the yellow pages in http://www.superpages.com. In contrast our mining system yielded 1718 emails and 950 urls of home pages.

4. Related Work

Extraction from semi-structured sources by *wrapper generation* methods is an extensively researched topic [10, 2, 8, 1, 11, 9, 12]. Wrappers have several disadvantages: (a) a significant amount of work is required to generate the rules, and (b) they are document specific as they rely on the syntactic relationship between HTML tags and the attribute value for proper extraction. Wrappers are therefore brittle to changes in the document structure. In contrast our extraction algorithms are independent of any page specific relationships between HTML tags and attribute values. All that is needed is an ontology for the intended service domain. With such an ontology extraction from any document relevant to that domain can be carried out. Information extraction techniques as embodied in [5, 4, 3] use supervised machine learning methods. Observe that the creation of the ontology is the only supervised step in our approach. Regardless of the ontology, our algorithm for associating attribute values to their corresponding service entity in a web document is unsupervised. Supervised machine learning techniques that will handle multiple entities in a document are as yet not known. Query languages for semi-structured documents constitutes an important class of extraction techniques. They all assume that the document schema is known a priori. In our approach we make no such assumptions. The work that comes closest to ours is [7, 6]. In this work the extraction problem is formulated as one of detecting boundaries between records and hence is applicable to only referral pages. The boundary detection is based on several different heuristics which can result in incorrectly identifying the entities.

5. Conclusion

Engineering an ontology is largely dictated by the the complexity of the identifier functions. In the case study reported in this paper we used regular expressions as the identifier extraction functions. Incorporating complex rules in the ontol-ogy can result in improving the precision of extraction considerably. This is an area worthy of investigation. Our requirement for the existence of a key to distinguish between home and referral pages resulted in misclassifying some referral pages. Relaxing this requirement is a topic of future work.

References

[1] N. Ashish and C. Knoblock. Wrapper generation for semi-structured internet sources. *ACM SIGMOD Record*, 26(4):8–15, 1997.

[2] P. Atzeni and G. Mecca. Cut & paste. In *ACM Symposium on Principles of Database Systems*, pages 117–121, Arizona, June 1997. ACM.

[3] M. E. Califf and R. J. Mooney. Relational learning of pattern-match rules for information extraction. In *Working Notes of AAAI Spring Symposium on Applying Machine Learning to Discourse Processing*, pages 6–11, Menlo Park, CA, 1998. AAAI Press.

[4] M. Craven, D. DiPasquo, D. Freitag, A. McCallum, T. M. Mitchell, K. Nigam, and S. Slattery. Learning to construct knowledge bases from the world wide web. *Artificial Intelligence*, 118(1-2):69–113, 2000.

[5] M. Craven, D. DiPasquo, D. Freitag, A. K. McCallum, T. M. Mitchell, K. Nigam, and S. Slattery. Learning to extract symbolic knowledge from the World Wide Web. In *Proceedings of AAAI-98, 15th Conference of the American Association for Artificial Intelligence*, pages 509–516, Madison, US, 1998. AAAI Press, Menlo Park, US.

[6] D. Embley, Y. Jiang, and Y.-K. Ng. Record-boundary discovery in Web documents. In *ACM SIGMOD Conference on Management of Data*, pages 467–478. ACM, 1999.

[7] D. W. Embley, D. M. Campbell, R. D. Smith, and S. W. Liddle. Ontology-based extraction and structuring of information from data-rich unstructured documents. In *Proceedings of the International Conference on Knowledge Management*. ACM, 1998.

[8] J. Hammer, H. Garcia-Molina, S. Nestorov, R. Yerneni, M. M. Breunig, and V. Vassalos. Template-based wrappers in the tsimmis system. In *ACM SIGMOD Conference on Management of Data*, pages 532–535. ACM, 1997.

[9] N. Kushmerick, D. S. Weld, and R. B. Doorenbos. Wrapper induction for information extraction. In *Intl. Joint Conference on Artificial Intelligence*, volume 1, pages 729–737, Nagoya, Japan, 1997.

[10] I. Muslea. Extraction patterns for information extraction tasks: A survey. In *AAAI-99 Workshop on Machine Learning for Information Extraction*.

[11] M. Perkowitz, R. Doorenbos, O. Etzioni, and D. Weld. Learning to understand information on the internet: An example-based approach. *Journal of Intelligent Information Systems*, 8(2):133–153, March 1997.

[12] S. Soderland. Learning information extraction rules for semi-structured and free text. *Machine Learning*, 34(1-3):233–272, 1999.

Reviewing RELIEF and its Extensions: A new Approach for Estimating Attributes considering high-correlated Features

Raquel Flórez-López

Department of Economics and Business Administration,
University of León, Campus de Vegazana s/n, 24071 León, Spain
e-mail: **dderfl@unileon.es**

Abstract

RELIEF algorithm [4], [5] *and its* extensions [8], [9] *are some of the most known filter methods for estimating the quality of attributes in classification problems dealing with both dependent and independent features. These methods attend to find all meaningful features for each problem (both weakly and strongly ones* [6]) *so they are usually employed like a first stage for detecting irrelevant attributes. Nevertheless, in this paper we checked that RELIEF-family algorithms present some important limitations that could distort the selection of the final features' subset, specially in the presence of high-correlated attributes. To overcome these difficulties, a new approach has been developed (WACSA algorithm), which performance and validity are verified on well-known data sets.*

1. Introduction

Feature Selection task means selecting a set of M relevant features from an original group of N variables (M≤N) so that the probability distribution of distinct classes considering these M features is as close as possible like the original distribution for the N original ones [10]. It presents three advantages for problem solving: (1) to simplify data description; (2) to make easier data collection; and (3) to improve the task of problem solving, both reducing its dimensionality and computation time. It is particularly relevant in classification problems, where an induction algorithm is used to decide if an unknown instance, described by a set of features, belongs to a certain class [13], so irrelevant and redundant features could confuse the class assignation; their removal improve the solution, reducing its complexity and the curse of dimensionality.

2. Feature subset selection

Although this problem has long been analysed by researchers coming from statistics and pattern recognition areas, who focus the investigation on linear regression problems, it has recently been analysed from the machine learning and knowledge discovery point of view, so that new algorithms have been developed divided into two main types: exhaustive and heuristic search, characterised for both search strategy and criterion function also distinguished between *filter* and *wrapped* methods.

2.1. The Filter Approach

Based on statistics, it uses a pre-processing step uniquely on the training data, so could be initially applied for many different classifiers. Some well-known instances of the filter approach are the FOCUS method (for noise-free Boolean concepts), the tree filters [1], the LVF algorithm [10] and two methods related with the feature weighting approach: the RELIEF algorithm [5], [6] and its extensions ("RELIEF-family" algorithms, see section 3) [8] and the EUBAFES technique [13]; these two last techniques differ in four important points: (1) the optimisation process (RELIEF uses an on-line optimisation strategy and EUBAFES employs a batch driven one); (2) the similarity measure (based on the weighted Euclidean distance for EUBAFES and on the L_1 metric for RELIEF); (3) the characteristics of weights (RELIEF gets continuous weights and EUBAFES lets obtain both binary and continuos ones) and (4) the final subsets (RELIEF gets an only one feature subset but EUBAFES proposed several subsets).

2.2. The Wrapper Approach

In this approach, induction algorithm is considered like a "black box" for calculating the relevance of each subset of features [7]. In addition, it is used to guide the search for the best attributes through the state space, so it acts as both heuristic and evaluation functions. Each state represents a feature subset, and both forward selection (adding attributes from an empty state) or backward elimination (reducing attributes from a full state) could be employed, together other alternatives. Some of the most known wrapper techniques are those developed by [3], known as BFS techniques ("backward/forward best-first search with compound operators") and HC techniques ("backward/forward hill climbing search with compound operators"), based on best-first search and hill climbing engines (respectively), considering C4.5 and Naive-Bayes induction algorithms as the heuristic/evaluation function.

Even though there is quite evidence that wrapper methods obtain good computational results [3] they can only be combined with low-complexity classifiers, being restricted by the time complexity of the learning algorithm, causing over-fitting too. As conclusion, we agree to [13] that filter techniques are preferable to wrapper methods, being more general and able to match complex classifier like artificial neural networks.

3. Reviewing RELIEF algorithm

3.1. RELIEF-family algorithms

The RELIEF algorithm [4], [5] is a filter method based on the feature weighting approach, that estimates attributes according their performance in distinguish near instances. RELIEF searches the two nearest neighbours for each instance: one from the same class ("nearest hit") and another from the miss class ("nearest miss"), defining weights through the expression:

$W[A]=P$(different value of A | nearest instance from different class)- P(different value of A | nearest instance from same class).

These weights denote the relevance of each feature A to the target concept. The pseudo-code of RELIEF is:

```
Set all weights W[A]:=0;
For i:=1 to m
    Randomly select an instance R;
    Find nearest hit H and nearest miss M;
    For A:=1 to all_attributes
        W[A]:=W[A]-diff(A,R,H)/m + diff(A,R,M)/m
    Next A
Next i
```

where diff(Attribute,Instance1,Instance2) is the difference between the attribute's values for instances 1 and 2 and m the number of neighbours, so that weights are all in the [-1,1] interval. Original RELIEF deals with both discrete and continuos attributes, but it is limited to binary problems, getting inefficient results for noisy and incomplete data. To avoid these difficulties, some extensions have been proposed for both classification [8] and regression problems [9]: RELIEF-A(considering k nearest hit and miss neighbours for each instance), RELIEF-B (treating with unknown values), RELIEF-C (similar to RELIEF-B but eliminating unknown values), RELIEF-D (calculating the posterior probability of unknown values), RELIEF-E (generalising RELIEF for multiple classes) and RELIEF-F (incorporating multiple classes in the weights' update scheme).

RELIEF-family algorithms are sensitive to correlations among attributes. They do not provide a definitive final subset of features, but user must select it (a rule of thumb considers weights being positive or higher than 0.1) and

parameters' selection is crucial for their final accuracy [8]. To avoid previous difficulties, a new feature-selection method has been developed, presented in next section.

4. The WACSA algorithm

The Weighted Adjusted-Correlation using Simulated Annealing (WACSA) algorithm is a new technique that combines the searching efficacy of the Simulated Annealing method with some of the best characteristics from RELIEF and EUBAFES. It takes into account the bi-variate correlation among variables, which is used to adjust the final subset of features. The WACSA algorithm is a feature weighting approach that generates successive Markov chains using SA; each chain ch has a length of $a.N$, $a \geq 1$ (being N the number of features) so that each piece ch_n represents a W vector with N components (one for each attribute), being w_i the relevance weight of the i-th feature. The algorithm treats to find the best W that maximise an evaluation function, defined for each instance R as: $f(W)=d_{Mc}(W)-d_H(W)$, where

$$d_H(W)= \sum_{\substack{l=1 \\ c \neq R(c)}}^{c} \left[\frac{\sum_{j=1}^{k} \sqrt{\sum_{i=1}^{N} w^A_i (R_i - M_{c_i})^2}}{k} \cdot \frac{1}{N_c} \right],$$

and $d_{Mc}(W)= \dfrac{\sum_{j=1}^{k} \sqrt{\sum_{i=1}^{N} w^A_i (R_i - H_i)^2}}{k}$,

being k the selected number of neighbours, m the number of instances, H_i the i-th variable for the hit neighbour, M_{ci} the i-th feature for the miss neighbour from the c-class [c distinct of R class or $R(c)$], N_c the number of examples belonging to c-class and w^A_i the i-th weight, adjusted for the correlation among the i-th feature and the S subset of features with weights $w_j > w_i$, $w_j \in W_S$ so that:

$$w^A_i = w_i \cdot \frac{\sum_{k=1}^{i-1} w^A_k |1 - correlation(i,k)|}{\sum_{k=1}^{i-1} w^A_k},$$

$$w^A_1 \geq w^A_2 \geq ... \geq w^A_N$$

Alternatively, it is possible to consider w_k instead w^A_k; and the adjusted-correlation $|1-correlation(i,k)|$ could be substituted for alternative expressions too, like the quadratic formula $(1-[correlation(i,k)]^2)$.

Both W and W^A weights vector are normalised so that $w_i, w^A_i \in [0,1]$ and $\sum_{i=1}^{N} w_i = \sum_{i=1}^{N} w^A_i = 1$; these conditions are necessary to ensure that both $d_{Hc}(W), d_{Mc}(W) \in [0,1]$, so $f(W) \in [-1,1]$. As it can be observed, f(W) seems similar to the adaptation rule for RELIEF, but it considers the weighted Euclidean distance proposed in EUBAFES.

The WACSA algorithm can be resumed as follows:

```
Set all weights w i=1/N, 1≤i≤N, w i∈ W
Initialice (t0)
h:=0
execute evaluation(W)
while stop criterion is not fulfilled do
    generate W', a neighbour of W
        Execute evaluation(W')
        If f(W')≤f(W) then
        W:=W'
        else
            generate q:=random[0,1)
            if q<exp( - (f(W') - f(W))/t_h )then
            W:=W'
            end if
        end if
    h:=h+1
    calculate t_h
end while
```

defining the *evaluation(W)* process as follows:
evaluation(W):

```
f(W):=0
for i:=1 to m
    randomly select an instance R;
    find k-nearest hit H(k)
        For c:=1 to number_classes_distinct_of_R(c)
            Find k-nearest miss M_c(k)
        Next c
    f(W):= f(W)+d_{Mc}(W)/m - d_H(W)/m,
Next i
```

Neighbour W' is generated through the change of an only one component w_i from W (selected through a random process) so that $w'_i := w_i$ + random[-s,s]. In our experiments, we have considered s=0.5, but other alternatives are possible, being interesting the employment of an adaptive scheme so that s decreases for each chain. It has been considered a double stop criteria: (1) a maximum number of chains (50 chains) and (2) a minimum number of non-changing chains (10 chains); the initial temperature was set using the approximation:

$$t_0 \approx \frac{-\Delta cost}{\ln \chi},$$

being Δcost the average cost change when worse solutions are generated from the current one, and χ the initial desired probability of changes; an exponential annealing process was used: $t_{k-1}=t_k \cdot p^k$, $0 \le p \le 1$; we established p= 0.9, with the Metropolis algorithm as the acceptation criterion. It was established a chain length of $a.N$, a=2.

The main limitation of WACSA algorithm is the absence of a deterministic subset of relevant features; on the contrary, a weight vector is proposed, so the user will subjectively decide the more important attributes. In spite of these limitations, the final vector is an adjusted one, so the effect of irrelevant and/or high-correlated attributes

has been reduced. In that way, decision about the "cut point" becomes much easier, being a rule of thumb the selection of the point such that $w_i \ge k.w_{i+1}$, with k=2 or k=3.

To evaluate WACSA's performance, we ran experiments on five artificial well-known data sets, taken from the UC-Irvine repository [12]; they were selected considering their accessibility and use in the feature selection literature, together to their recognised difficulty and the existence of evidence about relevant features: Monk1, Monk2 and Monk3 [14], CorrAL [3] and the binary data used for evaluating RELIEF [8].

- Monk 1, Monk 2 and Monk 3: These data sets have six binary features and two target binary concepts; in Monk1, if (att.1=att.2) or (att.5=1) then target is true, false otherwise; in Monk 2, target is true if exactly two attributes takes the value 1. In Monk 3, if (att.5=3 and att.4=1) or (att.5≠4 and att.2≠3) then target=true including a 5% additional noise. Results obtained with RELIEF-A and WACSA algorithms (k=10, m=124 – the number of training stages-) are resumed in Table 1; values in bold are those concerning to selected attributes (k=2 for the cut point of WACSA, positive weights for RELIEF-A), and values in both cursive and bold represent those features that would be selected for the RELIEF-A algorithm considering weights upper that 0.1.

	Att.1	Att.2	Att.3	Att.4	Att.5	Att.6
Monk1-WACSA	**0.384**	**0.410**	0.009	0.003	**0.168**	0.005
Monk1-RELIEFA	*0.111*	**0.006**	-0.018	-0.002	*0.102*	**0.002**
Monk2-WACSA	0.210	0.110	0.112	0.108	0.111	0.349
Monk 2-RELIEFA	**0.001**	**0.010**	**0.047**	**0.016**	**0.033**	**0.051**
Monk 3-WACSA	0.021	**0.463**	0.002	0.001	**0.392**	**0.120**
Monk 3-RELIEFA	-0.007	*0.190*	-0.016	**0.010**	*0.158*	**0.007**

Table 1. Feature selection for Monk1, 2 and 3

In the Monk1 problem, WACSA detects the three relevant attributes (giving to Att.1 and Att.3 a higher relative importance than Att.5 considering the information on the training data set), but RELIEF-A includes an irrelevant feature in the final subset (Att.6); if we consider weights higher than 0.1, it only identifies the Att.1 as relevant. In the Monk2 problem, WACSA has not a clear cut point (k=2), so all attributes could be relevant or irrelevant; if this condition is relaxed, features 1, 3 and 6 seem the most suitable (especially the last one), which could be surprising if we consider the primary relation: "target is true if exactly two attributes takes the value 1"; it seems that all features would be relevant for the problem, so the algorithm should select the overall set; nevertheless, if we analyse the specific training data set we could obtain the following conditional probabilities:

P(T1 | Att1=1)=0.3333;   P(T1 | Att2=1)=0.3333;
P(T1 | Att3=1)=0.3855;   P(T1 | Att4=1)=0.2885;
P(T1 | Att5=1)=0.3256;   P(T1 | Att6=1)=0.3374

In conclusion, WACSA algorithm seems to approximate these empirical distributions, except for Att3 which gets a lower weight than the empirical probability. RELIEF-A algorithm considers none attribute relevant for the problem (weights upper than 0.1).

About Monk3, WACSA identifies Att2 and Att.5 as relevant (according with the true relation), but RELIEF-A (positive weights) includes Att.3 and 6 too, being the last one irrelevant for the problem.

- CorrAL: There are six binary independent attributes: four of them are relevant, one is irrelevant and the last one is correlated to the output but affected with noise. Results obtained are resumed in Table 2:

	Att.1	Att.2	Att.3	Att.4	Att.5	Att.6
WACSA	**0..211**	0.036	**0.302**	**0.341**	0.001	0.092
RELIEF-A	*0.208*	*0.185*	*0.225*	*0.218*	-0.090	*0.198*

Table 2. Feature selection for CorrAL

RELIEF-A detects the irrelevant feature but includes the correlated–one in the final subset. WACSA excludes both the irrelevant and the noisy-correlated variables, but it does not maintains the rest of features, only Att1, Att3 and Att4. This result contrasts with the one from [3], who use a wrapper approach that only retains the two first attributes (Att1 and Att2); this difference is probably due to the limited length of the training.

- Binary data for RELIEF: It considers 2 binary target classes and 10 Boolean attributes, five of each are relevant and five random ones. For WACSA analysis it has been developed a new training data set: five attributes are relevant, three are correlated with these ones (100%, 90% and 80%) and five are random ones (Figure 1).

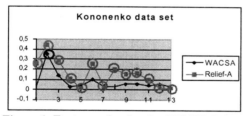

Figure 1. Feature selection for RELIEF dataset

RELIEF-A selects all relevant attributes (strongly and weakly ones), increasing unnecessarily the dimensionality of the problem. WACSA avoids this problem, considering only strongly variables and those weak that much increases the global accuracy of the classifier. As it can be observed, WACSA would select an only one feature, enough to characterise the problem, overcoming some limitations of RELIEF-family techniques.

4. Conclusions and future work

Two main conclusions can be extracted from this article: first of all, it has been developed a new filter feature selection algorithm that combines both Simulated Annealing paradigm and RELIEF-based techniques and that performs well on different training data (binary datasets).

Secondly, this algorithm lets overcome some of the most important limitations of RELIEF-family of techniques: their inefficiency against high-correlated variables and multiple irrelevant features.

We thought that this new technique could be helpful in the feature selection problem, so the future work would concentrate in their extension and validation using more diverse data sets and considering multi-class problems.

References

[1] Cardie, C. (1993): "Using decision trees to improve case-based learning". *Proceedings of the Tenth International Conference on Machine Learning*, pp. 25-32. Morgan Kaufmann.

[2] John, G. and Kohavi, R. (1995): "Feature subset selection using the wrapper model: overfitting and dynamic search space topology". *Proceedings of the First International Conference on Knowledge Discovery and Data Mining*, Menlo Park, august, pp. 192-197.

[3] John, G.H., Kohavi, R. and Pfleger, K. (1994): "Irrelevant features and the subset selection problem". Included in Cohen, et al (eds.): *"Machine Learning: Proceedings of the Eleventh International Conference"*. Morgan Kaufmann. San Francisco, pp. 121-129.

[4] Kira, K. and Rendell, L.A. (1992b): "A practical approach to feature selection". *Proceedings of the Ninth International Conference on Machine Learning*, Aberdeen, pp. 249-256

[5] Kira, K. and Rendell, L.A. (1992a): "The feature selection problem: traditional methods and new algorithms". *Proceedings of AAAI'92*, pp. 129-134.

[6] Kohavi, R. and John, G.H. (1995): "Wrappers for feature subset selection". *Artificial Intelligent Journal*, 97(1-2), pp. 273-324.

[7] Kohavi, R. and John, G.H. (1998): "The wrapper approach". Included in Liu, H. and Motoda, H. (eds.): *"Feature Selection for Knowledge Discovery and Data Mining"*. Kluwer Academic Publishers, pp. 33-50.

[8] Kononenko, I. (1994): "Estimating attributes: analysis and extension of RELIEF". *Proceeding of the European Conference on Machine Learning*, pp. 171-182.

[9] Kononenko, I. (1997): "Non-myopic attribute estimation in regression". *Applied Intelligence*, 7:1, pp. 39-55.

[10] Langley, P. (1994): "Selection of relevant features in machine learning". *Artificial Intelligence*, 97 (1-2), pp. 245-271.

[11] Liu, H. and Setiono, R. (1998): "Incremental feature selection". *Applied Intelligence*, 9:3, pp. 217-230.

[12] Murphy, P. (1995): *"UCI Repository of Machine Learning Databases"*. University of California, Irvine. Department of Information and Computer Science.

[13] Scherf, M. and Brauer, W. (1997): *"Feature Selection by Means of a Feature Weighting Approach"*. Technical Report No. FKI-221-97. Technische Universitat Munchen.

[14] Waltz, D. and Stanfill, C. (1992): "Toward memory-based reasoning". *Communications of the ACM*, 29, pp. 1213-1228.

ESRS: A Case Selection Algorithm Using Extended Similarity-based Rough Sets

Liqiang Geng and Howard J. Hamilton
Department of Computer Science, University of Regina
Regina, SK, Canada, S4S 0A2
{gengl, hamilton}@cs.uregina.ca

Abstract

A case selection algorithm selects representative cases from a large data set for future case-based reasoning tasks. This paper proposes the ESRS algorithm, based on extended similarity-based rough set theory, which selects a reasonable number of the representative cases while maintaining satisfactory classification accuracy. It also can handle noise and inconsistent data. Experimental results on synthetic and real sets of cases showed that its predictive accuracy is similar to that of well-known machine learning systems on standard data sets, while it has the advantage of being applicable to any data set where a similarity function can be defined.

1. Introduction

A *case selection algorithm* automatically derives a casebase from an available data set for future case based reasoning process. The goal is to select high quality cases, eliminate noisy data, and hence reduce the storage requirements and increase the speed of case based reasoning systems.

Aha et al. proposed a series of incremental instance-based learning algorithms (IBL), called IB1, IB2, IB3 and IB4 [1]. IB1 is similar to the k-nearest neighbor (k-NN) clustering algorithm, because it stores all the instances in the casebase and classifies unseen instances to the same class as the most similar instance in the casebase. IB2 reduces the size of the casebase by storing only the cases that cannot be correctly classified by the existing casebase. IB3 keeps track of the frequency with which stored cases, when chosen as one of the current object's most similar stored cases, matched the current object's decision value. If the matching frequency is lower than a given threshold, the case is discarded. IB4 incorporates weight learning and thus can tolerate irrelevant features better than IB3. The IBL algorithms have O(mn^2) worst-case time complexity for m attributes and n instances. Due to their incremental nature, the casebase generated by the IBL algorithms is strongly influenced by the order in which the objects are stored. No heuristics are used to select instances from a global point of view.

To overcome this limitation, competence measures can be used to order the instances before the selection process begins. Smyth and McKenna propose *relative coverage* to measure the competence of instances [11]. This measure is based on not only the coverage of an instance, but also on how many other instances cover the covered instances. This ordering process transforms IBL from an incremental method into a batch method.

Wilson and Martines [12, 13] propose a series of batch case pruning algorithms named *RT1*, *RT2*, and *RT3* (also called *Integrated Decremental Instance-Based Learning*). Instead of selecting good instances for inclusion, *RTx* selects bad ones for exclusion. *RT1* first constructs lists of neighbors and lists of associates for each instance. Then it checks to see if the absence of each instance *i* will improve the classification accuracy of its *associates*, which are the instances that have *i* as one of their nearest neighbors. If it does, this instance is eliminated, and the lists of neighbors and associates are updated to delete this instance from their lists. *RT2* does not update the associate lists; instead it keeps the deleted instances in the associate lists. Thus, the deleted instances continue to be considered during leave-one-out cross-validation. As well, *RT2* ranks the instances in descending order according to their distances to the border. This sorting attempts to delete central points and keep border points. *RT3* attempts to eliminate noisy instances before pruning by deleting all instances that cannot be correctly classified by their nearest neighbors.

Brighton and Mellish [2] propose a similar case pruning algorithm *ICF*. This algorithm uses the same method to identify and delete noisy instances as *RT3*. Then it calculates the reachable and coverage sets of each instance, which correspond to neighbors and associates in *RT3*. The difference between the reachable set and the neighbor set is that the neighbor set has fixed cardinality, while the reachable set has variable cardinality, which is determined by the *enemy* of the instance, i.e., the nearest neighbor of the instance that has a different decision value. The heuristic used here is that if the cardinality of the reachable set is greater than the cardinality of the coverage set, the instance is deleted. Although *RT3* makes only one pass, *ICF* performs multiple passes until no further instances can be removed.

Both *RT3* and *ICF* attempt to select border points. Brighton and Mellish [2] argue that border points have the ability to discriminate between classes. However, we think that when the decision boundaries are smooth and homogeneous, keeping representative center points rather than border points can reduce the storage significantly.

Yang and Wu propose that a clustering algorithm be used to divide a large casebase into several smaller ones [15]. Their method maintains a layered case base instead of selecting good cases. This method can improve the speed of case retrieval, but it may miss relevant cases and it does not reduce storage costs.

Our objective is to design a case selection algorithm that satisfies two requirements: it has a small number of user-specified parameters, selects a reasonable number of representative central points, and explicitly handles noisy and inconsistent data. This algorithm is based on extended similarity-based rough sets. Section 2 discusses similarity-based rough approximation. Section 3 describes the proposed algorithm. In Section 4, the results of testing the algorithms on well-known data sets and new synthetic data sets are presented. Section 5 gives conclusions and directions for future work.

2. Similarity-Based Rough Sets

Rough sets are a mathematical tool for dealing with vagueness and uncertainty used in data mining, decision making, and pattern recognition [7]. Similarity relation-based rough set is an extension of the standard rough set approach that replaces the indiscernibility relation with a similarity relation in the approximation process [10].

Given a finite non-empty set U of objects, called the *universe*, a binary relation R defined on $U \times U$ is a similarity relation if it is *reflexive*, i.e., if and only if aRa, where $a \in U$. From this definition, we can represent the relation R as a directed graph and define a similarity class for each object $x \in U$. The *similarity class* of x, denoted by $R(x)$, is the set of objects that are similar to x.

$$R(x) = \{y \in U / yRx\}$$

The *rough approximation* of a set $X \subseteq U$ is a pair of sets called lower and upper approximations of X, denoted by $R_*(X)$ and $R^*(X)$ respectively, where

$$R_*(X) = \{x \in X / R(x) \subseteq X\}$$
$$R^*(X) = \cup_{x \in X} R(x)$$

The lower approximation $R_*(X)$ of a set X is the set of objects whose similarity class belongs to X and the set consists of elements that can certainly be classified as elements of X, while the *upper approximation* $R^*(X)$ of X is the union of the similarity classes of objects in X and the elements in this set can possibly be classified as elements of X.

To enable it to deal with noise in a database, we propose the following *extended lower approximation* of a similarity-based rough set,

$$R_{*ext}(X) = \{x \in X / card(R'(x)) / card(R(x)) \geq ct\},$$

where $R'(x) = \{y / y \in R(x)$ and $d(y) = d(x)\}$ refers to the set of the objects that are similar to object x and have the same decision value as x. The *consistency threshold* $ct \in$

[0, 1] defines the degree to which noisy data are tolerated. It is a parameter that must be specified by the user for the ESRS algorithm. $R_{*ext}(X)$ is the set of objects which are classified, with certainty of at least ct, as elements of concept X according to the similarity relation R. If ct equals 1, $R_{*ext}(X)$ is identical to the standard similarity based lower approximation $R_*(X)$.

To conduct casebase generation, a source of data is represented as a *decision table*, i.e., a two-dimensional table where each row represents an object, and each column represents an attribute. Let $T = (U, A \cup \{d\})$ be a decision table where U is the universe, A is a set of condition attributes and d is a decision attribute [7]. Let V_a be a set of values of attribute a, where $a \in A$, $r(d)$ be the number of decision values, d_i be the ith decision value, and $Y_i = \{x \in U / d(x) = d_i\}$ be the set of objects that have the ith decision value in the decision table. $POS(R, \{d\}) = \cup_{i=1}^{r(d)} R_{*ext}(Y_i)$ is called the *positive region* of the partition $\{Y_i / i = 1, ..., r(d)\}$.

The coefficient $r(R, \{d\}) = card(POS(R, \{d\})) / card(U)$ is called the *quality* of approximation to the classification. It expresses the ratio of objects that can be correctly classified to all objects in the decision table. An object that cannot be classified is an *inconsistent object*.

To obtain the similarity class for every object, a similarity measure is needed for each kind of attribute, e.g., *interval-scaled attribute*, *ordinal attribute*, *nominal attribute*, *set attribute* and *text attributes*, and an aggregation method is needed to calculate the global similarity measure.

We say that object x is *similar* to object y if and only if the similarity measure between these two objects is greater than or equal to a similarity threshold st, i.e., xRy if and only if $S(x,y) \geq st$. The similarity threshold st determines the granularity of classification; a higher st value indicates a more refined classification of the data into clusters of representative cases.

3. The ESRS Algorithm

Based on the concepts of extended similarity-based rough sets and similarity measures, we propose the Extended Similarity-based Rough Sets (ESRS) algorithm to select representative cases from a database. First, in addition to the similarity threshold st and consistency threshold ct mentioned in Selection 2, some variables used in the algorithm are defined as follows.

1. *SimilarNo(i)*: the number of objects similar to the ith object O_i, including O_i itself.

2. *SimilarClassNo(i)*: the number of objects similar to O_i that have the same decision value as O_i, including O_i itself.

3. *Consistency(i)*: the fraction of the number of similar objects that have the same decision value as O_i. $Consistency(i) = SimilarClassNo(i) / SimilarNo(i)$. If

Consistency(*i*) is less than *ct*, O_i can be regarded as inconsistent with the database.

4. *r*(*R*, {*d*}): the quality of classification, i.e., the fraction of the all objects that are consistent.

The ESRS algorithm is shown in Figure 1.

```
ESRS(st, ct)
1. Based on st, compute the similarity measures between
all pairs of objects and create a similarity matrix, which
defines a similarity relation graph, with a node for each
object and an arc between each pair of objects with
nonzero similarity.
2. For each node i in the relation graph, {
        Compute SimilarNo(i), SimilarClassNo(i), and
        Consistency(i).
}
3. Compute r(R, {d}) as defined in Section 2.
4. Delete nodes that are considered inconsistent, i.e., those
which satisfy Consistency(i) < ct
5. Select isolated nodes, i.e., nodes whose SimilarNo is 1,
and place them in the casebase.
6. While the node set is not empty {
        Select a node with the maximum value for
        Consistency. If there is a tie, select one with the
        maximum value for SimilarClassNo. If there is a
        tie again, randomly select one node. Insert it into
        the case base.
        Delete the selected node and all its adjacent nodes.
}
```

Fig. 1. Algorithm ESRS

ESRS first constructs the similarity relation graph of the objects, where each node represents an object in the data set. Then it deletes the inconsistent nodes according to the value of *Consistency* and threshold *ct*. Next it selects all isolated nodes. Then, based on a global perspective, it repeatedly selects the most representative node in terms of *Consistency* and *SimilarClassNo* and deletes all nodes similar to it. It also determines the quality ratio *r*(*R*, {*d*}) of the objects that can be classified correctly to all objects. If the quality is too low, which means many objects cannot be classified, the user may want to increase *st* to refine the granularity of the clusters.

Let *m* denote the number of the condition attributes and *n* denote the number of the objects in the decision table. The time complexity for creating a similarity relation graph is $O(mn^2)$, for computing *SimilarClassNo*, *SimilarNo* and *Consistency*, and selecting nodes is $O(n^2)$, and for deleting inconsistent nodes is $O(n)$. Overall, the complexity of the ESRS is $O(mn^2)$. If $m \ll n$, the complexity is $O(n^2)$.

4. Experimental results

ESRS was implemented in Java and experiments were conducted on a 733MHz Pentium with 128Mb memory. Each run of ESRS on any testing data set took less than one minute. The average predictive accuracy (hereafter

accuracy) of the casebase when classifying unseen cases was determined using ten-fold cross validation.

In the first series of experiments, we compared ESRS to rule-based concept learning programs on UCIrvine data sets that are well structured with simple values (no sets, images, etc.) [6]. Results for ESRS on the Iris data set are shown in Table 1. The first number in each grid of Table 1 represents the number of selected cases and the second represents the accuracy on the test data set. Experimental runs were conducted using ESRS with different similarity and consistency thresholds. The results for the run(s) with the highest classification accuracy are shown in boldface. When the similarity threshold *st* increases, the granularity of the classification becomes finer, and the number of the selected cases increases. The accuracy reaches its highest value at the point (in this case, *st* = 0.7) where the granule size is most appropriate. When the consistency threshold *ct* increases, ESRS tends to identify more data as noisy and select fewer objects as representative cases; therefore, the number of the selected cases decreases. For the Iris data set, we did not observe any interdependency between *ct* and the accuracy. Similar results were obtained with the Glass and Pima data sets (not shown in detail).

Table 2 compares the classification accuracy of the ESRS algorithm with those of four well known data mining systems: the tree induction algorithm C4.5 [8], layered Artificial Neural Network (ANN) [9], Instance Based Learning 3 (IB3) [1] and rule induction algorithm LEM2 [4]. The data in the first four rows were obtained from [5]. The data in the last row are the best average accuracy for ESRS obtained using the testing methods described above in this section. The classification accuracy of ESRS approximates that of other well-known classification systems, provided the parameters are properly selected.

Ct\st	0.5	0.6	0.7	0.8	0.9
0.5	8, 92.7	13, 94.7	**20, 98.0**	40, 95.3	92, 93.3
0.6	8, 92.0	13, 96.0	**20, 98.0**	40, 96.0	92, 93.3
0.7	7, 88.7	13, 96.0	**20, 98.0**	40, 96.0	92, 93.3
0.8	6, 89.3	12, 96.7	**20, 98.0**	40, 96.0	92, 93.3
0.9	6, 90.0	10, 95.3	18, 96.7	38, 96.0	92, 93.3
1.0	6, 90.7	10, 94.0	18, 96.7	38, 96.0	92, 93.3

Table 1. Experimental results of running ESRS on the Iris data set.

Algorithm	Iris	Glass	Pima
C4.5	95.5	67.9	70.8
ANN	95.3	65.0	**76.4**
IB3	96.7	65.4	68.2
LEM2	94.0	66.8	62.0
ESRS	**98.0**	**69.7**	74.2

Table 2. Comparison of accuracy.

For the second experimental series, we tested ESRS on synthetic data. All synthetic data generated have 10 conditional attributes and 10 possible decision values. All conditional attributes range from 1 to 10,000. A case was chosen randomly, with a 90% chance of selecting each attribute to define the value of the case. Then 10 to 100 instances near the case were generated, with a maximum distance of 200 (or 1000) out of 10000 away from the value of each selected attribute in the case, and a random value for unselected attributes. In data sets Syn1 to Syn5, each case is based on a fixed subset of attributes, while in Syn6 to Syn8 each instance is based on a randomly chosen subset of attributes. Some parameters are shown in Table 3. The results are given in Table 4. We used C4.5 and k-NN, as implemented in Weka [14], on the same data. The results show that ESRS performs the best on this type of data.

Data Set	1	2	3	4	5	6	7	8
Cases	10	10	10	20	50	50	50	20
MaxRad	200	200	200	200	200	200	1000	200
MinRad	50	50	50	50	50	50	50	50
Instance per Case	10	20	100	50	20	20	20	50
Fixed Attribute	yes	yes	yes	yes	yes	no	no	no

Table 3. Synthetic data sets

	1	2	3	4	5	6	7	8
ESRS	93.0	91.0	92.7	95.1	95.4	91.9	89.8	93.7
C4.5	85.0	84.0	91.6	93.8	91.1	75.6	74.7	82.9
k-NN	93.0	91.0	92.7	94.8	94.4	87.9	87.5	90.4
ANN	87.0	88.0	92.5	89.9	71.2	60.7	60.6	81.2

Table 4. Classfication accuracy on synthetic data

For the third series we compare the performance of ESRS with other state of the art case selection algorithms, RT3 and ICF. Table 5 summarizes the classification accuracy (Acc) obtained and storage required using RT3, ICF, and ESRS on nine data sets. The results for RT3 and ICF were obtained from [2].

Dataset	RT3		ICF		ESRS	
	Acc	Storage	Acc	Storage	Acc	Storage
Balancescale	83.4	18.2	81.5	14.7	**90.0**	**5.2**
Breast-cancer-w	95.3	**3.1**	95.1	4.3	**96.4**	3.3
Ecoli	**82.8**	15.8	81.3	14.0	76.5	**6.6**
Glass	69.1	**23.3**	69.6	31.4	**69.7**	47.7
Iris	93.6	16.0	92.6	42.0	**98.0**	14.8
Pima	71.0	22.4	69.2	17.2	**74.2**	18.7
Voting	93.8	7.4	91.2	8.9	**94.0**	**1.3**
Wine	86.4	15.4	83.8	12.0	**95.5**	8.8
Zoo	87.1	26.1	92.4	52.8	**96.1**	26.4

Table 5. Comparison of accuracy and storage

5. Conclusion

In this paper, we proposed an extended similarity-based rough set algorithm called ESRS for selecting representative cases from data sets. This algorithm requires only two user-specified parameters, the consistency and similarity thresholds. The selected cases are representative in that they are central points and cover

all objects in the data set by means of the similarity relation, and they are not similar to each other. The experimental results indicate that the classification accuracy for this algorithm is comparable to classical machine learning algorithms on standard machine learning data and has better performance on synthetic data approximating sets of cases seen in practice.

In further research we evaluated automatic selection of the similarity threshold [3]. We will apply ESRS to data sets containing complex data types. We will add attribute reduction and weight assignment techniques to make the selected cases more compact. We will also improve ESRS's time complexity with efficient data structures.

References

[1] Aha, D.W., Kibler, D., and Albert, M.K., Instance based learning algorithms. *Machine Learning*, 6, 37-66, 1991.

[2] Brighton, H., and Mellish, C., Advances in instance selection for instance-based learning algorithms. *Data Mining and Knowledge Discovery*, 6, 153-172, 2002.

[3] Geng, L., and Hamilton, H.J., Automated Case Generation from Databases Using Similarity-Based Rough Approximation. A. Abraham and L. Jain (eds.), Recent Advances in Intelligent Paradigms, Physica (Springer) Verlag, Berlin. Forthcoming.

[4] Grzymala-Busse, J.W., LERS - a system for learning from examples based on rough sets. *Intelligent Decision Support*, Slowinski, R. (eds.), Kluwer Academic, 3-18, 1992.

[5] Krawiec, K., Slowinski, R., and Vanderpooten, D., Learning Decision Rules from Similarity Based Rough Approximations. *Rough Sets in Knowledge Discovery*, v2, L. Polkowski, A. Skowron (eds.), Heidelberg: Physica-Verlag, 37-54, 1998.

[6] Merz, C.J., and Murphy, P.M., UCI Repository of machine learning databases. University of California, Irvine, Department of Information and Computer Science, 1996.

[7] Pawalk, Z., *Rough Sets: Theoretical Aspects of Reasoning about Data*, Kluwer Academic, Dordrecht, 1991.

[8] Quinlan, J.R., *C4.5: Programs for Machine Learning*. Morgan Kaufmann, San Mateo CA, 1988.

[9] Rumelhart, D.E., Hinton, G.E., and Williams, R.J., Learning internal representations by error propagation. Rumelhart, D.E, McClelland, J.L., and the PDP Research Group (eds.), *Parallel distributed processing: Explorations in the microstructure of cognition*, MIT Press, Cambridge, MA, 318-362, 1986.

[10] Slowinski, R., and Vanderpoonten, D., Similarity relation as a basis for rough approximations. *Adv. in Machine Intelligence and Soft Computing* 4, 17-33, 1997.

[11] Smyth, B., and McKenna, E., Building compact competent case-bases. *Proceedings of the Third International Conference on Case-based Reasoning*, 329-342, 1999.

[12] Wilson, D.R., and Martines, T.R., An integrated instance-based learning algorithm. *Computational Intelligence*, 16(1), 1-28, 2000.

[13] Wilson, D.R., and Martines, T.R., Instance pruning techniques. *Proceedings of the Fourteenth International Conference on Machine Learning*, 404-411, 1997.

[14] Witten, I.H., and Frank, E., *Data Mining*, Morgan Kaufmann, 2000.

[15] Yang, Q., and Wu, J., Keep it simple: A case-base maintenance policy based on clustering and information theory. *Proceedings of the Thirteenth Canadian AI Conference*, 102-114, 2000.

An Algebraic Approach to Data Mining: Some Examples

Robert L. Grossman and Richard G. Larson
Laboratory for Advanced Computing, University of Illinois at Chicago
851 S. Morgan St M/C 249, Chicago IL 60607
{grossman, rgl}@uic.edu

Abstract

In this paper, we introduce an algebraic approach to the foundations of data mining. Our approach is based upon two algebras of functions defined over a common state space X and a pairing between them.

One algebra is an algebra of state space observations, and the other is an algebra of labeled sets of states.

We interpret H as the algebraic encoding of the data and the pairing as the misclassification rate when the classifer f is applied to the set of states χ.

In this paper, we give a realization theorem giving conditions on formal series of data sets built from D that imply there is a realization involving a state space X, a classifier $f \in R$ and a set of labeled states $\chi \in R_0$ that yield this series.

1. Introduction

Let R denote an algebra of functions formed by state space observations, that is, maps $f : X \longrightarrow k$. Classifiers will be elements of $f \in R$.

The second algebra of functions R_0 consists of state space observations with finite support, that is, maps $\chi : X \longrightarrow k$ with finite support. Labeled sets of states will be elements of $\chi \in R_0$.

Note that R and R_0 are k-algebras. We also assume that there is a pairing (the misclassification rate)

$$\ll f, \chi \gg \; \in \mathbf{R}, \qquad f \in R, \quad \chi \in R_0.$$

Fix a space D of labeled data elements. We define a labeled learning set to be an element of D^*, the set of words $d_1 \cdots d_k$ of elements $d_i \in D$. If k is a field, the $H = kD^*$ is a k-algebra with basis D^*. In this paper we study formal series of the form

$$p = \sum_{h \in D^\bullet} p_h h.$$

By a formal series, we mean simply a map $H \longrightarrow k$, associating each element of H with the series coefficient p_h. The coefficient p_h is the classification (or misclassification) rate for the learning set h. We make no assumptions about convergence. Formal series occur in the formal theory of languages, automata theory, control theory, and a variety of other areas.

Fix a formal series $p \in H^*$. Note that this is an object associated not with a single data set but with a family of data sets. For our applications, these may be thought of as associated with a series of experiments involving different, but related data sets. We address a standard question: given a formal series p, built from the data D, is there a state space X, a classifier $f : X \longrightarrow k$, and a set of initial states that yield p? This is called a realization theorem. The state space captures the essential data which are implicit in the series p. The formal definition is given below.

We now give two examples of formal series.

Example 1. The first example is motivated by the problem of learning a model to predict credit card fraud given transaction data, where each transaction is labeled fraudulent or not fraudulent. Let the set D consist of labeled data elements which are triples (p, a, f). Here p is an account ID, a bounded integer. The second component a is an integer between \$1 and \$1000 representing the transaction amount. The third component is a label 0 or 1, the first labeling a good transaction and the second a bad or fraudulent one. We assume that the first two components are distributed according to the uniform distribution, while 98% of the labels of the third component are 0, so that fraud occurs for approximately 2% of the transactions.

For this example, we let the state space $X = \mathbf{Z}^2$ which we think of as embedded in $\mathbf{R}^2$. A labeled set of states is a map $\chi : X \longrightarrow k$, with finite support. We assume that each state $x = (x_1, x_2)$ with $\chi(x) \neq 0$ is associated with a (unique) profile id or account id. The component x_2 is the transaction amount a of the last transaction associated with the account. There must be at least one such transaction or $x = 0$, which we assume is not the case. The component x_1 is the transaction amount a of the second to the last transaction associated with with the account. If there is no such transaction, then x_2 is 0.

Given a data set $d \in D^*$, consisting of words built from transaction triples (p, a, f), there is a natural action $\chi \cdot d$, which we think of the result of a data set updating a set of states. The profile in χ corresponding to p is left shifted by a and the resulting profile takes the label f.

We define a classifier $f : X \longrightarrow k$ as follows: $f(x) = 1$, if $x_1 = 1$ and $x_2 > 250$ and zero otherwise. This is motivated by the standard practice of testing a stolen credit card with a one dollar transaction and then buying an expensive item. Finally, we assume that 90% of credit card transactions for one dollar are fraudulent. Given these assumptions, the formal series $\sum_{d \in D^*} \ll f, \chi \cdot d \gg \cdot d$ is realizable by construction and the distribution of the coefficients can be computed easily as an exercise. Note that the series doesn't converge and though the coefficients may be arbitrarily close to 1, on average, they tend to be less than 0.2.

Example 2. For the second example, take the same data set D consisting of triples (p, a, f) as above and form words by as in Example 1.

Define a formal series

$$\sum_{d \in D^*} c_d \cdot d,$$

where this time the coefficient c_d is assumed to be a random variable on $[0, 1]$ which we assume to be independent of d. Assume that this formal series has a realization, say on a state space $\mathbf{R}^n$ so that there are functions $f, \chi : X \longrightarrow k$ with $c_d = \ll f, \chi \cdot d \gg$. Then either the action $\chi \cdot d$ is independent of d in which case the coefficients c_d are constant, which is a contradiction, or the coefficients $c_d = \ll f, \chi \cdot d \gg$ do in fact depend upon d, which violates our assumption that the c_d are a random variable independent of d. We conclude that this series doesn't have a finite dimensional state space realization.

Formal series elegantly capture the structure of a variety of infinite objects that arise in computation. Realization theorems use a finiteness condition to imply that the infinite object can be represented by a finite state space. One of the most familar realization theorems is the Myhill–Nerode theorem. In this case, the infinite object is a formal series of words forming a language; the finiteness condition is the finiteness of a right invariant equivalence relation, and the state space is a finite automaton. In our case of data mining, the infinite object is a formal series of learning sets comprising a series of experiments, the finiteness condition is described by the finite dimensionality of a span of vectors, and the state space is $\mathbf{R}^n$. The Myhill–Nerode theorem, and, more generally, languages, formal series, state space representations (such as provided by automata), and finiteness conditions play a fundamental role in the foundations of computer science. Our goal is to introduce analogous structures into data mining. We now briefly recall the Myhill–Nerode theorem following [4], page 65.

Let D be an alphabet. D^* is the set of words in D, and $L \subset D^*$ is a language. A language L defines an equivalence relation $\sim$ as follows: for $u, v \in D^*$, $u \sim v$ if and only if for all $w \in D^*$ either both or neither of uw and vw are in L. An equivalence class $\sim$ is called right invariant with respect to concatenation in case $u \sim v$ implies $uw \sim vw$ for all $w \in D^*$.

Theorem 1.1 (Myhill–Nerode) The following are equivalent:

1. L is the union of a finite number of equivalence classes generated by a right invariant equivalence relation.

2. The language $L \subset D^*$ is accepted by some finite automaton.

In the sections below, we point out further analogies between the Myhill–Nerode thereom and the data mining realization we prove below in Theorem 5.2. For now, we point out that a language $L \subset D^*$ naturally defines a formal series. Fix a field k and the k-algebra $H = kD^*$. Given a language L, define the formal series $p \in H^*$ as follows:

$$p(h) = \begin{cases} 1 & \text{if } h \in L \\ 0 & \text{otherwise} \end{cases}$$

In this paper, we prove a Myhill–Nerode type theorem for data mining. We have two innovations in this paper:

1. We introduce a realization theorem for data mining. In particular, we introduce a natural finiteness condition associated with an infinite series of data sets that comprise a series of experiments. As far as we are aware, realization theorems and these types of finiteness conditions in data mining have not been studied previously.

2. The distinction between data, states, data updates, data attributes, and derived attributes is usually ignored in alternative approaches. Rather one works with a classifier f on a data space D.

In our approach, we clearly distinguish the data $d \in D$, states $x \in X$ formed from the data using derived attributes, and the action of new data d' updating the states $d' \cdot x$.

2. Data, States, and State Space Observations

Let D denote a space of labeled data elements and D^* the set of words $d_1 \cdots d_k$ formed from data elements $d_i \in D$. We emphasize that each d_i is labeled.

Fix a field k. Let $H = kD^*$ denote the vector space witb basis D^*. Then H is an algebra whose multiplication is induced by the semigroup structure of D^*, which is simply concatenation.

Fix a space X. Elements $x \in X$ are called states and X is called the state space. Fundamental to our approach is the introduction of two algebras of functions defined over a common state space X and a pairing between them. Let R denote an algebra of functions formed by state space observations, that is, maps $f : X \longrightarrow k$. Classifiers will be elements of $f \in R$, that is, a classifier associates a value or label to each state.

The second algebra of functions R_0 consists of state space observations with finite support, that is, maps $\chi : X \longrightarrow k$ with finite support. By finite support we mean that the set $\{x : \chi(x) \neq 0\}$ is finite. Labeled sets of states will be elements of $\chi \in R_0$.

The other fundamental assumption is that there is an action of the data $h \in H$ on the functions $f \in R$ which satisfies

$$h \cdot (f + g) = h \cdot f + h \cdot g$$

$$h \cdot (\alpha f) = \alpha(h \cdot f) = (\alpha h) \cdot f,$$

for $f, g \in R$, $\alpha \in k$. That is, R is an H-module. Since the state space X and the function space R are closely connected, this is roughly equivalent to having an action of H on X. In addition, the action also satisifies the identity

$$h \cdot (fg) = \sum_{(h)} (h_{(1)} \cdot f)(h_{(2)} \cdot g),$$

where the map $H \longrightarrow H \otimes H$, $h \mapsto \sum_{(h)} h_{(1)} \otimes h_{(2)}$ is called a comultiplication. In this case R is called a H-module algebra. An algebra H with a comultiplication and units for both the multiplication and comultiplication, all of which satisfy certain compatibility conditions is called a bialgebra. See [1] and [3] for details.

We assume that

1. R and R_0 are H-module algebras.

2. There is a pairing

$$\ll f, \chi \gg \in \mathbf{R}, \qquad f \in R, \quad \chi \in R_0.$$

This is our setup for the analysis of data mining from an algebraic point of view. To summarize: we are given a bialgebra H, two function algebras R and R_0, and a pairing between them. We interpret H as the algebraic encapsulation of the data and the pairing as the misclassification rate when the classifer f is applied to the set of states χ. The process of updating and computing derived attributes is encapsulated in the action $\chi \cdot h$, for $h \in H$ and $\chi \in R_0$.

We now show how the same algebraic structure can be used to describe automata following [3]. As in the description of automata above, let D denote a finite alphabet, and D^* the set of finite strings of letters of D. Then D^* is a semigroup with operation concatenation, and with identity the empty string ϵ. $H = kD^*$ is a bialgebra. Let $L \subset D^*$ be a language, and let p be the characteristic function of L. Let M denote a finite automaton accepting the language L, let S be the set of states of the automaton, let s_0 be the initial state, and $F \subseteq S$ the set of accepting states. Then a word $w \in D^*$ is accepted by the automaton if and only if $s_0 \cdot w \in F$.

We now re-interpret this structure using the algebras R and R_0 introduced above. Let R denote the algebra of k-valued functions on the state space S. Then R is a commutative k-algebra. Let R_0 denote the set of characteristic functions on the set S which are 0 everywhere except at a single point where they are 1. Note that R_0 is an H-module defined by $h \cdot f(s) = f(s \cdot h)$ if $h \in D^*$.

Define
$$f(s) = \begin{cases} 1 & \text{if } s \in F \\ 0 & \text{otherwise} \end{cases}$$

Note that $w \in L$ if and only if $s_0 \cdot w \in F$ if and only if $f(s_0 \cdot w) = 1$ if and only if $p(w) = (w \cdot f)(s_0) = 1$. Define

$$\ll f, \chi \gg = f(s'), \qquad f \in R, \quad \chi \in R_0,$$

where s' is the point of S where $\chi(s') = 1$. Now if χ is the characteristic function of the initial state s_0,

$$\chi(s) = \begin{cases} 1 & \text{if } s = s_0 \\ 0 & \text{otherwise} \end{cases}$$

Then
$$p(w) = \ll f, w \cdot \chi \gg, \tag{1}$$

in case the language defined by $p \in H^*$ is accepted by some finite automaton. Equation (1) is the fundamental equation defining a realization. The left hand side contains the coefficients of a formal series, while the right hand side is based on a state space and functions defined on it. We give an analogous theorem (Theorem 3.4) for the formal series of learning sets arising in data mining in Section 5 below.

3. Realizations

We first define an algebraic finiteness condition on formal series of learning sets $p \in H^*$.

Definition 3.1 If H is a bialgebra, its primitive elements are defined by

$$P(H) = \{\, h \in H \mid \Delta(h) = 1 \otimes h + h \otimes 1 \,\},$$

where the map $\Delta : H \longrightarrow H \otimes H$, $h \mapsto \sum_{(h)} h_{(1)} \otimes h_{(2)}$ is the comultiplication.

Definition 3.2 The algebra H^* has a left H-module algebra structure given by $(h \rightharpoonup p)(k) = p(kh)$, for h, $k \in H$, $p \in H^*$. We say that the formal series of learning sets $p \in H^*$ has finite Lie rank if $\dim P(H) \rightharpoonup p$ is finite.

Finite rank is a naturally occuring condition and occurs in the Fliess theorem from control theory, in the Myhill–Nerode theorem from automata theory, and in hybrid systems [3].

In this section, we state and prove a simple realization theorem.

Let D denote a data space. More precisely an element of D is a triple whose first element is a Profile IDentifier (PID) chosen from a finite set $\mathcal{I}$ and used to keep track of the various states, whose second element is a label chosen from a finite set of labels $\mathcal{L}$, and whose third element is an element of S, a set of data associated with PIDs. In short, $D = \mathcal{I} \times \mathcal{L} \times S$, where $\mathcal{I}$ is the set of PIDs and $\mathcal{L}$ is the set of labels. We use heavily the facts that $\mathcal{I}$ and $\mathcal{L}$ are finite.

Recall that $H = kD^*$ denote the vector space with basis D^*. Let $U = kS$ denote the vector space with basis S. Then H is an algebra whose multiplication is induced by the semigroup structure of D^*, which is simply concatenation. Also $U = kS$ is an algebra whose structure is induced by the semigroup structure of S. We use the mappings from H^* to U^* induced by adjoiniing labels and PIDs to elements of S.

A simple formal learning series is an element $p \in U^*$. We can think of a simple learning series p as an infinite series $\sum_{s \in S} c_s s$. Essentially, a simple formal learning series is a formal labeled learning series without the labels and PIDs.

Definition 3.3 Let R be a commutative algebra with augmentation ϵ. We say that $p \in U^*$ is differentially produced by the pair (R, f) if

1. there is right U-module algebra structure on R;

2. $p(u) = \epsilon(f \cdot u)$ for $u \in U$.

The basic theorem on the existence of the state space is the following, in which the state space is the vector space with basis $\{x_1, \ldots, x_n\}$.

What Theorem 3.4 gives us is the existence of a finite state space based on a finiteness condition on the series p.

Theorem 3.4 Let $p \in U^*$. Then 1) implies 2).

1. p has finite Lie rank;

2. there is a subalgebra R of U^* which is isomorphic to $k[[x_1, \ldots, x_n]]$, the algebra of formal power series in n variables; there is $f \in R$ such that p is differentially produced by the pair (R, f).

Proof: See [2].

We end by revisiting the Myhill–Nerode Theorm:

Theorem 3.5 (Myhill–Nerode) Let D be a finite alphabet and $H = kD^*$. Let $p \in H^*$. Then 1) implies 2):

1. $\dim(H \rightharpoonup p)$ is finite and p takes on the values 0 and 1.

2. there is a finite state space S with k-algebra of functions R on S, and a function $f \in R$, such that $p_h = (h \rightharpoonup f)(s_0)$.

We see that the Data Mining Realization theorem (Theorem 3.4 above) is a generalization of the Myhill–Nerode theorem using a more general finiteness condition, a finite dimensional vector space for a state space, and a bit of added complexity because of the labels and the presence of a finite number of initial conditions.

References

[1] R. Grossman and R. G. Larson. The realization of input-output maps using bialgebras. Forum Mathematicum, 4:109–121, 1992.

[2] R. L. Grossman and R. G. Larson. An algebraic state space realization theorem for data mining. submitted for publication.

[3] R. L. Grossman and R. G. Larson. An algebraic approach to hybrid systems. Journal of Theoretical Computer Science, 138:101–112, 1995.

[4] J. E. Hopcroft and J. D. Ullman. Introduction to Automata Theory, Languages and Computation. Addison–Wesley, Reading, Massachusetts, 1979.

Wavelet Based UXO Detection

S. Hodgson, N. Dunstan and R. Murison
School of Mathematical and Computer Science,
University of New England, AUSTRALIA
email: mcs@turing.une.edu.au

Abstract

The detection and classification of Unexploded Ordnance (UXO) is considered a multi-dimensional pattern recognition problem. Standard techniques in solving multidimensional detection and classification problems involve using large sets of templates or libraries. This paper shows that by using Wavelet Transformation a single library will allow a particular class of ordnance to be classified over a range of depths.

1. Introduction

The debris left in old battle sites and disused artillery ranges is a significant environmental, economic, and humanitarian problem through-out the world. The ability to detect and discriminate between UXOs and non-UXOs with a high degree of accuracy decreases both the risk and cost of remediation. However false alarm rates remain unacceptably high [3]. In the Montana Remediation Project 65% of the subsurface metallic objects exhumed were non-UXOs. While at the Kaho'olawe clearance project only 3% of exhumed were UXOs. Many previous attempts to classify UXOs were made using the data in its raw form. Classifiers which use data in its raw form are in general known to perform poorly, particularly when the dimensionality of the signal is large[3]. It can be seen in Figure 1 that when one or more of depth, azimuth, or declination is varied the signal changes considerably. In this paper a wavelet transformation is applied to the signal of a 40mm grenade at a set depth and orientation. Then a calibration model is developed which allows the particular class of UXOs to be identified at a specific depth. The model is extrapolated to enabled identification over a range of depths. The training set of data consists of eight scans of a 40mm diameter grenade at depths 15cm, 20cm $\cdots$ 45cm. The original signals consisted of approximately 40 readings along a transect. These were interpolated to 64 equally spaced measurements using spline analysis as the proposed wavelet transformation requires data of lengths 2^n. The test set contains two scans of the 40mm grenade at each depth and 10 different types of ordnance objects and 39 different types of nonordnance. All sets of data were collected by Geophysical Technology Limited using their propriety TM-5EMu electromagnetic scanner[4]. It is known that the pulse response from a EMI scanner from a general conducting, permeable object is composed of N frequencies ω_i where $\omega_i \neq \omega_m$ when $i \neq m$. The amplitude of the signal is a function of several variables including the depth and orientation of the subsurface object[2].

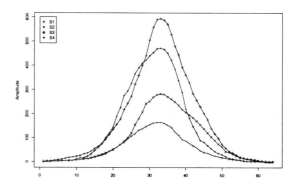

Figure 1. The Raw signal of a 155mm Shell at a Variety of Depths and Orientations

2. Wavelets

The discrete wavelet transform applied to a time series (signal) produces coefficients which are an alternate representation of the signal. For a signal of length $N = 2^p$, the signal is decomposed into p levels of resolution. The first is the scale of the signal. Subsequent levels $j = 1, .., p-1$ are interpreted as the smooth contribution to the signal from each dyadic block of length 2^{p-j}. Each coefficient is associated with a particular location and frequency so that a signal f can be expressed as a sum of products of coefficients $D_{j,k}$ and wavelet basis functions $\psi_{j,k}$ for $j = 1, ..., p$ levels of resolution and $k = 1, ..., 2^{j-1}$ locations within each level

$$f = \sum_{j=1}^{log_2 N} \sum_{k=1}^{2^{j-1}} D_{j,k} \psi_{j,k}$$

The wavelets $\psi_{j,k}$ are selected a priori and the choice is the type of wavelet which will best summarise the features of the signal. The coefficients are calculated by the inner product of the signal and wavelet [5]

$$D_{j,k} = < \psi_{j,k}, f >$$

The wavelet transform provides a decomposition of the energy of the signal into components associated with different levels of resolution and locations. Energy is the square of the coefficients and the total energy from frequency level J (crystal or subband) is

$$E_j = \sum_{k=1}^{2^{j-1}} D_{j,k}^2.$$

This is a measure of the amount of information about the signal contributed by crystal J. Our technique for detecting UXO uses the energies as summaries of features of the signal.

3. Classification at Discrete Depths

The data set consisted of scans from a 40mm grenade at depths d $(15, 20, ..., 45cm)$. Figure 2 illustrates the decay of $log(E)$ with $log(d)$ for crystals 1 to 5 and this linear relationship supports the power law $E \propto d^{-\beta}$. This profile in energies over depth is utilized in two ways for interpreting the source of a new test scan whose energies are $\varepsilon_1, \varepsilon_2, .., \varepsilon_5$. If the new object were in fact a 40mm grenade, the depth could be gauged. If the profiles $\varepsilon_1, \varepsilon_2, .., \varepsilon_5$ did not match that expected from a 40mm grenade, it would be classified otherwise.

3.1. The Calibration Model

From Figure 2 it can be seen that the mean energy of the low frequency components experience significant decay as the depth of the ordnance increases. In contrast the energy of the high frequency components of the signal experience little decay as the depth of the ordnance increases. The mean energy levels of the grenade at depth 15cm and two non-UXOs were calculated and plotted in Figure 3. If the energy of the low frequency components of the 40mm grenade displayed are used to characterize the ordnance at depth 15cm, then $S2$ would match the energy of the 40mm grenade. Similarly, if the highest frequency components where used $S1$ would match a 40mm grenade. If the energy

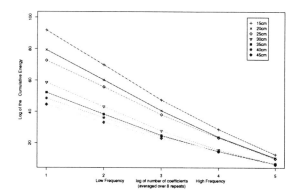

Figure 2. The Mean Energy Levels of the 40mm Grenade at 15cm, 20cm, $\cdots$,45cm

at all frequency levels were used then neither signal $S1$ nor $S2$ would match a 40mm grenade at that depth. Criteria 1 was proposed to detect and classify the 40mm grenade at discrete depths.

Criteria 1: An unknown signal is classified as a 40mm grenade at depth d iff its energy at subband level i falls within 2 standard deviation of the energy at subband level i of the 40mm grenade at depth d $\forall$ i

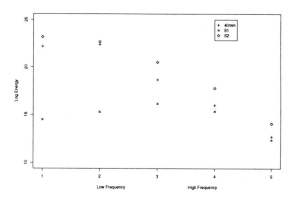

Figure 3. The Energy Levels of the 40mm Grenade at 15cm and Two non-UXOs

The accuracy of classification of a 40mm grenade using Criteria 1 is given in Table 2.

Category	% Classified as 40mm Grenades
Non-UXO	0.92%
UXO other than 40mm Grenades	4.6%
40mm Grenades	100%

Table 1. Scans classified as 40mm Grenades using Criteria 1

Subband	Intercept	Gradient
1	29.233	-4.301
2	37.033	-5.438
3	45.828	-6.839
4	52.938	-7.714
5	48.497	-6.757

Table 2. The values of a_i and b_i for the Energy equation of the 40mm grenade

4. Continuous Depths

In order to extend the discrete calibration model of the 40mm grenade into a continuous one it is necessary to determine the relationship between the energy level E_i and depth d. This was achieved by plotting the energy levels as the depth of the ordnance increases, as shown in Figure 4. With the aid of the power law $E \propto d^{-\beta}$ it can be seen that the relationship between $\log E_i$ and $\log d$ is linear. The log

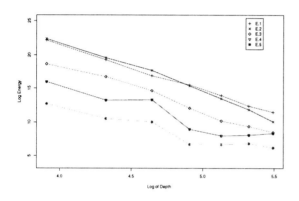

Figure 4. The Cumulative Energy of the 40mm Grenade at Depth 15cm, 20cm $\cdots$ 45cm

of the energy level E_i of the 40mm grenade as a function of log of the depth d may be modeled as

$$\log E_i = a_i + b_i \log d + \epsilon_i, \epsilon_i \sim N(0, \sigma_i^2) \qquad (1)$$

where a_i is the $log(energy)$ of the ordnance at depth 1cm, b_i gives the rate the energy of the scan decays as the $log(depth)$ of the ordnance increases and ϵ_i are independent and identically distributed normal errors. The values of a_i and b_i were determined for the eight scans in the training set and are displayed in Table 2. If the predicted depth at all subband levels is consistent then the unknown object is classified as a 40mm at that depth. If the predicted depths

differ significantly at each or any energy level then the object is deemed not to be a 40mm grenade. As an example the energy at each level i from two signals, Signal 5, a 40mm grenade at depth 15cm and Signal 6 an unknown sub-surface object are displayed in Table 4. The predicted

Subband	Signal 5		Signal 6	
	$\log E$	Depth cm	$\log E$	Depth cm
1	29.40	14.23	8.25	29.41
2	24.43	14.97	11.96	24.43
3	25.345	15.43	13.93	25.35
4	23.99	15.47	17.58	23.99
5	21.88	15.33	18.42	21.88

Table 3. Calculated Energies and Depths of Two Unknown Signals

depths for each energy level in Signal 5 is consistent so it is classified as a 40mm grenade at depth approximately 15cm. For Signal 6, the predicted depths at each energy level are significantly different so it is assumed not to be a 40mm grenade.

4.1. Prediction of Depth

Given new energy levels $\{E_1, E_2, \cdots, E_5\}$, the equation (1) relating energy to depth can be used to estimate depth and gauge the class of ordnance. When the individual regression of (1) are combined for multivariate calibration and estimation $log(E) \sim MVN(F(d), \sum)$ where $F(d)$ are the relationships of $log(E)$ to $log(d)$ in Table 3 and $\sum$ is the multivariate error matrix from these regressions. Given a new set of energy levels $\varepsilon = \varepsilon_1, ... \varepsilon_5$ a $100(1 - \alpha)\%$ confidence region for the estimate of $log(d)$ is given by [1]

$$[\varepsilon - F(d)]^T \sum{}^{-1}[\varepsilon - F(d)] \leq \frac{5}{(n-5)} F_{5,(n-5)}(\alpha) \qquad (2)$$

The value of d which minimizes the LHS of (2) is the least-squares estimate of the depth from which ε was observed. This can be found explicitly by

$$\widehat{log(d)} = (\hat{B} \textstyle\sum^{-1} \hat{B}^T)^{-1} \hat{B} \textstyle\sum^{-1} (\varepsilon - \bar{E})$$

where $\hat{B}$ is the matrix of regression coefficients in Table 3.

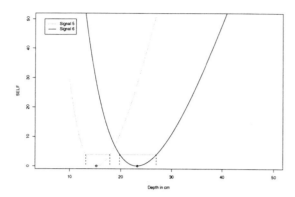

Figure 5. The SELF graphs of a 40mm grenade at depth 15cm (S5) and a unknown signal(S6)

4.2. Confidence Intervals and Envelopes

A plot of the quadratic from of (2), termed SELF[1], locates the least-squares estimate of depth graphically. For example when applying the 'SELF' function to the signals in Table 3 the plots produced are shown in Figure 5 If the 'SELF' function predicts the depth of the ordnance as not in its calibration range it can be automatically assumed the signal is not a 40mm grenade. If the 'SELF' function predicts a reasonable depth as, in Figure 5, further statistical analysis in the form of confidence intervals is used to differentiate 40mm grenades from non 40mm grenades. The values [2] of 'SELF' + Δ provide a $100(1-\alpha)\%$ confidence interval for the predicted depth d. The confidence limits of $log(d)$ are found in the following manner. A horizontal line is drawn at $\min(\mathrm{SELF}) + \Delta$. The points where this line cuts the profiles of SELF are the end points of the $100(1-\alpha)\%$ confidence interval. For Signal 5 'SELF' predicts the depth of the object at 15.25cm with a 95% confidence interval (12.5, 18.25) and the predicted depth for Signal 6 is 23.25cm with a 95% confidence interval (19.75, 27.50). The confidence intervals for each of the eight scans in the test set at each depth were determined in the manner described above. Then the mean of the upper and lower confidence intervals at each depth was calculated. The discrete bounds were converted to a confidence envelope by applying regression analysis to the

mean upper and lower confidence intervals. The resulting confidence envelopes were

$$L \geq -47.21 + 14.91 \log_2(d)$$
$$H \leq -75.40 + 23.99 \log_2(d)$$

Criteria 2: If the confidence intervals associated with the depth of a signal predicted by 'SELF' fell within the confidence envelop at the predicted depth the signal is classified as a 40mm grenade at the 'SELF' predicted depth.

So for a 40mm grenade at depth 15.25cm the confidence envelope is (11.39, 19.89) and at depth 23.25cm it is (20.46, 33.49). The confidence intervals for Signal 5 fall within the confidence envelope so it is classified as a 40mm grenade at depth 15.25cm. The lower confidence interval for Signal 6 fall outside the confidence envelope so the signal is classified as not being a 40mm grenade.

5. Conclusion and Further work

It has been demonstrated that by using wavelet transformations features can be extracted from the signal of a class of UXO at a given depth which allows the ordnance to be classified with a high degree of accuracy. The depth of the ordnance was also estimated accurately. It was then shown that a single model developed from the sub-energy levels of the response signal of the EMI scanner was sufficient to classify a given class of ordnance at a range of depths. Further work in developing a method to detect and classify ordnance would involve determining how the orientation of the ordnance effected the signal. Then extending the calibration model to identify the ordnance category at any depth or orientation.

This research is supported by the Australian Research Council and Geophysical Technology Limited.

References

[1] P. J. Brown. *Measurement, Regression and Calibration.* Oxford University Press, Oxford, 1992.

[2] L. C. P. Gao and L. Carin. An improved bayesian decision theoretic approach for land mine dectection. *IEEE Transactions on Geoscience and Remote Sensing*, 37(2), 1999.

[3] E. L. R. Grimm and P. Weichman. Detection and discrimination of uxo. In *UXO Forum*, 2000.

[4] G. T. Limited. State-of-the-art technologies for the detection of sub-surface unexploded ordnance. Technical report, Geophysical Technology Limited, 2001.

[5] D. B. Percival and A. T. Walden. *Wavelet Methods for Time Series Analysis.* Cambridge University Press, Cambridge, 2000.

---

[1] Squared-Error Loss Function

[2] Denote the R.H.S. of equation (2) by Δ

Ensemble Modeling Through Multiplicative Adjustment of Class Probability

Se June Hong, Jonathan Hosking, Ramesh Natarajan

IBM T.J. Watson Research Center

P.O. Box 218

Yorktown Heights, NY 10598

e-mail: sjhong@us.ibm.com, hosking@watson.ibm.com, nramesh@us.ibm.com

Abstract

We develop a new concept for aggregating items of evidence for class probability estimation. In Naïve Bayes, each feature contributes an independent multiplicative factor to the estimated class probability. We modify this model to include an exponent in each factor in order to introduce feature importance. These exponents are chosen to maximize the accuracy of estimated class probabilities on the training data. For Naïve Bayes, this modification accomplishes more than what feature selection can. More generally, since the individual features can be the outputs of separate probability models, this yields a new ensemble modeling approach, which we call APM (Adjusted Probability Model), along with a regularized version called APMR.

1. Introduction

The Naïve Bayes (NB) model is attractive for its simplicity, understandability, and classification accuracy ([3], [12], [7]). However, in many applications, it an accurate class probability estimate is desired; e.g., consumer promotions are based on the estimated response probability exceeding a certain threshold [16]. The accuracy of the NB model can be significantly improved by using a new approach given in section 2. This new model yields class probability estimates in which the prior probability of the class is adjusted by successive multiplicative factors arising from the independent items of evidence supplied by each feature, and importance parameters associated with each adjustment factor are estimated by fitting a logistic regression model. The NB model can be regarded as a simple ensemble model combining the weights of evidence from simple univariate predictive models. Therefore, the APM approach is also a new approach to model ensemble aggregation, based on multiplicative adjustments to the class probability predictions. This may be contrasted with the additive aggregation used in boosting or bagging.

Section 3 describes the training process for estimating the model parameters of APM and its regularized version APMR. Section 4 contains experimental results on problems from the UCI dataset. Finally, Section 5 provides a contrasts the present approach with other relevant techniques.

2. A new model for Naïve Bayes

Suppose that the data consist of n examples, and that the ith example has class label c_i and feature values in vector X_i. Let x_{ij} be the feature value of feature j in example i. The column vector of values of feature j will be denoted by x_j. The probability that the class is k given feature values X is

$$P(C = k|X) = P(C = k)\frac{P(X|C = k)}{P(X)}. \qquad (1)$$

Naïve Bayes makes the assumption that the feature values are independent given the class, and thus when comparing the possible classes for a given example we have

$$P(C = k|X) \propto P(C = k) \prod_j P(x_j|C = k). \qquad (2)$$

We note that this can be equivalently written as

$$P(C = k|X) \propto P(C = k) \prod_j \frac{P(C = k|x_j)}{P(C = k)}, \qquad (3)$$

which gives a new interpretation of NB: the class probability given the values of a set of features is proportional to the prior probability of the class adjusted multiplicatively by factors each of which reflects the influence of one of the individual features. Each adjustment factor is simply the ratio between the class probability given a feature value and the class prior probability. A natural extension of this interpretation is to permit the features to have different degrees of influence: importance parameters (weights) can be introduced as

$$P(C = k|X) \propto P(C = k) \prod_j \left(\frac{P(C = k|x_j)}{P(C = k)} \right)^{\alpha_j}, \quad (4)$$

which defines our Adjusted Probability Model, APM.

We can extend this insight by replacing $P(C = k|x_j)$ in (4) by $P^{(M_j)}(C = k|X))$, the output class probability from some predictive model M_j, with appropriate substitutions in (4) through (6) below. Used in this way, APM provides a new way of weighting and aggregating the predictions of several predictive models. See section (4) for an example.

The training process can be reduced to a logistic regression problem. From (4), after some algebra and for a given $X = X_i$, we have

$$\ln \frac{P(C|X_i)}{1 - P(C|X_i)} = q_0 + \sum_j \alpha_j q_{ij} \quad (5)$$

where

$$q_0 = \ln \frac{P(C)}{1 - P(C)}, \qquad q_{ij} = \ln \frac{P(C|x_{ij})\{1 - P(C)\}}{\{1 - P(C|x_{ij})\}P(C)}. \quad (6)$$

Equation (5) can also be written as

$$P(C|X_i) = \frac{1}{1 + e^{-q_0 - \boldsymbol{\alpha}^{\mathrm{T}} Q_i}} \quad (7)$$

where $\boldsymbol{\alpha}$ is a vector with elements α_j and Q_i is a vector with elements q_{ij} defined as in (6).

Equations (5) and (7) display APM in the form of a logistic regression model. Note that the term q_0 does not have an α coefficient: in statistical terminology it is an offset rather than an intercept. APM thereby differs from the usual logistic regression model for classification, as described for example by [19] and (sec. 4.1) in [13]. For a two-class problem, the model parameters α_j can be estimated by the method of maximum likelihood, as given in section 3. Extensions to multi-class problems are also possible, but are omitted here for brevity.

The probabilities needed to define the quantities q_0 and q_{ij} in equation (6) are naturally estimated from the data by

$$P(C = k) = \#\{i : c_i = k\}/n, \quad (8)$$

$$P(C = k|x_j = v) = \frac{\#\{i : x_{ij} = v \ \& \ c_i = k\}}{\#\{i : x_{ij} = v\}}, \quad (9)$$

along with suitable small-sample adjustments, such as the Laplace correction [15].

Since overfitting is possible in this scheme, we have also considered a regularized version of APM, APMR, by restricting the α_j coefficients in (5) to satisfy $\sum_j \alpha_j^2 = m$

where m is chosen to maximize the accuracy of out-of-sample predictions of class probabilities, similarly to ridge regression. The optimal value $\hat{m}$ is found by internal cross validation and binary search over the range of m. This is possible because the internal cross validation estimate of the loss in equation (10) below is generally a concave function of m. Model (5) is then fitted to the entire training set, with the restriction that $\sum_j \alpha_j^2 = \hat{m}$.

3. Optimization of the importance parameters

We assume a two-class problem with class labels 0 and 1, and consider the loss measure

$$\begin{aligned} \text{Loss} \ = \ & -n^{-1} \sum_i [c_i \log P(C|X_i) \\ & + (1 - c_i) \log\{1 - P(C|X_i)\}], \quad (10) \end{aligned}$$

where $P(C|X_i)$ is given by equation (7). This measure is the negative log-likelihood [9] (see also [2]), and it directly penalizes incorrect estimation of class probabilities: it is zero when the actual class has estimated probability 1, and increases as this estimated probability decreases. We use logarithms to base 2 in (10), so the loss is measured in bits.

The APM(m) model makes use of a Lagrangian multiplier λ and minimizes

$$\text{Loss} + \lambda \left(\sum_j \alpha_j^2 - m \right). \quad (11)$$

The minimization of (10) and (11) for the APM and APM(m) models is performed via the Newton-Raphson method; details can be found in [14].

4. Experiments

We present experimental results using the UCI data sets. Table 1 gives the means and standard deviations over 10 repetitions of 10-fold cross-validation (except for the DNA problem, which has a fixed train/test split). The small-sample adjustment that we used is indicated (details can be found in [14]). We mention, however, that only the problems with few examples, viz., breast and lymph, are sensitive to this correction.

For problems with more than two classes we report the results for each class (class k vs. rest is denoted as k for short in Table 1) and for "All" classes (which are computed by combining the class probabilities generated by independent APMR models for each individual class). We report the classification error rate and the loss measure (10), which is used for comparing the NB, APM, and APMR methods in this paper. In all cases, APMR produces a smaller loss than NB, often by a significant margin, and its classification

Table 1. Mean values of "Error" (misclassification rate) and "Loss" (from equation (10)) for NB, APM and APMR with std. dev. in brackets, obtained over 10 10-fold cross-validation runs. For APMR on DNA, the values are over 10 runs.

Class	Method	Error (%)	Loss
DNA: (no Laplace correction)			
1	NB	3.63	0.13
	APM	2.70	0.12
	APMR	2.50	0.10
2	NB	3.12	0.19
	APM	4.22	0.20
	APMR	3.51	0.17
3	NB	8.09	0.32
	APM	6.49	0.24
	APMR	6.41	0.23
All	NB	5.40	0.25
	APM	3.96	0.24
	APMR	3.49	0.24 (0.00)
SDNA (no Laplace correction)			
1	NB	3.12 (0.97)	0.13 (0.05)
	APM	2.65 (0.93)	0.13 (0.06)
	APMR	2.50 (0.75)	0.12 (0.05)
2	NB	2.99 (0.89)	0.18 (0.08)
	APM	3.27 (0.85)	0.17 (0.08)
	APMR	2.87 (0.77)	0.16 (0.07)
3	NB	7.78 (1.46)	0.30 (0.05)
	APM	6.28 (1.48)	0.24 (0.05)
	APMR	6.12 (1.36)	0.23 (0.03)
All	NB	4.36 (1.05)	0.25 (0.09)
	APM	4.27 (1.09)	0.25 (0.09)
	APMR	3.90 (1.09)	0.24 (0.08)
Mushroom (modified Laplace correction, $L = 1/n$)			
	NB	0.45 (0.23)	0.02 (0.01)
	APM	0	0
	APMR	0	0
Breast (full Laplace correction, $L = 1$)			
	NB	27.59 (7.36)	0.93 (0.23)
	APM	28.53 (7.54)	0.85 (0.13)
	APMR	27.97 (6.27)	0.82 (0.11)
Vote (modified Laplace correction, $L = 1/n$)			
	NB	9.72 (4.27)	0.94 (0.48)
	APM	4.66 (2.89)	0.29 (0.33)
	APMR	4.25 (2.75)	0.20 (0.16)
Lymph (full Laplace correction, $L = 1$)			
1	NB	2.00 (4.50)	0.13 (0.25)
	APM	0.67 (2.11)	0.16 (0.47)
	APMR	0.67 (2.11)	0.02 (0.04)
2	NB	15.52 (11.58)	0.58 (0.45)
	APM	19.62 (7.49)	0.93 (0.81)
	APMR	18.24 (11.90)	0.53 (0.30)
3	NB	12.14 (8.36)	0.57 (0.46)
	APM	16.33 (16.25)	0.77 (0.79)
	APMR	14.24 (14.59)	0.57 (0.42)
4	NB	2.00 (3.22)	0.07 (0.12)
	APM	0.67 (2.11)	0.02 (0.04)
	APMR	0.00 (0.00)	0.01 (0.02)
All	NB	12.81 (11.64)	0.64 (0.55)
	APM	19.62 (10.94)	0.88 (0.66)
	APMR	14.90 (11.01)	0.57 (0.36)

error rates are also often superior to those of NB and the other methods in the literature.

DNA: (3 classes, 60 features, 2000 training examples and a given test set of 1186 examples). In [8], the class 1 error rates range from 2.11% to 3.88%, depending on the specific SVM parameters used, while the APMR rate is 2.50%. The APMR all-class error rate of 3.49% compares well with 5.0% for bagged CART [1].

SDNA: (3190 combined "original" examples of DNA, with 15 examples containing missing values discarded). For "all classes", the APMR error rate is 3.9%, while [6] reported 4.9% for boosted C4.5 and 5.2% for bagged C4.5 models, [5] reported 3.7% for boosted C5.0, 6.0% for boosted stumps and 4.1% for AD-Tree, and finally [17] reported 5.58% for bagged C4.5 and 5.43% for boosted C4.5.

Mushroom: (2 classes, 23 features, 8124 examples). The APM and APMR error rates are zero, while [8] reported $4.23 \pm 0.75\%$ for NB and zero for the SVM based methods.

Breast(-cancer): (2 classes, 9 features, 286 examples). The APMR error rate of 27.97% compares with 27.59% for NB (but with smaller standard error, and with with significantly better average loss). For NB, [10] reported 26.88% (26.46% with feature selection), and [8] reported $26.88 \pm 7.48\%$. Also [8] reported $31.1 \pm 7.85\%$ for WBC$_{\text{SVM}}$, and $30.12 \pm 6.57\%$ for a linear SVM.

Vote: (2 classes, 16 features, 435 examples). The APMR error rate is 4.25%, while [17] reports 4.37% for bagged C4.5 and 5.29% for boosted C4.5, [6] report for 3.6% for bagged C4.5 and 5.1% for boosted c4.5, [5] reports 4.5% for boosted C5.0, 4.4% for boosted stumps, and 3.7% for AD-Tree, [10] reports 9.81% for NB (compared with our 9.72%) and 4.07% for NB with feature selection, [8] reports $9.81 \pm 3.92\%$ for NB, $4.14 \pm 3.13\%$ for WBC$_{\text{SVM}}$, and $3.77 \pm 2.77\%$ for a linear SVM.

Lymph:(4 classes, 18 features, 148 examples). APMR was worse than NB with a modified Laplace correction. Even with the full correction APMR is comparable to NB only for the loss. [17] reports error rates for bagged and boosted C4.5 of 20.41% and 17.43%. [10] report error rates of 16.76% for NB and 15.89% for NB with selection of best features. We infer that these results must have been obtained with a small Laplace correction. This problem has a fairly small number of examples and many features have values that are present in only one or two examples.

To demonstrate the use of APM for handling highly correlated features, and for aggregating multiple models, we performed the following experiment with the SDNA data. We generated 11 different Naïve Bayes models, one using all the original 60 features, and the other 10 generated by randomly selecting features from the original set, but with a bias towards including the more useful features. These 11 different probability models were combined using APM and APMR. The results in Table 2 show that even though the in-

Table 2. Comparison of APM and APMR for the SDNA problem using 11 input features, the class predictions from 11 Naïve Bayes models. Columns are as in Table 1.

Class	Method	Error (%)	Loss
SDNA (with 11 NB model outputs as inputs to APM/APMR)			
1	APM	2.77 (0.85)	0.12 (0.05)
	APMR	2.87 (0.92)	0.12 (0.05)
2	APM	3.02 (0.91)	0.15 (0.06)
	APMR	2.83 (0.86)	0.14 (0.05)
3	APM	6.52 (1.57)	0.24 (0.04)
	APMR	6.64 (1.47)	0.24 (0.04)
All	APM	4.0 (1.0)	0.24 (0.07)
	APMR	3.93 (0.95)	0.23 (0.06)

dividual model predictions are highly correlated, the APMR algorithm produced aggregated models that are comparable to the APMR model with all 60 individual features. We note that the individual models being aggregated need not be NB; they can be be decision trees, nearest-neighbor, or any technique that provides a class probability output.

5. Concluding Remarks

Many authors have shown the close connection between logistic regression and NB [4], [11], and a "weighted NB" method has also been used with fixed exponentiating weights in a text categorization application [18]. Closest to our approach is the weighted NB of [19] and the WBC_{SVM} model of [8]. In our notation, these models may be formulated analogously to model (4) as

$$P(C|X) \propto \{P(C)\}^{\alpha_0} \prod_j \{P(X_j|C)\}^{\alpha_j} . \quad (12)$$

In [8], the kernel is defined similarly to APM's q values in equation (6), and is optimized for minimum classification error rate using support vector machines. There is an important difference between APM and these methods: APM does not fit an importance measure α_0, because in APM the importance weights are used to only compensate for any class-conditional correlations among the explanatory features. In addition, we have shown how APM and APMR can use the output of any probabilistic model as an input feature. Our experiments show that compared with NB, the APM/APMR approach provides the same or better classification accuracy, with much better estimates of the class probability, which is desirable for many applications.

References

[1] L. Breiman. Bagging Predictors. *Machine Learning*, 24:123–140, 1996.

[2] A. P. Dawid. Probability forecasting. In S. Kotz, N. L. Johnson, and C. B. Read, editors, *Encyclopedia of Statistical Sciences*, volume 6, pages 210–218. Wiley, New York, 1982.

[3] P. Domingos and M. Pazzani. On the Optimality of the Simple Bayesian Classifier under zero-one loss. *Machine Learning*, 29:103–130, 1997.

[4] C. Elkan. Boosting and Naïve Bayesian learning. *Technical Report CS97-557, University of California, San Diego*, 1997.

[5] Y. Freund and L. Mason. The alternating decision tree learning algorithm. *Proceedings of ICML-99*, 1999.

[6] Y. Freund and R. Shapire. Experiments with a new boosting algorithm. In *Proceedings of ICML-96*, 1996.

[7] A. Garg and D. Roth. Understanding probabilistic classifiers. In *Proceedings of ECML-2001*, 2001.

[8] T. Gärtner and P. A. Flach. WBCsvm: Weighted Bayesian Classification based on Support Vector Machines. *Proceedings of ICML-2001*, pages 154–161, 2001.

[9] I. J. Good. Rational decisions. *Journal of the Royal Statistical Society, Series B*, 14:107–114, 1952.

[10] M. A. Hall and G. Holmes. Benchmarking attribute selection techniques for data mining. Technical report, Dept. of Comp. Sci., Univ. of Waikato, Hamilton, New Zealand, 2000.

[11] D. J. Hand and N. M. Adams. Defining attributes for score-card construction. *Journal of Applied Statistics*, 27:527–540, 2000.

[12] D. J. Hand and K. Yu. Idiot's bayes—not so stupid after all. *International Statistical Review*, 69:385–398, 2001.

[13] T. Hastie, R. Tibshirani, and J. Friedman. *The Elements of Statistical Learning*. Springer, New York, 2001.

[14] S. J. Hong, J. Hosking, and R. Natarajan. Multiplicative adjustment of class probability: Educating Naïve Bayes. Technical Report RC-22393, IBM Thomas J. Watson Research Center, Yorktown Heights, NY 10598, 2002.

[15] R. Kohavi, B. Becker, and D. Sommerfield. Improving Simple Bayes. Technical report, Data Mining and Visualization group, Silicon Graphics Inc., Mountain View, Calif., 1997.

[16] G. Piatetsky-Shapiro and S. Steingold. Measuring lift quality in database marketing. *SIGKDD Explorations*, 2:76–80, 2000.

[17] J. R. Quinlan. Bagging, Boosting and C4.5. In *Proceedings of AAAI-96*, 1996.

[18] J. D. M. Rennie. Improving Multi-class Text Classification with Naive Bayes. M.S. thesis, Dept. of Elec. Eng. and Comp. Sci., Carnegie-Mellon University, Pittsburgh, 1999.

[19] D. J. Spiegelhalter and R. P. Knill-Jones. Statistical and knowledge-based approaches to clinical decision-support systems, with an application in gastroenterology. *Journal of the Royal Statistical Society, Series A*, 147:35–77, 1984.

624

Mining A Set of Coregulated RNA Sequences

Yuh-Jyh Hu

Computer and Information Science Department
National Chiao Tung University
1001 Ta Hsueh Rd., Hsinchu, Taiwan
E-mail: yhu@cis.nctu.edu.tw

Abstract

Post-transcriptional regulation, though less studied, is an important research topic in bioinformatics. In a set of post-transcriptionally coregulated RNAs, the basepair interactions can organize the molecules into domains and provide a framework for functional interactions. Their consensus motifs may represent the binding sites of RNA regulatory proteins. Unlike DNA motifs, RNA motifs are more conserved in structures than in sequences. Knowing the structural motifs can help us better understand the regulation activities. In this paper, we propose a novel data mining approach to RNA secondary structure prediction. To demonstrate the performance of our new approach, we first tested it on the same data sets previously used and published in literature. Secondly, to show the flexibility of our new approach, we also tested it on a data set that contains pseudoknot motifs that most current systems cannot identify.

1 Introduction

RNA molecules serve not only as carriers of information, but also as functionally active units. They play an important role in post-transcriptional regulation. Like transcriptional regulation, post-transcriptional regulation is often accomplished by the binding of proteins to specific motifs in mRNA molecules [3]. What is different from DNA binding proteins, which recognize motifs composed of conserved sequences, is that RNA protein binding sites are more conserved in structures than in sequences. The motif prediction algorithms that only consider conserved sequence profiles [8] [11] [1] [14] [9] may fail to identify RNA motifs. A set of post-transcriptionally coregulated RNAs can be characterized by basepair interactions that organize the molecules into domains and provide a framework for functional interactions. If a new sequence is found to contain the common motifs, it may have the same characteristics

as those coregulated RNAs. We are interested in finding the consensus motifs in a family of coregulated RNA sequences.

Current main approaches to RNA secondary structure prediction include free-energy minimization [15] [13] and comparative sequence analysis [10] [7] . Although they show positive results of predicting secondary structures of a single sequence, it is questionable to use these methods to find common motifs in a set of sequences. Other approaches such as stochastic context-free grammars, e.g. COVE [4], and genetic algorithms [2] have been applied to multiple sequences, but they are aimed to find a global alignment instead of consensus motifs. A dynamic programming approach called FOLDALIGN, which takes into account both sequence similarity and structure constraints was first developed to discover RNA motifs in a set of sequences [5]. However, its time complexity is too high for practical use. Recently a new system called SLASH [6] has been developed. By combining FOLDALIGN and COVE, the time complexity of SLASH is acceptable for real applications, but it is currently limited to find stem-loop motifs.

In this paper we introduce a new approach for discovering structural motifs more complicated than stem-loop structures. To prove it is comparable to the latest approaches, we tested the new approach on the same data sets as used in the experiments of SLASH. Furthermore, we tested it on a published pseudoknot data set to demonstrate its capability that most current prediction methods lack.

2 Finding Consensus RNA Motifs

We consider motif prediction a supervised learning problem. Unlike most current approaches, we use both positive and negative examples. Positive examples are a family of coregulated RNA sequences; negative examples are the same number of sequences randomly generated based on the observed frequencies of sequence alphabet in positive examples. We learn the motifs that can be used to distinguish the given coregulated sequences from the random sequences.

As RNA motifs may vary in both sequences and structures, we need an expressive representation to describe a wide variety of motifs, and an effective strategy to search a large problem space for the right motifs. Because of its generality and effectiveness, we adapt genetic programming to find RNA motifs. Since RNA secondary structures are typically formed by basepairing interactions, we are focused on finding Watson-Crick complementary basepairs. There are three components in our approach. The first is a population of putative structural motifs. The second is a fitness function that measures the quality of each motif. The third is the genetic operators that simulate the natural evolution process. The details are described in the following sections.

2.1 How to represent individuals in a population

Each individual in a population is a putative motif. We use two kinds of segments to describe structural motifs. A segment is either a Watson-Crick complementary segment or a nonpairing segment. With different combinations of segments, a wide variety of RNA motifs can be easily represented.

To find the motifs from a family of RNA sequences, the user first specifies the maximum number of segments and the range of segment length allowed in a motif. According to the specification, we generate the initial population of putative motifs. The number of segments and the segment length in each motif are randomly assigned but conform to the user's specification. Besides, the pairing relation between complementary segments is determined at random. After the initial population is created, genetic operators are applied to the population to generate a better population of motifs. This evolution process is repeated until no improvement can be found.

2.2 How to measure the quality of individuals

We are interested in the motifs that can reflect the characteristics conserved in a family of coregulated RNA sequences, e.g. the RNA protein binding sites. We design a fitness function that assigns higher values to those motifs commonly shared by the given set of RNAs, and rarely contained in random sequences. We borrowed the idea of the F-score [12] to design our fitness function. The F-score is used in the field of information retrieval with the aim to balance the importance of two measures, recall (i.e. sensitivity) and precision (i.e. positive predictive value). Given a positive example set and a negative example set, we define the fitness function as follows:

$$Fitness(motif_i) = \frac{2 * Recall(motif_i) * Precision(motif_i)}{Recall(motif_i) + Precision(motif_i)}$$

$$Recall(motif_i) = \frac{no.\ of\ positive\ examples\ containing\ motif_i}{no.\ of\ total\ positive\ examples}$$

$$Precision(motif_i) = \frac{no.\ of\ positive\ examples\ containing\ motif_i}{no.\ of\ examples\ containing\ motif_i}$$

Which motif will be chosen to participate in the genetic operation, e.g. mutation, is dependent on fitness. Motifs with higher fitness have better chances of being selected. We adapt the tournament selection mechanism. It parallels the competition in nature among individuals for the right to take part in evolution. Unlike fitness-proportionate selection, tournament selection does not need a centralized calculation of the average fitness of the population, and it is somewhat faster than rank selection.

2.3 Genetic operators

Currently, we only apply three basic genetic operators in our method, reproduction, mutation and crossover. Reproduction simulates the self-replication process in nature. Instead of selecting one motif at a time, and passing it to the next generation, we accelerates the reproduction process by passing the better half of the population sorted by fitness from generation to generation.

Like the mutation operation in nature that causes sporadic and random alterations in the genetic materials, the mutation operator changes the segment configuration of a motif selected from the population. It first randomly picks a segment of the motif for alteration. If a complementary segment is selected, its corresponding pairing segment and its length range are then randomly changed. On the other hand, if a nonpairing segment is chosen, only its length range is changed. Note that the segment length can only be randomly altered within the range specified by the user.

Unlike mutation, the crossover operation is performed on two individuals. Its purpose is to exchange the segment configuration between two tentative motifs to generate two offspring. After two motifs are selected from the population, either a pair of complementary segments or a nonpairing segment is chosen at random for exchange.

3 Experimental Results

The purpose of our experiments is two-fold. The first is to demonstrate that our new approach is competitive with current RNA motif prediction systems. The second is to show that it can identify complicated motifs that most current systems cannot find.

To keep the consistency of a comparative study, It is important to use the same data sets in experiments. As SLASH (15) is the latest RNA motif prediction system, we first tested our approach on the same data sets as used in SLASH's experiments to show its competitive performance. Moreover, we used a published pseudoknot data set to demonstrate its flexibility that is lacking in most current systems, including SLASH. These data sets are described in the following sections.

3.1 Data sets

The first data set contains 34 archaea 16S ribosomal sequences and was previously used to test SLASH [6]. This data set was originally derived from a set of 311 sequences extracted from the SSU rRNA database (http://www-rna.uia.ac.be/ssu/). The archaea set of 311 sequences was further reduced to 34, filtering out the sequences that miss base assignments or are greater than 90% identical. To ensure that the sequences can only be aligned locally, Gorodkin *et al.* further randomly truncated each sequence at both ends by up to 20 nt (15).

The second data set is another data set used in the experiments of SLASH. It is the ferritin IRE-like data set (iron response element) constructed by Gorodkin *et al.* [6]. They first obtained 14 sequences from the UTR database. Since the selected IRE regions are significantly conserved not only in structure but also in sequence, even sequence motif finding algorithms can identify them within the UTRs. Therefore, they modified the IREs and their UTRs to make the search more difficult. By iteratively shuffling the sequences and randomly adding one nucleotide to the IRE conserved region, they obtained a set of 56 IRE-like sequences from the 14 IRE UTRs.

The third data set includes 18 viral 3'UTRs each of which contains a pseudoknot. Seven of the RNA sequences are the soil-borne rye mosaic viruses; the others are the soil-borne wheat mosaic viruses. We first retrieved the pseudoknot sequences from the PseudoBase (http://wwwbio.leidenuniv.nl/ ~Batenburg/PKB.html). Their accession numbers in PseudoBase are listed as PKB183-PKB189 and PKB194-PKB204. As the pseudoknots are relatively short, to make the search for the pseudoknots more challenging, we randomly include the flanking of 5 to 70 nt at both ends of each pseudoknot sequence.

3.2 Evaluation

As Gorodkin *et al.* [6], we applied the Matthews correlation coefficient (23) to quantify the agreement between the predicted motif and the actual structure assignment. For each sequence in the data set, two secondary structure assignments were compared by counting the number of true positives P_t (base pairs exist in actual assignment and are predicted), true negatives N_t (base pairs do not exist in actual assignment and are not predicted), false positives P_f (base pairs do not exist in actual assignment but are predicted) and false negatives N_f (base pairs exist in actual assignment but are not predicted), respectively. The Matthews correlation coefficient can then be computed as:

Table 1. The experimental results of three data sets. The first row shows the total number of sequences in each data set. Row 2 to 4 present the minimum, the maximum and the average sequence length respectively. The fifth row gives the standard deviation of sequence length. Row 6 and 7 provide the correlation coefficient averaged over 30 runs, and its standard deviation. In each run, we used a random negative set of the same size as the positive set.

Data set	archaea rRNA	IRE_like	viral 3'UTR
Total Sequences	34	56	18
Min Seq Length	90	117	37
Max Seq Length	108	330	137
Avg Seq Length	97.59	202.93	63.89
Seq Length std	3.77	59.31	25.95
Avg Coefficient	0.87	0.99	0.76
Coefficient std	0.02	0.02	0.05

Table 2. Tableau for RNA secondary structure prediction problem.

Objective:	Given a family of functionally related RNA sequences, predict the common structure motifs.
Terminal set:	User-specified pairing and non-pairing segment length ranges, and pairing segment indices.
Functional set:	Watson-Crick complementarity and structure element connections
Fitness measure	F-score based on precision and recall
Selection method:	Tournament selection
Parameters:	population size = 1000 maximum number of generations = 50 crossover rate = 50% mutation rate = 90% reproduction rate = 50%

$$C = \frac{P_t N_t - P_f N_f}{\sqrt{(N_t + N_f)(N_t + P_f)(P_t + N_f)(P_t + P_f)}}$$

Given that the sequence length is sufficiently large, the Matthews correlation coefficient can be approximated in the following way (15).

$$C \approx \sqrt{\frac{P_t}{P_t + N_f} \frac{P_t}{P_t + P_f}}$$

With the published/curated alignments, we can evaluate the performance of our approach by calculating the Matthews correlation coefficient. Due to its stochastic characteristics, our method was repeatedly tested 30 times on each of the data sets. The correlation coefficients averaged over 30 runs are presented in Table 1, and Table 2 is the GP tableau for the RNA secondary structure prediction problem.

4 Discussion

RNA molecules play an important role in post-transcriptional regulation. Knowing the common structural motifs in a set of coregulated RNA sequences will help us better understand the regulation mechanism. We developed a genetic programming approach to finding consensus structural motifs in a set of RNA sequences known to be functionally related. With flexible GP operators and structural motif representations, our new method is able to identify general RNA secondary motifs.

To show it is comparable to the latest RNA motif prediction systems, we tested the new method on the same data sets previously used in order to keep the consistency. We first tested it on a set of archaeal rRNA sequences that contain locally aligned stem-loop regions. By comparing with the curated database alignment, we were able to evaluate our new approach quantitatively by the Matthews correlation coefficient. We obtained a 0.87 correlation coefficient between the predicted structural alignment and the curated database alignment. This is similar to the published experimental results [6]. We also tested it on the ferritin IRE-like data set created by Gorodkin et al. [6], and obtained a 0.99 correlation coefficient. Our new method was further tested on a a set of viral 3'UTR pseudoknot regions extracted from the PseudoBase to demonstrate its capability that current RNA motif finding algorithms lack.

The future work can be carried out in two directions. First, we plan to enhance the fitness function by incorporating background knowledge such as thermodynamic or phylogenetic information. Second, our approach is currently limited to find basepairing structures. We will extend the motif representation and the genetic operators to deal with more complex structures, e.g. base triples and structures with multi-branch loops.

5 Acknowledgments

Thanks to Jan Gorodkin for providing the valuable archaea 16S rRNA sequences and the ferritin IRE-like data set. This project is partially supported by National Science Council, Taiwan (NSC 90-2213-E-009-169).

References

[1] T. Bailey and C. Elkan. Unsupervised learning of multiple motifs in biopolymers using expectation maximization. *Machine Learning*, 21:51–80, 1995.

[2] J.-H. Chen, S.-Y. Le, and J. Maizel. Prediction of common secondary structures of rnas: a genetic algorithm approach. *Nucleic Acids Res.*, 28:991–999, 2000.

[3] S. Cygi, Y. Rochon, B. Franza, and R. Aebersold. Correlation between protein and mrna abundance in yeast. *Mol. Cell Biol.*, 19:1720–1730, 1999.

[4] S. Eddy and R. Durbin. Rna sequence analysis using covariance models. *Nucleic Acids Res.*, 22:2079–2088, 1994.

[5] J. Gorodkin, L. Heyer, and G. Stormo. Finding the most significant common sequence and structure motifs in a set of rna sequences. *Nucleic Acids Res.*, 25:3724–3732, 1997.

[6] J. Gorodkin, S. Stricklin, and G. Stormo. Discovering common stem-loop motifs in unaligned rna sequences. *Nucleic Acids Res.*, 29:2135–2144, 2001.

[7] R. Gutell, N. Larsen, and C. Woese. Lessons from an evolving rrna: 16s and 23s rrna structures from a comparative perspective. *Microbiol. Rev.*, 58:10–26, 1994.

[8] G. Hertz, G. I. Hartzell, and G. Stormo. Identification of consensus patterns in unaligned dna sequences known to be functionally related. *Comput. Appl. Biosci.*, 6:81–92, 1990.

[9] Y. Hu, S. Sandmeyer, C. McLaughlin, and D. Kibler. Combinatorial motif analysis and hypothesis generation on a genomic scale. *Bioinformatics*, 16:222–232, 2000.

[10] A. Laferriere, D. Gautheret, and R. Cedergren. An rna pattern matching program with enhanced performance and portability. *Comput. Appl. Biosci.*, 10:211–212, 1994.

[11] C. Lawrence, S. Altschul, M. Boguski, J. Liu, A. Neuwald, and J. Wootton. Detecting subtle sequence signals: A gibbs sampling strategy for multiple alignments. *Science*, 262:208–214, 1993.

[12] D. Lewis and W. Gale. A sequential algorithm for training text classifier. *in Proceedings of the 17th Annual International ACM-SIGIR Conference on Research and Development in Information Retrieval*, pages 3–12, 1994.

[13] E. Rivas and S. Eddy. A dynamic programming algorithm for rna structure prediction including pseudoknots. *J. Mol. Biol.*, 285:2053–2068, 1999.

[14] J. van Helden, B. Andre, and J. Collado-Vides. Extracting regulatory sites from the upstream region of yeast genes by computational analysis of oligonucleotide frequencies. *J. Mol. Biol.*, 281:827–842, 1998.

[15] M. Zuker and P. Stiegler. Optimal computer folding of large rna sequences using thermodynamic and auxiliary information. *Nucleic Acids Res.*, 9:133–148, 1981.

Association Analysis with One Scan of Databases*

Hao Huang [(+)], Xindong Wu [(*)] and Richard Relue [(+)]

[(+)] Dept. of Math and Computer Science, Colorado School of Mines
Golden, Colorado 80401, USA

[(*)] Department of Computer Science, University of Vermont
Burlington, Vermont 05405, USA

Abstract

Mining frequent patterns with an FP-tree avoids costly candidate generation and repeatedly occurrence frequency checking against the support threshold. It therefore achieves better performance and efficiency than Apriori-like algorithms. However, the database still needs to be scanned twice to get the FP-tree. This can be very time-consuming when new data are added to an existing database because two scans may be needed for not only the new data but also the existing data. This paper presents a new data structure P-tree, Pattern Tree, and a new technique, which can get the P-tree through only one scan of the database and can obtain the corresponding FP-tree with a specified support threshold. Updating a P-tree with new data needs one scan of the new data only, and the existing data do not need to be re-scanned.

1 Introduction

An association rule is an implication of the form $X \Longrightarrow Y$, where X and Y are sets of items and $X \cap Y = \phi$. The support s of such a rule is that $s\%$ of transactions in the database contain $X \cup Y$; the confidence c is that $c\%$ of transactions in the database contain X also contain Y at the meantime. A rule can be considered interesting if it satisfies the minimum support threshold and minimum confidence threshold, which can be set by domain experts. Most of the previous research with regard to association mining was based on Apriori-like algorithms [1]. They can be decomposed into two steps:

1. Find all frequent itemsets that hold transaction support above the minimum support threshold.

2. Generate the desired rules from the frequent itemsets if they also satisfy the minimum confidence threshold.

Apriori-like algorithms iteratively obtain candidate itemsets of size $(k + 1)$ from frequent itemsets of size k. Each iteration requires a scan of the original database. It is costly

---

*This research is supported in part by the U.S. Army Research Laboratory and the U.S. Army Research Office under grant number DAAD19-02-1-0178.

and inefficient to repeatedly scan the database and check a large set of candidates for their occurrence frequencies. Additionally, when new data come in, we have to run the entire algorithms again to update the rules.

Recently, an FP-tree based frequent patterns mining method [2] developed by Han et al achieves high efficiency, compared with Apriori and TreeProjection [3] algorithms. It avoids iterative candidate generations.

The rest of the paper is organized as follows. We review the FP-tree structure in Section 2. In Section 3, we introduce a new FP-tree based data structure, called pattern tree, or P-tree, and discuss how to generate the P-tree by only one database scan. How to generate an FP-tree from a P-tree is discussed in Section 4. Section 5 deals with updating the P-tree with new data, and Section 6 provides a reference for our experimental results.

2 Frequent Pattern Mining and the Frequent Pattern Tree

The frequent-pattern mining problem can be formally defined as follows. Let $I = \{i_1, i_2, ..., i_n\}$ be a set of items, and D be a transactions database, where each transaction T is a set of items and $T \subseteq I$. An unique identifier, called its *TID*, is assigned with each transaction. A transaction T contains a pattern P, a set of items in I, if $P \subseteq T$. The support of a pattern P is the number of transactions containing P in D. We say that P is a frequent pattern if P's support is no less than a predefined minimum support threshold ξ.

A frequent pattern tree is a prefix-tree structure storing frequent patterns for the transaction database, where the support of each tree node is no less than a predefined minimum support threshold ξ. The frequent items in each path are sorted in their frequency descending order. More frequently occurring nodes have better chances of sharing the prefix strings than less frequently occurring ones, that is to say, more frequent nodes are closer to the root than less frequent ones. In short, an FP-tree is a highly compact data structure, "which is usually substantially smaller than the original database, and thus saves the costly database scans in the subsequent mining processes" [2].

After the construction of an FP-tree, we can use this data

structure to efficiently mine the complete set of frequent patterns with the FP-growth algorithm, which is a divide-and-conquer method performed as follows:

1. Derive a set of conditional paths, which co-occurs with a suffix pattern, from the FP-tree.

2. Construct a conditional FP-tree for each set of the conditional paths.

3. Execute the frequent pattern mining recursively upon the conditional FP-tree.

The study in [2] shows that the FP-growth algorithm is more efficient and scalable than both Apriori and TreeProjection [3]. The FP-tree based algorithm has some inherent advantages: the new data structure is desirably compact and the pattern growth algorithm is efficient with the data structure. But it also has the following problems:

1. A new FP-tree requires scanning the database twice.

2. Although a validity support threshold, watermark [2], is realizable, there is no guarantee of complete database information for the FP-tree when new data come into the database.

3. If the specific threshold is changed, we will have to rerun the whole FP-tree construction algorithm, that is, rescan the database twice to get the new corresponding frequent item list and a new FP-tree.

4. Even if the threshold remains the same, an FP-tree can't be constructed or updated at real-time. Each construction or updating needs to go from scratch, and scan the new and old data twice.

3 Patterns Generation with the Pattern Tree

The FP-tree based method has to scan the database twice to get an FP-tree, whose central idea is to get the list L of item frequencies in the first time and then construct the FP-tree in the second time according to L.

A Pattern Tree (P-tree for short), unlike FP-tree, which contains the frequent items only, contains all items that appear in the original database. We can obtain a P-tree through one scan of the database and get the corresponding FP-tree from the P-tree later.

The construction of a P-tree can be divided into two steps as well:

1. When retrieving transactions from a database, we can generate a P-tree by inserting transactions one by one after we sort the items of each transaction in some order (alphabetic, numerical or any other specific order), and meanwhile record the actual support of every item into the item frequency list L.

2. After the first and only scan of the database, we sort L according to item supports. The restructure of the P-tree consists of similar insertions in the first step. The only difference is that one needs to sort the path according to L before inserting it into a new P-tree.

This approach makes the best use of the occurrence of the common suffix in transactions, thereby constructing a more compact tree structure than FP-tree.

3.1 Algorithm

Algorithm 1 (P-Tree Generation)

Input: A transaction database DB and a minimum support threshold *minisup*

Output: A Pattern tree

The pattern tree can be created in two steps:

Step 1: Construct a P-tree P and obtain the item frequency list L.

(1) $P \leftarrow Root$
(2) $L \leftarrow \phi$
(3) For each transaction T in the transaction database
    a. Sort T into $[t \mid T_i]$ in alphabetic order. Here in each sorted transaction $T = [t \mid T_i]$, t is the first item of the transaction and T_i is the remaining items in the transaction.
    b. $Insert([t \mid T_i], P)$
    c. Update L with items in $[t \mid T_i]$

The function $Insert([t \mid T_i], P)$ performs as follows.

Function $Insert([t \mid T_i], P)$
  BEGIN
    FOR each of P's child node N
      IF $t.itemName = N.itemName$
        THEN
          $N.frequency \leftarrow N.frequency+1$
          IF T_i is not empty
            THEN
              $Insert(T_i, N)$
          ENDIF
          RETURN
      ENDIF
    ENDFOR
    Create a new Node N'
    $N'.itemName \leftarrow t.itemName$
    $N'.frequency \leftarrow 1$
    $P.childList \leftarrow N'$
    IF T_i is not empty
      THEN $Insert(T_i, N')$
    ENDIF
    RETURN
  END

Step 2: Restructure the initial P-tree P

(1) $newP \leftarrow Root$
(2) For each path p_i from the root to a leaf in the initial P-tree P, Until $p_i = \phi$ do:
    a. The common support of each item in p_i is that of the node next to the last branching-node. If there is no branching-node in p_i, the common support of each item is the actual support of each item in p_i.
    A branching-node is a node after which there exists more than one branch in the tree.
    b. Get a sub-path p_i' from p_i with the common support for every item.
    c. Sort p_i' according to L.
    d. Insert the sorted p_i' into the new P-tree, by calling function $Insert(p_i', newP)$.
    e. $p_i \leftarrow p_i - p_i'$.

3.2 Analysis

The P-tree generation algorithm needs exactly one scan of the database and one scan of the initial P-tree. The running time depends on how the patterns distribute in the database. The more high frequent patterns in the database, the faster the algorithm will be. The lower bound is the runtime of one scan of the database. In the contrary, the less the high frequent patterns in the database, the slower the algorithm will be. The upper bound is the runtime of two database scans.

3.3 Pattern Tree: A Formal Definition

A pattern tree (or P-tree for short) is a rooted tree structure, which has the following properties:

1. The root is labeled as "*Root*". All other items are either its children or its descendants.

2. Each node except the root is composed of three fields: *itemName*, *frequency* and *childList*, where *itemName* stands for the actual item in the transaction database, *frequency* represents the transaction support of the item in the database, and *childList* stores a list of its child nodes.

3. A path in a P-tree represents at least one transaction and the corresponding occurrence(s), which is the *frequency* of its least frequent item(s).

4. A node holds more or equal frequency to its children or descendants. Note that the root node doesn't have the actual meaning in transactions, so we don't consider its frequency.

5. A prefix shared by several paths represents the common pattern in those transactions and its frequency. The more paths share the prefix, the higher frequency it has.

4 FP-Tree Generation from the P-Tree

From the definition of the P-tree, we can observe that an FP-tree is a sub-tree of the P-tree with a specified support threshold, which contains those frequent items that meet this threshold and hereby excludes infrequent items. We will propose an algorithm and analyze it in this section.

4.1 Algorithm

After the generation of the P-tree, we can easily get the frequent item list given a specific support threshold. All we need to do is to get rid of those infrequent items from item frequency list L. Next, we prune the P-tree to exclude the infrequent nodes by checking the frequency of each node along the path from the root to leaves. Because the frequency of each node is not less than that of its children or descendents, we delete the node and its subtrees at the same time if it is infrequent.

Algorithm 2 (FP Generation from the P-Tree)
Input: A P-tree P, the frequency list L, & the support threshold ξ
Output: An FP-tree

1. Frequent Item List $FIList \leftarrow \phi$
2. For each item i in L
   If $i.frequency \geq \xi$
      Add i to $FIList$
3. Sort $FIList$ in frequency descending order
4. Invoke $check(P)$. The function $check$ is described as follows.
   Function $check(N)$
      BEGIN
         FOR each child c of the node N
            IF $c \in FIList$
               THEN
                  $check(c)$
               ELSE
                  Delete c (and the possible subtree starting from c)
            ENDIF
         ENDFOR
         RETURN
      END

4.2 Analysis

In practice, we can compare the user-defined minimum support threshold with the occurrence recorded in the item frequency list. So the pruning could be done according to the following two rules:

1. If the minimum support threshold is higher than the occurrence of most items, then we can check the items along the path beginning from the root as mentioned in Section 3.1. Once an infrequent item is found, its subtree including itself is deleted from the pattern tree.

2. When the occurrence of most items is above the minimum support threshold, we can check the items along the path beginning from the leaves, the inverse order with the first rule. As long as a frequent item is found, we keep it and prune its subtree.

Regardless of which rule is applied, the algorithm checks at most half amount of items in a pattern tree. In the mining process, the users always need to adjust the support thresholds to achieve an appropriate one. If the support threshold is set too high, the process may produce fewer frequent items and some important rules can not be generated. On the other hand, if the support threshold is set too low, the process may produce too many frequent items and some rules may become meaningless. One advantage of our approach is that we can easily get different FP-trees corresponding to different support thresholds. When the support threshold is changed, no further database scans are needed.

5 Updating the Pattern Tree with New Data

One concern with the P-tree is how to update it with new data. In this section, we will propose an algorithm to solve the problem and illustrate the process with an example.

As the database can always be updated, how to update the old rules is an important problem in data mining. There are two ways to update an FP-tree. One is to apply the construction algorithm to the new database, i.e. scan the updated database twice. In this case, the previous two scans of the old database are discarded. The other is to set "a validity support threshold (called watermark)" in [2]. The watermark goes up to exclude the originally infrequent items while their frequency goes up. But it may need to go down since the frequency of frequent items may drop when more and more transactions come in. This solution can't guarantee the completeness of the generated association rules. With new information the originally infrequent items may become frequent and vice versa.

Since we can generate the P-tree by scanning the database only once, we are also able to update the P-tree by one scan of new data without the need for two scans of the existing database and the second scan for the new data.

We can first insert the new transactions into the P-tree according to the item frequency list and meanwhile update the list. Then a new P-tree can be restructured according to the updated item frequency list. In the case there comes a new item, which does not appear in the existing database, we can assume its support is 0 and append it as a leaf node.

5.1 Algorithm

Algorithm 3 (P-Tree Updating)

Input: The original P-tree, *P1*, the original item frequency list, *L*, and a new transaction database *DB'*. (Note that with a compact format the original P-tree *P1* contains all items in the existing transaction database no matter whether or not they are frequent.)

Output: Updated pattern tree, *P2*

Step 1: Expand P1 using new data and meanwhile update L.

(1) For each transaction T in the new transaction database *DB'*

    a. Sort T according to the original frequency list L

    b. *Insert(T, P1)*

    c. Update L with items in T

(2) Sort L in frequency descending order.

Step 2: Restructure the expanded P-tree P1 into P2 according to the updated L.

(1) $P2 \leftarrow Root$

(2) For each path p_i in *P1*,

    Until $p_i = \phi$ do:

        a. Let s be the common support of each item in p_i.

        b. Get a sub-path p_i' from p_i with the common support for every item.

        c. Sort p_i' according to L.

        d. *Insert(p_i', P2)*.

        e. $p_i \leftarrow p_i - p_i'$.

5.2 Analysis

The most difficult problem concerning the FP-tree is to handle updates in the database. Once some new transactions are added, a new FP-tree has to be constructed to deal with these changes. The main advantages of the above algorithm in Section 5.1 are:

1. There is no further need to scan the existing database, because the original P-tree is already a compact version. Thus, the algorithm makes updating the P-tree more efficient by reusing the old computations on the original database.

2. We need to scan the new data only once. According to [2], an FP-tree is obtained by two scans of the entire database, including the existing and new database.

3. In the worst case, the cost of our algorithm is still $O(m * n)$, where m is the maximum length of transactions and n the number of the transactions in the database.

6 Tests and Results

We have performed experiments with multiple FP-tree generation and FP-tree updating while new data are added. Our test results show that the P-tree method outperforms the FP-tree method by an factor up to an order of magnitude in large datasets. The test environment, test databases, and detailed results are omitted in this paper due to size restrictions and can be found in [4].

7 Conclusions

We have proposed a new data structure, pattern tree or P-tree, and discussed how to obtain the P-tree by one database scan and how to update the P-tree by one scan of new data. Moreover, we have addressed how to get the corresponding FP-trees from the P-tree with different user-specified thresholds and also the completeness property of the P-tree. We have implemented the P-tree method and presented the test results in [4], showing that our method always outperforms the FP-tree method.

The key point of our method is to make best use of the P-tree structure, which presents a large database in a highly condensed format, and avoids the second database scan.

References

[1] M.-Y. Chen, J. Han, and P. Yu. Data Mining: An Overview from a Database Perspective. *IEEE Transactions on Knowledge and Data Engineering*. **8**(6): 866–883, 1996.

[2] J. Han, J. Pei, and Y. Yin. Mining Frequent Patterns Without Candidate Generation. *Proc. of ACM Int. Conf. on Management of Data (SIGMOD)*, 1–12, 2000.

[3] R. Agarwal, C. Aggarwal, and V. V. V. Prasad. A Tree Projection Algorithm for Generation of Frequent Itemsets. *Journal of Parallel and Distributed Computing*, **61**(3): 350–371, 2001.

[4] H. Huang, X. Wu and R. Relue. Association Analysis with One Scan of Databases. *University of Vermont Computer Science Technical Report CS-02-3*, 2002. http://www.cs.uvm.edu/tr/CS-02-03.shtml

Implementation of a Least Fixpoint Operator for Fast Mining of Relational Databases*

Hasan M. Jamil
Department of Computer Science
Mississippi State University, USA
jamil@cs.msstate.edu

Abstract

Recent research has focused on computing large item sets for association rule mining using SQL3 least fixpoint computation, and by exploiting the monotonic nature of the SQL3 aggregate functions such as **sum** *and* create view recursive *constructs. Such approaches allow us to view mining as an ad hoc querying exercise and treat the efficiency issue as an optimization problem. In this paper, we present a recursive implementation of a recently proposed least fixpoint operator for computing large item sets from object-relational databases. We present experimental evidence to show that our implementation compares well with several well-regarded and contemporary algorithms for large item set generation.*

1 Introduction

The importance and need for integrating data mining with relational databases have been addressed in several articles such as [7, 9]. The authors convincingly argue that without such integration, data mining technology may not find itself in a viable position in the years to come. To be a successful and feasible tool for the analysis of business data in relational databases, such technology must be made available as part of database query engines in a declarative way.

Declarative computation of association rules were investigated in works such as [6, 8, 9]. Meo et al. [6] proposes a new SQL like declarative query language for association rule mining which appears to be heavily oriented towards transaction databases[1]. In their extended language, they blend a rule mine operator with SQL and other additional features. The series of research reported in [8, 9] spear headed by IBM researchers mostly addressed the mining issue itself. They attempted to compute the large item sets by generating candidate sets testing for their admissibility based on their MC model, combination, and GatherJoin operators. Essentially, these works represent a faithful encoding of apriori like algorithms using SQL, and like [6], become too specific.

In a series of recent research [3, 4, 5], we have shown that association rules can be easily computed as ad hoc SQL3 queries without requiring any specialized relational operators or language constructs. SQL3's recursive view construct was particularly useful in developing the least fixpoint queries that involved the monotonic aggregate function **sum** inside

the recursion. Two approaches were proposed. In [3, 4], we have investigated computation of large item sets using a computationally expensive recursive join computation. But it was shown that unlike apriori like approaches, it can be made to compute only non-redundant large item sets. In [5], an apriori like fixpoint computation was also proposed. This approach required the development of a $\mathbf{T}_P$ like operator usually found in deductive database literature. The idea for such an operator was captured in the following representative SQL3 view definition for large item sets called the l_table. In the following SQL3 expressions t_table(TranID, Items) is supplied as the input transaction table where TranID is the transaction ID and Items is a set of items (readers may refer to [5] for a complete discussion on these expressions and the fixpoint computation approach).

```
create view f_table as
(select Items, count(Items)/m as Support
from t_table
group by Items);

create sequence seq increment by 1 start with 1;

create view recursive l_table as
((select Items, sum(Support) as Support
from (flatten(select sub(Items, {}, 1) as Items, Support
    from f_table))
group by Items
having sum(Support) ≥ δm)
union all
(select t.Items, sum(t.Support) as Support
from f_table as u,
    (flatten distinct(select sub(f.Items, l.Items, i.Degree)
        as Items
    from f_table as f, l_table as l,
        (select Seq.Nextval as Degree
        from iteration) as i,
    where sizeof(l.Items) = i.Degree − 1 and
    l.Items ⊂ f.Items)) as t
where t.Items ⊆ u.Items
group by t.Items
having sum(t.Support) ≥ δm));
```

What is interesting about these two approaches, specially the approach in [3, 4], is that unlike those in [6, 8, 9], only traditional SQL3 constructs were used and, in particular, no mining specific features were needed. And as such these approaches offer excellent opportunities for query optimization. Even the expressions above (and in [5]) use only one user defined function **sub** which implements the selection of a set with a specific cardinality and membership from a power set of a given set of elements.

---

* Research supported in part by National Science Foundation grants EPS-0082979 and EPS-0132618.

[1]It is important to note that association rules may be computed for virtually any type of database, transaction or not.

Initial experiments show that the SQL3 apriori approach just outlined outperforms the recursive join approach in [3, 4] as the former incorporates the stronger apriori pruning heuristics. In [5], the following recursive relational operator ϱ was also proposed to abstract the apriori type fixpoint encoding above.

Definition 1.1 (Fixpoint Operator) Let It and Su be two column names in a transaction database $\mathcal{D}$ with corresponding item set and support type domains, δ_m be the minimum support threshold, and n be the maximum cardinality of the item sets in It of $\mathcal{D}$. Then the large item sets operator ϱ is defined as follows:

$$\varrho^1_{It,Su}(\mathcal{D}) = \sigma_{Su \geq \delta_m}({}_{It}\mathcal{G}_{Su=sum(Su)}(\xi^1_{It}(\mathcal{D})))$$
$$\varrho^n_{It,Su}(\mathcal{D}) = \varrho^{n-1}_{It,Su}(\mathcal{D}) \cup (\sigma_{Su \geq \delta_m}($$
$${}_{It}\mathcal{G}_{Su=sum(Su)}((\xi^n_{It}(\mathcal{D})) \bowtie^1 \varrho^{n-1}_{It,Su}(\mathcal{D}))))$$

The large item set operator ϱ is defined in terms of two other operators ξ^k (called *strip*) and $\bowtie^k$ (called *distance-k item set join*) defined as follows. Let $\mathcal{I}$ be the set of all item and $\prec$ be a total ordering on the labels of the items in $\mathcal{I}$. Also let k-*sub* be a function that for any given item set $s \subseteq \mathcal{I}$ and k such that $1 \leq k \leq |s|$, it returns all distance-k subsets of s. For any two sets S and s, s is said to be a *degree-k* subset of S if $s \in \mathcal{P}(S)$ and $|s| = k$. Additionally, s is called a *distance-k* subset of S if $k = (|S| - |s|)$. Using this function we define the degree-k subsets of an item set relation as follows.

Definition 1.2 Let r be a relation such that its scheme includes a set valued attribute *Items*. Then for any $k \geq 0$, the degree-k subset of r is defined as

$$\xi^k_{Items}(r) = \{t \mid \exists u, v(u \in r \land v \in k\text{-}sub(u[Items]) \land$$
$$t = \langle v, u[R \setminus Items] \rangle)\}$$

For any two sets of item sets s_1 and s_2 in $2^{\mathcal{I}}$, s_1 is said to be a *strict distance-k* superset of s_2 if $s_2 \subset s_1$, $|s_1| - |s_2| = k$, and $\forall u, v(u \in s_1 \land v \in s_2 \land v \neq u \Rightarrow v \prec u)$. Intuitively, s_1 is an increasing superset of s_2. For example, abc is a strict distance-1 superset of ab, but not ac, when we consider the ordering $a \prec b \prec c \prec \ldots$. Let $\widehat{\supset}_k$ be a binary Boolean operator that returns true if s_1 is a strict distance-k superset of s_2, i.e., $s_1 \widehat{\supset}_k s_2 = \text{true}$. Finally, we define a *distance-k item set join*, $\bowtie^k$, operator as follows.

Definition 1.3 Let r and s be two relations on scheme $\{Items, Support\}$. Then the distance-k item set join of r and s is defined as

$$r \bowtie^k_{Items} s = \Pi_{r.Items,r.Support}(r \bowtie_{r.Items \widehat{\supset}_k s.Items} s)$$

Notice that $r \bowtie^k s$ returns all tuples in r such that there is a tuple in s that has an item set for which the item set in tuple of r is a distance-k superset. Other tuples are not selected. There is a more subtle issue here. By defining and using the notion of strict distance-k supersets, we have practically facilitated a "beamed" join of item sets. That is, item sets will join with only another item set that has an increasing cardinality and order. This is largely due to the ordering relation we insisted upon the item sets in $\mathcal{I}$ as a technical requirement.

Intuitively, the item set join based on strict distance-k supersets works as follows. Consider an input transaction table t_table and the corresponding large item set table l_table as shown below for a support threshold $\delta_m \geq 0.25$.

TranID	Items
t_1	{a,b,c}
t_2	{b,c,f}
t_3	{b,f}
t_4	{a,b,c}
t_5	{b,e}
t_6	{d,f}
t_7	{d}

transaction table — t_table

l_table

Items	Support
{a}	.29
{b}	.71
{c}	.43
{d}	.29
{f}	.43
{a,b}	.29
{a,c}	.29
{b,c}	.43
{b,f}	.29
{a,b,c}	.29

large item set table

Notice that, in this example, when a is a large item set (in table t_table), we need to generate the candidates ab and ac as b and c are also large. Also because there are database entries that contain ab and ac. This suggests that we need to consult the large item sets and the database entries to generate these candidates. In this way, we will not generate ad or af, for example. Again, when we consider b as a large item set, we may want to consider generating ab one more time because it is a possibility. But it is not necessary as we have already created ab as part of processing a. The question that remains, however, is how do we implement this "memory" in a set based setup such as relational algebra or SQL? One way to accomplish this is to apply SQL's **distinct** feature and make them unique, but this is an inherently expensive and wasteful operation. The strict distance-k supersets based item set join we have proposed help capture the idea by mimicking the affinity of the item sets (large or candidate) as shown in figure 1 during join processing in a set based setting.

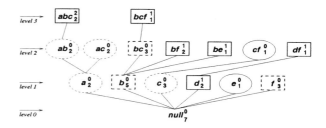

Figure 1: Exploration tree of input t_table showing beamed candidate generation path.

In the remainder of the paper, it is our goal to present a procedural implementation of ϱ and compare its performance with two leading approaches – FP-tree [2] and apriori [1]. We proceed as follows. In section 2 we present a recursive implementation of the operator followed by a comparative analysis in section 3, and conclusion in section 4.

2 Implementation of the Fixpoint Operator

In this section, we present a simple algorithm that implements the least fix point operator ϱ with the hope of demonstrating that even this primitive implementation performs well and is

634

comparable to leading algorithms and approaches in its class available in the literature (such as [9, 8, 6]).

2.1 A Depth-First Recursive Algorithm

The algorithm we are about to present exploits the so called "beamed" join technique for $\bowtie^k$ operator that not only facilitates faster join, but also allows us to explore the item set lattice (discussed in [3]) in a depth first manner (in fact it reduces to a forest of trees). Thus we trade time for space to avoid memory swaps. This also allows us to explore the forest one tree at a time. Let us first explain the basic idea of the algorithm using the example tables t_table and l_table, and a support threshold $\delta_m \geq 0.25$. The large item set operator ϱ necessitates that a set of distinct operations need to be performed in a sequence to compute the large item sets. First, we need to compute the large one item sets (the exit rule). We do so by scanning the database once and creating the list shown in figure 2. In this list, for every one item set, we list the record pointers to which an item set belongs. Notice that e is not a large item set since its support is less than δ_m (marked with a box around the node), and thus is taken out of the list L_1 (layer one list).

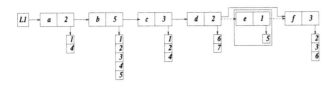

Figure 2: Generation of 1-item sets.

Then we take one node at a time in the list L_1 and explore its subtree in a depth first manner. Note that a node created in such a fashion will never be created in another branch in the forest and hence, there is no duplication of node expansion. To create the next level of a node we proceed as follows. We scan the tid list of the node X and fetch the item sets one at a time. We generate a new node with id Y only if the node id Y is larger than the current node id X in the $\prec$ relation, and it has not been created already. In the figure 3 below, we expand the tree for node a, followed by the tree for b in figure 4. Note that when we are at level 2 (figure 3), we discard node c, but continue to keep node b when we are exploring c. We delete both b and c when we exit from a, but keep a until we move below a.

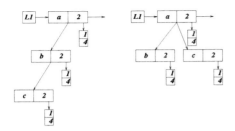

Figure 3: Exploring the a-tree – depth first expansion, shown from left to right.

The generation of next level nodes the way we did by checking for the satisfaction of the order relation $\prec$ among

the items, implements $\bowtie^1$ and ξ^k when we are at level k. The grouping is achieved by structuring the nodes in a tree, as we did, that always pushes an item set in one single branch of a tree. The summing of the support is done by counting the tids in the tid list and then checking if the node met the minimum threshold. If it did, then we expand it further; if not, we mark it dead (marked with a box around a node) and return to the parent node. If the node is large, we output the sequence from the root to the node as a large item set with its support count. The algorithm we have just described is presented in figure 5.

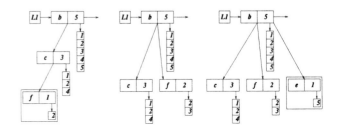

Figure 4: Exploration of the b-tree.

3 Performance Comparison

In this section, we present experimental evaluations of our framework as proof of its viability as a computing paradigm for association rules in relational databases. In our performance study, we compared our algorithm with apriori and FP-tree, two leading competitors. We have also implemented apriori and FP-tree ourselves to be fair, by eliminating the experience factor of the programmer in the comparison.

We developed our algorithm in C++ on a PC with AMD Athlon Processor 1.2G processor running Windows NT with 196 MB memory, 764 MB bytes virtual memory and 10GB hard drive. We have used the IBM data sets T25I10D10K and T25I20D100K for our evaluation. These synthetic datasets were extensively used almost as a benchmark to compare relative performance of most association rule mining algorithms. These data sets feature long patterns even for very small thresholds such as 0.1% and as such algorithms must explore almost all possible combinations of item sets. Also, these data sets intersect with each other (overlap) so heavily that the possible set of combinations is truly huge.

The graphs in figure 6 show the total execution times of our algorithm on these data sets and confirm that our algorithm performs better than apriori and almost approximates FP-tree. But so do many other algorithms. The real question is, does our algorithm perform better than other algorithms in its class – that is, those which also take an approach based on relational computation of large item sets? We would like to answer these questions in two steps.

First, we think our approach can only be compared with works such as [9]. Unfortunately, we could not run a comparative analysis using their data sets. But from the published literature, their method appears to be more expensive than our algorithm. Their running times are listed in excess of 10,000 seconds in some cases while ours are expected to be lower. As can be seen, even for the large T25I20D100K data set, our total running time is less than

```
algorithm: forest_expansion;
input: A transaction table D, support threshold δ_m.
output: Large item sets L_D (I_table).
begin
    scan D and generate a large 1-item set list L_1
        with a tid list for every item in which they appear;
    while L_1 is not empty do
        call the node pointed by L_1 X;
        call procedure node_expansion;
        remove node X from L_1
    endwhile;
end.


algorithm: node_expansion;
input: A node X and item list in the path I;
output: Void.
begin
    let the item in node X be u;
    count the tid list T;
    if the count is greater than δ_m then
        output large item set I ∪ u and its count;
        for every tid in the tid list T do
            fetch the item set s at T from D;
            for every item i in s do
                if u ≺ i and there is no child node Y at
                    X with item i then
                        create a node Y with item i;
                        copy the tids in Y from T in which
                            I ∪ u ∪ i appears;
                        call procedure node_expansion;
    else
        mark X dead;
    return;
end;
```

Figure 5: Algorithms for the large item set operator.

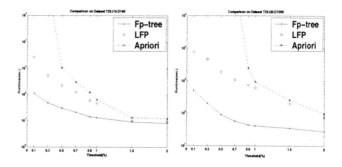

Figure 6: Total execution time of **fixpoint** on the data sets T25I10D10K and T25I20D100K as compared to apriori [1] and FP-tree [2].

8,000 seconds for 0.1% support threshold (note, however, that the hardware used is different).

Secondly, we believe that novel indexing techniques will help improve the performance of our algorithm significantly. We are currently developing an indexing scheme called the S^+ trees for set valued domains that aids fast set operations such as $\subset, \subseteq, \supset, \supseteq, =, \setminus, \cap$ and $\cup$. Recall that $\bowtie^k$ require such a join based on strict distance-k superset relationships. Our hope is that such an indexing scheme will help us locate specific portions of the database that is relevant for the computation at hand thereby increasing performance.

4   Conclusions

It was our goal to demonstrate that association rules can be computed using existing SQL3 machineries, which we believe we have done successfully. We have, of course, used a couple of built-in functions for set operations that current SQL systems do not possibly support, but we believe that future enhancements of SQL will. These functions can be easily implemented using SQL's create function statements as we have done. We have demonstrated that SQL's create view

recursive clause can simulate apriori effortlessly once the idea of a least fixpoint operator for apriori was at hand.

As a second step, we have also attempted to support our conviction with an implementation of the large item set operator ϱ that we have proposed. The initial performance results show that our algorithm does better than apriori and possibly better than [9]. We believe that new techniques for computing $\bowtie^k$ based on set indexing would be useful and efficient. In this connection, we are currently investigating query optimization issues involving ϱ and $\bowtie^1$ operators in relational algebra expressions.

References

[1] Rakesh Agrawal and Ramakrishnan Srikant. Fast algorithms for mining association rules in large databases. In *VLDB*, pages 487–499, 1994.

[2] Jiawei Han, Jian Pei, and Yiwen Yin. Mining frequent patterns without candidate generation. In *Proc. ACM SIGMOD*, pages 1–12, 2000.

[3] Hasan M. Jamil. Ad hoc association rule mining as SQL3 queries. In *IEEE ICDM*, pages 609–612, 2001.

[4] Hasan M. Jamil. Mining first-order knowledge bases for association rules. In *IEEE ICTAI*, pages 218–227, 2001.

[5] Hasan M. Jamil. On the equivalence of top-down and bottom-up data mining in relational databases. In *DaWaK*, pages 41–50, Munich, Germany, 2001.

[6] Rosa Meo, Giuseppe Psaila, and Stefano Ceri. An extension to SQL for mining association rules. *DMKD*, 2(2):195–224, 1998.

[7] Amir Netz, Surajit Chaudhuri, Usama M. Fayyad, and Jeff Bernhardt. Integrating data mining with SQL databases. In *IEEE ICDE*, 2001.

[8] Karthick Rajamani, Alan Cox, Bala Iyer, and Atul Chadha. Efficient mining for association rules with relational database systems. In *IDEAS*, pages 148–155, 1999.

[9] Sunita Sarawagi, Shiby Thomas, and Rakesh Agrawal. Integrating mining with relational database systems: Alternatives and implications. In *Proc. ACM SIGMOD*, pages 343–354, 1998.

Considering Both Intra-Pattern and Inter-Pattern Anomalies for Intrusion Detection

Ning Jiang   *Kien A. Hua*

School of EECS, University of Central
Florida
Orlando, FL 32816-2362
{njiang, kienhua} @cs.ucf.edu

Simon Sheu[1]

Department of Computer Science
National Tsing Hua University
101, Section 2, Kuang Fu Road,
Hsin-Chu, Taiwan 30013, R.O.C.
sheu@cs.nthu.edu.tw

Abstract

Various approaches have been proposed to discover patterns from system call trails of UNIX processes to better model application behavior. However, these techniques only consider relationship between system calls (or system audit events). In this paper, we first refine the definition of maximal patterns given in [8] and provide a pattern extraction algorithm to identify such maximal patterns. We then add one additional dimension to the problem domain by also taking into consideration the overlap relationship between patterns. We argue that an execution path of an application is usually not an arbitrary combination of various patterns; but rather, they overlap each other in some specific order. Such overlap relationship characterizes the normal behavior of the application. Finally, a novel pattern matching module is proposed to detect intrusions based on both intra-pattern and inter-pattern anomalies. We test this idea using the data sets obtained from the University of New Mexico. The experimental results indicate that our scheme detect significantly more anomalies than the scheme presented in [8] while maintaining a very low false alarm rate.

1. Introduction

Intrusion detection using trails of system calls (system audit events) has been studied extensively for many years. In the original works ([2][3][4][10]) of Forrest et al, the application under investigation is executed under various normal scenarios. System calls invoked by the application are captured and recorded in sequences, which are usually referred to as training sequences. Normal behaviors of applications are modeled by registering fixed-length subsequences (i.e. patterns) of these training sequences.

Intrusions are reported when there are significant deviations between the newly observed sequences (i.e. intrusion sequences) and the stored fixed-length patterns. The fixed-length pattern approach works well as long as the length of the pattern is properly chosen. Wespi et al proposed several schemes [7][8][9] to produce variable-length patterns. In particular, the technique, presented in [8], showed significant improvement over the fixed-length pattern methods. The main idea of the scheme involves discovering variable length *maximal* patterns and generating "building-blocks" to compose potentially any possible normal system audit sequences.

In this paper, we first refine the definition of maximal patterns in [8] and provide a pattern extraction algorithm to identify such maximal patterns. We then add one more dimension to the problem domain. In addition to examining the relationship between individual system calls (or system audit events), our technique also takes into consideration the relationship between patterns. We argue that an execution path of an application is usually not an arbitrary combination of various patterns; but rather, they overlap each other in some specific order. Such overlap relationship characterizes the normal behavior of the application. Finally, a novel pattern matching module is proposed to detect intrusions based on both intra-pattern and inter-pattern anomalies. We tested our technique using the data sets obtained from the University of New Mexico. The experimental results indicated that with approximately the same space and time efficiency, our scheme detected significantly more anomalies while maintaining a very low false alarm rate.

To the best of our knowledge, the proposed intrusion detection method is the first to exploit overlap relationship between patterns. In [2][3][4][10], overlap relationship between patterns is implicitly recorded by

---

[1]The author is supported by the MOE Program for Promoting Academic Excellent of Universities, Grant No. 89-E-FA04-1-4, Taiwan, R.O.C.

sliding a window over all the system calls and capturing unique sequences. However, the information is not utilized in the detection of attacks. In [8], the main idea is to identify "building blocks" to model normal application behavior. As a result of the pattern reduction operation, overlapping patterns are "flatted" and overlap relationship between patterns is no longer preserved.

2. System Architecture and Definition

In this section, we first give a brief description of the architecture of our intrusion detection system. Notations and formal definitions are then presented to facilitate further discussion.

2.1. System Architecture

The system consists of two parts: the offline training part and the online detection part. Operations of each component are described as follows:

1. Data collection module: The application under investigation is executed under various normal usage scenarios. During each execution, the application spawns one or many processes. System calls invoked by each of these processes are captured and recorded in a sequence. The output of this module is a number of system call sequences.
2. Data preprocessing module: First, each system call of the training trails is translated into a system call ID according to a predefined translation table. Identical consecutive system call IDs are then aggregated into one. After aggregation, there might be groups of identical system call sequences. For each group, we only keep one representative sequence and remove all other sequences.
3. Pattern extraction module: This module extracts *maximal* patterns from selected set of sequences generated by the data preprocessing module.
4. Pattern overlap relationship identification module: Patterns are organized into adjacency lists in which overlap relationship between patterns is located and maintained.
5. Pattern matching module: Incoming system calls of the application under protection are first subject to the same preprocessing operations as in 2. Pattern adjacency lists are then traversed at real time to identify both intra-pattern and inter-pattern mismatches. Significant deviations from the normal behavior cause the module to raise alerts.

In the following sections of the paper, we focus on the description of the last three components.

2.2. Notations And Definitions

Consider an alphabet Σ of size k, $\Sigma = \{e_1, e_2, ..., e_k\}$. In this paper, each element of Σ is a system call. A sequence s is defined as $s = (a_1, a_2, ..., a_n)$, $(a_i \in \Sigma, 1 \le i \le n)$. The size of a sequence s is represented by $|s|$. The input to the pattern extraction module is a set T of training sequences: $T = \{T_1, T_2, ..., T_m\}$. The ith sequence of T is defined as T_i, and the jth element of T_i is denoted as T_{ij}. Each element e_i of Σ can appear zero or more times in any sequence of T. Each such occurrence is referred to as an *instance* of e_i.

A pattern p is a subsequence of any sequence of T. Hereafter, a pattern with length i is referred to as an i-pattern. A pattern p can appear at various positions in different training sequences. We call each occurrence of a pattern in T an *instance* of that pattern. We use the notation $N(p,T)$ to denote the total number of instances of a pattern p in T. A pattern p is considered *frequent* with respect to the training set T if and only if $N(p,T) \ge 2$ and $|p| \ge 2$. In addition, we use a *location pair* $\langle d, f \rangle$ to record the position of a pattern instance starting at the system call T_{df} in a training sequence T_d. A set $L(p)$ is used to represent all the location pairs of a pattern p. Apparently, $|L(p)| = N(p,T)$.

Definition 1: Given a set T of training sequences and a frequent pattern p of T. Pattern p is *maximal* if and only if there exists at least one instance of p, such that it never appears in T as a subsequence of an instance of any other frequent pattern q. Suppose the length of p is i, p is also referred to as a maximal i-pattern.

Basically, Definition 1 states that a frequent pattern cannot be maximal if it always occurs as a subsequence of some other frequent pattern. For a given training set T, the set $P(T)$ represents all the maximal patterns of T.

We define a Boolean function *overlap* on two *location pairs* $\langle d_1, f_1 \rangle$ and $\langle d_2, f_2 \rangle$ of two maximal pattern p and q, respectively, as follows:

Definition 2: Consider two maximal patterns p and q (p and q can be identical) of a set T of training sequences. $\forall \langle d_1, f_1 \rangle \in L(p), \forall \langle d_2, f_2 \rangle \in L(q)$, a Boolean function is defined on the two location pairs as:

$$overlap(\langle d_1, f_1 \rangle, \langle d_2, f_2 \rangle) = \begin{cases} TRUE & \text{if} \begin{pmatrix} (d_1 = d_2) \wedge (f_1 < f_2) \\ \wedge (f_2 \le f_1 + |p| - 1 < f_2 + |q| - 1) \end{pmatrix} \\ FALSE & \text{otherwise} \end{cases}$$

If $overlap(\langle d_1, f_1 \rangle, \langle d_2, f_2 \rangle) = TRUE$, $p_{f_2 - f_1 + 1}$ is referred to as the *overlapping point*. As an example, suppose we have the following set T of training sequences:

$T = \{$"4 2 66", "4 2 66 105", "2 66 105" $\}$
According to Definition 1, $P(T)=\{$"4 2 66", "2 66 105"$\}$. The location pairs of both of the maximal patterns in T_2 are $<2,1>$ and $<2,2>$, respectively. Obviously, $overlap(<2,1>,<2,2>)=TRUE$. The system call "2" in pattern "4 2 66" is referred to as the overlapping point.

Definition 3: A maximal pattern p of a training set T is *terminable* if and only if there exists an instance of p such that it does not overlap with instances of any maximal pattern q. i.e.,

$$\exists loc \in L(p)\left(\forall q \in P(T)\left(\forall loc_1 \in L(q)\left(\begin{array}{c}\neg overlap(loc_1, loc)\\ \wedge\, \neg overlap(loc, loc_1)\end{array}\right)\right)\right)$$

For instance, the maximal pattern "4 2 66", in the last example, is terminable.

3. Pattern Extraction

In this section, we discuss how to compute $P(T)$ given a set T of training sequences. Numerous works [1][5][6] have been proposed to recognize patterns from sequences of events. However, many of them are aimed at discovering patterns that are more general with richer semantic meanings. Although it is feasible to revise some of them to generate maximal patterns as we defined, the performance of the revised algorithms will not be comparable to a specialized one.

We perform a sequential scan of the training sequences. For each never-inspected-before system call e, we determine all maximal patterns including e in an iterative manner. For each iteration, the following operations are performed:

1. We expand each instance of a frequent i-pattern in the "forward" direction of the respective training sequence to form $i+1$-patterns.
2. Certain i-pattern instances are expanded in the "backward" direction of the respective training sequence to generate maximal patterns.
3. Inspection of both directions is pruned based on a certain observation.

After all the maximal patterns are recognized, system call instances that never participate in any of the maximal patterns are identified and output. Details of the algorithm will be published in the future.

4. Discover Overlap Relationships Between Patterns

In the last section, we discussed how to identify maximal patterns from the training sequences. In the current section, we examine these maximal patterns to discover their relationships. More specifically, for each maximal pattern $p \in P(T)$, we find all the maximal patterns overlapping with p, and determine the corresponding *overlapping points*. We also identify all *terminable* patterns in $P(T)$. Internally, maximal patterns are organized into adjacency lists with each list corresponding to a maximal pattern. Overlapping and terminal information is also recorded for each maximal pattern.

5. Pattern Matching Module

In this section, we present a novel pattern matching module that detects both intra-pattern and inter-pattern mismatches.

During the intrusion detection stage, system calls of various processes of the application under protection are captured at real time. Before being sent to the pattern matching module, system calls are filtered, translated and aggregated, in the same way as in the training phase. The pattern matching module processes one system call at a time.

The pattern matching module verifies the intra-pattern and inter-pattern relationship by traversing the adjacency lists introduced in Section 4. Basically, a Pending Pattern Table (*PPT*) is maintained for each process of the application being monitored. The *PPT* records all legitimate traversing paths. A mismatch counter is incremented when it is impossible to further traverse the adjacency lists (i.e. the *PPT* is empty). An alarm is raised when at least l consecutive mismatches are encountered, where l is a user defined threshold.

6. Experimental Study

To assess the proposed technique, we compare it with an implementation of a building-block-based method similar to [8]. Hereafter, the building-block scheme is referred to as "the reference technique". In our experiments, we applied both techniques to system call trails of the *login* and *sendmail* applications executed under various scenarios. The test data sets can be downloaded from the website of the University of New Mexico (http://www.cs.unm.edu/~immsec/).

We compared both techniques based on their effectiveness, the size of the pattern database, and time efficiency. To measure the effectiveness, we count the number of sequences reported as abnormal. The length of a reported abnormal sequence must be greater than or equal to a predefined threshold, l. The sizes of the pattern databases are measured by counting the internal nodes of the respective data structures (tree for the referenced technique). The time efficiency of both pattern matching modules is determined by their average *PPT* sizes.

The *login* data set was used to test the ability of the proposed technique to detect Trojan horse attacks. We used all 24 normal traces to train the system. Two types of Trojan horse intrusion scripts were employed to attack the target system. One of the two scripts was recovered from an installation of Linux root kit based on a Linux version which is different from the one used to collect normal data. To achieve a stricter test, a second type of intrusion code was "home-grown" by UNM. The experimental result is very promising. With approximately the same time and space cost, our scheme detected at least 100% more anomalies than the referenced technique without raising any false alarm.

The *sendmail* data set has a total of 311 normal sequences, containing approximately 1.5 million system calls. 64 sequences remained after aggregation and duplicate reduction. Of these 64 sequences, 57 were selected to train the system, accounting for approximately 70% of all the system calls. The remaining trails were used to test for false alarm rate. Many intrusion scripts were implemented to generate anomalous behaviors. Again, with approximately the same time and space overhead, our approach detected on average 70% more anomalies than the reference technique. In particular, when the threshold l is set to 12, our scheme detected all the intrusions. The reference technique, on the other hand, failed to raise any alarm for one particular intrusion. However, in terms of false alarm rate, the referenced technique performed slightly better. It did not raise any false alarm while our scheme raised 2 false alarms when l is set to 12.

7. Concluding Remarks

In this paper, we propose a technique that detects intrusions based on both intra-pattern and inter-pattern anomalies. Our contributions are as follows:

1. We refined the definition of *maximal pattern* based on the definition given in [8].
2. An algorithm was proposed to identify maximal patterns in given training sequences.
3. Techniques were developed for identifying and storing overlap relationship between patterns.
4. An efficient pattern matching algorithm was designed.

The proposed technique was tested against a method similar to the one presented in [8] using the popular *sendmail* and *login* data sets. The experimental results indicate that our scheme

1. Detected significantly more anomalies with time and space efficiency similar to the technique proposed in [8],

2. Identified an intrusion missed by the technique proposed in [8], and
3. Achieved a very low false alarm rate.

We, thus, conclude that overlap relationship between patterns is important to intrusion detection. The concept is simple and inexpensive to implement.

8. References

[1] Rakesh Agrawal, Ramakrishnan Srikant. Mining sequential patterns. In *Proc. of the 11th International Conference on Data Engineering*, Taipei, Taiwan, March 1995.

[2] Stephanie Forrest, Steven A. Hofmeyr, Anil Somahaji, and Thomas A. Longstaff. A sense of self for Unix processes. In *Proceedings of the 1996 IEEE Symposium on Research in Security and Privacy*, pages 120-128. IEEE Computer Society, IEEE Computer Society Press, May 1996.

[3] Stephanie Forrest, Alan S. Perelson, Lawrence Allen, and Rajesh Cherukuri. Self-nonself discrimination. In *Proceedings of the 1996 IEEE Symposium on Research in Security and Privacy*, pages 202-212. IEEE Computer Society, IEEE Computer Society Press, May 1994.

[4] Steven A. Hofmeyr, Stephanie Forrest, and Anil Somayaji. Intrusion detection using sequences of system calls. Journal of Computer Security, 6(3):151-180, 1998.

[5] Heikki Mannila, Hannu Toivonen, A. Inkeri Verkamo. Discovery of frequent episodes in event sequences. Data Mining and Knowledge Discovery, 1997. 1(3): p. 259-289.

[6] Ramakrishnan Srikant, Rakesh Agrawal. Mining sequential patterns: generalizations and performance improvements. In *International Conference on Extending Database Technology (EDBT 1996)*.

[7] Andreas Wespi, Marc Dacier, and Hervé Debar. An intrusion-detection system based on the Teiresias pattern-discovery algorithm. In Urs E. Gattiker, Pia Pedersen, and Karsten Petersen, editors, *Proceedings of EICAR '99*, Aalborg, Denmark, February 1999. European Institute for Computer Anti-Virus Research. ISBN 87-987271-0-9.

[8] Andreas Wespi, Marc Dacier, and Hervé Debar. Intrusion detection using variable-length audit trail patterns. In Hervé Debar, Ludovic Mé, S. Felix Wu, editors, *Proceedings of RAID 00, Workshop on Recent Advances in Intrusion Detection*, Toulouse, France, October 2000.

[9] Andreas Wespi, Marc Dacier, Hervé Debar, and Mehdi M. Nassehi. Audit trail pattern analysis for detecting suspicious process behavior. In *Proceedings of RAID 98, Workshop on Recent Advances in Intrusion Detection*, Louvain-la-Neuve, Belgium, September 1998.

[10] Christina Warrender, Stephanie Forrest, Barak Pearlmutter. Detecting intrusions using system calls: alternative data models. IEEE Symposium on Security and Privacy. May 1999.

On Evaluating Performance of Classifiers for Rare Classes

Mahesh V. Joshi

IBM T. J. Watson Research Center
P.O.Box 704, Yorktown Heights, NY 10598
joshim@us.ibm.com

Abstract

Predicting rare classes effectively is an important problem. The definition of effective *classifier, embodied in the classifier evaluation metric, is however very subjective, dependent on the application domain. In this paper, a wide variety of point-metrics are put into a common analytical context defined by the recall and precision of the target rare class. This enables us to compare various metrics in an objective, domain-independent manner. We judge their suitability for the rare class problems along the dimensions of learning difficulty and levels of rarity. This yields many valuable insights. In order to address the goal of achieving better recall and precision, we also propose a way of comparing classifiers directly based on the relationships between recall and precision values. It resorts to a composite point-metric only when recall-precision based comparisons yield conflicting results.*

1. Introduction

Learning effective predictive models for rarely occurring events is an important problem with applications in many domains such as document categorization, network intrusion detection, web-log analysis, etc. Recently, new algorithms and insights have started appearing [1, 3]. However, the issue of evaluating the classifiers for these problems has not been properly addressed in a comprehensive, domain-independent manner. Various metrics exist in the literature to evaluate classifiers in general, primarily motivated by the domain in which they are applied [7, 6, 8, 5, 4, 9].

Our primary goal in this paper is to give a common objective perspective to various such metrics ranging from the traditional accuracy metric to a complex information theoretic metric [4]. An attempt is made to judge their suitability for evaluating the performance of the rare class prediction problem. We take a stand that for effective prediction a rare class, two metrics are crucial: recall and precision *with re-*

spect to to the rare class[1]. We translate many different metrics into this recall-precision perspective and evaluate their comparative relationships for varying levels of rarity of the target class and various difficulties of learning problems defined with respect to the recall and precision levels.

2. Evaluation Metrics

We focus on the binary classification problem involving two classes: C and NC. We assume that C denotes the rarer class. When the classifier is evaluated over a dataset T of n records, the confusion matrix of decisions is obtained as follows, where TP and FP are true and false positives, respectively, and TN and FN are true and false negatives, respectively.

	Predicted as C	Predicted as NC	Total
Actually C	n_{00} [TP]	n_{01} [FN]	n^c
Actually NC	n_{10} [FP]	n_{11} [TN]	n^{nc}
Total	$n_0 = n_{00} + n_{10}$	$n_1 = n_{01} + n_{11}$	n

FN and FP are also called type I and II errors, respectively. The terms "positive" and "negative" are defined w.r.t. C. Recall and Precision of the classifier w.r.t. C are defined as $R^c = n_{00}/(n_{00} + n_{01})$ and $P^c = n_{00}/(n_{00} + n_{10})$, respectively. Recall and precision w.r.t. NC are defined as $R^{nc} = n_{11}/(n_{11} + n_{10})$ and $P^{nc} = n_{11}/(n_{11} + n_{01})$, respectively.

Usually there is a tradeoff between achieving less number of type I errors versus achieving less number of type II errors. Realizing this, often a relative operating curve (ROC) characteristics of a classifier [7] is plotted by recording various combinations of type I and II errors obtained by a classifier algorithm on a given problem. When the target population of the classifier is expected to have significantly

---

[1]Given a binary classification problem of learning a model to distinguish a rare class C from the other class (NC), if a classifier is able to predict m cases of C correctly out of total n cases, then the Recall (R) of the classifier with respect to C is m/n. If the classifier makes total l predictions as class C (out of which only m are correct), then the precision with respect to C is m/l.

different class distributions and cost factors (on type I and II errors) than those assumed while training the classifier, a metric that quantifies the ROC curve as a whole is more suitable. However, the underlying assumption of this paper, just like most machine learning algorithms [6], is that the training and test samples are drawn from the same population and the costs of FP and FN are known and do not change from training to test scenarios. Under this assumption, we are interested in a classifier that can achieve the best single point on the ROC curve. Hence, we evaluate various *point-metrics*, which can be derived from the confusion matrix associated with each point in the ROC curve. In particular, we study the following point-metrics.

Accuracy (Acc): This metric is widely used in machine learning [6]. It is defined as $(n_{00} + n_{11})/n$.

F-measure (F): This is a metric used widely by the Information Retrieval community [8]. The generic form of F with respect to class C is: $F_\lambda^c = \frac{1}{\lambda \frac{1}{R^c} + (1-\lambda) \frac{1}{P^c}}, 0 \leq \lambda \leq 1$. With no a-priori knowledge of costs associated with either type of errors, we assign equal importance to recall and precision ($\lambda = 0.5$). Henceforth, we use F^c to refer to $F_{0.5}^c$, which simplifies to $F^c = 2 R^c P^c/(R^c + P^c)$.

Geometric Mean of Recall and Precision (GMRP): This metric is used by some in the information retrieval community [5]. It is also defined with respect to a particular class. For C, GMRP is $\sqrt{R^c P^c}$.

Sum of Recalls (SOR): This metric, sometimes referred to as the weighted accuracy, is simply $SOR = R^c + R^{nc}$.

Geometric Mean of Recalls (GMOR): This metric, defined as $GMOR = \sqrt{R^c R^{nc}}$, is also used by some researchers for the rare class problem [5].

Information Score (IS): A metric inspired from information-theoretic perspective is proposed in [4]. It caters to the rare class problems. Based on an assumptions that the classifier makes true and false predictions of C with 100% probability, and that the training and test samples are drawn from same population, one can derive the following expression for an average information score (I_a) for our confusion matrix (refer to [2] for detailed derivation):

$$I_a = -\frac{n_{00}}{n} \log(\frac{n^c}{n}) + \frac{n_{01}}{n} \log(1 - \frac{n^c}{n}) + \frac{n_{10}}{n} \log(1 - \frac{n^{nc}}{n}) - \frac{n_{11}}{n} \log(\frac{n^{nc}}{n}) \quad (1)$$

3. Comparison of Metrics

The point-metric used for comparing classifiers should reflect what is desired. For the rare class problem, we take a stand that it is desired to achieve a high value of recall (R^c) and precision (P^c) for the given rare class C. We now present an analysis of metrics Acc, F^c, $GMRP^c$, $SORP^c$, I_a, SOR, and $GMOR$, from the perspective of the weights given to the improvements in recall and precision.

Let α denote the ratio of number of NC examples to number of C examples in the test set; i.e., $\alpha = n^{nc}/n^c$. Higher the value of $\alpha > 1$, more rare is class C. Using definition of α, and the definitions of recalls and precisions given in the previous section, it can be verified that $R^{nc} = 1 - \frac{R^c}{\alpha}\left(\frac{1}{P^c} - 1\right)$. Using this expression of R^{nc}, one can express each of the metrics in terms of R^c, P^c, and α (refer to [2] for details).

We want to compare a classifier that achieves (R_1, P_1) values w.r.t. C with a classifier that achieves (R_2, P_2) values on the same test set. For each of the metrics (denoted generically by $\mathcal{M}$) being compared, we want to study the relationship required between P_1 and P_2 to ensure that $\mathcal{M}_1 > \mathcal{M}_2$, given that $R_1 > R_2$ holds[2]. Let $\beta = R_1/R_2$ ($\beta > 1$). Some algebraic transformations (a bit involved for some metrics) can be performed to show the following relationships between P_1 and P_2 for each metric:

$$F : \quad \frac{1}{P_1} < \frac{1}{P_2} + \frac{1}{R_2}\left(1 - \frac{1}{\beta}\right)$$

$$GMRP : \quad \frac{1}{P_1} < \frac{\beta}{P_2}$$

$$SORP : \quad \frac{1}{P_1} < \frac{1}{R_2(1-\beta) + P_2}$$

$$GMOR : \quad \frac{1}{P_1} < 1 + \frac{1}{\beta^2}\left(\frac{1}{P_2} - 1\right) + \frac{\alpha}{\beta R_2}\left(1 - \frac{1}{\beta}\right)$$

$$SOR : \quad \frac{1}{P_1} < \frac{1}{\beta P_2} + (\alpha + 1)\left(1 - \frac{1}{\beta}\right)$$

$$Acc : \quad \frac{1}{P_1} < 2 - \frac{2}{\beta} + \frac{1}{\beta P_2}$$

$$I_a : \quad \frac{1}{P_1} < 2 + \frac{1}{\beta P_2} - \frac{2}{\beta}$$

Let us denote by L_{P_1} the lower limit on P_1 value, that each of these above expressions is imposing. Interesting point to note is that although the expressions for I_a and Acc involve α, the expressions for L_{P_1} do not depend on α. Moreover, both I_a and Acc impose identical lower limit on P_1. Figures 1, 2 and 3 show plots of L_{P_1} for various metrics for different values of R_2 (constant over a column of graphs), P_2 (constant over a row of graphs), and R_1 (varies over the X-axis of each graph).

Figures 1 and 2 show that as the rarity goes up (α increases), the metrics SOR and $GMOR$ impose very little restriction on P_1, as L_{P_1} dips significantly below the P_2 level. Hence, these metrics can be maximized by just maximizing the recall for very rare classes, thus rendering them unsuitable. All the other metrics are independent of α. Using Figure 3, the following observations can be made about their relative performance.

---

[2]Note that similar analysis can be done by assuming $P_1 > P_2$, and checking the relationship between R_1 and R_2. We just present the analysis for the former case.

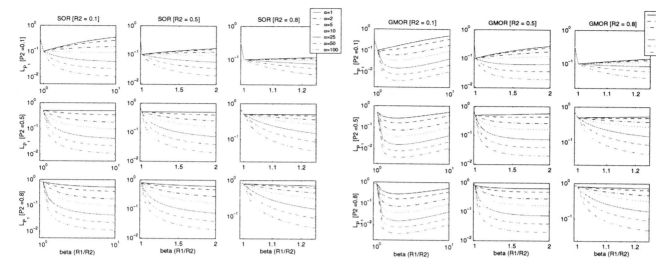

Figure 1. Behavior of Sum-of-Recalls (SOR).

Figure 2. Behavior of Geometric-Mean-of-Recalls (GMOR).

$SORP$ is not a good metric, because its performance varies dramatically over various plots. In most cases, except for combinations of higher P_2 values and lower R_2 values ($P_2 = 0.8, R_2 = 0.1$), it imposes one of the lowest restrictions on P_1.

For higher values of R_2, most other metrics are similar. F_1 imposes slightly higher limits on P_1 than $GMRP$ does.

I_a and Acc impose the most stringent requirements on P_2. For lower values of P_2 ($P_2 \leq 0.5$), there is a region in the graph where for any level of improvement in R_1 over R_2, even with $P_1 > P_2$, the metrics can be lower. For example, look at the row of $P_2 = 0.1$. This is not a desired property from rare class perspective, because improving both recall and precision (both significantly according to some statistical test) is an accomplishment when the problem is tougher; but, it is not getting rewarded by I_a and Acc. Another way to look at it is from the graphs in the row of $P_2 = 0.5$. They show that any value of $P_1 > P_2$ will improve the metric, irrespective of the level of improvement in recall. This stringent requirement tends to favor precision more than recall.

For lower values of P_2 and for higher values of R_2, F_1 achieves a balance between the limits imposed by $GMRP$ and I_a (or Acc). Only for higher values of P_2 and lower values of R_2, does $GMRP$ start getting better in some lower range of β, determined by a threshold that increases as P_2 increases. Here by *better*, we mean the L_{P_1} value for $GMRP$ lies between the F-measure and I_a and Acc. But, for most combinations of R_2 and P_2, F-measure is better than $GMRP$.

The above discussion indicates that ideally one should compare classifiers based on different metrics for different recall-precision combinations, but such comparison is dif-

ficult to justify in practice. Two metrics emerge as strong candidates: F metric for most of the regions in the recall-precision space, and $GMRP$ for the low recall (< 0.5) and high precision (> 0.5) combinations. F metric has some advantages over $GMRP$: its acceptability in many domains such as text categorization (where rare class problem are encountered very often) and it theoretical derivation in [8] to make it conform to the six conditions of an additive conjoint relational structure [8] imposed on two proportion-based quantities.

3.1. Proposed Classifier Comparison Strategy

One drawback of comparing classifiers using just the composite metric such as F-measure is that one cannot directly apply tests of significance to it to determine the confidence level of the comparison. Our primary goal is to achieve improvements in recall as well as precision for the rare class. In order to serve this goal more directly, we now propose a new classifier comparison strategy.

We use *p-test* [9] to compare improvements in recall and precision. On a given dataset with n^c examples of C, let classifiers A and B obtain (R_A, P_A) and (R_B, P_B) values of recall and precision w.r.t. C, respectively. Let A predict n_0^A examples as C (sum of true and false positives), and B predict n_0^B examples as C. Given this, the p-test is applied as follows:

$$Z_R = \frac{R_A - R_B}{\sqrt{2R(1-R)/n^c}},$$

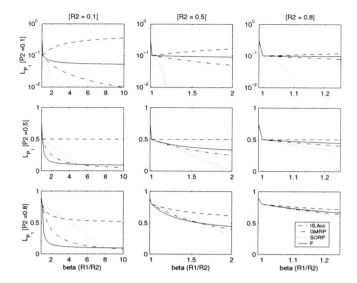

Figure 3. Behavior of various metrics that impose a lower limit on P_1 that is independent of rarity of C.

$$Z_P = \frac{P_A - P_B}{\sqrt{P(1-P)(1/n_0^A + 1/n_0^B)}},$$

where $R = \frac{R_A + R_B}{2}$ and $P = \frac{n_0^A \times P_A + n_0^B \times P_B}{n_0^A + n_0^B}$. Here, we are using the fact that P_A (resp. P_B) is a *proportion* obtained on population n_0^A (resp. n_0^B), and R_A and R_B are proportions on n^c. If $Z_R \geq 1.96$, then we regard R_A as being significantly better than R_B ($R_A \gg R_B$) at the 95% confidence level[3]. If $Z_R \leq -1.96$, then $R_A \ll R_B$. If $|Z_R| < 1.96$, then $R_A \sim R_B$. Similar tests are applied to compare P_A and P_B.

We call classifier A better than B ($A > B$) if either of the following criteria is satisfied: $R_A \gg R_B$ and $P_A \sim P_B$; or $R_A \gg R_B$ and $P_A \gg P_B$; or $R_A \sim R_B$ and $P_A \gg P_B$. Similarly, one can determine if $B > A$. If both conditions $R_A \sim R_B$ and $P_A \sim P_B$ hold, then $A \sim B$.

It may so happen that one metric (R or P) is significantly better and the other (P or R) is significantly worse. Only in such cases, we resolve the conflicts using a composite metric. From the earlier discussion, F-measure is a good choice for this purpose. F-measure does not have any probabilistic interpretation; hence, we cannot apply any significance test to its values. So, some heuristic needs to be applied, e.g. an improvement in F-measure by at least 1% is required to call a classifier better.

---

[3]Note that the confidence interval value of 1.96 for a confidence level of 95% is based on the z-test of statistical significance. If the values of n^C or $n_0^A + n_0^B$ are < 30, then the tables for t-test should be used to determine the appropriate confidence interval for a given confidence level. The size of the sample size can be used to determine the degrees of freedom required for applying a t-test.

4. Summary

We address the issue of evaluating the performance of a classifier when it comes to predicting rare classes effectively. We set a goal of rewarding a classifier when it achieves both higher recall and higher precision for the rare class. From this perspective, we have compared a wide range of metrics analytically and empirically, by deriving the dependency of each on the recall, precision, and rarity of the minority class. We have obtained various insights about the behavior of each metric over various ranges of these parameters. More detailed insights and extensive empirical comparisons between metrics on various real-world and synthetic rare class problems are given in [2]. In summary, we find that $GMRP$ and F-measure are the most suitable metrics that behave more or less similarly for moderately tough problems. However, $GMRP$ exhibits undesired behavior for significantly lower recall and precision values. Hence, F-measure is the more favorable metric for tougher rare class problems. We also propose a new classifier comparison strategy that addresses our primary goal more directly, while bringing in the composite metric of F-measure only to resolve conflicts.

References

[1] R. C. Holte, N. Japkowicz, C. X. Ling, and S. M. (eds.). Learning from imbalanced data sets (papers from AAAI workshop). Technical Report WS-00-05, AAAI Press, Menlo Park, CA, 2000.

[2] M. V. Joshi. On evaluating performance of classifiers for rare classes. Technical Report Under Preparation, IBM Research Division, 2002.

[3] M. V. Joshi, R. C. Agarwal, and V. Kumar. Mining needles in a haystack: Classifying rare classes via two-phase rule induction. In *Proc. of ACM SIGMOD Conference*, pages 91–102, 2001.

[4] I. Koronenko and I. Bratko. Information-based evaluation criterion for classifier's performance. *Machine Learning*, 6:67–80, 1991.

[5] M. Kubat and S. Matwin. Addressing the curse of imbalanced training sets: one-sided selection. In *Proc. 14th International Conference on Machine Learning*, pages 179–186. Morgan Kaufmann, 1997.

[6] T. Mitchell. *Machine Learning*. McGraw Hill, 1997.

[7] J. A. Swets. Measuring the accuracy of diagnostic systems. *Science*, 240:1285–1293, 1988.

[8] C. J. van Rijsbergen. *Information Retrieval*. Butterworths, London, 1979.

[9] Y. Yang and X. Liu. A re-examination of text categorization methods. In *22nd Annual International Conference on Information Retrieval (SIGIR'99)*, pages 42–49, Berkley, August 1999.

Learning from Order Examples

Toshihiro Kamishima and Shotaro Akaho
National Institute of Advanced Industrial Science and Technology (AIST)
Tsukuba Central 2, Umezono 1–1–1, Tsukuba, Ibaraki, JAPAN
mail@kamishima.net (http://www.kamishima.net/) & s.akaho@aist.go.jp

Abstract

We advocate a new learning task that deals with orders of items, and we call this the Learning from Order Examples *(LOE) task. The aim of the task is to acquire the rule that is used for estimating the proper order of a given unordered item set. The rule is acquired from training examples that are ordered item sets. We present several solution methods for this task, and evaluate the performance and the characteristics of these methods based on the experimental results of tests using both artificial data and realistic data.*

1 Introduction

In this paper, we advocate a new learning task that deals with orders of items, and we call this the *Learning from Order Examples* (LOE) task. The aim of the LOE task is to acquire the rule that is used for estimating the proper order of a given item set. The rule is acquired from training examples that are ordered item sets.

An example of performing the LOE task would consist of completing a questionnaire survey on preference in foods. The surveyor presents several kinds of foods to each respondent and requests that he/she sort the foods according to his/her preferences. By applying the LOE learning algorithm, for example, the surveyor will be able to determine the most preferred food, or to detect the degree of influence of attributes on respondent's preferences. For such a survey, it is typical to adapt the Semantic Differential method. In this method, the respondent's preferences are measured by a scale, the extremes of which are symbolized by antonymous adjectives. For examples:

[like] 5 4 3 2 1 [dislike].

Use of such a scale assumes that all the respondents share an understanding of its range, divisions and extremes. Such an unrealistic assumption can be avoided by introducing order scales and LOE techniques.

We present related works in Section 2, and formalize the LOE task in Section 3. Several LOE solution methods are presented in Section 4, and the experimental results in Sections 5 and 6. Section 7 summarizes our conclusions.

2 Related Works

Our LOE task is relevant to the work of Cohen et al. [1]. The inputs of their task are item pairs with the precedence information; that is information about which of the items should precede the other. From this set of pairs, their original algorithm derived a preference function $\mathrm{PREF}(I^x, I^y)$ measuring the confidence that item I^x precedes item I^y. They then attempted to find the order that maximizes the following function:

$$\sum_{x,y:I^x \succ I^y} \mathrm{PREF}(I^x, I^y), \qquad (1)$$

where $I^x \succ I^y$ denotes that I^x precedes I^y. The most basic difference between their study and ours is that inputs are item pairs with precedence information, whereas inputs of LOE tasks are sets of ordered items. Additionally, their goal was to obtain orders that preserved the pairwise precedence information as closely as possible, whereas ours is to estimate totally well sorted orders. These two orders are closely related, but are clearly distinguishable from one another, as indicated by an experiment described in Section 5. Further, Cohen et al. considered errors in the PREF function, not errors in final orders. We, on the other hand, explicitly examined the errors in final orders. Recently, Kazawa et al. [2] dealt with the similar problem to ours, but adopted another measures for errors in orders.

Several other previous studies have dealt with orders. Mannila and Meek [4], for example, tried to establish the structure expressed by partial orders among a given set of ordered sequential data. Sai et al. [6] investigated association rules between order variables.

3 Formalization of a LOE task

This section formally states the task of learning from order examples (LOE). This task is composed of two major stages: a learning stage and a sorting stage. In the learning stage, the rule for sorting is acquired from a training example set. In the sorting stage, based on the acquired rule, the true order of an unordered item set is estimated.

An item I^x corresponds to an object, entity, or substance to be sorted. Items are individualized by the attribute value vector, $A(I^x) = (a^1(I^x), a^2(I^x), \ldots, a^{\#A}(I^x))$ ($\#A$ is the number of attributes). In this paper, we concentrate on the case in which all the attributes are categorical. The domain of the s-th attribute is $v_1^s, \cdots, v_{\#a^s}^s$. The universal item set, $\{I\}_{All}$, consists of all possible items. An item set, $\{I\}_i$, is a subset of $\{I\}_{All}$. The number of items in $\{I\}_i$ is denoted by $\#I_i$.

An order is a sequence of items that are sorted according to some property, such as size, preference, or price. The order of the item set $\{I\}_i = \{I^x, I^y, \ldots, I^z\}$ is denoted by $O_i = I^x \succ I^y \succ \cdots \succ I^z$. To express the order of two items, $I^x \succ I^y$, we use the sentence "I^x precedes I^y." We assume an unobserved order of the universal item set, and call this the absolute order, O_{All}^*.

The example is a 2-tuple, $(\{I\}_i, O_i^*)$; an item set and its true order. In a noiseless case, the true order is consistent with the absolute order. In a realistic situation, however, true orders may be affected by noises, e.g., swapping of item positions or changes of attribute values. An example set, EX, consists of $\#EX$ examples, as follows:

$$EX = \{(\{I\}_1, O_1^*), (\{I\}_2, O_2^*), \ldots, (\{I\}_{\#EX}, O_{\#EX}^*)\}.$$

Note that there are items included in $\{I\}_{All}$ that do not appear in any examples.

The aim of the LOE task is to acquire the rule from the above training example set. The acquired rule is then used for estimating the true order of an unordered item set. We denote an unordered item set by $\{I\}_U$, and its estimated order by $\hat{O}_U$. Note that attribute value vectors of items in the unordered set are known.

In order to directly evaluate the errors in orders, we adopt the *Spearman's Rank Correlation Coefficient* or the "ρ" [3]. The ρ is the correlation between ranks of items. The rank, $r(O, x)$, is the cardinal number that indicates the position of I^x in the order O. For example, for the order $O = I^3 \succ I^1 \succ I^2$, the $r(O, 3) = 1$ and the $r(O, 2) = 3$. If no tie in rank is allowed, the ρ between two orders, O_i^1 and O_i^2, can be simply calculated as follows:

$$\rho = 1 - \frac{6 \times \sum_{I^x \in \{I\}} (r(O^1, x) - r(O^2, x))^2}{(\#I)^3 - \#I}.$$

The ρ becomes 1 if two orders are coincident, and -1 if one order is a reverse of the other order.

4 Methods

We describe two classification-based and one regression-based solution methods for the LOE task.

4.1 The LOE Methods Based on Classification Techniques

This method is similar to that of Cohen et al. The examples are decomposed into a set of item pairs, and the preference function is derived from these pairs. The unordered items are sorted based on this function.

In the learning stage, from the item set $\{I\}$ in the example $(\{I\}, O^*)$, all the item pairs, (I^x, I^y), are extracted such that I^x precedes I^y in the order O^*. For example, from the order $O^* = I^3 \succ I^1 \succ I^2$, three item pairs, $(I^3, I^1), (I^3, I^2)$, and (I^1, I^2), are extracted. Such pairs are extracted from all $\#EX$ examples, and these are collected into the set P.

Then the preference function, $\text{PREF}(I^x, I^y)$, is derived from the set P. This function, when given the attribute values of $A(I^x)$ and $A(I^y)$, outputs the confidence that I^x precedes I^y in the absolute order. To derive this preference function, we adopt the technique of the naive Bayesian classifier [5], as follows:

$$\text{PREF}(I^x, I^y) = \Pr[I^x \succ I^y | A(I^x), A(I^y)]$$
$$= \frac{\Pr[A(I^x), A(I^y) | I^x \succ I^y]}{\Pr[A(I^x), A(I^y) | I^x \succ I^y] + \Pr[A(I^x), A(I^y) | I^y \succ I^x]},$$

$$\Pr[A(I^x), A(I^y) | I^x \succ I^y] \approx \prod_{s=1}^{\#A} \Pr[a^s(I^x), a^s(I^y) | I^x \succ I^y].$$

Note that $\Pr[I^x \succ I^y] = \Pr[I^y \succ I^x] = 0.5$ is assumed. As the probability $\Pr[a^s(I^x), a^s(I^y) | I^x \succ I^y]$, we adopt the following Bayesian estimator with Dirichlet prior in order that the probability keeps non-zero:

$$\frac{\#(a^s(I^x), a^s(I^y)) + 1/(\#a^s)^2}{\#P + 1},$$

where $\#(a^s(I^x), a^s(I^y))$ is the number of all the pairs (I^z, I^w) such that $a^s(I^x) = a^s(I^z)$ and $a^s(I^y) = a^s(I^w)$, and $\#P$ is the number of pairs in P.

In the sorting stage, by using $\text{PREF}(I^x, I^y)$, the true order of $\{I\}_U$ is estimated. We examined the SumClass and ProductClass strategies, as follows.

SumClass (SC): The following greedy algorithm is designed so as to maximize the Equation (1); that is, the target function of Cohen et al.

1) $\hat{O}^{(0)} := \emptyset, \{I\}^{(0)} := \{I\}_U, t := 0$
2) $I^x := \arg\max_x \sum_{y:I^y \in \{I\}^{(t)}, x \neq y} \text{PREF}(I^x, I^y)$
3) $\hat{O}^{(t+1)} := \hat{O}^{(t)} \succ I^x, \{I\}^{(t+1)} := \{I\}^{(t)} - I^x$
4) if $\{I\}^{(t+1)} = \emptyset$ then output $\hat{O}^{(t+1)}$ as $\hat{O}_U$
            else $t := t + 1$, goto step 2

Simply speaking, this algorithm chooses, one by one, the most-preceding item. Note that this algorithm becomes equivalent to the greedy method of Cohen et al. if $\text{PREF}(I^x, I^y) = 1 - \text{PREF}(I^y, I^x)$ is satisfied.

ProductClass (PC): This strategy is the same as the Sum-Class strategy, except for this criterion of optimality. As the criterion, Cohen et al. adopted Equation (1), (i.e., the sum of the PREF's values), but they did not present any theoretical reason for adopting this sum. We therefore test the product of the PREF values, because this value represents the likelihood of precedence events under the independence assumption. Though these events are not in fact independent, we consider that on a theoretical basis, this criterion has an advantage over that of Cohen et al.

The algorithm is the same as the SumClass strategy, excepting for step 2, which is as follows:

2) $I^x := \arg\max_x \prod_{y:I^y \in \{I\}^{(t)}, x \neq y} \mathrm{PREF}(I^x, I^y)$

4.2 The LOE Methods Based on Regression Techniques

All the orders in the training example are integrated into one total order. By using regression techniques, the evaluation function used for estimating an item's rank is derived. Any unordered items are sorted according to the value of this function. We use the abbreviation "R" for this method.

At the Learning stage, all items that appear in the training example set are collected into one item set, $\{I\}_C$. Next, the system finds the combined order for the $\{I\}_C$ that is as consistent with the orders in the training examples as possible. To derive this combined order, O_C, make the set of item pairs P in the previous section, and calculate the following preference function:

$$\mathrm{PREF}'(I^x, I^y) = \mathrm{Pr}[I^x \succ I^y] = \frac{\#(I^x, I^y) + 0.5}{\#(I^x, I^y) + \#(I^y, I^x) + 1}$$

where $\#(I^x, I^y)$ is the number of the item pairs, (I^x, I^y), in P. By using the strategy ProductClass and the above function PREF', the combined order is derived. Note that the function PREF' is different from the previous PREF with regard to the dependence on attribute values.

From the order O_C, we then acquire the ranking function, RANK, that measures the tendency of precedence. This function is derived by a linear regression technique in which dummy variables are adopted, also known as the *Type I quantification method*. One categorical attribute, $a^s(I)$, is represented by $\#a^s - 1$ dummy variables. The first attribute value, v_1^s, is transformed into all the 0 dummy variables, and the other values, v_t^s, are transformed into dummy variables, the $(t-1)$-th element of which is 1 and the other elements of which are 0. For example, assume the attribute $a^s(I)$ can take 3 values. The values v_1^s and v_3^s are transformed into the dummy variables $(0, 0)$ and $(0, 1)$, respectively. All the variables in $A(I)$ are transformed into dummy variables, and these are concatenated into one vector, $d(A(I))$. For each element I in $\{I\}_C$, the $d(A(I))$ is derived. These vectors are combined into the matrix D whose i-th row is the

Table 1. The means of ρs

	ALL	3	5	10
SC	0.808	0.667	0.825	0.932
PC	0.808	0.667	0.825	0.932
R	0.802	0.617	0.837	0.950

$d(A(I^x))$ such that the rank of I^x is i in the order O_C. By using the following X, the function $\mathrm{RANK}(A(I^x))$ is defined as $X^T d(A(I^x))$:

$$X^T = (D^T D)^{-1} D^T (1, \dots, \#I_C)^T.$$

At a sorting stage, the true order of an unordered item set is estimated by sorting the values of $\mathrm{RANK}(d(A(I)))$.

5 Experiments on Artificial Data

We apply the three methods described in the previous section to artificial data in order to analyze the characteristics of these methods.

We prepared 9 types of universal item sets. The absolute order for these item sets was decided based on the linear weight function. For each type of universal item set, we randomly generated 10 different weights. Accordingly, 90 2-tuples of a universal item set and its absolute order were generated. Furthermore, from each of these tuples, we generated 9 example sets: $\#I$ (the numbers of items) was 3, 5, or 10, and the $\#EX$ (the numbers of examples) was 10, 30, or 50, respectively. In total, 810 example sets were generated. All the data sets were noiseless; that is, all the true orders were consistent with the absolute order.

As the testing procedure, we adopted a leave-one-out (LVO) test; that is, a $\#EX$-fold cross-validation test. As an error measure, we adopted the ρ between the estimated order and the absolute order.

Table 1 shows the means of the ρs. The column labeled "ALL" shows the mean over all 810 example sets, and the columns labeled 3, 5, and 10 show the means over the example sets composed of the item sets whose sizes were 3, 5, and 10, respectively. Overall, in accordance with increase in the size of the item sets, the more proper orders are estimated. For the ρ between two random orders lengths of which are $\#I$, it is known that

$$\rho \sqrt{(\#I - 2)/(1 - \rho^2)}$$

follows the Student t-distribution with degree of freedom $\#I - 2$. Based on this fact, we could check whether, on average, proper orders were estimated or not. All three methods can produce the proper orders when $\#I = 10$ at a significance level of 1%. In short, all three methods work well when item sets are large.

Table 2. The t-values between ρs

	ALL	3	5	10
$SC-PC$	-0.1472	-0.2709	0.3806	-1.5912
$SC-R$	1.4430	$\overline{4.4143}$	-2.2272	-8.5784
$PC-R$	1.4626	$\overline{4.4254}$	-2.3547	-8.5023

We next applied paired t-tests to determine the differences between methods. The $\alpha-\beta$ row of Table 2 shows the t-values for the α method's ρ minus the β method's ρ. The overline (underline) indicates that method α (β) is superior at the significance level of 1%. The columns are the same those in Table 1. The SC and the PC methods were approximately equal in terms of accuracy. However, we consider that the PC method is preferable because it has a theoretical advantage. Although the R method is significantly inferior when item sets are small, the R method surpasses the other two methods as the sizes of the item sets grow. From another experimental result not presented here due to lack of space, it seems that this phenomenon is due to the degree of transitive consistency among the precedence events.

Additional experimental results demonstrated the performance of the SC and the PC methods. These methods adopt a greedy search to find the order that maximizes the sum or the product of the PREF values; thus, the optimal solution may not be acquired. The degree to which the performance by this solution, compared with the optimal solution, is examined. By applying the paired t-test to the optimal ρ minus the greedy ρ, we obtain a t-value of -2.7915 for the SC and -2.9306 for the PC. Surprisingly, this means that the solution by the optimal search is significantly worse than that by the the greedy search. Namely, an effort to preserve the pairwise precedence information does not lead to an order minimizing the rank correlation. This result enhances the distinction between our LOE task and that of Cohen et al. as described in Section 2.

6   Experiments on Realistic Data

We applied the methods in Section 4 to more realistic data in the form of answers to a small questionnaire. We surveyed subjects on their preferences of *sushi* (Japanese food). We asked 52 people to sort 10 types of sushi according to his/her preference. Each item (i.e., a specific type of sushi) is described by five attributes, each of which can take three to five attribute values.

We first generated all possible combinations (i.e., $2^5-1=31$ combinations) of attributes. For each combination and each of the three methods, we applied the LVO test and derived the means of the ρs between the true orders and the estimated orders. For each method, we selected the best combinations of attributes based on these means of the ρs.

The means by using the best combinations are as follows:

SC	PC	R
0.451	0.454	0.455

For the orders estimated by all of the three methods, we observed a correlation between the estimated and the true orders at a significance level of 10%, on average.

The t-values for the differences between the ρs derived by two different methods are as follows:

$SC-PC$	$SC-R$	$PC-R$
-0.1807	-0.3098	-0.1002

We found no statistically significant differences among the three methods. An advantage of the R method was observed in the results on artificial data when the size of item sets are 10, but no such advantage was observed in this result. This is because sufficient examples are available relative to the size of the universal item set, and any method can therefore successfully derive high-quality orders. This was confirmed by the fact that all three methods estimated similar orders.

Finally, it should be noted that by observing the estimated orders and other related data, we can perform further analysis. For example, the survey answers revealed that the most preferred type of sushi is *toro* (fatty tuna). Since the ρ between the estimated order by the R method and my (the first author's) preference order is 0.842, it can be concluded that I have a highly typical tendency in terms of preference of sushi type.

7   Conclusion

We proposed a new learning task and presented its solution methods. We intend to develop the LOE technique so that it can be used to estimate order while directly minimizing the ρ error.

References

[1] W. W. Cohen, R. E. Schapire, and Y. Singer. Learning to order things. *J. of Artificial Intelligence Research*, 10:243–270, 1999.

[2] H. Kazawa, T. Hirao, and E. Maeda. Ranking SVM and its application to sentence selection. In *Proc. of 2002 Workshop on Information-Based Induction Sciences*, 2002. (in Japanese).

[3] M. Kendall and J. D. Gibbons. *Rank Correlation Methods*. Oxford University Press, fifth edition, 1990.

[4] H. Mannila and C. Meek. Global partial orders from sequential data. In *Proc. of The 6th Int. Conf. on Knowledge Discovery and Data Mining*, pages 161–168, 2000.

[5] T. M. Mitchell. *Machine Learning*. The McGraw-Hill Companies, 1997.

[6] Y. Sai, Y. Y. Yao, and N. Zhong. Data analysis and mining in ordered information tables. In *Proc. of the IEEE Int. Conf. on Data Mining*, pages 497–504, 2001.

A Personalized Music Filtering System Based on Melody Style Classification

Fang-Fei Kuo and Man-Kwan Shan

Department of Computer Science
National Cheng Chi University
Taipei, Taiwan, ROC
{g9008 , mkshan}@cs.nccu.edu.tw

Abstract

With the growth of digital music, the personalized music filtering system is helpful for users. Melody style is one of the music features to represent user's music preference. In this paper, we present a personalized content-based music filtering system to support music recommendation based on user's preference of melody style. We propose the multitype melody style classification approach to recommend the music objects. The system learns the user preference by mining the melody patterns from the music access behavior of the user. A two-way melody preference classifier is therefore constructed for each user. Music recommendation is made through this melody preference classifier. Performance evaluation shows that the filtering effect of the proposed approach meets user's preference.

1. Introduction

With the development of digital music technology, it is essential to develop the music filtering system which recommends music for users. The simplest recommendation is to recommend the new music. The advanced one is the personalized recommendation to make recommendation based on the personalized preference.

There are two major approaches for the personalized recommendation. One is the content-based filtering which analyzes the content of objects that the user has liked in the past and recommends the objects with relevant content. The other is the collaborative filtering which recommends objects that peer group of similar preference have liked. Much research has been done on developing the personalized recommendation technology. Research on recommended objects includes the news [3], web navigation, video [2] and music [4][8].

Ringo[8] is a pioneering music recommendation system based on the collaborative filtering approach. In Ringo, the preference of a user is acquired by the user's rating of music. Similar users are identified by comparing the preferences. Ringo predicts the preference of new music for a user by computing a weighted average of all ratings given by peer group of similar preference.

MRS is a system which provides music recommendation based on music grouping and user interests [4]. In MRS, music is grouped based on the extracted features – statistics of pitch, the tempo degree and loudness. Content-based filtering is achieved by recommending the music that belongs to the music groups the user is recently interested in.

The recommendation weight is computed where the latest accessed music has the highest weight. For collaborative filtering, users are grouped based on preferences. If the user's preference weight is lower than that of the user group, the weight difference is used to recommend.

In most approaches of the music recommendation systems, the identification of user's preference is based on the predefined music category. However, sometimes, it is not adequate to represent user's preference on the basis of the predefined category. For example, in the system providing two predefined music category, classic and jazz, what if the user who prefers classic jazz?

In this paper, we propose a new approach to recommend music based on users preference of the melody style. We propose the melody style classification approach to recommend the music objects. The system learns the user's preference by mining the melody patterns from the music access behavior. A two-way melody preference classifier is therefore constructed for each user. Music recommendation is made through this classifier.

2. Personalized filtering system

The proposed personalized filtering system provides the web service of filtering the dispreferred music and recommending the preferred new music. The system uses MIDI files as the raw data. The database contains both MIDI files and the extracted features. Users who first login the system should select their preferred categories from pre-defined categories. Music in the database is then divided into two parts according to the selection. The system mines user's preference and dispreference from both parts and builds the personalized two-way classifier. Then the music is ranked based on the classifier. The recommendation list contains the first *N* highest score songs. User can listen to and download music from the list. The history of the recommended and downloaded files is recorded as the users' profiles for mining the preference later. Figure 1 shows the system architecture.

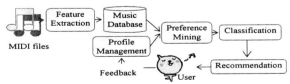

Figure 1. Architecture of Music Filtering System

3. Recommendation

3.1. Preference mining

In this work, we focus on the user's preference on the melody style. To build the preference classifier, we adopt data mining approach to obtain syntactic description of melody style. Issues about the preference mining include feature extraction, feature representation and mining techniques. In the following, we describe the issues in detail.

3.1.1 Feature extraction. In our work, we utilize the chord as the feature for mining the melody style. It is the chords that accompany and correlate closely with the melody. Hence, we can find the chords according to the melody. However, the MIDI files are often polyphonic, extracting melody from the MIDI file is necessary. We adopt the melody extraction method proposed in our previous work [7], which considers the instrument and volume information and keeps the highest note of simultaneous notes.

For the extracted melody, we propose a chord assignment algorithm, which is a heuristic method based on the music theory and Harmony [6]. We choose 60 common chords as the candidates and count score for each chord. The chords are represented in Roman numerals - I , II ,... VII. Figure 2 shows the chord assignment algorithm. To assign chords with appropriate frequency, the algorithm first decides the sampling unit SU according to the note density.

For each SU, the chord assignment contains two stages. In the first stage, we consider the relationship between melody and chords. We add scores for the following reasons: First, in most cases, music starts and ends with Tonic chord (chord I). Moreover, it would be more harmonious if melody sounds simultaneously with chords composed of the same pitches as melody. Last, the longer the pitch's duration in SU, the stronger influences on the chord assignment.

If the chord with the highest score in stage one is not unique and current SU is not the first of the music, we consider the relationship between adjacent chords by chord progression and root motion [6]. Root motion states that some interval of adjacent chords' roots sounds better than others (line 14, 15). According to chord progression (line 16 to 24), some chords are unstable and should progress to the stable chords to make the music sounds completely. Finally, if there is still more than one chord with the highest score, we assign a set of these chords, named as the chord-set.

3.1.2 Feature representation. After extracting the chord-set respective to each SU, melody can be represented as the following different types:

Itemset: melody is represented as a set of chord-sets.

Bi-gram set: melody is represented as a set of adjacent pairs of chord-sets extracted from a sequence of chord-sets.

Sequence: melody is represented as a sequence of chord-set.

3.1.3 Mining techniques. We adopted two melody mining methods with respect to the feature representation types.

Frequent Itemset. If the feature is represented as an itemset (or a bi-gram set), the concept of frequent itemset in the association rule mining is utilized. An itemset is frequent if the percentage of training songs which contain this itemset is larger than minimum support (*min_sup*). We implemented the Apriori algorithm to find the frequent itemsets.

Frequent Substring. For the chord-set sequence, to find the ordered patterns, we propose a new pattern - frequent substring. Frequent substring is modified from the concept of sequential patterns [1] in sequence data mining techniques. The substring is consecutive, which differs from the sequential patterns. A substring is frequent if the number of training songs that contains this substring is larger than *min_sup*. We modified the join step of the Apriori-based sequential mining algorithm to find frequent substring.

3.2. Music Style Classification

In our previous work of the music style classification [7], we adopted a modified associative classification algorithm [5] - Single-Type Uniform Support Classification (STUS). To improve the performance of STUS, we propose a new classification algorithm – Multitype Variant-Support Classification (MTVS).

3.2.1 Single-Type Uniform-Support Classification (STUS). The STUS classifier is an ordered set of rules. Each rule is of the form $l \Rightarrow y$, where $l \in \bigcup_k L_k$, l may be a frequent itemset, a bigram set or a substring and y is a category. Format of the classifier is $<r_1, r_2, ..., r_n, default\_class>$, where each rule r_i is ranked by the confidence and support. The confidence of a rule is the percentage of training songs that satisfy l belong to category y. The first rule that satisfies the test data is used to classify it. If there are no rules satisfying the test data, the classification is according to the default_class.

STUS contains two parts. In the first part, all the frequent itemset or substrings are found. Then, a classifier is built by several passes over the training data using heuristic method. Figure 3 shows the algorithm of part two.

3.2.2 Multitype Variant-Support Classification (MTVS). The algorithm described above employs the rules of one type of patterns and uniform *min_sup*. However, the uniform support may be not appropriate for all cases in the classification. For example, some composers whose style is diverse may have more number of rules but with lower supports.

On the other hand, for each category, the appropriate feature representation may differ from others and even may be a combination of multiple types of patterns. We propose Multitype Variant-Support Classification (MTVS) to build a classifier that contains rules of different types of patterns.

MTVS builds classifiers for all combinations of patterns with various *min_sups* and selects the most effective one. To evaluate the built classifiers, we take five-fold cross-validation. The algorithm trains five times on four of the five subsets and tests on the one left out (validation set). The classifier with highest average accuracy of testing on validation set is returned. Figure 4 shows the algorithm and Figure 5 gives an example of a two-way MTVS classifier.

Algorithm *Determine-Sampling-Unit*
Input: music object m
Output: sampling unit SU
1. Count the occurrence times C_n for all types of notes in m
2. if $\max_n C_n = C_{sixteenth-note}$ and $C_{sixteenth-note} \geq 2C_{eighth-note}$
   then SU = duration of half measure
3. else SU = duration of one measure
4. return SU

Algorithm *Chord-Assignment*
Input: previous chord-set pre_c, sampling unit SU
Output: chord-set CS
1. set scores of each chord c S_c to zero.
2. if $SU \cap (FirstMeasure \cup LastMeasure) \neq \phi$ then $S_{chord1} += 10$
3. for each distinct pitch p, accumulate the duration $D(p)$
4. $\mathbf{P} = \{all\ longest\ pitches\ p\}$
5. if $\max D(p) \geq 0.5 \times SU$ then $score = 2$
6. else if $|\mathbf{P}| = 1$ then $score = 1$ else $score = 0$
7. for each chord c do
8.   for each distinct pitch p in SU do
9.   if c contains p then S_c ++
10.   if $c \cap \mathbf{P} \neq \phi$ then $S_c += score$
11. if cardinality of $\{c|S_c = \max_i S_i\} = 1$ then return c
12.   else if $SU \cap FirstMeasure = \phi$ do
13.   for each chord c do
14.   if $root(pre\_c)$!= leading note and $root(c)$ is descending
               5th, descending 3rd or descending 4th of $root(pre\_c)$ then $S_c += 2$
15.   if $root(pre\_c)$ is subdominant, dominant or leading note
               and $root(c)$ is ascending 2nd then $S_c += 2$
16.   if pre_c = I 7 and c = IV or
17. pre_c = II 7 and c = V or
18. pre_c = III 7 and c = VI or
19. pre_c = IV7 $and\ c$ = V or
20. pre_c = VI7 $and\ c$ = II or
21. pre_c = VII 7 and c = III then $S_c += 2$
22.   if pre_c = V 7 then
23.   if c = I or c = VI then $S_c += 2$
24.   if c = V $then\ S_c += 1$
25.   if cardinality of $\{c|S_c = \max_i S_i\} = 1$ then return c
26.   else for each chord c do
27.   if $root(c)$ = lowest pitch in SU then $S_c += 2$
28.   return $CS = \{c|S_c = \max_i S_i\}$

Figure 2. Chord Assignment Algorithm

3.3. Personalized Recommendation

Once the personalized classifier is generated for the user, the recommendation engine then generates a ranked recommendation list, where the ranking score is based on the classifier. We define three types of recommendation:

(1) Boolean recommendation (BR)

The Boolean recommendation method (BR) makes recommendation by classifying the songs with the personalized classifier directly. The recommendation score of each music object m is defined as

$$BR(m) = \begin{cases} 1, & if\ m \in pc \\ 0, & otherwise \end{cases},$$

where pc is the preferred category of the user.

Among all matched rules, only the highest precedence one which belongs to preferred category contributes to BR. Each song is recommended only if it is classified into preferred category.

(2) Total rank recommendation (TR)

BR only makes use of single rule in the classifier, and all rules in the classifier have a uniform effect upon the ranking score. We propose another method which considers all matched rules and their ranks in the classifier.

The TR ranking score of music object m is defined as:

$$TR(m) = \begin{cases} \sum_{r \in R_{pc}} (|R| - rank(r)) - \sum_{r' \in R_{pc'}} (|R| - rank(r')), if\ \exists r, r'\ satisfies\ m \\ default\_rank, \qquad\qquad otherwise \end{cases},$$

Algorithm *Training-Classifier*
Input: music database MD, *frequent rules of all classes*
Output: *Classifier*
1. sort rules by confidence and support
2. for each rule r do
3.   for each music object m in MD do
4.   if r satisfies m then mark m to be classified
5.   if $\exists m$ be classified correctly by r then
6.   remove all marked m from MD
7.   insert r into the end of *Classifier*
8. $default\_class(r)$ = majority category of music in MD
9.   count total error of *Classifier*
10. remove rules after the first rule r' whose total error is lowest in *Classifier*
11. insert the $default\_class(r')$ to the end of *Classifier*
12. return *Classifier*

Figure 3. Training Classifier Algorithm

Algorithm *Multitype-Variant-Supports-Classification*
Input: music database MD, candidates of min_sup MS
Output: *Classifier*
1. divide training data of each category y into 5 subsets $T_{y,k}$
2. for each combination of min_sups and multiple patterns of all categories do
3.   for $k = 1$ to 5 do
4.   for each category y do
5. $training\_set_y = \bigcup_{i \neq k} T_{y,i}$
6. $validation\_set_y = T_{y,k}$
7.   mine frequent itemsets, bi-gram sets and substrings
               from $training\_set_y$
8.   for each type of patterns do
9.   calculate confidence of frequent patterns
10.   *Classifier* = *Training-Classifier*
11.   classify each $validation\_set_y$ by *Classifier* and store the accuracy a_k
12.   accuracy of all combinations = $\sum a_k / 5$
13. return the *Classifier* with the highest accuracy

Figure 4. MTVS Classification Algorithm

Set: { I , III , IV7} → class: A
Bigram: {(V I), (V 7 VII)} → class: B
Bigram: {(I II), (IV7 V), (II VI)} → class: A
Sequence: (V III II V I) → class: B
Default_class: class B

Figure 5. An two-way MTVS Classifier

$$with\ default\_rank = \begin{cases} 1, & if\ default\_class = pc \\ -1, & otherwise \end{cases},$$

where r and r' are rules in the classifier that satisfies m, R is set of all rules, R_{pc} and $R_{pc'}$ represent sets of rules that belong to preferred and dispreferred categories respectively. If confidences and supports of two rules are equal, the ranks of two rules are the same. If there is no rule satisfying m, TR is set to be $default\_rank$.

(3) Total confidence recommendation (TC)

Total confidence recommendation is modified from TR, which considers the confidences of all matched rules. The confidence not only reflects the strength of each rule but also contains the order information in the classifier. TC of music object m is defined as

$$TC(m) = \begin{cases} \sum_{r \in R_{pc}} conf(r) - \sum_{r' \in R_{pc'}} conf(r'), if\ \exists r, r'\ satisfies\ m \\ \pm default\_conf, \qquad\qquad otherwise \end{cases},$$

where $default\_conf = \dfrac{|remaining\_music \in default\_class|}{|remaining\_music|}$.

TC is set to be default confidence if there are no rules satisfying m. If the default class equals to preferred class, we give the default confidence a positive sign, and vice versa.

4. Experiments and results

The performance of the proposed recommendation mechanism is affected by two factors, one is the two-way MTVS classification, and the other is three recommendation methods described above. We performed two series of experiments for these influential factors.

4.1. Evaluation of Music Style Classifier

The experimental data in first part included four categories of MIDI files – Chinese folk song, Enya, Chopin and Bach. These categories are defined by various view points, including country, composer or singer. We collected Chinese folk songs from http://ingeb.org. Enya's music was gathered from several web sites of Enya. Chopin's music was acquired from the web site http://egalvao.com/chopin/. Bach's music was downloaded from http://www.bachcentral. com/. Each category contains 39 to 55 MIDI files.

The performance of the two-way MTVS classification is measured by the accuracy, which is defined as the percentage that the test songs are classified correctly. We took five-fold cross-validation to evaluate the performance.

Table 1 shows the results of the two-way MTVS classification. The categories A, B, C, D denotes Chinese folk, Enya, Chopin and Bach respectively. From the results of the classification, we can observe that music of Enya and Chopin (B-C) are less discriminating between each other because they are also peaceful. Other pairs perform well. This is consistent with our intuition.

4.2. Evaluation of Personalized Recommendation

In our recommendation system, the data set contains 245 MIDI files. Each file belongs to one of the pre-defined categories – Chinese folk, American folk, Enya, Elton John, Beatles, Chopin and Bach. Music of singer Elton John was collected from various web sites of Elton John. The album of Beatles was accessed from http://www.geocities.com/ SunsetStrip/Studio/7779/. American folk songs were collected from http://ingeb.org. The other categories are the same as the first part of experiments.

Ten users participated in our experiments. All users were requested to listening to all recommended songs to ensure the downloaded files being their preferences.

Performance measure of the recommendation is defined as

$$precision = N_{download} / N ,$$

where $N_{download}$ is the number of music files which are downloaded by user in the recommendation list, and N is the number of music files in the list. In our experiment, N is 20.

Table 2 and Table 3 show results of the recommendation based on three recommendation methods. Table 2 shows the average precision of each round. In Table 3, column 2 is average precision of all users over five recommendations. In addition, we average last 3 iterations to eliminate the influences from the predefined categories.

The results show that recommendation based on BR performed better than the other two ranking methods, and

there are no significant difference between the performances of TR and TC. TC improved as the recommendation times increased.

During the experiments, we made some observation about the users' behavior. Some users may feel impatient in selecting the preferred music. Furthermore, quality of MIDI files also affects users' selection. These external factors also affect the performance of recommendation experiment.

Table 1. Results of two-way MTVS classification

	A-B	A-C	A-D	B-C	B-D	C-D
Average accuracy	80.83%	83.32%	69.64%	58.93%	81.72%	81.89%

Table 2. Average precision for each round of recommendation

Recommendation rounds	1	2	3	4	5
BR	0.64	0.66	0.57	0.61	0.68
TR	0.67	0.51	0.49	0.52	0.67
TC	0.43	0.52	0.54	0.62	0.57

Table 3. Average precision of recommendation

	Total average	Average of last 3 rounds
BR	0.6328	0.6214
TR	0.57	0.56
TC	0.54	0.58

5. Conclusion

In this paper we presented a music filtering system by learning the user's preference on melody style. We proposed a modified melody style classification algorithm – Multitype Variant-Support Classification (MTVS) and described three recommendation methods based on the preference classifier. Experiments show that two-way MTVS classification performs well and the performance of recommendation method BR is better than other two methods.

References

[1] R. Agrawal and R. Srikant, "Mining Sequential Patterns," *Proc. of International Conference on Data Engineering ICDE'95*, 1995.

[2] C. Basu, H. Hirsh and W. Cohen, "Recommendation as Classification: Using Social and Content-Based Information in Recommendation," *Proc. of National Conference on Artificial Intelligence AAAI'98*, 1998.

[3] D. Billsus and M. Pazzani, "A Hybrid User Model for News Story Classification," *Proc. of International Conference on User Modeling*, 1999.

[4] H. C. Chen and A. L. P Chen, "A Music Recommendation System Based on Music Data Grouping and User Interests," *Proc. of ACM International Conference on Information and Knowledge Management CIKM'01*, 2001.

[5] B. Liu, W. Hsu, and Y. Ma, "Integrating Classification and Association Rule Mining," *Proc. of ACM International Conference on Knowledge Discovery and Data Mining KDD'98*, 1998.

[6] Percy A. Scholes, The beginner's guide to harmony, Oxford University Press, 1924.

[7] M. K. Shan, F. F. Kuo, and M. F. Chen, "Music Style Mining and Classification by Melody," *Proc. of IEEE International Conference on Multimedia and Expo ICME'02*, 2002.

[8] U. Shardanand and P. Maes, "Social Information Filtering: Algorithms for Automating 'Word of Mouth'," *Proc. of the Conference on Human Factors in Computing Systems*, 1995.

Solving the Fragmentation Problem of Decision Trees by Discovering Boundary Emerging Patterns

Jinyan Li   Limsoon Wong
Laboratories for Information Technology
21 Heng Mui Keng Terrace, Singapore 119613
{jinyan, limsoon}@lit.org.sg

Abstract

The single coverage constraint discourages a decision tree to contain many significant rules. The loss of significant rules leads to a loss in accuracy. On the other hand, the fragmentation problem causes a decision tree to contain too many minor rules. The presence of minor rules decreases accuracy. We propose to use emerging patterns to solve these problems. In our approach, many globally significant rules can be discovered. Extensive experimental results on gene expression datasets show that our approach are more accurate than single C4.5 trees, and are also better than bagged or boosted C4.5 trees.

1. Introduction

Decision trees, typically constructed by C4.5 [13], CART [2], or ID3 [12], are widely used in machine learning since their conception in the CLS framework [6]. A decision tree is a tree-based compact structure consisting of classification rules learnt from training data. These methods have two shortcomings. The first is the *fragmentation problem*. At the lower levels of a decision tree, the feature selection procedure uses fewer and fewer training data. This usually leads to the generation of many locally important but globally insignificant rules [11]. The second is the *single coverage constraint*. Every training instance is to be covered by exactly one rule. This leads to the loss of important rules. Sometimes, the number of rules contained in a decision tree is far less than the total number of rules inherent to the data, especially for gene expression datasets. Therefore, the accuracy of decision tree classifiers is overall inferior to other classifiers like neural networks and support vector machines (SVMs). Nevertheless, compared to neural networks and SVMs, decision tree classifiers have the advantage that their rules are easily comprehensible. This is particularly important in diagnosing a disease as medical doctors sometimes need to explain their decisions to colleagues and patients.

This paper proposes an emerging pattern (EP) approach [3] to solve these problems by discovering rules that are globally significant in a computationally efficient way. An EP is defined as a set of conjunctive conditions that most instances of a class satisfy and none of the other class satisfies. So an EP is also a classification rule. In this study, we compare EPs with decision trees. The EP approach outperforms decision trees on accuracy in general, and is competitive to that of SVMs. At the same time, the EP approach maintains the favorable comprehensibility of the rules derived from decision trees.

2. Decision Trees

The construction of a decision tree is a recursive process. The process involves determining the attribute which is *most* discriminatory and then splitting the training instances into groups. Each group contains multi-class instances or single-class instances, as categorized by this attribute. Next, a significant attribute of each of the subsets (groups) is used to further partition them and the process is repeated recursively until all the subsets each contain data of one class only. The resulting structure is called a decision tree, each node of which is an attribute discrimination test and each branch of which is a subset of the collection of training instances satisfying the test.

The main components of the tree—*leaves* and *nodes*—have distinct meanings. A leaf indicates a class name that is described in the training data. A node specifies a test to be carried out on a single attribute value with one branch and a subtree for each possible outcome of the test. A decision tree can be used to classify an instance by starting at the root of the tree and moving through it until a leaf is encountered. The class of the instance is predicted to be that stored at the leaf.

The key to constructing a decision tree is how to choose

an appropriate attribute as the root node, and subsequently some other attributes as the other nodes. For a training set, many alternative trees can be constructed by different feature selection metrics. Preferably, a tree should have a small number of leaves such that rules derived from it can be more readable and at the same time more reliable. Less leaves means that, on the average, there are more instances per leaf. This gives the derived rules a better statistical confirmation. Finding optimal decision trees is known to be an NP-complete problem [7]. C4.5 [13] is a heuristic algorithm for inducing decision trees. C4.5 uses an entropy-based selection measure to determine which attribute is most discriminatory. Most decision trees in the literature are constructed by this method.

Decision trees have these characteristics:

1. Single coverage of training data. Every instance in the training data must satisfy one and only one of the rules in the decision tree.

2. Fragmentation problem. In order to discover mutually exclusive parts of the original training data, C4.5 uses a top-down successive subdivision idea to recursively partition the training data. This strategy causes the *fragmentation problem* because towards the end of the subdivision process, the size of the underlying data becomes quite small, even though a statistical test requires a data of significant size [11, 5].

3. Locally reliable but globally insignificant rules. Due to the fragmentation problem, C4.5 trees always contain many "minor" rules. Eg., wrt the `Play` vs. `Don't Play` example of [13], the rule "if `outlook = sunny` and `humidity` $\leq$ `75` then `Play`", has only 22% (2 out of 9) coverage over all `Play` instances. Yet this rule has a 100% coverage (2 out of 2) over those `Play` instances that satisfy the condition "`outlook = sunny`". These minor rules may mislead the tree, and thus decrease the classification performance on independent test data.

Decision committee techniques such as AdaBoost [4] and Bagging [1] have been proposed to reduce the error rate of single trees. They both apply the C4.5 base classifier multiple times to generate a committee of classifiers. Each member classifier plays a particular role in classifying a test instance. Assume a training data of N instances be given, and a R number of repetitions or *trials* of the base classifier be applied.

By the bagging idea, for each trial $t = 1, 2, \cdots, R$, a bootstrapped training set is generated from the original instances. This new training set is the same size as the original data, but some instances may not appear in it while others appear more than once. Denote the R bootstrapped training sets as $B_1, B_2, \cdots, B_R$. For each B_t, a classifier C_t is

built. A final, bagged classifier C^* is constructed by aggregating $C_1, C_2, \cdots$, and C_R. The output of C^* is the class predicted most often by its sub-classifiers, with ties broken arbitrarily.

The boosting method also uses a committee of classifiers for classification by voting. Bagging builds the individual classifiers separately; but boosting builds them sequentially and each new classifier is influenced by the performance of those built previously. Those data incorrectly classified by previous models are always emphasized in the new model with an aim to let the new model become an expert for classifying those hard instances. Another difference is that boosting weights the individual classifiers' output depending on their performance, rather than giving equal weight to all the committee members.

3 Emerging Patterns

A *condition* (also called an *item*) is defined as a pair of an attribute and its a value. A *pattern* is simply a set of conditions. A pattern is said to *occur* in an instance if the instance contains this pattern. For two classes of instances, a pattern can have a very high occurrence in one class, but can change to a low or even zero occurrence in the other class.

Definition 3.1 Given two classes of data, an *emerging pattern* is a pattern whose frequency in one class is non-zero but in the other class is zero. A *boundary* EP is an EP whose proper subsets are not EPs.

If a pattern contains fewer items (conditions), then the frequency (probability) that it occurs in a class becomes larger. Removing any item from a boundary EP thus increases its home class frequency. However, by definition of boundary EPs, its frequency in the counterpart class becomes non-zero. Therefore, boundary EPs are maximally frequent in their home class. They separate EPs from non-EPs. They also distinguish EPs with high occurrence from EPs with low occurrence. Efficient discovery of boundary EPs has been solved in our previous work [3, 9].

In general, the EP approach has the following characteristics:

- A cluster of trees. Each EP is a tree with only one branch. Some EPs can be integrated into a bigger tree. However, these bigger trees usually cannot be combined into a single tree.

- Globally siginificant rules. Boundary EPs are aimed to differentiate one class from another by using as many instances as possible. The distinction is in terms of a whole class. However, some C4.5 rules are discovered based only on a fraction of a class and a fraction of another class. Globally, those locally discovered C4.5 rules may lose their significance. However, all top-ranked EPs are all globally important rules.

- Exponential number in size. By the greedy heuristic and the single coverage constraint, C4.5 always produces decision trees with small numbers of rules. In contrast, the number of boundary EPs can increase exponentially when the number of attributes and the number of discretized values for the attributes increase. This problem can be alleviated by selecting the most important attributes for EP discovery. Due to the removal of the less important attributes, many EPs are consequently missed. However, the most important EPs are still maintained.

PCL [15, 10, 8] is a way to aggregate the discriminating power of multiple EPs. Basically, the PCL classifier has two phases. Given two training datasets $\mathcal{D}_P$ (instances of class P) and $\mathcal{D}_N$ (instances of class N) and a test sample T, PCL first discovers two groups of boundary EPs from $\mathcal{D}_P$ and $\mathcal{D}_N$. Denote the ranked EPs of $\mathcal{D}_P$ as, EP_P_1, EP_P_2, $\cdots$, EP_P_i, in descending order of frequency. Denote the ranked boundary EPs of $\mathcal{D}_N$ as EP_N_1, EP_N_2, $\cdots$, EP_N_j, in descending order of frequency. Suppose the test sample T contains these EPs of $\mathcal{D}_P$: $EP\_P\_i_1$, $EP\_P\_i_2$, $\cdots$, $EP\_P\_i_x$, $i_1 < i_2 < \cdots < i_x \leq i$, and these EPs of $\mathcal{D}_N$: $EP\_N\_j_1$, $EP\_N\_j_2$, $\cdots$, $EP\_N\_j_y$, $j_1 < j_2 < \cdots < j_y \leq j$.

The next step is to calculate two scores for predicting the class label of T. Suppose we use k ($k \ll i$ and $k \ll j$) top-ranked EPs of $\mathcal{D}_P$ and $\mathcal{D}_N$. Then we define the score of T in the $\mathcal{D}_P$ class as

$$score(T)\_\mathcal{D}_P = \sum_{m=1}^{k} \frac{frequency(EP\_P\_i_m)}{frequency(EP\_P\_m)},$$

and similarly the score in the $\mathcal{D}_N$ class as

$$score(T)\_\mathcal{D}_N = \sum_{m=1}^{k} \frac{frequency(EP\_N\_j_m)}{frequency(EP\_N\_m)}.$$

If $score(T)\_\mathcal{D}_P > score(T)\_\mathcal{D}_N$, then T is predicted as the class of $\mathcal{D}_P$. Otherwise it is predicted as the class of $\mathcal{D}_N$. We use the size of $\mathcal{D}_P$ and $\mathcal{D}_N$ to break tie.

4   Comparison

We use a recently published gene expression dataset [14] for a comparison between C4.5 and PCL. The data was used to predict common clinical and pathological phenotypes relevant to the treatment of men diagnosed with prostate cancer. This dataset consists of 52 Tumor and 50 Normal

instances. All instances are described by 12600 attributes, each representing the expression level of a particular gene.

Using the 102 instances, C4.5 constructs a decision tree with 5 leaves. Of the 5 rules each corresponding to a leaf, 3 are not globally significant as they cover no more than 6 instances each. Using the EP approach, we discovered many significant rules. In fact, the top 20 rules all have coverage of about 70% of their home class. The EP discovery process is as follows. First, use the entropy-based discretization method to discretize the 12600 attributes. Then, select 20 most important discretized attributes such that they have the lowest entropy values. Then, remove the other attributes from the original data. Finally, use border-based algorithms [3, 9] to discover the boundary EPs.

Of the four genes selected by C4.5 in its 5 rules, only one (32598_at) is in common with the top 20 genes selected by our method. The list of our genes are ranked in a global manner. Thus, we can discover many globally important rules. The other three genes (34950_at, 33886_at, 40707_at) selected by C4.5 are at the 47th, 869th, and out of 1000 positions respectively in our list. The single coverage constraint and the fragmentation problem induce another problem that features selected by C4.5 can be far away from globally top-ranked features. To solve it and to improve accuracy of C4.5, we force C4.5 to select its favourable features within globally top-ranked features.

The accuracy of C4.5 and PCL are reported in Table 1. All experiments are conducted on the discretized data of the 20 most important genes, using the Weka package with its standard settings. We can see that the LOOCV (Leave one out cross-validation) and 10-fold CV accuracy of our PCL classifier is higher than C4.5, even after incorporating the Bagging or Boosting ideas. The accuracy of PCL is also very close to that of 3-NN, and much better than SVM. We note that the LOOCV accuracy of the single C4.5 tree, bagged C4.5 trees, and boosted C4.5 trees on the original data (without discretization and removal of features) is 87%, 92%, and 92% respectively with an error rate of 8:5, 3:5, and 3:5 (Tumor:Normal).

In C4.5, the decision tree is greedily constructed using an information gain idea and using a divide-and-conquer technique to stop the search of the most discriminatory features. As gene expression profiles often contain very large number of features, there exist many (tens of) good genes to separate two classes of cells. The greedily chosen genes from the training data may not be the optimal features for test data. There may well be many other equally discriminatory genes in the training data that got discarded. Thus, the accuracy of C4.5 can be sometimes greatly suffer from this problem. This problem can be partially solved by using a collection of decision trees constructed by the bagging and boosting ideas.

Table 1. The LOOCV and 10-fold CV accuracy and error rate of four classification models on the prostate disease datasets. Note that error rate $x:y$ means x number of Tumor instances and y number of Normal instances are mis-classified.

Method	Performance	PCL			C4.5			SVM	3-NN
		$k=5,10,15$			Single	Bagging	Boosting		
LOOCV	Accuracy (%)	95.1	95.1	95.1	91.2	94.1	93.1	90.2	96.1
	Error rate	3:2	3:2	2:3	6:3	4:2	5:2	5:5	1:3
10-fold CV	Accuracy (%)	97.1	97.1	95.1	92.2	92.2	93.1	90.2	96.1
	Error rate	2:1	2:1	2:3	4:4	5:3	4:3	5:5	1:3

The fragmentation problem of decision trees can be solved by discovering highly frequent boundary EPs in an efficient way. Extensive experimental results on high-dimensional gene expression data showed that our PCL classifier can outperform C4.5 (including bagged and boosted) on accuracy.

The bagging and boosting ideas can improve the accuracy of single C4.5 trees in most cases. However, sometimes, the boosting method cannot help C4.5 when the first tree make no mistakes on training data. The bagging method can sometimes decrease single tree's performance. This is because boostrapped samples can change much of the nature of the original training data. The rules provided by the bagged trees should be understood cautiously as the rules may not be valid when applied to the original training data.

By our EP approach, we have discovered many globally significant rules. These rules can have multiple coverage over training data. This step beyond the single coverage constraint let us make full use of important rules of training data. This is also a reason why our classifier is more accurate.

References

[1] L. Breiman. Bagging predicator. *Machine Learning*, 24:123–140, 1996.

[2] L. Breiman, J. Friedman, R. Olshen, and C. Stone. *Classification and Regression Trees*. Wadsworth International Group, Belmont, CA, 1984.

[3] G. Dong and J. Li. Efficient mining of emerging patterns: Discovering trends and differences. In S. Chaudhuri and D. Madigan, editors, *Proceedings of the Fifth ACM SIGKDD International Conference on Knowledge Discovery and Data Mining*, pages 43–52, San Diego, CA, 1999. ACM Press.

[4] Y. Freund and R. E. Schapire. Experiments with a new boosting algorithm. In L. Saitta, editor, *Machine Learning: Proceedings of the Thirteenth International Conference*, pages 148–156, Bari, Italy, July 1996. Morgan Kaufmann.

[5] J. H. Friedman, R. Kohavi, and Y. Yun. Lazy decision trees. In *Proceedings of the Thirteenth National Conference on Artificial Intelligence, AAAI 96*, pages 717–724, Portland, Oregon, August 1996. AAAI Press.

[6] E. B. Hunt, J. Marin, and P. T. Stone. *Experiments in Induction*. Academic Press, New York, 1966.

[7] L. Hyafil and R. Rivest. Constructing optimal binary decision trees in np-complete. *Information Processing Letters*, 5:15–17, 1976.

[8] J. Li, H. Liu, J. R. Downing, A. E.-J. Yeoh, and L. Wong. Simple rules underlying gene expression profiles of more than six subtypes of acute lymphoblastic leukemia (ALL) patients. *Bioinformatics*, page In Press, 2002.

[9] J. Li, K. Ramamohanarao, and G. Dong. The space of jumping emerging patterns and its incremental maintenance algorithms. In *Proceedings of the Seventeenth International Conference on Machine Learning, Stanford, CA, USA*, pages 551–558, San Francisco, June 2000. Morgan Kaufmann.

[10] J. Li and L. Wong. Geography of differences between two classes of data. In *Proceedings of the 6th European Conference on Principles of Data Mining and Knowledge Discovery, PKDD 2002*, pages 325 – 337, Helsinki, Finland, 2002. Springer-Verlag.

[11] G. Pagallo and D. Haussler. Boolean feature discovery in empirical learning. *Machine Learning*, 5:71–99, 1990.

[12] J. R. Quinlan. Induction of decision trees. *Machine Learning*, 1:81–106, 1986.

[13] J. R. Quinlan. *C4.5: Programs for Machine Learning*. Morgan Kaufmann, San Mateo, CA, 1993.

[14] D. Singh, P. G. Febbol, K. Ross, D. G. Jackson, J. Manola, C. Ladd, P. Tamayo, A. A. Renshaw, A. V. D'Amico, J. P. Richie, E. S. Lander, M. Loda, P. W. Kantoff, T. R. Golub, and W. R. Sellers. Gene expression correlates of clinical prostate cancer behavior. *Cancer Cell*, 1:203–209, March 2002.

[15] E.-J. Yeoh, M. E. Ross, S. A. Shurtleff, W. K. Williams, D. Patel, R. Mahfouz, F. G. Behm, S. C. Raimondi, M. V. Relling, A. Patel, C. Cheng, D. Campana, D. Wilkins, X. Zhou, J. Li, H. Liu, C.-H. Pui, W. E. Evans, C. Naeve, L. Wong, and J. R. Downing. Classification, subtype discovery, and prediction of outcome in pediatric acute lymphoblastic leukemia by gene expression profiling. *Cancer Cell*, 1:133–143, 2002.

Improving Medical/Biological Data Classification Performance by Wavelet Preprocessing

Qi Li
Department of CIS
University of Delaware
Newark, DE 19716
qili@cis.udel.edu

Tao Li , Shenghuo Zhu
Department of CS
University of Rochester
Rochester, NY 14620
{taoli,zsh}@cs.rochester.edu

Chandra Kambhamettu
Department of CIS
University of Delaware
Newark, DE 19716
chandra@cis.udel.edu

Abstract

Many real-world datasets contain noise and noise could degrade the performances of learning algorithms. Motivated from the success of wavelet denoising techniques in image data, we explore a general solution to alleviate the effect of noisy data by wavelet preprocessing for medical/biological data classification. Our experiments are divided into two categories: one is of different classification algorithms on a specific database (*Ecoli* [6]) and the other is of a specific classification algorithm (decision tree) on different databases. The experiment results show that the wavelet denoising of noisy data is able to improve the accuracies of those classification methods, if the localities of the attributes are strong enough.

1. INTRODUCTION

Noise is a random error or variance of a measured variable [3]. Many real-world datasets contain noise. There are many possible reasons for noisy data, such as measurement errors during the data acquisition, human and computer errors occurring at data entry, technology limitations and natural phenomena. Removing noise from data can be considered as a process of identifying outliers or constructing optimal estimates of unknown data from available noisy data. Various smoothing techniques, such as binning methods, clustering and outlier detection, have been used in data mining literature to remove noise. Most of these methods, however, are not specially designed in order to deal with noise and noise reduction and smoothing are only side-products of learning algorithms for other tasks. The information loss caused by these methods is also a problem.

Wavelet techniques have been successfully applied in image research area. The main idea of wavelet denoising is to transform the data into the wavelet domain, where the *large* coefficients are mainly the useful information and the *smaller* ones represent noise. By suitably modifying the coefficients in the new basis, noise can be directly removed from the data. Though wavelet techniques have been widely used for image data, little work has been reported on using wavelet techniques to denoise other kinds of data, say, medical/biological data which are mainly obtained by experiments or measurements and hence have a good chance of containing noise. This is because image data usually have strong (spatial) locality[1], but locality of medical/biological data is usually hidden. Although medical/biological data lack the spatial locality, in our recent investigation, we found that most medical/biological data contain a certain kind of locality which makes the use of wavelet techniques for denoising plausible. Take the *Ecoli* database [6] for example: the *Ecoli* database is used for predicting the cellular localization sites of proteins and it contains 336 instances with 8 attributes for each instance. The 6th attribute represents the score of discriminant analysis of the amino acid content of outer membrane and periplasmic proteins. It originally contains 8 classes where one class has 5 instances, two other classes have 2 instances each, 3 classes are subcases for a big class and 2 other classes are subcases of another big class. So we then simply the 8 classes into 4 classes: cytoplasm, perisplasm, inner membrane and outer membrane. We organize the data according to these four classes, i.e., the data in the same class are placed together and plot the distribution of their 6th attribute as shown in Figure 1. We observe good locality of the data from Figure 1 and hence it is plausible to use wavelet techniques to remove the noise.

2. WAVELET DENOISING

---

[1] By locality, we refer to continuity in the sense that the variance of the data is relatively small in its neighborhood.

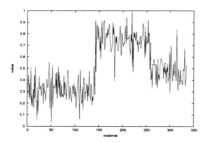

Figure 1: Locality of the 6th attribute in the _Ecoli_ dataset

Suppose observation data $y = (y_1, \ldots, y_n)$ is a noisy realization of the signal $x = (x_1, \ldots, x_n)$, $y_i = x_i + \epsilon_i$, $i = 1, \ldots, n$, where ϵ_i is noise. It is commonly assumed that ϵ_i are independent from the signal and are independent and identically distributed (_iid_) Gaussian random variables. A usual way to denoise is to find $\hat{x}$ such that it minimizes the mean square error (MSE), $MSE(\hat{x}) = \frac{1}{n} \sum_{i=1}^{n} (\hat{x}_i - x_i)^2$.

[2] has developed a methodology called _waveShrink_ for estimating x. It has been widely applied in many applications and implemented in commercial software, e.g., wavelet toolbox of Matlab. There are three commonly used shrinkage functions: the hard, soft and the non-negative garrote shrinkage functions:

$$\delta_\lambda^H(x) = \begin{cases} 0 & |x| \leq \lambda \\ x & |x| > \lambda \end{cases}$$

$$\delta_\lambda^S(x) = \begin{cases} 0 & |x| \leq \lambda \\ x - \lambda & x > \lambda \\ \lambda - x & x < -\lambda \end{cases}$$

$$\delta_\lambda^H(x) = \begin{cases} 0 & |x| \leq \lambda \\ x - \lambda^2/x & |x| > \lambda \end{cases}$$

where $\lambda \in [0, \infty)$ is the threshold.

Wavelet denoising generally is different from traditional filtering approaches and it is nonlinear, due to a thresholding step. Determining threshold λ is the key issue in waveShrink denoising. Minimax threshold is one of commonly used thresholds. The _minimax threshold_ λ^* is defined as threshold λ which minimizes expression

$$\inf_\lambda \sup_\theta \left\{ \frac{R_\lambda(\theta)}{n^{-1} + \min(\theta^2, 1)} \right\}, \qquad (2.1)$$

where $R_\lambda(\theta) = E(\delta_\lambda(x) - \theta)^2, x \sim N(\theta, 1)$. Interested readers can refer to [7] for other methods.

3. EXPERIMENTAL RESULTS

We use the minimax threshold to denoise since it has been reported to be very efficient. We also choose wavelet Db4 [1] in our experiments. The complete experimental results description can be found in our tech report [4].

3.1 Wavelet denoising for different classifiers

In this section, we investigate the effects of wavelet denoising for different classification techniques on _Ecoli_ database which is available from UCI machine learning repository [6]. We compare the performance of different classifiers on _Ecoli_ database between two cases: data with wavelet preprocessing and data without wavelet preprocessing. To further demonstrate the effects of wavelet techniques, we also derive several additional database by injecting noise into the _Ecoli_ database and perform the comparison across a range of noise levels.

The four classifiers we used are: decision tree, naive Bayes, PART rule learner, and oneR. The _Ecoli_ database is used to predict the cellular localization sites of proteins and it contains 336 instances with 8 attributes for each instance. We organized the data according the 6th attribute which represents the score of discriminant analysis of the amino acid content of outer membrane and periplasmic proteins and it may contain noise due to measurement errors. To denoise the database, we then preprocess data of 6th column with waveShrink technique before applying the classifiers on the database. We also derive 4 additional noisy databases from the original _Ecoli_ database by injecting different levels of noise. Denote the standard deviation of the 6th attribute of the original _Ecoli_ database as σ_6. The noise we add into the _Ecoli_ database satisfy Gaussian distributions with zero mean and standard deviations: $percentage_i \times \sigma_6$, $i = 1, 2, 3, 4$, where $percentage_i = 0.03, 0.05, 0.08$ and 0.1.

Figure 2 shows the comparisons between classification accuracies on data with wavelet preprocessing and data without preprocessing by decision tree, naive Bayes classifier, PART rule learner and oneR respectively. The accuracies are obtained by three-fold cross-validation. The improvements in decision tree, naive Bayes and oneR are obvious. There are about 1.6% improvement in decision tree, 1.4% improvement in naive Bayes and 3% improvement in oneR on average. And at different noise levels, the performance of decision tree, naive Bayes classifier and oneR on data with wavelet preprocessing is always better than those without preprocessing. The performance of PART rule learner on data with preprocessing before noise level 0.05 is better than those without preprocessing and after noise level 0.05, the former is beaten by the latter. This half-part success of wavelet preprocessing obviates our experience and intuition which tell us that the average performance

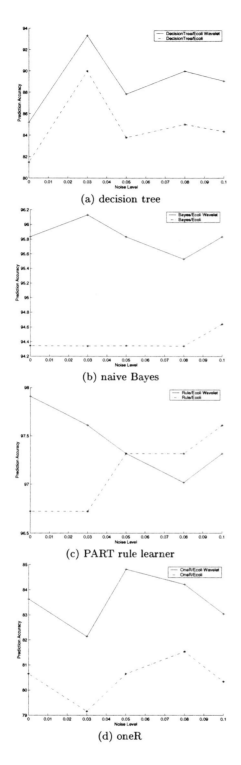

(a) decision tree

(b) naive Bayes

(c) PART rule learner

(d) oneR

Figure 2: The performance with four classifiers.

is usually degraded with the increasing noise levels. So we tend to see the performance comparison with PART rule learner on the *Ecoli* database a neutral result (neither positive nor negative).

In short, wavelet preprocessing is a promising method to improve the classification performance for different classifiers on the *Ecoli* database. But notice that the good locality (Figure 1) of the *Ecoli* database may not be owned by the other medical databases. So we need to study the effect of wavelet preprocessing on different kind of databases which is the task of Section 3.2.

3.2 Wavelet denoising on different databases

In this section, we investigate the effects of wavelet denoising on different databases with decision tree techniques. We compare the performance of decision tree classifiers on data with wavelet preprocessing and those without preprocessing. The databases we used are heart disease databases. They are also available in UCI machine learning depository [6]. We choose decision tree classifier since it is one of the most widely used techniques in practice.

Heart disease databases consist of real, experimental data from four international medical organizations, Cleveland Clinic Foundation, Hungarian Institute of Cardiology, the University Hospitals in Zurich and Basel in Switzerland, and V.A. Medical Center in Long Beach, California (VAMC). These databases have been widely used by researchers to develop prediction models for coronary diseases. There are a large amount of missing data of VAMC. 689 entries out of (200×13) are missing. Since missing values may seriously bias the threshold estimation, we will only consider the heart disease databases of *Cleveland, Hungarian and Switzerland*.

The arrangement of data is indexed by the monotonically increasing age of sampling people. The eighth column of the heart disease database is data on maximum heart rate. The maximum heart rate is affected by the activity and/or levels of fitness. The different activity may result a difference of $3-5$ beats in the number. For example, studies show that maximum heart rate on a treadmill is consistently $5-6$ beats higher than on a bicycle ergometer and $2-3$ beats higher on a rowing ergometer [5]. Also improper procedures introduce errors in the measurement. We also derive 4 additional noisy databases from the original database by injecting different levels of noise. The performances are obtained by randomly splitting the dataset into two: 80% for training and 20% for testing. Figure 3 shows the performances of decision tree classifier on the three heart disease databases with or without preprocessing on the eighth column. The results on *Cleveland* and *Hungarian* are positive. The classification accuracies with wavelet preprocessing are always higher than those without preprocessing on these two heart disease databases. The result on *Switzerland* is neutral. The classification accuracies are unchanged with preprocessing.

Similar results were observed on the fourth column of the heart databases. In addition, we did experiments on SPECTF and Pima Indians diabetes disease [6]. Readers could refer our tech report[4] for a complete description of all the experimental results.

4. CONCLUSIONS AND FUTURE WORK

In this paper, we study a general solution to reduce the noise sensitivity of by wavelet denoising. Two sets of experiments (on different classifiers and different databases) show that the preprocessing of noisy data is able to improve classification accuracies if the localities of attributes are strong enough.

Our experiments also show that lack of locality is the biggest hurdle for applying wavelet tool to the classification. Without locality or with weak locality, the wavelet domain (wavelet coefficients) is unable to characterize the noise accurately. Although most of medical/biological data have neither temporal locality nor spatial locality, it is still possible to arrange an artificial locality. For example, we may sort the data to bring continuity before wavelet denoising. We are currently exploring the techniques to discover/enhance localities of medical/biological data.

5. REFERENCES

[1] I. Daubechies. Ten lectures on wavelets. SIAM, Philadelphia, 1992.

[2] David L. Donoho and Iain M. Johnstone. Minimax estimation via wavelet shrinkage. *Annals of Statistics*, 26(3):879–921, 1998.

[3] Jiawei Han and Micheline Kamber. *Data Mining: Concepts and Techniques*. Morgan Kaufmann Publishers, 2000.

[4] Qi Li, Tao Li, and Shenghuo Zhu. Improving medical/biological data classification performance by wavelet preprocessing. Technical Report 788, July 2002.

[5] Londeree and Moeschberger. Effect of age and other factors on hr max. *Research Quarterly for Exercise and Sport*, 53(4):297–304, 1982.

[6] UCI. Machine learning databases. In *ftp://ftp.ics.uci.edu/pub/machine-learning-databases/*.

[7] Hong ye Gao. Wavelet shrinkage denoising using the non-negative garrote. *Journal of Computational and Graphical Statistics*, 7(4):469–488, 1998.

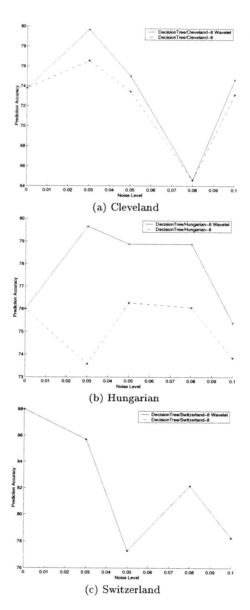

(a) Cleveland

(b) Hungarian

(c) Switzerland

Figure 3: The performances on three heart disease databases.

Progressive and Interactive Analysis of Event Data Using Event Miner

Sheng Ma, Joseph L. Hellerstein, Chang-shing Perng, Genady Grabarnik

IBM T.J. Watson Research Center

Hawthorne, NY 10532

{shengma, hellers, perng, genady}@us.ibm.com

Abstract—**Exploring large data sets typically involves activities that iterate between data selection and data analysis, in which insights obtained from analysis result in new data selection. Further, data analysis needs to use a combination of analysis techniques: data summarization, mining algorithms and visualization. This interweaving of functions arises both from the semantics of what the analyst hopes to achieve and from scalability requirements for dealing with large data volumes. We refer to such a process as a progressive analysis. Herein is described a tool, Event Miner, that integrates data selection, mining and visualization for progressive analysis of temporal, categorical data. We discuss a data model and architecture. We illustrate how our tool can be used for complex mining tasks such as finding patterns not occurring on Monday. Further, we discuss the novel visualization employed, such as visualizing categorical data and the results of data mining. Also, we discuss the extension of the existing mining framework needed to mine temporal events with multiple attributes. Throughout, we illustrate the capabilities of Event Miner by applying it to event data from large computer networks.**

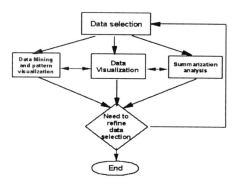

Fig. 1. Progressive Analysis

I. Introduction

Knowledge discovery is as an iterative process [2] that systematically discovers knowledge from data. Typically, the data volumes are large. Thus, to be scalable in practice, it is our experience that discovery must progress iteratively between data selection and data analysis. In that, analysis insights obtained results in refinement of data selection that starts a new analysis cycle. Further, the interweaving of three techniques–data visualization, summarization and mining– is needed for analyzing information from three granularities: raw data, summarization and pattern. Such iterative data selection and integrated data analysis form the foundation of progressive knowledge discovery. This paper discusses progressive analysis in detail and how it can be facilitated by Event Miner, a tool that integrates data selection, mining, and visualization.

The progressive analysis process arises both from the interactive nature of the process and from the scalability requirement for dealing with large data volumes. Our Event Miner has been successfully applied to analyzing many large data sets in computer system availability and performance management and computer intrusion detection applications. These applications require analyzing large volumes of temporal events through a combination of data selection, mining, and visualization. Actually, the commonalities between the analyses done is quite deep, which we illustrate by describing several commonly used scenarios.

- **Scenario 1: Top-Down Analysis:** The analyst first summarizes the data by one or more attribute (e.g. events per day; or events per event type). From this, he identifies attribute values that have an unusually high volume of events. To probe deeper, he looks for relationships between event types with a high frequency of occurrence. This is aided by using a combination of data visualization and mining.

- **Scenario 2: Bottom-up Analysis.** The analyst starts by mining for patterns. Interesting and/or frequent patterns are then studied to understand better how they relate with each other, something that is best done with a detailed, visual analysis.

- **Scenario 3: Knowledge-Driven Analysis.** The analyst identifies a suspicious pattern of events that occurs within a known context (e.g., time of day, system) based on domain knowledge (e.g. a security alert or a group of event types need to be investigated). Data that have the same context are then selected to look for other instances of the same pattern. This accomplished, the analyst next searches for occurrences of the same patterns that are not in the original context so as to assess the significance of the pattern.

A common theme in the foregoing scenarios is combined analysis at three granularities: event, pattern, and aggregation. Figure 1 depicts this approach and the interactions involved. A progressive analysis requires that users navigate freely between these information levels in order to solve complex problems. Further, insights obtained at one level can influence the selection and filtering of information at another level. An example of the latter is that event types of interest identified in summary analysis may determine the events selected in visualizations. Conversely, a time frame identified in data visualization can be used to restrict the scope of summary analysis. A second aspect of a progressive analysis is that analysis results from one analysis cause new data to be selected, thereby beginning a new analysis cycle. The latter is greatly facilitated by automatically constructing SQL queries from visualizations.

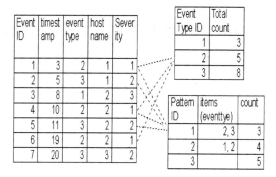

Event ID	timestamp	event type	host name	Severity
1	3	2	1	1
2	5	3	1	2
3	8	1	2	3
4	10	2	2	1
5	11	3	2	2
6	19	2	2	1
7	20	3	3	2

Event Type ID	Total count
1	3
2	5
3	8

Pattern ID	items (eventtye)	count
1	2, 3	3
2	1, 2	4
3		5

Fig. 2. Illustration of an internal data model and their relationship

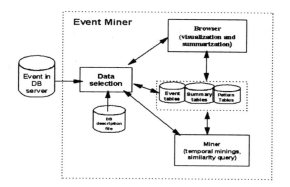

Fig. 3. Architecture of Event Miner

II. EVENT MINER

Event Miner is a tool designed to support such a progressive data mining process to effectively mine large scale categorical, temporal data. In the following, we first discuss the challenges to be addressed. We then discuss the data model as well as the architecture of Event Miner.

A. Challenges

Supporting progressive analysis for temporal, categorical data with multiple attributes requires addressing the following challenges:

(1) an interactive way to select new data from database server based on current previous analysis results (e.g., by knowing that a host generates extremely high volume of alarms on Monday, we would like to obtain alarms generated on Monday from this host for further analysis);

(2) a data model and an architecture that provide a modular way to "plug-in" to the architecture (e.g., to progress from data selection, to visualization, to mining);.

(3) scalable visualizations of categorical data; and

(4) capability to mine for temporal patterns with multiple attributes. Indeed, the progressive analysis may involve using visualization to identify data subsets to select.

For (1), we develop an interactive data selection module that can use current analysis results to define SQL constraints For (2), we introduce a data model for representing information at different levels: event, pattern, and summarization. The data model provides the means for integrating the phases of progressive analysis, allowing the output of one phase to be used as input to another. For (3), we develop new viewers that display categorical values effectively. We also study how to integrate results produced by different ordering methods. For (4), we extend the existing pattern definitions so as to handle multiple attributes and different types of patterns.

B. Internal Data Representation

Event Miner uses a tabular format as its basic data representation for different types of information. Two major types of tabular data can be created: temporal tabular data and non-temporal tabular data. Temporal tabular data called event table requires at least one attribute representing time. It is used to represent selected events by a SQL selection query. A non-temporal tabular

data is used to represent either the summary information obtained by an aggregation SQL query or patterns discovered by a mining algorithm. Figure 2 provides an example, in which there are three tables: event table (on the right), summary table (on the upper left) and pattern table (on the lower left). The event table is obtained by a selection SQL of the join of an external event table (with attributes event type, host name and time stamp) and an event type table (with attributes event type and severity). The summary table is obtained by an aggregation SQL of the external event table on event type. The pattern table is produced by a mining algorithm.

Both a summary table and a pattern table can be related to the corresponding event table. The events of the instances of patterns provides links between an event table and a corresponding pattern table. Clearly, a pattern has multiple instances; likewise an event may belong to instances of multiple patterns. For example, PatternID 1 consists of event type 2 and 3. It has two instances. The first instance contains EventID 1 and 2; the second one contains EventID 3 and 4. Similarly, many-to-one relationship can be established from an event table to a summary table. For example, EventID 1, 4 and 6 have the same event type that is corresponding to the second entry of the event type summary table.

We note that this unified data representation provides several advantages that will be further demonstrated in latter sections. First, we can apply the same visualization techniques to view events, patterns and aggregated information. Second, through the relationship of tables, we can link different analysis techniques and move from one analysis technique to another one. For example, a selection of a pattern can result in the selection of the events of the instances of the pattern, which can then be reflected to the event type summary table.

C. Architecture of Event Miner

Our objective in supporting progressive analysis naturally leads to the architecture of Event Miner as illustrated in Figure 3. Event Miner has three key components: data selection, Browser, and Miner. The data selection module provides an interactive way for a user to define two types of SQL queries with constraints: selection query that creates an internal temporal table; and aggregation (count) query that creates a summary table. More importantly, it provides a way to constructing SQL con-

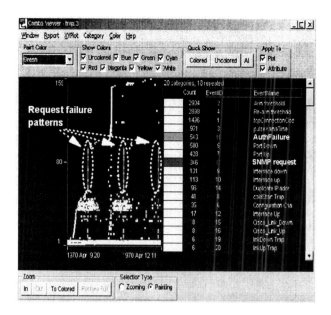

Fig. 4. Combo viewer. Left view: y-axis is host names and x-axis is time. Right view: a categorical table of Event type.

straints based on current analysis results. This allows us to load related data to refine the current analysis.

The Browser, built by using Diamond[10] APIs, provides visual, exploratory analysis of an internal table. Because of the unified internal data model, the Browser can be applied to analyze events, summary and patterns in a unified way. In addition to common data manipulation operations such as zooming, moving, sorting and scrolling, the Browser provides two core mechanisms –coloring/filtering and coordination– for supporting the progressive analysis. Figure 4 shows a combo viewer of an event data collected from a company's intranet. In this example, event types are colored. Its corresponding patterns can be clearly identified from the left side view.

The Miner integrates several data mining algorithms designed for mining temporal data including those for mining frequent temporal patterns, partial periodic patterns[8], and mutual dependence patterns[7], as well as the similarity query. The Miner provides a flexible way to define patterns and assists in better visualizing categorical data.

As we will soon demonstrate, Event Miner explores the synergy of these three components for progressive analysis. Due to the page limit, the foregoing discusses the concept of progressive data selection and the interaction between visualization and data mining, and leaves the detailed description of Browser and Miner in our long paper[9].

III. PROGRESSIVE DATA SELECTION

Progressive data analysis requires that data stored in database can be selected based on current analysis results. This implies two design considerations. First, the data selection module should be flexible in dealing with data stored in possibly multiple tables; while provide a coherent logical view to users. Second, it should provide a way that facilitate users to interactively

construct a SQL query based on current analysis results. For the first goal, we define a (analysis) logical view. A database description file is used to define the mapping from the logical view to the joint of physical tables. By doing so, the complicated database schema is transparent to an analyst.

Our second design goal is accomplished by two means. First, GUIs are provided to assist users to easily construct a SQL query with constraints. Second, a query can be constructed visually by extending previous operations performed in visualization viewers. The latter is essential for progressive data analysis.

To illustrate the progressive data selection, we detail Scenario 1. We recall that this scenario starts with the summary information, say summary by day. For this, a day-summary query is constructed to obtain the summary information that is represented as an internal table. Now, a data table viewer can be used, from which we can sort days by count and color days that have abnormally high event volumes. To continue our investigation on which hosts are responsible for such a high event volume, we construct a new host-summary query with constraint on the colored days. Once the host-summary information is loaded, we can identify and color hosts having significantly high event counts using a categorical attribute viewer. To further understand what may go wrong with these troublesome hosts in the selected days, we can construct a new selection query with the constraints on the colored hosts and days, and load all events related to the selected hosts and days into an internal event table. Now, data visualization and mining can be used for further analysis.

IV. INTERACTIONS BETWEEN VISUALIZATION AND DATA MINING

Data visualization and data mining can be used together to accomplish more complicated analysis task. Event Miner supports four types of interactions between visualization and data mining: (1) visualizing patterns found for analyzing relationships of patterns; (2) exploring the links between event table and pattern table to accomplish complex mining tasks; (3) mining for achieving better visualization effect; and (4) Visual similarity query. The foregoing briefly discusses (2) and (3). More discussion can be found in [9].

A. Data visualization and data mining interaction for complex mining tasks

By the interaction of data visualization and data mining, Event Miner can be used for complex mining tasks. We demonstrate this by two mining tasks (more details can be found in [?]. First, for selected events of interest, we would like to find those patterns that have at least one (or all) instance(s) in selected events. Second, for one or more patterns of interest, we would like to understand whether their instances are temporally related. The first task can be used for comparative analysis which allows users to find patterns that only occur or not occur in a segment of events (e.g. patterns occurring on Monday only). The second one provides additional evidences for validating patterns and understanding the temporal relationships of patterns.

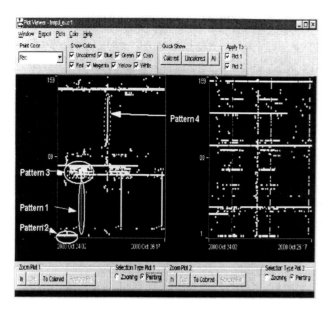

Fig. 5. Scatter plots resulted by different ordering algorithms. y-axis represents host names; and x-axis is time. Left plot is by an algorithm. Right one is by a random mapping.

B. Mining algorithms for achieving better visualization

Categorical data can be plotted in the same way as numerical data once categorical values are mapped into some numerical values. For example, we can map host names to integers as shown in Figure 4. However, one issue to be solved is how to choose such a mapping from exponentially many possible mappings. Often, a random order is not effective, especially when there are many values. The right view of Figure 5 shows the result of a random mapping of host names. Clearly, this plot does not reveal structures (or patterns) embedded in the data because data objects spread across the visual space. To resolve this issue, we have developed several algorithms [6][1] that clusters events first, and then orders hosts so that event clusters are better preserved. The left view of Figure 5 shows our result on the same data set. Here, many patterns of interest are surfaced and annotated in the figure.

As evidenced by Figure 4 and 5, different ordering methods provide different optimization trade-offs and lead to very different visual effects. In practice, the quality of ordering results may largely depend on users' preferences. Instead of determining which order is the best, the color linkage provides a practical solution. For example, we can color the first pattern in the left side view of Figure 5, and then see how this pattern appears in the right one. In this case, pattern 1 spreads along the y-axis in the right side view because of the use of the random ordering method.

V. RELATED WORK AND CONCLUSION

This paper describes a progressive data mining process with two aspects. First, the data selection and data analysis are done iteratively. Second, the data analysis is done by a combination of analysis techniques including data visualization, summarization and mining. There are three areas of work related to our current efforts: visualization in support of exploratory analysis [3][11], data mining systems that support visualization of the results [5], and integrated mining and visualization systems[4].

Event Miner is a tool designed to support such a progressive data mining process to effectively mine large scale categorical, temporal data. In particularly, Event Miner uses a unified data model and integrates three components: interactive data selection, visualization and summarization techniques, and data mining algorithms. The interactive data selection supports a friendly and flexible way for constructing a SQL query by extending analysis operations performed, and thus loading in related data fore further analysis. The Browser implements two powerful concepts: coloring/filtering and coordination, core mechanisms for achieving complex mining tasks by combining the mining algorithms and visualization.

We demonstrate the power of a progressive data mining through four types of interactions between visualization of events and data mining. First, visualization techniques can be applied to visualize patterns for a user to understand patterns. Second, the visualization of events can be used to interpret and select patterns of interest. Third, an algorithm can aid in better visualization through ordering categorical values. Last, visualization techniques can be used in a tight loop of a data mining process. In the visual similarity query, visualization not only enables users to select an interesting situation, but also helps determine the quality of returned results. In that, users can visually select a subset of data objects of interest for focused data mining. Users can also validate patterns found by visualizing instances of the patterns. Likewise, mining algorithms can find interesting patterns embedded in large data. Such patterns may provide a starting point for directing visual analysis of data records.

Our system has been used successfully to analyze large scale temporal data in many applications.

REFERENCES

[1] A. Beygelzimer, C. Perng, and S. Ma. Fast ordering of large categorical data for better visualization. In *KDD*, 2001.
[2] R. Brachmann and T. Anand. The process of knowledge discovery in databases: A human-centered approach.
[3] M. Derthick, J.A. Kolojejchick, and S.F. Roth. An interactive visualization environment for data exploration. In *Proceedings of knowledge discovery in databases*, 1997.
[4] D. A. Keim and H. Kriegel. VisDB: Database exploration using multidimensional visualization. *Computer Graphics and Applications*, 1994.
[5] B. Liu, W. Hsu, Y. Ma, and S. Chen. Discovering interesting knowledge using dm-ii, 1999.
[6] S. Ma and J.L. Hellerstein. Ordering categorical data for best visualization. In *InfoVis'99*, 1999.
[7] S. Ma and J.L. Hellerstein. Mining mutually dependent patterns. In *ICDM*, 2001.
[8] S. Ma and J.L. Hellerstein. Mining partially periodic event patterns. In *ICDE*, pages 205–214, 2001.
[9] S. Ma, J.L. Hellerstein, C. Perng, and G. Grabarnik. Progressive and interactive analysis of event data using event miner. Technical report, IBM T.J. Watson research center, 2002.
[10] D.A. Rabenhorst. Interactive exploration of multi-dimensional data. In *Proceedings of the SPIE Symposium on Electronic Imaging*, pages 277–286, 1994.
[11] R.J. Resnick, M.O. Ward, and E.A. Rundensteiner. FED – a framework for iterative data selection in exploratory visualization. In *Proceedings of Tenth International Conference on Scientific and Statistical Database Management*, 1998.

Toward XML-Based Knowledge Discovery Systems

Rosa Meo

Università degli Studi di Torino
Dipartimento di Informatica
Corso Svizzera 185 - I-10129 Torino, Italy
e-mail: meo@di.unito.it

Giuseppe Psaila

Università degli Studi di Bergamo
Facoltà di Ingegneria
Viale Marconi 5 - I-24044 Dalmine (BG), Italy
e-mail: psaila@unibg.it

Abstract

Inductive databases are intended to be general purpose databases in which both source data and mined patterns can be represented, retrieved and manipulated; however, the heterogeneity of models for mined patterns makes difficult to realize them. In this paper, we explore the feasibility of using XML as the unifying framework for inductive databases, introducing a suitable data model called XDM (XML for Data Mining). XDM is designed to describe source raw data, heterogeneous mined patterns and data mining statements, so that they can be stored inside a unique XML-based inductive database.

1. Introduction

Data mining applications are typically used in the decision making process; in fact, patterns mined from within the source raw data give an intuitive and synthetic representation of phenomena described by the data. However, the *Knowledge Discovery Process* (KDD process for short) is a typical iterative process, in which not only the raw data can be mined several times, but also the mined patterns might constitute the starting point for further mining on them.

These are the premises that lead Imielinski and Mannila in [3] to propose the idea of *inductive database*, a general-purpose database in which both the data and the patterns can be represented, retrieved and manipulated. The goal of inductive databases is to assist the deployment of the KDD process. Inside the context of inductive databases the KDD process is driven by the user as a querying sequence. Each query is an instance of a specialized query language, designed for a specific data mining or data analysis problem. Consequently, an inductive database should integrate several heterogeneous data mining and data analysis tools in the same framework.

However, data mining tools involved in the KDD process

deal with very different, heterogeneous and complex data models. For example, classification tools usually adopt a data model that is a classification tree [5], while tools for basket analysis usually represent patterns by means of set enumeration models [2].

In this paper, we propose a semi-structured data model specifically designed for inductive databases and, more generally, for *Knowledge Discovery Systems*. This model is called XDM (XML for Data Mining). It is based on XML and is devised to cope with several distinctive features at the same time. First, it is semi-structured, in order to be able to represent an apriori infinite set of data models. Second, it is based on two simple and clear concepts, named *Data Item* and *Statement*: a data item is a container of data and/or patterns; a statement is a description of a data mining operator application. Third, an inductive database modeled with XDM becomes both a collection of data items and a collection of statements, where the knowledge discovery process is represented as a set of relationships between data items and statements.

XDM provides several interesting features for inductive databases. Source raw data and patterns are represented at the same time in the model. The pattern derivation process is stored in the database: this is determinant for the phase of pattern interpretation and allows pattern reuse. Finally, the framework can be easily extended with new data mining operators, exploiting the notion of XML *namespaces*.

Thus inductive databases based on XDM really become open systems that are easily customizable according to the kind of patterns in which the user/analyst is interested in.

2. XDM Data Items

We now define the first basic element of the XDM data model, i.e. the *XDM Data Item*.

A *StructuralNode* is a generic node that composes the tree structure of an XML document or fragment. It can be either an *ElementNode* (that defines the structure of a tree fragment) or a *TextualNode* (with a textual content). An *ElementNode* n has a possibly empty set of *attributes*, i.e. pairs $(Name : String, Value : String)$, denoted as $n.Attributes$.

Definition 1: An *XDM Data Item* is a tree fragment defined in the following way.

• The root of a tree fragment is an *ElementNode*, here denoted as r, having the following properties: the element tag name, $r.Name$ ="DATA-ITEM"; the element content $r.Content$ is a sequence of *StructuralNodes*; the prefix associated to the name space, $r.Prefix$ ="XDM"; $r.NameSpace$, specifying the name space URI, is the standard XDM name space. Hereafter we will refer to the *ElementNodes* with the notation $Prefix:Name$.

• An *ElementNode* has a set of attributes, $r.Attributes$, denoting the data item information at creation time: Name, Date, Version, Derived (a boolean denoting whether the data item is derived by another data item), and Virtual, (a boolean denoting if the data item is materalized). □

Example 1: The start tag

```
<XDM:DATA-ITEM Name="Input" Version="1"
 Derived="NO" Date="..." Virtual="NO"
 xmlns:XDM="http://.../NS/XDM">
```

defines the attributes for the XDM data item named Input. This XDM data item is not derived and not virtual (it is materialized): it might contain the first version of input data to analyze.

In the above tag, notice the namespace definition xmlns:XDM="http://.../NS/XDM", which says that all element nodes prefixed as XDM belong to the namespace identified by the specified URI. □

Definition 2: The XDM:DERIVATION node is an element node defined on the standard XDM name space, here denoted as d. $d.Content$ is empty and $d.Attributes$ contains only one mandatory attribute select, which contains an XPath expression (see [1]) that refers to the XDM *statement* that generated the data item (see Section 3 and Section 4 for a detailed discussion on derivation). □

Definition 3: The XDM:CONTENT node is an element node defined on the standard XDM name space, here denoted as c. The XDM:CONTENT node has no attributes, and only one child *ElementNode* n in $c.Content$. □

Definition 4: The XDM:UPDATE-OF-ITEM node is an element node defined on the standard XDM name space, here denoted as u. $u.Content$ is empty, and $u.Attributes$ contains only one mandatory attribute select, which contains an XPath expression identifying the sequence of structural nodes that matches the expression, according to XPath semantics (see [1]). □

The *Content* of an *ElementNode* must match the following regular expressions: If Derived="NO" $r.Content$ = "XDM:UPDATE-OF-ITEM?, XDM:CONTENT" [1]. If Derived = Virtual = "YES" $r.Content$ = "XDM:DERIVATION, XDM.UPDATE-OF-ITEM?". If Derived="YES" ∧ Virtual="NO" $r.Content$ = "XDM:DERIVATION, XDM:UPDATE-OF-ITEM?, XDM:CONTENT". where DERIVATION, UPDATE-OF-ITEM and CONTENT are defined in the following.

Example 2: The following XDM code shows the first version of a derived XDM data item, named *Rules*, containing the association rules extracted from the source data given in input. These data items are shown in the left hand side of Figure 1 that shows a sample KDD process.

```
<XDM:DATA-ITEM Name="Rules" Version="1"
 Derived="YES" Date="..." Virtual="NO"
 xmlns:XDM="http://.../NS/XDM">
<XDM:DERIVATION select=
     "//XDM:STATEMENT[@ID='00128']"/>
<XDM:CONTENT>
<AR:ASSOCIATION-RULE-SET
 xmlns:AR="http://...NS/DATA/AssRules">
```
Actual association rule set
```
</AR:ASSOCIATION-RULE-SET>
</XDM:CONTENT>
</XDM:DATA-ITEM>
```

Notice that Derived is "YES" and Virtual is "NO". Therefore this data item will contain the actual data that is obtained by means of the derivation. The XDM:DERIVATION node specifies, with the XPath expression in the select attribute, the statement whose execution generated the item (statements will be described in Section 3). In particular, this item is generated by a statement based on the MR:MINE-RULE operator (see Section 3) which extract association rules from a data item. The generated set of association rules is included in the XDM:CONTENT section (inside AR:ASSOCIATION-RULE-SET tag). Note that this fragment is based on a specific namespace, (with prefix AR: and its own URI http://...NS/DATA/AssRules) defined for association rule sets descriptions. Note that the URI belonging to the standard XDM namespace could be different w.r.t. the host of the specific data mining operator. Indeed, XDM is independent w.r.t. the operators which can be added to the XDM-based system even in a following time. □

Example 3: The following XDM code fragment shows the initial part of the second version of the XDM data item named *Rules*. This is obtained by extracting rules from

---

[1]We use the XML notation for regular expression operators. In particular, "," denotes the sequence operator, while "?" denotes the optionality operator.

within an updated version of the source data item (see data items shown in the right hand side of Figure 1). The element node XDM:UPDATE-OF-ITEM shows that this current version is the update of the previous one. It makes use of an XPath expression in the select attribute.

```
<XDM:DATA-ITEM Name="Rules" Version="2"
 Derived="YES" Date="..." Virtual="NO"
 xmlns:XDM="http://.../NS/XDM">
<XDM:DERIVATION select=
 "//XDM:STATEMENT[@ID='00131']"/>
<XDM:UPDATE-OF-ITEM  select=
 "//XDM:DATA-ITEM[@Name='Rules']
 [@Version='1']"/>
   .   .   .
```

Notice that the UPDATE-OF-ITEM relationship is extremely useful, to keep trace of changing analysis results. In fact, if the data from which the analysis moves on changes, a cascade effect on derived data items generates a new set of data items which updates the previous ones; for example, changing the data from which association rules are extracted, a new data item with a new set of association rules is generated that updates the old association rule set. The presence of the UPDATE-OF-ITEM relationship may allow to investigate how association rules change in time, simply following the UPDATE-OF-ITEM chain. □

3. XDM Statements

The XDM model is devised to capture the KDD process and therefore it provides also the concept of *statement*. This one specifies the application of an operator (for data manipulation and analysis tasks) whose execution causes the generation of a new, derived data item.

Definition 5: An XDM statement s is specified by an XML fragment, whose structure is the following.

• The root of the fragment is an element node XDM:STATEMENT denoted as s. s has the attribute ID, which is the statement identifier (with $ID(s)$ we refer to its value).

• The content of each node XDM:STATEMENT has one single child node, describing the application of the operator.

• The operator application must specify (by means of an XPath expression) a non empty set of *source XDM data items*, which constitute the input for the operator application.

• The operator application must specify one single *output XDM data item*, which constitutes the output of the operator application. This occurs again by an XPath expression. □

Example 4: The following example shows the main features of the statement MR:MINE-RULE (see [4] for a complete description on the operator).

```
<XDM:STATEMENT ID="00128"
xmlns:MR="http://.../NS/MINE-RULE">
  <MR:MINE-RULE>
    <XDM:SOURCE-ITEM select=
    "http//XDM-DATA-ITEM[@Name='Item']
                  [@Version='1']"/>
... Nodes in the MR namespace ...
    <MR:OUTPUT>
      <XDM:OUTPUT-ITEM Name="Rules"
       Virtual="NO" Root="MR:RULE-SET"
       NS="http://.../NS/DATA/Rules"/>
    </MR:OUTPUT>
  </MR:MINE-RULE>
</XDM:STATEMENT>
```

Notice that the operator and its specific element nodes are defined in the namespace prefix MR:, corresponding to the URI "http://.../NS/DATA/Rules, because they are outside the standard XDM namespace. However, XDM:SOURCE-ITEM and XDM:OUTPUT-ITEM nodes, belonging to the *XDM* namespace appear in the content of the MR:MINE-RULE operator, as specified by the definition of statement. SOURCE-ITEM specifies the input of the operator providing Name and Version number of the XDM data item while OUTPUT-ITEM identifies the ouput node by means of the Name and the Root node of its tree fragment. Furthermore it specifies the attributes of the output node. □

XDM statements consist of the application of one operator. Operators are divided into two categories: *Data Manipulation Operators* and *Data Mining Operators*.

Data manipulation operators are useful for managing data items. Given the extensibility features of the XDM framework several (and the most common) operators can be defined on XDM data items, such as LOAD that insert a new data item into the database, DELETE, etc. For the sake of space we do not report them here, although the reader can easily guess that such operators allow the user to generate new data items by modifying or restructuring other data items.

4. XDM Database State

Database state is the last concept in XDM.

Definition 6: The state of an XDM database is represented as a pair

$$\langle DI : Set\ Of(DataItem), ST : Set\ Of(Statement) \rangle,$$

where DI is a set of XDM data items (see Definition 1), and ST is a set of XDM statements (see Definition 5). The following constraints hold.

• *Data Item Identity.* Given a data item d and its mandatory attributes Name, and Version, the pair $\langle$Name, Version$\rangle$

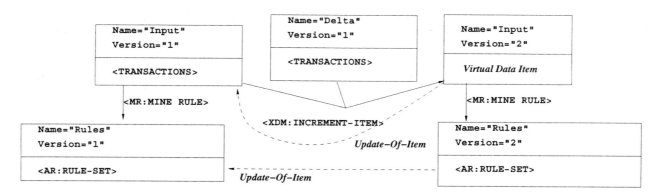

Figure 1. A typical knowledge discovery process based on XDM.

uniquely identifies the data item d in the database state.

- *Statement Identity.* Given a statement s and its mandatory attribute ID, its value uniquely identifies the statement s in the database state.

- *Relationship between statements and source data items.* Consider an XDM statement s. The XPath expression specified by the select attribute of each XDM:SOURCE-ITEM appearing in s must find one and only one XDM data item.

- *Relationship between derived data items and statements.* Consider a derived XDM data item d ($Derived(d) =$ "YES"). The XPath expression specified by the select attribute of the XDM:DERIVATION element must find one and only one XDM data item.

- *Update-of-item Relationship.* Consider an XDM data item d such that the XDM:UPDATE-OF-ITEM u appears in its content ($u.Name =$"UPDATE-OF-ITEM", $u.Prefix =$"XDM" and $u \in d.Content$). The value s of the select attribute must match one and only one XDM data item. □

Observations. The XDM database is then both a data item base and a statement base. When a new statement is executed, the new database state is obtained from the former one by adding both the executed statement and the new data item.

This structure represents the two-fold nature of the knowledge discovery process: data and patterns are not meaningful if considered in isolation; in contrast, patterns are significant if the overall process is described, because the meaning of data items is clarified by the clauses specified in the data mining operators that generate data items.

5. Conclusions

In this paper we presented a new, XML-based data model, named XDM. It is designed to be adopted inside the

framework of inductive databases.

XDM allows the management of semi-structured and complex patterns thanks to the semi-structured nature of the data that can be represented by XML.

In XDM the pattern definition is represented together with data. This allows the reuse of patterns by the inductive database management system. In particular, XDM explicitly represents the statements that were executed in the derivation process of the pattern. The flexibility of the XDM representation allows extensibility to new pattern models and new mining operators: this makes the framework suitable to build an open system, easily customized by the analyst.

One drawback of using XML in data mining, however, could be the large volumes reached by the source data represented in XML (due to the addition of mark-up tags and attributes).

References

[1] Xml path language (xpath), version 1.0. Technical report, World Wide Web Consortium, http://www.w3.org/TR/1999/REC-xpath-19991116, 11 1999.

[2] R. Agrawal, T. Imielinski, and A. Swami. Mining association rules between sets of items in large databases. In *Proc.ACM SIGMOD Conference on Management of Data*, pages 207–216, Washington, D.C., May 1993. British Columbia.

[3] T. Imielinski and H. Mannila. A database perspective on knowledge discovery. *Coomunications of the ACM*, 39(11):58–64, November 1996.

[4] R. Meo, G. Psaila, and S. Ceri. An extension to SQL for mining association rules. *Journal of Data Mining and Knowledge Discovery*, 2(2), 1998.

[5] R. Quinlan. *C4.5 Programs for Machine Learning.* Morgan Kauffmann, Los Altos, California, 1993.

Using Sequential and Non-Sequential Patterns in Predictive Web Usage Mining Tasks

Bamshad Mobasher, Honghua Dai, Tao Luo, Miki Nakagawa
{mobasher,hdai,tluo,miki}@cs.depaul.edu
School of Computer Science, Telecommunication, and Information Systems
DePaul University, Chicago, Illinois, USA

Abstract

We describe an efficient framework for Web personalization based on sequential and non-sequential pattern discovery from usage data. Our experimental results performed on real usage data indicate that more restrictive patterns, such as contiguous sequential patterns (e.g., frequent navigational paths) are more suitable for predictive tasks, such as Web prefetching, which involve predicting which item is accessed next by a user), while less constrained patterns, such as frequent itemsets or general sequential patterns are more effective alternatives in the context of Web personalization and recommender systems.

1. Introduction

Web usage mining techniques [9], that rely on offline pattern discovery from user transactions, can be used to solve scalability problems associated with personalization systems based on standard collaborative filtering. In addition, user models discovered through data mining, can capture more fine-grained information, such as the inherent ordering among accessed pages, than standard techniques afford.

However, using more fine-grained information about users' navigational histories as part of pattern discovery does not necessarily translate to more effective personalization. Furthermore, techniques that may prove effective for predictive tasks such as prefetching, may not necessarily be appropriate in the context of personalization.

In this paper we present a scalable framework for Web personalization based on both sequential and non-sequential pattern mining from clickstream data. Our framework includes efficient data structures for storing frequent itemsets or sequential patterns combined with algorithms which allow for effective real-time generation of recommendations.

We have conducted a detailed comparative evaluation,

based on real usage data, of both sequential and non-sequential patterns in terms of their effectiveness and suitability for personalization tasks. We distinguish between two different evaluation methodologies, one suited for evaluation of personalization effectiveness, and the other designed for evaluating the performance of predictive tasks such as Web prefetching (which involve predicting which item the user will access next during his/her navigation).

Our empirical results show that more restrictive patterns, such as contiguous sequential patterns (e.g., frequent navigational paths) are more suitable for predictive tasks such as Web prefetching (which involve predicting which item the user will access next during his/her navigation). On the other hand, less constrained patterns, such as frequent itemsets or general sequential patterns are more effective alternatives in the context of Web personalization.

2. Preprocessing and Pattern Discovery

The overall process of Web personalization, generally consists of three phases: data preparation and transformation, pattern discovery, and recommendation. In traditional collaborative filtering approaches, the pattern discovery phase (e.g., neighborhood formation in the k-nearest-neighbor) as well as the recommendation phase are performed in real time. In contrast, personalization systems based on Web usage mining [6, 7], perform the pattern discovery phase offline. Data preparation phase transforms raw web log files into clickstream data that can be processed by data mining tasks. The recommendation engine considers the active user session in conjunction with the discovered patterns to provide personalized content.

Web usage preprocessing [5] ultimately result in a set of n pageviews, $P = \{p_1, p_2, \cdots, p_n\}$, and a set of m user transactions, $T = \{t_1, t_2, \cdots, t_m\}$, where each $t_i \in T$ is a subset of P. Conceptually, we view each transaction t as an l-length sequence of ordered pairs:

$$t = \langle (p_1^t, w(p_1^t)), (p_2^t, w(p_2^t)), \cdots, (p_l^t, w(p_l^t)) \rangle,$$

where each $p_i^t = p_j$ for some $j \in \{1, \cdots, n\}$, and $w(p_i^t)$ is the weight associated with pageview p_i^t in the transaction t (usually binary weights are used in the context of association rule and sequential pattern discovery).

We focus on three data mining techniques: Association Rule mining (AR) [1, 2], Sequential Pattern (SP) [3], and Contiguous Sequential Pattern (CSP) discovery. CSP's are a special form of sequential patterns in which the items appearing in the sequence must be adjacent with respect to the underlying ordering. In the context of Web usage data, CSP's can be used to capture *frequent navigational paths* among user trails [10]. In contrast, items appearing in SP's, while preserving the underlying ordering, need not be adjacent, and thus they represent more general navigational patterns within the site. Frequent item sets, discovered as part of association rule mining, represent the least restrictive type of navigational patterns, since they focus on the presence of items rather than the order in which they occur within user session.

3. Personalization With Sequential and Non-Sequential Patterns

The recommendation engine takes a collection of frequent itemsets or (contiguous) sequential patterns as input and generates a recommendation set by matching the current user's activity against the discovered patterns. We use a fixed-size sliding window over the current active session to capture the current user's history depth. Thus, the sliding window of size n over the active session allows only the last n visited pages to influence the recommendation value of items in the recommendation set. We call this sliding window, the user's *active session window*.

The recommendation engine based on association rules matches the current user session window with frequent itemsets to find candidate pageviews for giving recommendations. Given an active session window w and a group of frequent itemsets, we only consider all the frequent itemsets of size $|w| + 1$ containing the current session window. The recommendation value of each candidate pageview is based on the confidence of the corresponding association rule whose consequent is the singleton containing the pageview to be recommended.

In order to facilitate the search for itemsets (of size $|w| + 1$) containing the current session window w, the frequent itemsets are stored in a directed acyclic graph, here called a *Frequent Itemset Graph*. The Frequent Itemset Graph is an extension of the lexicographic tree used in the tree projection algorithm of [1]. The graph is organized into levels from 0 to k, where k is the maximum size among all frequent itemsets.

Each node at depth d in the graph corresponds to an itemset, I, of size d and is linked to itemsets of size $d + 1$ that contain I at level $d + 1$. The single root node at level 0 corresponds to the empty itemset. To be able to match different orderings of an active session with frequent itemsets, all itemsets are sorted in lexicographic order before being inserted into the graph. The user's active session is also sorted in the same manner before matching with patterns.

Given an active user session window w, sorted in lexicographic order, a depth-first search of the Frequent Itemset Graph is performed to level $|w|$. If a match is found, then the children of the matching node n containing w are used to generate candidate recommendations. Each child node of n corresponds to a frequent itemset $w \cup \{p\}$. In each case, the pageview p is added to the recommendation set if the support ratio $\sigma(w \cup \{p\})/\sigma(w)$ is greater than or equal to α, where α is a minimum confidence threshold. Note that $\sigma(w \cup \{p\})/\sigma(w)$ is the confidence of the association rule $w \Rightarrow \{p\}$. The confidence of this rule is also used as the recommendation score for pageview p. It is easy to observe that in this algorithm the search process requires only $O(|w|)$ time given active session window w.

The recommendation algorithm based on association rules can be adopted to work also with sequential (respectively, contiguous sequential) patterns. In this case, we focus on frequent (contiguous) sequences of size $|w| + 1$ whose prefix contains an active user session w. The candidate pageviews to be recommended are the last items in all such sequences. The recommendation values are based on the confidence of the patterns. A simple trie structure is used to store both the sequential and contiguous sequential patterns discovered during the pattern discovery phase.

Depending on the specified support threshold and window size, it might be difficult to find large enough itemsets or sequential patterns that could be used for providing recommendations, leading to reduced coverage. This is particularly true for sites with very small average session sizes. In order to overcome this problem, we use *all-kth-order* method proposed in [8] in the context of *Markov chain models*. The *order* of the Markov model corresponds to the number of prior events used in predicting a future event.

Our recommendation framework for contiguous sequential patterns is essentially equivalent to kth-order Markov models, however, rather than storing all navigational sequences, we only store frequent sequences resulting from the sequential pattern mining process. The notion of all-kth-order models can also easily be extended to the context of general sequential patterns and association rule. We extend our recommendation algorithms to generate all-kth-order recommendations as follows. First, the recommendation engine uses the largest possible active session window as an input for recommendation engine. If the engine cannot generate any recommendations, the size of active session window is iteratively decreased until a recommendation is generated or the window size becomes 0.

4. Experimental Evaluation

We conjecture that more restrictive patterns, e.g., CSP, may be better suited for predictive applications such as Web prefetching which involve predicting a user's *next* immediate access to a page. This is in contrast to personalization tasks which involve prediction a (broader) set of pages to be recommended to the user based on his/her previous access patterns. Thus, we propose two different evaluation methodologies, which here we shall call *NEXT* and *ALL*, respectively. The NEXT method evaluates recommendation effectiveness by comparing the system's predictions with a user's immediate *next* action, while the ALL method compares the predictions against *all* of the user's remaining actions (accesses to pageviews) in the duration of a session.

The experiments were performed on real Web usage data from 3 different commercial and non-commercial sites. The results shown below represent selected experiments from only one of these data set; the full set of results and experiments are included in the full paper and available upon request.

For all experiments, we performed 10-fold cross-validation. In each iteration, each transaction t in the evaluation set was divided into two parts. The first n pageviews in t were used for generating recommendations, whereas, the remaining portion of t (*target set*) was used to evaluate the generated recommendations. Given a window size $w \leq n$, we select a subset (or a subsequence in the case of SP or CSP) of the first n pageviews as the surrogate for a user's *active session window*, denoted by as_t.

Both All and NEXT evaluation methods take as_t and a recommendation threshold τ as inputs and produce a set of pageviews as recommendations. The recommendation set contains all pageviews whose recommendation score is at least τ. The NEXT method compares the generated recommendations with the immediate next pageview in the remaining portion of the transaction t. On the other hand, the ALL method compares the recommendation set to all of the pageviews in the remaining portion of t. The *precision* measure represents the ratio of matches between the recommendation set and the target set to the size of recommendation set. The *coverage* measure represents the ratio of matches to the size of the target set. Finally, for a given recommendation threshold τ, the mean over all transactions in the evaluation set is computed as the overall evaluation score for each of the measures in both evaluation methods.

Figure 1 depicts the results for the all-kth-order versions of the three recommendation methods for both data sets. In these comparisons, we also included the precision and coverage of the standard k-Nearest-Neighbor (kNN) technique for standard collaborative filtering. The value of k was chosen based sensitivity analysis for the best performance in terms of coverage and precision.

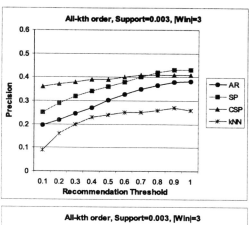

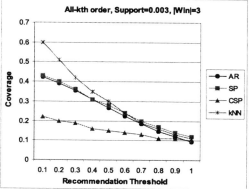

Figure 1: Recommendation Effectiveness Using Varying-Sized User Histories Based on the ALL Method

The results show that, in this case, SP will have similar (or better) performance than CSP in terms of both coverage and precision. This phenomenon is likely due to the fact that varying window sizes has a more dramatic impact on the precision of CSP than on SP or AR. The AR models also performs well in the context of personalization. In general, the precision of AR model is lower than SP, but it does provide better overall coverage. The comparison to kNN shows that all of the techniques presented in this paper, outperform kNN in terms of precision. In general, kNN provides good coverage (usually in par with the AR model), but the difference in coverage is diminished if we insist on higher recommendation thresholds (and thus more accurate recommendations).

We also compared the precision and coverage of AR, SP, and CSP based on the NEXT evaluation method. To provide a better basis for comparison of these results to those based on the ALL method, we use the same support threshold and window size parameters as those used in Figure 1. The results are shown in Figure 2.

The results show that, in this context, the CSP model provides much higher precision levels that both SP and AR,

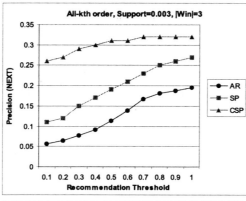

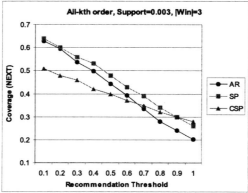

Figure 2: Comparison of Precision and Coverage Based on the NEXT Evaluation Method

while achieving coverage levels that are in par with the SP model. Indeed, at high recommendation thresholds, the coverage of CSP is similar to better than that of the SP model. The precision levels of the AR model are too low to make it a reasonable candidate for this type of application.

5. Discussion and Conclusions

Our overall conclusion based on the aforementioned results is that the SP and the AR models, generally provide the best choices for personalization applications. The CSP model can do better in terms of precision, but the coverage levels, in general, may be too low when the goal is to generate as many good recommendations as possible. On the other hand, when dealing with applications such as Web prefetching in which the primary goal is to predict the user's immediate next actions (rather than providing a broader set of recomendations), the CSP model provides the best choice. This is particularly true in sites with many dynamically generated pages (such as the one used in these experiments), where often a contiguous navigational path rep-

resents a semantically meaningful sequence of user actions each depending on the previous actions.

References

[1] R. Agarwal, C. Aggarwal and V. Prasad. A tree projection algorithm for generation of frequent itemsets. *In Proceedings of High Performance Data Mining Workshop*, Puerto Rico, 1999.

[2] R. Agrawal and R. Srikant. Fast Algorithms for Mining Association Rules. Proc. *20th Int. Conf. Very Large Data Bases, VLDB*, 1994.

[3] R. Agrawal and R. Srikant. Mining Sequential Patterns. *In Proc. of the 11th Int'l Conference on Data Engineering*, Taipei, Taiwan, March 1995.

[4] B. Berendt, B. Mobasher, M. Spiliopoulou, J. Wiltshire. Measuring the accuracy of sessionizers for Web usage analysis. In *Proceedings of the Web Mining Workshop* at the *First SIAM International Conference on Data Mining, SDM 2001*, Chicago, April 2001.

[5] R. Cooley, B. Mobasher and J. Srivastava. Data preparation for mining World Wide Web browsing patterns. *Journal of Knowledge and Information Systems*, (1) 1, 1999.

[6] B. Mobasher, R. Cooley and J. Srivastava. Automatic personalization based on Web usage mining. In *Communications of the ACM*, (43) 8, August 2000.

[7] B. Mobasher, H. Dai, T. Luo, M. Nakagawa. Effective personalization based on association rule discovery from Web usage data. In *Proceedings of the 3rd ACM Workshop on Web Information and Data Management (WIDM01)*, Atlanta, November 2001.

[8] J. Pitkow and P. Pirolli. Mining Longest Repeating Subsequences to Predict WWW Surfing. *Proceedings of the 1999 USENIX Annual Technical Conference*, 1999.

[9] J. Srivastava, R. Cooley, M. Deshpande, P-T. Tan. Web usage mining: discovery and applications of usage patterns from Web data. *SIGKDD Explorations*, (1) 2, 2000.

[10] M. Spiliopoulou and L.C. Faulstich. WUM: A Tool for Web Utilization Analysis. *In Proc. of EDBT Workshop WebDB'98*, Valencia, Spain, Mar. 1998.

Intersection Based Generalization Rules for the Analysis of Symbolic Septic Shock Patient Data

Jürgen Paetz

J.W. Goethe-Universität

FB Biologie und Informatik, Institut für Informatik

D-60054 Frankfurt am Main

paetz@cs.uni-frankfurt.de, www.informatik.uni-frankfurt.de/~paetz

Abstract

In intensive care units much data is irregularly recorded. Here, we consider the analysis of symbolic septic shock patient data. We show that it could be worth considering the generalization paradigm (individual cases generalized to more general rules) instead of the association paradigm (combining single attributes) when considering very individual cases (e.g. patients) and when expecting longer rules than shorter ones. We present an algorithm for rule generation and classification based on heuristically generated set-based intersections. We demonstrate the usefulness of our algorithm by analysing our septic shock patient data.

1. Introduction

The septic shock is of prime importance in intensive care medicine [1]. Most of the data in our database was symbolic data (therapies, operations, medication, admission data). Since the patients are very individual in their behavior the patient data is very inhomogenous.

Although association rules (a-priori [2]) are a common tool for analysing data, we tried a mechanism just the other way round: we generalize the patient data, beginning with the individual cases. We claim that it is worth and in fact reliable considering this generalization paradigm (see e.g. [3]). Our algorithm computes heuristically a kind of closed frequent itemsets [4] but not all of them and in a different, more natural way (using no backtracking or generators) [5].

In Sect. 2 we present the new set-based heuristic generalization algorithm "GenIntersect" [5] for classification, able to handle uncertain data with many attributes when expecting rather longer than shorter rules that should used not only for classification but also for medical interpretation. A winner-takes-all classification procedure that is based on a new measure "weighted confidence" is presented in Sect. 3.

With the help of this measure we evaluate the importance of the attributes and select features.

In Sect. 4 we discuss the main differences of our approach and the a-priori approach, mainly the robustness and the rule-context characteristics. We apply our algorithm in Sect. 5 to our symbolic septic shock patient database.

Additionally, we want to emphasize that our aim was not the comparison of several algorithms by evaluating benchmark data, although this is an important task. Our aim is to show that the fundamental idea of generalization (together with classification and feature selection) is useful in the medical domain.

2 Intersection Based Generalization Rules

Let us consider an example with two sets of items, $I_1 = ABC$ (short for $A \wedge B \wedge C$) and $I_2 = BCD$, e.g. $A =$ "green", $B =$ "big", $C =$ "4 doors", and $D =$ "fast." I_1 and I_2 describe the characteristics of two entities, e.g. two cars. What are the common characteristics of the two cars? Both cars are big and have 4 doors. Only car 1 is big and car 2 is fast. In set theoretic language we have generated an intersection of I_1 and I_2: $I_1 \cap I_2 = ABC \cap BCD = BC$. Thus, intersection theory is the natural access to rule generation. Of course, we can consider different classes for our itemsets. The sets of items need not to have the same number of elements. Hence, a missing item causes no problems when calculating intersections. Also we can reduce the number of attributes in one step much more than only one attribute. The intersection operator could be interpreted as a kind of *recombination operator*, known from evolutionary computing.

Example 2.1:

Let us consider the 8 itemsets $ABCD$, $AEFG$, $BEFG$, $CEFG$, $DEFG$, BE, CF, and DG. In [4] the *closure* cl(I) of an item with regard to itemset I is defined as the intersection of all the itemsets that contain I. Thus, the closure of A is $cl(A) = ABCD \cap AEFG = A$. If $cl(I) = I$, then an itemset I is called *closed*. In our example A is closed. Using the algorithm [4] we have to compute all the closures of frequent itemsets, successively for itemsets of length $1, 2, 3, \ldots$ Thus, the algorithm [4] computes as much candidates as a-priori. Using our intersection paradigma, building intersections directly from samples, we have a probability of $6/(7+6+5+4+3+2+1) = 6/28 \approx 0.21$ for generating the closed, more interesting, itemset EFG directly. The probability for generating the closed, less interesting, item A is only $1/28$. This example emphasizes that it is plausible and reliable to generate heuristically generalizations instead of generating a-priori-like candidates.

In the following we denote a finite set of itemsets as $\mathcal{IS}$. We will consider datasets where every sample is an itemset. Of course, identical samples may exist. We assume that identical samples are stored only one time in the database together with the frequency for every class. We call an intersection K of two sets I, J **nontrivial** if $K \neq I$, $K \neq J$ and $K \neq \emptyset$. We use the performance measures "frequency" and "confidence" for rules $I \Rightarrow c$, $I \in \mathcal{IS}$, c a class label, as introduced in [2], and we write $freq(I \Rightarrow c)$ resp. $conf(I \Rightarrow c)$.

2.1 Generalization Algorithm

Our aim is finding rules with high performance measures, obtaining a good classification by the rules that we generate and a reliable force of expression of the rules for physicians. The following algorithm, that is based on the principle of intersections, uses the set $\mathcal{IS}$ of all (training) itemsets as a starting point.

Algorithm 2.2: (GenIntersect)
Input parameters: Set of itemsets $\mathcal{IS}$, maxlevel, γ_i (minimum thresholds for the performance measures)
Output parameters: $\mathcal{IS}^F$ (generalized rules, including the initial rule itemset $\mathcal{IS}$), level, startlevel.

1. initialization
$\mathcal{IS}_{\text{new}} := \mathcal{IS}$;
level := 1;
startlevel(level) := 1;
endofalg := false;
2. generate level
while endofalg = false **do**
    startlevel(level+1) := $\sharp(\mathcal{IS}_{\text{new}})+1$;
    oldIS := $\sharp\mathcal{IS}_{\text{new}}$;
    pass through actual level
    for i = startlevel(level) **to** startlevel(level+1)-2
        pass through itemsets *without* considering itemsets of the preceding levels

        for $j = i + 1$ **to** startlevel(level+1)-1
            Inter := $\mathcal{IS}_{\text{new}}(i) \cap \mathcal{IS}_{\text{new}}(j)$;
            if Inter is a nontrivial intersection
                and (Inter $\notin \mathcal{IS}_{\text{new}}$) **then**
                $\mathcal{IS}_{\text{new}}(\sharp\mathcal{IS}_{\text{new}} + 1) :=$ Inter;
            end if, **end for** j, **end for** i
3. check termination
    if ($\sharp\mathcal{IS}_{\text{new}}$ = oldIS) **or** (level $\geq$ maxlevel) **then**
        endofalg := true;
        $\mathcal{IS}^F := \mathcal{IS}_{\text{new}}$;
    else
        level := level $+1$;
    end
end while
4. filter all the rules that have performance measures higher then all γ_i.

2.2 Heuristic Extensions

A disadvantage of the algorithm GenIntersect is the combinatorial explosion. Monotonic frequency pruning is not possible because the frequency is not monotone with respect to the generalization process. Thus, we should use adaptive heuristics. This makes sense, because we do not need all the optimal rules for classification. It is sufficient to go on with generalization until not much more rules are generated or until the classification result gets not much better within a level.

We introduce the *outer generalization index* to determine online if another generalization level makes sense. Additionally our *inner generalization index* determines within one level when an intersection process could be stopped, so that it can proceed with the next level.

The idea of the inner generalization index is the calculation of a sliding mean, using the number of newly generated itemsets per itemset. If this sliding mean value M becomes too small, we stop the intersection process within the actual level and proceed with another level. As our experiments showed, this is very performant in combination with a maximal number max_{new} of itemsets that one itemset is allowed to generate.

Definition 2.3:
We call the sliding mean M, mentioned above, the **inner generalization index** $G^{(in)} := M$.

How many levels do we need? A heuristic answer is our *outer generalization index*.

Definition 2.4:
Let m be the maximal possible number of new itemsets within one level and e the number of effectively generated new itemsets, that are not nontrivial and not already gener-

ated. Then, we define the **outer generalization index** as

$$G^{(out)} := \frac{e}{m} \ . \qquad (1)$$

If $G^{(out)} \in [0, 1]$ falls under a predefined threshold, then the algorithm terminates. If the index is approx. 1, then the algorithm should go on with another level.

More properties (use of negotiations, optimality) of our algorithm can be found in [5].

3 Classification

Now, we describe how we can classify a new (test) itemset $\mathcal{IS}$ using a generalized itemset $\mathcal{R}$ (representing a rule basis). One problem always arising in this situation is the different a-priori probability, e.g. 80% class 1 samples and 20% class 2 samples. The confidence measure is related to the a-priori percentage and is therefore not suitable for a classifier. We introduce an elegant way to solve this problem using an extension of the confidence, the *weighted* confidence.

Definition 3.1:
The **weighted confidence** $wconf$ for class c could be defined using the confidence together with the class proportions or easier as the proportion of the c-frequency (=class c coverage $\neq$ frequency!) considering all d-frequencies:

$$c\text{-}wconf(I \Rightarrow c) := \frac{c\text{-}freq(I \Rightarrow c)}{\sum_{d=1}^{m} d\text{-}freq(I \Rightarrow d)} \qquad (2)$$

The weighted confidence is ideal for a winner-takes-all classification. The best fitting rule with respect to the weighted confidence specifies the class. We call our algorithm "WeCoCl", abbr. for "Weighted Confidence Classifier." It is a classifier for itemsets with a multiple class alignment.

Algorithm 3.2: (WeCoCl)
Parameters: $\mathcal{IS}$ (all itemsets, that will be classified), $\mathcal{R}$ (with GenIntersect generated set of rule itemsets, filtered with the performance measures).

1. for all itemsets of the test itemsets calculate the sets of all "containing" weighted c_d-confidence values
   for all itemsets $I \in \mathcal{IS}$ **do**
       for all classes d **do** $WCONF_d := \emptyset$;
       for all itemsets (rules) $J \in \mathcal{R}$ **do**
           if $J \subset I$ **then**
               $WCONF_d = WCONF_d \cup \{d\text{-}wconf(J)\}$;
           end if, **end** for all J, **end** for all I
2. calculate the maximal weighted d-confidence per class; these values are noted as $maxWCONF_d$.
3. Be $maxind = index(\max_d\{maxWCONF_d\})$ and

$sindex = index(\max_{d, d \neq maxind}\{maxWCONF_d\})$.
if $maxWCONF_{maxind} - maxWCONF_{sindex} \geq \varepsilon$
   then classify I as class $maxind$, otherwise we
   classify I as "not classifiable." This is always the
   case if no itemset of the rule set is contained in I.
end

4 Discussion: Generalization vs. Association

A-priori generates great many, superfluous rules. Let us consider the rules ABC, BCD, both of the same class c. GenIntersect generates only the additional rule BC. A-priori considers the items A, B, C and D of length 1 and then the combinations of length 2. AD is an itemset, that is not contained in ABC or BCD. Frequent is the itemset BC, but also are the items B and C. We do not need to generate *all* frequent itemsets for classification. It leads to an effect, we call **context smearing**, resulting from the association process starting with the items, while the context is fixed by the itemsets.

Example 4.1:
Let B be the item "high blood pressure" and C "pH value." The important knowledge is the *combination* of both items BC. If we would choose only B or C as a classification rule, we claim that a high blood pressure or a low pH value are standalone interesting. This may be the case but it need not to be! If we present only B as a generalized rule to a physician, then he could conclude in a complete false way: he could think that giving a blood pressure lowering medicament is a benefit for the patient, although this medicament would again lower the pH value for the patient's disadvantage, because he was not aware of the complete information BC. A longer generalization rule is more useful to a physician.

How senseful is a rule set for the classification of *unknown* data, i.e. how **robust** is a-priori resp. GenIntersect?

Example 4.2:
Let us consider again the itemsets ABC und BCD (of the same class c). GenIntersect generates BC, an a-priori classifier would choose the rule B or C. Assume, the unknown itemset to classify is AB. It is $BC \not\subset AB$, i.e. AB would be classified as "not classifiable." In fact, AB could be of another class than BC, so that this decision is justified. But it is $B \subset AB$, i.e. AB would be classified as class d, although AB need not to be a class d itemset. There is no reason at all to classify in such a way. If we choose C instead of B, which seems to be an equal choice, we have $C \not\subset AB$. Thus, in fact B is not an equal choice compared to C, if we expect *unknown* itemsets, the usual case in medicine due to individual patients.

	mean result
number of rules (all, cl. s, d)	28.0 / 18.0 / 10.0
length of rules (cl. s, d)	12.8 / 11.6
correct, false, not classified [%]	67.96 / 18.42 / 13.63
specifity, sensitivity [%]	80.89 / 68.29
test confidence (class s, d) [%]	96.70 / 41.57
test wconf. (class s, d) [%]	83.83 / 78.70
test frequency (class s, d) [%]	27.00 / 12.44

Table 1. Results of the rule generation with GenIntersect and WeCoCl.

Shorter a-priori rule sets are not robust due to context smearing. We state that in the medical domain (e.g. rules for therapy planning) generalization rules are more reliable than association rules. Shorter association rules may even be harmful for patients!

5 Septic Shock Patient Data

Septic shock is of prime importance in intensive care medicine [1]. Our database consists of 362 septic shock patients. The data of each patient was given as admission data (e.g. chronic diagnoses) and daily measurements (e.g. acute diagnoses, medication and therapies).

We made three complete experiments with the patient data. The results were mean results of these experiments. We used the heuristics of Sect. 2.2. Initially we used 50% of the data for training our system, the other 50% for calculating the test results. Let us abbreviate the class "survived" by "class s" and the class "deceased" by "class d."

We made a first run of our algorithm with all the 96 items. After filtering the rules by the frequency and confidence thresholds 23 rules remained. Calculating the importance of the items by

$$imp_c(A) := \sum_{i=1, A \in I_i}^{r_l} freq(I_i \Rightarrow c) \ c\text{-}wconf(I_i \Rightarrow c) \frac{1}{|I_i|},$$

only 60 of the 96 items had an importance > 0 for one of the two classes. Only 27 items had an importance value that was noticeable > 0. With this 27 items we made three repetitions of the entire experiment. The mean results on the test data is shown in Tab. 1. The complete parameter and heuristics setting is documented in [5].

The NO items (e.g. not thrombocyte concentrate, not endoscopy, not min. 3 antibiotics given) appeared more often for class s, the YES items (e.g. respiration, catecholamines given) more often for class d.

An example for a rule of class d is:
"if not traumatic **and** number of organ failures > 2 **and** respiration **and** haemofiltration **and** not dialysis **and** catecholamines given **then** class d with $wconf = 89.73\%$ **and** $freq = 6.63\%$."

A comparison of GenIntersect to a-priori can be found in [5]. GenIntersect needs less memory (2MB instead of approx. 500MB). For class d a-priori was not reliable since for class d rules we need frequency thresholds less than 2%.

6 Conclusion

We presented an algorithm for generalizing itemsets. Using heuristics, it is reliable to generalize even larger data sets. The algorithm is very useful if classification tasks are considered. We confirmed our inventions by application to important medical real world data, the septic shock ICU patient data. A fundamental comparison to association rules was given. It showed that it does make sense to generalize instead of associate due to the two big problems context smearing and robustness, two important circumstances in medical applications. The whole work is documented in greater detail in [5].

Work for the future could be the invention of even more suitable adaptive heuristics.

Acknowledgment: The medical application was supported by the DFG (German Research Foundation).

References

[1] Hanisch, E., Encke, A.: Intensive Care Management in Abdominal Surgical Patients with Septic Complications, in: E. Faist (ed.) Immunological Screening and Immunotherapy in Critically Ill Patients with Abdominal Infections, Springer-Verlag (2001) 71–138

[2] Agrawal, R. and Skrikant, R.: Fast Algorithms for Mining Association Rules. Proc. 20th Int. Conf. on Very Large Databases (VLDB) (1994) 487–499

[3] Mitchell, T.M.: Machine Learning. McGraw-Hill (1997)

[4] Bastide, Y. et al.: Mining Minimal Non-Redundant Association Rules Using Frequent Closed Itemsets. Proc. 1st Int. Conf. on Computat. Logic (CL); 6th Conf. on Database Systems (DOOD) (2000) 972–986

[5] Paetz, J.: Durchschnittsbasierte Generalisierungsregeln Teil I + II. Frankfurter Informatik-Berichte Nr. 1 + 2/02, Institut für Informatik, FB Biologie und Informatik, J.W. Goethe-Univ. Frankfurt am Main, Germany, ISSN 1616–9107 (2002)

Exploring Interestingness Through Clustering: A Framework

Sigal Sahar

gales@post.tau.ac.il
Tel-Aviv University

Abstract

Determining interestingness is a notoriously difficult problem: it is subjective and elusive to capture. It is also becoming an increasingly more important problem in KDD as the number of mined patterns increases. In this work we introduce and investigate a framework for association rule clustering that enables automating much of the laborious manual effort normally involved in the exploration and understanding of interestingness. Clustering is ideally suited for this task; it is the unsupervised organization of patterns into groups, so that patterns in the same group are more similar to each other than to patterns in other groups. We also define a data-driven inferred labeling of these clusters, the ancestor coverage, which provides an intuitive, concise representation of the clusters.

1 Introduction

Determining which patterns are interesting is an important, but notoriously difficult problem [9, 13, 3]. Many approaches, requiring varying degrees of user intervention, have been formulated to tackle the problem, see [16] for a review. In this work we were motivated by the approach of [15] that identifies similar groups of rules to develop a first step in replacing a significant amount of the tedious, manual effort commonly involved when investigating interestingness. As [13] emphasize, the difficulty in analyzing the mined rules is in how to organize them effectively. We tackle this challenge by introducing a clustering framework that automates interestingness exploration of masses of rules by organizing them into groups by similarity. This can be seen as an example of higher order mining [17].

Clustering is the unsupervised organization of similar objects into meaningful groups, or clusters [7, 10, 8, 4], so that objects within a cluster are more similar to each other than to objects in other clusters. Since clustering does not require the pre-labeling of patterns it is ideally suited for exploring interestingness; the mining process outputs a list of unlabeled (as interesting/not-interesting) association rules.

In KDD clustering is frequently used to gain insight into the distribution of the *data* [7, 11]. In the context of association rules, clustering was previously used to partition intervals over numeric data domains, as input for mining algorithms as in [14]. In [12] association rules with two numeric attributes in the assumption were clustered by joining assumption attribute intervals. [6] proposed mining over sets of clustered data. In our work, we use clustering differently and for a different purpose. [18] were the first to use groupings to improve the understandability of rule covers with a common consequent over data domains constrained by a rule-confidence monotonicity assumption. In this work we introduce a *general* framework for clustering unconstrained association rules over unconstrained domains to enable exploring interestingness. To make the clusters easy to interpret we define a concise, data-driven cluster representation, the ancestor coverage, defined in Section 4. Additionally, we investigate the drawbacks and advantages of existing and new similarity measures, and the results of their application on real databases. [18] defined a similarity measure as the number of transactions two rules with equal consequents differ on. [3] proposed a distance metric to detect unexpected rules in a defined neighborhood, not for clustering. [5] proposed a measure to differentiate between attributes with overlapping/non-overlapping numeric values.

2 Definitions and Preliminaries

Let Λ be a set of attributes over the boolean domain and $\mathcal{D}$ be a set of transactions over Λ. For $A, B \subseteq \Lambda$, $A \cap B = \emptyset$, [1] define the **association rule** $A \to B$ to have support $s\%$ and confidence $c\%$ if $s\%$ of $\mathcal{D}$ contain $A \cup B$, and $c\%$ of $\mathcal{D}$ that contain A also contain B. Given support and confidence thresholds, [1]'s algorithm outputs all the association rules that have at least those thresholds. We refer to A as the **assumption** of the rule and to B as its **consequent**. We also use $\oplus$ to denote the xor operation: $X \oplus Y = (X \setminus Y) \cup (Y \setminus X)$. Let Ω be the list of association rules mined over Λ. Let $a, b \in \Lambda$, and $\rho = a \to b$. [15] defines the **family** of ρ in Ω as: $family_\Omega(\rho) \overset{\text{Def}}{=} \{r \in \Omega | r = A \to B, a \in A, b \in B\} \cup \{\rho\}$, and the **ancestor rule** of the family is defined to be ρ. An indicator of the size of a family is [15] $RSCL_\Omega(\rho) \overset{\mathbf{Def}}{=} \|family_\Omega(\rho) \setminus \{\rho\}\|/\|\Omega\|$, where $\|X\|$ is the number of elements in the set X. We introduce the **Relative Size of the Family of** ρ **over a Set of associ-ation rules** $\mathcal{C}$, which we define as $\mathbf{RSFS}_\mathcal{C}(\rho) \overset{\mathbf{Def}}{=} \|\{r \in \mathcal{C} | r = A \to B, a \in A, b \in B\}\|/\|\mathcal{C}\|$.

3 Interestingness Exploration Via Clustering

We introduce a clustering framework for grouping and naming of association rules, an effective automated tool for quickly exploring their interestingness. The clustering process typically includes the following steps [10, 8] (1) profiling, (2) similarity measure definition, (3) clustering algorithm, and (4) representing and evaluating the clustering.

3.1 Association Rule Profiles

A cluster of association rules is a set of similar rules. Before we can define the "similarity" of rules, we need to define what characterizes the rules, or their profiles. There are no theoretical guidelines to determine the features best suited for use in a similarity measure, how those features should be normalized or which is the most appropriate similarity measure to be used [10]. A skillful selection of the feature vector is necessary for simple and easily understandable clustering that will provide insight into the interestingness of the rules; a poor selection can yield to complex clustering that provides little or no insight. We choose to concentrate on the five characteristics that fully define an association rule $r = A \to B$: **(1)** A, **(2)** B, **(3)** the rule support, **(4)** the assumption support: the percent of $\mathcal{D}$ that contain A, and, **(5)** B's support: the percent of $\mathcal{D}$ that contain B.

3.2 Similarity Measures for Association Rules

We follow the reasoning in [4] and abandon the adherence to a distance metric and use a nonmetric similarity function[1]. We review two representative measures available in the literature in the context of our expectation of a good similarity measure: the dissimilarity between rules in the same cluster will be significantly less than that of rules in different clusters. Since neither of those measures satisfies this expectation, we introduce a new measure that does.

3.2.1 Support-Difference Measure

[18] defined a similarity measure between rules with an equal consequent as: $d(A \to B, C \to B) = [support(AB) + support(BC) - 2 \cdot support(ABC)] \cdot \|\mathcal{D}\|$,

which is naturally extended to unconstrained rules as: $d_{sd}(A \to B, C \to D) = support(AB) + support(CD) - 2 \cdot support(ABCD)$, but does not differentiate between attributes in the assumption and the consequent. For example, let $r_{tc} = t \to c, r_1 = t, a \to c, r_2 = t, c \to a$. A user classifying the family of r_{tc} as not-interesting indicates that r_1 is not-interesting. However, this user could be interested in r_2. The two rules r_1 and r_2 are therefore *not* similar to this user, and yet $d_{sd}(r_1, r_2) = 0$. This does not match our expectation of a good similarity measure: d_{sd} can rank rules that are *less* similar (r_1 and r_2) as closer than rules that are more similar, ($d_{sd}(r_{tc}, r_1) > 0$). Note that d_{sd} does not use all the profile features defined in Section 3.1.

3.2.2 Attribute Distance Measure

[3] introduced $d_{iset}(A \to B, C \to D) = \delta_1 \cdot \|(A \cup B) \oplus (C \cup D)\| + \delta_2 \cdot \|A \oplus C\| + \delta_3 \cdot \|B \oplus D\|$, and recommended: $\delta_1 = 1, \delta_2 = (n-1)/n^2$, and, $\delta_3 = 1/n^2$, where $n = \|\Lambda\|$. For the Grocery DB (Section 4), where $n = 1757, d_{iset}$ imposes an extremely strong similarity bias for rules over the same attribute sets. This property is *not* favored by all users. To avoid this problem we also used d_{iset} with equal δ_i weights. However, we still run across a problem where two rules, $r_3 = \langle \text{cucumbers} \wedge \text{tomatoes} \rangle \to \langle \text{onions} \rangle$ and $r_4 = \langle \text{cucumbers} \wedge \text{tomatoes} \rangle \to \langle \text{ctr\#3} \rangle$, such that $support(r_3) = 0.17, confidence(r_3) = 0.41, support(r_4) = 0.037$, and $confidence(r_4) = 0.09$, are ranked very closely by d_{iset}, whereas there is a significant difference between them, as marked by $d_{sd}(r_3, r_4) = 0.21$. Note that d_{iset} only uses the first 2 features of the association rule profile defined in Section 3.1.

3.2.3 New Similarity Measure

In Equation 1 we introduce a new similarity measure, d_{sc}, that addresses the drawbacks of the measures mentioned above to provide a natural similarity measure[2].

$$d_{sc}(A \to B, C \to D) \overset{\mathbf{Def}}{=} [1 + diff_{sup}(A,C)]\frac{\|A \oplus C\|}{\|A \cup C\|}\gamma_1 +$$
$$[1 + diff_{sup}(B,D)]\frac{\|B \oplus D\|}{\|B \cup D\|}\gamma_2 + \qquad (1)$$
$$[1 + diff_{sup}(A \cup B, C \cup D)]\frac{\|(A \cup B) \oplus (C \cup D)\|}{\|A \cup B \cup C \cup D\|}\gamma_3$$

where $diff_{sup}$ (difference-in-support) is defined as in d_{sd}: $diff_{sup}(A,B) = support(A) + support(B) - 2 \cdot support(A \cup B)$. 1 is added to the $diff_{sup}$ value for cases where $diff_{sup}(X,Y) = 0$ and at the same time $X \oplus Y \neq \emptyset$. As in [3], choices of values for the gamma-weights reflect preferences, in our case for inclusion. Sets $S, S' \subseteq \Lambda$ are

---

[1]In some scenarios the similarity of r and r' may be considered different from that of r' to r, necessitating non-symmetric similarity measures. However, clustering is normally performed using symmetric similarity measures, which we will adhere to.

[2]The dissimilarity between two rules is the weighted sum of dissimilarities between the assumptions, consequents, and attribute sets that make up the two rules, where each component is a weighted measure of the dissimilarities of the support ($diff_{sup}$) and the attribute set (xor ratio).

said to be **included** if $((S \subseteq S') \vee (S' \subseteq S))$. Rules $X \to Y$ and $Z \to W$ are said to be **included** if $((X \subseteq Z) \wedge (Y \subseteq W)) \vee ((Z \subseteq X) \wedge (W \subseteq Y))$. Inclusion is not captured by the xor relationship. For example, let $A_1 = \{a, b\}$, $A_2 = \{a\}$, $A_3 = \{a, b, d\}$, $A_4 = \{a, b, c\}$ be four assumptions. $\|A_1 \oplus A_2\|/\|A_1 \cup A_2\| = 1/2 = \|A_3 \oplus A_4\|/\|A_3 \cup A_4\|$. However, $A_2 \subset A_1$, whereas, $A_3 \not\subset A_4$ and $A_4 \not\subset A_3$. In that sense, A_1 and A_2 are closer than A_3 is to A_4. We therefore set γ_1 in Equation 1 to γ if $((A \subseteq C) \vee (C \subseteq A))$, and to 1 otherwise. Note that we do not treat $A = C$ differently since then $\|A \oplus C\| = 0$, and the assumption will not contribute to d_{sc}. Since the same analysis holds for consequents, we set γ_2 to the same value γ if $((B \subseteq D) \vee (B \subseteq D))$ and to 1 otherwise. Since for $r' = X \to Y$ and $r'' = Z \to W$, where $X \subseteq Z$ and $Y \subseteq W$, r' and r'' are not included in each other, even though their assumptions and consequents are included, we set γ_3 in Equation 1 to the same value γ if the two rules are included and and to 1 otherwise. For the rest of the paper we refer to the value $\gamma = 1/2$. Note that d_{sc} uses *all* the features of the association rule profile and the problematic similarities for the rules from previous sections are remedied. For reference, $d_{sc}(r_1, r_2) = 2.38$, $d_{sc}(r_3, r_4) = 1.96$.

3.3 Clustering Algorithms

There are two general types of clustering algorithms, hierarchical and partitional. Hierarchical algorithms create a hierarchical decomposition of the data, so that if two objects are in the same cluster at a certain level in the hierarchy, they will remain in the same cluster at all higher levels of clustering. Every hierarchical clustering spans out a dendrogram that shows how the objects are grouped. There are two main classes of hierarchical algorithms: (1) agglomerative algorithms that start with $\|\Omega\|$ singleton clusters and form the hierarchy by successively merging clusters, and, (2) divisive algorithms that start with one cluster that includes all the patterns and form the hierarchy by successively splitting clusters. Partitional algorithms find data partitions that optimize a chosen similarity criterion. See [7, 10, 8, 4] for detailed reviews of clustering methods. We chose to use the agglomerative hierarchical clustering method for exploring interestingness for several reasons: (1) the dendrogram that portrays the rule-grouping at each level is extremely useful for thorough investigation of the clusters, and, (2) we circumvent difficult questions that are part of partitional algorithms such as what is a good starting point for the iterative optimization and what is the ideal choice for a final number of clusters. For completeness, we outline the basic agglomerative hierarchical algorithm we started with: **(1)** Initialize $\|\Omega\|$ singleton clusters, each containing a single association rule. **(2)** Find the nearest pair of clusters using the chosen similarity measure. **(3)** Merge the rules in the two distinct

clusters into one cluster. **(4)** If all the number of remaining clusters is 1, stop. Otherwise go to step 2. See Section 4.2 for implementation changes made to the algorithm.

4 Discussion of Empirical Analysis

We used the following three databases for the analysis: (1) The **Grocery Database** that describes 67,470 shopping baskets of an online Israeli grocery store using 1,757 boolean attributes. We mined 3,046 rules from this DB using 3.5% thresholds. (2) The **Adult Database**, compiled from the 45,222 entries with no missing values from the Adult dataset [2], discretized into 171 boolean attributes. Mining this DB with 20% thresholds yielded 13,906 rules. (3) The **WWW Database** that describes the accesses of the 2,336 heaviest users to 15 site categories. Mining this DB with 6% threshold yielded 9,206 rules to be clustered.

4.1 Representation and Evaluation of Clustering

4.1.1 Cluster Representation and Interpretation

To provide a compact representation, clusters need to be abstracted or named. The rule covers of [18] will not serve as a representation in the general case since they only work in domains where there are no confidence rule exceptions, which is not always the case. Let $\mathcal{C}$ be a cluster of association rules. We define the **ancestor coverage** as the cluster representation of $\mathcal{C}$ to be the set of ancestor rules: $\{a \to b | a, b \in \Lambda, \forall r = X \to Y \in \mathcal{C}, r \in family(a \to b)\}$. For the representation to be effective, we need to find a minimal ancestor coverage set. For computational efficiency over large clusters we use a greedy algorithm. To find the minimal ancestor coverage we need to depart from $RSCL$ and use $RSFS$. Although the difference between $RSCL$ and $RSFS$ over $\mathcal{C}$ is at most $1/\|\mathcal{C}\|$, it can translate into a substantially larger ancestor coverage. For example, let $\mathcal{C}_1 = \{r_{ab} = a \to b, r_{abc} = a \to b, c\}$. Now, $r_{abc}, r_{ab} \in family(a \to b)$ and $r_{abc} \in family(a \to c)$. By definition, $RSCL(a \to b) = RSCL(a \to c)$, so either ancestor rule could be chosen to be in the ancestor coverage. However, if $a \to c$ is selected first, the ancestor coverage will include both ancestor rules, even though $\{a \to b\}$ is the minimal ancestor coverage. Using $RSFS$ ensures a minimal greedy ancestor coverage; we set the ancestor coverage of a cluster $\mathcal{C}$ by iteratively finding the ancestor rule with the largest $RSFS$ value of the rules remaining to be covered.

The ancestor coverage cluster representation is the desired concise, intuitive, entirely data-driven inferred cluster labeling or representation. For example, one of the larger clusters in the WWW Database after almost 8000 iterations, using d_{sc}, contained 1180 rules, but its cluster coverage contained only 20 ancestor rules. At that level in the hierarchical clustering, the average cluster size was 31.7 rules, and the average cluster coverage only contained 2.4 rules. The relative small size of the ancestor coverages remained the same over the other databases, and over the different iterations as well. For example, the average ancestor coverage was 5% of the cluster size for the Adult Database, and just over 18% for the very sparse Grocery Database. The ancestor rules are representative of the many rules they cover and their families are easy to understand [15], enabling a quick decision on whether to further explore the cluster. Further exploration of the cluster is enabled using the information from the dendrogram. Thus, users can drill into clusters that are potentially interesting and easily avoid spending time examining not-interesting clusters.

4.1.2 Outlier Analysis

An interesting application of clustering is in the discovery of "outlier" association rules, rules that are significantly different from the rest of the mined association rules (distance based outlier detection is mentioned in [7]). The rule outliers are manifested in the form of singleton clusters or very small clusters during an advanced stage of the clustering. These rules can be very interesting as they point out behavior that is unlike the "normal" behavior portrayed in the data, likely to describe a small portion of the population, and therefore is unlikely to be known to the database users.

4.1.3 Cluster Evaluation

An important part of the clustering process is the evaluation of the results. Although the final evaluation can only be provided by the users, measures of clusters quality can provide insight as to how legitimate vs. arbitrary the clustering is. The quality measure we used is the **votes of confidence measure**: the number of pairs of rules within a cluster (prior to its merging with the next cluster) that, according to the similarity measure, should be in the same cluster, that is, be the next candidates to be merged into one cluster that are already in the same cluster. For a measure of goodness we used this number with the maximum number of votes of confidence for a cluster of size m: $m(m-1)/2 - 1$.

4.2 Clustering Implementation Issues

The biggest challenge we have come across in implementing and running the clustering was in the processing-time and memory demands (we used a Compaq ProLiant DL580, 4 700MHz Xeon CPUs with 2GB RAM). Storing a similarity matrix ($n(n-1)/2$ proximity values), and determining the two most similar items in it over many iterations requires prohibitive amounts of memory and computational power/time. We therefore changed the algorithm to maintain only the similarity measures most likely to be used in the hierarchical clustering process to reach 1 cluster from

the $\|\Omega\|$ initial singleton clusters. Those are the smaller similarity measures. Their number is obviously larger than $\|\Omega\|$ since some measures will be between members of the same cluster, as in Section 4.1.3. Note that although this is a minor technical modification to the algorithm, it reduced the memory requirements and execution time by several orders of magnitude and was critical in making the clustering feasible over large number of rules. Other such technical modifications were made to enhance the algorithm runtime.

5 Conclusions

In this work we presented an association rule clustering framework exploring interestingness of rules. This clustering automates much of the tedious manual labor otherwise needed, and is an alternative to methods that require significant amounts of domain knowledge to determine interestingness of unconstrained rules. We introduced the ancestor coverage, a concise, data-driven representation of the clusters, as well as a new and natural rule similarity measure. From our analysis, clustering of association rules stands to be a very promising and fruitful venue for exploring interestingness, with many open areas for future research.

References

[1] R. Agrawal, M. Heikki, R. Srikant, H. Toivonen, and A. I. Verkamo. *Advances in KD and DM*, chapter 12, pgs 307–328. 1996.

[2] C. Blake and C. Merz. UCI repository of machine learning databases, 1998, http://www.ics.uci.edu/~mlearn/mlrepository.html.

[3] G. Dong and J. Li. Interestingness of discovered association rules in terms of neighborhood-based unexpectedness. *PAKDD*, pgs 72–86, 1998.

[4] R. O. Duda and P. E. Hart. *Pattern Classification and Scene Analysis*. John Wiley & Sons, 1973.

[5] P. Gago and C. Bento. A metric for selection of the most promising rules. *PKDD*, pgs 19–27, 1998.

[6] J. Han. Mining knowledge at multiple concept levels. *CIKM*, pgs 19–24, 1995.

[7] J. Han and M. Kamber. *Data Mining Concepts and Techniques*, chapter 8: *Cluster Analysis*, pgs 335–393. 2001.

[8] J. A. Hartigan. *Clustering Algorithms*. John Wiley & Sons, 99th edition, 1975.

[9] R. Hilderman and H. Hamilton. Principles for mining summaries using objective measures of interestingness. *ICTAI*, pgs 72–81, 2000.

[10] A. K. Jain, M. N. Murty, and P. J. Flynn. Data clustering: a review. *ACM Computing Surveys*, 31(3):264–323, 1999.

[11] G. Karypis, E.-H. Han, and V. Kumar. Chameleon: A hierarchical clustering algorithm using dynamic modeling. *IEEE Computer: Special Issue on Data Analysis and Mining*, 32(8):68–75, 1999.

[12] B. Lent, A. N. Swami, and J. Widom. Clustering association rules. *ICDE*, pgs 220–231, 1997.

[13] B. Liu, M. Hu, and W. Hsu. Multi-level organization and summarization of discovered rules. *SIGKDD*, pgs 208–217, 2000.

[14] R. J. Miller and Y. Yang. Association rules over interval data. *SIGMOD*, pgs 452–461, 1997.

[15] S. Sahar. Interestingness via what is not interesting. *SIGKDD*, pgs 332–336, 1999.

[16] S. Sahar. Interestingness preprocessing. *ICDM*, pgs 489–496, 2001.

[17] M. Spiliopoulou and J. F. Roddick. Higher order mining: Modeling and mining the results of knowledge discovery. *DM-II*, pgs 309–320, 2000.

[18] H. Toivonen, M. Klemettinen, P. Ronkainen, K. Hätönen, and H. Mannila. Pruning and grouping discovered association rules. *ECML Workshop on Statistics, Machine Learning and KDD*, pgs 47–52, 1995.

On Incorporating Subjective Interestingness Into the Mining Process

Sigal Sahar

gales@post.tau.ac.il

Tel-Aviv University

Abstract

Subjective interestingness is at the heart of the successful discovery of association rules. To determine what is subjectively interesting, users' domain knowledge must be applied. [7] introduced an approach that requires very little domain knowledge and interaction to eliminate the majority of the rules that are subjectively not interesting. In this paper we investigate how this approach can be incorporated into the mining process, the benefits and disadvantages of doing so, and examine the results of its application to real databases.

1 Introduction

[4] defined Knowledge Discovery in Databases (KDD) as "[...] the non-trivial process of identifying valid, novel, potentially useful, and ultimately understandable patterns in data." **Interestingness** distinguishes the "valid, novel, potentially useful, and ultimately understandable" patterns from those that are not. Since the problem of interestingness is ultimately subjective, subjective criteria that explicitly employ users' domain knowledge are needed to completely resolve this problem. Incorporating subjective interestingness into the mining process has obvious advantages: less patterns will be mined, and those are more likely to be interesting to the users. However, a drawback of this tactic is that the results may be tailored to match *only* the pre-specified subjective criteria; exploring slightly different interestingness criteria could require re-executing the entire mining process.

To reduce the number of mined patterns to make their post-processing easier, we need to incorporate into the mining *general* subjective interestingness criteria that (1) are very easy to define, and, (2) apply to the interests of a wide audience base. In

this work we tackle this task by incorporating the method of [7] into the mining process to create an algorithm that is simple, general and effective (see Section 3). We also examine the results and repercussions, both benefits and disadvantages, of the application of this method on the same databases used in [7]. Note that as in [7] our goal is to reduce, rather than eliminate, the number of not-interesting rules mined.

Related are works such as [1, 6, 9, 5] that incorporate subjective interestingness into the mining process, but rely on the availability of domain experts to express all the needed information in a predefined grammar. See [8] for a detailed review.

2 Definitions and Preliminaries

Let Λ be a set of attributes over the boolean domain, $\mathcal{D}$ be a set of transactions over Λ, and i-itemset denote an itemset of size i. For $A, B \subseteq \Lambda$, $A \cap B = \emptyset$, the **association rule** $A \rightarrow B$ is defined [2] to have support $s\%$ and confidence $c\%$ if $s\%$ of $\mathcal{D}$ contain $A \cup B$, and $c\%$ of $\mathcal{D}$ that contain A also contain B. We refer to A as the **assumption** of the rule and to B as its **consequent**. [2]'s algorithm outputs all the association rules that have at least predefined support and confidence thresholds. In this work we build on the AprioriTid algorithm [2].

Let Ω be the list of association rules mined over Λ. Let $a, b \in \Lambda$, and $\rho = a \rightarrow b$. The **family** of ρ in Ω is defined [7] as: $\mathbf{family}_\Omega(\rho) \overset{\mathbf{Def}}{=} \{r \in \Omega | r = A \rightarrow B, a \in A, b \in B\} \cup \{\rho\}$. ρ is then defined as the **ancestor rule** of the family of ρ in Ω.

We now define the **binuclear family** of a 2-itemset $\{a, b\}$ as: $\boldsymbol{biF}_\Omega(\{a, b\}) \overset{\mathbf{Def}}{=} family_\Omega(a \rightarrow b) \bigcup family_\Omega(b \rightarrow a)$. $\{a, b\}$ is referred to as the **ancestor itemset** and is said to **span** $biF_\Omega(\{a, b\})$. A binuclear-family is also be defined to be spanned by an ancestor rule: $biF_\Omega(\rho) \overset{\mathbf{Def}}{=} biF_\Omega(\{a, b\})$. Note that $biF_\Omega(a \rightarrow b) = biF_\Omega(b \rightarrow a)$.

3   The Algorithm

The goals of our algorithm are:
(1) Simplicity: keep the process simple by asking users only a few, easy classification questions.
(2) Generality: the results of the mining process with the integrated subjective interestingness will be general enough to be applicable to a wide user base for further interestingness post-processing.
(3) Effectiveness: integrating this type of subjective interestingness into the mining process will result in mining of much fewer association rules*.

[7] uses domain knowledge of the kind "*not interested in family$_\Omega(\rho)$*" for interestingness post-processing. The families of $a \rightarrow b$ and $b \rightarrow a$ cannot be distinguished during the mining process, when only itemsets are recognized. To integrate user preferences of the type used in [7] into the mining, we have to use generalized preferences of the type "*not interested in biF$_\Omega(\rho)$*". We can decrease the number of mined patterns by eliminating one or more of the frequent itemsets discovered during the mining. **The challenge** in deleting a frequent itemset $I = \{a_i, b_i\}$ is in ensuring that even though I is removed, rules of the type:

$$A \rightarrow D \text{ and } D \rightarrow A : a_i, b_i \in A \text{ and } a_i, b_i \notin D \quad (1)$$

that would have been mined had I not been deleted, will still be mined. An example for a rule in Equation 1 is $\langle$tomatoes,cucumbers$\rangle \rightarrow \langle$sugar$\rangle$ if $I_{ct} = \{$cucumbers,tomatoes$\}$ is deleted.

3.1   Selecting & Classifying Ancestor Itemsets

We only ask users a one-dimensioned classification question: is the ancestor itemset interesting or not-interesting to the user, that is, is the binuclear-family spanned by the ancestor itemset interesting/not-interesting. If a user classifies an ancestor itemset as not-interesting, it is marked for elimination (used in Section 3.2), otherwise, no action is taken on that ancestor itemset. We select ancestor itemsets for user classification to be the 1–3 most frequent 2-itemsets[†] in order of their frequency. These limited selection and classification processes naturally guaran-

---

*For example, integrating the first classification resulted, on average, in the mining of fewer than 80% of the rules that would have been mined otherwise (see Section 4 for details).

[†]Larger itemsets, itemsets with more than two attributes, are considered too complicated for the naive classification that we preserve: while the $biF_\Omega(\{a, b\}) = family_\Omega(a \rightarrow b) \cup family_\Omega(b \rightarrow a)$, the $biFamily$ of $\{a, b, c\}$ would be the union of the "families" of $a \rightarrow bc$, $ab \rightarrow c$, $b \rightarrow ac$, $bc \rightarrow a$, $ac \rightarrow b$, $c \rightarrow ab$, and possibly also of $a \rightarrow b$, $a \rightarrow c$, $b \rightarrow c$, $b \rightarrow a$, $c \rightarrow a$, and $c \rightarrow b$, with an even larger list for larger ancestor itemsets.

---

(1) Υ = ancestor itemsets classified for deletion;
(2) $\mathcal{I}_\Upsilon$ =new-attributes($\Upsilon, \mathcal{I}$); $\Lambda_\mathcal{I} = \Lambda \cup \mathcal{I}_\Upsilon$;
(3) L_1 = large 1-itemsets over $\mathcal{D}_\mathcal{I}$; $\widehat{C}_1 = database \mathcal{D}_\mathcal{I}$;
(4) C_2 = apriori-gen(L_1);
(5) determine-support($C_2, \widehat{C}_2, \widehat{C}_1$);
(6) delete-subjectively-not-interesting(C_2);

Figure 1. The Algorithm, Part I

tee our three goals: classifying an ancestor itemset is equivalent to classifying two ancestor *rules* as interesting/not-interesting. $biF_\Omega(\{a, b\}) = \mathcal{B}$ is easy to classify because it consists simply of $family_\Omega(a \rightarrow b) \cup family_\Omega(b \rightarrow a)$, and if $a, b \in X$ then $X \rightarrow Y, Y \rightarrow X \notin \mathcal{B}$. The other reason the classification is simple is that users only need to classify the 1–3 most frequent 2-itemsets. These itemsets are very likely to describe relationships known even to naive users, making them easy to classify. Since these most frequent 2-itemsets describe relationships that naive users are probably familiar with, a wide audience base is likely to classify them similarly, yielding generality. Finally, since the top three most frequent 2-itemsets are likely to have very large binuclear-families, likely to be classified as not-interesting (known), the limit on the number of ancestor itemsets also yields effectiveness[‡].

3.2   The Mining Process

The domain knowledge available to us is a list of pairs $\langle I, c \rangle$ where I is an ancestor itemset and c is its classification: interesting/not-interesting. For I classified as not-interesting we cannot simply limit the search space of large itemsets by deleting the itemset $\{a, b\}$ (see Equation 1), but we can *alter* the search space. Figure 1 outlines the first part of our algorithm. In line (1) we initialize Υ to be the set of ancestor itemsets classified by the user for deletion. Line (2) is described in Section 3.2.1, lines (3)–(5) in Section 3.2.2, and line (6) in Section 3.2.3. The second part of the algorithm, consisting of iterations for $k \geq 3$ and the rule generation, is performed as in [2]. We use the notations L_k, C_k and $\widehat{C}_k$ defined in [2].

3.2.1   Creating New Attributes

For any itemset $X = \{x_1, \ldots, x_n\}$, let v_X be a new attribute where the value of v_X on any transac-

---

[‡]In [7] prior to each classification, users can rely on the $RSCL$, defined in [7], as an indicator of the potential impact of the next classification they make. In our case, when interestingness is incorporated in one step, during the mining process, this kind of indication is not possible.

tion, τ, will be TRUE if and only if the value of every $x_i \in X$ is TRUE in τ. For each element in $\Upsilon = \{\{a_i, b_i\}\}_i$ where $a_i, b_i \in \Lambda$, we create a new attribute v_Y defined for $Y = \{a_i, b_i\}$ and for $n = 3$ for intersections as in Υ_2 below. We now define $\Lambda_{\mathcal{I}} \stackrel{\text{Def}}{=} \Lambda \cup \mathcal{I}_\Upsilon$, where $\mathcal{I}_\Upsilon = \{v_Y\}_Y$, and $\mathcal{D}_{\mathcal{I}}$ to be the extension of $\mathcal{D}$ spanned by $\Lambda_{\mathcal{I}}$.

We examine the creation of new attributes for two examples: for $\Upsilon_1 = \{\{a, b\}, \{c, d\}\}$, $\mathcal{I}_{\Upsilon_1} = \{v_{\{a,b\}}, v_{\{c,d\}}\}$. For $\Upsilon_2 = \{\{a,b\}, \{a,e\}\}$ three new attributes are created: $\mathcal{I}_{\Upsilon_2} = \{v_{\{a,b\}}, v_{\{a,e\}}, v_{\{a,b,e\}}\}$. The need for the third attribute will become clear in Section 3.2.3.

3.2.2 Starting the Modified Mining Process

In line (3) of Figure 1 we initialize L_1, the set of large 1-itemsets, from $\Lambda_{\mathcal{I}}$, the set of candidate large 1-itemsets. Since the ancestor itemsets in Υ are the most frequent 2-itemsets, almost all mining processes will discover all of $\mathcal{I}_\Upsilon$ as large 1-itemsets. During the same pass on $\mathcal{D}_{\mathcal{I}}$, $\widehat{C}_1$ is constructed. apriori-gen on line (4) and the elimination of the candidate large 2-itemsets that do not have at least the predefined support threshold on line (5) are executed as in [2], but over $\mathcal{D}_{\mathcal{I}}$ and $\Lambda_{\mathcal{I}}$.

3.2.3 Deleting Ancestor Itemsets

For $\Upsilon_1 = \{v_{ab}\}$, where there is only one ancestor itemset to be deleted, $\varrho = \{a, b\}$, we delete the following itemsets: **(1)** $\{a, b\}$, the itemset classified as not interesting, **(2)** $\{a, v_{ab}\}$, since it is equivalent to $\{a, a, b\} = \varrho$, and, **(3)** $\{b, v_{ab}\}$. Note that if ϱ is a large itemset, all three of the above 2-itemsets are large, and will actually be deleted from C_2. This observation holds for all the itemsets below as well.

For $\Upsilon_2 = \{\varrho_1, \varrho_2\}$, where $\varrho_1 = \{a, b\}$, $\varrho_2 = \{c, d\}$, one of two cases will occur:
Case 1: $\{a, b\} \cap \{c, d\} = \emptyset$ then $\Upsilon_2 = \{v_{ab}, v_{cd}\}$, and we delete: **(1)** $\{a, b\}$, **(2)** $\{a, v_{ab}\}$, **(3)** $\{b, v_{ab}\}$, **(4)** $\{c, d\}$, **(5)** $\{c, v_{cd}\}$, and **(6)** $\{d, v_{cd}\}$, using the same reasoning as for Υ_1.
Case 2: $\varrho_1 = \{a, b\}$, $\varrho_2 = \{a, d\}$, ($a \neq b \neq d$, $a = c$), then $\mathcal{I}_\Upsilon = \{v_{ab}, v_{ad}, v_{abd}\}$, and we delete the 14 2-itemsets: **(1–6)** $\{a, b\}$, $\{a, d\}$, $\{a, v_{ab}\}$, $\{b, v_{ab}\}$, $\{a, v_{ad}\}$, $\{d, v_{ad}\}$, **(7–14)** $\{a, v_{abd}\}$, $\{b, v_{abd}\}$, $\{d, v_{abd}\}$, $\{v_{ab}, v_{abd}\}$, $\{v_{ad}, v_{abd}\}$ $\{d, v_{ab}\}$, $\{b, v_{ad}\}$ $\{v_{ab}, v_{ad}\}$, where itemsets (7–14) are equivalent to v_{abd}. Note that deletions (7–14) are not symmetric as $v_{bd} \notin \Upsilon_2$. We examine this case in Υ_3 below.

Case 2 clarifies the need for v_{abd}. Without it, rules such as $a, b, d \rightarrow e$ will not be mined when users classify $\{a, b\}$ and $\{a, d\}$ as not-interesting.

Note that we do not need to eliminate any itemsets in the third iteration, when the 3-itemsets are constructed. Itemsets such as $\{a, x, v_{ab}\}$ that we would want deleted are automatically deleted during the pruning stage of candidate itemsets since at least one of its 2-itemsets, for example, $\{a, v_{ab}\}$, is not a member of C_2 as it has been deleted in one of the 14 deletions above.

Note that for $\Upsilon_3 = \{\{a, b\}, \{a, d\}, \{b, d\}\}$, $\mathcal{I}_\Upsilon = \{v_{ab}, v_{ad}, v_{abd}, v_{bd}\}$, and 21 2-itemset deletions are required: the 14 deletions of Case 2, and, **(15)** $\{b, d\}$, **(16–17)** $\{b, v_{bd}\}$, $\{d, v_{bd}\}$ (equivalent to v_{bd}), and **(18–21)** $\{a, v_{bd}\}$, $\{v_{ab}, v_{bd}\}$, $\{v_{ad}, v_{bd}\}$ and $\{v_{abd}, v_{bd}\}$ which are equivalent to v_{abd}.

4 Experiments With Real Data

We ran our algorithm on the same DBs used in [7] (1) The **Grocery DB** describes 67,470 shopping baskets, using 1,757 attributes, of an online Israeli grocery store (sparsest DB) (2) The **WWW DB** describes the accesses of the 2,336 heaviest users to 15 site categories (densest DB). (3) The **Adult DB** is based on the 45,222 entries with no missing values from the Adult dataset [3], discretized as in [7] into 171 boolean attributes. We mined each DB with zero, one, two and three ancestor itemsets classified for deletion. Not surprisingly, the ancestor itemsets corresponded to the ancestor rules used in [7], allowing us to readily compare the results.

4.1 Reduction in Number of Rules Mined

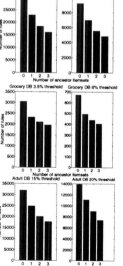

Figure 2 depicts the results of mining the WWW, the Grocery and the Adult DBs with 0–3 ancestor itemsets classified for deletion, and two mining thresholds each. Each histogram depicts the number of rules mined with a specific threshold, and each bar represents the number of rules mined when 0–3 ancestor itemsets were used in the mining.

The reduction in the number of rules mined as result of eliminating the first few ancestor itemsets is more substantial than that of eliminating latter ancestor item-

Figure 2.

sets (an average of more than 23% due to the deletion of the first ancestor itemset, just under 18%

and 12% for the second and third ancestor itemsets). This is parallel to the elimination of larger number of rules by the first few ancestor rules in [7] as compared to the elimination of latter ancestor rules. The explanation to both events is the same, captured by *RSCL* [7], and is the reason we limit the number of ancestor itemsets to a maximum of 3. Overall, the reduction in the number of mined rules due to the deletion of the three ancestor itemsets was approximately 47% for the WWW DB, 36% and 40% for 3.5% and 6% mining thresholds for the Grocery DB, and 45% and 47% for the Adult DB.

4.2 Resource Consumption

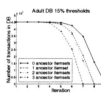

Figure 3.

Mining is normally dominated by the time it takes to calculate the support of the candidate itemsets, and Figure 3 depicts the size of $\widehat{C}_k$ for 0–3 ancestor itemsets deleted for the Adult DB. After the fourth iteration the size of $\widehat{C}_k$ decreases more rapidly when more ancestor itemsets are deleted, requiring less iterations to complete the mining when more ancestor itemsets are used. This behavior was manifested after the *second* iteration in the WWW DB. See Section 5 for conclusions.

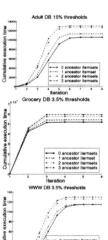

Figure 4.

Cumulative iteration runtimes in seconds on a Compaq ProLiant DL580 (4 700MHz Xeon CPUs) with 1GB RAM, running Solaris 7 and Perl 5.005_03, are depicted in Figure 4. Note the small number of iterations for the sparse Grocery DB, compared to the large number of iterations for the dense WWW DB.

Note that the relatively short mining times for the WWW DB combined with the large number of mined rules from this dense DB resulted in better *overall* runtimes when incorporating the first ancestor itemset into the mining. The modified AprioriTid runtime with 3.5% thresholds was 115 seconds with 0 or 1 ancestor itemsets. The total runtime, including `ap-genrules`, was 140secs when no ancestor itemsets were used, and 130secs when one ancestor itemset was used (with 29910 vs. 22932 rules). When mining with 6% thresholds AprioriTid took 51 seconds with 0 or 1 ancestor itemsets, 65 seconds total for 0 ancestor itemsets and 54 seconds total with 1 ancestor itemset (with 9206 vs. 6972 rules mined).

5 Conclusions and Future Work

To fully address the problem of interestingness, subjective interestingness criteria must be used. In this work we investigated how to incorporate [7] into a simple, general and effective mining process. The reduction in the number of rules outputted by the altered mining process is similar to the post-processing elimination in [7]. The domain knowledge we incorporate can only be used to alter the search space by flattening it, resulting in more itemsets discovered in the first few iterations, making those iterations' execution time longer. The execution time of later iterations is reduced, and the last one or two iterations are often eliminated. However, in general, the execution time of this new mining process, that outputs significantly fewer rules, is longer than that of mining the entire set of association rules. Our conclusion is that there is not always a benefit to incorporating subjective interestingness into the mining process. The output of the new mining process is significantly reduced, almost by a half, making post-processing easier, but post-processing can often achieve similar results with shorter runtime. Future work in this area includes investigating and formalizing types of domain knowledge that can be used to decrease the size of the search space.

References

[1] G. Adomavicius and A. Tuzhilin. Discovery of actionable patterns in databases: The action hierarchy approach. In *SIGKDD*, pages 111–114, 1997.

[2] R. Agrawal, M. Heikki, R. Srikant, H. Toivonen, and A. I. Verkamo. *Advances in Knowledge Discovery and Data Mining*, chapter 12, pages 307–328. 1996.

[3] C. Blake and C. Merz. UCI repository of machine learning databases, 1998, http://www.ics.uci.edu/~mlearn/mlrepository.html.

[4] U. M. Fayyad, G. Piatetsky-Shapiro, and P. Smyth. *Advances in Knowledge Discovery and Data Mining*, chapter 1, pages 1–34. 1996.

[5] R. Ng, L. Lakshmanan, J. Han, and A. Pang. Exploratory mining and pruning optimizations of constrained association rules. In *SIGMOD*, pages 13–24, 1998.

[6] B. Padmanabhan and A. Tuzhilin. Small is beautiful: Discovering the minimal set of unexpected patterns. In *SIGKDD*, pages 54–63, 2000.

[7] S. Sahar. Interestingness via what is not interesting. In *SIGKDD*, pages 332–336, 1999.

[8] S. Sahar. Interestingness preprocessing. In *ICDM*, pages 489–496, 2001.

[9] R. Srikant, Q. Vu, and R. Agrawal. Mining association rules with item constraints. *SIGKDD*, pages 67–73, 1997.

Exploring the Parameter State Space of Stacking

Alexander K. Seewald
Austrian Research Institute for Artificial Intelligence,
Schottengasse 3, A-1010 Wien, Austria
alexsee@oefai.at

Abstract

Ensemble learning schemes are a new field in data mining. While current research concentrates mainly on improving the performance of single learning algorithms, an alternative is to combine learners with different biases. Stacking is the best-known such scheme which tries to combine learners' predictions or confidences via another learning algorithm. However, the adoption of Stacking into the data mining community is hampered by its large parameter space, consisting mainly of other learning algorithms: (1) the set of learning algorithms to combine, (2) the meta-learner responsible for the combining and (3) the type of meta-data to use: confidences or predictions. None of these parameters are obvious choices. Furthermore, little is known about the relation between parameter settings and performance of Stacking. By exploring all of Stacking's parameter settings and their interdependencies, we intend make Stacking a suitable choice for mainstream data mining applications.

1 Introduction

When faced with the decision "Which algorithm will be most accurate on my classification problem?", the predominant approach is to estimate the accuracy of the candidate algorithms on the problem and select the one that appears to be most accurate. [7] has investigated this approach in a small study with three learning algorithms on five UCI datasets. His conclusions are that on the one hand this procedure is on average better than working with a single learning algorithm, but, on the other hand, the cross-validation procedure often picks the wrong base algorithm on individual problems. This problem is expected to become more severe with an increasing number of classifiers.

As a cross-validation basically computes a prediction for each example in the training set, it was soon realized that this information could be used in more elaborate ways than simply counting the number of correct and incorrect predictions. One such ensemble learning method or meta-classification scheme is the family of *stacking* algorithms [11]. The basic idea of Stacking is to use the predictions of the original classifiers as attributes in a new training set that keeps the original class labels. Stacking thus utilizes a *meta* classifier to combine the predictions from several *base* classifiers. Potentially, any classifier can be used as base and/or meta classifier. We shall refer to the type of meta-data consisting of base classifiers predictions as *preds*.

A straightforward extension of this approach is using class probability distributions of the original classifiers[1] which convey not only prediction information, but also confidence for all classes. We shall call the meta-data of this extension *class-probs*. This approach was evaluated and found to be superior to Stacking with predictions in [10], provided *multi-response linear regression* (MLR) is used as meta classifier.

While approaches such as boosting and bagging, which combine classifiers of the same type, have been used extensively in data mining, Stacking has not. In terms of performance on our datasets based on significant differences , the most recent scheme StackingCwins five times and loses only once against AdaBoostM1 with C4.5 as base classifier; wins six times and never loses against Bagging implementation with C4.5-clone as base-classifier; wins three times against selection by crossvalidation (X-Val) and never loses; and wins five times against majority vote while losing just once. So StackingCseems to perform slightly better than its competitors, even though much less research has been focused on improving Stacking! Why then has Stacking not been adopted more widely? Tentatively we can suggest some reasons: For one, Stacking requires an integrated workbench including common machine learning classifiers. As of the time of writing this paper, two of the largest commercially available data mining tools lack a basic machine learning classifier, NaiveBayes. Also, Stacking requires a lot of parameters: which base-classifiers to choose, which meta-classifier to choose and also the type of meta-data – either predictions *preds* or complete probablility distributions *class-probs*. We felt it was time to investigate parameter setting for Stacking systematically to see how various parameters contribute to Stacking's performance, in order to see where sensible areas for further improvement may lie, but also to give useful proposals for *all* parameter settings. We investigated both the original Stacking introduced in [11] and the extension by [10] here. In some cases we also relate their performance to that of the most recent scheme, StackingC.

2 Experimental Setup

For our empirical evaluation we chose twenty-six datasets from the UCI Machine Learning Repository [1]. These datasets include fourteen multi-class and twelve two-class problems, more details see [9]. Accuracy estimates are from a single ten-fold stratified cross-validation. Significant differences were evaluated by a χ^2-test after McNemar[2] with significance level of 95%, unless otherwise noted.

---

[1] Every prediction is replaced by a vector of probabilities, one for each class.
[2] [3] proposes this test when the investigated algorithm is run only once.

As base classifiers for Stacking we considered the following seven base learners, which were chosen to cover a variety of different biases. For figures, classifier numbers are used instead of their proper names.

1. J48: a Java port of C4.5 Release 8 [6]
2. KStar: the K* instance-based learner [2]
3. MLR: a multi-class learner which tries to separate each class from all other classes by linear regression (*multi-response linear regression*)
4. NaiveBayes: the Naive Bayes classifier using multiple kernel density estimation.
5. DecisionTable: a decision table learner.
6. IB1: the IBk instance-based learner with $K = 1$ nearest neighbors, to offset KStar with a maximally local learner.
7. KernelDensity: a simple kernel density classifier.

All algorithms are implemented in WEKA Release 3.1.8. Each of them returns a class probability distribution, i.e. they do not predict a single class, but give probability estimates for each possible class. Parameters for learning schemes which have not been mentioned were left at their default values.

These algorithms can be clustered into four natural groups by their internal structure, where the first member tends to give better results than the others.

- J48, DecisionTable
- NaiveBayes
- MLR
- KStar, IB1, KernelDensity

Surprisingly – as we found out during our experiments – this can also be supported empirically. In particular, the statistical correlation of accuracies within each group is always greater than 0.95 while it is much smaller between classifiers oferent groups. Thus, the structure of correlations allows us to determine these groups empirically.[3] So we considered not only the trivial set of all seven base classifiers, but also the set of four base classifiers J48, NaiveBayes, MLR and KStar by choosing from each correlated subgroup the classifier which performed best by geometric mean of accuracy ratio.

We define a variant as a specific Stacking algorithm of which all parameters – type of meta-data, meta-classifier, and the set of base classifiers – are known. Meta-data *class-probs* is signified by the prefix *St*, *preds* is signified by the prefix *StP*. After this prefix, *7B* refers to the full set of base classifiers while *4B* refers to the set of four diverse base classifiers mentioned in Section 2. After this, a hyphen precedes the meta-classifier's name or an abbreviation. E.g. *St7B-MLR* refers to Stacking with the full set of seven base classifiers, MLR as meta-classifier and *class-probs* as type of meta-data while *StP7B-MLR* refers to the same variant with *preds* as meta-data. In Section 4, we will define stacking groups as those variants which just differ in the meta-classifier. These are named without reference to the meta-classifier.

3 Base Classifier Choice

In this section we investigate Stacking variants with MLR as meta classifier[4] and any non-empty subset of our seven base

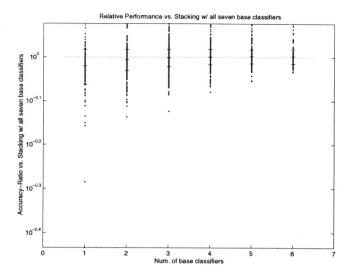

Figure 1. This figure shows the improvement of Stacking **variants with different numbers of base classifiers and** MLR **as meta classifier, where all possible subsets of base classifiers were considered, as** $\frac{Acc_{StVariant}}{Acc_{St7B-MLR}}$**. The dotted line indicates a ratio of 1.0. Each • shows the ratio from one dataset and variant. Average and standard deviation over all subsets with the same number of base classifiers are shown as error bars.**

classifiers as base classifiers. Because of the large number of comparisons, we used a significance level of 99% here to reduce our alpha-error. If we consider using all seven base classifiers (*St7B-MLR*) as gold standard, about one tenth of our variants are significantly better than *St7B-MLR* on any dataset; the rest shows no significant differences or are frequently even significantly worse. Figure 1 shows all our variants as accuracy ratios vs. *St7B-MLR*. One variant corresponds to a specific instantiation of Stacking with a non-empty subset from our seven base classifiers, always with MLR as meta-classifier, on *class-probs* meta-data. We have grouped the variants according to the size of the subset of base classifiers, from one to six.

Although at least some variants seem to offer considerable improvements on accuracy, this by no means assures a significant difference. We have considered two approaches to take significance into account.

At first we determined those variants which, over all datasets, never lose significantly against *St7B-MLR* and win as often as possible. It turns out that the maximum number of wins is only three, i.e. 11.5% of our datasets, which is somewhat disappointing. If we compare against *St4B-MLR*[5] instead, the maximum number of wins falls to zero. Concluding, dataset-independent variant resp. base classifier choice is not able to improve upon *St4B-MLR* here, even by hindsight.

If we were to consider a dataset-dependent choice of variants resp. base classifiers, i.e. possibly choosing a different variant for each dataset, the results are still quite disappointing.

---

[3]A preliminary analysis of the κ-statistic – a measure of diversity due to [4] – is also compatible with this finding.

[4]in the extension proposed by [10].

[5]Stacking with the set of our four diverse base classifiers.

While the maximum number of wins is 7 (26.9%) vs. *St7B-MLR*, it is only 2 (7.7%) vs. *St4B-MLR*.[6] Thus, even if we would resort to meta-learning and found a model which lets us choose variants as good as by hindsight – which is doubtful to say the least – the improvements would still be quite insignificant.

So, in the remainder of this paper, we just consider two sets of base classifiers: the trivial choice of using all seven (those used by *St7B-MLR*), but also the subset of four diverse ones (those used by *St4B-MLR*) we mentioned in the last section. This is motivated by the wish to investigate both meta classifier choice and base classifier choice, even if quite coarse-grained, in one setup.

4 Meta Classifier Choice

In this section, we investigate Stacking variants along three independent dimensions – which are indeed *all* possible dimensions for Stacking's parameters.

1. Different Meta-Classifiers, chosen from our set of four diverse classifiers from Section 2 (numbers 1-4).
2. Type of meta-data: either predictions = *preds* or complete class probability distributions = *class-probs*.
3. Base Classifiers: the set of four resp. seven base classifiers from Section 2, as maximally coarse-grained base classifier choice.

What concerns us most of all are the first two dimensions, i.e. to determine which meta-classifier is best, depending on type of meta-data; and whether or not one type of meta-data can be considered unconditionally superior. However, the third dimension can still roughly tell us the susceptibility of each meta-classifier to changes in its set of base classifiers and thus ... us the opportunity to also investigate coarse-grained base-... ifier choice at little additional cost.

... second and third dimension gives the name to our Stack-... up – i.e. *St4B*, *St7B* for *class-probs* meta-data[7] and ... *StP7B* for *preds* meta-data. The meta-classifier is usu-... n as an additional dimension in tables or figures, so ... ters are hereby accounted for.

... mine which meta-classifier is best, we resorted to ... anking of all meta-classifiers, separately for each ... p. Table 1 shows *wins* minus *losses* of each meta-... s all other meta-classifiers, for each group sepa-

... at the table reveals some insights: For *class-* ... MLR is clearly the best meta-classifier, which ... [10]. However, for *preds* meta-data *StP7B* ... – the latter considers NaiveBayes supe-... prefers MLR; with NaiveBayes and KStar ... second place. The wins and losses are ... and *St4B* which indicates that meta-... to make less difference for predictions ... xpected since most classifiers are best ... data, thus their performance as meta-... ince there is an upper limit on accu-... lar than for continuous data.

... is even just 1 (3.9%) for StackingC with

... case

Table 1. This table shows the significant wins minus losses for each variant, against the other three meta-classifiers.

Variant	J48	KStar	MLR	NB
St7B	2	-26	16	8
St4B	-2	-19	19	2
StP7B	-1	0	1	0
StP4B	2	-9	1	6

If we had to choose any one classifier for prediction meta-data, NaiveBayes seems the logical choice – it is not inconceivable that NaiveBayes ended up on second place because the ranking may be a little noisy; after all the difference is only one. A priori, the Bayesian approach inherent in Naive-Bayes seems a suitable way to combine confidences from the base classifiers, but in practice this seems to work well only for *preds* meta-data. It may be that the modelling of continuous attributes by multiple kernels is not appropriate for this task and that a simple normal distribution may be more useful. This would explain why in our case, NaiveBayes performs clearly better with *preds* – as does J48 – and not equally well on *class-probs* and *preds*, as [10] found. Interestingly, both KStar and IB1 do not perform better on *class-probs* meta-data – rather, they are those meta-classifiers with the highest number of significant losses on *class-probs* vs. *preds*. This also contradicts [10], who concluded that IB1 performs better on *class-probs*. Further work is needed to resolve these contradictory results.

Now we will investigate whether one type of meta-data can be considered superior. For this, we determined a ranking, see Table 2: While MLR performs better on *class-probs* meta-data, all other considered meta-classifiers perform better on *preds*, i.e. nominal, meta-data. The latter is to be expected since most machine learning algorithms are best suited to process nominal data.

This seems to contradict [10] who concluded that no meta-classifier on prediction meta-data offered satisfactory performance. However, their definition of MLR is different: each linear model had as input data only those partial class probability distributions concerned with the class it was trying to predict. So the dimensionality of the input data was smaller for MLR by a factor equal to the number of classes, which makes the mentioned comparison somewhat biased. If we try to replicate their results and replace MLR with their modified version, it is easily the best meta-classifier with a large margin – which explains their early dismissal of Stacking with *preds* meta-data. Concluding, Stacking with probability distributions (*class-probs*) is competitive to classic Stacking with predictions (*preds*). However, some Stacking variants based on *class-probs* perform significantly better than both, as shown in [8]. That is not to say that Stacking with predictions cannot be improved in the future – it remains an interesting research topic and should not yet be dismissed.

Now we were interested in the difference between using four base and all our seven base classifiers. In the former case, we see that *St4B* is usually better and in four cases even significantly better when using MLR as meta classifier. In the latter

Table 2. This table shows the improvements of *preds* vs. *class-probs* for various meta-learners in terms of significant wins and losses.

Comparison	J48	KStar	MLR	NB
St7B vs. *StP7B*	1/5	1/14	4/3	1/4
St4B vs. *StP4B*	1/4	1/11	2/0	1/4
St4B vs. *St7B*	2/2	3/2	4/0	1/2
StP4B vs. *StP7B*	2/0	1/3	2/1	3/4

case we see the same picture, but even less difference.[8] So we tentatively conclude that on average Stacking does seem to work better with a smaller set of less similar base classifiers, especially when using continuous meta-level data.

5   Conclusion

We have explored the parameter state space of Stacking. Concerning the choice of base classifiers, we have found a set of four base classifiers, chosen by a priori and a posteriori arguments, which performs best. However, using all available base classifiers also remains an acceptable option, although the performance may be worse[9] since the dimensionality of the meta-dataset is increased. When using predictions meta-data, the performance difference tends to be smaller, probably because most machine learning algorithms are better suited to deal with nominal data and therefore seem to exhibit less vulnerability to curse-of-dimensionality.

Concerning the choice of meta classifier and choice of metadata to be used, we have found that MLR is indeed the best meta-classifier for probability distribution data. We showed probability distribution meta-data and predictions meta-data to perform comparably. For predictions meta-data, the best meta-classifier has less advantage because of less performance variation among the meta-classifiers. NaiveBayes is a reasonable choice since it is once on first and once on a very close second place.

However, given that both StackingC [8] and sMM5 [5] outperform Stacking with *class-probs* meta-data and MLR as meta classifier, these two schemes can be considered the state-of-the-art in Stacking. Base-classifier choice is still applicable to both, so we propose using our set of four diverse base classifiers in both cases.

We believe that repeating our extensive base-classifier experiments with StackingC will not yield new insights. Because StackingC can be viewed as meta-classifier for probability distribution meta-data, we can see it as alternative meta-classifier. As such, we have investigated the distribution of accuracy ratios *St4B* by *St7B* and found it to be quite symmetric around 1.0, with the smallest standard deviation of all our meta-classifiers. Thus, StackingC seems to be least influenced by specific set of base classifiers, which leads us to expect that base cla

---

[8]We noted that for StackingC, the difference is even 1.0012±0.0117 for the accuracy ratio of 4B vs. 7B – making it the least susceptible to our coarse base classifier choice.

[9]In our case, a penalty of at most four significant losses on twenty-s datasets is observed. Dependent on the type of meta-data and meta-classifier which is used, this may be much less – e.g. for StackingC, it is only one loss.

fier choice has even less influence on StackingC than it has on Stacking. It still remains to be investigated whether this is also true for sMM5.

From preliminary experiments in [8], StackingC and sMM5 should perform comparably, so performance-wise there is no reason to prefer the one or the other. However, because of the simpler meta classifier and lower-dimensional meta-dataset we would expect StackingC to be faster by at most an order of magnitude.

We hope that future research in Stacking will stay as exciting and interesting as it has been in the past and that these new variants, among with our proposals as to their parameters, will bring the best-known meta-classification scheme Stacking nearer to main-stream data mining.

Acknowledgements

This research is supported by the Austrian *Fonds zur Förderung der Wissenschaftlichen Forschung (FWF)* under grant no. P12645-INF. The Austrian Research Institute for Artificial Intelligence is supported by the Austrian Federal Ministry of Education, Science and Culture. We would like to thank Elias Pampalk and an anonymous reviewer of the Machine Learning Journal for valuable comments.

References

[1] Blake, C. L., Merz, C. J: UCI repository of machine learning databases. http://www.ics.uci edu/~mlearn/MLRepository.html (1998). D partment of Information and Computer Science, Unive of California at Irvine, Irvine CA.

[2] Cleary, J. G., Trigg, L. E: K*: An instance-bas using an entropic distance measure. In Priedit sell, S., Proceedings of the 12th Internatior on Machine Learning (1995) 108–114, La'

[3] Dietterich, T.G.: Approximate Statisti paring Supervised Classification Neural Computation, 10 (7) 1895-

[4] Dietterich, T. G: Ensemble me In Kittler, J., Roli, F., First In tiple Classifier Systems (2

[5] Dzeroski S., Zenko B. than Selecting the Be ternational Confere Morgan Kaufma

[6] Quinlan, J. R gan Kaufm

[7] Schaffer valida

[8] See

Mining Associated Implication Networks: Computational Intermarket Analysis

Phil Tse and Jiming Liu

Department of Computer Science, Hong Kong Baptist University

philtse@alum.hkbu.edu.hk   jiming@comp.hkbu.edu.hk

Abstract

*Current attempts to analyze international financial markets include the use of financial technical analysis and data mining techniques. In this paper, we propose a new approach that incorporates implication networks and association rules to form an **associated network structure**. The proposed approach explicitly addresses the issue of local vs. global influences between financial markets.*

1. Introduction

Conventional wisdom has it that financial markets around the globe are interrelated. To cite an example, commodity prices and the U.S. dollar move in an opposite direction. This kind of intermarket actions can be further divided into two perspectives. In a local perspective, various markets in a certain country, such as stock, currency and bond markets, interact with each other. While in a global perspective, the same kind of markets (e.g. U.S. stock markets and other stock markets in the world) tends to be highly correlated. Current attempts to analyze international financial markets include the use of financial technical analysis and data mining. These efforts, however, do not make a clear distinction between the local and global perspectives of intermarket actions. In this light, we propose a new paradigm to analyze these intermarket actions by mining probabilistic networks and association rules. The discovered networks and rules form an **associated network structure** in which the distinction of local and global perspectives becomes possible.

1.1. Related Work

In our approach, we employ probabilistic networks to formulate interactions in a global perspective. Some traditional examples of inferring schemes over probabilistic networks are presented in Charniak's [3] work.

A number of algorithms were proposed to derive probabilistic networks. More modern works in this field include Liu and Desmarais [5], which proposed a method of learning implication networks from empirical data. Myers et al. [7] proposed a method of learning Bayesian networks from incomplete data using evolutionary algorithms.

2. Associated Network Structure and its Discovery

Liu and Desmarais [5] proposed a method for learning implication networks from a small number of empirical data samples. This approach emphasizes on inference accuracy rather than the actual topology corresponding to a knowledge structure.

Association rules are used for the proposed approach to connect the networks. As pointed out by Bowes et al. [2], causal inference algorithms extract relationships that are always stronger than association rules, because their elicitations are based on rigid statistical testing. The tests, however, are sometimes too rigid that some subtle but novel rules would be rejected during the testing process. Association rules, on the other hand, often represent more novel (e.g. support can be as low as 0.1, depending on the nature of the domain) but useful relationships. We, therefore, use a combination of these two techniques to form an associated network structure.

In summary, the components of an associated network structure are illustrated in Figure 1.

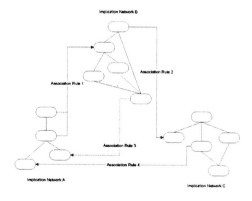

Figure 1. An associated network. The implication networks are connected by association rules.

2.1. Discovery of an Associated Network Structure

As pointed out by Liu and Desmarais [5], six types of implication relationship exist between any pair of nodes, i.e. A ⇒ B, A ⇒ ~B, ~A ⇒ B, ~A ⇒ ~B, A ⇔ B and A ⇔ ~B. The elicitations of these implication relationships are based on statistical examinations, which are referred to as hypothesis tests on empirical data [4].

The hypothesis testing works as follows: For any implication relation A ⇒ B, the following two conditions must be satisfied:

$$P(B \mid A) = 1 \qquad (1)$$
$$P(\sim A \mid \sim B) = 1 \qquad (2)$$

The hypothesis testing examines Conditions (1) and (2) by computing the lower bound of a $(1-\alpha_c)$ confidence interval around the measured conditional probabilities. This would allow the elicitation of implication relationship become possible under sampling errors.

The implication induction algorithm of Liu and Desmarais [5] is stated as follows:

Liu's and Desmarais' Implication Induction Algorithm
Begin
    Set a significance level α_c and a minimum conditional probability p_{min} for a network.
    For $node_i$, $i \in [0, n_{max}-1]$ and $node_j$, $j \in [i+1, n_{max}]$
    Begin
        For all empirical case samples
        Compute a contingency table

$$T_{ij} = \begin{array}{|c|c|} \hline N_{11} & N_{12} \\ \hline N_{21} & N_{22} \\ \hline \end{array}$$

        Where N_{11}, N_{12}, N_{21}, N_{22} are the numbers of occurrences with respect to the following combinations:
        N_{11}: $node_i = $ TRUE $\wedge$ $node_j = $ TRUE
        N_{12}: $node_i = $ TRUE $\wedge$ $node_j = $ FALSE
        N_{21}: $node_i = $ FALSE $\wedge$ $node_j = $ TRUE
        N_{22}: $node_i = $ FALSE $\wedge$ $node_j = $ FALSE
        For each implication type k out of the six possible cases
        Begin
        Test the following inequality:

$$P(x \leq N_{error\_cell}) < \alpha_c$$

        based on the lower tails of binomial distributions $Bin(N, p_{min})$ and $Bin(\overline{N}, p_{min})$, where N and $\overline{N}$ denote the occurrences of antecedent satisfactions in the two inferences using a type k implication relation, i.e., in *modus ponens* and *modus tollens*, respectively.
        If the test succeeds, then
          Return a type k implication relation.
        End
    End
End

Associated with each established relationship are weights representing the certainty of the relation. In order to facilitate the later inferences, the weights are estimated during the network structure discovery phase. Theoretically, two weights are associated with each type of implication relationship, as an inference can be made either in forward or backward direction. The weights are estimated from the empirical data samples. Specifically, the estimated conditional probability of the relation is used as the weight.

In our proposed approach, the Apriori algorithm [1][8] is used to mine the association rules. The nodes in each implication network are regarded as the items for the algorithm to generate itemsets which are required by the rules. After the itemsets are generated, rules with minimum confidence p_c and support s are discovered.

Note that in our proposed approach, it is only desirable to have association rules which connect different implication networks but do not connect the nodes in the same network. After the induction of implication networks and the mining of association rules, an associated network structure is ready for uncertainty reasoning purposes, such as analyzing intermarket actions.

3. Empirical Validation on Financial Market Analysis

In order to validate our proposed approach, we analyze several markets with an associated network structure discovered from empirical market data.

Murphy [6] points out the existing key relationships between the financial markets around the globe. Among others, there are four principal interrelated market sectors, namely currencies, commodities, bonds and stocks. Besides, interest rates also play a significant role in affecting the markets.

We are interested in finding out the relationships between the aforementioned markets. If the markets are correlated, some empirical data samples of these markets can be used to discover a proposed network structure which reflects their relationships. The empirically derived network structure can further be used to analyze the trends of the involved markets.

3.1. Settings for the Validation Experiments

The actual settings in our validation experiments are as follows:
1.   **Financial Market Selection.** With reference to the key intermarket relationships defined by Murphy [6], markets from the four principal market sectors from the United States and Japan are selected. Selected indexes for the markets are as follows:

U.S. Market
    a)   USD Index;
    b)   CRB Index;
    c)   Federal Reserve Fund Rate;
    d)   10-Year Treasury Bond Yield;
    e)   Dow Jones Industrial Moving Average;
Japanese Market
    f)   Japanese Discount Rate;

g) Nikkei 225 Stock Average;
h) Japanese Yen Real Effective Exchange Rate;
i) 10-Year Benchmark Bond Yield;
j) Composite Index of Business Indicators.

2. **Preparation of Empirical Data Samples.** Since the case study aims at investigating the long-term relationships of the selected financial markets, monthly data is chosen for the experiments. The data collected is within the period of December 1982 to December 2001 inclusively. The data gathered, however, is only in a form of numerical values. In the current study, we are interested in the relationships between the markets, e.g., if the greenback goes down, the commodities go up. Therefore, it is necessary to define what is 'up' and what is 'down' before any actual experiments can be carried out. Therefore, data has to be preprocessed to show the up and down trends of the markets.

The empirical data samples are further divided into a training set for the discovery of an associated network structure and a testing set for analysis and validation. In the case study, the training set includes empirical data samples from November 1983 to November 1992 inclusively. The testing set includes those from December 1992 to December 2001 inclusively.

3. **Discovery of an Associated Network Structure.** As pointed out by Murphy [6], the local financial markets influence each other more than the international markets do. In this connection, two implication networks will be generated: one for the U.S. market and one for the Japanese market. The implication relationships within implication networks show the stronger influences between the markets in a local perspective, while the association rules linking up the two implication networks show the weaker relations between the international markets. The significance level α_c and a minimum conditional probability p_{min} for the implication networks are 0.2 and 0.5 respectively. The minimum confidence p_c and minimum support s for the association rule mining are 0.6 and 0.1, respectively.

3.2. Experimental Results

This section presents the discovered network structure, and the analysis and validation results using the mined associated network structure.

3.2.1. The Discovered Network Structure

With the empirical data samples from the training set, the following implication networks representing the U.S. and Japanese financial markets can be discovered (Figure 2 and 3).

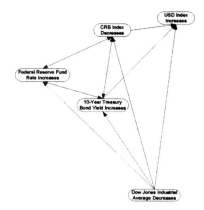

Figure 2. An implication network for the U.S. financial markets (p_{min}= 0.5, α_c= 0.2).

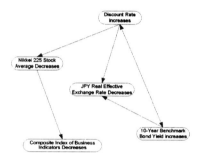

Figure 3. An implication network for the Japanese financial markets (p_{min}= 0.5, α_c= 0.2).

3.2.2. Association Rules Connecting the Networks

After the induction of the two implication networks, the selected financial markets are used to generate itemsets for mining association rules. The following association rules can be mined with the empirical data samples from the training set with the mining algorithm as stated in Section 2.

Rule 1: {Japanese Benchmark Bond Yield Increases/Decreases} → {U.S. 10-Year Treasury Bond Yield Increases/Decreases}
Rule 2: {Japanese Benchmark Bond Yield Increases/Decreases} → {U.S. CRB Index Increases/Decrease}
Rule 3: {Japanese Composit Index of Business Indicators Decreases/Increases} → {USD Index Decreases/Increases}
Rule 4: {Nikkei 225 Stock Average Decreases/Increases} → {USD Index Decreases/Increases}
Rule 5: {Nikkei 225 Stock Average Decreases/Increases, Composit Index of Business Indicators Decreases/Increases} → {USD Index Decreases/Increases}
Rule 6: {USD Index Decreases/Increases, Dow Jones Industrial Average Decreases/Increases} → {Japanese Benchmark Bond Yield Increases/Increases}
Rule 7: {USD Index Decreases/Increases, U.S. 10-Year Treasury Bond Yield Increases/Decreases, Dow Jones Industrial Average Decreases/Increases} → {Japanese Bond Yield Increases/Decreases}

The above association rules, along with the two implication networks, constitute an associated network structure as defined in Section 2.

3.2.3. Experiment to Evaluate the Overall Analysis Performance

In this experiment, two nodes from the U.S. markets are randomly picked from each monthly empirical data sample as observed evidence. When the observed value is TRUE, a belief value of 1 is given to the node; if the observed value is FALSE, a belief value of 0 is given. The beliefs of the other nodes in the two implication networks are revised accordingly with the implication relationships and association rules. When the updated belief value of a node is larger than 0.5, a TRUE value is assigned to the node, or vice versa. The estimated values of the updated nodes are further compared to the actual values in the same empirical data samples in the same month. Meanwhile, we record the total number of correct and incorrect guesses within the implication network corresponding to the U.S. financial markets, as well as the total number of correct and incorrect guesses using the association rules and the implication network corresponding to the Japanese financial markets. The above process is repeated five times, that is, five cycles. For each cycle, all the 109 monthly empirical data samples in the testing set are used.

The mean of the analysis accuracies using the U.S. market implication network is 58.4671%, with a standard deviation of 1.8453%. For the other nodes in the Japanese market implication network, the mean of the analysis accuracies is 66.6799%, with a standard deviation of 5.4041%. In general, the accuracies of analysis using the entire discovered network structure remain stable, with the mean accuracy 61.2508%, and a small standard deviation of 1.604%.

3.2.4. Experiment to Investigate the Effect of the Number of Observed Nodes on Analysis Performance

In this experiment, the number of nodes observed as evidences is controlled. The experimental procedure is similar to that in the preceding experiments, except the number of observed nodes which will be different. The means of the analysis accuracy with the U.S. markets implication network are 59.91%, 58.47% and 55.74% when 1, 2 and 3 node(s) is/are observed respectively. Surprisingly, the mean accuracy decreases slightly as the number of nodes observed increases.

4. Conclusion

This paper has presented a novel approach to analyzing financial intermarket actions with a combination of implication networks and association rules. The experiments show that the proposed analysis approach is able to model international financial markets with an automatic means of discovering an associated network structure.

The experiments further demonstrate the analysis ability of our proposed associated network structure. It is believed that the innate weakly correlated nature of the financial markets is accountable for the low accuracy. The stability of the proposed approach, however, is remarkably high (standard deviation of 1.604%).

One surprising result is that the analysis accuracy decreased as the number of observed nodes increased. The reason, subject to further examination, is that multiple-path traversal is allowed in the multiply connected implication networks in our study. An interesting extension of the present work, therefore, would be to investigate the optimal traversing method for implication networks.

References

[1] Agrawal, R., and Shafer, J. C. Fast Algorithm for Mining Association Rules, In *Proceedings of the 20th International Conference on Very Large Databases*, Santiago, Chile, 1994.

[2] Bowes, J., Neufeld, E., Greer, J. E., and Cooke, J. A Comparison of Association Rule Discovery and Bayesian Network Causal Inference Algorithms to Discover Relationships in Discrete Data. In *Canadian Conference on AI*, pages 326-336, 2000.

[3] Charniak, E. Bayesian Networks without Tears. *AI Magazine,* pages 53-61, 1991.

[4] Desmarais, M. C., Maluf, A., and Liu, J. User-expertise Modeling with Empirically Derived Probabilistic Implication Networks. *User Modeling and User Adaptive Interactions*, 5(3-4), pages 283-315, 1996.

[5] Liu, J., and Desmarais, M. C. A Method of Learning Implication Networks from Empirical Data: Algorithm and Monte-Carlo Simulation-Based Validation. *IEEE Transactions on Knowledge and Data Engineering*, 9(6), pages 990-1004, 1997.

[6] Murphy, J. J. *Intermarket Technical Analysis:Trading Strategies for the Global Stock, Bond, Commodity, and Currency Markets*. United States, J. Wiley, 1991.

[7] Myers, J. W., Laskey, K. B., and DeJong, K. A. Learning Bayesian Networks from Incomplete Data using Evolutionary Algorithms. In *Proceedings of the Genetic and Evolutionary Computation Conference*. Orlando, FL, Morgan Kaufmann, 1999.

[8] Srikant, R. Fast Algorithms for Mining Association Rules and Sequential Patterns, *Ph. D. Thesis*, University of Wisconsin-Madison, 1996.

Maintenance of Sequential Patterns for Record Modification Using Pre-large Sequences

Ching-Yao Wang[1], Tzung-Pei Hong[2] and Shian-Shyong Tseng[1]
[1]National Chiao-Tung University, Taiwan
[2]National University of Kaohsiung, Taiwan
tphong@nuk.edu.tw, {cywang, sstseng}@cis.nctu.edu.tw

Abstract

In the past, we proposed incremental mining algorithms for maintenance of sequential patterns based on the concept of pre-large sequences as records were inserted or deleted. Although maintenance of sequential patterns for record modification can be performed by usage of the deletion procedure and then the insertion procedure, twice computation time of a single procedure is needed. In this paper, we thus attempt to apply the concept of pre-large sequences to maintain sequential patterns as records are modified. The proposed algorithm does not require rescanning original databases until the accumulative amount of modified customer sequences exceeds a safety bound derived by pre-large concept. As databases grow larger, the numbers of modified customer sequences allowed before database rescanning is required also grow.

1. Introduction

Mining useful information and helpful knowledge from these large databases has thus evolved into an important research area [1][3]. Among them, finding sequential patterns in temporal transaction databases is important since it allows modeling of customer behavior [2][8][10].

Mining sequential patterns was first proposed by Agrawal and Srikant in 1995 [2], and is a non-trivial task. Although customer behavior models can be efficiently extracted by Agrawal and Srikant's mining algorithm, the sequential patterns discovered may become invalid or inappropriate when databases are updated. Conventional approaches may re-mine entire databases to get correct sequential patterns for maintenance. However, when a database is massive in size, this will require considerable computation time. Developing efficient approaches to maintain sequential patterns is thus very important to real-world applications.

In the past, some approaches were proposed to improve maintenance performance by previously mined information [4-9][11][12]. The common idea is that previously mined information should be utilized as much as possible to reduce maintenance costs. We proposed efficient incremental mining algorithms capable of updating sequential patterns based on the concept of pre-large sequences when new records were inserted or deleted [7][12].

In addition to record insertion and deletion, record modification is also commonly seen in real-world applications. Although maintenance of sequential patterns for record modification can be performed by usage of the deletion procedure and then the insertion procedure, twice computation time of a single procedure is needed. Developing efficient maintenance algorithms to update sequential patterns for record modification is thus necessary. In this paper, we attempt to apply the concept of pre-large sequences to solve this issue. The proposed algorithm doesn't need to rescan the original database until a number of original customer sequences have been modified. If the database is large, then the number of modified customer sequences allowed will be large too. This characteristic is especially useful for real-world applications.

2. The concept of pre-large sequences to maintenance for record modification

A pre-large sequence is not truly large, but promises to be large in the future. A lower support threshold and an upper support threshold are used to realize this concept. The upper support threshold is the same as the minimum support used in conventional mining algorithms. On the other hand, the lower support threshold defines the lowest support ratio for a sequence to be treated as pre-large. A sequence with a support ratio below the lower threshold is thought of as a small sequence. Pre-large sequences act like buffers and are used to reduce the movement of sequences directly from large to small and vice-versa in the maintenance process. Therefore, when few records are modified (i.e. few customer sequences are modified), the originally small sequences will at most become pre-large and cannot become large, thus reducing the amount of rescanning necessary. A safety bound for modified customer sequences is derived from the upper and lower thresholds and from the size of the database.

The modified records are first merged with the other records from the same customers to form the modified customer sequences. For example, the two original customer sequences shown in Table 1 will be transformed into the modified customer sequences shown in Table 2, when partial records of *Cust_id*=2 and *Cust_id*=3 are modified.

Table 1. The two original customer sequences

Cust_id	Customer sequence
2	<(C, D)(A)(E, F, G)>
3	<(A, H, G)>

Table 2. The two modified customer sequences

Cust_id	Customer sequence
2	<(D)(A)(E, F, G)>
3	<(A, E, G)>

The subsequences from the modified customer sequences and from the corresponding old customer sequences are then compared to obtain the subsequence differences resulting from record modification. Let modified candidate sequences for record modification be defined as the sequences mentioned above, with their count differences not being zero. For the above example, the candidate 1-sequences are shown in Table 3.

Table 3. The candidate 1-sequences with their counts

Candidate 1-sequences	
Candidate 1-sequence	Count difference
<(C)>	-1
<(E)>	1
<(H)>	-1
<(C, D)>	-1
<(E, G)>	1
<(A, E)>	1
<(A, H)>	-1
<(H, G)>	-1
<(A, H, G)>	-1
<(A, E, G)>	1

Considering the original customer sequences in terms of the two support thresholds, the modified candidate sequences may fall into the following three cases illustrated in Figure 1.

Case 1 may remove existing large sequences, and cases 2 and 3 may add new large sequences. If we retain all large and pre-large sequences with their counts in the original database, then cases 1 and 2 can be easily handled. Also, in the maintenance phase, the ratio of modified customer sequences to original customer sequences is

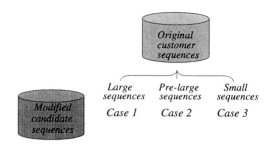

Figure 1. Three cases arising from modifying records in existing databases

usually very small. This is more apparent for a larger database. A sequence in case 3 cannot possibly be large for the entire updated database as long as the number of modified customer sequences is small when compared to the number of customer sequences in the original database. This point will be further described in section 4.

3. Notation

The notation used in this paper is defined below.
D: the set of original customer sequences;
T: the set of modified customer sequences transformed from the modified records and the other original records from the same customers;
U: the entire updated customer sequences;
d: the number of customer sequences in D;
t: the number of modified customer sequences in T;
S_u: the upper support threshold for large sequences;
S_l: the lower support threshold for pre-large sequences, $S_l < S_u$;
L_k^D : the set of large k-sequences from D;
L_k^T : the set of large k-sequences from T;
L_k^U : the set of large k-sequences from U;
P_k^D : the set of pre-large k-sequences from D;
P_k^T : the set of pre-large k-sequences from T;
P_k^U : the set of pre-large k-sequences from U;
C_k: the set of all candidate k-sequences from T;
I: a sequence;
$S^D(I)$: the number of occurrences of I in D;
$S^T(I)$: the number of occurrence decrements of I due to T;
$S^U(I)$: the number of occurrences of I in U.

4. Theoretical Foundation

In this section, we will show that if the number of modified customer sequences is small when compared with the number of original customer sequences, a sequence that is small (neither large nor pre-large) in the original database cannot possibly be large for the entire updated database.

Theorem 1: Let S_l and S_u be, respectively, the lower and the upper support thresholds, d be the number of original customer sequences, and t be the number of modified customer sequences. If $t \leq (S_u - S_l)d$, then a sequence that is small (neither large nor pre-large) in the original database is not large for the entire updated database.

The proof is skipped here due to the limitation of pages. From Theorem 1, the number of modified customer sequences allowed for efficiently handling case 3 is determined by S_l, S_u and d. It is easily seen that if d grows larger, then t will be larger too.

5. The proposed maintenance algorithm for record modification

INPUT: A lower support threshold S_l, an upper support threshold S_u, a set of large and pre-large sequences in the original database D consisting of d customer sequences, a set of t modified customer sequences, and a global variable c is used to accumulate the number of modified customer sequences since the last re-scan of the entire updated database.

OUTPUT: A set of sequential patterns for the updated database.

STEP 1: Calculate the safety bound according to Formula 1 as:
$$f = (S_u - S_l)d.$$

STEP 2: If $c + t \leq f$, then do the next step; otherwise, rescan the original database to determine large or pre-large sequences, set $c = 0$, and exit the algorithm

STEP 3: Set $k = 1$, where k is used to record the number of itemsets in the sequences currently being processed.

STEP 4: Find all the candidate k-sequences C_k^T with their count differences from the modified customer sequences.

STEP 5: Divide the candidate k-sequences in C_k^T into three parts according to whether they are large, pre-large or small in the original database.

STEP 6: Do the following substeps for each k-sequence I in the original large k-sequences L_k^D:

Substep 6-1: Set the new count $S^U(I) = S^D(I) + S^T(I)$. If I does not exist in C_k^T, $S^T(I)=0$.

Substep 6-2: If $S^U(I)/d \geq S_u$, then assign I as a large sequence, set $S^D(I) = S^U(I)$ and keep I with $S^D(I)$; otherwise, if $S^U(I)/d \geq S_l$, then assign I as a pre-large sequence, set $S^D(I) = S^U(I)$ and keep I with $S^D(I)$; otherwise, remove I.

STEP 7: Do the following substeps for each k-sequence I in the original pre-large k-sequences P_k^D:

Substep 7-1: Set the new count $S^U(I) = S^D(I) + S^T(I)$. If I does not exist in C_k^T, $S^T(I)=0$.

Substep 7-2: If $S^U(I)/d \geq S_u$, then assign I as a large sequence, set $S^D(I) = S^U(I)$ and keep I with $S^D(I)$; otherwise, if $S^U(I)/d \geq S_l$, then assign I as a pre-large sequence, set $S^D(I) = S^U(I)$ and keep I with $S^D(I)$; otherwise, remove I.

STEP 8: Form candidate $(k+1)$-sequences C_{k+1}^T from the originally large and pre-large $(k+1)$-sequences ($L_{k+1}^D \bigcup P_{k+1}^D$), each of which must be a $(k+1)$- sequence difference from the record modification.

STEP 9: Set $k = k+1$.

STEP 10: Repeat STEPs 4 to 9 until no large or pre-large sequences are found.

STEP 11: Modify the maximal large sequence patterns according to the modified large sequences.

STEP 12: Set $c = c + t$.

6. Experiments

Our proposed algorithm was implemented in C++ on a Pentium-III 800 dual-processor workstation with 512M RAM. The experimental datasets were generated by the program developed by Agrawal and his co-workers in [2]. 100000 customer sequences were generated at random, with each sequence having an average of 5 transactions of single items for a customer. The mean size of the maximal potentially sequential patterns was 4. Figure 2 shows the relationships between computational times and numbers of modified customer sequences for our proposed approach with the upper support = 0.6% and the lower support = 0.5%, and for the Aprioriall approach with minimum support = 0.6%.

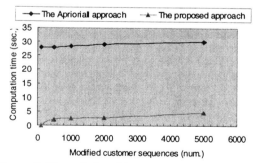

Figure 2. The relationships between computational times and modified customer sequences

From Figure 2, it is easily seen that the computational times by the proposed approach are much less than those by the Aprioriall approach for sequence modification when lower support thresholds are set at below 0.6%.

Experiments were then made for a comparison of different datasets. The relationships between computational times and numbers of customer sequences, when the number of modified customer sequences is 500 and the lower support threshold is set at 0.5%, are shown in Figure 3.

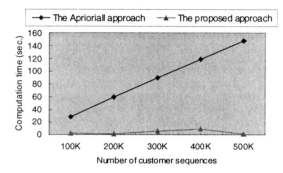

Figure 3. The relationships between computational times and different datasets

From Figures 3, it is easily seen that the execution times by the proposed algorithm for different datasets are very small. The execution times by the Aprioriall algorithm are much larger than those by the proposed algorithm and increase nearly proportionally along with the increase of customer sequences.

7. Conclusions

In this paper, we have proposed a novel efficient maintenance algorithm to sequential patterns for record modification. The concept of pre-large sequences is used to reduce the need for rescanning original databases and to save maintenance costs. The safety bound for not rescanning original databases is derived. If the size of the database grows larger, then the number of modified records allowed will be larger. These characteristics are especially useful for real-world applications.

Acknowledgment

This research was supported by the Ministry of Education and the National Science Council of the Republic of China under Grand No. 91-E-FA04-1-4, "High Confidence Information Systems".

References

[1] R. Agrawal, T. Imielinksi and A. Swami, "Database mining: a performance perspective," *IEEE Transactions on Knowledge and Data Engineering,* Vol. 5, No. 6, pp. 914-925, 1993.

[2] R. Agrawal and R. Srikant, "Mining sequential patterns," *The Eleventh IEEE International Conference on Data Engineering,* pp. 3-14, 1995.

[3] M. S. Chen, J. Han and P. S. Yu, "Data mining: an overview from a database perspective," *IEEE Transactions on Knowledge and Data Engineering,* Vol. 8, No. 6, pp. 866-883, 1996.

[4] D. W. Cheung, J. Han, V. T. Ng and C. Y. Wong, "Maintenance of discovered association rules in large databases: an incremental updating approach," *The Twelfth IEEE International Conference on Data Engineering,* pp. 106-114, 1996.

[5] D. W. Cheung, S. D. Lee and B. Kao, "A general incremental technique for maintaining discovered association rules," *The International Conference on Database Systems for Advanced Applications,* pp. 185-194, Melbourne, Australia, 1997.

[6] T. P. Hong, C. Y. Wang and Y. H. Tao, "A new incremental data mining algorithm using pre-large itemsets," *An International Journal: Intelligent Data Analysis,* Vol. 5, No. 2, pp. 111-129, 2001.

[7] T. P. Hong, C. Y. Wang and S. S. Tseng "Incremental data mining for sequential patterns using pre-large sequences," *The Fifth World Multi-Conference on Systemics, Cybernetics and Informatics,* Orlando, Florida, U.S.A, 2001.

[8] M. Y. Lin and S. Y. Lee, "Incremental update on sequential patterns in large databases," *The Tenth IEEE International Conference on Tools with Artificial Intelligence,* pp. 24-31, 1998.

[9] N. L. Sarda and N. V. Srinivas, "An adaptive algorithm for incremental mining of association rules," *The Ninth International Workshop on Database and Expert Systems Applications,* pp. 240-245, 1998.

[10] R. Srikant and R. Agrawal, "Mining sequential patterns: generalizations and performance improvements," *The Fifth International Conference on Knowledge Discovery and Data Mining,* pp. 269-274, 1995.

[11] S. Thomas, S. Bodagala, K. Alsabti and S. Ranka "An efficient algorithm for the incremental updation of association rules in large databases," *The International Conference on Knowledge Discovery and Data Mining,* pp. 263-266, 1997.

[12] C. Y. Wang, T. P. Hong and S. S. Tseng "Maintenance of Sequential Patterns for Record Deletion," *The IEEE International Conference on Data Mining,* pp. 536-541 2001.

Concept Tree Based Clustering Visualization with Shaded Similarity Matrices

Jun Wang   Bei Yu   Les Gasser
Graduate School of Library and Information Science
University of Illinois at Urbana-Champaign
501 E. Daniel St., Champaign, IL 61820, USA
{junwang4, beiyu, gasser}@uiuc.edu

Abstract

One of the problems with existing clustering methods is that the interpretation of clusters may be difficult. Two different approaches have been used to solve this problem: conceptual clustering in machine learning and clustering visualization in statistics and graphics. The purpose of this paper is to investigate the benefits of combining clustering visualization and conceptual clustering to obtain better cluster interpretations. In our research we have combined concept trees for conceptual clustering with shaded similarity matrices for visualization. Experimentation shows that the two interpretation approaches can complement each other to help us understand data better.

Keywords: Clustering Visualization, Conceptual Clustering, Shaded Similarity Matrix, Concept Tree

1. Introduction

One of the problems with existing clustering methods is that the interpretation of clusters produced may be difficult. To address this interpretation problem, on the one hand, people from statistics and graphics have focused on visualization approaches[4, 5]. On the other hand, researchers in machine learning (or artificial intelligence) have developed conceptual clustering[1, 10]. Clustering visualization can help users visually perceive the clusterings, and sometimes even hidden patterns in data. Conceptual clustering aims at representing the clusterings using symbolic knowledge. Clustering visualization utilizes people's perceptual ability (low-level information processing), while conceptual clustering exploits human inference ability (high-level information processing). However, these two different approaches have not previously been combined. The purpose of this paper is to combine conceptual clustering with visualization in order to obtain better intrepretations of clusterings.

Our approach is to use shaded similarity matrices[3] for visualization and concept trees[7] for conceptual clustering. Since there are exponentially many ways to order a set of objects, the key problem for the shaded similarity matrix approach is how to order the data or objects in a matrix so that similar objects are adjacent. Heuristic strategies are needed for generating a near-optimal ordering. Happily, concept trees provide not only an approach to conceptual clustering, but also a potential approach to solve the ordering problem, because *the more specific the concept shared by two objects, the more similar the two objects.* Our experiments (presented later) do show that concept trees are effective.

2. Shaded Similarity Matrices

Over the past forty years, shaded similarity matrices have been used in visual cluster anaylsis[8, 3, 11]. In a shaded similarity matrix[1], similarity in each cell is represented using a shade to indicate the similarity value: greater similarity is represented by dark shading, and lesser similarity by light shading. The dark and light cells may initially be scattered over the matrix. To reveal the potential clusterings visually, the rows and columns need to be re-organized so that similar objects are put in adjacent positions. If "real" clusters exist in the data, they should appear as symmetrical dark squares along the diagonal.

Here we will briefly show how shaded similarity matrices are constructed and how one looks through an example. The data used in the example is part of the *Iris* data from the UCI repository[9]. The *Iris* data set contains 150 instances, evenly distributed in 3 classes. We fetch 5 instances from each class, and thus obtain 15 instances (Table 1). The similarity matrix was computed based on Euclidean distance (Table 2).

The shaded similarity matrix is illustrated in Fig. 1. The right figure in Fig. 1 is generated from the original similarity matrix using the seriation algorithm which was pro-

---

[1]Some researchers use the term *shaded distance matrix, shaded proximity matrix,* or *trellis diagram.*

Table 1. Data matrix extracted from the Iris data set. *Abbreviations:* **sl: sepal-length, sw: sepal-width, pl: petal-length, pw: petal-width.**

Instance	sl	sw	pl	pw
e_1	5.1	3.5	1.4	0.2
e_2	6.3	2.9	5.6	1.8
e_3	7.0	3.2	4.7	1.4
...	...	...	...	...
e_{15}	6.5	2.8	4.6	1.5

Table 2. Similarity matrix corresponding to Table 1.

1.0	0.1	0.2	0.8	0.2	0.1	...	0.2
0.1	1.0	0.3	0.2	0.3	0.8	...	0.3
0.2	0.3	1.0	0.2	0.9	0.3	...	0.8
...	...						
0.2	0.3	0.8	0.2	0.8	0.3	...	1.0

posed in ClustanGraphics [11]. It works by weighting each similarity using the distance of the similarity cell from the diagonal. The algorithm tries to minimize the sum of the weighted similarities in the similarity matrix by reordering the pre-computed clusters in an agglomerative hierarchical clustering such as a dendrogram.

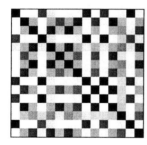

Figure 1. LEFT: *Randomly ordered* **shaded similarity matrix;** RIGHT: *Reordered* **shaded similarity matrix using a seriation algorithm.**

To display a similarity matrix of n objects, we need n^2 cells or $\frac{n^2}{2}$ cells (in the case of half matrix). In practice, usually it is not necessary to display all cells in a matrix. In this paper, only those cells are displayed whose similarity values are over a pre-specified threshold.

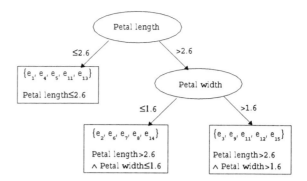

Figure 2. A concept tree on the Iris data set.

3. Concept Tree Based Clustering

3.1. Concept tree

A *concept tree* (also known as *concept hierarchy*) is composed of nodes and links with each node representing a concept[7]. The links connecting a node to its children specify an 'IS-A' or 'subset' relation. Fig.2 is an illustration of a concept tree generated by using the algorithm in Table 3 on the 15 *Iris* instances mentioned above.

3.2. Concept tree construction algorithm

Table 3 is a general algorithm for constructing a concept tree. The key part of the algorithm is how to select a *best* attribute using some split measurement. In this paper, we take the *within-group average similarity*[2] as the measurement. The best attribute is the one with the maximum within-group average similarity. Suppose an attribute a with k possible values splits a data set S into k subsets: $\{S_1, \cdots, S_k\}$. Let $\sigma(e_1, e_2)$ be the similarity of two instances e_1 and e_2. Then the *within-group average similarity* is defined as:

$$WAS(a) = \sum_{i=1}^{k} \frac{|S_i|}{|S|} \frac{\sum_{e_1,e_2 \in S_i} \sigma(e_1, e_2)}{|S_i|^2} \qquad (1)$$

3.3. Concept tree based ordering for shaded similarity matrices

Given that *objects sharing the same concept are probably similar*, if we put together all objects belonging to a concept, the ordering problem for shaded similarity matrices will be heuristically solved. Concretely speaking, given a tree with k leaves from left to right: $< L_1, L_2, \cdots, L_k >$. Each leaf represents a concept which covers a set of objects:

Table 3. Concept tree construction algorithm.

Inputs: The current node N of the concept tree,
an instance set S,
and an attribute set A .
Output: A concept tree.
Procedure: $CTree(N, S, A)$
If both S and A are not empty,
Then:
Select a best attribute $a \in A$ using some metric,
For each possible value v_i of a:
Form a node C, corresponding to the test $a = v_i$, [*]
Let S_{v_i} be the subset of S that have value v_i for a,
Make node C a child of Node N,
$CTree(C, S_{v_i}, A - \{a\})$.

[*] For numberical attributes, the test is represented as $a \leq v_i$ or $a > v_i$.

$L_i = \{e_{i_1}, \cdots, e_{i_n}\}$. Then the ordering of all objects will be:

$$< \{e_{1_1}, \cdots, e_{1_n}\}, \cdots \cdots, \{e_{k_1}, \cdots, e_{k_n}\} >$$

We don't care about the internal object ordering within a leaf. We assume that the objects within a leaf are similar enough, and if not the leaf node can be partitioned into smaller leaves until the objects within a leaf do become similar enough. Note that this ordering can only produce a partial order of the objects due to limitations of the tree structure.

4. Experimentation

To demonstrate the effectiveness of our approach, we have tested it on some UCI datasets. Here we use the full *Iris* dataset (150 instances) to generate a concept tree. Table 4 shows 3 concepts which are visualized as three square blocks along the diagonal from the left-top to right-bottom in the Fig. 3. Note that the concept tree here is a little bit different from the one in Fig. 2 because of the different dataset size.

Table 4. Concepts shown in Fig. 3.

Concept name	Square block	Concept description
concept-1	left-top	$pl \leq 2.5$
concept-2	center	$pl > 2.5 \land pw \leq 1.8$
concept-3	right-bottom	$pl > 2.5 \land pw > 1.8$

Among these 3 concepts, the concept-1 is the most clearly separated from other concepts. The concept-2 and

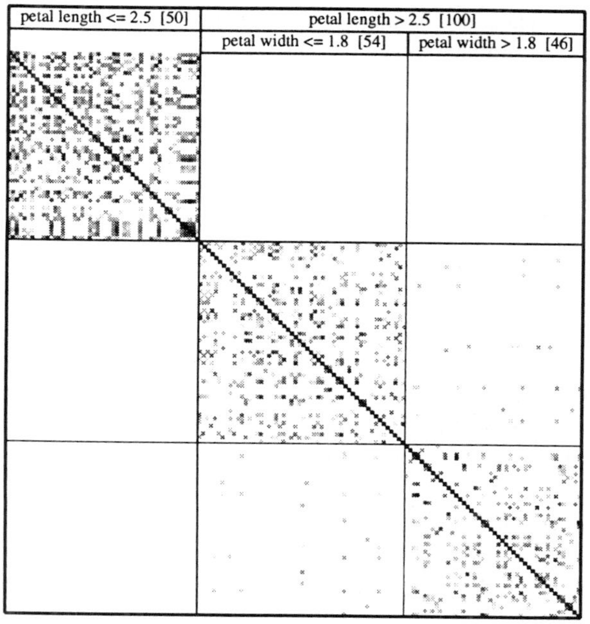

Figure 3. Concept tree based clustering visualization on the Iris dataset.

concept-3 are not perfectly separated. There are some instances covered by concept-2 which have high similarity[2] with the instances in concept-3 and vice versa.

Overall, the visualization result in the Fig. 3, allows us to discover two properties of the *Iris* dataset: 1) the dataset is naturally divided into three groups or clusters (there are three self-similar blocks); 2) each group can be described by a simple concept. In other words, we can say that both the visualization and the acquired concepts complement each other to help us better understand the data.

5. Discussion

First, it is apparent that the effectiveness of our approach depends on the definition of similarity, which is also a general problem for clustering methods. Second, our approach has an assumption that the data can be described conceptually, which does not always hold. However, if the data cannot be described conceptually, it is hard to say that the data are fully understood. Therefore, the problem becomes how to choose the right concept representation. Concept trees are only one kind of representation, and are not appropriate for all data.

Third, visualization based on shaded similarity matrices

[2] In the Fig. 3, if the similarity between two instances is over a threshold, a spot will be displayed for these two instances. In this situation we say that these two instances have high similarity.

has a scalability limitation. One solution is to use sampling and ensemble approaches. Using small sample sizes such as 100 or 200, we have tested the sampling approach on some Statlog datasets, including the *Shuttle* dataset which contains $43,500$ instances[6]. The results are promising.

6. Summary

This paper proposes a new approach for getting better interpretations for clustering results by combining visualization and conceptual clustering. This is achieved by using concept trees as a heuristic ordering strategy for shaded similarity matrices. Our experiment shows that the two clustering interpretation approaches can complement each other to help us better understand the data.

Acknowledgments

This work was partially supported by the Information Systems Research Lab (ISRL) of the Graduate School of Library and Information Science at University of Illinois at Urbana-Champaign. We are thankful to Dr. David Dubin, Professor Jiawei Han, and reviewers for valuable comments.

References

[1] F. Douglas. Knowledge acquisition via incemental conceptual clustering. *Machine Learning*, 2:139–172, 1987.

[2] B. S. Everitt. *Cluster Analysis*. John Wiley & Sons, Inc., New York, 1974.

[3] N. Gale, W. Halperin, and C. Costanzo. Unclassed matrix shading and optimal ordering in hierarchical cluster analysis. *Journal of Classification*, 1:75–92, 1984.

[4] P. E. Hoffman and G. G. Grinstein. A survey of visualizations for high-dimensional data mining. In U. Fayyad, G. Grinstein, and A. Wierse, editors, *Information Visualization in Data Mining and Knowledge Discovery*. Morgan Kaufmann, 2001.

[5] D. A. Keim. Information visualization and visual data mining. *IEEE Transactions on Visualization and Computer Graphics (Special Section on Information Visualization and Visual Data Mining)*, 8(1):1–8, 2002.

[6] R. King, C. Feng, and A. Shutherland. Statlog: comparison of classification algorithms on large real-world problems. *Applied Artificial Intelligence*, 9(3):259–287, 1995.

[7] P. Langley. *Elements of Machine Learning*. Morgan Kaufmann Publishers, 1996.

[8] R. L. Ling. A computer generated aid for cluster analysis. *Communications of the ACM*, 16(6):355–361, 1973.

[9] C. J. Merz, P. M. Murphy, and D. W. Aha. UCI repository of machine learning databases, http://www.ics.uci.edu/~mlearn/mlrepository.html, 1997. Dept. of Information and Computer Science, University of California at Irvine.

[10] L. Talavera and J. Bejar. Generality-based conceptual clustering with probabilistic concepts. *IEEE Transactions on Pattern Analysis and Machine Intelligence*, 23(2):196–206, 2001.

[11] D. Wishart. ClustanGraphics3: Interactive graphics for cluster analysis. In W. Gaul and H. Locarek-Junge, editors, *Classification in the Information Age*, pages 268–275. Springer-Verlag, 1999.

ΔB $^+$ Tree: Indexing 3D Point Sets for Pattern Discovery

Xiong Wang
Department of Computer Science
California State University, Fullerton
Fullerton, CA 92834-6870, USA
wang@ecs.fullerton.edu

Abstract

Three-dimensional point sets can be used to represent data in different domains. Given a database of 3D point sets, pattern discovery looks for similar subsets that occur in multiple point sets. Geometric hashing proved to be an effective technique in discovering patterns in 3D point sets. However, there are also known shortcomings. We propose a new indexing technique called ΔB$^+$ Trees. It is an extension of B$^+$-Trees that stores point triplet information. It overcomes the shortcomings of the geometric hashing technique. We introduce four different ways of constructing the key from a triplet. We give analytical comparison between the new index structure and the geometric hashing technique. We also conduct experiments on both synthetic data and real data to evaluate the performance.

1. Introduction

Three-dimensional point sets can be used to describe data in different domains, e.g. scientific data mining, computer-aided design, computer vision, etc. Pattern discovery is one of the problems that arise in these domains. It is concerned with similar substructures that occur in multiple point sets. For example, a motif is a substructure in proteins that has specific geometric arrangement and, in many cases, is associate with a particular function, such as DNA binding. Active sites are another type of patterns in protein structures. They play an important role through protein-protein and protein-ligand interaction, i.e. the binding process.

Similarity search in 3D point sets has been studied extensively. There are roughly three categories of approaches: volume-based approaches, feature-based approaches, and interactive approaches. Volume-based approaches use well-defined 3D structures to approximate the shapes of the point sets. They do not consider points inside the volumes. Thus they are not suitable for pattern discovery that is also con-

cerned with those points. Feature-based approaches capture the shapes of the 3D point sets by descriptors. The descriptors are essentially very high dimensional spaces and indexing them is a well known difficult problem, due to "the curse of dimensionality" [1]. The interactive approaches rely on the user to distinguish differences and provide feedbacks that were then used to refine the search. In molecular data, the differences between two molecules are often so subtle that bare eyes can hardly detect them.

We propose a new index structure called ΔB$^+$ Tree that facilitates pattern discovery in 3D point sets. We introduce three variants of ΔB$^+$ Trees and compare the effectiveness of them on both synthetic data and real data. The rest of the paper is organized as follows. In Section 2, we describe our approach to pattern discovery in 3D point sets. In Section 3, we present the structure of a ΔB$^+$ Tree. In Section 4, we compare ΔB$^+$ Trees with the geometric hashing technique. In Section 5, we report some experimental results. We conclude the paper in Section 6.

2. Finding Patterns in 3D Point Sets

The pattern discovery process consists of three phases: (1) decompose the point sets to candidate patterns; (2) index the candidate patterns to a ΔB$^+$ Tree; and (3) calculate the occurrence numbers of the candidate patterns.

The first phase is domain dependent. For example, chemical compounds often have substructures that are connected by double bonds. The building block of such substructures is referred to as a block in graph theory. We used an adapted depth-first search algorithm to identify these substructures [5]. These substructures are considered candidate patterns. To discover active sites on the protein surfaces, we extracted the surfaces of the proteins and constructed candidate patterns using the k-nearest neighbors of any given surface atom [3].

In the second phase, all the candidate patterns are indexed to a ΔB$^+$ Tree. The minimum match identified by the algorithm is a triplet match. A *triplet* is an ordered set of three points $\{P_i, P_j, P_k\}$, such that $d_{ij} \le d_{ik} \le d_{jk}$, where $d_{ij} = \|P_i - P_j\|$, $d_{ik} = \|P_i - P_k\|$, and $d_{jk} = \|P_j - P_k\|$ stand for the Euclidean distances between each pair of the points. Given a collection $\mathcal{D}$ of candidate patterns, we decompose each candidate pattern $D \in \mathcal{D}$ to triplets and index the triplets to a ΔB^+ Tree. The key of the ΔB^+ Tree is the three-dimensional vector (d_{ij}, d_{ik}, d_{jk}). Two keys are compared according to lexicographic ordering. For every triplet $\{P_i, P_j, P_k\}$ in D, A tuple in the ΔB^+ Tree has the structure $(CPID, GCF)$, where $CPID$ is the identification number of the candidate pattern and GCF is a 3×3 matrix. All triplets of the same shape share the same key and are grouped together. $CPID$ tells where this triplet comes from and GCF serves as a reference frame in constructing matches in the third phase. The tuples are stored in a disk file, called the tuple file. Tuples with the same key are stored contiguously.

In the third phase, each candidate pattern is used to access the ΔB^+ Tree to calculate its occurrence number. Let Q be a query pattern and ϵ a given range of tolerable errors. The algorithm decomposes Q to triplets and uses each triplet to access the ΔB^+ Tree. For each triplet $\{P_l', P_m', P_n'\}$ in Q, it looks for those keys (d_{ij}, d_{ik}, d_{jk}) in the ΔB^+ Tree, such that $|d_{ij} - d_{lm}'| \le \epsilon$, $|d_{ik} - d_{ln}'| \le \epsilon$, and $|d_{jk} - d_{mn}'| \le \epsilon$. Triplet matches are augmented together through comparison of the GCFs. For any query pattern Q, the process finds *all* possible matches of *any size* simultaneously. In other words, it identifies every possible alignment between Q and any candidate pattern within the range of tolerable errors. In contrast, volume-based and feature-based approaches do not provide alignment information.

3. ΔB^+ Trees

Recall that tuples with the same key are stored contiguously in the tuple file. The tuple file is indexed using a ΔB^+ Tree. Each distinct key has an entry in the leaf nodes of the ΔB^+ Tree. The ΔB^+ Tree is stored in a disk file, called the ΔB^+ Tree file. When building the internal node, we adopt the structure of CSB Tree [2]. The child nodes of each internal node are stored contiguously and only the pointer to the first child node is stored in the node. Notice that CSB Tree is a main memory index structure, while ΔB^+ Tree is disk based. The size of the node is set to the page size of the disk file.

Searching the ΔB^+ Tree with $\epsilon = 0$ is straightforward. For each triplet $\{P_l', P_m', P_n'\}$ generated from the query pattern Q, the searching algorithm seeks exact match with the key $(d_{lm}', d_{ln}', d_{mn}')$. When $\epsilon > 0$, starting from the root, the algorithm checks the keys in each level and filters out subtrees that are certainly out of the range. Essentially, the algorithm does a breadth first search. We also implement

another algorithm that uses a key $(d_{lm}' - \epsilon, d_{ln}' - \epsilon, d_{mn}' - \epsilon)$ to access the ΔB^+ Tree. The subsequent keys in the leaf nodes are then checked until a key (d_{ij}, d_{ik}, d_{jk}), such that $d_{ij} > d_{lm}' + \epsilon$. Those keys that are not within the range are filtered out. The breadth first approach performed slightly better.

Lexicographic ordering in essence partitions the keys using the first dimension first. It could be better if the values in the first dimension include information from all the three dimensions. We developed three variants of ΔB^+ Tree. They all use three-dimensional vectors as keys. The difference is in the values they use in the first dimension. Let $l = d_{ij} + d_{ik} + d_{jk}$. The first variant uses (l, d_{ik}, d_{jk}) as the key. We will call this ΔB^+ Tree-Length. Let a be the area of the triangle formed by the triplet $\{P_i, P_j, P_k\}$. The second variant uses (a, d_{ik}, d_{jk}) as the key. We will call this ΔB^+ Tree-Area. Let r be the radius of the circle that circumscribes the triangle formed by the triplet. The third variant uses (r, d_{ik}, d_{jk}) as the key. We will call this ΔB^+ Tree-Circle.

4. ΔB^+ Tree vs. Geometric Hashing

The framework we introduced in [4, 5] also has three phases. The difference is that we used a three-dimensional hash table to store the triplet information. The framework maintains two disk files, i.e. the header file and the tuple file. The tuple file is the same as discussed above. The header file stores a three-dimensional array. An entry in the header file has the format $(firstTuple, nTuples)$, where $firstTuple$ is the address of the first tuple and $nTuples$ is the number of tuples in that hash bin. For any tuple with key (d_{ij}, d_{ik}, d_{jk}), the hash bin addresses are calculated as follows:

$$
\begin{aligned}
l_1 &= Round(d_{ij}^2 \times Multiplier) \\
l_2 &= Round(d_{ik}^2 \times Multiplier) \\
l_3 &= Round(d_{jk}^2 \times Multiplier)
\end{aligned}
$$

$$
\begin{aligned}
index_1 &= (l_1 + l_2) \bmod Prime_1 \bmod Nrow \\
index_2 &= (l_2 + l_3) \bmod Prime_2 \bmod Nrow \quad (1) \\
index_3 &= (l_3 + l_1) \bmod Prime_3 \bmod Nrow
\end{aligned}
$$

where $Prime_1$, $Prime_2$, and $Prime_3$ are three primes. $Nrow$ is the cardinality of the hash table in each dimension. $Multiplier$ (e.g. 100) is used so that some digits after the decimal point can contribute to the distribution of the entries. It is set according to the range of tolerable errors. For example, if $\epsilon = 0.001$, $Multiplier$ is set to 1000. In the second phase, all candidate patterns are hashed to the hash table. In the third phase, each candidate pattern is used to probe the hash table to calculate its occurrence number.

We observed three shortcomings in the framework.

1. The hash functions (1) do not preserve accurate information of the data. It is not easy to determine an optimal value for $Multiplier$. Furthermore, once $Multiplier$ is fixed, the information stored in the hash table only approximates the raw data.

2. The hash function is not suitable for answering queries that allow variable ranges of tolerable errors when matching the points.

3. False matches have to be filtered out. Our experiments indicated that almost one quarter of the retrieved tuples are false matches. For large point set, efficiency deteriorates severely.

The first two shortcomings limit application of the framework to bioinformatics. Due to regularity of biological and chemical structures, dissimilarity is often very subtle. Inaccuracy introduced by the scanning devices adds noise to the data. It is extremely difficult to choose a fixed ϵ, i.e. the range of tolerable errors, especially, when the data are collected by different domain experts, using different equipments, such as in the case of Protein Data Bank [6]. It is highly desirable that ϵ be set to a tunable parameter, so that the domain expert can choose an optimal value according to the context. The ΔB^+ Trees overcome these shortcomings.

5. Experimental Results

We have implemented both the ΔB^+ Tree technique and the geometric hashing technique using GNU C++ Language. All experiments were conducted on a Sun Ultra10 workstation with 440 MHz CPU and 512 Megabyte memory. Two data sets were used in the experiments. The first data set includes 20 randomly generated point sets, each has 15,000 points. Since randomly generated point sets are rarely similar to each other, to make the experiments more interesting, we generated 2 point sets first. We then moved the X-coordinate of half of the points in each point set 0.001, 0.002, 0.003, 0.004, 0.01, 0.02, 0.03, and 0.04 respectively to generate 8 copies of these point sets. We generated 2 more point sets to make the total of 20 point sets. The second data set includes 140 proteins downloaded from the Protein Data Bank [6]. The proteins have 1,000 atoms on the average. We segmented both the point sets and the proteins to consecutive substructures of M points, namely the size of the candidate patterns was M. The parameters of ΔB^+ Tree were $PageSize = 1024$, $InternalNodeSize = 84$, and $LeafSize = 63$. The three primes of the geometric hashing framework were 276527, 387659, and 498761. $Nrow$ was 251 and $Multiplier$ was 1000.

We also implemented a typical bulkloading algorithm that keeps inserting sorted leaf entries into the rightmost path from the root. The heights of the ΔB^+ Tree for both data sets were 4. The heights of the ΔB^+ Tree with bulkloading were also 4 for both data sets, even though the ΔB^+ Tree files were much smaller. Our first observation in the synthetic data was that, although the size of the header file for geometric hashing was twice of the number of distinct keys, the number of non-empty bins was 23.1% less. These keys must have been hashed to the same hash bins of some other keys. In other words, about 23.1% of the matches were false matches in the third phase. Similarly, for the protein data, the header file for geometric hashing was 1.9 times larger than the number of distinct keys, while the number of non-empty bins was also 23.1% less.

Our first experiment compared ΔB^+ Tree with geometric hashing in terms of their response time in the third phase. Figure 1 shows response time as a function of M, the size of the candidate patterns for the synthetic data. Figure 2 shows the response time as a function of M for the proteins. Since all the variants had very similar response time, we only pictured one of them. The ΔB^+ Tree with bulkloading also performed very similarly, probably because they had the same heights.

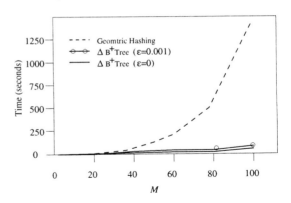

Figure 1. Response time as a function of M for the synthetic data

In the second experiment, we evaluated the performance of the ΔB^+ Tree technique with variable ranges of tolerable errors. We compared ΔB^+ Tree with its three variants. We fixed the size of the candidate patterns to 15. Figure 3 shows response time as a function of ϵ for the synthetic data. Figure 4 shows response time as a function of ϵ for the proteins. For all the variants, the ΔB^+ Tree with bulkloading did slightly better in answering range queries. We did not show the results here.

Notice that the response time for the protein data increased very fast when ϵ increased. This most likely is

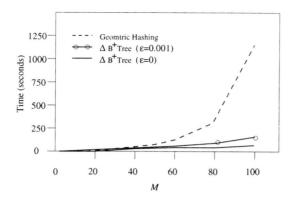

Figure 2. Response time as a function of M for the proteins

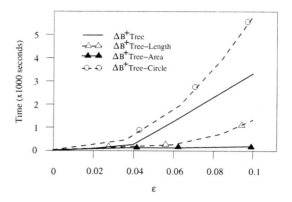

Figure 4. Response time as a function of ϵ for the proteins

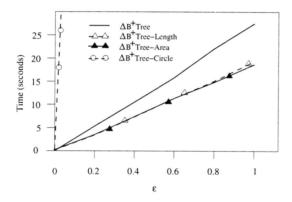

Figure 3. Response time as a function of ϵ for the synthetic data

caused by the fact that proteins are very similar in terms of inter-atom distances. There are some typical values of the bonds. This phenomenon makes it very difficult to set an optimal ϵ that is both large enough to cover data errors and small enough to detect the subtle differences among the data. This is the major motivation triggering the development of ΔB^+ Tree.

6. Conclusion

We have proposed a new index structure called ΔB^+ Tree. ΔB^+ Tree performs triplet matching and merging like in [4, 5]. In stead of using geometric hashing, we use a B^+ Tree to store the triplet information. The proposed indexing technique has all the advantages a B^+ Tree has compared with hashing techniques. We introduced three variants of ΔB^+ Tree and evaluate the effectiveness of them on both synthetic data and real data.

Our future work includes using three dimensional R^*-trees and other index structures to index the triplets and conducting experiments to compare the performance. We will conduct large scale experiments to index the Protein Data Bank for pattern discovery.

References

[1] S. Berchtold, C. Bhm, B. Braunmller, D. Keim, and H. Kriegel. Fast parallel similarity search in multimedia databases. In *Proceedings ACM SIGMOD International Conference on Management of Data*, pages 1–12, Tucson, Arizona, 1997.

[2] J. Rao and K. A. Ross. Making b$^+$-trees cache conscious in main memory. In *Proceedings of the 2000 ACM SIGMOD International Conference on Management of Data*, pages 475–486, Dallas, TX, 2000.

[3] X. Wang. α - surface and its application to mining protein data. In *Proceedings of the 2001 IEEE International Conference on Data Mining*, pages 659–662, San Jose, California, 2001.

[4] X. Wang, J. Wang, D. Shasha, B. Shapiro, I. Rigoutsos, and K. Zhang. Finding patterns in three dimensional graphs: Algorithms and applications to scientific data mining. *IEEE Transaction on Knowledge and Data Engineering*, 14(4):731–749, July/August 2002.

[5] X. Wang, J. T. L. Wang, D. Shasha, B. A. Shapiro, S. Dikshitulu, I. Rigoutsos, and K. Zhang. Automated discovery of active motifs in three dimensional molecules. In *Proceedings of the 3rd International Conference on Knowledge Discovery and Data Mining*, pages 89–95, Newport Beach, California, 1997.

[6] J. Westbrook, Z. Feng, S. Jain, T. N. Bhat, N. Thanki, V. Ravichandran, G. L. Gilliland, W. Bluhm, H. Weissig, D. S. Greer, P. E. Bourne, and H. M. Berman. The protein data bank: unifying the archive. *Nucleic Acids Research*, 30(1):245–248, 2002.

An Incremental Approach to Building a Cluster Hierarchy

Dwi H. Widyantoro & Thomas R. Ioerger
Texas A&M University
Department of Computer Sciences
College Station, TX 77843-3112 USA
dhw7942,ioerger@cs.tamu.edu

John Yen
The Pennsylvania State University
School of Information Sciences and Technology
University Park, PA 16802-2117 USA
jyen@ist.psu.edu

Abstract

In this paper we present a novel Incremental Hierarchical Clustering (IHC) algorithm. Our approach aims to construct a hierarchy that satisfies the homogeneity and the monotonicity properties. Working in a bottom-up fashion, a new instance is placed in the hierarchy and a sequence of hierarchy restructuring process is performed only in regions that have been affected by the presence of the new instance. The experimental results on a variety of domains demonstrate that our algorithm is not sensitive to input ordering, can produce a quality cluster hierarchy, and is efficient in terms of its computational time.

1. Introduction

Hierarchical clustering is an important tool in data *warehouse* analysis [8], ontology construction of a dynamic text collection (e.g., similar to the one in Yahoo!) and in interactive information retrieval [9]. As it involves a large data set that grows rapidly over time, re-clustering the data set periodically is not an efficient process. Due to the "information overload" phenomenon in recent years, the ability to perform a clustering process incrementally is increasingly appealing because it offers a viable option to a problem faced by a non incremental clustering process.

The sensitivity to input ordering is one of the major issues in incremental hierarchical clustering [6]. Previous works mitigate the effect of input ordering by applying restructuring operators, which can be broadly categorized into *local* and *global* approaches. Although relatively efficient to recover nodes misplaced at neighboring nodes, the local approaches [5, 11] in general suffer from their inability to deal with major structural changes. The global approaches [1, 4] alleviate these problems but these approaches are very expensive and make the algorithm non-incremental. By contrast, our method described in this paper represents a trade-off between the local and the global approaches while

preserving the incremental nature of the algorithm.

Incremental clustering algorithm has also been developed by Ester et al. from *Data Mining* perspective [2]. Specifically, they develop an incremental version of DB-SCAN, a density-based clustering algorithm. However, DB-SCAN and its incremental version are *partitional* clustering algorithms. Our approach is more related to the agglomerative hierarchical clustering techniques [3, 10], and therefore, can be viewed as the incremental version of the more traditional bottom-up hierarchical clustering methods.

2. Our Incremental Algorithm

Our approach aims to construct a concept hierarchy with two properties: *homogeneity* and *monotonicity*. Informally, a homogeneous cluster is a set of objects with similar density. A hierarchy of clusters satisfies the monotonicity property if the density of a cluster is always higher than the density of its parent. That is, the density of clusters monotonically increases along any path in the concept hierarchy from the root to a leaf node.

A cluster hierarchy is basically a tree structure with leaf nodes represent singleton clusters covering single data points. Each node in the tree maintains two types of information: *cluster center* and *cluster density*. The cluster density describes the spatial distribution of child nodes of a node. We define a cluster's density as the average distance to the closest neighbor among the cluster's members. A natural way of obtaining the distances to the nearest neighbors is by creating the minimum spanning tree (MST) of objects in the cluster. Specifically, the density representation of a node is a triple $D = \langle NDP, \mu, \sigma \rangle$ where $NDP = \{d_i \mid d_i \epsilon \Re\}$ is a population of nearest distance d_is, μ and σ are the average and the standard deviation of NDP. Each d_i in NDP is the length of an edge, measured by the distance between two nodes, of the MST structure connecting a node's child nodes. In general, the distance between two nodes, *w.r.t.* the nodes' cluster center, can be measured by using L^n distance function family.

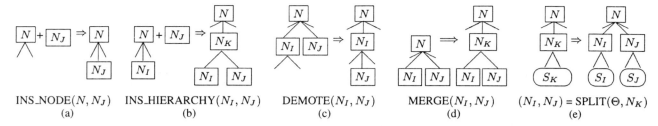

INS_NODE(N, N_J)　　INS_HIERARCHY(N_I, N_J)　　DEMOTE(N_I, N_J)　　MERGE(N_I, N_J)　　(N_I, N_J) = SPLIT(Θ, N_K)
　(a)　　　　　　　　　(b)　　　　　　　　　　(c)　　　　　　　　(d)　　　　　　　　　(e)

Figure 1. Restructuring operators: (a) node insertion operator, (b) hierarchy insertion operator, (c) demotion operator, (d) merging operator, and (e) splitting operator. S_K, S_I & S_J are the sets of child nodes of N_K, N_I & N_J, respectively; $S_K = \{S_I \cup S_J\}$ and $(S_I, S_J) = \Theta(S_K)$. Θ is a splitting function that separates S_K by disconnecting an edge in the cluster's MST structure into two disjoint sets S_I and S_J. (N_I, N_J) = SPLIT(Θ, N_K) splits N_K into N_I and N_J w.r.t. the splitting function Θ.

Definition 1 *Let $D_C = \langle NDP, \mu, \sigma \rangle$ be a density representation of a cluster C. Given a lower limit $L_L = f(\mu, \sigma) \leq \mu$ and an upper limit $U_L = g(\mu, \sigma) \geq \mu$, the cluster C is homogeneous with respect to f and g if and only if $L_L \leq d_i \leq U_L$ for $\forall d_i \epsilon NDP$.*

Definition 2 *Let C be a homogenous cluster. Given a new point A, let B be a C's cluster member that is the nearest neighbor to A. Let d be the distance from A to B. A (and B) is said to* **form a higher (lower) dense region** *in C if $d < L_L$ ($d > U_L$, respectively).*

Our approaches to incorporating a new data point into a cluster hierarchy incrementally can be divided into two stages. During the first stage, the algorithm locates a node in the hierarchy that can host the new data point. The second stage performs hierarchy restructuring. This two-stage algorithm is applied on observing the third and subsequent data points. The initial hierarchy is created by merging the first two points.

Locating the initial placement of a new data point during the first stage is carried out in a bottom-up fashion:

1. Find the closest point over leaf nodes.

2. Starting from the parent of the closest leaf node, perform *upward search* to locate a cluster (or create a new cluster hierarchy) that can host the new point with minimal density changes and minimal disruption of the hierarchy monotonicity. Let N be the node being examined at current level. The placement of a new point N_J in the hierarchy is performed according to the following rules:

   - if $L_L \leq d \leq U_L$ then perform INS_NODE (N, N_J) (see Figure 1a) where d is the distance from the new point N_J to the nearest N's child node.

   - if N_J *forms a higher dense region* on N, and N_J *forms a lower dense region* on at least one of N's

child nodes then perform INS_HIERARCHY (N_I, N_J) (see Figure 1b) where N_I is the child node of N closest to the new point N_J.

If none of the rules applies, the search proceeds to the next higher-level cluster. If the search process reaches the top-level cluster, a new cluster will be inserted at the top level using the hierarchy insertion operator.

The second stage aims to recover any structural changes that occur after incorporating a new data point. The following algorithm describes the hierarchy restructuring process.

Algorithm **Hierarchy Restructuring**
1. Let *crntNode* be the node that accepts the new point.
2. **While** ($crntNode \neq \emptyset$)
3. 　Let *parentNode* $\leftarrow$ Parent(*crntNode*)
4. 　Recover the siblings of *crntNode* that are misplaced.
5. 　Maintain the homogeneity of *crntNode*.
6. 　Let *crntNode* $\leftarrow$ *parentNode*

One of the most common problems is that a node is stranded at an upper level cluster. In such a case, a node N_J, which is supposed to be a child node of N_I, is misplaced as N_I's sibling. Line 4 addresses this issue by utilizing Definition 2 to detect the problem. Specifically, a node N_J, which is the sibling of N_I, is said to be misplaced as N_I's sibling if and only if N_J *does not form a lower dense region* in N_I. If such a problem is detected, we iteratively apply DEMOTE(N_I, N_J) (see Figure 1c).

Line 5 in the Hierarchy Restructuring algorithm repairs a cluster whose homogeneity property has been violated. Intuitively, the recovery process involves the elimination of both the lower and the higher dense regions, repeatedly, until all nearest distances in the cluster are within the cluster's bounds. The following algorithm describes the homogeneity maintenance process of a cluster. Working in a *divide and conquer* fashion, it receives a cluster N and replaces N by one or more homogeneous clusters.

Algorithm **Homogeneity Maintenance**(N)

1. Let an input N be the node that is being examined.
2. **Repeat**
3.   Let N_I and N_J be the pair of neighbors among N's child nodes with the smallest nearest distance.
4.   **If** N_I and N_J *form a higher dense region*,
5.   **Then** MERGE (N_I, N_J) (see Figure 1d)
6. **Until** there is no higher dense region found in N during the last iteration.
7. Let M_I and M_J be the pair of neighbors among N's child nodes with the largest nearest distance.
8. **If** M_I and M_J *form a lower dense region* in N,
9. **Then** Let (N_I, N_J) = SPLIT (Θ, N). (see Figure 1e)
10.   *Call* **Homogeneity Maintenance**(N_I).
11.   *Call* **Homogeneity Maintenance**(N_J).

3   Evaluation

Let $\mathcal{DATA}$ be the set of all data points, and $TC_i \in \mathcal{TC}$ be the ith target cluster in a set of target clusters $\mathcal{TC}$. Let $\mathcal{E}(TC_i)$ denote the set of data points belong to a target cluster TC_i such that $\mathcal{DATA} = \bigcup_i \mathcal{E}(TC_i)$ for $\forall\, TC_i \in \mathcal{TC}$, and $\mathcal{E}(TC_i) \cap \mathcal{E}(TC_j) = \emptyset$ for $i \neq j$. Moreover, let $N \in \mathcal{H}$ be a node in a cluster hierarchy $\mathcal{H}$ that is produced by a clustering algorithm using all data points in $\mathcal{DATA}$. Let $\mathcal{E}(N)$ denote the set of data points (i.e. leaf nodes) that are descendants of a node N. For each $TC_i \in \mathcal{TC}$, let N_i^* be the corresponding node in $\mathcal{H}$ such that:

$$N_i^* = \arg\max_{N \in \mathcal{H}} \left\{ \frac{\|\mathcal{E}(TC_i) \cap \mathcal{E}(N)\|}{\|\mathcal{E}(TC_i) \cup \mathcal{E}(N)\|} \right\}$$

Thus, N_i^* is a node in $\mathcal{H}$ that represents a target cluster TC_i. The quality of cluster hierarchy $\mathcal{H}$ is then calculated as an accuracy measure, which is defined as follows.

$$Acc_{\mathcal{H}} = \frac{\sum_{TC_i \in \mathcal{TC}} \|\mathcal{E}(TC_i) \cap \mathcal{E}(N_i^*)\|}{\|\mathcal{DATA}\|} \times 100\% \quad (1)$$

In all experiments, we use $U_L = \mu + \sigma$ as the upper bounds and $L_L = \mu - \sigma$ as the lower bounds of clusters with three or more cluster members. We set the upper bounds $1.5d$ and the lower bounds $(2/3)d$ for two-member clusters where d is the distance between the two clusters' members.

To test the sensitivity of our algorithm to input ordering, we use three natural data sets taken from the UCI repository: *Soybean Small*, *Soybean Large*, and *Voting*. The distance between two instances or clusters on these domains is calculated using the L^1 distance function. The experiments are performed in two settings: *random* and *bad* orderings [6]. We also run COBWEB [5] and ARACHNE [12] for performance comparison with other incremental systems.

Table 1. The performance of various incremental hierarchical clustering algorithms.

	Our IHC	COBWEB	ARACHNE
Accuracy (%) on Random Ordering			
Soybean Small	96.00	97.27	85.10
Soybean Large	69.49	64.27	60.80
Voting	85.55	84.37	79.40
Accuracy (%) on Bad Ordering			
Soybean Small	97.36	81.02	78.38
Soybean Large	71.97	60.13	64.26
Voting	85.58	77.81	66.75

Table 1 summarizes the experiment results, averaged over 25 trials. As indicated in the table, the performances of our algorithm are better than the other incremental systems in most cases. Our algorithm is also relatively not sensitive to the presentation of input ordering.

The next experiment is to test whether the performance of our IHC algorithm is still competitive with those of non incremental algorithms particularly the agglomerative hierarchical clustering methods [3, 10]. In this experiment we use a subset of the Reuters-21578 1.0 test collection obtained from the UCI KDD archive. We select only a subset of training stories that are assigned a single topic category. Each document is preprocessed (i.e. by removing stop words, performing features selection and weighting) and is represented by a feature vector. We measure the distance between two documents or clusters using the L^2 distance function. Because a document topic should be independent of the length of document, the feature vectors and cluster centers are normalized by L^2 normalization.

Table 2 depicts the best hierarchy quality produced by each clustering algorithm and the time needed to perform the clustering process. Because our IHC algorithm could produce different result on different input ordering, we average the result over 25 trials. As shown in table, the best result from the agglomerative methods is achieved by the *group-average* with the accuracy of 93.38%. This is only about 2.1% higher than the accuracy achieved by our IHC algorithm, which is 91.28%.

The last column of Table 2 reveals that the best result of our IHC algorithm is obtained by taking a much shorter time than those of the agglomerative approaches. While the best result of our algorithm requires only 56.1 seconds to perform the clustering process, the agglomerative methods need at least 5600 seconds, about 100 times longer than ours. Not only does our IHC algorithm offer an incremental process that can avoid data re-clustering, it also efficiently performs the clustering process.

Table 2. The performance on Reuter data set.

Clust. Method	Accuracy(%)	Execution Time (seconds)
IHC Algorithm	**91.28**	**56.1**
Single Linkage	81.60	5749.2
Complete Linkage	81.18	5692.3
Group-Average	**93.38**	5749.3
Centroid	80.55	5897.7
Ward	**91.27**	5820.7

4 Discussion

The worst case analysis of our IHC algorithm reveals that it needs $B^3 D \log_B n$ time to incorporate a single object, where B is the average branching factor of the tree, D is the dimension (e.g., #features) of objects, and n is the number of objects that have been previously incorporated in the tree. Tests on a variety of domains indicate that the tree branching factor is relatively small, ranging from 2 to 6. D can be associated with the cost for calculating the distance between two objects. The most expensive operation is re-calculating the distances among pairs of child nodes during the MST update[1], which is $B^2 D$ time. Given the incremental update time as above, the time complexity of our IHC algorithm is $\mathcal{O}(N \log N)$. This is better than the time complexity of an agglomerative method, which is $\mathcal{O}(N^2)$.

Our notion of density, which provides a basis for defining the homogeneity property, is based on a graph theoretic approach [10]. Despite the advantage of recognizing clusters of any shapes, using MST or a similar structure in a clustering process also has a drawback in that it easily chains several clusters together particularly in batch clustering such as the *single linkage* agglomerative clustering [3]. If there exists a formation of data points that could link clusters, the *single linkage* method tends to find those links because the underlying MST-like structure is formed over all data points. However, this problem is not necessarily the case in our algorithm. Because the calculation of distance between two nodes in our algorithm is based on the nodes' cluster center and the MST structure of a node is built over only the child nodes, the underlying MST structures are local to the nodes' levels. As a result, the MST structures in our IHC algorithm are scattered into several hierarchy levels and are dependent on the input ordering. The chance is therefore very small for encountering an ordering of several objects that can chain two clusters at the same hierarchy levels and clusters' parents. Hence, the clusters chaining problem that

---

[1]Currently we use *Prim*'s algorithm to rebuild the MST structure, which has an every-case time complexity of $\Theta(B^2)$. Fortunately, there exists an incremental MST algorithm [7] with $\Theta(\sqrt{(B-1)})$ update time that could be used to improve the efficiency of the MST update.

is deterministic in batch clustering is a random variable in incremental setting with very low probability of occurrence.

5 Conclusion

This paper highlights the inefficiency problem faced by non incremental hierarchical clustering methods in a dynamic environment. In response to this problem, we present a new incremental hierarchical clustering algorithm. Experiments conducted on a variety of domains indicate the effectiveness of our algorithm that illuminates its potential as a valuable tool for Data Mining task.

Acknowledgments

This research is partially supported by Contract DAAD17-00-P-0649 from the U.S. Army Research Laboratory (ARL) and by a grant from Dell Foundation.

References

[1] G. Biswas, J. Weinberg, and D. Fisher. Iterate: A conceptual clustering algorithm for data mining. *IEEE Trans. on Systems, Man, and Cybernetics*, 28(2):100–111, 1998.

[2] M. Ester, H.-P. Kriegel, J. Sander, M. Wimmer, and X. Xu. Incremental clustering for mining in a data warehousing environment. In *Proceedings of the 24th VLDB Conference*, 1998.

[3] B. S. Everitt, S. Landau, and M. Leese. *Cluster Analysis*. New York, NY: Oxford University Press Inc, 2001.

[4] D. Fisher. Iterative optimization and simplification of hierarchical clusterings. *Journal of Artificial Intelligence Research*, 4:147–180, 1996.

[5] D. H. Fisher. Knowledge acquisition via incremental conceptual clustering. *Journal of Machine Learning*, 2:139–172, 1987.

[6] D. H. Fisher, L. Xu, and N. Zard. Ordering effects in clustering. In *Proceedings. of the 9th International Conference on Machine Learning*, pages 163–168, 1992.

[7] G. Frederickson. Data structures for on-line updating of mst, with applications. *Siam J. on Comput.*, 14(4):781–798, 1985.

[8] J. Han and M. Kamber. *Data mining : concepts and techniques*. San Francisco : Morgan Kaufmann Publishers, 2001.

[9] M. Hearst and J. Pederson. Reexamining the cluster hipothesis: Scatter/gather on retrieval results. In *Proceedings of ACM SIGIR*, pages 76–84, 1996.

[10] A. Jain and R. C. Dubes. *Algorithms for Clustering Data*. Englewood Cliffs, New Jersey: Prentice Hall, 1988.

[11] M. Lebowitz. Experiments with incremental concept formation: Unimem. *Journal of Machine Learning*, 1:103–138, 1987.

[12] K. B. McKusick and P. Langley. Constraints on tree structure in concept formation. In *Proceedings of the 12th International Conference on Artificial Intelligence*, pages 810–816, 1991.

A Comparative Study of RNN for Outlier Detection in Data Mining

Graham Williams   Rohan Baxter   Hongxing He   Simon Hawkins

Lifang Gu

CSIRO Enterprise Data Mining

GPO Box 664, Canberra, ACT 2601, Australia

Firstname.Lastname@csiro.au

http://datamining.csiro.au

Abstract

We have proposed replicator neural networks (RNNs) for outlier detection [8]. Here we compare RNN for outlier detection with three other methods using both publicly available statistical datasets (generally small) and data mining datasets (generally much larger and generally real data). The smaller datasets provide insights into the relative strengths and weaknesses of RNNs. The larger datasets particularly test scalability and practicality of application.

1. Introduction

Outlier detection has regained considerable interest in data mining with the realisation that they can be the key discovery from very large databases [5, 4, 16]. Indeed, for many applications the discovery of outliers leads to more interesting and useful results than the discovery of inliers. The classic example is fraud detection but in customer relationship management (CRM) and other consumer databases outliers are often the most profitable group of customers.

In this paper we apply replicator neural networks (RNNs) to outlier detection [8]. RNNs have a flexible, non-parametric representation of clusters, which, in principle, should make them a useful, powerful outlier detection method. RNNs are compared with two parametric (from the statistical literature) methods and one non-parametric outlier detection method (from the data mining literature).

In Section 2 we review RNN outlier detection and briefly summarise the three alternative methods in Section 3. In Section 4 we describe the datasets and experimental design for performing the comparisons. Results are reported in Section 5, and Section 6 summarises the results and the contribution of this paper.

2. RNNs for Outlier Detection

RNNs for outlier detection [8]. employ feed-forward multi-layer neural networks with three hidden layers sandwiched between the input and output layers which have n units each, corresponding to the n features of the training data. The number of units in the three hidden layers are chosen experimentally to minimise the average reconstruction error across all training patterns. The neural network input variables are *also* the output variables so that the RNN forms an implicit, compressed model of the data during training—the RNN attempts to reproduce the input patterns in the output. A measure of outlyingness of individuals is then developed as the reconstruction error of individual data points.

A particular innovation is the activation function used for the middle hidden layer [8]. Instead of the usual sigmoid activation function for this layer (layer 3) a staircase-like function with parameters N (number of steps or activation levels) and a_3 (transition rate from one level to the next) are employed. As a_3 increases the function approaches a true step function, as shown in Figure 1.

This activation function has the effect of dividing continuously distributed data points into a number of discrete valued vectors, providing the data compression that RNNs are known for. For outlier detection the mapping to discrete categories naturally places the data points into a number of clusters. For scalability the RNN is trained with a smaller training set and then applied to all of the data to evaluate their outlyingness.

3. Other Outlier Detection Methods

Selection of the outlier detection methods used in this paper for comparison is based on availability and our intent to sample from distinctive approaches. The three chosen methods are: the Donoho-Stahel estimator [10]; Hadi94 [6]; and MML clustering [12].

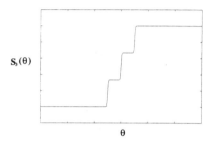

Figure 1. A representation of the activation function for units in the middle hidden layer of the RNN. N **is 4 and** a_3 **is 100 [8].**

Of course, there are many data mining outlier detection methods not included here [9] and also many omitted statistical outlier methods [13, 11]. Many of these methods are related to the three included methods and RNNs, often being adapted from clustering methods in one way or another and a full appraisal of this is worth a separate paper.

The Donoho-Stahel outlier detection method uses the outlyingness measure computed by the Donoho-Stahel estimator, which is a robust multivariate estimator of location and scatter [10]. It can be characterised as an 'outlyingness-weighted' estimate of mean and covariance, which down-weights any point that is many robust standard deviations away from the sample in some univariate projection.

Hadi94 [6] is a parametric bulk outlier detection method for multivariate data. The method starts with $g_0 = k + 1$ 'good' records, where k is the number of dimensions. The good set is increased one point at a time and the $k+1$ 'good' records are selected using a robust estimation method. The mean and covariance matrix of the 'good records' are calculated. The Mahalanobis distance is computed for all the data and the $g_n = g_{n-1} + 1$ closest data are selected as the 'good records'. This is repeated until the 'good' records contain more than half the dataset, or the Mahalanobis distance of the remaining records is higher than a predefined threshold value.

For the data mining outlier detector we use the mixture-model clustering algorithm where models are scored using MML inductive inference [12]. The cost of transmitting each datum according to the best mixture model is measured in nits (1.6bits = 1 nit). We rank the data in order of highest message length cost to lowest message length cost. The high cost data are 'surprising' according to the model and so are considered as outliers by this method.

4. Experimental Design

Each outlier detection method has a bias toward its own implicit or explicit model of outlier determination. A vari-

ety of datasets are needed to explore the differing biases and to develop an understanding of the appropriateness of each method for particular characteristics of data sets.

The statistical outlier detection literature considers three qualitative outlier categories: *cluster outliers* occur in small low variance clusters (where low variance is relative to the variance of the bulk of the data); *radial outliers* occur in a plane out from the major axis of the bulk of the data (if the bulk of data occurs in an elongated ellipse then radial outliers will lie on the major axis of that ellipse separated from and less densely packed than the bulk of data); *scattered outliers* occur randomly scattered about the bulk of data.

The datasets contain different combinations of outliers from these categories. We refer to the proportion of outliers in a data set as the *contamination level* of the data set and include datasets that exhibit different proportions of outliers. Statistical literature typically considers contamination levels of up to 40% whereas data mining literature typically considers contamination levels of much less ($< 4\%$), typical of the types of outliers in, for example, fraud (where it is even as low as 1% or less). Identifying 40% of a very large dataset as outliers is unlikely to provide useful insights into these rare, yet very significant, groups.

The datasets from the statistical literature and the data mining literature used in this paper are listed in Table 1.

Dataset	n	k	o	%	$\frac{n}{k}$	Description
HBK	75	4	14	21	19	Small cluster, some scattered.
Wood	20	6	4	20	3	Radial, small cluster.
Cancer	683	9	239	35	76	Scattered.
http	567497	3	2211	0.4	200K	Separate cluster.
smtp	95156	3	30	0.03	30K	Scattered, outlying.
ftp-data	30464	3	722	2	10K	Outlying cluster, some scattered.
other	5858	3	98	2	2K	Two clusters.
ftp	4091	3	316	8	1K	Scattered outlying and cluster.

Table 1. Statistical [14] and data mining outlier detection test datasets [2, 17]. Number of records = n, dimensions = k, outliers = o.

We can observe that outliers from the statistical datasets arise from measurement errors or data-entry errors, while the outliers in the selected data mining datasets are semantically distinct categories. Thus, for example, the breast cancer data has non-malignant and malignant measurements and the malignant measurements are viewed as outliers. The intrusion dataset identifies successful Internet intrusions. Intrusions are identified as exploiting one of the possible vulnerabilities, such as *http* and *ftp*. Successful intrusions are considered as outliers in these datasets.

It would have been preferable to include more data mining datasets for assessing outlier detection. The KDD intrusion dataset is included because it is publicly available and has been used previously in the data mining literature [17].

Knorr *et al.* [10] use NHL player statistics but refer only to a web site publishing these statistics, not the actual dataset used. Most other data mining papers use simulation studies rather than real world datasets.[1]

5. Experimental Results

We discuss here results from a selection of the test datasets we have employed to evaluate the performance of the RNN approach to outlier detection. Detailed results are available from the authors [15].

5.1. HBK

The HBK dataset is artificially constructed [7] with 14 outliers. Regression approaches tend to find only the first 10 as outliers. Data points 1-10 are "bad leverage" points—they lie far away from the centre of the good points and from the regression plane. Data points 11-14 are good leverage points—although they lie far away from the bulk of the data they lie close to the regression plane.

Donoho-Stahel and Hadi94 rank the 14 outliers in the top 14 places and the distance measures dramatically distinguish the outliers from the remainder of the records. MML clustering does less well, identifying the scattered outliers but missing the outlier records occurring in a compact cluster. Their compact occurrence leads to a small description length. RNN has the 14 outliers in the top 16 places and has placed all the true outliers in a single cluster.

5.2. Wood Data

The Wood dataset consists of 20 observations [3] with data points 4, 6, 8, and 19 being outliers [14]. The outliers are said not to be easily identifiable by observation [14].

We found that Donoho-Stahel clearly identifies the four outlier records, while Hadi94, RNN and MML all struggle to identify them. The difference between Donoho-Stahel and Hadi94 is interesting and can be explained by their different estimates of scatter (or covariance). Donoho-Stahel's estimate of covariance is more compact (leading to a smaller ellipsoid around the estimated data centre). This result empirically suggests Donoho-Stahel's improved robustness with high dimensional datasets relative to Hadi94. MML clustering has considerable difficulty in identifying the outliers according to description length and it ranks the true outliers last! MML clustering puts the outlier records in their own low variance cluster and so the records are described easily at low information cost. Identifying outliers by rank using data description length with MML clustering

does not work for low variance *cluster* outliers. For RNN, the cluster membership column again allows an interpretation of what has happened. Most of the data belong to a single cluster, while the outliers belong to various other clusters. Similarly to MML clustering, the outliers can, however, be identified by interpreting the clusters.

5.3. Wisconsin Breast Cancer Dataset

Our initial exploration of this dataset found that all the methods except Donoho-Stahel have little difficulty identifying the outliers. So we sampled the original dataset to generate datasets with differing contamination levels (number of malignant observations) ranging from 8.07% to 35% to investigate the performance of the methods with differing contamination levels. We found that the performance of Hadi94 degrades as the level of contamination increases, as one would expect. The results for the MML clustering method and the RNN method track the Hadi94 method closely. The Donoho-Stahel method does not do any better than a random ranking of the outlyingness of the data. Investigating further we find that the robust estimate of location and scatter is quite different to that of Hadi94 and obviously less successful.

5.4. Network Intrusion Detection

The network intrusion dataset comes from the 1999 KDD Cup network intrusion detection competition [1]. We follow the experimental technique employed in [17] to construct suitable datasets for outlier detection and to rank all data points with an outlier measure.

The dataset is divided into five subsets according to the five values of the *service* variable (*other*, *http*, *smtp*, *ftp*, and *ftp-data*). The aim is to identify intrusions within each of the categories by identifying outliers.

For the *other* dataset we observed that half the attacks are occurring in a distinct outlying cluster, while the other half are embedded among normal events. For the *http* dataset intrusions occur in a small cluster separated from the bulk of the data. For the *smtp*, *ftp*, and *ftp-data* datasets most intrusions also appear quite separated from the bulk of the data.

For the *other* dataset RNN finds the first 40 outliers long before any of the other methods. All the methods need to see more than 60% of the observations before including 80 of the total (98) outliers in their rankings. This suggests there is low separation between the bulk of the data and the outliers. For the *http* dataset the performance of Donoho-Stahel, Hadi94 and RNN cannot be distinguished. MML clustering needs to see an extra 10% of the data before including all the intrusions. For the *smtp* dataset the performances of Donoho-Stahel, Hadi94 and MML trend very

---

[1]A collection of data sets for outlier detection are available from http://datamining.csiro.au/outliers.

711

similarly while RNN needs to see nearly all of the data to identify the last 40% of the intrusions. For the *ftp* dataset the performances of Donoho-Stahel and Hadi94 trend very similarly. RNN needs to see $\approx 20\%$ more of the data to identify most of the intrusions. MML clustering does not do much better than random in ranking the intrusions above normal events. Only some intrusions are scattered, while the remainder lie in clusters of a similar shape to the normal events. Finally, for the *ftp-data* dataset Donoho-Stahel performs the best. RNN needs to see 20% more of the data. Hadi94 needs to see another 20% more. MML puts the intrusions in low variance clusters, where they have the shortest description length, and does not identify any scattered outliers with a high description length.

6. Discussion and Conclusion

The main contributions of this paper are:

- Empirical evaluation of the RNN approach for outlier detection;

- Using outlier categories: *cluster*, *radial* and *scattered* and contamination levels to characterise the difficulty of the outlier detection task for large data mining datasets (as well as the usual statistical test datasets).

- Understanding and categorising some publicly available benchmark datasets for testing outlier detection algorithms using outlier categories and contamination levels.

- Comparing the performance of three different outlier detection methods from the statistical and data mining literatures with RNN.

We conclude that the statistical outlier detection methods, Hadi94 and Donoho-Stahel, scale well and perform well on large and complex datasets. However they are parametric methods and lack the flexibility of non-parametric methods such as RNN and MML. MML clustering works well for *scattered* outliers and places *radial* and *cluster* outliers into their own clusters, requiring interpretation of clusters rather than a straight ranking based on an outlyingness measure.

The RNN method performed satisfactorily for both small and large datasets. It was of interest that it performed well on the small datasets since neural network methods often have difficulty with such smaller datasets. Its performance appears to degrade with datasets containing *radial* outliers and so it is not recommended for this type of dataset. RNN performed the best overall on the KDD intrusion dataset.

References

[1] 1999 KDD Cup competition. `http://kdd.ics.uci.edu/databases/kddcup99/kddcup99.html`.

[2] S. D. Bay. The UCI KDD repository, 1999. `http://kdd.ics.uci.edu`.

[3] N. R. Draper and H. Smith. *Applied Regression Analysis*. John Wiley and Sons, New York, 1966.

[4] W. DuMouchel and M. Schonlau. A fast computer intrusion detection algorithm based on hypothesis testing of command transition probabilities. In *Proc. of the 4th Int. Conf. on Knowledge Discovery and Data Mining (KDD98)*, pages 189–193, 1998.

[5] T. Fawcett and F. Provost. Adaptive fraud detection. *Data Mining and Knowledge Discovery*, 1(3):291–316, 1997.

[6] A. Hadi. A modification of a method for the detection of outliers in multivariate samples. *Journal of the Royal Statistical Society, B*, 56(2), 1994.

[7] D. M. Hawkins, D. Bradu, and G. V. Kass. Location of several outliers in multiple regression data using elemental sets. *Technometrics*, 26:197–208, 1984.

[8] S. Hawkins, H. X. He, G. J. Williams, and R. A. Baxter. Outlier detection using replicator neural networks. In *Proc. of the Fifth Int. Conf. and Data Warehousing and Knowledge Discovery (DaWaK02)*, 2002.

[9] E. Knorr, R. Ng, and V. Tucakov. Distance-based outliers: Algorithms and applications. *Very Large Data Bases*, 8(3–4):237–253, 2000.

[10] E. M. Knorr, R. T. Ng, and R. H. Zamar. Robust space transformations for distance-based operations. In *Proc. of the 7th Int. Conf. on Knowledge Discovery and Data Mining (KDD01)*, pages 126–135, 2001.

[11] A. S. Kosinksi. A procedure for the detection of multivariate outliers. *Com. Stat. & Data Analysis*, 29, 1999.

[12] J. J. Oliver, R. A. Baxter, and C. S. Wallace. Unsupervised Learning using MML. In *Proc. of the Thirteenth Int. Conf. (ICML 96)*, pages 364–372. Morgan Kaufmann Publishers, San Francisco, CA, 1996.

[13] D. E. Rocke and D. L. Woodruff. Identification of outliers in multivariate data. *Journal of the American Statistical Association*, 91:1047–1061, 1996.

[14] P. J. Rousseeuw and A. M. Leroy. *Robust Regression and Outlier Detection*. John Wiley & Sons, Inc., New York, 1987.

[15] G. Williams, R. Baxter, H. He, S. Hawkins, and L. Gu. A comparative study of RNN for outlier detection in data mining. Technical Report 02/102, CSIRO Mathematical and Information Sciences, 2002. http://datamining.csiro.au/papers/tr02102.pdf.

[16] G. J. Williams and Z. Huang. Mining the knowledge mine: The hot spots methodology for mining large real world databases. In A. Sattar, editor, *Advanced Topics in Artificial Intelligence*, volume 1342 of *Lecture Notes in Artificial Intelligenvce*, pages 340–348. Springer, 1997.

[17] K. Yamanishi, J. Takeuchi, G. J. Williams, and P. W. Milne. On-line unsupervised outlier detection using finite mixtures with discounting learning algorithm. In *Proc. of the 6th Int. Conf. on Knowledge Discovery and Data Mining (KDD00)*, pages 320–324, 2000.

Evaluating the Utility of Statistical Phrases and Latent Semantic Indexing for Text Classification

Huiwen Wu   Dimitrios Gunopulos
Computer Science & Engineering Department
University of California
Riverside, CA, 92521
{hwu, dg@cs.ucr.edu}

Abstract

The term-based vector space model is a prominent technique to retrieve textual information. In this paper we examine the usefulness of phrases as terms in vector-based document classification. We focus on statistical techniques to extract both adjacent and window phrases from documents. We discover that the positive effect of adding phrase terms is very limited, if we have already achieved good performance using single-word terms, even when SVD/LSI is used as dimensionality reduction method.

1. Introduction

The term-based vector space model is a prominent technique to retrieve textual information. The decision of appropriate "terms" in the vector as well as their weights is the most crucial step in the retrieval process, and can affect the retrieval accuracy drastically.

Phrases have intuitively been regarded as complex "terms" that should supply more information than single-word terms to increase the accuracy of text data retrieval. However, recent research shows that it is not the case. Some experimental results show that phrase-based terms may improve the effectiveness of retrieval, but only marginally. [2, 8] applied statistical phrases as entities in automatic text indexing procedures, and showed that the improvement of average precision ranged from -11.5% to +20.1%. [6] compared the usefulness of phrases from both statistical technique and syntactic methods, while [10] only examined the statistical phrases generated from non-NLP in vector-based retrieval. Both reported that phrases don't have major effect on precision. In [9], it was also reported that the overall retrieval performance of the phrases as search terms is reduced over the whole ranking.

In this paper, we analyze the impact of single-word terms and two-word (phrase) terms in text classification. We build two text classifier systems, DocClassifier and SVDClassifier, to evaluate the usefulness of phrase terms. Both systems use linear SVM to classify document from Reuters-21578 corpus. Each document is represented using single-word terms with or without phrase terms. The difference of two systems is that they use different dimensionality reduction methods for feature selection.

We also attempt to find a scheme to adjust the weight of phrase terms, since assigning an appropriate weight is critical in term-based statistical methods. The main contributions of this paper are:

- We perform a very general experiment to compare the effect of phrase terms with that of single-word term in a number of dimensionality reduction techniques.
- We evaluate window phrases and adjacent phrases, and show that window phrases have poorer performance than adjacent phrases.

The rest of the paper is organized as follows: In section 2, we introduce some backgrounds of our research. In section 3, we describe our two systems. And section 4 shows how we find phrases from documents. The concrete experimental setup, measures and results analysis are shown in section 5. Section 6 concludes the paper.

2. Background

Feature Representation (FR): A document is represented by a vector consisting of a number of features. Each feature is a representation of one term from a dictionary, which is built by analyzing training documents. There are various methods to represent a term, including term frequency (TF), TF multiplied by the inverse document frequency (TF-IDF), and binary representation (BR) [1].

Feature Selection (FS): It is highly desirable to reduce the size of the huge dictionary without sacrificing classification accuracy. Many feature selection techniques have been examined in [4, 5, 12]. We can calculate the document frequency (DF) or the information gain (IG) [1] for each term. Then a threshold is used to remove the less informative terms from the dictionary.

Latent Semantic Indexing (LSI): The goal of LSI is to extract the hidden semantic information behind the visible representation of a document. The key idea is to transform the original $m*n$ term-document matrix A to a $k*n$ factor-document matrix with $k<<m$. The mapping is computed by truncated SVD. First, we calculate $SVD(A) = U\Sigma V^T$. Then

we set all elements but the first k largest singular values in Σ to zero and get Σ_k. The LSI approximation of A is defined as $A_k = U\Sigma_k V^T$, which is rank-k optimal in the sense of both Frobenius norm and L_2 norm. Now that we have Σ_k and U_k (the first k columns of U), we can represent a document d in k-dimension latent space using $d_k^T = d^T U_k \Sigma_k^{-1}$. Compared to the original term vector space, the reduced latent semantic space is more accurate to estimate the similarity of documents due to the noise reduction nature of truncated SVD.

Support Vector Machine (SVM): SVMs are based on the Structural Risk Minimization principle from the computational learning theory. Recently they have been gaining popularity in text learning community [1, 4, 11, 13]. The idea is to find a hypothesis h to separate positive examples from negative examples with maximum margin [3]. In linear SVM, we use $w \bullet x - b = 0$ to represent the hyper-plane, where the normal vector w and constant b are learned parameters, x is the input vector. The margin is defined by the distance from the hyper-plane to the nearest positive and negative examples. Suppose we have the training set $T = \{x_i, y_i\}$, where x_i is the vector representation of the example and $y_i = 1$ or -1 stands for the positive or negative example. Now the problem is to find w and b that maximize the margin, or minimize $\|w\|$ subject to the constraint $y_i(w \bullet x_i - b) \geq 1$. Once we have the learned vector w and constant b, we can classify new test case x by checking if $w \bullet x - b > 0$ is true or false.

3. Methods

We design two text classification systems: DocClassifier and SVDClassifier, They are based on the same linear SVM learning machine, but with different format of document vector.

DocClassifier: We compare the effectiveness of single-word terms with that of phrase terms using different document vector formats: vector of single-word terms, vector of single-word terms and adjacent phrases, or vector of single-word terms and window phrases.

The system works as the following steps:

1) Scan the training documents to build the single-word dictionary, with preprocessing techniques like word stemming and stop-list word removal.
2) Represent each document as a vector using one combination of FR (TF, TF-IDF or BR) and FS (DF or IG) method; normalize the vector.
3) Scan the training documents again to generate the adjacent phrase dictionary; represent each document as a normalized adjacent phrase vector.
4) Represent each document as a normalized window phrase vector (see section 4).

5) Combine the single-word vector with the adjacent or window phrase vector using different phrase weight ([0, 1]) to get a mixed document vector.
6) Using SVM to train and test the classifier.

SVDClassifier: To further examine the usefulness of phrases in text retrieval, we apply the LSI dimensionality reduction technique to reduce the size of document vector before training the SVM. For the objective comparisons, we perform similar operations in SVDClassifier as in DocClassifier. The main difference is the feature selection method. In step 2), we apply SVD directly to the single word term-document matrix, without any FS methods like DF or IG. However, although SVD can handle large matrices, it is still necessary to eliminate some phrases from the original huge phrase dictionary. We use the IG selection method in step 3) to eliminate phrases before applying SVD to phrase term-document matrix.

4. Finding Phrases

In [2, 6, 8, 9, 10], phrases are applied to queries, and thus documents are not the only resource of the phrases. However, in both of our systems, all phrases are extracted from training documents. We only consider two-word phrases extracted using statistical techniques.

Adjacent Phrases: The adjacent phrase dictionary is extracted from training documents (after word stemming and stoplist word removal) using a simple statistical technique [6]. An adjacent phrase consists of two contiguous non-function words whose DFs are larger than or at least equal to a predefined threshold. The further operations on phrase term are all based on this original phrase dictionary.

Window Phrases: The window operation is used to explore more informative phrase terms. In our systems, if the distance between any two words is smaller than the predefined window size, we will check their DFs. If both of them have DFs larger than a predefined threshold, we will check if this phrase is an existing adjacent phrase. To extract more informative phrases, the adjacent phrase dictionary is first shrinked by IG before being checked. If this shrink dictionary contains the phrase, it is named a window phrase. Note that two phrases with same words and different word order are not identical, i.e., Phrase(A,B) $\neq$ Phrase(B,A).

When we extract window-phrases from documents, we only choose those that already exist in the shrink adjacent phrase dictionary. The reason is that the shrink adjacent phrase dictionary contains more informative phrases, which lead to more accurate result. Another reason is that if a two-word phrase is meaningful, it is more likely that two words appear adjacently than they appear in distance. So, if a window phrase is informative, it is very likely that it also appears in the shrink adjacent phrase dictionary.

Table 1. Performance summary

Exp	Num	Feature	Prep	Norm	FS	FR	miR	miP	miF1
1	6	Single	No	No	**IG**	**BR**	.7843	.8538	.8176
2	6	Single	Yes	No	**IG**	**BR**	.7948	.8680	.8298
3	6	Single	Yes	Yes	**IG**	**TF-IDF**	**.7988**	.8955	.8444
4	24	Single+Adj.Phrase(**0.5**)	Yes	Yes	**IG**	**TF-IDF**	.7948	.8953	.8421
5	24	Single+Win.Phrase(**0.5**)	Yes	Yes	**IG**	**TF-IDF**	.7945	.8945	.8415
a	9	Single	Yes	No	SVD(**300**)	**TF-IDF**	.7252	.8673	.7899
b	9	Single	Yes	Yes	SVD(**300**)	**TF-IDF**	.7862	.9056	.8417
c	36	Single+Adj.Phrase(**0.5**)	Yes	Yes	SVD(**300**)	**TF-IDF**	.7862	.9123	**.8449**
d	36	Single+Win.Phrase(**0.5**)	Yes	Yes	SVD(**300**)	**TF-IDF**	.7827	**.9138**	.8432

Num: the number of runs in this experiment series.
Feature: single-word only, or with adjacent phrase, or with window phrase. (phrase weight=1.0, 0.75, 0.5, or 0.25).
Prep(preprocessing): with or without word stemming and stop-list word removal.
Norm(normalization): with or without normalization. We normalize single-word vector and phrase vector separately.
FS(feature selection): DF or IG for DocClassifier; IG and SVD for SVDClassifier(factor = 100, 200, or 300).
FR(feature representation): TF, TF-IDF, or BR.

The weight of phrase term is another interesting issue to be considered. Suppose we have a selected phrase (i.e., it appears in the shrink adjacent phrase dictionary) with both of its components appearing in the shrink single-word dictionary. If the phrase weights equally to the single-word, the effect of these two component words will be doubled. How to adjust the phrase weight remains an open problem.

5. Experiments

Experiments Setup: We use Reuters-21578 corpus as our dataset. It collects in total of 21578 documents in 135 topics, with 9603 training documents and 3299 testing documents. We train and test SVMs using training and testing documents respectively. Our dictionaries are constructed only from the training dataset. The size of single-word dictionary is 19907 words. In DocClassifier, it is shrinked to 303 words by DF or 299 words by IG. The adjacent phrase dictionary has 244077 phrases, with a word DF threshold of 5. It is shrinked by IG to 21571 first. This shrink (adjacent) phrase dictionary is used in window phrase extraction and in SVDClassifier. While in DocClassifier, it is shrinked to a much smaller one of 203 phrases by DF or 201 by IG. For window phrase, we use a window size of 10 and minimal word DF equals to 5. To compare the effectiveness of single word and phrase objectively, it is necessary to use the same set of parameters for all the experiments.

Measures: We use micro average of recall, precision, and F1 as our measures [13]. Define:

B = number of positive documents found and correct;
C = number of misclassified positive documents;
D = number of misclassified negative documents;
Micro averaging recall: $miR = B / (B + C)$;
Micro averaging precision: $miP = B / (B + D)$;

Micro averaging F1: $miF1 = 2*miP*miR / (miR + miP)$.

Results and Discussion: We perform 9 experiment series, 5 in DocClassifier (exp 1-5) and 4 in SVDClassifier (exp a-d) (Table 1). Each series contains several runs using different options. From Table 1, we can obtain all the best result in each series. In DocClassifier, it shows that IG is better than DF for feature selection, and TF-IDF is the best feature representation method with vector normalization. Normalizing vector improves the retrieval accuracy dramatically in both systems.

Table 2 shows the comparisons between those best runs from statistical significance test view. We compare 13 pairs of runs in 9 experiment series using macro level s-test (sign test) and t-test [13]. P-value indicates if group A is better (or worse) than group B. We cannot conclude that phrase terms make significant improvement.

Table 2. Statistical significance test

GroupA	1	2	3	3	4	a	b	b	c	2	3	4	5
GroupB	2	3	4	5	5	b	c	d	d	a	b	c	d
s-test	<	<<	~	~	~	<<	~	~	~	>	~	~	~
t-test	~	~	~	~	~	<	~	~	~	~	~	~	~

"<<" means P-value ≤ 0.01; "~" means P-value > 0.05
">" or "<" means 0.01<P-value ≤ 0.05

We find that once the single word terms have already achieved a good performance, adding phrase terms can not make enhancement as they should be intuitively. The performance would be even worse if the phrase weight is inappropriate. Like the results of many works on phrases [2, 6, 7, 9, 10], we also discover that phrases make recall decreased on average (Figure 1). However, phrases in SVDClassifier can make improvement, although it is not significant. Table 1 and Figure 1 prove that phrases are only

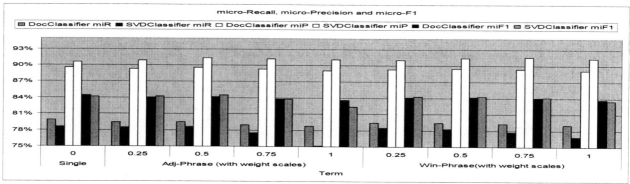

Figure 1. Comparison of overall performance with miRecall, miPrecision and miF1

auxiliary factor compared with single word terms. Window phrases are even worse than adjacent phrases. The reason is that meaningful phrases occurring apart have much less frequency than they occur adjacent. In DocClassifier, the number of phrases is reduced from 244077 to 201, so that the final document vector space is very sparse and thus contains lots of noise. However, in SVDClassifier, all phrases in vector before using SVD have contributions on the final selected phrases after SVD dimensionality reduction. Phrases still keep more information after SVD/LSI method than after feature selection method. Figure 1 also shows that with phrases as search terms, SVDClassifier performs better on precision and F1 than DocClassifier.

The phrase weight is another interesting and important issue. In our systems, a phrase weight of 0.5 leads to better performance. On the other hand, for micro-averaging recall, we find that the higher phrase weight is, the poorer the performance becomes. However, SVD/LSI with weighted adjacent phrases can make improvements in *mi*F1 and *mi*Precision, but not significantly.

6. Conclusions

We investigate the important issues of using phrase terms for textual information retrieval, i.e., phrase extraction, phrase representation and phrase weight.

Our empirical study shows that comparing with IG and DF, SVD/LSI has better performance working with phrase terms. However, phrases obtained by statistical techniques are not always useful on average. In some experiments like in SVDClassifier, they can improve precision with proper phrase definition and weight. We also come to the following conclusions:

- Useful phrases occur much less frequently than useful words; phrases thus don't have a major effect as search terms in vector space.
- Window phrases are less effective than adjacent phrases in our experiments, although they improve precision.

7. References

1. H. Drucker, D. Wu, and V.N.Vapnik. Support vector machines for spam categorization. *IEEE Trans. on Neural Networks*, 10(5):1048-- 1054, 1999.
2. J. L. Fagan. The effectiveness of a nonsyntactic approach automatic phrase indexing for document retrieval. *Journal of the American Society for Information Science*, 40(2):115-132, 1989.
3. M. A. Hearst. Trends & controversies: Support vector machines. *IEEE intelligent system*, 13(4):18-28, July/August 1998.
4. T. Joachims. Text categorization with support vector machines: Learning with many relevant features. *Technical Report 23*, University of Dortmund, LS VIII, 1997.
5. D. Mladenic, M. Grobelnik. Feature selection for unbalanced class distribution and Naïve Bayes. *ICML 1999*, pp.258-267.
6. M. Mitra, C. Buckley, A. Singhal, and C. Cardie. An analysis of statistical and syntactic phrases. In *Proceedings of RIAO97, Computer-Assisted Information Searching on the Internet*, pages 200-214, Montreal, Canada, June 1997.
7. M. Narita and Y. Ogawa. The use of phrases from query texts in information retrieval. In *Proceedings of SIGIR'2000*, Athens, Greece, July 2000.
8. G. Salton, C. S. Yang, and C. T. Yu. A theory of term importance in automatic text analysis. *Journal of the American Society for Information Science*, 26(1): 33-44, 1975.
9. F. Smeaton and F. Kelledy. User-chosen phrases in interactive query formulation for information retrieval. In *Proceedings of the 20th BCS-IRSG Colloquium, Springer-Verlag Electronic Workshops in Computing*, Grenoble, France, April 1998.
10. Turpin and A. Moffat. Statistical phrases for vector-space information retrieval. In *Proceedings of SIGIR'99*, Berkley, CA, USA, August, 1999.
11. D. Wu and V. N. Vapnik. Support vector machine for text categorization.
12. Y. Yang and J. P. Pedersen. A comparative study on feature selection in text categorization. In: Jr. D. H. Fisher (Eds.), *The 14th International Conference on Machine Learning*, pages 412-420, Morgan Kaufmann, 1997.
13. Y. Yang and X. Liu. A re-examination of text categorization methods. In *Proceedings of SIGIR'99*, Berkley, CA, USA, August, 1999.

Mixtures of ARMA Models for Model-Based Time Series Clustering *

Yimin Xiong   Dit-Yan Yeung
Department of Computer Science, Hong Kong University of Science and Technology
Clear Water Bay, Kowloon, Hong Kong

Abstract

Clustering problems are central to many knowledge discovery and data mining tasks. However, most existing clustering methods can only work with fixed-dimensional representations of data patterns. In this paper, we study the clustering of data patterns that are represented as sequences or time series possibly of different lengths. We propose a model-based approach to this problem using mixtures of autoregressive moving average (ARMA) models. We derive an expectation-maximization (EM) algorithm for learning the mixing coefficients as well as the parameters of the component models. Experiments were conducted on simulated and real datasets. Results show that our method compares favorably with another method recently proposed by others for similar time series clustering problems.

1. Introduction

Clustering is the unsupervised process of grouping data patterns into clusters so that patterns within a cluster bear strong similarity to one another but are very dissimilar to patterns in other clusters. Clustering problems are central to many knowledge discovery and data mining tasks. Many clustering techniques have been studied for data patterns that are represented as points in multidimensional spaces of fixed dimensionality. In this paper, we deal with sequential patterns such as sequences and time series possibly of different lengths.

Distance-based methods and *model-based* methods are two major classes of clustering methods. They are analogous to other nonparametric and parametric methods, respectively, in that the former category (i.e., distance-based or nonparametric methods) assumes only some weak structure of the data, but the latter category (i.e., model-based or parametric methods) assumes some strong structure. For time series data, model-based methods provide a principled

---

*A longer version of this paper can be found in `http://www.cs.ust.hk/faculty/dyyeung/paper/ps/yeung.icdm2002long.ps`.

approach for handling the problem of modeling and clustering time series of different lengths. In this paper, we will focus on model-based time series clustering methods. In particular, *mixture models* [9] will be used.

2. Related work

Finite mixtures of Markov chains [2] have been proposed for clustering time series. The *expectation-maximization* (EM) algorithm [3] is used to learn the mixing coefficients as well as the parameters of the component models. The number of clusters can be determined by comparing different choices of the number based on some scoring scheme. Another approach to the clustering of time series modeled by Markov chains is called Bayesian clustering by dynamics (BCD) [12] which can best be seen as a hybrid approach with both model-based and distance-based flavors.

While simple Markov chains are good enough for some applications, some time series can be modeled better using *hidden Markov models* (HMM) [11] due to their ability of handling temporal and spatial uncertainties simultaneously. Finite mixtures of HMMs have been studied. Similar to mixtures of Markov chains, the EM algorithm can also be used for HMM mixtures [14, 8]. To trade accuracy for efficiency, the k-means algorithm (used in [10]) and the rival penalized competitive learning (RPCL) algorithm (used in [7]) have also been used in place of EM.

In addition to Markov chains and HMMs, *autoregressive moving average* (ARMA) and *autoregressive integrated moving average* (ARIMA) models have also been used extensively for time series analysis [1]. Kwok *et al.* [6] applied mixtures of ARMA models as well as their special cases, mixtures of autoregressive (AR) models, for time series modeling and forecasting. However, clustering applications based on such mixture models were not studied by them. More recently, a method was proposed by Kalpakis *et al.* for clustering ARIMA time series [5]. This method is similar to the BCD method in that it is a hybrid method with both model-based and distance-based characteristics.

In the next section, we will propose a new time series clustering method based on mixtures of ARMA models.

3. Mixtures of ARMA models

The ARIMA model introduced by Box and Jenkins [1] is a combination of three types of time series data processes, namely, autoregressive, integrated, and moving average processes. A stationary ARIMA model with autoregressive order p and moving average order q is commonly denoted as ARMA(p, q). Given a time series $\mathbf{x} = \{x_t\}_{t=1}^n$, the fitted ARMA$(p, q)$ model takes the form

$$x_t = \phi_0 + \sum_{j=1}^p \phi_j x_{t-j} + \sum_{j=1}^q \theta_j e_{t-j} + e_t, \quad t = 1, 2, \ldots, n,$$

where n is the length of the time series, ϕ_0 is a constant term, $\{\phi_1, \phi_2, \ldots, \phi_p, \theta_1, \theta_2, \ldots, \theta_q\}$ is the set of AR(p) and MA(q) coefficients, and $\{e_t\}_{t=1}^n$ is a sequence of independent and identically distributed (IID) Gaussian white noise terms with variance σ^2. From [1], we can express the natural logarithm of the conditional likelihood function as

$$\ln P(\mathbf{x}|\boldsymbol{\Phi}) = -\frac{n}{2}\ln(2\pi) - \frac{n}{2}\ln(\sigma^2) - \frac{1}{2\sigma^2}\sum_{t=1}^n e_t^2,$$

where $\boldsymbol{\Phi} = \{\phi_0, \phi_1, \phi_2, \ldots, \phi_p, \theta_1, \theta_2, \ldots, \theta_q, \sigma^2\}$ is the set of all model parameters and e_t must be estimated recursively.

We now extend standard ARMA models to mixtures of ARMA models, or simply called ARMA mixtures, for time series clustering. Let us assume that the time series data are generated by M different ARMA models, which correspond to the M clusters of interest denoted as $\omega_1, \omega_2, \ldots, \omega_M$. Let $P(\mathbf{x}|\omega_k, \boldsymbol{\Phi}_k)$ denote the conditional likelihood function or density function of component model k, with $\boldsymbol{\Phi}_k$ being the set of parameters for the model. Let $P(\omega_k)$ be the prior probability that a time series comes from model k. The conditional likelihood function of the mixture model can be expressed in the form of a mixture density as $P(\mathbf{x}|\boldsymbol{\Theta}) = \sum_{k=1}^M P(\mathbf{x}|\omega_k, \boldsymbol{\Phi}_k)P(\omega_k)$, where $\boldsymbol{\Theta} = \{\boldsymbol{\Phi}_1, \boldsymbol{\Phi}_2, \ldots, \boldsymbol{\Phi}_M, P(\omega_1), P(\omega_2), \ldots, P(\omega_M)\}$ represents the set of all model parameters for the mixture model. For a time series $\mathbf{x}$, it is assigned to cluster ω_k with posterior probability $P(\omega_k|\mathbf{x})$, where $\sum_{k=1}^M P(\omega_k|\mathbf{x}) = 1$.

Suppose we are given a set $\mathbf{D} = \{\mathbf{x}_1, \mathbf{x}_2, \ldots, \mathbf{x}_N\}$ of N time series. Under the usual assumption that different time series are conditionally independent given the underlying model parameters, we can express the likelihood of $\mathbf{D}$ as $P(\mathbf{D}|\boldsymbol{\Theta}) = \prod_{i=1}^N P(\mathbf{x}_i|\boldsymbol{\Theta})$. Model parameter learning amounts to finding the *maximum a posteriori* (MAP) parameter estimate given the data set $\mathbf{D}$, i.e., $\widehat{\boldsymbol{\Theta}} = \arg\max_{\boldsymbol{\Theta}} [P(\mathbf{D}|\boldsymbol{\Theta})P(\boldsymbol{\Theta})]$. If we take a noninformative prior on $\boldsymbol{\Theta}$, learning degenerates to *maximum likelihood estimation* (MLE), i.e., $\widehat{\boldsymbol{\Theta}} = \arg\max_{\boldsymbol{\Theta}} P(\mathbf{D}|\boldsymbol{\Theta})$. This MLE problem can be solved efficiently using EM, which will be discussed in detail in the next section.

4. EM learning algorithm

The EM algorithm is an iterative approach to MLE or MAP estimation problems with incomplete data. It has been widely used for many applications, including clustering and mixture density estimation problems [13].

The likelihood of $\mathbf{D}$ can be rewritten as a function of the parameter vector $\boldsymbol{\Theta}$ for a given data set $\mathbf{D}$, i.e., $L(\boldsymbol{\Theta}; \mathbf{D}) = P(\mathbf{D}|\boldsymbol{\Theta}) = \prod_{i=1}^N P(\mathbf{x}_i|\boldsymbol{\Theta})$. Assuming a noninformative prior on $\boldsymbol{\Theta}$, the goal of the EM algorithm is to find $\boldsymbol{\Theta}$ that maximizes the likelihood $L(\boldsymbol{\Theta}; \mathbf{D})$ or the log-likelihood $\ell(\boldsymbol{\Theta}; \mathbf{D}) = \sum_{i=1}^N \ln P(\mathbf{x}_i|\boldsymbol{\Theta})$.

Since $\mathbf{D}$ is the incomplete data, we assume the missing data to be $\mathbf{Z} = \{\mathbf{z}_1, \mathbf{z}_2, \ldots, \mathbf{z}_N\}$, such that $\mathbf{D}$ and $\mathbf{Z}$ form the complete data $(\mathbf{D}, \mathbf{Z})$. Thus the complete-data log-likelihood function is $\ln P(\mathbf{D}, \mathbf{Z}|\boldsymbol{\Theta})$. If we knew the missing data (and hence the complete data), parameter estimation would be straightforward. Without knowing the missing data, however, the EM algorithm has to iterate between the Expectation step (E-step) and the Maximization step (M-step). In the E-step, we calculate the expected value $Q(\boldsymbol{\Theta}|\boldsymbol{\Theta}(t))$ of the complete-data log-likelihood with respect to the unknown data $\mathbf{Z}$ given the observed data $\mathbf{D}$ and the current parameter estimate $\boldsymbol{\Theta}(t)$, i.e., $Q(\boldsymbol{\Theta}|\boldsymbol{\Theta}(t)) = E[\ln P(\mathbf{D}, \mathbf{Z}|\boldsymbol{\Theta}) | \mathbf{D}, \boldsymbol{\Theta}(t)]$. In the M-step, we try to maximize $Q(\boldsymbol{\Theta}|\boldsymbol{\Theta}(t))$ with respect to $\boldsymbol{\Theta}$ to find the new parameter estimate $\boldsymbol{\Theta}(t+1)$.

In the context of using ARMA mixtures for clustering, the missing data correspond to the unknown cluster or group membership of each time series $\mathbf{x}_i$. The log-likelihood $\ell(\boldsymbol{\Theta}; \mathbf{D})$ can thus be expressed as $\ell(\boldsymbol{\Theta}; \mathbf{D}) = \sum_{i=1}^N \ln P(\mathbf{x}_i|\omega_{\mathbf{z}_i}, \boldsymbol{\Phi}_{\mathbf{z}_i}) + \sum_{i=1}^N \ln P(\omega_{\mathbf{z}_i})$. Given the observed data $\mathbf{D}$ and the current parameter estimate $\boldsymbol{\Theta}(t)$, the expectation of the complete-data log-likelihood becomes

$$Q(\boldsymbol{\Theta}|\boldsymbol{\Theta}(t)) = \sum_{i=1}^N \sum_{k=1}^M P(\omega_k|\mathbf{x}_i, \boldsymbol{\Theta}(t)) \ln P(\mathbf{x}_i|\omega_k, \boldsymbol{\Phi}_k)$$
$$+ \sum_{i=1}^N \sum_{k=1}^M P(\omega_k|\mathbf{x}_i, \boldsymbol{\Theta}(t)) \ln P(\omega_k).$$

The EM algorithm iteratively maximizes $Q(\boldsymbol{\Theta}|\boldsymbol{\Theta}(t))$ until convergence. For each iteration, we compute the posterior probabilities $P(\omega_k|\mathbf{x}_i, \boldsymbol{\Theta}(t))$ and $Q(\boldsymbol{\Theta}|\boldsymbol{\Theta}(t))$ using the current parameter estimate $\boldsymbol{\Theta}(t)$ in the E-step, and update the parameter estimate by maximizing $Q(\boldsymbol{\Theta}|\boldsymbol{\Theta}(t))$ with respect to $\boldsymbol{\Theta}$ to obtain $\boldsymbol{\Theta}(t+1)$ in the M-step.

5. Results on simulated datasets

As in [5], experiments were conducted on both simulated and real datasets. Instead of handling ARIMA time series directly, a preprocessing step of differencing was first applied to convert each nonstationary ARIMA time series into the corresponding stationary ARMA time series. Moreover, as discussed in [1], ARMA models can be converted into equivalent AR models. Thus, for simplicity, we in fact used mixtures of AR models in all our experiments, although the EM algorithm presented above can be used for general ARMA mixtures.

The cluster similarity measure [4] was used to evaluate and compare the clustering results obtained by Kalpakis *et al.*'s method (abbreviated in the tables below as CEP for cepstral coefficients) and our method (abbreviated as MAR for mixtures of AR models).

We first study the simpler scenario with simulated time series data generated by a known number of AR models. We consider two cases separately. The first case involves AR models with the same noise variance, and the second case involves AR models with different noise variances.

In the first experiment, we used two AR(1) models with their AR coefficients uniformly distributed in the ranges (0.30 ± 0.01) and (0.60 ± 0.01), respectively. The noise variance was 0.01 for both models. Each model generated 15 time series to form the dataset. As expected, both our MAR method and the CEP method worked very well because the two groups of time series are easily separable. The cluster similarity measure was always equal to 1.

We further conducted more experiments on time series generated by two closer AR(1) models. As before, the AR coefficient of one model was uniformly distributed in the range (0.30 ± 0.01), but that for the other model was set to four different ranges in four different experiments, varying from (0.55 ± 0.01) to (0.40 ± 0.01). In each experiment, each model generated 15 time series to form the dataset. Both methods were run 10 times on each dataset. The minimum, average, and maximum values of the cluster similarity measure over 10 trials were recorded. Table 1 summarizes the results obtained by the two methods. Our method is slightly better than CEP when the two AR(1) models are farther from each other, but CEP becomes slightly better when the range of AR coefficient of one model decreases to (0.40 ± 0.01), which is very close to that of the other model.

We repeated the experiments above under the same setup, except that the two AR(1) models had the same AR coefficient distribution range of (0.30 ± 0.01) but different noise variances of 0.01 and 0.02, respectively. Our method gives perfect clustering of the two groups of time series, but CEP, which makes no use of the noise variances, gives very poor results on this dataset with the cluster similarity values being $(0.51/0.59/0.67)$.

In the experiments above the number of component models was specified in advance. We further improve our algorithm by running the basic EM algorithm multiple times with an increasing number of component models until at

Table 1. Clustering results for time series generated by two AR(1) models with the same noise variance but different AR coefficient distribution ranges

Range of AR coefficient	Cluster similarity (min/avg/max)	
	MAR	CEP
(0.55 ± 0.01)	$(0.93/0.99/1.00)$	$(0.93/0.98/1.00)$
(0.50 ± 0.01)	$(0.83/0.93/0.97)$	$(0.80/0.93/0.97)$
(0.45 ± 0.01)	$(0.80/0.88/0.93)$	$(0.71/0.86/0.93)$
(0.40 ± 0.01)	$(0.63/0.77/0.90)$	$(0.63/0.79/0.93)$

least one redundant component model is found. When the number of component models specified is equal to or less than the actual number of clusters, the basic EM algorithm will converge. However, if the number of component models specified is larger than the actual number of clusters, the EM algorithm will not converge within a reasonably large number of iterations. Moreover, some component models will learn to become very similar to each other. Based on these characteristics, we can decide whether too many component models are specified. Hence the correct number of clusters can be determined and returned.

This set of experiments based on simulated datasets allows us to explore the strengths and weaknesses of the two methods under different controlled settings. While our method, like other EM-based methods, generally degrades in clustering performance when the underlying clusters are very close to each other, it is better than Kalpakis *et al.*'s distance-based method under more general situations. Specifically, our method is significantly better when the models have different noise variances. It is also more flexible in determining the number of clusters automatically.

6. Results on real datasets

For comparison, we conducted further experiments with the same four real datasets used by Kalpakis *et al.* [5]. The same preprocessing steps used by them were also applied to the datasets to remove the nonstationarity in the data. Moreover, due to differences in level and scale, a normalization step was applied to generate normalized data so that the time series values fall in the range $[0, 1]$. All the experiments were conducted on both normalized and unnormalized data. The cluster similarity values for the four real datasets are shown in Table 2.

Compared with the CEP method, our method can give the same (for two datasets) or better (for another two datasets) results when unnormalized data are used. Our method always works better on unnormalized data because

Table 2. Clustering results for real datasets

Dataset	Normalized		Unnormalized	
	MAR	CEP	MAR	CEP
Personal income	0.78	0.84	0.90	0.84
ECG	0.80	0.94	0.94	0.94
Temperature	0.58	0.65	1.00	0.65
Population	0.62	0.64	0.64	0.64

the variance information can be utilized in separating the clusters. However, both our method and the CEP method, due to their nature of modeling stationary ARMA processes only, do not learn the differences in trend of the time series and hence cannot give very satisfactory results for the population dataset. It should be noted, however, that the trends of the two groups of population time series are actually visually distinguishable. Extension of our method to address this issue will be discussed in the next section.

7. Conclusion and future work

In this paper, we have proposed a model-based method for clustering univariate ARIMA time series. This mixture-model method, based on mixtures of ARMA models, uses an EM algorithm to learn the mixing coefficients as well as the parameters of the component models. In addition, the number of clusters in the data can be determined automatically. Experimental results on both simulated and real datasets show that this method is generally effective in clustering time series, and that it compares favorably with the hybrid method proposed recently by Kalpakis *et al.* for similar time series clustering problems.

Our method can be improved in a number of aspects. One aspect is related to parameter initialization for the EM algorithm, which may affect the convergence speed of the algorithm and the quality of the solution found. Currently our method sets the initial prior probabilities of the clusters to be equal, and randomly picks M different time series to initialize the M component models. A possible improvement is to initialize the parameters of the mixture model based on the clustering results of some faster but less accurate method. This is analogous to the use of k-means for finding the initial parameter values for an EM algorithm.

Computational speedup can be achieved by pruning some models if their posterior probabilities become very close to 0, indicating that their significance is negligible. One problem with our method, like other EM-based methods, is that its clustering performance can degrade significantly when the underlying clusters are very close to each other. A possible extension to model ARIMA time series without removing the nonstationarity may also be explored.

References

[1] G. Box and G. Jenkins. *Time Series Analysis: Forecasting and Control.* Holden Day, San Francisco, CA, USA, 1970. Revised 1976.

[2] I. Cadez, D. Heckerman, C. Meek, P. Smyth, and S. White. Visualization of navigation patterns on a web site using model-based clustering. In *Proceedings of the Sixth ACM SIGKDD International Conference on Knowledge Discovery and Data Mining*, pages 280–284, Boston, MA, USA, 20–23 August 2000.

[3] A. Dempster, N. Laird, and D. Rubin. Maximum likelihood from incomplete data via the EM algorithm (with discussion). *Journal of the Royal Statistical Society, Series B*, 39:1–38, 1977.

[4] M. Gavrilov, D. Anguelov, P. Indyk, and R. Motwani. Mining the stock market: Which measure is best? In *Proceedings of the Sixth ACM SIGKDD International Conference on Knowledge Discovery and Data Mining*, pages 487–496, Boston, MA, USA, 20–23 August 2000.

[5] K. Kalpakis, D. Gada, and V. Puttagunta. Distance measures for effective clustering of ARIMA time-series. In *Proceedings of the IEEE International Conference on Data Mining*, pages 273–280, San Jose, CA, USA, 29 November - 2 December 2001.

[6] H. Kwok, C. Chen, and L. Xu. Comparison between mixture of ARMA and mixture of AR model with application to time series forecasting. In *Proceedings of the Fifth International Conference on Neural Information Processing*, pages 1049–1052, Kitakyushu, Japan, 21–23 October 1998.

[7] M. Law and J. Kwok. Rival penalized competitive learning for model-based sequence clustering. In *Proceedings of the Fifteenth International Conference on Pattern Recognition*, volume 2, pages 195–198, Barcelona, Spain, 3–7 September 2000.

[8] C. Li and G. Biswas. A Bayesian approach to temporal data clustering using hidden Markov models. In *Proceedings of the Seventeenth International Conference on Machine Learning*, pages 543–550, Stanford, CA, USA, 29 June - 2 July 2000.

[9] G. McLachlan and K. Basford. *Mixture Models: Inference and Applications to Clustering.* Marcel Dekker, New York, NY, USA, 1988.

[10] M. Perrone and S. Connell. K-means clustering for hidden Markov models. In *Proceedings of the Seventh International Workshop on Frontiers in Handwriting Recognition*, pages 229–238, Amsterdam, Netherlands, 11–13 September 2000.

[11] L. Rabiner. A tutorial on hidden Markov models and selected applications in speech recognition. *Proceedings of the IEEE*, 77(2):257–286, 1989.

[12] M. Ramoni, P. Sebastiani, and P. Cohen. Bayesian clustering by dynamics. *Machine Learning*, 47(1):91–121, 2002.

[13] R. Redner and H. Walker. Mixture densities, maximum likelihood and the EM algorithm. *SIAM Review*, 26(2):195–239, 1984.

[14] P. Smyth. Clustering sequences with hidden Markov models. In *Advances in Neural Information Processing Systems 9*, pages 648–654. MIT Press, 1997.

gSpan: Graph-Based Substructure Pattern Mining

Xifeng Yan   Jiawei Han
Department of Computer Science
University of Illinois at Urbana-Champaign
{xyan, hanj}@uiuc.edu

Abstract

We investigate new approaches for frequent graph-based pattern mining in graph datasets and propose a novel algorithm called gSpan (graph-based Substructure pattern mining), which discovers frequent substructures without candidate generation. gSpan builds a new lexicographic order among graphs, and maps each graph to a unique minimum DFS code as its canonical label. Based on this lexicographic order, gSpan adopts the depth-first search strategy to mine frequent connected subgraphs efficiently. Our performance study shows that gSpan substantially outperforms previous algorithms, sometimes by an order of magnitude.

1. Introduction

Frequent substructure pattern mining has been an emerging data mining problem with many scientific and commercial applications. As a general data structure, labeled graph can be used to model much complicated substructure patterns among data. Given a graph dataset, $D = \{G_0, G_1, ..., G_n\}$, $support(g)$ denotes the number of graphs (in D) in which g is a subgraph. The problem of *frequent subgraph mining* is to find any subgraph g s.t. $support(g) \geqslant minSup$ (a minimum support threshold). To reduce the complexity of the problem (meanwhile considering the connectivity property of hidden structures in most situations), only frequent connected subgraphs are studied in this paper.

The kernel of frequent subgraph mining is subgraph isomorphism test. Lots of well-known pair-wise isomorphism testing algorithms were developed. However, the frequent subgraph mining problem was not explored well. Recently, Inokuchi et al. [4] proposed an Apriori-based algorithm, called AGM, to discover all frequent (both connected and disconnected) substructures. Kuramochi and Karypis [5] further developed the idea using adjacent representation of graph and an edge-growing strategy. Their algorithm, called FSG, is able to find all frequent connected subgraphs from a

chemical compound dataset in 10 minutes with 6.5% minimum support. For the same dataset, our novel algorithm can complete the same task in 10 seconds.

AGM and FSG both take advantage of the Apriori level-wise approach [1]. In the context of frequent subgraph mining, the Apriori-like algorithms meet two challenges: (1) candidate generation: the generation of size $(k + 1)$ subgraph candidates from size k frequent subgraphs is more complicated and costly than that of itemsets; and (2) pruning false positives: subgraph isomorphism test is an NP-complete problem, thus pruning false positives is costly.

Contribution. In this paper, we develop *gSpan*, which targets to reduce or avoid the significant costs mentioned above. If the entire graph dataset can fit in main memory, *gSpan* can be applied directly; otherwise, one can first perform graph-based data projection as in [6], and then apply *gSpan*. To the best of our knowledge, *gSpan* is the first algorithm that explores depth-first search (DFS) in frequent subgraph mining. Two techniques, *DFS lexicographic order* and *minimum DFS code*, are introduced here, which form a novel canonical labeling system to support DFS search. *gSpan* discovers all the frequent subgraphs without candidate generation and false positives pruning. It combines the growing and checking of frequent subgraphs into one procedure, thus accelerates the mining process.

2. DFS Lexicographic Order

This section introduces several techniques developed in *gSpan*, including *mapping each graph to a DFS code (a sequence), building a novel lexicographic ordering among these codes*, and *constructing a search tree based on this lexicographic order*.

DFS Subscripting. When performing a depth-first search [3] in a graph, we construct a DFS tree. One graph can have several different DFS trees. For example, graphs in Fig. 1(b)-(d) are isomorphic to that in Fig. 1(a). The thickened edges in Fig. 1(b)-(d) represent three different DFS trees for the graph in Fig. 1(a). The depth-first discovery of the vertices forms a linear order. We use subscripts to label this

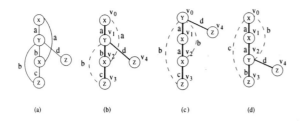

(a)　　　　(b)　　　　(c)　　　　(d)

Figure 1. Depth-First Search Tree

edge	(Fig 1b) α	(Fig 1c) β	(Fig 1d) γ
0	$(0,1,X,a,Y)$	$(0,1,Y,a,X)$	$(0,1,X,a,X)$
1	$(1,2,Y,b,X)$	$(1,2,X,a,X)$	$(1,2,X,a,Y)$
2	$(2,0,X,a,X)$	$(2,0,X,b,Y)$	$(2,0,Y,b,X)$
3	$(2,3,X,c,Z)$	$(2,3,X,c,Z)$	$(2,3,Y,b,Z)$
4	$(3,1,Z,b,Y)$	$(3,0,Z,b,Y)$	$(3,0,Z,c,X)$
5	$(1,4,Y,d,Z)$	$(0,4,Y,d,Z)$	$(2,4,Y,d,Z)$

Table 1. DFS codes for Fig. 1(b)-(d)

order according to their discovery time [3]. $i < j$ means v_i is discovered before v_j. We call v_0 the *root* and v_n the *rightmost vertex*. The straight path from v_0 to v_n is named the *rightmost path*. In Fig. 1(b)-(d), three different subscriptings are generated for the graph in Fig. 1(a). The right most path is (v_0, v_1, v_4) in Fig. 1(b), (v_0, v_4) in Fig. 1(c), and (v_0, v_1, v_2, v_4) in Fig. 1(d). We denote such subscripted G as G_T.

Forward Edge and Backward Edge. Given G_T, the forward edge (*tree edge* [3]) set contains all the edges in the DFS tree, and the backward edge (*back edge* [3]) set contains all the edges which are not in the DFS tree. For simplicity, (i, j) is an ordered pair to represent an edge. If $i < j$, it is a forward edge; otherwise, a backward edge. A linear order, $\prec_T$ is built among all the edges in G by the following rules (assume $e_1 = (i_1, j_1), e_2 = (i_2, j_2)$): (i) if $i_1 = i_2$ and $j_1 < j_2$, $e_1 \prec_T e_2$; (ii) if $i_1 < j_1$ and $j_1 = i_2$, $e_1 \prec_T e_2$; and (iii) if $e_1 \prec_T e_2$ and $e_2 \prec_T e_3$, $e_1 \prec_T e_3$.

Definition 1 (DFS Code) *Given a DFS tree T for a graph G, an edge sequence (e_i) can be constructed based on $\prec_T$, such that $e_i \prec_T e_{i+1}$, where $i = 0, \ldots, |E| - 1$. (e_i) is called a DFS code, denoted as $code(G, T)$.*

For simplicity, an edge can be presented by a 5-tuple, $(i, j, l_i, l_{(i,j)}, l_j)$, where l_i and l_j are the labels of v_i and v_j respectively and $l_{(i,j)}$ is the label of the edge between them. For example, (v_0, v_1) in Fig. 1(b) is represented by $(0, 1, X, a, Y)$. Table 1 shows the corresponding DFS codes for Fig. 1(b), 1(c), and 1(d).

Definition 2 (DFS Lexicographic Order) *Suppose $Z = \{code(G, T) \mid T$ is a DFS tree of $G\}$, i.e., Z is a set con-*

taining all DFS codes for all the connected labeled graphs. Suppose there is a linear order $(\prec_L)$ in the label set (L), then the lexicographic combination of $\prec_T$ and $\prec_L$ is a linear order $(\prec_e)$ on the set $E_T \times L \times L \times L$. For further details see [7]. **DFS Lexicographic Order** *is a linear order defined as follows. If $\alpha = code(G_\alpha, T_\alpha) = (a_0, a_1, ..., a_m)$ and $\beta = code(G_\beta, T_\beta) = (b_0, b_1, ..., b_n), \alpha, \beta \in Z$, then $\alpha \leqslant \beta$ iff either of the following is true.*

$(i) \quad \exists t, 0 \leqslant t \leqslant min(m, n), a_k = b_k \text{ for } k < t, a_t \prec_e b_t$

$(ii) \qquad a_k = b_k \text{ for } 0 \leqslant k \leqslant m, \text{ and } n \geqslant m.$

For the graph in Fig. 1 (a), there exist tens of different DFS codes. Three of them, which are based on the DFS trees in Fig. 1(b)-(d) are listed in Table 1. According to DFS lexicographic order, $\gamma \prec \alpha \prec \beta$.

Definition 3 (Minimum DFS Code) *Given a graph G, $Z(G) = \{code(G, T) \mid T$ is a DFS tree of $G \}$, based on DFS lexicographic order, the minimum one, $min(Z(G))$, is called* **Minimum DFS Code** *of G. It is also a canonical label of G.*

Theorem 1 *Given two graphs G and G', G is isomorphic to G' if and only if $min(G) = min(G')$. (proof omitted)*

Thus the problem of mining frequent connected subgraphs is equivalent to mining their corresponding minimum DFS codes. This problem turns to be a sequential pattern mining problem with slight difference, which conceptually can be solved by existing sequential pattern mining algorithms.

Given a DFS code $\alpha = (a_0, a_1, ..., a_m)$, any valid DFS code $\beta = (a_0, a_1, ..., a_m, b)$, is called α's **child**, and α is called β's **parent**. In fact, to construct a valid DFS code, b must be an edge which only grows from the vertices on the rightmost path. In Fig. 2, the graph shown in 2(a) has several potential children with one edge growth, which are shown in 2(b)-(f) (assume the darkened vertices constitute the rightmost path). Among them, 2(b), 2(c), and 2(d) grow from the rightmost vertex while 2(e) and 2(f) grow from other vertices on the rightmost path. 2(b.0)-(b.3) are children of 2(b), and 2(e.0)-(e.2) are children of 2(e). Backward edges can only grow from the rightmost vertex while forward edges can grow from vertices on the rightmost path. This restriction is similar to TreeMinerV's equivalence class extension [8] and FREQT's rightmost expansion [2] in frequent tree discovery. The enumeration order of these children is enhanced by the DFS lexicographic order, i.e., it should be in the order of 2(b), 2(c), 2(d), 2(e), and 2(f).

Definition 4 (DFS Code Tree) *In a DFS Code Tree, each node represents a DFS code, the relation between parent and child node complies with the parent-child relation described above. The relation among siblings is consistent*

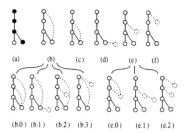

Figure 2. DFS Code/Graph Growth

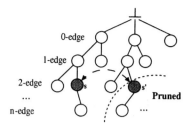

Figure 3. A Search Space: DFS Code Tree

with the DFS lexicographic order. That is, the pre-order search of DFS Code Tree follows the DFS lexicographic order.

Given a label set L, a DFS Code Tree should contain an infinite number of graphs. Since we only consider frequent subgraphs in a finite dataset, the size of a DFS Code Tree is finite. Fig. 3 shows a DFS Code Tree, the n_{th} level nodes contain DFS codes of $(n-1)$-edge graphs. Through depth-first search of the code tree, all the minimum DFS codes of frequent subgraphs can be discovered. That is, all the frequent subgraphs can be discovered in this way. We should mention that if in Fig. 3 the darken nodes contain the same graph but different DFS codes, then s' is not the minimum code (proved in [7]). Therefore, the whole sub-branch of s' can be pruned since it will not contain any minimum DFS code.

3. The *gSpan* Algorithm

We formulate the *gSpan* algorithm in this section. *gSpan* uses a sparse adjacency list representation to store graphs. Algorithm 1 outlines the pseudo-code of the framework, which is self-explanatory (Note that $\mathbb{D}$ represents the graph dataset, $\mathbb{S}$ contains the mining result).

Assume we have a label set $\{A, B, C, \ldots\}$ for vertices, and $\{a, b, c, \ldots\}$ for edges. In Algorithm 1 line 7-12, the first round will discover all the frequent subgraphs containing an edge $A \overset{a}{-} A$. The second round will discover all the frequent subgraphs containing $A \overset{a}{-} B$, but not any $A \overset{a}{-} A$. This procedure repeats until all the frequent subgraphs are discovered. The database is shrunk when this procedure continues (Algorithm 1-line 10) and when the subgraph turns to be larger (Subprocedure 1-line 8, only graphs which contains this subgraph are considered. D_s means the set of graphs in which s is a subgraph). Subgraph_Mining is recursively called to grow the graphs and find all their frequent descendants. Subgraph_Mining stops searching either when the support of a graph is less than $minSup$, or its code is not a minimum code, which means

this graph and all its descendants have been generated and discovered before (see [7]).

Algorithm 1 GraphSet_Projection($\mathbb{D}, \mathbb{S}$).

1: sort the labels in $\mathbb{D}$ by their frequency;
2: remove infrequent vertices and edges;
3: relabel the remaining vertices and edges;
4: $\mathbb{S}^1 \leftarrow$ all frequent 1-edge graphs in $\mathbb{D}$;
5: sort $\mathbb{S}^1$ in DFS lexicographic order;
6: $\mathbb{S} \leftarrow \mathbb{S}^1$;
7: **for each** edge $e \in \mathbb{S}^1$ **do**
8:     initialize s with e, set $s.D$ by graphs which contains e;
9:     Subgraph_Mining($\mathbb{D}, \mathbb{S}, s$);
10:     $\mathbb{D} \leftarrow \mathbb{D} - e$;
11:     **if** $|\mathbb{D}| < minSup$;
12:         **break**;

Subprocedure 1 Subgraph_Mining($\mathbb{D}, \mathbb{S}, s$).

1: **if** $s \neq min(s)$
2:     **return**;
3: $\mathbb{S} \leftarrow \mathbb{S} \cup \{s\}$;
4: enumerate s in each graph in $\mathbb{D}$ and count its children;
5: **for each** c, c is s' child **do**
6:     **if** $support(c) \geq minSup$
7:         $s \leftarrow c$;
8:         Subgraph_Mining($\mathbb{D}_s, \mathbb{S}, s$);

---

4. Experiments and Performance Study

A comprehensive performance study has been conducted in our experiments on both synthetic and real world datasets. We use a synthetic data generator provided by Kuramochi and Karypis [5]. The real data set we tested is a chemical compound dataset. All the experiments of *gSpan* are done on a 500MHZ Intel Pentium III PC with 448 MB main memory, running Red Hat Linux 6.2. We also implemented our version of FSG which achieves similar perfor-

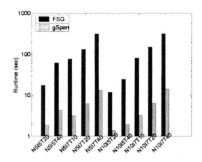

Figure 4. Runtime: Synthetic data

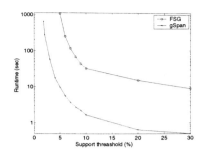

Figure 5. Runtime: Chemical data

mance as that reported in [5]. As shown in Figures 4 and 5, we compare the performance of *gSpan* with FSG [5] if the result is available; otherwise we show our own implementation result based on the same dataset. [5] did the test on a Linux machine with similar configuration.

Synthetic Datasets. The synthetic datasets are generated using a similar procedure described in [1]. Kuramochi et al. [5] applied a simplified procedure in their graph data synthesis. We use their data generator. *gSpan* was tested in various synthetic datasets with different parameters, $|N|$ (the number of possible labels), $|I|$ (the average size of potential frequent subgraphs-kernels), $|T|$ (the average size of graphs in terms of edges) and fixed parameters, $|D| = 10K$ (the total number of graphs generated), $|L| = 200$ (the number of potentially frequent kernels), and $minSup = 0.01 \times |D|$. As shown in Fig. 4, the speed-up is between 6 and 30.

Chemical Compound Dataset. The chemical compound dataset can be retrieved through this URL [1]. The dataset contains 340 chemical compounds, 24 different atoms, 66 atom types, and 4 types of bonds. The dataset is sparse, containing on average 27 vertices per graph and 28 edges per graph. The largest one contains 214 edges and 214 vertices. So the discovered patterns are much like tree, though they do contains some cycles. We use the type of atoms and bonds as labels. The goal is to find the common chemical compound substructures. Fig. 5 illustrates the runtime of *gSpan* and FSG as *minSup* varies from 2% to 30%. The total memory consumption is less than 100M for any point of *gSpan* plotted in the figure. For FSG, when the *minSup* is less than 5%, the process is aborted either because the main memory is exhausted or the runtime is too long. Fig. 5 shows *gSpan* achieves better performance by 15-100 times in comparison with FSG.

---

[1] http://oldwww.comlab.ox.ac.uk/oucl/groups/machlearn/PTE.

5. Conclusions

In this paper, we introduced a new lexicographic ordering system and developed a depth-first search-based mining algorithm *gSpan* for efficient mining of frequent subgraphs in large graph database. Our performance study shows that *gSpan* outperforms FSG by an order of magnitude and is capable to mine large frequent subgraphs in a bigger graph set with lower minimum supports than previous studies.

Acknowledgements. The synthetic data generator is kindly provided by Mr. Michihiro Kuramochi and Professor George Karypis in University of Minnesota. Dr. Pasquale Forggia, at Dipartimento di Informatica e Sistemistica Università di Napoli " Federico II ", provided helpful suggestions about the usage of VFlib graph matching library. We also thank Yanli Tong for her comments.

References

[1] R. Agrawal and R. Srikant. Fast algorithms for mining association rules. In *VLDB'94*, pages 487–499, Sept. 1994.
[2] T. Asai, K. Abe, S. Kawasoe, H. Arimura, H. Satamoto, and S. Arikawa. Efficient substructure discovery from large semistructured data. In *SIAM SDM'02*, April 2002.
[3] T. H. Cormen, C. E. Leiserson, R. L. Rivest, and C. Stein. *Introduction to Algorithms*. MIT Press, 2001, Second Edition.
[4] A. Inokuchi, T. Washio, and H. Motoda. An apriori-based algorithm for mining frequent substructures from graph data. In *PKDD'00*, pages 13–23, 2000.
[5] M. Kuramochi and G. Karypis. Frequent subgraph discovery. In *ICDM'01*, pages 313–320, Nov. 2001.
[6] J. Pei, J. Han, B. Mortazavi-Asl, H. Pinto, Q. Chen, U. Dayal, and M.-C. Hsu. PrefixSpan: Mining sequential patterns efficiently by prefix-projected pattern growth. In *ICDE'01*, pages 215–224, April 2001.
[7] X. Yan and J. Han. gspan: Graph-based substructure pattern mining. Technical Report UIUCDCS-R-2002-2296, Department of Computer Science, University of Illinois at Urbana-Champaign, 2002.
[8] M. J. Zaki. Efficiently mining frequent trees in a forest. In *KDD'02*, July 2002.

InfoMiner+: Mining Partial Periodic Patterns with Gap Penalties

Jiong Yang
UIUC
jioyang@cs.uiuc.edu

Wei Wang
UNC-Chapel Hill
weiwang@cs.unc.edu

Philip S. Yu
IBM T. J. Watson Research Center
psyu@us.ibm.com

Abstract

In this paper, we focus on mining periodic patterns allowing some degree of imperfection in the form of random replacement from a perfect periodic pattern. Information gain was proposed to identify patterns with events of vastly different occurrence frequencies and adjust for the deviation from a pattern. However, it does not take any penalty if there exists some gap between the pattern occurrences. In many applications, e.g., bio-informatics, it is important to identify subsequences that a pattern repeats perfectly (or near perfectly). As a solution, we extend the information gain measure to include a penalty for gaps between pattern occurrences. We call this measure as generalized information gain. Furthermore, we want to find subsequence S′ such that for a pattern P, the generalized information gain of P in S′ is high. This is particularly useful in locating repeats in DNA sequences. In this paper, we developed an effective mining algorithm, InfoMiner+, to simultaneously mine significant patterns and the associated subsequences.

1 Introduction

Periodic pattern discovery is an important problem in mining time series data and has wide applications. A periodic pattern is a list of ordered events, which repeat itself in the event sequence. It is useful in characterizing the cyclic behavior of the time series. In practice, not every portion in the time series may contribute to the periodicity. For example, a company's stock may often gain a couple of points at the beginning of each trading session but it may not have much regularity at later time. This kind of looser periodicity is often referred to as *partial periodicity*. Moreover, due to some random noise, a pattern may not always be repeated perfectly. In turn, the event sequence can be viewed as a series of perfect pattern repetitions with a few *random replacements*[1]. If the amount of "replacement" is below some reasonable threshold, we may regard that the pattern still exhibits in the event sequence.

As a newly developed research area, most previous work on mining time series data addresses the issue by creating a mapping to the association rule mining technique and therefore uses the support and confidence as the metrics to identify the

significant patterns from the rest. Most association rule mining algorithms favor frequently occurred event(s) due to the nature of the problem. However, patterns involving infrequent events may also be as significant as (or even more significant than) frequent events in an event sequence. This issue becomes more critical when different events occur at divergent frequencies.

Information gain is introduced in [3, 4, 5, 6] to measure the importance/significance of the occurrence of a pattern. The information gain of an occurrence of a rare event is high while the information gain of the occurrence of a frequent event is low. Thus, we are able to find the statistically significant patterns with the information gain threshold. However, the major limitation of this model is that it does not take into account where the occurrences are in the sequence. Let's take a look at two sequences: $S_1 = a_1, a_2, a_3, a_3, a_2, a_3, a_1, a_2, a_4, a_5, a_1, a_2$ and $S_2 = a_1, a_2, a_1, a_2, a_1, a_2, a_3, a_3, a_2, a_3, a_4, a_5$. The elements in the two sequences are identical. The only difference is the order of the events. The pattern (a_1, a_2) repeats perfectly in the first half of S_2 while it scatters in S_1. The two patterns have the same information gain in the two sequences. In some applications (e.g., repeats discovery in bio-informatics domain), a series of consecutive repeats are considered more significant than the scattered ones. That is, there is some "penalty" associated with the gap between pattern repeats [2]. As a result, we need a measurement that can make such a distinction. In this paper, we introduce the measure of generalized information gain (GIG) to capture the significance of a pattern in a sequence/subsequence. The occurrence of a pattern will be given a position GIG while a mis-occurrence (or a gap) will generate a negative GIG. The overall generalized information gain will be the aggregate of all occurrences and mis-occurrences of the pattern in a sequence/subsequence.

Since the characteristics of a sequence may change over time, many patterns may only be valid for a period of time. The degree of significance (i.e., generalized information gain) of a pattern may be diluted if we only consider the entire event sequence. In addition, a user may be interested not only in a significant pattern, but also where/when the pattern is significant as well. In a DNA sequence, researchers are also interested in which region a pattern is significant. The identification of significant pattern in a subsequence is of great importance in many applications. However, most previous research

---

[1] Or equivalently, the event sequence would become a series of perfect repetitions of some pattern after a few replacements (of events).

focused on discovering patterns that are significant over the entire data sequence[6]. In this paper, we relax the model by allowing a pattern to be significant during a contiguous portion of the entire sequence. A user is asked to specify the minimum GIG a significant pattern must carry over a subsequence of data. Upon satisfying this requirement, the subsequence(s) that maximizes the GIG of a pattern will be identified. In the previous example, the pattern (a_1, a_2) is very significant in the first half of S_2, but may not be significant over the entire sequence.

Although the generalized information gain is a more meaningful metric for the problems addressed previously, it does not preserve the *downward closure* property (as the *support* does). For example, the pattern $(a_1, a_2, *)$ may have sufficient GIG while both $(a_1, *, *)$ and $(*, a_2, *)$ do not[2]. We can not take advantages of the standard pruning technique developed for mining association rules. The observation that the *triangle inequality*[3] is still preserved by the generalized information gain motivates us to devise a threefold algorithm as the core of our pattern discovery tool, InfoMiner+.

1. First, the significant patterns involving one event are discovered.

2. Next, candidate patterns involving multiple events are generated based on the *triangle inequality*.

3. All candidate patterns are validated and for each pattern which is significant, the corresponding subsequence containing the pattern is also identified.

The remainder of this paper is organized as follows. The problem is formulated in Section 2 while our approach is presented in Section 3. We conclude this paper in Section 4.

2 Problem Formulation

Let $\Im = \{a_1, a_2, \dots, \}$ be a set of events and D be a sequence of events in $\Im$. We now introduce some notations that we will use for the remainder of the paper. As mentioned previously, we want to discover the patterns P such that there exists some subsequence D' of D, where P is significant in D'.

Definition 2.1 *A pattern with period l is an array of l events $(p_1, p_2, \dots, p_l)$, each of which is either an event in $\Im$ or *, i.e., $p_j \in \Im \cup * (1 \le j \le l)$. We say that the jth position is **instantiated** if $p_j \in \Im$. For any two patterns $P = (p_1, p_2, \dots, p_l)$ and $P' = (p'_1, p'_2, \dots, p'_l)$ of the same period l, P is a **superpattern** of P' (P' is a **subpattern** of P) if $p'_j = *$ or $p_j = p'_j$, for all $1 \le j \le l$.*

---

[2]We will explain it in more detail later in this paper.
[3]For example, the GIG of $(a_1, a_2, *)$ can not exceed the summation of that of $(a_1, *, *)$ and $(*, a_2, *)$.

Note that an event can appear at multiple positions in a pattern. For example, $(a_1, a_4, *, *, a_4)$ is a pattern of period 5 and its first, second and fifth positions are instantiated. It is also a superpattern of $(a_1, *, *, *, a_4)$.

We found that the *information* measure [1] which is widely studied and used in information theory field fulfills the first two properties. It is hence used to measure the amount of positive/negative influence to the overall significance of a pattern caused by each occurrence/absence. Based on it, we devise a novel measurement, *generalized information gain*, to quantify the significance of a pattern within a subsequence of events. The following is the definition of the information and the generalized information gain.

Definition 2.2 *For an event $a_j \in \Im$ and a sequence D of N events, let $Prob(a_j)$ be the expected probability that a_j occurs at any given position in D^4. Then the **information** of a_j with respect to D is defined as $I(a_j) = \log \frac{1}{Prob(a_j)} = -\log Prob(a_j)$. The information of the "eternal" event * is always 0^5.*

In the information theory community, information is originally used to quantify the *a priori* uncertainty that an event will occur or the "surprise" if the event occurs; and is defined as a continuous function of the probability that an event occurs. When the probability of an event occurrence approaches 1, the information of that event approaches 0. This enables us to handle the eternal event seamlessly. In addition, information is additive for independent events. This does not only provide a solid theoretical foundation, but also offer computational efficiency.

Definition 2.3
*The **information** of a pattern $P = (p_1, p_2, \dots, p_l)$ is the summation of the information carried by each individual position, i.e., $I(P) = \sum_{1 \le j \le l} I(p_j)$.*

Definition 2.4 *Given a pattern $P = (p_1, p_2, \dots, p_l)$ with period l and a sequence of l events $D' = d_1, d_2, \dots, d_l$, we say that D' is **in compliance with** P at position j ($1 \le j \le l$) iff either $p_j = *$ or $p_j = d_j$ holds.*

For example, the sequence a_1, a_1, a_2, a_3 is in compliance with the pattern $(a_1, a_2, a_3, *)$ at positions 1 and 4.

Definition 2.5 *Given a pattern $P = (p_1, p_2, \dots, p_l)$ with period l and a sequence of l events $D' = d_1, d_2, \dots, d_l$, we say that P **matches** D' (or D' **supports** P), iff D' is in compliance with P at every position j ($1 \le j \le l$).*

---

[4]For the sake of simplicity of exploration, we assume that, without additional qualification, a_j occurs equally likely at any position with probability $Prob(a_j)$. All results presented in this paper can be modified to apply to a more general scenario.
[5]Another way of looking at it is that $Prob(*) = 1$ at any time.

For instance, the sequence a_1, a_4, a_2, a_3, a_4 supports the pattern $(a_1, a_4, *, *, a_4)$ while the sequence a_1, a_4, a_2, a_3, a_6 does not support it since the sequence is not in compliance with the pattern on the last position.

Definition 2.6 *Given a pattern P with period l and a sequence D of $N(N \geq l)$ events: $d_1, d_2, \ldots, d_N$, the* **support** *of P within D is the number of subsequences $d_{l \times j+1}, d_{l \times j+2}, \ldots, d_{l \times j+l}$ that support P.*

Intuitively, the event sequence can be viewed as a list of segments, each of which consists of l contiguous events. There would be $\lfloor N/l \rfloor$ full segments, among which the segment that P matches will count for the support of P.

Definition 2.7 *Given a pattern $P = (p_1, p_2, \ldots, p_l)$ with period l and a sequence of l events $D' = d_1, d_2, \ldots, d_l$, the* **information loss** *of D' on position j with respect to P is the information of the event p_j iff D' is not in compliance with P at position j and there is no information loss otherwise. The overall information loss of D' with respect to P is the summation of the information loss of each position.*

Definition 2.8 *Given a pattern P with period l and a sequence D of $N(N \geq l)$ events: $d_1, d_2, \ldots, d_N$, the* **information loss** *of D with respect to P is the summation of the information loss of each segment $d_{l \times j+1}, d_{l \times j+2}, \ldots, d_{l \times j+l}$ with respect to P. The* **generalized information gain** *of D with respect to P is defined as $I(P) \times (S_D(P) - 1) - L_D(P)$ where $I(P)$, $S_D(P)$, and $L_D(P)$ are the information of P, the support of P within D, and the information loss of D with respect to P, respectively.*

In a subsequence, the first match of a pattern is viewed as an example, and only subsequent matches contribute to the generalized information gain[6].

Definition 2.9 *Given a pattern P, a sequence D and a generalized information gain threshold g, if there exists a subsequence D' of D so that the generalized information gain of D' with respect to P is at least g, then P is a* **valid pattern**.

Theoretically, the period of a valid pattern could be arbitrary, i.e., as long as the event sequence. In reality, a user can specify an upperbound of period length according to his/her domain knowledge. As a result, we use L_{max} to denote the maximum period allowed for a pattern. However, L_{max} can be arbitrarily large, e.g., ranging to several thousands. Now we can rephrase our problem model by employing the generalized information gain metric. For a sequence of events D, an information gain threshold g, and a period bound L_{max}, we want to discovery all valid patterns P whose period is less than L_{max}. In addition, for each valid pattern P, we want to find the subsequence

which maximizes the generalized information gain of P. In the remainder of this section, we give some more definitions which enable us to present our approach and communicate to readers more effectively.

Definition 2.10 *For any two patterns $P = (p_1, p_2, \ldots, p_l)$ and $P' = (p'_1, p'_2, \ldots, p'_l)$ of the same period l, P and P' are* **complementary** *if either $p_j = *$ or $p'_j = *$ for all $1 \leq j \leq l$.*

A set of patterns of the same period are said to be *complementary* if every pair of patterns in the set are complementary.

Definition 2.11 *Given a set Π of complementary patterns of the same period l, the* **minimum common superpattern** **(MCSP)** *of Π is the pattern P of period l, which satisfies the following two conditions.*

- *Each pattern in Π is a subpattern of P.*
- *There does not exist a subpattern P' of P $(P' \neq P)$ such that each pattern in Π is also a subpattern of P'.*

It follows from the definition that the information of the MCSP of a set, Π, of complementary patterns is the summation of the information of each pattern in Π.

For a given event segment $D' = d_1, d_2, \ldots, d_l$ and a set, Π, of complementary patterns, the information loss of D' with respect to the MCSP of Π satisfies the following equality

$$L_{D'}(MCSP(\Pi)) = \sum_{P \in \Pi} L_{D'}(P)$$

where $L_D(P)$ is the information loss of D' with respect to P. The rationale is that if D' is not in compliance with a pattern P in Π on position j, then the jth position must be instantiated and D' must not be in compliance with the MCSP of Π on position j either. In general, for any event sequence D, the overall information loss of D with respect to the MCSP of a set of complementary patterns Π is equal to the summation of the information loss of D with respect to each pattern in Π.

Definition 2.12 *A pattern $P = (p_1, p_2, \ldots, p_l)$ is a* **singular pattern** *if only one position is instantiated.*

Intuitively, a singular pattern of period l consists one regular event and $l - 1$ eternal events. The event may occur at one of the l positions. For example, $(a, *, *)$, $(*, a, *)$, and $(*, *, a)$ are all singular patterns of period 3 involving event a.

Proposition 2.1 (Triangle Inequality) *Given an event sequence D and two complementary patterns P and P' of the same period, let Q be the minimum common super pattern of P and P'. Then the generalized information gain of D with respect to Q is at most the summation of that of P and P'.*

Proposition 2.1 can be easily generalized to a set of complementary patterns, which is stated as follows.

---

[6]Since we aim at mining periodic patterns, only repeated occurrences of a pattern are used to accumulate the generalized information gain.

Proposition 2.2 *Given an event sequence D and a set of complementary patterns* Π, *let Q be the minimum common super pattern of* Π, *then the generalized information gain of D with respect to Q is at most the summation of that of each pattern in* Π.

3 General Approach

In this section, we outline the general strategy we use to mine patterns that meet certain generalized information gain threshold g. There exist three challenges for mining patterns with information gain: (1) The number of different patterns is

$$\sum_{0 < l \le L_{max}} (|\Im|^l - 1) = O(|\Im|^{L_{max}})$$

where $|\Im|$ and L_{max} are the overall number of distinct events and the maximum period length, respectively. Since L_{max} can be quite large, e.g., in the thousands, it is infeasible to verify each pattern against the data directly. Some pruning mechanism has to be developed to circumscribe the search space. (2) By definition, the generalized information gain measure does not have the property of downward closure as the traditional *support* measure does. This prevents us from borrowing existing algorithms developed for association rule problems to mine the qualified patterns. (3) The subsequence concept introduced in this paper poses a difficult challenge to determine when a subsequence should start and end. If a pattern misses some "matches", it is hard to tell whether this signals the end of a subsequence or this merely means some noise within a subsequence.

Fortunately, the *triangle inequality* holds for the generalized information gain. In other word, for a set of complementary patterns Π, the generalized information gain of the minimum common superpattern (MCSP) of Π is always less than or equal to the sum of that of each individual pattern in Π over the same subsequence of events. Inspired by this observation, we can first collect the generalized information gain of all singular patterns, and then generate candidate patterns by combining these singular patterns.

In the first phase, the valid singular patterns are discovered. The second phase generates the candidates of valid complex pattern based on the candidates of valid singular patterns via triangle inequality. Finally, InfoMiner+ verifies all candidates, and finds the corresponding subsequence for each valid pattern so as to maximize its generalized information gain. The first phase can be further divided into two steps: (1) identify the likely periods for each event and (2) find the valid singular pattern for each likely period. In the first step, the negative impact of gap penalties towards the overall GIG is taken into account to prune out disqualified periods of each event; while in the second step all possible format of singular patterns are considered and evaluated. For each likely period l of event a, there are l possible singular patterns, e.g., for $l = 3$, the three singular patterns are $(a, *, *)$, $(*, a, *)$, and $(*, *, a)$. After valid singular patterns are identified, the candidate complex patterns are generated according to the triangle inequality, and then verified. At the same time, for each significant pattern, we will find its associated subsequences. Due to space limitations, we omit the detailed description of the InfoMiner+ algorithm.

4 Conclusion

In this paper, we propose a new mining problem of partial periodic pattern with random replacement. To qualify significant patterns in a sequence, we introduce a new measurement: generalized information gain. This new metric can seamlessly accommodate the different frequency of event occurrences in an event sequence and the gap penalties and provides us with solid theoretical foundations. The triangle inequality preserved by the generalized information gain enables us to devise a linear algorithm to mine the significant pattern in any subsequence combinations.

References

[1] R. Blahut. *Principles and Practice of Information Theory*, Addison-Wesley Publishing Company, 1987.

[2] R. Durbin, S. Eddy, A. Krough, and G. Mitchison. *Biological Sequence Analysis: Probabilistic Models of Proteins and Nucleic Acids*. Cambridge University Press, 1998.

[3] J. Han, G. Dong, and Y. Yin. Efficient mining partial periodic patterns in time series database. *Proc. Int. Conf. on Data Engineering*, 106-115, 1999.

[4] E. Keogh, S. Lonardi, and W. Chiu. Finding surprising patterns in a time series database in linear time and space. *Proc. ACM Knowledge Discovery and Data Mining*, pp 550-556, 2002.

[5] J. Yang, W. Wang, and P. Yu. Mining asynchronous periodic patterns in time series data. *Proc. ACM SIGKDD Int. Conf. on Knowledge Discovery and Data Mining (SIGKDD)*, pp. 275-279, 2000.

[6] J. Yang, W. Wang, and P. Yu. InfoMiner: mining surprising periodic patterns. *Proc. ACM Knowledge Discovery and Data Mining*, 395-400, 2001.

FD_Mine: Discovering Functional Dependencies in a Database Using Equivalences

Hong Yao, Howard J.Hamilton, and Cory J.Butz

Department of Computer Science, University of Regina
Regina, SK, Canada, S4S 0A2
{yao2hong, hamilton, butz}@cs.uregina.ca

Abstract

The discovery of FDs from databases has recently become a significant research problem. In this paper, we propose a new algorithm, called FD_Mine. FD_Mine takes advantage of the rich theory of FDs to reduce both the size of the dataset and the number of FDs to be checked by using discovered equivalences. We show that the pruning does not lead to loss of information. Experiments on 15 UCI datasets show that FD_Mine can prune more candidates than previous methods.

1 Introduction

This paper proposes a new method for finding functional dependencies in data. Formally, let r be a relation on schema R, with X and Y subsets of R. Relation r satisfies the *functional dependency* (FD) X→Y, if, for any two tuples t_1 and t_2 in r, whenever $t_1[X] = t_2[X]$ then $t_1[Y] = t_2[Y]$.

FDs play an important role in relational theory and relational database design [3]. Current research is based on the fact that FDs may exist in a dataset that are independent of the relational model of the dataset. It is useful to discover these FDs. For example, from a database of chemical compounds, it is valuable to discover compounds that are functionally dependent on a certain structure attribute [2]. As a result, the discovery of FDs from database has recently become a popular research problem [1, 2, 4, 6, 7].

The remainder of this paper organized as follows. A statement of the problem is given in section 2. In section 3, the relationship among FDs is analyzed. The FD_Mine algorithm is presented in section 4. Next, the experimental results are shown in section 5. Finally, conclusions are drawn in section 6.

2 Problem Statement

Early methods for discovering of FDs were based on repeatedly sorting and comparing tuples to determine whether or not these tuples meet the FD definition. For example, in Table 2.1, the tuples are first sorted on attribute A, then each pair of tuples that have the same value on attribute A is compared on attribute B, C, D, and E, in turn, to decide whether or not A→B, A→C, A→D, or A→E holds. Then the tuples are sorted on attribute B and so on, until BCDE has been checked. In this paper, we say a FD is *checked* if data is used to examine whether or not a FD holds. Otherwise, we say a FD is *not checked*. A *candidate* is a combination of attributes over a dataset. All candidates of five attributes are represented in Figure 2.1 This approach is inefficient because of the extra sorting and because it needs to examine every value of the candidate attributes to decide whether or not a FD holds. As a result, this approach is highly sensitive to the number of tuples and attributes. It is impractical for a large dataset.

	A	B	C	D	E
t_1	0	0	0	1	0
t_2	0	1	0	1	0
t_3	0	2	0	1	2
t_4	0	3	1	1	0
t_5	4	1	1	2	4
t_6	4	3	1	2	2
t_7	0	0	1	1	0

Table 2.1 An example dataset.

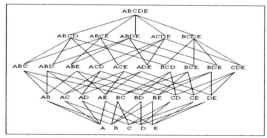

Figure 2.1 Lattice for 5 attributes.

Recent papers have proposed algorithms that do not sort on any attribute or compare any values. Mannila et al. [4, 5] introduced the concept of a *partition*, which places tuples that have the same values for an attribute into the same group. The problem of determining whether or not a FD holds on a given dataset can be addressed by comparing the number of groups among the partitions for various attributes. For *dataset r*, the data over the relational schema R, shown in Table 2.1, the partition for attribute A can be denoted as $\Pi_A(r) =\{\{t_1, t_2, t_3, t_4, t_7\}, \{t_5, t_6\}\}$. The partition for the attribute combination AD for Table 2.1 is $\Pi_{AD}(r) =\{\{t_1, t_2, t_3, t_4, t_7\}, \{t_5, t_6\}\}$. The *cardinality of the partition* $|\Pi_A(r)|$, which is the number of groups in partition Π_A, is 2, and $|\Pi_{AD}(r)|$ is 2 as well. Because $|\Pi_A(r)|$ is equal to $|\Pi_{AD}(r)|$, A→D can be obtained [2].

Our research addresses two related questions. First, can other information from discovered FDs be used to prune more candidates than previous approaches? Secondly, can this pruning be done so that the overall efficiency of the algorithm is improved? We address both these problems by further considering the theoretical properties of FDs, formulating algorithm FD_Mine, and testing it on a variety of datasets.

3 Properties of Functional Dependencies

In this section, the relationships among FDs are analyzed with particular attention to equivalent candidates and nontrivial closure.

Definition 3.1 Let X and Y be candidates over a dataset D, if X→Y and Y→X hold, then X and Y are said to be *equivalent candidates*, denoted as $X \leftrightarrow Y$.

Using Definition 3.1 and the Armstrong axioms [3], Lemma 3.1 and Lemma 3.2 can be obtained.

Lemma 3.1. Let X, Y and Z be candidates over D. If $X \leftrightarrow Y$ and XW→Z hold, then YW→Z holds.

Lemma 3.2. Let X, Y and Z be candidates over D. If $X \leftrightarrow Y$ and WZ→X hold, then WZ→Y holds.

Using Lemmas 3.1 and 3.2, the number of candidates and possibly the size of the dataset that needs to be checked can be reduced.

Example 3.1. In Table 2.1 the FDs A→D and D→A were discovered first. According to Definition 3.1, $A \leftrightarrow D$ holds. By examining all entries for attribute A, B, and C, we can determine that AB→C and BC→A hold. Without Lemma 3.1 and 3.2, we would need to examine all entries in Table 2.1 again to determine whether or not BD→C and BC→D hold. But with Lemma 3.1, BD→C can be inferred, and with Lemma 3.2, BC→D can also be inferred. Once the equivalence between A and D has been discovered, attribute D and all its values are redundant to further searching for FDs. FDs involving D can be inferred instead of being determined by checking the data. The result after removing D is shown in Table 3.1.

Definition 3.2 Let F be a set of FDs over a dataset D and X be a candidate over D. The closure of candidate X with respect to F, denoted Closure(X), is defined as {Y | X→Y can be derived from F by the Armstrong axioms}.

The *nontrivial closure* of candidate X with respect to F, denoted Closure'(X), is defined as Closure'(X) = Closure(X) – X.

Lemma 3.3. Let X and Y be two candidates of dataset D, Z = X$\cap$Y. If Closure'(X)$\supseteq$Y–Z, and Closure'(Y)$\supseteq$X–Z, then $X \leftrightarrow Y$.

According to the definition of an FD and the Armstrong axioms, the following properties can be inferred.

Property 3.1. Let X and Y be candidates over a dataset. Then Closure'(X)$\bigcup$Closure'(Y)$\subseteq$Closure'(XY) holds.

Property 3.2. Let R be a relational schema and X be a candidate of R over a dataset D. If X$\bigcup$Closure'(X) = R, then X is a key.

The downward closure property for itemsets can be described as follow: if any subset of size (k-1) of a k-itemset is not frequent then the k-itemset is also not frequent. A similar property exists concerning the FDs that need to be checked.

Definition 3.3. Let $X_1, X_2, \ldots, X_k, X_{k+1}$ be (k+1) attributes over a dataset D. If a $X_1X_2\ldots X_k \rightarrow X_{k+1}$ is a FD with k attributes on its left hand side, then it is called a *k-level* FD.

Property 3.3. [2,3] If $X_1X_2\ldots X_{k-1}X_k \rightarrow X_{k+1}$ is a k-level FD, then it needs to be checked when none of its (k-1)-level subsets $X_{i(1)}X_{i(2)}\ldots X_{i(k-1)} \subset X_1X_2\ldots X_{k-1}X_k$ satisfies $X_{i(1)}X_{i(2)}\ldots X_{i(k-1)} \rightarrow X_{i(k)}$.

	A	B	C	E
t_1	0	0	0	0
t_2	0	1	0	0
t_3	0	2	0	2
t_4	0	3	1	0
t_5	4	1	1	4
t_6	4	2	1	2
t_7	0	0	1	0

Table 3.1 Redundant Attribute D is removed from Table 2.1

4 The FD_Mine Algorithm

The FD_Mine algorithm uses the above properties to prune the dataset and the candidates.

The FD_Mine uses a level-wise search, where results from level k are used to explore level k+1. First, at level 1, all FDs $X \rightarrow Y$, where X and Y are single attributes, are found and stored in FD_SET F_1. The set of candidates that are considered at this level is denoted L_1. F_1 and L_1 are used to generate candidates $X_i X_j$ of L_2. At level 2, all FDs of the form $X_i X_j \rightarrow Y$ are found and stored in FD_SET F_2. F_1, F_2, L_1, and L_2 are used to generate the candidates of L_3, and so on, until no candidates remain, i.e., $L_k = \phi$ (k ≤ n-1).

Before introducing the FD_Mine algorithm, the following identifiers are introduced.

- *CANDIDATE_SET*: a set of candidates.
- *FD_SET*: the set of discovered functional dependencies, each in the form $X \rightarrow Y$.
- *EQ_SET*: the set of discovered equivalences, each in the form $X \leftrightarrow Y$.
- *KEY_SET: the set of discovered keys.*

Algorithm FD_Mine
To discover all functional dependencies in a dataset.
Input: Dataset D and its attributes $X_1, X_2, \ldots, X_m$
Output: FD_SET, EQ_SET and KEY_SET

1. Initialization Step
   set $R = \{X_1, X_2, \ldots, X_m\}$, set FD_SET = ϕ,
   set EQ_SET = ϕ, set KEY_SET = ϕ
   set CANDIDATE_SET = $\{X_1, X_2, \ldots, X_m\}$
   for all $X_i \in$ CANDIDATE_SET do
      set Closure'$[X_i] = \phi$
2. Iteration Step
   while CANDIDATE_SET $\neq \phi$ do
      for all $X_i \in$ CANDIDATE_SET do
         ComputeNonTrivialClosure(X_i)
         ObtaintFDandKey(X_i)
      ObtainEQSet(CANDIDATE_SET)
      PruneCandidates(CANDIDATE_SET)
      GenerateCandidates(CANDIDATE_SET)
3. Display(FD_SET, EQ_SET, KEY_SET)

Procedure **ComputeNonTrivialClosure**(X_i)
   for each $Y \subset R - X_i -$ Closure'$[X_i]$ do
      if $(|\Pi_{X_i}| = |\Pi_{X_i Y}|)$ add Y to Closure'$[X_i]$

Procedure **ObtaintFDandKey** (X_i)
   add $X_i \rightarrow$ Closure'$[X_i]$ to FD_SET
   if $(R = X_i \bigcup$ Closure'$[X_i]$) add X_i to KEY_SET

Procedure **ObtainEQSet**(CANDIDATE_SET)
   for each $X_i \in$ CANDIDATE_SET do
      for all $X \rightarrow$ Closure'$(X) \in$ FD_SET do
         set $Z = X \bigcap X_i$
         if (Closure'$(X) \supseteq X_i - Z$ and Closure'$[X_i] \supseteq X - Z$)
            add $X \leftrightarrow X_i$ to EQ_SET

Procedure **PruneCandidates**(CANDIDATE_SET)
   for each $X_i \in$ CANDIDATE_SET do
   if $\exists X_j \in$ CANDIDATE_SET and $X_j \leftrightarrow X_i \in$ EQ_SET
      delete X_i from CANDIDATE_SET
   if $\exists X_i \in$ KEY_SET then
      delete X_i from CANDIDATE_SET

Procedure **GenerateCandidates**(CANDIDATE_SET)
   for each $X_i \in$ CANDIDATE_SET do
   for each $X_j \in$ CANDIDATE_SET and $i<j$ do
      if $(X_i[1]=X_j[1],\ldots,X_i[k-2] = X_j[k-2], X_i[k-1]<X_j[k-1])$
         set $X_{ij} = X_i$ join X_j
      if $\exists X_i \rightarrow X_j[k-1] \notin$ FD_SET
         compute the partition $\Pi_{X_{ij}}$ of X_{ij}
         set Closure'(X_{ij}) = Closure'$(X_i) \bigcup$ Closure'(X_j)
         if $(R = X_{ij} \bigcup$ Closure'$[X_{ij}]$) add X_{ij} to KEY_SET
         else add X_{ij} to CANDIDATE_SET
   delete X_i from CANDIDATE_SET

Example 4.1: Suppose that FD_Mine is applied to dataset D, as shown in Table 2.1, with R = {A, B, C, D, E}.

Level 1				Level 2			
Candidate X	$|\Pi_X|$	Closure'(X)	FD	Candidate X	$|\Pi_X|$	Closure'(X)	FD
A	2	D	A→D	AB	6	E	AB→E
B	4	ϕ		AC	3	ϕ	
C	2	ϕ		AE	5	ϕ	
D	2	A	D→A	BC	6	ϕ	
E	4	ϕ		BE	6	A	BE→A
				CE	6	A	CE→A

FD_SET= (A→D, D→A)	FD_SET=(AB→E, BE→A, CE→A)
EQ_SET=((A, D))	EQ_SET= ((AB, BE))
PrunedSet = (A, B, C, E)	PrunedSet = (AB, AC, AE, BC, CE)
Next Level Candidates:	KEY_SET= (ABC)
(AB, AC, AE, BC, BE, CE)	Next Level Candidates: ( )

FD_SET = (A→D, D→A, AB→E, DB→E, BE→A, BE→D, CE→A, CE→D)
SAME_SET = ((A, D), (AB, BE))
KEY_SET = (ABC, BCE)

Table 4.1 Trace of FD_Mine Applied to the Table 2.1 Dataset

Table 4.1 summarizes the actions of FD_Mine. In iteration 1, since $|\Pi_A| = |\Pi_{AD}| = 2$, Closure'(A) is set to D, and A→D is deduced. In same way, D→A is discovered, so the equivalence A↔D is obtained. As a result, we only need to combine A, B, C, and E to generate the next level candidates {AB, AC, AE, BC, BE, CE}. At the same time, the nontrivial closure of each generated candidate is computed. For example, the closure'(AB) = closure'(A) $\bigcup$ closure'(B) = {D} $\bigcup \phi$ = {D}. In iteration 2, for candidate AB, only AB→C and AB→E need to be checked, because R−{A, B}−Closure'(AB) = {A, B, C, D, E}−{A, B}−{D}={C, E}. Since $|\Pi_{AB}| = |\Pi_{ABE}| = 6$, then AB→E is obtained. In the same way, at this level, BE→A and CE→A are also discovered, so the equivalence AB ↔ BE is obtained. As a result, we only need to combine AB, AC, AE, BC, and CE to form the level 3 candidates, which are {ABC, ACE}. Since CE→A, ACE is pruned by property 3.3. Since AB→E, then ABC→E. Since A ↔ D, then ABC→D, so ABC is a key, and ABC is also pruned by property 3.2. No other candidate remains, so the algorithm halts.

5 Experimental Results

FD_Mine was applied to fifteen datasets, obtained from the UCI Machine Learning Repository [8] and the results were compared to TANE [2]. TANE was selected for comparison because it establishes the theoretical framework for the problem. For the dataset given in Table 2.1, Figure 5.1(a) shows the semi-lattice for FD_Mine, and Figure 5.1(b) shows that for TANE. Each node represents a combination of attributes. If an edge is shown between nodes X and XY, then X→Y needs to be checked. Hence, the number of edges is the number of FDs that need to be checked. Both semi-lattices shown in Figure 5.1 have fewer edges than the lattice shown in Figure 2.1. In addition, the semi-lattice for FD_Mine has fewer edges than that for TANE.

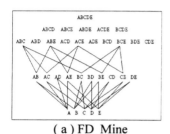 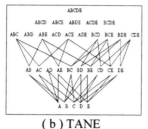

(a) FD_Mine   (b) TANE

Figure 5.1 Semi-lattices for the Data in Table 2.1

Table 5.1 compares the number of FDs that are checked on data by FD_Mine and TANE for 15 UCI datasets. Figure 5.2 shows more detailed results for the Imports-85 dataset. At levels 1 through 5, both algorithms check approximately the same number of FDs, but at levels 6 through 11, FD_Mine checks fewer FDs than TANE, because it prunes more unnecessary candidates than TANE by using the equivalences and FDs discovered at previous levels. For more results, see [9].

Dataset Name	# of Attr.	# of Rows	Total # of FDs Checked	
			FD_MINE	TANE
Abalone	8	4177	594	594
Balance-scale	5	625	70	70
Breast-cancer	10	191	5,095	5,095
Bridge	13	108	15,397	15,626
Cancer-Wisconsin	10	699	4,562	4,562
Chess	7	28,066	434	434
Crx	16	690	79,418	130,605
Echocardiogram	13	132	2,676	2,766
Glass	10	142	405	455
Hepatitis	20	155	1,161,108	1,272,789
Imports-85	26	205	2,996,737	3,564,176
Iris	5	150	70	70
Led	8	50	477	477
Nursery	9	12,960	2,286	2,286
Pendigits	17	7,494	223,143	227,714

Table 5.1 Comparison on UCI Datasets

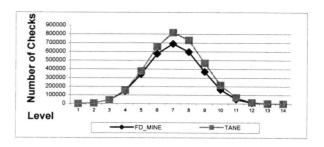

Figure 5.2 Graphical Comparison on Imports-85 Dataset

6 Conclusion

Based on our analysis of the theoretical properties of functional dependencies, equivalences among attributes were identified. Next, the FD_Mine algorithm, which finds functional dependencies in a dataset, is introduced here. Finally, FD_Mine was run on 15 UCI datasets. The results show that the FD_Mine is valuable because it reduces the size of the dataset or the number of checks required, but it does not to lead to loss of information or eliminate any valid candidates.

References

1. Flach, P. A., and Savnik, I., Database Dependency Discovery: A Machine Learning Approach. *AI Communications*, 12(3):139-160 1999.
2. Huhtala, Y., Kärkkäinen, J., Porkka, P., and Toivonen, H., TANE: An Efficient Algorithm for Discovering Functional and Approximate Dependencies. *The Computing Journal*, 42(2):100-111 1999.
3. Maier, D., *The Theory of Relational Databases*, Computer Science Press, 1983.
4. Mannila, H., and Räihä, K.J., Algorithms for Inferring Functional Dependencies from Relations. *Data and Knowledge Engineering*, 12(1):83-99 1994.
5. Mannila, H., and Toivonen, H., Levelwise Search and Borders of Theories in Knowledge Discovery. *Data Mining and Knowledge Discovery*, 1(3):241-258 1997.
6. Novelli, N., and Cicchetti, R., Functional and Embedded Dependency Inference: A Data Mining Point of View. *Information Systems*, 26(7):477-506 2001.
7. Roddick, J.F., Craske, N.G., Richards, T. J., Handling Discovered Structure in Database Systems. *IEEE Transactions on Knowledge and Data Engineering*, 8(2): 227-240 1996.
8. UCI Machine Learning Repository, http://www1.ics.uci.edu/~mlearn/MLRepository.html
9. Yao, H., Hamilton, H. J. and Butz, C. J., FD_MINE: Discovering Functional Dependencies in a Database Using Equivalences, University of Regina, Computer Science Department, Technical Report CS-02-04, August, 2002, ISBN 0-7731-0441-0.

Mining Genes in DNA Using GeneScout

Michael M. Yin
Department of Computer Science
New Jersey Institute of Technology
University Heights, Newark, NJ 07102, USA
mxy3100@njit.edu

Jason T. L. Wang
Department of Computer Science
New Jersey Institute of Technology
University Heights, Newark, NJ 07102, USA
wangj@oak.njit.edu

Abstract

In this paper, we present a new system, called GeneScout, for predicting gene structures in vertebrate genomic DNA. The system contains specially designed hidden Markov models (HMMs) for detecting functional sites including protein-translation start sites, mRNA splicing junction donor and acceptor sites, etc. Our main hypothesis is that, given a vertebrate genomic DNA sequence S, it is always possible to construct a directed acyclic graph G such that the path for the actual coding region of S is in the set of all paths on G. Thus, the gene detection problem is reduced to that of analyzing the paths in the graph G. A dynamic programming algorithm is used to find the optimal path in G. The proposed system is trained using an expectation-maximization (EM) algorithm and its performance on vertebrate gene prediction is evaluated using the 10-way cross-validation method. Experimental results show the good performance of the proposed system and its complementarity to a widely used gene detection system.

Keywords: Bioinformatics, Gene finding, Hidden Markov models, Knowledge discovery, Data mining

1 Introduction

Data mining, or knowledge discovery from data, refers to the process of extracting interesting, non-trivial, implicit, previously unknown and potentially useful information or patterns from data. In life sciences, this process could refer to finding clustering rules for gene expression, discovering classifications rules for proteins, detecting associations between metabolic pathways, predicting genes in genomic DNA sequences, etc. [6, 7].

Our research is targeted toward developing effective and accurate methods for automatically detecting gene structures in the genomes of high eukaryotic organisms. This paper presents a data mining system for automated gene discovery.

2 Our Approach

2.1 HMM Models for Predicting Functional Sites

Our proposed GeneScout system contains several specially designed HMM models for predicting functional sites as well as an HMM model for calculating coding potentials [8]. Often, the functional sites include (almost) invariant (consensus) nucleotides and other degenerate features. Thus, the invariant nucleotides themselves do not completely characterize a functional site. For example, a start codon is always a sequence of ATG and it is the start position in mRNA for protein translation, so the start codon is the first 3 bases of the coding region of a gene. ATG is also the codon for Methionine, a regular amino acid occurring at many positions in all of the known proteins. This means one is unable to detect the start codon by simply searching for ATG in a genomic DNA sequence.

It is reported that there are some statistic relations between a start codon ATG and the 13 nucleotides immediately preceding it and the 3 bases immediately following it [5]. We call these 19 bases containing a start codon a *start site*. We build an HMM model, called the Start Site Model, to model the start site. Figure 1 illustrates the model. As shown in Figure 1, there are 19 states for the Start Site Model. Except for states 14, 15 and 16, there are four possible bases at each state, and a base at one state may have four possible ways to transit to the next state. States 14, 15 and 16 are constant states (representing a start codon), and the transitions from state 14 to 15 and from state 15 to 16 are also constant with a probability of 1. With the Start Site Model, we can use the HMM algorithms described in our previously published paper [9] to detect a start site.[1]

---

[1] In the previously published paper [9], we presented HMM models and algorithms for detecting splicing junction donor and acceptor sites. The HMM model for a donor site contains 9 states whereas the HMM model for an acceptor site contains 16 states. The algorithms used for training the HMM models for start sites, donor sites and acceptor sites and for detecting these functional sites are similar. Please see related publications [8, 9] for details.

733

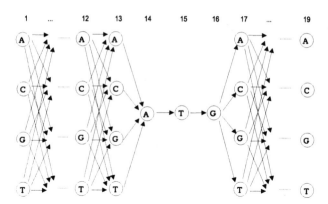

Figure 1. The Start Site Model.

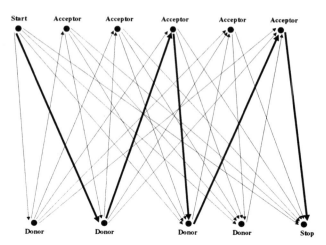

Figure 2. A site graph for gene detection with the boldface edges representing real exons-introns.

2.2 Graph Representation of the Gene Detection Problem

The goal of GeneScout is to find coding regions. The main hypothesis used in our work is that, given a vertebrate genomic DNA sequence S, it is always possible to construct a directed acyclic graph G such that the path for the actual coding region of S is in the set of all paths on G. Thus, the gene detection problem is reduced to the analysis of paths in the graph G. We use dynamic programming algorithms to find the optimal path in G.

Consider a directed acyclic graph G where vertices are functional sites, and edges are exons and introns (Figure 2). All the edges from the top vertices to the bottom vertices in the graph G are candidate exons, and the edges from the bottom vertices to the top vertices are candidate introns. There must be a path on G representing real exons-introns as shown by the boldface edges in Figure 2. So, given a vertebrate genomic DNA sequence with detected sites, it is always possible to construct a directed acyclic graph G such that the path for real exons-introns is in the set of all paths on G. Thus the gene detection problem is reduced to the analysis of paths in the graph G [4].

2.3 A Dynamic Programming Algorithm

Consider again the graph G in Figure 2. A candidate gene is represented by a path in G. Let S_G denote the set of all paths in G. We assign a score to each functional site based on the HMM models and algorithms described in Section 2.1 [8, 9]. The score is used as the weight of the corresponding vertex v in S_G, and we denote that weight as $W(v)$. We associate each edge (v_1, v_2) in S_G with a weight $W(v_1, v_2)$. The weight $W(v_1, v_2)$ equals the coding potential of the candidate exon or intron corresponding to the

edge (v_1, v_2) (the modeling and calculations of the coding potential are described in [8]).

Now, let v be a vertex in S_G and let $(v_1, v), \ldots, (v_k, v)$ be all edges entering v. Let $S(v)$ be the set of all paths entering the vertex v. We can calculate the weight of the optimal path in $S(v)$, denoted $\Theta(S(v))$, as follows:

$$\Theta(S(v)) = \max_{i=1}^{k}(\Theta(S(v_i)) + W(v_i) + W(v_i, v)) \quad (1)$$

This recurrence formula can be used for computing $\theta(S(v))$ given the set of weights $\theta(S(v_i))$, $i = 1, \ldots, k$. Thus a dynamic programming algorithm can be used to find the weight of the optimal path and locate the path itself in the graph G. This path indicates the real exons (coding region) in the given genomic DNA sequence.

In the testing (prediction, respectively) phase where an unlabeled test (new, respectively) sequence S is given, GeneScout first detects the functional sites on S and then builds a directed acyclic graph G using the detected functional sites as vertices. Next, GeneScout finds the optimal path on G and outputs the vertices (functional sites) and edges on the optimal path, which displays the coding region on S.

3 Experimental Results and Discussion

In evaluating the accuracy of the proposed GeneScout system for detecting vertebrate genes, we adopted the database of human DNA sequences (570 sequences in total) originally collected by Burset and Guigo [2].

We applied the 10-way cross-validation method [9] to evaluating how well GeneScout performs when tested on sequences that are not in the training data set. The GeneScout system is trained using the training data set (i.e., all sequences excluding those in the test data set are used as the training data) and then is tested on the sequences in the test data set. For each run, the training data set contains 90% of the total exons and the test data set contains 10% of the exons. Notice that each of the 570 sequences is used exactly once in the test data set.

Table 1 shows the results obtained in each run of cross-validation, and the average over all the ten runs. We estimate the prediction accuracy at both the nucleotide level and the exon level. At the nucleotide level, let TP_c be the number of true positives, FP_c be the number of false positives, TN_c be the number of true negatives, and FN_c be the number of false negatives. A *true positive* is a coding nucleotide that is correctly predicted as a coding nucleotide. A *false positive* is a non-coding nucleotide that is incorrectly predicted as a coding nucleotide. A *true negative* is a non-coding nucleotide that is correctly predicted as a non-coding nucleotide. A *false negative* is a coding nucleotide that is incorrectly predicted as a non-coding nucleotide. The sensitivity (S_c^n) and specificity (S_c^p) at the nucleotide level described in Table 1 are defined as follows:

$$S_c^n = \frac{TP_c}{TP_c + FN_c} \quad (2)$$

$$S_c^p = \frac{TP_c}{TP_c + FP_c} \quad (3)$$

The approximation correlation (AC) [2] is the measure that summarizes the prediction accuracy at the nucleotide level. AC ranges from -1 to 1. A value of 1 corresponds to a perfect prediction, while -1 corresponds to a prediction in which each coding nucleotide is predicted as a non-coding nucleotide, and vice versa. At the exon level, let TP_e be the number of true positives, FP_e be the number of false positives, TN_e be the number of true negatives, and FN_e be the number of false negatives. A *true positive* is an exon that is correctly predicted as an exon. A *false positive* is a non-exon that is incorrectly predicted as an exon. A *true negative* is a non-exon that is correctly predicted as a non-exon. A *false negative* is an exon that is incorrectly predicted as a non-exon. The sensitivity (S_e^n) and specificity (S_e^p) at the exon level described in Table 1 are defined as follows:

$$S_e^n = \frac{TP_e}{TP_e + FN_e} \quad (4)$$

$$S_e^p = \frac{TP_e}{TP_e + FP_e} \quad (5)$$

The result in Table 1 shows that, on average, GeneScout can correctly detect 86 percent of the coding nucleotides in

Run	Nucleotide			Exon	
	S_c^n	S_c^p	AC	S_e^n	S_e^p
1	0.86	0.78	0.77	0.51	0.49
2	0.85	0.79	0.77	0.50	0.48
3	0.86	0.80	0.78	0.52	0.50
4	0.85	0.78	0.75	0.49	0.51
5	0.87	0.78	0.78	0.53	0.48
6	0.85	0.79	0.77	0.53	0.49
7	0.84	0.80	0.77	0.52	0.49
8	0.87	0.77	0.76	0.49	0.47
9	0.86	0.78	0.77	0.51	0.48
10	0.86	0.80	0.77	0.52	0.50
Average	0.86	0.79	0.77	0.51	0.49

Table 1. Performance evaluation of the proposed GeneScout system for gene detection.

System	Nucleotide			Exon	
	S_c^n	S_c^p	AC	S_e^n	S_e^p
GeneScout	0.86	0.79	0.77	0.51	0.49
VEIL	0.83	0.72	0.73	0.53	0.49
FGENEH	0.77	0.88	0.78	0.61	0.64
GeneID	0.63	0.81	0.67	0.44	0.46
GeneParser 2	0.66	0.79	0.67	0.35	0.40
GenLang	0.72	0.79	0.69	0.51	0.52
GRAIL 2	0.72	0.87	0.75	0.36	0.43
SORFIND	0.71	0.85	0.73	0.42	0.47
Xpound	0.61	0.87	0.68	0.15	0.18
GenScan	0.93	0.90	0.91	0.78	0.81

Table 2. Performance comparison between GeneScout and other systems for gene detection.

the test data set. Among the predicted coding nucleotides, 79 percent are real coding nucleotides. At the exon level, GeneScout achieved a sensitivity of 51 percent and a specificity of 49 percent. This means GeneScout can detect 51 percent of exons in the test data set with both of their 5' and 3' ends being exactly correct.

Table 2 compares GeneScout with other gene finding tools on the same 570 vertebrate genomic DNA sequences. The performance data for the other tools shown in the table are taken from the paper authored by Burset and Guigo [2] except for the VEIL system, whose data is taken from the paper authored by Henderson *et al.* [3] and GenScan, whose data is published by Burge and Karlin [1]. It can be seen from Table 2 that GeneScout beats or is comparable to these other programs except GenScan.

It can be seen from the table that GenScan is more accurate than GeneScout at both the nucleotide level and the

Prediction Results	# of coding nucleotides	% of coding nucleotides
GenScan predicted correctly	414,049	93.2%
GeneScout predicted correctly	382,712	86.1%
GeneScout and GenScan both predicted correctly	361,821	81.4%
GeneScout predicted correctly and GenScan missed	20,891	4.7%
GenScan predicted correctly and GeneScout missed	52,228	11.7%
GenScan and GeneScout both missed	9,558	2.2%

Table 3. Complementarity between GenScan and GeneScout.

exon level. However, as indicated by GenScan's inventors Burge and Karlin [1], many of the 570 sequences collected by Burset and Guigo [2] were used to train the GenScan system. This means that a portion of the test sequences were used in GenScan's training process. In contrast, GeneScout is tested on the sequences that are completely unseen in the training phase. We ran GenScan on the 570 sequences and got the same performance data as shown in Table 2. Table 3 shows the complementarity between GenScan and GeneScout. For the 570 sequences that contained 444,498 coding nucleotides totally, GenScan correctly predicted 93.2 percent of the coding nucleotides, while GeneScout correctly predicted 86.1 percent of the coding nucleotides. If both systems are used together, one can correctly predict (81.4% + 4.7% + 11.7%) = 97.8% of the total coding nucleotides. This is higher than the sensitivity of either individual system. We also found out that GenScan did not correctly predict any coding nucleotides in eight of the 570 sequences. In contrast, GeneScout did not miss any of the test sequences and , for the eight sequences GenScan missed, GeneScout correctly detected about 85% of the coding nucleotides. GeneScout runs much faster than GenScan. For example, it takes GeneScout 0.8 seconds to predict the gene structure on a 5 kb sequence. For the same sequence, GenScan needs several seconds to finish. Run time for the GeneScout program is $O(NV^2)$ where N is the length of the input sequence and V is the number of vertices on the site graph constructed during the gene predicting process. In practice, the run time grows approximately linearly with the sequence length for sequences of several kb or more. Typical run time for a X kb sequence on a Sun Sparc10 workstation is about $0.1 \times (X + 3)$ seconds.

Future work includes the incorporation of more parameters or criteria into GeneScout. One source of possible new parameters could be obtained from the analysis of potential coding regions, such as preferred exon and intron lengths, and positions of exon-intron junctions relative to the reading frame. We may also model more functional sites such as those in the upstream or downstream of a coding region. These efforts will further improve GeneScout's performance to make it more accurate for vertebrate gene detection.

References

[1] C. Burge and S. Karlin, "Prediction of complete gene structures in human genomic DNA," *J. Mol. Biol.*, 268:78–94, 1997.

[2] M. Burset and R. Guigo, "Evaluation of gene structure prediction programs," *Genomics*, 34(3):353–367, 1996.

[3] J. Henderson, S. Salzberg, and K. H. Fasman, "Finding genes in DNA with a hidden Markov model," *Journal of Computational Biology*, 4(2):127–141, 1997.

[4] M. A. Roytberg, T. V. Astakhova, and M. S. Gelfand, "Combinatorial approaches to gene recognition," *Computers Chem.*, 21(4):229–235, 1997.

[5] S. L. Salzberg, "A method for identifying splice sites and translational start sites in eukaryotic mRNA," *Computer Applications in the Biosciences*, 13(4):365–376, 1997.

[6] J. T. L. Wang, S. Rozen, B. A. Shapiro, D. Shasha, Z. Wang, and M. Yin, "New techniques for DNA sequence classification," *Journal of Computational Biology*, 6(2):209–218, 1999.

[7] J. T. L. Wang, B. A. Shapiro, and D. Shasha, editors, *Pattern Discovery in Biomolecular Data: Tools, Techniques and Applications*. Oxford University Press, New York, New York, 1999.

[8] M. M. Yin, *Knowledge Discovery and Modeling in Genomic Databases*. Ph.D. Dissertation, Department of Computer Science, New Jersey Institute of Technology, 2002.

[9] M. M. Yin and J. T. L. Wang, "Effective hidden Markov models for detecting splicing junction sites in DNA sequences," *Information Sciences*, 139(1-2):139–163, 2001.

Clustering Spatial Data when Facing Physical Constraints

Osmar R. Zaïane
University of Alberta, Canada
zaiane@cs.ualberta.ca

Chi-Hoon Lee
University of Alberta, Canada
chihoon@cs.ualberta.ca

Abstract

Clustering spatial data is a well-known problem that has been extensively studied to find hidden patterns or meaningful sub-groups and has many applications such as satellite imagery, geographic information systems, medical image analysis, etc. Although many methods have been proposed in the literature, very few have considered constraints such that physical obstacles and bridges linking clusters may have significant consequences on the effectiveness of the clustering. Taking into account these constraints during the clustering process is costly, and the effective modeling of the constraints is of paramount importance for good performance. In this paper, we define the clustering problem in the presence of constraints – obstacles and crossings – and investigate its efficiency and effectiveness for large databases. In addition, we introduce a new approach to model these constraints to prune the search space and reduce the number of polygons to test during clustering. The algorithm DBCluC we present detects clusters of arbitrary shape and is insensitive to noise and the input order. Its average running complexity is O(NlogN) where N is the number of data objects.

1. Introduction

Recently, we are witnessing a resurgence of interest in new clustering techniques in the data mining community, and many effective and efficient methods have been proposed in the machine learning and data mining literature [7]. Those methods have focused on the performance in terms of effectiveness and efficiency for large databases. However, almost none of them have taken into account constraints that may be present in the data, or constraints on the clustering. These constraints have significant influence on the results of the clustering process of large spatial data. In a GIS application studying the movement of pedestrians to identify optimal bank machine placements, for example, the presence of a highway hinders the movement of pedestrians and should be considered as an obstacle, while a pedway

over this highway could be considered as a bridge. To the best of our knowledge, only two clustering algorithms for clustering spatial data in the presence of constraints have been proposed very recently: COD-CLARANS [6] based on a partitioning approach, and AUTOCLUST+ [2] based on a graph partitioning approach. COD-CLARANS [6] and AUTOCLUST+[2] propose algorithms to solve the problem of clustering in the presence of physical obstacles to cross such as rivers, mountain ranges, or highways, etc. The algorithm we propose, DBCluC (Density-Based Clustering with Constraints, pronounced DB-clu-see), is based on DB-SCAN [1] a density-based clustering algorithm that clearly outperforms the effectiveness and efficiency of CLARANS [5], the algorithm used for COD-CLARANS. In this paper, we also introduce a new idea for modeling constraints using simple polygons.

2. Modeling Constraints

DBSCAN, which is extended to DBCluC, is a clustering algorithm with two parameters, Eps and $MinPts$, utilizing the density notion that involves correlation between a data point and its neighbours [1]. In order for data points to be grouped, there must be at least a minimum number of points called $MinPts$ in $Eps - neighbourhood$, $N_{Eps}(p)$, from a data point p, given a radius Eps. In DBSCAN, the density concept is introduced by the notations: Directly density-reachable, Density-reachable, and Density-connected. These concepts define "Cluster" and "Noise". The detailed figures and discussion are found in [1].

The following definitions introduce the spatial relation between data objects and obstacles in a two dimension planar space before modeling obstacles represented by polygons.

Definition 1. (Visibility) Let $P(V, E)$ be a polygon with V vertices and E edges. Given two data objects o_i and o_j, *Visibility* is the relation between o_i and o_j in two dimension planar space, if an edge joining o_i and o_j is not intersected by P. Given a database D of n data objects D={d_1, d_2, d_3, ..., d_n}, an edge l joining vertices d_i and d_j where d_i, d_j

∈ D, i≠j, and i and j ∈ [1..n], d_i is *visible* to d_j, if l is not intersected by any e_k ∈ E.

Definition 2. (Visible Space) Given a set D of n data objects with a polygon $P(V, E)$, a visible space S is a space that has a set D' of data objects satisfying the following

(1) Space S is defined by three edges: the first edge(edges) $e∈E$ connects two minimal convex points v_i, v_j ∈V, the second edge f is the extension of the line connecting v_i and its other adjacent point v_k ∈V, and the third edge g is the extension of the line connecting v_j and its other adjacent point v_l ∈V.

(2) ∀ p, q ∈D', p and q are visible from each other in S. Thus, $D'⊆D$.

(3) S is not visible to any other visible space S'. Thus, $S∩S' =∅$.

2.1. Obstacle Modeling

While we model obstacles with polygons, a polygon is represented with a minimum set of line segments, called obstruction lines, such that the definition of visibility (Definition 1) is not compromised. This minimum set of lines is smaller than the number of edges in the polygon. This in turn reduces the search space. The obstruction lines in a polygon depend upon the type of polygon: convex or concave. Note that an obstacle creates a certain number of visible spaces along with the number of convex points. Before we discuss the idea to convert a given polygon into a set of primitive line segments (obstruction lines), we need to test if a given polygon is convex or concave. For the purpose, we have adopted a convexity test that determines a class of polygon as well as a type of all points in the polygon. There are two principle approaches to label a class of a point in a polygon: Summation of external angles and Turning direction [4]. Since Turning direction approach is more efficent than Summation of external angles approach, we adopt the Turning direction apporach.

2.1.1 Polygon Reduction

In order to model a polygon with a set of primitive edges, we have initially categorized the type of the polygon by the convexity test we presented in the previous section. Once we have labeled the type of a polygon as well as the type of vertex for all vertices in a polygon, we construct a set of primitive edges to maintain visible spaces (Definition 1). It is clear that a convex polygon should have the same number of visible spaces (Definition 2) as the number of vertices in the convex polygon since each convex vertex blocks visibility against its adjacent visible spaces. We observe the fact that two adjacent edges sharing a convex vertex in a polygon are interchangeable with two edges such that one of

them obstructs visibility in a dimension between two adjacent visible spaces that are created by the convex vertex and the other impedes visibility between two adjacent visible spaces and the rest of visible spaces created by the polygon. As a consequence, the initial polygon is to be represented as a loss-less set of primitive edges with respect to visibility (Definition 1). The loss-less conversion of the Polygon Reduction algorithm is proved in [4]. We introduce the following definition to model obstacles (polygons).

Definition 3. (An Obstruction line) Let P (V, E) be a polygon with a set of V vertices and a set of E edges. An obstruction line l is an edge whose two end vertices are two convex points v_i ∈ V and v_m ∈ V, while it is interior to P and not intersected with e ∈ E. An obstruction line of a convex point v ∈ V from the polygon P obstructs in a dimension the two visible spaces A_j and A_k created by two adjacent segments of v.

The detailed discussion about Polygon Reduction Algorithm is illustrated in [4]. Now, we define the concept of "Cluster" to extend from [1] since the problem this paper investigates considers obstacles and formalize their concept. The following notions are necessary to take into account disconnectivity constraints. Note that the definition of "Noise" is equivalent to DBSCAN. The illustration of examples of each notion is shown in [4].

Definition 4. (Directly obstacle free density-reachable) A point p is directly obstacle free density-reachable from a point q with respect to *Eps, MinPts* if

(1) p ∈ $N_{Eps}(q)$

(2) p is obstacle-free from q, where "obstacle-free" denotes that an edge joining p and q is not intersected by any obstacle.

(3) $|N_{obstacle-free}(q)| ≥ MinPts$, where $|N_{obstacle-free}(q)|$ denotes the number of points that are obstacle-free from q in the circle of radius *Eps* and centre q

Definition 5. (Obstacle free density-reachable) A point p is obstacle free density-reachable from a point q with respect to Eps and MinPts if there is a chain of points p_1, .., p_n, p_1 = q, , p_n = p such that p_{i+1} is directly obstacle free density-reachable from p_i.

Definition 6. (Obstacle free Density-connected) A point p is obstacle free density-connected to a point q with respect to *Eps* and *MinPts*, if there is a point o such that both p and q are obstacle free density-reachable from o with respect to *Eps* and *MinPts*.

Definition 7. (Cluster) Given a set D of n data objects D={d_1, d_2, d_3, . . ., d_n} with respect to a set of obstacles, a cluster is a set C of c data objects C={ c_1, c_2, c_3, . . ., c_c }, where C ⊆ D. Let D be a database of points. A cluster C with respect to *Eps* and *MinPts* is a non-empty subset of D satisfying the following conditions: Let i and j ∈ [1..n] such that i ≠ j.

(1) Maximality. $\forall$ d_i, d_j if d_i ∈ C and d_j is obstacle free density-reachable from d_i with respect to *Eps* and *MinPts*, then d_j ∈ C.

(2) Connectivity. $\forall$ d_i, d_j ∈ C, d_i is obstacle free density-connected to d_j with respect to *Eps* and *MinPts*.

2.2. Modeling Crossing

In this section, we present a modeling scheme of a constraint *Crossing (Bridge)* in a two dimension planar space. Before formalizing a crossing that can connect data points from different clusters, we need a modeling scheme to consign connectivity functionality of a bridge as well as to control connectivity flow for a wide range of applications. For this purpose, we introduce "*Entry point*" and "*Entry edge*" notions. An *Entry point* is a point on the perimeter of the polygon crossing when it is Eps-reachable given point *p* with respect to *Eps*, where $Eps - reachable$ of an Entry point is any data point which is in an Eps-neighbourhood. As a result *p* becomes reachable by any other point *x* Eps-reachable from any other Entry point of the same crossing with respect to *Eps*. In other words, given two different Entry points, p_1 and p_2, at two extremities of a crossing; a point *a* is Eps-reachable to p_1 with respect to *Eps*; and a point *b* is Eps-reachable to p_2 with respect to *Eps*, *a* and *b* are then connected by Definition "density-connected [1]". An *Entry edge* is an edge of a crossing polygon with a set of Entry points starting from one endpoint of the edge to the other separated by an interval value i_e where $i_e \leq Eps$. The descriptions of Entry points and Entry edges are amalgamated with the definition of crossings as follows.

Definition 8. (Crossing) A crossing (or bridge) is a set *B* of *m* points generated from all Entry edges. By definition any point b_m ∈ B is reachable by all other points in *B*.

Before a bridge is modeled, the bridge *B* is denoted by *B(P, E)*, where *P* is a set of Entry points and a set of Entry edges *E*. Thus a bridge *"connects"* objects such as clusters or data points that are $Eps - reachable$ from all Entry points generated from the bridge. The $Eps - reachable$ are not affected by any obstacle entities. In other words, crossing entities have a priority over obstacle entities, unless otherwise specified.

3. DBCluC Algorithm

Once we have modeled obstacles using the polygon reduction algorithm and modeled crossing constraints, DB-CluC starts the clustering procedure from an arbitrary data point. This is the advantage of DBCluC in that the performance is not sensitive to an input order. Due to the arbitrary selection of an initial starting point, DBCluC can consider crossing constraints *after or while* clustering data points. This enables DBCluC to be flexible in revising discovered clusters. The clustering procedure in DBCluC is similar to that of DBSCAN [1], with respect to the density notion. Hence, all definitions introduced in Section 2 are extended to DBCluC. Using the Polygon Reduction algorithm, DB-CluC efficiently performs the clustering of data objects with obstacles. In addition, DBCluC groups distant clusters with crossing constraints, which maximize the density-reachable by *Entry edges* and *Entry points*.

Input : Database, Crossings, and Obstacles
Output : A set of clusters
1 // While clustering, bridges are taken into account;
2 Start clustering from Entry points of crossings ;
3 **for** *Remaining Data Points Point from Database* **do**
4   **if** *ExpandCluster(Database...)* **then**
5 | ClusterId = nextId(ClusterId);
    endif
endfor

Algorithm 1: DBCluC

In Algorithm 1, crossing constraints are taken into account while clustering data objects. *DBCluC* maximally expands a set of clusters such that all data points that are reachable by crossings are grouped together. Note that *DB-CluC* can also consider crossing constraints after clustering. However, when it comes to dynamic evaluation of correlations between data objects and constraints, the crossing constraints must be processed in the course of clustering. "Database" is a set of data points to be clustered in Algorithm 1. In this paper, the database is limited to two dimensional space for experimental purposes. Line 1 initiates the clustering procedure from a set of entry points that are modeled from crossing constraints. Thus, a set of data objects is maximally grouped according to the crossing connectivity defined by a set of entry points in crossing constraints. Once a maximum set of clusters is discovered after Line 2, Line 3 builds up a cluster from data objects that are not reachable by the crossing connectivity in the database. In the course of clustering, Line 5 assigns a new cluster id for the next expandable cluster. The ExpandCluster in Algorithm 1 may seem similar to the function of the DBSCAN. However, the distinction is that obstacles are considered in RetrieveNeighbours (Point, Eps, Obstacles). Given a query point, neighbours of the query point are retrieved using SR-tree [3].

4. Performance

In this section we evaluate the performance of the algorithm in terms of effectiveness and scalability on a Pentium III 700Mhz machine running Linux 2.4.17 with 256MB memory. For the purpose of the experiments, we have generated synthetic datasets. Due to the limited space, we report evaluations varying the size of the dataset and the number of obstacles in order to demonstrate the scalability of DBCluC. More experiments are available in [4]. Figure 1 represents the execution time in seconds for eight datasets varying in size from 25K to 200K showing good scalability. The execution time is almost linear to the number of data objects. Figure 2 presents the execution time in seconds by varying the number of obstacles. According to our experiments, DBCluC is scalable for large databases with complicated obstacles and bridges in terms of size of the database and the number of constraints running in $O(N \cdot \log N)$, where N is the number of data objects in a database, if we adopt an indexing scheme for obstacles.

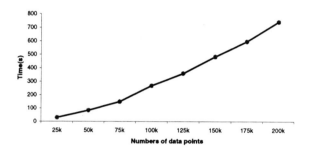

Figure 1. Algorithm Run Time by varying the number of data points

5. Conclusions

In this paper we have addressed the problem of clustering spatial data in the presence of physical constraints: obstalces and crossings. We have proposed a model for these constraints using polygons and have devised a method for reducing the edges of polygons representing obstacles by identifying a minimum set of line segments, called obstruction lines, that does not compromise the visibility spaces. The polygon reduction algorithm reduces the number of lines representing a polygon by half, and thus reduces the search space by half. We have also defined the concept of reachability in the context of obstacles and crossings and have used it in the designation of the clustering process. Owing to the effectiveness of the density-based approach, DBCluC finds clusters of arbitrary shapes and sizes with minimum domain knowledge. In addition, experiments

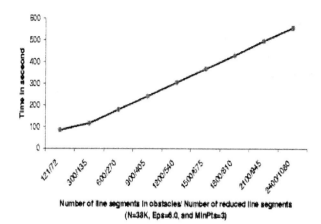

Figure 2. Algorithm Run Time by varying the number obstacles

have shown scalability of DBCluC in terms of size of the database in number of data points as well as scalability in terms of number and complexity of physical constraints.

References

[1] M. Ester, H.-P. Kriegel, J. Sander, and X. Xu. A density-based algorithm for discovering clusters in large spatial databases with noise. In *Knowledge Discovery and Data Mining*, pages 226–231, 1996.

[2] V. Estivill-Castro and I. Lee. Autoclust+: Automatic clustering of point-data sets in the presence of obstacles. In *International Workshop on Temporal and Spatial and Spatio-Temporal Data Mining (TSDM2000)*, pages 133–146, 2000.

[3] N. Katayama and S. Satoh. The SR-tree: an index structure for high-dimensional nearest neighbor queries. In *Proc. of the 1997 ACM SIGMOD Intl. Conf.*, pages 369–380, 1997.

[4] C.-H. Lee. Density-based clustering of spatial data in the presence of physical constraints. Master's thesis, University of Alberta, Edmonton, AB, Canada, July 2002.

[5] R. Ng and J. Han. Efficient and effective clustering methods for spatial data mining. In *Proc. of VLDB Conf.*, pages 144–155, 1994.

[6] A. K. H. Tung, J. Hou, and J. Han. Spatial clustering in the presence of obstacles. In *Proc. 2001 Int. Conf. On Data Engineering(ICDE'01)*, 2001.

[7] O. R. Zaïane, A. Foss, C.-H. Lee, and W. Wang. On data clustering analysis: Scalability, constraints and validation. In *Sixth Pacific-Asia Conference on Knowledge Discovery and Data Mining (PAKDD'02)*, Lecture Notes in AI (LNAI 2336), pages 28–39, Taipei, Taiwan, May 2002.

Mining Surveillance Video for Independent Motion Detection

Zhongfei (Mark) Zhang
Computer Science Department
Watson School of Engineering and Applied Science
State University of New York (SUNY) at Binghamton
Binghamton, NY 13902, USA
zhongfei@cs.binghamton.edu

Abstract

This paper addresses the special applications of data mining techniques in homeland defense. The problem targeted, which is frequently encountered in military/intelligence surveillance, is to mine a massive surveillance video database automatically collected to retrieve the shots containing independently moving targets. A novel solution to this problem is presented in this paper, which offers a completely qualitative *approach to solving for the automatic independent motion detection problem directly from the compressed surveillance video in a faster than real-time mining performance. This approach is based on the linear system consistency analysis, and consequently is called* **QLS**. *Since the* **QLS** *approach only focuses on what exactly is necessary to compute a solution, it saves the computation to a minimum and achieves the efficacy to the maximum. Evaluations from real data show that* **QLS** *delivers effective mining performance at the achieved efficiency.*

1 Introduction

A target in motion from a surveillance video may be interpreted as a potential suspicious activity. If the camera is still, the problem of automatic detection of motion from the video is trivial. However, in many applications, it is *not possible* to have a still camera. An example is in the automatic data collection in military surveillance using unmanned aerial vehicles (UAVs), such as US Predators. In this case, the surveillance goal is to detect any military maneuvers, which are typically manifested as the target motion in the video. Note that since in this case the cameras in UAVs are also in motion, the problem of detecting any target motion is consequently translated to the problem of detecting *independent motion* (IM) — the motion other than the camera motion. Fig. 1

shows exemplary frames from the real US Predator surveillance videos that represent two different scenarios: a scene with IM and a scene without IM. Due to the fact of large scale, automatic data collection (multiple Predators in nonstop data collection) in a typical military surveillance, the data volume is *massive*. It is noted that due to the fast development of unmanned surveillance and data collection technologies, the existence of such massive surveillance databases is ubiquitous. On the other hand, manual mining for the detection of IM is painfully proven to be extremely tedious and prohibitively expensive. Consequently, solutions to automatically mining video data to retrieve shots containing IM are in high demand. This paper addresses this data mining problem, and motivated by this demand, a highly efficient and effective data mining algorithm is developed in this research for automatically retrieving any shots that contain IM from a surveillance video.

There are two scenarios related to IM detection. Given a video sequence, *quantitative IM detection* refers to *temporal* segmentation into those shots that contain the scene in which one or more independently moving targets are present, and *spatial* segmentation and delineation of each of the independently moving targets in each of the frames of these shots. *Qualitative IM detection*, on the other hand, refers to only the *temporal* segmentation of the video sequence to return those shots that contain IM; it does not perform spatial segmentation to identify the independently moving targets in each frame. The focus of this paper is primarily on qualitative IM detection. Taking the motivated applications of the US military surveillance data shown in Fig. 1, once the shots containing IM are *automatically* detected and retrieved, the major painstaking and tedious mining effort (i.e., manual searching the massive video data to detect those shots containing IM) is saved because the

741

majority of the video does not have IM. Therefore, in terms of the data mining concern for detecting IM, the objective is qualitative IM detection from the temporal sequence of the video, as opposed to quantitative IM detection in all the frames.

Motion analysis has been a focused topic in computer vision and image understanding research for many years [8, 3, 2]. IM analysis deals with multiple motion components simultaneously, and therefore, presumably is more challenging.

Most of the existing techniques for IM detection in the literature aim at quantitative detection [7, 4, 1]. Due to this fact, very few of them can afford efficient performance, as their solutions to temporal IM detection depend on spatial IM segmentations. While quantitative detection is useful in general, due to the specific applications that have motivated this project, a qualitative approach is sufficient. This is based on the following two reasons. (i) In the military and intelligence applications, the time issue, i.e., the detection efficiency, is always an important concern. Obviously the qualitative approach saves time as the spatial segmentation in the image domain in each frame is avoided. (ii) It is not necessary to take a quantitative approach in these applications. Even if the independently moving targets are all segmented and identified in each frame in the quantitative approaches, given the current status of computer vision and artificial intelligence in general, it is *not possible* to have a fully automated capability to interpret whether the segmented and identified IM in the frames indicates any military or intelligence significance without human expertise' interaction. Therefore, these detected shots must be left to the Image Analysts for further analysis anyway, *regardless* of whether or not the independently moving targets are segmented and identified in each frames of these shots.

The other observation is that in the literature, most of the existing techniques for IM detection are based on image sequences, as opposed to compressed video streams. This restriction (or assumption) significantly hinders these techniques from practical applications, as in today's world, information volume grows explosively, and all the video sequences are archived in compressed forms. This is particularly true in the applications this paper concerns, in which the data volume is *massive* and they must be archived in a compressed form, such as MPEG.

Based on these considerations, we have developed a completely *qualitative* approach to solving for the automatic IM detection problem *directly* from the compressed surveillance video in an *efficient* performance. By an efficient performance, it is meant that the data mining speed is faster than the real-time performance. This capability allows two possible application scenarios for this technology. The first is to equip this algorithm with the sensors to allow real-time data mining while the sensors are in surveillance. The second is to mine an archived surveillance video database in which all the video data are stored in a compressed format; the fast scanning performance allows efficiently automatic mining the data to retrieve shots containing IM. This qualitative approach is based on the linear system consistency analysis, and consequently is called **QLS**.

2 QLS

Assuming that the camera model is a 3D to 2D affine [5], it can be shown [10] that given n macroblocks in a frame of an MPEG compressed video stream, we can build a linear system:

$$D_m = \xi_m b_m \tag{1}$$

with the following theorem:

Theorem 2.1 *Given n macroblocks in a video frame represented in the linear system in Eq. 1, if there is no IM with any of these macroblocks, then the linear system is consistent.*

The consistency of Eq. 1 is defined by determining the value of the statistic R:

$$R = \frac{\sigma_{min}(D_m)}{\sigma_{min}(D_m b_m)} \tag{2}$$

where $\sigma_{min}(D_m)$ and $\sigma_{min}(D_m b_m)$ are the smallest singular values of the coefficient matrix D_m and the augmented matrix $D_m b_m$, respectively, assuming Eq. 1 has unique solution if it is consistent; multiple solution cases may be handled similarly. Consequently, Eq. 1 is consistent *iff* R is above a threshold.

In MPEG compression standard, for each macroblock in a frame, if this macroblock is inter-coded, there is a motion vector available. Since the macroblock information (including the motion vector and the center coordinates) can be easily obtained directly from a compressed MPEG video stream, we have a linear system Eq. 1 that can directly work on the MPEG compressed data without having to depend on a specific algorithm to compute the correspondence or optical flow between the two frames, and without having to decompress the video stream [6]. If the macroblock is intra-coded, we just exclude this macroblock from the linear system of Eq. 1. If the frame is an I frame in which all the macroblocks are intra-coded, $R = 1$. This could be a false positive, which can be easily removed by filtering the R statistics, resulting in rejection of this false positive in the final detection.

We use the normal flow [9, 7] to detect IM. The rationale is that if the normal flow is low, the motion vector is probably not accurately estimated; consequently this macroblock should be rejected from Eq. 1.

Now the **QLS** algorithm is summarized as follows, which takes four parameters: the normal flow threshold T_n, the scan window width r, the R statistic threshold T_R, and the defined minimum number of frames T_f of a segment that contains IM.

Scan an input video stream in compressed MPEG
For every pair of consecutive frames
    Start to build up the linear system Eq. 1
    For each macroblock M of frame l of the pair
    Estimate the normal flow $\nabla I(M)$ of M
    If $\nabla I(M) > T_n$
        Incorporate M into Eq. 1
    Compute R of the linear system Eq. 1
Compute the median filtered $\bar{R}$ over a window of r
If $\bar{R} - 1 > T_R$
    Label l as no IM (NIM)
Else, label l as a frame with IM (IM)
Any IM segment $> T_f$ is retrieved

3 Experimental Evaluations

We have implemented the **QLS** as a stand alone version in a Windows2000 platform with Pentium III 800 MHz CPU and 512 MB memory. Fig. 1(c) and (d) show the *original* R statistics computed at every frames for the two shots from two surveillance videos in Fig. 1(a) and (b), respectively. The statistics are obvious to tell whether and where there is IM in the video. The first shot containing 1119 frames describes an IM of a missile launcher moving to its destination. The mean of the original R is 1.0 and the deviation is 0.00122 over the 1119 frames. The second shot containing 1058 frames surveys an area of ground terrain with no IM. The mean of the original R is 1.389 and the deviation is 0.169 over the 1058 frames. A separate evaluation with over 160,000 frames of real

surveillance data indicates an 81.27% precision and a 93.6% recall of **QLS** [10].

Since **QLS** essentially just needs to compute the R value for each frame, and since in each frame there is typically a very limited number of macroblocks, the complexity of **QLS** is very low. The current implemented version of **QLS** scans a compressed MPEG video with a typical frame resolution of 240 by 350 at the speed of 35 frames/second under the current platform, which is already faster than real-time. Note that this implementation is just for proof of the concept and the code has not been optimized. This shows that **QLS** holds great promise and vitality in the future applications in both proposed scenarios: real time data mining equipped with the sensors and fast data mining for an archived database.

4 Conclusions

This paper presents an efficient and effective approach to automatically mining surveillance video data for IM based on a qualitative, linear system approach called **QLS**. As compared with the existing techniques and available technologies, the **QLS** has the following distinctive advantages: (i) No camera calibration is required or necessary, i.e., image coordinates directly from the video frame may be used without having to convert them into calibrated coordinates. (ii) The statistics computed in the algorithm are stable due to the *Low condition numbers* of the matrices, resulting in avoiding the unstable matrix computation problem of high condition numbers typically existing in many computer vision and image understanding techniques. (iii) No specific motion model is assumed, i.e., **QLS** is able to detect IM for any motion models, either planar or parallax motion, or either dense parallax or sparse parallax camera motion. (iv) **QLS** is able to detect IM only based on two frames, as opposed to some techniques in the literature requiring more than two frames. (v) Due to the qualitative nature, the **QLS** complexity is very low, and is able to have efficient detection. (vi) **QLS** directly works on the compressed data; it does not need to decompress a video before applying the detection. (vii) **QLS** only requires one camera video stream to be able to detect IM, as opposed to some techniques in the literature that require stereo video streams.

Acknowledgment

This work is supported in part by NEC Research Institute, Inc. at Princeton, NJ, DARPA, and AFOSR. The author acknowledges Stoyan Kourtev and Xunyin Wang at SUNY Binghamton, Binghamton, NY, for part of the implementation of **QLS**. The author is also grateful to David W. Jacobs at NEC Research Institute for many useful and enlightening discussions.

References

[1] A.A. Argyros and S.C. Orphanoudakis. Independent 3D motion detection based on depth elimination in normal flow fields. In *Proc. International Conference on Computer Vision and Pattern Recognition*. IEEE Computer Society Press, 1997.

[2] O. Faugeras. *Three-Dimensional Computer Vision: A Geometric Viewpoint*. MIT Press, 1993.

[3] T.S. Huang and C.H. Lee. Motion and structure from orthographic views. *IEEE Trans. Pattern Analysis and Machine Intelligence*, 11:536–540, 1989.

[4] M. Irani and P. Anandan. A unified approach to moving object detection in 2D and 3D scenes. In *Proc. of IUW*, 1996.

[5] D.W. Jacobs. *Recognizing 3-D Objects Using 2-D Images*. Ph.D. Dissertation, MIT AI Lab., 1992.

[6] S-W. Lee, Y-M. Kim, and S.W. Choi. Fast scene change detection using direct feature extraction from MPEG compressed videos. *IEEE Trans. Multimedia*, 2(4):240–254, 2000.

[7] R. Sharma and Y. Aloimonos. Early detection of independent motion from active control of normal image flow patterns. *IEEE Trans. SMC*, 26(1):42–53, 1996.

[8] S. Ullman. *The Interpretation of Visual Motion*. MIT Press, 1979.

[9] A. Verri and T. Poggio. Motion field and optical flow: qualitative properties. *IEEE Trans. Pattern Analysis and Machine Intelligence*, 11(5):490–498, 1989.

[10] Z. Zhang. Qualitative independent motion detection. *Computer Science Tech Report*, 2002.

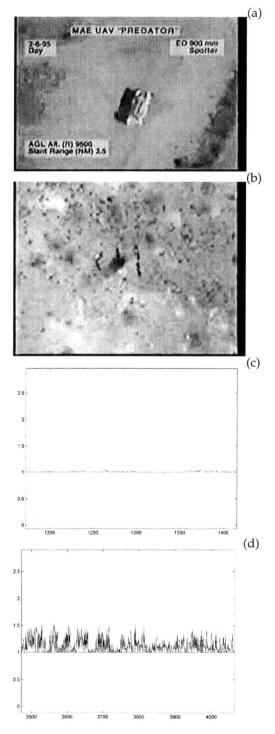

Figure 1: (a) An example of a shot containing an independently moving target (a missile launcher) (b) An example of a shot containing no IM (terrain) (c) The original R statistics computed for the shot in (a) (1119 frames) (d) The original R statistics computed for the shot in (b) (1058 frames).

Adaptive Parallel Sentences Mining from Web Bilingual News Collection

Bing Zhao, Stephan Vogel

Language Technologies Institute, School of Computer Science, Carnegie Mellon University
{*bzhao, vogel+*}@cs.cmu.edu

Abstract

In this paper a robust, adaptive approach for mining parallel sentences from a bilingual comparable news collection is described. Sentence length models and lexicon-based models are combined under a maximum likelihood criterion. Specific models are proposed to handle insertions and deletions that are frequent in bilingual data collected from the web. The proposed approach is adaptive, updating the translation lexicon iteratively using the mined parallel data to get better vocabulary coverage and translation probability parameter estimation. Experiments are carried out on 10 years of Xinhua bilingual news collection. Using the mined data, we get significant improvement in word-to-word alignment accuracy in machine translation modeling.

1. Introduction

Parallel corpora are major resources for many natural language processing systems like cross-lingual information retrieval and statistical machine translation, which heavily rely on word-level translation equivalences. Existing parallel data resources available through organizations like the Linguistic Data Consortium are often limited in size, limited to major languages and not representative for specific tasks. Therefore, the Web is seen as an important source for bilingual corpora [2, 5, 6]. The focus so far has been to find parallel web pages, i.e. pairs of web pages where one is the translation of the other. For parallel corpora, which were created by translating existing text into some other language, a number of alignment approaches has been proposed [3, 5]. Using sentence length information or bilingual dictionaries proved efficient for this task.

Very often one can find data, which is not parallel in this strict sense but still closely related by conveying the same information. We call such data comparable. An example of such a resource is the news stories published by the Xinhua news agency in Chinese and English, which we used in our experiments. Building a sentence aligned bilingual corpus from such data is a much harder task than generating a sentence alignment for parallel data. The sentence alignment algorithm has not only to cope with sentences that have no translation at all, i.e. with insertions and deletions, but it also has to evaluate the sentence pairs how good translations they are. That is to say, we need to have an alignment model that gives reliable scores for all

sentence pairs, which allows filtering out those that are not proper translations.

In our approach, a maximum likelihood criterion is proposed, which combines sentence length models and a statistical lexicon model. Specific models are formulated for insertions and deletions. The statistical lexicon can be extracted from an already existing sentence aligned parallel corpus. For sentence aligning the comparable corpus, which may be from a different domain, this poses the problem of low coverage resulting in less reliable alignment scores. To alleviate this problem we propose an iterative process that adapts the lexicon towards the new corpus, thereby giving higher vocabulary coverage and more reliable sentence alignment.

The paper is structured as follows: Section 2 presents the sentence alignment model. The translation lexicon based and sentence length based models are described in section 3 and 4. In section 5 experiments on a comparable bilingual news collection are demonstrated. Discussion and conclusions are given in section 6.

2. Alignment Model

Let S denote a news story in the source language (Chinese) and T a news story in the target language (English). Each story can be represented as a sequence of sentences as follows:

$$S = \{s_1, s_2, ..., s_j, ..., s_J\}, \qquad T = \{t_1, t_2, ..., t_i, ..., t_I\},$$

where s_j and t_i are sentence appearing in order in S and T respectively. The sentence alignment model is to calculate the distance between all possible parallel pairs (s_j, t_i) and to align them. The distance is based on both a translation lexicon and sentence length models. Dynamic Programming (DP) is applied to find the Viterbi path aligning the two sentence sequences in (S, T), and all aligned pairs are extracted and filtered from the alignment.

2.1. Maximum Likelihood Criterion

Let A denote the alignment between S and T. We want to find the sentence alignment $A^*_{[1:J][1:I]}$ that gives maximum likelihood of aligning S and T as follows:

$$A^*_{[1:J][1:I]} = \arg\max_A \{P(S:T \mid A)\} \qquad (1)$$

A consists of sub-alignments, $a_{(j,x)(i,y)} = \{[s_j, \cdots; s_{j+x}] : [t_i, \cdots; t_{i+y}]\}$, where x sentences in S are aligned to y sentences in T. Both x and y can be larger than 1 indicating one-to-many alignments, or zero indicating insertions/deletions. There are seven types allowed in our approach as defined in section 2.2. Under the assumption that the $a_{(j,x):(i,y)}$ are independent of each other, the probability in (1) can be approximated as follows:

$$
\begin{aligned}
P([1,s_j]:[1,t_i]\,|\,A) &= \prod_{a_{j,x):(i,y)}\in A} P(a_{(j,x)(i,y)}\,|\,A) \\
&= \prod_{a_{j,x):(i,y)}\in A}(P(A\,|\,a_{(j,x)(i,y)})P(a_{(j,x)(i,y)})/P(A)) \\
&= \prod_{a_{j,x):(i,y)}\in A}(P(A\,|\,a_{(j,x)(i,y)})P([s_j\cdots s_{j+x}],[t_i\cdots t_{i+y}])/P(A)) \\
&= \prod_{a_{i,x):(i,y)}\in A} P(A\,|\,a_{(j,x)(i,y)})P([s_j\cdots s_{j+x}]\,|\,[t_i\cdots t_{i+y}])P([t_i\cdots t_{i+y}])/P(A)
\end{aligned}
\tag{2}
$$

We assume that all possible alignments A between story S and story T are equally probable, thus $P(A)$ is a const and can be omitted during the maximization in (1). Again, under the independence assumption regarding the $a_{(j,x):(i,y)}$, the maximization process can be implemented via a standard dynamic programming strategy depicted as follows:

$$
\begin{aligned}
A^*_{j+x,i+y} &= \arg\min_A\{-\log P([s_1\cdots s_{j+x}]:[t_1\cdots t_{i+y}]\,|\,A)\} \\
&\cong \arg\min_A\{D(([s_1\cdots s_{j+x}]:[t_1\cdots t_{i+y}]\,|\,A)\} \\
&= \arg\min_A\{D([s_1\cdots s_{j-1}]:[t_1\cdots t_{i-1}]\,|\,A^*_{j-1,i-1}) + d([s_j\cdots s_{j+x}]:[t_i\cdots t_{i+y}]\,|\,A)\} \\
d([s_j\cdots s_{j+x}]:[t_i\cdots t_{i+y}]\,|\,A) &= -\log(P(a_{(j,x)(i,y)}\,|\,A)) \\
&= -\log(P(A\,|\,[s_j\cdots s_{j+x}])P([s_j\cdots s_{j+x}]\,|\,[t_i\cdots t_{i+y}])P([t_i\cdots t_{i+y}]))
\end{aligned}
$$

In (2), there are two types of probabilities: the *translation* probability $P([s_j:s_{j+x}]\,|\,[t_i:t_{i+y}])$ and *non-translation* probabilities: $P(A\,|\,a_{(j,x)(i,y)})$ and $P([t_i:t_{i+y}])$. These probabilities are to be approximated using lexicon-based models stated in section 3 and two sentence length models as stated in section 4.

2.2 Alignment types in Dynamic Programming

There are seven alignment types of $a_{(j,x):(i,y)}$ allowed in our dynamic programming approach as shown in Figure 1.

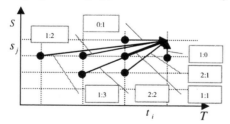

Figure-1 *Seven alignment types in DP*

The different alignment types $(x{:}y)$ we use are: 1:1 (substitution), 1:0 (deletion), 0:1 (insertion), 1:2 (expansion), 2:1 (contraction), 1:3 (tri-expansion), and 2:2 (merge). For different language pairs and other corpora additional alignment types such as 3:1 and 3:3 might prove helpful.

3. Translation Lexicon Models

We used a statistical translation lexicon known as *Model-1* [1, 4] for both efficiency and simplicity. Detailed information can be found in [1].

Model-1 is the conditional probability that a word *sw* in the source language is translated given word *tw* in the target language: *t(sw|tw)*. The translation probability can be reliably estimated using the EM algorithm. The probability for an alignment of source sentence *s* given target sentence *t* is calculated as:

$$
P(s\,|\,t) = \frac{1}{(l+1)^m}\prod_{j=1}^{m}\sum_{i=0}^{l}t(sw_j\,|\,tw_i)
\tag{3}
$$

where l and m are the corresponding sentence length measured as number of words in the sentences *s* and *t*.

In our approach, probability (3) is further normalized so that the probabilities for different lengths of sentence *s* are comparable at the word level:

$$
\overline{P}(s\,|\,t) = \left[\frac{1}{(l+1)^m}\prod_{j=1}^{m}\sum_{i=0}^{l}t(sw_j\,|\,tw_i)\right]^{1/m}
\tag{4}
$$

This sentence alignment probability can be shown to reach global maximum [1], and leads itself to adaptation. We can use the mined parallel data to retrain *model*-1 and update the alignment with better vocabulary coverage and better sentence alignment probability estimation in (4).

3.1. Explicit Alignments

The explicit alignments $a_{(j,x):(i,y)}$ are those alignments of which x and y are non-zero, including 1:2, 1:3, 2:2, 2:1, and 1:1. The calculation of the *translation* probability $P([s_j:s_{j+x}]\,|\,[t_i:t_{i+y}])$ in (2) is now explicit and straight forward. Let $s=[s_j:s_{j+x}]$ and $t=[t_i:t_{i+y}]$, and equation (4) is applied directly in this case.

3.2. Implicit Alignments: Background Models

Implicit alignments $a_{(j,x):(i,y)}$ are needed for deletions and insertions, where a text segment is aligned to Empty text. These correspond to the noises in the alignment, which have no translation counterpart in the comparable text. They are expressed by setting x or y zero.

One possibility is to align all words to an imaginary empty word "*NULL*", then apply (4). But this probability of aligning a word to *NULL* is very unreliable to be estimated; also both *t(fw|NULL)* and *t(NULL|ew)* need to be estimated, which will introduce more computation load and uncertainty; third, the length of the "empty text" in equation (4) is problematic to define.

In our approach, we build two background models, where the empty text is defined as all of the words in the vocabulary of a language. By this we actually assumed a large "sentence" consisting of all of the words in that vocabulary. The sentence length is then the vocabulary size of that language. The insertion and deletion can now be defined as follows:

For deletion, the probability of aligning text s to empty text segment $\overline{P}(s \mid NULL)$ is defined via equation (4):

$$\overline{P}(s \mid NULL) = \left[\frac{1}{\mid V_T \mid^m} \prod_{j=1}^{m} \sum_{i=0}^{\mid V_T \mid} t(sw_j \mid tw_i) \right]^{1/m} \quad (5)$$

where $\mid V_T \mid$ is the vocabulary size of target language eg. English. For insertion, we have correspondingly:

$$\overline{P}(NULL \mid t) = \left[\frac{1}{(l+1)^{\mid V_S \mid}} \prod_{j=1}^{\mid V_S \mid} \sum_{i=0}^{l} t(sw_j \mid tw_i) \right]^{1/\mid V_S \mid} \quad (6)$$

Intuitively, common words in English are more likely to be insertions, and common words in Chinese are more likely to be deletions. Equations (5) and (6) are based on such intuitions.

By defining the empty text in this way, we can model insertion/deletion using the same equation as the other explicit alignment types. However, we expect that in (6), for a given tw_i, most of $t(sw_j \mid tw_i)$ can be very small. Therefore the product over the whole vocabulary V_S will be too small to be discriminative. In our approach, for a given tw_i, we only keep those $t(sw_j \mid tw_i)$ which are larger than a floor during our training of model-1.

4. Sentence Length Models

In equation (2), the two non-translation probabilities: $P(A \mid a_{(j,x)(i,y)})$ and $P([t_i : t_{i+y}])$ can be approximated by sentence length models, which were also tested on French-English [3]. Assuming the posterior probability of $P(A \mid a_{(j,x)(i,y)})$ is only related to the length of the aligned segments, we have:

$$P(A \mid a_{(i,x)(j,y)}) = P(A \mid [s_j : s_{j+x}], [t_i : t_{i+y}])$$
$$\approx P(\mid [s_j : s_{j+x}] \mid : \mid [t_i : t_{i+y}] \mid \| [s_j : s_{j+x}], [t_i : t_{i+y}])$$
$$\approx P(\mid [s_j : s_{j+x}] \mid - \mid [t_i : t_{i+y}] \mid) = P(\delta(x,y))$$

The length difference $\delta(x,y)$ is assumed to be a Gaussian distribution [3] and the normalized difference in equation (7) is considered to be normal distribution $N(0,1)$.

$$\overline{\delta} = \frac{y - x \cdot c}{\sqrt{(x+1)\sigma^2}} \quad (7)$$

where c is a const indicating the average length ratio between target and source sentences. For Chinese-English, x is dependent on word segmentation, and in our experiment c is 1.067. σ^2 is the variance of the sentence length difference, in our case, 0.197 shown in Table-1.

For the distribution of $P([t_i : t_{i+y}])$, one can use a target language model (n-gram) to approximate it. Here, to save the computation, we actually choose the Poisson distribution to model it. The Poisson distribution is a good approximation of the sentence length distribution and can be estimated from a monolingual corpus.

$$P([t_i \cdots t_{i+y}]) = \frac{\lambda_a^{\| t_i \cdots t_{i+y} \|}}{[t_i \cdots t_{i+y}]! \, e^{\lambda_a}} \quad (8)$$

λ_a is the expectation of the Poisson distribution. In our case, λ_a is the expectation of the length of segment $[t_i \cdots t_{i+y}]$. Following [5] we set λ_a to be different for different alignment types $a_{(j,x):(i,y)}$. $\lambda_{1:1}$ can be estimated using the English part of the Hong Kong news parallel corpus. The other λ_a are tied as follows:

$$\lambda_{1:0} = \lambda_{0:1} = \frac{1}{2}\lambda_{1:1} = \frac{1}{3}\lambda_{1:2} = \frac{1}{3}\lambda_{2:1} = \frac{1}{4}\lambda_{2:2} = \frac{1}{4}\lambda_{1:3}$$

Both (7) and (8) can be directly applied for insertion and deletion. In (7), x or y can be zero, indicating insertion and deletion. In (8), y can be zero, indicating deletion. Intuitively, a sentence pair with very large length difference is unlikely to be parallel, and abnormally short or long sentences are relatively more likely to be insertion/deletion (noise), as reflected in our sentence length models.

5. Experiments

Our work is motivated by the need to mine parallel sentences from the 10 years (1992~2001) Xinhua Web bilingual news corpora collected by Language Data Consortium (LDC). The collection is open-domain and comparable, with roughly similar sentence order of content. The English stories focus mainly on international news and the Chinese stories on domestic news. Most of the stories have no corresponding story in the other language. The first step was therefore to find comparable story pairs [2, 6]. This resulted in 17310 story pairs which were then used for the sentence alignment experiments. Each story has between 3 and 80 sentences, and the ratio of the number of sentences between English and Chinese stories is 1.36:1.

Preprocessing included word segmentation for the Chinese stories, separation of punctuation characters, and removal of web junk text. The Chinese full-stop '。' and the English period "." were used in sentence boundary detection. Table-1 shows the statistics of the sentence length models.

Table-1 *Sentence length model: word vs character*

	Word-based	Character-based
Mean	1.067	1.468
Var	0.197	0.275

The character-based model has a larger variance than the word-based model. No punctuations are counted in our sentence length models.

5.1. Parallel Sentence Alignment Models

First, we tested different alignment models, a character-based length model only (CL), a word-based length model only (WL), a translation model only (TB), and the proposed maximum likelihood criterion combining WL and TB (WL/TB) as shown in Table 2.

Table-2:*Alignment types(%) in alignments resulting from different alignment models*

Models	0:1	1:0	1:1	1:2	2:1	2:2	1:3
CL	10.9	4.38	19.3	20.4	7.94	28.1	8.9
WL	4.63	2.99	57.5	18.3	3.45	5.11	8.05
TB	9.62	3.92	60.8	14.7	4.8	0.04	6.1
WL/TB	5.33	3.0	66.5	15.8	2.2	0.01	7.2

The length models (CL and WL) generate a large number of 2:2 alignments. While both TB and WL/TB give more reliable alignments from our close and detail examination. It showed necessary to incorporate the word translation identity information for robustness and accuracy. The combined WL/TB under maximum likelihood gives our best result.

5.2. Adaptive Parallel Data Mining

In a second experiment we used the mined data to re-train the translation lexicon. Results are shown in Table-3. There is no very large variation of the alignment type's proportion, but the aligned sentence-pair's perplexity changed significantly as shown in figure-2.

Table-3 *Alignment types (%) in adaptive extraction*

Iter	0:1	1:0	1:1	1:2	2:1	2:2	1:3
1	5.33	3.00	66.5	15.8	2.20	0.01	7.21
2	4.86	2.69	66.9	16.0	2.26	0.01	7.29
3	4.81	2.65	66.6	16.3	2.38	0.01	7.26
4	4.81	2.64	66.6	16.2	2.39	0.01	7.28

Table-4 *Vocabulary coverage of each iteration*

iteration	1	2	3	4
Chinese	65%	83%	85%	86%
English	57%	73%	80%	81%

There is a big increase of vocabulary coverage from iteration 1 to 2, shown in Table-4.

The sentence pair's perplexity pp is defined as:

$$pp = d([s_j : s_{j+x}] : [t_i : t_{i+y}] \mid A) = -\log(P(a_{(j,x)(i,y)} \mid A))$$

The distribution of the sentence-pairs perplexity in each iteration is shown in Figure 2. Sentence pairs, which have a perplexity less than the given threshold, are selected as training data for the next iteration.

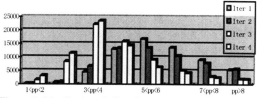

Figure-2. *Distribution of aligned sentence pairs' perplexities*

Our approach got 110K (44MB) aligned parallel sentence-pairs, which are used to train word alignment models. The quality of the mined data is evaluated by word alignment accuracy of the models according to a gold-standard manually labeled test set.

5.3. Word-to-word Alignment Accuracy

A direct evaluation of the quality of mined parallel data is to test their effect in training word alignment models. We used GIZA++ [4] to build translation models up to model-3. Word alignment accuracy was then evaluated using a hand-aligned test set containing 365 sentence pairs with 4094 word-to-word alignments.

Table-5 *Word alignment of translation models*

Baseline	Model-1	Model-2	Model-3
Precision	43.43%	44.98%	43.65%
Recall	50.98%	53.81%	49.66%
F	46.90%	49.00%	46.46%
With mined data	Model-1	Model-2	Model-3
Precision	48.94%	48.88%	48.88%
Recall	58.97%	58.55%	56.84%
F	53.49%	53.28%	52.56%

The baseline models were trained using 290K sentence pairs from the Hong Kong News corpus available from LDC. The additional mined data was 57K sentence pairs (pp<5.0) selected after iteration 4. There is a consistent improvement for all three word alignment models. The harmonic mean F value of *Model-1* has a 14.05% relative improvement, showing better vocabulary coverage and high parallel quality of the data we mined.

6. Discussion and Conclusions

We described our approach of generating a high quality parallel corpus from a very large Chinese-English bilingual web text collection. Lexical information and sentence length information is combined to find reliable sentence alignment. The extracted parallel data was used to train word-based alignment models. The improved quality of the resulting word alignment proves the effectiveness of the sentence alignment method.

7. References

[1] Brown, P. F. and Della Pietra, S. A. and Della Pietra, V. J. and Mercer, R. L, "The Mathematics of Statistical Machine Translation: Parameter Estimation", *Computational Linguistics*, 19-2, pp 263—311, 1993.

[2] Bing Zhao and Stephan Vogel, "Full-text Story alignment models for Chinese-English Bilingual Corpora", *International Conference on Spoken Language Processing*, Sep. 2002.

[3] Church, K. W. "Char_align: A Program for Aligning Parallel Texts at the Character Level". In *Proceedings of ACL-93*, Columbus OH. 1993.

[4] Franz Josef Och and Hermann Ney. "Improved Statistical Alignment Models". In *Proceedings of ACL-00*, pp. 440-447, Hongkong, China, 2000.

[5] Stanley Chen. "Aligning sentences in Bilingual corpora using lexical information". In *Proceedings of the 31st Annual Conference of the Association for computational linguistics*, pages 9-16, Columbus, Ohio, June 1993.

[6] Xiaoyi Ma, Mark Y. Liberman, "BITS: A Method for Bilingual Text Search over the Web". *Machine Translation Summit VII*, 1999.

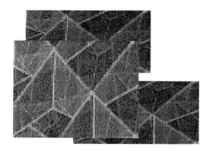
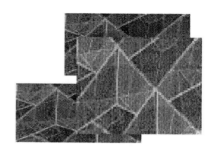

Industry-Track Papers

Telecommunications Strategic Marketing - KDD and Economic Modeling

Stefano Cazzella
DIS - Univ. di Roma "La Sapienza"
cazzella@tin.it

Luigi Dragone[*]
DIS – Univ. di Roma "La Sapienza"
dragone@dis.uniroma1.it

Stefano M. Trisolini
TELECOM Italia
stefano_trisolini@virgilio.it

Abstract

The Italian deregulation process of telecommunications market in the last years has produced a large economic impact since it has altered equilibriums that were established for a long time. In this framework, we notice a strong need for adequate tools to analyze the market and its trends and, at the same time, a lack of specific solutions within the scientific literature, due to the new technical challenges issued by the problem.

In particular, in the context of building a Decision Support System (DSS) for the strategic marketing unit of TELECOM Italia (TI) we have devised a new methodology to profitably combine most powerful tools from KDD and Economic Sciences. We have tested our approach by analyzing the residential telecommunications market demand in Italy during the transition from a monopolistic structure to an oligopolistic one.

In this paper, we first address the state of the art in DSS design, then we describe the proposed methodology and its application in the case study.

1. Introduction

The availability of methodologies and tools to support decision making activities at various levels, both tactical (e.g., CRM) and strategic (e.g., investment planning), is certainly a major need for enterprises. Such tools must be able to take into account the knowledge about the organization and its surrounding environment to simulate the impact of decisions taken in order to optimize the return for the enterprise itself.

To answer this need, in the field of Economic Sciences, a large number and variety of theories have been devised to model and to explain the economic agent behavior. At a practitioner level, these theories need a large amount of data about the addressed phenomenon that are usually gathered by soundings and processed using econometric techniques [4].

Meanwhile, one of most significant industrial field applications of KDD research results is the exploitation of Data Mining techniques and tools in the building of CRM system. In particular, an enhanced CRM system adopts different Data Mining techniques to support market segmentation and customer behavior prediction in order to select the optimal set of actions to undertake w.r.t. each customer, implementing a DSS for tactical marketing.

However, these methodologies turn out inadequate to build a DSS for the strategic marketing. In fact, a strategic decision can concern a large number of customers, or the whole market, whereas the formal tools generally adopted in Data Mining-based CRM systems focus on individual customer. Consequently, they cannot help to analyze the whole underlying system (the market) and to predict its aggregated behavior. Moreover, the use of *universal approximators* (e.g., neural nets, decision trees) tends to reduce the need of complex model analysis and to ignore contributions form specific literature.

We also need to point out that enterprise data, despite of their correctness and accuracy, are subject to two unavoidable sampling distortions: (1) data are incomplete, since they keep track of the observed customer behaviors from the enterprise perspective only; (2) data are partial, since they keep track only of the customer features relevant to the business. Consequently, they do not offer a complete view of the market and of customers.

We argue that a naïf application of KDD techniques to strategic marketing DSS design is quite inadequate, and, on the other hands, the traditional techniques that rely on market soundings do not fully exploit the enterprise information asset.

To cope with these issues, we have devised a strategy that exploits the most relevant contributions of both KDD and economic modeling approaches. Specifically, the goals of our methodology are the followings:

- to rely on Microeconomic theories to model the system;
- to employ unsupervised Data Mining learning techniques and aprioristic knowledge to compensate, at least partially, sampling distortions;
- to exploit supervised Data Mining learning techniques to fit a Microeconomic model, in order to exploit their scalability features.

The design of a DSS for strategic marketing requires the ability to infer the preferences of each customer, since this information is generally not available to an economic operator. It is a very delicate issue and its solution is generally very complex, but we can address it satisfactorily, by relying on peculiarities of this market.

At a high level of abstraction, the proposed

751

methodology is divided in four subsequent steps:

1. Problem analysis and model selection;
2. Data acquisition and sampling compensation;
3. Model fitting;
4. Model analysis.

Each step exploits specific theoretical and software tools w.r.t. the context, but some results can be generalized to other ones where similar hypotheses hold. From a KDD perspective this methodology can be thought as an attempt to improve learning result understandability through domain knowledge (i.e., economic models) [7]. Another proposal to exploit KDD in strategic marketing is presented in [8], where the problem of the discovered knowledge profitability is addressed.

2. Case study

The Italian telecommunications market deregulation process has developed in various steps: during the period that we have analyzed (2000/01) every customer was enabled to use different carrier providers that supplied telecommunication services to specific destinations (e.g., international, long distance). In any case, the customer has to subscribe a contract with TELECOM Italia because it was the only provider of wireline base services (e.g., local-loop, local area calls).

From our preliminary analysis of the business problem, we can assume that:

- the market is composed of different services (call destinations) with their own consumption level;
- the market is undertaking a transition from a monopolistic structure to an oligopolistic one;
- TI is still the only basic services provider, consequently every customer is a TI customer;
- TI cannot observe its own customer preferences (i.e., a customer choices a different provider) since there is no formal contract resolution;
- the overall service consumption levels are quite stationary;
- the product differentiation does not rely on the rates only, because otherwise, since each competitor is cheaper than TI on at least a service, then no customer should use TI as a provider for these kind of services.

In the following sections, we show the application of our methodology to the analysis of the *customer churn* phenomenon in telecommunications market. A more traditional approach to churn analysis with KDD techniques is illustrated in [11].

2.1. Model selection

Neoclassic Microeconomic market theories rely on the analysis of two main functions: *demand and supply functions* that, due their interactions, determine, w.r.t. the selected model, the market equilibrium in terms of consumption of goods, their sale prices, etc..

The economic decision theory, on which demand functions are modeled, relies on the fundamental assumption of the *consumer's instrumental rationality*, that states that a consumer takes a decision in order to maximize its own interest assessing costs and benefits.

Given a market made up of n goods, we define a *basket* as the n-uple of their consumption levels $z \in \Re^n$. We express the *utility* that a consumer gains from the consumption of a basket through a utility function $u : \Re^n \to \Re$. Despite the fact that the absolute utility value of a basket does not have any intrinsic meaning, the comparison of the utility values of two or more baskets defines an order relation on the space of the baskets. In fact, every consumer selects the basket that maximizes its own utility given its liquid assets (*budget constraint*). The consumption levels obtained as solution of the utility maximization problem define the so-called demand functions for each good. We can define a demand function for each consumer and, by means of aggregation, for the whole market [4].

In this case, we are interested in the modeling of a demand function that concerns the decision of replacing the current ex-monopolistic supplier (TI) with one or more competitors (churn). The economic literature suggests adopting a *Discrete Choice Model* (DCM) to deal with this problem [1].

In theory, we do not know which factors are involved in the consumer's selection process and we are also not able to know them exactly, but we argue that there are some non-monetary aspects involved. To cope with this issue we have selected a *random component hedonic DCM* that aims to capture the effect of consumer's specific characteristics in its selection process bringing accordingly them into the utility function. The utility function, consequently, represents the specific consumer satisfaction level. The unobservable characteristic contribution on the consumer's utility can be modeled as a random variable that we are able to estimate [2, 10].

Given x_j, the j-th consumer's vector of observable features, and ε_j, the vector of unobservable ones that are random variable realizations, the utility of the i-th good for the j-th consumer is expressed as:

$$u_{i,j} = u_i(x_j, \varepsilon_j) = w_i \cdot x_j + \xi_i \cdot \varepsilon_j =$$
$$= w_i \cdot x_j + e_{i,j} = u_i(x_j, e_j) \qquad i = 1, \cdots, k$$

where: k is the number of goods in the market, w_i and ξ_i are two vectors of coefficients that express the degree of influence of each consumer's characteristic (the observable and unobservable ones respectively) on the utility of the i-th good, and e_j is the j-th consumer's idiosyncratic vector concerning the k goods.

The i-th good demand function depends on the observable consumer's characteristics x and its own idiosyncratic e and can be expressed as:

$$z_i(x,e) = \begin{cases} 1 & i = i(x,e) = \underset{h=1...n}{\arg\max}\, u_h(x,e) \\ 0 & \text{otherwise} \end{cases}$$

Since it is a *Linear Random Utility Model* (LRUM) function, the i-th good market share is the expected value of the corresponding demand function given variable probability distribution functions of the features [1].

2.2. Data acquisition and sampling compensation

The information system of TI includes a centralized Enterprise Data Warehouse system that provides an historical and integrated view of organizational data to management and decision support systems. It provides a detailed description of each customer in terms of service consumption patterns (see [3, 14]).

Here, we do not address data management issues, but we focused the details of the sampling distortion problem.

In order to correctly model the relationship between the service demand and the customer features we need to compensate in a suitable way the incompleteness of available data. In fact, since the data belong to only one supplier, even the ex-monopolistic one, they lack information about two critical facts: (1) it is unknown whether and which customers employ competitor services (i.e., who the churners are) and whether we observe the whole consumption profiles; (2) it is unknown what the competitor consumption profiles are.

Nevertheless, if we can periodically observe the customer behaviors for a long enough time period (i.e., 6 months or more) we can, from a theoretical perspective, reconstruct the preferences of ex-monopolistic supplier customers. Since the underlying phenomenon is very complex, it is very hard to summarize the whole consumption behavior in a set of measures, on which we can impose some discrimination criteria without introducing aprioristic and arbitrary hypotheses.

Another approach is the behavioral partitioning of customers into homogeneous groups w.r.t. their usage profiles. In order to minimize the number of aprioristic hypotheses, we have adopted a clustering algorithm to discover the most relevant behavioral patterns. In particular, we have employed the *demographic clustering algorithm* [6] implemented in the tool *IBM Intelligent Miner* because it is able to automatically detect the optimal number of groups w.r.t. a partition likelihood criterion. To increase the result quality we have selected a minimal set of maximally independent features.

We have analyzed the usage patterns of each group that we have interpreted in terms of corporate marketing: behavioral patterns has been partitioned w.r.t. their usage

of services subject to competition and, consequently, the churning likelihood. On this basis we have periodically evaluated the position of high risk customers in the consumption space to detected abnormal behaviors that provide good evidences of a churning behavior in act.

In such way, we are able to reconstruct the consumer preferences (churn or not churn) of the most profitability market share, because high-risk customers produce the largest quantity of communications on critical services. Consequently, we have focused our attention in subsequent analysis on these ones, taking into account only the behavioral patterns observed before the churn event as suitable proxies of the service consumption.

2.3. Model fitting

The fitting of the consumer preference model is reducible to a classification problem, since the demand function is a classification function that maps points from a multi-dimensional space into a finite set of values.

Given a training set composed of pairs $< x_j, i_j >$ where the observable feature vector of the j-th consumer is combined with its own preference we can train a classifier that is able to approximate and to generalize the function $i(x,e)$ even without the unobservable components. The problem can be stated as a search for a classification function $i(x)$ agreeing with the $i(x,e)$ on the largest number of examples. Let $y_h(x) = w_h \cdot x + \delta_h$, the classification function can be expressed as:

$$i(x) = \underset{h=1..k}{\arg\max}\, y_h(x)$$

This kind of classification function is implemented by a neural network known as *linear machine* [12], that we have adopted to fit our model. This network is composed of as many perceptrons as classes, and its output is the index of the perceptron with the maximum output level.

In fact, if we bind each model variable to a network input, we bind each network weight to the corresponding model coefficient [16]. The network is able to predict the possible customer behavior from its own consumption pattern by classifying it as a possible churner or a faithful customer. In addition, the Microeconomic theory provides us a way to give an interpretation to the trained network and to insight the customer's selection process.

If the classes of the training set are linearly separable we have that each example $< x, h >$ is such that $i(x) = i(x,e) = h$. The mean utility of each class can be stated as the $y_h(x)$ mean value, so:

$$\overline{u_h(x,e)} \approx \overline{y_h(x)} \Rightarrow \overline{w_h \cdot x + e_h} \approx \overline{w_h \cdot x + \delta_h}$$

Under the hypothesis that x and e are statistically independent we have that $\delta_h \approx \overline{e_h}$. We argue that the bias value δ_h of each perceptron approximates the mean of the customer idiosyncratic w.r.t. the h-th choose and it captures the influence of unobservable characteristics.

We have employed the *thermal perceptron algorithm* to train the linear machine [5] that has been minimized exploiting a *variable elimination technique* [15].

2.4. Model analysis

The consumer's utility function fitted by the linear machine training can be analyzed by a large number of techniques specific of the economic literature [1, 4], but we have focused on the followings [15]:

- *Internal analysis*, that aims at establishing for each preference the relative significance of each feature;
- *Comparative analysis*, that is used to point out the most relevant features w.r.t. the overall selection process.

The internal analysis orders the model features according to their absolute weight values, where the absolute value approximates the feature relevance and the weight sign states how the feature is related to the utility level. The comparative analysis relies on the *weight dispersion* that measures the relevance of each feature on the overall selection process, because it is more affected by features that have greater difference between homologous coefficients in different utility functions.

In particular, we have observed that, among the 27 features employed in the model fitting step, it is sufficient to take into account only the bias and the 6 features with highest dispersion values to statistically explain more than 90% of demand determination (see Table 1). We have also found that high consumption levels and enhanced service subscriptions (e.g., ISDN) are deterrent to churn, that is, instead, joined to presence of Internet access services.

3. Conclusions

Our experience in design a DSS for strategic marketing has shown several limitations of the KDD techniques. Consequently, we have devised a new approach to accomplish our task that aims at exploiting some Microeconomic theory elements as previous domain knowledge and KDD techniques to fit the model.

We have experimented our methodology by analyzing the deregulated Italian telecommunications market. The model obtained is able to explain 65% of consumer's selection process, despite it is built on the available data of one market operator only, without turning to external information sources, but accordingly exploiting domain knowledge. It is a very interesting result in term of intelligence capabilities of marketing department.

The relationship between our model and the traditionally built ones is currently under investigation, we aim at pointing out new data requirements in order to improve the model quality and reduce the contribution of unobservable characteristics. We intend besides extend the model to take into account the customer migration to mobile telecommunications networks.

Table 1 Model feature dispersions

Rank	Feature	Dispersion (%)	Cumulative dispersion (%)
1	Unobservable characteristics (bias)	35.36	35.36
2	ISDN service	31.36	66.72
3	Total charge	11.63	78.35
4	No. of long-distance off-peak calls	3.57	81.92
5	No. of mobile peak calls	3.15	85.07
6	Use of TELECOM Italia ISP	3.00	88.07
7	Use of another ISP	2.53	90.60

References

[1] S. Anderson, A. DePalma, J. Thisse, *Discrete choice theory of product differentiation*, MIT Press, 1992.

[2] S. Berry, J. Levinsohn, A. Pakes, "Automobile Prices in market Equilibrium", *Econometrica*, 60(4), 1995.

[3] D. Calvanese, L. Dragone, D. Nardi, R. Rosati, S. M. Trisolini, "Enterprise Modeling, Data Warehousing and Data Mining in TELECOM Italia", To appear on *Information Systems*.

[4] A. Deaton, "Demand Analysis", *Handbook of Econometrics*, Elsevier Science, 1986.

[5] M. Frean, "A thermal Perceptron Learning Rule", *Neural Computation*, 4(6), 1992.

[6] J. Grabmeier, A. Rudolph, "Techniques of Cluster Algorithms in Data Mining", Tech. Rep. of IBM Informationssysteme GmbH, 1998.

[7] V. Kavakli, P. Loucopoulos, "Goal Driven Business Analysis: An Application in Electricity Deregulation", *Proc. of CAiSE*98*, Pisa, 1998.

[8] J. Kleinberg, C. Papadimitriou, P. Raghavan, "A Microeconomic View of Data Mining", *Journal of Data Mining and Knowledge Discovery*, 1999.

[10] D. McFadden, "Econometric models of probabilistic choice", *Structural Analisys of discrete data with econometric applications*, MIT Press, 1981.

[11] D. R. Mani, J. Drew, A. Betz, P. Datta, "Statistics and data mining techniques for lifetime value modeling", *Proc. ACM SIGKDD'99*, 1999.

[12] N. J. Nilsson, *The Mathematical Foundations of Learning Machines*. Morgan Kaufmann, 1990.

[14] S. M. Trisolini, M. Lenzerini, D. Nardi, "Data Integration and Warehousing in TELECOM Italia", *Proc. of ACM SIGMOD'99*, 1999.

[15] P. Utgoff, C. Brodley, "Linear machine decision trees", Tech. Rep. 91-10 of Dept. CS, Univ. of Massachusetts, 1991.

[16] B. Warner, M. Misra, "Understanding neural networks as statistical tools", *The American Statistician*, 50, 1996.

* Now at *CM Sistemi – luigi.dragone@gruppocm.it*

webSPADE: A Parallel Sequence Mining Algorithm to Analyze Web Log Data

Ayhan Demiriz
Information Technology, Verizon Inc.,
919 Hidden Ridge, Irving, TX 75038
E-mail:ayhan.demiriz@verizon.com

Abstract

Enterprise-class web sites receive a large amount of traffic, from both registered and anonymous users. Data warehouses are built to store and help analyze the click streams within this traffic to provide companies with valuable insights into the behavior of their customers. This article proposes a parallel sequence mining algorithm, webSPADE, to analyze the click streams found in site web logs. In this process, raw web logs are first cleaned and inserted into a data warehouse. The click streams are then mined by webSPADE. An innovative web-based front-end is used to visualize and query the sequence mining results. The webSPADE algorithm is currently used by Verizon to analyze the daily traffic of the Verizon.com web site.

1 Introduction

This paper introduces an algorithm to analyze click streams from raw web logs. Click streams are collections of hits from specific user sessions. Assuming that user sessions in web logs are constructed by appropriate technology, we must first clean the web logs to remove redundant information. Parsing the cleaned web logs and inserting the data into a repository (data warehouse or relational database) is the next step in the analysis process. Data stored in a repository is easily used for frequency analysis with proven database technologies to create excellent summary reports. However, when it comes to analyzing the sequences, even with well defined process flows, the number of nested queries required to follow the processes step by step within a relational database framework makes the analysis prohibitively expensive. This ex-

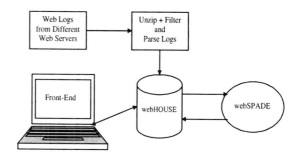

Figure 1. System Architecture

pense, combined with the fact that simple database queries are unlikely to discover hidden sequences and relationships within the data, make it important to use an effective sequence mining algorithm to analyze the data contained within the web logs.

We propose a parallel sequence mining algorithm based on [3, 4]. There are several major differences in this paper compared to earlier work [3, 4]. Differences and improvements can be summarized as follows: 1- webSPADE is a Wintel-based parallel implementation. 2- It only requires one full scan of the data compared to three full scans in previous algorithms. 3- Temporal joins are used in webSPADE contrast to the non-temporal joins in the original algorithm. 4- The design of webSPADE achieves data and task parallelism simultaneously. 5- The current system has been in production since Mid-October of 2001 without any major problem. 6- Click stream data is analyzed daily and sequences are stored in a relational database. 7- A user-friendly front-end is used to visualize and mine stored sequences for a user-determined time range and support level. 8- By using front-end, it is possible to analyze click-

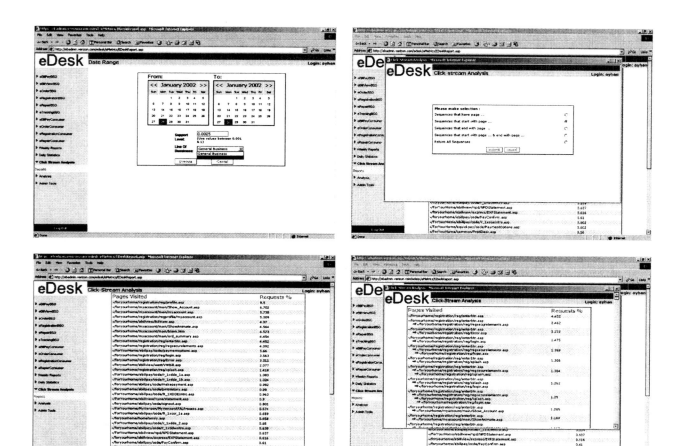

Figure 2. (A)- Parameter Selection Screen, (B)- Frequent Pages

Figure 3. (A)- Analysis Selection, (B)- Sequences

stream data from a very large time period (e.g. whole year) in a short time.

We propose an integrated solution for performing click stream analysis in this paper. A simplified system architecture is shown in Figure 1. The parser feeds the data into webHOUSE, a data warehouse. The sequence mining algorithm, webSPADE, reads daily data from webHOUSE and inserts the daily sequences into webHOUSE. The front-end is used to query the webHOUSE to analyze sequences.

The nature of the sequence mining problem makes massive computation unavoidable. This situation is the ideal application for parallel programming. Parallel sequence mining algorithms are generally derived from sequential ones by introducing load balancing schemes for multiple processors and

distributed memory. Since the data warehouse is built on MS SQL Server in our implementation, webSPADE has been developed in the Wintel environment, simplifying the parallelization of the serial programs.

The core point of our implementation is to modify the SPADE algorithm for the purpose of performing click stream analysis. The details of the original SPADE algorithm can be found in [3]. The main advantage of using this algorithm is the use of join operations instead of scanning all the data to count certain item sets. The original SPADE algorithm proposed in [3] requires three full scans of the data. Note that both SPADE and webSPADE may require large number of scans on intermediate partial data.

The paper is organized as follows: We introduce an analysis oriented front-end in Section 2. An analysis of web log data from Verizon.com during the month of January of 2002 is given in Section 3 for illustration purposes. Computational times are also reported in Section 3. The paper wraps up with a conclusion. Interested readers are advised to read the full version of this paper available at http://www.rpi.edu/~demira/research.htm.

2 Front-End

We present a very innovative way of scaling up any sequence mining algorithm by utilizing the database technology to analyze very large datasets spanning a large time window e.g. a quarter. A user friendly front-end enables users to choose three different parameters: support levels, time window(start and end date of analysis) and line of business (LOB) to query the sequences. Similar visual pattern analysis techniques are introduced in [1, 2] in the context of the "mine and explore" paradigm using episode and association mining.

Our approach is very simple. webSPADE runs **daily** with a predetermined support level to find sequences based on different lines of business; Support level is set to 0.1% for General Business and 0.25% for Consumer in our application. **Daily sequences** are then stored in a relational table. By design, webSPADE limits the length of sequences and, in this particular application, the maximum length of sequences is set to ten. Thus the relational table is composed of ten fields to determine the sequences, analysis date, line of business, frequency of sequence and total hits on analysis date.

Stored sequences can be used to analyze click streams between user specified dates. As seen from Figure 2(A), users can specify any support level and dates for a given line of business allowing a great degree of flexibility. **It should be noted that webSPADE is run daily and results are stored; there is no on-the-fly computation when the user selects parameters using the parameter selection screen.** In fact, stored results are aggregated and presented to the user. This point is the major difference from the previous work introduced in [1, 2]. On the other hand, our methodology requires mining efforts on a portion of data (for one day). Resulting patterns are then aggregated and presented to the user for visual analysis and pattern search. Moreover, our approach scales up the underlying mining algorithm and visualizes the results simultaneously. This is a significant improvement in

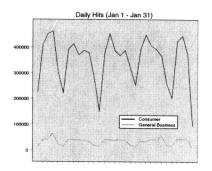

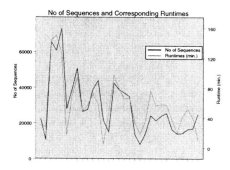

Figure 4. (A) Daily Hits, (B) Number of Sequences and Runtimes

terms of computation efficiency.

After selecting the parameters, frequent pages are shown to the user as seen in Figure 2(B). Further analysis can be deployed by clicking on any page name in frequent page list (see Figure 2(B)). Once clicked, a pop-up window appears as seen in Figure 3(A). There are five options to choose on this screen. Users can select to see sequences that contain a selected page, start with a selected page, or end with a selected page. Users can list all the sequences as well. There is another option to list all the sequences starting with the selected page and ending with another page. Each option corresponds to a different stored procedure in the database. Having results stored in a relational table gives tremendous flexibility to report and query the results. Once an option is chosen, the resulting sequences are listed in the browser window as seen in Figure 3(B).

webSPADE and the web-based front-end, depicted in Figure 2 and 3, can be used for other time dependent sequential data. To illustrate the practical usage of sequence mining and to assess the performance of webSPADE we analyze all the data from January 2002 in next section.

3 An Illustrative Example

webSPADE has been used for analyzing web log data since mid-October of 2001. We can now analyze virtually all the frequent sequences since then by using the front-end reporting tool mentioned in the previous section. So far there are approximately 480M cleaned hits in the datawarehouse. Based on this data, webSPADE has found approximately 6M frequent sequences. To illustrate the usage of the webSPADE algorithm, we consider the data from January 2002. As we mentioned above, certain pages on Verizon.com are tagged to collect session information and our analysis covers only these pages. As we also mentioned above, the pages of two different lines of businesses are analyzed separately. Total daily hits during January are depicted in Figure 4(A). When we consider the whole month, there are approximately 12 million hits (requests) from both lines of business. This is a relatively large dataset.

The number of sequences and daily runtime of webSPADE in minutes is depicted in Figure 4(B). Reported times are the sum of runtimes for both lines of business. As expected, the number of sequences depends on number of daily hits (requests). Although webSPADE is not run on a dedicated server, the example runtimes of webSPADE can be considered close to reality. Note that runtimes also include both database access time and insertion time of sequences into the relational table.

The operational value of sequence mining is undeniable. For example, it is easy to monitor the traffic to understand whether a web page is functioning well or not. More specifically, certain pages might experience heavy traffic but the following pages may experience very low traffic. Sequence mining can easily catch such patterns. Some design problems might cause such patterns e.g. a misplaced next button at the bottom of the page; many people may not be able to see the next button because of smaller monitors. Such changes are requested in the light of sequences mining findings.

Sequence mining can also be used to find out who comes to a certain page and where they go after that page. For example, although bill view and bill pay processes are independent from each other in General Business pages, a significant portion of customers first view their bill and then pay it in the same session. It is also found that the bill view process sometimes fails to show bills due to the database access timeout. So, if we can increase the reliability of the bill view process, some of our customers will pay their bills in the same session. This is a very simple conclusion but it might take some time to come up with plain SQL analysis. Large scale sequence mining enables us to come to a conclusion on this matter more rapidly.

4 Conclusion

We successfully applied a parallel sequence mining algorithm to perform click stream analysis. webSPADE requires only one full scan of the database, but several partial scans of the database. Data and task parallelism are easily achieved using multi-threaded programming. Load balancing is left to the operating system. Post-implementation tunings are still ongoing to speed up the process even more. An innovative analysis technique to scale up sequence mining algorithm is also used for value-added business analysis.

Acknowledgments

I would like to thank Dr. M. J. Zaki for his helpful comments and directions on improving this paper and work.

References

[1] M. Klemettinen, H. Mannila, and H. Toivonen. Interactive exploration of discovered knowledge: A methodology for interaction, and usability studies. Technical Report C-1996-3, Department of Computer Science, University of Helsinki, 1996.

[2] M. Klemettinen, H. Mannila, and H. Toivonen. Interactive exploration of interesting patterns in the telecommunication network alarm sequence analyzer tasa. *Information and Software Technology*, 41:557–567, 1999.

[3] M. J. Zaki. SPADE: An efficient algorithm for mining frequent sequences. *Machine Learning Journal*, 42(1/2):31–60, Jan/Feb 2001. Special issue on Unsupervised Learning (D. Fisher, editor.).

[4] M. J. Zaki. Parallel sequence mining on shared-memory machines. *Journal of Parallel and Distributed Computing,*, 61(3):401–426, March 2001. Special issue on High Performance Data Mining (V. Kumar, S. Ranka and V. Singh, editors.).

Mining Online Users' Access Records for Web Business Intelligence

Simon Fong
Faculty of Science and Technology
Universidade de Macau
Macao
simon@enetique.com.sg

Serena Chan
Omron Asia Pacific
e-Business Development Team
Singapore
serenachan@omron.com.sg

Abstract

This paper discusses about how business intelligence on a website could be obtained from users' access records instead of web logs of "hits". Users' access records are captured by implementing an Access-Control (AC) architectural model on the website. This model requires users to register their profiles in an exchange of a password; and thereafter they have to login before gaining access to certain resources on the website. The links to the resources on the website have been modified such that a record of information about the access would be recorded in the database when clicked. This way, data-mining can be performed on a relatively clean set of access records about the users. Hence, a good deal of business intelligence about the users' behaviors, preferences and about the popularities of the resources (products) on the website can be gained. In this paper, we also discussed how the business intelligence acquired, in turn, can be used to provide e-CRM for the users.

1. Introduction

Nowadays most companies have moved into e-business where they use Internet as a platform to interact with their customers. This has created more touch points than the traditional face-to-face visits, and therefore we have a new realm called Web Business Intelligence to deal with.

In Web Business Intelligence, for targeting the business areas of decision support and personalized service, we have identified three main technologies namely Data-warehousing (that includes data-mining modules and decision support modules), Web log analyzer [1] and Web spy [2]. Each one of them provides certain insight or understanding of one of the many aspects of a business respectively. In particular, we state that having a web log analyzer alone is not sufficient to provide a complete picture of business intelligence. Nevertheless, web-log analysis gives very good detailed reports on web site traffic statistics. Other information such as competitors, market positions, and most importantly the customers and their behaviors on the

website needed also to be known. In our case, e-Personalization that means personalizing web-content according to the customer's interest/needs will be guided by the knowledge that we have on him.

To realize the objectives of Web Business Intelligence, we propose an Access-control (AC) architecture that can progressively built upon a basic website. The objective is to distribute the functions of e-CRM and business intelligence using an agent-architecture and to monitor users' accesses on the website.

2. Hybrid AC Architecture

We present in this section our hybrid model for e-CRM and data-mining for business intelligence, that is tailored to meet the requirements for easy integration and upgrade for some primitive web-server to operate in e-business environments. The distinguishing features of this architecture are the integration of the distributed software agents each takes a specific role for producing a particular result, and the users' access monitoring system on the website. It supports the ability for mining to be performed at remote sites using mobile agents provides insightful business intelligence reports, and it also feeds back the results to some rule-based systems residing at the server for doing e-Personalization. This helps it to be easily adopted by most existing web-sites who want to have complete functions of e-CRM and BI, but yet reluctant to replace the whole e-business platform.

The hybrid model operates on the principle of letting the website with only some slight modification to act as the portal for capturing the user's particular, their trails, and also for providing them a better online service via e-Personalization. Thus, it has the option of using the client-server model or the mobile-agent model or an integrated approach involving both. We suggest that a web business should evolve progressively by taking a phrasal approach. The difference in performance between the three models are how fast the BI can be obtained and how much real-time the e-CRM can take place. The components of the hybrid AC architecture illustrated in Figure 1 are as follows:

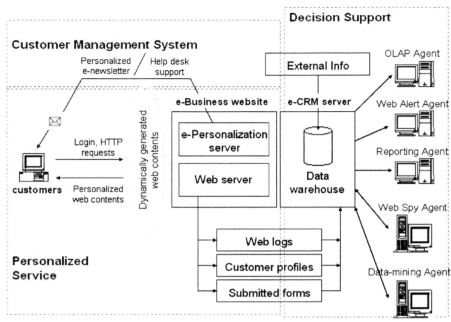

Figure 1. Agent-based Framework for BI and e-CRM

3. Access-Control Mechanism

It can be seen that with all the components working together, the three business areas are covered, as shown in the figure. The highlight of this paper is on about how a login and access control mechanism is implemented on the web site; thereafter Web business intelligence can be discovered.

AC mechanism is a prerequisite for implementing an e-CRM enabled website with customer-centric business intelligence. It works, basically by requiring a user to login, in order to identify himself before he is granted access to certain protected resources. It is assumed that a user would think it is fair that they would have to be bothered about logging in for getting some invaluable resources in return. At the first time, he would have to sign up a registration form with a user-name and a password of his choice.

On the website, the hypertext links to the protected resources such as a free-trail of software, a product's manual, etc., would have to be modified. Upon clicking on any one of these protected hypertext links, not only a user would be challenged with a password for checking access rights, the event of that "click" will be recorded in a database. Specifically, we record down who, at what time, on which website (in the case of a multi-regional website), have accessed to what resources from which web page. This recording event happens from when the user has logon (both success failure cases) to every time he clicks on a protected link. The idea of doing so is that we want to be able to keep track of which resources have been accessed by whom, when, and how often, on our website. Hence we can derive insights on what is happening on the website rather in terms of accesses than merely traffic hits per visit. The information obtained are more insightful than those from web-logs, since we beforehand have kept a full demographic details about the users when they registered, compare to the information obtained from web-logs which are only IP addresses. We will later discuss about how the records of user access will be analyzed for web business intelligence. The technical implementation flows for login procedure and thereafter access procedure are shown in Figures 2 and 3 respectively. For both cases, a record is generated in two different database tables namely login and access. The AC architecture has three distinguishing features:

1. Instead of using web log data "GET" that is relative only to the name of a web page, we can more accurately pinpoint which "resources" on the page that we want to monitor. It can be a link, a JPG file, a PDF file, or a movie clip. Access to them requires the user to login. We have the flexibility to design which links require the users to login and therefore we can monitor the access patterns on them.
2. Users can be uniquely identified by their login ID
3. Before the analysis, we can have relatively clean user profiles because the data fields of an access record are carefully chosen.

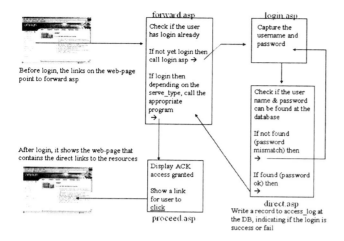

Figure 2. Logical flow for login procedure

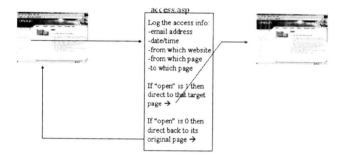

Figure 3. Logical flow for access procedure

4. Web Business Intelligence

Web business intelligence refers to the ability to make better business decisions in running a website through intelligent use of collected data, mostly from the same website. It is about gathering, managing, and analyzing data. Then the data are transformed into useful, actionable information to run an information-driven e-Business.

With the AC mechanisms implemented, at the appropriate links at which the company wants to monitor about their popularity, a wealth of good business intelligence (BI) can be obtained. In essence, we would be able to obtain a new realm of BI with the information about when and what the users have access and login to the website. We suppose that the web business intelligence can be obtained at two levels; one with and the other one without the aid of data-mining. At the first level, where simple statistics are used, we can show the following information as business intelligence about the products and the website:

(1) **Customer profiling (demographics).** When integrated with web traffic, one can tell the online customers behaviors. However, this requires some advanced techniques like web log mining. At the first level, for example, we can tell about the top 10 (or top 5, 100, etc) of the countries, the industries where the users come from, or their designations;

(2) **Customers' interests.** The top customers' interests on the products can be listed out. In a simple way, this information is obtained from the registration form when the users signed up. There is other more sophisticated technique to estimate the user's interest of a web page without directly asking the user. This method [3] is proposed for locating multi-word phrases in order to estimate interests on certain pages.

(3) **Product popularity.** The web pages of products that have been accessed most could be ranked and displayed as vital business information. This is a relatively fair approach when compare to measuring web page hits as each page may have different hit count per access

(4) **Technical knowledge base.** Over a certain period of time, the online inquiry forms posted by the customers have been collected, organized that form a searchable technical knowledge base. The base can made to be searchable that stores the past problem cases and the appropriate solutions. In a simpler form, it could be provided to the users as a set of frequently asked questions.

So far the task of obtaining the BI at the first level is limited to a single or only a few sources of data. Data-mining plays an important role in analyzing complex sometimes unorganized data from multiple sources. For instance, we can merge the data from different dimensions such as the attributes about the customers, the aspects about the products, different places or the schemes of the website, traffic patterns and time. From this huge pool of complex merged data with a diversity of dimensions, data-mining could help discovering some hidden patterns that may be of business values. Finding correlation among data and doing prediction are beyond the capability of simple statistical calculation.

5. Pattern Discovery under AC Architecture

Web usage mining, which is also known as pattern discovery is a process of mining for user browsing and access patterns. With our AC architecture, mining is an important backend process for deriving business intelligence at the second level. In AC environment, we record only those user accesses taken from the links that we chose. It is assured that the user must have logged in, given us his unique user-id and then granted the access.

So each access record stored in the database contains vital information of the user's identification, time of access, the website's identity, from which page he is making the access, and which "item" he is accessing. The item or the place of tracking can be a graphics, a movie clip, a PDF file or a hypertext link. Each user-id can be easily linked to the user registration table in the database; that implies a full set of information about that user is available. The problems of user identification as with web log processing no longer exist. We can take for granted that the user is readily identified as he has passed the password challenged. The recording of his trail is made almost instantly by our program code embedded at the link as soon as he mouse clicked on it. Besides the flexibility of choosing whichever resources we want to monitor, the biggest advantage is that the effort for data preprocessing is minimal. This AC method is believed to be more reliable because there is no missing or ambiguous value, and no need to remove any reluctant information. However, this requires a good design in setting up the links that we want to trace in advance. A non-technical drawback however, would be the difficulty in luring the users to sign up, and then get them perform the login action at every first time he wants to access a resource during a session. The value of the resources that the user seeks must be able to justify the trouble of login.

6. A Generalized Data-mining Model for AC

With our AC model, we attempt to generalize the discovery attributed to the following format: *who -> when/how visited which parts of the website -> for what -> why*. Obviously, the format contains pivots of natural clauses such as who, when, what, etc. These pivots would be easily derived from the attributes or fields of the AC records, except the last two: for what and why.

Who: attribute of the user-id in AC record. Knowing the user-id, the rest of the demographic information about that user can be obtained from the user registration records.

When: time stamp information in AC record. A hierarchical time dimension model will need to be created later on, e.g. year, quarter, month, week, etc. prior to mining.

How: this information can either be a case in the form of patterns obtained through the analysis discussed in the previous section, or a simple path formed by the "From" and "To" fields in the AC records. Other abstract forms of taxonomical representation could be "through a promotion", "from a link in a newsletter" or "from a search engine".

Which parts: this is usually the destination information in the AC records plus the preceding trails if any. The destination information could be a single resource file or a page that is obtained from the "To" field

of the access table. The preceding trails would have to be obtained from Path Analysis. Each one of the preceding trails is a paths a user during one visit has traversed within the physical web site layout.

For what: this is tacit information inferred from the results of Association and Clustering analysis. Alternatively, an analyst may have a conjecture for the groups and explicitly set a value for this variable with his subjective judgment. In an information-only website, the ultimate purposes for the users may be to obtain certain information in the form of a report, a product brochure, some free software download or to post a technical question. Furthermore, the users may want to purchase something in the case of an online shopping website.

Why: this is the concluding remark that an analyst draws for the patterns. This is a continuous review process with largely human intervention since the data-mining system would not be able to explain why such has happened. It would only reveal the hidden patterns from a large pool of data. The explanation of the outcomes would have to be first answered by a human expert. Subsequently, prediction using a decision tree will be possible as an extension to this model.

7. Conclusion

Access Control (AC) technique is based on this key innovation: obtaining data from the resource links at the web server instead of web-server log files. It is a password-based forcibly method for capturing customers' trails. It is based on the assumption that the users are willing to login in exchange of some valuable resource from the website. By virtue of this innovation, AC architecture provides better information than log-file analysis, gives site owner more reliable business intelligence. Web log tells mostly about traffic statistics and treating each user anonymous (because it is difficult to identify a user by its IP address). Access records with unique user identification and exact navigated locations, would be more suitable for data-mining for customer-centric Web Business intelligence.

8. Reference

[1] WebTrend Weblog Analyser, www.webtrend.com

[2] S. Fong, A. Sun, K. Wong, "Price Watcher Agent for E-Commerce", Int. Conference on Intelligent Agent Technology, World Scientific, pp.294-300, 2001.

[3] P. Chan, "A Non-invasive Learning Approach to Building Web User Profiles", KDD-99 Workshop on Web Usage Analysis and User Profiling, pp.7-12, 1999.

Discovery of Interesting Association Rules from Livelink Web Log Data

Xiangji Huang
School of Computer Science
University of Waterloo
Waterloo, Ontario N2L 3G1 Canada
jhuang@cs.uwaterloo.ca

Aijun An
Department of Computer Science
York University
Toronto, Ontario M3J 1P3 Canada
aan@cs.yorku.ca

Nick Cercone
Faculty of Computer Science
Dalhousie University
Halifax, Nova Scotia B3H 1W5 Canada

Gary Promhouse
Open Text Corporation
Waterloo, Ontario N2L 5Z5 Canada
gary@opentext.com

Abstract

We present our experience in mining web usage patterns from a large collection of Livelink log data. Livelink is a web-based product of Open Text, which provides automatic management and retrieval of different types of information objects over an intranet or extranet. We report our experience in preprocessing raw log data and post-processing the mining results for finding interesting rules. In particular, we compare and evaluate a number of rule interestingness measures and find that two of the measures that have not been used in association rule learning work very well.

1 Introduction

The use of internet technology permits organizations to generate and collect large volumes of electronic data in their daily operations. Open Text's Livelink is a web-based product that is designed to facilitate the storage, sharing and management of critical information and processes for an organization. We describe two challenges that we faced in mining Livelink usage patterns from a large volume of unique Livelink log files. The first challenge is preprocessing the raw log data to extract information that is relevant to our task. We present our techniques for preprocessing the log data. In particular, we describe the need for identifying information objects from log entries and methods for identifying users and sessions from the logs. The second challenge we faced is filtering the mining results to present rules or patterns that are potentially interesting. To find interesting rules, we use seven interestingness measures to rank the generated association rules, two of which have not previously been used to evaluate association rules. Pruning techniques are also applied to eliminate rules that are considered

redundant according to structural relationships among the rules and their interestingness values. To determine which interestingness measures work well in our application, we conduct evaluation of the seven interestingness measures by evaluating the top-ranking rules from each measure using the feedback from domain experts. We also compare these interesting measures by looking at the correlation between each measure and the ϕ-coefficient that describes the correlation between the antecedent and consequent of a rule.

2 Livelink Log Files

The log files used in our experiments contain Livelink access data for a period of two months. The size of the data is 7GB. The data describe more than 3,000,000 requests made to a Livelink server from around 5,000 users. Each request corresponds to an entry in the log files. The entry contains: 1. the IP address the user is making the request from; 2. the cookie generated by the Livelink server on the user's machine; 3. the time the request is made and the time the required page is presented to the user; 4. the name of the request handler in the Livelink program; 5. the name of the method within the handler that is used to handle the request; 6. the query strings that can be used to identify the page and the objects being requested, and some other information that are irrelevant to our task, such as the URL addresses that are useful for error-handling.

3 Data Preprocessing

The objective of data preprocessing is to transform the raw log data into the data that can be used for learning patterns. The following tasks are performed in the data preprocessing step of our project: identifying the user from each entry of the log files, identifying the information objects that the user requests from each log entry, removing noisy entries, which are the entries in which no interesting objects are requested, and finally grouping entries into sessions. We use IP addresses to identify users of Livelink. Even though the same user can log into Livelink through different IP addresses, the chance for this to happen is considered to be smaller than the chance that cookies are disabled because in almost all the time a user accesses Livelink from the desktop in his/her office. Therefore, instead of using cookies to identify users, IP addresses are used. The unique part of data processing in our project is object identification. In previous works on web usage mining, it is the pages that were identified from log entries. At the beginning of this project, we identified all the pages involved in the log files. Because almost all of the pages in Livelink are dynamic, the number of such pages is huge[1]. However, the problem is not in the number of pages, but in the usefulness of dynamic pages. When we analyzed the discovered patterns that describe access relationships among pages, we found that many of those patterns reveal the *program patterns* within Livelink. For example, two pages are found to be always accessed together because one is the frame within the other, which is defined by the Livelink program. These patterns are not considered to be interesting by our domain experts. In addition, there could be great similarities in the contents of different dynamic pages. Two dynamic pages may be considered to be different pages even though they contain the same set of information objects. In order to discover truly interesting and unexpected patterns, we conducted object identification from each dynamic page and build the session file based on the objects. An object could be a document (such as a PDF file), a project description, a task description, a news group message, a picture and so on. Different types of objects have different domains of identities. Based on the domain knowledge about Livelink, identities of the objects being requested can be extracted from the parameters in the query string of the log entry. Most entries contain only one object, but some entries have zero or more than one object. We ignore all the entries with no information object. After objects are identified, we group the requests made by each user into sessions. In our case, a session consists of a sequence of sets of objects requested by a single user such that no two consecutive requests are separated by an interval more than a predefined threshold. In our experiments, the threshold is set to be 10 minutes.

4 Learning Interesting Association Rules

We implemented the Apriori algorithm [1] to learn association rules from the session file. An association rule describes the association relationship between information objects. For example, an association rule

$$\langle o1, o2, o3 \rangle \rightarrow \langle o4, o5 \rangle \ [support = 0.01 \ confidence = 0.6]$$

means that 1% of the sessions contain objects $o1, o2, o3, o4$ and $o5$, and that 60% of the sessions containing $o1, o2$ and $o3$ also contain $o4$ and $o5$. The number of discovered association rules depends on the *support* and *confidence* thresholds. On our data set, we found that the number of generated rule is not affected much by changing the confidence threshold. However, the number of rules greatly depends on the support threshold. At low support regions, a very small change in support threshold can lead to a super exponential growth in the number of rules. Table 1 shows how the number of rules varies with the support threshold given a confidence threshold. To avoid missing interesting rules or generating too many rules, we set the support and confidence thresholds to be 0.0028 and 0.5, respectively, in our later experiments. The number of rules generated under this setting is 4556. Although 4556 is much less than 74,565 (which is the number of rules for the support threshold of 0.0025), there are still too many rules and not all of them are interesting. Therefore, we are facing both the *rule quantity* and *rule quality* problems. To solve the problems, we rank the rules according to some interestingness measures and prune the rules according to both structural relationships of the rules and their degrees of interestingness.

4.1 Interestingness Measures

The goal of data mining is to find patterns that are interesting and relevant to the task at hand. Various interestingness measures have been proposed. They generally fall into two categories: *objective* and *subjective* [8]. Objective measures are statistical measures whose values are calculated based on the data used in the mining process. Examples of objective measures include RI [6] and IS [9]. Subjective measures can be defined according to the unexpectedness and actionability of the discovered patterns [8]. A rule is unexpected if it is surprising to the data analyst, and actionable if the analyst can act on it to his/her advantage. In our experiments, we use both objective and subjective measures. Seven statistical measures are used as objective measures to rank the generated rules. Subjective measures that measure the unexpectedness and actionability of rules are used to verify the top-ranking rules produced by the objective measures. Our objective of using subjective measures is to determine which objective measures are best suitable for our application. Given an association rule $A \rightarrow B$, we use the following objective measures to the measure the interestingness of the rule:

1. Support and confidence (SC). Rules are ranked according to their support value as the main key and their confidence value as the secondary key.

2. Confidence and support (CS). Rules are ranked according to their confidence value as the main key and their support value as the secondary key.

---

[1]we identified nearly 200,000 pages from the two-month data.

Support threshold	0.02	0.01	0.008	0.005	0.003	0.0028	0.0025	0.0023	0.0021	0.002
Number of rules	2	14	39	88	723	4556	74,565	392,670	1,677,442	4,800,070

Table 1. Number of generated rules versus support threshold (confidence threshold = 0.5)

3. RI [6]. This rule-interest measure is defined as $RI = P(AB) - P(A)P(B)$.

4. IS [9]. Derived from statistical correlation, the IS measure is defined as $IS = \sqrt{\frac{P(AB)P(AB)}{P(A)P(B)}}$.

5. MD [2]. The MD measure was inspired by a query term weighting formula used in information retrieval and has been used to measure the quality of classification rules [2]. We adopt the formula to measure the extent to which an association rule $A \rightarrow B$ can discriminate between B and $\overline{B}$: $MD = log\frac{P(A|B)(1-P(A|\overline{B}))}{P(A|\overline{B})(1-P(A|B))}$.

6. C2 [4]. The C2 formula measures the agreement between A and B. It has been evaluated as a good rule quality measure for learning classification rules [2]. It can be defined as $C2 = \frac{P(B|A)-P(B)}{1-P(B)} \times \frac{1+P(A|B)}{2}$.

7. Conviction (CV) [3]. Conviction tests the independence between A and $\overline{B}$. It is defined as $Conviction = \frac{P(A)P(\overline{B})}{P(A\overline{B})}$.

The values from some of these measures (such as RI, MD and C2) can be zero or negative, indicating A and B are not correlated or they are negatively correlated, respectively. In our association rule program, rules with this kind of interestingness values are considered uninteresting and are pruned.

4.2 Pruning Rules

The use of an interestingness measure can help identify interesting rules by ranking the discovered rules according to the measure. However, it cannot be used to identify redundant rules. By redundant rules we mean that the same semantic information is captured by multiple rules and hence some of them are considered redundant. Shah *et al* [7] discuss some pruning techniques for detecting redundant rules. We adopt two of their *pruning rules* and adapt the rules to use with interestingness measures. Our pruning rules are as follows.

- **Pruning Rule 1:** If there are two rules of the form $A \rightarrow C$ and $A \wedge B \rightarrow C$, and the interestingness value of rule $A \wedge B \rightarrow C$ is not significantly better than rule $A \rightarrow C$, then rule $A \wedge B \rightarrow C$ is redundant and should be pruned.

- **Pruning Rule 2:** If there are two rules of the form $A \rightarrow C_1$ and $A \rightarrow C_1 \wedge C_2$, and the interestingness value of rule $A \rightarrow C_1$ is not significantly better than rule $A \rightarrow C_1 \wedge C_2$, then rule $A \rightarrow C_1$ is redundant and should be pruned.

Rank	SC	CS	IS	RI	CV	MD	C2
1	33(-)	304(-)	868(+)	33(-)	33(-)	867(+)	868(+)
2	34(-)	868(+)	867(+)	34(-)	20(-)	868(+)	867(+)
3	20(-)	167(-)	866(+)	20(-)	34(-)	866(+)	866(+)
4	21(-)	254(-)	209(-)	21(-)	72(-)	1578(+)	209(-)
5	72(-)	271(-)	210(-)	72(-)	73(-)	2054(+)	2838(+)
6	73(-)	157(-)	869(+)	73(-)	21(-)	1580(+)	2840(+)
7	36(-)	302(-)	447(+)	36(-)	213(-)	688(+)	210(-)
8	29(-)	246(-)	18(-)	60(-)	60(-)	60(-)	18(-)
9	60(-)	221(-)	19(-)	61(-)	37(+)	209(-)	2848(+)
10	61(-)	256(-)	70(-)	213(-)	70(-)	168(-)	70(-)

Table 2. Ranking of Rules by Different Interestingness Measures

A rule R_1 is significantly better than rule R_2 if $\frac{IV(R_1)-IV(R_2)}{IV(R_2)} > 5\%$, where $IV(R_1)$ and $IV(R_2)$ are the interestingness values for R_1 and R_2, respectively.

5 Experimental Results and Analysis

In our experiments, we set the support and confidence thresholds to 0.0028 and 0.5, respectively. 4556 association rules were generated under this setting. Each generated rule is attached with 7 interestingness values calculated from the 7 interestingness measures. The rules are ranked according to their interestingness values, resulting in 7 ranked lists (one for each measure). We then apply our pruning techniques to remove all the rules whose antecedent and consequent are uncorrelated or negatively correlated, and the rules that are redundant according to the two pruning rules described in section 4.2.

We observed that none of the 4556 rules generated from our program is an uncorrelated or negatively correlated rule. However, many of them are redundant rules. By applying the two pruning rules, the number of rules is reduced dramatically for all the interesting measures. For example, if IS, IR or Conviction is used as the interesting measure, the number of rules is reduced from 4556 to 449, 361 or 396, respectively. Table 2 shows the top 10 rules ranked by each of the 7 measures after pruning. The numbers in the table are rule IDs. These top-ranking rules were presented to our domain expert who evaluated these rules according to the unexpectedness and actionability of the rules. Based on his feedback, we classify these rules into interesting (marked with +) and uninteresting (marked with -) rules. We can observe from the table that IS, MD and C2 produce similar top-ranking rules, and that the top-ranking rules from SC, RI and CV are also similar. The top ranking from CS is different from others. We also observe that MD and C2 work the best on the data set. IS is also a good measure. However, SC, CS, RI and CV either fail to identify any or identify only one interesting rule in their top 10 lists.

	SC	CS	IS	RI	CV	MD	C2
Correlation coefficient	0.3075	-0.2289	1.0000	0.3312	0.1437	0.8610	0.8340

Table 3. Correlation between different interestingness measures and ϕ-coefficient

Another way to compare the various measures presented in this paper is by determining their correlation with respect to the ϕ-coefficient [9]. ϕ-coefficient is an estimate of correlation coefficient between two random variables on finite samples. A correlation is a special kind of association: a linear relation between the values of two random variables. Correlation coefficient measures the degree of linearity between two random variables. Theoretically, it is defined as the covariance between two variables divided by their standard deviations. ϕ-coefficient can be used as an interestingness measure for association rules, which measures the degree of linearity between the antecedent and consequent of a rule. Tan *et al* [9] gives an exact formula for calculating a rule's ϕ-coefficient and uses it as a reference metric for comparison with other interestingness measures. We use the same method to evaluate our interestingness measures on the Livelink data set. We calculate the ϕ-coefficient for each generated association rule and then calculate the correlation coefficient between an individual interestingness measure and ϕ-coefficient based on the top-ranking rules for that interestingness measure. Table 3 illustrates the correlation values between each rule interestingness measure and ϕ-coefficient. According to the table, IS has a very high correlation with ϕ-coefficient, which is not surprising because it is derived from the correlation coefficient itself. On the other hand, CS has a negative correlation with ϕ. In between IS and CS, MD and C2 have high correlation with ϕ, while RI, support (SC) and Conviction (CV) have low correlation with ϕ. Based on both Table 2 and Table 3, we can cluster the 7 interestingness measures into four groups. The first group contains IS; the second includes MD and C2; the third consists of RI, SC and CV; and the fourth group contains CS. The measures in each group produce similar top-ranking results and have similar correlations with ϕ-coefficient.

6   Conclusions

In our project for mining association rules from Livelink log files, we faced two major challenges: preprocessing the raw data to provide an clear picture of how Livelink is being used, and filtering the mining results to present only the rules and patterns that are potentially interesting. This paper described our experience in meeting these two challenges. In data preprocessing, information objects that are contained in each requested page are identified from the log files. Session files are built upon objects instead of pages. For identifying interesting rules from the mining results, we used both pruning techniques and interestingness measures to filter the generated association rules. A great amount of redundant rules were removed by the pruning technique that uses two pruning rules based on structural relationships of the rules. We evaluated and compared seven interestingness measures in our experiments. Our results indicate that MD, C2 and IS are good interesting measures. Among the three good measures, MD and C2 work better and have weaker correlations with ϕ-coefficient than IS. However, MD and C2 have stronger correlations with ϕ-coefficient than other measures that do not work well.

References

[1] Agrawal, R. Srikant, R. 1994. Fast Algorithms for Mining Association Rules, *Proc. of the 20th Int'l Conf. on Very Large Databases*, Santiago, Chile.

[2] An, A. and Cercone, N. 2001. "Rule Quality Measures for Rule Induction Systems: Description and Evaluation", *Computational Intelligence*, Vol. 17 No. 3.

[3] Brin, S., Motwani, R., Ullman, J. and Tsur, S. 1997. "Dynamic Itemset Counting and Implication Rules for Market Basket Data", *Proc. of 1997 ACM-SIGMOD Int. Conf. on Management of Data*, Montreal, Canada.

[4] Bruha, I. 1996. "Quality of Decision Rules: Definitions and Classification Schemes for Multiple Rules", in Nakhaeizadeh, G. and Taylor, C. C. (eds.): *Machine Learning and Statistics, The Interface*. Jone Wiley & Sons Inc.

[5] Hilderman, R.J. and Hamilton, H.J. 2001. Evaluation of Interestingness Measures for Ranking Discovered Knowledge. In Cheung, D., Williams, G.J., and Li, Q. (eds.), *Proc. of the 5th Pacific-Asia Conf. on Knowledge Discovery and Data Mining*.

[6] Piatetsky-Shapiro, G. 1991. "Discovery, Analysis and Presentation of Strong Rules". *Knowledge Discovery in Databases*, AAAI.

[7] Shah, D., Lakshmanan, L.V.S., Ramamritham, K. and Sudarshan, S. 1999. "Interestingness and Pruning of Mined Patterns". *ACM SIGMOD Workshop on Research Issues in Data Mining and Knowledge Discovery*.

[8] Silberschatz, A. and Tuzhilin, A. 1996."What makes patterns interesting in knowledge discovery systems". *IEEE Trans. on Knowledge and Data Eng.*, 8(6).

[9] Tan, P. and Kumar, V. 2000. "Interestingness Measures for Association Patterns: A Perspective", *Technical Report TR00-036*, Dept. of Computer Science, Univ. of Minnesota.

Mining Optimal Actions for Profitable CRM

Charles X. Ling   Tielin Chen
Department of Computer Science
The University of Western Ontario
London, Ontario, Canada N6A 5B7
E-mail: {ling, tchen}@csd.uwo.ca

Qiang Yang
Department of Computer Science
Hong Kong University of Science and Technology
Clearwater Bay, Kowloon Hong Kong
E-mail: qyang@cs.ust.hk

Jie Cheng
Global Analytics
Canadian Imperial Bank of Commerce (CIBC)
Toronto, Ontario, Canada M5J 2S8
E-mail: jie.cheng@CIBC.ca

Abstract

Data mining has been applied to CRM (Customer Relationship Management) in many industries with a limited success. Most data mining tools can only discover customer models or profiles (such as customers who are likely attritors and customers who are loyal), but not actions that would improve customer relationship (such as changing attritors to loyal customers). We describe a novel algorithm that suggests actions to change customers from an undesired status (such as attritors) to a desired one (such as loyal). Our algorithm takes into account the cost of actions, and further, it attempts to maximize the expected net profit. To our best knowledge, no data mining algorithms or tools today can accomplish this important task in CRM. The algorithm is implemented, with many advanced features, in a specialized and highly effective data mining software called Proactive Solution.

1 Introduction

There are two aspects for Enterprises to build a strong CRM (Customer Relationship Management). One is "enabling CRM", which focusses on the infrastructure, database management, multiple touch-point information integration, and system integration. That is, enabling CRM facilitates and enables the basic functionality of CRM. The other aspect is "intelligent CRM", which emphasizes on making better decisions on improving customer relationship based on customer data. Data mining has been applied to intelligent CRM with a limited success.

A common problem in current applications of data mining in intelligent CRM is that people tend to focus on, and be satisfied with, building up the models and interpreting them, but not to use them to get profit explicitly. More specifically, most data mining algorithms (predictive or supervised learning algorithms) only aim at constructing customer profiles, which predict the characteristics of customers of certain classes. For example, what kind of customers (described by their attributes such as age, income, etc.) are likely attritors (who will go to competitors), and what kind are loyal customers? This knowledge is useful but it does not directly benefit the Enterprise. To improve customer relationship, the Enterprise must know what *actions* to take to change customers from an undesired status (such as attritors) to a desired one (such as loyal customers). To our best knowledge, no data mining algorithms or tools have been published or are available to accomplish this important task in intelligent CRM.

The task is not easy. First of all, actions cost money to the Enterprise. A customer of an insurance company could be given a new car (action) in exchange of the policy renewal (from possible attritor to loyal customer), but it is clearly not worthwhile. Therefore, one must take into account the cost of actions to the Enterprise. Second, customers are different in their values to the Enterprise. An action worthwhile to one customer may not be worthwhile to another. Third, many actions are possible but which ones are optimal? The key question is what actions are best to each different customer such that the potential benefit of taking these actions is optimal (after taking into account the cost of actions).

In this paper, we will describe a novel procedure that utilizes decision-tree models to find optimal actions to take to change customers from the undesired status to the desired one while maximizing the expected net profit (after taking away the cost of actions). We will also describe our data mining software called Proactive Solution that implements the algorithm, along with many advanced features. Applications of Proactive Solution will be briefly discussed.

2 Building Decision Trees for Actions

We describe a new data mining system that utilizes decision tree to discover actionable solutions for the status change problem in CRM. The algorithm is implemented in a data mining system called "Proactive Solution", a data mining software for intelligent CRM.

The overall process of Proactive Solution can be briefly described in the following four steps:

1. Import customer data: data collection, data cleaning, data pre-processing, and so on.

2. Build customer profiles: using an improved decision-tree learning algorithm [7] to build customer profile from the training data.

3. Search for optimal actions for each incoming customer (see Section 2.1 for details). This is the key and novel component of our data mining system Proactive Solution.

4. Produce reports for domain experts to review the solutions and selectively deploy the actions.

In the next subsection, we will mainly discuss components of the step 3 (search for optimal actions) in details.

2.1 Search for Optimal Actions

The basic idea for searching optimal actions in decision tree is quite simple. After a customer profile is built, the resulting decision tree can be used to classify, and more importantly, give probability of customers in the desired status (such as being loyal or high-spending). When a customer (can be either an training example used to build the decision tree or an unseen testing example) falls into a particular leaf with a certain probability of being in the desired status, the algorithm tries to "move" the customer into other leaves with higher probabilities of being in the desired status. The probability gain can be converted into an expected gross profit. However, moving a customer from one leaf to another means some attribute values of the customer must be changed. The attribute value changes are viewed as actions, and actions incur costs. The algorithm searches all leaves in the tree to find a best leaf to move the customer to such that the gross profit minus the cost of the corresponding actions is maximal.

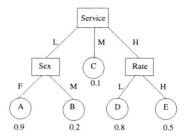

Figure 1. An example of customer profile

Here is an overly simplified example to show the working of the algorithm. Figure 1 represents a hypothetical decision tree as the customer profile of loyal customers built from a bank. The tree has five leaf nodes (A, B, C, D, and E), each with a probability of customers' being loyal. The probability of attritors is simply 1 minus this probability.

Let say a customer, Jack, with Service (service level) being L (low), Sex being M (male), and Rate (mortgage rate) being L, is classified by the decision tree. Clearly, Jack falls into the leaf B, which predicts that Jack will have only 20% chance of being loyal (or Jack will have 80% chance to churn in the future). The algorithm will now search through all other leaves (A, C, D, E) in the decision tree to see if Jack can be "replaced" into a best leaf with the highest net profit.

1. Consider leaf A. It does have a higher probability of being loyal (90%), but the cost of action would be very high (Jack should be changed to female), so the net profit is a negative infinity.

2. Consider leaf C. It has a lower probability of being loyal, so the net profit must be negative, and we can safely skip.

3. Consider leaf D. There is a probability gain of 60% (80% − 20%) if Jack falls into D. The action needed is to change Service from L (low) to H (high). Assume that the cost of such a change is $200 (given by the bank). If the bank can make a total profit of $1000 from Jack when he is 100% loyal, then this probability gain (60%) is converted into $600 ($1000 \times 0.6$) of the expected gross profit. Therefore, the net profit would be $400 ($600 − 200$).

4. Consider leaf E. The probability gain is 30% (50% − 20%), which transfers to $300 of the expected gross profit. Assume that the cost of the actions (change Service from L to H and change Rate from L to H) is $250, then the net profit of moving Jack from B to E is $50 ($300 − 250$).

Clearly, the node with the maximal net profit for Jack is D, with suggested action of changing Service from L to H.

Notice that actions suggested for customer status change imply only correlations (not causality) between customer features and status. Like other data mining systems, the results discovered (actions here) should be reviewed by domain experts before deployment. This is the Step 4 discussed at the begining of this Section.

The algorithm for searching the best actions can thus be described as follows: for each customer, search every leaf node in the decision tree to find the one with the maximum net profit using the formula:

$$P_N = P_E \times P_{gain} - \sum COST$$

where P_N denotes the net profit, P_E denotes the total profit of the customer in the desired status, P_{gain} denotes the probability gain, and $COST$ denotes the cost of each action involved.

In the following subsections, several features of Proactive Solution are described in more details.

2.2 Cost matrix

Attribute value changes will incur costs in most cases, and such costs can only be determined by domain knowledge and/or domain experts. For each attribute used in the decision tree, a cost matrix is used to represent such costs. Users of Proactive Solution must provide values in the cost matrix. In most domains, values of many attributes (such as sex, address, number of children,etc.) cannot be changed with any reasonable amount of money. Those attributes are called "hard attributes". In this case, users must assign a very large number to every entry in the cost matrix. This would naturally prevent Proactive Solution from suggesting any changes on the hard attributes. If some value changes are possible with reasonable costs, then those attributes (such as the Service level, Rate, promotion packages, etc) are called "soft attributes". Note that the cost matrix needs not to be symmetric. One can assign $200 as the cost of changing service level from low to high, but infinity (a very large number) as the cost from high to low, if the bank does not want to "degrade" service levels of customers as an action.

One might ask why hard attributes should be included in the tree building process in the first place, since they can prevent customers from being moved to other leaves. This is because that many hard attributes are important in accurate probability estimation of the leaves. When the probability estimation is inaccurate, the reliability of the prediction would be low, or the error margin of the prediction (see Section 2.4) would be high. In addition, even if a customer falls into a leaf with some hard attributes on the path from the root to the leaf, the customer can still be moved to other leaves where the hard attributes have the same values, or the hard attributes are irrelevant. The example given in Figure 1 is such a case. Customer Jack falling into leaf B can be moved to leaves D or E without changing the hard attribute "sex".

One might argue that the cost of attribute value changes is hard to give. Exactly how much does it cost to a bank to open a new loan account? To address this problem, we allow users to input action costs in a fuzzy term in the format of *(mean, deviation)*: users can specify the mean and the deviation of the mean of the cost. Proactive Solution will calculate lower and upper bounds of the cost according to the mean, deviation, and the confidence level given by the users (see Section 2.4). Note also that all costs are relative; exact amounts are not important for obtaining optimal actions of each customer.

2.3 Building Multiple Decision Trees

Another improvement we have made in Proactive Solution is to build multiple trees using the same training data but with different subsets of hard attributes (all soft attributes are included). Figure 2 shows two decision trees with different hard attributes. As discussed in Section 2.2, hard attributes do sometimes prevent customers from being moved to other leaf nodes. Trees with different hard attributes provide more chances for customers to be moved to leaves with positive net profits. For each customer, the optimal actions are taken from the best tree with the highest net profit. Experiments show that Proactive Solution with multiple trees often doubles the total sum of net profits of all customers compared to a single decision tree.

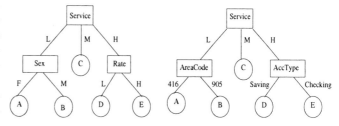

Figure 2. Multiple trees with different subsets of hard attributes.

2.4 Error Margin

To produce realistic solutions, we used a sophisticated statistical method to calculate the reliability of the solution, measured by error margins. The error margin is related to the confidence level (set by the users) of the results, the accurate probability estimation of the decision tree, and the number of examples falling into the leaves. For example, if the confidence level is set to 95%, and Proactive Solution predicts a net profit of $800 with an error margin of $200 for a particular customer, then with probability 95%, the actual net profit would be within $600 $(800 - 200)$ and $1000 $(800 + 200)$.

Section 2.2 discussed reasons for including hard attributes for reducing the error margin. If all hard attributes are excluded in the decision tree, the error margin can be very large, and the lower bound of the net profit can be small or even negative, making the benefit of taking the actions uncertain.

3 Applications of Proactive Solution

We have implemented the novel action-searching algorithm and features discussed in the previous subsections in Proactive Solution. Many other advanced features have been implemented but are not discussed here due to space limitation.

Proactive Solution has been applied to various intelligent CRM tasks in financial institutions and insurance companies with satisfactory results. One task is to promote the purchasing of financial products (from low-spending to high-spending). The dataset contains about 100 attributes. The hard attributes include customer personal and demographic information. The soft attributes include account types, fee charges, agent information (such as agents experience, agent management style, etc.), other products, promotional information, etc. Proactive Solution increases substantially the total spending of customers when compared to a control group of customers.

Proactive Solution is a software for mass customization in CRM, since actions for different customers can be different. It is action-oriented since it suggests actions needed for improving CRM. It is proactive, since it suggests actions before the situation is getting worse. For example, Proactive Solution suggests actions to prevent customers from leaving before they actually leave. It is profit-driven since it aims at maximizing the net profit for the Enterprise (instead of some data mining evaluation measure such as error rate or lift). It is highly effective since it deploys many advanced features to accomplish this task extremely well.

4 Summary

Intelligent CRM improves customer relationship from the data about customers. Unfortunately, very little work has been done in data mining on how to improve (actions) such relationship of customers (changing customers from an undesired status to a desired one). Proactive Solution is the first such system that proposes proactive actions while maximizing the net profit. It offers effective solutions to intelligent CRM of any Enterprises.

References

[1] Stephen J. Smith Alex Berson, Kurt Thearling. *Building Data Mining Applications for CRM*. McGraw-Hill, 1999.

[2] Jill Dyche. *The CRM Handbook: A Business Guide to Customer Relationship Management*. Addison-Wesley, 2001.

[3] Barton J. Goldenberg. *CRM Automation*. Prentice Hall, 2002.

[4] C. X. Ling and H. Zhang. Toward Bayesian classifiers with accurate probabilities. In *Proceedings of The Sixth Pacific-Asia Conference on Knowledge Discovery and Data Mining (PAKDD)*. Springer, 2002.

[5] Tom Mitchell. Machine learning and data mining. *Communication of the ACM*, 42(11), November 1999.

[6] F. Provost, T. Fawcett, and R. Kohavi. The case against accuracy estimation for comparing induction algorithms. In *Proceedings of the Fifteenth International Conference on Machine Learning*, pages 445–453. Morgan Kaufmann, 1998.

[7] J.Ross Quinlan. *C4.5 Programs for machine learning*. Morgan Kaufmann, 1993.

[8] Padhraic Smyth Usama Fayyad, Gregory Piatetsky-Shapiro. From data mining to knowledge discovery in databases. *AI Magazine*, 17(11), Fall 1996.

Visually Mining Web User Clickpaths

Teresa Mah, Ying Li

Microsoft Corporation
One Microsoft Way, Redmond, WA
teresam,yingli@microsoft.com

Abstract

As powerful as clickpath mining methods can be, they often lead to huge incomprehensible and non-interesting result sets. Our clickpath mining practice at MSN was faced with challenges of keeping analysts closer to the data exploration process, revealing powerful insight from clickpath mining that business owners can directly act upon. These challenges stressed the importance of an interactive and visual representation of clickpath mining results. Most products today that can perform clickpath visualization do so by presenting massive cross-weaving web graphs. We present a new type of clickpath visualization which focuses only on clickpaths of interest, simplifying the visualization space while still retaining the same degree of mineable knowledge in the data. We also describe visualization techniques we have used to enhance the detection of interesting clickpath patterns from data, and provide a real-life case study that has benefited from the use of our implemented clickpath visualizer PAVE.

1. Introduction

Understanding how users navigate the web helps site designers improve site design and thus provide a better user experience. Traditional methods do not easily lend themselves to providing powerful insight into how users traverse sites. This makes it difficult for site designers to both understand and take action on the results. To address this need, we researched a new type of web usage mining called funnel analysis or funnel report mining and presented our methods at KDD-2001 [1].

As pointed out in [2], as we develop the ability to extract complex structures such as funnels from data, we are faced with the challenges of keeping consumers of data mining analyses closer to the data exploration process, giving them the ability to visualize results to reveal the insight gained from mining exercises. The power of our funnel mining methods identifies huge amounts of patterns in clickstream data which leads to very large result sets. Feedback from business owners, while positive, has stressed on many occasions the importance of a visual representation of funnels in order to more easily absorb the mined results and provide the

visual impact necessary for real business action. Since one can view a funnel mining analysis as a specialized type of clickpath mining, the research described in this paper is a natural progression of our work in [1], where now we focus on the visual representation of a funnel and the knowledge that can be derived from it.

Two issues in clickpath visualization need to be addressed: structure and detection. The fundamental nature of the problem of clickpath visualization is inherent in the nature or structure of the web itself. A clickpath is a connection between a number of different points (i.e. URLs, websites) in a network, and discerning between clickpaths entering and exiting a point becomes more problematic when dealing with an entity as large as the web. The second issue with clickpath visualization is how to present clickpaths of interest and facilitate visual detection of previously unknown patterns, thus making mining of the clickpaths an almost effortless task.

In our clickpath viewer PAVE, we solve problem one by focusing the visualization on a number of starting points, and looking only at clickpaths/funnels from these starting points, in a relatively linear manner rather than the ad-hoc nature of the web. The problem of visual pattern detection is more difficult in that no one technique can be used to detect all types of patterns; therefore, we introduce a package of visual techniques that can be used to enhance the mining of clickpaths.

The rest of the paper is organized as follows. Section 2 presents our framework for the visual mining of clickpaths. In Section 3, we describe different visual techniques enabling users to detect, explore and drill down on clickpaths of interest. Section 4 contains a case study using our clickpath viewer to mine patterns from an MSN clickpath data set. Section 5 lists some related work in the field of web clickpath visualization, and Section 6 concludes the paper and describes some future projects.

2. Visual Representation of a Clickpath

Of today's business intelligence products, not many have attempted to address the problem of clickpath visualization. Of those that have, the main structure in their product for clickpath visualization is a multi-directed graph. Unfortunately, this type of structure becomes too complex to analyze and mine as the number of clickpaths increases. In our method, we narrow down the scope of the visualization, focusing only on subpaths of interest. The primary structure of clickpath visualization then becomes a tree. This simplifies the visualization space while retaining the same degree of mineable knowledge in the data. We have implemented this visualization in our clickpath viewer PAVE (PAth ViEwer).

Instead of showing all clickpaths in the display space, we ask the user to choose a set of starting pages. This set of starting pages defines the funnels/subpaths that will be displayed in the clickpath visualizer. From our experiences, site managers are only interested in subpaths that start at their home page or at key pages within their site; they are usually not interested in looking at all clickpaths within their site.

Given a clickpath data file, and the starting pages of interest, we run the funnel analysis algorithm SPNAV described in [1] on the data to extract all subpaths (starting with the pages entered) and their corresponding frequency. These subpaths are then imported into PAVE. Using this data, we can visually represent all subpaths starting with the same page as a tree, where the node at the root of the tree is a starting page of interest that the user selected. Users can select multiple starting pages, in which case each starting page will be the root node of a new tree.

Each node will display the corresponding page's URL, and will represent the subpath that started at the root of the tree and ended at that node. Each node will also contain an associated value or measure. The measure type is selected by the user, and can be changed at any time. Different value types/measures can be: the number of times a subpath was navigated (subpath views), number of unique users or total time spent on a subpath, and retention/drop-off percentage with respect to the number of subpath views or navigating users (relative to the frequency of the root or the parent nodes).

Having a tree structure as the underlying component for clickpath visualization makes navigation a much simpler task. We discuss three different methods to interactively explore subpaths of interest in a tree:

1) *Expanding all children in the next level* – At any one node, a user can execute a simple left mouse click on a node to expand and display (or collapse) all children in the next level. In this type of visualization, users can easily expand levels at specific nodes to follow only clickpaths of interest. This attention to focus simplifies the visualization space, at the same time as maintaining the same degree of mineable knowledge in the data. In Figure 1, all two level subpaths that start with a hit on the Portal page are displayed. Retention values relative to the root node are displayed as the measure. Clicking on the "Portal" root node reveals all pages that were hit after a "Portal" page view. Here we see that of all hits on Portal,

47.6% of them were followed by another hit on Portal, 11.6% were followed by a hit on Hotmail and 11.5% were followed by a hit to other MSN sites.

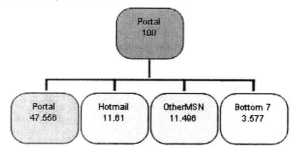

Figure 1: A two-level subpath tree

2) *Expanding children one at a time* – In some cases, the user may be interested in expanding a select number of children under a node. In PAVE, we provide a technique called "funnel previewing" which gives analysts a sneak peak of what funnel values and shapes look like for subpaths represented in the next level. A user can right click on a node to display visuals of all funnels in the next level, allowing one to choose the particular "next page" of interest instead of expanding all children. In Figure 2, the user is previewing second level subpaths starting with the root node "Portal". The lengths of the bars in each funnel window represent the retention of each step of the subpath relative to the frequency of hits on the root node. Clicking on a funnel will display the selected child in the next level.

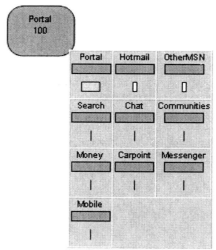

Figure 2: Funnel previewing

3) *Expanding all levels* – To provide a bird's eye view of all clickpaths, PAVE has the option to look at all subpaths by expanding every level, or limiting depth by specifying a certain number of levels to fully display. Zooming capabilities are provided to view subpath trees at various zoom values. In the majority of cases, the analyst will

want to expand all levels, and through the detection tools provided, get an idea of where the relevant clickpaths are, and then zoom into these areas of interest.

3. Visual Mining of Patterns

The previous section describes the underlying structure PAVE presents for exploring and interactively navigating clickpaths. This section describes the package of tools we provide to facilitate the visual mining of patterns and trends from these clickpaths.

Detection by Color

In PAVE, we use color density to detect significant retention and/or drop off rates within a subpath tree. Nodes have different color densities depending on frequency or retention/drop-off values of the subpath represented by the node. Using color density detection, one can fully expand all levels in a subpath tree and easily spot which funnels have the highest density/dropoff/retention without having to look at any subpath in detail. Different color density schemes can be provided. In PAVE, nodes can be colored based on their absolute frequency/time spent values and retention or drop-off rates relative to the root/parent node. Base colors for each subpath tree can also be changed by the user.

Detection by Exploratory and In-Place Zooming

The largest number of nodes within a subpath tree is displayed when the zoom value is smallest; however, in such a case, the URL and retention/frequency value of the node cannot be shown since the node itself is so small. We provide two different techniques to zoom in on local areas of interest while navigating a large subpath tree.

"Exploratory Zooming Mode" enlarges nodes in a neighbourhood as a user mouses over an individual node. Once the mouse leaves the node the zoomed-in nodes will revert back to their original sizes. With "In-Place Zooming Mode", a user can permanently enlarge the size of a node by clicking the node and selecting a zoom value.

Detection by Sorting and Filtering

By default, PAVE unveils children in each level by descending retention/frequency order. Providing a sort function can help to detect areas of i.e. high retention as well as areas of high drop-off. Sorting a tree by higher drop-off rate can be extremely useful when the site designer needs to know where he/she is losing users within the site.

To further assist analysts in the visual mining of trends and patterns, any clickpath visualization package should provide some core filtering capabilities. Types of filtering we have identified as being prudent to the clickpath space are depth filtering (i.e. only display clickpaths < 4 levels deep), retention/frequency filtering, URL filtering, and top/bottom subpaths filtering. With these types of filters, analysts can easily prune the display space to contain only subpaths that have the exact depth, frequency, or URLs desired. Many site managers are interested in the top or bottom X clickpaths, in which case one can apply top/bottom filtering.

Detection by Activation

To explore and mine a subpath tree for the first time, one can make use of the "activation" technique. "Activating" a subpath tree sets the color of all its nodes to clear. Once a tree is activated, the user can specify interest criteria on subpaths and/or nodes; those satisfying the activation criteria will be colored differently from those that did not satisfy the criteria. The user can specify different colors to be applied for each activation criteria. Types of activation criteria can be URL, frequency/retention, and top/bottom activation.

Reversing a Subpath Tree

Up to this point, our clickpath visualization has been uni-directional. That is, given a starting page of interest, PAVE can display all subpaths beginning with a page. Clickpath analysis, on the other hand, is a bi-directional problem when evaluating individual pages at a time. Therefore, how can we visually focus on all clickpaths entering a certain page?

To provide this functionality, we need to perform a reverse funnel analysis on all starting pages to generate reverse clickpath funnels that will tell us how website users navigate to a particular page. Then, the visual representation of a reverse subpath tree is literally that. In PAVE, a user can click on any subpath tree and reverse it visually (upside-down tree) to show subpaths entering, rather than exiting a node. All other visual detection and navigational techniques can be applied to this "reversed" tree; however, the data within the tree will be different, reflecting entry subpaths. With this functionality, the analyst has full flexibility in visualizing and mining all subpaths leading to and leaving from points of interest in his/her website.

4. Application of Visual Mining on MSN Network Clickstream Data

For the purposes of this paper, we ran the funnel analysis algorithm SPNAV (described in [1]) on a particular non-random sample of international users who came to the MSN network of sites on three separate days, and imported this data into PAVE. We wanted to know: for sessions starting with a Hotmail hit, what do the more popular clickpaths look like?

To answer this question using PAVE, we looked at subpaths (with a maximum depth of four) starting with Hotmail. We sorted this tree in descending order to display only the more popular subpaths. We saw Portal hits within many of these top subpaths, so we set the tree in activation mode, activating all "Hotmail" nodes with the color red and all "Portal" nodes with the color yellow. The results are shown below.

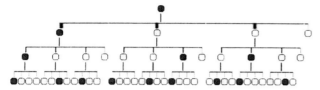

Figure 3: Activated Hotmail and Portal nodes

Here we see that a majority of the more popular subpaths starting with a Hotmail hit also contain a Portal hit. This information is useful when product planning for the Portal site. With this information, the business can justify leveraging the MSN Portal as a prime advertising spot for i.e. MSN's Hotmail Extra Storage product.

5. Related Work

Research related to our work here falls in the area of web usage mining, and in particular, sequential pattern discovery in web usage mining. Srivastava et al [3] presented a good survey of web usage mining up to January 2000. In the area of sequential pattern discovery related to web usage mining, Wu et al [4] presented SpeedTracer as a tool for discovering most frequented traversal paths and most frequently visited page groups. Kato et al [5] proposed a tool for discovering the gap between web site publisher expectations and user behavior. Berendt [6] presented a tool, STRATDYN, that builds on top of and complements an older well known tool WUM (Web Utilization Miner). Berendt [7] proposed stratograms to visualize web usage at different degrees of detail. Cadez et. al. [8] presented an approach of exploring and analyzing navigation patterns that we have used in our data mining service for MSN.

6. Conclusions and Future Work

A clickpath/funnel analysis is the most direct foreclosure of how a site directs traffic within its own set of pages, as well as to its partners. These types of analyses generate much excitement in business due to the revenue making possibilities that can be derived from the yet-to-be mined data. However, to generate even greater impact, the raw analysis and mining needs to be combined with effective visualization. We have presented a new method of visualizing clickpath information, by focusing and drilling down on specific clickpath sets of interest, rather than presenting all clickpaths, which is often either overwhelming or not interesting. We use a tree rather than a multi-directional graph structure as the foundation for visualization, simplifying the display space while still maintaining the same amount of information. Combined with different pattern detection tools such as visual color density, activation, filtering and tree reversal techniques, we have developed the framework for a clickpath visualization package that makes exploration both flexible and interactive, maximizing the visualization experience for the end user.

One direction for future work is to combine clickpath information with product category hierarchy data so that site owners can interactively visualize funnels at different levels of product hierarchy. Another direction is embedding product revenue data in funnels so that the revenue impact of clickpath variations can be easily revealed to business owners.

7. References

[1] T. Mah, H. Hoek, Y. Li, "Funnel Report Mining for the MSN Network", KDD-2001, August 2001.

[2] U. Fayyad, G. G. Grinstein, and A. Wierse, "Information Visualization in Data Mining and Knowledge Discovery", Morgan Kaufmann, 2002.

[3] J. Srivastava, R. Cooley, M. Deshpande, P-N Tan, "Web Usage Mining: Discovery and Applications of Usage Patterns from Web Data", SIGKDD Explorations, Volume 1, Issue 2, Page 12 – 23, 2000.

[4] K-L Wu, P. S. Yu and A. Ballman. "Speedtracer: a web usage mining and analysis tool". IBM Systems Journal, 37(1), 1998.

[5] H. Kato, T. Nakayama, Y. Yamane, "Navigation Analysis Tool based on the Correlation between Contents Distribution and Access Patterns", WEBKDD-2000

[6] B. Berendt, "Web usage mining, site semantics, and the support of navigation", WEBKDD-2000

[7] B. Berendt, "Understanding web usage at different levels of abstraction: coarsening and visualizing sequences", WEBKDD-2001.

[8] I. Cadez, D. Heckerman, C. Meek, P. Smyth, and S. White, "Visualization of Navigation patterns on a web site using model-based clustering", KDD-2000.

Experimentation and Self Learning in Continuous Database Marketing

James E Pearce[1]
MarketEaze Solutions
jpearce@ozemail.com.au

Robin N Shaw
Deakin University
rshaw@deakin.edu.au

Geoffrey I Webb
Monash University
webb@csse.monash.edu.au

Brian Garner
Deakin University
brian@deakin.edu.au

Abstract

We present a method for continuous database marketing that identifies target customers for a number of marketing offers using predictive models. The algorithm then selects the appropriate offer for the customer. Experimental design principles are encapsulated to capture more information that will be used to monitor and refine the predictive models. The updated predictive models are then used for the next round of marketing offers.

1. Introduction

Continuous database marketing is an extension of database marketing where customers are either targeted periodically based on changes in behaviour, or made marketing offers at a touch point [1-3]. The key difference between a continuous campaign and a one-off campaign is that a continuous campaign will continue to be active for a period of time, which allows for the collection of data and ongoing modification of the campaign structure based on analysis of the results collected to date.

Our work in data mining for continuous database marketing has led to the realisation that new marketing processes are required. This paper encapsulates our thinking on the various issues that arise. The processes currently used in industry often fail to integrate data mining with other aspects of marketing campaign management. By addressing this problem and providing an experimental framework over the lifetime of the marketing campaign, our methodology allows optimised offers to be made and improves the quality of predictive models. Our particular innovations are to maintain multiple marketing models in parallel, and to institute systematic, statistically well founded processes to evaluate and refine those models.

We give a brief review of the issues surrounding continuous database marketing, and outline the usual methods employed to address them. We then examine some of the issues in more detail and propose methods of addressing them within an overall framework of a continuous database marketing campaign.

2. Background

Database marketing plays a strategic role in many organisations, particularly for business-to-consumer organisations that interact directly with their customers.

Database marketing practice is becoming increasingly complex. Companies are introducing additional channels beyond direct mail, such as outbound telemarketing, outbound email, SMS and web. Marketing campaigns are shifting from being one-off efforts to being continuous programs where customers are targeted opportunistically, based on changes in behaviour. This means that the processes such as data mining need to adapt to the continuous paradigm.

The complexity of the decision process has also increased. Rather than omitting customers unlikely to respond from a mailing list, companies now need to decide whether to make an offer, when to make an offer, which channel to use, and which offer out of many potential offers to make.

2.1. Data mining in database marketing

Data mining for database marketing has been dominated by supervised learning techniques, including logistic regression, artificial neural networks and decision-tree models [4-6]. A typical use of a model built by one of these techniques is to reduce the size of a list of customers who are to be contacted by omitting those customers unlikely to respond. This issue has been examined many times in the literature [4, 7-15].

---

[1] The principal author is enrolled in a research doctorate at Deakin University and acknowledges financial support from the School of Computing & Mathematics to enable him to participate in ICDM 2002.

2.2. Experimental framework

In order to test the effects on offer uptake of different factors that can be influenced by marketers, and to quantify the effects of these offers, database marketing employs an experimental framework. This framework also serves as a data collection mechanism for building new predictive models and refining existing predictive models.

Experimentation used in database marketing can vary from a very simple design to complex fractional-factorial experimental designs, where thousands of offers can be tested by varying the levels of a few factors [16, 17].

When predictive models are being used, a control cell can be formed by the inclusion of a 'random' cell. A random selection of customers are included in this cell regardless of the outcome of the predictive model usually used to determine whether an offer should be made to a customer [18]. This allows the effectiveness of predictive models to be measured.

3. Current issues in database marketing

Database marketing is shifting from a static model, where marketing campaigns were one-off exercises, to continuous marketing, where successful initiatives continue to be made over time and ongoing assessment can be used for progressive campaign refinement [2].

3.1. Continuous marketing

Continuous campaigns aim to make an appropriate offer to customers at a particular time when customers are seen to be receptive. They can take one of two forms. The first, known as 'event-triggered' marketing, is a batch process. Periodic checks of significant events in customers' attributes and behaviour are made, resulting in a relevant offer being made to all customers who match the specified criteria at regular intervals.

The second form, known as 'opportunistic marketing', occurs when an offer is made to a customer at an interactive touch point [19]. With this type of campaign the customer's visit to the touch point itself triggers the campaign; the company does not know that the customer will visit during a particular period. The decision and selection process must be performed quickly so that a dialogue can be maintained.

3.2. Decisions in continuous campaigns

To perform a continuous campaign effectively there are a number of issues that need to be addressed. They include the selection of an appropriate and significant 'event', definition of eligibility criteria that decide whether a customer is eligible to receive a particular offer, a decision on whether a particular offer should be made to a customer, incorporation of an experimental framework, a decision on which offer should be preferred for each customer, and refinement of predictive models based on the uptake of the offer.

The criteria that govern whether a customer is eligible to receive an offer are determined by business policy; for example, a credit card customer may not be eligible for an offer of an increased credit limit if a recent statement is overdue. Such policies need to be taken into account within our framework. Different offers can be expected to have different eligibility criteria, and not all customers may be eligible for any offer.

The decision of whether a specific offer should be made to a specific customer can be aided by the use of a predictive model to select customers if the probability of uptake is greater than a threshold value [8, 9]. In this paper we assume that a model has been built for each specific offer.

4. A continuous marketing framework

Our framework covers the use of predictions and prediction intervals to determine whether a customer should receive an offer; offer selection, based on comparison of the estimated probability of response for a number of offers; the inclusion of an experimental design framework within the decision process; and a requirement to update predictive models and estimates of model accuracy with current response information.

Our innovations are to consider the outcomes of multiple predictive models when selecting an offer, to use statistical experimental design principles to augment existing models with causal data, and to evaluate and refine these models continually.

The basic procedure followed in applying the framework is outlined below. The first step is to identify those customers who are to be made an offer. The next step is to determine which offers a customer is eligible for in terms of business policy. Next we determine the customer's probability of take-up for each of those offers by using predictions from a model. These probabilities are compared with a threshold probability for each offer to determine whether a customer is to be made an offer. The next stage is to decide which offer to make to the customer. Experimental design principles are utilised to capture more information that will be used to monitor and refine the predictive models. Once the offer is made to the customer, the take-up is recorded, and the relevant predictive model updated. The updated predictive models are then used for the next round of marketing offers.

4.1. Customer eligibility

Typically decisions concerning whether a customer is eligible to receive an offer compare the estimated prob-